THE ZIONIST CONNECTION II

What Price Peace?

THE ZIONIST CONNECTION II

What Price Peace?

ALFRED M. LILIENTHAL

"To the Jew as a man—everything:
to Jews as a nation—nothing."
—*Count Stanislas Clermont-Tonnerre*
to the French Assembly, October 12, 1789

"Peace in Palestine cannot be achieved by
force, but only through understanding."
—*Albert Einstein*

"The fault, dear Brutus, is not in our stars,
but in ourselves, that we are underlings."
—*William Shakespeare*

NORTH AMERICAN
New Brunswick, New Jersey

Manufactured in the United States of America.

6   7   8   9   10

Library of Congress Cataloging in Publication Data

Lilienthal, Alfred M.
   The Zionist connection II: what price peace?

   Includes bibliographical references and index.
   1. Jewish-Arab relations. 2. United States—
Foreign relations—Near East. 3. Near East—
Foreign relations—United States. I. Title.
DS119.7L52   327.5694'017'4927   82-061135

This is a revised and updated edition of
The Zionist Connection: What Price Peace?
published four times by Dodd Mead and once by
Middle East Perspective, Inc.

This is the first paperback edition.

Published by: North American, Inc.
              P.O. Box 65
              New Brunswick, NJ 08903, U.S.A.

*To Christians, Jews, Muslims and Non-Believers,
living and dead, who have had not only the courage to
place their concern for mankind above their allegiance
to any group or sect but also the willingness to do
battle in behalf of this conviction*

Contents

PART FOUR•POLITICS OR POLICY

Introduction

If some compelling justification was required for bringing a most controversial book, with a most unorthodox approach, before a world in which the human psyche has become far more attuned to the pleasant process of being softly lulled by Big Brother than to the painstaking task of absorbing upsetting, nonconsensus material, then the astounding November 19–20, 1977, pilgrimage of Egyptian President Anwar el-Sadat to Jerusalem supplied the reason. The Middle East imbroglio, always complex, had now become "curiouser and curiouser," to borrow words from *Alice in Wonderland.*

Euphoric Americans clung to their video sets over that weekend. Sadat was addressing the Knesset—Egyptians and Israelis were not only talking to one another, but smiling. The "A-rabs" were at last willing to give up war. Peace, surely, must be on the way.

This wishful thinking of course overlooked the fact that since 1948 there had been two wars going on simultaneously in the Middle East. The one between Israel and the Arab states was only a secondary consequence of what Syrian President Hafez al-Assad has called the "mother question"—the conflict between the Israeli Zionists and the Arab Palestinians. While there was some possibility of a separate agreement ending the Egyptian-Israeli war, a solution for the core of the dangerous Holy Land conflict seemed as distant as ever.

The November 10, 1975, U.N. resolution equated Zionism with racism and racial discrimination, and for the first time placed the genesis of the continuing Middle East struggle squarely before a startled American public. But fervent supporters of Israel, Christians as well as Jews, reacted with unprecedented furor to the overwhelming U.N. censure and stirred the media to direct an equally unprecedented

1

onslaught against the U.N., the Arab states, and the Third World bloc. The supporters of the resolution were denigrated with the charge "emulators of Hitler." The pro-Israel American public was led to believe that this was indeed but another attack on Jews and Judaism, a Nazi renaissance. The pertinency of this U.N. action to the continuing Arab rejection of the State of Israel was totally covered over by whipped-up emotionalism.

What is Zionism, and what is its connection with the Middle East conflict? How, if at all, is it differentiated from Judaism? Why has Organized Jewry, invariably an unequivocal exponent of the separation of church and state, condoned their union in an Israeli state demanding the allegiance of everyone everywhere who considers himself a Jew, whether he be an observant practitioner or not? What validity is there to the insistence of a persistent minority that anti-Zionism is the equivalent of anti-Semitism? Such questions may mystify 90 percent of Americans, yet the answers go to the very heart of the Middle East conflict.

It was the serious confusion between religion and nationalism that led directly to the 1948 establishment of the Zionist state of Israel in the heart of the Arab world, causing disastrous consequences for all concerned, including Americans whose government had played a major role in that nation-making. The resultant uprooting of Palestinian Arabs, whose numbers today have swollen to more than 1.6 million, many exiled for thirty years to refugee camps living on a U.N. dole of seven cents per day, brought down on the U.S. the enmity of an Arab-Muslim world, eroding a measureless reservoir of goodwill stemming from the educational and eleemosynary institutions America helped found. The creation of Israel, likewise, led to the penetration of the area for the first time by the Soviet Union, endangered the security interests of the U.S., and thrust the burden of a premature energy crisis into every American home.

However much the essence of Judaism may have remained as distinct as ever from Zionism, the nationalist shadow has so overtaken the religious substance that virtually all Jews have, in practice, become Israelists, if not Zionists. Many who mistrust the Zionist connotation can still have their cake and eat it, through Israelism.

While the vast majority of Jews in the Diaspora (the aggregate of Jews living outside of Palestine) do not believe in Zionist ideology, out of what is mistaken for religious duty they have given fullest support, bordering on worship, to Israel. Such worship of collective human power is just about as old as Pharaonic Egypt, and was practiced by the

Sumerians, pre-Christian Greeks, and Romans as well. As Dr. Arnold Toynbee pointed out in *A Study of History:*

The prevalence of this worship of collective human power is a calamity. It is a bad religion because it is the worship of a false god. It is a form of idolatry which has led its adherents to commit innumerable crimes and follies. Unhappily, the prevalence of this idolatrous religion is one of the tragic facts of contemporary human life.

And these Jewish Zionists-Israelists have been joined by a large segment of articulate Christian opinion in the new worship of the State of Israel, which has been accorded the same privileges and immunities that have been vouchsafed to religionists who follow a genuine faith.

On every other issue of concern to Americans, both sides have invariably been publicly presented, no matter how controversial: the cigarette lobby vs. cancer research, the drug alarmists vs. the upholders of pot, traditionalists-oldsters vs. Beatles-hippies, civil rights gradualists vs. extremists, hawks and doves over Vietnam, pro-Watergate outcome vs. Nixon apologists—to mention but a few. It has only been on the subject of Jews, Zionism, and Israel that the U.S. and most of the Western world have had a near-total blackout. The mere presence of the powerful Anti-Defamation League, even before the fearsome "anti-Semitic" label might be brandished, has imparted a sensitivity so powerful as to smother any idea of private discussion, let alone public debate, on the grave issues involved.

The record of pressures, suppression, and terrorization practiced against many—including Presidents of the U.S., who in undisclosed memoranda, letters, and documents have entertained serious doubts about the course upon which Zionism has embarked—is massive and yet incomplete. The more submissive of the victims of Jewish nationalist pressure have usually been either too ashamed or too afraid to publicize their experiences.

Rarely has the deceit of so few been so widely practiced to the disastrous detriment of so many, as in the formulation and implementation of U.S. Middle East policy. Guilt, fear, and the preoccupation with domestic politics rather than consideration of policy, justice, and security interests have molded the direction of the deep U.S. involvement. And if John Q. Citizen was unmindful of what was really taking place, it was largely due to the inordinate power of the media to penetrate the inner sanctum of every home with its slantings, distortions, and myth-information. "T'ain't people's ignorance," as Artemus Ward once quipped, "that does the harm, 'tis their knowin' so much that ain't so." Barnum notwithstanding, the media has been able to fool the people most, if not all, of the time.

The Watergate cover-up has to play second fiddle to the concealments in the Middle East fiasco for more than thirty years, involving, as it has, the continuous serious threat to world peace manifested by four regional wars and three serious Big Power confrontations, which only narrowly missed becoming World War III. The stationing of American technicians in the Sinai to help supervise the second Egyptian-Israeli disengagement accord may have been a step in the making of a new Vietnam. " 'One day,' predicted a senior U.S. diplomat," according to *Newsweek* magazine, " 'there will be a congressional investigation into how we lost the Middle East that will make the great China debate seem trivial.' "

This book, it is hoped, will contribute to a great Middle East debate that should take place before, rather than after, catastrophe strikes again in that already harassed portion of the globe. Certain basic questions require answers: "Whose legal and moral claim to Palestine is stronger, the Israeli Zionists or the Arab Palestinians? How, if at all, may these claims be reconciled? How may the U.S. protect its vast political and economic stake in the area and simultaneously continue to foster its special, unique relationship with Israel? Will the undeniable, overwhelming public statement of "never again," as to another Vietnam, be meticulously regarded in our pursuit of Middle East peace? And above all, this clincher: Will President Reagan and his policy advisers cease avoiding and openly face the central issue in the entire problem—not the existence of an Israeli state, nor even the nonexistence of a Palestinian state, but the kind of a state Israel has to become so as to bring lasting peace to the area?

For some time it has been apparent that someone would have to assume the burden of carefully examining the historical record of the Arab-Israeli conflict, starting with the "original sin" in uprooting the indigenous Arab Palestinians, and daring to articulate conclusions seldom aired. As Norman Thomas once observed, one of the Jewish faith is perhaps able to speak with "the necessary moral authority that no Gentile can express."

However strong the temptation may be for any author to succumb to the prevailing mood of his surroundings and to indulge in indiscriminate stereotyping, heightened by clichés and slogans, I have tried to maintain a fair perspective and not to allow personal experiences to dull the observer's vision, nor instill too deep-seated a passion. It is out of sadness, not anger, that I am forced to conclude that in embarking upon the new path that Organized Jewry has hewn for it, prophetic Judaism has incurred an incalculable loss in moral values, which author Moshe Menuhin has described as "the Decadence of Judaism in Our Times." What else can account for the anomaly by which the once-persecuted have adopted the philosophy of their chief persecutor?

In doling out incarceration and death while sweeping through conquered Europe, did not the Führer undo the laws of emancipation for which so many Jews had so long struggled, as he decreed: "You are not a German, you are a Jew—you are not a Frenchman, you are a Jew —you are not a Belgian, you are a Jew"? Yet these are the identical words that Zionist leaders have been intoning as they have meticulously promoted the in-gathering to Israel (Palestine) of Jews from around the globe, even plotting their exodus from lands in which they have lived happily for centuries.

If at times this book seems unduly critical of Israel, and neglects to place in balance the oft-repeated arguments in its favor, it is simply because the gigantic propaganda apparatus of Israel-World Zionism has spun such extensive and deeply ingrained mythology that there is hardly enough space to refute widely accepted theses and expose the picture as it really is. The reader, however, is particularly cautioned to keep in mind at all times the very vital distinction between the State of Israel and the people of Israel. Nor can he overlook the fact that one of Western man's most precious possessions is the inalienable right to dissent. As Thomas Jefferson expressed it, "For God's sake, let us freely hear both sides."

This new, updated paperback edition has been published as an answer to the widespread demand to learn more about the untold side of a subject, the understanding of which may be vital to man's very existence.

In giving fair consideration to what to many will come as an astounding recital, my readers are asked to display what William Ellery Channing once defined as the free mind:

I call that mind free which jealously guards its intellectual rights and powers, which calls no man master, which does not content itself with a passive or hereditary faith, which opens itself to light whencesoever it may come, and which receives new truth as an angel from heaven.

PART ONE

THE ORIGINAL SIN

". . . If we had invested in the Arab problem a tenth of the energy, the passion, the ingenuity, the resourcefulness which we developed in order to gain the support of Britain, France, the US and Weimar Germany, our destiny in the development of Israel may have been quite different. . . . We were not ready for compromises; we did not regard it as a major problem. . . . We did not make sufficient efforts to get, if not the full agreement of the Arabs, at least their acquiescence to a Jewish state, which I think would have been possible. That was the original sin."

DR. NAHUM GOLDMANN,
*President of the World Jewish Congress
writing in* New Outlook,
November-December 1974

THE ARAB WORLD

I   Sixty-seven Words: One Man's Dream, Another's Nightmare

We study the day before yesterday in order that yesterday may not paralyze today and today may not paralyze tomorrow.

—F. W. Maitland

How far back into history must we go to start untangling the basic and relevant roots of the Israeli-Arab conflict? So much has been written and said on this subject that the pursuit ultimately vanishes into the distance like perspective lines. As each side pushes its competing and parallel claim farther and farther back, the words tend to merge into an indistinguishable blur.

Thus, if post-1967 claims matter, why not pre-1947? If post-Balfour claims, why not pre-Ottoman? If pre-Masada, why not pre-Moses? If post-Abraham, why not pre-Semite? Continuing in this vein, we would eventually end up in some Stone Age, and then who would inherit the earth? The Basques? The Kenyans?

Absurd? Perhaps. Yet few protested when Moshe Dayan, speaking to the World Assembly of the Jewish Agency in Jerusalem on February 7, 1973, said in all seriousness that "any peace agreement Israel concluded with Jordan should include the right of Israelis to settle anywhere on the West Bank of the Jordan River." Dayan, then Defense Minister of Israel, noted, "The West Bank—I prefer to call it Judea and Samaria—is part of our homeland. As it is our homeland, we should have the right to settle everywhere without visas or passports from anyone else. The Israeli government should make sure that any peace agreement it signs includes that right."

It was only natural for Menachem Begin, after the stunning May 1977 victory of his Likud alignment over the Labor party, to designate Moshe Dayan as Foreign Minister. The two men shared an identical attitude toward the land wrested by Israel from Jordan in the six-day

9

October 1967 War and occupied since. But the history of this region is a far cry from the Zionist mythology to which the Western world has been continuously exposed.

Palestine, with its 10,000 square miles of mostly desert and rocky hills, derives its name from the Philistines, who were pushed out of the Aegean islands by the Greeks and settled on the Canaanite coast. Palestine became an Arab country in the seventh century A.D., having long since ceased to be Jewish in religion or rule, for the Jewish state had fallen in the first century A.D. From the 16th century the Arabs in Palestine were part of the Ottoman Empire, under whose rule they enjoyed a certain degree of self-government. Palestine was at that time part of Greater Syria.

Hebrew, Israelite, Judean, and the Jewish people (and Judaism) have been used by the mythmakers to suggest an historic continuity. In fact, they were different people at different times in history with varying ways of life. And the earliest of these reputed pre-Christian-era forebears of present-day Jews intermarried with the Amorites, Canaanites, Midianites, Phoenicians, and other Semitic ancestors of the present-day Arabs whom they found there and with whom they shared their lands.

Neither the Jews nor these forebears ever constituted a race or even a distinctive pure ethnic grouping. The very word *Hebrew* does not indicate a derivation from a land or a region, but comes from the word *Ibhri,* "one who crosses over." It was first used in reference to Abraham when he crossed over the Jordan from his home in Ur of the Chaldees into the Holy Land.

Jews not only have a mixed ancestry, but Judaism was a tremendous proselytizing force before and even after the coming of Jesus. It was in the face of growing competition from the new Christian faith that the rabbinate and other Jewish leaders ceased proselytization, turned inward, and began to make "a racial hoard of God," to use the words of H. G. Wells.[1] But in so doing they did not succeed either in wiping out their past history or in making an ethnic nation of themselves.

Even the Jewish concept of being the chosen people of God has been distorted. God chose the Hebrews to be the special messengers of monotheism, the belief in one deity. They were "the chosen" not in the sense of being superior but to carry out the task of spreading the word of one God. Soon the Jews had to share this mission with others, as the followers of Christianity and Islam also made monotheism the central theme of their religions.

As to the rightful ownership of Palestine, nothing can be proven in any absolute sense. Both sides can quote Scripture from any one of a number of holy books. Palestinian Arabs of today certainly have, at the very least, as valid a claim to what is Israel now as do the Israeli Jews. But sharing the land is not in accord with the nationalist dream of the modern political movement known as Zionism, whose ambitions and ideology have triggered the chain of events leading to the present crisis.

The early 19th-century Jewish settlements in Palestine were completely nonnationalist in motivation. Political Zionism, spurred by the writings of Moses Hess (*Rome and Jerusalem*, 1862) and Leo Pinsker (*Auto-Emancipation*, 1882) and the inspired, dedicated leadership of Theodor Herzl, did not succeed in winning wide support among the Jews of Europe or America. The 9,000 Jews whom Sir Moses Montefiore found in Palestine on his first visit in 1837 had barely reached 50,000 at the turn of the century. The settlements that he founded, and Baron Rothschild generously supported after him, benefited only the new colonists and posed no threat to the indigenous Arab population.

On the other hand, Jewish students in Russia formed clubs.[2] Organizations for political nationalism such as the society BILU with its motto "House of Jacob, come let us go" and the Hovovei Zion (Lovers of Zion) were among the forerunners of the World Zionist movement organized by Herzl in 1897. But verbal support of Jewish nationalism was not translated into immigration to Palestine.

When Herzl sought the establishment of a Jewish state in Palestine and turned to Sultan Abdul Hamid,[3] the Turkish overlord told him: "I cannot agree to vivisection . . . my people fought for this land and fertilized it with their blood . . . let the Jews keep their millions."[4]

The Kaiser, approached by avid Zionist leaders with the bait that Palestine would become "an outpost of German culture if it were a Jewish Palestine," was then cultivating the Sultan, and he gave an emphatic "no," as did the Czar of Russia. They resisted this despite the fact that Herzl dangled before the potential overlords of a Jewish Palestine all kinds of monetary advantages, from a university to long-term credits.

When Herzl turned to Britain, Colonial Secretary Joseph Chamberlain made the offer of what is today Kenya. Most political Zionists could not envision a Jewish state anywhere but in biblical Zion. The Kenya proposal,[5] and Baron Hirsch's plan for an autonomous community in Argentina, revealed the conflict between those Jews who would look to the establishment of a haven-home for Jews anywhere they could prosper, and those who would insist upon a state designed to be the revival of old Zion in Palestine. The impetus for this latter nationalist fervor came from the masses and middle-class Jews, not from the wealthy and more successful who appreciated the importance of taking no step through a nationalist movement that would interfere with the unmistakable trend toward integration.

Although Herzl's story of personal dedication to his dream of a Jewish homeland has been told often and fulsomely, and the mere mention of his name serves as a reminder to many contemporary Jews, there are some little corners to his life that many of those who followed his precepts have been only too happy to forget. Herzl had been willing to accept the Chamberlain offer of Kenya as the site for the Jewish homeland, but he was overruled by the leadership in the movement he had brought into being, which forty-four years after his death proclaimed, under his portrait, the Zionist state in Palestine. Herzl, as Desmond Stewart pointed out in his revealing biography,[6] had been only too willing to serve as an instrument of Britain's vast colonization effort at the end of the century. Ironically, one of the alternate situs for the Jewish Eastern Company, which he proposed to found, as he suggested in his meeting with Chamberlain, was El Arish in the Sinai. It was at this very place in the 1973 October war that U.S. planes landed their airlift to the then harassed Israeli army. Uncle Sam was following a policy in support of Jewish colonialism, which London seventy-two years earlier had refused to do in rejecting Herzl's scheme.

Herzl had only the most meager knowledge of what Palestine was actually like—its geography and more especially, its demographic composition. He had to be told by one of his close associates during one of his few visits to the country that there were Arabs living there. This attests to Herzl's visionary, but unrealistic, state of mind.

Adding to the Herzl paradox was the fact that he had begun his career as a political assimilationist who was not afraid to say that "the Jew must get rid of certain nasty social habits and remake himself in the image of the Gentile—then the curse of anti-Semitism would wither and die." Yet he gave birth to the most segregational of movements.[7]

Herzl's traumatic reaction while reporting the treason trial in Paris of Captain Alfred Dreyfus, the victim of clerical anti-Semitism (made famous by Émile Zola's "J'accuse"), coupled with his failures as a playwright, caused him to turn to Zionist exclusivism. His utopian novel *Altneuland* was followed by his classic, *Der Judenstaat* (The Jewish

State), and led to his convening the Basel Zionist Congress with its ensuing call for "a publicly recognized and legally secured Jewish home in Palestine."

As a tactical move to win broader support and to throw off suspicions of their ultimate aims—a tactic also employed later in drafting the Balfour Declaration—the Zionists carefully limited their claim: "Not a Jewish state, but a home in the ancient land of our forefathers where we can live a Jewish life without oppression or persecution." To critics they responded: "Only those suffering from gross ignorance or actuated by malice could accuse us of a desire of establishing an independent Jewish Kingdom."

The word "home" quieted the fears of non-Zionist Jews. Meanwhile, through the realization of their demands for unlimited immigration into Palestine, the Zionists hoped eventually to become a majority in Palestine.

For the next twenty-five years the Zionist movement dedicated itself to the practical aspects of buying land, establishing schools, and building up its position in Palestine rather than achieving the creation of a political entity.

With the outbreak of World War I, the Zionists moved their central headquarters from Berlin to Copenhagen, from where they could woo both the Central and the Allied powers. In the face of the hostility of Jamal Pasha, the Turkish Commander for Palestine, they continued to remind the Germans and Turks of the advantages of a pro-Zionist Palestinian regime and of the need for a "counterweight" to the Arab demand for autonomy. The Zionist argument, as expressed by one of their spokesmen, ran as follows: "We wish to establish on the eastern shores of the Mediterranean a modern cultural and commercial center which will be both directly and indirectly a prop of Germanism."[8]

Certain Zionist leaders contended that their "legally secured home" could be more readily obtained from Britain than from Turkey or Germany. With the objective of building a claim against Britain, the revisionist Vladimir Jabotinsky offered to form a Jewish Corps, and eventually three Jewish battalions of Royal Fusiliers rendered service to Palestine in 1918.

Dr. Chaim Weizmann was the key figure in what turned out to be the Zionists' successful operation in Britain. Weizmann managed to meet with Foreign Secretary Arthur Balfour and with the influential editor of the Manchester *Guardian*, C. P. Scott, to gain the cooperation of these and other important Christian figures in organizing a strong British Palestine Committee. These men, convinced that a Zionist settlement in Palestine would be a political asset to the British Empire, urged support of Weizmann on political, military, and humanitarian grounds.

The two most powerful Jewish organizations in Britain—the Board of Deputies of British Jews and the Anglo-Jewish Association—as well as many American Jews sympathized with the cultural aspects of Zionism and supported a Jewish community in the Holy Land that would be secure in the enjoyment of civil and religious liberty and would "receive equal political rights with the rest of the population and reasonable facilities for immigration."[9] However, they were unalterably opposed to any recognition of Zionism on a political basis. They objected to "recognition of Jews as a homeless nationality" and to the investment of "Jewish settlers with certain special rights in excess of those enjoyed by the rest of the population."

Led by Secretary of State for India Edwin Montagu, who insisted that Jews be regarded as a religious community and himself as a Jewish Englishman, these anti-Zionist Jews fought the establishment of any Jewish nation. They maintained it would have the effect of "stamping Jews as strangers in their native land and undermining their hard won position as citizens and nationals of those lands."[10] With prophetic vision, opponents of Zionism held the proposal for a Jewish state all the more inadmissible "because the Jews are and will probably long remain a minority of the population of Palestine and because it might involve them in the bitterest feuds with their neighbors of other races and religions which would seriously retard their progress."

The efforts of the British-Jewish Conjoint Committee and their spokesman in the British War Cabinet bore fruit in the final wording of the Balfour Declaration:

His Majesty's Government view with favour the establishment in Palestine of a national home for the Jewish people[11] and will use their best endeavours to facilitate the achievement of this object, it being clearly understood that nothing shall be done which may prejudice civil and religious rights of existing non-Jewish communities in Palestine, or the rights and political status enjoyed by Jews in any other country.

The safeguarding clauses protecting the status of Jews outside Palestine and of the Arabs in Palestine were important limitations upon the grant to Zionism, making the Declaration a conditional credit rather than a blank check. What the Declaration actually would make possible, as expressed by the Hebrew philosopher and leading cultural Zionist Ahad Ha-am, was the establishment of an "international

spiritual center of Judaism, to which all Jews will turn with affection
. . . a center of study and learning, of language and literature, of bodily
work and spiritual purification."[12]

A national home without political sovereignty in Palestine would
be achieved by the very fact that the mandated territory would attract
hundreds of thousands of Jews, which would give it a higher percentage of Jews than anywhere else in the world. The limited character of
this home was conveyed not only by the verbiage employed and the
restrictive safeguarding clauses, but also by the necessity of reconciling the Declaration with other pledges and guarantees given by the
British government to the Arabs.

The Balfour Declaration was set forth in the monumental letter of
November 2, 1917, from Britain's Foreign Minister to Baron Lionel
Rothschild. Arthur James Balfour had no way of realizing that decades
later the world would keenly feel the impact of what he had written.
Subsequent events, which have moved the Middle East to the center
of the world stage, are intimately related to the ambiguous sixty-seven-
word Balfour Declaration set forth in that letter. The meaning of the
Declaration must be interpreted against the background of relations
between the British government and the Arab peoples of the Middle
East.

The outbreak of World War I found Arab nationalism vigorously
stirring. Several secret nationalist societies increased their activity, and
leaders from Arab provinces took advantage of their position as delegates in the Turkish Parliament to further exchanges regarding liberation tactics. The key figure at this time in the Arab picture was Hussein,
the great-grandfather of King Hussein of Jordan, Sharif of Mecca,
descendant of the Prophet and custodian of the Holy Places. His influence was widespread. In his varied activities to bring Arab nationalism
to a head, he was assisted by his two able sons, Abdullah and Faisal.

Lord Kitchener, first as British Agent in Egypt and then as Secretary of State for War, was alert enough to appreciate the considerable
help that the Arabs could give Britain in the Allied effort against
Turkey. On October 31, 1914, he sent a message to Hussein, pledging
support of the Arab struggle for freedom should they enter the war on
the side of the Allies.

The British call to the Sharif found Hussein willing but cautious.
While Arab nationalists wished to be free of Turkish rule, they retained
a certain amount of self-government and had no desire to exchange
one type of rule for Western European domination. Before acting, they
wished to make certain that they could win outright independence.

Hussein pretended to join the Turks in their jihad (holy war), which had been proclaimed by the Sultan against the Allies, meanwhile seeking out Arab support among nationalist leaders in Syria and Iraq.

On May 23, 1915, Arab nationalist leaders agreed upon what is now known as the Damascus Protocol. This called for the independence of all Arab land in Asia (with the exception of Aden) and the abolition of the Capitulations giving foreigners special rights, but provided economic preference for Great Britain in the liberated areas as well as a defense alliance with her. These were the terms upon which the Arab leaders were prepared to support a revolt under the leadership of Hussein and to enter the war against Turkey.

The British were worried about the effect of the Sultan's jihad and were hard-pressed elsewhere in Europe when the correspondence began between General Sir Henry McMahon, the British High Commissioner for Egypt, and Hussein. The entire correspondence, eight letters in all, was characterized by the British desire to avoid any direct commitment and the Arab insistence on a clear promise of independence before throwing their people into the war. McMahon's first position[13] was that "it is inopportune to discuss the area of Arab independence." But the next note expressed Britain's readiness to recognize and uphold the independence of the Arabs in all regions lying within the frontiers proposed by the Sharif "save certain stipulated districts," and without detriment to the interests of France. Palestine fell clearly within this British pledge of independence, dated October 24, 1915. As State Department consultant Professor William Yale expressed it, to exclude Palestine from being one or part of an Arab state was "contrary to the wishes, hopes, and expectations of the Arabs."[14]

For some years, because of the nuances in Sir Henry's drafting, it was contended by certain Zionist academicians, supported by the British government, that the independence pledge was purposely vague and never intended to pertain to Palestine. But the publication in 1964 by scholar Dr. Fayez Sayegh[15] of two British documents, the twenty-page "Memorandum on British Commitments to King Hussein" and the twelve-page "Appendix of Previous Commitments of His Majesty's Government in the Middle East,"[16] clearly revealed that Palestine unmistakably was contained within the McMahon independence promise.

The third note from Sir Henry expressed pleasure in Hussein's efforts "to gain all Arab tribes to our joint cause and prevent them from giving assistance to our enemies. We leave it to your discretion to choose the most suitable opportunity for the initiation of more decisive measures." The last word from the British High Commissioner came on February 12, and the Arab revolt broke out in the Hejaz on June 5, 1916.

Aided by the entrance of Arab forces on their side, the British were able to withstand the German effort to take Aden and blockade the Red Sea and the Indian Ocean. "Had the result done nothing else than frustrate that combined march of Turks and Germans to Southern Arabia in 1916, we should owe it more than we have paid to this day," wrote British archaeologist D. G. Hogarth, of the staff of the Arab Bureau.[17]

The Arabs drew off considerable Turkish forces that had been aimed against British General Murray in his advance on Palestine. The General noted that "there were more Turkish troops fighting against the Arabs" than there were fighting against him. The Arab contribution to the British victory in the area was termed by General Allenby an "invaluable aid." By repudiating their allegiance with Turkey and throwing in their lot with the Allies in exchange for pledges of independence, the Arabs had redressed the balance in the Middle East.

In the light of the terror inflicted upon the Arabs by their Turkish overlords in a frenzied effort to suppress the revolution, the contribution must have been considerable. As the countryside rose to aid the Arab forces under Faisal, Arab nationalist leaders were taken from their homes in Damascus, brought to public squares, and hanged. Food was withheld from the people in Palestine and Lebanon, and tens of thousands died of starvation. Everywhere Arab patriots paid with their lives. When Hussein called upon all Muslims to join in the revolt, and Ibn Saud took the lead in the Arabian Peninsula, Jamal Pasha, leader of the Turkish forces, was compelled, to use his own words, "to send forces against Hussein which should have been defeating the British on the Canal and capturing Cairo."[18]

Had the Arabs been aware of secret diplomatic agreements then being negotiated, it is highly unlikely any revolt would have taken place. Secret exchanges between Russia, Britain, and France resulted, on May 16, 1916, in the Sykes-Picot Agreement, named for the negotiators, Sir Mark Sykes of Britain and Charles François Georges Picot of France. The spoils of the Ottoman Empire were divided among the three countries (Russia's share being of no concern here as it fell outside the scope of the Arab world). Under the agreement, France was to receive western Syria with the city of Mosul, while the rest of Mesopotamia (Iraq) from Baghdad to the Persian Gulf went to

England. In the desert between there was to be a future Arab state, the northern part under French control and the southern under British domination. Although the French had insisted on all of Greater Syria including Palestine, the British, concerned over Suez and the need for a base near this strategic artery, forced agreement on internationalization of most of the Palestine area while reserving Haifa and Acre in the north for themselves. The ultimate future of areas in which spheres of influence had been demarcated was left undecided.

The French were as much in the dark as to the Hussein-McMahon correspondence as the Zionists were to this Sykes-Picot provision for the internationalization of Palestine. And the Arabs, of course, knew nothing of any of this secret diplomacy, which constituted a complete repudiation of all the promises to Hussein, until Russian revolutionists published the secret Czarist arrangement found in the Imperial Archives. It was the Turks who brought the information to the Arabs in February 1918 in an effort to win their withdrawal from the war. The Turks were now willing to recognize the independence of the Arab countries if the Arabs signed a separate peace agreement. In alarm, Hussein notified the British government. Balfour replied: "His Majesty's Government confirms previous pledges respecting the recognition of the independence of the Arab countries."

Continued Arab distrust of Allied intentions led to the request by seven exiled Arab leaders living in Cairo that Britain state frankly her policy toward the Arab future. On June 16, 1918, came the British "Declaration to the Seven," which confirmed the previous pledges of freedom and independence contained in the Hussein-McMahon correspondence and gave additional assurances of a regime acceptable to the wishes of the population. This policy statement, coming after the Balfour Declaration, added to other governmental statements delineating the meaning of a "national home."

While the safeguarding clauses in the Balfour Declaration protected the "civil and religious" rights of the Arab communities in Palestine, it was the promise delivered by Commander D. G. Hogarth that protected the "political and economic" rights. The British archaeologist had been sent to Jedda a few weeks after the promulgation of the Balfour Declaration to reassure Sharif Hussein that "as far as Palestine is concerned we are determined that no people shall be subjected to another" and that the return of the Jews to Palestine was to be permitted but only "insofar as compatible with the freedom of the existing population, both economic and political."[19]

According to Hogarth's own account, Hussein was willing to welcome Jews to all Arab lands but would not accept an independent Jewish state. "Nor was I instructed to warn him," continued Hogarth, "that such a state was contemplated by Great Britain." Hussein assented both to Jewish settlement in Palestine as a refugee-haven from persecution and to free access to the Holy places.[20] Writing later in an introduction to Graves' *Palestine: The Land of the Three Faiths,*[21] Hogarth noted that the spirit in which nationalism was preached to the Arabs could not be reconciled with any political implications read into the Balfour Declaration. "It was not realized," he stated, "by our government of 1917 how far it [Palestine] was a settled land in occupation of a people Arab in tradition and hope, which had not been oppressed so greatly by the Turks as to welcome liberation at the price of a new subjection."

The Zionists, whose own hopes now rested on Allied victory, also attempted to allay Arab fears regarding their ultimate designs. As Nahum Sokolow had calmed the doubts of the anti-Balfour Declaration Jews in 1917 by denying that Zionism had any intent to establish a state, so now Weizmann attempted to dispel the doubts of the Arabs. On April 27, 1918, he stated that Arab fears of being ousted from their present position indicated either a "fundamental misconception of Zionist aims or the malicious activities of our common enemies." Weizmann visited Faisal in his camp near Aqaba and gave the Arab leader assurances that Zionism was not working for the establishment of a Jewish government in Palestine. This meeting was a forerunner to the London agreement between Faisal and Weizmann, signed early in January 1919, in which full cooperation was pledged toward joint efforts in the upbuilding of Palestine. But Faisal consented with a stipulation inscribed by him on the text of the agreement he signed, conditional upon the fulfillment by Great Britain of her pledges respecting Arab independence.[22] (In his Knesset speech on November 20, 1977, following President Sadat's address, Prime Minister Menachem Begin referred to the agreement but totally ignored the Faisal condition, the non-fulfillment of which as to Palestine vitiated the agreement.)

With the successful culmination of the war, Arab nationalist leaders met and organized the election of the General National Syrian Congress. This first Arab Parliament with representatives from all parts of Syria, including Palestine, convened in Damascus on July 2, 1919. The delegates favored a constitutional monarchy under Sharif Hussein's son, Faisal, as King of a united Syria. The U.S. was the choice as the power to give economic and technical assistance to the new

Syria. Britain was also viewed in the role of friend, but no help was wanted from France. In citing Woodrow Wilson's condemnation of secret treaties, the delegates pointed out: "We may look to Wilson and the liberal American nation, who are known for their sincere and generous sympathy with the aspirations of weak nations."

This Syrian Congress, after opposing Jewish immigration into Palestine and Zionist claims for the establishment of a Jewish common-wealth, stated that "our Jewish fellow citizens shall continue to enjoy the rights and bear the responsibilities which are ours in common." It was the belief of this Arab parliamentary body that the Paris Peace Conference would recognize that "we would not have risen against Turkish rule, under which we enjoyed civil and political privileges as well as the right of representation, had it not been that the Turks denied us our rights to a national existence."[23]

While the Arab nationalists were proclaiming the independence of Syria as a sovereign state with Faisal as King, the Allied Council of Four was proceeding to divide the Ottoman spoils at the San Remo Peace Conference. In the Allied formula, announced May 5, 1920, Britain forgot her promise to Faisal and recognized the partition of Syria, in exchange for which she won from France and Italy the right to rule over Palestine. Greater Syria was divided into three spheres: Syria, over which France was to have the mandate; Lebanon, over which France was likewise to have the mandate; and Palestine, which was to go to the British. A rider was attached to the effect that the mandate for Palestine carried with it an obligation to apply the Balfour Declaration, but there was no recognition of the ultimate independence of this territory. The territory east of the Jordan River had been added to the Mandate of Palestine, and the British were willing to apply the promise of independence contained in the Hussein-McMahon Agreement to what was to become the kingdom of Transjordan.

In ignoring the wishes of the people of Palestine, Britain had committed an open breach of faith. In Arab eyes it was another "Et tu Brute." T.E. Lawrence in *Seven Pillars of Wisdom* did not hesitate to refer to the Arab betrayal and "the revolt that had begun on false pretenses." He bitterly noted, "Had I been an honorable adviser, I would have sent my men home and not let them risk their lives for such stuff."[24]

Hussein, whose sons Faisal and Abdullah were destined to sit upon thrones created by the British in Iraq and in Transjordan, rejected to his last days friendship with Britain, on the grounds that the promise of Arab independence in Palestine had been broken.

In subsequent years Zionist leaders were wont to minimize the binding force of these British pledges to the Arabs. They argued that these promises had been superseded by the Balfour Declaration, promulgated to serve the Zionist interest of creating a political state. History does not bear out this contention.

British self-interest was the primary motivation. At the time of the Balfour Declaration in 1917, the Allied military position was seriously threatened, and this was intended as a cold war move. The Germans were reported to be considering a similar gesture to win Zionism to their side. While undoubtedly the British government, and Lloyd George in particular, felt a sense of gratitude to Weizmann for his ingenious process of developing trinitrotoluene (TNT), more important was that, to quote the words of a former President of the Zionist Organization of America:

Britain, hard pressed in the struggle with Germany, was anxious to gain the whole-hearted support of the Jewish people: in Russia on the one hand, and in America on the other. The non-Jewish world regarded the Jews as a power to reckon with and even exaggerated Jewish influence in unity. Britain's need of Jewish support furnished Zionist diplomacy the element of strength and bargaining power which it required to back its moral appeal.[25]

The Declaration was issued at the time of lowest Allied fortunes: "Revolutionaries had been crushed, Russian army demoralized, French unable to take offensive on a large scale, and the Italians had sustained the great defeat at Caporetto."[26] It was felt that the support of American Jewry at this stage could make a substantial difference to the Allied cause. It was also hoped that the British move would lessen world Jewish hostility toward Russia, and give those Jews who had been active in overthrowing the Czar's regime a real incentive to keep Russia in the war on the Allied side.[27]

Another most practical consideration motivated the British government. The Suez Canal needed a protective base in a nearby territory where "important elements would not only be bound to Britain by every interest but would command the support of world Jewry."[28] The strength that a Jewish Palestine could add to the position of Great Britain in the area was an argument the Zionists themselves had stressed with the British, as they had previously with the Turks and the Germans. Winston Churchill, speaking of the Balfour Declaration in the House of Commons in July 1937, said:

It is a delusion to suppose this was a mere act of crusading enthusiasm or quixotic philanthropy. On the contrary, it was a measure taken . . . in due need of the war with the object of promoting the general victory of the Allies, for which we expected and received valued and important assistance.[29]

Even as the British acquiesced to Zionist wishes by issuing the Balfour Declaration, they negated the illusion that the motivation for their action had been Zionist interests and they admitted the limitations imposed on the scope of the ambiguously worded document by their pledges to the Arabs. In a War Cabinet debate over the Balfour Declaration in 1917, Balfour declared that he understood the words "national home" to mean:

. . . some form of British-American or other protectorate under which full facilities would be given to the Jews to work out their own salvation and to build up by means of education, agriculture and industry a real center of national culture and focus of national life. It does not necessarily involve the early establishment of an independent Jewish state, which was a matter for gradual development in accordance with the ordinary laws of political evolution.[30]

And one week before the Declaration, in a memorandum of October 26, 1917, Lord Curzon, who was to succeed Balfour as Foreign Secretary, stated to the Cabinet that the administration "cannot be Jewish, but should secure to the Jews, but not to the Jews alone, equal civil and religious rights with other elements in the population."[31]

The June 1922 policy statement by the Secretary of State for the Colonies, known as the Churchill White Paper, sheds additional light: "It is contemplated that the status of all citizens of Palestine in the eyes of the law shall be Palestinian, and it has never been intended that they or any section of them should possess any other juridical status."[32] The future Prime Minister stated that the Jewish community in Palestine should be able to increase its number by immigration, but such an increase was not "to exceed whatever may be the economic capacity of the country at the time to absorb new arrivals." The White Paper talked of the "further development of the existing Jewish community 'of Palestine' to become a centre."[33]

As to the Arab demand for an independent government, the White Paper had this to say:

It is not as has been represented by the Arab delegation that during this war His Majesty's Government gave an undertaking that an independent national government should be *at once* established in Palestine. [Italics added.]

In this manner the adroit Churchill did not negate the possibility of future independence for the Arabs. He also took the occasion to refute specifically the repeated assertion, first advanced by Weizmann at the Peace Conference and often thereafter reiterated, that "Palestine would become just as Jewish as America is American and England is English." On June 27, 1923, the Colonial Secretary, the Duke of Devonshire, told the House of Lords that while the intention had been from the beginning to make a national home for the Jews, "every provision has been made to prevent it from becoming in any sense of the word a Jewish state or a state under Jewish domination."[34]

Churchill, who was later to become an ardent Zionist supporter, also tried to assure a deputation of Arabs that a Jewish national home did not mean "a Jewish government to dominate Arabs. We cannot tolerate the expropriation of one set of people by another."[35] The Arabs, however, were not reassured by these words or by those of Earl Balfour, now sitting in the House of Lords, that he disagreed with those "who hope and those who fear that . . . the Balfour Declaration is going to suffer substantial modifications . . . the fears are not justified, the hopes are not justified . . . the general lines of policy stand out and must stand."[36] In the absence of any new guarantees, they feared the "disappearance or subordination of the Arabic population, language and culture in Palestine."

The mandatory instrument adopted in 1923 by the League of Nations did not enlarge the scope of the grant contained in the Balfour Declaration in incorporating the British policy statement, including the clauses safeguarding the rights of Arabs and non-Zionist Jews. If anything, Arab rights were broadened by the reference in Article VI against prejudicing "the rights and position of other sections of the population." The word "position" envisions the protection of economic and political rights, as well as the civil and religious rights covered under the Declaration.

Few British statesmen were willing to face up to the fact that the Balfour Declaration was a definitely limited and conditional grant. It was one thing for British officials to hold out the hope that, in the course of normal political developments, a Jewish majority might develop in Palestine. It was quite another matter to accept the Zionist claim that the Balfour Declaration was a grant to ensure a Jewish majority and Jewish rule. The Jewish population never could have overtaken the Arab population advantage without the displacement of hundreds of thousands of Arabs that subsequently occurred.

Lord Grey, who had been Foreign Secretary at the time of the Hussein-McMahon correspondence, singularly pointed to Britain's dilemma in the House of Lords on March 27, 1923:

The Balfour Declaration promised a Zionist home without prejudice to the civil and religious rights of the population of Palestine. A Zionist home, My Lords, undoubtedly means or implies a Zionist government over the district in which the home is placed, and as 93 percent of the population are Arabs, I do not see how you can establish other than an Arab government without prejudice to their civil rights.

Lord Grey asked his fellow Lords to study all pledges and come to a decision regarding "what is the fair thing to be done."

Zionist interpretations of the Balfour Declaration were as varied as types of Zionists themselves. Ahad Ha-am felt that the final wording of the Balfour Declaration was a rejection of Jewish historic rights to Palestine:

If you build your house not on untenanted ground, but in a place where there are other houses, you are sole master only as far as your front gate. National homes of different people in the same country can demand only national freedom for each one in the internal affairs, and affairs of the country which are common to all are administered by all householders jointly.[37]

"Our leaders and writers ought to have told the people this," significantly added this spiritual Zionist.

In contrast, Ahad Ha-am's close friend and pupil, Weizmann, while admitting that the final wording of the Balfour Declaration represented a "painful recession" to the limited character of "a national home in Palestine," was convinced:

. . . that the political work was far from finished. The Balfour Declaration and the San Remo decision were the beginning of a new era in the political struggle, and the Zionist organization was our instrument of political action.[38]

Some Zionist zealots did not see that the establishment of a national home for one people in a country already the national home of another could only mean the limited nature of a second home or the expropriation of the first people. Others saw the obvious, and planned the expropriation. It was at their private meetings, rarely publicized, that the political Zionists spelled out their plans of expanding from a national home to a state and ultimately to a larger state.[39] The outspoken revisionist Vladimir Jabotinsky, the mentor of Menachem Begin, referred to the Balfour Declaration as providing "a corner of Palestine, a canton, how can we promise to be satisfied with it? We cannot, we never can . . . should we swear to you that we should be satisfied, it would be a lie."

The Zionists had been astute enough to bring about an increase in the size of the mandate over Palestine to include the territory east of the Jordan. Their careful plans of moving into this territory were revealed by Weizmann at the 1921 Zionist Congress: ". . . The future would be decided when Cisjordania is so full of Jews that a way is forced into Transjordania."[40] Only the establishment of the Kingdom of Transjordan under Abdullah frustrated the Zionist design.

Through the Zionist Commission appointed to implement the Balfour Declaration and serve as a link between the British authorities and the Jewish population, and through the Jewish Agency, the successor body under the mandate, the Zionists pushed their drive for control of Palestine. Having got one foot in the door, the Commission opened new schools and took other steps to develop the Jewish community, then some 70,000 strong. The appointment under the Mandate of ardent Zionist Sir Herbert Samuel as first High Commissioner for Palestine greatly facilitated their aim of becoming in fact a subnational government and in this way ensuring the acceptance of their meaning of the Balfour Declaration. The Jewish Agency became a Jewish government within the mandatory government, exerting political influence and drawing both propaganda and financial support from all over the world.

The mandatory power increasingly was squeezed between Jewish nationalism, on the one hand, and resisting Arab nationalism on the other. In this battle the peculiar status enjoyed by the Jewish Agency under the mandate gave it the upper hand. Several attempts by the British government to devise a settlement reconciling the conflicting obligations resulted in total failure.

There were many Jewish nationalists who did not insist on Zion as the only acceptable site for the Jewish state. But for Chaim Weizmann and the Eastern European Zionists, it was Palestine or nothing. Their concept of nation was one of fated racialism. To them, what made a person a Jew was not practice of the Judaistic faith (many of them being, in point of fact, unabashed agnostics and atheists); suffice he was *born* "a Jew"—and once a Jew, always a Jew. Underlying that concept was a deep despair, a cult of exclusivity combined with a sense of doom. Its central tenets were the axiomatic conviction that anti-Semitism cannot be erased from this earth, and the equally axiomatic assumption that Jews cannot live a normal life outside their own state, Israel.

Such despair has remained the philosophy of Zionism. The Israeli state was created by a movement that believed Jews could live in dignity only when settled in a land of their own, a land totally Jewish in language, custom, culture, and government. Religion has not been perchance omitted from this listing: Zionism is more than ever profoundly indifferent to the Judaist faith. But in order to sell itself in a Western world that had long ago liberated the Jews from ghetto confinement, that political cult of doom assumed the vernacular of compassionate humanitarianism and faith. Power politics were made up to look like philanthropy.

Weizmann was a most adept and practical manipulator, not to say ruthless, willing to employ even devious tactics. One does not know whether to be amazed or appalled to hear Weizmann himself say:

We Jews go the Balfour Declaration quite unexpectedly. In other words, we are the greatest war profiteers. . . . The Balfour Declaration of 1917 was built on air and a foundation had to be laid for it through years of exacting work; every day and every hour these last ten years when opening the newspapers I thought: "Whence will the next blow come?" I trembled lest the British government would call me and ask: "Tell us, what is this Zionist organization? Where are they, your Zionists?" For these people think in terms different from ours. The Jews, they knew, were against us. We stood alone on a little island, a tiny group of Jews with a foreign past.[41]

The majority of American Jews, the non-Zionists, were trapped into support on the basis of not knowing the facts, exactly as other Americans neither know nor have been given the facts regarding the Middle East. Weizmann himself explained the precise manner in which the Jewish minority pulled off its coup:

Those wealthy Jews who could not wholly divorce themselves from the feeling of responsibility toward their people, but at the same time could not identify themselves with the hopes of the masses, were prepared with a sort of left-handed generosity, on condition that their right hand did not know what their left hand was doing. To them the university-to-be in Jerusalem was philanthropy, which did not compromise them; to us it was nationalist renaissance. They would give—with disclaimers; we would accept—with reservations.[42]

A closer look at the realities of that period reveals that the Zionist movement obviously owes its success at least as much to the political turmoil, conflict, and disintegration known as World War I as it does to any "vision" of Herzl or even the machinations of Weizmann. Indeed, the genesis of the Israeli state can be traced to the conflicts between various warring states and a by-product of the breakup of empires going back several centuries. As Bert deVries, Professor of history at Calvin College in Michigan, put it:

The source of the conflict between Israel and the Arab nations is the ambiguous formation of these nations after World War I. Prior to the war the whole area was a part of the Ottoman Turkish Empire. National boundaries were largely absent. All the modern nations of the Middle East had their origins in the dismantling of the Turkish Empire. The haphazard and contradictory way in which this empire was dismembered is responsible for many of the ingredients of the Middle East crisis of the 1970's.[43]

But there is something more involved in this type of Big Power politicking. This was still a time when the Big Powers took very little notice of the individuals affected by their grand designs. Territories and populations were traded around like so many bolts of cloth. Only this can account for the subsequent adoption of the Balfour Declaration despite a deep, obvious flaw in what Israelists claim constitutes the legal underpinning for their state in Palestine, and which the British government hid from the British people: the population breakdown in Palestine at the time they granted a national home to the Zionists. In expressing what appeared to be a liberal concern for the minority, they hoped to conceal the fact that 93 percent of the population was then Christian or Muslim Arab and but 7 percent Jewish. The reference to the overwhelming Arab majority as "the existing non-Jewish communities," whose rights allegedly were being safeguarded, was akin to going into a room where there are 100 people and referring to 93 of them as the "non-7."

In *Palestine: The Reality,* author J. N. Jeffries described the aim of the framers of the Balfour Declaration:

By an altogether abject subterfuge, under colour of protecting Arab interests, they set out to conceal the fact that the Arabs to all intents constituted the population of the country. It called them the "non-Jewish communities in Palestine!" It called the multitude the non-few; it called the 670,000 the non-60,000. . . .

But, of course, there [this] is more than mere preposterous nomenclature. . . . It is fraudulent. It was done in order to conceal the true ratio between Arabs and Jews, and thereby to make easier the suppression of the former. It was as though in some declaration Highlanders and Lowlanders had been defined as "the existing non-Irish communities in Scotland" in order that dispossessive action [from Scotland] against the Scots could be attempted more easily.[44]

It is hard to find a document that has wrought more tragedy to the world than the Balfour Declaration. The British failed to view in the armed disorders of 1920 and 1936 signs of deep and unalterable Arab resentment. The British error—and that of the U.S., which blindly followed her lead—led to deteriorating relations climaxed in the fatal Suez invasion of October 1956, hastening the reduction of a once proud empire to a third-rate power and helping bring on four hot wars and a global oil embargo. How the U.S. became swiftly saddled with grave area responsibilities and, as a result, faced the very real danger of World War III erupting in the Middle East, requires a new chapter.

II   America Picks Up the Torch

No one means all he says, and yet very few say all they mean, for words are slippery and thought is viscous.

—Henry Brooks Adams

Arab hopes for national independence rested heavily on the declarations of President Wilson. His promulgation to the American Congress on January 8, 1918, of the Fourteen Points by which he postulated how the postwar world ought to be governed included the following twelfth point: "The other nationalities which are now under Turkish rule should be assured an undoubted security of life and absolutely unmolested opportunity of antonomous development." At Mount Vernon on July 4, 1918, President Wilson declared (that) one of the primary aims for which the United States had entered the war was:

the settlement of every question whether of territory, sovereignty, of economic arrangement or of political relationship, upon the basis of the free acceptance of that settlement by the people immediately concerned and not upon the basis of a material interest or advantage of any other nation or people which may desire a different settlement for the sake of its own exterior influence or mastery.

This Wilsonian principle of self-determination sharply conflicted with the position later attributed to the President by a March 1919 news story that the President had "expressed his personal approval of a declaration respecting the historic claims of the Jews regarding Palestine and that he was persuaded that the Allied nations with the fullest concurrence of the American Government were agreed that the foundation of a Jewish Commonwealth should be laid in Palestine."

The Peace Commissioners' meeting in Paris doubted that the President had made such a statement. Through Secretary of State Robert Lansing they requested that Wilson, who had returned to the

U.S., be questioned as to the authenticity of the statement. On April 16 came the President's reply:

Of course I did not use any of the words quoted in the enclosed, and they do not indeed purport to be my words. But I did in substance say what is quoted, though the expression "foundation of a Jewish Commonwealth" goes a little further than my idea at that time. All that I meant was to corroborate our expressed acquiesence in the position of the British Government in regard to the future of Palestine.[1]

What Middle East policy the U.S. had at the time was merely to follow and support the British. How far Wilson would have acquiesced in the position of the British when this conflicted with his deep-seated political philosophy is a matter of considerable conjecture. In order to achieve his dream of a League of Nations, the American President had been forced to accept the Versailles Treaty, entailing the sacrifice of some principles. But other evidence indicates a determination that so far as the future of the Arabs was concerned, he was still determined to stick to his basic formula of the "consent of the governed."

At a meeting of the Council of Ten held in Paris on May 22, 1919, Wilson declared he "had never been able to see by what right France and Great Britain gave this country [Syria] away to anyone." The President favored sending a Commission of inquiry to ascertain the wishes of the people of Syria, Palestine, and Iraq. This suggestion stemmed from his Mount Vernon address and a proposal by Faisal. But the British, following the lead of the French, backed away from this idea, and the Four Power Inquiry never took place. In 1919 President Wilson dispatched Oberlin College President Dr. Henry C. King and industrialist Charles R. Crane as the American section of the International Commission on the Mandates in Turkey.

The findings of the King-Crane Commission,[2] based on a six-week inquiry in the areas concerned, were withheld from the public until late December 1922, after the provisions of the Peace Treaty had been established. It was only then that the ailing Wilson gave permission for full publication of the Commission report. The findings made it obvious why Balfour, the Zionists, and Clemenceau had all opposed any inquiry into the Middle East. The American Commissioners reported:

No British officer consulted by the Commissioners believed that the Zionist program could be carried out except by force of arms . . . only a greatly reduced Zionist program should be attempted by the Peace Conference and then only very gradually initiated.

The Commission proposed that one mandate be established for all of Syria, including Palestine, within which Lebanon should be given autonomy, and recommended that Faisal be made King of Syria with another Arab ruler to be found for Iraq. Noting that while they had been frankly predisposed to Zionism at the start, the Commissioners called for a serious modification of the extreme Zionist program of unlimited immigration, looking to Jewish statehood. "The actual facts in Palestine coupled with the force of the general principles proclaimed by the Allies and accepted by the Syrians" had driven them to new recommendations.

Regarding the Balfour Declaration, King and Crane wrote:

A national home is not equivalent to making Palestine into a Jewish state nor can the erection of such a Jewish state be accomplished without the gravest trespass upon civil and religious rights of existing non-Jewish communities.

During the course of the Commission's investigation, Jewish representatives had never attempted to conceal the ultimate goal of completely dispossessing the present non-Jewish inhabitants of Palestine by various forms of purchases. Nine-tenths of the inhabitants, the Commission reported, were against the entire Zionist program. "To subject the people so minded to unlimited Jewish immigration and to steady financial and social pressure to surrender the land would be a gross violation" of Wilsonian principle, they wrote, "and of the people's rights, though it be kept within the forms of law."[3]

The American Commissioners endorsed the program that had been announced by the General Syrian Congress as a basis on which the Syrians could unite and the mandatory power could propitiously inaugurate a new state. The rationale advanced for a unitary Greater Syria (i.e., the territory was too limited; the population too small; the economic, geographical, racial, and language unity too manifest for the establishment of a separate independent state) takes on dramatic meaning today in the light of the region's continuous conflict and the disastrous Lebanese civil war, which are direct consequences of carving up the territory into the independent states of Syria, Lebanon, Jordan, and Israel.

The Commissioners warned that anti-Zionist feeling among the Arab people of the liberated Turkish provinces "is intense and not lightly to be flouted." The colonial powers, Britain and France, were in great disfavor. More than 60 percent of these people had indicated their choice of the U.S. as the mandatory power, no other nation receiving more than a 15 percent choice in the petitions submitted to the Commissioners. America had earned this popularity among the Arabs through her unselfish record, untainted by territorial or imperialist ambitions, the philanthropic and educational institutions she had set up, and her past record of good treatment of backward areas in permitting Cuba and the Philippines to move toward full freedom.

Although Article 22 of the Covenant of the League of Nations stated that the wishes of the communities formerly belonging to the Turkish Empire must be a principal consideration in the selection of the mandatory power, the British and French had other definite plans for this territory even had the U.S. not debarred herself in donning the mantle of isolationism. American postwar isolationism became an ideal instrument in the hands of the new, powerful alliance between the Washington politicos and the Zionist lobby. The vacuum created by the absence of American foreign policy was eagerly filled with a spate of resolutions supporting the ever-increasing Zionist appetite.

Considerations of domestic politics rather than area foreign policy governed. In routine manner national and state legislative declarations continued to advocate the establishment first of a Jewish national home and then later a Jewish commonwealth in Palestine. Whereas the British were pursuing their pro-Zionist tactics for reasons of empire, the principal motivating force behind American actions in the Middle East remained political. The essential differences between home and state, between haven and sovereignty, were glossed over in the U.S. as politician and lobbyist worked hand in hand to mold inexorable support for Zionist nationalist aspirations.

Starting with the joint resolution of June 30, 1922, support of Zionism was voiced in one form or another by successive Congresses. But basically the United States had retreated into isolationism and was far more preoccupied with its own domestic affairs—first the inflationary years of the 1920s and then the depression years of the 1930s. There still was no specific Palestine policy save aping the British. The Middle East issue had not yet become a point of competition between the two major parties or the nation's politicians to see who could promise more to obtain "the Jewish vote."

Then, in 1933, two men stepped onto the stage of modern history who were to dominate events for the next twelve years. When it came to the Jews and modern Israel, both played roles, but it was Adolf Hitler, not Franklin Delano Roosevelt, who, unfortunately, assumed the major role.

The increasing flow of Jewish emigrants from Europe with the advent of Hitler caused a stiffening of opposition and increased fear on the part of the Arabs that Britain would never honor her pledges. The 1936 six-month strike by the Arabs in Palestine led to the Peel Royal Commission to Palestine and their June 22, 1937, report recommending partitioning Palestine into Arab and Jewish states.[4] The continued Arab insurrection against this recommendation forced the British government to send the Woodhead Commission to further investigate the partition plan, which was found impracticable.

A virtual state of war continued for three years; even exiling Arab leaders to the Seychelles did not halt it. At the London Conference of 1939 the British government sought to end the strife and consulted separately with representatives of the Arabs, both of Palestine and other Arab countries, and then with Jewish leaders. During his participation in this Conference, the Lord Chancellor, Vincent Caldecot, upon examining the McMahon-Hussein correspondence, admitted that the Arab point of view proved to have greater force than had appeared heretofore.[5] The Committee on which the Lord Chancellor served with Arab delegates unanimously reported that "His Majesty's Government had not been free to dispose of Palestine without regard for the wishes and interests of the inhabitants of Palestine." The occasion of the London Conference served to make public for the first time the Hogarth message to King Hussein of twenty-one years previous, which contained the official interpretation of the Balfour Declaration shortly after its final drafting.

The MacDonald White Paper of 1939[6] pointed to the ambiguity in the expression "a national home for the Jewish people" as the fundamental cause of unrest and hostility between Arabs and Jews. Affirming the 1922 interpretation given by Colonial Secretary Churchill that the government "at no time contemplated the subordination of the Arabic population, language, or culture in Palestine," this White Paper declared "it was not part of their policy that Palestine should become a Jewish State. . . . This would be contrary to their obligations under the Mandate, as well as to the assurances which have been given to the Arab people in the pact that the Arab population of Palestine should not be made the subjects of a Jewish state against their will." The goal was described as an independent Palestine state within ten years, in which "Arabs and Jews could share in such a way as to ensure that the essential interests of each are safeguarded." In such a Palestinian state, it was envisioned that "Jews and Arabs would be as Palestinian as English and Scottish in Britain are British."

As a concession to the Zionists, the White Paper did call for the admission of 75,000 more Jews over the next five years, with no further immigration thereafter "unless the Arabs of Palestine are prepared to acquiesce in it." At the same time the British pledged they would check the ever-increasing illegal immigration into the Holy Land.

The reaction to the new British decree in Jewish Palestine circles was violent. Demonstrations took place, a British constable was killed, and the Grand Rabbi tore up the White Paper before the congregation in Jerusalem. As Chairman of the Executive of the Jewish Agency, David Ben-Gurion said on August 25, 1939, "For us the White Paper neither exists nor can exist. We must believe as if we were the State in Palestine until we actually become that State in Palestine."

Sir John Hope Simpson, a British expert sent to the mandated territory in May 1930 to report on the riots that had heightened tension between Arabs and Jews living in the Holy Land, wrote the following in a 1944 article regarding the Zionist determination to expand the national home established for them by the British government under the Balfour Declaration into a Jewish state:

Had the Jewish authorities been content with the original object of settlement in Palestine—"a Jewish life without oppression and persecution" in accordance with Jewish customs—the national home would have presented no difficulty. The Jews could have entered and settled as so many did in the P. I. C. A. [Palestine Jewish Colonization Association] settlements—founded in many cases long before the Balfour Declaration—in friendly relationship with their Arab fellow-citizens, and themselves loyal citizens of Palestine. The unfortunate fact is that the Jewish immigration today is not composed of Jews who, on religious grounds, wish to return to the land of Zion, in order to lead a Jewish life, without oppression and persecution, in accordance with Jewish customs. Rather is it composed of Jews, largely devoid of religious conviction, animated by a spirit of political nationalism, and determined to secure domination in Palestine, the home land of the Arab for at least 1,300 years.

No effort has been made to coalesce with the existing population. On the contrary, there is extreme divergence between the virile occidentalism of the immigrant and the conservative orientalism of the mass of the resident population. After its description of the organization of Jewish policy in Palestine the Royal Commission writes: "It would be difficult to find in history a precedent for the establishment of so distinct an *imperium in imperio*.[7]

With the outbreak of open hostility between Nazi Germany and the Allied free nations, British efforts to find a solution to the Palestine dilemma were temporarily shelved. But the Zionists in the U.S. did not halt for one second their intensive campaigning for statehood. The American Palestine Committee, numbering hundreds of U.S. senators, representatives, Cabinet members, governors, and other influential personalities from all walks of life, were exerting pressure everywhere it counted; in a joint statement of December 1942 signed by 63 senators and 181 congressmen they called on Roosevelt "to restore the Jewish homeland."

President Roosevelt had dispatched Brigadier General Patrick J. Hurley (later to become Ambassador to China) to the Arab Middle East as his personal representative to report directly to the White House. General Hurley informed the President of the Zionist insistence on increased immigration into Palestine and concrete plans for expansionism, although opposed by Arabs and some Palestinian Jews:

For its part, the Zionist Organization in Palestine has indicated its commitment to an enlarged program for:
(a) A sovereign Jewish state which would embrace Palestine and probably Transjordan;
(b) An eventual transfer of the Arab population from Palestine to Iraq;
(c) Jewish leadership for the whole Middle East in the fields of economic development and control.[8]

With the Jews of Europe facing the onslaught of Hitler genocide and Nazi crematoriums, President Roosevelt hoped that the rescue of 500,000 could be achieved by affording a generous worldwide political asylum. In line with this humanitarian idea, Morris Ernst, a New York attorney and a close friend of the President, went to London in the middle of the war to see if the British would take in 100,000 or 200,000 uprooted people. The President had reason to assume that Canada, Australia, and the South American countries would gladly open their doors. And if such good examples were set by other nations, Mr. Roosevelt felt that the American Congress could be "educated to go back to our traditional position of asylum."

The key was in London. Would Morris Ernst succeed there? He came home to report, and this is what took place in the White House as related by him to a Cincinnati audience in 1950:

ERNST: We are at home plate. That little island [it was during the second blitz that he visited England] on a properly representative program of a World Immigration Budget will match the United States up to 150,000.
ROOSEVELT: 150,000 to England—150,000 to match that in the United States —pick up 200,000 or 300,000 elsewhere, and we can start with half a million of these oppressed people.

A week or so later, Ernst and his wife again visited the President.

ROOSEVELT: Nothing doing on the program. We can't put it over because the dominant vocal Jewish leadership of America won't stand for it.

ERNST: It's impossible! Why?

ROOSEVELT: They are right from *their* point of view. The Zionist movement knows that Palestine is, and will be for some time, a remittance society. They know that they can raise vast sums for Palestine by saying to donors, "There is no other place this poor Jew can go." But if there is a world political asylum for all people irrespective of race, creed, or color, they cannot raise their money. Then the people who do not want to give the money will have an excuse to say "What do you mean, there is no place they can go but Palestine? They are the preferred wards of the world."

Ernst, shocked, first refused to believe his leader and friend. He began to lobby among influential Jewish friends for this world program of rescue, without mentioning the reaction of the President or the British. As he himself put it: "I was thrown out of parlors of friends of mine who very frankly said, 'Morris, this is treason. You are undermining the Zionist movement.'[9] He ran into the same reaction among all Jewish groups and their leaders. Everywhere he found "a deep, genuine, often fanatically emotional vested interest in putting over the Palestinian movement" in men "who are little concerned about human blood if it is not their own."[10]

This response of Zionism ended the remarkable Roosevelt effort to rescue Europe's displaced persons.

By mid-1942 London and Washington had reached an agreement on the tactic of restraining local political foment over the Palestine question by delaying a settlement of the issue until the conclusion of the war, meanwhile assuring both Arabs and Jews that no decision would be reached without prior consultation with both.[11] As tensions in the Holy Land increased, a joint Anglo-American statement to this effect, and emphasizing that "no changes brought about by force in the status of Palestine or the administration of the country would be permitted or acquiesced in," was prepared for release to the public. The White House, under constant Zionist bombardment, hoped to ward off further public agitation and domestic political activities relative to Palestine while the war was in progress.

A leak occurred, however, before the Anglo-American joint statement could be issued, and Zionists immediately flooded high government officials with protests.[12] At this point Secretary of State Cordell Hull believed that the matter should be decided not on a diplomatic basis but on a military one. Secretary of War Henry L. Stimson concluded that the military situation was not serious enough to warrant any statement on Palestine. The plan was canceled. The joint declaration, earlier agreed upon as being in the national interest by the highest political authorities of both countries, thus had been killed by American Zionist pressure groups.[13]

The need for an alleviative joint declaration was given greater urgency by the State Department following the lengthy meeting in Riyadh between Saudi Arabian King Abdul Aziz Ibn Saud and Colonel Harold B. Hoskins, who had headed a special mission to the Middle East and North Africa in early 1943, then was dispatched to see whether the Saudi monarch might suggest any basis for a settlement of the torrid Palestine question. It was felt that Colonel Hoskins, a close student of the problem who spoke Arabic fluently, could best approach Ibn Saud with the suggestion of meeting with Dr. Chaim Weizmann, then President of the World Zionist Organization.

In line with the previous advice of U.S. Resident Minister James Moose, Ibn Saud was vehemently opposed to further Jewish immigration into Palestine, let alone the creation of a Jewish state there. This was confirmed in the week-long daily meetings held with Hoskins in August 1943. The King rejected the American proposal that he meet with Weizmann on the ground that his position of leadership in the Arab world did not permit him "to speak for Palestine, much less deliver Palestine to the Jews even if he were willing for even an instant to consider such a proposal."[14] Hoskins said the Saudi King, whose anti-Zionist stand had brought him "a flood of telegrams and congratulations" from Arabs and Muslims all over the world, "could never afford to support Jewish claims to Palestine."

The Arab world rocked in protest when the Wright-Compton and other resolutions calling for unrestricted Jewish immigration and the establishment of a Jewish commonwealth in Palestine were introduced in Congress in 1944. The year before all Jewish groups, save one, had enunciated the Biltmore program in an all-out appeal for a Zionist state. Lengthy hearings were held before the Foreign Affairs Committee, but a letter from Secretary of War Henry L. Stimson to Committee Chairman Sol Bloom asked that the resolution be shelved "since such action would be prejudicial to the successful prosecution of the war" by vastly complicating the Middle East picture.

Presidential approval was received once more in March for the Anglo-American joint statement on Palestine. But within a few days of approving the issuance of the statement—Zionist intelligence within the White House was again doing its job well—the President was forced on March 9 to receive Rabbis Wise and Silver, who then announced to the press an affirmation of the President's support of the Zionist position. Even as he was a master in the art of statesmanship, FDR was equally the politician par excellence. He knew just when he had to subordinate the idealism behind a concern for the national interest to the realities of getting elected, and this was the outset of the 1944 national campaign.

The Wise-Silver announcement provoked an immediate protest throughout the Arab Middle East and street riots in Damascus, Homs, and Jerusalem. It became necessary for the State Department to issue a confidential interpretation of the rabbis' statement for the use of U.S. Chiefs of Mission in Arab countries, explaining that U.S. policy on Palestine was based on consultation with both Arabs and Jews.[15] This was in line with Roosevelt letters to Ibn Saud and other heads of Arab governments late in 1943. But such assurances to the Arabs had never been made public, whereas the Zionists continued to spread throughout the media any and all encouragement received from the President or any other administration official.

In the 1944 campaign pro-Zionist planks were included in both major party platforms. Under the impact of the Zionist Biltmore Declaration, the Democratic plank spoke of "a free and democratic Jewish commonwealth" in Palestine. The Republicans used the phraseology "a free and democratic commonwealth," but Governor Thomas E. Dewey in the campaign had unmistakably indicated that such a commonwealth was to be a Jewish one. At first there had been a general disposition in Arab capitals, including Riyadh, to write these off as merely party politics. But on October 15 the President addressed a letter to New York Senator Robert F. Wagner in which he endorsed the Democratic Palestine plank, therefore making the matter appear more serious and raising grave doubts in the minds of the Arabs regarding the pledges previously given them by the President.

After the election the President sent Secretary of State Edward R. Stettinius, Jr., to tell Rabbi Wise and congressional leaders that the reintroduction of the Palestine resolution in Congress at that time would be undesirable. Nevertheless, resolutions were introduced in both houses, and it took the personal appearance of Secretary Stettinius before the Senate Foreign Relations Committee to defeat the legislation. The FDR position was never put in writing but was made known orally to Rabbi Wise, House Foreign Affairs Chairman Congressman Sol Bloom, and others. Moreover, the President sent a message to Senator Wagner in which he pointed out that the passage of the resolutions could lead to bloodshed between Jews and Arabs and should, therefore, be averted at this time, although he significantly added: "Everybody knows what American hopes are."

Killing the resolution did not halt an intensive Arab anti-American press campaign and the subsequent boycott by Palestine Arabs of the Culbertson Economic Mission, the purpose of which had been to improve economic relations between the United States and certain Arab countries.

The Arab attitude was otherwise stiffening, and the State Department was very aware of this. In signing the October 7, 1944 Pan-Arab Protocol, better known as the Alexandria Protocol, which led to the subsequent formation of the Arab League, King Ibn Saud urged a joint military committee to defend Arab Palestine by force if necessary. And in a January 9, 1945, memorandum to the President, Secretary Stettinius noted how significant it was that Ibn Saud should "regard himself as a champion of the Arabs of Palestine and would himself feel it an honor to die for their cause."[16]

James Landis, American Director of Economic Operations in the Middle East, one-time Dean of Harvard Law School and an outstanding liberal, warned the President early in 1945 that any presidential action regarding Palestine that did not go to the root of the matter "was not likely to advance very far and that, for this reason, it might be well for the President to avoid the issue entirely unless he was prepared to make some far-reaching proposals."[17] Landis insisted:

. . . a vacillating policy with reference to Zionism as in the past twenty years has proved to be equivalent of no policy . . . the approach to the problem must start from an insistence that the objective of the Jewish commonwealth or the Jewish state as distinguished from the Jewish national home must be given up. The political objective implicit in the Jewish state idea will never be accepted by the Arab nations and is not consistent with the principles of the Atlantic Charter [the joint statement of FDR and Churchill of August 14, 1941], nor is the Jewish state idea demanded by the mandate. But given an adequate conception of the Jewish national home, together with the political limitations that must be placed on that conception, it should be possible to sell that to the Jews and Arabs as well.

Of course, the one great stumbling block is the question of immigration. That question at the present possesses a significance that it should not possess because of its relationship to the political as distinguished from the economic future of Palestine. *In other words if the extent of immigration can be related to the economic absorptive capacity of Palestine rather than to the political issue of the Jewish minority or majority, there is hope of striking an acceptable compromise even on the immigration question with the Arabs. This is particularly true now, for I believe the economic absorptive capacity of Palestine has been grossly exaggerated.* [Italics added.]

Seeking to increase the certificates of immigration into Palestine, which according to the limitations set by the British White Paper would be exhausted in four months, the Zionists in the U.S. opened up their heaviest barrage on the State Department[18] and the White House on the eve of the February Yalta Conference where the Big Three—Roosevelt, Stalin, and Churchill—were scheduled to discuss all outstanding problems including Palestine. Following this conclave, both the British and American leaders were due to have meetings with King Ibn Saud. The Zionists were fearful that the ambivalent Chief Executive, under pressure from the pro-Arab State Department, might abandon the Democratic party's commitment to Zionism and renege on what they considered binding promises of the previous March made to Rabbis Wise and Silver.

At Yalta nothing was said about Palestine, but at the colorful meeting of February 14 with Ibn Saud aboard the U.S.S. *Quincy* in Great Bitter Lake in the Eastern Mediterranean, Roosevelt made a significant promise in answer to the Saudi monarch's full exposition of the Arab side in the Palestine dispute and the claim that continued Jewish immigration and purchase of lands constituted a grave threat to the Arabs. The President replied that he wished "to assure His Majesty that he would do nothing to assist the Jews against the Arabs and would make no move hostile to the Arab people. He reminded His Majesty that it is impossible to prevent speeches and resolutions in Congress or in the press which may be made on any subject. His reassurance concerned his own future policy as Chief Executive of the United States Government."[19]

According to the memorandum of conversation, the two Chief Executives were in agreement that Jewish homeless survivors of Hitler might well be resettled in the lands from which they were driven. The President, according to a conversation upon his return from the meeting, had been deeply impressed by the "intensity of the Arab feeling with regard to Palestine."[20] The President is reported to have remarked that he had learned more about the Arab Jewish situation from Ibn Saud in five minutes than he had understood all his life.[21]

Churchill had indicated at Yalta that he was as strongly pro-Zionist as ever, and in his talk with Ibn Saud a week after Roosevelt's, the British Prime Minister suggested that the Jews be placed in Libya, a country with a lot of room and few people.[22] (Roosevelt's mention of this suggestion to Ibn Saud had brought forth the strong objection that such a step would be unfair to the Muslims in North Africa.) Churchill, according to the words used by the Saudi ruler in later confiding details of the meeting to U.S. Minister to Saudi Arabia William Eddy, had opened the discussion on Zionism "confidently wielding a big stick."[23] He referred to the subsidization Saudi Arabia had received from Britain for more than twenty years, which the Arabian monarch admitted had enabled "my reign to be stable and fend off potential enemies on my frontiers." The King now wanted assurances that Jewish immigration to Palestine would be stopped. But Churchill refused to give any such promises, although he assured His Majesty that "he would not drive the Arabs out of Palestine or deprive them of their means of livelihood there."

To the Churchill request for Arab moderation and a realistic compromise with Zionism, the King stated (as paraphrased by Minister Eddy) that what the Briton proposed was not gratitude or help itself, "but to wipe out my honor and destroy my soul. I could not acquiesce and in the preposterous event that I was willing to do so, it would not be as a favor to Britain, since the promotion of Zionism from any quarter must indubitably bring bloodshed and widespread disorder in the Arab lands with certainly no benefit to Britain or anyone else."

The Saudi narrator told his American listener that "by this time Mr. Churchill had laid the big stick down." The British Prime Minister was firmly reminded that "the British and their allies would be making the wrong choice between a friendly and peaceful Arab world and a struggle to the death between Arabs and Jews if unreasonable immigration of Jews to Palestine is renewed. *In any case the formula must be arrived at by and with Arab consent.*"[24] (Italics added.)

After his Great Bitter Lake meeting with Ibn Saud, the President on March 16 authorized Rabbi Wise (to whom the doors of the White House were invariably wide open) to state that the President was still in favor of unrestricted Jewish immigration and a Jewish state. Or as Richard H. S. Crossman, British Parliamentarian, sarcastically noted, "The President then hurried back from the Crimea to Washington to assure the Zionists that his attitude toward them remained unchanged."

As the Arab Middle East once more angrily reacted, FDR soared to the heights of double-talk. He approved of the Department of State's telegraphed explanation to its Middle East posts of the presidential authorization to the Zionist rabbi: the statement referred only to possible action at some future date and the President had very much in mind his pledges to Ibn Saud and other Arab heads of state that they would be consulted as well as the Jews on any U.S. move relative to Palestine.

Foreign Service officers in the State Department continued to call for an enunciation of a definitive Palestine policy that would give full consideration to U.S. long-term interests. The public, meanwhile, was being kept entirely in the dark as to the continuing presidential assurances of consultation on Palestine that were being given to Arab leaders.

On March 10 the President received letters simultaneously from the King of Saudi Arabia, the Regent of Iraq, the President of the Syrian Republic, the King of Yemen, and the Lebanese Prime Minister. These communications all followed the same lines in presenting Arab claims to Palestine, marshaling moral, historical, and political arguments. The State Department recognized that the Arabs, and particularly King Ibn Saud, were determined to fight if necessary in defense of their position on Palestine. "The President's continued support of Zionism may thus lead to actual bloodshed in the Near East *and even endanger the security of our immensely valuable oil concession in Saudi Arabia.*"[25] (Italics added.)

This warning from Wallace Murray, Director of the Office of Near Eastern Affairs in the State Department, foreshadowing the oil boycott of 1973, twenty-eight years later, also included a reminder to the President that it would not be wise to reach a settlement on Palestine without the full agreement of the Soviet government, which at that writing (March 20, 1945) was opposed to establishment of a Jewish state. "The continued endorsement by the President of Zionist objectives could throw the entire Arab world into the arms of the Soviet Union," added the career diplomat who had just been designated Ambassador to Iran.

In replying a week before his death[26] to the letter from Ibn Saud, Roosevelt indicated clearly, as he had communicated to the King in person, that no decision would be taken with respect to the basic Palestine situation "without full consultation with both Arabs and Jews," and reassured the Saudi monarch that he "would take no action as Chief of the Executive Branch of this Government which might prove hostile to the Arab people."

This was more presidential double-talk—saying one thing for external diplomatic affairs and quite another for internal public consumption—which persisted through his death on April 12 at Warm Springs, Georgia. The U.S. had developed no clear-cut policy toward Palestine, which of course only contributed materially to the instability of the political situation and the growing friction between Arabs and Jews.

Within the confines of the White House, the President was willing to be quite open in his criticism of Zionism, and the biography *Eleanor and Franklin*[27] is most revealing as to the First Family's differences on Zionism. Mrs. Roosevelt referred to "the wonderful work that had been done by the Zionists in certain parts of Palestine." The President noted that except along the coastal plain, Palestine had looked extremely rocky and barren to him as he flew over it on his way to the Cairo Conference. Mrs. Roosevelt commented on the fact that the Zionists felt much stronger and were willing to run the risk of a fight with the Arabs over Palestine. The President agreed that this was a possibility, but reminded her that "there were fifteen or twenty million Arabs in and around Palestine and, in the long run, he thought these numbers would win out."

It is surprising to learn that intrepid Zionist Eleanor Roosevelt herself had earlier been an advocate of trusteeship, not statehood, and that only later did she become a rabid, avid supporter of Israel. It is even more interesting to note in this excellent biography that Eleanor Roosevelt was not exempt from Richard Crossman's famed observation that "everyone harbors a soupçon of anti-Semitic prejudice."[28] We astonishingly read of Eleanor Roosevelt saying that she had to attend a party given by Admiral William Harris for Bernard M. Baruch "which I'd rather be hung than seen at," as she complained in a letter to her mother-in-law, "mostly Jews." Two days later she wrote, "The Jew party [was] appalling. I never wish to hear money, jewels . . . and sables mentioned again."[29] Henry Morgenthau, with whom she and the President later became warm personal friends when he served as Secretary of the Treasury in the first Roosevelt Cabinet, and Louis Brandeis were exempted from this dislike, sort of "some of my best friends are. . . ." Her mother-in-law, Sara, wrote from Hyde Park after meeting the Morgenthaus, "Young Morgenthau was easy, and yet modest and serious and intelligent. The wife is very Jewish but appeared very well." The persistent strivings of Mrs. Roosevelt, particularly as former First Lady, to advance the Israeli cause could have stemmed from an unconscious atonement for her secret feelings of earlier years. So many other persons of her social class and era likewise jumped from a near-anti-Semitic stance to a virulent pro-Israel position.

While FDR publicly was most sympathetic to Jews and intent on rescuing those who were trapped by the Nazi movement in Europe, privately the wartime President had no interest in Jewish-Zionist statehood. A refined student of history who was both concerned with

American national interests and worried about possible Communist gains, he personally found the idea of Jewish statehood repugnant.

The full extent of the Roosevelt coolness toward Zionist aspirations for statehood was never completely realized until the State Department in May 1964 disclosed heretofore classified documents bearing on 1943 U.S. policy in the Middle East. President Roosevelt had at that time been urging a "trusteeship for the Holy Land with a Jew, a Christian, and a Moslem as the three responsible trustees." This proposal had come forward after negotiations between King Saud and Zionist chieftain Weizmann had come to naught. The categoric rejection by the Saudi monarch of the Roosevelt suggestion that he meet with the Zionist leader, according to presidential emissary Harold Hoskins, stemmed from the fact that "during the first year of the war, Dr. Weizmann had impugned his (the King's) character and motives by an attempted bribe of 20 million Pounds Sterling."[30] Apparently the King had been told that the Weizmann promise of payment had been guaranteed by the President himself. And FDR was highly irritated at the use of "his own name as guarantor of payment as there was no basis in fact for doing so."

In 1972 when the letters and cablegrams between the two leaders of the wartime British-American alliance, Churchill and Roosevelt, were made public to researchers at the Hyde Park Memorial Library, the two sides of FDR on the Middle East were confirmed again. The many published versions had suggested that Roosevelt in his meetings and correspondence with the Saudi monarch had urged him to admit more Jews to Palestine, whereas in fact the President had indicated an agreement with Churchill that survivors might well be resettled in the lands from which they were driven, particularly Poland.[31]

Nor did Roosevelt really fool the leading Zionists of his time.[32] In Ben Hecht's autobiography, *Child of the Century,* he even called Roosevelt "an anti-Semite." In 1953 Zionist chieftain Rabbi Emanuel Neumann admitted that the late President's friendship toward Jews had been indisputable, but noted that "for the Zionist cause he had little time and thought."[33] The movement, therefore, directed its principal pressures on the leaders of both parties in Congress, fully realizing that to attack FDR would have been disastrous:

To the Jewish masses in America and throughout the world, Roosevelt loomed as the great friend and champion of their people. How could such a friend oppose or ignore Jewish national aspirations? Not only was it difficult to accept such a painful thought—there was a strong psychological need to reject it. In a tragic hour and a hostile world there simply had to be a champion and protector. If it was not Stalin or Churchill, it had to be Roosevelt. This emotional dependence on Roosevelt was reinforced by eminently practical considerations. He might be re-elected, and he was re-elected for a fourth term. His would be the power to shape the postwar settlement. To cross him, to offend him, to alienate his affection was to court disaster for the Zionist cause.[34]

Roosevelt's sudden death found the Zionists quite prepared to challenge his successor, upon whom they now concentrated their pressure while not abandoning in any way their rewarding efforts on Capitol Hill. Their task with President Truman proved to be immeasurably simpler than with his predecessor, even though the new incumbent in the White House was immediately put on notice by the Department of State of the dangers and complexities of the Palestine question.

In a personal and confidential letter of April 18, 1945, to President Truman, Secretary of State Edward R. Stettinius attempted to put the Palestine problem in true perspective:

It is very likely that efforts will be made by some of the Zionist leaders to obtain from you at an early date some commitments in favor of the Zionist program, which is pressing for unlimited Jewish immigration into Palestine and the establishment there of a Jewish state. As you are aware, the government and people of the United States have every sympathy for the persecuted Jews of Europe and are doing all in their power to relieve their suffering. *The question of Palestine is, however, a highly complex one and involves questions which go far beyond the plight of the Jews in Europe.* . . . There is continual tenseness in the situation in the Near East, largely as a result of the Palestine question, and as we have interests in the area which are vital to the United States, we feel that this whole subject is one that should be handled with the greatest care and *with a view to the long-range interests of the country.* [35] [Italics added.]

The Stettinius letter was followed by a lengthy memorandum of May 1 from Acting Secretary of State Joseph C. Grew, fully briefing the incoming President with the history of the relations between President Roosevelt and the Arab Chiefs of State, including the pledge given to King Ibn Saud of prior consultation on Palestine and assurances "that he would make no move hostile to the Arab people and would not assist the Jews against Arabs."[36]

In the face of the unmistakable views of his predecessor and of clear warnings from the State Department, Truman nevertheless proceeded to lend his support to the establishment of a Jewish state in Palestine. He inched the Zionists closer to their goal by his admixture of the humanitarian problem of refugeeism with the political question of statehood.

III   The Creation of Israel Revisited

A bad beginning makes a bad ending.

—Euripides

With the death of FDR in April 1945, the entire international picture changed overnight, and nowhere more so than in America's dealings with the Jews and the Middle East situation. For all the gutsy qualities that Harry S. Truman possessed, which have now become enshrined in contemporary legend, he had neither the strength nor the vision of FDR.

Much was made of the cocky, confident "man from Independence," but in those early months Truman was extremely insecure, susceptible to whoever got to him. And no one knew this better than the Zionists. In the words of *The American Zionist*, the "going became easier" after Harry Truman took office. The successor to FDR, we are told:

. . . was a far less complex personality than his illustrious predecessor—less adroit and sophisticated, simpler and more straightforward. He accepted the Zionist line reluctantly and under pressure, at first, but having accepted it, he followed through honestly and firmly. In the end he found himself in direct conflict with Britain's Bevin. He did not shrink from the encounter, but, supported by popular opinion, he stuck to his guns and forced the State Department to acquiesce in his pro-Zionist policy.[1]

Indeed, Truman became the pivotal figure in the establishment of Israel. For obvious reasons he has been honored by the Zionists, the Israelists, and the Jews of a whole generation. It was during his administration that the State of Israel came into being. It was under Truman that the U.S. committed itself to the maintenance of that state, and it was Truman's policies that initiated the special and unique U.S.-Israel relationship, which still governs American Middle East policy.

46

The story of Truman and the creation of the State of Israel is a matter of public record now. Yet most Americans have paid little attention to the evident facts. Essential to the maintenance of the status quo in Israel, and to U.S. relations with Israel, is a selective version of the Truman story. Interestingly enough, many individuals, organizations, and elements in the media usually so active in bringing revelations and reappraisals of "inside stories" to the attention of the American public have shown, in this particular instance, no interest in publicizing this episode. Truman committing errors at Potsdam—that is acceptable book material. But Truman making mistakes over Israel is taboo.

Truman's first action on the Palestine question was to reply to messages of March 10 sent by Emir Abdullah, the ruler of Transjordan, to President Roosevelt, which had never been answered. In his letter to the grandfather of King Hussein, the President reiterated the assurances FDR had given just prior to his death to Ibn Saud: "I am glad to renew to you the assurances which you have previously received to the effect that it is the view of this government that no decision shall be taken respecting the basic situation in Palestine without full consultation with both Arabs and Jews."[2] This promise of consultation prior to any decision was repeated by Truman in a separate message to Prime Minister Mahmoud Fahmy Nokrashy of Egypt, who had joined other Arab heads of government in communicating with Roosevelt in March.[3]

On June 16 Undersecretary Joseph C. Grew again cautioned Truman that the Zionists would be exerting pressure anew and would no doubt desire to confer with the President regarding Palestine prior to his meeting with Churchill and Stalin at Potsdam, scheduled for July 16 to August 2, 1945. Grew advised the President to receive any materials with thanks, give assurances that Zionist views would be given careful consideration, and reiterate that the matter of settlement would eventually come before the United Nations Organization.[4]

Meanwhile, the Zionists had stepped up their lobbying campaign directed to the new occupant in the White House, and were warning the State Department that unless a forthright U.S. position was taken, more extreme elements in the Zionist movement would be replacing the moderate leadership of Rabbi Stephen Wise and Dr. Nahum Goldmann. The militant elements were then allegedly led by Rabbi Abba Hillel Silver.

In another meeting, on June 27, Evan Wilson, the Desk Officer for Palestine, reported on a lengthy conversation held at the State Department between his chief, Loy W. Henderson, new head of the Office of

Near Eastern and African Affairs,[5] with several Zionists, including Goldmann and David Ben-Gurion. The future Prime Minister of Israel stated at the meeting:

The Jews were to be allowed to set their own house in order without interference from outside elements. . . . They objected to a situation in which their demands in Palestine, which they regarded as legitimate, would not be met because Lord Killearn [the British Ambassador in Cairo] had to appease some Egyptian pasha. The Jews could not recognize that an Egyptian pasha or a Bedouin sheikh or an Iraqi bey had any right or interest in the Palestine question. The Arabs of Palestine, of course, were legitimately interested in that country and there was no intention of disturbing them or calling their rights into question. Jews and Arabs had lived there in amity for many years and there was no reason why they should not continue to do so, provided the Arabs elsewhere left them alone.[6]

Even as he picked up the British tactic of "divide and rule," Ben-Gurion warned that the pledges made by Allied leaders to the Jews had to be carried out and that his people would fight if necessary to defend those rights. He and his companions expressed complete confidence in their ability to deal with the Arabs, whom he said he knew well, and whom he predicted "would not really put up any kind of a fight." The bedouins of the desert were of course good fighters, but it was well known that they had no interest in the Palestine question. So the leaders of the Arab states would not be successful in rallying their people to support the Arab position in Palestine.

Ben-Gurion and his colleagues made clear from the beginning that reducing the bars on immigration would not answer the problem. The immediate establishment of a Jewish state was the only answer. On July 24, Truman handed Churchill a memorandum in which he stated that the U.S. was interested in the British "finding it possible without delay to take steps to lift the restrictions of the White Paper on Jewish immigration into Palestine."[7] The President asked the Prime Minister to send him his views on the settlement of the Palestine question.

The emphasis was now on immigration to Palestine and, of course, the rescue of the Jews, which came after the fact—the war had ended and there was far less need for this rescue. The matter had obviously become a political ploy.

At Potsdam, Churchill and Clement Attlee, present as Britain's newly designated Prime Minister, discussed with Truman the question of a Jewish national state. But just as Roosevelt had avoided bringing up the matter at Yalta, similarly the new President did not take up the issue with Stalin because, according to Truman, "there was nothing Stalin could do about it." At this time the Soviet position on Palestine was not fixed. While Czechoslovakian Foreign Minister Jan Masaryk had assured Washington that the Soviet Union favored creation of a Jewish state in Palestine, a public address by Middle East expert Professor Evgueny A. Korovin in Moscow had declared that the Soviet Union was supporting the Arabs in Palestine. The President later explained at an August 16 press conference: "It was the American view put forward at Potsdam that we want to let as many Jews into Palestine as it is possible, and that the matter will have to be worked out diplomatically with the British and the Arabs, and it would have to be on a peaceful basis, *as we had no desire to send half a million American soldiers to keep the peace in Palestine.*"[8] (Italics added.)

Truman's avoidance of a discussion with Stalin came under great criticism from Dr. Fadhil Jamali, the Director-General of the Ministry of Foreign Affairs in Baghdad, who protested the President's endorsement of immigration into Palestine of as many Jews as possible, and was irked by the statement that "the Soviet Union could do nothing about it." The Iraqi diplomat pointed out that the U.S.S.R. had an interest in the immigration problem if it was to be considered of an international nature; if it was a problem of a domestic nature, then neither the U.S. nor the U.S.S.R. had any interest.

The President's approach to the subject of immigration at the Potsdam Conference won him warm congratulations in a telegram from Rabbi Wise, who reiterated the view that no large military forces would be "especially required in Palestine to keep the Arabs in check in case it should be decided to permit unlimited Jewish immigration." But a telegram of August 22 from Chargé d'Affaires Moose in Baghdad to the Secretary of State pointed out that every time the question of Palestine—i.e., Zionism—was brought up, there were local disturbances, and that the Arabs all stood together on this important subject.[9]

The position of the State Department at this time was outlined in a lengthy, detailed, and meticulously written memorandum by Henderson to the Secretary on August 24 in which he discussed four possible plans for Palestine: (1) an independent Jewish commonwealth, (2) an independent Arab state, (3) partition under the trusteeship system, and (4) proposed trusteeship agreement for Palestine. This paper ruled out the first possibility, creation of a Jewish commonwealth, as dangerous to the interests of the U.S., a violation of the wishes of a large majority of the local inhabitants, and "jeopardizing American economic interests including our oil interests in Saudi Arabia and other Arab countries."[10]

The position preferred by this Foreign Service officer was a trusteeship agreement to be reached by Britain, the U.S., and the Soviet Union—and, if possible, France—under which Palestine would be given special status as an international territory with Great Britain as the administering authority.[11] Such a plan, it was recognized, would be opposed by both the Arabs and the Jews, but with less intensity than any of the other alternatives.

In the meantime, the end of World War II in Europe had created a new problem: the epitome of distress of the displaced person. These refugees from Hitler's gas chambers were actually, not theoretically, homeless. They came from many lands: Austria, Germany, Poland, Hungary, Rumania, the Baltic countries. They were of all faiths: about 500,000 Catholics, 100,000 Protestants, and 226,000 Jews.[12] Of these Jews, some 100,000 were in the assembly camps of Germany, Austria, and Italy; 50,000 were undetained in the United Kingdom; 12,000 were in Sweden and 10,500 in Switzerland; the rest were scattered over the Continent.

On August 31 Truman wrote Prime Minister Attlee that issuance of 100,000 certificates of immigration to Palestine would help alleviate the refugee situation. He enclosed a copy of the very moving report by the President's special representative, Earl G. Harrison, on the conditions in the refugee internment camps in Central Europe. This was one of the most persuasive documents used by the Zionists in gaining the support of the President and other Americans for the immediate evacuation of the Jews in the camps to Palestine.

The Truman top-secret communication, handed by Secretary of State James Byrnes to Attlee in London, fell into the hands of Iowa's former Senator Guy Gillette, an officer of the American League for a Free Palestine, and was made public three days later. Immediately U.S. radio and newspaper reports picked up the Truman request for the admission of further Jews into Palestine. In the Middle East a great howl was raised. The Arab countries, particularly Saudi Arabia, alleged that this major step, affecting Palestine so importantly, had been taken without the promised consultation assured by President Roosevelt in person in letters to King Ibn Saud and repeated by him to other Arab chiefs of state, and later reiterated by President Truman to Emir Abdullah and to Prime Minister Nokrashy.

In the ensuing uproar against the U.S. for prodding Britain into admitting 100,000 immigrants into Palestine, Truman was attacked for his "generosity at the expense of the Arabs." He was further assailed for allegedly stating at a press conference that a search of the FDR papers had failed to discover any record of the pledge made by the late President to King Ibn Saud regarding prior consultation over Palestine. For this reason the Saudi Arabian monarch cabled Truman and proposed to publish conversations and a memorandum of the conversation held with FDR aboard the U.S.S. *Quincy* on February 9, 1945, as well as the later controversial letter of April 8, together with the King's original letter to FDR that had prompted the presidential response.

The Ministers (they were not as yet accorded the rank of Ambassador) of the four Arab governments then accredited to Washington— Egypt, Iraq, Syria, and Lebanon—registered an angry complaint to Undersecretary Dean Acheson on the failure of the United States government to live up to its promises. The Zionists joined in protesting the latest Truman suggestion on Jewish immigration, claiming they, too, had not been consulted. They feared that the administration was trying to kill the possibilities of a Jewish state by granting 100,000 Jewish visas.

The uproar in Arab countries over the U.S. immigration proposal and the alleged failure to consult with the Arabs, followed by the release of the FDR-Ibn Saud and the parallel FDR-Regent of Iraq letters, led the American Ministers in Arab countries to cable warnings to the Department of State of "severe blows to American prestige and threats to vital U.S. interests from a hostile Arab world."[13] Added to the seriousness of the Truman proposal was the estimate of the War Department that it would take as many as 400,000 soldiers, half of whom would probably have to come from the U.S., to maintain order if Palestine was opened to Jewish immigration.

In reply to the Truman letter of August 31, British Ambassador in Washington Lord Halifax, in a memorandum of October 29, personally handed to Secretary Byrnes and in the ensuing conversation, set forth Attlee's suggestion for the urgent establishment of a joint Anglo-American Committee of Inquiry[14] to examine the question of Jewish immigration to Palestine and elsewhere.[15] Lord Halifax took extreme exception to the conclusions reached in the Harrison report that "Jews [in Europe] are at present living under worse conditions than any other victims of the persecution," and insisted that the committee should explore the possibilities of Jewish emigration to countries other than Palestine.[16] The British felt it was most important that

"Jews should be enabled to play an active part in building up the life of the countries from which they came in common with other nationals of these countries."[17]

Faced with the deteriorating position in the Holy Land as the fighting between Arabs and Jews increased, Foreign Minister Ernest Bevin instructed his Washington emissary to push for urgent action, suggesting October 25, six days later, for the joint U.S.-U.K. announcement of the establishment of the Anglo-American Committee. This was the immediate U.S. reaction to the British suggestion:

LORD HALIFAX: The last day Parliament meets in that week you see. They don't want to miss another weekend. That would be their thought.

BYRNES: Quite frankly, I am thinking of the New York City elections the following Tuesday, and when this is submitted to the President he has to think about that.

LORD HALIFAX: Would this not be rather good?

BYRNES: I am wondering whether it would or not. I have not followed it, but I know that other people do. I know it has a lot to do with that election and I am going to read about it with much interest.

LORD HALIFAX: Is it the following Tuesday—the New York election?

BYRNES: Yes. We will have to think that one over. I am thinking of the alternative. The alternative is that for the present nothing would be done. I had thought that when Mr. Attlee came over here, there would be a discussion by the President and Mr. Attlee. That, however, will be some weeks. That date is uncertain.[18]

The British Ambassador also pointed out "that the Zionists are using every possible form of intimidation to stop Jews from leaving Palestine to go back to Europe and play their part in its reconstruction."[19] In a further conversation with Byrnes three days later, he again addressed himself to the urgency of convening the Anglo-American Committee.

On his part, Byrnes did not hide the fact from Lord Halifax that he had been subjected to intensive and continuing Zionist pressures. Both Eugene Meyer, the editor and publisher of the *Washington Post*,[20] and Administrative Assistant to the President David K. Niles[21] had thrust themselves on him that morning.[22]

While the Washington-London impasse continued, the situation in the Middle East worsened. A concentration of bomb outrages, in which many were killed and wounded and all communications in Palestine came to a halt, was carried out throughout the mandate territory by 3,000 Jews under the combined operations of the Irgun, the Stern Gang, and the Haganah. November 5 found the British and Americans still fighting over the terms of reference. Pressures accounted for the Truman adamancy, for he could not alter his stand lest he be interpreted as seeking homes for Jewish refugees other than in Palestine. Two days later Secretary Byrnes indicated to Lord Halifax that the proposed British changes would be "construed as turning the focus of attention away from Palestine."[23]

At this time there were additional complications. A strong memorandum from the Arab League, submitted to the Department of State through its representatives in the Arab countries, noted that the proportion of Jews over the preceding twenty years had decreased from ten-to-one to two-to-one, and called upon the British Mandatory Power to carry out its previous pledge to stop all immigration to Palestine "after five years of the issue of the White Paper of 1939." The statement declared that the Truman suggestion to permit 100,000 Jews to enter was a violation of both the 1939 White Paper pledge and British and U.S. government promises "that they shall not take decisions on resolutions regarding immigration or settling of the Palestine problem without full consultation and agreement with Arab states."[24]

In Saudi Arabia Emir Faisal asked U.S. Minister William Eddy whether U.S. promises to seek no change in the basic situation in Palestine without prior consultation with Arabs meant without prior "agreement" of Arabs.[25] The wily Foreign Minister in his talk with Eddy gave his first indications of his deep understanding of the international political scene and expressed deep concern for U.S.-Saudi Arabian relations:

I assure you that the British were telling us officially that they favor the Arab case against Zionism, but that they are being pushed by you into pro-Zionist moves. The very real admiration and respect which all Arabs held for America is evaporating rapidly and may soon disappear altogether, along with our many mutual interests and cooperation.

We Arabs would rather starve or die in battle than see our lands and people devoured by the Zionists, as you would do if we were giving them one of *your* states for a nation. [Italics added.] Do not think we would yield to Zionism in the hope of survival or property elsewhere. If it develops that the USA and the British will aid the Zionists against our will and to our destruction, we shall fight Zionism to the last man. In the meantime, don't forget that the British are blaming the initiative on the Americans.[26]

A compromise was finally reached by the American and British governments as to terminology and the terms of reference for the Anglo-American Committee. Announcements of the forthcoming inquiry were made by Foreign Minister Bevin in the Commons and by Truman in Washington on November 13. The British and American members of the committee were announced simultaneously in London and Washington on December 10. Zionists in London and New York attacked the news simultaneously, calling it a fresh betrayal to which they would never submit.[27] Riots followed in Tel Aviv. The Anglo-American Committee of Inquiry on Palestine, with six American and six British members, was empowered "to examine political, economic and social conditions in Palestine as they bear upon the problem of Jewish immigration and settlement therein"[28] and "to examine the position of European Jews" in terms of estimating the possible migration to Palestine or elsewhere outside of Europe.

Among the committee members were U.S. Federal Judge Joseph C. Hutcheson, Chairman; Dr. Frank Aydelotte, Director of the Institute of Advanced Studies at Princeton; former American Ambassador to Italy William Phillips; attorney Bartley C. Crum; James G. McDonald (later to be the first American Ambassador to Israel); and R. H. S. Crossman, prominent Laborite member of Parliament.[29] The first meeting was held in Washington early in January 1946. Representatives of Jewish organizations as well as those who expressed the Christian and the Arab viewpoints were heard. Sessions were resumed in London later that month, and several subcommittees carried on investigations in various countries of Europe. The full committee held further sessions in Egypt, and subcommittees also visited the capitals of Syria, Lebanon, Iraq, Saudi Arabia, and Jordan. These exhaustive deliberations were completed in Switzerland. A report, unanimously signed at Lausanne, was made public in London and in Washington on April 30, 1946.[30]

The principal recommendation (No. 2 in the committee report) called for immediate issuance of entrance certificates into Palestine for 100,000 Jews "who had been the victims of Nazi and Fascist persecution." Had these 100,000 admissions actually been granted, the overwhelming majority of Jewish displaced persons whose situation required immediate action would have been saved and the revolting D.P. centers could soon have been closed. The report went on to state: "Jew shall not dominate Arab, and Arab shall not dominate Jew in Palestine. . . . Palestine is a Holy Land, sacred to Christian, to Jew and to Moslem alike, and because it is a Holy Land, Palestine is not, and can never become a land which any race or religion can justly claim as its very own."[31]

Two of the six American members, James G. McDonald and Bartley Crum, who later became ardent advocates of Jewish statehood, joined another political Zionist-to-be, British member R. H. S. Crossman, in unequivocably expressing the view that while

. . . the Jews have a historic connection with the country, they embodied but a minority of the population. . . . Palestine is not and can never be a purely Jewish land. It lies at the crossroads of the Arab world, its Arab population, descended from the long-time inhabitants of the area, rightly looks upon Palestine as their homeland. It is therefore neither just nor practicable that Palestine should become either an Arab state in which an Arab majority would control the destiny of a Jewish minority, or a Jewish state in which a Jewish majority would control that of an Arab minority.

This section of the committee's report was Recommendation No. 3, entitled "Principles of Government: No Arab, No Jewish State."[32] Palestine's government, as envisioned by the members of this committee, was ultimately to be placed under international guarantees in order to protect and preserve the interests òf Christiandom and of the Muslim and Jewish faiths alike, and to "accord to the inhabitants, as a whole, the fullest measure of self-government."

The committee found that Palestine alone could never meet Jewish emigration needs and that the U.S. and Britain, in association with other countries, must endeavor to find new homes for displaced persons.

While willing to endorse the committee's plea for the admission of 100,000 Jews to Palestine, Organized Jewry opened fire on the report's other nine recommendations, of which the acceptable one was an integral part. The American Zionists in New York, the British Zionists in London, and the Jewish Agency in Jerusalem insisted, as they had at the committee's hearings, on nothing less than Jewish statehood in accordance with the Biltmore Program adopted in New York four years earlier at the conclave of Jewish organizations in New York's famed hotel.

The Morrison-Grady Plan,[33] drawn up by representatives of the Secretaries of State, Treasury, and War from the U.S. and their British counterparts, recommended a federal state for Palestine with separate Jewish and Arab cantons, a district of Jerusalem and a district of the Negev. The question of immediate Jewish immigration was made conditional upon Arab acceptance. The Zionists screamed, "Sellout." Paul Fitzpatrick, New York State Democratic Committee Chairman, wired Truman this warning: "If this plan goes into effect, it would be useless for the Democrats to nominate a state ticket for the election this Fall.

I say this without reservation and am certain that my statement can be substantiated."[34]

In early 1947 a last British attempt to conciliate the Arab and Zionist positions called for admission into Palestine of 4,000 Jews per month for two years, and subsequent admissions depending on the future absorptive capacity of the country. This second offer for the rescue of almost 100,000 Jews was also spurned. The Jewish Agency denounced it as incompatible with Jewish rights to immigration, settlement, and ultimate statehood.

Meantime, on December 22, 1945, Truman had directed the Secretaries of State and War, and certain other federal authorities, to speed in every possible way the granting of visas and to "facilitate full immigration to the United States under existing quota laws." Congress, which had often shown its vulnerability to Jewish pressure groups, did not implement the President's request regarding the application of unused quotas to uprooted Europeans. Finally a bill was introduced by Congressman William G. Stratton in the so-called "Do-Nothing" 80th Republican Congress, in 1947, to admit displaced persons "in a number equivalent to a part of the total quota numbers unused during the war years."[35] Under the Stratton bill up to 400,000 displaced persons of all faiths would have been permitted into the U.S.

The hearings on this legislation (HR 2910) lasted eleven days and covered 693 pages of testimony. There were exactly eleven pages of testimony given by Jewish organizations, who seemed profoundly uninterested. In 1944 when the House Foreign Affairs Committee was considering the Wright-Compton resolution calling for establishment of a Jewish commonwealth, scarcely a Zionist organization did not testify, send telegraphed messages, or have some congressman appear in their behalf. In support of the Wright-Compton resolution, 500 pages of testimony were produced in four days, the vast bulk by Zionists and their allies.

Yet on the Stratton bill, which would have opened America's doors to 400,000 displaced persons, the powerful Zionist Washington lobby, otherwise most articulate, was virtually silent. Only one witness appeared for all the major Jewish organizations—Senator Herbert Lehman, then ex-Governor of New York. In addition to Lehman's statement, there was a resolution from the Jewish Community Councils of Washington Heights and Inwood, and the testimony of the National Commander of the Jewish War Veterans. Not a single word was volunteered in behalf of displaced persons by any of the Zionist organizations that at that moment were recruiting members and soliciting funds "to alleviate human suffering."

During a meeting at the Shoreham Hotel in Washington, Congressman Stratton expressed his surprise at the lack of support from certain organizations that normally ought to have been most active in liberalizing the immigration law. Obviously the Illinois Representative had never heard the President of the Zionist Organization of America exhort his membership:

I am happy that our movement has finally veered around to the point where we are all, or nearly all, talking about a Jewish state. That was always classical Zionism. . . . But I ask . . . are we again, in moments of desperation, going to confuse Zionism with refugeeism, which is likely to defeat Zionism? . . . Zionism is not a refugee movement. It is not a product of the second World War, nor of the first. Were there no displaced Jews in Europe, and were there free opportunities for Jewish immigration in other parts of the world at this time, Zionism would still be an imperative necessity.[36]

The generous admission of Jewish displaced persons to the U.S. and to other countries would have eradicated the necessity for a "Jewish state." Yet the human flotsam in former concentration camps impressed the Zionists only in two respects: as manpower and as justification for Jewish statehood.

This is what a Yiddish paper had to say on the distressing subject:

By pressing for an exodus of Jews from Europe; by insisting that Jewish D.P.'s do not wish to go to any country outside of Israel; by not participating in the negotiations on behalf of the D.P.'s; and by refraining from a campaign of their own—by all this they [the Zionists] certainly did not help to open the gates of America for Jews. In fact, they sacrificed the interests of living people—their brothers and sisters who went through a world of pain—to the politics of their own movement."[37]

In Europe a well-organized movement, supported by large financial contributions from Zionist sources, had set up "the underground railway to Palestine." Jews from all over Europe were moved down to ports on the Mediterranean. There they were placed on ships, often overcrowded and unseaworthy, under conditions of utmost privation and squalor. A very large proportion of this human freight was brought from countries of Communist-dominated Eastern Europe. For indeed, the Kremlin had begun to play its Middle East game of sowing unrest in the Arab world and pushing Britain out.

To most Americans, however, the struggle in Palestine was merely a drama of refugees fighting for homes, this time against their new English oppressors. When the British terminated all entry into Palestine, anti-British feelings mounted in the U.S. There was no movie house in America that did not carry a newsreel shot of the distraught

Jewish faces aboard the SS Exodus '47, which was intercepted by the British and its passengers prevented from illegally entering the Holy Land.

Organized American Jewry exerted utmost pressure on public opinion and politicians. This, they reminded everyone, was the same kind of war the American Revolutionists had waged against the very same imperialist power. The tactics of the British in Palestine were compared with those used for a long time against Ireland's fighters for freedom. The blowing up of the King David Hotel in Jerusalem by the Irgun Zvai Leumi and the mob hanging of two British sergeants at Nathanya elicited from Hollywood's Ben Hecht: "Every time you let go with your guns at the British betrayers of your homeland, the Jews of America make a little holiday in their hearts."

It was perhaps unfortunate that throughout this trying period Britain's Foreign Minister was Ernest Bevin. This onetime Welsh miner's temperament was hardly suited to the task of reconciling two such intransigent forces as the Arabs and the Zionists. Nor was he able to demonstrate, particularly in the U.S., just how Britain was being squeezed between two flaring nationalisms. At Bournemouth before a Labor party gathering in 1946, Bevin charged that the U.S. was pressing Britain to allow more Jews into Palestine—because we did not want to allow them into America. While he meant to attack the political exploitation of human suffering, he unwittingly brought down upon himself the totally unjustified charge of being anti-Semitic. His quick temper constantly handicapped his efforts to separate the problem of displaced European Jewry from the political question of Palestine.

By early 1947 events in Palestine clearly demanded international intervention. Zionists were more than ever insisting on a Jewish majority in Palestine in order to secure a Jewish commonwealth. The British were resisting all efforts to force them into a new policy. The Arabs, fighting both the British and the Jews, were demanding an independent Palestinian state.

Audible public opinion in the U.S. supported illegal immigration. Such organizations as the American League for a Free Palestine, the Hebrew Committee for National Liberation, and the Political Action Committee for Palestine were each raising funds for their own Palestinian terrorist group. Their competitive advertisements defended terrorism and stressed the tax exemptability of contributions for terrorist organizations. Congressman Joseph C. Baldwin, scion of one of New York's oldest families and public relations adviser to the Irgun Zvai Leumi, condoned the flogging of four British soldiers and assured

Menachem Begin, Irgun leader (now Israel's Prime Minister), that he, Baldwin, would do everything to make Begin's position clear in this country.

And then the British decided to give up the Palestine ghost. The Anglo-Arab Conferences, which had started in September 1946 and had adjourned to January 1947, proved a total failure, as did the so-called Bevin Plan which, revising the earlier Morrison-Grady Plan, suggested semiautonomous Arab and Jewish cantons for a five-year period and the admission into Palestine of 100,000 displaced persons. Both parties vehemently objected, whereupon Britain announced it was not her intention to enforce any plan. At the same time the Zionist Jewish Agency proclaimed its refusal to cooperate with Mandatory authorities in any action against terrorists.

Britain felt there was nothing left to do but to place the controversy before the U.N. A special session of the General Assembly was called by Secretary-General Trygve Lie.

Submitting the dispute to international adjudication, Bevin let loose with a characteristic barrage of words. He accused American politicians of wrecking any chance for an amicable solution of the Palestine problem and, quite undiplomatically, pointed the finger at the White House when he explained to the House of Commons:

I did reach a stage, however, in meeting the Jews separately . . . when things looked more hopeful. There was a feeling . . . when they left me in the Foreign Office that day, that I had the right approach at last. I went back to the Paris Peace Conference, and the next day . . .—I believe it was a special day of the Jewish religion—my right honourable friend, the Prime Minister, telephoned me at midnight and told me that the President of the United States was going to issue another statement on the hundred thousand. I think the country and the world ought to know about this. . . .[38]

Bevin was referring to the 1946 Day of Atonement plea of President Truman to admit 100,000 refugees. The Paris Peace Conference was then in session, and Bevin implored Secretary Byrnes to intercede with Truman not to issue a statement that might upset current delicate negotiations. Whereupon the Secretary of State told him that "if the President did not issue a statement, a competitive statement would be issued by Dewey." The New York Governor, who was the Republican standard-bearer in 1944 and 1948, was leading the fight for a G.O.P. Congress.

In the *New York Times* of October 7, 1946, political columnist James Reston disclosed that several administration advisers had opposed the Truman statement because Britain was alleged to be on the verge of reaching a truce with the Zionists. Attlee himself had asked the President to withhold the statement, but Truman refused to heed the British request. It was believed that Mead and Lehman, the Democratic candidates for Governor and Senator in New York, would be helped by the Truman declaration. On October 6 New York Governor Thomas E. Dewey outbid Truman by declaring the British would admit "not 100,000 but several hundred thousand Jews." Ohio's Senator Robert A. Taft, Dewey's conservative rival in the Republican party, also joined in the fun by raising the ante.

Whether the British talks with the Zionists would have been successful if domestic American politics had not interfered is questionable. But the whole episode was extremely characteristic of the political pattern the U.S. government has inevitably followed whenever Israel and the Middle East are involved.

The Arabs were as clearly inept in propaganda techniques as the Jewish Nationalists were masters. No publicity was given to King Ibn Saud's protest to the President that the Yom Kippur declaration on Jewish immigration was a violation of the promised consultation "whenever the basic situation in Palestine" was involved.[39] But American national politics being what they are, the chances of impressing this country with the Arab world's point of view were at best slim: There is a rather negligible Arab vote in the U.S. Whatever the rights of Palestine's indigenous inhabitants may have been, these were completely dismissed, as were the ineffectual murmurings of anti-Zionist Jews, in the worldwide propaganda battle between the Mandatory administration and the Jewish Agency.

The British were determined to maintain law and order pending the U.N. decision over the ultimate fate of the Holy Land. The Zionists continued to present their power play to the confused world in terms of humanitarianism. Continuous clashes between wretched would-be immigrants and the armed British authorities were the only issue really discussed in the American press. The S.S. *Abril,* Ben Hecht's boat, crowded with refugees, was seized by the British; three British were killed and several were injured in an effort "to rescue or capture" (as the U.S. press reported) refugees who plunged into the sea. Terrorists blew up the Iraq Petroleum Pipeline. The Irgun declared open warfare. Dov Gruner and three other terrorists who had attacked a Palestine police station were hanged. The Stern Gang promised retaliation.

During all that time the only contribution of the U.S. government was words. There was much talk about displaced persons and human suffering, but no real effort to bring them into the U.S. Everybody knew, and said, what Britain should or should not do. Every politician hurried to get in on the act, to exploit "humanitarianism" for votes. Everybody favored unlimited immigration to the Holy Land. Eleanor Roosevelt urged a luncheon meeting of the Women's Division of the United Jewish Appeal to speak out. "The time has come," she said, "when we have to stand up and be counted. You have not told Congress so they would hear one unmistakable voice."

Organized Jewry hardly needed such a reminder. Day in and day out the press carried headlines such as "The American Jewish Congress demands——," "Senator Lehman Again Renews His Plea to Open Up Palestine," "Congressman Javits of Manhattan Suggests a Congressional Junket to Palestine to Foster Establishment of a Jewish Commonwealth." The British Empire building in Rockefeller Center in New York was picketed; the city's Mayor William O'Dwyer, not yet a refugee in Mexico, excoriated the British before the National Council of Young Israel. Zionists flooded the capital with letters trying to link Palestine with aid to Greece and Turkey. "Tell the British," some letters said, "there will be no aid for the British policy in Greece and Turkey unless they follow the United States lead on Palestine."

The State and War Departments, it is true, were constantly cautioning the White House and Congress that an irresponsible vote-chasing policy for Palestine might irreparably damage the American position in one of the world's most strategic areas. But politicians following the scent of "blocs" are beyond the reach of reason, and both parties were convinced that their eloquent support of statehood for Israel was a prerequisite for conquest of pivotal states. There was, in fact, no need for the Zionists to refute the solemn warnings that were coming from War and State. All the Zionists had to do was make sure the politicians remained hypnotized by "the Jewish vote." Perhaps for the first time in history, a decisive battle could indeed be won with the tools of propaganda.

It is to the credit of the Zionists' acumen that they grasped their chance. But it is perhaps less to the credit of America's non-Zionist Jewry that it permitted its self-appointed Zionist leaders to bet the future of American Judaism on the roulette of power politics.

And so it was that on April 28, 1947, the Special Session of the General Assembly of the United Nations convened in New York to consider Palestine. The Zionists had succeeded in forcing the issue into a forum where they could control events independent of the Palestinians and the Arabs in general. What happened in the next

months led to the fateful U.N. vote on November 29, 1947, partitioning Palestine.

Both the Truman *Memoirs* and the Margaret Truman biography of
her father[40] are very clear and unambiguous in detailing the pressures
that forced the U.S. to whip other U.N. members into line to assure
passage of the partition resolution.[41] In his own *Memoirs,* the man from
Independence is the number-one witness to the tremendous Zionist
coercion:

The facts were that not only were there pressure movements around the
United Nations unlike anything that had been seen there before, but the White
House too was subjected to a constant barrage. I do not think I ever had as
much pressure and propaganda aimed at the White House as I had in this
instance. The persistence of a few of the extreme Zionist leaders—actuated by
political motives and engaging in political threats—disturbed and annoyed
me. Some were even suggesting that we pressure sovereign nations into favorable votes in the General Assembly. I have never approved of the practice of
the strong imposing their will on the weak whether among men or among
nations.[42]

Truman's daughter in her book fell victim to the same general
misconception to which nearly every writer and even every historian
on the subject has been prey: namely, that the term "national home,"
not used previously in diplomatic parlance, nor since, was equivalent
to "national state." She thus construed the Anglo-American Committee report as supporting Jewish sovereignty. She also added importantly to her father's story of Zionist pressures. Truman's mother, for
example, had sent the White House a letter she received from "a
Jewish friend of a friend" requesting her to influence the President to
have the Palestine problem put on the agenda of a conference then
going on in London. The President, daughter Margaret related, "came
very close to blowing up at this attempt to involve his mother in
international politics."

There was also a very significant letter of December 2, 1947, to
Henry Morgenthau, Jr., who had served as Secretary of the Treasury
under Roosevelt, in which Truman wrote:

I wish you would caution all your friends who are interested in the welfare of
the Jews in Palestine that now is the time for restraint and caution in an
approach to the situation in the future that will allow a peaceful settlement.
*The vote in the U.N. is only the beginning, and the Jews must now display tolerance and
consideration for the other people in Palestine with whom they will necessarily have to be
neighbors.*[43] [Emphasis added.]

These later two references to the President's growing impatience with Zionists, which did not appear in the New York *Daily News* summary[44] of the biography, were published, for example, by the upstate Binghamton (N.Y.) *Press*[45] and elsewhere where Zionists did not wield so strong an axe and the Jewish readership did not mean so much.

Also mindful of potential readers, the Truman biography tried to convey the impression that the pressure on the White House came equally from both Zionist and anti-Zionist Jews. President Truman's meetings with Rabbis Stephen S. Wise and Abba Hillel Silver of the Zionist Emergency Committee were alleged to have been balanced by those with certain "anti-Zionists," including Joseph Proskauer and Jacob Blaustein of the American Jewish Committee (AJC), who "called to tell Dad that not all Jews supported the Zionist program." The most that could ever be said about the AJC was that its membership originally included non-Zionists and a very few anti-Zionists. The latter soon became convinced by their colleagues that to oppose the creation of the State of Israel was heretic, and the potent AJC became, as it has been since, an all-out supporter of Israel while proclaiming not to be Zionist. The only militant anti-Zionist group at the time, the American Council for Judaism, was denied permission to see the President.

As a matter of fact, if Judge Proskauer ever did so caution the President as to the views of certain non-Zionist and anti-Zionist Jews, he himself soon was singing another song. For the judge was not only one of those who helped put the squeeze on smaller U.N. members when the critical 1947 vote at the General Assembly was nearing, but it was he who insisted shortly thereafter that the U.S. sell arms to the Haganah, the military arm of the Jewish Agency, for "those who are defending the decision of the United Nations."

In its reaction to the Margaret Truman book, the Zionist organ *Near East Report* indicated just how supersensitive Zionists were, twenty-five years later, to the charge of political pressures. Editor I. L. Kenen claimed that such accounts, including Truman's expression of resentment, were grossly exaggerated: "It is true that Zionists worked hard to win American support, but in this campaign they were joined by a great majority of the American people."[46] Kenen claimed that there had been "a multitude of diverse pressures" at work and that the President had been in a much more significant conflict at the time with his own Department of State over Palestine. According to him, after opting in 1946 for partition, these counterpressures forced Truman into silence in 1947, leading to an agreement that the U.S. delegation at the U.N. "would reserve its position from campaigning with other delegations."

There were wide differences between the President and the Department of State as to what course of action would best protect the national interests of the country, and the Truman Cabinet itself was divided on this. Defense Secretary James Forrestal bitterly opposed partitioning Palestine because of the Arab antagonism that would be aroused. The Secretary's military advisers were convinced that withdrawal of the British from Palestine would result in serious trouble in the area, which could only help the Soviet Union. His chief, President Truman, who survived Forrestal by some twenty-two years, lived to see the emergence of the Soviet Union for the first time as a Mediterranean power and the area turned into a caldron of regional war and hatred, ever-threatening global conflict, and the diminishing American position in a part of the world that is deciding the energy consumption to be enjoyed by his daughter and his grandchildren.

Truman's Secretary of State, George Marshall, was less than enthusiastic regarding the U.S. position on partition. Hence, when recognition of Israel was under consideration in May 1948, Marshall was not trusted by the President with the decision-making. In fact, Truman had problems with all his Secretaries of State on this single issue. James Byrnes, who had held the post prior to Marshall, had, in his own words to Forrestal, "disassociated himself from President Truman's decision in 1946 to turn down the Grady report which had recommended either a federated state for Palestine, or a single Arabian state,"[47] but not an exclusively Zionist Jewish state.

In 1969, twenty years after succeeding Marshall as Secretary of State, Dean Acheson in his book *Present at the Creation: My Years at the State Department* bared for the first time his own opposition to establishment of the Israeli state in what he called "Arab Palestine." The differences over the Palestine question marked his only major disagreement with his chief, President Truman. Here is how Acheson described it:

I did not share the President's views on the Palestine solution to the pressing and desperate plight of great numbers of displaced Jews in Eastern Europe. The numbers that could be absorbed by Arab Palestine without creating a grave problem would be inadequate, and to transform the country into a Jewish state capable of receiving a million or more immigrants would vastly exacerbate the political problem and imperil not only American but all Western interests in the Near East. From Justice Brandeis, whom I revered, and Felix Frankfurter, my intimate friend, I had learned to understand, but not to share, the mystical emotion of the Jews to return to Palestine and end the Diaspora. In urging Zionism as an American Government policy, they had allowed, so I thought, their emotion to obscure the totality of American interests.[48]

While many of those closest to the President were either opposed to or unenthusiastically going along with his design for Palestine, those outside the government were exercising the pressures, the existence of which apologists today deny. The Zionists were reaching boldly into the chancelleries of foreign countries. "Operation Partition" was executed by a strategy board of immense international influence; the three American masterminds were New York's Judge Joseph Proskauer, Washington economist Robert Nathan, and White House Assistant "for minority affairs" David Niles.

These three, speaking to foreign governments and diplomats always as "mere private citizens," were men of impressively good connections in public affairs. Robert Nathan, for instance, knew precisely how to weaken Liberia's objections to partition. The Liberian delegate was simply told that Nathan would go after his good friend, Edward R. Stettinius, Truman's first Secretary of State, who at that time was attending to his enormous business interests in Liberia. The Liberian diplomat considered this attempted intimidation and so reported to the Department of State. In the final moment, however, by some strange coincidence, Liberia's vote was cast in favor of partition. And informed hints to various South American delegates that their vote for partition would greatly increase the chances of a Pan-American Road project, then under consideration, greatly improved Zionist traffic in the General Assembly.

Eleanor Roosevelt, too, inexhaustibly worked on the many friends she had among the foreign delegates at the U.N., and she was incessantly prodding her husband's heir to put pressure on the State Department, whose officers were properly limiting their efforts to peaceful debates with foreign delegates.

When partition prospects looked particularly grim, Bernard Baruch was prevailed upon to talk with the French, who could not afford to lose interim Marshall Plan aid. Through former Ambassador William Bullitt, the adviser to Presidents passed a message in a similar vein to the Chinese Ambassador in Washington.[49] Other important Americans "talked" to countries such as Haiti, Ethiopia, the Philippines, Paraguay, and Luxembourg, all dependent on the U.S. Drew Pearson, an old friend of the Zionists, told in his "Merry-Go-Round" column how Adolph Berle, legal adviser to the Haitian government, "talked" on the phone to Haiti's President, and how Harvey Firestone, owner of vast rubber plantations in Liberia, "talked" with that government.

In discussing the partition vote at the Cabinet luncheon on December 1, 1947, Undersecretary of State Robert Lovett said that "never in his life had he been subjected to as much pressure as he had in three days beginning Thursday morning and ending Saturday night. Herbert Bayard Swope and Robert Nathan were among those who had importuned him."[50] The Firestone Tire and Rubber Company, according to Lovett, made use of its concession in Liberia and had transmitted "a message to their representative there, directing him to bring pressure on the Liberian Government to vote in favor of partition."[51] Lovett remarked that Jewish zeal was so intense that it "almost resulted in defeating the objectives" sought.[52]

Bribes as well as threats had been used. One Latin American delegate had changed his vote to support partition in return for $75,-000 in cash and another, a Costa Rican, declined a $45,000 bribe but eventually voted for partition in accordance with orders from his Government.[53]

And no pressure was sadder, or more cynical, than that put on the Philippines. War hero and head of the delegation, General Carlos Romulo, left the U.S. for Manila shortly after delivering a fiery speech against partition on the floor of the General Assembly. Ambassador Elizalde had spoken by telephone to President Manuel Roxas and told him of the many pressures to which Romulo and the delegation had been subjected. The Ambassador's own view was that although partition was not a wise move, the U.S. was determined to see it happen and it would be foolish to vote against a policy so ardently desired by the U.S. Administration at a time when seven bills were pending in the U.S. Congress in which the islands had a tremendous stake. The Ambassador and President Roxas agreed that the Philippines must not risk antagonizing the U.S. when support could be so easily gained by a proper vote on Palestine. This was all subsequently reported in a lengthy cable from the U.S. Ambassador in Manila to the State Department.

A joint telegram from twenty-six pro-Zionist U.S. Senators, drafted by New York's Robert F. Wagner, was particularly important in changing the Philippine vote. The senatorial telegram, sent a few days before the decisive ballot to twelve other U.N. delegations, changed four votes to yes and seven votes from nay to abstention. Only Greece, despite pressures from prominent Greek-American businessmen, including film mogul Spyros Skouras, largely because of her traditional friendship with Egypt, risked antagonizing the U.S. Senate and stuck to no.

Sir Muhammed Zafrullah Khan, at the time Pakistani Foreign Minister, expressed the feelings of so many of his fellow U.N. delegates when he declared in a post-vote statement:

We entertain no sense of grievance against those of our friends and fellow representatives who have been compelled under heavy pressure to change sides and to cast their votes in support of a proposal the justice and fairness of which do not commend themselves to them. Our feeling for them is one of sympathy that they should have been placed in a position of such embarrassment between their judgment and conscience, on the one side, and the pressure to which they and their Governments were being subjected, on the other.[54]

It is true Truman had expressed the wish that the U.S. delegation at the U.N. not use threats or improper pressure of any kind on other delegations. As Undersecretary Lovett expressed it, "We were willing to vote for that partition report only because it was a majority report." But unofficial representatives in the name of the U.S. government had nevertheless exerted tremendous pressures.

Dean Rusk, then Director of the State Department's Office of United Nations Affairs, admitted to a meeting of representatives of national organizations a few months after the partition vote that, while the U.S. "never exerted pressure on countries of the U.N. in behalf of one side or another, certain unauthorized officials and private persons violated propriety and went beyond the law" to exert the needed squeeze. As a result, Rusk pointed out, partition was "construed as an American plan" in the eyes of certain countries, and the decision was robbed of whatever moral force it might otherwise have had.

In explaining the U.S. position to King Farouk of Egypt and to King Ibn Saud, the U.S. Ambassadors in Cairo and Jeddah were instructed in messages of December 26, 1947, and February 3, 1948, to state that the U.S. had taken the stand it had because of "expressions of policy by responsible American officials, resolutions of Congress, and Party platforms of the last thirty years. They came to a conclusion that unless there was some unanticipated factor in the situation, the trend of public opinion and policy based thereon practically forced it to support partition." The message also took pains to answer the Arab charge that the U.S. delegation had been under pressure to take its stand and had pressured other governments.

Furthermore, Acting Secretary of State Lovett informed the Kings:

It is understood that one of the reasons for Arab resentment at the General Assembly decision is concern lest the Zionists intend eventually to use their state as a base for territorial expansion in the Middle East at the expense of the Arabs. It is the conviction of the US Government, based on conversations with responsible Zionist leaders, that they have no expansionist designs and are most anxious to live with the Arabs in the future on cordial terms and to establish with them relations of a mutually advantageous character. . . . *If, at a later time, persons or groups should obtain control of the Jewish state who have aggresive designs against their neighbors, the US would be prepared firmly to oppose such aggressiveness in the United Nations and before world opinion.*[55] [Italics added.]

(Someone somehow seems to have forgotten these pledges, which were initialed by the President.)

Official records disprove the attempt to refute charges of coercion. The actual extent to which pressures played the dominating role in the drama at Lake Success was revealed not only by Truman in his diaries, but more clearly in the 1947 State Department papers released late in 1971, one quarter of which dealt with Palestine.[56] At the same time the President was calling publicly for adoption of the U.N. Partition Plan and the creation of Israel, he was vigorously opposing other behind-the-scenes pressures. In a memorandum from Truman to Undersecretary of State Lovett dated December 11, 1947—some two weeks after the deciding vote at the U.N.—the President repeated previous orders that no one in the administration should state any preference on the Palestine question during further U.N. discussions:

It seems to me that if our delegation to the U.N. is to be interfered with by members of the United States Senate and by pressure groups in this country, we will be helping the United Nations down the road to failure. I have a report from Haiti in which it is stated that our Consul in Haiti approached the President of that country and suggested to him, *that for his own good,* he should order the vote of his country changed, claiming that he had instructions from me to make such a statement to the President of Haiti. It is perfectly clear that pressure groups will succeed in putting the United Nations out of business if this sort of thing is continued.[57] [Emphasis added.]

This threat had worked. The affirmative vote of Haiti, whose representative only twenty-four hours previously had been fiercely attacking the proposal during the Lake Success debate, was one of the three last-minute shifts (the Philippines and Liberia were the other two) to bring about the 33-to-13 two-thirds majority the partition plan required.

The publication of State Department papers dealing with Palestine developments of 1948 was delayed for more than two years and then came out in one 1,730-page volume. The documentary evidence of the subordination of the national interest to domestic political pressures proved to be almost too hot to handle.

In a paper delivered December 28, 1976, in Washington before the annual meeting of the American Historical Association (at a session held jointly with the Jewish Historical Society), Truman's Special Counsel Clark Clifford assailed what he called the argumentation advanced by "a school of revisionist historiography" that the Truman Palestine policy had been motivated "entirely by the purely political consideration of wooing the Jewish electoral vote" and the "portrayal of the birth of Israel, one of the most seminal events of modern times, as somehow illicit and ignoble."

That the prestigious American Historical Association should have set the stage for the Clifford performance—in which avid Israelists Barbara Tuchman, Eugene Rostow, and Howard Sachar (historian and son of the President of Brandeis College) also participated as part of a panel whose one-sidedness even moderator Professor Jacob Hurewitz, invariably a supporter of Israel, was forced to note—further attests to the unbelievable influence wielded by Zionism in the U.S. Obviously, the damaging effect of the long-awaited publication of Volume V of *Foreign Relations of the United States* for 1948 and the subsequent publicity given the Marshall memorandum therein had to be quickly counteracted.

Clifford charged that "the State Department repeatedly attempted to undermine President Truman's policy on the Middle East,"[58] and that the "evidence which includes documents that are not found in the recently published volume of *Foreign Relations,* confirms that the President was not being well served on the implementation of American policy regarding Palestine. The trusteeship proposal was a case in point."

On March 19, 1948, U.S. Ambassador to the U.N. Warren Austin had dropped what Clifford called a "bombshell" when he read a statement calling for temporary shelving of the partition resolution and establishment of a U.N. trusteeship over Palestine (the solution privately favored by FDR).

In her 1973 biography of her father, Margaret Truman claimed that he never formally committed himself to the trusteeship plan and that the State Department had engaged in what she described as a "conspiracy" behind her father's back.[59] With the Secretary and the Undersecretary out of the country, the Austin statement, in the eyes of the President's daughter, constituted a gross betrayal. The State Department had reversed his Palestine policy, she added, and "the third and fourth levels of the Department had succeeded in cutting his throat." In support of the viewpoint of the President's daughter, Clifford adduced his own evidence of State Department "machinations" undermining the partition plan and the President's "humanitarian" design.

Truman's calendar diary entry for March 19, 1948, read:

The State Department pulled the rug from under me today. I did not expect that would happen. In Key West, or en route there from St. Croix, I approved the speech and statement of policy by Senator Austin to the U.N. meeting. This morning I find that the State Department has reversed my Palestine policy. The first I know about it is what I see in the paper. Isn't that hell? I am now in the position of a liar and a double-crosser. I never felt so in all my life. There are people on the third and fourth levels of the State Department who always wanted to cut my throat.[60]

The President apparently had overlooked, or forgotten, the vital details. While on board the *Williamsburg* in the Caribbean on February 21 he had received a detailed top-secret telegram[61] from Secretary Marshall setting forth the U.S. position on the Palestine question and the procedure to be followed by Ambassador Austin at the Security Council.[62] It was clearly stated that if the Security Council was unable "to give effect to the General Assembly resolution on Palestine [i.e., partition] . . . and if the Security Council is unable to develop an alternative solution acceptable to the Jews and Arabs of Palestine, the matter should be referred back to a special session of the General Assembly." The Secretary considered it would "then be clear that Palestine is not yet ready for self-government and that some form of U.N. trusteeship for an additional period of time will be necessary."[63]

Truman sent a telegram February 22 to the Secretary of State from St. Thomas stating: "Your working draft of recommended basic position for Security Council discussion received. I approve in principle this basic position."[64] The "working draft" to which he referred was contained in the Secretary's telegram to the President of February 21. The contents of Senator Austin's speech of March 19 was in accord with the policies proposed in that telegram.

In pursuance of these policies, the Department had taken a series of other steps, all leading up to the speech of March 19, which one by one were approved by Truman. For instance, the President approved telegrams 107 and 108 sent by the Department on March 5 authorizing the kind of speech Senator Austin might make when there was clear evidence before the Security Council that the Jews and Arabs and the Mandatory Powers were not prepared to implement the General Assembly plan of partition through peaceful means.[65] On March 8 the Secretary informed Senator Austin that the President had approved the draft statement on the situation in Palestine "as set forth in DEP-TEL 107 for use if and when necessary."[66]

This is why Secretary Marshall could unhesitatingly tell a March 20 press conference in Los Angeles: "The course of action with respect to the Palestine question which was proposed on March 19 by Ambassador Austin appeared to me, after the most careful consideration, to be the wisest course to follow. I recommended it to the President, and he approved my recommendation."[67]

Four weeks earlier the President had given his approval to the Marshall proposals.[68] Yet when Ambassador Austin delivered his remarks to the U.N. temporarily reversing U.S. policy, Truman was outraged at the action of the "striped-pants boys," as he referred to the foreign service officers in his memoirs, and regarded the timing of the release of the proposal as an attempt to force his hand.

Documentary evidence is overwhelmingly to the contrary.

It so happened that on the two days preceding the speech of March 19, both the Secretary and Undersecretary Lovett were not in Washington. They were the two members of the Department who had been keeping the President informed of developments and who were most closely acquainted with the President's feelings and views. The Acting Secretary was Willard L. Thorp, Assistant Secretary for Economic Affairs, who had had nothing to do with the Palestine problem and unfortunately little contact with the White House. Thus the responsibility for making decisions with regard to Palestine rested primarily with those senior officers of the Department who had been working on the problem, including Norman Armour, the Assistant Secretary for Political Affairs; Charles Bohlen, the Counselor of the Department; Dean Rusk, Director of the Office of United Nations Affairs, and his Special Assistant Robert McClintock; John Hickerson, Director of European Affairs; and Loy Henderson, Director for Near Eastern and African Affairs. Senator Austin in New York, who had been working closely with the Secretary and the Undersecretary and had maintained contacts with the White House, had the knowledge and experience that caused these officers of the Department to respect his judgment and listen to his suggestions.

During this particular period Dean Rusk and Robert McClintock, his Special Assistant, in view of the fact that their office was the entity in the Department through which U.N. problems were usually handled, "carried the ball" along with Senator Austin. They worked closely, however, with the other concerned officers of the Department, and all of them shared responsibility for such actions as were taken.

All evidence based on available documents and on interviews with surviving participants[69] sustains the view that each believed he was doing his share in carrying out the policies agreed to by the Secretary, the Undersecretary, and Senator Austin, and approved by the President. Carlisle Hummelsine, Director of the Executive Secretariat, Office of the Secretary of State, kept in daily touch by telephone with Lovett in Florida, informing him of the events of the day and passing his suggestions and comments along to the other responsible officers.

The Clifford accusation that State Department officers "disobeyed White House instructions"[70] to avert partition has also been vigorously denied by foreign service officers involved. That there had been little enthusiasm from the outset for the Palestine partition plan by these foreign service experts has never been denied. Writing with a pen of prophecy, Loy Henderson expressed these views in a September 1947 memorandum to Secretary Marshall:

An advocacy on our part of any plan providing for the partitioning of Palestine or the establishment in Palestine of a Jewish state would be certain to undermine our relations with the Arab, and to a lesser extent with the Moslem World at a time when the Western World needs the friendship and cooperation of the Arabs and other Moslems. . . . The resources and geographical position of the Arab countries are of such a character that those countries are necessarily factors of importance in the international economic field. Arab friendship is essential if we are to have their cooperation in the carrying out of some of our vital economic programs. During the next few years we are planning to draw heavily on the resources of the area, not only for our use, but for the reconstruction of Europe. Furthermore, we are intending to make important use of the communications facilities in the area.[71]

Henderson, who over the years has been the chief target of much Zionist criticism, answered the Clifford allegation of State Department obstruction:

We might be criticized for failure to keep in close touch with the White House, but it is ridiculous to charge that these officers would deliberately conspire among themselves to take action which might embarrass the President whom we were conscientiously endeavoring to serve. We felt that it was our duty to apprise him if, in our opinion, he might be about to take action which would not be in the best interest of the United States. Since we were convinced that he wanted to do what was in the country's interest, we considered that such advice as we might give was in his interest as well as in that of the country.[72]

In "President Truman's Recognition of Israel," an article in the December 1968 *American Jewish Historical Quarterly,* Ian J. Bickerton declared flatly that Truman had agreed to the suggestion of his Secretary of State that Palestine be placed under a temporary U.N. trusteeship but had given no specific directive for the implementation of this U.S. policy reversal.[73]

John Snetsinger states bluntly in his revealing book, *Truman, The Jewish Vote and the Creation of Israel,* that Truman "directly and knowingly approved the change in American policy on Palestine."[74] Secretary Marshall likewise pointed out that the President had agreed to the statement but was exercised over the fact that he "had not been advised that Ambassador Austin was going to make his Security Council statement at that particular time."[75] This is supported by several pages of penciled notes dated May 4, 1948, in the handwriting of Clifford, which can be found among the papers in the Harry S. Truman Library at Independence, Missouri. These notes, by Clifford's own admission, were prepared by him for the May 12 conference at the White House at which recognition of the Jewish state was discussed. Clifford indicated that the President had approved the Austin draft statement on March 8, asking the U.N. to set aside partition and establish a temporary U.N. trusteeship in Palestine, and that Secretary Marshall had directed Austin to make the speech "as soon as possible as Austin believed appropriate." The Clifford notes also admitted that while the final text of the speech Austin delivered had not been shown to the President, "it was the same substance as the draft previously submitted to the President" and that "Marshall and Lovett [who were out of Washington] left no word that the President was to be informed when Austin was to speak."[76]

Truman stated in his *Memoirs* that "the suggestion that the mandate be continued as a trusteeship was not a bad idea."[77] Presidential Aide Matthew J. Connelly confided to some of his colleagues that "the President had approved some agreement, during the Caribbean trip, setting forth the new policy."[78]

What had infuriated Truman was the timing of Austin's pronouncement of the American policy reversal at the U.N., for it had come the day after a secret White House meeting with Dr. Chaim Weizmann, the President-to-be of Israel. Truman and Weizmann, who had entered unnoticed through the East Gate, met together for forty-five minutes. The President assured the Zionist leader that the U.S. was staunchly supporting partition and would stick to this position. (Truman, incidentally, was not the only political figure to have been strongly influenced by Weizmann. Arthur Balfour, to whom the Zionist leader was introduced in 1917 by Prime Minister David Lloyd George, was said to have been "won over completely by his charm, his persuasiveness, and his intellectual power."[79] The Balfour Declaration followed later that year.)

Neither Secretary Marshall nor anyone else at the State Department had any knowledge of Truman's secret meeting. And the very next day the new U.S. policy shift to trusteeship was announced without the President having been advised in advance of the speech that he had approved in principle in the Virgin Islands.

The reversal, which Weizmann undoubtedly viewed as a deliberate breach of faith on Truman's part, followed exactly the procedure laid down in the memorandum approved eleven days earlier by the White House. Further consultation with the President, who was in the Caribbean, had not been envisioned, nor was this necessary. Truman had passed along to the Secretary and his assistants, and to Senator Austin, the responsibility for the detailed wording of the speech in the framework of approved policy, leaving to them the timing of the delivery once the agreed preconditions for reversal to trusteeship had been met.

The initial U.S. attempt to gain support in the Security Council for the necessary implementation of the General Assembly partition resolution failed on March 5, receiving support of only five of the seven needed members on a preliminary vital vote. The U.S. draft resolution calling on the Security Council "to do everything it can under the Charter to give effect to the recommendation of the General Assembly,"[80] was doomed to defeat, although not put to a final vote.[81]

U.S. foreign policy makers as well as other U.N. members were divided over the question of whether the Security Council, empowered to act to prevent threats to the peace, could move with military force to impose a General Assembly plan, namely, partition. Maintenance of peace was generally held not to be the same as enforcement of the partition recommendation. These uncertainties accounted for the failure of Ambassador Austin to recruit countries other than the Soviet

Union, Belgium, France, and the Ukraine to support the U.S. resolution, thus in effect vitiating partition.

The Security Council did provide for establishment of a committee composed of its permanent members (U.S., U.S.S.R., France, and China—Britain would not serve) to find ways of implementing the General Assembly resolution. It was only after ten days of failure of the consultations by this committee that Secretary Marshall authorized Ambassador Austin in a top-secret message on March 16 to present his speech and draft resolution of March 19 to the U.N. "since no party to the Palestine problem believes partition can be carried out except by the use of force."[82]

Dean Rusk in New York indicated his agreement with the Secretary's decision:

The plan proposed by the General Assembly is an integral plan which cannot succeed unless each of its parts can be carried out. There seems to be general agreement that the plan cannot be implemented by peaceful means. This being so, the Security Council is not in a position to go ahead with efforts to implement this plan in the existing situation.[83]

Britain as the Mandatory Power absolutely refused to participate in any implementary measures to effectuate partition. The general consensus of the Security Council indicated opposition to carrying out the General Assembly Resolution of November 29, thus in effect vitiating partition. Unless the U.S. took some action for establishment of an administration to govern Palestine, chaos threatened.

As the bitter battling between the Jewish Agency and the Palestine Arab Higher Committee accelerated—the Arab states indicated they planned military intervention on May 15, the date of the Mandate's end—the U.S. proposed a temporary trusteeship, setting aside partition "without prejudice to the character of the eventual political settlement," and called for a special session of the General Assembly.

Impelled by reports from many quarters, Truman for some time had been entertaining serious private doubts, never publicly expressed, as to the sagacity and practicability of the partition decision. In a blunt report to the Security Council on February 16, 1948, the United Nations Palestine Commission pointed out that it would require "military forces in adequate strength" in order to be able to implement the partition resolution. The hopes of a peaceful transfer of responsibility from the British Mandatory Power to the Arab and Jewish states had vanished when the Arab Higher Committee, the most authoritative spokesman for Palestine's Arab community, indicated they were deliberately planning "to alter the plan by force." The commission feared that May 15, the date set for the transfer, would usher in "a period of uncontrolled widespread strife and bloodshed."

In a February 24 report preparatory to the policy reversal to trusteeship, the State Department Policy Planning Staff under George Kennan (later Ambassador to the U.S.S.R.) emphasized the necessity of "preventing the area from falling under Soviet influence":

> . . . we are deeply involved in a situation which has no direct relation to our national security and where the motives of our involvement are solely in part commitments of dubious wisdom and in our attachment to the UN itself. If we do not effect a fairly radical reversal of the trend of our policy to date, we will end up either in the position of being ourselves militarily responsible for the protection of the Jewish population in Palestine against the declared hostility of the Arab world, or of sharing that responsibility with the Russians and thus assisting in their installation as one of the military powers of the area. In either case, the clarity and efficiency of a sound national policy for that area will be shattered.[84]

Secretary Marshall had informed the President that the U.S. had three options: abandonment of the partition plan; vigorous support for implementation, including the use of force; and referral back to the General Assembly for a review of the entire question.[85]

It was the unanimous opinion of the military, including Secretary of Defense Forrestal and General Alfred Gruenther, that the U.S. was in no position militarily to commit armed forces to an international peace force to enforce partition. Gruenther declared partial mobilization would be required if more than 15,000 troops (a division) were needed for the international policing.[86] And the President had given public assurances that he would not send American troops to Palestine. Truman steadfastly refused to consider establishment of an international constabulary to police the area, which would bring the Soviet Union, long knocking at the door, directly into the area for the first time. He was opposed to any commitment that would tie down American troops in Palestine, for such a move would leave him less leverage to handle Europe's pressing unresolved postwar problems.[87] The security risks posed by the possible necessity of use of force in the Middle East deeply concerned him.

The National Security Council had submitted a report to Secretary of Defense Forrestal indicating the extent to which the Palestine turmoil was acutely endangering the security of the U.S.[88] This report, prepared by the CIA, emphasized both the strategic importance of the Middle East and its vast untapped oil resources.[89]

Increasing international tensions were another factor prompting the President to support temporary abandonment of partition. On February 24, 1948 the Czechoslovakian coup d'état took place. One week after this pro-Soviet move, a top-secret telegram was received in Washington from General Lucius Clay in Berlin, warning that within the last weeks he had felt "a subtle change in the Soviet attitudes," which meant that war, previously felt by him to be "unlikely for at least ten years, may come with dramatic suddenness."[90]

These developments only tended to confirm the fears, expressed in the many memoranda submitted by almost all concerned officers of the State Department ever since the Palestine problem had come to the fore at the U.N. the previous September, that implementation of partition would undermine U.S. relations with the Arab-Muslim world and might even create the risk of involvement in a war against the Arabs, one the U.S.S.R. would be sure to take advantage of.[91]

If, as Margaret Truman insisted, the President did not wish an open break with Secretary Marshall and did not feel free to tell the whole story of the alleged State Department "perfidy," even in his *Memoirs,* this was because of the President's deep ambivalence on the subject. Publicly he talked about Jewish immigration to Palestine and eventual partition. At the same time, behind the scenes, he shared the State Department's view that partition was unworkable, and he gave complete cooperation to the efforts at the U.N. to win additional support for a U.N. trusteeship directed to the maintenance of peace pending a political settlement.

In his *Memoirs* Truman described the March 19 trusteeship statement by Ambassador Austin not as a rejection of partition but as an effort to postpone its effective date until conditions were more propitious.[92] (From the very outset the new U.S. approach had invariably been referred to as a "temporary trusteeship.") The President conceded that his policy on Palestine did not mean commitment to any set of dates or circumstances, but was dedication to internal obligations and relief of human misery. Hence Truman could reconcile the trusteeship proposal with his own policy, despite his angry calendar entry, so long as it was not interpreted as abandonment of the partition plan, which Clifford claimed certain members of the State Department were doing.

Failing in the immediate prerequisite task of bringing about a truce between Jews and Arabs in their escalating warfare, the U.S.

could win little support for the trusteeship proposal. While the Security Council was struggling to arrange a truce, a special session of the General Assembly convened "to consider further the question of the future government of Palestine." Impeding any solution was U.S. reluctance to commit troops either to act on its own or as part of an international police force.[93] (Anomalously, the Soviet press at this time was critical of the U.S. shift to trusteeship, calling the "repudiation of the partition resolution an open violation of U.S.A. international obligations" and quoting the *New York Post*'s criticism that Forrestal was obstructing partition in behalf of American oil companies.[94])

The President, Secretary Marshall, and other officers in the State Department were in total agreement that the U.S. was "not prepared to join in enforcement measures in Palestine for the maintenance of international peace and security until U.N. trusteeship had been established and then only to maintain the integrity of trusteeship as a bulwark of international peace and security,"[95] not to implement partition. It was Washington's general fear that the tactic of the Soviets, who were wooing the Jewish Agency, was to seek enforcement of peace to the exclusion of the establishment of a framework within which a peaceful solution of the Palestine problem might be found.

The President would make no specific commitment to contribute armed forces to the U.N. for maintenance of law and order in Palestine even as part of a truce and trusteeship.[96] At his press conference March 25, Truman stated that "our policy is to back up the U.N. in the trusteeship by every means necessary," but that did not necessarily mean that American troops would be used. Following Clifford's advice,[97] the President made clear that the trusteeship proposed was not a "substitute for the partition plan, but an effort to fill a vacuum soon to be created by the termination of mandate on May 15" and "does not prejudge the character of the final political settlement."

It was in this March public statement that the President clearly rebutted the Clifford charges that the State Department had undermined his resolve to support partition:

This country vigorously supported the plan for Partition with Economic Union recommended by UNSCUP and by the General Assembly. *We have explored every possibility consistent with basic principles of the Charter for giving effect to that solution. Unfortunately, it has become clear that the partition plan cannot be carried out at this time by peaceful means. We could not undertake to impose this solution on people of Palestine by use of American troops, both on Charter grounds and as a matter of national policy.*[98] [Italics added.]

The President concluded: "If the U.N. agrees to trusteeship, peaceful settlement is yet possible; without it, open warfare is just over the horizon."[99]

The kind of gross distortion in which Clifford and his researchers[100] indulged to prove malevolence on the part of the State Department can be seen through one comparison of his version of what took place in 1948 with official U.S. documents. The former Special Counsel to President Truman and the Secretary of Defense under President Johnson told his American Historical Society audience:

But the basic attitude of the department remained the same. On May 11, *one of its senior officers,* in a telephone call to Henderson and Wadsworth in New York, made the comment that Jews in Palestine were running their own affairs, which "was not according to plan."[101] [Italics added.]

Volume V of the *Foreign Relations of the United States,* published in 1976, reveals that this senior officer was Dean Rusk, that his telephone conversation had in fact not been with Ambassadors Henderson and Wadsworth but with Ambassador Philip C. Jessup and Jack Ross.[102] Here is what actually was said:

Phil, I think what is likely to come out from down here, particularly across the way [the White House], is the idea that something has happened in fact over there. It is not according to plan, but nevertheless there is a community in existence over there [the Jewish community in Palestine] running its own affairs.[103]

By reporting the phone conversation out of context, Clifford imputed State Department subversion of policy and placed at the door of a former Secretary of State an implication of an anti-Semitic remark, the credibility of which was increased by making Loy Henderson, the favorite bête noire of the Zionists, a party to the conversation.

Final insight on the controversy over the U.S. reversal to trusteeship can be gleaned from the memorandum to Charles E. Bohlen of March 22 from Secretary Marshall affirming that the timing of the Austin U.N. speech was "the reason he [the President] was so much exercised. He had agreed to the statement but said that if he had known when it was going to be made, he could have taken certain measures to have avoided the political blast of the press."[104] Like President Carter twenty-eight years later, after the issuance of the October 1, 1977, joint communiqué with the U.S.S.R. regarding "Palestine rights," Truman seemed to have failed to anticipate the fury with which Organized Jewry would react to the shift in policy.

As the impossibility of the pacification of the Holy Land became increasingly evident and the end of the mandate approached, Zionists everywhere mounted new offensives. In a letter of April 9, 1948, to Truman, Weizmann warned of the consequences of not implementing partition, declaring that "the choice of our people is between statehood and extermination."[105] With the cooperation of White House aide David Niles and Clark Clifford, domestic politics again raised its ugly head.

The stunning victory in a special Bronx congressional election of American Labor party candidate Leo Isacson over Boss Ed Flynn's Democratic organizational candidate in a district in which there was a 55 percent Jewish constituency provided the excuse. This was attributed to the militant pro-Zionist stand taken by the victorious candidate in whose behalf Henry Wallace had spoken frequently in the district. Wallace had declaimed, "Truman still talks Jewish, but acts Arab.[106] The voters had soundly repudiated the Truman administration's lack of enthusiasm in implementing partition and giving all-out support to the creation of a Jewish state.

The outcry against the sell-out of partition and Jewish statehood increased. The administration's embargo on the shipment of all arms to the Middle East was attacked as hurting the Jews far more than the Arabs. The Truman administration was assailed for its "vacillation and inadequacy" by the Republican party to which the press, then preponderantly Republican, added the charge, "betrayal of humanitarianism." In the large cities organized Jewry once again mobilized public opinion. The story of the courageous fight of the Palestinian Jews crowded newspapers and radio. In New York City, Communist and left-wing labor leaders ran a "Palestine Protest Rally" in Madison Square Park, attended by 10,000, at which "oil politics" was attacked. Special services were held in more than 8,000 Jewish houses of worship throughout the nation to protest the U.S. stand on Zion. The President was personally bombarded with appeals to support partition from political leaders all over the country, notably Chairman of the House Foreign Affairs Committee Sol Bloom and powerful Chicago Democratic chieftain Jacob Arvey.

Clifford was now convinced that his plans for Truman's 1948 national presidential campaign were being jeopardized by U.S. reversal of its Palestine policy. Previously Clifford had vacillated between idealistic statements that in the long run "there is likely to be a greater gain if the Palestine problem is approached on the basis of far-reaching decisions founded upon intrinsic merit" and his full awareness of the political importance of the Jewish bloc vote, particularly in New York State. Although no President since 1876, except Woodrow Wilson in 1916, had lost New York with its forty-seven electoral votes and still won the election, the presidential adviser had not been convinced that the best way to win this Jewish vote was through the adoption of pro-Zionist policies. But as November 1948 grew nearer, Clifford bowed to political forces and gave unstinting recognition to the inter-relationship between the administration's stand on the Palestine issue and presidential success at the polls. By May 4 he was convinced, according to his papers,[107] that a Jewish state "will be set up shortly," and he avowed forthright recognition of the state.

On May 7 Max Lowenthal, closely associated with the Jewish Agency, a consultant to the White House, and a confidant of both Clifford and Niles, sent a confidential memorandum "FOR MR. CLIF-FORD ONLY. This is for the protection of the Administration, not to be shown in written form, to anyone else, *under any circumstances.*"[108] Low-enthal called for recognition of the Jewish state even before May 15 as that "would free the Administration of a serious and unfair disad-vantage" in the November elections.[109]

Other Zionists were satisfied with asking for prompt recognition once the state came into being. Within the State Department itself, long-time Zionist supporter General John Hilldring, who had been appointed by the President as Special Assistant to the Secretary on Palestine Affairs,[110] was doing everything to undermine the influence of those foreign service officers who continued to caution against premature recognition of the Zionist state.

With the help of Democratic National Chairman Howard McGrath, Undersecretary of the Interior Oscar Chapman, Federal Se-curity Agency Administrator Oscar Ewing, and other politicos, over-whelming additional pressures were brought on the President. Secre-tary Marshall's influence was waning as Clifford's advice became Truman's important guidestone. The hope was that a dramatic gesture of support to Israel would be amply repaid by Jewish votes and contri-butions.[111]

A decisive White House meeting was held on May 12 at 4 P.M., attended by seven others in addition to the President: Marshall, Lovett, Clifford, Niles, White House Aide Connelly, and State Department veteran Foreign Service Officers Robert McClintock and Fraser Wil-kins. Clifford pressed for approval of a presidential statement, stating it was his intention to recognize the Jewish state once it came into being. Clifford openly admitted that his support of such a policy was based upon consideration of the political implications involved in such a course, and also claimed that it would "steal a march on the U.S.S.R."[112]

Niles, Clifford, and Lowenthal, as the key contact with the many Zionist groups, had prepared well for the meeting. Following conferences starting May 6, Niles had prepared the initial draft of this statement and had sought guidance and approval from Benjamin V. Cohen, who had served as Counselor in the State Department under Secretary Byrnes. The final draft read by Clifford at the White House meeting had been revised by Clifford's assistant, George Elsey, to include suggestions set forth in a Lowenthal memo of that day,[113] the seventh memo in five days.

Secretary Marshall had done nothing to hide his deep resentment over the fact that Clifford was even present. "Mr. President," he protested, "this is not a matter to be determined on the basis of politics. Unless politics were involved, Mr. Clifford would not even be at this conference. This is a very serious matter of foreign policy determination."[114]

According to Elsey's notes, the Clifford statement received "a violent reaction from Marshall: 'This is just straight politics. You wouldn't get my O.K.' Clifford was enraged, and Marshall glared at Clifford."[115] The White House Counsel later angrily recalled: "He said it all in a righteous God-damned Baptist tone."[116]

In opposing the course suggested by Clifford, Undersecretary Lovett maintained that it would be

. . . highly injurious to the U.N. to announce recognition of the Jewish State even before it came into existence and while the General Assembly, which had been called into special session at the request of the U.S., was still considering the question of the future government of Palestine . . . Furthermore, such a move would be injurious to the prestige of the President. It was a very transparent attempt to win the Jewish vote but it would lose more votes than it would gain. Finally, to recognize the Jewish State prematurely would be buying a pig in a poke. How did we know what kind of a Jewish State would be set up?[117]

In his own memorandum of conversation, which received wide publicity in 1976 when Volume V of the 1948 *Foreign Relations of the United States* was finally printed, Marshall expressed sharp disagreement with Clifford:

I remarked to the President that speaking objectively, I could not help but think that the suggestions made by Mr. Clifford were wrong. I thought that to allow their suggestions would have precisely the opposite effect from that intended by Mr. Clifford. The transparent dodge to win a few votes would not in fact achieve this purpose.

The great dignity of the office would be seriously diminished. The counsel offered by Mr. Clifford was based on domestic political considerations, while the problem which confronted us was international. I said bluntly that *if the President were to follow Mr. Clifford's advice and if in the elections I were to vote, I would vote against the President.*[118] [Italics added.]

Following the spirited exchange of views, the President, who had remained neutral, according to all reports, concluded the meeting by suggesting that he "was inclined to side with Secretary Marshall and we would sleep on it."[119] According to Clifford, the President also stated, after the others had left, that "following a short cooling period, we would get into it again."[120]

Indicating that he had not as yet made up his mind to recognize the incipient state, the President refrained from using the Clifford draft statement at his scheduled press conference on May 13. Meanwhile, following the White House conference, Lovett arranged to have Legal Adviser Ernest A. Gross immediately send a memorandum to Clifford noting that any premature recognition of a new state's existence "is wrongful in international law because it constitutes an unwarranted interference in the affairs of the previous existing State."[121] Even recognition immediately after the state came into being could not meet the State Department's standard requirements for recognition.[122]

As Weizmann noted in his diary, the mandate had but a few more days to run when "I strengthened our contacts with *our friends* in Washington, and affirmed my intention of going ahead with a bid for recognition of the Jewish State as soon as it was proclaimed."[123] (Italics added.) Then, on May 13, 1948, he wrote a personal letter to Truman asking that the U.S. "promptly recognize the Provisional Government of the new Jewish State." Up to that day, the General Assembly had neither revoked nor reaffirmed the November partition resolution and was still wrestling with the problem of how to bring about a truce that would save lives in Palestine. A U.S. resolution, approved by the President, had been introduced in the General Assembly calling for the appointment of a U.N. Commissioner for Palestine to mediate between the parties and to "promote agreement on the future government of Palestine."

The documentary evidence would seem to show that at some point after the fateful White House meeting of May 12 the President decided to go ahead, regardless of the views of his Secretary of State, and recognize Israel as soon as the latter declared itself a state. No doubt he was affected by the eloquence of Weizmann and the persuasiveness of Clifford that something had to be done to get the Democratic party off the election hook. Immediate recognition of Israel was needed to recoup the political losses stemming from the violent reaction to the shift to trusteeship. While the President was closeted on May 14 with intimate advisers—one of the few callers he received that day was B'nai B'rith President Frank Goldman—and the White House maintained a rigid silence, Clifford took the necessary action.

Around eleven-thirty the representative of the Jewish Agency for Palestine, Eliahu Epstein, (later, as Eliahu Elath, the first Israeli Ambassador to the U.S.) was telephoned by Clifford from the White House[124] and told that the U.S. was prepared to accord the new state recognition (de facto, if it was to be a provisional government that was being formed) upon the declaration of Israel's independence, but that a formal request for such recognition would have to be received from the new government that afternoon. Epstein pointed out quite reasonably that the new state could not send such a request prior to its birth (which was not expected before midnight May 14, 6 P.M. Washington time).[125]

According to the Snetsinger account, Clifford demanded and received "a pledge of secrecy" from Epstein, which precluded his contacting Jewish Agency officials in Palestine. Furthermore, there was the important time factor. Epstein assumed full personal responsibility for drafting and delivering the required recognition request as soon as possible. He called Benjamin V. Cohen, who was expert in such matters because of his drafting experience in the State Department, to come over to the office of the Jewish Agency and assist him in composing the draft. When it came to the name of the state, which had as yet not been announced by the Jewish Agency in Tel Aviv, it was Cohen who suggested, "We'll have to use the designation referred to in the U.N. Resolution—simply 'the Jewish State.' "[126] Accordingly, the draft was typed, signed, and rushed by Agency press attaché Harry Zinder in his car to the White House.

A few minutes later Elath's secretary reported that she heard on the radio that "they've named it the 'State of Israel.' " According to this version of events, she sped in a cab, "caught up with Zinder at the White House entrance, removed the letter from the envelope, and with a ballpoint pen crossed out references to 'the Jewish State,' substituting the words 'State of Israel.' "[127]

The letter stated that "the State of Israel has been proclaimed as an independent republic" and that "I have been authorized by the provisional government of the new State . . . to express the hope that your government will recognize and will welcome Israel into the community of nations." Not only had the request for recognition, when delivered that afternoon at the White House, not been authorized by those who were to become the provisional government, but there was no provisional government until eight hours after the request, allegedly from that provisional government in Tel Aviv, had been received.

Apparently both the President and Clifford, as he told Lovett two days later, had been impressed by the Undersecretary's arguments at the May 12 meeting with regard to the disadvantages and dangers of premature announcement of the U.S. intent to recognize Israel. To minimize the risks, Clifford had been careful to ask Epstein to state the boundaries the new state would accept when he presented the request for recognition. Epstein took upon himself the responsibility of declaring that Israel would accept the boundaries as defined in the November 1947 resolution.

Meanwhile, Clifford had decided to keep the President's decision of recognition from Secretary Marshall and everyone else[128] in the Department of State until the afternoon to avoid a leak and any objections Marshall or Lovett might raise to the move. He wished to preclude any attempt to persuade the President to delay the recognition. The Secretary was only told sometime between three and four that afternoon.[129]

According to Undersecretary Lovett's memorandum of conversation with Clifford, which took place following lunch at the F Street Club on May 14, he was informed that "the President was under unbearable pressure to recognize the Jewish state promptly." He also was told by Clifford to draft "appropriate language to put into effect recognition in the event the President decided upon it."[130] Clifford brushed aside Lovett's caution against "indecent haste" until "we could confirm the details of the [State's] proclamation." The Undersecretary was concerned about proper notification of the British, French, and Belgium governments and of Ambassador Austin in New York. Clifford declared that the President could not afford "to have any such action leak."

The documents show that once the President ordered the process of recognition to go ahead, both Lovett and Marshall accommodated themselves to the decision, never questioning the presidential power to do so. According to Dr. Forrest Pogue, Director of the Dwight D. Eisenhower Institute for Historical Research and former Executive Director of the Marshall Foundation, "There is much evidence to show that Marshall, apart from being unswervingly loyal to President Truman, always had a healthy respect for the Presidential prerogative, according to the Constitution, to make foreign policy decisions, and regardless of his own views on any given issue which he did not hesitate to express to the President beforehand, always deferred to the President's position once the decision was made."[131]

What Marshall and Lovett chiefly opposed to was not recognition per se but the Clifford proposal to have the President announce on May 13 that the U.S. would recognize the new state as soon as it declared itself on the 14th.

At twenty minutes to six the Undersecretary was notified that the President was to make the recognition announcement shortly after six and that he could now notify Ambassador Austin in New York. The Lovett memorandum of this memorable day ends thus:

My protests against the precipitate action and warnings as to consequences with the Arab world appear to have been outweighed by considerations unknown to me. But I can only conclude that the President's political advisers, having failed last Wednesday afternoon to make the President a father of the new State, have determined at least to make him the midwife.[132]

At six o'clock Eastern Daylight Time the British mandate expired. At 6:01 P.M. the new State of Israel came into existence, promulgated "in the name of the Jewish people." And at 6:11 P.M. the U.S. accorded recognition. Charles Ross, presidential press secretary, read to reporters summoned to his office Truman's two-paragraph announcement that accorded de facto recognition.[133]

As the administration in Washington was recognizing the sovereignty of Israel, U.S. representatives at the U.N. were still discussing the internationalization of Jerusalem and were trying to reach "an agreement on the future government of Palestine." Vera Weizmann, widow of the first Israeli President, in her book *The Impossible Takes Longer,*[134] describes how U.S. Mission member Professor Philip C. Jessup had to ring up the White House from a public phone booth at Lake Success to obtain confirmation of the rumored presidential announcement of recognition of the Israeli state while the question of the internationalization of Jerusalem was being debated on the floor of the General Assembly.

Notified by Dean Rusk of the President's move, Ambassador Austin shut himself up in his Waldorf Astoria Towers apartment in disgust. It was not until half an hour later that a member of his mission read the statement of recognition to the General Assembly, reportedly obtained from an Associated Press ticker tape.

The delegates at the U.N. were stunned by this latest abrupt U.S. policy reversal, which now sanctioned partition after beating the drums so long for trusteeship. Cuban Ambassador Guillermo Belt had to be restrained from going to the podium and announcing his country's withdrawal from the U.N.[135]

George Barrett of the *New York Times* reported that one delegate, when asked exactly what the U.S. position was on Palestine, replied that he did not know because he had not seen an announcement for twenty minutes. This humiliating undercutting of such distinguished Americans as Ambassador Austin, Deputy U.S. Representative Francis B. Sayre, Sr., and Professor Jessup further emphasized the magic hold exercised by Israel in political quarters. Even Eleanor Roosevelt, although strongly favoring the recognition of Israel, wrote Secretary Marshall on May 16 complaining about the way this had been done because it "created consternation in the United Nations."[136] Dean Rusk was dispatched to New York by Secretary Marshall to "prevent the U.S. delegation from resigning en masse."[137]

Internecine disputes between former allies strangely brought to light additional pertinent, heretofore missing details regarding this saga. Margaret Truman, supported by I. L. Kenen, tried to make light of any influence that Eddie Jacobson, the President's former haberdashery partner in Kansas City, might have had in supporting the idea of a Jewish state. She called "an absurd myth" the allegation that "Eddie saw Dad secretly innumerable times during his White House years, using his friendship to bring Dad over to a pro-Jewish point of view. I don't believe they ever discussed politics except in the most off-hand fashion," she wrote.[138] But Acheson, Truman's Secretary of State after Marshall, in a television interview and in his autobiography indicated that the President was moved by "the repeated entreaties of Eddie Jacobson," who "talked to the President a great deal about it" and whose "ideas appealed to the President very much."[139]

Frank J. Adler, administrative director of Kansas City's (Missouri) Temple Congregation Ben Jehuda, issued through the Jewish Telegraphic Agency a strong statement concerning Margaret Truman's denigration of "one of our boys," contending that she "was completely in error when she dismissed as inconsequential the influence of Eddie Jacobson on the President's decision with regard to the Palestine situation." According to Adler, official White House records of the Truman administration at the Truman Library include references to twenty-four appointments in the President's office for Eddie Jacobson, thirteen of which are marked "off-the-record."[140] Adler's research for his book, *Roots in a Moving Stream,* a centennial history of his congregation, had sent him to the library in Independence. In addition, Jacobson was with Truman on the 1948 election whistle-stop train for three days. And, quoting Truman Library sources, Adler stated that "they engaged in private discussions, largely U.S. policy on Israel."[141] "His way of making an appointment with the President was unique," according to another source. "He often asked for the meeting to be made that day or the next, and usually the answer was 'Come right over.' "[142]

In his *Memoirs* published in 1965, the former President referred to Jacobson as his late "great and irreplaceable friend." Jacobson's widow was one of the very select few at the final burial service for Truman on December 28, 1972, in Independence, Missouri.

In the same book, Truman notes that Jacobson *never* asked for a single favor for himself but recalls that Jacobson did intervene when Chaim Weizmann found the doors to the White House closed to him at a critical moment. Edward E. Grusd in his book *B'nai B'rith: The Story of a Covenant* fills in the details on this incident:

The word got out that the White House door was bolted against all Zionist leaders, and it is a fact that although many knocked, none was admitted. Meanwhile the United Nations halted all partition implementation measures. During this period, however, the President and Secretary of B'nai B'rith had an audience with Mr. Truman. It had no visible effect, however, and President Goldman called on the lodges and chapters to express themselves by letters to Mr. Truman and the United Nations.

At this critical juncture, B'nai B'rith was able to make an important contribution which broke the logjam. Dr. Chaim Weizmann, internationally famous scientist and head of the World Zionist Organization, although he was over seventy and ill, came to the United States to make a personal appeal to President Truman. While he lay bedridden in a New York hotel, American Zionist leaders again tried to make an appointment for him at the White House. But President Truman refused.

It came to Frank Goldman's knowledge that one of the President's oldest and dearest friends was an Eddie Jacobson of Kansas City, Missouri. He got in touch with A. J. Granoff of Kansas City, a prominent attorney and a past President of District No. 2. It turned out that Mr. Granoff was Mr. Jacobson's attorney, and he gladly introduced his client to the President of B'nai B'rith. Mr. Jacobson told him he was not a Zionist, and that B'nai B'rith was the only Jewish organization to which he belonged. He had been Harry Truman's close buddy in the Army during World War I, had served in the same artillery unit with him in France, and after the war he and Mr. Truman had been partners in a Kansas City haberdashery. He was so close to the President that all he had to do to see him in the White House was to come to Washington, call up, and immediately be invited to "come on over, Eddie."[143]

It was not exactly that cut-and-dried, according to the President's own account of the meetings. A telegram from Jacobson to the White House pleading that the Chief Executive see Weizmann brought no results. But when his former haberdashery partner called him on the morning of March 13 and expressed a desire to come to the White House, the President said to him, "Eddie, I'm always glad to see old friends, but there's one thing you've got to promise me. I don't want you to say a *word* about what's going on over there in the Middle East. Do you promise?" And he did.[144]

Here is how Truman described the meeting with Jacobson, who was shown into the Oval Room after being "begged by Matthew Connelly"[145] not to discuss the Palestine question with the President:

Great tears were running down his cheeks and I took one look at him and said, "Eddie, you son of a bitch, you promised me you wouldn't say a word about what's going on over there." And he said, "Mr. President, I haven't said a word, but every time I think of the homeless Jews, homeless for thousands of years, and I think about Dr. Weizmann, I start crying. I can't help it. He's an old man and he's spent his whole life working for a homeland for the Jews. Now he's sick and he's in New York and he wants to see you, and every time I think about it, I can't help crying."

I said, "Eddie, that's enough. That's the last word." And we talked about this and that, but every once in a while a big tear would roll down his cheek. At one point he said something about how I felt about old Andy Jackson, and he was crying again. He said he knew he wasn't supposed to, but that's how he felt about Weizmann.

I said, "Eddie, you son of a bitch, I ought to have thrown you out of here for breaking your promise; you knew damn good and well I couldn't stand seeing you cry."

And he kind of smiled at me, still crying, though, and he said, "Thank you, Mr. President." And he left.[146]

Truman, says Grusd, was "sick of the way the Zionists had badgered and unjustly condemned him" for his actions in regard to Palestine and he was so angry that Jacobson later wrote, "I suddenly found myself thinking that my dear friend the President of the United States was at the moment as close to being an anti-Semite as a man possibly could be,"[147] It took all of Eddie Jacobson's friendship and persuasive powers; Truman was finally induced to arrange a secret meeting with the Zionist leader.

According to Merle Miller's autobiographical version, after Jacobson left, Truman called the State Department (Loy Henderson and others working on the problem in the Department deny this) and told them he was going to see Weizmann:

> Well, you should have heard the carrying on. The first thing they said—they said Israel wasn't even a country yet and didn't have a flag or anything. They said if Weizmann comes to the White House, what are we going to use for a flag?
>
> And I said, "Look here; he's staying at the Waldorf-Astoria in New York and every time some foreign dignitary is staying there they put something out. You find out what it is and we'll use it. And I want you to call me right back."[148]

That meeting on March 18 not only led to the warm Truman-Weizmann friendship that played a vital part in the later Truman act of recognizing Israel, but also brought about inclusion of the Negev within that portion of Palestine assigned by the U.N. to the new Zionist state. Jacobson did not go with the scientist to the White House, as he was told by Weizmann he should be "saved" in case he was needed for another emergency. "You have a job to do, so keep the White House doors open."[149]

A year later the Chief Rabbi of Israel came to see the President and told him, "God put you in your mother's womb so that you could be the instrument to bring about the rebirth of Israel after two thousand years." At these words, we are told that "great tears started rolling down Harry Truman's cheeks."[150]

During former Israeli Premier Ben-Gurion's last visit to the States, Truman visited him at his New York hotel. Ben-Gurion is said to have remarked, "I do not know how you will stand in American history, but you have a secure place in the history of Israel." As an embattled Israel struggles to hold onto that initial inheritance with which the late President endowed it, who can quarrel with this assessment on both counts?

As he revealed many years later in one of his hundreds of hours of taped interviews with author Miller for the book *Plain Speaking,* Truman shared some of his vilification of the State Department in a White House meeting with Zionist state builder Rabbi Stephen Wise, whom "he referred to as the most courteous man I have ever seen."[151]

> I told him I knew all about *experts.* I said that an expert was a fella who was afraid to learn anything new because then he wouldn't be an expert anymore.
>
> And I said that some of the *experts,* the career fellas in the State Depart-

ment, thought that they ought to make a policy, but that as long as I was President, I'd see to it that *I* made policy. Their job was to carry it out, and if there were some who didn't like it, they could resign any time they felt like it.[152]

Truman's nice words about the Rabbi did not jibe with what has appeared elsewhere in his writings, particularly in his *Memoirs,* where we learn that he later closed the door completely to this intense Zionist leader and would not see him because of his "emotional tantrums" in their meetings. These Zionist pressures on the White House were described in this interesting passage:

Well, there had never been anything like it before and there wasn't after. Not even when I fired MacArthur, there wasn't, and I said I issued orders that I wasn't going to see anyone who was an extremist for the Zionist cause, and I didn't care who it was. . . . I had to keep in mind that much as I favored a homeland for the Jews, there were simply other matters awaiting . . . that I had to worry about.[153]

During the year following the narrow Zionist victory at Lake Success, a temporary U.N. trusteeship for Palestine emerged as a possible alternative to partition. The political pressures exerted on the President (and the Congress) more than balanced his concern for the national interest. As Truman noted:

The Jewish pressure on the White House did not diminish in the days following the partition vote in the U.N. Individuals and groups asked me, usually in rather quarrelsome and emotional ways, to stop the Arabs, to keep the British from supporting the Arabs, to furnish American soldiers, to do this, that and the other. I think I can say that I kept my faith in the rightness of my policy in spite of some of the Jews.[154]

One of the problems that Truman increasingly "had to worry about"—and undoubtedly wished to worry about—was the Palestinian Arabs. As the President concerned himself over the plight of the new refugees, his relations with the Zionists and the Israeli state cooled considerably. The President was deeply disturbed.

According to previously classified State Department diplomatic letters and cables for 1949, Truman sent a strong, angry note to Israel on May 28 demanding that Israel withdraw from territories captured during the 1948–49 war with the Arabs and urging the government to take back a certain number of refugees. He expressed "deep disappointment at the Israeli refusal to make any of the desired concessions on refugees or boundaries at the Lausanne Conferences" (April 27 to

September 15, 1949). The President interpreted Israel's attitude "as dangerous to peace in opposition to U.N. General Assembly resolutions."[155] The May 28 note ended with the toughest stance taken by the American government thus far, warning that if Israel continued in her attitude, "the U.S. government will regretfully be forced to the conclusion that a revision of its attitude toward Israel has become unavoidable."[156]

Ten days later, in a formal note of June 8, Israel rejected the American demand. The Israelis insisted that "the war has proved the indispensability to the survival of Israel of certain vital areas not comprised originally in the share of the Jewish state." As far as the plight of the Palestinian refugees was concerned, the note termed them "members of an aggressor group defeated in a war of its own making. History does not record a case of large-scale repatriation after such experience."[157] (What was the creation of the State of Israel but a "large-scale repatriation"?)

In his summation of the Israeli note, Deputy Undersecretary of State Rusk wrote, "With regard to the refugees, the note repeats the familiar arguments blaming the Arab states for the plight of these people. . . . The note maintains that Israel has gone as far as it is possible for it to go under the present circumstances in regard to repatriation and reiterates the position that nothing more can be done until a final peace settlement is reached." Rusk also underlined Israel's continued rejection of any territorial settlement and pointed out that "the basic positions of the United States and Israel thus remain unchanged, and there is no reason for the United States to abandon the firm position it has taken as regards Israel."[158]

A top-secret State Department memorandum to Truman two days later called upon the U.S. to adopt a hard-line attitude toward Israel in an attempt to pressure her to return to the partition lines. Among other things the memorandum suggested:

(1) Immediate adoption of a generally negative attitude towards Israel by refusing Israeli requests for U.S. assistance, such as for the training of Israeli officials in this country and the sending of experts to Israel; by maintenance of no more than a correct attitude toward Israeli officials in this country and towards American organizations interested in promoting the cause of Israel; and by failing to support the position of Israel in international organizations.

(2) Holding up allocation of $49 million of a $100 million export-import bank loan earmarked for Israel.

(3) Lifting the tax-exempt status of the UJA and other American Jewish fund-raising organizations.[159]

The U.S. Ambassador to Israel, James G. McDonald, cabled Clark Clifford to inform him that Truman's note had "embittered Israeli opinion" and that Premier David Ben-Gurion and Foreign Minister Moshe Sharett might be forced "despite their will and better judgement to resist demands." The envoy suggested that "Israeli concessions with refugees are possible if request for these are not again put in form of demand, but under no circumstances except use of overwhelming force will Israel yield any part of Negev."

It was this exceedingly pro-Israel American Ambassador to Israel who later reported the subsequent U.S. retreat: "The [next] American note abandoned completely the stern tone of its predecessor. . . . More and more Washington ceased to lay down the law to Tel Aviv."[160] And as a corollary, it may be added, it became axiomatic that more and more it was Tel Aviv that seemed to be laying down the law to Washington. To the Arab world, this all too ready presidential acceptance of the Israeli leaders' prompt rejection of American requests demonstrated a lack of sincerity in the original rebuke administered by Washington to Tel Aviv.

To the very end Truman insisted consistently that his own actions in helping Israel arose not from outside influences, which he never denied were all too present, but from his own deep concern for the persecuted Jews of Europe. The ambivalence inherent in all of the President's actions was brought out in the statement he made to a group of diplomats called home in 1946 to report to the State Department on the deteriorating U.S. position in the Middle East: "I am sorry, gentlemen, but I have to answer to hundreds of thousands who are anxious for the success of Zionism. I do not have hundreds of thousands of Arabs among my constituents."[161]

Clifford in no way ever substantiated his serious charges against officers of the State Department, including former Secretary of State Dean Rusk and, by implication, George Marshall, who presided over the Department during the period in question. The Clifford role in the creation of Israel and in nurturing the relationship during the subsequent Truman administration, which has developed into our overriding, special commitment to the Zionist state, could never be squared with the moral code set down by Marshall in 1948. He declined to answer any questions on Palestine at a February 28 press conference, declaring that such statements should come from Ambassador Austin at the U.N. lest "there be any confusion as to what is being stated."[162] Then, in a secret and completely off-the-record confidential message to Ambassador Austin in New York, Marshall stated:

As far as I am concerned and the State Department is concerned, but particularly as far as I am concerned, in this highly emotional period of extreme bitterness and violent attacks, my intention is to see that nothing is done by the State Department in guidance for the action of its delegates to the U.N., in response to either military threats or political threats, one or the other, nothing whatever. My intention is to see that the action of the U.S. government is to be on a plane of integrity that will bear inspection and a common review and that there will be no bending to any military threat or to any political threat so long as I am Secretary of State.[163]

The unbelievable pressures exerted and the affluence brought into play by the ubiquitous Zionist machinery prevented Truman from attaining the "high plane of integrity" set by his Secretary of State. While the President insisted consistently to the end that his actions in helping Israel stemmed from his own deep concern for the persecuted Jews of Europe, his memoirs and papers attested to an untold story of the many influences at work not only from the outside but more importantly even from within the White House: Samuel Rosenman, special counsel to FDR and for a year Truman's contact man with Weizmann; Benjamin V. Cohen; Max Lowenthal; Eddie Jacobson; and a host of additional Jews as well as such Christians as Eleanor Roosevelt and General John Hilldring. But David K. Niles was the big Zionist connection. A protégé of Harry Hopkins, Niles (born Neyhaus) had become an executive assistant to President Roosevelt after the 1940 election and was a member of a select group of confidential advisers with an often-quoted "passion for anonymity." FDR, weighed down by war responsibilities, turned over to Niles the handling of problems relating to minorities. Thus Niles soon became what amounted to the first Jewish Ambassador to the White House, and when Truman succeeded Roosevelt, the Palestine issue was placed in his lap.

Niles, unknown to the public although occasionally publicized as "Mr. Truman's Mystery Man,"[164] was in a unique position to further Zionist interests.[165] He made possible the continual unique access to the White House enjoyed by Eliahu Epstein and helped channel to the President the opposition against the Morrison-Grady Plan, which the President had considered to be fair.[166] Niles often conveyed Eddie Jacobson's views directly to the President.

The man from Independence was constantly being torn between his desire "to work for the best interests of the whole country" and the overriding necessities of domestic politics, of which he was constantly being reminded by the many Zionists around him.

In response to James G. McDonald and New York Senators Robert F. Wagner, Sr., and James Mead, who had brought a memorandum attacking the Morrison-Grady Plan, the President, according to Vice President Henry Wallace, snapped: "I am not a New Yorker. All these people are pleading for a special interest. I am an American."[167] Subsequently that year at a Cabinet meeting, when Wallace warned Truman that the plan was "loaded with political dynamite," the President blurted out, "Jesus Christ couldn't please them when he was here on earth, so how could anyone expect that I would have any luck."[168]

Just as Zionist pressures were being mounted prior to the decisive meeting of the General Assembly on partition, Truman wrote to Mrs. Roosevelt, "I feel very much that the Jews are like all underdogs when they are on top, they are just as intolerant and as cruel as the people were to them when they were underneath. I regret this situation very much because my sympathy has always been on their side."[169]

Truman's final explanation for his own ambivalency on the Palestine question was expressed in a 1947 memorandum to Niles: "We could have settled this Palestine thing if U.S. politics had been kept out of it. Terror and [Rabbi] Silver are the contributing causes of some, if not all, of our troubles."[170]

In retrospect, the truth seems to be that the late President was governed in his Palestine thinking by two considerations not inherently in conflict: his concern for votes as the head of his party, and his humanitarian feeling as a great liberal, which was described by former Secretary Dean Rusk:

I doubt that there are fewer people who hold Harry Truman in higher esteem than do I. On this particular issue, however, I think that it would be fair to say there were two Harry Trumans.

The one was the man who considered George Marshall the greatest living American and who was strongly inclined to back Marshall's judgment. Marshall himself was very anxious to find a settlement in Palestine with which both sides could live and which would not be the basis for prolonged fighting in that critical part of the world. Some of the criticism aimed at Loy Henderson should really be aimed at Marshall himself; on this issue he was in no sense merely a puppet of his various advisers. You may recall, for example, that with President Truman's full knowledge, I, myself, tried to negotiate with Arabs and Zionists a military and political "standstill" to take effect with the expiration of the British mandate in order to give a little more time to try to find a more permanent solution. My negotiations failed over the issue of the rate of Jewish immigrants into Palestine during the "standstill."

The other Harry Truman was the man accurately described as having strong personal feelings about a homeland for the Jewish people and strong sympathies for the Zionist cause. He, as all Americans, had been deeply shocked by the full exposure of the frightful atrocities of the Hitler regime. Mr. Truman was strongly impelled toward a homeland for the Jews where such things could not be repeated, and this view was politically reinforced by a large, active and dedicated group in this country who were working very hard on behalf of a Jewish State in Palestine. It would be naive to think that these domestic political considerations played no part in Mr. Truman's own thinking and decisions.

These two Harry Trumans caused the man himself considerable anguish and produced on occasion some actions and instructions which appeared to have inner-contradictions. I do not fault him unduly for this because high political office is filled with similar problems.[171]

British historian Dr. Arnold Toynbee similarly referred to the Truman dichotomy:

The Missourian politician-philanthropist's eagerness to combine expediency with charity by assisting the wronged and suffering Jews would appear to have been untempered by any sensitive awareness that he was thereby abetting the infliction of wrongs and sufferings on the Arabs; and his excursions into the stricken field in Palestine reminded a reader of the Fioretti di San Francesco [The Little Flowers of St. Francis of Assisi] of the tragic-comic exploit there attributed to the impetuously tender-hearted brother Juniper, who, according to the revealing tale, was so effectively moved by a report of the alimentary needs of an invalid that he rushed, knife in hand, into a wood full of unoffending pigs and straightway cut off a live pig's trotter to provide his ailing human being with a dish that his soul desired, without noticing that he was leaving the mutilated animal writhing in agony and without pausing to reflect that his innocent victim was not either the invalid's property or his own.[172]

Others in Britain have not been as charitable to the President's motivations as the famed British historian. In *A Prime Minister Remembers,* published in the spring of 1961, Earl Clement Attlee, former British Prime Minister, charged that "U.S. policy in Palestine was molded by the Jewish vote and by party contributions of several big Jewish firms."[173] The one-time leader of the British Labour party insisted that Truman had been swayed by political considerations in calling for the immediate admission of 100,000 Jews into Palestine in the midst of the 1946 congressional campaign. In defending his foreign minister against charges of anti-Semitism (Zionist pundits called Ernest Bevin the "Haman of the Forties," a reference to the Old Testament villain of Queen Esther's days), Attlee alleged that Truman had gone against the advice of his own State Department and military people: "The State Department would tell us one thing, then the President would come out with the exact opposite."[174]

In Britain only to a slightly lesser degree than in the U.S., Israel enjoyed for a long time[175] a strange, abnormal political position little affected by the political party in power. Perhaps Christian expiation for Jewish persecution and biblical fundamentalism, buttressed by a powerful, assimilated Jewish community whose social ties reached even into Buckingham Palace,[176] were the important factors in winning British support for Zionism at the outset of the Palestine problem. But British foreign policy likewise reflected the absence of an Arab vote and a deliberate consideration for the "Jewish vote."[177]

As a member of the House of Commons pointed out in a parliamentary debate:

There are no Arab members in Parliament. There are no Arab constituents to bring influence upon their members in Parliament. There is no Arab control of newspapers in this country. It is difficult to get a pro-Arab letter in the *Times.* There are in the City no Arab financial houses which can control amounts of finance. There is no Arab control of newspaper advertising in the country. There are no Arab ex-colonial secretaries."[178]

Time never settled Anglo-American differences over the major responsibility for the Palestine debacle. From his home in Independence, the peppery former President had acidly commented on the criticism directed against his administration by Attlee: "The British were highly successful in muddling the situation as completely as it could possibly be muddled." To which Lord Attlee promptly retorted: "There is no Arab vote in America!"

Anglo-American concern for the Jewish vote forged the final disastrous and unjust decision. The appropriateness of comparing the U.S. intervention in Palestine to St. Francis's Juniper action leaving the "mutilated animal writhing in agony" is clearly manifest from these undisputed figures. At the time of the partition vote there were only 650,000 Jews in Palestine while there were 1.3 million indigenous Palestinian Arabs, either Christian or Muslim. Under the partition plan, 56.4 percent of Palestine was given for a Zionist state to people who constituted 33 percent of the population and owned about 5.67 percent of the land. Nothing so totally illustrates the devastating abnegation of the Western professed ideal of self-determination than these U.N. maps on Palestine's land ownership (1945) and population distribution (1946). This is the "original sin," which underlies the entire Palestine conflict.

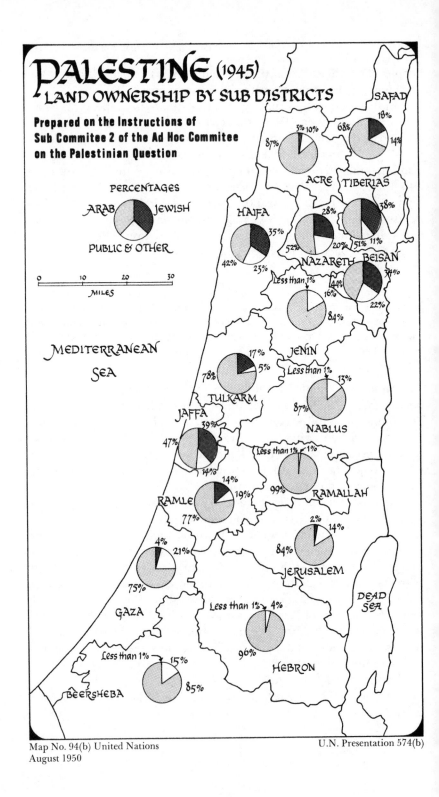

PALESTINE (1945)
LAND OWNERSHIP BY SUB DISTRICTS

**Prepared on the Instructions of
Sub Commitee 2 of the Ad Hoc Commitee
on the Palestinian Question**

PERCENTAGES

ARAB   JEWISH

PUBLIC & OTHER

0   10   20   30
MILES

MEDITERRANEAN
SEA

SAFAD   18%   14%
68%
3% 10%
87%

ACRE   TIBERIAS
HAIFA   28%   38%
35%   52%   20% 51% 11%
42%   23%
NAZARETH   BEISAN
Less than 1%   44%   34%
16%   22%
84%

JENIN
17%   Less than 1%   13%
78%   5%
TULKARM   87%
JAFFA   NABLUS
39%
47%   Less than 1%   1%
14%   99%   RAMALLAH
14%
RAMLE   19%
77%   2%   14%
84%   JERUSALEM
4%   21%
75%   DEAD
SEA

GAZA   Less than 1%   4%
96%   HEBRON

Less than 1%   15%
85%
BEERSHEBA

Map No. 94(b) United Nations
August 1950

U.N. Presentation 574(b)

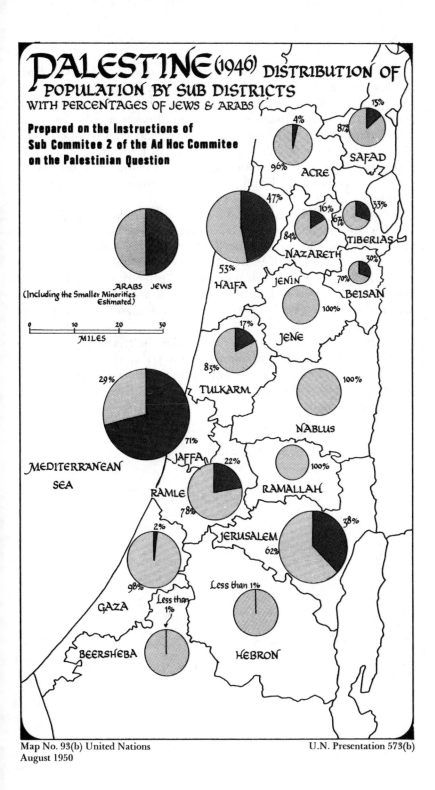

PALESTINE (1946) DISTRIBUTION OF
POPULATION BY SUB DISTRICTS
WITH PERCENTAGES OF JEWS & ARABS

**Prepared on the Instructions of
Sub Commitee 2 of the Ad Hoc Commitee
on the Palestinian Question**

ARABS JEWS
(Including the Smaller Minorities
Estimated.)

0   10   20   30
MILES

4%
96% ACRE

15%
87% SAFAD

47%
53% HAIFA

16%
84% 6% NAZARETH

33% TIBERIAS

JENIN
100%

70% 30% BEISAN

17%
83% JENE

100% NABLUS

29%
71% JAFFA

22%
78% RAMLE

100% RAMALLAH

38%
62% JERUSALEM

TULKARM

2%
98% GAZA

Less than 1%

Less than 1% HEBRON

MEDITERRANEAN
SEA

BEERSHEBA

Whatever motivation history may finally ascribe to the "Man from Independence" for his role in the affair, what is already shatteringly clear is the crying injustice inflicted upon the Arabs, the deep harm wrought to Jews and Judaism, and the inordinate price the American people have paid for the handsome dowry Truman bestowed on fledgling Israel. History has already recorded how far short the President fell of his stated goal of reconciling "regard for the long-range interests of our country with helping those unfortunate victims of persecution find a home."

No doubt what reluctance the "Missourian politician-philanthropist" might initially have had in equating "home" with "state" was driven from him by the facts of life. Certainly his training under the Pendergast machine had, above all, taught him to be a political realist. But in ignoring the advice of three of his Secretaries of State—James Byrnes, George Marshall, and Dean Acheson—and of Secretary of Defense James Forrestal, Truman may have written U.S. foreign policy's "American Tragedy."

Why and how such basic facts regarding the creation of Israel, so vital to the survival of their country and to civilization, have been so successfully secreted from the American people requires a careful examination of a cover-up and a cover-over that have few parallels in the annals of man.

PART TWO

THE COVER-UP

It is a catastrophe when evil triumphs, but it is an even greater catastrophe if it compels the just to resort to injustice in order to combat it. Unless the world returns to moral conscience, to the value of the spirit and its primacy over force, power is only a source of destruction.

Paul Tournier

IV   Inside Israel

Things are seldom what they seem
Skim milk masquerades as cream.
                    —Gilbert and Sullivan, *H. M. S. Pinafore*

On November 10, 1976, the General Assembly of the U.N., meeting in plenary session, fired a new shot heard 'round the world. By the overwhelming vote of 72 to 35, representing 73 percent of the world's population, the international body reaffirmed the earlier overwhelming committee vote of a resolution terming Zionism "a form of racism and racial discrimination."

In the debate preceding the count, Zionists hysterically ranted against the U.N. and, supported by the *New York Times*, charged that adoption of the resolution "would encourage anti-Semitism in other countries." U.S. Permanent Representative to the U.N. (and Senator-to-be) Daniel Patrick Moynihan angrily assailed the resolution and its sponsors, particularly venting his Irish spleen in a flow of venom directed against Idi Amin,[1] Uganda's controversial Chief of State and President of the Organization of African Unity. Member countries of that organization, together with the Arab and Eastern blocs, constituted the principal sponsors of the most serious indictment of the Israel state since its founding in 1948. For the first time the legitimacy of the state was being challenged.

After the result of the vote was announced by the President of the Assembly, Ambassador Moynihan rose from his seat, strode over to Israeli Ambassador Chaim Herzog and, as if in total defiance of the onlooking members of the international body, warmly embraced him.[2]

In banner headlines the press screamed: "Shame of the U.N." "Repugnant." "Anti-Semitic." The Western world recoiled in varying degrees of shock, anger, and amazement. To the man in the street, the

103

action conveyed little meaning save that "the Arabs are ganging up on the Jews again." To only a handful of Americans did the word "Zionism" ring the slightest bell.[3] Even to most of those who followed the course of the U.N. debate, the censure of Israel with the charge of racism, normally leveled against the Nazi and Fascist enemies of the Jews, was totally unintelligible. The Zionist movement, still hiding behind the facade of refugeeism and humanitarianism, had not surfaced on its own; "Palestinians" was still but another word for Arabs, connoting a cross between wild-eyed terrorists and Cadillac-owning bedouins, whose avarice was increasingly responsible for the inaccessibility of reasonably priced gasoline and oil.

Jews and Israelis were easily identifiable, but not so Zionists. The claim that the State of Israel had come into existence primarily to provide a home for the victims of Hitler's persecution had gone unchallenged. That the 1947 demographic makeup of Palestine, two-thirds Arab (Muslim or Christian) and but one-third Jewish, necessitated an abnormal sovereignty and an abnormal nationalism for the new nation occurred to only a few observers. Nor was there awareness that behind the splendid facade of refugeeism, the need to end the perennial homelessness of "the Jewish people"—the nationalist excuse for establishing a state—was being advanced by a scarcely recognized, powerful worldwide movement, Zionism.

It mattered little or not at all that Judaism, the faith, was in fact far from identical to Zionism, the political movement, and that all Jews were not Zionists. Some Jews, including members of the Neturei Karta, who observed all the tenets of religious observance most meticulously, vehemently opposed the nationalist concept. The Zionist movement, ushered in by Theodor Herzl, had called only for a "legally secured home in Palestine" at its Basel Congress of 1897, but then used all-out world sympathy for the oppressed Jews as a sub rosa cover for achieving its real goal, Zionist statehood. And the World War II holocaust removed the last obstacles to the creation of the Jewish state in what was once Palestine.

The new white flag with a single blue six-pointed star, hoisted on May 15, 1948, on a mast on the east coast of the Mediterranean Sea, meant one thing to the Zionist leadership inside the new state and quite another to the world outside. Even as Christian and Jewish supporters were viewing Israel as a state for refugees, the President of the World Zionist Organization, Rabbi Abba Hillel Silver, was openly declaring what he had been saying behind closed doors for years to his followers: "Zionism is not refugeeism. Refugees or no refugees, we still have to realize our ancient goal of recreating a Jewish state in Palestine."

Zionists had always talked of the necessity of "the redemption of the Jewish people through the in-gathering of the exiles," insisting that the tag "exiles" be applied to all Jews outside Israel. U.S. Zionists refused to accept personal residence in Israel as the sole criterion for being a good Zionist and exercising some control over Israeli policy. This issue came to a head at the 23rd World Zionist Congress of 1951, where a compromise was reached whereby the call for "in-gathering" was toned down to make it only one task of Zionism rather than the sole instrument of Jewish redemption. In this way those who did not wish to be "in-gathered" themselves, at least not for the moment, were able to continue their proselytizing among others of American Jewry and remain in good standing in the party.

From the outset of the drive to win a state for themselves, the Zionists had to hide their true nationalist, political ambitions beneath the outer garment of philanthropy in order to win the support of the wealthy and influential Jewish families who were non-Zionist, if not anti-Zionist, at that time. A forthright exposition of true Zionist goals would have endangered the success of the movement.

However successful Zionist leadership may have been in hood-winking other Jews in the West into support of statehood on false grounds, deception was of little avail in trying to solve the far more complicated questions confronting Zionism in the Middle East itself. The 1948 demographic makeup of the new Israeli state, with its 42 percent Arab minority, exposed the Jewish majority to the much higher Arab birth rate and to the very real possibility that the Arabs of Israel might one day become the majority and the Jews a minority within their own state. The Zionist leaders who took over the helm of Israeli government on May 15, 1948, made crystal clear that they would never permit this to happen. "Israel is the country of the Jews and only of the Jews," David Ben-Gurion told Ibrahim Shabath, editor-in-chief of *Al-Mersad*.[4] Golda Meir declared to the Knesset: "I want a Jewish state with a decisive Jewish majority which cannot change over-night. . . ." These remarks of two Israeli Prime Ministers reflected the identical outlook of Israel's founder, Theodor Herzl, who had written in his *Diaries:* "We must expropriate gently the private property on the estates assigned to us. We should try to spirit the penniless Arab population across the borders by procuring employment for it in the transit countries, while denying it any employment in our country."[5]

Such remarks, if uttered by other than Jews and Israelis, would have been forthrightly condemned as racist. But by commanding world sympathy—invoking the specter of Hitler whenever necessary—and talking in terms of security to defend actions taken within the state, Israel continued to hide from the outside world the truth on what was going on within the country. Ignorant, misled Americans insisted on judging the Middle East conflict in terms of the survival of refugees from Hitler, never as the Zionist building of a nation that required expulsion of the overwhelming majority of the Palestinian people from their country, along with expropriation of their lands, homes, and property. (A controversial television documentary showing Israeli soldiers expelling Arabs from a border village in the 1948 war was first banned by the Minister of Education but then shown in Israel on February 13, 1978.)

The new Israeli state moved swiftly to ensure a permanent Jewish majority in the country and to become the exclusivist state for which their dogma called. The Zionist leadership set in motion a simultaneous dual flow: immigration of Jews into the country and emigration of Arabs from the country. The Diaspora Jews were incessantly reminded of the dangers of anti-Semitism. To push out Arabs, to "fear-in" Jews, and to wipe out in the Western world any meaningful differentiation between Jews and Zionists became the imperatives of the supranationalist movement working in cooperation with the government of Israel. "Greater Israel," the slogan of the expansionist opposition Herut party of Menachem Begin, quietly and gradually was taken over by the Labor Establishment as part of its own program during its May 1948 to May 1977 rule.

Israel's quest for "Lebensraum" (living room)—and without Arabs—has remained immutable from the outset, first in Israel proper and then after 1967 in the occupied territories. The fear in Israeli circles has been that between the 1.4 million Arabs who live on the West Bank and in Gaza, and the 574,000 within Israel proper—and with the comparative fertility rate of 3.2 per 100 for Jews, 7.1 for "non-Jews," and 8.3 for Moslem Arabs, according to the *Jerusalem Post* of October 3, 1977—the Israeli Jews by the end of the century would be outnumbered by the Palestinian Arabs. The grave dilemma was how to keep the land without the people so as not to become a minority within their own state.

Forcing out the Arabs was one way of accomplishing this. The June war of 1967 helped. For example, the 43,000 refugees subsisting in the Akabet Jabeer refugee camp had been reduced to 3,000 after the Palestinians were driven across to camps on the east side of the Jordan

River. An additional 55,000 other refugees from the West Bank registered with the United Nations Relief and Works Agency (UNRWA)
also fled in wild panic.

While plotting the further emigration of Palestinians out of the
country, the Israelis had to rely on the cheap labor force provided by
the Palestinian farmers. The Israelis made it more difficult for these
farmers remaining on the land by barring them from cultivating certain
lands as a security risk. By thus forcing the Palestinians off the land,
they naturally decreased Palestinian agricultural products on the market, which was a consequent boost for those Israeli products managing
to reach Arab markets.

Further, in order to lure from their fields the bulk of the Arabs
working on the land to serve as a cheap labor force for building the
industrial side of Israel, particularly in construction projects, the Israelis offered the farmers an incentive of a higher living wage than they
had ever received. This brought them off the farms and into the human
traffic crossing over the Jordan River. Robbed of this cheap labor, and
already drained by calls to military service, Israel would have been
even more hard-pressed for manpower.

By taking manpower from Palestinian agriculture and diverting it
to Israeli industrial development, the Palestinian agricultural base has
been endangered. Plantations lie fallow, and large-scale Palestinian
migration has ensued—precisely the Zionist aim of holding Arab land
without its people.

The Zionists enjoy their cake and are able to eat it, too—to the
applause of the unknowing world. The widely publicized "open
bridge" policy, permitting the flow of Palestinians to and from the
West Bank into Jordan, was believed by world public opinion to indicate Israeli goodwill toward its conquered people. But this policy has
not been carried out in any way for the sake of the Palestinians. Without the daily flow into Israel of 55,000 Palestinian Arab refugees,
earning a daily wage of less than $350,000 but buying roughly some
$30 million in Israeli products, the Israeli economy would have come
to a halt.

The share of Arab labor in Israel's productive industries, according to the *Jerusalem Post*'s economic editor Moshe Ater, by mid-1976
approximated one-quarter, divided equally between Arabs from within
Israel proper and commuters from the administered territories.[6] In
agriculture and building it is one-half. Even in manufacturing, the
share of Arab labor exceeds 10 percent. Arabs constitute about half of
the unskilled workers employed in manufacturing, and virtually all the

farmhands. Arabs also dominate in a number of service industries, such as hotels and garages, which involve inconvenient hours or "dirty" work. As Israeli Jews continue to retreat from productive activity to services and middle-class professions, the Arabs' economic role continues to far exceed their numerical share of the population. And this economic imbalance has accentuated tensions between Arab and Jewish Israelis.

The "open bridge" policy also made possible a flow of Israeli goods, particularly agricultural products, across the Allenby Bridge from the West Bank into Jordan. Produce was usually carried in Israeli-registered trucks with the license plates covered over on arrival in Jordan. This permitted Israel to export its own products into the Arab world through the use of Palestinian middlemen, to whom they offered a good fee for their services plus a bonus, depending on the profit earned. This explains the huge uproar when a consignment of oranges stamped "Jaffa" found its way to the Amman market and the Arabs discovered visible proof that they had been subsidizing their Israeli enemy for years.

It should not be forgotten that the "open bridge" policy also permitted a counterflow of tourist traffic into Israel with the invaluable dollars of American Christians who were visiting Jordan and the Holy Land simultaneously.

The "open fences" established by Israel with South Lebanon represented a move toward achieving the Zionist goal of a "Greater Israel" to include what is now southern Lebanon up to the Litani River, with its invaluable waters. This aspiration had been expressed in maps presented to Versailles Treaty conferees in 1919 by Zionist representatives.

The Book of Leviticus gives this biblical command: "The stranger who sojourns with you shall be unto you as the native among you, and you shall love him as yourself; for you were strangers in the land of Egypt.[7] This, like so much else in the Holy Scriptures, was ignored from the outset by the government of the fledgling Israeli state. If the Arabs, who were themselves amost pure Semites, could be accused of anti-Semitism, as they have been because of their intense and unrelenting opposition to Zionism and to Israel, the show of bigotry fits far more appropriately on the Israeli foot. The 180,000 Arabs who remained and did not flee the new state upon its establishment in 1948 (now grown to 570,000 plus), and the 700,000 Jewish Arabs who emigrated to Israel from Yemen, Iraq, Egypt, and the North African countries, have been the victims of anti-Semitism, to use the popular parlance. As the editor of the *Jewish Newsletter* reported, they "have been subject to a series of discriminations and persecutions which would shock the civilized world, if they were fully known."[8]

While Israel is almost universally regarded as the shining example of "democracy" in the Middle East, Israel's 1952 Nationality Act codified discrimination into law and made the Arabs second-class citizens. Under this legislation all Jews in Israel automatically became citizens of the state, but not one of the more than 240,000 Arabs by that time in the country could gain citizenship without first proving that he had been a Palestinian citizen before May 14, 1948, and that he had lived in Israel continuously since the establishment of the state, or that he had entered Israel legally after its establishment.

To become a naturalized Israeli citizen, the Arab had to meet six requirements, including providing documentary proof of residence in Israel "for three of the five years preceding the application" and knowledge of the Hebrew language. A Jew, from no matter where in the world, is exempt from these requirements as part of "the Jewish people." This grouping (in official Israeli government and Zionist organization declarations the term is invariably followed by a verb in singular form) has won increasing acceptance and a certain legal status: "A national home for *the Jewish people*" in the 1917 Balfour Declaration and "the historic connection of *the Jewish people* with Palestine" (italics added) in the 1922 preamble of the League of Nations covenant were derived from the Basel program of the First Zionist Congress in 1897, forerunners to the careful and purposeful wording used in the declaration of the establishment of the State of Israel on May 14, 1948:

We appeal to the Jewish people throughout the Diaspora to rally round the Jews of Eretz Israel in the tasks of immigration and upbuilding and to stand by them in the great struggle for the realization of the age-old dream—the redemption of Israel.[9]

To preserve the "Jewish people," imperiled by emancipation and assimilation, Prime Minister David Ben-Gurion declared in the *Israel Government Year Book 1952:*

The State of Israel is a part of the Middle East only in geography, which is, in the main, a static element. From the more decisive standpoint of dynamism, creation and growth, Israel is a part of world Jewry.[10]

The Law of Return codified this Jewish people concept: "The State of Israel considers itself as the creation of the Jewish people"[11] and endowed any Jew (only in recent years have criminals, such as

Meyer Lansky, and drug addicts been denied the right to immigrate to Israel for permanent settlement). Without exception, Israeli spokesmen continued to proclaim, as did the Israeli High Court in January 1972, "There is no Israeli nation apart from the Jewish people residing in Israel and the Jews in the Diaspora." And if Jews outside were to be considered part of the state and were to be "ingathered," the other side of the coin was that more Palestinians had to be removed, let alone not permitted to return home, to make room for incoming Jews. Under this law a Jew may become a citizen of Israel after one minute in the land, a status that can be denied to an Arab although he may have been born in the land and his forebears been there for a thousand years. When Israel annexed the eastern Arab portion of captured Jerusalem in 1967, thousands of Palestinian Arabs fell within the borders of the enlarged State of Israel—but ten years later many were still being denied Israeli citizenship.

The Israeli Nationality Law makes it possible for a non-Jew to be born within Israel's pre-1967 territory and yet be doomed to inherited statelessness. The Israeli Ministry of Interior has yet to publish official statistics on the number of stateless Palestinian Arab residents living under Israeli law. The State of Israel created two classes of citizens, Jews and non-Jews, with differing legal rights. This implemented the Zionist thesis that theirs was a Jewish state belonging to the "Jewish people" everywhere and only to Jews—in accord with Ben-Gurion's dicta.

Arabs who were granted citizenship in Israel were treated quite differently from the Jewish settlers. Many were removed from villages along the border in the interests of security and paid but nominal compensation for their property. Those permitted to remain in their villages were subject to strict regulations and military rule. Until 1966 they were confined under curfew restrictions to certain areas. With no access to civilian justice, they were subject to court-martial. They faced restrictions on their comings and goings. They had to obtain a permit to travel away from the border or to visit Jewish settlements, and Jews were not permitted to enter Arab villages without written permits from the government. Arabs in Israel held distinctive identity cards, different from those held by Jews. The official Israeli explanation for this strict rule over Arab Israelis was the necessity of security: "Arab states still threaten Israel with war, and Arab villages are situated near Israel's borders."

A motion by opposition parties in the Knesset calling for abolition of discriminatory military rule was defeated by the ruling Mapai party and its Religious party allies by a narrow margin in February 1962. The relaxations of military rule then permitted were characterized by the *London Times* as "not amounting to much. . . . It is the principle of military rule that has been challenged rather than details of its application."[12] Zionist organizations in the U.S., then and since, have been very sensitive to the charge raised incessantly in U.N. debates of discrimination against the Arabs of Israel, even bringing certain Arabs to the U.S. to make appearances on radio and TV and to hold press conferences as a refutation to these allegations.

The underlying assumption of the system of military government imposed upon Israel's Arab citizens for eighteen years after the creation of the state was that every Arab was a security risk whose movements and activities had to be constantly monitored and controlled. Arabs could not travel within the country without special passes from the military government. They could be summarily exiled from their home villages and restricted to special zones, all at the discretion of local military governors and without recourse to the courts. In some cases entire villages were forcibly emptied and the land then turned over to nearby Jewish settlements for cultivation. All this was done in the name of military security.

Under this military arrangement, an unresponsive bureaucratic apparatus was bred, totally unrelated to any military concerns and interfering in every aspect of the communal life of the Arabs. Military governors were known to cultivate and promote their own favored Arab leaders, of course preferring those who would foster the interests of the ruling Labor party.

Israel's growing security problem, buttressed by the Israeli Masada complex, underlay the decision to refuse to permit the Maronite Christian inhabitants of tiny Kafr Baram and Ikrit to return to their deserted villages. These Christian Arabs, who had always sympathized with the Israeli government, had left during the 1948 war when the Israeli army asked them to evacuate their villages for two weeks; an Arab counteroffensive was feared and the towns were situated in a very strategic position a few miles from the Lebanese border. They locked their homes, collected their herds and stables and sheds, left eighteen men to guard their property, and set out for temporary shelter in a village two or three kilometers away. Thereafter, the Knesset passed the Land Acquisition Act giving retroactive legality to the transfer of the land of Kafr Baram to the Development Authority, ending any hopes on the part of the evacuees for their return. The army then blew up the houses in the village, and the next day trucks came to remove the ruins. Baram was wiped off the face of the earth. As the explosive charges were placed around the walls of the houses, the evacuees gathered on a hill above their village for one last look; it is called by them the "hill of tears."

In a 1974 letter to Prime Minister Golda Meir, the head of the Greek Catholic community , Archbishop Joseph Raya, protested the treatment of Christian Arabs in Israel:

There is not enough justice in this country. There is neither democracy nor liberty. No ￢nd justifies injustice whether the end is to be the good of the state or the nation. If you base security on the denial of justice, there is no accumulation of money which will guarantee that security; not even an army as strong as the Romans will ensure it.[13]

Promises had been given to the inhabitants of the two villages at the time of the 1948 war that they would be allowed to return. Israel's Supreme Court in a 1951 decision ruled that the citizens of Ikrit were not refugees but Israelis, and as their property had not been abandoned, there was no legal right to include it with enemy absentee property. But the military declared they could not return for "security reasons," the area having been declared "closed territory."

A letter to the Israeli daily newspaper *Ha'aretz* made the telling point:

If the Israeli government is not capable of reaching a just and free agreement with Arab inhabitants who are under its rule and with local refugees within the boundaries of the state, and on the basis of respecting their basic rights, how will it be able—on the basis of its present policy—to reach a just and lasting agreement with neighboring Arab countries, in a solution of the Israeli-Arab conflict by peaceful means in joint agreement?

One of the writers for another of the Israeli newspapers, *Yediot Aharonot,* viewed this problem from a very opposite and sentimental viewpoint:

There is another point which Kafr arouses a spiritual attachment in the people of Kafr Baram and Ikrit despite the lack of historical proof and only by intuition. It seems to me that most of the Maronites in the Galilee and Lebanon are the survivors of Jewish villages whose inhabitants converted to Christianity in the oppressive period of the Byzantine authority. The inhabitants of Baram and Ikrit have very Jewish eyes, and the Aramic language in which their prayers are written also strengthens this supposition. Finally, all my sensitive spiritual motivation whispers to me, "They must be treated well and returned to their inherited land." But here I find myself in a difficult conflict with my Zionist conscience.

This same writer went on to admit that there was a basic unresolved conflict inasmuch as the Arabs, as well as the Israelis, have a deep sentimental attachment to the land of their fathers, "which lights the fires of hatred against us." He then decided that he must put aside his sentimental feelings and permit his Zionist inclinations to win out because if these people were permitted to return to their land it would mean the "uprooting of the Zionist theory."

What really decided the fate of the citizens of these two little villages was that their moral right to return was subordinated to government fear of permitting more Arabs to live near the troublesome Lebanese border. Even seven hours of intense conversation between Meir and Israel's intelligentsia could not alter the mind of the Prime Minister, who was worried lest a precedent be established for the return of other Arabs to lands taken from them, both in sensitive regions and elsewhere. Even the public admission by Tel Aviv University Law School Dean Amnon Rubinstein that the return of the villages would not demand "the addition of a single soldier in the region" was of no avail.

The tragedy of the village of Baram is not unique. It is an example of how much of Palestine was expropriated by force. General Chaim Bar-Lev stated in *Yediot Aharonot* on August 8, 1972:

It's first and foremost a security matter. The minority (non-Jewish villages on the Lebanese borders) are extremely important, and we have no wish to add to their number. . . . If we now allow the return of Kafr Baram, we would be creating a precedent, and there are several other villages whose inhabitants have also been evicted.

More direct and blunt was Yoram Bar Porath, writer for the same newspaper:

It is the duty of the Israeli leaders to explain to the public with clarity and courage a number of facts that have been submerged with the passage of time. *The first of these is the fact that there is no Zionism, settlement, or Jewish State without eviction of the Arabs and expropriation of their lands.*[14] (Italics added.)

Baram's 200 families, who now live in nearby Gush-Halav, want only to have the uncultivated land returned to them, thus ending their thirty-year exile. "Baram is where I grew up and laughed," said Maronite Argoub Mtanes. "That is where we want to live."[15] Although the Prime Minister's Adviser on Arab Affairs, Shmuel Toledano, long ago conceded the loyalty of the inhabitants of the villages and agreed that they posed no security threat, the government has remained firm in its decision. The massive demonstration, supported by most of the liberal forces within Israel and clerical groups, was reported in the Western press, but to no good effect.

When Begin came to power he stated, as part of his new alliance with Maronite forces in Lebanon, that he wished the return of the people of Kafr Baram and Ikrit to their homes[16] but as yet this wish remains but a devout hope to the dispossessed people of the two villages.

The London *Times* noted that military rule was not the sole handicap under which Arabs in Israel lived:

A greater source of complaint for the younger generation is the lack of adequate higher education and, still more, the shortage of jobs when education is complete. Except in teaching, there is still not the scope for Arabs in public service that their numbers or abilities warrant . . . they are worse off in commerce and industry.[17]

Nationally, economic and social disabilities also remain unaltered. As far back as 1961, *Christian Science Monitor* correspondent in Israel Moshe Brilliant reported that Arabs were barred from jobs even in positions not remotely connected with national security, for private enterprise regarded them as security risks.[18] Arab students often attended university only after being granted travel permits limiting them to one route and forbidding them to stop off on their way or to stir from Jerusalem, except with the express written permission of the military governor in their place of residence. Jewish doctors were barred from residing in Arab communities where they were employed at government health centers. This left such villages without medical care after sundown. Every Arab or Druze working in Tel Aviv or Haifa, even if he were a veteran, would have to commute daily from his village to the city, where he might spend the night only if he had obtained a special permit from the military governor, who was free to act completely at his own discretion.

Military governors controlled labor relations, awarded building and business permits and marriage certificates, approved appointment of teachers and municipal council members and religious officials. These military rulers were known to force Arabs to sell to Jewish purchasers from a nearby settlement by refusing permission to go to town to sell their property. Permission was required to look for work or to obtain medical help, and Arab children were known to die in the arms of their mothers while waiting in the corridor of the governor for a permit to see the doctor.

Many Israelis were shocked by a letter in the *Jerusalem Post* February 3, 1964, written by an eminent Israeli, Dr. Peter Ben. He attributed the death of twenty-four Arab children in a measles epidemic to the fact that most Arab villages had no regular doctors at all. He accused the Israeli Ministry of Health of negligence in treating the Arab minorities, whom he referred to as "the country's 20 percent of uninsured citizens."

In calling for an end to military rule, former Minister of Justice Pinhas Rosen said, "We must turn the Arabs in Israel into citizens with equal rights in compliance with the principles of a really democratic state."[19] But when military rule formally came to an end, the life of Arab Israelis was still marred by other serious discriminatory actions in force since the creation of the state.

Most of the Arab farmer-peasants lost their land during the first (1948) Arab-Israeli war. In the wake of the armed forces, nearby kibbutzim seized additional farmland from Arab villages. Under the 1950 Absentee Property Law, absolute power to declare any property or person absentee was vested in the Custodian of Absentee Property Land, and other property of absentees could be confiscated. Held to be "absentee" was any Arab who "left his place of residence and went [for any duration of time, even days or hours] to another place which was, at that time, held by forces that tried to hinder the establishment of the State of Israel." Thirty thousand Palestinians who had fled from one part of Israel to another during the fighting were thus declared absentees and lost their property. For example, half of the Arab inhabitants of Kafr Elut remained in their village, but the other half took refuge in Nazareth. All were declared absentees, and those who remained in their homes were required to make payment to the Custodian for use of their own lands.

The Land Acquisition Law of 1953 legalized seizures of Arab lands that had taken place to date. Arabs who owned land in Israel and remained behind, but had moved or been moved elsewhere, were compensated in cash based on the 1950 value, which ranged between 15 and 25 Israeli pounds per quarter acre (dunum) rather than the 1953 value, which was somewhere between 250 and 350 Israeli pounds per quarter acre. The pound had depreciated from $2.80 in 1950 to $1 at the time of the new legislation. Jewish writer Derrick Tozer described these laws as "extraordinary, even in modern times." The Tel Aviv newspaper *Ha'aretz* protested: "There is no reason to legalize the fact that certain farms exploited the victory of the state and seized for their own benefit the lands of their neighbors."[20]

While serving as Minister of Agriculture, Moshe Dayan introduced in 1961 in the Knesset the Agricultural Lands Condolidation Law, allegedly designed to consolidate scattered land parcels in Galilee and permit the establishment of twenty new Jewish settlements there (even then the Israeli Establishment was worried about a possible Arab majority in this heavily Arab region). Commenting in *Ner*, Dr. Shimeon Shereshevsky declared that the purpose of this law was to bring about the same result as the 1953 legislation, under which "innumerable acts of injustice were perpetrated against those whose lands were thus 'acquired,' including the land values fixed for them, compensations which have not been paid in many cases to this day." This Israeli further noted, "The bad and insulting attitude toward the Arab land owners, whose lands and those of their ancestors were confiscated, quite simply because Jewish kibbutzim and moshavim[21] wanted to increase their holdings." In the words of *Ha'aretz*, "Under the right of expropriation, more and more land was being added to one section of the population at the expense of another which happens to be weaker."[22]

An ingenious use of other laws helped in the grab of Arab lands. Under the right given to the Minister of Defense, an area could be declared a "security zone," which Arab cultivators were not permitted to enter. Under the Cultivation of Wastelands ordinance, the government was authorized to take over land not cultivated. Since the declaration of a security zone results in the area not being cultivated, it could then be taken over by the government and given to Jewish settlers, who were permitted to enter and cultivate it. By these and similar means, as early as 1965 some 3,125,000 acres (12,500,000 dunums), more than 60 percent of the land of Arab Israelis who had never left Israel, had been confiscated. Critic Shereshevsky stated that the Israeli government was concerned with only one thing: "to remove the Arab rural settlers from their homes and uproot them from their lands, so as to force them to leave Galilee and the Triangle and go elsewhere, to the large cities such as Haifa, where they would live in the slums as proletarians deprived of hope."

Not only did the Palestinians lose their land, they also lost the right to work on the land. During the mandate, the Jewish Agency, the Keren Kayemet, the Keren Hayesod, the Histadrut (whose official name is General Federation of Jewish Labor in Palestine), and almost all Jewish public and private institutions made it a rule that no Arab was to be employed. Under the Mandate, according to a British High Commissioner report, "the principle of persistent and deliberate boycott of Arab labor had been set in force, although it was contrary to the Mandate . . . and an increasing source of danger to the country."[23]

Article 3 of the constitution of the Jewish National Fund, which holds most of the agricultural land in Israel, declares that land "is to be held as the inalienable property of the Jewish people," and "in all works and undertakings carried out or furthered by the Jewish Agency, it shall be deemed to be a matter of principle that Jewish labor shall be employed." This proviso appears as Article 23 in standard land leases, along with the proviso that the "employment of non-Jewish labor shall constitute adequate proof as to damages." Near civil war and bloodshed ensued when certain Jewish owners of orange groves tried to hire the cheaper and sometimes better trained Arab laborers for their groves. When this racist clause was incorporated into Israeli law on August 1, 1967, as part of the Agricultural Settlement Law, Knesset opposition member Uri Avnery stated, "This law is going to expel Arab cultivators from the land that was formerly theirs and was handed over to the Jews. We shall be acting in accordance with the verse which says, 'Hast thou killed and also inherited?' " It was only in 1959 that the monolithic Histadrut began to accept Arab labor members into its ranks.

Even after the controls imposed by military rule had been removed, the Israeli Arabs were still treated as a conquered and suspect population. In 1948 and 1949 Israel adopted the Emergency Defense Regulations from the British World War II decrees, absolutely restricting the movement of all Palestinians, both Arab and Jewish. This became the most feasible instrument of oppression and eviction that the Zionist regime could muster. Supplemented by travel limitations and expulsions, it served as a cloak for the plunder of lands.

Here is a sampling from these far-reaching presently existing laws:

Articles 109 and 110 give power to enter anyone's home at any hour, day or night.

Article 119 empowers the Military Commander to destroy a house if under his suspicion.

Article 120 gives the power to confiscate private property.

Article 121 gives the power to expel from the country.

As mentioned above, the Minister of Agriculture under Regulation 125 has been permitted to expropriate "fallow" lands. First, the owner is told he cannot work the land; after a certain period of time the area becomes fallow and the Agricultural Minister can then expropriate it. A former Minister of Defense said regarding this regulation:

"The 125th paragraph on which the military government bases itself in great measure is a direct continuation of the struggle for Jewish settlement and immigration."

Although the Jewish community in Palestine fiercely resisted the same British mandatory laws before statehood, Israel now continues their use against the Arabs. Israel's one-time Minister of Justice Yaacov Shapiro described these regulations in 1946 as "unparalleled in any civilized country; there were no such laws even in Nazi Germany." And then the Zionist government applied them both to the Arab inhabitants of the 1967 occupied territories and to Arab citizens of Israel.

Other Zionist leaders, including former Premier Ben-Gurion, just prior to his death, defended the Emergency Regulations as the prop on which the military government rested: "The military government comes to defend the rights of Jewish settlement in all parts of the country." Through such regulations, thousands of Arabs have been dispossessed of their rightfully owned lands and tens of settlements have been built on these closed areas, with the new immigrants arriving from the Soviet Union and elsewhere.

While the American media continued to draw a picture of a contented Arab population enjoying the greatest benefits of "democratic Israel," far better off and far happier than their own brethren under Arab rule, Arab youth in Israel were being brought up in an atmosphere of total oppression in which threats of house arrest, demolition of their homes, eviction, or expulsion often forced them to deal closely with police security officers. Young Arab students who refused to serve as informers were told they could not receive the jobs they sought, as was the case of one Nebil Saath, who could not obtain a job at the Broadcasting Service in the early 1960s because he would not play the role of a quisling. Thereafter, while living in his village of Um-El-Fahum, southeast of Haifa, he was forced to renew his permit monthly in order to leave the village for studies and for work.

It was under the cover of war that the mass displacement of indigenous Arabs could be most effectively carried out. In order to create a larger Jewish majority, thousands of Palestinians had been forced to flee from their homes during the initial fighting in 1948, and they were then joined in exile by others who were expelled after the war had ended. This policy enacted during what Israel called its "War of Independence" was equally so in the June 1967 six-day war. Reduction of the Arab population in Israeli-occupied areas in 1967, as in 1948, became a dire necessity and official Israeli policy. U.N. Chief of Staff Odd Bull reported: "The Israelis encouraged their departure by various means just as they had in 1948."[24] In 1967 the 1.5 million Arabs in Israel proper and in the conquered territories, with the almost three-to-one edge in birthrate, obviously posed the threat of an eventual Arab majority within a few decades. Direct annexation of people as well as territory could only challenge Israel's racially exclusivist state. *US News and World Report* indicated that Israel was considering "a variety of schemes that would in one way or another prevent the Arabs in the occupied territories from becoming Israeli citizens to save Israel from 'conquest' by the Arabs from within."[25] Leaders of Israel debated alternate "democratic" procedures for liquidating the problem.

In a report released in December 1970, the U.N. Special Committee to Investigate Israeli Practices Affecting the Human Rights of the Population of the Occupied Territories found that there was much "evidence of mass deportation and of the creation of conditions which leave no option to the individuals except to leave the territory." The committee further found that the inhabitants of the occupied areas were being "deprived of leadership by the deportation or detention of a considerable number of those persons looked upon by the inhabitants as leaders."

Declaring that any law is invalid if such law violates the provisions of the Geneva Convention, the Special Committee rejected the defense by Israel of its actions under the authority of the Defense Emergency Regulations of 1945. On the basis of "considerable evidence, eyewitness accounts, and newspaper reports," the committee held:

There is a policy of collective and area punishment being imposed indiscriminately on the civilian inhabitants in the occupied areas . . . that such punishment is, in most cases, inflicted by way of reprisal for acts of sabotage of which the resistance movement is suspected . . . the collective and area punishment takes the form of destruction of houses, curfews and mass arrests. A common feature of these forms of collective punishment appears to be the lack of proportion between the act committed and the punishment imposed. It is an established fact that Halhul was the scene of extensive destruction, that the destruction was inflicted as a collective punishment by way of reprisal, and that the Israeli authorities were responsible for the destruction that took place.[26]

The committee was composed of representatives of Sri Lanka (Ceylon), Somalia, and Yugoslavia, whose findings were in line with those of the International Committee of the Red Cross.

Later on in the same year, the committee warned that Israel was continuing to violate the rights of Arab inhabitants in the occupied territories and expressed concern that the "measures taken by Israel all tend to show they will make the occupied territories socially, economically, politically and judicially part of Israel unless some form of supervision of the occupation is put into effect."

Long after the stunning military victory of 1967, Israel continued to pursue a policy of outright expulsion of the Arab civilian population through deliberate intimidation, oppression, economic strangulation, and psychological warfare. The goal was to keep most of the seized territory but somehow be rid of the Arabs living there. In June and July 1968 alone, thirteen months after the 1967 war, 4,116 refugees were driven across the River Jordan onto the East Bank, clearly indicating the extent to which Israeli policy was being implemented by local military governors. By August 1968 the refugee flow into the Kingdom of Jordan had risen to 408,000, of whom 351,000 had come from the occupied West Bank and the remainder from the Gaza Strip. Official UNRWA figures indicated 80,000 refugees were squeezed into six camps where conditions were appalling. The rest subsisted in Jordanian cities, suffering acute social and economic problems.

The flight from Israel of the original Arab Palestinian refugees, who by 1976 numbered 1.5 million, has long been a matter of dispute. Propaganda accepted by most Americans insists that the Arabs left voluntarily, on their own accord at the behest of their leaders with the intent of returning home with the "victorious Arab armies." Aside from the fact that no such "behest" has ever been recorded, the 1967 war exposed this as pure myth-information. History does sometimes repeat itself, and 1967 pointed up what Christopher Sykes had written in *Crossroads to Israel,* a book not unfriendly to the Zionist case, in describing the 1948 flight: "But if the exodus was by and large an accident of war in the first stage, in the later stage it was consciously and mercilessly helped on by Jewish threats and aggression towards Arab populations."[27]

In an article in the London *Times,*[28] two members of the British House of Commons spelled out details of the psychological warfare used in 1967 to "persuade" Arab Palestinians to leave their homes and flee across the Jordan. Many left their camp in Jericho because of sheer panic, but "rifle butts do seem to have been used in some cases (we saw their imprint on some refugees)," according to the parliamentarians.

These two House of Commons members, Ian Gilmour and James Walters, had upset the Israeli officials by arriving unexpectedly and were thus able to view the true conditions of the crossings over the

Allenby Bridge. Their comment is pertinent: "The contrast between the indulgence granted to Israeli trippers and the attitude of guards towards the Arabs was shocking. Tourists can go to the Israeli end of the bridge and photograph the departing refugees. Arabs who have been separated from their families are not allowed to go to the same spot to see if their children are alive." The two British parliamentarians were convinced that "the bulk of the refugees have been and still are being forced out."

Expert psychological warfare served in other instances. Residents of Bethlehem were informed that "unless they left within hours, they and their homes would be blown up. They left." In another village a rumor was spread that anyone remaining in the village one hour later would be killed. The entire populace evacuated their homes and, just by chance, found buses outside their village to transport them across the river. Such a desertion of a village has often just preceded demolition and the rebuilding of an Israeli paramilitary settlement in its place.

As reported in *There Goes the Middle East,*[29] the little town of Qalqilya, lying in the hills of Samaria, boasted luxuriant orange groves in the coastal plain nearby. In 1949 an armistice line divided the town from its groves. At the time of the first orange-picking season, many people from Qalqilya went over the line to pick oranges from their own trees. The Israelis concealed patrols in the groves and killed the pickers. The resulting incidents were described to Western readers as "armed incursions of bandits." These trying times, endured by the Arabs for eighteen years, ended in 1967 when Qalqilya, as well as neighboring Zeita, Habaleh, Deir Ghosun, Latrun, and Beit Yalu, all captured in the six-day war, were bulldozed and the latter two villages all but eradicated from the map.

The refusal of Israel to permit the indigenous Palestinian population to return to their homes and the flagrant violation of civil and human rights visited on its Arab minority, who at best could be considered second-class citizens (in fact, third-class because the Oriental Jews from the Arab world were accorded second-class treatment), was kept far from the attention of Israel's many admirers in the West. American Jews and Christians had been sold the notion that the Israeli state was a modern "bastion of democracy" (some bastion—without U.S. money and arms, Israel would totally collapse). Indeed, Israel was democratic in the sense that its representative form of government was far advanced over that of its neighbors. But out of abysmal ignorance and a gnawing sense of guilt for the holocaust, the Western community willingly accepted in toto the idealized Zionist fairytale, including the myth that the Arabs of Palestine were being well treated.

On paper, the Israeli Arabs, whose numbers have increased from 125,000 in 1949 to 574,000 in 1977, appear to be full-fledged citizens with the same rights and duties as the 2.6 million Jewish residents. They may vote, pay taxes, own land, run businesses, go to their own public schools, hold union cards, carry Israeli passports, sit in the Knesset, and, as *New York Times* correspondent Terrence Smith noted, "occasionally even die in the same indiscriminate terrorist attacks on the streets of Jerusalem."

On the other hand, these Israeli Arabs are not called to serve in the armed services, nor are their kin entitled to automatic citizenship as Jews are under the Law of Return. And even in highly vaunted "democratic" Israel, there are political discriminations. The Arabs are grossly under-represented. For their 14 percent of the population, they should have sixteen or seventeen seats, in the parliament; they have five. Arab political parties, as such, are prohibited; only the Communist Rakah party is free of Zionist control, so the Arabs give their support to it.

But it is in practical economic, human, and social terms that Israeli Arabs are demonstrably second-class citizens. Their per capita income is significantly less than the average of Jewish Israelis; their educational level is far inferior. While representing 14 percent of the total population, they constitute only 3 percent of the university population, and the proportion of Arabs in civil service is far lower than what they would be entitled to on the basis of their share of the population. Of a total of 48,792 civil servants in 1961, only 500—approximately 1 percent—were Arabs. This situation has not substantially improved since then.

Politically, it was only in 1972 that Israeli Arabs won the right to join the ruling Labor party, after years of being barred. By 1977 only about 4,000 of the 300,000 party members were Israeli Arabs, and in the 120-seat Knesset, there were but five Arabs. With the exception of these few elected officials, there are no Israeli Arabs in the high ranks of the Israeli Establishment, no Cabinet members. There are, of course, none in the army, and while Arabic is the official language with Hebrew, few government officials speak it. There is no universal level of instruction in Arabic. Public telephone directories are issued in Hebrew and English, not in Arabic. There are many other benefits and advantages provided by the government to Jews only.

Arab schools in Israel have suffered from a serious shortage of books, forcing teachers and pupils to use old ones. And the situation regarding school buildings is also sad. Most are not fit to be used as schools: old, with small, dark rooms and few sanitary amenities. Playing fields, furniture, and other equipment are inadequate. But the Ministry of Education has turned a blind eye to these conditions, adding the pretext that he was unable to provide such aid to villages that had no local authority (a municipality or a local council); of course, the Minister of Interior has not yet established any form of local government in 40 percent of Arab villages, inhabited by 60 percent of the Arab population of Israel.

In the course of ten fiscal years, 1960–1970, the state allocated the paltry sum of ten million Israeli pounds (less than $2 million, three quarters of which were repayable loans) for the improvement of Arab schools in the country. This constituted only a minuscule proportion of the Ministry of Education's budget which totals tens of millions of Israeli pounds.[30]

It may be claimed that the Israeli Arabs are better off than their brethren had been on the West Bank under Jordanian rule and in most other Arab countries, that their standard of living is higher, their infant mortality lower, and other social services improved. But they certainly are far less free under Israeli rule than they used to be.

Israel's treatment of her Arab citizens led the great Socialist leader Norman Thomas to declare in early September 1961: "An Arab, without too much exaggeration, can complain that the Jews are practising Hitlerism in reverse. The Arabs have been made second-class citizens."[31] But few Americans read this sincere observation, and none would have dreamt of linking it with the troubles in Israel that broke out on September 22, 1961.

The alleged well-being of the Arab community in Israel was shattered on that date when antigovernment demonstrations broke out in Nazareth, Haifa, Acre, and other Arab population parts of Israel. The uprising continued for five days following the killing of five Arab youths who had attempted to cross into then Egypt-held Gaza and were apprehended by the Israeli border patrol. The *New York Times* was obliged to carry an account of the incidents on the front page, with correspondent Laurence Fellows closing his report on this note:

The bitterest pill for the Arabs in Israel by far is a military government. Perhaps 180,000 of the 220,000 Arabs in Israel live under army rule. They are under curfew restrictions and are confined to certain areas. . . . In addition, they are not given access to civilian courts under ordinary circumstances, but are subject instead to courts-martial."[32]

However contemptuous of the Palestinians most Israelis may be, they are also deeply disturbed and worried about a vital demographic factor they cannot control, either within Israel proper or in the occupied territories. The Arab population, already being 67 percent in Galilee's western portion and only 39,000 less than a majority by mid-1975 in the northern district (in 1974 but 759 Jews were added to the population while the Arab population increased by 9,035), threatened to constitute a majority of the total population of the district. This led to the plan set forth in a secret memorandum submitted to Prime Minister Rabin by the Northern District Commissioner of the Ministry of Interior, Israel Koenig. "According to this rate of increase, by 1978 Arabs will constitute over 51 percent of the total population of this district," Koenig pointed out, which will "endanger control of that area and create possibilities of military forces from the north infiltrating in proportion to the acceleration of the nationalistic process among Israeli Arabs and their willingness to have help [from their co–Arabs]."[33]

Reminiscent of another secret, racist report—the Klausner Memorandum of 1946, submitted to the Jewish advisers in the occupied German zone so as to prevent Jews in the World War II concentration camps from going to countries of their own choice rather than to Israel —the 1976 Koenig plan for Galilee proposed to thin out the Arab population through varied measures. To meet the challenge of the Palestine Liberation Organization (PLO) and the rise of Arab nationalism in the country, Koenig proposed "to redress the drastic situation by giving Arabs no more than 20 percent of the available jobs; by changing the selection system to reduce the number of Arab students in the universities and encouraging the channeling of these students into technical professions, physical and natural sciences and thus to leave them with less time for dabbling in nationalism—also to make trips for students easier while making the return and employment more difficult, which is to encourage their emigration."[34]

Further, this plan would have the Israeli government "neutralize and encumber Arab agents in the northern areas in order to avoid the dependence of the Jewish population on those agents and otherwise disassociate the population from its present leadership."[35] To bring the "rebels" under national control, payment of "big family grants to Arabs should be transferred from the national insurance system to the Jewish Agency or the Zionist Organization." Never has Israel's Zionist system of classifying its citizens into Jews and non-Jews been more nakedly exposed.

A blind eye continued to be turned for years to Israel's intercommunal and interreligious relationships, particularly since the military rule in Israel had been relaxed. On the surface, the Arabs of Israel and the Israeli government seemed to have worked things out so that visitors on conducted tours gained the impression that "everything was coming up roses." Then in the spring of 1976 savage rioting erupted in several towns of the Galilee region of Israel.

In the face of the Israeli decision to expropriate 375,000 acres (1.5 million dunums) of Arab-owned Galilee land, and governmental encouragement of Jews to settle there, the threatened Arab villages and defense committees declared March 30, 1976, as "Day of the Land" and launched a general strike in which the whole Arab population of Israel participated. Normally passive in the face of denial of full civil and democratic rights, the Israeli Arabs suddenly came to life. The establishment of settlements in the occupied territories had long been a thorn in the side of the Arabs of the West Bank and Gaza, but this time the aggrieved protestants were the Israeli Arabs. The progressive confiscation of Arab lands for Jewish development inside Israel was keeping pace with Jewish civilian settlements in the occupied lands.

The Israeli Arabs were joined by a mass strike in the occupied West Bank and Gaza, where protest demonstrations had been held the three previous months. All sectors of the Palestinian people—students, workers, peasants, and women—united to express their condemnation of twenty-eight years of Israeli takeover and misrule. Thousands of Arab teenagers blockaded roads and stoned military vehicles. Israeli soldiers responded with firearms. When it was all over, seven Israeli Arabs were dead, with scores on both sides injured. Among those killed was the teenage daughter of the prominent Nabulsi Palestinian family, who had been shot in the back of the neck.

It was the worst outbreak of communal violence in Israel's history and created shock waves throughout the already beleaguered country. Having previously convinced themselves that "their Arabs" had been reconciled to the Jewish state, many Israelis had to wonder for the first time about a new Palestinian nationalist time bomb within their own borders.

The lid had been blown off Pandora's box, exposing to the outside world for the first time the true state of the Palestinian Arabs and the actual facts of the Israeli occupation of Arab lands. What had previously been considered pure Arab propaganda regarding the oppressive rule in the occupied territories and the third-class citizenship in Israel proper was now exposed to world public opinion in a manner even the U.S. media could not ignore. Previously, Israel had been able to appear as a benign occupier of Palestinian lands, but when news services circulated pictures of Israeli soldiers and police grabbing teenage Israeli-Arab schoolgirls by the hair, clubbing others to the ground, and even shooting one in the back, it was difficult for the Zionists to live up to their image as an open society and the only "democracy" in the Middle East.

Many events had been helping to coalesce the rising tide of nationalism among Arab Israelis with the continuing resistance of Palestinians Arabs in the occupied territories. In Gaza an agricultural packaging plant had been destroyed by four masked commandos, involving losses estimated from two to five million Israeli pounds ($400,000 to $1 million). More importantly, in Nablus, even as the Israeli military occupying forces continued to blow up homes of Palestinians suspected of aiding the fedayeen, Palestinian flags began to flutter over public buildings and minarets, and leaflets appeared calling on the population "to continue the combat of chasing the enemy from all the occupied territories." In Jerusalem 500 prominent Arabs, including the muftis of Amman, Jerusalem, and Hebron, attended a rally protesting the occupation and Israeli reprisal raids on Palestinian refugee camps. "Israeli murderers" was one of the slogans shouted to the gathering. The December 1975 election of an Israeli Arab Communist as mayor of Nazareth had been followed by the overwhelming PLO victories in the local elections throughout the occupied West Bank and Gaza. In this voting, temporizers and the old-line politicians were thrown out, forced to give way to intense PLO nationalists.

Inside Israel, demonstrators marked the Prime Minister's visit to Nazareth, and slogans of solidarity with the PLO were shouted during student demonstrations. Arab students in the universities, not permitted arms or to serve in the military forces, refused to take guard duty at the universities. As a show of independence, the inhabitants of Nazareth were called by its Arab mayor and council to help the municipality pay off its pressing debts.

The "Day of the Land" outbreak was the consequence of longsimmering grievances of Israel's Arab minority. Even as attempts to bring about a dialogue on the U.N. resolution equating Zionism with racism and racial discrimination were being totally suppressed, *Pi Ha-Aton*, [36] the weekly student paper on the campus of Jerusalem's Hebrew University, was publishing an article on the subject in Hebrew from the pen of the country's leading civil rights defender, Dr. Israel Shahak.

Professor of Organic Chemistry at Hebrew University and survivor of the Bergen-Belsen concentration camp, Shahak chaired the Israel League for Human and Civil Rights. Citing laws and regulations in force in Israel and known to everyone due to their rigorous enforcement, he contended that "the State of Israel is a racist state in the full meaning of this term because people are discriminated against, in the most permanent and legal way and in the most important areas of life, only because of their origin . . . one who is not a Jew is discriminated against, only because he is not a Jew." Starting with the right to live, to dwell, or to open a business in the place of his choice, Shahak dissected racism in Israel as it is today:

Most of the land in Israel belongs to or is administered by the Jewish National Fund (JNF), which forbids non-Jews to dwell or to open a business, and sometimes even to work on its lands only because they are not Jews! Such policy not only enjoys here perfect legality (in contrast to a similar discrimination against the Jews which is illegal in most countries of the world), but is supported by all the instruments of the Israeli rule. In such a manner many whole towns were created in Israel, which are as the phrase goes "clean of Arabs" and this legally, or rather as we should say *"clean of Gentiles (goyim)."* In other towns, like Upper Nazareth, only one special quarter is "devoted" to the dwelling of Arabs. Any attempt of an Arab to buy or to rent a flat from a Jew is opposed openly and legally by all the branches of the government (the Ministry of Housing, Municipality, etc.) and also by the illegal opposition of the Jewish inhabitants, which is nevertheless supported by the Israeli police. I can only remind you that nobody opposes an operation of the sale or the rental of a flat in Nazareth, if the buyer or the lessee is a Jew, which means, according to the racist definition of this word employed legally in Israel, a human being who can prove that his mother, his grandmother, his great-grandmother and the grandmother of his grandmother were Jewish. If he can prove this, such an operation becomes all right all of a sudden and nobody opposes it, neither the government nor the inhabitants. There is opposition only if the mother of the buyer is not Jewish.

Shahak pointed out that Muhammad Ma'aruf, an Israeli citizen from the village of Dir-el-Assad, tried to open a factory in Carmiel but was prohibited from doing so because that town was "out of bounds" to non-Jews and he had to build outside the "pure" boundries. However, a Jew may dwell or open a business in any place of his choice, but only because his mother was a Jew; right is denied to those whose mother was not Jewish.

This discrimination did not stem from any "security" reasons. It is imposed on *all non-Jews,* including those who have served in the Israeli army and may have been wounded. Ma'aruf, a Druze, and all his family "were obliged to serve a compulsory service in the Israeli Defense Force, just as Jews are. *But he has not the right given to every Jew to dwell in Carmiel."* (Italics added.) And as Shahak notes, "a Jewish thief or robber or murderer, who has completed his sentence, has the right to dwell in Carmiel. But a 'goy,' a Druze, a Circassian, a Bedouin, or a Christian cannot dwell in Carmiel because he happened to be born to the 'incorrect' mother."

In the eyes of this civil rights defender, the worst racists in Israel are the kibbutzim members who will not accept into membership an Israeli citizen who is not a Jew "even in cases where a daughter of a kibbutzim has fallen in love with one of its hired non-Jewish workers. Any discrimination of that kind, if it is inflicted on Jews in other countries, encounters—and rightly so—the shout of 'anti-Semitism' . . . the Zionist State of Israel does exactly the same thing as anti-Semites attempt—usually without success—to do in other countries."

According to the teachings of the Israeli Ministry of Education, Jewish pupils from kindergarten on are taught the concept of the "Salvation of the Land": Land is "saved" when it is transferred to Jewish ownership. Personnel of the Jewish Nation Fund, with "the most forceful support of the Israeli government and especially of its 'security arms,' are employed continually in 'saving' land both in Israel and in the occupied territories."

Israeli Arabs have no right to settle in the new town of Yamit, established in occupied Egyptian Sinai, while non-Jews are being expelled from "saved" land. To Shahak, Zionism in this respect is worse than the apartheid South African regime where whites are forbidden to buy land in a "black" area and blacks are forbidden to buy in a "white" area. But Zionism strives to "save" as much land as it can without any limit in all areas of the "Land of Israel," turning the land "saved" into "one big apartheid in which human beings who were born of non-Jewish mothers have no right to live."

Regarding the right to work, the Shahak article called attention to the story of July 3, 1975, in *Ma'ariv* under the heading: "The Israeli settlement authorities are taking action against the leasing of lands to Arabs":

The Ministry of Agriculture and the Settlement Department of the Jewish Agency have recently launched a vehement campaign to *eradicate the plague* of land-leasing and orchard leasing to *Bedouins and Arab farmers* in the Western Galilee. The Director of the Galilee area for the Jewish Agency, Mr. Aharon

Nahmani, said that his office sent a circular notice to all settlements, in which they are warned that the leasing of national lands for cultivation by Arab share-croppers, as well as renting of the orchards for picking and marketing by Arabs *contradicts the law and the regulations of the settlement authorities and the settlement movements.* The management of the Galilee area enjoins the settlements to abstain from this practice, and stresses that last year already, the department pressed legal charges against settlements which did not abstain. [Italics added.]

Shahak, remembering his concentration camp experience, angrily writes:

Pay attention, please: Because I am a Jew, I am allowed to lease orchards for picking or marketing, but an Arab, only because he is an Arab, is forbidden this! The Ministry of Agriculture of the State of Israel together with the settlement authorities will persecute and prosecute the Jewish settlements, for doing things which are completely legal when done between Jews and Jews and become a grave offence when done between Jews and Arabs! And truly enough the settlements were punished. But since in this country "the settlements" are a holy cow, because they are racist, a special privilege was granted to those offenders who "broke the law." They were not brought to court, on the accusation of this most horrible "crime" of not being racists, but made "a deal" and bought themselves off by giving "donations" to a mysterious fund!

The Israel paper *Al-Hamishmar* of July 21 the same year related the end of this story:

The Ministry of Agriculture mentions a number of agricultural settlements which were "caught" for breaking the law and leasing their lands for cultivation, or for the picking of their crop. Since they committed that offence for the first time, they were not fined but were obliged to give donations in money to a special fund which stands to be established in the near future, and the aims of which have not yet been defined. The sum of the "donations" was £ 750,000 ($75,000). If a settlement is caught once again leasing lands, all form of state support will be interrupted. That settlement will not receive water-allotments, will not obtain credit, and will not enjoy development loans.

The struggle of the government against the right of its own Arab citizens to work and gain their means of livelihood had been opened by the declaration of Minister of Agriculture Aharon Uzan that "the domination of Jewish agriculture by Arab workers is a cancer in our body."

Apparently the Israeli Ministry of Housing has a special unit called "Department for the Housing of Minorities." While the Housing Ministry is engaged in building flats for Jews only *inside* Jerusalem, its minorities department is doing the reverse: it "thins out" Muslims and transfers them *out* of Jerusalem and further, according to Shahak:

The racist state of Israel has no human housing policy, as it exists in varying manners in the U.S.S.R., in the U.S.A., and in Britain. The State of Israel does not pretend to care about housing for a human being because he is a human being, for a poor family, or one that has many children, because decent housing is a human need. No! The State of Israel because of its Zionist aims, such as the "Judaization of the Galilee," is carrying out two contradictory sets of policies at the same time: One of maximum care for Jews and the other of discrimination against and oppression of the "non-Jews."

Health has been dealt with in a similar manner through the appointment of a "Deputy Minister of Health for the Minorities." Similarly, in almost every area of life there exists a racist separation between "Jews" and "non-Jews," leading to gross discrimination. Israeli society can be defined as a society in which there are no Israelis, only Jews and non-Jews.[37] Calling the Israeli Mission to the U.N. in New York for a population quote, one is asked, "Do you want the population with Arabs or without Arabs?" There are even separate statistics for infant death rate, the 1972 tables showing the figures to be 18.8 for Jews and 40.2 for non-Jews. Almost all Israeli statistical data are set forth in terms of "Jews" and "non-Jews." In every way it is legally crucial for a citizen of Israel to be officially defined as a Jew in order to qualify for major privileges accorded only to Jews.

As Shahak pointed out, the State of Israel was not the only racist state nor the Zionist organization the only racist organization. He, as have others, deplored a paragraph in the 1968 Palestinian Covenant (since amended) that could be considered a racist declaration, but this Israeli progressive insisted that "justice first begins at home," linking the struggle against racism with that for peace:

Only a state which will abolish inside itself all forms of racism, beginning with those it enforces itself, is capable of effectuating a policy which can bring all of us to a stable peace. Such peace can only be one in which people will not be discriminated against because of their origin, nor in their right to live or work where they wish, nor in any other area of their lives, *and in which the government will treat everyone in the manner in which all human beings deserve to be treated.* [Italics added.]

Government-decreed racism was reflected in the attitude of Israeli citizens toward their Arab neighbors. A 1971 Harris Poll revealed that two-thirds of the Israeli Jews assumed their Arab "fellow citizens" to be lazier, crueler, crookeder than themselves, and fully 84 percent of the Jews opposed marriage to Israeli Arabs.

*   *   *

Although in the face of surrounding Arab enemies Israel gave the impression of being a united monolithic whole, there was far less internal cohesion even among its Jews than an outsider would ever imagine. With people drawn from over 100 nations around the world, the Israeli community is not homogeneous and is divided into many conflicting groups. Aside from their third-class Arab citizens, the Jews themselves are divided into the Sephardic or Oriental Jews from the Arab and North African countries, and the Ashkenazi, whose background is European. The former already outnumber the latter and are increasing at a faster rate, but it is the Western and Eastern European Jews, rather than the Oriental Jews, who control the reins of the country and have made the Sephardim second-class citizens.

The leaders of Israel have been of European or non-Middle East origin. Chaim Weizmann, David Ben-Gurion, and Golda Meir were born in Russia, Abba Eban in South Africa. Menachem Begin and Shimon Peres were born in Poland, while Yigal Allon and Moshe Dayan are the sons of settlers from Eastern Europe. Yitzhak Rabin was the first sabra-Israeli-born Prime Minister.

Israel, despite the imposition of Hebrew as a common language, is coming apart at the seams, even before the seams have been securely joined. The history of more than 2,000 years of living separately under varying cultures and rules in the Diaspora cannot be wiped out. The community of persecution hardly makes a common bridge to transform people who are, in essence, Iraqi, German, Turkish, French, etc., into the common denominator, namely, Israelis. The now simmering struggle of the Sephardim against the Ashkenazi Establishment is evidence of this. This split runs deep because it is not only a cultural fragmentation but goes to the very essence of the individual being.

Imagine an Eastern Arab Jew, originally from Morocco or elsewhere in North Africa, living in the slums of Jerusalem for more than twenty years, looking out and seeing recent immigrants from Moscow, Kiev, or Leningrad and noting the advantages showered on these new arrivals. While those immigrants from the Soviet Union, settling by 1972 at the rate of 3,000 per month, were assigned apartments as soon as they stepped off the plane, and were provided extremely favorable mortgage rates, thousands of poor Oriental Jews who had arrived years earlier were not eligible for subsidized rents and were still confined to slum housing. Nor were they given cash grants, tax-free incentives in terms of cars, refrigerators, television sets, stereos—all luxury items.

Israel's Black Panthers are those Oriental Jews who have banded together under that name to dramatize their protest against the second-class citizenship imposed on the darker-skinned Jews from Arab countries. It took this Madison Avenue approach to overcome the obvious reluctance of foreign correspondents to report on this long-existing, simmering discrimination. Although some of their leaders, including Kochavi Shemesh, have been jailed because of their participation in protests and public demonstrations—some featured by violence and Molotov cocktails—violence has not been their aim. These protestants are not revolutionaries.

Virtually nothing of the story of bigotry against the "black Jews" of Israel had ever been carried previously by the American media, even though the *New York Times,* as well as other major newspapers and press associations, have long had permanent representatives based in Jerusalem and/or in Tel Aviv. The 60 percent Sephardim (from North Africa or Asia) have had to content themselves with 3 percent of all top executive government posts and just 20 percent of the seats in the Knesset. Under the premiership of Golda Meir, the eight-man Cabinet included only Iraqi-born Police Minister Shlomo Hillel to represent the Arab-speaking Jews (Iraqis, after the Poles and Rumanians, constitute the largest Israeli ethnic group).

Many of these Oriental Jews are the very ones who were transported from Yemen in operation "Magic Carpet" and viewed the planes as flying birds sent by God to bear them to the Promised Land. These Arab Jews are educationally and socially backward, and many have been unable to pull themselves up by their bootstraps. Some cannot afford to send their children to high school, which costs about $300 a year (1973 figures). It is estimated that at least 60,000 Israeli families live in poverty, almost all of whom are Arab. About 67 percent of Israel's enrollees in elementary school are Orientals, but because of the huge high school drop-out rate, they make up only about 18 percent of high school graduates and a mere 5 percent of university graduates. Somehow, the grants given out for college scholarships have not gone to these Jews from Arab countries.

As far back as July 1951, Iraqi Jews had been holding mass demonstrations in Tel Aviv against racial discrimination. These were reported in the *Alliance Review,* the organ of the American Friends of the Alliance Israelite and Universitè, but nowhere else. Other unpleasant outbursts followed, to the point where Prime Minister Ben-Gurion felt compelled to assail "Israeli anti-Semitism" publicly. Many of the B'nei Israel sect—the brown Jews from Bombay, Rangoon, and Calcutta—found themselves the object of discrimination. At one point Israel's rabbinate even banned marriages between Indian-born Jews of this sect and Jews of other communities. When this stigma was finally removed, these particular Jews were still required to prove the purity of their forebears before marrying out of their community.

A large group of these Jews sought repatriation to India because, they claimed, they were being forced to do the lowest kind of labor and were called "black" by the rest of the populace. Whenever assaults of an unknown origin took place on dark streets, Tel Aviv papers almost automatically reported "the assault is thought to have been committed by a North African," referring to the latest dark-skinned Jewish immigrants from Morocco, Tunisia, and Algiers.

A most serious race riot broke out in the summer of 1959 in the slum district of the port city of Haifa. The battle between "black Jews" from Arab countries and "white Jews" from Europe lasted four days, resulting in eleven Israeli policemen wounded, thirty-two rioters arrested, and considerable property damage.[38] While Arabs in Tel Aviv in 1961 were demonstrating against the government, 400 Yemeni Jews paraded through the streets wearing black armbands to protest discrimination "they contend is practiced against them by the lighter-skinned Jews of the country," according to a far-back-page, small *New York Times* item. Thousands of Christian and Jewish Americans visiting Israel rarely bother to go beyond the conducted tour, or they turn a blind eye to what has been going on in Israel's intercommunal and interracial relationships. How could they dare ever question anything about the "land of milk and honey"?

The reaction at that time of the Israeli government to the Jewish Panthers was most enlightening. After meeting with their leaders, Prime Minister Meir was reported by *Time* magazine as taking an instant dislike to them. "Perhaps they were good boys once," was her comment, "and I hope they will be good in the future, but they are certainly not good boys now."[39] The Minister of Housing placed the blame for the clash on the poverty of the Sephardim, mainly because they "spent money they could not afford on bar mitzvahs, weddings, and TV sets" instead of saving for housing.

The vast differences among the component ethnic groups making up Israel are, of course, invariably obscured by the common front that the Arab threat has created. But the mark of history has left an indelible imprint that cannot be patched together through a brotherhood based on outside hostility, although this is an almost irresistible unifying force within the new state. Israel comprises citizens from 102 lands speaking eighty-one languages. Even Meir was forced to admit that hundreds of thousands of Israelis live poorly and "dangerous strains have appeared in the inner fabric of Israeli society." While she denied deliberate discrimination against Orientals, she charged that they have brought a feeling of discrimination "with them in their suitcases [not unlike the answer that Christians have given to Jewish complaints of discrimination in the U.S.]. . . . But disadvantages exist, and they make the problem very difficult."[40] In 1973 Georgian Jews from the Soviet Union, the newest immigrants at that time to Israel (many of whom settled in Ashdod after Soviet authorities had eased emigration restrictions), organized protest demonstrations, hunger strikes and riots against alleged discrimination. Their fellow Israelis called them "backward, arrogant, clannish, and stiff-necked," or worse.

Israel is faced continuously with an increasing number of strikes and demonstrations. There are sharp and real differences between the white Jews and the darker, or black, Jews from Africa and Asia, between Ashkenazim and Sephardim, atheist and theocrat, rich and poor, new immigrants and new settlers, rising new cities and old villages, those living on the kibbutzim and those living in the capitalist cities. Conflicts are contained and a superficial impression of unity appears because of the outside danger, the struggle for survival and the manner in which this has been reported, or rather not reported, by the Western media.

In late 1977 charges of racism were leveled against Israel by a group of Black Jewish Americans, who filed a complaint with the U.N. The group was jailed and deported from Israel for demanding access to the community of Dimona in the Negev Desert, where more than 1,000 other American Black Hebrews live. According to Asiel Ben Israel, minister of the Hebrew Nation of Israelites—Black Americans of the Jewish faith, "The state of Israel is racist to the core."[41] As examples of this discrimination, Ben Israel contended that the Israeli government "since 1971 has refused to give work permits to Black Hebrew Americans, and although 350 children have been born to the group, refused to issue birth certificates." In addition, he insisted, "They are kept in total, complete isolation. They cannot leave and any person who tries to visit them is refused entry. If they persist, they are jailed and deported as we were."

Cultural and economic differences are not the only ones that divide the Israelis. The pervasive nature of religious law in Israel has been kept out of sight under the cover of progressive achievement. But with the election of Begin and a share of power in his cabinet resting both with the ultrachauvinist National Religious party (NRP), which has served in every preceding government since the inception of the state (the dismissal of the party from the coalition in December 1976 by Prime Minister Rabin helped weaken the Labor government), and with the ultraorthodox Agudat Israel, the concealment has ended. Too, the new Prime Minister is religious himself and unhesitatingly makes liberal use of biblical quotations in his political posturings.

Through their control of the Ministry of Religion, the orthodoxy of the NRP has emerged in the past with many controversial victories over secular forces, whereby laws and customs of the Middle Ages have been made part of Israeli marriage law. Jews cannot marry non-Jews; male Jews thought to be descended from the ancient priests (Cohanim) are not allowed to marry divorcees; and marriages performed by civil authorities outside Israel are declared invalid, making the children illegitimate. In addition to Sabbath blue laws and the strict dietary regulations of orthodoxy, reform and conservative rabbis have not been permitted to perform the most sacred rites of religion, marriage, circumcision, etc.

Because these rabbis do not carry out the orthodox Halachah they have, with the exception of a handful of conservative rabbis, been barred from practicing their vocation in Israel, despite the vigorous public demands of their rabbinical organizations in the U.S. for "equal rights and recognition."[42] Meanwhile Reform Jews of American or Conservative Jews of Anglo-Saxon backgrounds find themselves chafing at the strict orthodox laws of the country, which make it so difficult for them to worship.

The new Likud government immediately antagonized their fervent Conservative and Reformed Judaism supporters by endorsing legislation introduced by its two religious components that revised the Law of Return to exclude Jews and their families who have been converted to Judaism by nonorthodox rabbis. This strict construction of defining who is a Jew complicated further the status of immigrants from the Soviet Union, where civil marriages are the norm and many have intermarried with no conversion at all.

Another part of Israeli religious law bars a woman from obtaining a divorce without written consent from her husband. A widow must obtain consent to remarry from her husband's brother. She may have to pay part of her inheritance to get her brother-in-law to give up his right of "livirate" and, if he is a minor, the widow may have to wait until he comes of age before he releases her. Children born of a married woman's affair or a common-law marriage are bastards and as adults are not allowed to marry under Israeli law.

The noted feminist Letty Cottin Pogrebin, in a markedly pro-Israeli article appearing in *Ms.* magazine, was forced to admit that the role of women in "the promised land" is not enviable. She writes of a woman who had moved from the West side of Manhattan and who "describes a life that sounds like the worst of both worlds. She has communal self-denial, hard work and lost individuality, but she hasn't been relieved of time-consuming exhausting family chores." According to Pogrebin, "even though women comprise one third of the Israeli work force, they're concentrated in the familiar female ghettos of clerical work, nursing, and teaching . . . they earn 25 to 40 percent less than men . . . and the kibbutz prototype of communal child care is enjoyed by less than 4 percent of the population; most parents can't find or afford baby-sitters."[43]

The few Israelists who do know what has been going on in the Israeli state are most unhappy about the situation and usually keep silent. But in 1975 I. F. Stone, editor of the famed newsletter that bore his name, spoke out:

Israel is creating a kind of moral schizophrenia in world Jewry. In the outside world, the welfare of Jewry depends on the maintenance of secular, nonracial, pluralistic societies. In Israel, Jewry finds itself defending a society in which mixed marriages cannot be legalized, in which non-Jews have a lesser status than Jews, and in which the ideal is racial and exclusionist. Jews must fight everywhere for their very security and existence against principles and practices they find themselves defending in Israel.

Ironically, one of the groups that has been most at odds with the state is its most Orthodox element. Within the Mea Shearim sector of Jerusalem there is bitterness toward Zionism that surpasses in intensity all Arab oppostion. The ultra-Orthodox Neturei Karta regard the creation of the State of Israel as usurpation by man of an act that God was to bring about with the coming of the Messiah. This small, militant group literally observe all the oral and written laws of the Torah.

When Meir addressed an Israel Bond meeting in New York in December 1971, Neturei Karta members were joined in picketing the Americana Hotel by a larger contingent of men and women from the National Committee of Orthodox Jewish Communities, who were opposed to Israel's conscription of girls under the Military Draft Act. American Zionists were shaken up when TV news programs depicted Jews with beards and peyes (long sideburns), who by no stretch of the imagination could be written off as anti-Semites, in militant opposition to Israel's policies. This small group of religious zealots, who have on occasion reacted violently by overturning cars entering their area in Jerusalem on the Sabbath, vigorously expressed its view through its late leader, Rabbi Amram Blau:

We in the Holy Land find ourselves in an unfortunate position, both materially and spiritually. Materially, we are against our will included in an independent, nationalistic state, labeled Jewish, whose entire foundation and ways are opposed to our faith. Our sages warned us against such a phenomenon two thousand years ago. The state has, since its establishment, been in a constant state of war and bloodshed. Jewry has always lived in peace with its Arab neighbors, and we are certain that we could have continued living in the Holy Land in peace with our Arab neighbors. We decry bitterly the bloodshed of these wars, diametrically opposed to our will and our faith. We look forward with trepidation and horror to the future predicted by our Sages for this independent state.

Spiritually, we find ourselves under the rule of Jews, devoid of faith, who aspire to live in permissiveness and abandon. The education and culture in like manner are leading our youth astray in our Holy Land. The situation is to us more bitter than death itself, may G-d spare us.

Our Jewish brethren in exile among the nations of the world live under no comparable awful threat, neither material nor spiritual. We find no formula to turn back the wheels of confusion that have run down Jewry in the Holy Land.

. . . Let the state's power be unable to drag children of these Jews away from their heritage. Do all that is possible to rescue these Jews from the lot of this state; for they are not part of it—they opposed its establishment and oppose its existence. Let these Jews be enabled to lead their lives as Jews and bring up their future generations in the ways of their heritage, protected from the general education and culture of the state.[44]

Outside of small, inconspicuous ads that American members of this group have placed in *The Times,* little of this philosophy reached the American public. A rare *Washington Star* May 13, 1978 religious page article on the Neturei Karta was headed "This is a Story I Wish Someone Else Would Tell," and ended:

With great trepidation I have told their side of the story given the volatile nature of writing in such a vein about Israel, the next time I hope I don't have to write about Neturei Karta. . . . It's safer that way.

The already overburdened American taxpayer, facing the exorbitant inflationary cost of living (hardly offset by pro forma tax cuts), is certainly entitled to see "Inside Israel" so as to learn why the U.S. government is spending so many billions for a special, unique relationship with a small Middle East enclave, which has been more than a little complicating the peace process. Behind the propaganda facade, aside from the Arab question, what is Israel like for Jews themselves? Is it the utopia Zionists would have the world believe?

The Israeli public must put up not only with rampant inflation and the perpetual war economy, but with the highest taxes in the world. As far back as 1971, before the October war that only made matters worse, *Time* magazine reported that a man earning $15,000 a year would wind up with a mere $4,500 after paying income, municipal, property, and service taxes, and handing back money for compulsory government loans. This same man had to pay 75 cents a gallon for gas. His English Ford sold for $7,000 in Israel as against $2,880 in Britain, and his black-and-white television set cost him a minimum of $600. In addition to the high taxes, Israelis were obliged after the 1973 war to purchase a compulsory war loan in the amount of 10 to 20 percent of their income.

By June 1977 the inflation rate had increased to the second highest in the world, surpassed only by Uruguay and six times the rate in the U.S. During 1976 it had varied only a few points below this. On November 3, 1976, Israelis awoke to discover that basic food prices had increased 20 percent and the already high cost of fuel had risen 11 percent. Within the following two weeks public transportation increased 20 percent and electricity and water rose 11 percent.

The already high consumer price index was up 5 percent, and the sharp price increases all but wiped out the 12 percent cost-of-living increment for salaried workers that went into effect at the beginning of October. To partially meet a budgetary gap, it had been necessary for the government to slash state subsidies for such staples as milk, bread, butter, eggs, frozen chickens, and cooking oil.

The new economic policies of Finance Minister Simha Ehrlich under the Menachem Begin administration led to street marches by thousands of Israeli workers protesting the latest price increases. In October 1977 restrictions on trading in foreign currency were removed (a violation had resulted in the unseating of Yitzhak Rabin); this made the Israeli pound freely convertible and sent it plummeting down to 7½ cents from a once-high of $4. Commodities subsidized by the government cost the consumer 15 percent more, the value-added tax (akin to sales tax) rose 50 percent, and inflation hit the 40 percent mark before the end of the year. The cost of most imported goods jumped 45 percent.

Israel's estimated defense budget for 1976 was $3.3 billion, about 40 percent of the total budget. In 1976 Israel spent 35 percent of its gross national product on defense-related items, an inordinately high amount when compared, for example, with the U.S., which spends about 7 percent of its G.N.P. on defense. And this was at a time when the country was enjoying a relative calm on its borders as the Arabs were preoccupied in slaughtering one another in Lebanon.

Israel's economic plight was becoming so desperate that one of its famed reporters quipped: "They tell us we are going to have to tighten our belts until we get by with a Size 0." It is a matter of proven experience that Diaspora Jews give more money when the danger of war is greater. The Israeli government, therefore, also has a great vested interest in not making peace. In early 1967, for instance, economic controls had produced a major unemployment problem. Investment was at a low ebb, and there was little demand for imports. Out of that economic crisis and recession, war was the only way out. And "Oh, What a Lovely War!" it was. World Jewry came across as never before. Five hundred million dollars were brought into the coffers of the Israeli treasury through the Special Emergency UJA Fund and Israel Bonds. It remained to be seen whether, once again, with emotionally minded American Jews both footing the bill and fighting Washington pressures on Israel to become more flexible, war might not be the ultimate method chosen by this U.S. ward both to break out of her dire economic conditions and to resolve the peace negotiations. The Israeli economy is perpetually confronted by two unusual internal factors working against it: heavy dependence on outside gifts (largely from the U.S.) and total dependence on a slave-worker population composed of Arabs and Oriental Jews.

On the political front, Israel has proved no different than any other nation. Zionist politicians differ not one whit from politicians all over the rest of the world in their pursuit of a single goal: The quest for power is the name of the game. Israeli politicians, as elsewhere, indulge in their share of infighting, splinter parties, and power ploys, and have been caught with more than their portion of corruption. The scandals that have rocked the Tel Aviv establishment since 1974 included a prison sentence for an ex-national health service chief (who was about to be placed in charge of the Bank of Israel), convicted of siphoning off public funds to his own Labor party; the suicide of Housing Minister Avraham Ofer under a cloud of suspicion of land fraud; and the arrest of a Rabbinical Court judge for unlawful currency manipulations.

Israel's Watergate was the investment fraud involving the business conglomerate of Tibor Rosenbaum. Israeli and foreign Jewish capital, estimated as high as $8.5 million, had been deposited without authorization in the International Credit Bank of Geneva, which failed along with Rosenbaum's Inter-Credit Trust of Liechtenstein. (The Geneva bank was being used to finance arms purchases for Israel in Europe.) Involved was France's Baron Edmund de Rothschild, who, with associates, had injected some $100 million in capital and long-term loans into the Israel Corporation, the country's largest investment organization, in order to strengthen the sagging economy. Tied into these investments were 300 wealthy non-Jews (Holland's Prince Bernhard was also involved) as well as Kuhn Loeb & Company and Samuel Rothberg, a top Zionist leader in the Israel Bond drive in the U.S. for years. Underworld figure Meyer Lansky reportedly had funds in the collapsed bank. The corporation had been formed at the celebrated Tel Aviv "Millionaires' Conference" of 1968 when Israel was basking in the security won by the six-day war and was pushing her economic recovery in the wake of the recession, which had impelled the launching of the conflict. The new company had been established to promote the development of basic industry and manufacturing and was formed by the conferees who, in addition to Baron de Rothschild from Paris, included London's Sir Isaac Wolfson, another equally well-known Zionist, and Sir Sigmund Warburg. The usual incentives for foreign investment had been granted the new company. At the outset each million-dollar participation brought with it a directorship; at one point there were 175 directors, illustrating the breadth of the project. The new refinery at Ashdod in the south to process the 1967 war-captured oil, petrochemical shipping, and hotels were some of the investments into which the Israel Corporation had placed its funds. Israeli shipping line Zim Navigation and the Haifa Refineries, both owned in part by the Israel Corporation, had deposits in the bankrupt Rosenbaum enterprises.

This sad state of affairs had been at least noted by a leading Israeli weekly news magazine, which had earlier sarcastically commented: "The contributors and donors to the UJA and the Israeli Bond investors would be quite interested in knowing that a great part of their contribution and investments are now safe and well-protected in numbered bank accounts of Israeli employees and officials in the 'Promised Land'—Switzerland."[45]

Millionaire property speculator Shmuel Flatto-Sharon, arrested by the Israeli government in December 1976 at the request of the French government but released on bail the following day, proceeded to run for and win a seat in the Israeli Knesset. An Israeli resident since

1971, Flatto-Sharon had been sentenced by a French court to five years in prison. His parliamentary immunity to criminal legal proceedings effectively blocked the French government's request for his extradition on fraud charges. Although he claimed to be willing to return to France "at any time," Flatto-Sharon was widely photographed by the Israeli press, while sick in bed, studying Hebrew in order to assume his parliamentary duties, and conferring with his lawyers. According to the Newsletter *Israel and Palestine* (published in Paris by Maxim Ghilan) Flatto-Sharon was praised in Tel Aviv as a "true prophet. Most of our politicians smuggle abroad the money they steal from here. He, at least, took to Israel money taken abroad."

To climax Israel's fall from integrity, Prime Minister and Mrs. Yitzhak Rabin, prior to the 1977 elections, were discovered to have maintained illegal savings bank accounts in Washington, dating back to his Ambassadorship. They were charged in court; she was fined heavily ($20,000) and he resigned, turning over the government to Shimon Peres.

This long wave of corruption was a factor—if not the major one —in the downfall of the Labor government in the May 1977 elections. As one foreign journal pointed out:

This preoccupation with scandal great and small, comes at a time when there should be preoccupation with the possibilities of obtaining a peace agreement in the Middle East. But the brutal Israeli taxes (which incite tax avoidance) and the maze of rules and regulations on, for example, overseas bank accounts, stem from the inordinate—and probably in the long term untenable—expenditure on defense that Israel requires.[46]

Israeli internal politicking, at the very least, adds to U.S. financial liabilities and often threatens the whole world. In trying to consolidate their own political positions, Israeli leaders continue to vie with one another in exploiting the troubles with the Arabs. One learns from the book *The Middle East: Quest for an American Policy* that "of the Middle East actors, Israel has maintained the highest level of reported military action during the 64-month period of January 1966 through April 1971. It has generated more hostile behavior to the Arab nations than they have directed to Israel."[47]

As University of California political scientist Malcolm Kerr pointed out in 1968, and it still holds true: "Any border incident . . . could initiate a series of increasingly violent retaliatory actions on both sides. Every threat uttered against Israel, whether or not it was accompanied by serious intent, and every commando raid . . . gave credence to the views that the Israelis were merely retaliating."[48]

Because so few take the trouble to look "inside," Israel is still not infrequently depicted to the world as a small, confined country of peace-loving kibbutzim, content to scratch out an existence on the desert-come-to-bloom if only the Arabs would leave them alone. Her aggressive posture, stemming from the Zionist number-one goal of "ingathering the exiles," bringing all Jews from the Diaspora "home," remains carefully concealed from her many supporters abroad, particularly innocent-minded coreligionists. If there were Jews from the West taking advantage of the Law of Return or from the Soviet Union "seeking asylum," there had to be more land—preferably without inhabitants, but land, above all. Expansionism and new frontiers were the inevitable concomitants of Zionist dogma, which remained immutable and sacrosanct even as change otherwise appeared to be an indispensable *sine qua non.*

Ben-Gurion always insisted that the "boundaries of the state would have been larger had Moshe Dayan been the commander-in-chief in 1948," while Foreign Minister Yigal Allon, who commanded the army in that first Arab-Israeli war, countered with the claim that Ben-Gurion had ordered the cease-fire. These Israeli leaders were in agreement that Israel ought to have "occupied the Litani River in the north and the Sinai desert in the south and also liberated the whole of our homeland," to use Allon's words.

Moshe Dayan gave expression to this same expansionist dogma when he stated after the six-day war:

Our fathers had reached the frontiers which were recognized in the Partition Plan. Our generation reached the frontiers of 1949. Now the six-day generation has managed to reach Suez, Jordan and the Golan Heights. That is not the end. After the present cease-fire lines, there will be new ones. They will extend beyond Jordan—perhaps to Lebanon and perhaps to central Syria as well.[49]

Nobel Peace Prize winner S. Y. Agnon was among the fifty-four signators to an advertisement in a 1968 edition of *Ha'aretz* proclaiming the birth of a new movement called EVERYTHING (i.e., Everything is Ours) and demanding the retention of every inch of territory won in the June 1967 war. The hawk faction, in Israel as in other countries, invariably has a political appeal that doves and other elements lack. They are able to unite the people behind simplistic slogans against the outside "enemy." Thus an aggressive stance and an aggressive behavior have become necessary to many aspects of Israeli internal life and to relations abroad with Diaspora Jewry, particularly those in the U.S. Yoel Marcus, writing in *Ha'aretz* in 1975, had this to say:

We shall have to mobilize American Jewry, still a powerful force. . . . We shall have to explain again and again that a strong Israel is not only in the American interests, but also still the only way to convince the Arabs to find some form of coexistence with her.

We must make clear—and first of all to ourselves—that we do not necessarily intend to play according to Arab rules. We shall determine which Arab move is from our point of view a *casus belli,* and at what point we shall play the game differently from the way others expect us to. If the Free World is frightened and the West is in the process of decline, it may be that *we have a number of means available to terrorize it more than the Arabs could.* A word to the wise is enough.[50][Italics added.]

Such veiled threats alluding to Israel's possession of an estimated minimum of twelve atom bombs, when combined with the Masada complex which has so deeply permeated Israeli thought, makes for a highly combustible compound, particularly under the command of a Begin. Masada was the fort where the last of the Jewish Zealots of the first century held out in their mountain fortress against the Roman legions, and when faced with the choice of surrender or death, chose suicide rather than submit to enemy subjugation. Junior Israeli officers are administered their oath of loyalty into the army at the site of the Masada Memorial. This kind of public ideal—although present as one of a number of patriotic images in many cultures, as in the American "Remember the Alamo"—can be dangerous when permitted to invade and dominate, particularly when combined with a determination to take their enemies with them this time, as hinted in the Marcus piece but spelled out more explicitly in *Commentary* editor Norman Podhoretz's article, "The Abandonment of Israel."[51]

Modern Jewish zealots, inside and outside the Israeli state, were often being reminded of Masada as the high point of Jewish history. This was reflected in the 1969 speech of then Defense Minister—now Foreign Minister—Moshe Dayan to the graduates of the Cadet School: "The Arabs do not agree to our venture. If we want to continue our work in Eretz Israel against their desires, there is no alternative but that lives should be lost. It is our destiny to be in a state of continual warfare with the Arabs. This situation may well be undesirable but such is the reality."[52]

It was inevitable that arch expansionist Menachem Begin, who had been rejected six times, should seize upon the propitious moment for capturing the imagination of the Israeli people and come to power on a program that his predecessors had been quietly espousing as well as gradually implementing. It was equally inescapable that his "peace" cabinet increasingly should assume the appearance of a Jewish military junta with its five[53] Israeli generals (as of the end of 1977): Deputy Prime Minister Yigal Yadin, Foreign Minister General Moshe Dayan, Defense Minister General Ezer Weizman, Minister of Agriculture General Ariel Sharon, and Transport and Communications Minister Meir Amit.

Yadin, as leader of the Democratic Movement for Change, had refused for five months to join the new government because of its policy of insisting on continued settlements in the occupied territories. But he succumbed to the mood of the new Establishment, overwhelmingly backed by popular acclaim, whose philosophy had been eloquently set forth by Dayan earlier in eulogizing a kibbutz leader killed by the Arabs in a border dispute:

In front of their (the Palestinians) eyes, we are taking possession of the land and villages in which they and their forebears have dwelled. . . . Let us not draw back at the sight of the burning hatred which fills the lives of the hundreds of thousands of Arabs surrounding us. . . . This is the destiny of our generation.[54]

But a new force had emerged to pose the first real challenge to Zionist ambitions to hold onto land already seized and to grab more of "Eretz Israel" (Old Israel). In losing the six-day 1967 war, the Arab confrontation states of Egypt, Syria, and Jordan showed that their hearts were not really in the battle. They had been only standing in as proxies for the Palestinian people whose plight always constituted the very heart of the Middle East conflict. But the Palestinians could scarcely field a fighting force of their own, let alone command international attention, until March 1968, when the battle of Karameh drastically changed the picture.

Out of this unexpected strong showing by Palestinian commando units defending their camp on the East Bank of the Jordan against an Israeli invasion force emerged the Palestinians and their political-military organization, the Palestine Liberation Organization, which had been in the making since 1964. It was the very existence of these Palestinians, not the hostile Arab armies, that constituted the growing Israeli nightmare and challenged the very being of the state. Nasser's blockade of the Straits of Tiran played right into Zionist hands, providing them with the excuse to launch the 1967 conflict. The seizure by Israel of the West Bank and of Gaza during that war anticipated the eventual Palestinian transmutation from refugee to political status, demanding nationhood in at least a part of Israel and its occupied territories.

Then, even as Tel Aviv insisted they did not exist, the frustrated Palestinians seized on violence to bring their untold tragedy to the center of the world stage.

V   What Palestinians?

Against the agony,
The world is adamant,
The sun's eye is gouged,
The world is lost and torn!

The world, my Lord,
Has not raised a single candle,
Has not shed a single tear,
To wash away
Jerusalem's grief.

—Fadwa Tuqan

Former Israeli Prime Minister Levi Eshkol stated in a 1969 interview in *Davar:*

What are the Palestinians? When I came here there were only 250,000 non-Jews, mainly Arabs and Bedouins. It was desert—more than underdeveloped. Nothing. It was only after we made the desert bloom and populated it that they became interested in taking it from us.[1]

Until very recently, much of the world accepted without questioning such statements as that of Prime Minister Eshkol, or declarations such as these by another Israeli Prime Minister, Golda Meir:

How can we return the occupied territories? There is nobody to return them to.[2]

There was no such thing as Palestinians. . . . It was not as though there was a Palestinian people in Palestine considering itself as a Palestine people, and we came and threw them out and took their country away from them. They did not exist.[3]

Although the fate of the Palestinians today, as always, constitutes the heart of the Middle East conflict, for many reasons the very exis-

146

tence of these people has been ignored, let alone brought into true focus. The objective observer was sidetracked because he could not help but be moved to great compassion by even the most casual examination of the circumstances under which so many of the Jewish refugees escaped the hell of Hitler to find a home in Palestine. Their vast accomplishments in fashioning their new land were bound to elicit great admiration. But the plight of the Jews in Europe ought not to have been considered by itself, as if the state for the surviving victims had been set up in a vacuum. Unfortunately, this fallacy underlies the perspective held by most American Jews who have so copiously supported Israel in a myriad of ways and, at the same time, bear a personal, intense hatred, scorn, and disdain—a racism exceeded by no Nazi Gauleiter—for their vicarious foes, the Arabs, and in particular the Palestinians.

Likewise, American Christian liberals have managed until recently to overlook almost completely the Arab presence in the Holy Land. Their reaction, when confronted with the dire consequences wrought upon the Palestinians by Israel's creation, is most reminiscent of the early Zionists when they realized "the land without a people for a people without a land" to which they aspired actually had people—and people, incidentally, whose own national aspirations were definitely already forming.

This discovery of the other occupants of Palestine, the 93 percent indigenous populace, came as a rude shock to the early settlers. Max Nordau, one of Theodor Herzl's closest associates, came crying to him one day in 1897, "But there are Arabs in Palestine. I did not know that!"[4]

This was fifty years before the founding of Israel. In this same early Zionist period, the father of modern Hebrew, Ben Yehuda, was similarly dismayed upon his arrival in 1882 and "faced a crisis of conscience," in the words of Israeli author Amos Elon in his valuable book *Israelis: Founders and Sons.*[5] Ben Yehuda saw himself coming to Palestine

". . . as a proselyte, a stranger, the son of a foreign country and a foreign people; in this, the land of my forefathers, I have no political and no civil right. I am a foreigner . . . I suddenly broke. Something like remorse rose in the depths of my soul. . . . My feet stood on the holy ground, the land of the forefathers, and in my heart there was no joy . . . I did not embrace the rocks . . . I stood shocked. Dread! Dread!"[6]

The unrealism of these Zionist settlers has been brilliantly captured by Elon:

There are few things as egocentric as a revivalist movement. For decades the Zionist leaders moved in a strange twilight zone seeing the Arabs and the same time not seeing them. Their attitude was a combination of blind spots and naiveté, of wishful thinking, paternalistic benevolence, and that ignorance which was often a factor in international events and sometimes their cause. It may very well be that without this ignorance most Zionist leaders would not have ventured on their task in the first place.[7]

Former head of the Jewish Agency Dr. Nahum Goldmann, in a 1974 article in *The New Outlook*,[8] wrote of the total unawareness of the Arabs on the part of most early Zionist settlers and of their importance in establishing any Zionist state. Goldmann referred to an article he had published for a German Jewish newspaper several months after the Balfour Declaration of November 1917, in which he had stated that while the Declaration was an important historical document, "if the day comes when the Arabs issue a Balfour Declaration, it will be ten times more important." It had been his belief at the time that "without an agreement with the Arab world there was no future for the realization of the Zionist idea." His colleagues laughed at him and asked how could he ever compare the poor Arab bedouins with the British Empire. Very few of them were aware of the Arabs, and those who were did not attach the necessary significance to them.

Great statemaker David Ben-Gurion was another Zionist pioneer who was taken aback by the Arab presence in Palestine. At the outset he and some of his more liberal colleagues were willing at least to talk in terms of granting the Arab minority some voice in the projected Jewish state, while firmly rejecting any Palestinian claim to nationhood. For their part, some Palestinians feared the intense nationalism of Ben-Gurion. After being arrested by Turkish authorities in 1915 for Zionist agitation, the future Premier of Israel, upon his release, ran into a fellow law-school alumnus who, when told that the Turks wished to expel the budding Zionist from the country, remarked to Ben-Gurion, "As your friend, I am deeply sorry. But as an Arab, I am pleased." It was then that the future Prime Minister of Israel first became slightly aware of anti-Zionist feeling among Palestinian Arabs, but he did not believe the Arab nationalist political movement had any real roots in Palestine. He felt it was concerned only with the desire of the people of Lebanon and Syria to break free from the foreign yoke.

The Arab Palestinians as a whole failed to recognize the European Jewish émigrés as a threat until it was too late, largely because they had looked upon the Jews in past historic terms as nothing more than a small, docile minority thriving in the region under the special protection of Muslim Arab rulers, traditionally provided to nonbelievers by the Koranic right of El Dimha with the payment of a tax.

The history of the land known traditionally as Palestine bares the almost totally Arab nature of the country, until the Zionist arrival. The name Palestine was derived from "Philistia," for this was the land of the biblical Philistines, or people of the sea, who occupied the southern coastal area in the 12th century B.C. On the basis of an examination of human remains, anthropologists have found that 50,000 years ago the Palestinians were of mixed racial stock. From the 4th millenium B.C. until 900 B.C., the predominant indigenous stock were the Canaanites. Towns such as Jericho, Megiddo, and Beth-Shan were centers of civilization in Palestine in the early Bronze Age; by the middle of that age, links had developed between the people in Palestine and the civilization of Phoenicia.

Throughout its long history Palestine has always been the target of successive invaders and has continuously changed rule. This land has rarely been free of great-power domination. After the Canaanites came the Egyptians and Hittites; then a combination of Canaanites, Philistines, and Hebrews; the Hebrew kingdom of the North and Judea in the South; Babylonians, Persians, Greeks, Ptolemies, Seleucids, Maccabees, Seleucids, Romans, Persians, Romans, Arabs, Turks, Crusaders, Egyptians, Mamelukes, Turks, Britons; and now Israelis and Jordanians.

The Hebrew-Israelite-Judean-Jewish (as it has been successively referred to) community never totally predominated even in the more than nine centuries of the two kingdoms and the united nation. As Dr. Julian Morgenstern has pointed out, there were "only two brief simultaneous periods in the life of each kingdom, neither lasting more than fifty years, when there was any indication of national strength and glory."[9]

The mythmakers have insisted that Palestine was once an uncultivated land without people, and that the miracle of Zionism developed a state with modern technology and "turned the desert into green hills." While some Jews continued to live in Palestine since their original entrance circa 1000 B.C., in contemporary times the Jewish population of Palestine at the time of the Balfour Declaration in 1917 was a mere 7 percent of the 700,000 inhabitants. The rest were Muslim (570,000) and Christian (70,000) Arabs.

Israeli Ambassador to the U.N. Yosef Tekoah insisted before the Security Council on May 4, 1968, that Jerusalem is "no more Arab because of the Arab occupation than it was Turkish because of the

Turkish occupation," and that "the very name is Hebrew, meaning city
of peace." Actually Jerusalem had been overwhelmingly Arab from the
7th century until the modern influx of Westerners began toward the
end of the 19th century. As for the name of the city, it first appears as
"Urushalimma" (Jerusalem) in Egyptian texts of the 19th century B.C.,
more than 800 years before King David occupied the city. The name
meant "foundation of Shalem," that same Semitic god whose name
appears in "Shalmaneser," the Assyrian king.

But the Zionist, in his desire for exclusive possession of what he
referred to as his "ancestral home," and in his mistaken belief that he
alone had a right to it, ignored the existence of the Palestinians and
romanticized his own. Within Israel only a few voices attempted to
kindle the Jewish conscience. One was that of Judah Magnes, first
president of the Hebrew University, who helped bring into being the
Ihud (Brotherhood), a movement dedicated to Arab-Jewish friendship.
During the bitter conflict prior to the creation of Israel, Magnes, bold
champion of binationalism, said: "We seem to have thought of everything—except the Arabs. . . . But the time has come for the Jews to take
into account the Arab factor as the most important factor facing us.
. . . If we wish to live in this living space, we must live with the Arabs."[10]

Then there was Moshe Smilansky, one of the first settlers, who
expressed deep disappointment at the neglect of the indigenous population. He wrote in the publication *Ner:* "Where are you, Jews? Why
do we not at least pay compensation with a generous hand to these
miserable people? . . . Did a single Jewish farmer raise his hand in the
Parliament in opposition to a law that deprived Arab peasants of the
land? How solitary does sit the Jewish conscience in the city of Jerusalem!"[11] And Zionist philosopher Ahad Ha-am, in one of his last letters,
commented: "If this be the Messiah, then I do not wish to see his
coming."

Such few protestants, speaking out humanistically in behalf of the
universal dogma of Judaism, were at the outset overwhelmed by the
pioneering zealot majority and later by the specter of Hitler. There
emerged a new Israeli trauma combining an overriding concern for
security, the psychological vestiges of the Masada complex, and a
feeling of guilt (mixed with fear) stemming from the growing awareness of the Arab-Palestinian community. Exclusivity increasingly became the mark of narrow Zionist dogma in which there was little room
for pluralism. Party members and sympathizers alike in the U.S. picked
up and embroidered this theme.

In the face of the Palestinian refugee flight precipitated by the

1948 war and planned terror, the Israeli government maintained a consistent propaganda stand: The Palestinians had fled of their own accord in the hope of returning home victorious, and the other Arab states should take care of these people, who had never really owned but were only squatters on the land that had been given 3,000 years earlier to the Jews by God.

Typical of this attitude was a statement by Joseph Weitz, one-time head of the Jewish Agency Colonization Department, who wrote:

Between ourselves, it must be clear that there is no room in this country for both peoples. The only solution is Eretz Israel . . . without Arabs, and there is no other way but to transfer the Arabs from here to the neighboring countries—to transfer all of them—not one village, not one tribe should be left.[12]

This intent, reiterated in *Davar* after the six-day war, updated the philosophy behind Herzl's original plan to uproot and displace the Arab population by any and all means possible. As told in his Diaries, the father of Zionism envisioned this role for the indigenous populace: "If we move into a region where there are wild animals to which the Jews are not accustomed—big snakes, etc.,—I shall use the natives, prior to giving them employment in the transit countries, for the extermination of these animals." Herzl would also have had the "natives drain the swamps" inasmuch as they were "accustomed to the fever."[13]

There was total absence of any reference to Arabs in the first Zionist Congress. The attitude of Jewish nationalist leaders reflected the views of Herzl and of Vladimir Jabotinsky, the leader of the expansionist-revisionist Greater Israel movement and the idol of young Menachem Begin. At an early conclave, Jabotinsky referred to the Palestinians as "a yelling rabble dressed up in gaudy, savage rags."[14]

Some Israelis later even went so far as to justify Israeli exclusivism on moral grounds. In 1970 a Hebrew University professor, Eliezer Schweid, observed in an official Zionist publication, *Dispersion and Unity:*

. . . The general policy of Zionism based itself upon the certainty and primacy of the right of the Jewish people to its homeland. From this point of view, the opposition of the Arabs was a stumbling block *that must be overcome, and not a moral problem that must be dealt with. We must emphasize again that one should not see in this approach disregard for truth and righteousness. This approach had a factual and moral basis.* Arab nationalism in the land of Israel appeared from its beginning, not as a movement whose purpose was to realize or defend the right of an existing national entity, but rather as a movement that realizes its very being in defiance of Zionism.[15] [Italics added.]

For their part, American Jews have sincerely believed they were safeguarding the very existence of their coreligionists in Israel, never dreaming it was Zionist exclusivism for which they were giving their dollars, political support, and moral aid, and betraying their single loyalty to their own country.

And today, when the thesis of binationalism is raised by Arabs in advancing their rights to a Palestinian state and in calling for a secular, pluralistic Israel, the Jews in America see this only as a threat "to destroy the State of Israel." They see no reason why there should be, nor do they believe there can be, a de-Zionization or restructuring of the Israeli state, in line with the universal thesis of Judaism and the thinking of universalists such as Magnes, Buber, Einstein, and others.

Jews have been adamant in refusing to recognize even the possibility of any other claims to Palestine aside from their own. This conviction was infinitely strengthened by Hitler and the holocaust. Palestine was theirs by right and theirs alone, to be shared with no one. Few in America even recognized, let alone were willing to discuss, the need to redress any past wrongs. But Nathan Chofshi of Herzlia, one of the pioneer Jewish settlers in Palestine, wrote:

We came and turned the native Arabs into tragic refugees. And still we dare to slander and malign them, to besmirch their name instead of being deeply ashamed of what we did and trying to undo some of the evil committed. . . . We justify our terrible acts and even attempt to glorify them.[16]

The great tragedy was that the few voices from the Jewish side spurred by ethical universalism to call for binationalism in Palestine found little echo among the Arabs, whose emotional initial response to Zionist policy was to rule out any possibility of sharing. The Arabs missed their great opportunity for a unitary Palestinian state when their representatives at the 1947 U.N. debate at Lake Success showed no official support for a minority report suggesting a single state with a federal structure rather than the partition of the mandated territory.[17]

And yet these Palestinians could point with dignity and pride to a history in which they and other Arabs had perennially extended a warm shelter to Jews fleeing persecution in Christian Europe, to Christian Armenians escaping oppression in Turkey, and to other harassed peoples. Most Palestinians always honestly believed in a pluralistic state in which Arabs and Jews could live together in a democratic society of one man, one vote.

With the partition of 1947 under the auspices of the U.N. and the unilateral declaration of the State of Israel in May 1948, the fate of these Palestinians was sealed. The Zionists of Palestine had seized the initiative, and backed by the U.S. in particular and world opinion in general, they moved inexorably to extend their control over the land of Palestine. The total inequity of this action was self-evident from the small Jewish percentage of the total population of Palestine at the time (33 percent) as well as from the minuscule percentage of the total land they owned (7 percent). This is a matter of record—the U.N. figures have never been in dispute. Present-day Israelis simply rely on the fact that no one will take the trouble to consult these figures, giving the Zionists the opportunity to cultivate a number of myths that have come to take precedence over any statistics, even when bared.

One such Israeli myth has been that the Palestinians all fled from their homes and land of their own volition, intending to return under the banner of victorious Arab armies recruited in neighboring Arab lands. According to this mythology, those few Palestinians who might have owned anything have only themselves to blame, for they had gambled on force and lost.

However, the responsibility for the Palestinian refugee problem rested squarely with the Zionist military forces, particularly the "freedom fighters," as they were called at that time, the Begin-led Irgun Zvai Leumi, which with the Stern Gang were the two principal terrorist groups. The Irgun perpetrated many acts of violence and terror. Far worse than the more celebrated King David Hotel incident, in which only ninety-five British and Arabs were killed, and the garroting-hanging of two British sergeants at Nathanya, was the attack on the small village of Deir Yassin in which 254[18] women, children, and old men were killed and their bodies thrown down a well on April 9, 1948. This particular village, hugging a rocky promontory west of Jerusalem, had managed to keep out of the turmoil of fighting and excesses of nearby Jerusalem until that moment; Haganah commander David Shaltiel noted that Deir Yassin had been "quiet since the beginnings of disturbances . . . not mentioned in reports of attacks on Jews, and one of the few places which has not given a foothold to foreign bands."[19] Harry Levin in *Jerusalem Embattled*[20] wrote: "When an Arab band tried to make its base there [Deir Yassin] last month the villagers themselves repulsed them, at the cost of the Mukhtar's (headman's) son."

Deir Yassin had done nothing to provoke this attack and had lived peaceably in a sort of agreement with the Jewish suburbs surrounding it.[21] The village had on occasion actually collaborated with the Jewish

Agency[22] and was said by a Jewish newspaper to have actually driven out some Arab militants.[23] It was the Muslim sabbath when the attack was launched on the little village by the combined forces of the Irgun and the Stern Gang.

No warning had been given to the villagers, as was later claimed (Begin has stated that all victims of Irgun attacks had been warned beforehand), because the armored truck with its loudspeaker had tumbled into a ditch and been tossed on its side far short of the first houses of the village. Advised by a night watchman of the approaching Jewish raiders, some inhabitants, with only a robe thrown around them, managed to flee to the west.

The initial resistance of the men of Deir Yassin to the attack was soon overcome, and all of the town's inhabitants were ordered out into a square, where they were lined up against the wall and shot. According to the recital in *O! Jerusalem* by Larry Collins and Dominique Lapierre, the daughter of one of the principal families of Deir Yassin, declared that she saw "a man shoot a bullet in the neck of my sister Salhiyeh, who was nine months pregnant. Then he cut her stomach open with a butcher's knife."[24] Another woman was killed when she tried to extricate the unborn infant from the dead mother's womb. A sixteen-year-old survivor, Naaneh Khalil, claimed she saw a man take "a kind of sword and slash my neighbor Jamil Hish from head to toe and then do the same thing on the steps to my house to my cousin Fathi."[25]

According to the accounts of survivors, the female members of the two terrorist groups matched the savagery of their male counterparts. "Bit by bit, Deir Yassin was submerged in a hell of screams, exploding grenades, the stench of blood, gunpowder and smoke. Its assailants killed, they looted, and finally they raped."[25] Another survivor, Safiyeh Attiyah, saw one man open his pants and leap on her. "I screamed," she said, "but around the other women were being raped, too. Some of the men were so anxious to get our earrings they ripped our ears to pull them off faster."[27]

Fifteen houses in Deir Yassin were dynamited to drive out the owners, and when the terrorized survivors fled to those homes still standing, the Irgun commanders began to systematically work their way through these remaining buildings with Sten guns and grenades.

Most of the men of the village were absent because they worked in Jerusalem. When the terrorists entered, there were only women and children and older people. For two days afterwards, while they tried to tidy up the mess they had made, the Irgun allowed no one else to enter except a Jewish policeman, who reported that one Arab had been killed.[28]

When the British authorities refused to investigate the incident, the Arabs of Jerusalem prevailed upon the International Red Cross to look into the facts. Swiss representative Jacques de Reynier led the first party to reach the site and found 150 bodies thrown into a cistern and another 40 or 50 at one side. In all, he counted 254 dead, including 145 women, of whom 35 were pregnant. He found a six-year-old girl still living under the heap of corpses. Eyewitnesses said later that it was not possible to go near the village without becoming nauseated.[29]

In his diary, the International Red Cross representative indicated that when he arrived the terrorists had not completed their work. According to his entry that night:

The first thing I saw were people running everywhere, rushing in and out of the houses, carrying Sten guns, rifles, pistols and long ornate knives. . . . They seemed half mad. I saw a beautiful girl carrying a dagger still covered with blood. I heard screams. The German member of the Irgun explained, "We're still mopping up." All I could think of was the SS troops I'd seen in Athens.[30]

And then to his horror de Reynier noted he saw "the young woman stab an elderly man and woman cowering on the doorstep of their hut." When he entered one of the first houses, he noted that "everything had been ripped apart and torn upside-down. . . . There were bodies strewn about. They had done their 'cleaning up' with guns and grenades and finished their work with knives. Anyone could see that." The Swiss Red Cross representative rushed the wounded to the nearest hospital. The other surviving women and children were stripped and paraded in three open trucks, their hands over their heads, up and down King George V Avenue, where they were spat on and even stoned.[31]

Shaltiel and his Haganah command had been occupied in fighting on other nearby fronts. We are told by writer J. Bowyer Bell[32] that when he arrived at the edge of Deir Yassin, "a smoking ruin filled with corpses of men, women and children" greeted him. When Irgun Commander Mordechai Ramaan announced the village was completely under control and a Haganah unit should be sent in to take over, Shaltiel replied, "We're not going to take responsibility for your murders."[33] The claim later made by the Irgun that those killed had been fiercely resisting was totally disproved by another Haganah member commander of the youth organization, Eliyahu Arieli, who stated: "All of the killed, with very few exceptions, were old men, women or children. The dead we found were all unjust victims, and none of them had died with a weapon in their hands."[34] Shaltiel's adjutant was said to have told the commander of the Stern contingent of attackers, "You are swine."

While the Jewish Agency for Palestine and the Haganah publicly disassociated themselves from the outrage, the latter took military advantage of the victory by eventually taking over the village, and the former accepted other spoils. The Jewish Agency posted leaflets descriptive of the massacre in many Arab villages. Loudspeaker vans toured Arab Jerusalem broadcasting in Arabic, "Unless you leave your homes, the fate of Deir Yassin will be your fate."[35]

A group of American correspondents who attended a press conference given by the Irgun and the Stern Gang were told that it was "the beginning of the conquest of Palestine and Trans-Jordan."[36] The Israelis took advantage of the massacre, which has compared with the Nazi atrocities at Oradoursur-Klane and Lidice, or even "a horror worse, for in Lidice only the men and boys were slaughtered."[37]

Most of the information of Collins and Lapierre in *O! Jerusalem* was obtained from de Reynier's report to the International Red Cross and several reports on the incident forwarded to the Chief Secretary of the Palestine government, Sir Henry Gurney, by Richard C. Catling, Assistant Inspector General of the Criminal Investigation Division, on April 13, 15, and 16, 1948. Bearing the dossier number 179/110/17/GS under the designation "Secret" and signed by Catling, they contained the interrogation reports of the massacre survivors by a team of British police officers together with corroborating physical evidence obtained through medical examinations of the survivors by a doctor and a nurse at the government hospital in Jerusalem.

Israelis today, and Begin defenders in particular, deny that the Israelis in any way instigated the flight of the Palestinians, whom they insist left voluntarily as a result of Arab broadcasts urging them to leave "so that the Arab armies could sweep through." But other sources indicate contrarywise. Jon Kimche, the Zionist writer, calling the incident "the darkest stain on the Jewish record throughout the fighting," stated, "The terrorist justified the massacre of Deir Yassin because it led to the panic flight of the remaining Arabs in the Jewish state area."[38] Jewish writer Don Peretz described the result of Deir Yassin as a "mass fear psychosis which grasped the whole Arab community."[39] Arthur Koestler wrote, this "bloodbath . . . was the psychologically decisive factor in the spectacular exodus of Arab refugees."[40]

Moshe Sharett, in a letter to U.N. Conciliator Count Folke Bernadotte, referred to "a mass exodus, mostly spontaneous, a cataclysmic phenomenon which, according to the experience of other countries, changes the course of history." In his own report, Bernadotte stated: "The exodus of Palestinian Arabs resulted from panic created by fighting in their communities, by remorse concerning real or alleged acts of terrorism, or expulsion." Dr. Chaim Weizmann, the first President of Israel, referred to the Deir Yassin incident as "a miraculous simplification."[41] A policy of deliberate terrorism, "adopted by the Zionist forces in an attempt to cow the Arabs into submission and break their will to further resistance,"[42] was how a Canadian writer phrased it. This precipitated the mass Arab flight, not the orders of the Arab Higher Committee, as Israelists contended.

According to Erskine Childers' article "The Other Exodus"[43] and Professor Maxime Rodinson's *Israel and the Arabs,*[44] there is very little evidence to support the Israelist contention that the Arabs left their homes at the orders of Arab leaders and the Arab Higher Committee. Research clearly indicates that those not incited to leave by Zionist propaganda fled at the bayonet point of the Israeli army, joining the tide of those who "were made to leave by deceit, lying, and false promises," to use the words of one Jewish witness to the flight who described the manner by which "we, Jews, forced the Arabs to leave cities and villages."[45]

Begin denied responsibility for the tragedy (at the time Prime Minister Ben-Gurion sent an apology to Jordan's King Abdullah, the Jewish Agency deplored the "commission of such brutalities by Jews as utterly repugnant" and the Chief Rabbi of Jerusalem took the unusual step of excommunicating participants in the attack) and claimed that "this atrocity charge was a combined Jewish Agency-Arab propaganda story" (quite a combination!). However, in *The Revolt: The Story of the Irgun,*[46] Begin boasted of the daring deeds he committed. He referred to "the military victory at Deir Yassin," greatly simplifying the task of transforming Israel into an exclusively Jewish state and admitted that the "subsequent tales of 'Irgun butchering' " had resulted in

maddened, uncontrollable stampede. Of the about 800,000 Arabs who lived on the present territory of the state of Israel, only 165,000 are still there . . . In the rest of the country, too, the Arabs began to flee in terror . . . All the Jewish forces proceeded to advance through Haifa like a knife through butter. . . . The Arabs, who began fleeing in panic, shouting 'Deir Yassin!' . . . The political and economic significance of this development can hardly be overestimated.

And the President of the Zionist Organization of America, Rabbi Abba Hillel Silver, was quoted as having said, "The Irgun will go down in history as a factor without which the State of Israel would not have come into being."[47]

It is true, as the Zionists allege, that many Palestinians left thinking they might return as soon as the war was over. They fled without any idea of permanency. Many left all their clothes behind. As one told me in a refugee camp, she "left her things to sew, pictures, the paintings and photographs"—things people would not leave behind if they did not intend to return, or indeed if they even had time to plan their departure. But once the war was over, the way home was closed to them—perhaps forever if the Zionists of Israel continue to have their way.

Some Arabs fled because of deliberate acts of terrorism, others because the war was on their doorstep, explosions everywhere and civilians were under fire. From the outset the incoming Israelis employed terror and fear to drive the Palestinians from their homes. These Israelis were even then determined that the world reecho their cry, "What Palestinians?" As the London *Times* reported on one of hundreds of such incidents: "On April 22, 1948, Zionists attacked Haifa after midnight, occupied buildings, streets and public buildings. The Palestinians taken by surprise moved their women and children to the Port area for evacuation to Acre. While in full flight the Arab refugees were attacked by advanced Jewish posts. 100 Arabs were killed and 200 wounded."[48]

This does not mean that the Arabs, in turn, did not commit atrocities of their own. But it is vital to understand the manner in which the land was emptied of Palestinians who had lived for centuries in their homeland.

Moshe Dayan, now a self-proclaimed critic of terrorism, played an important part in the early Zionist terror campaign against the indigenous peoples. On July 11, 1948, forces led by Dayan attacked the Arab town of Lydda, now the location of the Tel Aviv airport. Pro-Zionist writers Jon and David Kimche in their book *A Clash of Destinies* describe exactly what happened: "Dayan drove at full speed into Lydda shooting up the town and creating confusion and a degree of terror among the population. . . . Its Arab population of 30,000 either fled or were herded on the road to Ramallah. The next day Ramleh also surrendered and its Arab populous suffered the same fate."[49]

Another Israeli myth: The Palestinians had owned the land and over the years had never done anything with it. They had hardly any settlements, only a few miserable farms. Whatever you see in Israel— villages, towns, cities, farms, and the rest—have all been built up by the Jews, and principally since 1948. So goes the myth.

This is an outright perversion of the truth, and those Israelis who have the courage to speak out will verify that Palestine was being developed in line with the times and its regional culture long before the Jews took over. What the Israelis did, in fact, was to *destroy* most of the Palestinian villages. Prior to the Zionist seizure of Palestine in 1948 and the establishment of the state, an industrious Palestinian Arab community lived in developed cities and villages scattered throughout the country.

Concentration camp survivor Dr. Israel Shahak, who organized the Israeli League for Human and Civil Rights, tells us in his 1973 report "Arab Villages Destroyed in Israel"[50]: "The truth about Arab settlements in the area of the State of Israel before 1948 is one of the most guarded secrets of Israeli life. No publication, book or pamphlet gives either their number or location. This is done on purpose so that the accepted official myth of an 'empty country' can be taught in schools and told to visitors."

In Palestine's fifteen districts before 1948 there were 475 villages (not including areas inhabited by a certain number of nonmigratory Arab tribes, which were not considered villages). Since 1948 no less than 385, three-fourths of the original number, have been completely destroyed by the authorities, leaving only 90 of the original villages. The chart on the following page from the Shahak report shows that in many districts, such as Ramleh with its thirty-one villages, every Arab settlement was demolished by the Israelis. In the district of Jaffa, outside Jerusalem, only Jaffa City remained.

Annex 1 to the report lists by district the names of all the villages that existed before 1948 and those existing in 1973. Almost all of the 385 destroyed villages, even with their cemeteries and tombstones, were literally bulldozed away. Passing visitors are told: "That was all a desert."

Minister of Defense Moshe Dayan, addressing students of the Haifa Technion School in March 1969, stated: There is not a single Jewish village in this country that has not been built on the site of an Arab village. The village of Nahalal took the place of the Arab village of Mahloul. Gifat took the place of Jifta. . . ."[51]

Name of District	Number of Villages Before 1948	Number of Villages Now	Number of Destroyed Villages
Jerusalem	33	4	29
Bethlehem	7	0	7
Hebron	16	0	16
Jaffa	23	0	23
Ramleh	31	0	31
Lydda	28	0	31
Jenin	8	4	4
Tul-Karem	33	12	21
Haifa	43	8	35
Ako	52	32	20
Nazareth	26	20	6
Safad	75	7	68
Tiberias	26	3	23
Beisan	28	0	28
Gaza	46	0	46
TOTAL	475	90	385

According to a 1968 report made by delegates of the National Council of Churches, headed by Rev. Raymond E. Maxwell,

. . . the destruction of villages appears to be a particular expression of articulated Israeli policy that the Arabs must be taught by prompt, destructive reprisals that insubordination will not be tolerated . . . as evidence of the existence of Yalu, Beit Nuba and Imwas, there remains only a scrap of wood, a bent rod, scattered here and there . . . and a broken water pump which has been installed with ecumenical relief funds. Eucalyptus trees have been planted and are rapidly covering the ground where the villages had stood for hundreds of years.

This policy of physically destroying Palestinian settlements within territory controlled by Israel has never ceased. To solidify their gains after the 1967 war, according to U.N. figures, the Israelis destroyed during the period between June 11, 1967, and November 15, 1969, some 7,554 Palestinian Arab homes in the territories seized during that war; this figure excluded thirty-five villages in the occupied Golan Heights that were razed to the ground.[52] In the two years between September 1969 and 1971 the figure was estimated to have reached 16,312 homes.

Israeli journalist-soldier Amos Kenan was so shocked by his experiences in occupied territories that he had to write:

The unit commander told us that it had been decided to blow up three villages in our sector [in the Latrun area], Beit Nuba, Imwas, and Yalu. . . . Unarmed people were to be allowed to pack up their belongings and were told to go to the nearby village of Beit Sura. We were ordered to block the entrances of the village and prevent inhabitants from returning. The order was to shoot over their heads. At noon the first bulldozer arrived and pulled down the first house at the edge of the village.[53]

On the site of the Arab village of Imwas, a "national park" was opened in September 1975. In describing the dedication of the park, a writer for *Ma'ariv* stated there had been Arab villages there "but in June 1967 the villages were 'abandoned.' "[54] Michael Adams, editor of *Middle East International* and former *Guardian* correspondent in Beirut, related the comment by a rival journalist in *Ha'aretz* "that the use of the simple word 'abandoned' was a wonderful expression, very Zionist, sounding like 'to give oneself the sack.'" [55] This journalist went on to warn that it might be better not to let the children playing in the park dig in the ground in case they came across the remains of the houses that had been destroyed, which would, however, be passed off as "the remains of a 12th-century synagogue." He then sarcastically concluded:

Originally, there were Jews here and then came the bulldozers of the Jewish National Fund. In between there was—nothing; and if there was anything, well, it was abandoned and destroyed. Now there's a national park, and that's all that's important. Truthfully what is nicer: a nationalist Arab village or a Jewish national park?[56]

As for the Israeli claim that the "Jews came and made the desert bloom," a Palestinian Arab still living within the borders of pre-1967 Israel noted that the orange groves were there before the Jews:

Before I was born, my father had two orange groves and was exporting some 23 million boxes by 1948 from Jaffa. And yet, the tour directors taking Jews from all over the world, including Americans, through our cities and countryside, keep talking about these orange groves that the Israelis had planted since 1948. You know, it's funny, there was a little American lady on the bus and as the tour director went on to talk about the great achievements of the Israelis in orange planting, she remarked, "Nonsense. That orange grove is certainly older than twenty years."

Israeli apologists invariably insist that the Palestinian Arabs never had it so good. They call it "a benign, enlightened occupation." It is true that 40–50,000 from the West Bank work in Israel daily. They are mostly unskilled workers who come from their towns and villages by bus or walk as much as three miles to work. They are paid more than they ever received under Jordanian rule. The pay may be good for them, but it is Israel that benefits most from this boon. Israel depends totally today on this cheap labor to operate machines in the new factories of the kibbutzim and to build houses, schools, and roads.

According to the Israeli daily *Ma'ariv* (March 14, 1974), "hundreds of Arab children, 14–16 years of age, work in West Jerusalem. The work they do involves no learning and in many cases borders on shameful exploitation." Noting that the problem was not a new one, the Israeli newspaper pointed out "that the phenomenon has now become an inseparable part of the social and economic fabric of the capital. In the past, a garage owner was ashamed to employ a boy for 4 Israeli pounds a day ($1.20); today there is no shame. The explanation given is that no one compels him to stay, and some argue that they are doing these boys a favor."

"What relevance does economic prosperity have to people's happiness?" asked novelist Amos Oz in the same *Ma'ariv* article. "We were much more prosperous under the British Mandate than the first years of our independence." This Israeli could understand what Anwar Nusseibeh, former Jordanian Minister of Defense, meant when he talked after the Israeli conquest of "the terrible frustration for the Palestinians in this occupation—the frustration of being an outsider in one's land."

Well-educated, suave, and moderate, Nuseibeh analyzed the problem confronting his fellow Palestinians:

It's not a matter of food or clothing. We have enough of that. It's a question of having to deal with an alien bureaucracy, of receiving orders in a language I do not understand, of getting notices under my door in writing I cannot read. The other day a police officer arrived to tell me that the fine for a traffic ticket I received has been doubled because I did not pay it on time. Of course I never knew that I'd been charged with it in the first place because I could not read the writing [in Hebrew].[57]

What actually took place during the June 1967 Israeli takeover of Arab lands has never been recited in any of the plethora of books published on the "wondrous" six-day Israeli victory.

The Bab el-Maghraba District of Arab Jerusalem, for instance, was a pleasant and architecturally distinctive quarter of freshly white-washed roof terraces, gardens, and neat unattached houses built in North African style several hundred years ago to house Moroccan soldiers garrisoned in Jerusalem for the Ottomans. Shortly after sunset on June 8, 1967, the night following the takeover of the Old City by Israeli paratroopers in the six-day war, demolition of the district began. The occupants were evicted on one-hour's notice. One woman, deaf and alone, not hearing the order, was buried alive beneath the ruins. Within a few days more than 130 buildings, including two mosques, were eradicated—the equivalent of three city blocks.

Widespread sequestrations of Arabs also took place in the Sharf Quarter leading to the mosque and in the Daraq Tabouni region. Not less than 3,500 persons residing there were given scant notice to leave, a procedure likewise used against large groups of Arabs who had dwelt for centuries in the region of French Hill and Mt. Scopus near the British Cemetery. There were other isolated instances of sequestration by the Israelies in their continued effort to Zionize Jerusalem. Condemnations by the U.N. Security Council for these expropriations going back to May 1968 had no effect in bringing about any change of position by the Israelis.

Although the Arabic language is given to gross hyperboles, the following account of a Christian Arab living in occupied Jerusalem still must make the reader pause:

Early in June, 1967, the people of the West Bank of Jordan, including Jerusalem, suddenly found themselves under Israeli occupation, and the same tragedy of 1948 has been repeated. Their nationality and personality as a nation has again been the subject of doubt.

Terror reigned when the Israeli army entered Jerusalem. Looting on a large scale commenced, and ninety percent of the shops were broken into. Both military and civilian Israelis ransacked houses and emptied them of all valuables. Residents of Jerusalem did not realize at the beginning what was happening, many of them, who for the first time now seeing Israeli soldiers, mistook them for Iraqis coming to the rescue. Due to this mistake many civilians were killed in welcoming such soldiers.

For the next five days, the curfew was relaxed only two hours a day. When it was lifted, the first impression one gained when leaving his house was the vast destruction of houses and commercial centres and the number of bodies of both military and civilian Arabs that were in the streets. People were running about inquiring as to their relatives. Everyone appears to have missed somebody. In some houses the number of missing came up to ten. Hundreds of young innocent men were carried by force in trucks and detained without any offense. Their fate is still doubtful.

Arab Jerusalem was not prepared for war for the simple reason that it was thought that as a holy city, the town would be spared the catastrophes of battle. Not a single sandbag was prepared and no shelters built. The civilian population was not trained for civil defense.

During the five days of fighting in Jerusalem the population could understand that it was war, but worse was coming after the fighting had stopped. Every officer and soldier acted on his own initiative and took the law in his own hand. The following are some examples of what took place.

Israeli soldiers entered the house of the Sandouka family whose head was a sick man in bed for two years. Without warning they shot dead four of his family, injured two grandchildren aged eight and twelve and a cousin who happened to have been taking shelter with them. The tragedy was completed when the head of family was shot and killed and dumped over the bodies of his family.

The Hindiyeh family lost two sons aged twenty and twenty-four. When the younger brother was shot and killed at the doorstep of his house, his elder brother tried to pull him in, but he was in no better luck, and another shot penetrated his stomach. The second son could have been saved if medical attention was available. The mother tried first aid but without success and he died of hemorrhage. His mother had no water even to wash up the blood of her sons.

Two girls of Khashram family, aged nineteen and twenty, were victims of Israeli cruelty. The first was hit by a shrapnel. The other sister decided to take her to the nearest first aid centre and carried a white flag to show that they are innocent civilians. Immediately when they proceeded from the house, they were met by an Israeli tank which shot both sisters dead on the spot.

Jerusalem has since become a special victim of Israeli expansionist policy. Following the 1967 war, the Israeli government embarked on a program of Zionizing East Jerusalem. For this purpose a company for restoring and developing the Jewish quarter was established, and expropriation orders were submitted. The company took over existing buildings, reconstructed them, and then sold them to Jews, out from under the Arab ownership. The purpose, of course, was to cause the immediate evacuation of hundreds of Arab families. The inhabitants were offered the ridiculous sum of £ 15,000 ($1,500) as compensation, which was never sufficient to purchase any alternative housing.

Many refused to move, in which case pressure was put on them, often by compensating one or two families much above the official price. When they left, reconstruction began on their apartment, turning the lives of the other tenants into a nightmare as walls were broken down, sewage pipes broken, and the building became unlivable.[58]

The story of how "thousands of Arab residents since 1967 have lost their family homes to Israeli-directed redevelopment" was detailed by the *Christian Science Monitor* March 5, 1975:

Since 1967, thousands of Arab residents have lost their family homes to Israeli-directed redevelopment. . . . Property developers in Israeli-annexed East

Jerusalem are continuing pressure to evict and "relocate" Arab inhabitants of the old walled city and to "modernize" it. Evicted Arab families see box-like contructions of new Israeli housing rising from the debris of their demolished homes. . . . When Mr. Saifi refused to sell his home in Jerusalem, bulldozers demolishing nearby houses pushed high mounds of rubble around his house, making access nearly impossible. The foundations were undermined by digging on two sides. Israeli police, at this writing, were pounding frequently on the door and warning Mr. Saifi's elderly mother, the only person still living there, to leave because the house was unsafe . . . Mr. Muhammad al-Maghrebi refused any compensation for his house . . . and is holding on. . . . Another house . . . belongs to three families named Shaheen and houses twenty people. Demolition on three sides has already undermined the foundations, but some of the Shaheens are staying until they are forced out. . . .

In Jerusalem Zionist expansionism took the form of outright destruction and usurpation, then total annexation. "Now that the Jews have got Jerusalem, they cannot give it up without losing their soul," said Mayor Teddy Kollek.[59] The status of Jerusalem was not even negotiable and, according to its Chief Executive, internationalization was a bad solution, dividing the city to an even greater degree.

Defending his position, Kollek claimed, "The Arabs in Jerusalem already have functional independence. They enjoy a greater degree of physical security, prosperity, and freedom of expression than citizens of Arab countries. They have their own schools. They can attend Arab universities. . . . They have freedom of movement. . . ." The *Times* correspondent interviewing the Mayor added, "In fact, they have everything except the right to be their own masters."[60] To the individualistic, independent-spirited Arabs, this right was first, last, and above all.

The Jewish Mayor indicated that he understood "how this must rankle." But he defended Israeli conduct in the Holy City: "The Arabs had been occupied for hundreds of years by the Turks, the British, the Bedu from Jordan, and now Israel." Kollek admitted that there were "many Arabs who hope for eventual independence, but not just now."

It is in the Holy City more than anywhere else in the occupied territories that the visitor is overwhelmed by visible evidence of the Israeli "fortress" mentality, which has, unfortunately, supplanted any sincere search for peace. One cannot help feel deeply saddened, then angered, to see the ugly high-rise hotels, offices, and concrete-block tenement apartments (often with wash flapping in the breeze) looking ominously down upon the Old City and breaking the beautiful, peaceful contour of surrounding hills. The enthralling, uplifting feeling that once pervaded every believer here, whether sauntering on the Via Dolorosa on which Jesus trod under the burden of the Cross, gazing at the Al-Aqsa Mosque, the spot from which Muhammad ascended to heaven, or standing by the Wailing Wall so sacred to the Jews, has been stilled by the ominous presence overshadowing the holy places.

It was this "Zionization" of Jerusalem that led to the highly publicized censure and ban of Israel by UNESCO and the counterboycott. Such musical luminaries as Artur Rubinstein and Leonard Bernstein publicly called upon Yehudi Menuhin, Chairman of the executive committee of the International Music Council, an affiliated body of UNESCO, to join in the counterboycott of UNESCO organized by Zionist groups. But Menuhin declined to follow their advice. In a response to a cable sent to him in Paris, the noted violinist declared Jerusalem, because of its "universal meaning, must be treated as a trust for humanity at large and not as the province of a single power." He added that "a broader attitude" was essential "if Jewish people everywhere and Israelis in particular are to command international support and sympathy, which is now at a low ebb."[61] "The Rape of Jerusalem," as some called it, went forward despite the advice of the international development consultants who bitterly opposed such modern constructions as the proposed twenty-four-story Hyatt House in East Jerusalem.

And everywhere the contrast prevailed between the two combatants: the neon advertisements in Hebrew versus the Arabic scriptures in stone. The houses of 100 Arab families were torn down to create a plaza in front of the Wailing Wall. And lest any visitor become momentarily unmindful as to who was the appropriate and rightful possessor of this Holy City, a terrace has been erected facing the wall where the tourist might pick up a telephone-phonograph apparatus and with the payment of a nominal sum have poured into his ears all the customary Zionist propaganda.

Elsewhere, the former Jewish quarter of the Old City was emptied of its Arab inhabitants, most of whom were Palestinian refugees from lands taken by Israeli forces in 1948. Eight hundred acres of the best land in the Old City were expropriated, old homes bulldozed, and trees cut down so the land could be used for Jewish settlements. An Arab woman with tears in her eyes pointed to the places where once she played as a child under the shadow of lovely old olive trees. Land requisitioning continued to go forward, takeovers to satisfy so-called security requirements, archaeological needs, or just plain Israeli demands. The continued digging, to bring to light the original Wailing

Wall, endangered the mosque of Al-Aqsa as well as other Muslim and Christian places of worship. Despite Mayor Kollek's vaunted promise of nonintention to create a monoculture, whenever Arab cultural rights conflicted with alleged Israeli "needs," Arab rights inevitably had to give way.

Israeli propaganda would have Americans believe that Arabs and Jews were equals in the new "united Jerusalem." How could this flamboyant claim be squared with the facts? Car plates for Arabs were distinguished by the first three digits; Arab taxis had to be painted in a distinctive manner. American visitors to Jerusalem who rode in Arab cars and taxis have found themselves harassed at checkpoints. Phone numbers of Arabs were all given the initial digit "8" to distinguish them from others. Arab identification cards carried this notation: "This identification does not represent verification with relation to the law of entry into Israel" (literal translation). This vague caveat could only mean that an Arab leaving Israeli territory was not sure of readmittance.

Inside the occupied West Bank and Gaza, the atmosphere fairly bristled with conflict. An announcement that the military government for the West Bank was informing landowners in the northern regions of the Jordan Valley between Nablus and Jenin that over 500 acres (2,000 dunums) of their lands would be declared a closed area for military purposes, would mean very little to Americans. But the history of Israeli colonization to date indicates this has been the standard first step for securing lands for new Jewish settlements. This was no "paper tiger." This move had a direct impact on human beings, as I learned during my travels.[62]

I saw rich, agricultural land pushed aside, acres of fertile farming giving way to ghetto-like, blockade-type Eastern European multiple dwellings. The claim that the Zionists made the desert bloom falls apart when one can see the green productiveness of the old terraced Arab farms reaching as far as the eye can see on both sides of the road. Forty-five kilometers out of Jerusalem are flourishing vineyards. Then come the new, fortresslike buildings at Hebron for Jewish resettlement, in sharp contrast to the small Arab houses with their arches, olive trees, little gardens, and distinctive architecture.

The Arab Palestinians, no matter how cozy a picture the media continued to draw, still deeply resented the occupation. Just when the Gaza Strip had become a bit less turbulent and the situation of the Arabs there slightly more tolerable, largely thanks to the efforts of Gaza City's Arab Mayor Rashid al-Shawa, the Israeli Military Governor ordered him to incorporate the neighboring Shati refugee camp within the city limits and provide it with municipal services. The Palestinians feared that such a change in the legal status of the strip would result in the permanent integration of the area with its 400,000 refugees within Israel. Mayor al-Shawa pointedly refused to obey the order and was dismissed. Nine members of the eleven-man city council resigned. A *Christian Science Monitor* editorial quoted what Michael Adams had written in the *Guardian Weekly,* stated: "I had my ups and downs during four years of war in Germany, but the Germans never treated me as harshly as the Israelis are treating the Arabs of the Gaza Strip, the majority of whom are women and children."[63]

Traveling through the West Bank in 1974, I met with Adel Ahmed Shakaar, Deputy Mayor of Nablus, the West Bank's largest city. One of his top assistants, Engineer Hamdi Qasas, having read my books, proceeded to talk freely at great length about the latest series of outrages committed by the Israelis against the Palestinians. More than 100 houses had been blown up in the past months, often on the basis of mere suspicion of collaboration with the Palestinian Fatah. We were taken to see the most recent example of Israeli oppression, a home that had housed seventeen persons but had been ruthlessly blown to pieces when one of the young residents was accused of collaborating in the kidnapping of an Israeli soldier. While the American press still reported in rhapsodic terms the alleged good relations between the occupiers and the occupied, the contrary was apparent to any inquiring viewer. The ruthless control being exercised over the Palestinians was all too evident.

This house had been blown up only two weeks previously. After the Israeli military had done their job, the members of the family refused to move, insisting on sitting near the main road so everyone could see what had happened. The military government had requested that the Mayor take care of these new refugees so that they did not continue to make a public display of their situation. His response was that they should have thought of this before they destroyed the home of seventeen people. The family was divided into two or three groups and taken in by other families. To add insult to injury, the Israelis forbade a homeowner to rebuild in the same location, or anywhere else —as a practical method of getting rid of the Palestinians. With the motto "I won't help you, and I won't let anyone else help you," the Israeli Establishment continued its pushing-out process of the indigenous population.

Indiscriminate destruction of homes enforces collective punishment against the Palestinian community. The chief victims often have been children and babies, women and old men, whose only crime consisted of having some kind of blood relationship with a man merely suspected by the authorities of sympathizing with the fedayeen. Demolition of homes, carried out even in the middle of severest winters, such as that of 1973–74, resulted in whole families, who were not even permitted to remove their personal belongings, being thrown out into the freezing cold lacking adequate dress as well as shelter.

Antagonism against the occupier reached new heights when the many friends of Kamal Nasser, the poet-PLO leader assassinated in the cunning Israeli commando raid on Beirut, overcame security obstacles to gather together in April 1973 from all over the region to mourn with his family in the little church at Bir Zeit on the West Bank. (The Israelis would not permit the body to be sent across the Allenby Bridge. The slain Palestinian was buried in Beirut, with tens of thousands marching through the streets to the cemetery there.)

The subsequent arrest of two editors of the Jerusalem Arabic weekly *Al Fajr,* charged with evading censorship and inciting to revolution, stirred additional unrest. These editors had audaciously printed a poem, written by the mother of the late Kamal, in an editorial in which Jordanian and Israeli intelligence officers were charged with planning the Beirut attack at a meeting in Eilat.

Earlier, five young dissident Jews had been sentenced by a military court to a fine or six months in prison merely for protesting Israel's seizure of an area on the occupied West Bank near Akraba for Jewish settlement. A paramilitary colony had been quickly established there, and a civilian settlement called Gitit was being built. The 4,000 peasants of Akraba, a small Palestinian village six miles southeast on Nablus, had refused to sell their lands. Then, according to *Le Nouvel Observateur* and the *Christian Science Monitor,* the Israelis took this drastic action:

On April 28, an Israeli Piper plane overflew Akraba spraying a chemical defoliant over the villagers' wheat fields. In one night all the wheat sown the previous December (200 hectares or 494 acres) had changed its color: the green turned brown, burnt by chemical products. . . . The Israelis do not deny these facts. They admit having sprayed the fields with chemicals, but only "to teach a lesson to these villagers" who were stubbornly continuing to work lands to which the army had forbidden them access. . . . One can't help wondering why, in the midst of these arid hills, cultivated fields were chosen as training grounds (for the Israeli military). The answer is no mystery: the idea is to prepare for the arrival of the Israeli settlers. In any case, Akraba is not the only village of the occupied West Bank where pressure is exerted on the villagers to sell their lands.[64]

This shocking action aroused the ire not only of the Arabs but of their Jewish sympathizers. At a New Left rally in front of the Knesset, the five accused youths had distributed pamphlets that vividly proclaimed: "We are loyal to our people and our country, but we refuse to accept the confiscation of land belonging to the Arabs, the destruction of their crops, and their replacement with a Jewish village."

Any objective examination of what was taking place could not help reveal the unmistakable Israeli motivation to push Arabs off their property and take over. Medical centers for blood and TB and laboratory facilities, which had been servicing the Arabs of Jerusalem and twenty-nine Arab villages, were ordered closed on April 1, 1973, and moved to Ramallah, greatly inconveniencing people who needed quick help. One of the four centers was thereafter reopened, but nothing was heard further of the other three. The claim was also made that the Sharia, the Muslim courts, were very gradually being closed down. The Kadi in charge, we were told, was just another stooge who was forced to swear to the Israeli Establishment that appointed him. Thirteen new quarters were being established by Israelis in and around Jerusalem, planned to accommodate eventually 122,000 new Jewish immigrants. This did not at all end the Arabs' fear. It was rumored that 1,000 additional square miles (80,000 dunums) would also be used for Jewish populating of the area so as to link up Bethlehem, Jericho, and the Dead Sea.

Arrests, trials, and deportations of West Bank Arabs increased. Even as Israel was vehemently protesting the treatment of prisoners of the October 1973 war and the Syrian-Egyptian reluctance to exchange prisoners as violations of the Geneva Convention, oppressions against the inhabitants of the conquered territories, clearly forbidden by the Geneva Convention, continued and were being ignored.

The Amman Committee of Expelled Palestinians, claiming to represent sixty-eight exiled Palestinians—"men and women of prominence and influence, Muslim and Christian religious leaders, doctors, lawyers, pharmacists, engineers, teachers, students, union workers, farmers, and heads of municipalities"—submitted a memorandum to the Jordanian Prime Minister in 1969 stating:

"It is clear that the . . . expulsion of people of influence or leadership is intended to fragment the people's unity, lower their morale, and undermine their resistance to the occupation. . . ."[65]

Most of the allegations against the deportees concerned activities normally considered within the realm of human rights, such as: "publicly opposed the annexation of East Jerusalem," "incited students to demonstrate," "planned merchant strikes," "leaflets found in his house," "active in Communist party," "collected funds for PLO," "caused unrest in school," "urged people not to work in Israel," "demonstrated on Human Rights Day," "is wife (or son or daughter) of——(suspected or actual Palestinian activist)," etc.[66]

When the Israeli policy of deportation without trial was just beginning, a critical article appeared in *New Outlook* (Tel Aviv):

To the best of our own personal knowledge, at least some of the personalities deported had not occupied themselves with sabotage or terror, but had, within the limits of the given situation, voiced their opposition to Israeli rule on the West Bank. If that is a crime that warrants deportation, we may not be far from the day when thousands of others will have to be treated the same way.[67]

The magazine's prediction soon became a fact, and the deportations never ceased; if anything, it became more brazen. On December 10, 1973, which coincidentally is celebrated in Israel as the Day of Human Rights, eight[68] Palestinian intellectuals and community leaders of the West Bank were expelled to Jordan, the expulsions being carried out in the most brutal manner. The men were arrested at night and taken from their homes, without the victims or their families being told what the charges were. In each home from which the father of the family was taken for expulsion, a security man was left, whose task was to prevent the family from having immediate contact with the outside world, even with an attorney.

The arrested men were kept in the dark as to the exact reason for their apprehension. As one of them, Dr. Walid Kamhawi, later detailed:

An officer climbed into the vehicle in which we were being transported, read a paper he held in his hands, and then we knew—the Israeli occupying authorities had ordered our expulsion from our homeland, because we "constituted a danger to Israeli security." It was so funny, that in spite of the "secure borders" and the ultra-modern war machinery of "invincible Israel" we, a doctor, a mayor, a trade-unionist, two lawyers and three teachers, were a threat to Israeli security, though none of us had carried a pistol in his life. No court, no trial, not even a charge was brought against any of us.[69]

They were taken into the desert area of the Araba Valley and compelled by threat of force to cross over into Jordan. Abd al-Jawad Saleh,[70] the Mayor of the town of El-Bireh, refused to obey the order to cross over the border and was wounded with a bayonet by one of the Israeli soldiers. To force them to advance further into Jordanian territory, shots were fired in their direction. A few weeks later, when the father of Mayor Saleh died, the son was not allowed to cross back even for a brief visit to attend his father's funeral.

Jewish Israeli lawyer Felicia Langer described another deportation as it was related to her by one of her many Palestianian clients:

There were twelve of us. On 1 July 1970 we were taken to the Beersheba prison. The guards told us that this was the first stage of our release. When we arrived in Beersheba we were told it was banishment. Next morning at six o'clock we were handcuffed and blindfolded and our feet were chained. In reply to our questions we were told that we were going home. They put us in a truck and we travelled for about four hours. When the truck stopped we were taken to another vehicle and travelled about three hours more. We didn't know where we had been taken to. When the vehicle stopped the cloth was taken off our eyes. We saw then that we were in an armoured car. We were surrounded by other armoured cars loaded with armed soldiers. We were on the road, and around us extended the desert. An officer came and ordered us in a threatening voice: "Now you walk towards the East," and he pointed at the dunes of the endless desert. "Anyone coming back will be shot. Anyone coming back in a month, a year, or any other time must know that only death awaits him here." To the east the burning sands of the desert were waiting for us. It was mid-day in July. Our heads had no cover; our shoes were plastic slippers. We each had a water-bottle with lukewarm water and a bag with sand-covered food. We started walking in the terrible heat of noon without knowing where our steps would take us. We were afraid of getting lost in the desert. We remembered the Egyptian soldiers who died in the Sinai sands after suffering hunger, thirst and sun stroke. We walked for more than two hours until suddenly we met a first-line post of the Jordanian army. They thought we were spies and started shooting at us. By a real miracle none of us were wounded, and finally we succeeded in convincing them, and we were taken to Amman. As you know, the Jordanian authorities refused to accept people deported across the bridges. So the Israeli authorities wanted to confront them with facts. I think they expected the Jordanians to kill us. We were told later that we had been banished near the Al-Dahl region, in Wadi Araba. Our feet were inflamed when we arrived in Amman. The skin of my shaved head had peeled off because of the sun. The desert was a nightmare.[71]

The Israeli government has used deportation as a means of ridding itself of outspoken Palestinian nationalists, including the mayors of Jerusalem and Ramallah, the editor of *Shaab* newspaper, former members of Parliament, and doctors and lawyers. Dr. Hanna Nasir, president of Bir Zeit College, was expelled from his Ramallah home on November 21, 1974. He was a member of a distinguished Palestinian family, including his father, Musa, who had served as Jordan's foreign minister, and his cousin, Kamal, the assassinated PLO spokesman-poet. Nasir had been an outspoken nationalist. With no notice whatsoever, he and four others were awakened and bodily removed from the West Bank, accused of inciting recent demonstrations and of being members of "hostile organizations." Yet *New York Times* correspondent Terence Smith, in a November 22 story, wrote that Nasir "did everything he could to avoid a confrontation" between the marching, protesting students of his college and the Israeli soldiers sent in to keep the area quiet.

In an American Friends Service Committee Report of April 1977, Ann Lesch indicated that between June 1967 and February 1976 nearly 1,500 Palestinians had been deported from the occupied territories, most of them community leaders, and some 110 political activists. The study[72] lists by name 1,136 individuals with the exact date of deportation and the route by which they were dispelled—by the River Jordan bridges into Jordan, across the Lebanese border or set loose in the desert region between the Dead Sea and the Gulf of Aqaba.

Some nationalists have not been deported. Ramallah-born Raymonda Taweel was placed under house arrest in August 1976. She can see people, but their names are carefully noted by policemen guarding her door. Her crime: She passed word along to foreign correspondents on what was really happening. For this she was accused of poisoning the foreign media. She defied Israeli officials in the military government, saying: "This is supposed to be an open society. There is a price for democracy and I am going to continue." She refused to write a letter of apology and the authorities refused to bring charges, even permitting her to leave the country to visit the U.S. during the meeting of the U.N. General Assembly in 1976. But, contrary to Israeli hopes, she returned to carry on her battle. On March 22, 1978 at 1:30 A.M., Israeli military police knocked at her door and took her off "for interrogation." She was not permitted to contact her lawyer nor were the charges against her revealed.

The claim widely spread by the Zionist Establishment that the occupation of Sinai, Golan, the West Bank, and Gaza has been "the most liberal occupation in history" is not borne out by independent correspondents. The London *Times* (June 17, 1974) declared: "It is a curious form of 'liberalism' with hundreds of new prisoners in the past few months crammed into Israeli jails in addition to the thousands already there for several years." And four years later, according to *Time* magazine of June 19, 1978, Arab students were being arrested for such vaguely defined crimes as "indiscreet talk." Brother Joseph Lowenstein, President of Bethlehem University, who kept a log of undergraduates called in for interrogation, noted that 104 out of a student body of 400 had been questioned.

Were this occurring anywhere else in the world, liberals in America would have been the first to voice strongest objections to the fact that there is no legal way of opposing the occupation by Israel. Peaceful demonstrations, protests, strikes, distribution of leaflets are all heavily punishable by law. Thousands are currently in prison for having chosen these forms of resistance. Prison sentences are meted out for any type of help given to a person suspected of antioccupation activities. In late 1976 there were estimated by the Middle East Resources Center to be 3,200 security prisoners in Israel and the occupied territories, many being held without charges or a trial date.

According to one particularly harsh law, anyone who suspects that another person intends or is about to commit an offense against the military laws in force in the occupied territories, and does not prevent him from doing so, or inform the authorities at once, is himself guilty of an offense punishable by up to five years in prison or a fine of £1,000.

In *With My Own Eyes,* Felicia Langer detailed the treatment of prisoners, the violence, beatings, and torture to which suspects are subjected during interrogation by members of the Shin Beth (Israeli Security Service).[73] There has hardly been a trial whose records do not contain testimony in which the accused complains of beatings and torture, and the evidence is all too visible to those such as Langer who have access to these prisoners. Israel was indeed continuing practices that cultural Zionist leader Ahad Ha-Am had observed back in 1891: "They treat Arabs with hostility and cruelty, deprive them of their rights, offend them without cause and even boast of these deeds, and nobody among us opposes these despicable inclinations."

The Israeli officials set up a category of West Bank Palestinians, calling them "Temporary Residents" despite the fact that many of these Arabs were born in the place where they now live and where their families have lived for a number of years. There was the case of Mrs. Ratibe El-Basha of the village of Beit Iba. She had come back from Kuwait with the body of her husband for burial in her village. She was forthwith declared a "Temporary Resident" in the very village in which she had been born and lived all her life prior to forced exodus with her husband to the Arabian Gulf for employment after the 1967 war. She shared the house with her ten-year-old son, her aged father, and the rest of the family. Each month she was compelled to ask for a permit to live in the village, which meant that she had to go to the Allenby Bridge, cross over to the East Bank, return, and apply for a new permit on the spot. It is quite difficult to describe in words the brutality, humiliation, and cruelty of this treatment, which had been repeated for several months. Protests to the Israeli authorities in an attempt to alleviate some of these hard conditions imposed on this widow were of no avail. And this was only one of many similar cases.

In an attempt to acquaint the American people with these facts of life within Israel and the occupied territories, Shahak came to the U.S. in 1974 to lecture and to visit newspaper offices. He did shake up some people, particularly when he detailed how the Jewish National Fund had been engaged in the process of buying up all inhabitable land in Israel (except in the cities of Haifa, Tel Aviv, and Jerusalem), following which restrictive covenants were slapped on the purchases so that Arabs might never rent or buy them. And amazingly enough the Israeli courts have enforced with fines any attempted breach of these covenants.

The survivor of Hitler's concentration camps returned a year later to testify before the House Subcommittee on International Organizations and Movements of the Foreign Affairs Committee. He told the members: "I did not have any such experience in my life that shocked me so much as witnessing the blowing up of Arab houses by Israeli demolition squads in the occupied territory of the West Bank of the Jordan River." The professor stated that it has been "the standard practice of Israeli authorities ever since the 1967 war to seize Arabs whom they deem undesirable on the West Bank or in the Gaza Strip and deport them, after which their homes are destroyed." Shahak challenged the eight representatives, who were taking his testimony, to go out to the area and "see if you think these things are correct for yourselves and express your own opinion." Congressman Jonathan B. Bingham of the Bronx and Lester L. Wolff of Long Island, both stalwart Zionists, countered with the suggestion that such time would be better spent dealing with charges of Arab abuse of Israelis.

Even though the truth was easy to obtain, these legislators and others of their equally uninformed and prejudiced colleagues in both houses of Congress did not really wish, or were afraid, to understand what lay at the core of the Middle East conflict. When the counsel of the Senate Subcommittee on Refugees and Escapees and two other staff members were sent on a Middle East fact-finding mission to review the dire situation facing the Palestinians, the report containing the findings was bottled up and efforts to obtain a copy were met with refusal from the Chairman of the Senate Judiciary Subcommittee on Refugees, Senator Edward Kennedy.[74]

Some little light on the treatment of Palestinian political prisoners, held indefinitely under administrative detention, had previously been shed by international agencies and the European press. A report to the U.N. by one of its special working groups declared that the "vast majority of detainees are held in detention by virtue of administrative orders and that persons under administrative detention are deprived of any guarantees concerning the length of detention and fair trial."[75]

The International Red Cross reported:

On a visit which was carried out without the presence of an observer, 81 prisoners were found huddled in one cell. The prisoners all declared that they were not allowed to leave their cells, even to use the toilets or the washing facilities. They had to use the cell tap which was situated only 15 centimeters from the level of the floor.[76]

Shortly thereafter *Le Monde* informed its readers:

Two thousand eight hundred Palestinian Arabs and around a hundred and ten Israeli Arabs are presently detained in Israeli prisons, Israeli official sources declared Tuesday. Among the Palestinian prisoners there are a few dozen women. . . .[77]

Somehow more courageous than any of the larger English or U.S. journals, the London *Sunday Times* exposed the Israeli practice of administrative detention:

Ishak Ali el-Marari was arrested on March 7, 1969, in Jerusalem. After two months of interrogation, during which he claimed he had no access either to his wife or his lawyer, he was charged with having been a member of an illegal organization. Interestingly, though he is still in prison, the charges against him were dropped on June 6, 1969. . . . This does not mean under the system of administrative imprisonment which is now widely used that there is anything to prevent his remaining in prison for an indefinite period.[78]

The Economist reported that the official Israeli figure in 1970 of "non-Israelis in prison was 3,700 (Arab estimates put the number at up to four times the Israeli figure)," more than 1,000 of whom were "under administrative detention, that is without charge, some of them for periods of more than two years." This writer was most perspicacious in pointing out the shape of things to come:

By subjecting to the same treatment confessed saboteurs, those condemned for political activity and innocent members of the Arab public who happen to fall under suspicion, the authorities are in fact achieving the one thing they presumably would like to prevent: a consolidation of Arab opinions inside Israel behind the commando movement.[79]

Another noxious practice, kept out of sight but carried on by the Israelis against the Palestinians, was collective punishment. A memorandum received by the U.N. Special Committee on Human Rights in the Occupied Territories discussed this:

Ever since the beginning of the Israeli occupation in 1967, collective punishment has been a principle of wide application—blowing up houses, taking of hostages, expulsion of Palestinian leaders and notables, curfew, etc. The man personally responsible for the Israeli policies in the occupied territories is Defense Minister Moshe Dayan. When asked by Knesset member Uri Avneri, "Is the Ministry of Defense acting in such cases according to principles of collective responsibility of the whole family for one of its members?" Minister Dayan answered, "Yes."[80]

When oppresion against inhabitants was stepped up after the October 1973 war, huge mass arrests were carried out. In the town of Nablus alone 550 people (all males) were arrested in two days, including high-school age youths and even elementary school youngsters.[81] Five of the prisoners taken on January 5, 1974, disappeared from sight.

In an interview reported in the Norwegian *Arbuderbladet* (April 4, 1970), Arne Haaland, a member of the Executive Committee of Amnesty International, the London-based organization that attempts to monitor human rights worldwide, stated: "We never claimed that the allegations about torture had been proved . . . but we have in our possession very extensive material to support the assumption that torture does in fact occur. We have rarely—if ever—had such reliable material on which to base the establishment of the fact in relation to torture taking place—or not taking place—in a particular country."

The Amnesty report, "Israeli Methods of Torture," uncovered these practices:

a. Police dogs let loose on the prisoner who is usually handcuffed with hands behind back. The dogs are trained to throw the prisoner on the ground. The prisoner is then ordered to get on his feet, and so on.
b. Finger placed on the end of an open door, and then the door is slammed on them.
c. Finger nails are pulled out with ordinary pincers.
d. The prisoner is injected with pepper solutions.

e. The prisoner is injected with solutions which he is told induce instant insanity. He is shown what he is told is an antidote, which would be given to him if only he confessed in time.

f. A large metal container is fitted over the head and neck and held firm to the body by extension. The container is then hit with sticks on the outside, at first slowly and in routine fashion, and then with increasing tempo. The more battered the container, the more difficult it is to remove.

g. Match sticks are inserted into the penis. Sometimes they are lit.

h. A certain chemical substance (possibly a nerve irritant) is put in the hand of the prisoner who is ordered to clench it. The substance gives the effect of an electric shock.[82]

After inspecting an Israeli prison where 370 Arab hunger-strikers were protesting jail conditions, Gaza's Mayor Shawa declared: "The conditions in the Ashkelon prison are terrible. They are kept 16 men to a cell and are locked up 22 hours a day. They sleep on the floor and have few winter clothes." The inmates, imprisoned for security offenses, demanded they be treated as prisoners of war. A representative of the International Red Cross agreed that living conditions in the prison were terrible, but comparable with those at other prisons in the occupied territories.

Where Shahak and Langer failed to win any meaningful media coverage on the gross maltreatment and torture of Palestinians, The London *Sunday Times* succeeded in its June 19, 1977, four-page spread based on the exhaustive study of its prestigious "Insight" team of Paul Eddy and Peter Gilman. Working inside the West Bank, they interviewed forty-four Palestinian Arabs who had been arrested by Israeli security forces and who stated they were tortured during interrogation to extract confessions of crimes. In twenty-two of these cases the Arabs questioned agreed to be named even though they still live under Israeli occupation. The others asked to remain anonymous.

Corroborating the Shahak and Langer charges, *The Times* found that torture was so "systematic that it cannot be dismissed as a handful of 'rogue cops' exceeding orders" and "implicated all of Israel's security sources." The six principal conclusions reached were:

1) Israel's security and intelligence services ill-treat Arabs in detention.

2) Some of the ill-treatment is merely primitive: prolonged beatings, for example. But more refined techniques are also used, including electric-shock torture and confinement in specially constructed cells. This sort of apparatus, allied to the degree of organization evident in its application, removes Israel's practice from the lesser realms of brutality and places it firmly in the category of torture.

3) Torture takes place in at least six centers at the prisons of the four main occupied towns of Nablus, Ramallah, and Hebron on the West Bank, and Gaza in the south; at the detention center in Jerusalem known as the Russian compound; and at a special military intelligence center whose whereabouts are uncertain, but which testimony suggests is somewhere inside the vast military supply base at Sarafand,[83] near Lod Airport on the Jerusalem-Tel Aviv road.

4) All of Israel's security services are implicated: the Shin Beth, roughly Israel's MI-5 and Special Branch in one, which reports to the office of the Prime Minister; Military Intelligence, which reports to the Minister of Defense; the border police; and Latam, Israel's "Department for Special Missions," both of which report to the Police Minister.

5) Torture is organized methodically. It appears to be sanctioned at some level as deliberate policy.

6) Torture seems to be used for three purposes. The first is, of course, to extract information. The second motive, which seems at least as common, is to induce people to confess to "security" offenses of which they may, or may not, be guilty. The extracted confession is then used as the principal evidence in court: Israel makes something of the fact that it has few political prisoners in its jails, only those duly convicted according to the law. The third purpose is to persuade Arabs in the occupied territories that it is least painful to behave passively.

During their exhausting task the two reporters compiled 110,000 words of recorded testimony, interviewing their subjects for hours, making certain each interviewee could "withstand detailed cross-examination" of incidents covering the ten years of Israeli occupation in the West Bank and Gaza. They ended their field investigations in December 1976, but this highly authoritative source poignantly stated in its summation of the effort that "there is no reason to believe it [the torture] has ceased; the allegations are continuing."

The experiences of individual victims of Israeli interrogation, repulsive as they are, provide a sharper insight into the seriousness of the charges. The first case in the London *Times* was that of Omar Abdel-Karim, a thirty-five-year-old carpenter from Beit Sahur, just south of Bethlehem. He was arrested on October 3, 1976, as he was crossing eastward over the Allenby Bridge into Jordan. Upon his apprehension, according to the *Times*, "he was fit, happy, and holding down a job." When released, after five months in the hands of Israeli security, "he looked like an old man" and was carried over the bridge to Jordan on a stretcher because he could not walk.

Upon admission to the King Hussein Hospital immediately following his release, a medical examination showed this to be his condition, according to the *Times:*

He complained of pains in the chest and found it hard to breathe out. He had an infection of the urinary tract. He talked of severe head pain and showed signs of giddiness. And his difficulty tended to confirm his complaint that his joints, especially his knees, were painful too. Chest x-rays then showed that Abdel-Karim's ribs had at some point been fractured. Abdel-Karim continued to bear marks of having come through some traumatic experience. With the aid of antibiotics, multi-vitamins and a high protein diet, Abdel-Karim has slowly recovered, though two months later, he could still barely walk.

During eight hours of questioning by the "Insight" reporters in mid-April, he said his ordeal began in the 'Russian Compound'—the detention and interrogation center in Jerusalem that houses Shin Beth and Latam and occasionally the border police. He was beaten on the soles of his feet, hung up by his wrists, and kicked around during his first week of interrogation, but continued to insist he was innocent of the charges against him, namely that he was a member of the fedayeen. He was then transferred to another location, blindfolded, and there his torture ordeal began. Among other things, he was suspended by his wrists from a pulley and beaten until his ribs broke; a bottle was forced up his rectum; his wife was beaten in his presence until he confessed falsely to the crime. When his interrogators discovered he lied to save his wife, and no explosives were found in his home as he had confessed, he was kept under a cold shower, jammed into a barrel of freezing water, and suspended from his wrists while his interrogator squeezed his genitals.

Other details, which hardly make for edifying reading, relate to five other prisoners, who were variously set on by dogs; had their testicles squeezed; had a ball-point pen refill pushed into their penis; were beaten on the head, the body, and the genitals; or were "raped" by a trustee prisoner, at the connivance of the Israelis.

Israel's denials were not long in coming. In a rambling 3,500-word reply published in the *Times* on July 3, 1977, Israel categorically denied all charges and regretted that the Sunday *Times* "found it fit to print such an article."[84]

In the case of Omar Abdel-Karim, the Israeli reply claimed that he was ill before his arrest and that upon his release from prison "he happily appeared at the press conference and on Jordanian television." On July 10, in a rejoinder, the *Times* flatly refuted both claims. It said: "Not true. He was fit, happy and holding down a job. By contrast, he left Israeli hands a stretcher case." To the claim that he appeared on television, the "Insight" team said: "The Director General of Jordanian TV, Mohamed Kamal, stated: 'I have personally searched through all our records; there was no such interview.' Nor was there a press conference. Summoned by the hospital doctor in Jordan, two reporters went to Karim's bedside, one from Reuters and the other Daniel Southerland of the *Christian Science Monitor.* Southerland recalled that Karim was mostly in bed, propping himself on one elbow to talk: 'He was rather weak and frail and very thin, and obviously suffering physical pain.' He had 'difficulty walking' even with a cane. 'Seen from the rear . . . he looked like an old man,' Southerland wrote at the time. And he concluded that Karim had been 'badly beaten.' "

Commenting on the overall Israeli response, the *Times* said: "Israel's reply to our investigation dealt with the central points by flat denial, rather than with detailed evidence; it raised side issues; it devoted great energy to attacking two of its own citizens (lawyers Felicia Langer and Lea Tsemel, who defended some of the accused) who were by no means our principal witnesses; it contained a number of untruths."

Perhaps the most unsavory reading of all, however, was the account of a certain Josef Odeh and his daughter Rasmiah, which in the words of the London *Times* "is terrible—though by no means unique." The story stated that it squares with the pattern of other testimony and that some corroboration is available. According to the testimony of Josef Odeh:

After his daughter Rasmiah was arrested, she was beaten. She was lying on the floor and there were blood stains on her clothes. Her face was blue and she had a black eye. Odeh was then taken into an interrogation room to find Rasmiah naked and handcuffed. One of the interrogators, he said, "Asked me to sleep with her," and I said: "Don't even think of that. I would never do such a thing." They were beating me and beating her and we were both screaming. . . . And they spread her legs and shoved the stick into her. She was bleeding from her mouth and from her face and from her end.

In explaining how the Israeli authorities handle their security problem in occupied Arab lands, the *Times* traced the development of these oppressive measures since 1967 after Israel's victory in the six-day war. "Israel has never denied that its battle against the Palestinian resistance has involved tough measures." The *Times* said: "It has demolished homes (16,212 between July 1967 and August 1971, according to an independently kept log) and deported 'known agents of subversion' (1,120 to Jordan since 1967, according to Jordanian police records).''

As the number of arrests swelled in 1967 and 1968 there was no alternative to overcrowding the jails of Israel, the West Bank, and Gaza with Palestinian prisoners. In the months after the 1967 war the number of detained Palestinians passed the 2,000 mark.

Ten years after the occupation began, only thirty-seven "detainees" remain, thus allowing Israel to demonstrate to itself and to the world that it has no political prisoners, only convicted terrorists. The number in 1977 was 3,200 Palestinians guilty of security offenses and 2,600 guilty of other offenses. Convictions in political cases were always handed down by military courts, which have become the fulcrum of Israel's claim to rule the occupied territories according to the rule of law. But as the *Times* pointed out, convictions were always based on confessions, which the "Insight" team charges were obtained by torture—at least in the forty-four cases investigated.

To corroborate this point and the hopelessness of obtaining any justice in a military court, the *Times* investigators said: "We have talked with six lawyers—two Israelis and four Palestinians—who regularly appear in the courts to defend those accused of security offenses. The mechanism is, in its way, elegant, almost syllogistic. Most convictions in those courts are based on confessions by the accused; most of those confessions, the lawyers are convinced, are extracted by ill treatment or torture; *almost without exception the courts reject that contention.''* (Italics added.)

In describing how rigged the entire process was against the Palestinian defendants, the *Times* detailed the following: "The suspect can be held for up to eighteen days before being taken before a military judge. He can order further detention of up to six months. In this time, the suspect is interrogated. When eventually he is brought to trial—up to a year later—the prosecution is almost invariably equipped with a statement, signed by the suspect, confessing to at least some of the charges." During the interrogation time, the *Times* said defendants have no access to a lawyer and in most cases are detained at locations unknown to their relatives.

When allegations of torture are brought up in court to refute the confession of a defendant, a "little trial" takes place. According to the *Times'* account, this is what happens:

The defendant tells the court that he was ill-treated or tortured. The prosecution then produces the policeman or army officer who took the confession.

According to the young Israeli-born advocate Lea Tsemel, the officer tells the court: "I sat with the suspect, we had coffee together, I gave him cigarettes, he talked freely, and everything was normal." And this officer is almost always telling the truth. The catch is that the policeman may indeed have taken the statement. But he did not conduct the interrogation. Many of the former prisoners we questioned said that, after they had agreed to make a statement, they were passed from interrogators to the police, together with a note of the offenses they were admitting. The new officer then composed the statement for the court.

In the editorial "A Case for Concern," which appeared the same day as the "Insight" report broke on the front page, the Sunday *Times* declared:

. . . Torture must be condemned wherever it is practiced. But in the occupied lands of Israel the people are dependent on international protection and only respect for international convention can help them . . . the justification of torture for the control of populations cannot be accepted by nations with claims to Western values, whatever the provocations. It is self-defeating. . . . It demoralizes those who practice it. . . . Mr. Begin suffered in a Russian prison in his youth, had a price on his head under the British, and has written with great emotion in condemnation of British methods of interrogation, and trial of his comrades in the Irgun Zvai Leumi. Unless his convictions have cha ıged, he cannot be satisfied that since 1967 Israel has used against Arab prisoners the British mandate laws and regulations he so bitterly denounced. . . .

The Israeli press, normally so "vigorous and outspoken," observed a strange silence as to just what was happening in the interrogation centers. With the exception of *Ha'aretz*, the Israeli media have rarely mentioned assertions of ill-treatment by Arabs in Israeli-occupied territories, thus giving the military administration authorities virtual carte blanche to do as they have pleased.

The *Observer* gave its approval to the findings of its rival London journal. Twenty-seven Members of Parliament representing all parties introduced a motion calling for a detailed investigation of the Sunday *Times'* allegations. David Watkins, one of the sponsors of the motion, wrote: "The Zionist lobby has gone into action in its usual fashion, unable to refute the *Times'* evidence and therefore descending to attempts to discredit this very reputable and internationally known newspaper."

Four months before the Sunday *Times* story had broken, the *Christian Science Monitor*[85] had a lengthy piece, datelined Amman, on the "brutality which persists in the current no-war, no-peace situation." The subject was Omar Abdul Ghani-Salameh, described as a "badly beaten, frail-looking Palestinian" who had been permitted, despite Arab policy of disapproving of the deportation of any Palestinians from Israeli-occupied area, to make the 50-mile trip from the prison in Nablus to the King Hussein Hospital in Salt.[86]

The Chief Surgeon and Director of the hospital found Salameh, whom Israeli military authorities described as a "convicted guerrilla," suffering from "ill health," having difficulty walking, and suffering from fractured ribs, multiple "contusions" or bruises, and a general weakness due to loss of weight. Salameh, from a town near Bethlehem, told two reporters that his "ill health" stemmed from torture after his arrest as he was about to cross the river into Jordan with legal permission on family business. According to the account of correspondent Daniel Southerland, the Palestinian claimed that "Israeli soldiers handcuffed and blindfolded him, threw him into a car, and began punching him with their fists even before he reached the 'Russian Compound' (in Arabic *Moscobiya*, the place in West Jerusalem where Arab dissidents from the occupied West Bank are beaten up). Here his interrogators attempted to force him to admit his connection with Palestinian resistance groups by forcing him to lie down on the floor while three men beat him on the soles of his feet with sticks."

The torture during the next nearly five months included electric shocks throwing him into convulsions and "suspensions from the ceiling by a system of chains and pulleys which rendered him unconscious." One of his "easy" tortures, according to Salameh, was to "clean a floor full of dirt and glass with his tongue and then swallow the filth afterwards." When he protested to his torturers and begged them "in the name of God" to desist, their reply was, "Your God is under my feet."

Except for this article, there was a near-total blackout on this subject by the U.S. media, save the most limited *New York Times* coverage of the London disclosures. When Shahak and three Palestinians testified before a Senate subcommittee in October 1977 as to the brutal deprivation of human rights on the West Bank and Gaza, it was only a small Minnesota paper that noted in an editorial: "Deportation, confiscation, racial discrimination, detention without trial—these are ugly words for ugly practices."[87]

Minute coverage was paid (on a back page of the *New York Times*) to the release of a report after a three-week fact-finding trip to the Middle East by a ten-member delegation of American lawyers from the National Lawyers Guild. These representatives of a national organization of progressive attorneys, with seventy chapters and 5,000 members, had studied the Arab-Israel conflict and conducted a particular investigation of Israeli human rights practices in the occupied territories at their August 1, 1977 press conference. The returning Guild members confirmed the charges that Israeli military interrogators frequently torture to extract confessions and that no lawyer may be present until the questioning has ended. Beyond a confession, the returning lawyers reported, little evidence was required for conviction, and these confessions were originally drafted in Hebrew, which most detainees do not know.

The Guild delegation had been told by the Mayor of Ramallah that in April and May 1977, for a period of forty-five days, Jewish settlers went every night into a Palestinian village and fired shots, broke windows and door handles, and shouted obscenities at sleeping villagers, claiming the land was theirs and urging the villagers to leave. The Mayor said the Jewish settlers had been accompanied by Israeli soldiers, who provided protection for them.

The findings of the delegation were summed up in the words of Attorney Malea Kiblan, contained in the August 1 press statement:

Before I came, I had never fully understood the U.N. Resolution that equated Zionism with racism, and I came here with an open mind to have personal access to the facts of the situation. When I saw things firsthand, I was totally overwhelmed by the way the Arabs are treated as inferior people. I didn't really understand institutional racism until I made this trip, although we have racism in the United States. Israel is built on an exclusivist system, and the Arabs racially cannot qualify as equal citizens in the West Bank or in Israel in any area, including health, education, personal treatment, and every other area.

In September 1977 the Swiss League for Human Rights confirmed the pattern of violation of Palestinian rights that had been observed, investigated, and recognized by responsible organizations concerned with the defense of human rights: Amnesty International (1977 Nobel Peace Prize) in March 1972; the Israeli League for Human and Civil Rights in February 1973; and a fact-finding mission of the American National Lawyers Guild in August 1977. The Swiss League report concluded:

. . . the Israeli occupation of the West Bank caused repeated violations of the provisions of the Universal Declaration of Human Rights including numerous arbitrary arrests, prolonged cases of detention and deportations (a contravention of Article 3 of the Declaration); enforced residence, serious restrictions on border crossing and prohibiting return (a contravention of Article 13 guaranteeing right of free movement and free choice of residence); arbitrary expropriation, prohibiting of construction and demolition of buildings (contravention of Article 17 stipulating that "no one shall be arbitrarily deprived of his property"); common and systematic practice of torture (in contravention of Article 5); and the flagrant inequalities between Jews and Arabs in the West Bank (in contravention of Article 2, Paragraph 2).

At the end of its report the Swiss League stated: "Finally, our delegation cannot but feel concern with respect to the right to a nationality cited in Article 15 of the Human Rights Declaration. In effect, the very status of an occupied territory results in the denial of a nationality to its inhabitants."

In presenting the League's report in October to the U.N. Special Committee to Investigate Israeli Practices Affecting the Human Rights of the Population of the Occupied Territories, President of the Swiss League for Human Rights Denis Payot stated: "I felt it necessary to come in person to New York. The cause of one man is a very worthy one, but the cause of a whole people in distress is much more so."

Human rights reports prepared by the Department of State in February, 1978, in accordance with the provisions of the Foreign Assistance Act, clearly indicated that Israel has grossly violated the Fourth Geneva Convention in its occupation of the West Bank and Gaza. Noting the Insight Team report of the *Sunday Times,* the rapporteurs stated that while there was no evidence "of consistent practice or policy of torture, there are documented reports of the use of extreme and psychological pressures during interrogation and instances of brutality by individual interrogators cannot be ruled out."[88] The State Department further noted the "selective expulsion of West Bank and Gaza residents *suspected* of engaging in terrorism or anti-Israel political agitation" [Italics added.] "Collective punishment" has been meted out to other individuals convicted of or suspected of terrorism and to their families through the demolition or sealing up of homes. Some 3,100 non-Israeli Arabs were said to be under arrest or in prison in Israel proper. While freedom of religion is unqualified, freedom of expression and of assembly are restricted by Israeli interpretation of security requirements."

On February 14, 1978, the U.N. Human Rights Commission condemned Israel for the eighth straight year on for alleged atrocities in occupied territories. Of the 32 member nations, only the U.S. and Canada dissented; seven abstained. And Freedom House's 1978 *Comparative Survey of Freedom* ranks Israel at the bottom of the scale for political rights and civil liberties in foreign administered areas; only Chile and South Africa rated lower.[89]

One comment can best sum up these shocking revelations of what has been transpiring to Palestinian Arabs inside the occupied territories and in Israel proper. On the day after the U.N. had voted partition of Palestine in November 1947, Israel's first President-to-be, Dr. Weizmann, stated: "I am certain that the world will judge the Jewish state by what it shall do with the Arabs."

As part of their "push out the Arabs and bring in the Jews" program, directly after the 1967 war, the Israeli government gave impetus to new settlements throughout the conquered areas. Although they were in defiance of Article 49 of the Fourth Geneva Convention, of which Israel is a signatory, providing that "Occupying powers shall not deport or transfer parts of its own civilian population into the territories it occupies," the settlements were welcomed by Israeli hawks[90] who wished to create a situation that would inhibit any move on the part of any Israeli government to withdraw from the Arab territories occupied in the six-day war.

In his detailed paper "Signposts to Destruction: Israeli Settlements in the Occupied Territories," former long-time Middle East *Guardian* correspondent Michael Adams noted that "settlements which were initiated in 1967 as military or paramilitary outposts, like the first settlements on the Golan plateau and the Jordan valley, have been gradually turned over to civilian occupation, emphasizing their permanency in the eyes both of the government and of the settlers themselves, while a growing proportion of the more recently established settlements dating from the early 1970s, like those in Sinai and around Jerusalem, have had from the outset an openly civilian character."[91] Pressure from the Golan Heights settlers, who had been disturbed by the uncertainty of their status, led Golda Meir as Prime Minister to state that the Golan Heights was "an integral part of Israel." Even the *New York Times* was forced reluctantly to admit:

These settlements, which range in size from paramilitary agricultural hamlets on the Golan Heights to incipient cities, represent the reality of Israeli policy. They are the tangible evidence of Israel's determination to carve out new borders of the territory taken in 1967.[92]

The Zionist land-grabbing was the natural consequence of their previous history of colonization in Palestine prior to the creation of the Israeli state and the necessary concomitant of the Law of Return designed to bring in hundreds of thousands of Diaspora Jews from their "exile." It was soon quite apparent that these new colonies were being established in locations Israel already considered part of her territory and as a shield against counteraction that could be expected from those they had displaced. In 1971 Prime Minister Meir told a group of Soviet immigrants who had been settled in the Golan Heights that "the border is found there where Jews live and not by a line on a map."[93] Ten days earlier General Dayan had expressed it this way: "In every place where we have established a settlement, we will never abandon that settlement or the place itself."[94] And even as the *New York Times* carried a banner five-column headline: "Eban Tells UN Israel Is Flexible Regarding Mid-East Boundaries," the Zionist state continued to tighten its occupation of Arab lands and to add to the number of faits accomplis.

The Israeli Foreign Minister had only to tell the General Assembly in October 1972: "We have not sought to determine the final peace boundary, and we have drawn no ultimate maps," for its New York organ to proclaim Zionist flexibility. But at that very moment in the fall of 1972 Israel was bringing to forty (not including major developments in Hebron and Jerusalem) the number of new communities of Israeli settlers, which had begun in 1967 with five, in the occupied territories on the West Bank, the Golan Heights and Sinai, and the Gaza Strip—actions quite contrary to U.N. resolutions as well as to international conventions. Strategically placed throughout the occupied territories, these settlements included fourteen Nahal or paramilitary settlements.

Before the outbreak of the 1973 war, two more settlements were added, and plans were underway for building in occupied Sinai the city of Yamit, with an estimated quarter of a million persons, as the centerpiece of a complex of settlements between El Arish and the Gaza Strip. This ambitious program in the heart of Egyptian territory—aimed "as a buffer between concentrated Arab populations in the Gaza Strip and in Egypt"[95]—was no doubt an important factor in spurring President Sadat to strike, after much hesitancy, in October 1973. Well-known journalist, former editor of *Al-Ahram,* and author, Mohamed Hassanein Heikal, who served some time in the Sadat Cabinet as Minister of Information, in his memoirs quoted the Egyptian leader as saying, "Every word spoken about Yamit is a knife pointing at me personally and at my self-respect."[96] A few weeks before the war, Defense Minister Dayan had openly admitted on Israeli radio that his proposal for the establishment of Yamit was "to serve as one of the factors enabling us to establish the borders further to the west."

This Sinai project and a complex of settlements in Israel, the Rafah Approaches, caused the displacement of a large number of heretofore very friendly bedouin Arabs. Thirty thousand residents were told (and this was stamped on their I.D.s) that "for security reasons" they would have to leave their ancestral homeland by January 15, 1975. Their lands were expropriated, their groves bulldozed, their homes, schools, and mosques leveled.[97] General Ariel Sharon undertook to evict ten tribes, only one of which had been involved in actions that could point to any of its members as security risks.[98]

As the modern Jewish city began to emerge on the sands of northeastern Sinai, Sharon, according to one observer, ordered his troops to "eject the reluctant . . . and move them to resettlement sites. . . . Under the shadow of the cranes and scaffoldings of the urban construction site here, remnants of the former population have been trying to stay put in a cluster of mud and stucco houses."[99]

By the end of 1975 the number of settlements had risen to sixty and the following year to sixty-eight, in which, according to an article by William Drummond of the *Los Angeles Times,* 7,500 Jews were living. The location of these settlements were: twenty-five in the Golan Heights, seventeen in the Jordan Valley, five in Hebron vicinity, four in the Jerusalem area, fourteen in Gaza-Rafah region, and three in the Gulf of Aqaba. And twenty-two more were on the drawing board despite the strong opposition from the newly-formed progressive party, the Yaad, in which such iconoclasts as writer Amos Kenan, former Histadrut Secretary-General Ben-Aharon Yitzhak, Knesset member Uri Avnery, civil rights champion Mrs. Shulamit Aloni, Mayor General Matityahu Peled, and ex-secretary of the Labor party Arie Eliav had joined forces to oppose further expropriations and territorial expansion.

The West Bank settlements formed a "cordon sanitaire" around large Arab towns and villages, and served as a defense buffer against any possible incursions across the Jordan River. (This defense system underlay the peace plan that Israeli Foreign Minister Yigal Allon had long enunciated and which he set forth in detail, with a map, for the readers of *Foreign Affairs* in the fall of 1976.)

While Israel's leading independent newspaper, *Ha'aretz,* admitted that additional settlements in the "administered territories" (the term used by Israel for the "occupied territories") would most definitely limit the area regarding which negotiations would be possible, U.S. columnists Evans and Novak heard a much different point of view from Israelis. In talking to members of a small settlement in the Jordan Valley, the Americans were told by a youthful member: "Nobody gives a damn about a just peace and secure borders. That is only a dream. The reality is military strength along the present borders."[100]

And the Greater Israel Movement, arguing that the creation of further faits accomplis would prove to the Arabs that time was against them and would force the intransigents to negotiate, continued to push the government to move faster in its new settlements program.

Although earlier in an interview with *Ha'aretz* Prime Minister Rabin had stated that "what happened in the past year in the administered territories was one area of foreign policy I am not proud of," in speaking to a meeting of anxious delegates from Merom Ha-Golan and other settlements on the Golan Heights at a time when rumors were rife that the Israeli government might pull back, he said (and this was reported only by the *Jerusalem Post*, [101] not by the U.S. press, so as not to handicap Secretary Kissinger's efforts at disengagement): "If there are any who have doubts on the matter, they would do better to disregard them and remove worry from their minds. No government has established a settlement just in order to evacuate it, and therefore members of the Golan Heights settlements can be completely confident."

This was a clear indication that the permanent settlements in the Golan Heights had not been established just to be dismantled again. The Prime Minister concluded: "We stand here with a sense of confidence and security which is due to the formidable increase in the strength of our army. Your unwavering determination to put down roots in this place against all the odds is encouraging." Ten months earlier General Rabin had declared that the Golan Heights would remain an indivisible part of Israel.[102]

Israeli expansionists were led by the Gush Emunim (literally "bloc of the faithful"), a paramystical, ultrachauvinist movement insisting that as the Chosen People and through biblical revelation, the Jews have the right to all of Palestine, and that Israel must hold onto all the occupied territories, with the possible exception of portions of the Sinai. Drawn from the extreme right-wing Likud party, the successor to the Jabotinsky Revisionist movement of the 1930s and Menachem Begin's Irgun Zvai Leumi of the 1940s, the Gush commanded the support of some Cabinet members, but sometimes found themselves clashing with the Israeli army. But they succeeded in establishing certain unauthorized new settlements on the West Bank and Golan Heights. In some instances they were forced to return home, despite the rabid oratory of their leader, Rabbi Moshe Levinger. International attention focused on the attempted settlement at Kadum Camp, where politically hard-pressed Premier Rabin arranged a compromise under which some forty to fifty settlers were permitted to remain unofficially.

The Gush leader in the Knesset was Mrs. Geula Cohen, who proudly proclaimed she had been a member of the Stern Gang responsible in Israel for the murder of Count Folke Bernadotte, U.N. conciliator, and of many British officers. Mrs. Cohen in June 1976 told an American visitor that Gush Emunim had not "occupied" but "liberated areas on which they settled. It belongs to us because the Bible says so. When we won the six-day war, that very day in 1967 we should have truly annexed all these territories."[103] When asked how she would deal with the problem of the Palestinian people, this fierce ultranationalist responded: "Who are the Palestinian people? We are the Palestinian people—not the Arabs!" A more sophisticated member of the group, also holding a seat in the Knesset, is thirty-year-old Ehud Olmert. He would grant each Arab Palestinian the right to choose whether he wishes to vote for members of the Jordanian or Israeli Parliament and to which of the two governments he would prefer to pay taxes. This tough, brash expansionist refused to use the word "annexation." "Since the West Bank is part of the historic home of the Jews, it is my right to have it."

During campaigning in the May 1977 elections, Prime Minister Begin left no doubt that he shared these views. He referred to settlements on the West Bank in biblical terms of "Judea and Samaria," insisting they were "liberated" and not "occupied" nor even "administered" territory. And he purposely chose to make his first post-election appearance in a synagogue ceremony at the then not yet legalized Kadum settlement. During his visit to Washington that July President Carter had urged the new Israeli Prime Minister to refrain from starting new settlements until after the Geneva peace talks, following his return to Israel. But Begin granted official recognition to Kadum and two other already-launched settlements although Washington called this move "an obstacle to progress in the peacemaking process." Some three weeks later, on August 17, the Israeli government authorized establishment of three new settlements in the occupied sector upon the recommendation of a committee headed by new Agriculture Minister Ariel Sharon, whose two-man bloc in the Knesset helped give Begin his initial majority of one. Sharon, well-known for his spectacular counter-crossing of the Suez Canal during the 1973 war, had also been responsible for the October 1953 massacre of sixty-six Palestinians in the attack by Israel's notorious Unit 101 on the border village of Kibya.

One of the new settlements was to be on a site south of Hebron assigned to Gush Emunim, a second in the Judean foothills for the ultraorthodox Agudat Israel, and the third near Petah Tikva, just across the West Bank border in Israel proper near the Zur Nathan kibbutz of the left-wing Hashomer Hazair. The presence of the Gush near Hebron could only exacerbate existing Israeli-Palestinian tensions in the Arab city of 60,000, where a twelve-day military curfew had been imposed during interreligious violence that had flared the previous October. The Tomb of the Patriarchs, where Abraham allegedly is buried and long a Muslim sanctuary (the Ibrahim Haram) because Islam reveres the Hebrew prophets, was converted after the 1967 capture of the West Bank into half a synagogue and half a mosque. A Zionist magistrate passed a ruling allowing Jews to pray in the holy mosque, and the Arabs exploded. An argument that broke out between Muslim worshipers and Gush extremists from the nearby existing Qiryat Arba, an Israeli settlement, led allegedly to the desecration of the Koran and to retaliatory acts against Torah scrolls. (The "funeral service" for the desecrated Jewish holy books, a regular orthodox ritual, including the recitation of the Kaddish, was attended by Defense Minister Shimon Peres and received three-column headlines in the *New York Times* on October 7. The story of the acts of Jewish vandalism against the Koran was buried in the back pages.)

Settlement Qiryat Arba, abutting Hebron, had been the scene of many demonstrations at which Rabbi Levinger had harangued militant supporters with fiery chauvinism: "We should look above us to the heavens and see that these cities are ours. The government of Israel, if it doesn't take its orders from on high, is in trouble." On such occasions leaflets were circulated calling for the relocation from the West Bank of Hebron's Palestinians Arabs. While that goal had not yet been achieved, Begin now had provided for a second wedge into the heart of the city.

Anomalously enough, an Israeli public opinion poll taken in September 1977 by Louis Harris[104] showed that a large majority of Sephardim (of Arab background) expressed a willingness to leave in the hands of Begin, whom many had supported at the polls, the question of allowing more religious settlements in the occupied territories, even though only 18 percent of these Sephardic respondents were themselves avowedly "religious." By this time, Israel had established 113 new settlements, seventy-seven in the occupied Arab areas, the remainder within the borders of Israel as created in 1948. On the drawing boards were settlement plans for the next fifteen years calling for 186 new communities, of which forty-nine were to be in the occupied territories.[105]

As the Palestinians strove to rivet world attention to their political rights and their identity as a people, even the slight attention that had been paid to their plight as refugees faded from view. Their suffering had become accepted. It seemed that the only time the humanitarian aspects of the Palestinian problem made the news was when UNRWA would announce a further reduction in the funds made available to this agency charged with the responsibility of keeping the refugees alive.

Their villages destroyed, their property seized, and their lands turned over to Jewish immigrants—no compensation had ever been paid for the tens of millions of pounds in movable and immovable property taken from the initial Palestinian refugees in 1948—the refugees found themselves the victims of new world animosity stemming from the reaction to acts of terrorism, often committed by guerrillas in their name. The appropriate image of homeless, hungry victims of injustice had never been created, as the Zionists had so successfully done with their refugees from Hitler.

The Palestinians had earned contempt, if not hatred, and gained little of the love called for by an understanding French-Catholic cleric, Bishop Menager of Meaux:

There is a Palestinian problem one cannot ignore. Hundreds of thousands of men and women, torn from their villages, have lived for more than twenty years in refugee camps. Situations of injustice are breeding grounds of war and violence. It is at this level that political action ought to be stronger than hate.

During the Lebanese civil war, which saw the Palestinians further victimized, attention invariably focused on the political rather than the humanitarian aspects of the struggle. The violence, marking this unprecedented, suicidal fratricide in which 60,000 lost their lives, tended to rekindle Western public opinion of Palestinian terrorism directed at innocent people in supermarkets or airports—violence never to be condoned however understandable. Strange that it should have been Yael Dayan, Moshe's authoress daughter, who declared that if she had been born a Palestinian Arab she would most certainly have been a commando. It took twenty-seven years from the time of the U.N. partition decision at Lake Success in November 1947 before the Palestinians could return to the U.N. and be granted a full hearing. And without their terrorism, they would have remained the forgotten people.

What a sad commentary on Western civilization, and on the U.S. in particular, which has opened its heart to every other oppressed, dispossessed, and disadvantaged people. When it came to the Palestinians, whose plight stemmed directly from the American act of opening its heart, its purse strings, and its political power to redressing the wrong done by Hitler, America immediately slammed the door and cried "terrorism."

While it is unfair to draw stereotypes and make overgeneraliza-tions, the Palestinians, as a whole, are not a violent people. Given to gross verbal exaggerations, they seldom follow through with deeds the words they utter in the heat of anger. Terror does not come naturally to them. But frustrated, oppressed, having no obvious alternative, they have taken to arms, guerrilla warfare, and fedayeen activities, hitting the enemy—the Israelis—whenever and wherever they find them.

The Palestinians launched themselves on this terrorist road by following in the path of other successful liberation movements. It worked in China, in Cuba, among the Portuguese colonies, for Algeria; and it had worked for the Zionists in their creation of the Jewish state. Thus the freedom fighters of Palestine had good examples on which to model their own activities. They could see that the Western media was not opening the slightest to them. Therefore they went to desper-ate lengths to find a means of breaking down the barriers so as to communicate with the outside world. For example, the principal aim behind the kidnapping of three ambassadors—two Americans and one Belgian—from the Saudi Arabian Embassy in the Sudan in 1974, an incident in which the three lost their lives, was to get these ambassa-dors out of the country, onto a plane, fly them to Washington, and there at the Washington airport, with the three hostages at gunpoint, hold a press conference the world could not ignore. Whose disgrace is it that such violence was needed in order to tell the human story of the clear-cut injustice the Palestinian people have so long endured?

With very few exceptions there has been no effort made in the U.S. to present the "why" behind the Palestinian resort to violence. When in America, for instance, are people exposed to the kind of sentiment expressed by Professor Ya'cov Talmon, an Israeli educator, in an open letter to Minister of Information Yisrael Galili, published in *Ma'ariv* in May 1969? Professor Talmon had this to say:

Don't forget, Your Excellency, that the Jewish national home and the establish-ment of the State of Israel were the result of an agreement between the great Powers imposed upon the Arabs. When, therefore, you state that you do not recognize the Arabs of Palestine as a moral or legal entity in Palestine with specific national and popular characteristics, you are in fact saying that they are 'natives,' with no identity of their own. In other words, Your Excellency, they have no rights as a community. Why should you, therefore, wonder when the Arabs or others describe you as colonizers and claim that they cannot reach an agreement with you, because you simply do not recognize the principle of mutual respect, but look only toward expansion? Words are more painful than physical pain, and they are long remembered, even after the human body has been cured of its pain. . . .

And I ask you, in your capacity as Minister of Information, what shall I answer the thinkers and educated people of other nations, when they ask me: why should not the Arabs join the ranks of the freedom fighters, when he hears the words of Galili? You deprive him of his right to national existence and self-determination. When the British attempted to do the same with you, didn't the Haganah, the Irgun and the Stern Group resort to terror and violence? Yes, Mr. Minister, I ask you most sincerely: What do you expect my answer to be? And I assure you most genuinely that I did not fabricate these questions, nor did I invent them. The duty of the historian impels him to see all aspects of the problem and not to be a liar or a propagandist.

When the CBS television network carried its program "The Palestinians" to a large, prime-time viewing audience (10 P.M., June 15, 1974), Americans, perhaps for the first time, were given a somewhat fair view of the problem as presented by a good cross-section of the people concerned. CBS interviewer Bill McLaughlin, at the outset, introduced a member of one of the fedayeen groups, the Popular Front for the Liberation of Palestine (PFLP, the group most responsible for most of the acts of terrorism):

Palestinian Guerrilla Ramez: As we understand that innocent people from my people is dying, I do understand that innocent people from other nations might die. I don't feel glad about it, but as well I can tell you that this does take place all over the world and it did take place all over history.

About the "guerrillas," McLaughlin had this to say:

When the Arab armies went down to humiliating defeat in 1967, the guerrillas kept Arab pride alive. This teenager stumbling across a dried-up creek is reaching for manhood; at the same time, he is learning to kill. When guerrillas do kill, the cycle of terrorism and counter-terrorism will begin all over again. And guerrilla guns threaten more than Israel. As long as the guerrillas are supported by the people, no Arab government could attack them and survive politically.

And, most significantly, McLaughlin added:

Guerrillas consider all Israelis part of the military establishment. But, in fact, killing civilians makes headlines; killing soldiers does not. Sooner or later, guerrillas like Ramez justify terrorism. And these guerrillas are mostly the sons of farmers whose homes were in Palestine until their defeat in 1948. They live frustrated and homesick lives in refugee camps or guerrilla bases. They have almost no control over their own future, they can be sold out by the great powers, and they expect to be.

Maher Yamani, a twenty-four-year-old fedayeen who took part in the machine-gunning of an airliner in Athens and spent a year and a half in a Greek jail, stated:

What could we do? We tried all ways possible, until we found the way of the gun. As long as it is in our hands, we will continue fighting until we perish, all of us. We will continue fighting, me, myself and my son and my grandsons as well, my daughters and their children and all the Palestinians. We Palestinians cannot accept a piece of our own land as charity from another country.

This same determination to return home exists among those Palestinians who have done far better in life than young Yamani. The commercial elite of the Palestinians have made good in their exile. Today they actually dominate the Jordanian middle class and the Kuwaiti civil service; they play important roles in helping to modernize Saudi Arabia and the other Gulf States. They have specialized in management and finance, controlling the huge Arab Bank and the money exchanges and owning much valuable downtown real estate in cities like Amman and Beirut (before the 1975–76 civil war).

Hasib Sabbagh is a civil engineer who, until the disastrous civil war, lived in the Lebanese capital. In his lovely home his favorite possession was said to be a small glass bottle containing soil from Jerusalem brought to him by a friend after the 1967 war. Sabbagh fled to Lebanon in 1948 nearly empty-handed, but in 1950 he and two partners obtained a $50,000 loan, as he told the CBS viewing audience. Now their company, the Construction Company (CCC), boasts assets of $50 million and serves as economic consultants without fee to the resistance movement, helping to plan for a future state. When asked whether he would give this all up to go back to Palestine, Sabbagh replied: "If I can go back as I was before, I would give it all up and go back to where I was brought up, where I had my childhood, where my father is buried and my family was. There is more than materialistic things to life. This is something sentimental." If a new West Bank state were to be established, this industrialist would like to go there and help his people develop the country.

When queried about the guerrilla organizations, Sabbagh pointed out heatedly:

They are not guerrillas. They are people asking for their rights. We have been waiting for the world to help us regain our rights for twenty-five years, and nobody listens to us. Even our Arab countries did not listen to us. Only after the 1967 war did they start listening to us.

Palestinian women revealed to their American audience that their feelings were equally intense. Violet Costandi, the wife of a forty-eight-year-old refugee who had successfully rebuilt his life in Beirut in the television production field, had this explanation for her attachment to Palestine:

I was born there, it is my homeland. How would you ask me such a question? I don't belong here, I belong to the land there . . . I as a child running through the grape yards and the orange groves. I had grape yards and the orange groves and everything. And that was mine, I want to go—I want to live—I want to be there, it belongs to me. If you—if something belongs to you, like a suitcase, and somebody steals it from you, you feel so bad about it. How come "your home town, your house"? I have two houses in Bir Zeit. They are beautiful to me. If I live in a place, if they make me a queen, I will not have the same feeling like when I go back to them. And it is still—and I still have the memory of them and to me it is only yesterday that I left, only yesterday. I will never forget.

How many Americans have ever been given the chance to understand that the Palestine Liberation Organization is a legitimate organization, part of a general effort by the Palestinians to organize their people? The disrupted Palestinian nationalism has concealed the simple truth of the similarity of the Palestinians' likeness to all other peoples as well as the uniqueness of their circumstances.

When cornered occasionally by a knowledgeable liberal to explain their harsh treatment of the Palestinians, Israelis resort to the familiar mythology that these Palestinians hardly existed as a people or as a culture, that they were at best an inchoate and amorphous mass of peasants. Thus when the Israelis destroy houses and villages and seize lands, etc., it scarcely matters. As the myth goes, the Palestinians are barely human beings, let alone cultured human beings, and one need not waste any time thinking of them as a modern society or as a civilized people.

The facts are as follows: The total estimated Palestinian population is 3.3 million, of which half are officially classified by the U.N. as refugees dependent on U.N. services for aid and shelter in refugee camps. There are 950,000 in Jordan, 693,000 in the West Bank, 390,000 in Gaza, 574,000 in Israel; the rest are scattered throughout the Arab world, including Lebanon, Syria, Kuwait, Egypt, Iraq, the Gulf, Libya, and Saudi Arabia. There are an estimated 7,000 in the

U.S., 5,000 in Latin America, and about 150,000 in Europe. The UNRWA records show 1,706,486 receiving aid and shelter from that agency as of June 30, 1977.

While many of the Palestinians remain as wards of the U.N., the majority have fanned out into the Arab world and overseas and are leading useful, if in some cases difficult lives. In their Diaspora they have become the teachers of the Arab world, the engineers, the builders, the commercial leaders. A high percentage have entered the professions. Universities are well equipped with Palestinian doctors and technicians; Palestinian engineers and architects are laying down roads and constructing bridges. Above all, their dispersion has driven them in search of higher education, and they are the best educated of all Middle East peoples, the Israelis not excluded.

The 1967 war, the subsequent Israeli occupation of the rest of Palestine, and then the spectacular stand of the commandos at Karameh transformed the Palestinians' individual struggle for survival into a collective struggle for the preservation of a national identity. It is the new Palestinians, with feelings of self-awareness and self-reliance and a great pride in themselves, that emerged from the twenty-nine years of suppression and banishment.

Far from vanishing, as the Zionists hoped, with their rebirth the Palestinians have emerged as the principal physical as well as psychological force in the area. In oil-rich Libya, distant from the fighting zone, Palestinian children were being taught in Red Crescent schools the history of their native land and its meaning to them. They sang their national anthem, the haunting *Baladi* ("Homeland") as their mothers worked on knitting uniforms for the commandos. The Palestinians had come alive and were no longer going to permit the Egyptians, Syrians, or any other Arabs to wage war—a losing war—in their behalf, as they had for twenty years. They were determined to carry the burden themselves. The spirit was contagious and helped electrify the Arabs in the countries in which these Palestinians had taken shelter—and, of course, also vastly complicated the problem of finding peace. No Arab leader, even one as strong as Nasser, had been able to accept a settlement for the 1967 war and take back his own occupied territories without providing for a political—not merely a humanitarian—settlement of the older 1948 war. This was the grave problem that confronted President Anwar el-Sadat in the peace initiative he started in November 1977.

It was only in 1965 that a small group of Palestinian commandos for the first time crossed the cease-fire lines separating Israel from

Lebanon and conducted the first military raid into Israel. They were under the command of an engineer turned soldier-commando by the plight of his people. Nine years later Yasir Arafat, as head of the Palestine Liberation Organization and the only person apart from Pope Paul VI who did not represent a government to address a plenary meeting of the U.N. General Assembly, informed the members of that international body of the goals, ambitions, and aspirations of his people for an independent Palestinian nation. That November 1974 day, in distant Cairo and Beirut, people gathered on streets listening to transistor radios. A holiday was declared in the refugee camps.

Arafat had studied civil engineering at Cairo University (then Fuad University) and then, after being commissioned a lieutenant at the Egyptian Military Academy, he served as a demolitions expert in fighting the invading Israelis, British, and French forces in 1956.[106] Moving to Kuwait to work as an engineer, Arafat helped train commandos for raids against Israel and soon joined the commando group Al Fatah, which under his leadership in 1969 took over the dormant Palestine Liberation Organization (PLO).

The PLO had begun to represent the interests of the Palestinian people in 1963, but its military wing, the Palestine Liberation Army, had played only a most minor role in the crushing Arab defeat of 1967.

Under Arafat's leadership the dormant PLO sprang to life. The Palestine National Council (PNC) was enlarged to 293 members, to include various sectors of the Palestinian community—not only the different commando groups with their varying political ideologies, but also independent political leaders, representatives from camps and communities throughout the Middle East, the occupied West Bank and Gaza and beyond, as well as representatives of various specialist groups such as students, lawyers, doctors, women, trade unions, and independent Palestinians attached to no group. This Council meets at least once a year, but a Central Council of fifty-five members serves as the legislative body for the larger group. Day-to-day PLO policies are formulated by its fourteen-member Executive Committee.

Through vibrant leadership, the Palestine identity emerged and the people in exile became more closely associated with the resistance movement. Such important functions as scholarship aid for young Palestinians, feeding of families whose bread winners had been killed, providing medical treatment and research soon followed. The Palestine Red Crescent opened clinics and modern hospitals and paid for specialist medical treatment at European clinics; pensions and scholarships were provided and schools opened in the refugee camps to supplement U.N.-financed institutions. The PLO Research Center was formed and books relating to the conflict were published. A planning center was set up to work on long-term strategy, including political and diplomatic campaigns, and to prepare a detailed study on the viability of a Palestinian state and on manpower resources of the Palestinian people, as well as to review the military strategy of the resistance movement. It was at the 1974 Arab summit meeting at Rabat that the PLO earned the recognition of being designated the sole representative of the Palestinian people.

The history of the PLO has been marked by constant internecine struggles, often armed conflict among its divergent seven major organizations: Al Fatah; the Popular Front for the Liberation of Palestine (PFLP); the Popular Democratic Front for the Liberation of Palestine (PDFLP); the Popular Front for the Liberation of Palestine—General Command, which under the leadership of Ahmed Jabril broke off from the PFLP; the Al Saiqa, led by Zuhair Mohsen, formed in 1967 of Palestinians sympathetic to the Syrian Ba'ath party; the small Arab Liberation Front, which is allied to the Iraqi Ba'ath party; and the Palestine National Front, formed in 1974 by Palestinians living under Israeli occupation, many of whose leaders were quickly deported by the Israeli government. In addition, there emerged a faction in Iraq under the leadership of Abu Nidal.

Within the Palestine Liberation Organization[107] are the Palestine Labor Organization, the Palestine Women's Organization, Students' Organization, Artists' Organization, Writers' Organization, Palestine Red Crescent, Palestine Orphans Trust, Palestine Youth Organization, Palestine Research Center, Palestine Medical Organization, Palestine Lawyers' Organization, Architects' Organization, Teachers' Organization, and Artisans' Organization. In the movement are many prominent Christians, including the Reverend Ilya Khoury; George Habash, leader of the Popular Front for the Liberation of Palestine; and Nayef Hawatmeh, leader of the Popular Democratic Front for the Liberation of Palestine.

Arafat, known to his people as Abu Ammar, has said: "What we have done is to make the world and the Palestinian himself realize that he is no longer U.N. refugee number so-and-so, but a member of a people who hold the reins of their own destiny and are in a position to decide their future." As Chaim Weizmann and David Ben-Gurion brought about the vivid emergence of the "Jewish people" into the field of Palestine, so Arafat was forging an entry of his people into that same field, now presently exclusively occupied by the State of Israel.

But the PLO leader has had a far rougher road to hoe than any of his Zionist opposite numbers, even Herzl, who also faced the monumental task of launching a movement. Arafat, too, may not survive to see his dreams realized. During the Lebanese civil war and even at the Ryadh and Cairo conferences that brought an end to the fighting, it was more than rumored that Syrian President Hafez al-Assad sought his "scalp." The 1975–1978 happenings in Lebanon proved, as Arafat once noted, that "Palestine is the cement that holds the Arab world together, or it is the explosive that blows it apart."

The tremendous task undertaken by the PLO leader of building his people into a nation and obtaining a situs for their identity has faced no end of complexities. Driven from Jordan in 1970, the Palestinians had to face in Lebanon opposition against the presence of heavily armed guests bordering upon a "state within a state." Without the overpowering personal charisma of a Nasser or Qaddafi, invariably wearing dark glasses and white checkered kaffiyeh headdress and often unshaven Arafat has had to contend with the Arab normal congenital incapacity for collaboration and continuous attempts to fragment the Palestinian movement into smaller groupings with particular social and political philosophies.

The internecine Palestinian disputes—sometimes erupting into armed conflict, particularly between the Fateh supporters of Arafat in the PLO and George Habash's Marxist PFLP (Popular Front for the Liberation of Palestine)—led Brigadier-General Misbah Budeiri, Chief of Staff of the virtually inactive Palestinian Liberation Army, to remark: "I don't approve of these left-wing groups. I am just here to liberate my land—as a soldier. What's the use of being a Socialist or a Communist when you've got no land where you can put your ideals into practice?"

When he heeded pleas of Lebanese and of Arab moderates to halt fedayeen attacks on Israel so as not to draw further Israeli retaliatory aerial raids on southern Lebanon, Arafat was beset by cries of "subservience to the Arab regimes," as the more violence-minded Palestinian guerrilla groups stepped up their attacks on Israel. It was such taunts that forced him to enter the Lebanese civil war and risk the very existence of the PLO by throwing his entire military strength in with Lebanon's leftist coalition and finding his armed forces looking right into the muzzles of the well-equipped, eager Syrian army.

Yet even after the disastrous confrontation in Lebanon with the intervening Syrian armies and with the Maronite Christian forces, which nearly crushed him militarily and politically, Arafat managed to survive. The scenario outlined by Senator James Abourezek on the Op-Ed page of the *New York Times* in January 1975 still applied, perhaps only to a slightly lesser degree:

Very little imagination is needed to write the script for the chain of events if Yasir Arafat is eased out of his leadership of the PLO. It is not difficult to outline the step-by-step escalation of violence until finally the United States and Russia discover that the "vital interests" of each require their active participation in a Middle East shooting war.

An oil embargo would result from even a minimum military confrontation. Our present economic condition makes the U.S. vulnerable to an outbreak of anti-Semitism against both Jews and Arabs, manifesting itself in a total cutoff of aid to Israel, an attempted take-over of Arab oil fields, or a combination of both.[108]

How many Americans have been allowed to listen to Yasir Arafat? How many really read what he said when he finally had a chance to address the U.N. General Assembly on November 13, 1974? Many remembered the holster he wore—what media follower was allowed to forget this?—but never heard or read one vital word he uttered.

Referring to the emigration of Soviet Jews to Israel, the PLO chieftain told a capacity audience in the General Assembly hall:

Why should our Arab Palestinian people pay the price of such discrimination in the world, Mr. President? Why should our people be responsible for the problems of Jewish immigration if such problems exist in the minds of some people? Why don't the supporters of these problems open their own countries, which can absorb and help these emigrants?

Arafat continued:

Mr. President, if the emigration of Jews to Palestine had had, as its objective, the goal of enabling them to live side by side with us, enjoying the same rights and assuming the same duties, we would have opened our doors to them as far as our homeland's capacity for absorption permitted. Such was the case with thousands of Armenians and Circassians, who still live among us in equality as brethren and citizens. But that the goal of this emigration should be to usurp our homeland, disperse our people, and turn us into second-class citizens—this is what no one can conceivably demand that we acquiesce to.

"Since its inception," Arafat explained, "our revolution was not motivated by racial or religious factors. Its target was never the Jew as a person, but racist Zionism and undisguised aggression. In this sense, ours is also a revolution for the Jew as a human being as well. We are struggling so that Jews, Christians, and Muslims may live in equality and enjoy the same rights and assume the same duties, free from racial or religious discrimination."

The PLO leader then made this crucial point relative to religious tolerance:

Mr. President, we do distinguish between Judaism and Zionism. While we maintain our opposition to the colonial Zionist movement, we respect the Jewish faith. Today almost one century after the rise of the Zionist movement, we wish to warn of its increasing danger to the Jews of the world, to our Arab people, and to world peace and security. For Zionism encourages the Jew to emigrate out of his homeland and grants him an artificially created nationality.

The Palestinian traced the fate of his people:

Zionist terrorism which was waged against the Palestinian people to evict it from its country and usurp its land is registered in our official documents. Thousands of our people were assassinated in their villages and towns, tens of thousands of others were forced at gunpoint to leave their homes and the lands of their fathers . . .

No one who in 1948 witnessed the catastrophe that struck the inhabitants in hundreds of villages and towns—in Jerusalem, Jaffa, Lydda, Ramleh, and Galilee—no one who has been a witness to that catastrophe will ever forget the experience even though the mass blackout has succeeded in hiding these horrors as it has hidden the traces of 385 Palestinian villages and towns destroyed at the time and erased from the map. . . . That terrorism fed on hatred, and this hatred was even directed against the olive tree in my country, which has been a proud symbol and which has reminded them of the indigenous inhabitants of the land, a living reminder that the land is Palestinian. Thus, they sought to destroy it. How else can one explain the statement by Golda Meir, which expressed her disquiet, about the Palestinian children born every day. They see in the Palestinian child, in the Palestinian tree, an enemy that should be exterminated.

While countless acres of olive groves have been burned by the Zionists in an effort to further eradicate his presence, the ceaseless love of the Palestinian for his village is such that even if all the houses are gone, the placement of every tree is still vividly remembered. The Zionists must have learned by now that perhaps it is far easier to uproot a tree than to quiet the spirit of a Palestinian Arab.

Exemplifying this unconquerable spirit, Arafat represents no personality cult, and he defies the Western norm of charisma. Should the PLO chieftain be chopped down, there will be others to come forward and take his place in the continuing bitter struggle for freedom and identity. For the Palestinians do have a strong sense of nationhood. Even children who have never been there talk vividly about life in the

Old City of Jerusalem or the beauty of Mount Carmel and the orange groves of Jaffa. The Palestinians' collective memory of homeland and the dream of return are kept alive, in part, by a large body of nostalgic poetry, which as *Time* magazine once noted, was written by "angry young lyricists who know both the harshness of Israeli prisons and the despair of life in refugee camps."[109]

Tawfiq Zayad's poem, "The Impossible," epitomizes Palestinian national determination:

> It is much easier for you
> To pass an elephant through a needle's eye,
> Or catch fried fish in a galaxy,
> Plough the sea,
> Force a crocodile to speak
> Than to destroy by persecution
> The shimmering glow of a belief,
> Or check our march,
> One single step.
>
> As if we were a thousand prodigies
> Spreading everywhere
> In Lydda, in Ramallah,
> 　in the Galilee . . .
> Here we shall stay,
> A wall upon your breast,
> And in your throat we shall stay,
> A piece of glass, a cactus thorn,
> And in your eyes,
> A blazing fire.

Just two days before his death in 1970 in his ninety-eighth year, Bertrand Russell, still fighting for justice for all peoples and particularly concerned about the fate of the Palestinians, wrote: "We are frequently told that we must sympathize with Israel because of the sufferings of the Jews in Europe at the hands of the Nazis. . . . What Israel is doing today cannot be condoned, and to invoke the horror of the past to justify those of the present is gross hypocrisy."[110] And the famed philosopher asked this question: "How much longer is the world willing to allow this spectacle of wanton cruelty?"

But the world was powerless. Washington had seemed to be inching closer to some recognition of the PLO in the spring of 1976. The thanks offered publicly by Secretary Kissinger and President Ford to Arafat and his organization for assisting in the evacuation of endangered civilians in Lebanon worried the Zionists greatly. Then along came the escalation of the Lebanese civil war and the Entebbe affair, the reaction to which was magnified by abysmal Arab public relations. The revulsion that had followed from seeing Arab youth being beaten by Israeli soldiers was driven from American minds, and Palestinian raids into Israel, baldly presented out-of-context by the media, alienated American public opinion. The U. S. under President Carter struggled to shake off its tethers—a giant under the control of the strongest organized minority in the world, which knew exactly how to get what it wanted through the right connections.

VI   The Jewish Connection:
       Numbers Don't Count

Numbers are not crucial to any struggle. Strength and purpose
are.

—Mahatma Gandhi

When so much is at stake, inevitably the question must arise: How has
the Zionist will been imposed on the American people? Far from all
Jews believe in the concept of a Jewish state, and the Jews themselves
constitute a very small minority of the American population, some 3
percent, a little over 6,000,000. Is it possible that Americans have
become so apathetic that 6,000,000 can manipulate the other 207
million?

There are many compelling reasons why population figures are of
little relevance to the Zionist success story, why neither numbers nor
wealth alone can account for the strength of pro-Israel sentiment in the
U.S. and in the Western world. This strength, qualitative and not
quantitative, can be summed up in one word: power. They are able
either to muster fantastic muscle at the right moment and at the right
place, or instill the fear that it might be used.

It is the Jewish connection, the tribal solidarity among themselves
and the amazing pull on non-Jews, that has molded this unprecedented
power. Although many Jews were initially opposed to the creation of
Israel, the Zionists were able to use the Hitler tragedy to obliterate
anti-Zionist opposition and non-Zionist indifference in capturing every
aspect of organized Jewish life.

There has swiftly emerged in the Jewish ethos of the post-World
War II era a universally and inflexibly supported movement, Israelism,
which embraces many variations of "Friends of Israel." The Jewish
communities had been subdued, Jewish connections manipulated by
Washington's most potent lobby to achieve nationalist goals.

When it comes to organization and depth, the Zionist apparatus is unparalleled. The philanthropic, political, religious, educational, and cultural branches all work in a total cooperative effort in extracting money and full political support from all American Jews. None are exempt from the call. Many who were queasy about being labeled "Zionist," sensing a connotation they did not quite like, found multifold ways of becoming Israelists and thus supporting the cause. Nor have psychological ties been neglected.

Semites, as anti-Semites, have frequently resorted to the aged cliché, "Once a Jew, always a Jew." And this has served to bring the many minimal Jews—those whose mother or father or both were Jewish but who had few, if any, ties with the religion or Jewish communal life—into Israelist ranks. The further removed from Judaism, the religion, a Jew may become, the more he is likely to compensate through support of the state. The rabbinate and other Jewish religious leaders have warned—and figures bear out these fears—of the serious flight from Judaism, evidenced both by the decline in formal religious observance and by steadily increasing marriages outside the faith. But the greater the escape into religious nothingness, the greater the converse worship of the State of Israel as a substitute for the worship of Yahweh.

The synagogues may be virtually empty on a Friday evening or a Saturday morning, but on the three big Holy Days[1] they are overcrowded to hear the pulpit reverberating with appeals for increased purchases of Israel Bonds as a renewal of faith in Israel. And those who abstain completely from attendance satisfy their guilt feelings for having run from the faith of their fathers by contributing to the UJA or by purchasing an Israel Bond. Thus they are able to convince themselves that they are still "on the team."

Wherever there is intermarriage, invariably the minimal or marginal Jew proves his loyalty to his religion by means of a rabid avowal of the Israeli cause. That is one simple way of expiation for having disobeyed Mother's admonition: "You must marry a nice Jewish girl." His—or her—"goy" partner can, in the same way, similarly demonstrate a total lack of bigotry by expression of a common love of Israel so as to avoid domestic strife stemming from any past denominational differences.

This letter from the Christian wife in a mixed marriage says a great deal:

Since the war started, my husband and I have discussed the Middle East problem quite a lot. He listens to what I say, but having grown up with

Orthodox grandparents and extremely conservative (religion-wise) parents, his responses to the questions are, quite naturally, pretty much automatic. So my function in the matter becomes more or less merely to present food for thought.

We have another friend who is Jewish, and I have had a few discussions with him. He is more open to another point of view, but the automatic pro-Israel reaction is still there basically. There is certainly no question of my not being able to discuss the subject with my husband. He is certainly willing to listen, if not particularly willing to agree.

Having married out of his religion to the great dismay of his family, I do not think his response is the product of having thought the matter out in a logical manner. It's an emotional reaction. Besides, he's stubborn.

With few exceptions, Jews who intermarry, who change their names to a more Christian-sounding appellation (there has been an increasing number of these), or who otherwise wish to escape from being considered a Jew find an exit hatch in Israel. Their support of Israel somehow helps calm their internal stirrings of guilt. The noticeable change in editorial policy, foreign news emphasis and the strict censorship exercised over anti-Zionist advertisements on the part of the *Wall Street Journal* marked another conquest for the Jewish connection.[2] Warren H. Phillips, successor to William F. Kerby as President and Chief Executive Officer of Dow Jones & Company, which owns the *Journal,* was born to Jewish parents but married out of the faith. His employees, aware of his background, bowed to his purported support of Israelism.

The story has often been told of Clare Boothe Luce's first visit to the Vatican following her conversion to Catholicism. She started detailing to the Holy Father the many things she was doing as a devout follower of her new faith until the Pope himself interrupted her to say, "Madame Luce, you know I am a Catholic, too." Apocryphally, converts have always been more devout than those born into the faith. Shortly after Elizabeth Taylor, who had become a Jewess following her marriage to Mike Todd, had taken former Navy Secretary John Warner as her sixth husband, the Hollywood trade papers announced in big type a "Salute to John Warner." The ad stated that the salute would be "the greatest gala dinner in Hollywood's history" and would aid the Jewish National Fund (it would also do Warner no harm in his race in Virginia for the U.S. Senate). More than 100 top stars attended this very successful affair. And the last visitor received by Menachem Begin at the Waldorf Astoria before returning home after his first meeting with President Carter was the beautiful Liz Taylor.

The Jewish connection covers all areas and reaches every level. Most Americans may not even sense this gigantic effort, but there is scarcely a Jew who is not reached by its tentacles. The stranglehold of the Zionist minority over the majority is exploited to the hilt in an infinite number of ways and often most subtly. The advertisements of the United Jewish Appeal (tax-deductible, of course) continue to be replete with Zionist jargon cleverly tucked away in sad accounts about Jewish refugees. It is almost impossible to discredit a charity drive which, under the caption "The Big Meal," runs a most appealing full-page picture of pathetic, hungry-looking children sitting down to "a solid meal—courtesy of you—the contributor to the United Jewish Appeal."[3] And the humanitarian-religio appeal is often loaded with political ploys stamped on the envelope: "Keep Israel Alive—Passover Campaign." An infinite number of innocent Jews are sucked into this kind of giving through the clever admixture of politics and humanitarianism.

The very definitive ties set out in Israeli legal compacts between the Jewish Agency, a public body operating in the U.S., and the government of Israel subject American citizens and taxpayers to direct influences of a foreign government. This came out clearly in the legal action brought in 1968 by Saul E. Joftes, the former Secretary-General of B'nai B'rith's International Council, against that organization, whose employee he had been for more than twenty years. Joftes charged that the B'nai B'rith, an organization accepting tax-free contributions, was being developed "more as an adjunct of a foreign power than as a voluntary agency."

In the course of the litigation, it was brought out that one of the responsibilities of a B'nai B'rith "volunteer worker" named Avis Shulman was to "arrange with Jewish Agency tourist officials to meet with tourists who were going to Eastern Europe and to brief them on what the state of Jews was in Eastern Europe." In a confidential May 7, 1974, memorandum intended "for the eyes of members of the Board of Governors only," the B'nai B'rith's Washington representative, Herman Edelsberg, asked for increased funds "to enlarge our program of instruction for American tourists visiting the Soviet Union to include non-Jews as well as Jews."[4]

Of even greater significance was the role Israeli Consul Uri Ranaan and the Israeli Consul General apparently played in Mrs. Shulman's employment by B'nai B'rith. They even picked up the tab for her to work out the balance of the year. When Theodor Herzl urged the Zionist organizations "to capture the Jewish communities," he probably never imagined so sophisticated a tactic as this kind of apparent penetration of the oldest and one of the most powerful of Jewish organizations.

Indicative of the far-reaching activities of the Zionist organizations was a 1970 report by the Chairman of the Department of Information of the American Zionist Council. Some of the salient points are given below, in the Council's own words:

I. MONITORING AND COUNTER-ACTION OF PRINTED MATERIALS

The office staff monitors the daily press, the Negro press, the Protestant and the Catholic Church press, the academic press, magazines of all kinds and books. When hostile attacks on Israel or the Zionist movement appear anywhere, material is prepared and sent, either directly to the editor or from the office as draft material to our friends in groups throughout the country who might have better access to the particular publication involved. The advantage of having local Zionist Councils is that we are immediately informed by them of any unfriendly attack on Israel from any part of the United States, either directly from the communities or via our Field Offices. Because of our extensive monitoring service, the routine job of preparing replies to hostile material goes on constantly.[5]

II. THE SPEAKERS BUREAU

There is a very well organized Speakers Bureau which,[6] with an absurdly small staff, does an amazing job.

The largest part of these [speaking] engagements is before non-Jewish groups, although at times a request from a Jewish group is serviced at a nominal fee. Where do we get the speakers? The representatives of the Israel government, visitors from Israel, American men and women—Jews and Christians—who have been to Israel on organized tours, or through personal visits, especially equipped Israelis who are invited here to attend some international conference and whose presence in this country is utilized by our Bureau for addresses before meetings arranged by us.

III. RESEARCH BUREAU

. . . We cannot expect every Zionist organization to have available the kind of material which is called for at every moment to answer attacks, to give information, to send materials to friends and potential friends. For instance, Dr. Sidney Marks, Executive Director of the Zionist Organization of America had a letter from one of its leaders in Houston asking urgently for information in four specific areas in order to help him prepare an answer to the attack made upon Israel and the Zionist movement in his community. Dr. Marks turned to us, and we were able to get the material to Houston in a matter of hours.

The Research Bureau also analyzes books and articles which deal with Israel or the Middle East. When the book is favorable, it is recommended. When it is unfavorable, it is analyzed and distortions are pointed up by providing the factual data required, so that our local councils will be prepared to react to the impact which these books make on the communities. We also stimulate book presents to libraries, both community and university libraries.

IV. VISITORS TO ISRAEL

Firmly convinced that an experience in Israel gives the visitor an understanding and appreciation of the problems and progress of that country for which there is no substitute, a good part of staff time is devoted to stimulating visits to Israel on the part of public opinion molders, either as individuals or groups. In some cases, subsidy is involved.

V. SPECIAL ISSUES PROJECTS

Our Department also has the responsibility for the preparation of memoranda and for informing the local Zionist Council leaders and Jewish community leadership as to our recommended position and steps for action on issues such as the Arab refugee problem . . . etc.

B. VOLUNTEER COMMITTEES

The Commission on Inter-Religious Affairs[7] is responsible for our effort in gaining friends in the Protestant and Catholic religious communities. The work concerns itself with monitoring the Christian church press, stimulating articles presenting Israel and Zionist ideology, answering the hostile attacks very often found in the publications of the Protestant and Catholic Church, as well as cultivating key religious leaders and editors.

Seminars for Christian Clergy: This has been an extremely successful project. There have been ten seminars during the past year, held in important communities throughout the United States.

The Inter-University Study Tour to Israel: A very successful tour has just been completed, made up of 49 participants who for the most part paid their own way. Two Negro participants were sponsored by B'nai B'rith and the Anti-Defamation League.

Writers planning a European visit are invited to sessions of the Committee and encouraged or helped to go to Israel. There is a discussion of the kind of story they should look for, one which may likely bring forth an article in a magazine with which the writer has contact.

The TV-radio Committee[8] . . . arranges for talks and interviews on radio and TV; submits ideas for possible programs to stations and networks so as to give a better and more sympathetic understanding of Israel to the viewing American public. . . .

The Zionist-Jewish connection draws for its strength upon every strata of life, every political point of view, and every religion. Contrary to what most people believe, all Zionists are not Jews; many of the most devout supporters of Israel are Christians. That is why Rudolf G. Sonneborn, key man in the American wing of the Jewish underground movement in Palestine before the establishment of the Zionist state, was able to boast back in October 1947: "We have at least one person in virtually every community in America."[9]

The extent and depth to which organized Jewry reached—and reaches—in the U.S. is indeed awesome. When Secretary of State William P. Rogers embarked in late 1969 on a new peace initiative to meet the dangers of the escalating Israeli-Egyptian war of attrition and called for the withdrawal of Israel from occupied areas, a grand national offensive was waged by Hadassah, the Women's Zionist group, allegedly concerned with welfare and humanitarian advances in Israel. President Faye Schenk urged members to "write, wire, and call" not only the President and Secretary of State, but Congressmen and Senators. The new U.S. peace proposal, she claimed, "endangers Israel's future and fails to offer her any valid guarantees." At one time or another, the myriad of Jewish groups are organizing locally and nationally some citizen action, some public protest in behalf of Israel.

The Israelist cause draws its power not alone from its meticulous organization but from the fact that many Jews hold positions that give them greater visibility, prominence, and potential influence than their numbers would suggest. The mere presence of American Jews in all urban communities—and even in some of the most rural ones—lends inestimable strength to the all-powerful connection. Six million, most very well situated, stand ready and willing, and also are most able to use their talents as well as their connections to advance the Israeli cause. Every Christian living in an urban area has a banker, a butcher, an accountant, a candlestick maker—a doctor, a lawyer, a supplier, a neighbor, or just a plain fellow club member—who is Jewish, whom he above all does not wish to offend, and certainly not for the sake of some people 5,000 or 6,000 miles away with whom he has little in common. It is on this basic fact of life that the Israelist movement has fattened itself and that latent opposition to Zionism has died stillborn. Arab lands are distant. Jews are very much in everyone's back yard—or just over the fence—which, in the long run, means infinitely more than even an occasional energy shortage.

One of the loveliest ladies that I ever knew—I loved her dearly—used to take an hour's trip to the office annually to renew her own and her Christmas gift subscriptions to the newsletter *Middle East Perspective,* bringing her payment in cash. On one occasion when she brought her annual donation in the midst of a heavy snowstorm, I could not help but ask, "Isabel, you know how much I love to see you, but why in the world didn't you mail this check instead of driving into the city in this horrible weather?"

"Alfred, I can't have Henry Ackerman, my Jewish accountant, draw a check to your newsletter. You are too well known, and I just can't afford to lose him. So I take the money from my Christmas cash check and bring it personally into you."

But whereas New York City, with its almost one-third Jewish population, is firmly in the grip of the Zionists, this influence by no means stops there, nor does it have any intention of so doing. From my own experiences lecturing around the country, I can attest to the pervasiveness of this Jewish connection. I had hardly finished a lecture to the Spokane (Washington) Central Lions Club when three members pounced upon the president and demanded equal time. Of course Zionists only get 99 percent of the time devoted to this issue, and no sooner is 1 percent given to the opposing viewpoint than they try to cut it down to half a percent by asking time for themselves. This was in Spokane, a city of 200,000 with only 180 Jewish families. But again, size has nothing to do with influence, particularly when the Christian president happened to be in a business where Jews controlled his supply.

A letter from the gentleman who made the introductory presentation noted, "Your talk certainly set the cat among the canaries as far as Spokane is concerned. I have had telephone calls from the president of B'nai B'rith and also the presidents of the Jewish Men's Club, both of whom were rather upset at my having introduced you at the Lions."

On that same lecture tour, which had taken me to the West Coast, I lectured in Kansas City at William Jewell College and was afterward interviewed by the *Kansas City Star.* The story that appeared the following day omitted any reference to charges of press slanting, discussed at great length in the lecture and backed up by substantial documentation. The article appeared only in the edition distributed in North Kansas City. A look about the city the next day explained a lot. Everything is surely "up-to-date in Kansas City," as Rodgers and Hammerstein once noted, and no small part may be due to names like Hertzberg, Wolf, Lerner, and Altman, who own important stores there. Here was Jewish affluence in still another city. The same *Star* contained an ecstatic review, covering half a page, of a new book entitled *Israel's Survival Is a Holy Thing*, and the following day ran a prominently placed picture-story headed "Reunion in Israel," a detailed account of a Russian Jew who had brought his family from Moscow to Tel Aviv.

On this same tour the chairman of the Republican County Committee, under whose auspices I spoke at a Reno, Nevada, luncheon, was later warned by Zionist contributors that "the party must entice a speaker to challenge Dr. Lilienthal's remarks in the very near future." A stroll through the famed gambling city indicated the usual influence: large stores owned by Ginsburg, Leeds, Lerner, etc.

Irvington-on-the-Hudson in wealthy Westchester County, like so many other suburban New York City communities, is also subject to the same influences: UJA fund-raising and other Jewish nationalist activities, together with coverage of Middle East news items invariably favoring the Israeli side, prominently appear in the local newspaper. And the Irvington Library, too, reflected this bias. In the card index for the Middle East there was one book by Dr. Sidney Fisher and a few books under "Arab" and "Egyptian," most of them, of course, dealing with the ancient history of Egypt and having nothing at all to do with the Arab-Israeli conflict. But under "Israel" there was a wide variety of books on the political history, travel, and social conditions of that country. These included all kinds of pro-Israel books, including Leonard Slater's *The Pledge,* Robert St. John's latest book on Israel as well as his earlier distorted biography of Gamal Abdel Nasser, *The Boss*[10]; Harry Golden's *The Israelis,*[11] replete with oversimplifications and clichés; and Israeli Amos Elon's *The Israelis: Sons and Founders,*[12] the eminently fair attempt at presenting his people. Yael Dayan, daughter of Moshe Dayan, and Miss Ruth Gruber, an old-time Zionist propagandist, were also represented.

Prominently displayed on the shelves also was a book by Gerold Frank, *The Deed,*[13] a sympathetic treatment of the two young killers of Lord Moyne, Britain's High Commissioner in Egypt whose 1944 death marked the opening of the incessant violence and terrorism that has since overtaken the Middle East and has engulfed the entire world.

Zionist zeal can manifest itself in the least suspected place on the most unsuspected occasion. New Orleans Mayor Moon Landrieu had been one of the hundred young top national leaders listed by *Time* magazine in the fall of 1975 to whom *Middle East Perspective* sent complimentary subscriptions. On official New Orleans stationery, we received the following letter:

Dear Dr. Lilienthal:

The nice thing about America is that one can say and write pretty much what he thinks. Therefore, you have the right to express your comments in your publication.

I also have the same right. With my right, I simply want to say that you are a fool. If you think Israel is causing the problem in the Middle East, you are a complete fool. If you are nothing more than anti-Semitic, then I can better understand why you would write such trash.

Sincerely,

JAY HANDELMAN
Assistant Director,
Public Relations Office

In a letter to the Mayor (sent in a plain white envelope to avoid another interception), I wrote to ask whether he had seen the letter advising him of the complimentary subscription and had authorized the Handelman response. In reply, Mayor Landrieu expressed appreciation "for calling the letter to my attention. Please understand that Mr. Handelman was not authorized by me to send this letter, and the thoughts he expressed should not have been under city letterhead." Just one of the innumerable examples of the harm the Jewish connection in high places can so easily wreak!

Leaders often cooperate unwittingly in Zionist suppressive tactics in order to save themselves trouble or embarrassment. Without due consideration for the erosion of free speech, they sometimes agree to requests for the postponement or elimination of speakers, programs, or articles relative to Zionism or Israel lest they be offensive to their Jewish friends. A Zionist Unitarian in Rockford, Illinois, seriously opposed a study of the Palestinian question because "it might lead to anti-Semitism." No sooner had a lecture by a critic of Zionism been scheduled by the Rotary Club on the island of Nantucket, thirty miles out at sea, than a stiff demand for cancellation or "equal time" was presented. The club's president, the owner of the island's largest hardware store, felt instantaneously obliged to promise to schedule a Zionist speaker. Program chairmen of service clubs are loathe to rise above demands thrust upon them that non-Zionist speakers be canceled, or not booked, because "if you insist on letting them talk, it will make your Jewish friends very unhappy." The implied threat is very obvious.

Aside from the superb organization and mobilization of the Zionists, the impact of money provides another reason for the lopsided attitude toward the Middle East in every corner of the U.S., and sometimes beyond its borders, too.

On lovely St. Thomas in the Virgin Islands, tourists on Main Street, seeking bargains as they pour onto land from cruise ships in the port of Charlotte Amalie, cannot miss the well-located Bolero Shop. No matter which door they enter, they are met by large signs, "Visit the Israeli Shops," and in the rear again are posters leading to exhibits of the most mediocre pottery and brass. The principal owner of the store happens to be the largest contributor on the island to the UJA, Henry Kimmelman, once chief fund-raiser for Hubert Humphrey's presidential campaign.

The St. Thomasite Zionists raised a vast sum of money during the 1973 war, largely through the donation of a free ad in the local paper. The Arab merchants were denied an equal opportunity to appeal to the populace. They were simply told by the newspaper that their fund was "political, not humanitarian," and therefore could not be run free.

Nearby at the Dutch end of St. Marteens on the main shopping street is the Windmill, a quality jewelry shop. On one of its two big windows is painted "Shalom—Welcome." The store that sells paperbacks has two travel books on Israel.

In Britain, too, the Jewish connection has been powerful and all-encompassing. Marks & Spencer (hereafter referred to as M&S), the largest chain store organization in the United Kingdom with some 251 stores and sales of just under $1.5 billion in 1973, also owns a chain of stores in Canada and is opening up throughout Europe. M&S does not manufacture any of their own goods, but they lay down certain regulations and specifications that must be followed by manufacturers regarding quality. Some of these manufacturers do not supply any firm except M&S and are therefore wholly dependent upon the goodwill of that company and its dictates. Whenever possible, M&S sells Israeli and South African goods. Their counters are always stocked with produce, vegetables, and fruits from these two countries. The range of goods sold in M&S stores includes clothing of all types, foodstuffs of all kinds, toiletries, household goods, and so forth.

During the 1973 war, as in other previous crises involving Israel, the company sent telegrams to all M&S Jewish suppliers "summoning" them to a meeting. They were then told how much they would have to donate to Israel. Several manufacturers complained to their friends about this, but said that the firm made it clear (although perhaps not in so many words) that their contracts would be terminated if they did not "cough up" sufficient money. Since many factories supply no other firm but M&S, no manufacturer would risk losing his livelihood.

Also, Jewish members of the company's staff are regularly pestered to give money to various Zionist appeals. The sales promotion department, which looks after publicity and advertising, frequently has assigned staff members to design and prepare Zionist appeal brochures and other such material during office hours, at the expense of the shareholders. In addition, an executive of the company, paid by the firm, is employed full time in promoting the interests of Israel. Hannah House, a building in Manchester Street, London W1, which was built to supply recreation and canteen facilities for staff members of the firm, housed in part of its premises an Israeli government office that promotes trade and commerce.

A firm called Triumph, one of the largest bra and girdle manufacturers in the world and one of the biggest suppliers of M&S, has, in the past, produced their goods in factories in Austria. M&S bullied the firm to open a factory in Israel. M&S is now bringing pressure to bear on Triumph to close down all their Austrian interests and to manufacture solely in Israel.

During the December 1973 demonstrations in London outside the Syrian Embassy over the Israeli prisoners of war being held by Damascus, Jewish staff members were told that they were free to go during working hours, without deduction of pay, to demonstrate outside the Syrian Embassy. An observer who was inside the embassy while the demonstrations were taking place wrote: "Several hundred British Jews, all yelling hysterically, 'Release *our* boys! Set *our* soldiers free!' " (Italics added.)

Another firm that makes a point of promoting and selling Israeli goods of all kinds—clothing, jewelry, food, etc.—is prestigious Selfridges, the large department store that recently opened an adjoining hotel. It is owned by Charles Clore, who like the heads of M&S, is intensely Zionist and has donated a small fortune to Israel.

Zionist flexibility permits the solicitation and acceptance of support from any and all sources. It used to be said at the outset of the Middle East conflict when Israel was first established that the anti-Semites, along with the Arabists, constituted the bulk of what little American opposition there was to Israel. And perhaps this may have been initially true of certain extreme right-wingers who rushed to Arab offices —and to the anti-Zionist Jews, too—and pledged their verbal backing (and very little more). But since then there has been a marked shift. By way of a gross anomaly, one finds that the more a Christian—or a Jew—possesses even a soupçon of prejudice, the more he is likely to support the State of Israel. He feels that in this way he can compensate for his bias. Consequently, the real anti-Semite can often be found in the ranks of those singing Israel's praises.

When Israel came into being and campaigned for immigrants to supply manpower, the idea of relegating "these nonintegratable Jews" to the foreign State of Israel and to do so with popularity became a bigot's dream come true. Support of Israel now began to earn him a gold star on his otherwise sullied escutcheon.

After the heightening of the area cold war in the 1960s with Big Power polarization, which saw the Russians supporting Nasser and the Arabs, and the U.S. backing Israel, conservatives joined other right-wingers and liberals in support of Israel. Concerned with the containment of Communism, they fell for the gambit directed at them by Israelist propagandists and fellow Jewish conservatives. They were unable to recognize the difference between Communist controlled, indoctrinated, or oriented countries, such as the Soviet satellites of Eastern Europe, Cuba, or North Vietnam, and those who have been forced to look to the Soviet Union for temporary diplomatic, military, or economic assistance without buying Communist ideology. The Arab socialist countries, including Egypt under Nasser, even as they were forced by the U.S. "Israel First" policy to look to the Soviet bloc for vital multifold assistance, remained virulently anti-Communist, as evidenced by the Egyptian leader's banning of the Communist party and the large number of Communists jailed.

Bedeviled by their own inadequate grasp of the realities of the area conflict and egged on by important Jewish connections, the right-wing press, *Human Events, National Review,* and the publications of the Birch Society, often competed with Zionist newspapers in anti-Arab slogans and in applying the label "Communist." Paradoxically, this anti-Communist attitude, which was contributing to the molding of American public opinion in favor of Israel, was at the same time driving basically anti-Communist peoples, the Arabs whose strong theism constituted a natural bulwark against Communism, into greater reliance on the Soviet Union.

Tel Aviv's 1967 victory greatly assisted this movement of conservatives, right-wingers, and bigots toward the Israeli camp. Americans of all shades of political opinion like a winner, of course. Likewise, the conservatives' proclaimed advocacy of law and order intuitively aroused strong opposition to the many acts of violence committed by Palestinian commandos and their allies.

One-sided reportage on terrorism, in which cause was never related to effect, was assured because the most effective component of the Jewish connection is probably that of media control. It is well known that American public opinion molders have long been largely influenced by a handful of powerful newspapers, including the *New York Times,* the *Washington Post,* and the *St. Louis Post-Dispatch*—owned respectively by the Sulzbergers, Eugene Meyer and now his daughter Katharine Graham (half-Jewish, who also owns Newsweek), and the Pulitzers, a Hungarian Jewish family. The New York *Post,* until recently when it was sold to Rupert Murdoch, was in the capable hands of Dorothy Schiff, the granddaughter of banker Jacob Schiff.

Walter Annenberg, who served as Nixon's Ambassador to Britain, owned the *Philadelphia Inquirer, The Morning Telegraph, Seventeen,* and *TV Guide* (estimated advertising revenues of $55 million), as well as several television stations. Samuel Newhouse, of Jewish background, owns some forty-nine newspapers, including the influential *Newsday* on Long Island, four television stations, a number of radio stations, and a cluster of vital magazines, including *Vogue, Glamour, Mademoiselle,* and *House and Garden.* In smaller communities around the country, exercising large influence, are such Jewish-owned or operated organs as the Las Vegas *Sun* and the *Carolina Israelite.*

Other newspapers, not Jewish-owned, have top editors, directors, and advertising chiefs who are Jewish, such as the *Los Angeles Times* and the *International Herald Tribune,* an amalgam of the *New York Times,* the *Washington Post,* and the old *New York Herald Tribune.* In 1978 the *Washington Star's* owner was *Time Magazine* and the publisher until June 1 was Joe L. Allbritton, but the views of the executive editor Sidney Epstein and associate editor Edwin Yoder, Jr. were clearly reflected in its editorials and articles during the critical Middle East developments.[14]

All of the leading magazines, ranging from *Commentary, Esquire, Ladies Home Journal, New York Review of Books, New Yorker,* and *U.S. News and World Report,* have Jews in key positions as publishers, editors, or managing editors. These people, at the very least, have the veto power over whatever appears in their publications. No one is about to criticize Jews—or even take Israel to task—for fear of being out of line with the boss, who is likely to fire him. The boss himself may not be a screaming Zionist, but scarcely ever will walk out of step with the overwhelming articulated opinion by expressing his own views on this subject, which in turn makes his Christian friends and contacts keep whatever criticism they may harbor under full wraps. There is also the constant overriding concern of the media about losing advertising, so vital to every publication, at times making a mockery of the vaunted "freedom of press." Power is thus very often exercised by default.

Parade, the Sunday newspaper magazine with a circulation of close to 20 million and a claimed readership of twice that number, has Christian ownership, but editor Jesse Gorkin, two senior editors, and many writers, until 1977 staff changes, were Jewish. Lloyd Shearer, its editor-at-large in California, has worked actively with Zionist groups, including the Anti-Defamation League and the Jewish Defense League, and used his pen either to subtly attack the Arabs whenever possible through his column, "Personality Parade," or to advance Zionist propaganda. For example, a Shearer piece blamed brainwashing and the fear of war for the refusal of emigrating Soviet Jews to go to Israel, while not mentioning Israeli taxes, bureaucracy, inflation, corruption or fear of conscription—the reasons why so many other Israelis were leaving the country.[15]

It would be futile to list the number of top Jewish editors and writers across the country. Many of the largest book publishers, including Knopf, Random House, Holt, Liverwright, Viking Press, Simon and Schuster, Van Nostrand Reinhold, and Lyle Stewart are Jewish-owned, directly or by Jewish-controlled interests (including CBS, RCA, Music Corporation of America, Litton's, and Gulf and Western). In other firms such as Macmillan and Grosset & Dunlap, one will find editors-in-chief or presidents who are Jewish. Three years ago, one large Christian publisher showed far greater regard for the possible emotions of his Jewish editor-in-chief than he did for a sure-hit manuscript that severely criticized Zionism. A call for a review copy to a smaller house, the Dial Press, led to a connection with a Mimi Garfinkle. This all explains why such a pitifully small number of anti-Zionist or pro-Arab books ever see the light of day.[16]

An additional source of Zionist strength flows from the control of the distribution field of paperbacks, magazines, and newspapers. A near monopoly in the news distribution field in New York lies in the hands of Henry Garfinkel Corporation National Services, which owns the Union News Company. Few pocketbooks or paperbacks they oppose can be brought to the attention of the reading public. The Book of the Month Club, which has distributed close to 250 million books in the last forty years, was founded by the late Harry Sherman, who was of Anglo-Welsh-Jewish parentage. Many of the wholesale book firms are Jewish controlled.

In radio and television, again one finds almost an overwhelming presence of key Jews. Chairman of the Board of CBS until very recently was William Paley; RCA's David and Robert Sarnoff for a long time ran their subsidiary, the National Broadcasting Company (NBC) whose present chairman is Julian Goodman; and Leonard Goldenson headed the American Broadcasting Company (ABC) until succeeded by Fred Silverman. A few officials in three offices all located on the east side of Sixth Avenue in Manhattan between 49th and 54th Streets select most of the ideas, experiences, and news reaching most of the American people. Each of these three major networks has a separate news subsidiary with offices responsible only for news programs. Reuven Frank ran NBC's, Richard Salant CBS's, and Martin Rubinstein served under Goldenson, with Avram Westin as executive producer. They dictated pretty much what 200 million Americans learned of what had happened in the nation and in the world each day. Virtually all national and international news is filtered, edited, and broadcast by these three corporations.

Not only is television chock-full of Jewish producers, but many of the commentators, news reporters, editors, and directors of news programs are Jewish. Look at the influential national talk-interview programs where, among others, David Susskind, Mike Wallace, Lawrence Spivak, and Irving Kupcinet have reigned supreme. For a long time Stuart Schulberg of NBC sat on top of the popular "Today" show, under Hugh Downs and then under Barbara Walters, to make certain that while every Tom, Dick, and Harry might appear, nothing was to be aired that might upset the continued brainwashing of their viewers as to the Middle East. Try and get something that is anti-Zionist, no less pro-Arab, through the blockade of the three networks and you will quickly find out just how many producers and assistants are of the chosen faith. Calling from Nantucket, at the outset of the October 1973 war, to protest one of the many viciously slanted CBS news broadcasts of that time, I was three times connected with someone bearing an obvious Hebraic name. It has been estimated that close to 70 percent of the important posts in the media are held by Jews, and there are an infinite number of Judith Epsteins, as at Channel 13, guarding the gateways to the top echelon.

Taxicab drivers, insomniacs, and other night hawks have for a number of years been regaled by the competing radio talk shows of Jewish loyalists Barry Gray and Barry Farber and Zionist converts Long John Nebel and Bob Grant. Their lame excuse for letting their bias show has been the fear of loss of all-necessary advertising. The same holds true for the incessant appearances of Dr. Martin Abend on Metromedia's news outlet in New York and environs.

One need not point to the total control of the motion picture industry to understand why the film *Exodus*, based on the famed Leon

Uris book, with its subtle distortions of the Palestinian issue and glorification of Zionist terrorism, is still being shown as a repeat in some
theaters and on late-night television programs across the country. The
alliance between television and the motion picture industry has been
very close, one feeding into the other. Metro-Goldwyn-Mayer, 20th-
Century Fox, Paramount Pictures, Columbia, Warner Bros., Universal
and United Artists have all been headed, founded, and controlled by
well-known Jews such as Goldwyn, Fox, Laemmle, Schenck, Lasky,
Zukor, Thalberg, Cohen, Mayer, and Warner. Little wonder that Bob
Hope once equipped that "Hollywood is the only place where Catholics give up matzoh balls for Lent."

In addition, during the last several years Hollywood has closely
collaborated with and assisted the budding Israeli movie industry.
Richard Boone (Paladin), while not Jewish himself, promoted Israel's
potential as a film-making center and in one of his earlier efforts
starred Hannah Meron, the Israeli actress who lost her left leg in the
1970 bombing of an El Al plane in Munich.

Likewise, the American theater headed by Broadway—and this
has been equally true of the entire entertainment world, including
music and other forms—has been dominated by Jewish names, too
numerous to list. No opportunity is lost by Israelists to push their
wares through the arts. These words, for instance, from a 1973 review
of the *Poseidon Adventure,* the film based on the novel of the same name
by Paul Gallico, deserve attention: "An amazingly fat Shelley Winters
and Jack Albertson as the couple en route to Israel and their grandchildren contribute a touching vignette or two in a big cast largely seen
in bit roles." A careful reading of the Paul Gallico book shows that this
couple, Belle and Manny Rosen, play an important role, but there was
no mention of their going to Israel. In the film this was brought in very
prominently by the screenplay writers, Stirling Silliphant and Wendell
Mays. An Israeli travel folder was held up by the couple as they sat on
deck and talked about going to see their grandchildren in the Holy
Land for the first time—a gratuitous boost by Hollywood screenwriters
for Israeli tourism, which had slumped badly in 1972. Could the film
writers' change of names, à la my grade-school classmate Ming Toy
Epstein, not have contributed to their Zionist outlook?

Propaganda was further insidiously injected into the movie scenario when the dying Belle handed a swimming medal to her husband,
pointing to the Hebrew letters on the rear, standing for "light"—the
scene that was plugged on television ads for the film. The characteriza-
tion of the screenplay by *New York Times'* reviewer Vincent Canby as

"burrowing into some new foolishness with all the intensity of a mad mole digging through soap chips" did not prevent the film from becoming a big success and further advancing the Zionist saga.

As their contribution to public edification during the growing crisis in U.S.-Israel relations, Hollywood and Broadway were always doing more than their bit for Zionism. Otto Preminger, producer and director of *Exodus,* announced production of a film on Israel's history. The tentative name of this feature was *The First 25 Years: Dayan's Israel,* to be based on the Israeli Foreign Minister's autobiography, *Story of My Life.*

Although the movie *Exodus* was an unqualified success, the musical version was a flop on Braodway; it closed after a disastrous three weeks despite a Uris-paid Sunday *Times* appeal to keep the play going. In a piece entitled "The Last Straw," *Women's Wear Daily* reviewer Arthur Gottfried called *Ari* "a disgrace . . . a primitive production." Certain emotional themes do not lend themselves to stage dramatization, as was proven when the play based on the life of Theodor Herzl also quickly closed. But the Zionists kept pushing their wares. Few plays have been so widely heralded in advance as *Golda,* based on the life of Israel's former Prime Minister and written by William Gibson, whose wife is Jewish. For seven months before its November, 1977 opening, major dailies and magazines were flooded with ads, feature articles, and pictures of the lead, Anne Bancroft, with and without Mrs. Meir, on the news as well as the theatrical pages, including notices placed in the middle of the *Times'* theatrical directory. Although the play came to New York with a $250,000 advance sale and a super-deluxe opening night, new advertising, and free publicity, it closed after ninety-three performances and the entire investment of a half a million dollars was lost, although rumored prospects of a film or television special might retrieve part or all of this.

Maybe because she was English, actress Vanessa Redgrave was totally naïve about the meaning of the Jewish connection. In New York in October, 1977 for promotion of the new screen hit *Julia,* in which she starred with Jane Fonda, the self-admitted Trotskyite also tried to create interest in a moving, two-hour documentary about the PLO filmed with BBC cameramen that summer in Lebanon and containing an interview with Yasir Arafat. Vanessa phoned Joey Adams (who, despite his name, is a member of the tribe and had raised $200-million for Israel) and asked help for getting her film on television. When she told him what the movie was about, he exploded, "Lady, you're very sick," and hung up.

According to the *New York Post*, Redgrave said the film demonstrated that Israel was a "fascist, racist nation" (which was her lingo) and should be eradicated" (which was definitely not hers).[17]

The film star had roused the hornets. Picketing began outside Cinema I in Manhattan, and at one performance the Jewish Defense League unleashed dozens of mice. *Show Business* sounded the clarion call for war by printing this fiery caption on a reprint from the earlier *New York Post* story: "Vanessa Redgrave Urges Extermination of Israel."[18] A full-scale "hate war" erupted which was joined by radio station WINS, the *Soho Weekly News, Our Town,* for whom Cindy Adams wrote a column, Mayor Edward Koch, and well-known producer and former president of the Anti-Defamation League, Dore Schary. What burned the Zionists and their friends in Hollywood and on Broadway was that her documentary had the potential of arousing sympathy for the Palestinians and exposing the manorial splendor in South Lebanon of Christian Phalangist leaders, Israel's allies.

The war accelerated when Vanessa was nominated as best supporting actress for her role in *Julia* in which she, ironically enough, played an anti-Nazi heroine in a story based on the memoirs of Lillian Hellman. Enormous pressures were brought to bear by the Jewish Defense League, the American Jewish Committee and everyone they could commandeer to bar her from winning. *New York Times* critic Vincent Canby pontificated that "great actresses are not those who go around trying to find distribution outlets for films on behalf of the PLO."[19]

Outside the Los Angeles Music Center the night of the Fiftieth Annual Academy Awards, vying demonstrations by the Jewish Defense League and the Palestine Liberation Organization came close to open conflict over Miss Redgrave. The neo-fascists carried signs reading "PLO Murders Jewish Children," "Redgrave and Arafat—A Perfect Love Affair." On the other side, the PLO supporters carried a placard "Vanessa—A Woman of Conscience and Courage."

In one of the most dramatic moments in filmdom history, the Tel Aviv-Broadway-Hollywood axis was soundly defeated when Vanessa Redgrave took home the Oscar. Beautifully gowned and coiffed, Miss Redgrave's acceptance speech was fiery and impassioned. Accepting the Oscar, which she held aloft in triumph, she said: "You should be proud that in the last few weeks you stood firm and you refused to be intimidated by the threats of a small bunch of Zionist hoodlums, whose behavior is an insult to the stature of Jews all over the world and to their great and heroic record of struggle against fascism and oppression. I salute that record and thank you, and I pledge to you that I will continue to fight against anti-Semitism and fascism."

This was one of the few, even temporary, setbacks for the Zionist connectors, but Hollywood on this occasion had wished to prove how non-political, pro-art they were. But the battle against the winner was hardly over. Later at the Awards, writer Paddy Chayefsky, an active Zionist and leader in the "Free the Soviet Jewry" movement, sharply attacked Miss Redgrave; her own producer, Richard Roth, sounded off at a lavish post-Academy party at which she was shunned by the leaders of the entertainment industry, according to the *New York Post.* Comedian Alan King breathed fire: "I am that Zionist hoodlum she was talking about. It's just a pity I wasn't on the platform tonight. I would have gone for the jugular." Few words could have more appropriately expressed the murder pathology of the Begin-led world Zionist movement than these. The vast abyss between Judaism and Zionism had been openly exposed to a hundred million people around the world, and the subsequent Adams-King effort to gather signatures for an imposing *Variety* advertisement against the actress fell flat on its face.

There is little doubt that the Anti-Defamation League and the other so-called "defense organizations" will be calling for a book burning campaign when this volume hits the book stores. At the time of the outcry against Chairman of the Joint Chiefs of Staff General George Brown for his Duke University charge of undue Jewish influence through "ownership" of the media, these organizations and other critics of the General pointed out that of the total number of daily papers in the U.S., only a small percentage are Jewish-owned (3.1 percent of the 1,748 U.S. dailies), and that even where the ownership is Jewish, as in the case of the *New York Times,* the *Washington Post, Newsweek,* and the Newhouse chain, many of the editors are not Jewish. It has also been pointed out that there is no Jewish ownership of the wire services, nor of *Time* magazine (the Chairman of the Board, Andrew Heiskell, is married to Marion Sulzberger Dryfoos, sister of the present *New York Times* publisher and widow of his predecessor). But the decisive factor has always been control, not ownership.

It is fear and pressure that govern. Publishers and editors are constantly concerned about their advertising—Jewish or otherwise—are worried about calls from the Anti-Defamation League, and are directed by their own inner compulsions, so often fed by the Holocaust. And when the AP, UPI, the *Washington Post,* the *New York Times,* the news magazines, the networks, and the two major polls—Gallup and Harris—agree on the same general viewpoint, as they have on the

Middle East, forget it—it's the "ball game."

Even if, as has been alleged, the major networks, NBC, CBS, and ABC, which grew out of the heavily Jewish-dominated entertainment and advertising businesses, do happen to have a majority of anchormen, commentators, and analysts who are not Jewish, they are nevertheless most concerned about their future and will not do anything to risk antagonizing their Jewish overseers. Hence the news has been consistently, overwhelmingly pro-Israel and anti-Arab, any expression of anti-Zionism being practically verboten.

The fact that the pro-Israel stance of Jewish-owned papers is scarcely distinguishable (perhaps only to the extent of degree) from the bias of the rest of the press is but a corollary of the famed advertisement: "You don't have to be Jewish to love Levy's Rye Bread." You do not have to be a Jewish publisher to bow to the juggernaut of power behind the State of Israel. Christians in all forms of media endeavor, as in all walks of life, have often been more fervent supporters of Israel than their Jewish prototypes.

The final proof is said to be in the eating. Any unbiased survey of news reportage and commentary, whether on radio-television, in magazines or newspapers, as well as of letters to the editor appearing on the opinion-making editorial page, would unmistakably reveal the extent of control exercised through the Jewish connection. While the dramatic 1974 appearance of the PLO's Yasir Arafat before the U.N. could scarcely be ignored, and hence was accorded fuller coverage than usually given the other side, whenever did Jewish columnists such as C. L. Sulzberger, William Safire, Theodore White, Max Lerner, Joseph Kraft, and Walter Lippmann ever do more than mildly slap the Israelis on the wrist and chide them for some relatively inconsequential wrongdoing, while resolutely refusing in any way to even remotely "repudiate the anachronism of Zionism in the modern world and the madness of attempting to establish a theocratic state in the swarming beehive of Islamic Palestine."[20]

Outside of government, media experts such as David Garth and Charles Guggenheim, pollsters Louis Harris and Daniel Yankelovich, fund-raisers Max Fischer for the Republicans and Arthur Krim for the Democrats, and presidential speech writers Democrats Richard Goodwin and Adam Walinsky, and William Safire for the Republicans, have exercised a potent political influence.

All it takes is one good connection, and the Zionists produce a great "deal." The connectors are never daunted, never ever stop—either giving Treasury Secretary William E. Simon the annual civil leadership award of the American Jewish Committee at a $175-a-plate Waldorf Astoria dinner[21] or the sports division honoring Yankee player Phil Rizzuto for his contribution to baseball.

And the Zionist links are everywhere. Edgar M. Bronfman, scion of the wealthiest Canadian Zionist family, presented the Synagogue Council of America's Covenant of Peace Award (including $18,000) to Lillian Carter, mother of the president, at a dinner in September 1977. Ambassador to the U.N. Andrew Young was the keynote speaker at the dinner affair.

All types of Christians are wheedled into all types of support. At a Chestnut Hill, Massachusetts, reception, Rose Kennedy bought some $15,000 worth of Bonds, qualifying her for the Israeli Ambassador's "Society of Trustees." The Jewish Connection is very effective in Britain, too. The Duke of Devonshire, as Chairman of the Conservative Party's "Friends of Israel" Committee, toured the U.S. to raise funds for "little Israel."

A favorite gambit is to make love of Israel part of the popular culture, to make us all feel a little bit "Jewish" without our knowing what hit us. An annual event in New York City has been the "Salute to Israel" parade with national, state, and city officials, along with honored Israeli guests such as Jerusalem Mayor Teddy Kollek or Chief Rabbi Shlomo Goren on the reviewing stand, and marching school bands—Protestant, Catholic, and nonsecular schools—swinging by. The students participate because of the exposure and publicity offered by the national band competition, which is adroitly scheduled as part of the "Salute." When questioned, the director of a high school band from Matawan, New Jersey, professed total ignorance of any political implication to the parade or the presence of his youngsters. "We could be playing for the Greeks or the Poles, on their day. Why not for the Jews?" Thus, unwittingly, the innocent help magnify in the press and on TV the strength of support for Israel.

In California, too, there are many who zealously serve the connection. Milton M. Gordon, a key figure in the mortgage broker industry, with more than a passing interest in pending state legislation, arranged for free all-expense trips in 1975 to Israel of California's State Treasurer Jesse Unruh, Democratic State Chairman Charles Manatt, Assembly Speaker Leo McCarthy, Senate President pro-tem, and twelve other legislators, from both parties. Part of the funds came from Israel, "the rest from business and labor leaders," according to the Sacramento Bee.[22]

The following year there was another all-expense junket for ten other California legislators, estimated to cost in excess of $13,000. On their return, these legislators had nothing but paeans of praise for Israel and its "militancy." Ironically, the Judah L. Magnes Memorial Museum of Berkeley, which had sponsored what Director Seymour Fromer called a "cultural exchange fellowship," had been established to honor the first president of the Hebrew University in Jerusalem, Dr. Judah L. Magnes, a devout anti-Zionist and a fervent believer in Holy Land binationalism; he was forced to end his days in exile in the U.S. out of fear of Begin-like terror, which struck down his driver and narrowly missed taking his life.

Jews, toughened by centuries of persecution, have risen to places of prime importance in the business and financial world. By 1955 18.9 percent of all Americans with an annual income of $10,000, and more than 20 percent of all American millionaires, were Jews.[23] Their wealth and resultant influence provided a weapon for advancing the interests of the Israeli state and a shield from censure-criticism of the most-favored-nation position that was accorded the new Mediterranean state. While there were, at the outset of the Palestine question, pockets of resistance to the concept of a Jewish state, and the founding members of some of the great Jewish financial institutions considered Zionism quite abhorrent, the doubters soon quickly learned to keep such opinions to themselves. Their opposition was whittled down to an occasional, scarcely whispered disparagement of Jewish nationalism, even as they raised funds for or used their enormous influence on behalf of Israel. It was no accident, then, that the greatest amount of giving, not only for charitable but for political purposes, has come from Jews, some of the more affluent of whom have even contributed to the candidates of both major parties so as to ensure a favored position for the interests of Israel.

Jewish wealth and acumen wields unprecedented power in the area of finance and investment banking, playing an important role in influencing U.S. policy toward the Middle East. While not true of the commercial banks, the financial houses of Wall Street have been and are dominated by Jews or are worried about Jews who may be their biggest customers. The great investment banking houses—led by Goldman, Sachs; Kuhn, Loeb & Company; Lazard Frères; Lehman Brothers; Salomon Brothers; and Loeb Rhoades & Company—have played a large role in financing modern corporate America and have exercised a great influence on the nation's economy. A vertiable Who's Who in American industry and corporate life can be obtained by listing the corporations on which these Jewish bankers have representation on the Boards of Directors. Any listing of inherited wealth cannot overlook the older families—the Warburgs, Kahns, Guggenheims, Seligmans, Gimbels, and Strausses—or such well-established San Francisco families as the Fleischakers, Haases, Lilienthals, Sutros, and Schwabackers.

Loeb Rhoades has also a considerable brokerage business and processes security transactions for some sixty correspondent firms around the country.[24] That is why this investment house was in a position to volunteer in 1974 to be of substantial assistance to the Zionist cause. Congress had placed a $730 million ceiling on military sales made on credit, which required Israel to borrow $300 million to cover part of her military purchases. Several commercial banks, anxious to curry favor with the Arabs, had balked at floating these securities. The U.S. government then did the unprecedented by guaranteeing for the first time an offering by a foreign country, a lengthy story the *New York Times* unabashedly broke on its front page.[25] Undertaking the chore at a much lower lending rate, Loeb Rhoades quickly sold the twenty-year securities to many of its customers across the country. Even as Secretary of State Henry Kissinger was pledging U.S. evenhandedness in an effort to persuade Anwar el-Sadat and Hafez al-Assad to proceed with disengagement, another branch of the government was guaranteeing a loan to complete the purchase of Israeli military procurements in the U.S.

No protest was registered, only praise was voiced, when Controller Harrison J. Goldin of New York City, then a bankrupt municipality, announced the $30 million, monthly installment purchase of these securities from the pension funds of the New York Teachers Retirement System. Los Angeles County, the City of Chicago, and the states of Michigan, Oregon, Tennessee, and Wisconsin announced purchase plans of the securities, as did the International Ladies Garment Workers Union (Secretary-Treasurer Sol C. Chaikin stated: "We're interested in it because it's for a good cause. But we wouldn't have done it if it had not been backed by the full faith and credit of the U.S. Government."). The Israeli Permanent Representative to the U.N. hailed the armament investment as a "significant contribution in the best American tradition of justice."[26]

In the larger metropolitan areas, the Jewish-Zionist connection thoroughly pervades affluent financial, commercial, social, entertainment, and art circles. In most cases there is not the slightest chance of bringing any reasonable persuasion to bear on people in these circles.

Nathan Cummings, the man who built Consolidated Foods Corporation and Sara Lee into a national institution, has more than 100 additional companies with which he is connected in some important manner. In the spring of 1977 he invited 700 people to be his guests on the occasion of his eightieth birthday in the grand ballroom of the Waldorf Astoria Hotel. Attending were such outspoken international Zionists and benefactors of Israel as British industrialist Sir Charles Clore, Canadian Edgar M. Bronfman of Seagram's, and Baron Edmund de Rothschild of Paris. Others present at the party included Charles G. Bluhdorn of Gulf & Western, Leonard Goldenson of American Broadcasting Company, Senator Jacob Javits, New York's Mayor Beame, Israeli Ambassador Simcha Dimitz, etc., etc.

At this $200,000 affair Bob Hope popped out of the 1,000-pound, 6-foot by 12-foot cake, to the applause of gathered notables from such companies as U.S. Steel, Coastal States Gas, Heinz's, Dillon Reed, Norton Simon, Bianca Commerciale Italiana, etc. No officer of these companies would ever dare think of uttering one word against Israel or Zionism, because they would instinctively think of "Nate Cummings." Although his precise views on Zionism might not be known to them, the evidence was there for all to see that he was a generous benefactor of Israel, and good business sense would compel any business acquaintance of his to fall in line with the thinking of "Our Crowd."

And there are tens of thousands of counterparts to the Cummings' connections. When one of his Jewish depositors withdrew his account (with only a $250,000 line of credit) in protest after David Rockefeller had allegedly joined other business leaders in warning President Nixon of the need for a new Middle East policy, the Chase president was forced to make a public statement that the U.S. "must do all it can to safeguard security and sovereign existence of Israel."

In the midst of the 1973–74 Middle East crisis, Charles Bluhdorn called on the Motion Picture Association of America to assume the lead in repricing "commodities unique to us that are exported to the oil-rich nations of the Middle East." The Viennese émigré was highly critical of American businessmen "quaking, fearful, afraid of anybody," who were bowing to the Arabs. The control of the Motion Picture Association, whose receipts hit a record high of $1.9 billion in 1974, rests heavily in Jewish hands. But Bluhdorn's influence extends far beyond the film industry. In addition to Paramount Pictures, Simon and Schuster and Pocket Books, this huge $3.39 billion (as of 1976) conglomerate has its fingers into manufacturing and production of auto and consumer appliances and energy products; raw sugar and cigars (Dutch Masters and El Producto); zinc and other metals; apparel products (Kayser-Roth); paper ("Paper Maid"); building products and automative replacement parts; as well as supplying a wide variety of financial services (group health and other insurance).

For many years readers of the *New York Times* have been intrigued by the full length, two-columned ads in behalf of Israel placed by A. N. Spanel. After disappearing for some months, Spanel suddenly re-emerged with his latest "public service" contributions signed by Spanel International, Ltd. His many previous ads had been under the auspices of International Latex, which became a part of the large, financially-troubled Rapid American conglomerate owned by multi-millionaire Meshulam Riklis. According to the *Wall Street Journal,* Riklis sets aside 20% of his income for donations to Jewish-Israeli groups and in 1972 loaned Hubert Humphrey $150,000 (of which he has been repaid only $6,000) for the Minnesota Senator's unsuccessful bid for the presidential nomination. Riklis' conglomerate also runs Schenley Industries, Lerner Shops and McCrory Variety and controls Kenton Corporation, among other companies.

A descendant of ten generations of rabbis and ordained himself before entering the business world, Eli M. Black was chairman of United Brands, one of the largest food processing companies, when he made the front-page headlines on February 4, 1975, by his 44-story plunge to death. A director of the PEC Israel Economic Company and very active in many Israelist organizations, the fifty-year-old suicide's varied business and art connections had included the American Securities Corporation, the American Seal Cap Corporation, John Morrell & Company (the fourth largest meat packer in the U.S.), United Fruit, Foster-Grant, and American Hoechst Corporation. Other interests of the Black empire, which reached into several Central and Latin American countries, included petrochemicals, the A&W International chain of drive-in restaurants, which are second only to McDonalds in the fast-food business; the Inter Harvest lettuce growing; and the TRT Telecommunications operating in Latin America and the U.S. President of the United Farm Workers Cesar Chaves was one of many from all walks of life paying tribute to the dead executive. It was on the ubiquitous contacts of the many Eli Blacks that the State of Israel constantly drew.

While *The French Connection* won an Oscar, a far more interesting film, but one that Hollywood dares not make, would be *The Jewish Connection.* Jewish bank directors not only have been serving as "pushers" for Israel Bonds but have on occasion boldly placed Israel's interests above those of their shareholders. In 1973 the Arabian Gulf Emirate of Abu Dhabi sought a substantial five-year loan from a consortium of European banks, which in turn invited the First National Bank of Chicago to take $25 million of the loan. The Chicago bank, in turn, asked a large Midwest regional bank to participate to the extent of $5 million. The regional bank, checking and finding that Abu Dhabi's credit was absolutely first-class, committed itself to the loan. When word of this reached two Jewish directors of the regional bank, they stormed in and demanded that the bank cancel the projected loan and buy Israel Bonds instead. The bank's officers acceded to the request that the loan commitment be withdrawn, at the same time refusing to put the money into Israel Bonds. It was disclosed that the bank would have enjoyed a $375,000 profit on the loan in the five-year period. As a result of the action of these two Jewish directors, the bank's stockholders lost that profit. However, no stockholders' action has been brought against the directors for betrayal of their trust in placing private political loyalties and the interests of a foreign state above those of its fiduciaries.

The right man in the right place in the Pentagon can perform wonders, particularly when he has some help from the Secretary of State. An amazing kind of politicking in U.S.-Israel relations at the highest level was revealed in an April 17, 1974, newspaper report by Saul Friedman of the *Philadelphia Inquirer*. The article centered on a swap between U.S. Jewish leadership and the Defense Department: support of a big budget for the Pentagon, something liberal-affiliated Organized Jewry usually opposes, in return for pledges to Israel from the U.S. government of a military, political, and economic nature.

A number of dinners and social functions had been given at which Secretary Kissinger and Admiral Elmo R. Zumwalt, Jr., outgoing Chief of Naval Operations, were alleged to have served as prime lobbyists among Jews on behalf of the Defense Department. Attending these meetings and buying the "deal" were such prominent leaders as David M. Blumberg, President of B'nai B'rith, and Ira Silverman, Director of the Institute for Jewish Policy Planning & Research, an arm of the Synagogue Council of America. The frank swapping of Jewish support for the Pentagon budget in return for U.S. support given Israel in the October 1973 war was referred to by Silverman, according to the Friedman story, "as the Pentagon lobbying of the Jewish lobby." There was nothing subtle about the approach of the military to the

Jewish leaders, according to Silverman: "We helped you; now you help us."

The Synagogue Council representative was also quoted as stating:

At the practical level, the case is made in more objective terms of self-interest, that just as the C-5 transport planes and aircraft carriers, items previously opposed by the would-be military budget slashes, were invaluable in support of Israel during the war, so will American military capacity in the future determine Israel's security.

The Friedman report continued as follows:

One Jewish leader, Herman Bookbinder, Washington representative for the American Jewish Committee, is among those who are rethinking their traditional views against defense spending. On his own initiative, Bookbinder called together colleagues in other Jewish groups "to take another look at the military budget."

Bookbinder was further quoted by Friedman as parroting the Defense Department's "propaganda" about its needs, caused by the fact that "more than a third of our [the USA] total inventory was chewed up in just a few weeks" (for Israel in the October war). Friedman had this striking observation to make about the previous similar experience of Jews: "The Jewish community was in a similar fix when the Johnson and Nixon administrations put pressure on Jewish leaders to moderate their opposition to the Vietnam War in exchange for support of Israel."[27]

The Friedman report as published merely touched on a tiny tip of the iceberg of an abysmal corrupting process that has been pervading the nation's capital wherever Israel has been concerned. The use of aid to Israel as bait in an international power play debased the corrupter and the corrupted alike. The promises to Israel were not only dangerously injurious to a sound national defense and the national economy, but illustrated the extent to which Israel had in fact become the fifty-first state, not as William Buckley once humorously referred but in dead seriousness.

Nor has the Pentagon been impervious to penetration, as the strange history of Joseph Churba illustrates. A childhood friend of Jewish Defense League's Rabbi Meir Kahane, their professional association began in 1965 when they set up Consultant Research Associates.[28] One of their first ventures was the Fourth of July Movement, an attempt to mobilize campus support for the war in Vietnam, for which they also co-authored the book *The Jewish Stake in Vietnam.* Churba was then an instructor at Adelphi College, studying for his doctorate at Columbia.

As far back as 1967, it was reported that he was part of the intelligence bureaucracy, a rumor Churba always denied. However, in 1971, he was employed as a professor of Middle East Studies at the U.S. Air Force University, Maxwell Air Force Base in Montgomery, Alabama. It was on a visit here that Major General George J. Keegan, Chief of Air Force Intelligence, met Churba, and the super-hawkish views of the general meshed perfectly with the vehement pro-Israel, anti-Soviet sentiments of the professor to build instantaneous bonds of friendship.

December 1972 found Churba in the most sensitive post of Special Advisor (on the Middle East) in Keegan's headquarters in Washington, where he speedily and avidly attempted to win proselytes for the Zionist cause. While there are scores of pro-Israel moles in the Pentagon, it has been the Air Force that has benefited most from the Israeli connection and the many area armed conflicts. Air warfare is in such a continual state of flux and its weapons so ephemeral that every bit of intelligence helps. Like the Israelis, the U.S. Air Force has always nursed a "first strike" mentality.

In a widely publicized New York Times interview of October 20, 1976, Churba accused the Pentagon of being unfair to Israel. He assailed Chairman of the Joint Chiefs of Staff George Brown's view that Israel was a "burden" as "dangerously irresponsible," claiming that this indicated a growing "tilt against Israel in the Defense Department." At this time, the Intelligence officer admitted to being an ordained rabbi, but vigorously denied this "biased his view in support of Israel."[29]

Churba resigned from his position after General Keegan was forced to strip him of his special security clearance for having spoken out publicly on security matters despite due warning. Shortly thereafter, the Times published a lengthy Churba letter arguing that Israel was of great strategic importance to the United States. On March 24, 1977, together with avid Israelist Joseph Sisco,[30] former Under Secretary of State and then president of the American University in Washington, he appeared on the televised "MacNeil/Lehrer Report," on which he criticized President Carter for presenting specific proposals as to the nature of a Middle East settlement favoring the Arabs. He declared that the Palestinians should not be included in the negotiations: "They are not relevant to the table."

The Times on August 25, 1977, carried a Churba letter, "West

Bank Settlements: Legality is not the Issue." That same month his former supervisor, General Keegan, shortly after he had retired from his post, was a guest of the Israeli government and was quoted in a lengthy *Jerusalem Post* front-page article praising the Zionist state as an outpost of Western democracy and an asset to US strategic military goals. Keegan called for more military aid for Israel, in particular F-15s, in order to make certain that there are no "deficiencies that are going to compromise the long-term position of Israel."[31]

In the Fall, the General and the professor teamed up in a crusade to reignite the cold war using Israel as "the single key to balancing Soviet imperialism in the Mediterranean," as Churba declared in *The Politics of Defeat: America's Decline in the Middle East*, a small "Vanity Fair" published book[32] which was widely reviewed due to the efforts of the American-Israel Public Affairs Committee in Washington whose assistance was gratefully acknowledged by the author. Churba's book, described by reviewer Mark Bruzonsky as "a historical interpretation, colored by devotion to Israel and near-paranoid anti-Soviet impulses,"[33] opposes de factor alliances with Egypt and Saudi Arabia, assails the notion of "Palestinian rights" as a fallacy, and calls for recognition of the thesis "that the pillars of stability in the region are Turkey, Iran and a secure Israel . . . bolstered by the fostering of a strongly independent Christian Lebanon."

The Jewish connection on the political level has been of even far greater consequence. Starting at least with the Franklin D. Roosevelt administration, important decision-making echelons of the U.S. government have been filled with many Jews. The New Dealers contained the broadest kind of list, ranging from Henry Morgenthau, Jr., Herbert Lehman, David Niles, and Samuel Rosenberg to Morris Ernst and Robert Nathan. Bernard Baruch played a unique role as adviser to five Presidents. David E. Lilienthal[34] and Lewis H. Strauss[35] were Chairmen of the Atomic Energy Commission. Under the brief rule of John F. Kennedy, Arthur Goldberg served as Secretary of Labor and Senator Abraham Ribicoff as Secretary of Health, Education and Welfare. The presence of Abe Fortas on the Supreme Court, until his resignation, was in the tradition of Justices Frankfurter, Cardozo, and Brandeis, who had previously served on the highest court in the land.

President Nixon used Henry Kissinger, Herbert Stein, Leonard Garment, Murray Chotiner, and other Jews in key positions. President Ford retained Garment's services and added to key White House posts Milton Freedman, L. William Seidman[36] and Alan Greenspan, among many. When Ford gave his State of the World speech on April 10,

1975, to a joint session of Congress, the TV eye that settled on the Cabinet was revealing. There was Secretary of State Kissinger, Secretary of Defense Schlesinger (born a Jew and now an Episcopalian), Attorney General Edward Levi, and HEW Secretary Casper Weinberger (Jewish grandfather). And to this extraordinary lineup of Jewish affluence could then be added for all practical purposes the President himself and Vice President Nelson Rockefeller, whose deep commitment to Zionism could be matched by no one, Jew or Gentile.

In critical 1977 as the new Carter administration turned major attention to the Middle East, the Zionist lobby in Washington was employing its wiles on the new 95th Congress, with its increased very friendly Democratic majority, and on the new occupant at the White House and on the Carter Cabinet, whose composition augured well indeed. W. Michael Blumenthal, the Secretary of the Treasury, was a Presbyterian whose parents were Jewish; Harold Brown, the Secretary of Defense, claimed no religious affiliation but likewise had a Jewish background. The same held for James Schlesinger, the former Secretary of Defense under Nixon and Ford and the first Secretary of Energy, who was a convert to Christianity. All three, because of their backgrounds, were even more vulnerable to Zionist pressures than if they had remained in their ancestral faith. Subject to blackmail from without and guilt from within, the easiest way to defend their flight from Judaism and show that they still "belong" in the family was to give fullest support to Israel's position. Two of the seven top aides of President Carter were his counsel Robert J. Lipshutz, once head of the B'nai B'rith in Atlanta, and Stuart E. Eizenstat, Assistant to the President for Domestic Affairs. Dr. Mark Siegel, top aide to Hamilton Jordan, President Carter's chief political adviser, served as liaison with Jewish groups (the position held in previous administrations by David Niles, Maxwell Rabb, Myer Feldman and Leonard Garment) until his resignation over Middle East policy on March 9, 1978.

At sub-Cabinet levels were other key Zionists, such as Deputy Secretary of the Treasury Kenneth Axelson, Undersecretary of the Treasury Anthony M. Solomon, Assistant Secretary of State for Economic and Business Affairs Julius M. Katz, and C. Arthur Borg, Executive Secretary of the State Department. The $1,000- to $5,000-a-plate Waldorf dinner, which replenished the Democratic party coffers to the tune of more than $1 million and was attended by President Carter, was cochaired by Krim, Steve Ross, and Mary Lasker.

While some of them had only minimal links with Zionist-Israelist organizations or their lobby, none wished to "rock any boats"; they were only too willing to quietly advance the interests of Israel, and conversely were appalled or frightened by anything pro-Arab or anti-Zionist that might pass over their desks.

Former Chairman of the Democratic National Committee Robert S. Strauss was appointed the President's special U.S. trade representative, and Arthur J. Goldberg, who had served under three Presidents, was designated Ambassador-at-large and Chairman of the American delegation to the October 1977 East-West Belgrade Conference on Human Rights. Goldberg, an avowed Zionist, became Board Chairman of the United Nations Association. Formerly known as the American Association for the United Nations, this group had played a key role in swinging U.S. public opinion behind the 1947 partition plan and since that time had followed the same staunch, unwavering pro-Israeli line. In 1975 association President James Leonard was one of the four panelists on the televised MacNeil-Lehrer Report who excoriated the U.N. for its resolution equating Zionism with racism.[37]

In 1968 the association had been given a $400,000 grant by the Ford Foundation to make an assessment, among other things, of the crisis in the Middle East. This grant was reminiscent of an analogous 1959 situation when the Senate Foreign Relations Committee let out a $25,000 contract for an impartial study of U.S. Middle East policy to the Institute for Mediterranean Affairs. By the time the Zionist composition of the Institute (mostly American and Israeli followers of Menachem Begin) was brought to the attention of Senator Fulbright and other members of the committee, it was too late to upset the contract. The committee subsequently discarded the obviously biased $25,000 report and reassigned the study to its own staff.

Other powerful groups and rich foundations have also been penetrated by the connectors. The Carnegie Foundation's Commission on the Middle East was allegedly a bipartisan group with both staunch pro-Israelis and pro-Arabs on it, according to Dr. Joseph E. Johnson, the former head of the foundation and "convenor" of the commission. On one side were such unquestionably devout Zionists as Senators Javits and Kennedy, and Brookings Institute President Kermit Gordon. The purported "balance" consisted of Chase Manhattan's David Rockefeller and former *Time* publisher James Linen, both of whom had some business interests in the Arab world but many more with Israel and American Israelists, and never dared lift a finger against Zionism. The commission's Executive Director was Larry L. Fabian, another Zionist.

Nowhere, however, has it been more apparent that the connection, not numbers, is what counts, than in the conduct of U.S. elected representatives in Congress, who have so thoroughly exemplified the maxim: Plus ça change, plus c'est la même chose (the more things change, the more they remain the same).

VII   Whose Congress: Thwarting the National Interest

> It could probably be shown by facts and figures that there is no distinctly native American criminal class except Congress.
>
> —Mark Twain

The reason for the remarkable political success achieved by the Jewish connection and the Zionist connectors lies deep in the American political system. Our system of representative government has been profoundly affected by the growing influence and affluence of minority pressure groups, whose strength invariably increases as presidential elections approach, making it virtually impossible to formulate foreign policy in the American national interest. And the Electoral College system has greatly fortified the position of the national lobbies established by ethnic, religious, and other minority pressure groups, the Jewish-Zionist Israel lobby in particular.

An added tower of strength to the Jewish connection has been the Jewish location: 76 percent of American Jewry is concentrated in sixteen cities of six states—New York, California, Pennsylvania, Illinois, Ohio, and Florida—with 181 electoral votes. It takes only 270 electoral votes to elect the next President of the U.S. Our Chief Executive is chosen by a plurality of the Electoral College votes, not of the popular vote. Under this system the votes of a state go as a unit to the candidate winning a plurality of voters, which endows a well-organized lobby with a powerful bargaining position. For example, in the presidential election of 1884 in the State of New York, Democratic candidate Grover Cleveland received 563,015 popular votes while his Republican rival, James G. Blaine, received 562,011 votes. With a bare 1,004 plurality, Cleveland received all of New York's electoral votes, resulting in his election. A change of 503 votes would have shifted the election to Blaine. This explains why the politicians have been mesmerized by fear of the "Jewish vote" and by those who claim they can deliver the "swing vote" in a hotly contested state.

The will of the majority has often been frustrated. Three Presidents—John Quincy Adams in 1824, Rutherford B. Hayes in 1876, and Benjamin Harrison in 1888—were elected with fewer popular votes than their leading opponents.[1] But it is the Cleveland 1884 election that is the classic example, under the prevailing system, of how a minority group such as the Zionists possesses a potent bargaining strength by pandering the votes of a bloc.

The inordinate Israelist influence over the White House, the Congress, and other elected officials stems principally from the ability to pander the alleged "Jewish vote" as well as fill the campaign coffers of both parties with timely contributions on a national as well as local level, while taking full advantage of the anachronistic system by which American Presidents are elected.

None of the many powerful political lobbies in Washington is better entrenched than the meticulously organized brokers of the "Jewish vote." The individual Jew who might not go along with Zionist ideology or Jewish nationalism is too cowardly to speak up and take the usurpers of his voice to task, and so the peddling of his vote goes forward. Hence the happy alliance dating back to World War I between the supine American politicians and the Zionists, who have controlled the Congress in its near 100 percent pro-Israel stance.

Occasionally a member of the House of Representatives has earned a Congressional Medal of Honor for bravery, as did Silvio O. Conte of Pittsfield, Massachusetts, in 1970 for exposing a most sordid legislative deal involving the Middle East. Conte revealed that the House had accepted a Senate $2.5 billion proviso covering grants for various specified institutions in Israel in exchange for senatorial acceptance of the authority to extend easy credit to foreign countries purchasing American arms (including Israel, of course). The Senate had done the unprecedented in voting grants for specific institutions of a foreign country: $500,000 for the Weizmann Institute; $1,250,000 for Igud Leiluf Hanoar; $500,000 for Hahaiyim Girls College; and $250,000 for the Vocational School of the Underprivileged.

The House and Senate versions of the foreign aid appropriations bill were as yet unreconciled when the Conference Committee came up with a deal accepting the appropriation for Israeli institutions against an allowance of money for military sales. At this juncture Conte proposed that the conference recess for twenty-four hours so "I can go out and get a school in Israel and get a piece of the action."

"Are you insinuating . . . ?" Wyoming Senator Gale McGee, Chairman of the subcommittee, started to ask indignantly. Conte interjected: "I am not insinuating anything." He continued, "I just don't understand how these projects, never requested by the State Department, got into the bill, and I think the whole procedure stinks."

In late June 1973 the same kind of venal scene was repeated when Republican Senate leader Hugh Scott tried to push through an amendment that would have restored reductions to the military aid bill and included a proviso for "supporting assistance" (a form of military aid) to Israel. The Scott Amendment would have increased the new support of Israel from $50 million to $70 million. But three Democratic Senators—Frank Church of Idaho, Birch Bayh of Indiana, and Stuart Symington of Missouri—outbid the Republican leader by introducing a substitute amendment that raised the grant to Israel to $85 million and at the same time preserved the Senate Foreign Relations Committee's reductions in the overall military program.

Both sides unabashedly accused the other of engaging in a "bidding contest." Senator Scott, who owed his presence in the Upper House in no small way to his ceaseless exploitation of the "Jewish vote," complained bitterly when he was being outmaneuvered, his favorite weapon being used against him. The Church substitute, the Pennsylvania Senator charged, "tries to increase the amount for Israel, hoping all Senators who are motivated by the Jewish vote will immediately rush in and support the substitute. . . . This is simply an attempt to say to the Senators, as they walk through the door just before the vote, 'We raised the amount of money for Israel. You want to vote for that, don't you?' "

Senator Bayh countered: "It appears almost as if this very important authorization to help sustain democracy in Israel is being used as a blackmail effort to get several times that amount to spend we know not where and we know not for what."

The attempt to table the Church substitute failed 37 to 35. The substitute then was adopted by a margin of 54 to 21. On the final ballot fourteen members of this "fearless" body, who had voted with Scott and the administration on the tabling resolution, deserted because they adamantly refused to appear on the record as against the larger $35 million increase for Israel.

Obviously, one group of politicians who are most likely to be under the control of the Zionist lobby are those who represent populations with a large percentage of Jews. And no place fits this description more than New York City and New York State. Of the approximately

6.3 million Jews in the U.S., 2 million live in Greater New York City and some 2.2 million in New York State. As one New York City congressman expressed it to a reporter for *The New Yorker,* "support of military aid for Israel was about the same to his district as support of dams and reclamation projects was to a congressman from the West.[2] It is hardly surprising to find that most of New York's politicians, whether they be Christians or Jews, have virtually been speaking as ambassadors of Israel.

This has taken many forms. In 1968 a bloc of congressmen, principally from New York State and led by Representative Seymour Halpern, initiated action in the House to prevent any resumption by the U.S. of normal diplomatic relations with the United Arab Republic. The "sense of Congress" resolution for which the Representative from Queens gained the support of twenty-four congressmen would have required the Nasser government first to enter "into meaningful negotiations with the government of Israel" before Washington and Cairo restored relations.

A spate of critical speeches in the House in the wake of the U.N. censure of Israel for its March 1968 attack on Jordan led the vote-conscious Halpern to give vent once more to his Arab-phobia and prove that he was the number-one Zionist protagonist in the House. On several previous occasions Congressman Halpern had labored to attract the attention of his Queens constitutents by excoriating the Jordanians and introducing other "sense of Congress" resolutions, either seeking to bar the U.A.R. from membership on the Security Council or to halt American aid to Arab nations "which discriminate against American citizens." (A charge of juggling income tax returns forced a premature retirement from the Congress of this stalwart Zionist.)

When Catholic Robert Kennedy decided to move and represent New York in the Senate, he had to assume an even more pro-Israeli stance than he had in his home state of Massachusetts. It was in that 1968 campaign that the "Support Israel Above All" campaign moved into high gear, and tragedy eventually ensued. In a frantic quest for votes, Robert Kennedy became more Jewish than any rabbi. This Irish Catholic, appearing in synagogues wearing a yarmulke and prayer shawl, called for an end to any aid for Arab countries and, at the same time, for the sale of fifty Phantom jets to Israel, to replace those lost in the 1967 war. Since Israel had bombed and napalmed Palestinian refugee camps and seized masses of Arab territory, including all that remained of Palestine, young Palestinian refugee Sirhan Sirhan, who was watching the Senator on television, fled the room in angry tears, his hands covering his ears, and scribbled in his notebook: "RFK must die."

Kennedy's assassination did not, unfortunately, deter other politicians from pandering to Zionist interests in varied and sundry ways. No one could have been the least surprised when the Nelson Rockefeller drive for reelection as Governor of New York was launched in the late spring of 1970 by means of a full-page advertisement on Middle East policy under the signature of a new "American Committee for a Lasting Peace." Rocky's idea of creating stability in the area was to "strengthen Israel's capacity to cope with the Soviet-Arab strategy of attrition being waged against her." In the ad the word "Palestinian" did not appear once. Rockefeller was competing with the ever-alert Ambassador Arthur Goldberg, the Democratic nominee, for the Jewish vote. With a choice like this, between the proverbial Tweedledum and Tweedledee, the people of New York State had little option in that year of Middle East crisis.

When congressmen start indulging in their favorite sport of vying for the "Jewish vote," one can be sure it is another election year without even consulting the calendar. Although leading economists, including Federal Reserve Board Chairman Arthur Burns, had called for a cut in government spending as a means of halting inflation and the growing recession, the House Foreign Affairs Committee[3] in the summer of 1974 increased economic grants in aid to Israel from $50 million to $250 million. Where the administration had recommended $300 million in military credit sales, the committee altered this by approving $200 million in credit and $100 million in the form of a grant. Florida Congressman Dante Fascell (from the Miami district) justified the increase by referring to the "massive Soviet supply to Egypt and Syria and Israel's mounting external debt and declining foreign exchange reserves."

The interjection of the Arab-Israeli conflict into the local political scene has often been tortuously and ludicrously accomplished.[4] In his 1974 campaign to oust New York Republican Jacob Javits, who has often appeared to be Israel's delegate to the U.S. Senate, former Attorney General Ramsey Clark embarrassed would-be supporters with his gross ignorance of both the causes of the energy crisis and other facts of the Middle East conflict. In his half-page advertisement in the New York Sunday *Times,* the Democratic candidate emulated every other politician's chauvinistic approach as he foolishly attempted to outbid his opponent for the Jewish vote. Every cliché ever invoked by endless rhetoricians on this subject was used, including a categorical downgrading of the Palestinian problem as "more the symptom than the cause of the area's unrest."

In the gubernatorial campaign of that same year, the *New York Post* ran the headline "Gov. Candidates Woo Ethnic Vote" and the subhead "Wilson: I Am All Out For Israel." This story included a picture of the staid New York Governor Malcolm Wilson, a Catholic, wearing a yarmulke on his head as he attended a fund-raising Waldorf Astoria dinner given by the Orthodox Shaarez Zedek Hospital in Jerusalem. Wilson was quoted as saying: "I, like other Americans, rejoice in Israel's victories over her enemies"—this even as Secretary Kissinger was winding his way through the Arab Middle East in an effort to prove that the U.S. was hewing to its announced new evenhanded course, so necessary for maintaining the peace momentum and, even more importantly, for any hope of lowering oil prices and stemming the economic collapse of the Western world. On the day before the elections, Wilson had a full-page *New York Times* ad proclaiming: "Protest Against Terror and Injustice Day."

His rival, Hugh Carey, managed to outbid Wilson in his support of Israel, and won the election handily. The following June Israeli Premier Yitzhak Rabin, who was in the U.S. for talks with Secretary Kissinger, made a point of coming through New York to confer with two of his top delegates in America, the Governor of New York State and the Mayor of New York City. It was something of an "I'll puff up your political image and you'll fill up my coffers" deal. Carey, interviewed on television news as he emerged from his conference with Rabin, shamelessly informed the assembled reporters: ". . . and I told [Rabin] not to pay any attention to what the polls might show . . . the people of the state have not wavered in their support of Israel and will continue to give that support."

Here was an elected American official telling the head of a foreign government that it is this foreign state's interests that will prevail, even over the expressed will of a majority of Americans. If any other country but Israel had been given such a blank check, Carey would have been up for treason the next morning.

A year earlier, in 1973, during the New York Democratic mayoralty primary contest, the four candidates had made the customary foreign policy interjections into the campaign. The winner, Controller Abraham Beame, called the proposed sale of American Phantom jets to Saudi Arabia "a dangerous action" that could "escalate the belligerent Arab rhetoric to actual war." The other B's—Blumenthal, Badillo, and Biaggi—competed with the victorious Beame in various paeans of praise for Israel, not one of which related cause to effect. And in the ensuing election campaign, Republican John Marchi could not refrain from attempting to outbid his rival on this critical issue.

Needless to say, Beame never let his side down. One of his first acts upon assuming the office of Mayor was to hold a fund-raising gala for Israel at Gracie Mansion, the Mayor's official residence. Only when reproached by an Arab group, and reminded that Arab-Americans also pay taxes in the city, did he half apologize for using the official residence to raise money for a foreign government, and promise never to do it again.

As his successor, Edward Koch, was to do, Beame's predecessor, John V. Lindsay, throughout his terms of office conducted himself more like the Mayor of Tel Aviv than of the largest city in the U.S. In 1966, when King Faisal of Saudi Arabia was invited to Washington as the personal guest of President Johnson for important talks, the Mayor dishonored the White House in the same manner as had his predecessor, Mayor Robert F. Wagner, Jr., on the occasion of the earlier visit of the then ruling King Saud, by making it understood that the Saudi Arabian monarch was not welcome in the city. Plans for a large reception at the Metropolitan Museum of Art were canceled by Mayor Lindsay after the invitations had been sent out. King Faisal had told a luncheon press gathering in Washington that Jews in America who followed Zionist leadership in assisting Israel were the enemy of his country. For some weeks previously, Zionist groups had been pressuring Lindsay to turn his back on the Saudi king. The Mayor took advantage of the monarch's Washington remarks to cancel the reception and to compete with Republican attacks on the visiting Saudi leader.

A page out of this venal political book was reenacted when President Georges Pompidou visited the U.S. in February 1970 after his bitter dispute with the Israelis over the planes and submarines the French government refused to release. John Lindsay's behavior raised a very real question. His boycott of President Pompidou's first visit to the U.S. as chief executive exposed the ambitions of New York's mayor for office far beyond the confines of the Hudson River. Only this could have prompted him to act as he did in the face of a guest of the President of the U.S. on a very important visit. After the assumption of the Presidency by Richard Nixon, U.S. relations with France had improved, and the New York Mayor did his very best to destroy the new ties.

In between the insults to Faisal and Pompidou, Lindsay lavishly received and entertained Golda Meir, Israel's Prime Minister. More taxpayers' money was spent on her entertainment than had ever been expended by the city for the many fabulous receptions held under Grover Whelan or Robert Patterson, former V.I.P. official greeters.

The blatant Lindsay performance even led columnist William F. Buckley, Jr., normally a strong Israeli proponent, to comment in his column "On the Right":

Jewish leaders in New York City should surely speak out against the vulgarization of diplomacy by Mr. Lindsay. "I do not think it is fitting that our great City pay homage to a foreign President Georges Pompidou who displayed such contempt for world peace," commented the Mayor, seconded by Congressman Podell of Brooklyn. Can anyone imagine his saying the same thing if the French had just finished sending 100 million dollars worth of jet planes to Israel? It is humiliating for a proud people to be subject to the social and diplomatic equivalent of currying favor by eating blintzes.[5]

After Lindsay threw his hat into the presidential arena in 1971, the affairs of the City of New York went from bad to worse. At city expense, accompanied by *city* employees still on the *city* payroll, Lindsay commuted between City Hall, Florida, and other primary states, vying in blatant appeals for the "Israel-First" vote with the other Democratic senatorial aspirants for the White House—Humphrey of Minnesota, Jackson of Washington, Muskie of Maine, McGee of North Dakota, and Hughes of Iowa. The result was the Florida "bagels and lox" primary, a disgraceful exhibition on how low candidates for high office will bow in the quest for votes.

In switching over to the Democratic party, Lindsay apparently had failed to do his homework. Otherwise he could never have been so totally unfamiliar with these strong words of Woodrow Wilson, his new party's standard-bearer in 1912 and 1916: "A man who thinks of himself as belonging to a particular national group has not yet become an American. And the man who goes among you to trade upon your nationality is not worthy to live under the Stars and Stripes."

In choosing the Florida primaries as the initial test of strength in his bid for the presidential nomination, New York's not-too-unbright John V. Lindsay was well aware of the large bloc of former New Yorkers who had fled to the sunshine of the South and were not immune to a blatant pro-Israel stand. But the Mayor ran a poor fifth in the Florida sweepstakes won by George Wallace, with Hubert Humphrey, the only candidate who had called on Washington to recognize Jerusalem as Israel's capital and insisted it was "wrong not to have done so in the beginning," coming in second.

Meanwhile the city, which had elected him and paid him a hand-some salary, continued to suffer from sordid scandals in connection with the Development Program, the Police Department, the Municipal Loan and Housing Program, etc., as well as sundry deficiencies and incompetencies—all of which were the precursors of the city's near-bankruptcy in 1976.

In pursuit of the Jewish vote, Lindsay never failed to advance Israelist propaganda, even when it added to the existing dangers ad-herent in the Middle East conflict. His verbal intervention in behalf of Soviet Jewry at the time of the Leningrad trials was another manifesta-tion of the venal politician grasping for votes, helping only to encour-age the Soviet Union's hard stand. This incessant interference in the lives of Jewish nationals in other countries, marked by an educational campaign to encourage emigration to Israel as well as to instill a primary loyalty for Israel through the mischievous equation of political Zionism with spiritual Judaism, was exceedingly dangerous. The ensu-ing harsh Leningrad sentences could be partly attributed to the Soviet reaction to the interference by worldwide Jewish leaders and the su-pine politicians holding the mayoralties of large U.S. cities.

Pursuing the same politics on the Israeli question to the bitter end, the Mayor early in 1973, in cooperation with the Metropolitan Museum of Art, brought an exhibit of previously unshown archaeolog-ical treasures from Jerusalem as the pièce de résistance, the center-piece in the New York celebration of the twenty-fifth anniversary of Israel's independence. It seemed to matter very little to the Museum, and less, of course, to the Mayor, that most of the major elements in the proposed exhibition were taken during the six-day war from Jor-danian territory and legally belonged to non-Israeli owners. This scheme had been cooked up while Lindsay was in Jerusalem on a goodwill trip as guest of Mayor Teddy Kollek.

There were other Lindsay counterparts with their own fancy poli-ticking making peace in the Middle East more impossible. Despite attempts by fair-minded citizens and inept Arab-Americans on the West Coast to stop him, Los Angeles Mayor Sam Yorty allocated $25,000 for the partial underwriting of the costs of extra internal security at the Jerusalem fair held in his city to celebrate Israel's quar-ter of a century. The date had been moved up to suit the convenience of the city, just as has been done so often with our own holidays. In his memorandum to the City Council, Yorty also indicated that an additional $25,000 would be asked from the County of Los Angeles.

Despite a vigorous protest against this wanton abuse of power in the disbursement of public funds, both legislative bodies yielded to the pressure applied and voted for the needed monies.

Recession or no recession, energy crisis or no energy crisis, Israel managed to retain its fifty-first-state status, as far as Congress was concerned. In 1974, at the same moment that the President was slashing appropriations for the health and education of the American people and vetoing legislation that would have increased veterans' benefits, a rump meeting of the Israeli hawks on the Senate Foreign Relations Committee met and upped the appropriations to Israel for the next fiscal year some $389 million over what the administration had requested. Chairman Senator J. William Fulbright, other key members, and staff were never apprised of the meeting that was held under the leadership of Senator Humphrey, whose coconspirators included such well-known Zionist Senators as Jacob Javits, Clifford Case, and Gale W. McGee.

Politics, it has been said, makes strange bedfellows, but the Middle East conflict makes even stranger ones. Senators who on almost every other issue were a million miles apart have found themselves in agreement when it came to Israel. In an April 1975 CBS television interview, South Dakota's Senator George McGovern and Idaho's Frank Church, doves on Vietnam, were at swords point with New York's Senator James Buckley as to U.S. policy in Southeast Asia. But all was milk and honey when the Senators discussed the virtues of Israel vis-à-vis the Arab world, and all concurred that "our only ally must never be deserted." At the time of the oil embargo, liberal Senators once violent Vietnam doves, and "progressive" academicians, including four Nobel economic laureates, joined with conservative Senators and right-wingers in pronouncements bristling with antagonism toward the Arabs.

The extent of the inconsistency brought out on Capitol Hill by the Middle East conflict is illustrated in an apocryphal story told by General Ira C. Eaker:

The Javits fighter, closely resembling the F-4 Phantom, is a multi-purpose airplane named for its designer, the senior Senator from New York. When it flies over Hanoi, it is clearly provocative and likely to initiate World War III. But when it flies over Cairo, with Israeli markings, it is obviously in defense of freedom[6]

One of the stars of the pro-Israel troupe is a man who, on the face of it, might be excused from duty on the front lines. He comes from a state as far from Israel or the Middle East as possible, and one with a negligible Jewish population. He has taken on many other causes and issues as his own, so he could hardly be said to "need" Israel as a talking point. But Israel has had no greater friend in all of the U.S. than Senator Henry (Scoop) Jackson, a Democrat from the State of Washington.

At the Century Plaza Hotel in Los Angeles, where 1,100 people gathered in rich regalia, Jackson launched his 1976 presidential campaign on January 26, 1975. Many prominent California Jewish philanthropists and political angels were present; some paid the minimum $250 into the war chest for the privilege of attending, others paid much more. A five-minute documentary on Jackson was created by producer David Wolper to boost the uninspiring image of the Senator, to whom Zionist supporter James Wechsler of the *New York Post* had referred as "the insistent bore."

The Washington Senator's greatest contribution to Israel had come in 1970 when he drafted Section 501 to the Defense Procurement Act[7] giving the President blanket authority to grant unlimited military purchase credits for Israel. House Speaker John McCormack, himself always a dedicated Zionist supporter, was forced to admit: "I have never seen in my forty-two years as a member of this body language of this kind used in an authorization or an appropriation bill. . . ." The investment of such power in the President of the United States obviously made him the number-one target of the Israeli lobby.

In 1970 President Nixon had used this authorization to give Israel $500 million. When the President only asked for $582 million military aid for fifteen countries, including Israel, under the next year's budget, Jackson criticized the Nixon action as "wholly inadequate both as to amount and terms." Israel was slated to receive only $300 million of this, and her many friends, led by Jackson, were up in arms. Under the impetus of stories carried by the Jewish Telegraphic Agency and *Near East Report,* picked up by the *New York Times* and the media in general, a vast campaign was opened to bypass Senator Fulbright's Foreign Relations Committee, which had jurisdiction over routine military sales, and to force the President to invoke the authority under Jackson's Section 501 so as to give Israel much more. This tour de force was successful.

In 1972 part of the bidding for presidential primary votes centered on competitive legislative efforts to increase resettlement aid for would-be emigrant Soviet Jews. While the Jackson proposal, which called for $250 million for a two-year period, was defeated in the

Senate Foreign Relations Committee by a more modest $85 million bill of Senator Edmund Muskie of Maine, the spectacle of who could offer most in support of Zionism's Soviet Jewry gambit was all too reminiscent of the voting auction in which Governor Dewey, Senator Taft, and President Truman had vied in the 1946 congressional elections to see who would offer more visas to Palestine.[8]

Senator Fulbright protested even the smaller amount: "Here, we are proposing to give $85 million to Israel when I am having trouble getting $8 million for a road in Arkansas because funds are short." Similarly, Democratic Senator Stuart Symington of Missouri, usually a strong proponent of Zionist legislation, noted that the Israeli lobby might be "overreaching itself."

The Jackson-Vanik Amendment to the 1972 U.S. trade agreement with the U.S.S.R. linked the granting of trade privileges for the Soviet Union to the removal of emigration barriers imposed on Soviet Jews. With Senators Javits and Ribicoff, Jackson pressed for the barring of credit to the Kremlin as additional leverage to force Moscow to release Jews. While making votes for Jackson at home, these restrictions spelled rejection by the U.S.S.R. of the long-negotiated agreement. Although President Ford expressed sympathy for the "plight" of Soviet Jewry, in his "State of the World" address in April 1975 he called for the rejection of the amendment so that progress toward increased détente between the U.S. and the U.S.S.R. might continue. Jackson stood firm as the foremost champion of the Israel lobby and continued to clamor in behalf of Soviet Jewish emigration.

The question naturally arises: Why should Senator Jackson go to such trouble for Israel and the Jews? Why is he such a determined, not to say hysterical, activist on their behalf? Or, as Saudi Arabian Ambassador to the U.N. Jamil Baroody once expressed it, "Who is this Henry Jackson 6,000 miles away who is more Jewish than the Jews, and more Zionist than the Zionists?"

At least to an ex-Senate colleague it was quite obvious what made "Scoop" tick. One of the Republican stalwarts in the upper House, Vermont's George D. Aiken, who retired after thirty-four years, having served long on the Foreign Relations Committee, spoke up very frankly in his published Senate diaries:

Senator "Scoop" Jackson got about 70 of his colleagues to join in a resolution which would sharply restrict trade with Russia just as a better understanding between Russia and the U.S. is developing and more tolerance towards the Jews by the U.S.S.R. is beginning to appear. Ostensibly, my Senatorial colleagues condemned Russia for charging an excessive exit fee to Jews who wished to leave the Soviet Union, but Russia permitted over 30,000 to leave last year, a figure many times the number that used to be permitted to leave annually. . . .

Frankly, I believe that the leaders of this move to incite more trouble and probable war in the Middle East, which would involve both Russia and the U.S., are prompted by two principal motives. First, as leaders of what some folks might call the "War Party" in the U.S., they were defeated in their efforts to keep the conflict in Indochina continuing at high speed until a military victory was won. Their position on Indochina, of course, would have meant a lot more business for the manufacturers of war materials in the U.S. The second reason lies in the fact that if Russia could be taunted or persuaded to give more aid to the Arabs and more trouble to Israel, then these stalwart champions, several of whom have high political ambitions, could rush to the aid of Israel, competing with each other to see who could offer the most, militarily and otherwise, in support of that small independent country.

Why are they so devoted to Israel? In my opinion, it is because the Jewish people in America are among this country's most spectacular campaign fundraisers and staunchest political workers, and certainly could be expected to be most generous in their contributions of support to those who promised the most American assistance to their brethren in the Middle East. I think my most ambitious colleagues are making a mistake. Mrs. Meir and other top officials know the differences between real friends and allies and those who are making loud noises and promises for the purpose of getting support for the next election campaign.[9]

And "Scoop" was running for the Presidency of the United States. His many services for Israel won him the unflagging support of Zionists and Israelists alike. The contribution lists in both his presidential efforts were studded with names of Jewish contributors from New York, Miami, and California. It was estimated that as much as 80 percent of the money he raised in 1975 for his 1976 bid came from Jews.[10]

Among Jackson's principal Jewish contributors were oil man Leon Hess of Amerada Hess, who allegedly channeled some $225,000 to Jackson, directly or indirectly. Among the other important contributors, who gave nearly $1.5 million, were Leon Davis of the Colonial Penn Group of New York and his wife; Max Karl of NGIG Investment Corporation of Milwaukee; investment banker William R. Solomon; and Charles Wolstetter, chairman of Continental Telephone Corporation of Virginia. People helping in the Jackson campaign at the topmost level included Stanley Golub, a wealthy jeweler and a stalwart supporter of Israel, but more on the liberal side than the Senator, and

Jerry Hoeck, a wealthy retired Seattle advertising executive who had met Jackson during the 1972 campaign.

Under new federal legislation, the U.S. government matches, up to $5 million, funds raised by presidential nominees if they can raise $5,000 in gifts of under $250 in twenty different states. It was very simple for UJA legmen to get Jackson the needed twenty contributors in any state in fifteen minutes.

While he had a falling out with George Meany, determined opponent of détente, over the Soviet trade bill, Jackson worked very closely both with labor leaders who were on most intimate terms with the Zionist Establishment and, more importantly, with the Israel lobby, which has become intrinsic to the warp and woof of the U.S. political system for the past thirty years.

This lobby has fully infiltrated and integrated itself within our national elective process. Show me a man who is running for President, and I will show you invariably a politician who will not dare offend this potent lobby. Show me a legislator in either branch of the Congress, and I will show you an officeholder who invariably bows to this powerful pressure group.

The ability of the American Israel Public Affairs Committee (AIPAC), the Zionist lobby established in Washington under the dedicated, able leadership of I. L. (Si) Kenen, to hard-sell Representatives and Senators of both parties, is a matter of record. The entire American Jewish community is represented in AIPAC through the presence of the potent umbrella grouping, the Conference of Presidents of Major Jewish Organizations.[11] Kenen's weekly *Near East Report,* with a claimed circulation in excess of 30,000 subscribers, goes to every congressman (as well as every Arab embassy) on a paid or free basis, and maintains links with every important member on the Hill. When an issue important to Israel comes before Congress, Kenen alerts at least 1,000 Jewish leaders scattered across the country, who in turn activate their own web of friends, letter writers, and important campaign contributors. Such a system cannot be denied.

The Jewish connection is invaluable to the work of the lobby. Where Kenen wished to obtain a conservative Southern WASP as cosponsor of the Jackson-Vanik Amendment so as to facilitate passage, the American Jewish Committee's Washington representative, Hyman Bookbinder, phoned this organization's chapter chairman, who was a law partner of Georgia's Senator Herman Talmadge, and the deal was swiftly consummated.

Whereas other pressure groups on other subjects may have to

comb congressional offices arguing the merits of certain proposals in order to gain the necessary affirmative votes, the Israel lobby channels information to its many allies in Congress, rounds up scores of assured votes when they are needed, and has the pleasant task of urging well-intentioned, overly eager members not to wander off with their own competing legislation in support of Israel.

In 1969, on the occasion of Israel's twenty-first birthday, a group of 59 Senators[12] and 238 Representatives lent their names to an advertisement that appeared in the Sunday *New York Times* (May 11, 1969), reproduced "as a public service by the American Israel Public Affairs Committee." This congressional Israel birthday declaration, one of the most vociferously pro-Israel and anti-Arab pronouncements then to have been publicly promulgated, attacked U.N. resolutions censuring Israel, called for face-to-face negotiations, and contained no reference whatsoever to the humanitarian needs, let alone the political rights, of the Palestinian Arabs. This categorical and cynical outpouring included no single word that even implied that the Middle East struggle was a two-sided dispute and that the Arabs, as well as the Israelis, had a case.

As shocking as it was to the most hardened cynic to see 297 legislators lend their names in support of a document drafted in the interests of a foreign country and reproduced as an advertisement for public consumption, some explanation can be found in the increased activities and growing power of this lobby on the one hand, and the abject fear of the legislators on the other. The Zionists were now extending their influence beyond the larger electoral college states into the heartland of the country.

But sometimes there is more to a political outpouring like this than meets the eye. The truth was exposed when Paul W. Lapp of the Pittsburgh Theological Seminary called the attention of his congressman, Robert J. Corbett, to a basic contradiction between the opinions expressed in a letter written him by Corbett on May 1 and his signature on the birthday declaration. Lapp pulled no punches in his documented letter. Congressman Corbett's reply stated that he had been invited, through a phone call to one of his staff, "to join in a birthday greeting to the State of Israel," to which he readily agreed. But as the congressman went on to say, he had not agreed "to be part of any policy statement nor of any newspaper ad" and still stood by his earlier statement to his constituent "that our best interests are not served by taking a strong stance in favor of either side in the Middle East dispute."

During the height of the 1973 war a thirty-six-hour "phone blitz," to quote Kenen himself, by AIPAC on October 18 resulted in the immediate introduction of legislation in both Houses to transfer "Phantom aircraft and other equipment in the quantities needed by Israel to repel aggressors" in the amount of $2.2 billion. This resolution was cosponsored by 67 Senators, including Humphrey, Jackson, Ribicoff, and Javits, while in the House there were 237 cosponsors. A massive campaign led to passage of this military aid bill, as well as defeat of an attempt to strip $500 million from the legislation. Firing off ninety-five telegrams to members of the House Appropriations and Foreign Affairs Committees, Kenen saw to it that the proposed cut was immediately restored. All told, the Israeli aid package, including $400 million that had been voted earlier, came to a thumping $2.6 billion.

Of particular help to the Israelist lobbying were conservatives who, Kenen liked to point out, regard Israel as a source of strength against Communist-backed regimes and "a bulwark against the totalitarian threat." Liberals, of course, pointed to the "democratic way of life in Israel." Thus this alert lobby played both sides of the political street, and successfully.

Even the influential Chairman of the House International Relations Committee (the new name for the House Foreign Relations Committee) found himself forced to bow to Zionist power. The views of Wisconsin's Democratic Representative Clement J. Zablocki, favoring across-the-board reductions in military exports to the Middle East, including Israel, repeatedly clashed on the House floor with members of the "Israel First" bloc. Direct confrontations between him and New York's Democratic Congressman Benjamin S. Rosenthal came to a head when Zablocki countered a Rosenthal resolution calling for the veto of a proposed $1.5 billion military sales package to Saudi Arabia by introducing a resolution to veto a proposed sale of F-15 planes to Israel, reportedly amounting to $600 million for twenty-five aircraft and support (both sales were ultimately cleared by the House). Believing in "calling a spade a spade,"[13] the Wisconsin Democrat had also invariably protested labeling military grants to Israel as "credit sales." Repayment of half of the $2.7 billion program for fiscal years 1976 and 1977 as military credit sales to Israel was to be forgiven. Zablocki also voted on June 28, 1976, against the foreign aid bill of which Israel was to be chief beneficiary.

Rosenthal, with the aid of other "Israel-Firsters" and the AIPAC boys, moved to block Zablocki from assuming chairmanship of the Committee for International Relations in the 95th Congress. After a bitter behind-the-scenes conference, an amicable arrangement was worked out. Zablocki has not since opposed any of Israel's ambitions on Capitol Hill. In March 1977 he even addressed a meeting of the Zionist Organization of America, explaining that his disdain for "excessive military amounts of foreign aid did not undermine his commitment to the freedom, independence, and security of Israel." He expressed the hope that ". . . the United States would enter into a formal security commitment with Israel. . . ."[14]

During the important debate on the anti-Arab boycott legislation, of which his "friend" Rosenthal was an important sponsor, the now safely confirmed Chairman did not say a word that would have displeased his former adversaries. And when, in the course of the debate on this measure, Democratic Congressman Lee Hamilton of Indiana took the floor, and after first pointing to his ofttime support of Israel, reminded the legislators that as members of the U.S. Congress, not of the Israeli Knesset, "the interests of the U.S. should be our primary concern," Zablocki did not blanch.

What Zablocki had once been preaching and what Hamilton had said in the House might have been particularly addressed to Hubert Humphrey with real meaning. As a member of the Senate Foreign Relations Committee, the former Vice President voted against the sale of 650 Maverick missiles to Saudi Arabia because, as he wrote a constituent: "I do not believe that the U.S. should provide this technologically sophisticated offensive weapon to countries *which could be in a potential state of belligerency with an American ally in the Middle East.*"[15] (Italics added.) Never once had the Senator opposed sending to Israel any of the billion dollars of offensive weapons voted by the Congress over many years.

Another of the lobby's fervent supporters in Washington, Congressman Robert Drinan, the first Roman Catholic priest elected to Congress, unwittingly revealed his Israeli ties to Nick Thimmesch of the *Los Angeles Times*, who asked him the following question in December 1973: "If such [anti-personnel] weapons are intrinsically evil, aren't they evil everywhere, including the Middle East?" Thimmesch described the Congressman's response: "The most confused comment came from Congressman Drinan . . . who said such weapons were 'horrible in Vietnam,' but his moral decision was to vote them for Israel as 'the lesser of two evils.' Very Jesuitical."[16]

Long defying the lobby, Senator Foreign Relations Committee Chairman Fulbright brought down upon his head the wrath of the Israeli lobby when he stated on October 7, 1973, on the CBS show

"Face the Nation" on national television: "The Israelis control the policy in the Congress and the Senate. . . . Somewhere around 80 percent of the Senate of the United States is completely in support of Israel—of anything Israel wants. . . ."

The Senator had made the remark in answer to the question as to what would be the best way to settle the Arab-Israeli war, which had broken out two days before, and whether it would not be in everyone's interest for the U.S. and the Soviet Union to refrain from furnishing either side with aid. Fulbright had responded: "Yes, but the U.S. government alone is not capable of doing that, because the Israelis control the policies of the Congress and the Senate, and unless we use the U.N. and do it collectively, we know that the U.S. is not going to do that. The emotional and political ties are too strong. I have witnessed that, and I can speak from my own experience." When pressed on this matter by his interviewers, he said that on every test on anything in which the Israelis were interested in the Senate, "the Israelis have seventy-eight to eighty votes."

The furious outcries following the Fulbright remark only pointed up the truth of his statement, and the phenomenon was all but admitted when Kenen boasted in the *Congressional Quarterly* that he had almost instantaneously mustered sixty-seven senatorial signatories to the resolution calling for the shipment of Phantoms to Israel. In serving as a substitute for Kenen in testifying on December 13, 1973, at the Senate Foreign Relations Committee hearings on the emergency $2.2 billion aid bill for Israel, Rabbi Philip Bernstein of Rochester conceded that the personal presence of Kenen was no longer needed, as the Senate was "all wrapped up." Kenen, who was in California lecturing, explained his absence from this important hearing: "I rarely go to the Hill. There is so much support for Israel that I don't have to."[17]

While acknowledging their consistent strength in the Congress, Kenen and other AIPAC representatives insisted this was only because senators and representatives realized that a strong Israel was in the American interest. Accusing Fulbright of being "consistently unkind to Israel and our supporters in this country," *Near East Report* assailed the Senator for questioning the motives of his colleagues. The Zionists were determined to "get" Senator Fulbright, and they poured money into Arkansas for his rival, Governor Dale Bumpers, in the May 1974 Democratic primary.

Philip Kaplan, a Little Rock attorney, blasted Fulbright on behalf of Arkansas Jews: "We were shocked at his saying the Jews control

Congress," and he added, "Fulbright is a Neanderthal."

Philip Back, Arkansas chairman of Bonds for Israel, said that Fulbright's statement that Congress was controlled by Israel was "uniformly disliked by Arkansas Jews."

The *Chicago Tribune* reported on May 12, 1974: "Fulbright's positions on the Middle East have not endeared him to American Zionists, who have declined to contribute 'a single dime' to his campaign." The *Tribune* added that a Bumpers lieutenant boasted:

> I could have bought central Arkansas with the offers of money from the Jewish community. . . . The Jews obviously are very unhappy with Fulbright, starting with Golda Meir. The offers of assistance came from people in New York and California, who have raised a lot of money in the Jewish community for political purposes.

Senator Fulbright was defeated in the primaries and returned to private life.

This has been one of the prime methods used by the American supporters of "little Israel," itself but a tiny splinter state, in exercising its inordinate control over the legislative body and the Presidency of one of the world's two superpowers. The loss of the experience, wisdom, courage, and perspicacity of Senator Fulbright was nothing short of another disaster to U.S. foreign policy interests, but a very great victory for Israel and her supporters.

While Kenen vehemently denied in 1975 that he and the Washington Anti-Defamation League representative received daily briefings from the Israeli Embassy, the close relationship between this Washington lobby and Tel Aviv has long been a matter of record. Kenen will admit, when asked, that Jewish money plays a real part in this process of winning friends in Congress. In the 1972 and 1976 presidential elections Jews donated more than half the contributions of over $10,-000 to Democratic candidates. AIPAC, supported by nondeductible contributions, operated in 1974 on a $400,000 annual budget[18] while representing major Jewish organizations on Capitol Hill. The UJA and other fund-raising organizations are not ostensibly a part of the AIPAC umbrella because it might endanger their own tax-deductible status.

When an issue would come up in Congress, according to Kenen, "We would send out a notice to the leadership of the American Jewish community letting them know what developments are occurring and they, in turn, would do what they could." The committee has a staff of seventeen full-time employees and maintains extensive files on matters concerning Israel, especially materials to rebut what

Kenen called "the Arab propaganda apparatus."

On the occasion of his twentieth year of service in Washington, Kenen was honored in April 1972 with a testimonial dinner at which Israeli Foreign Minister Abba Eban paid tribute to the "partnership" AIPAC had welded between the U.S. and Israel.

When Morris Amitay succeeded veteran Kenen in 1975 as head of this most successful of Washington lobbies, the young, dynamic leader boasted confidently that his pressure group would continue to be as effective as it had been in the past: "We have been systematically visiting the freshman class of ninety-one congressmen and ten new men in the Senate. Our relations are very friendly, stronger with the freshman class than with the House as a whole."[19]

The new director soon showed how completely in control he was of the situation on the Hill. At a time when President Ford genuinely seemed to be departing from his congressional practice of leading the "Israel-First" bloc, the rest of his former colleagues still carried on in their accustomed fashion. Under the direction of this small, highly effective Israel lobby, steps were taken to thwart the efforts of the White House to move toward evenhandedness. This was all revealed in an amazing article, astonishingly spread over page 2 of the *New York Times*,[20] frankly analyzing the activities of this most powerful of pressure groups (all of the *Times'* top brass must surely have been on summer vacation at the time or this story never could have appeared in print!).

President Ford had agreed, as a demonstration of the new U.S. impartiality, to sell Jordan improved Hawk missiles with the NAS systems worth $256 million. But the lobby went immediately to work. A secret confidential communication about the proposed sale, based on a classified[21] Defense Department document and sent by the White House to members of the Senate Foreign Relations and the House Foreign Affairs Committees, was leaked by Zionist aides of Senator Clifford P. Case (Dem.-N.J.) and of Representative Jonathan B. Bingham (Dem.-N.Y.) to Amitay. Immediately the lobby mobilized their organizations in 197 major cities and 200 smaller cities across the country, warning of the dangers to Israel in a two-page memorandum and letter, which described the scope and nature of the proposed Hawk sale to Jordan and concluded that it was capable of "providing cover for offensive operations against Israel." (Metromedia's famed and controversial commentator, Dr. Martin Abend, parroted the thrust of this memorandum on Channel 5 in New York, as did other Israelist pundits around the country.)

The communities were called upon to act at once and to apply their forceful, capable pressures. The memorandum was also mailed to all members of Congress. This Zionist committee claimed a nation-wide membership of 12,000, not including, of course, the membership of its many cooperating national organizations.

Within twenty-four hours of the distribution of the memorandum, the congressmen were besieged with phone calls, telegrams, and mail-grams from constituents urging them to oppose this Hawk sale to Jordan. Congressman Edward J. Derwinski (Dem.-Ill.) revealed he had received several pressuring calls and that he had argued, "The military security of Jordan could be an asset, not a liability." The congressman added, "I was absolutely firm so they backed off," and he complained vigorously of an "overpresence" of the Israel lobby and of its "steady pressures. It's as if they were saying, 'If you don't agree with us now, whatever you did before for us does not count,' " he noted.

To this alleged claim by the Illinois congressman of overkill, chief-tain Amitay of the Israel lobby quickly replied: "Better to overkill than to underkill if you're trying to achieve something. If we have to make a case solely on the basis of the interests of Israel, we've had it. Basi-cally, I think we are effective because we have a good cause . . . we are effective as a lobby because we've got a lot of people we can call on immediately." And this lobbyist brazenly concluded: "We've never lost on a major issue." (This was to hold true until May 15, 1978, when President Carter's package jet deal for Saudi Arabia, Egypt and Israel was not upset in the Senate despite the efforts of the Israel lobby.)

And so they did not lose on the Jordan issue of the Hawk missiles. Congress offered the Amman government a little less than half of the missile system sought, and imposed restrictions on their use. Despite the threat that Hussein might turn elsewhere (even to the Soviet Union), the legislators stuck by their guns, and the matter was put off.[22] One unidentified Democratic Senator was quoted in the *Times'* explosive article as saying that he would only talk off the cuff about the Israel lobby and the quotation could not be attributed to him "because they can deliver votes and they control a lot of campaign contributions. That's why I cannot go on the record, or I'd be dead.

"It's the strongest lobby," the Senator added, then he went on to say: "It doesn't dilute its strength by lobbying on other issues—a lot of members resent it, but they don't feel they can do anything about it. That lobby wants to do Congress's thinking on Israel—they don't want any independent judgments."[23]

"Last spring the Israel lobby rounded up the seventy-six Senators to sign the petition backing Israel," another member of Congress recalled. He further said: "A lot of guys stated they were afraid not to sign it, even though they didn't want to. Some of them told me it was the last time they would sign such a petition. But if another comes, I'll bet they'll be just as scared of the lobby and sign up again—but don't quote me by name." Iowa Senator John Culver, according to syndicated columnist Tom Tiede, had first decided not to sign the petition of support for Israel, but in the end changed his mind because, as he told friends, "they put too much pressure on me."[24]

Three American organization heads,[25] two of them Jewish, asked the Justice Department to probe the circumstances under which the contents of a classified document sent by the White House to the Senate Foreign Relations Committee and the House Foreign Affairs Committee was transmitted to an agent of the State of Israel. A telegram addressed to Attorney General Edward Levi, calling for an immediate, thorough, and impartial investigation of the *New York Times* disclosure that Senator Case, Representative Bingham, and their respective aides had passed the information to a registered Israeli agent was never even acknowledged, let alone any action taken on it.

Amitay's connections with staff members of key congressional committees and with aides to the legislators are close and intimate. Michael Kraft in Senator Case's office has consistently backed Israel's cause and is in almost daily contact with Amitay. Foreign Relations Committee staffer Stephen Bryen[26] is in close touch with the AIPAC, as is Senator Charles Percy aide, Scott Cohen. Zionist Richard Perle from Senator Jackson's staff, probably the closest ally of the lobby, launched the spring 1975 letter signed by seventy-six Senators warning the President against a foreign policy reassessment to the disadvantage of Israel. The Senator Bayh/Javits "Dear Colleague" letter said, "Recent events in Indochina underscore America's need for dependable and stable allies as well as greater participation by the Congress in formulating our foreign policy."

When Amitay served as Administrative Assistant to Senator Ribicoff, he and Perle coalesced key Senate staff people to work on behalf of Israel and Soviet Jewry. Included in this group, according to Stephen D. Isaacs in his book *Jews and American Politics,* were

. . . Richard D. Siegel (an aide to Pennsylvania's Richard Schweiker); Mel Grossman (an aide to Florida's Edward J. Gurney); Albert A. ("Pete") Lakeland (an aide to Javits); Daniel L. Spiegel (an aide to Senator Humphrey); Mel Levine (an aide to California's John V. Tunney); Jay Berman (an aide to

Indiana's Birch Bayh); and Kenneth Davis (an aide to Minority Leader Hugh Scott of Pennsylvania). All but Lakeland are Jewish. This group has worked quietly drafting legislation and other materials and mounting "backfires" to insure support of the legislation, while Jackson, in particular, and Javits and Ribicoff have worked "out front" to garner support among fellow senators.[27]

Also working very closely with the lobby was Dan Spiegel, Legislative Assistant to Hubert Humphrey, who to the end remained the staunchest Zionist. And much of the credit for delaying the Carter-Begin confrontation over the disposition of the West Bank during the first 1977 visit of the Israeli Prime Minister to Washington must go to Amitay's boys on the Hill. As the lobbyist indicated to *Washington Post* journalist Stephen Isaacs, "Jewish legislative staff members very definitely keep their Jewishness in mind."[28]

When President Carter planned to meet secretly with four key Senators who automatically back Israel, the word was somehow passed to Amitay, who then called on each one to shore up his support prior to the meeting with the President. There is no question that this lobby possesses the most unusual political savvy. "They are plugged into the Washington-based network," a veteran congressional staffer noted. "They are well armed with the usual vehicles that lobbyists need; they are adept and intelligent—and they know how these cats meow."[29] And they have other powerful Zionist oriented groups working side by side, often plowing a path for them.

The Anti-Defamation League does its share cooperating in "converting" congressmen at critical moments. Opposition to sending the deadly C-3 concussion bombs to the Zionist state immediately brought overt suggestions from this group that the opponents were secretly anti-Semitic. "That's the pervasive force they strike in the hearts of members up here," one Capitol Hill aide was quoted as saying.[30] "If you're in opposition to anything Israel wants, you get a big white paintbrush that says you're anti-Semitic." Congressman David Obey (Dem.-Wis.) expressed it this way: "If you question their programs, they say you are for their enemies and against them. . . . I defend Israel, but not irrational policies that would lead to war for both of us."[31]

While some legislators resented this kind of coercion, most bowed to the powerful pressure. Congressman Thomas Downey from Long Island in suburban New York City, who was one of the youngest men ever to serve in the lower house of Congress, had serious doubts about the 1976 foreign aid bill, which contained more than $1.7 billion for the Zionist state. His constituents, judging from their mail, were against foreign aid, and although Downey had been—and still was—

a strong supporter of Israel, he was inclined to vote against the bill. Soon some concerned rabbis came to call upon him, demanding a positive vote on Israel. Downey defended his position but stated that he would go along with their demands, despite his convictions, if there was a "show of support" from his own district, where only 5 percent of the voters were Jewish. Two days later he received 3,000 telegrams from constituents in his district, and when the roll call came on foreign aid, Congressman Downey registered an emphatic "yes."[32]

In addition to pressures from and fear of the lobby, heavy donations to their campaign funds, and an occasional overseas junket, members of Congress have other very practical reasons for their deeply rooted pro-Israelism. Financial disclosures of income earned by members of the Senate for speeches, public appearances, and writings, published from time to time in the *Congressional Quarterly*, clearly indicate how potent a language dollars speak, even in the upper house of Congress. In 1969 Jewish organizations paid out more money than any other interest group for speaking engagements by U.S. Senators. Twelve Senators received $29,250 in handsome fees, ranging from $5,000 to $2,500, for saying—sometimes written for them—nice things about Israel before audiences across the country.

There cannot help but be some small connection between the largesse handed out as honoraria and the overwhelming support given in the Senate at that time to the Israeli request for more Phantoms. This pro-Israeli posture was not accidental or coincidental. The twelve Senators (Bayh of Indiana, Muskie of Maine, Harris of Oklahoma, Cranston of California, McGovern of South Dakota, Mondale of Minnesota, Packwood of Oregon, Tydings of Maryland, Williams of New Jersey, Moss of Utah, Ribicoff of Connecticut, and McGee of Wyoming) had enthusiastically supported the open letter that year addressed to Secretary Rogers urging additional jet aircraft for Israel, and the latter two were among the Senators circulating the letter for signatures.

Maine's Senator Muskie led the Zionist list with $13,500 earned for seven speeches, topped by his $2,500 speech before the Jewish National Fund. In 1967 before the Senator became the Democratic Vice Presidential candidate, Jewish groups showed no interest in him. And after former Vice-President Hubert H. Humphrey returned to the Senate, he received $52,500 for twenty-four speeches to Jewish organizations between January 1971 and February 1974. These financial reports as filed with the Secretary of the Senate did not give full credit to Israelist activity. The business of senatorial flesh-peddling has been a highly lucrative one for certain lecture bureaus. Often a Senator was booked through a bureau, which contracted with him at one price and sold him to the sponsoring group at a considerably higher figure. Hence it was the bureau that paid the Senator and that alone was listed in the report to the Senate, not the Jewish organization. Likewise, frequently Zionist-oriented individuals exerted quiet pressure to bring a Senator to a campus, and only the name of the university or college appeared in the report. Other conduits undoubtedly also were employed in providing the Washington lawmakers with important and lucrative engagements.

Such a use by tax-deductible organizations of tax-free dollars to woo the taxpayers' representatives was more than a bit reminiscent of the 1963 disclosure (in 300 printed pages of testimony taken that year in May and August) by the Senate Foreign Relations Committee of what *Newsweek* magazine described as "one of the most effective networks of foreign influence." More than $5 million masked tax-free UJA dollars had been distributed through "conduits" of the Jewish Agency in Jerusalem and the Jewish Agency's American Section, a registered foreign agency, in order to mold public opinion and exert pressures in favor of Israel.[33]

Again in 1973, the publication of lecture earnings by pro-Israel Senators revealed that it was not only votes that made such fervent Zionists of legislators, but an even more practical consideration—the payoff! For speaking to such groups as the United Jewish Appeal, the Development Corporation of Israel, the B'nai B'rith, or a synagogue, Senator Birch Bayh received $21,500 for fifteen appearances; Hubert Humphrey $27,500 for only eleven turns; Henry Jackson $9,700 for seven; Edmund Muskie $14,650 for seven; Gale McGee $13,500 for twenty-two; Mike Gravel $7,200 for eleven; former Democratic Committee Chairman Fred Harris $8,000 for eight; etc. Between 1971 and 1974 "Scoop" Jackson had netted a cool $41,000 in Zionist speaker fees on the chicken-soup circuit.

Honoraria from Zionist groups, Israeli philanthropic and development organizations, synagogues and Jewish clubs paid fourteen senators $108,028 in 1976.[34] At a time President Nixon was being increasingly engulfed by the growing disaster of Watergate's payoffs, no one was interested in or dared make the slightest allusion to these facts and figures, least of all columnist Jack Anderson, who was so constantly engrossed in bringing to light so many other interesting exposures, even the amount of money Jackie Onassis spent for her honeymoon.

This is why New Yorkers were surprised when the press reported that newly-elected Senator Daniel Patrick Moynihan, who had built his political reputation as a defender of Israel during his stormy U.N. career as U.S. Ambassador, had earned in 1976 $75,000 for twenty speeches to such Jewish groups as the Zionist Organization of America, the UJA, the Jewish National Fund, and the Jewish Federaion of Cleveland.[35] The disclosure was made in reports filed with the Secretary of the Senate in Washington. The $3,750 per talk given to Moynihan was far more than Oregon's Wayne Morse used to receive as a speechmaker when he was, as one Florida editor put it, "virtually in the employ of several major Jewish fund-raising organizations."[36]

In assuming his Senate seat, Moynihan was making a big financial sacrifice. The growing dependence of members of Congress on outside income, admittedly a likely source of influencing legislation, led Congress to enact legislation in 1975. A $25,000 annual ceiling was placed on such outside honoraria in 1977; the ceiling drops to $8,625 under the new ethics code effective January 1, 1979.

Sometimes money is transferred more subtly and more indirectly to the legislators by way of contributions to political campaigns. It was none other than Joseph Alsop, long one of the most ardent, frenetic supporters of Israel, who wrote: "With the possible exception of Senator Edward Kennedy, no liberal Democrat gets less than 50 percent of his campaign financing from the Jewish community. In certain cases, the percentage reaches a very much higher figure." This had been true for all campaign chests and candidates, save that of all the Kennedys, who had their independent means.

The list of funds contributed by mid-1971 to the presidential primary races of Senators Edward M. Muskie,[37] George S. McGovern,[38] Birch Bayh,[39] and Harold Hughes,[40] four leading candidates, showed they were overabundantly saturated with Jewish big givers, further demonstration of the leverage employed by the Israeli cause in the U.S. at the very seat of power. As the *Times* noted, "close to half of the big political givers are in the New York City area."[41]

Money and power do talk, and potently. It was a little hypocritical in 1974 and 1975 for Zionist supporters in Congress—and even the President of the U.S.—to shout "Arab oil blackmail" when they are most aware of the kind of blackmail-bribery that has permeated the halls of Congress and the entire aura of Arab-Israeli-U.S. relations.

It is not surprising, therefore, that one can count almost on one hand the members of Congress who have dared defy the lobby and speak out for a more balanced Middle East policy in the national interest. In a speech to the Senate in 1970, Senator Mark Hatfield (Rep.-Ore.) criticized the blind obeisance to the Israeli cause:

We must squarely confront the third rising force, the Palestinian movement. The issue of Palestine must be understood, and its meaning in the eyes of all the Arab world must be grasped. Our viewpoints must become sensitive to the injustice that the Palestinians feel so deeply, and our policies must be constructed to deal with this sense of injustice.[42]

In 1970, as seventy-four members of the Senate joined together in calling upon Secretary of State Rogers to "provide Israel with the aircraft so urgently needed for its defense," Senator Henry Bellmon (Rep.-Okla.) called for a more "balanced debate" on the Middle East, which could prevent a second Vietnam. Bellmon queried his Senate colleagues as to whether "a military answer in the Arab-Israeli conflict is in the long-range interest of any of the countries concerned." And the Oklahoma Republican put these significant words into the record:

It is in keeping with the U.N. resolutions that the refugees of Palestine be offered the choice of repatriation. . . .

Indeed, there are many friends of Israel who are fearful that the constant need to demonstrate military prowess will render the nation into a modern Sparta, a nation devoid of a soul.[43]

On the floor of the House on October 18, 1973, Denver's freshman Representative James Johnson questioned the wisdom of stepping up U.S. arms shipment to Israel and suggested the action was an "act of war" against the Arabs. He warned that we will "make a grave mistake if we continue to alienate the Arabs and drive them into the Soviet bloc by continuing to provide aid to Israel under terms which can inevitably lead to a commitment of our forces." The congressman noted that American troops had been placed "on a military alert during the latest crisis just two or three days after assurances that they would not be sent to the Mideast."

Leonard Larsen, chief of the Washington Bureau of the *Denver Post,* which has always been a stalwart supporter of Israel, detailed the story of Johnson's courageous statement and the consequences thereof. He told of Johnson receiving a batch of vituperative mail "threatening any future he might be entertaining in politics and portraying him as anti-Semitic, pro-Communist, and a beast to rival Hitler."

Early in 1975 George McGovern—no longer a presidential aspirant and now a bit more concerned about the interests of the people of South Dakota, whom he continued to represent in the Senate, than in the Jewish vote—visited the Middle East as Chairman of a Senate Foreign Relations subcommittee. After actually talking with some Palestinians for the first time, the Senator began to realize that there was, indeed, "another" side to the issue, one that apparently made sense to him, and he brought down on himself the wrath of the Zionists by advocating the creation of a Palestinian West Bank state. In his meeting the following day with Golda Meir in Israel, he received the frostiest of receptions, from which he had not quite recovered when I later talked with him at a U.N. reception while the Senator was serving with the U.S. delegation for that General Assembly session. Apparently the former Prime Minister, emotionally wrought, had practically called him an anti-Semite for his espousal of justice for the Palestinians.

At about the same time that McGovern made his statement favoring a Palestinian state, Senator Charles Percy (Rep.-Ill.) also expressed some change of heart. Percy's stay at the U.N. as part of the U.S. delegation during the General Assembly in the fall of 1974 had exposed him to much of the international thinking regarding the Palestinian question. This was followed by a twelve-country tour the following mid-January. Upon his return, the senior Illinois Senator declared that there were "limits to U.S. support for Israel" and that Israeli leaders were unrealistic in believing they could avoid contact with the PLO. Percy had found Yasir Arafat relatively moderate and, more significantly, he struck a theme practically unheard of in the Senate: "We cannot support Israel, right or wrong." And, the Senator added, if the Israelis were responsible for launching a new Middle East war, "it is not clear that the U.S. support would be with them."

Only a few weeks earlier, Senator Percy had been one of the seventy-one Senators who, in an open letter to President Ford circulated by AIPAC, called for support of Israel and attacked both granting U.N. observer status to the PLO and sending an invitation to Yasir Arafat to address the General Assembly. The Percy turnabout supported the thesis long propounded by some friends of the Middle East: Make it possible for anyone to visit the Arab world as well as Israel, and there is a 90 percent chance that he will come home sensing the justice of the Palestinian position.

But the Zionists refused to permit this conversion to stand. Lobbyist Amitay had declared at the time of the Illinois Senator's controversial remarks: "Percy is not irredeemable." The continuous campaign, spurred by blistering criticism in *Near East Report* and the Anglo-Jewish press, resulted in a speedy receipt of 20,000 pieces of mail by the Senator, and six months later he was still receiving fifty letters a week. When Senator Javits attacked President Carter for his "the Palestinians should have a homeland" approach in June 1977, Percy picked up the attack on Carter in a speech before the Anti-Defamation League in Chicago. Amitay had brought the Illinois Senator, now a real 1980 presidential aspirant, back into the fold.

The most consistent opponent of Washington's "Israel-First" policy, aside from Senator Fulbright, has been South Dakota's Senator James Abourezk, the first person of Arabic descent ever to sit in the upper house of Congress. In his maiden speech on foreign affairs to the Senate on October 18, 1973, Abourezk said:

As a compassionate people, we can no more tolerate the inhumanity in the continuation of the Palestinian refugee camps than we could the mistreatment and genocide practised against the Jews by Hitler. Until the refugee matter is dealt with, we must realistically face the fact that even the most brilliantly drawn border agreements will fail in the face of continued terrorism.

We cannot stop by showing compassion only for homeless Jews. Our compassion must extend to the Palestinians who have found themselves without a homeland.

Mr. President, the job of this body and this nation is to do everything within our power to bring peace to the Middle East. *Let us forego the easy posturing for our constituents.* Let us put aside partisan divisions that have nothing to do with the Middle East. Let us demonstrate in our actions the kind of even-handed restraint to change the course leading to disaster. [Italics added.]

Abourezk has won wide respect in Washington as an outspoken Senator willing to risk displeasure in behalf of issues he believes are right. He was an early opponent of the war in Vietnam and an active advocate of reforms based on the Watergate scandals. It was logical that the Colorado Democratic State Committee should invite the Senator to address its traditional 1977 "Jefferson-Jackson Day" dinner in Denver. But a high-pressure campaign to dump him immediately swung into gear once the invitation had been issued. Colorado Zionist Federation Director Arnold Zaler announced he was "disappointed" in the choice of speakers. Dinner Committee member Betty Christ moved to withdraw the invitation. Denver labor leader John Mrozek announced he was canceling his large ticket purchase and blustered: "He is pro-Arab and anti-Israel. The labor movement is pro-Israel. As a Democrat, I object to inviting someone who goes against the state and national party platform, which is pro-Israel."

Only by the narrowest margin was the motion to withdraw Abourezk's invitation defeated. By the time he arrived in Denver on March 25, tensions had increased. At the airport the South Dakotan told a press conference: "As a U.S. Senator, I have sworn to uphold the Government of the U.S., but I never dreamed that I would be required to swear allegiance to any other government."

Before a dinner audience of more than 700, Abourezk reviewed the attempts to suppress him. Once, he said, his appearance at Yeshiva University (New York City) had been prevented, and in November 1976 prior to an appearance in Rochester, New York, people threatened to bomb the auditorium where he was to speak. The Senator minced no words:

The point of the controversy surrounding this dinner has been my refusal to take an absolutist position for Israel. There is extreme danger to all of us in this kind of absolutism. It implies that only one position—that of being unquestionably pro-Israel—is the only position.

Senator Abourezk went on to describe the pressures of the Zionist lobby:

For several years now, I have been extremely skeptical of the extraordinary influence which the Zionist lobby has in this country. Its ability to accomplish virtually any legislative feat involving military or economic assistance to Israel is legend.

When one reads in headlines of the public outrage at attempted manipulation of our government, directed by a foreign country, one can only wonder that so little is written about the most powerful of all foreign government lobbies, the Israeli lobby. The Israeli lobby is the most powerful and pervasive foreign influence that exists in American politics. And one must never forget that Israel, despite its status as an ally, is still a foreign power with its own national interests to preserve. It is not an American protectorate or territory, and for it to have the enormous legislative influence in the U.S. Congress that it does is dangerous. It is dangerous because the United States, and its Middle East foreign policy, is likely to become, if it has not already, a captive of its client state.

I do not represent Israel in the United States Senate nor do I represent any of the Arab states. I represent South Dakota, and the interests of the people of the United States.

Winding up his address with a warning that suppression of dialogue was something which "we as Americans should all fear," the Senator was greeted with a standing ovation, according to the *Rocky Mountain News*, "although there were pockets of people who sat on their hands."[44] In an editorial the same Denver newspaper stated:

"James Abourezk is not a fanatic screaming for the blood of Israel. Colorado Democratic leaders should be proud to have him as their speaker. He is better than they deserve."[45]

While McGovern was losing his home state by a wide margin in 1972 in the presidential election, Abourezk carried South Dakota with 57 percent of the vote. That is why the announcement in January of 1977 that the popular Senator would not be a candidate for reelection when his term expired in 1978 shocked his many constituents at home and dismayed his many friends around the country. The Senator's retirement statement only cited "family responsibilities." Some months back when Abourezk asked one of his fellow Senators how he generally voted on Middle East matters, his colleague responded that "he found it to be less troublesome for him personally to vote the Israeli side." He explained that he had once voted against Israel, after which he "spent most of his time explaining the vote to hostile Jewish constituents and to lobbyists for the government of Israel."

Because Abourezk had not taken the easy road, he could undoubtedly foresee many troubles ahead, with which he might not be able to cope. As they had done with Senator Fulbright, the Israeli lobby was prepared to pour tens of thousands of dollars into South Dakota in 1978 to defeat the Senator who had so adamantly refused to take on a dual allegiance.

As early as 1974 the Israel lobby started gunning for him. As Jim Abourezk expressed it, "the Israeli lobby is intimidating. If you get on their hit list, you spend a lot of time defending yourself from 'intellectual terrorism.' "[46] Before retiring as AIPAC Chairman, Kenen wrote letters to Abourezk's Senate campaign contributors noting that the Senator had gone "to great lengths to support the Arab cause and to undermine American friendship in Israel. . . . I consider the question important enough to write to you and others who supported Abourezk."

Only a few voices have reverberated through the halls of Congress in an effort to keep alive the thesis so brilliantly advanced in 1969 on the Senate floor by Senator Fulbright. In talking of the picketing by the Seafarers' International Union and the Longshoremen's International Association of the Egyptian (then U.A.R.) passenger-cargo ship *Cleopatra,* in protest against the denial of free navigation for all ships through the Suez canal, the Foreign Relations Committee Chariman had assailed certain minority pressure groups for "whipsawing foreign policy" to the detriment of the national interest. With a profound historical vista, in words that will stand as a perpetual monument to the thinking of a true American, Fulbright addressed himself to the broader aspects of this particular incident:

It is the problem of the development in this nation of organized groups which bring into American political life the feuds and emotions that are part of the political conflicts of foreign nations. This is one of the things that our founding fathers came here to avoid when they created this nation. . . .

Mr. President, this nation has welcomed millions of immigrants from abroad. In the 19th century we were called the melting pot, and we were proud of that description. It meant that there came to this land people of diverse creeds, colors and races. These immigrants became good Americans, and their ethnic or religious origins were of secondary importance. But in recent years, we have seen the rise of organizations dedicated apparently, not to American, but to foreign states and groups. The conduct of a foreign policy for America has been seriously compromised in this develoment. We can survive this development, Mr. President, only if our political institutions—and the Senate in particular—retain their objectivity and their independence so that they can serve all Americans.[47]

There has always been a wide difference of opinion as to whether a congressman was to represent in Washington the interests of his district or the totality of American interests. For the first time a new concept has been advanced and, sadly, almost unanimously accepted. American federal legislators are to represent the interests of the foreign state of Israel and to comport themselves as if they were members of the Knesset. In becoming, wittingly or unwittingly, lackeys of the Israeli lobby, the members of Congress have abysmally betrayed the trust of the American people whom they represent. The same and more can be said of the other arch-villain in the Middle East tragedy, the media, whose continuous myth-information has provided the total cover-up for the improbity of Washington in its unique relationship with Israel.

VIII Slanting the Myth-Information

Four hostile newspapers are more to be feared than a thousand bayonets.

—Napoleon

Does the mass media in America personify freedom and democracy, or does it deliberately restrict some voices and exclude exposure of others? Does it expose and condemn all glaring acts of injustice, or does it make particular exceptions? Does it act as a watchdog on abuses in our domestic and foreign policy, or does it recoil from certain politically sensitive issues? To what extent do biased reportage and cartoon-drawing foster false stereotypes of the outside world and encourage U.S. public opinion to political hostility against or friendship toward other countries?

Loaded questions, yes, but ones that ought not to be ignored. The radio, television, newspapers, and magazines (and books, too) are in many cases the only adult sources for information about foreign countries. They play a decisive role in shaping public attitudes toward the formulation of foreign policy, especially the Arab-Israeli conflict and the Palestine question.

While most Americans probably would concede that the nation's radio and television networks, newspapers, and magazines fall short of perfection, they would argue in the same breath that their media have few equals in extensive coverage of events, balanced presentation of controversial issues, and talent for exposing scandals of Watergate proportions. Americans, who have come to trust the media after losing faith in their leaders, would accept the suggestion of a media cover-up in the Middle East with the greatest reluctance.

But evidence points unmistakably to the pro-Israeli and anti-Arab bias of the mass media for many varied reasons: the religio-ethnic pressures of the powerful Jewish community and its potent lobby, exercised through advertising and otherwise; the general Western atti-

271

tude finding empathy with people of European culture such as Israelis[1] while at the same time looking suspiciously on non-Western peoples, and the ever-present Christian guilt feeling for the Nazi genocide.

There are no set rules or guidelines as to what constitutes news. What is held to be news by the press, television, and radio is decided by reporters on the spot, by news personnel in charge at the time the story breaks, and by the editor. And editors have been given carte blanche even by the Supreme Court. In the words of Chief Justice Burger: "For better or worse, editing is what editors are for, and editing is the selection and choice of material." While the Fourth Estate never lets up on its reminders about freedom of the press, the corresponding responsibility of the press is rarely ever mentioned. Few question what editors do or do not pass as news.

There are admittedly a "disproportionate number of Jews in the American media, relative to the population," according to Ronald Koven, Foreign Editor of the *Washington Post.* Many reporters are Jewish; their version of an event is accepted by the foreign news desk editor, who may also be Jewish or, if Christian, may not thoroughly understand the development and will yield to the "knowledge" of his reporter. In television, Jewish reporters "often want their stories on Israel done and go and ask that they be done," observed NBC correspondent Marilyn Robinson.[2]

The presence of so many Jews in the media was attributed by Koven "not to a Zionist plot" but to the fact Jews, like Irish immigrants before them, "went onto places where they made more money and had more prestige." No matter for whatever reason they may have entered the media, they are there in force and prestigiously located. Many networks and news magazines assign Jews as correspondents in Israel —such as Bill Seaman of ABC-TV, Jay Bushinsky who represents Metromedia and Westinghouse TV, and Michael Elkins of BBC. Objectivity from such representation is not possible.

Aside from the news itself, commentary—or analysis—provides further opportunity for slanting, as Harry Reasoner illustrated during the Israeli 1975 demonstrations against the Kissinger disengagement mission. The ABC commentator justified these actions by saying that the Arabs started all the wars, and he placed the blame on them alone for the 1948, 1956, 1967, and 1973 conflicts.

The media bias may stem from a Christian reporter or correspondent's fear of being accused of being anti-Semitic or a Jew's fear of losing popularity. Stanley Siegal's meteoric rise through ABC-TV's 9 A.M. talk show has brought him to the top of the television ratings; the *New York Times* hailed him as an "uninhibited terror that stalks the local ABC studios, the man who had the nerve to ask Angie Dickinson whether she had an affair with President Kennedy, the man who asked Renée Richards, point-blank, whether she was enjoying her sex life. . . ."[3] But Siegal has adamantly refused to air anti-Zionist or pro-Arab opinion. *New York Times* correspondent Tom Wicker, outspokenly fearless in advancing the civil and human rights of the oppressed anywhere a few years back, admitted that he was staying afield from reportage on the plight of the Palestinians because he did not wish to lose the support of so many followers who were needed "for battles on other fronts."[4]

Fear of pressure and actual pressure also play a vital role. As James McCartney, foreign and security affairs specialist of the Knight newspaper chain in Washington, explained it: "I don't think any chief editorial writer for a paper in Philadelphia or Detroit goes for many months without a visit from someone representing the Jewish community and with a pro-Israel view, or a luncheon or something of that sort."[5] Neither the Arabs nor their friends have begun to enter this arena.

There is no question that the large Jewish population in major cities where there is a built-in audience for what is happening in Israel has produced in editors the automatic reaction to view the Middle East situation in terms of what readers (or listeners) would want to know. Peter Jennings, ABC news commentator, admitted, "There is definitely an anti-Arab bias in America, and I regret it."[6]

Some of the abundant pro-Israel and anti-Arab reportage has stemmed from the media failure to place permanent correspondents in Arab countries prior to the 1973 war and the oil embargo as they did in Israel. The difficulty of access of American correspondents in the Arab world to news and news sources, even as these were literally foisted upon them in Israel, as well as the careful, remarkable Israeli (plus American Zionist) public relations in contrast to an Arab neglect and disdain of this modern communications technique, has also contributed to one-sided reportage. Still, much of the bias has been deliberate.

The atmosphere against which John Doe judges the day-to-day happenings in the Middle East has been poisoned or sweetened by the use of stereotypes, "the fixed and oversimplified conceptions which people hold about each other"[7]—that Irish fight, Orientals are inscrutable, Jews are grasping, Swedes are stolid, and Arabs are nomadic, backward, sneaky, and villainous. In a typical stereotype slur, Marvin

Kalb, reporting on the assasination of Faisal in a CBS Special from Saudi Arabia, commented that while he was with Henry Kissinger in Riyadh, he saw many people with "shifty eyes."[8]

The influence of stereotyping in molding American attitudes toward the Middle East has taken on greater significance because so little space is given to and there are so few readers of foreign news, as shown by *The American Institute of Public Opinion's Readership Survey* of fifty-one newspapers, conducted for the International Press Institute.[9] Anti-Arab stereotyping begins in elementary schools[10] and its acceptability has been made simpler by the historic Christian antagonism toward Islam. The distorted image, built from many innocent and purposeful misconceptions about the religion, history, and socioeconomics of the Arabs, has gone side-by-side in media reportage with the pro-Israel glorifications.

Innocent stereotyping, for example, simply uses the word "Arab" to refer equally to Egyptians, Saudis, and Libyans as well as to Palestinians. The Arab has been an easy victim for the cartoonist, who invariably portrays Arabs as the Jews were portrayed by the Nazis: somebody dirty, with a long nose, either a terrorist or an old sheikh, gas pump in hand, and dripping with petrodollars. At best, it is a person with Arab headdress and flowing robe, usually riding a camel or a Cadillac.

Far less innocently motivated has been the plethora of stories covering the armed conflict which inevitably never fails to refer to, if not to show, Palestinians carrying Russian Kalshnikovs. While the Communist label is tied to the Arabs, scarce mention is made that it is U.S. Phantoms that have been the instrumentalities for Israeli bombing of Lebanese villages and Palestinian refugee camps.

To counter the bad Arab image, the Information Center of the League of Arab States has four regional offices in the United States, but, Zionist scare propaganda to the contrary, is underfinanced as well as inexpert and understaffed. This puny, ineffectual Arab effort in no way has begun to match the acumen and skill shown in the information operations of the Israelis, let alone those of their Zionist and Israelist supporters.

The Zionists, of course, have a press totally of their own. The Anglo-Jewish press, comprising approximately 140 newspapers with a combined circulation of 3.75 million, is headed by *Hadassah* magazine (360,000), New York *Jewish Press* (210,000), and *National Jewish Monthly* (200,000). As if the Israeli cause needed another publication in the U.S., the American Jewish Committee started in 1976 a new quarterly,

Present Tense, "to broaden understanding of world Jewish affairs"—i.e., Israeli affairs. Zionists have also had their own Herzl Press working out special arrangements for co-publication and/or distribution with McGraw-Hill, Doubleday, and other major publishers.

Israeli positions are always quickly explained and accessible; the Palestinians are made out to be nothing more than a collective group of "terrorists," rather than a liberation movement. Only very occasionally has the plight of a million and a half refugees been presented, because just the mere recital of that story is certain to arouse some feeling for these people. At the same time, the human aspects of the Israelis, ever intermixed with some reference to the holocaust, is daily unfolded in most loving detail.

To compress the media's misrepresentation of the Middle East conflict into one chapter is no easy task, so vast and complex is the subject. From stacks of material accumulated over the past ten years, examples of distortion have been selected. Most of the slantings presented here were obtained from careful monitoring of the media over these years; some few are based on personal experiences with editors, publishers, and commentators.

As television focused on the clashes between Israel and the Arab world, stereotyping intensified. The Arab was depicted on entertainment programs and on documentaries as "pimp, cheat, and backstabber, whether lurking among the shadows in the bazaar of Cairo or sitting in a tent in the middle of the desert surrounded by oil wells."[11] All the worst possible images of the Arab from the blood-feuding bedouin to the oil blackmailer are offered. As Southern Illinois University Professor Jack G. Shaheen pointed out in his study,[12] this image of the Arab goes forward on television while Americans have matured to a point where degrading caricatures of blacks, Chicanos, Jews, or homosexuals are no longer socially acceptable. In 1976, on prime time network television, the producers of "Cannon"[13] were almost obsessed with depicting the Arab as the scoundrel, who was similarly depicted on "The Six Million Dollar Man,"[14] "Medical Center,"[15] and NBC's monthly show "Weekend."[16] During the quiz show "To Tell the Truth," Peggy Cass commented that Arabs now illegally occupy space on American Indian reservations and sell Indian jewelry.[17] "Mystery Theater" has been used to advance anti-Arab propaganda.[18] In the annual NBC Christmas special "The Little Drummer Boy," the stereotyping was obvious when the young hero youth wore a yarmulka and the only scoundrel was an oversized Arab who blatantly exploited the young boy.[19]

On July 24, 1976, St. Louis public television station KETC-TV, according to the station's program guide, *TV Guide,* and local newspaper listing, was to air on "Documentary Theater" the show "Palestinians and the PLO." Viewers were instead subjected to "Dateline Israel," with the Anti-Defamation League's Arnold Forster and the Israeli Ambassador to the U.N. discussing the sensitive Palestine issue. And the station never indicated the name of the organization or organizations providing the operating funds for the program aired, as they invariably do.[20]

Popular television host Merv Griffin was given a trip to Israel. On his return, he had two shows about his visit, which started with a Mayor Ted Kollek-conducted tour of Tel-Aviv and Jerusalem. An American couple and three children from San Diego were shown at an absorption center; they had moved to Israel because they wanted "to live a full Jewish life—the quality of life, they knew, was superior." At the end of each night's program, the announcer stated, "We wish to thank the UJA for their assistance and help in producing this show." And then these words were flashed on the screen: "WE ARE ONE."

A closer look at radio and television coverage of the Middle East reveals how the media-controllers have made a mockery of responsible journalism. The Federal Communications Commission's Fairness Doctrine, which has been in force since July 1, 1966, is invariably cited by television and radio broadcasters as a defense against charges of bias. But it only provides that whenever "there is a discussion of controversial issues of public importance, a licensee is under obligation to ensure that proponents of opposing viewpoints are afforded reasonable opportunity for the presentation of contrasting views." This doctrine, often confused with the equal-time requirement for political candidates, unfortunately does not apply to news coverage, only to talk and opinion shows. And the FCC has given a very narrow, rigid interpretation to this obligation, being most reluctant to interfere with the licensee and force him to present the views of petitioners.

In reply to a complaint about a grossly one-sided panel presentation on Menachem Begin directly after his election, the FCC declared there had been no substantiation of the claim that the "Israeli elections, Mr. Begin's book and his career and character, the desirability of his heading the Israeli government and the Israeli treatment of Arabs, etc.," constituted a "controversial issue of public importance."[21] The networks and individual stations have likewise been given a free hand in deciding what is a "reasonable opportunity" of reply. This has allowed for slanting of their coverage of an event or selecting segments of the news in order to satisfy particular interest groups. Where the Middle East is concerned, this boils down to preferential treatment of pro-Israel spokesmen and a blackout of news unfavorable to Israel. On occasion an Arab spokesman, normally with little grasp of the English language and with whom the viewer or listener can scarcely relate, will be invited to join a panel to debate with an American Jew who has a distinct advantage.

The ABC program "Directions" on Sunday, March 5, 1978, presented the President and Executive Vice President of the Synagogue Council of America, Rabbis Saul Teplitz and Henry Siegman. Four weeks later the same half-hour show brought the views of Chairman of the Conference of Presidents Alexander Schindler and former President of the American Jewish Committee Morris Abrams. The moderator Herbert Kaplow did not even attempt to hide his total support of Israel and Zionism as he asked the correct "tough" questions of the four participants who were all 100 percent pro-Zionist and pro-Israel, save that Abrams two minutes before the program ended stated that the settlements on the West Bank "are not essential to Israeli security" and therefore fall within the framework of U.N. Resolution 242 (hence subject to negotiations). This one shading of difference among the four officials of Organized Jewry, plus the Abrams declaration that American Jews may not be "willing to bend with every vagary of Israel foreign policy" constituted to ABC attorney Thomas H. Wolf a sufficient enough of a contrasting viewpoint to satisfy the requirements of the Fairness Doctrine and to deny requests to present quite different views.

There are other methods, too, of showing bias. Consider how the media handled the televised appearances of Egypt's President Nasser in February, 1970 and PLO leader Yasir Arafat in November, 1974. Nasser appeared on New York City's Channel 5 in an hour interview by William Touhy of the *Los Angeles Times* and columnist Rowland Evans. Under the TV listings in the *New York Times* for that Sunday there was a complete blackout for the hour—as if Channel 5 had gone off the air; somehow all the other programs on the Arab-Israeli issue that week won a listing. The CBS show "The Newsmakers," whose guest was ardent promoter of Israel Senator Jacob Javits, managed to appear on page two of the first section of the *Times* in the late TV listings. Programs featuring Senator Charles Goodell, then competing with Javits as a number-one pro-Israel spokesman, Congressman Emmanuel Celler, and even David Ben-Gurion were also listed for that week.

On the very evening after Nasser's appearance, on the 10 P.M. news program of this same Channel 5, Bill Jorgensen brought in none other than Israeli Ambassador to the U.S. General Yitzhak Rabin, allowing him to present a rebuttal to President Nasser.

On the morning of November 13, 1974, Arafat addressed the U.N. —a momentous occasion marking the first time the Palestinian view-point was put before the General Assembly and a world listening audience. He found himself sandwiched between Zionist spokesmen. Channel 5 had scheduled a telecast of the event, but deliverance of Arafat's speech was delayed. Under the closest security precautions since the famed 1960 General Assembly session attended by so many heads of state, the PLO leader and his colleagues literally had to be smuggled into the U.N. compound by helicopter, and then more time was needed in which to work out the translation of his speech from Arabic to English.

In filling the time originally scheduled for Arafat, the program directors of Channel 5 took full advantage of the situation. Israeli former Foreign Minister Abba Eban, then teaching at Columbia University, was asked to take up the forty minutes. He proceeded to tear apart the PLO point of view even before the viewers had heard a single word of the Palestinian position that morning—or, for that matter, any other morning. Arafat's speech was then telecast. Following his ad-dress, Channel 5 gave a one-sided panel enough time to finish the job of demolishing the Palestinians' ideology. One of the panelists who was presented as a neutral academician was Professor J. C. Hurewitz of Columbia University, who in fact has been a supporter of Israel from the time of the 1950 publication of his first book, *The Struggle for Palestine*.[22]

The coverage of Arafat's speech by much of the media hit a low point, even for journalistic distortions. In referring to the PLO leader's proposal for a secular, democratic, binational state, *Time* magazine gratuitously commented: "That proposal implicitly requires the disso-lution of Israel, which goes against a long series of U.N. and other international affirmations."[23] The magazine continued: "Arafat *tried* to distinguish his respect for the Jewish faith from his hatred of Zionism." (Italics added.) Several specific references in Arafat's talk indicated that he and his Palestinian followers differentiated sharply between Zionism and Judaism. But *Time*, the *Times*, and other stalwart Israeli supporters refused to report this.[24]

As a climax in its coverage of the important Arafat appearance at the U.N., *Time* magazine latched onto his words: "Many of you who are in the assembly hall were [once] considered terrorists." Admitting that his statement was more than rhetorical, the *Time* writer pointed to other terrorists who now had become respectable statesmen despite their initial use of violence. At this juncture it would have been appropriate, if not necessary, for *Time* to mention Israel's terrorism along with the examples given of Ireland, Mexico, and Algeria. But not a word was said of Israeli violence in establishing the state that had sparked the Palestinians' counterterrorism. The magazine referred only to the Israelis as "victims of violence who have suffered through years of wanton attacks by Palestinian bombers and gunmen."

This was written in November 1974, thirty months before the election to the Israeli Premiership of Menachem Begin, the arch-terrorist of the Middle East. Well documented in the excellent research files of this news magazine was the record of Deir Yassin, the King David Hotel, and other Irqun acts of terrorism without which, boasted the former Israeli leader, there would have been no State of Israel.

The NBC "Today" show has been chock-full of "back from the Promised Land" pro-Israel interviews.[25] Scarcely, if ever, have anti-Zionists or pro-Arab Americans been similarly privileged with an interview or even been given the benefit of fair play, as the anatomy of a 1974 radio program illustrates. On March 11 on the "Barry Gray Show" over radio station WMCA, Arnold Forster and Benjamin Epstein, respectively Counsel and Vice President of the Anti-Defamation League, were permitted for 2½ hours to label every critic of Zionism and the State of Israel as anti-Semitic. The pretext for this lengthy interview was their recently published book, *The New Anti-Semitism.* Substituting for the usual moderator of this show, who himself was vehemently pro-Zionist, was William Scott, little more than a baseball pitcher in batting practice, helping Forster and Epstein hit the ball out of the park every time at bat. I promptly sent a telegram of protest to Peter Straus, President of WMCA, demanding under the rules of the FCC that an opportunity be given to present "a contrasting view by a responsible element." It so happened that Dr. John N. Booth, a former journalist and a distinguished Unitarian minister from the West Coast, was due East at this time, and the telegram asked that he appear with me.

The show's producer, Paul Zelden, called to say that some arrangement would be made to balance the coverage. After considerably more prodding, Zelden agreed that Booth and I would be given time to air our views, but not by ourselves. To this we replied, again by telegram: "We would be happy to debate with Forster and Epstein, although their reappearance is not required under the Fairness Doctrine. We would, of course, prefer to be given a reasonable opportunity to present another point of view on this all-important issue by ourselves, as the other two gentlemen were originally permitted to do." Zelden then agreed to get either Forster or Epstein to appear for two hours with us.

The next word came from the station that both declined to appear, and that we would have to appear with "two or three other people," whom the station would designate. This idea was entirely unacceptable, particularly when we were informed that the "two other people" would be an assistant Peace Corps director who had served in Israel and the head of some Zionist organization or other. Not only had we been denied permission to present our position alone, but our views were to be downgraded by the caliber of persons chosen to debate with us. Booth and I declined to appear on such a program. Had we agreed to participate, our audience would have been oblivious to WMCA's subtle flouting of the Fairness Doctrine and impressed, no doubt, by the apparent fair numerical balance—two for, two against.

A blistering letter was sent to Straus indicating that all our communications were being presented to the FCC in Washington. At this time WMCA was encountering some other troubles in the Capital and did not wish to make waves. Two weeks later WMCA reluctantly aired a two-hour slam-bang Forster-Lilienthal debate.

The art of slanting is practiced by media people the public would least suspect. Some of the best-known network commentators and reporters, generally trusted by Americans of many persuasions as objective and fair, have taken advantage of their status by plying the pure-Israeli line.

This was clearly the case in a "Face the Nation" interview with Tunisian President Habib Bourguiba in the spring of 1965. The interview was taped in the Carthage palace of Tunis and conducted by Martin Agronsky, Winston Burdette, and George Herman. Also present were the son of the President, Foreign Minister Habib Bourguiba, Jr., and myself, a guest in the country. Judging from a few cracks made by Agronsky, my presence as the only outsider was not appreciated. Small wonder! During the lengthy period in which Bourguiba, Jr., translated from English into French for his father and back again into English for the panelists, I took copious notes of both languages to enable me to compare the actual taping session with the edited program appearing on TV.

The telecast seen by American audiences showed Bourguiba

mouthing his answers in French with his son's translation used as a voiceover. Everything that the President had said against Egypt's Gamal Abdel Nasser appeared in the carefully edited program as presented over the network, while everything the Tunisian leader had said against Zionism and Israel was deleted so as to give the impression that he was more pro-Israel than even Jewish Defense Leaguer Meir Kahane. The blissfully ignorant and somewhat naïve American viewers had no way of knowing the truth.

A "Sixty Minutes" program narrated by Mike Wallace on January 6, 1974 provides another typical example. The program covered the oil embargo as well as pro-Zionist and pro-Arab groups in the U.S. American Jewish groups were pictured around a table, calmly plotting their activity on behalf of Israel. The sole opposition to Zionism and U.S. Middle East policy was depicted as coming from the Arab League and the Action Committee headed by Iraqi Dr. Mohamed Mehdi. Most of the program centered on the latter, who presented the typical Arab stereotype[26]—loud, blustering, emotional—in vivid contrast to the calm, sympathetic demeanor of the American Jewish leaders in their exposition of how to meet the challenge of Arab propaganda. In the filmed interview, Mehdi talked of demonstrations (the picture of Arab violence again) and boasted of oil power, but made no mention of how the average American was affected by the U.S. policy being followed. CBS's presentation concealed any indication that indeed there were many Americans (including some Jews), some organized in small groups across the country, others unorganized and inarticulate, but nevertheless opposed to Washington's position.

Throughout the program Wallace tried to imply that oil companies were financing what little American opposition there was to Israel. The CBS veteran went out of his way to point out that four or five oil company representatives were present at a large Washington reception for Saudi Arabian Oil Minister Sheikh Zaki Yamani and, of all the many personages that were greeted by the guest of honor, Wallace let the cameras focus on Yamani warmly shaking the hand of the Soviet Ambassador on his arrival at the Embassy gathering.

A Wallace interview with Foreign Relations Committee Chairman Fulbright in his office at the time he was opposing the $2.2 billion bill for special aid to Israel was cut to the bone, limited to the Senator's concern over threats that Zionists were going all-out to defeat his bid for reelection. Fulbright's presence at the Saudi Arabian reception was of course given special attention, which helped complete the picture of the gathering of all evil forces to defeat "little Israel."

The pièce de résistance in slanting, came at the program's end in a bald statement by Wallace that a CBS News poll reported that 60 percent of the 1,231 persons polled by phone wanted "little or no pressure on Israel" to relinquish captured Arab lands so as to promote resumption of Arab oil shipments, and only 35 percent wanted substantial pressure. The next day the *New York Post* carried this public opinion rating in bold headlines.

The actual breakdown of responses revealed how CBS had subtly distorted the results of this poll. On the question of applying pressure on Israel, 12 percent had answered "a great deal", 23 percent "a fair amount," 13 percent "very little," and 47 percent "none at all." In announcing the results, CBS had lumped those who had responded "very little" and "none at all" to get the 60 percent majority figure they wished, whereas CBS should have indicated that 47 percent wanted no pressure while 48 percent favored some kind of pressure—very little, a fair amount, and a great deal—with 5 percent giving no answer.

A little sleuthing turned up further evidence of foul play: The responses of those interviewed by telephone to a pretest question had been overwhelmingly against the Zionist-Israeli position. The original, more direct question was: "The Arabs have said that they will resume oil shipments when Israel gives up lands acquired in the 1967 war. Should or should not the U.S. put pressure on Israel to return these lands? "Twenty-six percent had responded that the U.S. should put pressure, and 15 percent had responded in the negative.[27] As a result of this preliminary survey, the test question was changed to eliminate any reference to the vital matter of the resumption of oil shipments. And then the figures were manipulated by Wallace to give the desired pro-Zionist result.[28]

Lest any media fairness should manifest itself, the "what have you done for us lately" attitude of Zionism has generally kept a firm control. Even Mike Wallace found himself on the spot for allowing CBS cameras to tell the truth.

On February 16, 1975, the CBS "Sixty Minutes" special interviewed Syrian Jews who attested to the gross exaggerations concerning their lot and stated that their situation had greatly improved, even in the face of the continuing war with Israel. The American Jewish Congress brought charges of "excessive, inaccurate, and distorted representations." Don Hewitt (Jewish himself) was threatened and received a nasty letter, a copy of which was sent to the FCC. A protest was also filed with the National News Council.

Quite accustomed to criticism, the CBS commentator noted that this had been the first time he had "come up against a conscientious campaign by the so-called Jewish lobby—against a mimeograph machine rampant. We were swamped!"[29]

Complaints from the Jewish Congress persisted throughout the spring of 1975, while CBS maintained the charges were groundless. As Wallace pointed out, "the world Jewish community tends somehow to associate a fair report about Syria's Jews with an attack on Israel because Syria happens to be Israel's toughest enemy. But the fact is there is not one Syrian Jew in jail today as a political prisoner."[30]

On June 7 CBS relented and repeated the segment on Syrian Jews from its previous program, adding a new introduction and a five-minute epilogue responding to the Zionist criticism. The Jewish Congress was still not satisfied. In December 1975 the *New York Post* reported Wallace as saying, "I'm going back to Syria to find out how the Jews are faring there." Wallace continued, "I did not say back in February of 1975 that Jews were living like kings. What I said was, 'It is apparent that the Syrian Jewish community is kept under close surveillance.'"

In 1976 Wallace returned and did a second program, which confirmed the findings of the first. He is definitely no longer the darling of the Israelis' cult. He learned the hard way what others have taken for granted: Investigation of sensitive matters concerning Israel, directly or indirectly, is a risky business. The alternative to full disclosure is silence or slanting, and the latter route is often the safest.

Lest CBS seem alone to be inordinately biased, let us turn to Radio WRFM and Jim Branch's treatment of the complex Middle East problem on a program in December 1971:

You have a very suspicious Israel—suspicious that the U.N. is stacked against it and with some good reason. . . . In 1967 Israel could have moved on to Cairo. They could have finished the Arab war capability once and for all, but they didn't despite the fact that the Arabs made it abundantly clear that they never would consider Israel a legitimate nation and therefore were going to totally destroy them.

Commentator Branch continued: "Why didn't the Israelis finish the job, especially when history indicated that the Arabs would just try it again later?"

History indicates no such thing. When effect is not related to cause, one obtains a picture entirely out of perspective. What Branch was alluding to, of course, was the old, oft-quoted canard that Nasser would "drive the Israelis into the sea." (When Member of Parliament

Christopher Mayhew in 1970 offered on television to pay £5,000 to anyone who could produce any evidence of the statement attributed to Nasser, no claimant came forward with legal proof—the quotation was wrongly translated, or wrongly attributed, or invented, "usually culled straight from some pro-Israeli publication.")[31]

The WRFM gem continued:

The United Nations took off where the Arabs left off, taking the Egyptian position on almost everything. That would not necessarily be so bad except that the Arabs were clearly the precipitators of the Middle East War [a comment in sharp contrast to U.S. Ambassador to the U.N. Charles Yost's lengthy article in *Foreign Affairs*, February 1968] . . . and the U.N. is not supposed to be on the side of those who precipitate wars . . . and instead of maintaining peace and guaranteeing Israel rights to sovereignty, the U.N. has allowed the Arabs to rebuild their armies.

An ABC-TV special on the Arab-Israeli crisis presented on June 2, 1969, was a dead giveaway of the network's sympathies. The network chose syndicated columnist Drew Pearson—a long-time, hard-line Zionist exponent—as producer and narrator of the program. Pearson approached the subject with customary disdain for the Arabs.

In his presentation of the Arab side of the question, Pearson's commentary and footage almost exclusively emphasized Palestinian preparations for war, with repeated references to fedayeen identification with revolutionaries of Communist countries, and Arab backwardness. Many less feet of film on guerrilla training and more on the conditions that had existed for the refugees for over twenty years, with appropriate commentary, would have been more informative. As for the backwardness, his scenes followed the rampant Hollywood stereotyped image of the Arab as an uncivilized, unwashed, camel-riding, illiterate bedouin in the desert. (The bedouins, incidentally, constitute no more than 5 percent of the total Arab population.)

The Israelis, in contrast, were depicted as technologically well advanced and strongly desiring peace. Unmentioned was the fact that the only peace treaty the Tel Aviv government sought was one that would have enabled her to keep her captured land intact at the expense of Arab territorial rights and Palestinian self-determination. Nothing was said of the essential role of private "charitable," tax-deductible dollars supplied by world Jewry in supplementing European technological skills.

Pearson's narration about child life in the bomb shelters of Israeli kibbutzim was touching, but his sympathetic approach did not extend to the Arab refugee child living for *years* in flimsy tents under unimaginable conditions of poverty and privation.

The Pearson allegation that the Israelis were inferior in military equipment to the Arabs was his ultimate distortion. Nothing could have been further from the truth at the time. It was generally accepted that the Israelis possessed the military capability to overrun the entire Arab world with no difficulty whatever. They possessed the entire range of defensive and offensive weapons of the most up-to-date design, while the Arabs, although rearmed after 1967, still only possessed weapons of a defensive nature whose quality was at best questionable.

Despite a reputation for presenting more balanced, fuller, and generally less simplistic coverage of issues and events, even public television and educational broadcasting falls by the way when the Arab-Israeli situation appears on the horizon.

National Educational Television seemed ready to make an exception when it announced in May 1970 its network presentation of "The Advocates," a two-part special featuring debate on U.S. support for Israel. Participating in the program were Professor Roger Fisher, who argued against further support, and his pro-Israel Harvard Law School colleague, Allan Dershowitz, who presented the affirmative viewpoint

Hopes of an impartial show were scuttled from the outset by the history of the conflict presented by film clips, playing upon the Nazi persecution and shaded in this manner (italics added):

1939 . . . World War II brings Hitler's vicious campaign of genocide. Six million Jews are murdered. For most Jews fleeing Europe *there is no refuge except Palestine.* . . .

1947 . . . The U.N., *over Arab protests,* decides to partition Palestine into separate Jewish and Arab states.

May 14, 1948 . . . Israel proclaims its independence . . . in a matter of hours it is attacked by Egypt, Iraq, Jordan, Lebanon, and Syria. The Israelis defeat the Arab forces. More than half a million Arab Palestinians leave their homes.

1949 . . . *Contrary to agreement,* Jordan occupies parts of Jerusalem, denying Jews access to their Holy places.

1956 . . . President Nasser of Egypt nationalizes the Suez Canal, *blocking Israel's shipping through the Canal and the Gulf of Aqaba.* Israel, with British and French support, launches a surprise attack across the Suez penninsula to the Canal and the Gulf. After a truce, Israel is *persuaded to withdraw* from the Sinai *under assurances* that she will have access to the Suez and the Gulf of Aqaba, and that a U.N. peacekeeping force will be moved into the Sinai.

May 1967 . . . As Arab *terrorist activities* from Syria become more vicious,

Israel threatens drastic *reprisal.* Egypt mobilizes troops in the Sinai. Nasser orders the U.N. peacekeeping group out and once again moves to block Israel's shipping.

June 6, 1967 . . . Diplomacy fails to open the Gulf of Aqaba. Israel again strikes at Egypt in the Sinai. Jordan and Syria attack Israel. In a six-day war Israel defeats all Arab forces. Israel occupies the Sinai, etc.

If this constituted an objective, impartial recital of the facts leading to the 1970 crisis, then the words "objective" and "impartial" should be taken out of Webster's dictionary.

The four occasions on which Victor Palmieri, the moderator, interrupted during the first Sunday evening's program clearly indicated how neutral he was. He broke in on Palestinian Abu Omar during the heated Dershowitz cross-examination to help the Israeli protagonist by stating, "Isn't it true Palestine as such was never a national state?" He did not permit Abu Omar to reply to this, and interrupted him to repeat: "Isn't it true it was never a Palestinian state? Why isn't it true, then, that it [the conflict] is just as much a movement for the national liberation for the Israelis as it is for Palestinians?"

After Professor Fisher finished his interview of Nasser, Palmieri queried: "Mr. Fisher, if Egypt loses she survives. If Israel loses, she is destroyed. Wouldn't it be a reasonable first step for the Arabs to pledge control over the Palestinian commando terrorist acts and then seek the pledge that you want from Israel, a pledge of withdrawal?"

In June 1977 Public Television presented the first of four James Michener "visual" essays, "Israel: A Search for Faith," produced by the Reader's Digest Association. The famed author, a strong protagonist for Israel and equally anti-Palestinian, ludicrously presented Israel as a land of faith, although more than 60 percent of its population was either atheistic or agnostic.

In the film Michener continually misled his viewers not only by invariably using Zionism, the nationalist movement, interchangeably with Judaism, the faith, but by conveniently substituting the country Israel for the people of Israel. He equated Hebrew, Israelite, Judean, Jew, and Israeli as one, so as to draw a continuity for Jews from 2000 B.C. to date. Everyone watching Michener was led to believe there has always been an Israel, and by implication that the Zionists have every right to hold onto this land. But in fact, aside from the 250-odd years the Kingdom of Israel existed in the 8th century B.C., there was no entity called Israel in the Middle East until 1948.

To boot, the photography placed emphasis on what Israel had done with its land, but showed in no way how the holy city of Jerusalem, surrounded by Israeli high-rises, has lost much of its spirituality. This hour-long presentation was effective Zionist political propaganda, all the more so because it was provided the subtle tonings of skilled causist Michener.

Educational TV could not ignore the controversial 1975 U.N. resolution on Zionism and racism, which had much of the nation in an uproar. New York's Channel 13 began its coverage in a detached enough manner: cameras followed the voting to the end, recording the decision of every member state. The station then relayed the speeches of Chaim Herzog, Israeli Ambassador to the U.N.; Dr. Fayez Sayegh, speaking on behalf of Kuwait and the Arab bloc; and U.S. Ambassador Daniel P. Moynihan—in that order. The Israeli and American speeches, both of which denounced the resolution in near-hysterical terms, ran a combined total of twenty-six minutes, as compared to the nine minutes accorded to Sayegh.

These speeches were followed by the Robert MacNeil Report (now the MacNeil-Lehrer Report), which presented a panel of "specialists" to "analyze" the outcome of the vote. The panelists were all Zionist-oriented. Freelance journalist Anthony Astrachan called the resolution an "obscenity." The other panelists—Charles Maynes, Jr., from the Carnegie Endowment; Professor Anthony Gaglione, political scientist from East Stroudsburg State College in Pennsylvania; and James Leonard, President of the U.S. Association for the U.N.—joined together in a continuous chorus of outrage against the U.N. resolution. "Moderator" MacNeil was no less restrained.

In the fall of 1976 ABC's "Accent On" program had a one-hour presentation (aired on two successive Sundays) in which six panelists discussed the Arab boycott of Israel. Out of the six, three were officers of the United Jewish Appeal and the American Jewish Committee, one was the son of the leading Zionist lobbyist in Washington, and the fifth was a Jewish law professor. Time was demanded under the Fairness Doctrine to present another viewpoint, and after several telegrams, phone calls, and two meetings, it was reluctantly granted.

Six weeks later, the perpetually active Dr. Mehdi and I were finally given a half hour. In *TV Guide,* the *New York Times,* and *New York Post* the program was listed as an "Arab Perspective of the Arab Boycott." It was obviously ABC's hope that the potential audience would react: "Well, who's interested in an *Arab* perspective of the Arab boycott."

At the first opportunity I let the audience know that I was presenting an *American* perspective, explaining why it was vital to the economy of the U.S. that the antiboycott legislation be defeated.[32]

My point was clearly made, much to the chagrin of moderator Bob Lape and producer Carrie Van Zile. But the last word was theirs. As our program ended, the station played an advertisement for Leon Uris's *QB VII* (starring Ben Gazzara and Leslie Caron), which was shortly to appear on ABC. And the illustrations for this advertisement were a minute of Nazi concentration camps! Anti-anti-Semitism was intended to blanket out any effect the presentation of the third point of view on the Middle East conflict, the American, might have had.

When network or local television feels pressed hard enough to make some display of fair play, invariably an Arab League representative or an Arab Ambassador is dug up to balance a raft of pro-Israel appearances, because even if his presentation should happen to be good, it can be totally discounted as coming from someone with an axe to grind. This was true when Arab League Ambassador Amin Hilmy was pitted in 1976 on WNET's MacNeil-Lehrer Report against Anti-Defamation League Chairman Seymour Graubard in New York and Congressman James Scheuer in Washington, plus moderator MacNeil, in a discussion of the Arab boycott.[33] The fact that many Muslim and Arab firms were on the boycott list, whereas Jewish companies were doing business in the Arab world, was totally obfuscated behind charges of anti-Semitism.

When an American anti-Zionist does manage to fight his way onto educational TV, the scales are tipped heavily in his opponent's favor. A classic example was the November 29, 1975, program of William Buckley's "Firing Line," on which I debated the Zionism resolution with Paul Riebenfeld, Co-Chairman of the Public Affairs Committee of the Zionist Organization of America.[34] From the very outset, Buckley bent over backwards to assist Riebenfeld in strengthening his arguments against mine. At one point Buckley cautioned a flustered Riebenfeld, "Don't be so defensive. I'm on your side." Our host's bias was further demonstrated by his quiet deference to the Zionist leader's lengthy harangues extolling Zionist policy, including the Israeli treatment of the occupied Arab territories, in contrast to Buckley's constant interruptions, bordering on outright hostility, whenever I managed to get a word in edgewise. In one memorable exchange, Buckley tried to discredit my position by asking if it was not true that Israel had accomplished far more during its twenty-eight years of existence than the Arabs had done in 2,000 years.

Buckley's careful manipulation of time in favor of Riebenfeld, and his shrewd interjections, served to reinforce the prevailing Zionist-induced image that Israel is sacrosanct. On any other issue, this irrepressible iconoclast, who had been more than fair to me on a previous occasion, would have deemed such onesidedness unforgivable. But when Israel is on the stand its halo must be preserved at all costs.

Israel's glowing image stems in part from the work of journalists writing from Israel. The International Press Institute at Zurich, in its very complete survey of 1970 "News from the Middle East," made the following observation, quoting an American correspondent (and because of the sensitivity of the subject the name of this correspondent was withheld, as were the names of all others quoted in this report): "Most correspondents in Israel are won over by the Israelis because of the little state's valiant struggle for existence, and they give little emphasis to the bleaker side. For example, one seldom reads about sub-standard living conditions, exorbitant prices, black markets, inefficient and insulting municipal workers, discrimination against Israeli Arabs and the lack of religious devotion except among the small orthodox minority. Instead we get a picture that is all 'milk and honey.' " This carefully nurtured blackout of Israeli defects, this "missing information," contrasts vividly to the widespread myth-information personified in the "desert recaptured" theme.

While it was Israel that launched the combined air, land, and sea assault on Egypt, Jordan, and Syria on the morning of June 5, 1967, it was several days before the American public was told who had attacked whom. Many Americans still believe that the Egyptians started the war, because the media so grossly and repeatedly exaggerated Nasser's threats. Very few stories of Arab suffering appeared in the American media. The horrible ordeal of Egyptian soldiers cut off in the desert, forced to march for miles barefooted under the blazing sun and dying in their tracks, if not already strafed by Israeli aircraft, was only portrayed in one brief *Life* magazine account. Totally ignored was the destruction of the cities of Suez and Ismailia, where virtually every important building was leveled, forcing out a population of more than 100,000.

There were countless examples of "distortion through omission" during the reportage of the October 1973 war. As in 1967, the airwaves were incessantly filled with the Israeli version of what was taking place. Foreign Minister Abba Eban was heard, Golda Meir was quoted verbatim, Moshe Dayan was paraphrased. CBS's Providence outlet stated it was in close touch with both Arab and Israeli Missions at the U.N., then proceeded to present interviews with two Israelis. Monitoring of something like forty news programs far into the night on the Saturday of the attack and on Sunday morning revealed that there was not a single radio station that failed to mention that the "attack had taken place on Yom Kippur, when Israelis were in the crowded synagogues." Similarly, not one program mentioned that this was also Ramadan, the month in which Muslim Arabs do not eat or drink, observing a strict fast from sunup to sundown. And Muslims have a far higher degree of religiosity than their Israeli counterparts. The media promptly called it the "Yom Kippur war."

Americans who are cognizant of this double standard and distressed by the pro-Israel bias in the media find it difficult to get their views in print. Their principal outlet is, of course, the Letters to the Editor column, long recognized as an important part of the American media and certainly an essential part of our democratic forum. Even in rural and small urban areas, there is evidence that this forum also falls prey to the scarcely believable Zionist control.

After many unsuccessful attempts, Grace Kerrish finally saw one of her letters, critical of Zionism, printed in the *Chippewa Herald Telegram* of Chippewa Falls, Wisconsin (population 12,000).[35] Hers was a Pyrrhic victory; an editor's note appeared in the same issue, alleging that her letter contained "factual untruths." The editor repeated the hackneyed Zionist propaganda that the Israelis requested the Palestine Arabs not to flee but to remain in their homes, and he further flatly declared that "it was proven beyond the shadow of a doubt that the Arabs are already in the Russian fold."

This was by no means an isolated instance. Dr. John N. Booth, who daily studied the Letters column in the *Independent Press Telegram* of Long Beach, California, encountered similar hostility when he wrote a letter of protest to Editor William W. Broom.[36] In his letter Booth complained of a "prejudiced selection of letters to the editor," noting "there appears to be a definite effort to keep out non-Zionist or critical-of-Zionist communications." Booth made reference to subtle Zionist pressures on "newspapers, clergymen, writers, and others," and suggested that "a newspaper should be the first to expose and condemn this."

In three curt sentences Editor Broom dismissed the matter: "Letters expressing opinions on issues and events meet our criteria for the editorial page. Letters complaining about beastly remarks from those disagreeing do not. The space is simply not ample to handle the airing of personal vendettas, and I doubt many readers would be interested in the denouement."

One would like to admire such decisiveness had it come from an objective editor. But Booth's study of the paper's letters to the editors over an eighteen-month period revealed that letters "complaining about beastly remarks" did appear regularly. One Samuel Whitman, a frequent "correspondent" to the Long Beach paper, had been certainly successful in venting his spleen against sympathizers with the Arabs. In one letter he singled out eminent historian Dr. Arnold Toynbee for "uttering the most ridiculous nonsense." In another, he expressed his chagrin that the U.S. did not tell Nasser to "go drink seawater."

Booth's study showed that in one eight-week period alone, five slanted Zionist letters from other writers were published. One lone communication, correcting some falsehoods in one of the five polemical letters, was allowed to appear on the other side of the issue.

In the course of his study Booth paid close attention to the paper's standards of selection and decided that superior literary skill or insights were hardly the criteria for determining the type of letters appearing in the newspaper. The majority of letters, he reported, "rewrote history, defamed the Arab peoples, or were sheer propaganda efforts." Booth noted that one letter (October 8, 1969) defending Israel's seizure of all Jerusalem, despite U.N. condemnation, was signed by "Joel Moskowitz." Investigation proved that the author of the letter was a 15-year-old boy. His father, Dr. Irving Moskowitz, was a known writer of letters to editors. Shortly thereafter (December 12, 1969), the parent himself was published again by the paper's editors in a letter charging that the Arabs "have terrorized the United States" and, according to Booth, offered other curious views of Middle East events.

Booth discovered that editorial approval even extended to letters from apparently phony organizations. A Rev. M.F. Carlsgaard of Paramount, California, signed his anti-Arab letter, "President, Christian Ministers to Prevent Communist Domination in the Middle East." Booth's inquiry of the local representatives of the National Council of Churches brought this reply: "This group is unknown to our clergy associates." Further investigation failed to locate this group, but it had been honored with space by the *Independent Press Telegram.*

The Unitarian minister's study concluded:

There is an almost rhythmic publication of Zionist letters. On the other hand, it is easier to drive a camel through the eye of a needle than to persuade the Long Beach editors to publish a carefully researched letter that is less than congratulatory of Israel's position. The few exceptions deserve a nod for tokenism. Letter after letter, from knowledgeable writers, interpreting the Middle Eastern situation from the non-Zionist side, moderately, thoughtfully and concisely, disappear into the maw of the local editorial page office never to see print. Two young students, Roger Malstead and Nancy Gallagher, who have lived in the Middle East and are leaders of the American Students for Justice in Palestine at UCLA, dramatize the newspaper's prejudices. Their thoroughly documented letter to the *Independent Press Telegram* detailing corrections for errors in two published letters by Israeliphiles Eleanor Stein and Sol Rankel never saw print. The anti-Arab mis-statements in the local paper by Stein and Rankel still stand.

Illustrative of the kind of treatment the Letters to the Editor column too often receives, on June 7, 1977, the *Washington Post*[37] printed under the heading "Israel Today: The Election, The Pressures" four vehement pro-Begin, pro-Zionist letters from Jack S. Cohen (Rehovot, Israel), Steven Mispsick (Washington, D.C.), Mark Klein (Jerusalem), and Joseph B. Axelman (Alexandria, Virginia). And the illustration appearing in the center for this three-columned spread of Zionist letters was the flag of Israel—this in the leading paper in the capital of the United States.

Editorials are of course opinionated by nature, leaving the reader the option of agreeing or disagreeing. But the reader seldom exercises this option when confronted with firsthand accounts written in vivid "I was there, you better believe it" terms. Charles S. Gregg, a private American citizen reporting on his brief trip to the Middle East for the *Sunday News* of Ridgewood, New Jersey, wrote what he saw through Zionist-tinted glasses. For all his readers knew, he was demonstrating a flair for accurate observation when he wrote:

It did not take long to discover that the entire populace [of Egypt]—cab drivers, hotel clerks, policemen, shopkeepers, etc.—had found their escape from Egypt's abject social and economic misery through a fanatical hatred of Israel as the cause of all its ills, including Uncle Ahmed's toothache and yesterday's bad weather. The people have been so propagandized by wily Arab dictators like Nasser intent on making them forget social injustice through anti-Semtism.[38]

This was his comment on Israel: "All the Greggs were deeply moved by our five days in this miraculous nation. Israel's miracle is that it exists although for 20 years surrounded by hostile forces which thrice have been thwarted in invasion attempts—and still fantastic internal progress has been attained." By printing this piece, the *Sunday News* had bestowed upon Gregg the trappings of authoritativeness, when in fact the writer was merely a tourist giving a highly subjective and one-sided account of the areas he visited.

The press can use any number of pretexts for mounting some form of fanfare for Israel or against the Arabs. The *Boston Globe* in 1973 on the back page of its first section under the heading RELIGION, "The Jewish People—40 Centuries Strong," had an article six columns long distributed by the United Press. No objective observer could ever claim this was a news story, let alone one dealing with religion. It belonged, if anywhere, on the editorial page. Under the byline of Lewis Cassels, the propaganda started: "For more than 4,000 years a variety of enemies with a variety of motives have tried to exterminate the remarkable people who call themselves Jews."

Support for Israel—both financial and moral—always peaks when Israel is at war with the Arabs. In the aftermath of the October 1973 war, while I was on a speaking engagement in Salt Lake City, Utah, I was not surprised to see a fervent "Aid-Israel" campaign developing in the local press. Salt Lake City's Jewish community of some fifty families was small but powerful.[39] In the Sunday Edition of the *Salt Lake Tribune,* the United Jewish Council made the front page with its boxed-off announcement of a community rally to "demonstrate the Salt Lake Jewish community's solidarity with Israel." On the back page of this same section, a full-length column appeared under the heading "Our Fight," then "Fund Rally Slated to Aid Israel." The entire article, empathizing with the Israelist cause, carried this statement of the Chairman of Salt Lake City's Jewish Council:

The sympathy of non-Jews has been forthcoming. Salt Lake City is distinguished by a lack of anti-Semitism. I think the little man is on the side of the Israelis. It's just the governments who play politics. . . . There is little fear that the Arab oil will determine American support. Only about 5% of American energy is supplied by the Arabs.[40]

The front page of this important Sunday edition ran a two-column, six-inch picture of Israeli mothers "searching through photographs made available by foreign film crews for photos of sons who are reported missing," with a prominently placed two-column story, "Missing Israelis? Film Provides Kin Clue." There was nothing to indicate that Arab mothers counted for anything or that the Arabs were also human. Here in Salt Lake City, the capital of the Mormon world, one not only encountered avid sympathy for Israel based on myth and misinformation, but also the Mormon propensity to favor Israel because their theology, as set forth in the Book of Mormon, views the Israeli return as part of prophecy. The followers of this religion consider themselves to be the Ten Lost Tribes of Israel.

However slanted the *Salt Lake Tribune* was, far more distorted were the columns that appeared syndicated in that city's *Deseret News,* which is owned by the church. One was a General Features syndicated article by Jim Fiebig, "Arabs Can Keep Oil," including the following:

> It's blackmail—but things aren't all that dark. The United States depends on the Arabs for no more than 6% of its oil and Federal officials say we could offset this by turning our thermostats down one degree and squeezing more production from domestic wells. Let's start turning and squeezing. What the Arabs have suggested with their dirty little game is that America's commitment to its friends goes no deeper than an oil well.[41]

There has never been a shortage of excuses for trumpeting Israel. In December 1968 the *Denver Post* brought out an eight-page supplement on the country at a time when Executive City Editor Robert Pattridge was on a trip to Israel sponsored by the United Jewish Appeal. The supplement contained such objective headlines as "Israel Progressiveness Draws Immigrant Flow" . . . "Israelis Have 'Nowhere to Run'" . . . "Bitter Battle Remembered—Golan Heights Quiet" . . . "Arab Has Freedom in Israel" . . . "UJA Director Believes Jewish Appeal Aid Vital" . . . "Denver Helps Build Dollar Bridge to Aid Israel."

When all-expense trips were not arranged, the Zionists were providing inexpensive visits by the media. *Broadcasting* magazine carried an advertisement by the American Zionist Federation announcing a "Media Tour of Israel for Editors-Writers."[42] At an inclusive cost of $331, "TV Radio and News and Program Directors and Commentators" were given a ten-day in-depth study tour and were introduced to their counterparts and to top Israeli personalities.[43]

News slanting by the press, along with presenting a plethora of "myth-information," has been as true in smaller urban areas as in the largest cities. On the basis of a lengthy study of Middle East coverage during the year 1975 by the *Sacramento Bee* in California's capital, Ombudsman Thor Overson admitted the correctness of the judgment of Mary Bisharat, herself the wife of a displaced Palestinian and an acknowledged Palestinian advocate, that her hometown paper had taken on an "anti-Arab, pro-Israel image."[44] The detailed Bisharat study did not suggest the entire *Bee* coverage was distorted, but rather that it failed in its incompleteness and was faulted by insensitive editing.

The Bisharat critique covered four categories: charges of Israeli-centered reporting; the unreported; the underreported; illustrations, including pictures. Cutting across the categories was the coverage of the wire service report of July 31, 1975, that Israel had built up a stockpile of ten atomic weapons. The *Bee* played the story on page 3 and gave it five inches—many major dailies played it on page one— with the headline "Israel's A-Bomb Hoard?" Three months earlier the *Bee* had quoted Egyptian President Anwar Sadat saying that if Israel added nuclear weapons to its arsenal, so would Egypt. The head on that story was quite different. It ranged over a three-column spread, reading: "Sadat Rattles Atomic Sword at Israelis."

Of the seven packets of newspaper clippings for 1975 in the *Bee* library on the Mideast concerned strictly with the Israel-Arab conflict, five are indexed "Israel." This suggests that the conflict was seen, even if subliminally, from the Israel point of view. (The Ombudsman placed the blame on wire service coverage but admitted "it could involve selection, editing of the wire report, and *Bee* processing."[45]) For that year there were 173 articles on the war indexed "Israel," against 41 found in the packet labeled "Palestinians." One story carried the headline: "Israel May Have Big Oil Deposit." Bisharat noted: "The deposit is in land occupied by Israel and therefore not Israel's but under siege. The deposits are in Ramallah in Palestinian land, sixteen miles northwest of Jerusalem."

The January 12 headline was "Palestinian Guerrillas Ambush Israelis." The story described how Israelis shelled three Lebanese villages with mortars and systematically destroyed crops there. Bisharat: "For those readers who do not get beyond the headline, quite another picture is created by 'Palestinian Guerrillas Ambush Israelis.' "

In reporting the Sinai withdrawal, a headline reads: "Israel Loses Territory," not "Egypt Regains Territory." Again, the story and headline are seen exclusively from the Israeli point of view.

On July 14 the story was: "Israeli Planes Go On Attack; Enemy's 2-Hit Claim Denied." "Whose enemy?" asked Bisharat. "Is it so firmly implanted in us who the 'enemy' is? Have we been so conditioned we accept Israel's 'enemy' as our 'enemy'? It would be an appropriate headline in the *Jerusalem Post* but not in the *Bee.* "

In reporting the Mideast arms buildup, no reference is found to Israeli weapons in headlines. For Israeli reports on the Arabs, the word "arms" is employed October 19, November 6, and November 18.

In the headlines of twenty-three stories on the Israel-Lebanese border crisis from January 5 through December 1, fifteen begin with "Israel," two with the reference "Lebanon" or "Lebanese." Of the same twenty-three, only four begin with "Arab"—and two of these employ the term "Arab Guerrillas." There were no references in the clips referring to Israeli "Guerrillas" or Israeli "Terrorists."

Bearing out the Bisharat contention that references to Palestinians were "all negative, pejorative," Ombudsman Overson observed:

In 16 articles reporting conflict on the Israeli-Lebanese border, Israelis are "Troops," "Commandos," "Security Forces," all neutral to positive terms. References to Palestinians include "Guerrillas," "Infiltrators," "Raiders," all negative to pejorative terms. Yasir Arafat is a "Guerrilla Chieftain."

In Israel incursions-invasions into Southern Lebanon (12 were reported from January to September) the reader rides along with Israeli "Commandos" and "Troops" as they "cross the frontier" or "slip across the border." There are no "invasions," no "incursions."

Arab invasion-incursions are reported less delicately, and usually are told from the Israeli point of view: July 18—"Israel security forces today kill 3 Arab Guerrillas who infiltrated." September 18—Israeli soldiers killed a "raiding party of 3 Palestinian guerrillas." And a story on May 11: Israelis "crossed into southern Lebanon in an anti-terrorist operation" during which Israelis "captured five suspected guerrillas."

Another image created by selective terminology was the November 22 wire service story reporting that Arab raiders were on a "head-hunting mission."

On the unreported, Bisharat was quoted by the *Bee* as noting:

Journalists might be expected to be interested in censorship of the press. They have been in India, yet the closing down of the chief daily newspaper in Arab Jerusalem by Israeli authorities was not reported in the *Bee*.

In addition, there is a tendency to omit important development realities. For one: The recognition by some in American Jewry that there is a "real desire for peace in the Arab world." The quote is from Israel Mowshowitz, prominent New York rabbi, in commenting on a three-week tour of Egypt, Syria and Lebanon, as well as Israel—a fact-finding tour encouraged by Representative Lester Wolff. When a New York rabbi says that, by golly it is news, and we should hear it. We did not.

Local U.S. newspapers are not alone in their devotion to Israel. America's best known weekly, *Time* magazine, gave a rousing salute to Israel in an editorial March 16, 1970:

Israel is a democratic, modern, stabilizing force in a chaotic and brutally backward corner of the world. The Israelis have created a nation and made the desert bloom, thereby more than earning their right to national existence. Israel needs U.S. support to survive, and if Israel were some day to fall, U.S. interests would suffer.

The issue at that time, after the Israeli triumph in the six-day war, was not whether Israel would be able to survive, but whether she would set forth concessions she was willing to make in order to bring peace to the area. With this glowing editorial *Time* only encouraged the Golda Meir government to stand pat on its occupation of Arab lands and to wait for its enemies to come and beg for peace.

Norman Cousins, founder of the original and new version of the reputedly liberal[46] *Saturday Review,* was more explicit in stating the editorial policy of his publication vis-à-vis the Middle East. In a letter explaining his reasons for rejecting several article possibilities I had submitted to him ("Who Has Been Sending the Letter Bombs," "The Creation of Israel Revisited"), he replied bluntly, "We will never publish anything that questions the right of Israel to exist."

Meanwhile, Cousins' publication had run three vigorously pro-Israel pieces in the first seven months under its new format, to wit, Rafael Rothstein's "Undercover Terrorism—The Other Middle East"; "Munich—Was it Worth It?" by the magazine's editors; and in their initial issue, a piece by Teddy Kollek, the Mayor of Jerusalem, "Who Owns Jerusalem?" Nor was there any subsequent change in direction of its coverage (Cousins, at one point a quiet anti-Zionist who opposed the creation of Israel, had somehow to square his escapism from Judaism).

Katharine Graham's *Newsweek* paid tribute to Israel in its issue of November 24, 1975. Responding to the Zionism-equals-racism vote at the U.N., the magazine attempted to explain Zionism in a dramatic two-page spread entitled "The Birth of a Nation." The authors of the article—Angus Deming, Phyllis Malamud, and Lynn James—were careful to include what they considered to be the Arab interpretation of Zionism, thus achieving a balanced look to their explanation. Their bias was discernible nonetheless. In describing the Arab point of view, they noted that "because Israel is by definition a Jewish State, most of its Arab residents *regard themselves* as second-class citizens." (Italics added.) Absent was any reference to Israel's discriminatory policies toward the indigenous Arab population on such matters as labor, land ownership, and education or to the Law of Return giving Jews from anywhere the right to become citizens, whereas Arabs who had lived in the land for centuries had been forced out and are not permitted to return. Included was this stock piece of Zionism:

Israel is their country—has, in fact, been so for 4,000 years—and sizable Jewish communities have lived there throughout the centuries. The Zionist movement, in this view, aimed at restoring a moribund state, not at harming other people. Zionists concede that Israel has an established religion, but note that other countries do too. And they maintain that Arabs freely live, vote and take office in Israel.

As the facts were presented, this Zionist explanation came across to the readers as most reasonable.

The sympathy for Zionism was all too transparent. Whatever restraint the writers may have exercised in the name of objectivity was overcompensated for by the layout of the article—complete with four large pictures of Theodor Herzl, 19th-century Jewish settlers in Palestine, Ben-Gurion, and Israeli troops at the Wailing Wall. Conspicuously absent from the photo display were the victims of Zionism, the Palestinian Arabs.

Benjamin D. Sherman in the Letters column of *Newsweek* July 4, 1977 disputed the magazine's profile of Menachem Begin in its May 30 International issue, which blamed him for many atrocities including the Deir Yassin killings and contended both that the village had "been used by Arab forces as a base of operation" and that "prior warning had been given to inhabitants to evacuate." An editorial note (as lengthy as the protesting letter) agreed with the letter writer, preposterously stating that "most contemporary scholars find no evidence that the Irgun engaged in widespread or systematic atrocities and that 200 villagers had died in the ensuing battle between the Irgun and Arab forces." As for alleged "acts of rape and mutilation, both the Arabs and the British had ample reasons for wanting to discredit the Irgun."

In answer to a protesting letter from Dr. J. Calvin Keene, former head of the Religious Department at St. Lawrence University, that no battle, but a massacre comparable to Lidice had taken place, Madeleine Edmonson responded on August 19: "There was no massacre. And we'll stand by the accuracy of that account." To support her position she cited "highly reputable reporters" A. J. Heckelman, author of *American Volunteers and Israel's War of Independence,* Dan Kurzman, author of *Genesis,* both staunch Zionist apologists, and J. Bowyer Bell. The latter in his book specifically refers to the "massacre of Deir Yassin" and the total abhorrence felt by the Haganah commander,[47] scarcely sustaining her contentions. The overwhelming weight of evidence of the International Red Cross, the United Nations, Ben-Gurion, the Chief Rabbi, Collins and Lapierre, Koestler, Kimche, Levin, and others previously cited (see pages 153 to 158) was simply dismissed by *Newsweek* as "anti-Jewish" propaganda.

The final word on this tragedy appeared on May 2, 1972 in the Tel Aviv newspaper *Yediot Aharonot*, which carried a letter from an Israeli who claimed to have been a Haganah officer:

> I saw the atrocities committed. I saw corpses of women and children who were cold-bloodedly murdered with bullets in their homes with no signs of fighting or house explorations. From my experience I know there is no war without killing and that not only soldiers get killed. I saw much in war, but I have not seen such a thing as Deir Yassin. And that is why I cannot forget what happened there.

Far less subtle in its handling of articles dealing with Israel has been *New York* magazine. From top to bottom this publication, prior to the 1976 Murdoch takeover, was Jewish-Zionist owned, controlled, and directed (Publisher Clay S. Felker; Editorial Directors Sheldon Zalaznich, Byron Nobell, and Jack Nessel; Design Director Milton Glaser, etc., etc.). This was reflected in the bias of the October 28, 1974, Tad Szulc *New York* magazine article "The Inexorable Drift Toward the Next Arab-Israeli War," portraying Israel one year after the "Yom Kippur" conflict as still "under siege" by Palestinian terrorists, while commemorating the anniversary of those killed in 1973. A typical notice in the *Jerusalem Post*, announcing the unveiling of the tombstone of one Raphi Unger, was reprinted in full in the article. Senator Javits was attacked for not really being pro-Israel in fact because, according to this writer, he had labeled President Nixon's alleged anti-Semitic remarks "irrelevant."

It was no surprise to anyone for *New York* magazine to run a four-page advertising supplement in the *New York Times*, the front page of which was adorned by a large and evil caricature of Saudi Arabia's King Faisal with the bold, inflammatory caption, "Are you going to let this man make you miserable?"—this was at a time Secretary Kissinger was trying to convince the Arabs of U.S. sincerity.

Well-known political author Richard Reeves[48] poured forth in *New York* magazine, "If Jews Will Not Be *For* Themselves, Who Will Be For Them?" This hysterical plea for more Zionist information propaganda noted that "if non-Jews have no idea how much the state of Israel means to American Jews, that is a Jewish fault."

When it concerns Israel or its leadership, magazines depart from their typical format and television commentators forget their accustomed deep and often embarrassing probing to indulge in ecstatic elegies. Such was the introduction of *The Saturday Evening Post* (April

1976) to an article on "The Palestinians" by former Israeli Prime Minister Golda Meir: "A pioneer in the work that made a vigorous productive nation out of barren desert asserts the rights of her people to their native land" and the equally one-sided interview granted her by Barbara Walters on the ABC $1 million, well-publicized news program to which the former NBC commentator had just switched. The otherwise tough, caustic interviewer presented easy, leading questions to help the Zionist leader implant more propaganda.

Pictures have been exploited to arouse compassion for Israelis and Jews. As an illustration, one need only refer to the tremendous photographic publicity given to the nationwide Jewish demonstrations protesting discrimination against Jews in the U.S.S.R. on the occasion of the Moiseyev Ballet's visit to this country in 1970. (In Seattle an eight-column spread was given to a photo of the demonstrators.)

It so happened that about this same time a sizable demonstration was launched against visiting Prime Minister Meir. As she was about to address a large gathering of the United Jewish Appeal at the New York Hilton, 200 militantly chanting protesters marched in front of the ABC building across the street in a show of solidarity with the Palestinian guerrillas. The picketers chanted, "No GIs to the Middle East" and "Sixth Fleet—Keep Out." This was quite an imposing turnout— particularly so for the Israelists and Zionists attending the function. They had seldom been the butt of such a well-organized protest in their capital city. Yet not a single photo appeared in the New York press of the demonstration.

While protests against Israel are ignored, the most minuscule demonstrations against the Arabs get blown out of proportion in the media, as happened on New Year's Day 1975 when WPIX Channel 11 (New York) 10 o'clock news reported the following:

Fifteen members of the Jewish organization called "Save Our Israel" held a noisy demonstration near the Lebanese Mission to the U.N. on East 76th Street. The protesters say it is a myth that Jews came to Palestine in 1948 and threw out the Arabs. They claim Lebanon and other Arab states helped create the Palestinian refugee problem by encouraging them to leave Palestine. Now they say the Arab states should take in the refugees. There was no comment from the Lebanese.

This "news" commentary was based on a press release, sent out by SOIL (Save Our Israel) and falsely captioned "Solidarity with the Arab Refugees."[49] The twelve-line mimeographed release gave no indication of how many people would take part. As it happened, there were exactly fifteen participants, engaged in "very dispirited, futile picketing," to use the words of the Lebanese Consul General.

It should not surprise anyone familiar with this media bias that American book publishers are also one-sided in their presentation. As I. F. Stone expressed it in "Confessions of a Jewish Dissident", his controversial article for *The New York Review of Books,* "finding an American publishing house willing to publish a book which departs from the standard Israeli line is about as easy as selling a thoughtful exposition of atheism to the *Osservatore Romano* in Vatican City."[50] Although books are not burned as they were in Nazi Germany of 1933 to the tune of the "Horst Wessel Lied" or Chopin's Funeral March, in America the same end result—i.e., forcing conformity to an imposed pattern of thinking—has been achieved. The book burners of 1977 have discovered other means of destroying ideas, far more subtle and more refined than using a common match. And the result has been near-catastrophic.

The university and academically oriented firms and the smaller publishers probably have the best record for fairness, but those catering to the mass American market have long abandoned impartial representation. As with the media, the distortions take many forms. The basic one is simply in the choice of books printed, promoted, and sold. For example, while browsing through the bookstands in the Tucson airport en route to Spokane during a 1971 lecture tour, I came across several recently published paperbacks dealing with the Middle East—all Zionist, of course—including *Hammer and Sickle* by Arie Eliev, an Israeli writer, and *Forged in Fury* by Michael Elkins. The eye-catching jacket of the latter book included a brilliant imprint of a Nazi flag into the center of which had been plunged a knife topped by a Star of David insignia. In bold type was printed: "This is a book about Jews. When you read it, you will understand the fiery heart that holds Israel together."

It is generally conceded that Americans purchase more books than they actually read. Heavily illustrated books, in particular, usually get only a quick glance. The illustrations are often selected and captioned by the publishing house, which consequently has a chance to distort the meaning of the text for readers who look only at the pictures. This might explain the masterly use of illustrations in *O Jerusalem!*[51] by Larry Collins and Dominique Lapierre, authors of the bestseller, *Is Paris Burning?*

One does not have to go beyond the dust jacket to learn the opinions of the publisher, Simon and Schuster, if not of the authors.

The comments, gauged to quickly woo potential Jewish purchasers, begin with a slanted contrast:

The Jews: some of them descendents of the old rabbinical families that had dwelt in Jerusalem for centuries—others the offspring of Zionism's early pioneers who had come to Palestine to reclaim their lost homeland by sweat and sacrifice; still others the remnant of the Six Million, trying to rebuild their shattered existence in new surroundings.

The Arabs: resentful of what they felt to be an effort to seize a land they believed theirs in the name of a crime they had not committed—the persecution of the Jews in the Christian West; driven to disaster by incompetent politicians, deeding the world the seeds of a new tragedy in their refugee camps.

Within this frame of reference the reader is introduced to the struggle for the Holy City, and sympathies are naturally guided in the direction in which the authors wish them to turn. One picture being worth a thousand words, the authors very pointedly use their photographs, in conjunction with accompanying captions and explanatory writing, to impart their kind of history. The selection of pictures, with few exceptions, helps depict the Arabs as bloodthirsty renegades and the Jews as a valiant people capable of enduring the most inhumane suffering in order to fulfill their goals of a Jewish state. The photographs in *O Jerusalem!* from pages 388 to 404 serve as an excellent example. "The Indomitable Architect of a Jewish State" is the Ben-Gurion caption; "It was thanks largely to his foresight in preparing his people for conflict with five Arab armies that the state of Israel was able to survive the first critical weeks of its existence in May–June, 1948." As usual, it is always little Israel, always the senseless numbers game instead of the quality, background, education, and support from the outside that underlie the figures.

Golda Meir's picture bears "Political Secretary of the Jewish Agency in 1948—The Woman Whose Mission Saved the Nation. She arrived in New York with ten dollars in her pocketbook and left a month later with fifty million dollars." Even pictures of lesser Zionist personalities are invariably captioned with words of glowing praise.

The first Arab picture is headed "A Terrorist's Harvest," dealing with "the cruel war in the streets of Jerusalem." This is what is said about the Arab leadership: "The principal technician of the Arab attacks was a thirty-year-old Palestinian Arab named Fawzi el Kutub, a graduate of an SS commando course in Nazi Germany. On February 1, 1948, he succeeded in destroying the *Palestine Post* building with a booby-trapped police truck." And there are pictures of the buildings he helped destroy in Jerusalem with bombs. Of another Arab leader, whom they refer to "as the most effective one in 1948," Abdul Khader Husseini, these are his words: "We will strangle Jerusalem." And this is on the same page with a picture of Jews lining up for "Food for Jerusalem's Famished Jews—At a Terrible Price." The story continues:

For weeks the city's 100,000 Jews endured the ordeals of a siege, their meager water ration distributed by tank truck, as illustrated above. Few convoys managed to struggle past the Arab ambushes, while the Haganah strove to claw a relief route, baptized the "Burma Road," across the Judean Hills. Most Jewish trucks, like the burning vehicle (below) fell victim to the Arab's ambushes. Their rusted ruins (below) still stand along the highway to Jerusalem, silent memorials to the sacrifices of the young men and women of the Haganah, made to keep the Jews of the City of David alive.

Included in this particular group of pictures is the familiar one of Ben-Gurion proclaiming the State of Israel on the afternoon of May 14, 1948, with a glowing caption so oft reiterated: "The Accomplishment of a 2,000-year-old Dream: The Rebirth of Israel." The Zionist leader is shown at the head of a table surrounded by others in the movement, proclaiming the beginnings of Israel. Above him is a photograph of Theodore Herzl, the father of Zionism.

To heighten the contrast, the two photographs on the opposite page (348) show a group of Arabs with guns in the act of seizing the Israeli kibbutz of Kfar Etzion, the Haganah's outpost south of the city. And below them is a picture of Arab Legion Commander Major Abdullah Tell with another officer, posed with "two of the four survivors of the 150 Jewish men and women who had defended the kibbutz's principal settlement."

On few subjects can anyone produce a group of photographs and captions so carefully chosen to impart so slanted a view. Apparently author Collins, who had represented the United Press in Beirut, had been influenced by his coauthor Lapierre or his publisher had his way with the photo section to make sure the Zionist story came through and readers would not be offended by the book's lurid, detailed description of the Deir Yassin massacre of Palestinians.

Many successful books today do not simply "make it" on their own. They become bestsellers when the publisher decides to make a major commitment in advertising and promotion. Because few books get this special promotion, a *New York Times* advertisement for *If Israel Lost the War,* a so-called "documentary novel,"[52] is significant and worth comment. The simulated front-page story of June 9, 1967, described the death and destruction wreaked by the Arabs as they rolled over Israel, with King Hussein of Jordan giving instructions to "Kill all the Jews!" This presentation from a respectable publishing firm (Coward-McCann) repeated aged Zionist propaganda that Arabs are fanatical anti-Semites who wish to outdo Hitler by pushing all Israelis into the sea. King Hussein's actual words were altered and taken out of context, as has been done time and time again to the statements of other Arab leaders.[53] This fictional documentary attempted to portray Arabs as neo-Nazi fanatics. Published just after the public hangings in Iraq, it was easier to pass off as credible.

But that was relatively mild. A much more high-pressure case involved the publication by Simon and Schuster in 1971 of *Red Star Over Bethlehem,* by self-styled Middle East "expert" Ira Hirschmann. To begin with, the book was widely advertised. Both the *New York Times* and *Commentary* referred to the author as an "international mediator and State Department emissary." When *Middle East Perspective* ran an open letter as a full-page *Times* advertisement on the day that President Nixon took office, every "i" dotted in the ad and every "t" crossed was meticulously checked for accuracy by the *Times* prior to publication. But Hirschmann's claims, which also appeared on the book's jacket, were never investigated by the paper.

Thirteen years earlier the now defunct *Look* magazine had featured an article by Ira Hirschmann, "The Case of the Missing Arab Refugees," in its September 17, 1968 issue. The article accused the United Nations Relief and Works Agency (UNRWA) of "supporting nonexistent Arab refugees with U.S. tax dollars." Unsubstantiated charges of the misuse of funds in the publication of "anti-Israel and anti-Jewish hate propaganda" were intermixed with Hirschmann's other allegations. The publication was timed to coincide with the U.N. consideration of both the Arab-Israeli conflict and the new budget for UNRWA, which had just published an effective photo pamphlet, "Twice in a Lifetime," dealing with the latest exodus of Palestinians.

In the aftermath of Hirschmann's outrageous article, *Look* magazine was inundated with letters noting that indeed the Arab refugees do exist and that their plight is a dire one, as well as challenges to publish the other side of the problem. The response of *Look* was to run six letters, four of which took issue with Hirschmann and two that defended his viewpoint. But the last word was given to a letter from Hirschmann himself, in which he noted that he had written the report on the refugees in an office and with the help of a secretary loaned him by the American Embassy in Beirut in accordance with instructions from Washington "to provide me with cooperation and facilities."

That was not the end of the Hirschmann article. It contained so many errors and distortions that UNRWA, which had been looking after the humanitarian aspects of the Palestine Arab refugees, issued a statement through its New York office to the press, which said in part:

> The 180,000 children who attend UNRWA/UNESCO schools every day certainly exist, and so do the 113,000 children who drink a glass of UNRWA milk daily, and the 46,000 young children who daily eat a hot meal provided by UNRWA. The inhabitants of UNRWA camps, for whom water and sanitation services are provided, also exist.
>
> All these services, by their very nature, cannot be provided for non-existent persons. Together they account for two-thirds of UNRWA's expenditures.

Hirschmann had sought to give himself credentials as an expert, alleging he had worked for UNRWA. Dr. John Davis, former UNRWA Commissioner-General, in a letter to *Look* Editor William B. Arthur had this to say:

> As a matter of fact, Mr. Hirschmann's only connection with UNRWA was that of consultant (without remuneration) for fundraising during part of the World Refugee Year, a position he held from October 1960 to April 1961. Mr. Hirschmann was employed on this basis because he contended that he had wide contacts in terms of potential sources of funds within the United States. I regret to add that he never succeeded in raising *any funds whatsoever.* [Italics added.]

It should come as no surprise to anyone familiar with Zionist tactics that Hirschmann never had been given any assignment by the State Department, as Deputy Assistant Secretary of State for Public Affairs Robert J. McCloskey revealed:

> Ira Hirschmann says he received a "commission" to do a survey of the refugee problem. That statement is incorrect. Hirschmann was received at his request at the State Department, prior to and following his trip to the Middle East, but at no, repeat no, point was he given any assignment or "commission" from the State Department. The views presented in his article, therefore, are his own and do not represent the position of the State Department.[54]

Both the ads and the jacket asserted that Hirschmann was the only American Jew to have been granted an exclusive interview with the late President Nasser. C. L. Sulzberger of the *Times,* Eric Rouleau, and this writer had interviewed the U.A.R. leader on several occasions. When this was pointed out to the publishers, they replied that they were "objective and responsible" and apologized for "the oversight on the part of the advertising agency for preparing that copy." But no public retraction was made and the harm had been done.

American publishers have almost invariably refused to publish books not written from a pro-Israeli standpoint. General Sir John Glubb, the internationally known and respected Englishman who commanded Jordan's Arab Legion, has written numerous books about the history of the Arabs and about the current crisis. He has unique knowledge of and experience in the Middle East, but while Hodder and Stoughton, his distinguished London publishers, have usually found American outlets for his historical works, no American publisher will touch those books that are critical of Israel. When Sir John wrote about topical issues, American publishers would not accept it. But General Glubb's biography of Muhammad was brought out in America by Stein and Day of Chicago, Muhammad being a "safe" Arab, a "good" Arab, a dead Arab.

The general cowardice is not confined to "conservative" elements in our society. The liberal community—otherwise so outspoken and fearless when it comes to unpopular issues—has almost totally abrogated its responsibilities in this area. When Dr. Booth tried to place his article, "How Free and Courageous Is the Liberal Church?" with the official organ of the Unitarian Universalist Ministers Association, *The Journal of the Liberal Ministry,* one of the editors told him they could not publish it because it would create "unbearable dissention [*sic*]" in ministerial ranks.

The Beacon Press, once so courageous and forthright but now viewed in some quarters as a "paper tiger press," has assiduously avoided the hot seat. Without much contemporary validity, it still rides the reputation for boldness achieved by Paul Blanchard's exceedingly critical books on Catholicism, the handiwork of an earlier brand of editors. The spring 1972 book catalog abounded in safely analytical books on all subjects: twenty-one on world affairs, twenty-seven on national affairs, ten on general history, twenty-two on European history, and twenty on the Third World. But not one volume had been published since 1957 on the powerful Zionist movement or the Middle East imbroglio.

I know of two volumes, including one published in Great Britain, which Beacon was offered, but the director rationalized his negative decision on this vital political/religious matter in these words: "We know the subject is delicate, sensitive, dangerous, and so we have to respect arguments made against bringing it out." Yet this was the same publishing house that received numerous accolades when it defied various orders by publishing Senator Mike Gravel's copy of *The Pentagon Papers*. Indeed, the Middle East/Zionist issue is the one that has separated the men from the boys.

This kind of Zionist cover-up is aided even by so well-known an author as James Michener, who advances Zionist ideas in *The Drifters*. One of the epigraphs that heads each chapter states:

Following World War I, the countries of Europe absorbed 1,500,000 refugees. Following the Greek-Turkish war, Greece absorbed 1,400,000 refugees thrown out of Turkey. Following World War II, the countries had to adjust to 13,000,000 refugees. Following the Indian-Pakistan war, the two sides absorbed upwards of 15,000,000 refugees. But in the wake of the Arab-Israeli war, the Arab countries prove themselves totally incapable of absorbing a few hundred thousand refugees for which they were themselves largely to blame.[55]

Michener, as a student of the Middle East who has visited there many times, knew full well that it has never been a question of the Arab countries being willing to absorb refugees, but rather the insistence of the Palestinian Arabs on not being absorbed into the Arab countries and having a country of their own.

In *The Drifters* the reader meets Yigal, the American, who chooses to settle down in Israel with his pioneering parents rather than with his wealthy grandparents in the States and who, as a lad of sixteen, goes into the six-day war and proceeds single-handedly to dispose of six Egyptian tanks. When he steps into a bar at Torremolinos, the fun-loving, depraved young people there, of course, recognize him on sight as the "great Israeli war hero." An earlier Michener *Look* cover story,[56] "Israel: A Nation Too Young to Die," was made of similar cloth, featuring an attractive photograph of stone houses, which had been built by Arabs before the Zionist colonization of Palestine had ever begun, and of olive trees, planted and cultivated by Arabs for centuries—all passed off as Israel's "making the desert bloom."

Even libraries have been affected. A visit a few years back to the USIS Library in Tel Aviv showed how Uncle Sam's own information service exhibited its partiality toward Israel. The USIS Library contained many outspoken Zionist authors and Zionist-oriented books, including works by Ludwig Lewisohn, Nadav Safran, David Ben-Gurion, Waldo Frank, James G. McDonald, Leon Uris *(Exodus)*, James Michener *(The Source)*, Walter Lacquer, and others. A look in the card catalog of the USIS Library in Beirut the same year did not produce one single book that could remotely be described as anti-Zionist in the way the many books in Tel Aviv were pro-Zionist.

The *Reader's Digest,* which has followed a predictable course in its choice of articles on the Middle East conflict, provides a logical bridge for any discussion of slanting in books and mass-circulation periodicals. Not long after the creation of the Jewish State in 1948, the *Digest* carried my article, "Israel's Flag Is Not Mine." But as the years passed and the *Digest* began to see which way the flag was waving, its editors soon lost all interest in even giving the other side a small piece of their valuable territory. My first book, *What Price Israel?,* published in 1954, was considered for condensation at that time, and three staff editors even did the necessary and difficult cutting. Then, suddenly, the project was vetoed,[57] and no condensation of that book or anything close to it has ever appeared; the *Digest* had joined the club.

In 1968 the Digest carried the condensation of Lester Velie's *Countdown in the Holy Land,* a book that rivals Leon Uris's *Exodus* in dispensing myth-information about Israel. *Countdown* deals extensively with the June war of 1967 and the events that brought the State of Israel into being in !948. In the *Digest* condensation, the words "Palestinian Arab refugees" do not appear once, but much attention is given to the homeless survivors of the holocaust, put at the grossly exaggerated figure of more than a million. (The official figure of the 1946 Anglo-American Committee of Inquiry was 226,000.)

In April 1969 the *Digest* found space for an article entitled "Jerusalem: The Sacred City." Its author, noted journalist John Gunther, calls Jerusalem a "City of Peace" but fails to mention the numerous blown-up and bulldozed houses that belonged to Arabs suspected of collaborating with the Fateh guerrilla movement. Israel's "Muslim neighbors invaded the little republic, determined to kill it off at birth," Gunther writes, without a word of reference to four previous months of incessant warfare and terrorism carried out by Zionist terrorist organizations, the Irgun and the Stern Gang, and by the Jewish Agency's regulars, the Haganah and the Palmach. The plight of the Palestinian Arab refugees is totally ignored in Gunther's article.

Cleveland Amory, who as a columnist and TV commentator has specialized on society life and authored *The Proper Bostonians,* visited Israel under the aegis of the *Reader's Digest.* In a complete departure from the field in which his expertise lies, Amory wrote a piece entitled, "Israel in Siege," which was Little Israel and the Big Bad Arabs all over again. People of Amory's background, and Wasps in general, prefer to regard Jews as belonging to a foreign state, as quasi-foreigners. Hence support of Israel is an ideal way out for some prejudice against Jews *qua* Jews.

The *Digest* has made a contribution to slanting in still another direction. An almanac is supposed to be a reference book, presenting the reader with an objective survey of facts and statistics. But the 1977 edition of the *Reader's Digest Almanac* (published by W. W. Norton Co.) contains outright Zionist propoganda masquerading as information. It demonstrates a glaring lack of objectivity by the amount of space assigned to each of the Arab states as compared to Israel and by the distortions in the data itself. "Information" about Israel occupies four columns, while "data" on Egypt and Syria together does not exceed five columns. In the opening paragraph of the so-called profile on each country, the editors betray their pro-Israeli basis. The following excerpts are direct quotes from the introductions to each section:

> *Israel Today:* "About the size of New Jersey, Israel is a small Middle Eastern nation on the east coast of the Mediterranean Sea. It is the only nation in the world in which Judaism is the official religion. Most of the people are the families of Jewish immigrants who came to their biblical homeland in the past 50 years from Europe, Africa, Asia and America.
>
> Surrounded by Arab nations that wish to destroy the Jewish state, Israel has fought four wars for its existence since declaring its independence in 1948. Its troops occupy over 25,000 square miles claimed by Palestinian Arabs. The nation remains continually on the alert against attack from its neighbors and spends two thirds of its national budget for military preparedness.
>
> *Egypt Today:* Egypt is the largest and most powerful of the Arab countries of the Middle East. But it has lost four wars in the past three decades with neighboring Israel, a Jewish State with a population only one-ninth the size of Egypt's.
>
> *Syria Today:* A militant Arab state, Syria has joined in four wars in three decades against its neighbor Israel.

Like other information aids, where the subject of Israel is concerned, this volume also makes no mention of the vast sums of money the tiny state receives from the U.S. and elsewhere. The problem of the Palestinian refugees is acknowledged, but the editors avoid even a hint of the truth—that the creation of Israel caused the native Palestinian inhabitants to flee or be driven from their homes and lands. Also included in this section is mention of "the daring rescue of passengers" at Entebbe. The operation is ridiculously described as "the most dramatic development in international affairs in 1976" and is given almost as much space as the U.S. presidential debates.

In addition to the U.S., the only other part of the world cited in another section for an "historical survey" is the Middle East area. The period covered spans the centuries from 3200 B.C. to the present. Even though it is presented as a chronology of developments, the pro-Israeli slant is flagrant and obvious, as can be seen from the following excerpts:

> *1929*—Arabs attack and kill Jews in Jerusalem, Palestine, in dispute over Wailing Wall.
>
> *1948*—First Arab-Israeli war: all of Israel's Arab neighbors attack and attempt to destroy new nation but Israel with help of military armament from U.S. is able to drive back Arab forces.
>
> *1964*—Palestine Liberation Organization founded by Arab nations to conduct terrorist raids on Israel.

In the manuscript given by my publisher to the copy editor for a thorough going-over prior to publication, I had expressed astonishment that "such a magazine as the *Digest* with its wide circulation and highly experienced staff should stoop to such a slanted presentation." Attached to this page when the editor's work had been done was a note shedding light on what certainly was a 100 million to one shot. She informed me that she had served for five years (1968–72) as chief copy editor of this very Almanac, but beginning in 1973 it had been freelanced. She had even graciously researched the 1972 edition to find the following Israel section, which must be compared with "Israel Today" and the chronology set forth above regarding the 1977 almanac:

> The politically conscious Arab elite opposed the national-home policy as an obstacle to their independence, which they felt should follow logically on the collapse of the Ottoman Empire. As Jewish migration increased under the pressure of Nazi German persecuion, an Arab rebellion caused Britain to heed Arab objections by limiting Zionist immigration and land purchases during WW II. But after the war Britain was forced to give in to the twin pressures of its own desire to find a haven for Jewish survivors of Nazism and a savage campaign of terrorism by Palestinian Jews. . . . The two most important issues still blocking genuine peace in the area are the resettlement of hundreds of thousands of displaced Arab refugees from Palestine and adamant Arab refusal to acknowledge Israel's right to exist.[58]

In the aftermath of the 1967 war, one publication that bore promise of a more balanced interpretation of events was *Atlas*. Although published in the U.S., *Atlas*'s outlook was purportedly international since its pages were devoted exclusively to translated excerpts and summaries of the world press. Yet its selection of articles on the war, and particularly its introductory explanations preceding each translation, left no room for doubt that its sympathies lay heavily in the Israeli camp.

The lead article of the July 1967 issue, "The Embattled Middle East," carried the subheading: "The War Game that Went Wrong: The Case of Keeping Israel Alive." The comment introducing pieces from the London Sunday *Times* and *Le Nouvel Observateur* (Paris) read: "With a flash of gunfire, war had pitted the Arab world (nearly 100 million people) against Israel (about 2.5 million people joined to build a homeland on the soil of their ancient beginning.)" The French piece, written by Jean Daniel, was described as "a most remarkable article written on the eve of war on the importance—to mankind—of Israel's survival." Articles by London *Times* correspondent David Holden[59] were to be included in this *Atlas* issue, according to prepublication blurbs, but they were not. Judging from the November 19 piece that Holden wrote in the *Times*, "Military Occupations Are Apt to Be Nasty for the Occupied," one could understand this omission from *Atlas*.

The war was scarcely over when the September 1967 issue of *Atlas* carried four articles from the Arab-Israeli press, introduced under the title "The Middle East: The Irony, the Anger" in this manner: "Peace in the Middle East was far away, if in truth a lasting peace was possible. Belligerent Arab leaders met in saber-rattling conferences. The Israelis kept wide-awake on the long cease-fire lines."

In October *Atlas* endeavored to bring Black America into a racist onslaught on Nasser and the Arab world by means of a cover-featured article: "Slaughter in Africa—Arabs Against Blacks," a piece translated from *Stern*, Hamburg. In its "editorial" introduction, blame is placed at the door of the U.A.R. leader for "the extermination in the Sudan of thousands of negroes at the hands of Nasser's puppet Arab leaders." Not one single word in the original piece, itself written by two top reporters for this widely circulated German weekly, remotely related the Egyptian leader to what was alleged to have taken place.

Today *Atlas* is under different ownership and presents a more balanced selection of articles. One-sided accounts favoring the Israeli position are still the norm, however, in national mass-circulation periodicals. Any dramatic shifts would invoke the wrath of powerful pro-Israel groups, and could easily induce large-scale cancellations of subscriptions and removal of advertisements from the publication, resulting in serious economic losses.

Even the mildest form of criticism has been known to elicit hostile reactions from Zionist quarters. For instance, when *Life*[60] magazine once ventured to make just a few cautionary remarks about Israel, it received this reaction from the Minneapolis, Minnesota, Jewish periodical *The American Jewish World.*

But if one brainwashed negro spews out his ignorant torrent of illwill, what are we to say of a supposedly informed, responsible, and nationally influential source such as *Life* magazine when it, too, flops over on to the side of anti-Israelism? Especially on the damp and disgusting grounds of pragmatism. . . .

To justify its contemptible appeal to economic greed, *Life* throws in a couple of indictments, 1) accusation of adventurism and 2) the charge that Israel has violated Arab boundaries ever since the June war. *Life* must be reading the U.N. Security Council's mail from Cairo, Amman and Beirut. Or, it has taken it upon itself to serve as the mouthpiece of the Arab-odored State Department.

In either case we must say with a sense of grievous desertion that, with friends like the black extremists and *Life* magazine, we don't need Nasser.[61]

When Harold R. Piety, Associate Editor of the *Dayton Journal Herald,* wrote in December 1975 a remarkable article, "Who Speaks for Judaism?" in the *Journal Herald* Forum, he was roundly criticized and received many blasts from the local Zionists despite the objectivity of the article and the deep sympathy expressed for the victims of Nazi Germany. In this lengthy article the Ohio editor expressed the view that the General Assembly should have dealt with the Zionist issue as an essentially internal issue and admitted that many of the nations that voted in support of the resolution at the U.N. did so cynically. But his main emphasis was to express the view that

. . . the anti-Zionism of the Arab nations is not anti-Semitism. The Arabs themselves are Semites, and the Muslim world historically was hospitable to Jews when Christians were murdering them. When the terrible pogroms in Czarist Russia in the 1880's and 1890's terrorized Jews in the Pale, Jewish communities were living in harmony with Muslims throughout the Arab world, including in the Old City of Jerusalem. *Zionism, not anti-Semitism, changed that.* [Italics added.]

Piety was prohibited from writing further Middle East articles, and his frankness may even have cost him a deserving editorial promotion.

Occasionally there are some slight indications that Israel's stranglehold over the American media might be weakening ever so slightly. Israeli Defense Minister Shimon Peres, appearing on "Face the Nation" on December 15, 1975, encountered some tough questioning with regard to the bombing attacks on Lebanon, new settlements in the Golan Heights, and Israel's refusal to debate with the PLO in the U.N. Security Council. The same may be said regarding the February 12, 1978, "Meet the Press" appearance of Foreign Minister Moshe Dayan, when Israeli policy on the settlements was given a blistering going-over. Then there are inevitably sharp reversions to the norm, at moments of crisis when pressure on the media mounts from inside as well as outside.

It will take eons of time before Americans realize the extent of the media's irresponsible coverage of the Middle East, whereby the most complex issues have been presented only in terms of sweeping blacks and whites, the good guys and the bad guys, cowboys and Indians—in short, the impeccable Israelis and the abominable Arabs.

Within the mass media a few publications—a very rare few—resisted Zionist pressures and succeeded in presenting both sides of the Arab-Israeli dispute, notably the *Christian Science Monitor.* Many foreign correspondents who covered the area over the years also reported on and analyzed the news with honesty and objectivity. These included not only John Cooley of the *Monitor* and John Law of *U.S. News,* who covered the Middle East for twenty-two consecutive years, but such other correspondents, whose organizations tended to have a pro-Israeli bias, as Wilton Wynn of *Time,* Kennett Love of the *New York Times,* and Barry Dunsmore and Peter Jennings of ABC.

The views of Rabbi Elmer Berger, leader of American Jewish Alternatives to Zionism, expressed before Southeastern Massachusetts Technological Institute in November 1967, are still valid:

It must be clear . . . that, in a democracy where enlightened public opinion is essential for the formulation and implementation of a national foreign policy, one of the first problems confronting American policy-makers for the Middle East is this long history of formidable pro-Zionist and pro-Israeli propaganda. The central proposition, the rock upon which this democracy is founded, can be summed up in four words: "Let the people know." These words apply as precisely to our national interest in the Middle East as they do to any of our domestic liberties and responsibilities. If we are to match policy with our national interests in the Middle East, the American people will need to be more critically alert. *The American press has been almost criminally negligent* in helping to provide such vigilance. [Italics added.]

The *New York Times* is the ultimate case in point.

Número Uno: *The New York Times*

There's villainous news abroad.

—Shakespeare, *Henry IV*

The founder of the *New York Times,* Adolph S. Ochs, wrote the following for the editorial page of his first issue, on August 19, 1896:

It will be my earnest aim that the *New York Times* give the news, all the news, and in concise and attractive form in language that is parliamentary in good society, and give it as early, if not earlier, than it can be learned through any other reliable medium; to give the news impartially, without fear or favor, regardless of party, sect or interest involved; to make of the columns of the *New York Times* a forum for the consideration of all questions of public importance and, to that end, to invite intelligent discussion from all shades of opinion.

Those words are emblazoned in large letters behind the bust of Ochs at the *Times* office, and are frequently carried in advertisements promoting the *Times.*

Throughout this volume endless examples are cited illustrating the enormous extent to which this powerful newspaper has deliberately strayed from the goals of its founder and scarcely ever presents the Middle East impartially, let alone fearlessly. But why should the *Times* be singled out in a chapter to itself?

In these days where control of the media is concentrated in fewer and fewer hands, there is even greater meaning to the title of the George Seldes book written in the 1930s, *Lords of the Press.* Today the *New York Times* is indeed the superlord by virtue of its 854,000 daily circulation and its 1.4 million readership of its four-pound, 400-page Sunday issue reaching every part of the country, as does its syndicated news service, which competes with the Associated and United Press and is carried by more than 100 papers in the U.S., Canada, and overseas.

The *New York Times* Company, now on Wall Street's good-buy lists, owns nine smaller dailies, four weeklies, six magazines, two broadcasting companies, three book-publishing companies, and part of three Canadian paper mills. Current publisher Arthur O. Sulzberger was planning to add two new magazines in 1978, one on fishing and the other on outdoor pursuits, and hopes to purchase more broadcasting stations, among other possible acquisitions. The *Times* employs the nation's largest full-time news staff: 550 journalists in New York, 32 outside the U.S., 40 in Washington, and 19 throughout the country. One has to travel across the country and abroad, too, to appreciate fully the influence and uniqueness of the *Times*.

To a certain extent all news in America, particularly foreign, is what the *Times* calls news. This, as syndicated columnist Nicholas Von Hoffman pointed out, is because the *Times* spends on foreign correspondents the kind of money other papers, magazines, and networks will not.[1] It is also because "so few print or broadcast editors are able to make independent judgments of their own on the news, simply lack the character and stature to have an opinion of their own, and prefer the safety of letting the nation's most prestigious paper do their decision-making for them." This, adds Von Hoffman, is particularly so on the Israeli issue, where any adverse publicity can bring down on the editor vociferous abuse from the nation's most meticulously organized lobby.

There is no newspaper in the world that can compare with the *New York Times* for sheer coverage of news, both domestic and foreign. One feels completely lost when not seeing it, but equally aggravated while reading it.[2] But from the headlines on the front page to the letters column and the Op-Ed page, and most subtly in the Sunday "Week in Review," there is no opportunity lost to advance the prejudices and predilections of its ruling clique. Editorializing is scarcely confined to the editorial page. To give an appearance of impartiality, it will even run a highly emotional or badly written letter to represent the opposing point of view, which then entitles the *Times* to run three or four more letters supporting its own viewpoint. To understand what is really taking place requires the major task of reading the paper from cover to cover day in and day out.

There is increasing world reliance on its news dispatches. *Times* columnists such as James Reston, Anthony Lewis, C. L. Sulzberger, and Russell Baker appear nationally. High schools as far west as the State of Washington read summaries of the Sunday section "Week in Review" in their current events classes, and this section is as much read as the Bible by midwestern wives who wish to catch up with the news in one place and at one sitting.

Another important influence of the *Times* derives from the often reported fact that it has long been read by many of our elected officials, from the President down. They may curse it, or toss it into the wastebasket, but they cannot entirely ignore it. And even when they disagree violently with its editorial positions—as overtly expressed—they probably depend on the *Times* for both "objective" and in-depth reporting as do so many students of world affairs.

There are other reasons why the *Times* must be singled out and analyzed, indeed exposed. For one, there is its reputation as an intelligent, thinking person's publication. This also carries the implication that it is somehow objective, nonpartisan, unemotional. All of that simply means that the *Times* ends up being more insidious, cunning, and ultimately dangerous than, for instance, the blunt, unsubtle *Daily News,* one of its rivals in New York City. With the *News* and its like, the reader always knows where the paper stands, and thus knows where he or she, in turn, should stand. With the *Times,* and its reputation for objectivity, the reader is lulled into accepting each story as *"the* truth."

Another aspect of the *Times* that has a direct bearing on our concern is its reputation, gained and enhanced in recent years, as a fearless exposer of scandals in high places and public life. One thinks of its role in printing the *Pentagon Papers* and in exposing the Nixon administration. It has been zealous in exposing the CIA over the years and was influential in airing the New York nursing home scandals, as well as many instances of corruption in local government.

This, coupled with its own motto—"All the News That's Fit to Print"—has set up an image. The concomitant of this reputation and motto is: If it's not in the *Times,* it's not happening.

By any standards, every aspect of Israel has been "overcovered" in the *New York Times.* Any cursory examination of the daily, let alone of the Sunday editions, will yield a plethora of articles of kibbutzim, travel, Israeli folk dances, the Israeli "economic miracle," etc. It is interesting to compare this coverage with the paper's reportage on pre-Qaddafi Libya, which had an economic miracle of its own—a miracle, incidentally, that was entirely homespun, not artificially stimulated from abroad as has been the case of Israel.

The *New York Times* Index of January 1968 to March 1969 (well after the June 1967 war, so that information directly relating to the hositilies would not predominate), reflected the following coverage for "Israel" and "Libya." These statistics of course do not take into consideration the many items listed under the headings beginning

"Jewish" and "Zionist," nor under the names of the many component groups in the Zionist-Israelist movement.

State of Israel	*Libya*
30 Headings	14 Headings
161 Main Subheadings	0 Main Subheadings
9 Secondary Subheadings	0 Secondary Subheadings
878 Lines in Index	36 Lines in Index

The bias of the *New York Times* is carried out through a myriad of devices. The greatest harm has been wrought not by fully reporting one side of the coin and completely neglecting the other, nor by the gross partiality in editorials and in the letters to the editor. What is more dangerous is the subtle means of distortion, including slanting by labeling ("Hitler of the Nile" and "Communist puppet" are but two of the infinite number); by headlining ("Israel Will Aid New Thant Move" headlines a story on page one[3] while the statement that U.A.R., Jordan, and Syria had earlier so agreed was lost somewhere in the account); by strategic placement (a pro-Israeli story appears on page 1 while the rebuttal the next day is buried on the bottom of page 11); by explanation (an editorial refutation inserted in brackets in the middle of an otherwise 100 percent news story, downplaying an attack by the American Council for Judaism on Zionism by citing the small number of Council members in contrast to the large figure of Zionist membership[4]); by contrast (in its coverage follow-up of the Israeli attack on the Karameh refugee camp pictured Prime Minister Eshkol at the bedside of a wounded Israeli soldier while King Hussein is shown inspecting a captured Israeli tank.[5]).

The *Times* invariably prominently displays that news which fits its viewpoint and conceals the developments toward which the paper is not well disposed. A classic example of this occurred when philosopher Jean-Paul Sartre, who in the past had rejected all honors including the Nobel Prize, accepted an honorary doctorate from the Hebrew University of Jerusalem. The *Times* carried the following words, reporting Sartre's response to this reward: "My acceptance of this title, which I regard as an honor, has a political significance. It expresses the friendship I feel for Israel since its birth, and my desire to see that nation prosper in peace and security." This was the end of the *Times* quotation. But the very next sentence, quoted in the *Christian Science Monitor* and cut out by the *Times*, read: "*I consider that such a peace can only exist if the Israelis start talking with the Palestinians, for I am also concerned over the fate of the Palestinian people. . . .*" (Italics added)[6]

Another striking example of the many distortions "by omission" was the *Times'* reportage the day after President Sadat's appearance on the "Sixty Minutes" Mike Wallace-moderated show of March 27, 1977. While extracts from the Egyptian President's remarks were quoted, there was not one word about what Yasir Arafat had said on the same program, let alone that he had appeared. The PLO leader's words showing his people to be warm human beings, not desiring to kill Jews, and his adroit handling of the customary tough Wallace questioning, was intentionally kept from *Times* readers. On the most important question of why the PLO was not prepared to recognize Israel at that time, Arafat had noted on CBS that it was first up to Israel (and the U.S.) to recognize the Palestinians, who have been the victims since 1948 of the original injustice that brought the Zionist state into being and their simultaneous displacement.

There had been a similar near-total blackout in the coverage of Senator Fulbright's historic farewell address at Westminister College, in November 1974, viewed by many as one of the most important speeches of the century. The Hearst *San Francisco Examiner,* as well-known anti-Zionist writer Moshe Menuhin in a rejected letter to the Sulzberger paper noted, printed important passages, including the Senator's acute warning of the "danger of a fifth Middle East war," but the *Times* in its minimal coverage omitted any reference to "Israel's strange influence in getting all the money she needs from America."

In addition to its across-the-board slanting, this powerful newspaper helps create a general atmosphere in which brainwashing can more easily take place, and the more obvious instances of distortion can be kept from being recognized. A shining example was the Sunday issue of February 8, 1970, when the *Times* ran a front-page, left-hand-column story headed "5 Arab Countries Begin Cairo Talks on War Strategy." Adjacent was a two-column lead of an interview with Golda Meir, "Air Raids Show Nasser Is a Failure."

Between these two stories was an article headlined "Israeli Jet Sale Not Set, U.S. Says." This was a denial by the State Department of the *Times* story of the previous day. These articles were intended to raise speculation over the jet sale and to spur an increase in the tempo of Zionist pressures that were already mounting on Washington to supply Israel with twenty-five Phantoms and eighty Skyhawks for delivery in 1971. (Whether calculated to have that effect or not, this widespread publicity on the alleged sale made Secretary of State William Rogers' visit to Morocco and Tunisia, then in progress, most unpleasant.)

The Meir interview, running over to an inside page with a five-column head, presented the reasoning for Israel's continued air attacks into the very environs of Cairo. But even the most sympathetic treatment at the hands of writer James Feron could not conceal the obvious Israeli motivation behind the raids—to force Nasser to make peace or to quit his office. No mention, however, was made of what was well known to Meir and to the reporter: that no Arab government could then have survived five minutes if it entered into direct negotiations for peace while Arab territories still remained in Israeli hands. Sadat could do this in 1977 only after the Arab show of strength in the 1973 war.

In "The Week in Review" section of that same date, an editorial, "Jets for Israel," prematurely defended the U.S. supplying additional jet planes to Israel as "a tragic but necessary decision." On the same page was an article from Jerusalem by James Reston, "Jerusalem: Surrounded, Outnumbered, and Defiant," which helped advance the theme of the editorial.

The same section carried a piece datelined "Jerusalem," also from the pen of James Feron, which gave expression to Israeli thinking about her war of attrition, and its "risky premise that many moderate rulers have followed fallen strong men," speculating "whether this might not be the case someday of Cairo." Next to this was a chart illustrating the "Strategic Importance of Golan Heights," bearing this weighted, over-caption: "Israel seized Syria's Golan Heights during the six-day war in 1967 to insure the safety of Israeli towns and farm settlements that have come under bombardment from Syrian guns on the heights. . . ."

Filling out the page was an article datelined "Cairo" and headlined "Arabs Pin Hopes on Moscow," which described the alleged jubilation in the Egyptian capital in the wake of Kosygin messages warning the West that Israeli air strikes against Egypt had become dangerously provocative. As on other occasions, *Times* reportage here was furthering the polarization of U.S.S.R.-Arabs vs. U.S.-Israelis. A news report from Hong Kong on page 4, noting a message of support from Chou En-lai to President Nasser, further tied the Arabs to Communism, as did the prominent mention that Red China was supplying arms to the Al Fateh guerrillas.

In the travel section, crowded in by photographs, a four-column headline read: "Tourists in the Land of the Twilight War . . . And Still They Come to Israel." Authored by the ubiquitous James Feron, the article started from the subcaption to insist that "tourists from Kansas, as above, and New York continue their invasion of Israel and the Holy

Land, nonchalantly accepting the signs and symbols of a nation at war." Only deep in the article did one read that there had been a tourist decline in 1969. The largest photograph, incidentally, was unmistakably that of Christians, for the tourist decline had been more marked among non-Jews. The full page endeavored to show that Israel was still a fine tourist spa to visit just then, and the theme was carried over to a lengthy continuation inside the paper.

The first piece in the magazine section was "Israel's Early Warning System in the Arab World," an article by Paul Jacobs dealing with the vital role played by Israeli intelligence, "a major factor in Israel's survival." This interesting article, written with the greatest of sympathy for Israel, was previewed by continued announcements on WQXR, the *Times*-owned radio station. While the famed abortive Lavon spy affair was briefly mentioned, nothing was said of the other many instances in which Arab governments, notably Syria, had apprehended Israeli spies, to which the world usually responded: "Anti-Semitism." The bold heading atop one of the last pages of the Jacobs article, "World Anti-Semitism Has Given Israel Agents Who Know Cairo As Well As They Know Tel Aviv," sought to justify the Israeli spying and spread the *Times'* favorite cult. And in the Book Review section reviewer Professor Rubin Rabinovitz dissected an Iris Murdoch novel in which the evil acts of the villain, a survivor of Belsen, were the results of "the evil he himself suffered during his imprisonment."

That day's *Times* might seem, by now, rather remote in time, but chances are you could take almost any Sunday *Times* of the past twenty years and find the same pattern of distortion, bias, slanting, and coloring, if not to the same extent, as that particular Sunday.

Sunday, July 8, 1973, involved coloration in the Sports section. On page 4 under a Tel Aviv byline (the writer was not identified nor was it a "Special to the New York Times," indicating it was probably a reprint from a Zionist handout), was a four-column heading: "Maccabiah Games: Somber Occasion." The article noted that the quadrennial sports event, which "brings together leading Jewish sportsmen of the free world," was to open the following Monday evening in Tel Aviv. The article went on:

You will also recall the murder of members of the Israeli contingent to the Munich Olympics last year. A memorial prayer composed by the Chief Rabbi will be intoned, and eleven torches will be lit in succession as each victim is named. Most of the victims had won medals at Maccabiah Games. . . . The organizers invited two non-Jewish Dutch athletes who, in sympathy with the Israelis, withdrew from the Olympics after the murders.

The front page of that *Times* almost gleefully carried in large capitals: "Iraq Executes 23 for Coup Attempt," while in the center of the first news section was a lengthy story about Libya's Colonel Qaddafi "giving Egyptian leaders a foretaste of difficulties under the merger," in which the problems facing the scheduled Libyan-Egyptian union were detailed. While these stories were accorded solid, noticeable space, two days previously, buried in an inside *Times* page and set in a single column on the far left, completely overshadowed by seven columns of advertising, was a lengthy story "Jews Ask Kosygin to Permit Return." This concerned sixty Soviet Jews who, in a reversal of their exodus, were pleading to return to the Soviet Union and had petitioned Premier Alexei Kosygin, then visiting Vienna. The "News Summary and Index" of that day listed this story in a most misleading fashion so as not to attract attention: "Sixty Jews in Vienna Petition Kosygin." (What Jews? Petition for what?), The Libyan-Egyptian troubles over their merger had been spelled out in the same Index over no less than sixteen lines.

On June 10, well before the October 1973 war and the Arab oil embargo, the *Times* contended in an editorial that there was no connection between U.S. policy in the Middle East and the enrgy crisis: "American governmental and oil officials are hardly so naïve as to believe that a change of policy in the Arab-Israeli dispute could significantly affect the long-term trend toward nationalization among all of the Arab oil states, although the Libyan example may accelerate that trend." Three years later the *Times* was taking the same tack in editorials and news stories when the Saudi Arabians broke the price front in OPEC and limited themselves to a 5 percent rise. Israel's media champion would recognize this action only as a gesture of restraint and a sign of goodwill toward the incoming Carter administration, not as leverage on Washington to exert pressure on Israel in future peace negotiations so as to move toward peace terms the Arabs could accept.

Photographs in a newspaper such as the *Times* are a very potent part of the journalistic imprint. Every aspect—the selection, size, placement, caption—you may be sure is never left to chance. The use of photojournalism may often be most subtle, a means of concealing covert sympathy for Israel and antipathy for Palestinians and Arabs.

In May 1964 when Egypt's Gamal Abdel Nasser was being courted by Nikita Khrushchev, the *Times* ran a picture on the front page of a

Sunday issue of the the Egyptian and Soviet leaders riding together in the same automobile in a welcoming parade in Cairo. Fair and good; it was certainly a major event for that day. But then on the front page of their "Week in Review" section of the same *Times,* the news editors inserted (and this is normally put to bed in New York before the Soviet leader had even set foot on Egyptian soil) virtually the same photograph. The point was made—if you did not get the message on page 1 of the *Times,* here it is: Nasser, Israel's greatest foe, is a Communist —Egypt is going along with the Soviet Union. (Nasser's incessant battle against the Communists at home in Egypt where most of them were jailed, while accepting enormous military aid from the Soviet Union, was scarcely ever related to *Times* readers.) Such slanting by repetition has often been employed.[7]

On May 14, 1969, on page 3 appeared a picture four columns 5½ inches deep, with caption, of a wounded Israeli soldier receiving a blood transfusion after being shot by Egyptian snipers while on duty on the East Bank of the Suez Canal. There were no pictures of any size of Egyptians or Syrians wounded in this war of attrition.

Again, in May 1970 the photo of the bombing of the Egyptian school in Bahr al Bakr was relegated to a back page under an ambiguous headline and appeared only after the *Times* previously had all but accepted the Israeli excuse that this was a military installation. On June 4 there was a three-column front-page spread of the Israeli school at Beisan that had been hit. The Palestinian statement that this was an accident was given no attention.

When Secretary William P. Rogers visited the Arab countries of Saudi Arabia, Lebanon, Egypt, and Jordan in 1971, there was no picture with any of his hosts on the front page of the *Times,* even though this was the first visit to this part of the world of a U.S. Secretary of State since John Foster Dulles journeyed to that part of the world in 1953. But as soon as Rogers stepped into Israeli territory, the *Times* carried a four-column front-page photo (the story appeared on page 10) of the Secretary with Foreign Minister Abba Eban and Premier Golda Meir.[8]

Photojournalism exposed its uglier side even more recently. When a Palestinian rocket killed two Israelis November 9, 1977, the picture of grieving relatives appeared on page 1 of the *Times*[9] and was repeated on page 2 of the "Week in Review."[10] The photos following the Israeli retaliatory air attack in which 110 Lebanese and Palestinian were killed showed a broadly smiling worker carrying an indistinguishable body from the rubble on the same page 1, and in the "Week in

Review" a seemingly relaxed Arab mother and children resting in a hospital.

In the 1977 exchange between Israel and Egypt of forty-seven Arab prisoners for the bodies of nine Israeli soldiers and two spies, the *New York Times*[11] displayed a prominently-placed heartrending picture of the coffins of the Israeli dead under a U.N. flag. But there was no explanation as to how or why it was that the two spies had been executed in Cairo in 1955. One had to read the *Jerusalem Post*'s international edition six days later to learn the facts. As pointed out there, both of the Israelis had been instrumental "in helping to organize a group of young Jewish activists in Egypt into a sabotage ring aimed at undermining the developing relationship between Egypt and the U.S. and instilling terror in the Egyptian public." The *Times* had simply referred to the "so-called Lavon affair," and supplied no other details. A third member of the group committed suicide in his cell, and three others were freed in a prisoner exchange with the Egyptians after the 1968 war.

Instead of reciting these facts about this ugly sabotage attempt at disrupting U.S.-Egyptian relations, the *Times,* quoted this emotional outpouring of one of the spy survivors: "It is the end of a very sad story and the realization of a dream. Their dream was to come and live in Israel. They fought for it and gave their lives for it, and today they come in the saddest way possible." Their deaths had in no way been related to their coming to Israel. Both Dr. Moshe Marzouk and Shmuel Azar were Egyptian-born, but then had gone to Israel and received training at intelligence schools as intelligence agents for what the *Times* had previously only referred to as a "disastrous adventure."

In contrast to the use of incessant pictures of Jews behind barbed wires or with Nazi guns at their backs to keep alive pro-Israel sentiment, a *Times* Marvine Howe story (July 3, 1977) covering the full "family style" page bore the heading, "Beirut's Children: They Survived the War, but Cannot Forget it" and was dominated by two large photos (covering precisely half of the space given the article). Palestinian children during the Lebanese civil war were shown above these captions: "Left, playing with a human skull (held aloft) found in the ruins of the city and Moslem youths, at right, patrolling a corner checkpoint while showing a small girl how to hold an automatic rifle." The boys bearing automatics and holsters were between thirteen and sixteen years, and the girl, who could barely shoulder the weapon, no more than seven.

Following the outbreak of the February 1978 fighting between

Syrian members of the Arab peacekeeping force on one side and Lebanese army regulars and Christian militiamen on the other, the *Times* ran a six-inch, two-columns appealing picture on page 3 of an anguished woman holding a baby and another youngster by her side with this caption: "A Lebanese Christian seeking shelter with her children Friday in Beirut where Syrian gunners shelled the Christian sector of the capital."[12] This appeared the following Wednesday—*five days* after the alleged shelling and after fighting had ceased, but at a time when public sentiment was building against Begin and the Israelis after Sadat's successful public relations visit to the U.S. and Zionists were waging a counterpropaganda offensive. The Israeli-Lebanese Christian alliance was solidifying, and the tactic was to woo Christians in the U.S.

The *Times,* an implacable foe of President Nasser, on every possible occasion totally misrepresented his goals, even as he was striving to bring about the ceasefire of 1970. That year the Egyptian President delivered a May Day speech at Shubra Al Kheima. Three papers reported this talk differently. The *Washington Post* of May 2 carried this headline: "Nasser Urges Nixon Peace Move in Mideast." The first paragraph noted that Nasser called upon Washington to salvage peace by ordering Israel to withdraw, and the third paragraph contained his observation that "President Nixon's failure to achieve an Israeli withdrawal would undermine American influence in the Arab world for decades or centuries." The *Christian Science Monitor* story from the pen of John Cooley, under a Beirut dateline, headlined: "Nasser Asks Nixon to Press Israeli Retreat." The story carried a picture of the U.A.R. leader with the caption: "Puts onus for Mideast solution on the United States."

From the *Times* coverage it was impossible to believe that this was the same speech. The headline was: "Nasser Warns US on Aid for Israel—Declares Delivery of Planes Would Be 'Dangerous'—Scorns Foe's Charges." Rarely had a chief of state addressed a more humble appeal to the Chief Executive of another country as had Nasser, and rarely had headlines so completely warped the vital remarks of a head of state.[13]

Time and again, Israelis-Zionists use their favorite newspaper to send up trial balloons or to beat the Israeli war drums. In May 1973 the *Times* prominently reported and bemoaned the alleged transfer to Egypt of French-built Mirage jets from Libya and British-built Hunter interceptors from Iraq. The story headline on page 1: "Egyptian Air Bases Reported Equipped for Libyan Planes"; the continuation on page 6 bore this misleading heading: "Air Preparations in Egypt Reported." The great protagonist for Israel was laying the propaganda groundwork to excuse a possible Israeli preemptive strike against Egypt before Anwar Sadat could become strong enough either to renew the war of attrition across the Canal or to strike into occupied territory, as he had implied he might be forced to do and actually did do five months later. The mere possible presence of a few Libyan planes was built up as a threat in the minds of readers, totally unaware that the Israeli Air Force had 450 jet fighters, including 110 U.S. Phantoms and 50 Mirages of its own and was, in the words of a weekly news magazine, "patently superior to Egypt's lackluster, low-profile air force."[14]

At no moment in its recent history has the *New York Times* so significantly earned its real slogan—"All the News That's Fit to Slant" —as it did by its coverage of the passage of the 1974 U.N. resolution permitting the Palestinians the right to appear before the General Assembly in November that year. The twenty-nine-paragraph story of October 15, 1974, starting on page 1 and concluding on page 3, detailed the arguments of the opposition to the U.N. resolution, including the claim of U.S. Ambassador John A. Scali that passage would hamper rather than promote a settlement of the Middle East question, and many allegations of Israeli Ambassador Yosef Tekoah. The only indication why 105 nations (only four had opposed and twenty abstained) had given their support to the resolution was relegated to the last two short paragraphs. In one, Syria's Ambassador Hissam Kellani defended the right of the Palestinians, "like any other revolutionary people" (the exact label the *Times* wished to stamp on the Palestinians) "to choose their leaders." And in the final paragraph, Cuban Ambassador Ricardo Quesada, whose very support of a resolution could drive many of the *Times* readers to the other side, asserted that "all liberation movements in the world at one time or another have been labeled terrorist." During the debate twenty-two other speakers rose to support the resolution, but not one single word of their remarks appeared in *The Times*.

To minimize this overwhelming vote in favor of granting the Palestinians the first step on the road to the recognition of their political rights, the *Times* misleadingly stated that "members of the European economic community engaged in a European-Arab dialogue were split in their vote." In fact, none of these countries voted against the resolution. France, Ireland, and Italy voted aye; Britain, Belgium, Denmark, Luxembourg, the Netherlands, and West Germany abstained. The article contained no listing of the votes, which would have betrayed to the reader the tremendous diversity of the 105 nations supporting the Palestinians and would have indicated the extent to which U.S.-Israel isolation was growing. The four holdouts were the U.S., Israel, the Dominican Republic,[15] and Bolivia.

The *Times* did its utmost in every possible way to downgrade the significance of the invitation to the Palestinians, even as many new elements throughout the world were granting recognition to them. As if their front-page subtle distortion was not enough, there was in the same issue a four-column picture, 6½ inches deep: "Israelis Mourn War Dead—At Mt. Herzl Military Cemetery in Jerusalem, Women Pray at Small Grave of One of 2,600 Soldiers Killed in Last Year's War. Services Mark the First Anniversary of War's End."[16]

Likewise, the *Times* conveniently moved the anniversary of the October (Yom Kippur-Ramadan) war up twelve days by following the Israeli rather than the Julian calendar, which would have placed the commemoration on October 6, in order that the observance would actually fall on Yom Kippur 1974, thus giving it a vital religious symbolism. Starting with the evening papers of September 25 and then the daily papers of September 26, the American media spilled over with praise of Israel's fortitude and recalled the Yom Kippur war, as they simultaneously ran pictures of Jews observing the Holy Day. The *Times'* front page carried a three-column spread of soldiers wearing the tallith (religious shawl), even though the majority of Israeli soldiers, like a comparable portion of their countrymen, were well known to be agnostics or atheists.

Had the anniversary been noted on October 6, the *Times* and the rest of the media would have been reduced to mere words of praise of Israel's fortitude and might even have been forced anew to come up with a justification for calling it the "Yom Kippur war" rather than the Ramadan or October war.

This bastion of Zionist strength left no stone unturned in evoking more pity, sympathy, and support for the Israeli cause. Mourning Arabs on the anniversary of the war or on any other day somehow never appealed to *Times* photographers.

While the U.N. was indicating to the world that there were indeed Palestinians, this journal was adding its own version of the Golda Meir cry, "What Palestinians?" In an editorial of October 5, 1974, entitled "Into the Mine Field" (a description of a trip by Secretary of State Kissinger into the danger zone of the Arab world), the *Times* pontificated: "Yesterday's vote to recognize the PLO as the refugees' [even the use of "refugees" rather than the more political "Palestinians" carried an implication] official spokesman is another in a long series of acts that has discredited the General Assembly as a peaceful instrument of conciliation." The chief publicist for the State of Israel seemed as much upset as Tel Aviv over the turn of events.

As spelled out in its news reportage and editorials, the *Times'* idea of a settlement had been for Israel to make some minor concessions by giving back some unspecified small amount of the occupied territory while retaining its role as the dominant and expansionist force in the area. To advance this viewpoint, the Op-Ed page[17] had been opened to Yale Professor and former Assistant Secretary of State Eugene Rostow's insistence that Security Council Resolution 338 (of 1967) required an Arab peace treaty before any Israeli withdrawal, a viewpoint that could not be sustained by any possible interpretation. And the *Times* was closed to the publication of any realistic analysis that did not fit this yardstick. Accordingly, chief editorial writer John B. Oakes, placed the entire burden for the future of peace "on how successfully the moderate Arab leaders can restrain their colleagues from closing the doors on the concessions that alone can lead to peace,"[18] while mentioning nothing as to what Israel might be required to do or the pressures the U.S. ought bring on Israel.

The hatred against the PLO spewed in the news and editorial pages alike must have embarrassed even the most rabid supporters of Israel. Not only did the *Times* vent its spleen editorially again that fall against the U.N. for voting to permit the PLO to present its case to the General Assembly, but it did not neglect the specialized agencies of the international organization. When UNESCO baldly censored and barred Israel from membership in regional groups (and cut off $28,-000 in assistance), Oakes in a blistering editorial assailed the action as a "vindictive ploy" by the Arabs and the underdeveloped countries. The editorial, "UNESCO vs. UNICEF," made the distinction between "the good organization, UNICEF," (which has indeed a most worthy program on behalf of undernourished and neglected children) and UNESCO, which had "amassed votes of vengeance against Israel."[19]

The facts behind the UNESCO action was *Times* missing information. In the face of many U.N. and auxiliary body warnings and censures, Israel had not only unlawfully annexed Old Jerusalem, but continued to carry out its virtual "rape" of the holiest city in the world. Everywhere the old, belonging to the Arabs—whether an ancient olive tree, the little fountain, or the quaint houses in the Moroccan quarter with their distinctive architecture and tiny gardens—had been torn down or plowed under, giving way to the new Israeli ugly cement-block buildings.

Prior to the UNESCO condemnation of Israel, renowned designer Buckminster Fuller, sculptor Isamu Noguchi, and architect Louis I. Kahn—members of the Advisory Council of the Jerusalem Committee appointed by Mayor Teddy Kollek to help guide the development—unqualifiedly condemned the trend of construction within view of the Old City and called for a halt to many projects already approved. Kahn declared:

These high buildings are as ominous as an invasion. They loom over the Old City like a band of Indians on the hilltops ready to charge. . . . Jerusalem is something special, a kind of trust from all mankind. These high-rise towers are money buildings, and they are all the worse for being among buildings that aspire to a spiritual awareness.

On his part, Fuller objected to blocking the whole mystery of Jerusalem, "which is wrapped up in the vistas out to the Judean wilderness," and he assailed "the high-rise walls of greed, erected by avaricious landowners who will put anything up so long as it makes money." Even *Times* correspondent Terence Smith had earlier admitted that the "graceful contour of the surrounding hills is being broken by a proliferation of high-rise hotels, offices and apartment buildings."[20]

Adjacent to the critical *Times* editorial, eight inches of space contained a letter from the president of the U.S. committee for UNICEF further distinguishing her "fine group" from the disreputable UNESCO. Two years later the U.S. exerted sufficient pressure on UNESCO by withholding funds (amounting to nearly $15 million, or one quarter of its modest budget) to permit Israel to join the European regional group. The *Times* in an editorial, "Progress in UNESCO,"[21] still took the occasion to criticize the policies of the organization because the delegates had on two successive days at its conference in Nairobi, Kenya, overwhelmingly voted in favor of resolutions accusing Israel of "systematic, cultural assimilation" of the Arabs in the occupied areas and charging the Zionists with policies "contrary to human rights and fundamental freedom" and the architectural Zionization of Jerusalem.

Aspects of the *Times'* reportage of the 1973 war maintained the pattern of distortion. The *Times* scarcely deviated from what, in effect, was warmongering for Israel. It persisted in presenting a picture of good "little Israel" besieged by the many "bad oil-rich Arab states." Large headlines (in the *New York Post* as well) carried accounts at the height of the war of the rumored transfer from the Soviet Union to Cairo of atomic warheads, which could be used on missiles and could wipe out Israel's cities. But nothing was said of the fact that Israel not only had warheads—and she had not obtained these from the U.S.— but had two atomic reactors, one provided by the U.S. plus the Dimona reactor in the Negev Desert, clandestinely obtained from France in the early 1950s, existence of which was kept from Washington until 1960.

Every intelligence service in the world acknowledges that Israel has had nuclear capability for a number of years. A denial by Defense Minister Shimon Peres that "to the best of my knowledge, Israel is just in the scientific part of this program"[22] meant only that certain key components were not assembled but were, for the moment, being stored separately—as was brought out in French and other non-*Times* stories. With the first shipment of Phantoms sent by Lyndon Johnson, Israel had been receiving nuclear equipment including bomb racks and special computers. Israeli scientists had been long obtaining from the U.S. many kinds of direct and indirect assistance in developing its own nuclear research, and this increased proportionately as U.S. and Israeli intelligence organizations worked in closer unison.

Long before 1973 Israel allegedly had from six to ten atomic devices, not totally sophisticated bombs but still capable of wiping out tens of thousands of people. The front page of the *Buffalo Evening News* back on May 9, 1969, had carried a Reuters story based on West Germany's *Der Spiegel* account that Israel had become the world's sixth nuclear power and had six Hiroshima-type bombs of 20-kiloton power produced at Dimona. According to an April, 1976 *Time* magazine story, Golda Meir gave Defense Minister Moshe Dayan permission to activate the atomic bombs on October 9, 1973, after he reported that Israeli forces were being routed by Syrians on the Golan Heights and had been repulsed by Egypt along the Suez Canal.

On December 3, 1974 the *Christian Science Monitor,* carried a lengthy front-page article quoting Israeli President Ephraim Katzir that "if Israel needs nuclear weapons, it will have them." This statement (with photo of the President) took on greater significance because the Chief of State had been one of the founders of Israel's major defense center and because he had spoken at an informal meeting with international science writers. President Katzir stated that Israel had the research "know-how" to put together bombs within a reasonable time. The *Monitor* article also noted that according to experts Israel had sufficient plutonium to make a number of bombs.

Buried away at the bottom of page 11 of the *Times* on December

3 were six lines, exactly twenty-seven words, noting that the Israeli Chief Executive had stated Israel "would not be the first to introduce nuclear weapons to the Middle East"—that was all the New York paper would publish on this sensitive subject.

Israel's nuclear capacity gain came dramatically to world attention in May 1977 when Paul L. Leventhal, a former staff nuclear weapons expert for the Senate Government Operations Committee, told a Salzburg Conference on a Non-Nuclear Future that 200 tons of natural uranium (enough to build forty-two nuclear weapons), placed on a ship that vanished nine years ago, had ended up in Israel. The Hamburg-registered *Scheersberg*, which had been carrying the precious ore under the control of Euratom, the European Economic Committee Atomic Energy Agency, disappeared in the Mediterranean between Antwerp and Genoa in November 1968. The ship had been commanded by a British captain and first officer; when it later turned up it had a new name, a new crew, and no uranium.

In Oslo ten days after the Salzburg bombshell, Norway's former chief prosecutor revealed that Israeli agent Dan Aerbel had admitted taking part in the operation to divert the uranium-laden ship. Aerbel had been seized in 1974 by the Norwegians with four other members of Israel's Mossad secret service for the killing of a Palestinian guerrilla leader in the small town of Lillehammer, given a five-year jail sentence, and then pardoned one year later "for psychiatric reasons." Aerbel, known to be a key member of the Israeli "hit team" responsible for the murders of eleven Arab-Palestinians in Europe, denied any involvement in the uranium affair. Israeli intelligence had previously displayed its mettle in stealing five gunboats in 1973 out of the Cherbourg harbor in defiance of the French embargo and in the famed 1976 rescue of the Air France hostages at the Entebbe airport in Uganda.

Six months later *Rolling Stone* magazine[23] in a sensational story revealed the Israeli government "had raised a secret nuclear arsenal." The story confirmed the hijacking of European uranium and told of the smuggling of 200 to 400 pounds from the Nuclear Materials and Equipment Corporation (NUMEC) plant in Apollo, Pennsylvania.[24] The article stated both Presidents Johnson and Ford had been aware of the smuggling from an American nuclear plant. Unidentified government officials and a former CIA official were quoted as saying that Johnson ordered Director Richard Helms not to investigate.

The authors of the article, magazine Associate Editor Howard Kohn and Washington correspondent Barbara Newman, stated at an October 24 news conference that a CIA estimate that Israel had fifteen nuclear bombs was conservative; they had unconfirmed reports of up to 150 bombs. While the *New York Post* of October 24 on page 4 headlined "Israel's Nuclear Arsenal—Says West Shut Eyes to Uranium Hijacks," the *Times* headlines and story on page eight the next day passed it all off as left-wing magazine sensationalism: "Rolling Stone Magazine Says Israelis Stole Uranium for Nuclear Arms."

The most serious nuclear safeguards case the U.S. ever faced broke into the open in late February 1978 when the Nuclear Regulatory Commission (NRC) released a 550-page report in response to a House committee inquiry over previous testimony given by NRC Executive Director Lee V. Gossick. In revealing that Gossick had "testified incorrectly," the report confirmed that the CIA had evidence Israel had the atomic bomb by 1968 and that bomb material in fact had been diverted from the Apollo plant. Equally important to the report was that CIA third-ranking official Carl Duckett had informed a closed meeting of the NRC in 1976 that President Johnson had been told eight years earlier that Israel had atomic weapons. The President had told CIA Director Richard M. Helms, "Don't tell anyone else, not even Dean Rusk or Robert McNamara" (then the Secretaries of State and Defense respectively).

The story was broken by the *Washington Post* in a March 2 page-one story, "Ex-CIA Aide Says Johnson Quashed Israel A-Bomb Data," but the page-five *Times* version read: "Ex-CIA Man Says Johnson *Heard* in '68 Israel Had A-Bombs" (italics added). Duckett had apparently also told members of the NRC in 1976 that CIA evidence pointed to the fact that Israel had obtained atom bomb material in the mid-1960s; circumstantial evidence pointed to the Apollo plant, which had reported a "loss" of 202 pounds of highly enriched uranium in 1965. Plant president Zalman M. Shapiro, an enterprising scientist and "dedicated Zionist," according to *Newsweek*,[25] had been active in the Zionist Organization of America and the American Technion Society, which raised funds for Israel's "MIT" in Haifa. The Atomic Energy Commission on February 14, 1966, privately told Congress that it was not possible to reconstruct "the specific events which resulted in this high loss." An examination of the records of NUMEC revealed that twenty-six of them were "incomplete, inaccurate, or missing."[26]

The head of the nuclear processing plant had early felt "strongly about the need for an independent Jewish state." NUMEC had extensive business ties with Israel and three foreigners, including an Israeli, actually worked at the plant. The FBI uncovered some "pretty astounding things . . . as to how this fellow Shapiro dealt with the Israeli Intelligence Service."[27]

No direct evidence of diversion or unlawful activity was produced by the CIA or the FBI in its limited probe ordered by President Ford in 1976. Shapiro, minus his former government clearance, went back to his post at Westinghouse. Nothing of this would have surfaced had not young analyst James Conran, in putting together a history of the nation's efforts to protect nuclear materials since the 1954 Atoms for Peace program, run into a blank wall in his research when he discovered one file involving NUMEC and its president missing. He protested the refusal of NRC safeguard officials to allow him to examine the file. When Conran pressed the matter and even wrote to congressmen and to President Carter, the director of the NRC's Office of Internal Inspection "produced a report that suggested Conran might have psychiatric problems."[28]

Conran was removed from his safeguards post. Two House investigating committees, under Morris Udall and John Dingle, are still looking into the matter. The title of the *Newsweek* article, "Mystery of Israel's Bomb," became obsolete with the publication in late June 1978 of *The Plumbat Affair*, authored by three *Sunday Times* journalists, two of whom were part of the paper's "Insight" team, which has exposed the existence of Israeli torture in the occupied territories. The book details how Israel obtained its 200 tons of uranium sufficient to make a dozen atom bombs, and how the plutonium extracted from the uranium was used to manufacture nuclear warheads designed by Yuval Ne'eman, who had been primarily responsible for the computerization of the files of Israel's secret police, the Mossad. Advised by the CIA in the early stages of the October 1973 war that Israel, facing defeat, was "on the point of resorting to nuclear weapons," Secretary Henry Kissinger and President Nixon speedily "authorized the airlift of U.S. weapons and ammunition to Israel."

No one should have been surprised, save the readers of the *Times,* when the Israelis in 1975 requested Pershing missiles from Washington to be used for atomic warheads. Secretary of Defense Schlesinger promised that as soon as the U.S. went back into production of these weapons, the Israelis might receive theirs—in 1977 or 1978. Through headlines and otherwise the *Times* poured out an entirely different story of threats to Israel, rather than the threat Israel had long posed to the Arab countries in the atomic field as a mini super power holding them at bay, and used as additional leverage with Washington to ward off pressure to yield the occupied territories. Israel has adamantly refused Washington's request to become a party to the atomic Non-Proliferation Treaty, to which the U.S., U.S.S.R., and 103 countries were party.

When Mohamed Hassanein Heikal, then editor of the influential Egyptian newspaper *Al-Ahram,* urged that it was necessary for the Arab world to "build, buy or borrow nuclear weapons as a deterrent to any use of such weapons by Israel, who already had such weapons," the headline in the *New York Times* on November 24, 1973, was: "Top Cairo Editor Urges Nuclear Arms for Arabs."[29] To the headline reader it was the Arabs who were using the nuclear arms threat, as the *Times* presented a new version of the perennial "Arabs want to drive the Israelis into the sea." Only five paragraphs from the end of the Heikal story did the *Times* admit: "Policy makers in Washington were reported a few years ago to have evidence that Israel had perfected the technology for nuclear weapons."

Even before any resolutions could be adopted by the first Arab summit meeting at Rabat after the October war, the *New York Times* in big front-page headlines on November 25, 1973, cried: "Arab Talks Open with Attack on Israel." The Egyptian Foreign Minister was quoted as saying: "We must preserve all our weapons for our combined military strength. The battle has not yet ended. This requires an integrated Arab front. . . ." Nothing unusual about such Arab polemics. But the headlines breathed the story that its makers wished the readers to get: insidious and continuous hostility toward Israel.

Another way in which the *Times* maintained the cover-up was through slanting by position—simply relegating unfavorable news to the back pages, if in the paper at all. As an example, on April 4, 1975, at the bottom of page 35 in the lower left-hand corner, the *Times* reported that Senator George McGovern had come out in favor of an independent Palestinian state; television and radio news programs mentioned it several times during the day. Buried away on the obituary page was this important change of heart by the 1972 Democratic presidential nominee, whose candidacy the *Times* had strongly supported. A week previously the *Jerusalem Post* featured in large headlines: "McGovern Meets Arafat/Urges PLO Recognition." But it was only after he had held a press conference in Jerusalem that the *Times* gave even minimal notice to this important pronouncement.

On another occasion, in front-page stories on two successive days (August 19 and 20, 1974), the *Times* detailed the growth of suppressive power exercised by the military courts of South Vietnam, whereby defendants' rights and rules of evidence had been totally eliminated.

In pursuit of the paper's "liberal" line, the reporter had meticulously investigated civil terror under President Nguyen Van Thieu, to the point of citing specific incidents and presenting charts showing the abuse of martial law in this alleged police state. But three days later, on the *Times'* front page, Israeli military suppression of Palestinian civil rights on the West Bank was depicted by Terence Smith not in terms of Israeli repression, but of Palestinian terrorism: "ISRAEL IS COMBATING A TERRORIST SURGE . . . Have jailed hundreds of Arabs."[30] The resistance movement "that had surfaced in the past six months" had never previously been brought to the attention of its readers in the plethora of *Times* stories emphasizing only improved Arab-Israeli relations, disrupted by occasional attacks on Israel allegedly launched from outside the country, from Syria or Lebanon, but never by Palestinians from within Israel.

Now, suddenly, a growing half year's rising tide was admitted, but speedily discounted: "The core of the resistance, according to the Israeli officials, was the Jordanian Communist party, which was outlawed by King Hussein," whose membership "was estimated at no more than 400, but is a tightly organized, well-disciplined network of small cells."

Unlike reportage on Vietnam, there had been no effort to investigate the facts, no charts made on Israel's military and police force, and particularly no mention of the application by the Israelis of British World War II mandatory regulations aimed to suppress all civil rights of the indigenous Palestinian Arab population. Torture and mistreatment of Palestinians were dismissed by the *Times* as "accusations unsupported, save by attorney Felicia Langer," who, it was pointed out, "was a member of the Israeli Communist party" and was representing more than fifty of the prisoners. Her charge of torture was summarily written off by citing denials by Israeli officials, including "Defense Minister Shimon Peres and other government ministers that the accusations of mistreatment are unfounded." The account noted that "privately Israeli officials acknowledge that some of the prisoners may have been roughed up during arrest or interrogation 'by the Shin Beth,' the notoriously efficient and ruthless Israel security service, which may have applied 'psychological pressure.' " But this was said to be "standard police techniques for getting information out of people who are unwilling to talk. There is no torture." The *Times* subhead, "Standard Police Techniques," further exculpated the Israelis of any guilt.

Unlike the South Vietnamese account, no prisoners were interviewed, no statements obtained of alleged torture. The findings of the

International Red Cross were summarily dismissed: The group was said to have "refused to discuss the situation." There were no comparable four-column photographs of "South Vietnamese students accused of being Communists arriving for trial before a military court in Saigon" depicting what seemed to be drugged or tortured prisoners. This cover-up by the *Times* of West Bank resistance and Israeli repression was soon bared by the increasing violence which was difficult to conceal.

The U.N. Human Rights Commission at a meeting in Geneva on February 15, 1977, adopted by a vote of twenty-three to three (the U.S., Canada, and Costa Rica), with six abstentions, a resolution accusing Israel of practicing "torture" and the "pillaging of archaeological and cultural property" in the Arab territories under occupation. The *Times* buried the report in six sentences at the very bottom of a page 6 column (the rest of the page was all advertising) under the smallest point heading used in the paper. Most of the brief account was taken up by a listing of those countries that voted "nay," including the U.S., and those abstaining. (In contrast, the visit by Lady Bird Johnson during the summer of 1976 to the Lyndon Baines Johnson Forest near Jerusalem to plant "two saplings in the forest of 1,000 six-foot pines" received prominent coverage, including a two-column picture of the ceremony.[31])

At this Geneva meeting chief U.S. delegate Allard Lowenstein vigorously contended that the resolution adopted was based on unproven allegations, despite the well-researched inquiry of the London Sunday *Times* "Insight" team (see pages 178–183). But the *New York Times* revealed its selective bias by reporting the London *Times* story on June 20 in a short fifteen-line item, carefully tucked away on page 14 and coupled with an Israeli London Embassy denial of equal length. Two weeks later the *Times,* now responding to the furor the London story had raised, carried a lengthy 158-line story providing an outline of the tortures charged; but the headline read: "Israelis Deny a London Paper's Charges of Torture." Before the readers were acquainted with the charges, they were flooded with the denial. Then, on July 8, the *Times* carried a Reuters story titled "Arab Captives in Gaza Say Israelis Beat Them but Don't Torture Them," based on interviews with Palestinians security offenders detained in the Gaza Strip jail. The article suggested Arabs were being badly roughed up but that no torture occurred. The London *Times* rejoiner had pointed out that its story concerned West Bank jails where the alleged torture took place, and not in Gaza where things had relatively improved the previous few years. Israeli censors had deleted 110 lines from the Reuters story "on the grounds that they disclosed army interrogation techniques." The reader was being neither unfair nor unreasonable in wondering what these techniques might be and where to draw the demarcation line between "beating and maltreatment" and "torture."

On June 2, 1978, the *Times* devoted an unprecedented one half of its Op-Ed page to an article by two Zionist law professors,[32] "disproving" charges that torture had been used by Israel against an Arab-American student who had been arrested while visiting his dying father in Ramallah on the West Bank and accused of training in Libya with the Popular Front for the Liberation of Palestine, a PLO group. The three-column headline, "Israeli Torture, They Said," and a box, "Two observers at the trial of Sami Esmail, an Arab, draw conclusions about charges of human rights violations," indicated that this was the New York paper's answer to the varied, substantiated charges of Israeli use of torture in the occupied territories. (U.S. citizen Esmail was convicted and sentenced to a year and a half in prison for his alleged associations which took place wholly outside of Israel.)

In vivid contrast to the *Times* treatment of the torture of Palestinians was the page 2, August 24, 1977 two-column coverage in fifty lines of "Militant Moslems on Trial in Cairo," with attention drawn by a photo of equal size showing the leader of the Egyptian extremists shouting, mouth wide open, his hand raised in a frenzied gesture. This trial of a small sect accused of the murder of a former little-known Cabinet minister had drawn little attention elsewhere than in Egypt, but provided an opportunity to further stereotype the Arabs as fanatics at the time when the question of PLO participation at a Geneva Conference was being hotly discussed (and who would make a distinction between Egyptian and Palestinian extremists?). This was before Sadat had won the status of a "good Arab."

During the serious spring 1976 uprisings by the Arabs in Israel and in the occupied territories, the editorials of the *Times* as well as of the *Washington Post* and the *Los Angeles Times* mildly chided the Israelis for "military excesses" and were concerned only lest this "sudden" Israeli behavior tarnish the Zionist image of an otherwise "benevolent" occupation.[33] It was hard to guess where these would-be guardians of American morality—on other issues, of course—had been during the arrests, blowing up of houses, deportations of Palestinian leaders, and varied flagrant brutalities heaped upon the Palestinians in the occupied areas since the 1967 occupation and later in Israel proper. And these Goliaths had their own permanent correspondents based in Israel and in Lebanon.

The *Times* has also excelled in the more subtle ways of presenting myth-information to its readership. In headling on August 15, 1977, "Israel Is Extending Services For Arabs," the *Times* implied great benefits for the Palestinians, whereas the government had taken action to further annex the occupied territories. To justify Tel Aviv's latest onslaught, the four-column heading of November 9, 1977 read: "Israel Shells South Lebanon, Reportedly in Response to Rocket Attacks."

Toning, placement, invention, raising trial balloons, and publication of out-of-date stories given an appearance of present-day relevancy—all these techniques play an important role in stimulating what is passed off as Middle East "news." The *Times* of August 23, 1974, on page 6 had a two-column lead: "US Hears Report That Arabs Sought to Bar It from Azores." The State Department was the source for reports that "some unidentified Arab nation" had offered Portugal $400 million to deny the U.S. use of the Lagens base in the Azores, which served as a refueling point for the American airlift to Israel during the October 1973 Arab-Israeli war.

What was newsworthy for prominent publication—even if verified, and it never was—about a ten-month-old attempt on the part of the Arabs to block, if they could, the flow of military supplies to Israel during a war in which Egypt and Syria had been fighting for their very existence? Was this cricket? Congressman James Johnson of Denver on the floor of the House had called the U.S. resupply effort flowing to Israel "an act of war." Had not several NATO allies of the U.S. refused to have their territory or airspace violated by the shipment of military supplies to Israel? What made this worthy of a two-column, twelve-inch story, unless it was part of the cold war waged against the Arabs by the media, the *Times* in particular?

The following week, the "Business and Finance" section of the Sunday *Times* carried a five-column, half-a-front-page spread, replete with illustration and concluded on half an inside page, "How Arabs Turn Oil into Armaments." A gross fear of what the Arabs might do with their hundreds of millions of petrodollars underlies the article written by Pranay Gupte. The multimillion-dollar defense purchases by Iran, a non-Arab but oil-producing country, were cited as a possible pattern for what the wealthy Arab oil-producing countries might do.

The entire tone of the article was calculated to inspire fear of the Arabs and to supplement speculation being raised by *Times* columnists as to the possibility of armed intervention to assure both access to oil and the security of Israel. The Institute on Human Relations, an organ of the American Jewish Committee and part of the Zionist apparatus, was used as the source for figures on direct foreign investment in the

U.S., which had increased from $3 billion in 1973 to over $6 billion. The Arab share of this was not precisely given but was insinuated to be very high and, of course, excessive. The article elsewhere bore unmistakable signs of having been Israelist inspired. The Institute was also quoted as "warning that Middle East oil revenues in 1974 could reach $110 billion" and that a significant quantity of this Arab revenue was going into military purchases.

Again trying to confuse the reader into believing Iran was an Arab nation, it was noted that in 1973 foreign military sales amounted to $8.26 billion, of which the Iranians purchased $4 billion and Saudi Arabia $587.6 million. And only by reading elsewhere on the page a box listing the arms sales to all countries did the reader learn that Israel in 1974 had purchased $2.1 billion in military equipment, exceeded only by Iran's buying and almost four times Saudi Arabia's purchases.

To heighten fear of the Arabs, the writer quoted from a Lebanese representing Kidder, Peabody, the American brokerage firm, in Beirut: "There is no reason why we Arabs should not control U.S. companies. We can hire the best lawyers, the best public relations people and the best accountants. I think we should make a major take-over in the States as a matter of opinion." This view of one Roger Tamraz was held to be "a growing one, according to observers."

The Tamraz quote appeared verbatim in the August 28 issue of *Near East Report,* as part of an analysis paralleling the *Times* on the Arab "investment threat." This, once again, clearly indicated the close connection between the *New York Times* and this Zionist Washington organ.

The *Times* has always prided itself on its open-mindedness, presenting divergent and even unpopular views, traditionally through its "Letter to the Editor" column and then through the newer institution of the Op-Ed page. Spokesmen for all kinds of opposing viewpoints, causes, and positions on any and all subjects have almost universally been able to obtain space, even a Clifford Irving to comment on Judge Sirica's honesty and morality. When it has come to the Arab-Israeli conflict, however, there has been a slight departure from normal liberal practice.

The *Times* has published a totally disproportionate number of Zionist, pro-Israel letters. This finding was supported by a survey, "Stands on the Arab-Israel Conflict: Letters to the Editor and Op-Ed Articles Published by the *New York Times.* "[34] The periods covered for the letters were the years 1975 (January through December), 1976

(January through June), and 1977 (January through September). In the first period there were 140 pro-Israeli letters published as against 41 pro-Arab or anti-Zionist ones and 25 neutral. The overall findings for the twenty-seven months: pro-Israeli 286, pro-Arab 86, neutral 50.

However, the comparative quantified results do not convey all of the real impact of the stands taken, as the figures alone do not reveal the extent of the underlying bias—in favor of Israel—with all its subtleties. The editors of the *Times* have used various manipulative mechanisms designed not only to highlight the presentation of pro-Israeli stands but also to undermine pro-Arab and/or neutral stands. For example, those whose letters defended the Arab-Palestinian position were usually most carefully selected. Very often it was someone clearly identifiable as of Arabic lineage, or an Arab Ambassador who obviously had an axe to grind and therefore whose credibility was instantaneously challenged, and with whose mode of expression the readers often could not relate.

It was rare that a pro-Arab letter was allowed to appear without an accompanying rebuttal, or one shortly thereafter. Usually, as in the instance of the Abu Daoud affair in January 1977, the letters critical of the French were twice as long as the letters deploring the hysteria and expressions of outrage over the release of the suspected Palestinian perpetrator of the attack at Munich.

The survey showed that "Letters to the Editor" were most of the time much longer for pro-Israel stands[35], and significantly longer in some instances.[36] Additionally, pro-Arab or neutral stands were usually followed by their immediate pro-Israel counterparts, while the reverse did not necessarily take place. Furthermore, in some instances a pro-Arab letter was temporally and spatially separated[37] (i.e., placed in a later issue) from its pro-Israel counterpart, despite the proximity of the dates the letters were written. On the other hand, Arab stands presented are *immediately* followed by their specific pro-Israel response, regardless of the fact that the latter may have been written at a much later date.[38]

In addition to the variable of relative length of letters (advantageous to the pro-Israel stand), other devices have been used by the editors, such as sandwiching a pro-Arab and/or neutral stand between three or more pro-Israel ones,[39] as well as the cumulative presentation of a number of pro-Israel stands—thus strengthening their impact—and relegating the pro-Arab rejoinder to the end.[40]

Incidences of title-slanting (i.e., not representing the essence of the pro-Arab view) have occurred, but such has never been the case when the editors selected titles for pro-Israel letters.[41] The editors' layout has also frequently been used to favor pro-Israel letters; for example, by boxing their titles and not that of a pro-Arab letter appearing simultaneously.[42] The editors have resorted to other prejudicial tactics by sometimes giving a single heading to both pro-Israel and pro-Arab stands, when such is questionable and not necessarily applicable to the latter.[43] (The findings of this survey hold true for the first six months of 1978, when letters published were only slightly less preponderantly pro-Zionist due to the sentiment for Sadat: 54 pro-Israel, 19 pro-Arab, 23 neutral.)

The survey covered Op-Ed articles printed between January 1 through the end of September 1977. There were thirty-one pro-Israel articles, seven neutral, and four pro-Arab. In this way the *Times* enforced the view that the only people who could possibly take issue with its pro-Israel stance were "those Arabs"—a view strengthened by occasional articles in the *Times* Magazine section such as the Joseph Kraft hate piece, "Those Arabists in the State Department."[44] Letters expressing concern for the totality of American interests or opposition to the subordination of Judaism to political Zionism never appeared. Jewish iconoclasts, it was feared, might perhaps inspire a revolt of the "enslaved" Jewish masses, many of whom have themselves harbored distinct doubts about Israelism but, without leadership, have resorted to the herd instinct.

I also personally endeavored to set the *Times'* record straight on one rather important matter—the exploitation of Dr. Albert Einstein by the Zionist movement. When the greatest scientist of our age died on April 18, 1956, at the age of seventy-six, the *Times* in the course of its eulogy referred to "Israel, whose establishment as a state he had championed." This "kidnapping" of Einstein for Israel was one of the most extraordinary coups ever perpetrated by any political group anywhere, but with the help of the omnipotent *Times* anything is possible. The great mathematician had vigorously opposed the creation of the State of Israel, but a myth to the contrary has been widely spawned by the media, and was repeated sixteen years later.

In late March 1972 the *New York Times* published a series of articles dealing with the life and thought of Albert Einstein as allegedly revealed in the collection of his manuscripts, letters, and other papers, which were to be published by his estate. The third of the series included on the front page a three-column photograph of Einstein with Israeli Premier David Ben-Gurion, and the caption read: "Einstein papers tell of scientist's efforts toward the creation of Israel."

The article further referred "to his long efforts in behalf of the creation of a Jewish national state and of his sad refusal" to accept the Presidency upon the death of Chaim Weizmann.

Einstein, despite the *Times'* incessant recitals to the contrary, clearly opposed the creation of the State of Israel. A clear understanding of the position taken on Palestine by the great mathematician, himself a refugee from Nazi Germany, will not only set the record straight and correct journalistic inaccuracies, but is most relevant to the continuing quest for a just peace in the Middle East.

In his testimony in January 1946 before the Anglo-American Committee of Inquiry, and in answer to the specific question whether refugee settlement in Palestine demanded a Jewish state, Einstein stated: "The State idea is not according to my heart. I cannot understand why it is needed. It is connected with narrow-mindedness and economic obstacles. I believe that it is bad. I have always been against it." He went further to deride the concept of a Jewish commonwealth as an "imitation of Europe, the end of which was brought about by nationalism."

Then, in 1952, in a message to a "Children to Palestine" dinner, Einstein spoke of the necessity of curbing "a kind of nationalism which has arisen in Israel if only to permit a friendly and fruitful co-existence with the Arabs." When this portion of the Einstein message was censored in the organization's press release so as to impart the impression of all-out support of Israel, I went to Princeton to seek the Professor's views on the incident. Einstein then told me that he had never been a Zionist and had never favored the creation of the State of Israel.

It was then that he also told me of a significant conversation with Weizmann. Einstein had asked him: "What of the Arabs if Palestine were given to the Jews?" And Weizmann replied: "What Arabs? They are hardly of any consequence."

Einstein referred me to his book *Out of My Later Years,* published in 1950, in which he had expanded on his philosophy: "I should much rather see a reasonable agreement with the Arabs on the basis of living together than the creation of a Jewish state. Apart from practical considerations, my awareness of the essential nature of Judaism resists the idea of a Jewish state with borders, an army, and a measure of temporal power, no matter how modest. I am afraid of the inner damage Judaism will sustain."[45]

In subsequent years he vigorously supported many Israeli cultural activities, in particular the Hebrew University and the Weizmann Institute, to which he was deeply dedicated. According to biographer Dr.

Philip Frank, the professor had a "good hearted weakness" and was hesitant to rebuke Zionists for their frequent manipulations of his views and unauthorized use of his name in order to enhance their prestige and fill their political purse. His hesitation to disassociate himself from political Zionism helped confuse the American press.

In his modest manner, he publicly declined the Israeli Presidency, as Weizmann's successor, on the given grounds that he was not qualified in the area of human relationships. But, in fact, that acceptance of high office in nationalist Israel was hardly in keeping with the basic philosophy of this great humanist and universalist.

Attempts to tie the renowned scientist to political Zionism continued. First there were the welter of public tributes from Israeli and Zionist leaders, published at the time of his death. And two weeks later in a story prominently published by the *Times,* the Israeli Consul in New York claimed that Einstein had been preparing a laudatory speech for nationwide television in commemoration of the seventh anniversary of Israel. Not only was the evidence of Einstein's Zionist intent scarcely substantiated, but it was in direct conflict with the professor's last statement about the Israeli state, given in an interview with Dorothy Schiff, pro-Israel publisher of the *New York Post.* She quoted him as saying: "We had great hopes for Israel at first. We thought that it might be better than other nations, but it is no better."[46]

In the third of its articles on Einstein, the *Times* nevertheless repeated the myth of his support of the creation of Israel without indicating any new proof. Were the good professor alive today, there is every reason to believe that he would be in the forefront of those condemning the deprivation of the rights of the Palestinian Arabs. As far back as January 28, 1930, Einstein had warned in the Palestinian newspaper *Falastin* that "oppressive nationalism must be conquered" and that he could "see a future for Palestine only on the basis of peaceful cooperation between the two peoples who are at home in the country . . . come together they must in spite of all." And from the outset he had fully supported the idea of Dr. Judah Magnes, President of the Hebrew University, of an Arab-Jewish binational state. In a letter to the *Times* with Rabbi Leo Baeck of Germany, he wrote: "Besides the fact that they [Magnes and his followers] speak for a much wider circle of inarticulate people, they speak in the name of principles which have been the most significant contribution of the Jewish people to humanity." Such statements are hardly consonant with the *Times'* allegation of the scientist's support of the creation of a Zionist state.

The *Times'* revival of this Einstein mythology led me to call Op-Ed page editor Harrison E. Salisbury and suggest that it would be appropriate for him to run a piece presenting the true views of the learned scientist on this subject. Although every type of opinion has been presented on this important page, Salisbury refused to commission such an article, as is customarily done. He stated he would be happy to look at the finished product if it were written on speculation.

Even this I did, and here is his letter rejecting the article, the substance of which has been set forth in the above pages:

I'm sorry to say that we decided against your article concerning Professor Einstein. As I told you when we discussed this matter on the telephone, I was dubious about the idea of elaborating on this particular aspect of Dr. Einstein's career, and I confess on reading the article my feeling was strengthened. You may feel that I overstate the case, but it would seem to the casual reader like myself that Dr. Einstein's views, as one might expect, underwent a series of changes over the years and the picture does not come out so strongly in your article as to compel its publication.

How possibly could any subsequent Einstein "change over the years"—and his basic attitude toward political Zionism never altered one iota—affect what he did or did not do about the creation of Israel, an act which took place in 1948? The cultural Zionism in which Einstein believed was a far cry from Jewish nationalism embodied in the Zionist State of Israel, which he decried to his very death in 1956.

Likewise, the *Times* sees to it that Middle East books for its Sunday Book Review Section fall in the proper hands. The revised edition of Prime Minister Begin's *The Revolt* and of Joseph Churba's *America's Decline in the Middle East* were reviewed by Wolf Blitzer, Washington correspondent for the *Jerusalem Post* and editor of *Near East Report,* the Zionist lobby's official publication. *For Jerusalem,*[47] written by Mayor Teddy Kollek and his son Amos, was placed in the safe care of ardent Zionist, Saul Bellow. Still another biography on Begin,[48] along with Anwar Sadat's autobiography, was given to Nadav Safran, an Egyptian Jew who emigrated to Palestine and fought in the Israeli army before coming to the U.S. from Israel to study and teach at Harvard.

The most pitiful thing about the *Times'* handling of the Middle East is that it did not have to be so. The progressiveness and integrity of its founder, Adolph S. Ochs, and his son-in-law, Arthur Hays Sulzberger, who succeeded him upon his death in 1935, established a tradition in which fair reportage and legitimate dissent were unquestioned. The *Times* was obligated to raise and face questions about Israel in the same courageous manner as Sulzberger had done when, as publisher, he publicly declared in 1946: "I dislike the coercive methods of Zionists who, in this country, have not hesitated to use economic means to silence persons who have different views. I object to the attempts at character assassination of those who do not agree with them."

In the same spirit, the *Times* publisher declared at the commemoration of the eightieth anniversary of the Miztah Congregation at Chattanooga, Tennessee, "I cannot rid myself of the feeling that the unfortunate Jews of Europe's D.P. camps are helpless hostages for whom statehood has been made the only ransom."[49] But then the *Times'* anti-Zionism came under attack as the Zionists launched their devastating 1946 boycott, which brought the paper to its knees. Ideology abruptly went out the window. Overnight the editorial policy shifted from anti-Zionism to non-Zionism, and later to Zionism. And the news pages soon succumbed to the predilections of its editorial overseers.

The details of that boycott were hidden away in a file in Sulzberger's safe and remained for many years one of the guarded secrets of Times Square. It was in *The Kingdom and the Power*,[50] Gay Talese's interesting book on the *Times,* that some light was shed on what had only been referred to as *the* frightening experience. It had been known that pressure from the large department store advertisers had brought the paper to its knees, but what had not been revealed was that it had been the cancellation of an advertisement submitted by the American League for a Free Palestine, the American alter ego and fund-raiser for the terrorist Begin-led Irgun Zvai Leumi, which had aroused Zionist ire and helped usher in the boycott.

Sulzberger had explained, according to Talese's account, that while his paper in the past often had run the ads of organizations it opposed editorially—it had, in fact, once lent the *Daily Worker* newsprint when the Communist daily was in short supply—and had previously published many Zionist ads without question, the decision to cancel on this occasion was based on the *Times'* conviction that the League was directly connected with the Irgun terrorists in the Middle East and, secondly, on the anti-British charges in the advertisement not supportable by facts. For these reasons the *Times* publisher felt he could not be responsible for the ill will the contemplated advertisement would stir between Britain and the U.S. " 'We happen to believe that the British are acting in good and not in bad faith,' Sulzberger wrote to one of the Zionist leaders. 'From our standpoint, therefore, your advertisement is not true. Since there is no yardstick by which truth of this kind can be proved, it means that we are putting our judgment ahead of yours—something of which you will not approve and which we do only with the greatest hesitancy.' "51

Thirty-one years later, when the publishership rested in the hands of his son, Arthur Ochs Sulzberger (in the interim son-in-law Orville Dryfoos had directed the paper until his death in 1963), the *Times* joined in the greatest whitewash in journalistic history by welcoming to this country Israel's new Prime Minister, Menachem Begin, for opposition to his terrorist activities had led to the 1946 ad cancellation, the boycott, and the paper's conversion to Zionism. The vicious circle had been closed as the U.S. "began the Begin." No one reading the *Times* could ever imagine that the world, to recall Nevil Shute, was really "On the Beach."

Probably the person most responsible for the paper's shift from anti-Zionism to non-Zionism to an almost outright Zionism52 is Executive Editor Abe Rosenthal. Fanatically devoted to the *Times,* he was first hired as a $12-a-week stringer at New York City College, spent nine years as a foreign correspondent, and became Metropolitan Editor in 1963. Under the patronage of Sulzberger, he became Managing Editor in 1969 and was elevated to Executive Editor in 1977.

According to most reports, Rosenthal can do no wrong in the eyes of his boss. As a result he does exactly what he likes with the paper. A 1977 *Time* report claimed that he has "done more to re-shape the paper than any editor since Carr Van Anda (first Managing Editor under Adolph Ochs)." As one reporter claimed: "It's not that Abe doesn't tolerate dissent, it's that he rarely hears any."53

He has ruthlessly shifted and rearranged the staff, installing his own men as editors, including Managing Editor Seymour Topping, Deputy Managing Editor Arthur Gelb, Assistant Managing Editor James Greenfield, News Editor Allan Siegal, and Foreign Editor Robert Semple. There has been a gradual disappearance of Christians on the staff; those who remain, like Washington Bureau Chief Hedrick Smith or Assistant Foreign Editor Terence Smith, show a distinct Zionist leaning. (Smith recently returned from a four-year stint as the *Times* correspondent in Israel.)

The whole trend under Rosenthal has been manifested in the final shift to all-out support of Israel, a position with which no Zionist could possibly find fault. Publisher Sulzberger wishes to avoid any personal involvement in this subject and leaves it all to his Executive Editor, who indulges in all kinds of ploys, ranging from trial balloons to contrived articles, to advertise the Israeli cause. Writer Pranay Gupte, who penned the August article on Arab oil and armament purchases, was brought back as a lad from Bombay by Rosenthal and pushed up the ladder. Gupte maintains closest ties with Jewish groups and publications, even doing occasional writing for the American Jewish Committee, which manages to find its way into the pages of the *Times*.

The editorial policy of the paper on the Palestine issue, reflected in its news reportage, was first to attack the Arafat proposal for a secular, binational state to include Israel and occupied Palestine, and then to oppose a Palestinian state on the West Bank and in Gaza when the PLO had opted for this solution. The Palestinian organization succeeded Nasser as the number-one bête noire of the *Times* writers, who could see little wrong in efforts to bar the PLO from any participation in deciding the fate of its own people. And friends of the PLO such as President Assad became the target of specially prepared critical articles.[54]

Led by the *Times*, the U.S. media, with few notable exceptions,[55] greeted Begin's election in an expected manner, referring in large print to his banalities in behalf of peace and to his intrepid defense of Palestine as an "early liberator," and only in small type in back pages to his record as a terrorist leader. (When the *Times* in December felt obliged to print on its Op-Ed page a photo of the Irgun blown-up King David Hotel, the type used for the caption was half the normal size.[56]) Columnists Alexander Cockburn and James Ridgeway of the *Village Voice*[57] uniquely referred to "the Disastrous Victory of Menachem Begin, because he is reactionary in every way. He has created his own reality. He lives in a different century, on the other end of the political totem pole." But *Human Events*[58] hailed Begin as "Israel's Ronald Reagan" and applauded his strong anti-Communist position exemplified by his opening "of the gates to a group of Vietnamese refugees fleeing Communist rule" and sending for economist Milton Friedman to solve the country's economic difficulties. (The appointment of Friedman, who had helped bolster the financial position of the Chilean military junta that had ousted the Allende government, one of the darlings of the *Times*, drew no critical comment from that paper.)

The *Times* was far from alone in handling Begin with kid gloves. Once again, New York's Channel 13 revealed its idea of an objective panel discussion: permit the view of an American Jewish Congress representative, an Israeli-born journalist,[59] and of a former Begin aide to go unchallenged. Peter Bergson, who had run the Irgun's stateside organization, the American League for a Free Palestine, described his old chieftain as a "kind, gentle man." In its May 18 edition on the May victory of Begin's Likud party, the *New York Post* referred to "Victory by Hawk," but its only page-one reference to Begin's terrorist background was a quotation from exaggerated Damascus commentary. Relegated to the bottom of an inside page was a brief reference to his "tough militancy," including his "raid" on Arab villages and the King David Hotel incident.

The *Times* of that day carried on page one: "Israel's Labor Party, Dominant Since 1948, Loses to Rightist Bloc." In paragraph four it stated: "The Likud is headed by Menachem Begin, a hard-line 64-year-old politician who has been a Labor Party critic for years." Throughout the story, continued in depth onto page 8, there was not a single word about Begin's past terrorist history. Nor did the following day's stories in the *Times* (three on page one, including a picture of the victorious candidate with Mrs. Begin) in which the newly elected Prime Minister was referred to as a "courtly, baldish figure" who kisses women on the hand or cheek on introduction and is particular about his attire,"[60] make any allusion to his past background save to depict Begin as a "freedom fighter" in a "liberation movement." The fearful Arab reaction to the Begin triumph, shunted to page 14, was made to appear paranoic, as another of the usual gross exaggerations from that part of the world.

From the second day after the elections to his arrival in the U.S. in July, *Times* reportage focused on the *new* Begin. His peaceful demeanor was portrayed in his post-election call on Presidents Sadat and Assad and on King Hussein "to meet him as soon as possible in face-to-face peace talks" and in his well-publicized efforts to achieve Cabinet participation by both the Labor party and Yigal Yadin's Democratic Movement for Change. Israeli pledges of "caution on its rule in Gaza and the West Bank" made front-page headlines on May 23. In contrast, Arab statements, which at this moment were at a minimum, presented them as bellicose; the many Arab internecine quarrels, whether between the PLO and the Syrians or between Sadat and Qaddafi, were built up into booming headlines, such as in a Sunday "Week in Review" feature, "The Arabs Can't Seem to Stop Fighting."[61]

Reported at length was the shuttling back and forth to Israel of Rabbi Alexander M. Schindler, chairman of the Conference of Presidents of Major American Jewish Organizations, who upon his return was received "at the White House by Robert J. Lipshutz, Counsel to the President, and Stuart Eizenstat, head of the Domestic Council, the two most prominent Jews on Mr. Carter's staff."[62] Schindler insisted that the Israeli leader was no "raving extremist"[63] and might "soften his policies." On June 7 the *Times* reported, "Jews in US Seeking Unity

Behind Begin." Between Schindler's efforts and those of Shmuel Katz, Begin's personal representative and Minister of External Information, who had been dispatched to the U.S., the *Times* by June 26 could carry the headline "Begin Gaining Support of the Jewish Community as His Visit to US Nears." Jews had discarded their doubts and were now, according to the *Times,* solidly behind Israel's new chieftain, as was the *Times* editorial page, which called for a "real" peace to include Arab normalization of relations with Israel, but was absolutely silent about any counterpart normalization of Israeli nationalism.[64]

Photojournalism again played its important role here. The day Begin actually took over the reins of government and appeared in the Knesset as Prime Minister, his picture, nattily attired with tie, appeared on the front page of the *Times.*[65] The very next day another picture from the takeover proceedings appeared, with no additional news backup, showing the neat Begin with tie in sharp contrast to his predecessor, Rabin, with open-necked shirt and tieless.[66] A lengthy front-page story, "66 Vietnam Refugees Reach Israeli Haven," with an imposing headline and most sympathetic picture, helped the image of the new leader.[67]

In its half page devoted to the "questions and answers on the background and main issues of the Middle East conflict" the day before the July 1977 Carter-Begin meeting,[68] there was the briefest mention of the Palestinians, an expression of doubt as to what they wanted, but nothing about the beginnings of the problem (the original sin) to indicate what they deserved. The image of spoilers and terrorists was left intact.

In its editorial that same day, "Mr. Begin Comes to Washington," the *Times* justified Israel's refusal since 1967 to pull back so as to "provide security against attack, which their neighbors have never been willing to foreswear," suggesting future withdrawals to be staged "only gradually and behind a variety of residual defense arrangements." If Begin were willing to accept this, the *Times* argued that the President "might shift some of the recent American pressure to the Arab nations, which have yet to articulate even to their own peoples their readiness to contemplate peace."

The Sunday two days before Begin's meeting with Carter in Washington, the *New York Times* Magazine[69] carried a cover photo of Menachem Begin, identifying him (on page 4) as "the leader of the Irgun underground in Palestine," and two articles on "The New Face of Israel." Four photos of a younger Begin, introducing the articles, carried this large caption: "The lives of a founding father of Israel—

Menachem Begin as the leader of the *Jewish underground military organization,* the Irgun Zvai Leumi, in the late 1940's." (Italics added.)

The longer article contained the diaries of a June 8–22 visit to Israel by CBS Diplomatic Correspondent Marvin Kalb, who had gained renown as the admiring publicist for Henry Kissinger but had now turned his magic pen—and his voice, too—to the new Israeli leader. Prior to his *Times* piece, Kalb had complained, in a lengthy interview in the Jerusalem *Post,*[70] of the hysterical reaction of portions of the American news media to the election victory of Begin, and he had criticized fellow CBS news commentator Walter Cronkite for opening an evening program with the words "Begin, former terrorist." Kalb had also assailed *Time* magazine for alleging that "Jews raped Arabs at Deir Yassin, a claim the PLO never made." His contribution to image building could scarcely have been outdone by the most rabid Israeli journalist.

For his call for a Palestinian homeland and eventual return to the 1967 borders, President Carter was portrayed as the object of greatest hostility in Israel from the new as well as the old Labor party leadership, to the point that even Golda Meir "has hinted to friends that she may have to abandon her retirement from public life and 'open up on the American President.' " Here and elsewhere in the article it was *"Aux armes, citoyens"* (to arms, citizens) as American Israelists were rallied to Begin's side.

Kalb held nothing back: a recital of Masada and the wiping out of its 900 Jewish defenders in A.D. 73; Israeli writers and Cabinet ministers sounding their fears of Carter policy; new Defense Minister Weizman insisting "Carter will understand why we talk about 'Judea' and 'Samaria' not the 'West Bank' "; Begin mouthing Zionist dogma that " 'The land of Israel' belongs to the Jewish people," and that "Israel's right to exist comes from God." Accompanying the Kalb piece was a large cartoon reprinted from the *Jerusalem Post* magazine offering Begin's sarcastic plan for an American "withdrawal from occupied territories," showing what the U.S. would look like as it withdrew successively from Mexican, Northwest, Texas, and Florida "annexations."

The deft Kalb analysis ended on this note: "Hundreds of Israelis crowded around the grave of young Natanyana, the young paratrooper who was killed on July 4, 1976, during the Israeli rescue mission at Entebbe." After the chanting of the commemorative "kaddish," Begin delivered a brief eulogy and, as we are told by this admiring writer, as his eyes "swept over the crowd, only one thought could be reverberating in the mind of the leader of Israel—in a sense of the Jewish people —the security of Eretz Israel would be the security of the Jewish people. Surely the President would understand."

The shorter article, "Hawk on a Mission of Peace," by *Times* correspondent in Jerusalem William E. Farrell, further fashioned the new image of the Israeli Prime Minister. Tracing his Zionist career in Poland and presenting him as a near-victim of both Nazi and Soviet totalitarianism, the author portrayed Begin as a man of peace (a picture showed him smiling broadly as he patted the hands of a bedouin sheikh in an Arab encampment in the Negev Desert), who had battled the British oppressor in Palestine and upon whose shoulders the blame for blowing up the King David Hotel had been placed, although the British had refused to heed warnings to abandon the building (Begin in 1948 had confided to Walter Deuel of the *Chicago Daily News* that the British had all of thirty minutes to evacuate their headquarters).[71]

The Farrell piece rallied the readership with the confident conclusion that Begin, while a stubborn "politician," was ready to meet the Carter challenge over the West Bank and the Palestinian issue, and that he "may be the right man at the right time to persuade the Israelis that major territorial concessions must be made." Regarding the atrocity of Deir Yassin, Farrell exculpated the former Irgun chieftain of blame in this manner: "Begin was involved in a *battle* [italics added] in which 200 Arabs, including women and children, were killed after a 'warning' to non-combatants."

The warm and enthusiastic reception accorded Begin on his July 1977 visit to the US, in no small part due to the *Times*, was all too reminiscent of his first celebrated visit in 1948 after the Israeli state had come into existence on May 15. The Reception Committee for Menachem Begin, formed by his American League for a Free Palestine, exploited the American weakness of prominent citizens to promiscuously join any organization smart enough to pick a sweet-sounding name. A group of important Christian Zionists, including the Senators of Kansas, Rhode Island, and Maryland, a score of Governors, men of letters, and clergymen of all faiths, were founding members of the Reception Committee. The invitations, calling upon the recipient to add his name to the list of distinguished Americans welcoming Menachem Begin to the U.S., read:

A Commander-in-Chief of the Irgun Zvai Leumi, he led one of the most glorious and successful resistance movements in history. A little defenseless community, a people who, in the course of almost two thousand years of dispersion, had lost the art of military defense, was transformed under the miracle of his leadership into a fighting and heroic nation. It was through the Hebrew Underground under his command that the hitherto pariah people of the world, the Jews, won back their dignity and self-respect and the respect of the civilized world. It was because of the valiant fight waged by the Irgun that the whole structure of the British regime in Palestine collapsed, making possible the proclamation of Hebrew sovereignty and the establishment of the State of Israel.

The two-page letter neglected to mention even one small word about Begin's bloody exploits save his determination to drive the British out of Palestine (thus endowing his terror with an anticolonist cast). According to the Reception Committee, Begin was the hero of Israel and the Freedom Movement's candidate for Prime Minister. This, coincidentally, was the fall of 1948—the time of an important national election in the U.S. As a member of the House Foreign Affairs Committee remarked, "Put any petition with the name Jew on it before a candidate in an election year, and you can get anyone to sign anything!" At any rate, within a few weeks the Welcoming Committee had grown to include eleven Senators, twelve Governors, seventy-odd congressmen, seventeen justices and judges, and educators, public officials, and mayors by the scores.

These celebrated names emblazoned a huge advertisement in the *New York Times* under the headline: "The Man Who Defied an Empire and Gained Glory for Israel—Menachem Begin, former Irgun Commander-in-Chief, Arrives on Goodwill Mission Today." By now the *Times* was no longer questioning Zionist ads. The usual Waldorf Astoria dinner and an official welcome at City Hall was to follow. The main object of the visit was to obtain funds for electing Begin Prime Minister of Israel. His political platform called for incorporation of most of Jordan and other adjacent territories into Israel so that the new state would include the original boundaries of biblical Canaan.

Begin's record was well known in the State Department and his visa application was rejected, until President Truman, vacationing in Key West, issued a presidential order to grant entrance. But the arrival in the U.S. of a man who had carried out wanton criminal acts and even was seeking to overthrow the U.N. partition proposal because not enough land had been ceded to the Zionists was exuberantly heralded by U.S. officialdom. The Welcoming Committee disintegrated only after well-known Protestant clergyman Dr. Henry Sloane Coffin, Catholic Father John La Farge, and Rabbi Morris Lazaron, alerted by this author, publicly warned the duped U.S. politicians and called for the repudiation of Begin.[72]

Kansas Senator Arthur Capper claimed he did not know how his name happened to appear in a newspaper advertisement concerning Begin. Senator Herbert R. O'Connor, Democrat of Maryland, asserted he had never approved acts of terrorism and that the only possible connection he had with the Begin shindig was his concern with "the general Palestinian problem in furthering the U.S. policy on the new State of Israel." Congressman John F. Kennedy from Massachusetts wired the Chairman of the Committee, author Louis Bromfield: "Belatedly and for the record I wish to withdraw my name from the reception committee for Menachem Begin, former Irgun Commander. When accepting your invitation, I was ignorant of the true nature of his activities, and I wish to be disassociated from them completely." The office of Congressman Joe Hendricks of Florida revealed that the congressman had been out of town and thus his name "mistakenly" had been given to the Begin Committee. Several other Congressmen could not recall later whether they, or their office, had ever authorized the use of their names. Dr. Harry C. Byrd, President of the University of Maryland, said: "Some people I know asked me if they could use my name as a member of the reception committee and I said they could. I didn't know who he was. I am not going to New York." And so it went —after the damage had been done.

Albert Einstein, Sidney Hook, Hannah Arendt, and Seymour Milman were among the signatories to this letter, which appeared in the *Times* on December 4, 1948.

Among the most disturbing political phenomena of our time is the emergence in the newly created state of Israel of the "Freedom Party" . . . a political party closely akin in its organization, methods, political philosophy, and social appeal to the Nazi and Fascist parties. It was formed out of the membership and following of the former Irgun Zvai Leumi, a terrorist right-wing chauvinist organization in Palestine.

The current visit of Menachem Begin, leader of this party, to the United States is obviously calculated to give the impression of American support for his party in the coming Israeli elections, and to cement political ties with conservative Zionist elements in the United States. Several Americans of national repute have lent their names to welcome his visit. It is inconceivable that those who oppose fascism throughout the world, if currently informed as to Mr. Begin's political record and perspectives, could add their names and support to the movement he represents. . . . A shocking example was their behavior in the Arab village of Deir Yassin . . . this incident exemplified the character and actions of the Freedom Party. Within the Jewish community they have preached an admixture of ultranationalism, religious mysticism, and racial superiority. Like other Fascist parties, they have been used to break strikes, and have themselves pressed for the destruction of free trade unions.

The discrepancies between the bold claims now being made by Begin and his party, and their record of past performance in Palestine, bear the imprint of no ordinary political party. This is the unmistakeable stamp of a Fascist party for whom terrorism (against Jews, Arabs, and British alike) and misrepresentation are means, and a "Leader State" is the goal.

In the light of the foregoing considerations, it is imperative that the truth about Mr. Begin and his movement be made known in this country. It is all the more tragic that the top leadership of American Zionism has refused to campaign against Begin's efforts, or even to expose to its own constituents the dangers to Israel of support to Begin. The undersigned therefore take this means of publicly presenting a few salient facts concerning Begin and his party, and of urging all concerned not to support this latest manifestation of fascism.

The reference to unions made Philip Murray, then President of the CIO and one of the original members of the Welcoming Committee, suddenly realize that he had never authorized the use of his name —after it had appeared for weeks on thousands of letters, let alone advertisements.

What made the *Times'* complicity in building a different face for Begin so patently dishonest twenty-nine years later was that the editors and writers of a newspaper so steeped in foreign affairs could not help know of the connection between the Irgun massacre at Deir Yassin and the Palestinian problem, the continuing core of Middle East turmoil. Journalistic history reveals few parallels to the cover-up of the past record of the head of the Israeli government. Without the *New York Times*, no new Begin would have ever been created for the American people.

In the face of the overwhelming evidence of inescapable facts, the *Times* with its enormous influence continued to provide otherwise the most effective cover-up for the Israeli occupation. Its editorial and news pages vigorously opposed the PLO at every turn, not only the long term goal of a binational Palestine but also the immediate goal of an independent entity on the West Bank. When Secretary Vance in the summer of 1977 was in Jordan looking for "Palestinian dignitaries" to supplant the PLO, it even gave credence to denials that the Arafat-led group reflected the sentiments of the Palestinian people.

A Flora Lewis (European correspondent sent to the Middle East) dispatch from Tel Aviv[73] declared "West Bank Arabs Favor UN Trusteeship Over Area." The impression was conveyed that the Secretary had met at a garden party at the home of Foreign Minister Moshe Dayan with a representative group of West Bank Arabs who had presented him a petition denying that the PLO was representative of West Bank Palestinians. Although only a small group of dissidents, led by the son of former Hebron Mayor Sheikh al-Jaabari, were identified in the article, Lewis simulated a "balance" between them and the group of West Bank Arab Mayors of major towns who had made clear their total support of the PLO in a letter earlier delivered to Vance's staff in Jerusalem.

It was more than slightly ironic that Secretary Vance at this stage should have advanced the trusteeship concept President Truman had contemptuously attributed to the "striped-pants boys" when State Department career officers had suggested this as a solution in 1947 and again in 1948 after international support for partition had failed. (See Chapter I.) Had not the President precipitately recognized Israel, a Palestinian trusteeship might then have been effected and much of the ensuing turmoil avoided.

In a September 9, 1977, article datelined "Ramallah, Israel-Occupied Jordan," *New York Times* Senior Editor and former Editorial Page Editor John B. Oakes still was writing that "though no Arab will admit it, this is surely one of the mildest military occupations in history."[74] Downgrading the PLO, as he had when he wrote many of the *Times'* editorials, Oakes pointed to the alleged "lack of unanimity to the PLO claim to be the 'sole and legitimate representative of the Palestinian people' " in contrast to the "solid determination of the 40 families at the new Kudum settlement 'to establish our rights to this land forever.' "

Oakes enthused about the "far higher wages" enjoyed by Arab labor in Israel than outside and about the "building boom," but remained totally blind to Palestinian oppression. His observation that "Israeli troops are hardly to be seen" was in direct conflict with the article "Permanent State of Siege," from the pen of a fellow journalist of the *Philadelphia Inquirer* three months earlier: "Uniforms are everywhere. Jeeps with anti-tank guns roll down Ben Yehuda Street without attracting attention. Young men and women carrying submachine guns stroll down the street, or clamber aboard buses.[75]

During the 1977–78 peace talks ushered in by the Sadat initiative, the *Times'* opposition to the PLO, editorially and on the Op-Ed page, intensified as Egyptian-Israeli differences centered on the issues of settlements and Palestinian self-determination. A John Oakes article devoted an entire column, "Defying the PLO," to a refutation of the right of the Arafat group to speak for West Bank Arabs, using as his authority a "prosperous Palestinian businessman (passing through New York) who did his own share of bomb-throwing and terrorism against the Israelis 30 years ago" and who now has "no use of the PLO's extreme position and terrorist tactics and fears its radicalism."[76]

In building up Abdel-Nour Khalil Janho as a "tough, energetic entrepreneur who was typical of the West Bankers who have no love for the PLO's extreme position," former top editorial writer and nephew of the founder of the *Times* Oakes told his readers only part of the story. Janho, as a letter to the editor subsequently pointed out,[77] was a close friend of Jerusalem's Mayor Teddy Kollek and was notorious for his intimate relations with both Jordanian intelligence and Israeli military authorities. The years of collaboration led to special privileges and favors, including the monopoly in the bottling and distribution of gas, bringing him a purple Cadillac and wealth. Badly defeated in the spring 1976 elections on the West Bank, this dissident was involved in a shooting in broad daylight over a gambling debt in which he killed one man and wounded another, but was absolved by a military court although this was a civil matter. Although receiving military protection from the Israeli army, Janho himself was assassinated early in 1978, an act of which Oakes and the *Times* took no notice at all.

When the peace talks broke off principally over the issues of Israeli settlements and the "self-rule" offered Palestinians, *Times* editorials refused to censure Israel or place the blame on Begin: "The issue over what has come to be called the 'self-determination' of Palestinians is a tragic legacy of rival nationalisms and the failure of the Arabs to accept the partition of Palestine when it was offered by the world 30 years ago."[78] In March even after the full-scale invasion of southern Lebanon, the *Times* insisted that the ball rested in the Arab's court: "Only by showing that they understand Israel's need for elementary security can they logically presume peace on the return of lost territory."[79] Again, total disregard for the Zionist nature of the Israeli state!

To maximize Israeli compliance with the UN March 19 resolution calling for forthright, complete withdrawal, a bold two-columned *Times* headline on page one of April 12 and repeated three days later proclaimed the "2-Stage Pullback." Both stories were accompanied by large maps of South Lebanon on which names of towns and hamlets from which withdrawal had been made were set in boxed large print giving the false impression that this was a meaningful withdrawal. Twenty-two square miles of the 500-square-mile area occupied in March, or five percent, had been relinquished.

The role of the *Times* in molding public opinion by means of such persistent deceit and bias cannot be exaggerated. This giant possesses a tremendous, monolithic influence directly on the public, as well as on opinion-molding leaders, although a 1978 Harris poll showed that the people "running" the press stood sixteenth in public esteem in a listing of twenty professions and occupations. How to curtail this power without breaching the prohibition against interference with freedom of the press constitutes one of the great challenges of our times, a problem which Chief Justice Warren E. Burger touched upon in a concurring opinion of April 26, 1978, when he declared that "large media conglomerates had no special claim on First Amendment rights of free expression or other constitutional liberties."[80] For the major peril that now faces Americans has been spawned by widespread missing information and myth-information underlying their country's Middle East policy, no small part of which has been caused by the double standard applied to terrorism.

X   Terror: The Double Standard

And so, to the end of history, murder shall breed murder, always in the name of right and honor and peace, until the gods are tired of blood and create a race that can understand.

—George Bernard Shaw, *Caesar and Cleopatra*

It is nearly impossible to pick out the one particular subject of Middle East reportage the media has most slanted and distorted. But certainly the manner in which the use of violence has been presented probably has had the most influence in formulating American public opinion.

The media has succeeded in getting Western man to accept a double standard: one, that Jews and Zionists have been freedom fighters in pursuit of a moral, legal, historical imperative—namely, the establishment of their own state, Israel. On the other hand, the media has stressed that when Palestinians resorted to armed violence to regain their homeland, they were terrorists. Whereas the Hitler experience was readily invoked to condone Zionist intemperate acts, the desperate frustration of being deprived of their homes for thirty years, and any hearing for their grievances, was deemed no excuse for Palestinian excesses.[1] The choice of words and pejorative adjectives, the shadings, the explanatory material spelling out the particular incident, and the amount of sympathy employed in describing the victims were all instrumentalities in applying this double standard.

As an example, few voices were allowed to be heard in dissent of the totally accepted Zionist labeling given the October war. One of these appeared on WEEI, the CBS outlet in Boston, three days after the fighting erupted. Following four callers, who were to varying degrees pro-Israel, the moderator introduced a soft-spoken voice unmistakably Indian or Pakistani, who complained of the use of slanted language by the reporters. He stated that the moderator had no right to call the war an act of aggression when all Egypt and Syria were trying to do was get back their own territory. Moderator Howard Nelson tried unsuccessfully to rebut the gentleman by reading the dictionary meaning of the word "aggression," totally refusing to take into consideration the initial 1967 Israeli seizure of Arab lands. The persistent questioner countered by pointing to the persistent media slantings: "Why is it, when Israelis hijack a Lebanese plane and force it to land in Israel, newscasters call it a 'diversion,' but when the Palestinians engage in air thievery, it is called 'hijacking.' Why," he asked again, "is there this double standard?"

A study[2] made of U.S. press reportage showed that although all acts of terrorism were generally bemoaned, Israeli actions were usually justified as responses to "intolerable situations." The *Washington Post,* for example, justified the 1973 Israeli assassinations in Beirut as "the best kind of terrorism," since they killed "the worst kind of terrorists."[3] In editorials dealing with the commandos, 95.2 percent of the coverage by the *New York Times,* 91 percent by the *Washington Post,* and 100 percent by the *Detroit Free Press* was against commando terrorist activity. While condemning the commandos, the *Times* did manage to publish three features indicating sympathy for the plight of the Palestinian refugees as refugees. The *Washington Post* had three editorials and one feature on the refugee problem.

Under rules of the media, the Israelis are "freedom fighters" and the Arabs are "terrorists," the Israelis "make reprisals" while the Palestinians "commit atrocities," the Arabs constantly stand vilified, the Israelis glorified. As stated in an October 1968 "Letter to Christians" signed by sixty-six ministers from nine denominations:

Westerners in general are already aware of what the Israeli feels: pride that he is once more, after so long, master in Palestine, where he no longer need apologize for being Jewish. But Westerners are not so aware of what the Arab feels: resentment at losing his land, humiliation at military losses, frustration at being unable to make his claims understood to the rest of the world. . . . Westerners should understand that the Arabic term for the underground fighters, *fedayeen,* means "those who sacrifice themselves," and that the Arabs compare them to the underground fighters in Europe during the Nazi occupation.[4]

This double standard came into play long ago and slowly permeated reporting from the outset of the struggle in Palestine, helping to mold the popular impression of events there. Most people became conditioned to believe that it was the Arabs alone who resorted to violence. But the record of the Zionist use of violence in behalf of their cause, carefully blacked out from public surveillance,[5] is a lengthy one that could be traced back to the days of the British mandate.

Violence was often used against their own, as on November 25, 1940, when the S.S. *Patria* was blown up in the Haifa harbor, killing 276 illegal Jewish immigrant passengers. At the time of the incident these deaths were attributed to the British, and it was not until ten years later that the responsibility for this disaster was placed at the door of the Zionists. David Flinker, Israeli correspondent of the Jewish *Morning Journal* (the largest Yiddish daily) described what had happened:

. . . It was then that the Haganah General Staff took a decision at which their leaders shuddered. The decision was not to permit the *Patria* to leave Jaffa. The English must be given to understand that Jews could not be driven away from their own country. The *Patria* must be blown up. The decision was conveyed to Haganah members on the *Patria* and in the hush of night, preparations had begun for the execution of the tragic act. On Sunday, November 26, 1940, the passengers were informed by the English that they were being returned to sea. The Jews remained silent, save for a whisper from man to man to go "up the deck, all up the deck." Apparently, the signal did not reach everybody, for many hundreds remained below—never to see the light again. Suddenly an explosion was heard and a panic ensued. . . . It was a hellish scene; people jumped into the water, children were tossed into the waves; agonizing cries tore the heavens. The number of victims was officially placed at 276. The survivors were permitted by the High Commissioner to land.[6]

Fifteen months later the S.S. *Struma* exploded in the Black Sea, killing 769 illegal Jewish immigrants. The Jewish Agency described it as an act of "mass-protest and mass-suicide," and the U.S. media once more placed the responsibility for these deaths at the door of the British and their Palestine immigration policy.

There followed the assassination in Cairo on November 6, 1944, of Lord Moyne, the British Minister Resident; the Irgun's blowing up of the King David Hotel in Jerusalem, killing ninety-one and injuring forty-five British and Arabs (subsequent evidence indicated the involvement of the Haganah and the Jewish Agency), and the 1947 dispatch of letter bombs to British Cabinet Ministers and the bomb attacks of December 11, in and near Haifa, killing eighteen Arabs and wounding fifty-eight others. In subsequent years the Arab-owned Semiramis Hotel in Jerusalem was blown up, killing twenty persons, among them the Viscount de Tapia, the Spanish Consul. The Haganah admitted responsibility for the outrage.

In 1948, following the adoption of the U.N. partition resolution but prior to the May 15 promulgation of the Israeli state, Irgun, Stern Gang,[7] or Haganah terrorists repeatedly struck with bombs, loads of explosives, or even armed forces at Arab civilians in villages, towns, and cities. The grossest outrage, of course, was the April 9 massacre at Deir Yassin of 254 women, children, and old men.

On September 17, 1948, U.N. Palestine Mediator Count Folke Bernadotte, nephew of Swedish King Gustav V, and his aide, Colonel André Pierre Serot, were assassinated by members of the Stern Gang while driving in the Israeli-controlled sector of Jerusalem. American Ambassador Stanton Griffis, convinced that the identity of the assassin was well known to the Israeli government, commented in his memoirs: "The murder of Bernadotte will remain forever a black and disgraceful mark on the early history of Israel."[8]

During a February 1977 press conference marking the publication in Israel of a new book on David Ben-Gurion, *The Secret List of Heinrich Roehm,* it was definitely admitted by author Dr. Michael Bar Zohar (writing in the U.S. under the name of Michael Barak) that the late Prime Minister had the names of the three who had carried out the assassination; one of them, Yehoshva Zeitler, was one of Ben-Gurion's best friends.[9] Zeitler explained that "we executed Bernadotte because he was a one-man institution who endangered the status of Jerusalem by his declared intention of turning her into an international city. He was hostile to Israel from the moment the state was established and actually laid the foundation for the present U.N. policy of supporting the Arabs." The decision to kill Count Bernadotte had been taken by three Stern Gang leaders, Nathan Yelin-Mor, Dr. Israel Eldad-Scheib, and Zeitler, commander of activities in Jerusalem and an intimate friend of the first Prime Minister.

In 1950 Zionist agents in Baghdad threw bombs at a synagogue and at other Jewish targets in order to pressure Jews into emigrating to Israel. In 1953 the small Jordanian hamlets of Kibya and Nahalin, and the UNRWA refugee camp at Bureij in the Gaza Strip, were attacked; 102 villagers and refugees were killed. Between 1952 and September 1956, prior to the first Suez war, the Arab villages of Beit Jalu, Falame, Rantis, Bani Suhaila, Baheya, Gharandal, Wadi Fukin, and Gaza were shelled on raids, killing 118 civilians.

A few hours after the Israeli army began its march into Sinai on October 29, 1956, a curfew from 5 P.M. to 6 A.M. was imposed on Kafr Kassem and other villages of the Little Triangle within Israel. This curfew advance of one hour was transmitted at 4:45 P.M. to the Mayor of the village, who informed the Israeli officer in charge that a large number of villagers were working in the fields and could not be notified of the change; forty-nine villagers returning after 5 P.M., including fourteen women and small children in the arms of their mothers, were mowed down without any warning whatsoever by machine guns as they came in from their work.

These facts, suppressed for a long time, seeped through when the border policemen were finally brought to trial. The proceedings lasted more than two years, and the Israeli High Court passed light sentences: one officer received seventeen years, another fifteen years, three were acquitted, and five constables received sentences of seven years. All were set free one year later by government amnesty. And from the ever intensely active libertarian-human rights movement in the U.S., only silence. Identical reaction followed the 1966 Israeli armed force attack, including tanks and armored cars, practically wiping out the small Jordanian village of Es-Samu'a, killing eighteen and wounding fifty-four others.

By 1972, with the emergence of the PLO movement, Israeli espionage agencies concentrated their attention on individual Palestinians, who were struck down by letter bombs, regular bombs, and machine guns in Beirut,[10] Los Angeles,[11] Rome, [12] Tripoli,[13] Stockholm,[14] Copenhagen,[15] Paris,[16] Cyprus,[17] and in Oslo.[18]

The task of seeking out and destroying Palestinians known to be connected with recurring fedayeen attacks on Israelis rested with the Mossad, the Israeli version of the CIA, known familiarly as the "Institute." A special branch within Mossad, set up in 1972, had been responsible for the April 10, 1973, raid on Lebanon and the assassination of the three PLO leaders, Kamal Nasser, Mohammed Yusuf Najjar, and Kamal Adwan. The meticulously executed operation was part of a plan, "Operation: God's Wrath," under the command of Prime Minister Meir's Special Adviser on Security Affairs, General Aharon Yariv, whose goal had been the elimination of the 1,000 Palestinians capable of providing leadership to the movement. The elimination of this select number, it was thought, would liquidate the movement itself. And the outbreak of fierce fighting in Lebanon's civil war in the spring of 1975 facilitated other raids by the Israeli secret service, which soon added twenty-three victims to its roster.[19]

Starting with the December 28, 1968, helicopter raid on the Beirut Airport, Lebanon was the continuous site for Israeli attacks on civilians and civilian targets, most of which occurred in the south of the country. These commenced with a number of small raids in 1969 and 1970, reported to the U.N. but generally ignored. In 1972 the Israeli armed forces began their serious raids with an attack on the Arkoub region, in which two civilians were killed; on the Nabatiyeh refugee camp, in which ten were killed; on Nahr al-Bared and Rafed and Rashaya-al Wadi camps, causing the deaths of sixteen; on Baddawi and Nahr-al Bared, killing twelve.

In April 1974 six South Lebanese villages were attacked by Israeli armed forces, and in May the village of Kfeir was bombed with four persons killed, including a woman and her seven-year-old daughter. Eleven days later Israeli planes again raided the refugee camp of Naba-tiyeh and that of Ein-el-Helweh as well, killing fifty and wounding 200, and completely obliterating the former Palestinian site. On the 19th of the same month, Israeli naval units bombarded the Rashidiyeh refugee camp, killing eight civilians. The next month the Israeli planes returned to bomb three U.N. camps, killing seventy-three and wounding 159. In July Israeli naval units raided Tyre, Sarafund, and Saida, sinking twenty-one fishing boats. The aerial bombing and ground raids of Lebanese towns and U.N. refugee camps in the south of the country continued into 1975.

The idealization of Zionist terror, far beyond mere condonation, assumed its inexorable course when twenty-two-year-old Egyptian Jew Eliahu Betzouri and his seventeen-year-old friend Eliahu Hakim slew Lord Moyne in 1944. Years after the conviction, David Ben-Gurion admitted "his reverence for the dedicated patriots who were hanged in Cairo" for this assassination of Great Britain's Resident Minister. (Israel's first Prime Minister also referred to terrorist Abraham Stern, the poet who founded the group bearing his name, as "one of the finest and most outstanding figures of the era.")

The reportage on the trial by such illustrious newsmen of the day as the *Times'* C.L. Sulzberger, AP's Relman Morin, and UP's Samir Souki featured the defense counsel and the defendants' condemnation of the British administration for graft, anarchistic rule, and acts of injustice. Popular sympathy was established in the U.S. with the young "heroes," even though in his House of Commons eulogy of the slain British Minister of State, Prime Minister Winston Churchill referred to "the shameful crime" and boldly declared: "If our dreams for Zionism are to end in the smoke of assassins' guns and our labors for its future to produce only a new set of gangsters worthy of Nazi Germany, then many like myself will have to reconsider the position we have maintained so consistently and so long in the past." No wonder that political adviser to the Jewish Agency Leo Cohen, after listening to the Churchill BBC broadcast, stated:

When I think how proud we have been that Zionism could come before the world with clean hands as a creative movement of the highest order, and when I think of what those boys have been led to do . . . it is something so exasperating, so awful and dreadful.

But Churchill's reassessment never reached fruition, and the Western world's honeymoon with Zionism continued. Chaim Weizmann had written at the time to Churchill: "I can assure you that Palestine Jewry will, as its representative bodies have declared, go to the utmost limits of its power to cut out, root and branch, this evil from its midst."[20] Two years after that assurance, the Anglo-American Committee of Inquiry in its report was still requesting the Jewish Agency "to resume active co-operation with the Mandatory Authority in the suppression of terrorism and of illegal immigration and in the maintenance of that law and order throughout Palestine which is essential for the good of all, including the new immigrants."[21]

Author Gerold Frank, who ghosted Bartley Crum's *Behind the Silken Curtain* and Jorge Garcia-Granados' *The Birth of Israel,* both extremely pro-Israel books, had the final word to say in his elegy to the Moyne assassins in his book, *The Deed.*[22]

Here in the remote corner [the cemetery of Bassatin which contains the bodies of such great Jews as Moses Maimonides], amid the debris and neglect of ages one finds a single square stone, not large—two feet high, three feet wide—no names on it, but in Hebrew "pray for their souls." Beneath it, Eliahu Hakim and Eliahu Betzouri sleep together, as they were buried in one coffin, curled in each other's arms as children. They lie curled together like sleeping children under the eternal stone. No one guards their grave now. The sands of the desert blow, nothing grows there, and no weeds, no foliage. Only the sifting, creeping yellow dust over everything, and in the cloudless sky a molten sun. In the ancient earth in the nameless grave they lie together under the imperishable stone. Few remember them now.

This is how the people have been prepared to accept Zionist acts of violence and to judge the continuing conflict. Thus when the Irgun led by Menachem Begin[23] blew up the King David Hotel and some of his followers were apprehended, the compassionate but often misled Eleanor Roosevelt wrote to Lady Reading, a friend in England: "If these young people are killed, there will be without any question a sense of martyrdom and a desire for revenge which will only bring more bloodshed. A generous gesture will, I think, change the atmosphere."

A special variation on the double standard is to be seen in the handling of espionage activities by the Israelis and their Arab counterparts. As to the Israeli cause, the end always justifies the means. The Zionists and Israelis are admired no matter what dirty tricks they use, often by the very people who are the first to condemn the use of "dirty tricks" at home, by the CIA or other American intelligence-espionage agencies. The Zionists and Israelis are allowed to break all the rules of international law, and to make their own. The kidnapping of Adolph Eichmann from Argentina was only the best publicized of many instances of how the Israelis have been able to get away with defying international edict. Imagine if the CIA were to kidnap some wanted criminal for crimes against the American people! Imagine if the Arabs were to abduct an Israeli for crimes against the Palestinians! Yet so long as it is Jews, Israelis, Zionists—everything goes.

This has long been true in the attitudes toward Israeli spies. One of the major instances of this, now forgotten by most of the few people who ever knew about it, was the Lavon Affair that once rocked Israel to the very core.

After the Egyptian revolution of 1952, relations between the U.S. and the new Gamal Abdel Nasser government steadily improved. Cultural and economic agreements between Egypt and other Arab states and the U.S. were being discussed, and it was sincerely hoped that the U.S. would aid the projected Aswan Dam development program. By 1954 American Ambassador Henry Byroade's personal friendship with Nasser seemed likely to produce results. A U.S. aid program of $50 million had been started.

The situation was viewed in high Israeli quarters as a grave threat to the continued flow of American dollars into Israel from public, if not private, sources. A direct severance of relations between Egypt and the U.S. was deemed desirable. An Israeli espionage ring was sent to Egypt to bomb official U.S. offices and, if necessary, attack American personnel working there so as to destroy Egyptian-U.S. relations and eventually Arab-U.S. ties. The creation of simulated anti-British incidents was calculated to induce the British to maintain their Suez garrison. Several bomb incidents involving U.S. installations in Egypt followed.

Small bombs shaped like books and secreted in book covers were brought into the USIA libraries in both Alexandria and Cairo. Fishskin bags filled with acid were placed on top of nitroglycerin bombs; it took several hours for the acid to eat through the bag and ignite the bomb. The book bombs were placed in the shelves of the library just before closing hours. Several hours later a blast would occur, shattering glass and shelves and setting fire to books and furniture. Similar bombs were placed in the Metro-Goldwyn-Mayer Theater and in other American-owned business buildings.[24]

In December two young Jewish Egyptian boys carrying identical bombs were caught as they were about to enter U.S. installations. Upon their confession, a sabotage gang of six other Jews was rounded up. Five more were implicated in the plot. The conspirators, who received sentences ranging from fifteen years to life, were the objects in the U.S. of multifold sympathetic editorials and articles. Nothing appeared in print at the time to refute the image that this had been but another Nasser conspiracy to unite his country against Israel. The cry "anti-Semitism" widely reverberated.

In 1960 an investigation in Israel called attention to the forgery of an important document in what had been announced as a "security mishap" that had precipitated the resignation of Pinhas Lavon as Minister of Defense in 1955. Shimon Peres, then Deputy Minister of Defense, and Moshe Dayan had, with the forgery, attempted to place the legal responsibility for the unsuccessful 1954 sabotage attempt at Lavon's door. Ben-Gurion had fought the reopening of the case, but a subsequent rehearing revealed that Lavon had been an innocent victim of the machinations of Peres, Dayan, and Brigadier Abraham Givli.

Even though the army, through censorship, attempted to cover up its own blunders, the affair led to a Cabinet crisis and the resignation of the Ben-Gurion government in 1961. As late as December 29, *1960,* the *Times* was still referring to the scandal only as "a disastrous adventure in 1954." As the already abnormal ties between Israel and the U.S. grew stronger, scant attention was paid to the disclosure in Israel of this blatant attempt to torpedo U.S.-Arab relations.

In 1971 one of the spies who figured in the Lavon Affair, Marcelle Ninio, broke into the headlines of Israel and of the satellite Israeli press in the U.S. Ninio, the only woman involved in the affair that so rocked the political life of Israel, had been exchanged for Egyptian prisoners of war after the June 1967 war, along with Victor Levy, Robert Dassa, and Philip Nathanson, her cosaboteurs, and "Champagne Spy" Wolfgang Lotz, who had been apprehended in 1965 after four years of spying in Egypt. According to a five-paragraph story in the *New York Times* of November 16, 1971, Premier Golda Meir was to attend the wedding of a girl "who at the age of 16 was convicted of espionage for Israel and spent 10 years in an Egyptian jail." The Lavon Affair was referred to as a "mysterious sabotage mission inside Egypt" in 1954, about which "full details remain a secret."

The entire tone of the article suggested innocence on the part of Israel and of the bride-to-be. It had been just another case of those "hating Egyptians" trying to put a spy rap on a nice Jewish girl. The *New York Post* carried a four-column story on page 4, "Israeli Heroine to Marry," and referred to the "dark-haired woman who spent fifteen years in a Cairo prison for alleged sabotage activities."

Both newspapers slanted the reportage, withholding undisputed facts in this true spy story. Although the so-called "heroine" had been deeply involved in proven espionage, seventeen years later the same "editorial papers" were compounding the felony they had originally committed. To avoid presenting the established facts of Israeli sabotage against the U.S., which had involved Israeli Cabinet ministers Dayan and Peres, the *Times* covered up the affair in this fashion: "The mission quickly was shown to be a far-fetched idea."

When Israeli spy Elie Cohen, alias Kamal Amin Tabas, was uncovered by Syrian intelligence and hanged in Damascus, an angry hue and cry arose in the West, led by the media with photos (front page of the *New York Times*) of the condemned's body hanging in the public square. Two popular books, *Our Man in Damascus*[25] by Eli Ben-Hanan and *The Silent Warriors*[26] by Joshua Tadmor translated from the Hebrew by Israeli *Ha'aretz* U.S. correspondent Raphael Rothstein, made a martyr of the spy (the latter tome was dedicated ironically enough to Elie Wiesel, the godfather of anti-anti-Semitism) and attacked the lack of a fair trial to which the press was not admitted. In the course of their glorification of the Israeli superspy, the authors unwittingly further proved his guilt. Cohen had been arrested in Egypt as part of the Lavon Affair spy ring but held only for two years, released, and then had joined Israel's Secret Service as a trained espionage agent with Damascus to be the base of his operations. As an Oriental Jew he was fluent in Arabic and was scarcely distinguishable from any Muslim or Christian Arab. Most of the important Israeli spies were Arab Jews.

Cohen cleverly worked his way into affluent social and political circles in Damascus, even becoming acquainted with General Amin el-Hafez, who was to come into power in March 1963. Through his contacts Cohen was able to ascertain the number, type, and placement of MIG-21 planes, T-54 tanks, and other Soviet armament, which Syria was receiving from the Soviet Union, as well as Damascus plans for the construction of a canal as counterdiversion of the Daniyas, one of the principal sources of the Jordan River.

The incalculably invaluable information smuggled out to Israel until his apprehension was an important factor in his country's success in the six-day war. This was never alluded to in any way by the American press in their accounts of the "martyred" spy. But author Rothstein sharply pointed this up: "Now the peaceful Golan Heights, where Russian tanks lie rusting and concrete fortifications are piles of rubble, is a tourist attraction, and much of the credit for this turn of events belongs to Israel's silent hero, Elie Cohen."

In the fall of 1972 the major capitals in Europe, the Middle East, and the U.S. were rocked by a spate of letter and package bombs. This phase of the lethal-letter war opened with the letter-bomb killing of an Israeli diplomat in his London office. Coming on the heels of the Munich tragedy, biased world public opinion was only too ready to believe that these acts had been the responsibility of the Palestinian Black September group, although the strict security watch at the Israeli Embassy had intercepted seven other letters, only one of which contained a leaflet boasting Black September sponsorship. Upon close examination it remained very much of an open question who had been sending what bombs to whom.

According to neutral observers in Britain, while the popular press tended to lean sympathetically toward the Israelis, "the serious press was more objective. After the thirteen letter bombs intercepted in London in November, British Jewry was talking of retribution, but so far as can be seen, there is no evidence to support the theory that Black September is behind the current wave of incidents." British writers, including those of the London *Times,* viewed evidence of the Palestinian complicity as "uneasy." Yet in the U.S. there was no indecision. The minds of the public were made up for them by the American press and the politicians, although a New York City episode took on the aura of a Hitchcock movie gone awry.

In October, letter bombs addressed to two retired officials of Hadassah (Women's Zionist Organization) were discovered when they failed to detonate. Mrs. Rose Halprin, who had not been president since 1952, allegedly received one at her East Side home. There were fifteen Halprins in the 1972 Manhattan telephone directory, eighteen in the edition a year earlier. There was no listing for Rose Halprin. It was difficult to understand how a group of Palestinians 5,000 miles away could ever have obtained her name let alone her address.

The second letter had been addressed to a one-time executive director (one newspaper referred to her as Hannah Goldberg and another as Mrs. Hannah Rosenberg) and was opened under police supervision without it exploding.[27] Following the apprehension of the letter bombs addressed to the New York women, Mayor John Lindsay released this statement: "Terror by mail is the latest, and in some ways, the most vicious technique yet devised by conspirators against Israel. To direct it at two outstanding ladies of Hadassah here reaches a low in the politics of terror."

At the same time a number of letter bombs sent to the Israeli Mission to the U.N. were also intercepted. (One of these was supposedly addressed to a diplomat not even as yet listed in the U.N. directory.) A spokesman for the Israeli Embassy was quick to be quoted: ' The letters sent to New York show that the terrorist organization is not just anti-Israeli, as they claim, but anti-Jewish throughout the world." And to further this impression that the Palestinians posed a threat to all Jews, two letter bombs, also mailed from Penang, appeared in Rhodesia, sent to residents of Bulawayo. One had been addressed to prominent young Zionist leader Colin Raizon, another to the mother of Rhodesian Olympic weight lifter John Orkin. Both were intercepted by the police.

Was it more than a coincidence that the letter bombs, sent to the Hadassah and to the Israeli Mission, all of which were intercepted, were received at a time when Israel was doing its best to coordinate its efforts with those of the U.S. in forcing the Legal Committee of the U.N. to adopt an antiterrorist pact with muscle as a means of further restraining the operations of the Palestinian guerrillas?

This alleged introduction of bombs into the U.S., following in the wake of the Munich Olympics incident, played a major role in moving federal authorities to initiate a "dragnet" investigation and interrogation and surveillance of Arab residents and students in the country. Cracking down on Arabs and restrictive measures against all travelers passing through the U.S. was the inevitable result.

On October 26, on page 2 in a five-column headline, the readers of the *New York Times* were told: "Israel Intercepts Letter Bombs Mailed to Nixon, Rogers and Laird." The story pointed out that the latest letter bombs were "similar to those mailed to Jews in various countries from Amsterdam last month by the Arab guerrilla organization known as the 'Black September.' One letter bomb killed an official in the Israeli Embassy in London."

Two days later a UPI story, carried on certain radio stations, revealed that an American tourist, twenty-two-year-old Dennis Feinstein from Stockton, California, had been arrested by the Israeli police as he attempted to cross over into Lebanon. He was being held on suspicion of mailing letter bombs to top American officials. The story appeared in some papers, including the *Washington Post.*

The *Times* News Summary and Index of the city edition on October 28 listed for page 3 under "International": "Israel holds American in mailing of letter bombs." But not one line of the story appeared in that edition. In the later edition the listing was deleted from the Index. In page 3 of the earlier edition there had been an unclear, meaningless photo of "men with opposing views scuffling on a Santiago, Chile, street," which appeared to have been dropped in as a last-minute filler replacement in a spot where the Israeli story might have initially been intended to go. New copy replaced this photograph on page 3 in the later edition.

It took the *Sunday Times* of December 24, 1972 in a lengthy article, "How Israelis Started the Terror by Post," to place the responsibility for the spate of bombs. As noted by other European observers, it was out of character for the Black September not to have claimed "credit" for these incidents, as they had done instantaneously at the time of Munich and invariably on other occasions.

With the exception of the first London bomb, which just missed detection, the bomb in the Bronx post office, and the one mailed from India, which injured jeweler Vivian Prins in London, all the other numerous letter bombs sent in Europe and the U.S. to Jews and Jewish organizations were somehow intercepted or proved to be duds. In contrast, almost all of the bombs addressed to Arabs and Palestinians worked successfully. The device for these bombs is very simple, and they have been generally termed to be uniformly deadly. In the words of the police in New York regarding the Hadassah letters: "They failed to detonate even though the trigger was lying directly against the blasting cap." And the Palestinians proved on many occasions their ability to handle infinitely more sophisticated weapons than these.

While the invention of the letter bomb went back to a brilliant but unbalanced Swedish chemist, Martin Eckenberg, who killed himself at the age of forty-one in a London prison in 1910, Zionist terrorists, the Stern Gang and the Irgun, had brought the weapon to the Middle East. In 1947 letter-bomb campaigns were directed against prominent British politicians believed to be unsympathetic to the Zionist goal of establishing a state in Palestine, and figured in the internationally publicized incident in which the brother of a British officer, Roy Farran, who had been acquitted of murdering a Jewish youth in Palestine, was killed by a parcel bomb admittedly sent by the Stern Gang.

The Zionist apparatus literally exploded when a *Times* front-page story headlined an excerpt from Margaret Truman's book alleging a 1947 letter-bomb attempt by the Stern Gang on the life of her father.

The Anglo-Jewish press across the country reverberated with criticism, one newspaper going so far as to make the familiar charge of "anti-Semitism." In a *New York Times* Letter to the Editor, Benjamin Gepner, who identified himself as the U.S.-Western Hemisphere leader of the "Stern Group," insisted that it was absurd even to think that there could have been such a plot against the President. The letter-bomb attempt apparently had taken place at a time when the Chief Executive was urging Zionists to be more restrained in their demands and to become more sensitive to the Palestinian plight. Aside from the fact that the authoress had little reason to pull this assassination attempt out of the air, the Stern Gang's own long record of terror supported the plausibility of the story.

Explosive devices were widely used by the Israelis in a broad campaign directed against German scientists working in Egypt in 1962 and 1963. A bomb placed in a gift parcel exploded, killing scientist Michael Khouri and five others with him, and an attempt was made on the life of Dr. Hans Kleinwachter, another scientist. Another package addressed to a West German scientist working in Cairo blew up when opened, blinding his German secretary. The daughter of German scientist Dr. Paul Goerke was threatened with a similar fate.

The Israelis succeeded in their reign of terror. Almost to a man, the West German scientists working on the development of rockets for President Nasser's army quit their Egyptian positions and returned home. This is recounted in detail in *The Champagne Spy*,[28] authored by Israeli spy Wolfgang Lotz, who boasted of having sent messages out of Cairo on the wireless hidden in his bathroom scales to his chief, saying that he was "sure we can induce additional German scientists to leave by dispatching more threatening letters and seeing that they are published in the German press." After a public reprimand by Prime Minister Ben-Gurion, Israeli Security Chief Iser Halprin resigned in an admission of Israeli complicity in the campaign against the Germans.

There were still other bomb varieties in which the Israelis excelled. Prior to the June 1967 war, the Chief Intelligence Officer in the Gaza Strip and the Egyptian Military Attaché in Jordan were both killed by book bombs. In the wake of the 1972 Lydda Airport massacre, the Palestine Popular Front's spokesman, Ghassan Kanafani, was blown up when a plastic bomb attached to the exhaust of his car exploded. And a series of booby-trapped letters, sent that fall, killed or badly injured a dozen senior Arab guerrillas and prominent Palestinians in Beirut.

Following the Kanafani death, *Ma'ariv*, the Israeli daily, wrote:

"The terrorists' statement linked the death of Kanafani to Israel and accused her of mounting this operation. Israel does not deny this or confirm it." Some eleven days following this incident, Anis Sayegh, a Director of the Palestinian Research Institute in Beirut, received an envelope ostensibly addressed to him from the Islamic Higher Council. When he opened it, it exploded, causing him partial blindness and the loss of three fingers. Within the same time period, another mail parcel exploded in the hands of the Director of a Beirut bank and the security officers of the Fateh in Beirut. (One had to closely scan the small print and the back pages of the *Times* to find a line or two, if that, about these incidents.)

In putting together all the pertinent bits of this tragic history, this observation is very much in order: The terrorists of yesterday have since become Prime Ministers, Foreign Ministers, Generals, and other VIPs of the Israeli state of today, and the armies that brought Israel its "liberation" and widely employed terror—the Haganah, Irgun, and the Stern Gang—have become the victorious armies of Israel today. While letter bombs and other forms of terrorism have been used by both sides, it was the Israelis who introduced them into the Middle East and made, as usual, the perfect propaganda use of the deadly explosives. For it was the exploitation of terror, above all, that continued to provide the public excuse for the adamant Israeli refusal to recognize the PLO, which for so long was supported by the Nixon, Ford, and Carter administrations and greatly complicated the task of reaching a Middle East settlement.

No single act so totally equated the Palestinians with terror than the killing of the Israeli athletes at the Olympic games in Munich. In the early morning of September 5, 1972, eight Palestinian guerrillas (newspapers more often referred to them as "Arabs" because that word evoked stronger sparks of hatred) invaded Olympic Village in Munich by climbing over a fence and forcing their way into the dormitories of the Israeli team, where they killed two athletes and took nine others as hostages. The guerrillas demanded the release of two hundred of their compatriots held in Israeli jails and an airplane to take them to an unspecified Arab capital. Israel, consistent with her long-standing policy, refused to negotiate with the Palestinians, but high German authorities attempted to do so, offering to pay unlimited ransom and even to substitute four of themselves for the hostages.

After lengthy parleying and three extensions of the original noon deadline, the Arab guerrillas and their Israeli hostages were flown fifteen miles by helicopters from Olympic Village to the NATO Fuer-

stenfeldbruck Airport, where they had been told they could board a
Lufthansa jet for an Arab airport. Five German sharpshooters backed
up by police waited to confront the eight Palestinians. Two guerrillas
left the helicopter to inspect the Boeing 727 on which they planned to
head for Tunisia. The Germans opened fire. One of the three helicopters was set afire by an exploding grenade thrown by one of the Palestinians as he jumped from the helicopter. But a German government
spokesman reported that the hostages were all safe. Three hours later
the Olympics Committee announced that all the hostages had been
killed.

In the course of the official government inquiry into the airport
shootout, Police Chief Manfred Schreiber admitted he had lost control
of the situation during the shooting.[29] The original police announcement claimed that the guerrillas had fired first, but most eyewitnesses
agreed that the sharpshooters had opened fire. Under dispute, until
today, was how the Israeli hostages died: Was it when the Arabs blew
up the helicopter, or had they already been killed by Arab machine-gun
fire? It also was not beyond the realm of possibility that some had died
at the hands of German bullets intended for the guerrillas.

It has never been established that the airport battle was necessary.
All discussion of this very moot point was summarily dismissed by
Police Chief Schreiber—and by the U.S. media—with the unsubstantiated allegation that the Arabs would have murdered the hostages en
route had they been allowed to leave the airport. This presumption
was in no way supported by the meticulous care and consideration
shown their hostages by the Palestinian hijackers of the U.S. and European planes in the September 1970 incident in Jordan (or by the
treatment accorded in other later hijackings up through Entebbe in the
summer of 1976).

Five and a half months later, on February 21, 1973, a Libyan
Boeing 727 with 113 civilians aboard was callously clawed out of the
sky by Israeli fighter planes over Israeli-occupied Egyptian territory of
the Sinai, about twelve miles from the Suez Canal. Some 102 passengers and 8 crewmen were killed immediately or later died, including
27 women and children. The plane had overflown Cairo, losing its way
in a terrible sandstorm, when it was intercepted by Israeli fighters,
whom the French pilot mistook for a friendly escort of Egyptian MIGs.
The aircraft had already turned around and was headed toward Cairo,
nine minutes away, when it was shot down.

The Israeli version, supported by Moshe Dayan press conferences, insisted that the plane had penetrated "probably the most sensi-

tive area held by Israel," that warnings had been given, that instructions to land had been ignored by the pilot, and that the 727 was not shot down but crashed after landing. The Defense Minister contended that the Israeli fighter pilots had signaled the Libyan plane pilot for fifteen minutes (in that time the plane would have been past Israel and well over the Mediterranean). And from the outset this Israeli fairy tale was accepted—even embroidered upon—by the American press, radio, and television.

If the media had indulged a bit more in research and study and less in generating hysteria and hatred, they would have discovered a perfect precedence in Israel's 1955 stand when an El Al plane, which had strayed into Bulgarian airspace, was shot down and fifty-eight lives were lost. In a lawsuit brought in the International Court of Justice at Geneva, Israel successfully argued:

It is the duty of any person who seeks to interfere with the normal flying of civilian aircraft by ordering it to land at a designated airport not to deliberately and unreasonably increase the inherent risks and certainly not to provoke completely new and unwarranted hazards inevitable when modern armaments were intentionally brought into play. The Bulgarian admission shows that these safeguards were not discharged. The heart of the present case is that fire was opened on the 4XAK which in the space of a few minutes was callously clawed out of the sky and destroyed. The Israeli government contended that no rule of law, not the liberal interpretations of any provision of the Chicago convention governing international aircraft, nor the rules of general international law, would permit such a degree of violence.

The generally accepted practice is to try to "box" the plane in and lead it in the correct direction. And the Libyan Boeing was already moving out of the danger zone when it was blown to smithereens.

The language used in page-one headlines of the *New York Times* the day after the incident carefully concealed what had taken place: "Israelis Down a Libyan Air Liner in the Sinai, Killing at Least 74— Say it Ignored Warnings to Land . . . Jet Crash-Lands." The *Times,* the *Post,* and other big-city presses avoided the use of the words "shot down," trying to give an impression that the jet crashed on its own after warnings to land.

The media's obvious aim was to exculpate Israel of any possible guilt and place the guilt on the French pilot, who had been on loan to Libyan Airways, for his refusal to listen to the warnings. Varied types of the art of slanting went into the reportage to the American people. There was, for example, slanting by placement—whatever the Arabs said, including Cairo and Libya, was relegated to unimportant positions; whatever Israel said went into headlines. In other previous air tragedies the papers invariably showed pictures of pretty stewardesses; There were no pictures of the Libyan airline stewardesses in this instance. In fact, there was no picture at all of survivors, which might have evoked some sympathy for the Arab victims. All one saw or read was condonation and excuse of the Israelis.

At the time of the Munich killing of Israeli athletes, banner headlines carried "the expression of horror by leaders around the world." Bold headlines ran: "Head of UN Condemns Raid as Dastardly." But Secretary-General Kurt Waldheim's statement that he "deplored" the fact that a civilian plane had been shot down, and his expression of shock, concern, and condolences on the shooting down of the Libyan airliner, were reported only in the early editions of the *New York Post* and buried away, the seven-line account obscured under a tiny head: "Waldheim [his name without his title is not familiar] Expresses Shock."[30] The quoted Israeli fear that "the Israelis could not guarantee that it was not a kamikaze plane loaded with explosives headed for an Israeli city" was featured prominently and made to sound plausible. And the only mention of the terrible blinding sandstorm, which caused the Libyan plane to lose its way, was as an incidental reference to the more than two-hour delay to Israeli helicopters taking off with wounded survivors.

The front page of the *Daily News* in New York[31] carried this bold headline: "Israelis Down Arab Jet." The readers had to turn to page 2 to discover that it had been a civilian airliner. The *New York Post* headlines were also of interest. The first was: "Israel Forces Down Libya Jet—70 Die." A little later in the day: "Israel Downs [never "shoots"] Libya Airliner; 70 Killed." And then in the continuation off this first page, they reverted to the original headline of the earlier edition: "Israel Forces Down a Libyan Jet; 70 Die."

Where the *Times'* story on the Israeli emergency Cabinet meeting featured the Israeli claim that the pilot had acknowledged the warnings and interception signals, the *New York Post* even went further into the realm of the fanciful, quoting an Israeli newspaper account that the pilot had radioed his pursuers: "We cannot obey your orders because of the political situation. This area does not belong to you." While this yarn was being spread through the combined wire services across the country, the correspondent of Israeli journal *Ha'aretz* was spreading other propaganda on a two-hour talk show over New York radio station WMCA. Under the usual "fair" media arrangements, the former

President of the Zionist Organization of America, another articulate Israelist, and this Israeli writer were pitted against the editor of *Middle East Perspective*. The "moderator" of this program three days later was among the six commentators of the same station who interviewed prominent guests from Israel, representatives of Israeli-oriented national and international organizations, and their American counterparts in a continuous twenty-five-hour broadcast tribute to Israel's first quarter century.

The *Times,* which scarcely waits minutes to execute moral judgment editorially, remained silent the day after the plane shooting, although the tragedy had been known in the U.S. before noon the day before. On the third day the editorial page spoke out under the title: "Tragic Blunder." Its words, "horrifying blunder" and "act of callousness," like slapping a child on the wrist for eating too much candy, could be contrasted to those used in its editorial six months earlier on the Olympics tragedy, "Murder in Munich": "Arab fanatics . . . homicidal hatred . . . indiscriminate murder . . . innocent lives snuffed out."[32] The editorial reluctantly conceded that the tape of the pilot's exchange with the Cairo control tower "lent credence, though not conclusive evidence" that the pilot had no idea that he would be subject to an air attack if he did not land. The publication's principal concern appeared to be the effect the incident would have on Israel's image and its case before the U.S. public.[33]

The murder in Khartoum on March 2, 1973, by the Black September movement of one Belgian and two American diplomats was as sickening an act as the shooting down of the Libyan plane and in no way condonable. As the author of *The Game of Nations,*[34] Miles Copeland, noted in *National Review,* "The Palestinian movement is a breeding ground, as is any homeless, idle and hungry population, for what we might call 'unstructured rebellion'—that is, rebellion against things in general, toward no clear goal."[35]

Whereas the *Times* waited three days to publish its editorial on the Libyan incident, less that six hours after the Khartoum deaths had been announced, the editorial page was attacking the act as "lunacy at large."[36] Bias was shown not only in the speed with which the paper reacted but in the words of its editorial: "The Palestinian extremists made their move just as Arab propaganda machinery was spinning forth outrage against Israel for the shooting down of an unarmed Libyan airliner . . . *Such talk now is even less appropriate than ever. . . .*" (Italics added.)

Where the plane had been obviously shot down on what was still

Egyptian territory but occupied by Israel, not a single news program on the three major television networks mentioned this fact. CBS' Walter Cronkite declared the plane had been shot down over Israeli territory.[37]

After the Israeli government reluctantly admitted that the crucial black box, recording communications between the Libyan plane and the ground control tower and conversations among those in the pilot's cockpit, had revealed that the French pilot had actually thought he was surrounded by friendly Egyptian MIGs showing him the way home, the *New York Times* continued to cover up Israeli guilt. The front page of February 24 contained two six-column photos, one captioned "Five Israeli military chaplains read psalms as the coffins [crude, unpainted fruit crates with crooked nails protruding and shrouds showing] of victims of the downed plane are placed on a boat." The other, "A military cortege on the Egyptian side of the Suez Canal waiting for the first boat." The glowing headline, "100 Bodies of Jet Victims Taken Over Suez to Egypt," the reportage, and the publication of the Dayan offer of partial compensation endowed the Israelis with great acts of magnanimity.

The sole headlined reference to the important revelations of the flight recorder was ambiguously set forth in this manner: "Israel Confirms Cairo Data." This admission only followed the substantiation by U.S. intelligence sources, which had also monitored the conversation. One had to read well into the article to discover that the important black box had confirmed the control tower tape, played at the press conference two days earlier, the authenticity of which the *Times* had then questioned.

In his endeavor to exculpate the Israelis from the guilt the International Civil Aviation Organization had voted 105 to 1 to fasten upon them, the *Times'* Robert Lindsey, in a June 7 article headlined: "Sinai Crash Study Notes Confusion," unwittingly blew up another Israeli myth widely circulated at the time of the tragedy by his paper: that the curtains of the windows of the Boeing had been closed and therefore the Israelis could not see that the plane carried passengers.

As on so many other occasions, the *Times* proved to be more Israelist than the two leading Israeli papers, *Ma'ariv* and *Ha'aretz.* One Israeli columnist noted that the downing of the plane had been kept secret for three or four hours before publication of any announcement, which in itself created at the outset a number of question marks. It was the first time in the history of civil aviation that a plane had crashed in an area easily reachable and yet, for twenty-four hours, it was impossible to get a picture of the wreckage. Requests to visit the site were rejected without explanation. Emergency arrangements for the press were refused. Nor was the spokesman for the Israeli defense forces available for any queries or questions until twenty-four hours later, when reporters had a right "to ask themselves what had taken place and what had been erased in the interim."

Further, according to Israeli accounts, it was only three days after the incident that General David Elazar, the Chief of Staff, spoke to the public. He had, according to the official version, received the report on the Libyan plane "after some minutes of contacts between the planes—apparently between 14:03 and 14:05, and the contact was finished at 14:11 when the flaming Libyan plane touched the ground." Actually, as revealed by the all-important little black box, the contact ended at 14:09 when the bullets were fired at the wings of the Boeing to force it to land. Therefore the contact had not lasted more than from four to six minutes. As one Israeli newspaper saw it, "the reception of the information from the air force commander and his pondering, as well as the decision, were all executed within a single three-minute connection. Why, they ask, was not more time given for the decision? Why did the Chief of Staff hear, think, and decide almost simultaneously?"

Perhaps the excuse made by the Israeli fighter pilot at a press conference sheds some light. "When I hit him, he was at a minute's flight distance from the canal." This fear that the plane might have crossed back safely into Egypt was in line with the Chief of Staff's remarks that he had "to decide immediately." If the latter had waited to contact Defense Minister Dayan, the Libyan plane could have slipped away, which apparently would have been contrary to his instructions.

Air Force Commander Mordechai Hod, who had directed the June 1967 air strikes against Arab airfields, claimed that the Libyan pilot could see the airport but had disregarded all signals. Hod ascribed certain words to the pilot that were totally disproved, again by the black box. There was no basis, according to the Israeli press accounts, for the Chief of Staff's statement that the Boeing pilot saw and understood the signals made by the Israeli Phantom pilots, disregarded and stubbornly refused to follow them. The pilot's words of confusion, as recorded, directly contradicted such a version.

The first signal to land was given by the Israeli Phantom jets two minutes after the Libyan plane was identified. The first warning shots came a minute and a half later. In this briefest interim, Hod came to the conclusion that "there is no doubt that the Boeing crew understood what we were asking from them and that the crew saw the airport and refused to land there." But again according to irrefutable evidence, the Libyan crew did not see any airport. The first warning shots were fired at a time when the plane was moving away from the airport in a westerly direction toward the Suez Canal and Egypt. And Hod talked to his Chief of Staff after the plane had turned away from the Bir Gafgafa Airport, where the Israelis wished it to land, and perhaps even before the first warning shots were fired.

It was established that the Chief of Staff had acted only after it was clear that the Boeing had not—and could not—cause any harm in its mistaken course into Sinai. Fears that the plane had aggressive intentions were groundless. Aggressive intentions are carried out while moving toward a target and certainly not while going away, back to one's home base. Yet the *Times* continued to allude to this repudiated contention that the destructive design of the Libyan plane was a genuine possibility. Because of the impossible weather conditions, Israeli suspicion that the enemy might be taking air photos was likewise totally unjustified.

While a *Daily News* editorial called the incident "a wantonly brutal downing, which shocked and horrified Israel's warmest friends,"[38] in the four days following the wanton attack on the Libyan plane, not a single columnist in any of the New York papers carried a single reference to the incident. Moralists such as Peter Hamill, who spouted every time someone was killed in Vietnam or Israel, were glued to their chairs in total silence. Where Tom Wicker had written about the seeds of terrorism on the previous September 7, nothing now came from his fertile pen on Israeli brigandage.

This U.S. reaction was in marked contrast to the hysteria that raged for ten days after the Israeli athletes had been killed—the endless, overwhelming, nationwide media reportage detailing the mourning, tributes to the dead, and vituperative censure of the Arabs.[39]

The media's gross romanticization of the Munich tragedy was exposed in a column by Shirley Povich in the *Washington Post:* "It is time to deflate that guff about the great brotherhood the Olympics promote. They are torn by constant bickering among team officials of all the nations, and political alignments influence the judging in events like boxing, diving and gymnastics." In contrast to the sensationalism in U.S. newspapers that ran photos showing mourning athlete Jesse Owens, handkerchief in hand, and grieving Israeli teammates of the deceased,[40] the Washington writer noted:

Olympic Village was a shame to behold on Tuesday afternoon, after the first shock at the news that two Israelis were dead and nine held hostage by Arab raiders. A few hours after the initial excitement subsided, you couldn't find an empty ping pong table in the village, rock music was blaring as usual, and it was just another day in Olympic Village. There was other evidence of boredom all around, even with their Israeli comrades having all that trouble in Building 33.[41]

The funeral services both in Israel and in the U.S. for the one athlete who had been born American, but at the time of his death held Israeli citizenship, received the widest coverage. An Associated Press story out of Cleveland, Ohio, indicated that Governor John J. Gilligan, at that time a presidential hopeful, had ordered state flags to be lowered to half-mast in memory of this weight lifter who was one of the nine Israeli hostages "killed by Arab commandos" (two athletes died in the original attack at Olympic Village). The bereavement of the parents of David Berger overflowed onto every television set in the U.S.[42]

The *Times'* recital of the return of the bodies of the Arab victims of the Libyan plane incident to Cairo noted that six bodies, which were neither Egyptian nor Libyan, had been sent to the governments concerned: five to France and one to the U.S. This, three days after the incident, was the first reference whatsoever to the fact that an American had been among the victims. Only on the last six lines on page 8 of the *New York Times*[43] did the name of the American appear—Wladyslaw Boysoglebski, sixty-two years old, of Chicago, an American who had taken out citizenship after immigrating from Poland. No flags were ordered to be set at half-mast by Illinois Governor Richard B. Ogilvie when the body of this American was returned, in contrast to the honor accorded in Ohio to a half-American, half-Israeli serving on the Olympic team of a foreign country. A call to the cable desk of UPI to find out whether they knew anything about the disposition of the body that was being shipped via Tel Aviv embassy to the States yielded a total blank.

While the responsibility or necessity for the German attack killing the Munich hostages was never established, at no point did the media ever call attention to this doubt. However, in the reportage of the Libyan plane incident, every sort of innuendo, excuse, or explanation was indulged in, either by the media on its own or by publicizing the views of the Israeli pilots, the Israeli army, and the Israeli government. Where the Munich story had received banner headlines right across the front page and was continued with large five-column *Times* headlines on the second day, the 110 innocent victims of trigger-happy Israeli pilots received, on the first day, three columns, and the third line of the heading gave the Israeli point of view, and that was that.

More than four years later, the Zionists were continuing to exploit the 1972 Olympics affair. ABC national television provided unpaid prime time (December 1976) at a cost of close to $2 million for a specially produced Sunday evening television film, *Twenty-One Hours at Munich*, under the meticulous direction of coproducers Edward Feldman and Robert Greenwald (illustrating once more the Zionist connection). The greatest liberties were taken with the facts to portray the Palestinians as the blackest villains, even attributing sorrowful last words to one Israeli athlete, who had died all alone. The ABC press releases, replete with pejorative adjectives, further spawned anti-Arab hatred.

Everywhere this double standard prevailed[44] with but a few dissenting voices. Robert Pierpoint, CBS White House correspondent, was one of a handful to point out that the U.S. had lost its sense of fair play. He noted that in February 1973, when the Israelis carried out a commando raid deep in the heart of Lebanon, striking at Palestinian refugee camps 130 miles from their own territory with planes and tanks and wiping out thirty-seven lives in the process, "there was next to no outcry in this country." It was on this occasion that an entire Lebanese family of six was crushed to death as they sat in their car, by an Israeli tank. Many other innocents were killed in this same raid, along with a few Palestinian guerrillas, allegedly part of the Black September movement.

Pierpoint on this CBS telecast declared that the shooting down of the Libyan airliner had drawn some official regrets, but not expressed publicly nor at the level of the White House. He continued:

Nor did any U.S. official ever indicate that the U.S. might think twice before it dispatched more American-built Phantom jets to Israel of the type that had shot down the Libyan airliner. Indeed, the very next week, President Nixon let it be known after his talk in the Oval Office with Israeli Prime Minister Golda Meir that more such Phantoms would soon be on their way. Contrast these events with what happened after the Arab Black September's massacre of Israeli athletes at Munich. The U.S., from President Nixon on down, expressed outrage, and the President ordered steps taken to see that no such terrorism could strike at Israelis in this country . . .

Senator Hugh Scott, after meeting with President Nixon to discuss domestic problems, standing at a White House podium, in response to a question on what should be done to the Arabs who had participated in the murders in

Khartoum, responded, "I hope they shoot them all, and the sooner the better." No mention was made of a trial, or the possibility that if a fair trial were held, it might turn out that not all the terrorists were guilty of the murders.

For so long Americans have become used to thinking of the Israelis as the good guys and the Arabs as the bad guys that many react emotionally along the lines of previous prejudices. The fact is that both sides have committed unforgivable acts of terror, both sides have killed innocents, both sides have legitimate grievances and illegitimate methods of expressing them. Perhaps the Arabs' action was more irrational—sheer terror. At least it was not backed by a relatively rational government which justifies its actions as necessary. The Israelis have and utilize a formidable political propaganda force in this country in the form of six million Jews. The Arabs have only slightly less than a million descendants in America just beginning to organize a nationwide counterforce. Perhaps this will help bring balance. *In the meantime, the rest of us might apply more steady balance and fair play to the difficult problems of the Middle East.* [Italics added.]

The broadcast was no sooner on the airwaves and reprinted in the *Christian Science Monitor*[45] than the usual hue and cry was raised. Pierpoint was, of course, charged with anti-Semitism, and his head was demanded. Telegrams and letters poured into the network. The CBS President and Vice President in charge of news were importuned to exercise some control over Pierpoint's judgment. The CBS correspondent had this to say about the smears and fears that were raised: "As you can imagine, some of the criticism was highly emotional if not downright hysterical. I was not surprised at this since the subject is a highly emotional one. I was mildly surprised at the manner in which the critics are so well organized that within hours people who had not heard the broadcast were protesting by phone or writing letters. In any case, the opposition to this kind of broadcast was and is formidable."[46]

The treatment of the Ma'alot affair soon thereafter clearly indicated that the Pierpoint call for press fair play had fallen on deaf ears. On May 15, 1974, three fedayeen from the Popular Democratic Front for the Liberation of Palestine (PDFLP) stole across the Lebanese-Israel border (an Israeli nurse testified that one had been living nearby in Safad for a long time) and at six in the morning seized a Ma'alot school in which ninety teenage members of the semimilitary Nahal[47] had been spending the night after some training.

Fifteen youngsters escaped through an open door at the time of the takeover, and two were allowed to leave because they were ill. The guerrillas sent two more youths out with a list of twenty-six prisoners held in Israeli jails whose release they demanded in exchange for the hostages. They asked that the French and Rumanian Ambassadors serve as mediators.

The prisoners—twenty-three Palestinians, two Israelis, and one Japanese—were to be flown to Damascus, according to the guerrilla demand. As soon as the arrival of the released prisoners had been confirmed in the Syrian capital, the mediating Ambassadors would receive through Paris and Bucharest a code word with which to identify themselves before starting negotiations for the release of the hostages. But if no code word was received by 6:00 P.M., the guerrillas "would not be responsible for the consequences," they warned.

While negotiations were being carried on between the Palestinians, Israelis, Cairo (from where the plane to carry out the Palestinian prisoners was to come), and the Ambassadors, Israeli military forces attacked the school half an hour before the guerrilla deadline. In the ensuing battle the fedayeen were wiped out, but sixteen children were killed, victims of either exploding Palestinian grenades or Israeli bullets. And the Zionist-media alliance both in the U.S. and Britain (where I happened to be at the moment) went absolutely wild, even as the facts surrounding the tragedy's final moments became increasingly beclouded. While nothing could ever condone the brutal killing of innocent children, much evidence was adduced that the Israeli government had far from done everything in its power to avoid the tragic loss of life and that the military had overreacted. And it was the French Ambassador to Israel who cast the principal doubts on the oversimplified story disseminated by the Western press.

Ambassador Jean Herly was waiting at the French Consulate in Haifa throughout the afternoon for the Israeli authorities to call him to Ma'alot. At 2:00 he had been informed by the Israelis that he was not to receive the code word permitting him to negotiate with the fedayeen until the prisoners held by Israel had been freed and had reached Damascus. At 3:22, according to Israeli Foreign Ministry documents, the Ambassador had requested permission to proceed to Ma'alot. The answer was delayed. Realizing at 4:45 that it was now impossible to organize the release of the Palestinian prisoners and get them to Damascus in time for the 6:00 deadline, the Ambassador had himself flown by helicopter to Ma'alot to plead with the Palestinians to extend their ultimatum.

Upon his arrival, a high-ranking Israeli officer asked the French Ambassador if he had the code word. He replied in the negative, and then, as he told Agence France Presse, asked to meet the Minister of Defense or the Chief of Staff, "thinking that I could perhaps, even without the code word and through my diplomatic pass, get into contact with the fedayeen and try at least to postpone the expiration of the ultimatum." But he was informed it was "too dangerous." A few minutes later, at 5:30, in the words of the Ambassador to the press, he heard shots and explosions. "I was told that it was all over and asked to return to Tel Aviv." Acting on the direct orders of the Chief of Staff, forty minutes before the ultimatum's expiration at 5:20 P.M., the Israeli military forces stormed the building.

Herly, a diplomat to the end, stated that he was certain that the authorities "had not willfully sought to prevent him from speaking to the terrorists, but I still ask myself and wonder: What could have been done that wasn't done between five o'clock and six o'clock?" He had been denied permission to talk to the Palestinians on the grounds that he had not received the code word from Palestinian headquarters in Damascus. But as the Ambassador later told the *Jerusalem Post,* there must have been a "grave misunderstanding" because he was, in fact, not supposed to receive the code word until the released prisoners had arrived safely in Damascus. Israeli Information Minister Shimon Peres insisted that Herly never could have talked to the Palestinians without having the code word in his possession.

According to *Ha'aretz* of May 17, the government had decided early in the morning to reject the clearly understood Palestinian conditions. But to buy time, Moshe Dayan and General Mordechai Gur informed the fedayeen that they agreed to their terms, meanwhile formulating plans for the military rescue of the hostages. Fully aware of the overwhelming sympathy of the Western press, both the Prime Minister and the Minister of Defense saw an opportunity to take a chance, even at the expense of children's lives, of making important favorable international propaganda at a time when Israel's public relations standing in the world had gravely plummeted. The die was cast, and French mediation efforts were not permitted to upset the carefully calculated Israeli planning.

As at Munich, the Israelis justified the decision to storm the school on the conviction that the Palestinians intended, in any event, to kill their young hostages when their demands were rejected and the ultimatum ran out. Again, guerrilla action did not sustain this thesis. As PDFLP spokesman Yasser Abed Rubbuh later declared, the three terrorists had orders to prolong the original deadline by two hours in the event no agreement was reached. The Palestinians maintained that at no time did they plan to harm the hostages if their demands were met. Their plan had been to bargain the first half of the hostages for the release of the prisoners on their list, and then the second half for the safe passage of the three Palestinians out of Israel.

It was the Palestinian contention that the political decision to storm the school "whatever the consequences" had been made long before the 1600 GMT deadline was reached. According to the PDFLP version, "the Rumanian and French Ambassadors were told by the Israelis they do not have any aircraft available to take the prisoners to Damascus." But the Rumanian government had been notified at 1530 GMT, half an hour before the deadline and the exact time the Israelis stormed the school, that the prisoners had actually taken off for Cyprus.

The Popular Front openly admitted responsibility for Ma'alot, but at the same time, in a statement appearing in the London *Times*,[48] PDFLP leader Nayef Hawatmeh challenged Israel to submit to a public postmortem to determine who, in fact, had been responsible for the bloodshed. This the Israeli government ignored, and the media declined to follow up the matter.

Had there been a careful investigation, it would have been revealed that the border settlement of Ma'alot had been carefully chosen by Hawatmeh for this raid on the twenty-sixth anniversary of the establishment of the Israeli state. This village, once the Arab village of Tarchiha, as part of western Galilee, was to have been included under the 1948 U.N. partition plan in the Arab state, but was attacked and occupied before May 15, then annexed by the Israeli state. The Arab villagers fled during the fighting, and after the 1949 armistice their return was barred. The village was razed to the ground, and on its ruins the Israeli village of Ma'alot had been built.

The U.S. media was totally uninterested in any exposition of Palestinian thinking. By the sheerest of coincidences, in the late evening of May 14 as the attack on Ma'alot was taking place, I was in Beirut taping a conversation with Palestinian Abu Nidal (a pseudonym), leader of a group that had split off from the PDFLP and is Iraq-oriented. This twenty-five-year-old Palestinian expressed himself frankly and violently:

We believe that Palestine is ours, and the only way to get back what is ours is to fight. . . . I am not Mr. Sadat. I am a Palestinian, and I am not concerned with world opinion, including American, which has done nothing for our very fair cause through more than twenty-six years. The world can respect you only when you are strong enough to stand in the face of the world and fight for your cause. . . . We showed we were serious in our attack on Qiryat Shemona, and we will strike again.

His reference was to the Palestinian attack six weeks earlier on an Israeli border village in which eighteen Israelis had been killed and sixteen injured, but three of his companions had lost their lives, the oldest of whom was just twenty years old.

The following day when I reached London, this pertinent tape was used on BBC television and radio. But on arrival in New York, forty-eight hours after Ma'alot, there was the accustomed total blackout from television-radio news and talk shows. No one dared put into question the Israeli-Zionist propaganda that the sole Palestinian aim was to murder the innocent and spread terror without cause.

At Ma'alot little children had been involved, and hysteria ruled the American Jewish community. Brooklyn District Attorney Eugene Gold and companions chained themselves to a fence in front of the U.N. in protest. New York's Mayor Beame addressed a large emotional rally, urging the U.N. to adopt immediate sanctions against Arab countries to avert further acts of terrorism. *New York Post* columnists Max Lerner and Peter Hamill far outstripped in narrow, vindictive one-sidedness the efforts of other media pundits. Hamill screamed:

And now they were killing children, Israeli children. . . . People were dying in the deserts of the Middle East. Israel, which initially had allied itself with the U.S. on a moral basis, had discovered that it was just another colony, its fate in the hands of Henry Kissinger whose wife kept Arab swag in a wall safe in her bedroom.[49]

In Jerusalem Premier Golda Meir claimed her government had been prepared to submit to the commandos' demands to free the prisoners, but that they had not had enough time to act. In an angry television address she vowed that Israel "will do everything in its power to chop off the hands that intend to harm a child or an adult in any city or village." The Meir caretaker government, which was soon replaced by the Yitzhak Rabin Cabinet, came under increasingly angry attack from many quarters for its handling of the affair, as more and more of the facts began to leak out.

One of the freed Ma'alot students, sixteen-year-old Rachel Lagziel, told reporters that the captives were allowed to listen to their transistors and to hear all the news broadcast in Hebrew. "We were allowed to drink our water and eat our provisions," eighteen-year-old Tamara Ben-Hamu later said. "Don't be afraid" one commando said. "If Israel gives us the prisoners, you will not be harmed." (This, of course, never appeared in the U.S. press—only in Israel.)

Angry Israelis assailed Dayan. "You have made us the stepchildren of Israel," Ma'alot Council Chairman Eli Ben Yaacov screamed at him. "It's because most of us are from Morocco," he added.

Before a day after the incident had passed, the Israelis had struck back against South Lebanon in a retaliatory raid. Air attacks against civilian targets brought death to fifty-two in an impoverished refugee camp and in Lebanese villages. Ain El Helweh and Bowry El Barajneh, refugee camps north and south of Beirut, were the targets of the Israeli air attacks carried out by thirty-six U.S.-supplied Phantoms. On the second successive day the "reprisal" for Ma'alot found the Nabitieh refugee camp in South Lebanon literally razed to the ground.

The following is from a dispatch filed by Paul Martin, which appeared in the London *Times* on May 18:

Rescue workers had just dug up the bodies of the young woman and her four small children from the rooms of their tiny house when I arrived in this Palestinian refugee camp today. The bodies were mutilated almost beyond recognition. Nobody knew the woman's name, but one refugee said he thought her husband had been killed during last night's Israeli bombing raids as well.

The house was one of about 60, lining the camp's main street, which were flattened by three separate air strikes in two and a half hours. Half the camp, which holds 5,000 people, had been completely destroyed by direct hits on houses in no way connected with the Palestinian guerrillas. I counted more than 40 craters from 1,000-lb. bombs peppering an area of less than 400 square yards.

Eight children, between the ages of 8 and 12 were killed when bombs showered down on the camp's school. Their bodies were taken to Sidon Hospital because their parents could not be found in the confusion. More bodies are expected to be recovered from the debris of twisted and crumbled buildings. The death toll so far in Nabatieh alone is 25 civilians killed and nearly 60 wounded.

On the outskirts of the camp there was an endless string of pathetic processions to the sedate little cemetery. There were no demonstrations of overt grief or anger—just looks of shock and fear. Men, women and children, who died in Israel's reprisal, were taken at short intervals to hastily prepared graves. Their bodies were borne on open stretcher-like coffins, draped with a flower arrangement resembling the Palestinian flag.

Nabatieh was the worst hit in Israel's wave of air strikes launched yesterday afternoon on Palestinian refugee camps and villages at 4 P.M. as the streets were filled with people. The bombing and strafing lasted 10 minutes. Then, as rescue workers began to drag the dead and wounded from the debris, they struck again at 5 P.M.; the final and most devastating strike came at 6:45 P.M.

As I arrived in Nabatieh today, the last refugees were fleeing with mattresses and the bare essentials of survival: "This is the third time in the past three years that we have been driven out of here by Israeli air raids," an old villager said, "Each time we have had to build up all over again, but we will be back, perhaps in a week, perhaps in a month; but, God willing, we will be back."

The presence of armed guerrillas in Palestinian refugee camps is no new phenomenon. However, at Nabatieh there clearly was no evidence in the camp itself of any guerrilla military bases. What is obvious from this latest Israeli blow against Lebanon is that civilians suffered the most. Little or no damage was done to the guerrillas and, if anything, they stand to gain much politically from what has happened.

Such events tend to create militants. At one point a group of refugees who had lost a relative gathered around me when I was introduced as a British correspondent, a man of about 40 snapped angrily: "Curse you and your Balfour. Curse America. Curse you all."

A U.N. report on Nabatieh listed "60 percent destroyed, 20 percent badly damaged, 20 percent partly destroyed. Not one house had a roof left," the international organization noted. Yet such acts of terror against civilian populations were relegated to inconspicuous coverage, and the pretext for the merciless retaliation, that fedayeen were based in this area, was accepted as an extenuating circumstance for the killings in the retaliatory onslaughts on refugee camps.

As planes brought death to 200 innocents in these latest May raids in South Lebanon, which had begun in 1968 and accelerated to almost daily attacks, the same politicians, ministers, rabbis, priests, and writers who had condemned the "cowardly methods" employed in the killings at Munich and Ma'alot found themselves acquiescing in the more sophisticated Israeli means of terror used in Lebanon. Exploding dolls dropped from planes "to entice" children to their deaths brought no outraged outcries. Lebanese villages such as Rashaya Fuqhar, once a prosperous town of 2,000 Christian Arabs and a handful of Palestinian refugee camps in the Arkoub region of Lebanon, were subjected to attacks by airplane, artillery, tanks, and gunboats. Israeli commandos invaded villages and camps alike, "forceably checking identifications, blowing up houses, killing villagers, and taking prisoners."[50] Still, certain American newspapers called this tragedy—the forerunner to the Lebanese civil war—a lesson that should serve as "an ultimatum to the Lebanese government to rid themselves of the Palestinians within their midst."

It was very obvious that the "lords of the press" were not interested in striking an equal balance by reporting these as "atrocities" as they had so labeled Ma'alot. In the face of the Israeli aerial onslaught on innocent Lebanese and Palestinian refugees, all that the *New York*

Times would do was to administer another mild slap to the Israel wrist and ask for "a determined show of restraint on both sides":

The fully justified anger and determination of Israel to resist terrorist assaults that have caused 49 deaths, mostly among children in ten weeks, nevertheless affords no sound basis for resort to counterterror from the air, especially when such indiscriminate tactics, also involving the death of many innocents, have repeatedly proved ineffective. In the present context, the Israeli response is especially *unfortunate* since it directly serves the Palestinian extremists' objectives.[51] [Italics added.]

The principal concern of the *Times* was that the Israeli savagery was counterproductive.

Unmatched continued Israeli and U.S. Zionist-induced media hysteria over the thirty-eight victims of the March 11, 1978, Palestinian raid served as a cover for Begin's retaliatory blitzkreig into southern Lebanon. First reports two days later in the *New York Post* mentioned 250 deaths and 100,000 refugees.[52] In Saturday's *New York Times,* Marvine Howe quoted "reports" of 100,000 refugees. In fact, there were some 260,000 refugees and approximately 2000 deaths. For noting that "apparently a dead woman in Lebanon is not worth as much as a dead woman in Israel," Jimmy Breslin of the *New York Daily News* was bitterly assailed, and the next week an entire Sunday letters column was devoted to ten angry writers tearing him to pieces.

Two *Times* editorials flayed "the senseless terror against Israel" and averred that, "beyond messages of condolence," the world "owes Israelis sympathy and partnership in measures to punish terrorism on every front,"[53] and as late as May 7 correspondent William Farrell was writing about the "terrorist rampage in the March carnage." James Wechsler's front and editorial pages in the *Post* alternately spared no language in attacking the Palestinian raiders, bemoaned the "lost peace," and then gloried with across-the-page headlines: "Guerillas Routed In All-Out Retaliation."[54] As the air bombardment of fleeing innocent Lebanese and Palestinian civilians continued, the *Times* referred to the "justified Lebanese retaliation."[55]

The *Washington Post* carried an AP picture of a machine-gunned car and reported the ambushing at Aadloun by Israeli commandos of two taxi-loads of Tibnine villagers. According to reporter Jonathan Randal, "one taxi was riddled with machine-gun bullets, the other hit by the fin of a rocket with Hebrew lettering on it. As many as 20 villagers—most of them women and children—were killed."[56] Marvine Howe of the *Times* simply reported that fifteen civilians had been killed and two wounded in circumstances that were "unclear,"[57] while the

Daily News briefly referred to an AP report of civilian deaths. The *Time* correspondent described the "ghastly" sight of the taxis, noting that fourteen in all had been slaughtered. Correspondent Dean Brelis referred to the "indiscriminate" bombing of the port city of Tyre, where, with the exception of one Palestinian anti-aircraft gun, "no military target had been hit . . . What had been hit, and hard, was the civilian dwellings. Was this deliberate counter-terrorism on the part of the Israelis? It certainly looked that way."[58] Nothing of this was even hinted at in the *Times* or other U.S. dailies. And the State Department, which had quickly condemned what it called "a brutal act of terrorism against Israeli civilians," refused to issue any censure of Israel for its invasion of Lebanon.

During an Israeli air bombardment of Lebanon the previous November in which more than 100 civilians were killed, a man in his sixties, as told by an American newsman, "lost everyone he had in the world at Hazziyeh—his wife, six children, his brother, his brother's wife, his brother's four children. Numbed by grief, he walked like a robot around a Palestinian Red Crescent hospital near Tyre. He knelt among the bodies of his family, crouched over the dirty mutilated face of his smallest son, kissed him and said, 'Darling, go. It doesn't matter, God is great.' "[59]

This man, if possible, was perhaps more fortunate than other defenseless parents in unarmed Lebanese villages and Palestinian refugee camps upon whom, as Thomas Kiernan describes in the prologue of *The Arabs*, American-made Phantoms showered phosphorous bombs made of wax and acid—wax which stuck to the skin while the acid ate it away:

A human figure materialized out of the gloom, an eerie, unintelligible chant issuing from what was once its lips. Stumbling, weaving, then falling to its knees and crawling, it crept towards us. It was a child—boy or girl I couldn't tell—and its charred skin was literally melting, leaving a trail of viscous fluid in its wake. Its face had no recognizable features. The top of its skull shone through the last layer of scorched membrane on its head. Not more than ten yards from us it fell on its side, its kneecaps exposing like the yolks of poached eggs. It twitched once or twice in the dust, gave a final wheeze, then went still in the puddle of molten flesh that formed around it in the dust. . . . Later it was run over by a car. No one would ever know what had happened to that child.[60]

While the unparalleled destruction in Lebanon has since become a recognized fact, only the primary cause remaining in contention, the total devastation of Quneitra, the one-time capital of Syria's Golan

Heights, remains one of the world's best-kept secrets.

Under the terms of the Syrian-Israeli disengagement accord, the return of Quneitra to the Syrians was the principal *quid pro quo* for President Hafez al-Assad's reluctant acceptance of the fruits of Henry Kissinger's thirty-day shuttling. The southern quarter of the town, the hills surrounding it on three sides, and the rich cultivated land—east, west, and south—still remained in Israeli hands, allegedly to protect Israeli settlements in the Hulah valley. Three Israeli settlements built since 1967, in defiance of U.N. resolutions, lay within four miles of the town. Without these Israeli settlers in the Golan, Kissinger might have been able to make a more satisfactory arrangement. But as one settler in Merom Golan boasted, "By our very presence we are proving once again the importance of settlement to Israel. Where we settle, there we shall remain."[61]

The Syrian returnees in June 1967 were greeted by a Hebrew inscription on a demolished wall: "You wanted Quneitra. You will have it in ruins." This threat was carried out.

Kurt Waldheim, Secretary-General of the U.N., after visiting the former capital of the Golan Heights, remarked: "I was very shocked by what I saw at Quneitra." For the Soviet Ambassador to Syria, Quneitra revived memories of Stalingrad at the end of the last war. And to Father George Muhassal, when he and his flock were finally permitted to reenter the city, it was Hiroshima all over again.

In a statement released through the Near East Ecumenical Bureau in Beirut, this pastor of the Greek Orthodox Church in Quneitra charged the Israelis with bulldozing 80 percent of the city and with desecrating-looting Christian churches and the cemetery just prior to their withdrawal on June 26: "The concrete tombs were opened by machine-gun fire and, in some cases, hand grenades. The bodies were brought outside and systematically looted. Hands were broken off to get bracelets, teeth with gold were taken, and parts of the bodies were not put back in the proper coffins."

Such accusations coming from a priest of a church in the city might be dismissed as exaggerations. But Irene Beeson, writing in the *Guardian,* was most explicit in her description of the systematic Israeli destruction before leaving. These are the words, as recounted by Beeson, of one of the ten inhabitants who alone had remained under the Israeli occupation in 1967:

They had about eleven bulldozers stationed in the town, but they had to bring in reinforcements to cope with the huge task. The smaller houses collapsed under a single thrust. For the larger two, three and four-story villas and buildings, they had to build earth ramps so that the bulldozers could reach the upper floors.

They worked from dawn to dusk for several days with grim determination and great expertise. It took them practically a whole day to finish off the three-story house down the street. Only the houses of the ten Arab inhabitants who had not fled were intact. Left standing, also, was the gutted, bullet-ridden 300-bed hospital which the Israelis used for target practice. One of the town's churches was destroyed. Others left standing and only slightly damaged structurally, but had been stripped of everything—marble facings on the walls, furnishings, precious 4th-century icons, statues, lamps.

The shell of the Officers' Club is another landmark. What remains of this wall is riddled with bullet holes, decorated with sexy murals, insulting and pornographic graffiti. . . . Generators were removed and carted away by the Israelis, who made off with all the town's pumps for drinking and irrigation water. Into the water reserves and wells the Israelis had poured diesel oil, petrol and garbage, making good the inscription they had left behind.[62]

You can always read what others have to say, but that is not the same as viewing for yourself, as I did a year later, the utter emptiness and desolation of Quneitra, a city that had been bulldozed in its entirety. The tracks of the machines were still evident everywhere. Smaller houses had collapsed under a single thrust, while the larger villas and buildings had obviously been bulldozed in the manner described by Irene Beeson.

Such dark devastation visited by man upon man has had few equals. The only signs of life were the stray, hungry-looking cat streaking across the road and a few wild red poppies that had sprung up beside the burnt-out framework of what once had been Quneitra's proud hospital. To me came a flashback to childhood:

> In Flanders Field the poppies grow
> Between the crosses row on row
> That mark their place.

My visit to Quneitra was on a cold May afternoon, but the temperature in no way could match the frigidity of the scene—dramatized by nearby snow-capped Mount Herman, where so many fierce aerial battles between the Syrians and the Israelis had occurred. The approaches to Quneitra were guarded by the Austrian U.N. peacekeeping force.

This tragedy can best be seen through neutral eyes. However, despite continued widespread coverage of violence and terrorism in the U.S. media, there were no reports on Quneitra. In July 1974 an Australian delegation comprised of two members of Parliament, two

Labor leaders, two journalists, and the Federal Secretary of the Young Labor Association visited the Golan Heights. Leader of the delegation George Petersen wrote an article, "The Town That Used To Be," for the Australian publication, *Nation Review:*

The most striking feature of the Quneitra buildings is that, in most cases, there are no walls and the roofs are resting on the ground. How this was done is only too apparent by the caterpillar tracks on the ground near the destroyed buildings.[63]

After describing the conditions he found in the city, Petersen concluded:

Quneitra was destroyed for the same reasons that most of the original inhabitants were expelled from Palestine—because the Zionists intend to take over the land, expel the original inhabitants and use it for their own purposes. . . . Looking across the cease-fire lines to Ain Zivan kibbutz in Israel, I know whom I would hate the most if I were a native of Quneitra. Not the soldiers, not even the bulldozer operators, but the men, women and children living on that kibbutz for the benefit of whom and of others like them the destruction of Quneitra was instituted at an enormous cost to the native inhabitants. And I know that I would want to cross the cease-fire line and kill those usurpers.

In the same publication, many letters from Zionists who knew nothing whatsoever about Quneitra emotionally reacted to the Petersen article. In a reply to one of the letters signed by five persons, Petersen struck back:

When I was at Quneitra on July 5, the bulldozer tracks were clearly visible. . . . I am puzzled why the apologists for the Israeli government deny that Quneitra was destroyed by bulldozers and explosives! The Israeli practice of bulldozing Arab villages to the ground is well substantiated in past reports by such impartial parties as the International Committee of the Red Cross and the Israeli League for Human and Civil Rights. . . . Why should the Zionists have made an exception of Quneitra? I would particularly like your five correspondents to explain how they justify the forcible eviction to Syria of over 100,000 native inhabitants of the Golan Heights area. Does Israel's right to exist justify turning the civilian residents into homeless refugees? Or are your correspondents' concepts of humanity confined only to people who describe themselves as "Jews"?

Zionists contend that Quneitra had been destroyed during the 1967 and 1973 wars rather than methodically bulldozed at the time of the Israeli withdrawal. But a BBC documentary film showed Commentator Peter Snow some three or four days before the Israeli evacuation in a very alive city with many houses all intact—further proof that the city had been calculatingly destroyed, house by house, church by church.

Another eyewitness from the Australian delegation was Stewart West, President of the South Post Branch of the Waterside Workers Federation of Australia. Under the title "The Destruction of Quneitra," he wrote as follows:

In most war-damaged cities, you see heaps of rubble, bomb and shell craters, burned-out buildings, with walls still standing and sometimes whole streets left undamaged. But not in Quneitra. The city was completely destroyed in a couple of days immediately prior to the Israeli withdrawal on June 25, 1974. Most of the houses were demolished with explosives or pushed down with bulldozers. . . . The destruction of Quneitra must be in the same category *as the destruction of ancient Carthage, as the destruction of European cities by the Huns, and the Mongols, and with Hiroshima and the Nazi destructions during World War II.*[64] [Italics added.]

Australian trade union newspaper *Scope,* in a special twenty-eight page supplement of August 1, 1974, devoted two of its pages to the Quneitra atrocities with a lead that read: "Syrian city of Quneitra used to be half-way between the Israeli border and Damascus. In June of this year, Israeli bulldozers destroyed the last of its houses, ripped down the last of its trees and orchards and pulled back up the hills of the Golan Heights." The main piece, presumably written by *Scope*'s Editor, George Coote, added in part:

June 26 was days after the disengagement between Israeli and Syrian troops, and the last Arab house in Quneitra was destroyed minutes before UN peace-keeping forces moved in. . . . Quneitra was smashed with dynamite and bull-dozers which made sure nobody would live there again. . . . This was a puzzle for the Australian delegation visiting the city. Did the Quneitra story hit the Australian media?

The answer to this question and to the query posed by British journalist Kathleen Evan's contribution to the same special issue, "Had You Really Heard About Israel's Genocide?" was identical. Next to nothing had appeared in Australia and Britain—and nothing in the U.S.—on the story of a gutted city where nearly 45,000 people once had happily lived.

Zionist terror also reached the sidewalks of New York. One Sunday afternoon in January 1972, the relative stillness of Seventh Avenue was broken by the angry bellow of voices crying out in unison "Free Soviet Jews," alternating with "Six Million—Not One More." Carnegie Hall, where the Osipov Balalaika Orchestra was performing with stars of the Bolshoi Ballet and the Bolshoi Opera Company, was under siege. Two busloads of Mayor John Lindsay's police were keeping an angry threatening mob from ticket holders who had to pass the picket lines to enter the famed music hall.

The ugly, tastelessly clad pickets who were alternately cursing, hissing, and spitting at other Americans, many of whom were themselves Jews, were members of Rabbi Meir Kahane's Jewish Defense League. Most of them were wearing buttons bearing their organizational emblem, "Never Again," while some had buttons reading "Free Syrian Jews." One woman in a fur coat had a cloth emblem with the flags of Israel and the U.S. joined together—symbolizing the duality of these rabid ultramilitants. And on that Sunday miscreants of the same ilk were picketing the Syrian Mission in another section of Manhattan. That evening the Egyptian Tourist Office at Rockefeller Center was bombed. And two days later a fire bombing of "unknown origin" erupted in the offices of impresario Sol Hurok and Columbia Artists, killing his secretary and injuring many. An anonymous caller to the Associated Press said: "Cultural bridges of friendship will not be built over the bodies of Soviet Jews. Never again." On this occasion the leaders of a few rival Israelist organizations in muffled voices related their disapproval to the press. But no action was taken, and history was being allowed to repeat itself.

The case of Meir Kahane would require a long examination. All that may be noted here is the way he has benefited from the imposition of the double standard. The five-year suspended sentence given him in 1971 after his admitted manufacture of bombs, harassment of Soviet diplomats, and acts of violence against American and Arab citizens was scarcely believable. Only in a Brooklyn District Court presided over by Judge Jack Weinstein and in an America under Zionist domination could this have happened.

In a news conference following the sentencing, the brazen Rabbi forthrightly disavowed the court's injunction against further breaches of the peace by stating that he would use violence if he determined it to be "necessary." He announced that he would divide his time between New York and Jerusalem, where he was opening an international center, and would "maintain dual citizenship as permitted under Israeli law."

The militant Rabbi vacated the leadership of the group he founded after his defeat in the December 1973 Israeli parliamentary elections. The Israeli government deported him after he and other Israeli militants were arrested following a Gush Emunim demonstration during the summer of 1976 in an off-limits Hebron hospital on the West Bank. Kahane cried out to his followers living in the nearby Jewish settlement of Kiryat Arba, which looks down on the Arab city from a promontory: "This is a Jewish city. Abraham lived here, and so will we. This is the building where Jews were murdered by Arabs." The six-columned *New York Times* report on page 2 showed a smiling, charismatic Kahane sitting in an Israeli army truck after his arrest.[65]

Upon release from prison in his country of adoption, Kahane returned to the U.S. to face criminal charges. Convicted, he kept newly enthralled followers in line through his arrogant behavior from his "country club prison," as he used his demand for kosher food and religious observance to move freely in and out of confinement.

His 1975 book, *The Story of the Jewish Defense League,*[66] was reviewed in the Sunday *Times* book section by Herbert Gold[67] (on the same page as Elie Wiesel was reviewing *The Blood of Israel: The Massacre of the Israeli Athletes*), and the reputedly sensitive novelist referred to Kahane as a "lively rabbi with a baroque mind" whose "new book, ill-written, shrill and without nuance, nevertheless gets at a truth about contemporary Jewish experience which is generally missed by both the un-Jewish popular mind and the established Jewish organizations." The reviewer found Kahane at times "almost loveable," supporting the publisher's jacket blurb "that militance is and will be necessary to assure the future physical and spiritual existence of the Jewish people."

Little wonder that Kahane and his breed in the JDL, despite an occasional rap on the knuckles, have been permitted to break the laws, shoot at the innocent, deface property, and attack with impunity. When Dr. Mohamed Mehdi of the Action Committee was attacked by JDL members with a lead pipe in May 1974 and sent to the hospital with a broken back,[68] it took nearly a year for the police to make an arrest although a perpetrator appeared on television to boast of the deed. This same arrogant defiance of the law was manifested in an ugly attack on me when I lectured February 5, 1975 at William Patterson College at Wayne, New Jersey, in a rebuttal to an address made there by former Israeli Foreign Minister Abba Eban.[69] Neither of these incidents received any media attention. Shortly thereafter, Mehdi's offices on East 44th Street in Manhattan were set afire and almost totally gutted. The *New York Times* relegated this obviously vicious arson to five short paragraphs on page 40, referring only to a "suspicious fire" resulting in "medium damage to office equipment."[70] Yet this same newspaper had often given prominent coverage to the many Mehdi demonstrations and his often zany statements which did not put the

Palestinian position in the best light.

Frustration and desperation breed desperation and frustration. The grim reaction to the devastation suffered by the Palestinians in Jordan in 1970 led to an increase in violence and in the arenas in which force was applied. There emerged more desperate and intransigent guerrillas, groups such as the Black September tied to the internationalist terrorist-revolutionary movement. The Japanese Red Army, the Bader-Meinhof, and other groups cooperated with Palestinians on whose strong moral position they drew to achieve their own ends in Europe. Terrorist acts served as a sad reminder that these Palestinians just would not disappear. As Dr. Elmer Berger, expressed it:

Right or wrong, the exploits of the Palestinians stir an Arab world which knows that if the president of the United States calls them "outlaws," no power has done more to put these people outside the "law" than the United States. For no power is as responsible as the United States for Israel's persistent defiance of the "law" as it has been inscribed in every international agreement ever written on the Palestine problem."[71]

The vilification of Palestinians goes forward without placing their terrorism in the tragic context of the struggle for their right of self-determination. This refusal of Western communications media to relate cause to effect has made the growth of violence inevitable and the ensuing harrowing conflict in Lebanon unavoidable. The die was first cast for that lovely country with Israel's December 1968 reprisal attack on the Beirut Airport.

For this double standard the *New York Times* must bear a heavy responsibility, riveting so much attention, as it has, on the subject of terrorism and refusing (even in a piece "Terrorism or Liberation Struggle? Violence Begets Many New Nations"[72] in which the PLO was discussed but not a word said about Begin's Irgun) to place any blame on Israel for the use of violence from the onset of her successful struggle for "legitimacy," but on every occasion detailing the rise of the PLO through alleged stages of terrorism.[73]

In a June 22, 1974, editorial following the Palestinian attack on the Israeli border villages of Kiryat Shemona, Ma'alot, and Shamir[74] in which fifty-one in all had been killed, the *Times* placed the responsibility for the "stepped-up Palestinian terrorist attacks and Israeli counter-attacks" at the door of "die-hard Palestinian extremists, infuriated by the rapid erosion of the support for their intransigent stand among their own people as well as in Arab capitals . . . these frustrated fanatics have resorted to repeated acts of barbarism in a desperate effort to reverse the accelerating momentum toward accommodation." (Worried indeed they were, as were all Palestinians, that there might be a Middle East accommodation that did not take into consideration their "inalienable rights.")

It is the saddest commentary on the decadence of the world in which we live, that the only way these people could be heard was to launch repeated terrorist attacks. Who knew about the Palestinians before Munich? Who cared one whit about the rights of Palestinians before Ma'alot? The answer is obvious—no one! There have been myriad stories about the poor Jewish refugees from everywhere coming into Israel and building up "the desert," but what humanitarian pieces broke into print about the Palestinians who had been thrown out from their ancient homes, until they struck and struck hard? And did not Winston Churchill in his *History of the English Speaking Peoples* once write, "It is in the primary right of man to fight and to kill for the land they live in."[75]

Parade compounded the *Times'* felonies with its own piece: "Terrorists: How They Operate a World-wide Network" in which it was made to appear that most terrorism stems solely from the Arab Middle East where "a gusher of Arab oil money is available" and "President Qaddafi, an unpredictable Big Daddy, subsidizes terrorism to the tune of $90 million a year."[76] In an October 1976 interview, "Our Very Existence Depends on the U.S.," with *Parade* writer George Michaelson, Prime Minister Rabin complained that the media had blown up the West Bank demonstrations. The article contained the subhead, "An Exaggerated Picture," above reports of Israeli mistreatment of Palestinians, together with a photograph captioned: "Israeli Soldiers Grab West Bank Rioter."[77] But four months later, an expansive, flattering Michaelson outpouring on President Sadat (the cover showed the Egyptian holding a rose) discussed every aspect of war and peace in the Middle East without the word "Palestine" appearing once.[78] And in two other articles dealing with the West Bank problem, this writer further attached the terrorist label to the Palestinians and dismissed the PLO with an unsubstantiated blanket statement that "among older, wealthier and more traditional West Bankers, the PLO's militancy is suspect."[79]

Few in the media cared to distinguish between terror as carried out by private groups or individuals and terror as executed as part of governmental policy. Neither the leaders of the Irgun nor of the Stern Gang had ever been prosecuted by the Israeli government after the establishment of the state. These terrorist groups were absorbed into the Israeli army intact as special units and their leaders elected to the Knesset. And shortly after he took over as chief of state, Begin issued a postage stamp honoring Abraham Stern, whose group had helped him in the assault on Deir Yassin and had masterminded the assassination of U.N. mediator Folke Bernadotte.

As South Dakota Senator James Abourezk noted in a speech on the Senate floor prior to the Ma'alot incident, the village of Kfeir in South Lebanon where his parents had been born "was bombed by Israeli Phantoms, fueled by American bombs and American money." In that attack four civilians had been killed: a six-month-old baby, a five-year-old and an eight-year-old child, and the mother of one of the children. Coming two days prior to Ma'alot, the Israelis could not claim "retaliation." And if ever there were heartrending details that lent themselves to dramatic rendition, here they were. But no NBC spectaculars, no *New York Times* Sunday magazine or *Parade* renditions ever sobbed out this tale.

Senator Fulbright added his comments to those of his South Dakota colleague, noting that these persistent attacks cast doubt on Israeli's sincerity for peace, a capital reason for the U.S. media reticence to publicize Israeli raids on civilian sites in South Lebanon and on defenseless refugee camps. The standard Israeli justification for these raids had invariably been to bomb "terrorists" who had committed previous acts of violence against them. Yet the "terrorists" who committed the Ma'alot atrocity had died at Ma'alot.

Nor had other Israeli "retaliations" scarcely ever been visited upon those Palestinians who had perpetrated the provocative raids. Rather, the Israeli alleged "responses" were aimed at eradicating any chance of a peace settlement according recognition to the Palestinians. A spiraling sequence of violence and terrorism was hardly likely to muster the respect from the world the displaced Palestinians so desperately needed in order to win acceptance of their rights—rights which, if granted, might jeopardize the existing character of the Israeli state.

What added insult to injury for the handful of protesting Senators was that these Israeli raids had been all carried out with armaments supplied by the U.S. through a vote of the very legislative body in which they served. As Senator Abourezk pointedly reminded his colleagues in the Senate (scarcely reported outside of the Congressional Record):

If we in the United States are to furnish Phantom jets, bombs, napalm, fire bombs and money to fuel the planes when they do the bombing and the killing in southern Lebanon, then we must be held accountable for the deaths that will result from what I consider to be official Israeli Government terrorist activities—no less terrorist in nature than an act of three or four individual Arabs who kill civilians in Israel.

Mr. President, this raises one important question: "Where are the doves in the United States today who cried and who agonized over the killing in Vietnam—the killing that was carried out in the very same manner as it is being done now in southern Lebanon? Where are these people today who protested that same kind of killing in Indo-China?"

The answer is obvious, Mr. President; they are deathly silent and in some cases, those very same doves are cheering on the Israelis in their bombing raids that result in the slaughter of so many innocent people.[80]

The significance of the role played by the issue of terror in achieving the Middle East "cover-up" has been surpassed only by the contribution of the syndrome of anti-anti-Semitism to the "cover-over," which shall now be examined.

PART THREE

THE COVER-OVER

Jews have suffered, and Christians have suffered. Mankind has suffered. There is no group with a monopoly on suffering, and no human beings which have experienced hate and hostility more than any other. I must say, however, that it is my impression that Jewish history has been taught with a whine and whimper rather than with a straight-forward acknowledgement that man practices his inhumanity on his fellow human beings . . . Out of this peculiar emphasis on suffering there has developed a new attitude of vicarious suffering—a feeling among numbers of Jews today that because other Jews have suffered and died they, the living, are somehow entitled to special consideration.

RABBI RICHARD E. SINGER
Highland Park (Illinois)
Lakeside Congregation

XI   Exploiting Anti-Semitism

In a democracy every group that affects public policy must be accountable to the entire citizenry. A democracy cannot survive if Iron Curtains are placed around groups, secular or religious, that intervene in public affairs.

—Paul Blanchard

Throughout history, important civilizations have fallen due to reasons ranging from external overexpansion to internal corruption. Should the Western way of life, of which the U.S. is the chief progenitor, fall victim to the ravages of time, future historians might well ascribe the downfall to a scarcely known disease, "labelitis." The "label" has contributed to the paralysis of individual thinking and has led to the concomitant mass conformity which, together with fear, has helped transform America into a nation of sheep years before "1984."

The influence of the label and slogan is infinite. The unadorned cliché parades forth shamelessly and unchallenged, sweeping politicians everywhere in and out of office. Slap the word "liberal," "Fascist," "reactionary," or "Communist," as the case may dictate, on any point of view you do not like, and a sure, quick victory can be yours immediately.

Nothing has accounted more for the success of Zionism and Israelism in the Western world than the skillful attack on the soft underbelly of world opinion—"Mr. Decent Man's" total repugnance toward anti-Semitism. The charge of this bias, instantaneously bringing forth the specter of Nazi Germany, so totally pulverizes the average Christian that by contrast calling him a Communist is a pleasant epithet. It was the Christian revulsion toward anti-Semitism in the wake of Hitlerian genocide, not the superiority of Zionist over Arab rights, that first created and then firmly entrenched the Israeli state, even permit-

403

ting the occupation of conquered territories in the face of the U.N. charter and international morality. So strong has become the general aversion to anti-Semitism that even the full-blooded Semite, the Arab, absurd as it may be, has difficulty defending himself against this charge. The Jerusalem peace talks in January 1978 were disrupted when Prime Minister Begin hurled accusations of "anti-Semitism" at both President Sadat and his Foreign Minister.

The emotional reaction, engendered by Nazi genocide, has given rise to an eleventh commandment, "Thou shalt not be anti-Semitic," and to a corollary twelfth commandment, "Thou must be anti-anti-Semitic." No Christian wishes to run afoul of these supplements to the interdictions handed down by Moses from Mount Sinai. In their zeal to carry out the new commandments, the anti-anti-Semites, guided by Organized Jewry, have rejected the basic distinction between those who are against Zionism-Israelism because they deplore its political precepts and abhor the consequences wrought by its measure, and those who are against Jews because they simply dislike Jews. Christian anti-Zionists and even Jewish anti-Zionists are alike denounced as anti-Semites—discussion, muted doubts, and debate on Middle East policy are crushed.

As Harvard's Dr. David Riesman noted some years ago in the *Jewish Newsletter:* "The Zionists can muster not merely the threat of the Jewish vote and the no-less important Jewish financial and organizational skills, but also the blackmail of attacking anyone who opposes their political aims for Israel, as anti-Semitic."[1] For writing that "it is a sign of mediocrity in people when they herd together," Boris Pasternak, the Russian author of *Dr. Zhivago,* was immediately stigmatized by responsible Zionists, including the then Prime Minister of Israel, David Ben-Gurion, as an anti-Semitic Jew.

That there are bigots and haters, that there was a Nazi Germany whose unparalleled genocide still stings the conscience of Man, and that there still is anti-Semitism, no one but the most irrational would deny. It is one of an infinite number of prejudices that ought to be eradicated. However, the presence of this sociological phenomenon should not give inviolabihty to the ruthless suppression of even the most constructive criticism of the State of Israel and of the multifold Zionist organizations. Anti-Zionism can no more be equated with anti-Semitism, the racist ideology directed against Jews as Jews, than Zionism can be equated with Judaism.

Leading the high-pressure, efficiently organized, continuous campaign to keep anti-Semitism in the limelight through the pursuit of alleged anti-Semites, as well as to suppress all dissent with Washington's "Israel First" policy, is the well-financed offspring of the 130-year-old B'nai B'rith, the Anti-Defamation League, which was founded in 1913. Known as the ADL, this most powerful organ is supported on most occasions by other Jewish organizations. The ADL's earlier emphasis on stamping out genuine prejudice and bigotry gave way long ago to acts of defamation, spying, and publishing spurious literary productions, motivated by support of Israel and effected by eliminating critics of Zionist tactics.

The ward of the oldest and most powerful Jewish organization in the world, the ADL backs up its New York City national headquarters with an annual budget of $7.4 million (1975); twenty-eight regional offices around the country and two in Canada; a professional staff of 300, including specialists in the fields of human relations, communications, education, urban affairs, social sciences, religion, and law. It has representatives in hundreds of communities from coast to coast, and has thousands of secret dossiers on citizens of Canada and of the U.S. According to its own pamphlet: "Each regional office has its own board drawn from leaders and prominent citizens in its areas. Thus, in hundreds of communities throughout the nation, the ADL is able to cooperate as a neighbor to solve important local problems. . . ." Through its multifold private and public reports, allegedly directed against prejudice and bigotry, the ADL exerts enormous prejudice, often bordering on blackmail.

In a *True* magazine interview in February 1971, three top leaders of the ADL, Benjamin Epstein, Seymour Graubard, and Dore Schary, boasted of their use of undercover agents and entrapment through impersonation. "ADL must have a pretty extensive spy network to do all this," the interviewer commented. *Newsweek,* trying to be as inoffensive as possible, called the ADL's methodology "highly selective" and "never a total portrait."[2] A review of ADL "Reports," often issued in book form by outside publishing houses, revealed the organization "straining to fit the products of its own espionage into the procrustean bed of its own personal predilections," to use the words of Unitarian minister and author Dr. John Nicholls Booth, a victim and a critic of that same organization. While sounding plausible, many of the charges leveled by this group were full of half-truths, inaccurate and questionable. The secret and confidential reports of the ADL, widely distributed in liberal circles, often resorted to placing the stock apology "but some of my best friends are Jews" in the mouths of critics to impute an innuendo of anti-Semitism. Odious impressions were often created by twisting a few words, distorting the original text.

Increasingly, the B'nai B'rith and the ADL have directed their activities, allegedly against bigotry, toward assisting Israel. When Israel's Ministry of Tourism decided to offset adverse 1967 headlines in the American press about the constant aerial bombing of Arab lands by inviting 1,200 foreign newsmen to Israel for a visit, the B'nai B'rith not only recruited journalists but organized their subsidized tours.[3] The ADL continuously employed its "nonprofit organization" postal permit to disseminate Israeli propaganda publications, as it did during the June 1967 war[4] and on an infinite number of occasions since. As former B'nai B'rith officer Saul E. Joftes brought out in his suit against the brotherhood, which he carried successfully to the Supreme Court despite efforts of attorneys to stall adjudication for almost four years, charitable, tax-deductible funds were diverted into Israel-related projects of a political or quasi-political nature.

Americans who have recently shown how sensitive they are to threats to their privacy and liberties when CIA wiretapping and spying were revealed have never been told about the building of what might be called the Jewish Gestapo or the largest nongovernment spy system functioning in the Western hemisphere. In his book *The Pledge,*[5] Leonard Slater, a staunch Zionist sympathizer, detailed the many illegal programs devised to assist in bringing Israel into being. Starting in 1945, Zionists enlisted key Jews and Gentiles in many countries around the world; connived with judges, custom officials, and politicians; and according to FBI reports, even smuggled weaponry and men out of the U.S. and Europe, past the British into Palestine for the day of reckoning with the Arabs. Washington economist Robert Nathan interceded with J. Edgar Hoover to help free Zionist agents arrested at the Canadian border for smuggling arms destined for Israel.[6] Cases of rifle barrels were stolen from the U.S. Naval Supply Depot in Hawaii.

Under the lead of the "Sonneborn Institute," named after U.S. Haganah leader Rudolf Sonneborn, the quest for an armament industry was realized. Material was gathered for Palestine into depots from Zionist organizations across the U.S. From Wisconsin came 350,000 sandbags, from Ohio 92,000 flares, from New Jersey 25,000 helmets. Chicago supplied 100 tons of barbed wire and ten tons of khaki paint, while New Orleans sent salt tablets and penicillin. San Francisco offered mosquito netting, Minneapolis 600 mine detectors, and from the port city of Norfolk, Virginia, two corvettes, an ice cutter and, "to guide the naval strategists of the future Jewish state, the complete memoirs of Admiral von Tirpitz."[7]

Under the guise of Talmudic studies in New York City, attorney Nahum Bernstein was teaching espionage and hand-to-hand fighting. This intelligence school met in an Orthodox religious tax-exempt institution which called itself the National Council of Young Israel.

Through the B'nai B'rith, the ADL, the American Jewish Committee, and varied Zionist and pro-Israel groups, Israeli intelligence continued to penetrate into every part of the U.S. Temples, synagogues, and rabbis unabashedly cooperated. In fact, there was a cynical joke that is said to have circulated in the Pentagon: Every confidential military memo apparently was typed in triplicate, "one for the White House, one for the State Department, and one for Tel Aviv." At one point the Israeli navy was a photocopy of the U.S. Navy even as far as training from the Blue Jackets Manual.

Outside of the U.S., too, secretive surveillance and purchased support for Israel went forward. The February 1970 hearings of the U.N. Non-Governmental Organization Committee heard a report that there was "a clandestine program of quasi-espionage in Eastern European countries, through American Jewish tourists, conducted by the Israeli government and paid for by the Israeli government, but run from inside B'nai B'rith, which was used as a cover-up."

There are many ways of using anti-Semitism as an instrument to compel agreement with the Zionist position and to still any criticism of the Israelis. Foreign Minister Abba Eban, on the occasion of one of the many Israeli reprisals against Lebanon, defended Israel's actions: "The attitude of foreign countries cannot be entirely divorced from the traditional attitude of the non-Jewish world to the Jewish world." According to this theme on which the eloquent Israeli spokesman elaborated in 1974 and 1975 after he had retired from his Cabinet post and was lecturing on American university campuses while teaching at Columbia University, any and all criticism of Israel could only be considered anti-Semitic.

Dr. Willard Oxtoby, writing in *Presbyterian Life,*[8] had this to say on the effect of the anti-Semitism labeling:

Hopefully, anti-Semitism may soon become a sin of the past, but for the time being, it is still an emotionally potent word and nobody wants to be caught being anti-Semitic. . . . Like the news media, and for the same reasons, the Christian critic of Zionism is paralyzed. He cannot condemn Israeli armed conquest because he must pussyfoot in the delicate area of religious prejudice. As a result, Zionism is a subject on which in the United States there is more effective suppression of freedom of speech than any other.

Since criticism of Jews by blacks automatically became labeled anti-Semitism; since censure of Israel by Christians ranging from President Charles de Gaulle to the General Assembly and Security Council of the U.N. was held by the world Jewish community to be but another "manifestation of perennial anti-Semitism," according to Abba Eban; since anti-Zionism was declared by the Rabbinical Council of America to be but a new guise for anti-Semitism, it was inevitable that freedom of expression in the U.S. became totally restricted. Veteran Zionist leader Dr. Nahum Goldmann alleged there was a new kind of anti-Semitism that had sprung up in Communist countries and elsewhere among those whom he chose to term "members of the left wing." This variety of anti-Semitism, he asserted in February 1969, was being propagated in the form of anti-Israeli and anti-Zionist positions.

Exploitation of prejudice reached unheard of heights in the 1974 study of the Anti-Defamation League (ADL), *The New Anti-Semitism,* written by its high priests of the cult of anti-anti-Semitism, General Counsel Arnold Forster and National Director Benjamin R. Epstein. According to the press release, headed "Searchlight on Hatred," widely distributed by publisher McGraw-Hill, the new anti-Semitism is based on the old, only it emanates from different and surprisingly respectable sources. "The hostility of the Radical Left, the Radical Right, pro-Arab groups, black extremists, and a malingering anti-Jewish hate-mongering that has plagued the United States since the early twenties" has allegedly now been augmented by "others within the government, the media, the clergy and the arts, who are insensitive to Jews and Jewish concerns, particularly to the needs and wants of the State of Israel."

And as authors Forster and Epstein indicated in their two-hour, unopposed radio interview on New York's popular WMCA Barry Gray talk show, anyone who does not go along 100 percent with their views of Israel is deemed "insensitive" and therefore "anti-Semitic." The ADL leaders made it very clear that "any threat to the security of the State of Israel" must be considered a threat to the Jews of the U.S. and hence must be viewed as anti-Semitism. The reason given by them for this new bigotry: "The hard-won status of American Jewry."

The publication of this much ballyhooed study and book just happened to coincide with the growing feeling in many parts of the country that Zionist pressure, influence, and financial power had been responsible for the energy crisis that brought gas shortages and grave dangers. The cultists bitterly complained that Jews were no longer protected by the "moral indignation that followed the holocaust."

Apparently, they wished to extend a protective curtain over the Zionist-imposed Middle East policy and other positions espoused by the Jewish Establishment.

This was the seventh of the books on which these same authors had collaborated.[9] As usual, the book was released to the press first as a study one month before publication to lay the groundwork for a vast publicity follow-up. The *New York Times* obliged, as customary, with solid three-column coverage headed "Report by Anti-Defamation League Sees Example of New Kind of Anti-Semitism."[10]

This latest ADL work contained no index, probably purposely because it would have quickly revealed an imposing roster of respectable people listed as "anti-Semites." The tightly woven volume, set in smaller than usual type, contained infinite words and multifold unproven charges based on innuendo and insinuation. The names of those who were vilified were interwoven with those of a few recognized bigots and were adroitly dropped among members of the Radical Left, the Radical Right, Arab, and black extremists—a perfect example of the deceptive method of affixing guilt by juxtaposition.

While the Foreword of its latest "study" set forth the ADL's long-term goal to "fight against prejudice, bigotry and descrimination" with "the weapons [of] law, education and public persuasion . . . to seek justice and fair treatment for all citizens alike," this widely accepted image of the organization was destroyed by the repeated insistence of the authors that "American Jews regard attacks on the existence of Israel as the ultimate anti-Semitism." As stated in the last paragraph of the Epilogue, "the heart of the new anti-Semitism abroad in our land" lies in the "widespread incapacity or unwillingness to comprehend the necessity of the existence of Israel to Jewish safety and survival throughout the world." Therefore, the mildest criticism of Israel or of Zionist activities was viewed as offensive "insensitivity" or "callous indifference" and was equated to anti-Semitism, distinguishable from the traditional kind, the authors averred, in that "the new anti-Semitism is not necessarily deliberate in character and is more often expressed by respected individuals and institutions here and abroad—people who would be shocked to think of themselves or have others think them as anti-Semites."

In this Foreword ADL National Chairman Seymour Graubard laid the groundwork for old, recognizable tactics:

While the memory of the Nazi Holocaust was fresh in mind, anti-Semitism was silenced. As that memory fades, however, as Jews are more and more being considered a part of the Establishment, there are new growths of anti-Semitism. They are being nurtured in a climate of general insensitivity and deterioration of morality and ethics, the kind of climate, history reminds us, in which anti-Semitism grows best.

Having recalled the past to build fear and to invent present hostile situations, the ADL was ready to apply the smear and vilification so as to censor and silence, thus building an iron curtain over America that would bar any criticism, however constructive, of Israel, Zionists, or Jews (Judaism is rarely, if ever, involved). Even the *New York Post*'s James Wechsler, long an avid friend of Israel, was objective enough to write that the latest Forster-Epstein ADL work is "grievously flavored by an intolerance of their own in equating criticism of Israel with anti-Semitism." Calling the presentation "illegitimate and uncivil," the columnist described a standard

which requires a kind of political psychiatry to isolate hidden intent, by proceeding from a well-documented dissection of the frenzies of Gerald L. K. Smith to a loose indictment of Senator J. William Fulbright and columnists Evans and Novak. They do not explicitly apply the label anti-Semitic to the latter three. But the context in which the attack appears—indeed their inclusion in the volume—carries, to borrow their words, "an unmistakable message" and inescapable "innuendo."[11]

The assumption of the simultaneous role of judge, prosecutor, witness, and juror brought this sole protest from the "brave" band of liberals who are otherwise frothing at the mouth at such stifling of freedom. All of the ADL books, with the tremendous publicity given to them before, during, and after publication (they were widely promoted on radio and otherwise by among others, Walter Winchell, during his days of fame) and the extensive advertising, ought long ago to have earned for the organization its appropriate name, "The *Defamation* League."

The growth of anti-Semitism, which the ADL and other Israelist groups allegedly feared, suited the needs of the Zionists who wished to make Jews more conscious of their Jewishness. The worship of ethical universal Judaism, in their eyes, was for the few skull-capped old men and Talmudic scholars. But for the masses, who were turned off by the tedium of synagogue worship, there was the new exciting Israelism and the worship of anti-anti-Semitism.

From its outset the Zionist movement had clearly indicated the extent of its vested interest in prejudice. Herzl expressed the hope that any anti-Semitism would "act as a propelling force which, like the wave of the future, would bring the Jews into the promised land."[12] At the same time he also wrote: "Anti-Semitism has grown and continues to grow—and so do I."[13] The father of Zionism predicted: "The governments of all countries scourged by anti-Semitism will be keenly interested in assisting us to obtain the sovereignty we want."

The rabbinate had long employed anti-Semitism as a means of keeping the flock within the fold, and since the creation of Israel, support in the Diaspora has been continuously and easily enlisted by depicting the new Jewish state as a kind of insurance policy in case of a renaissance of anti-Semitism. Consequently, Zionist leadership has cared little about how much anti-Semitism their own separatist activities might generate.

The late British Parliamentarian Richard H. S. Crossman, an ardent Anglo-Saxon proponent of Zionism, cited Dr. Chaim Weizmann's contention that "anti-Semitism is a bacillus which every Gentile carries with him wherever he goes and however often he denies it."[14] At this first meeting Dr. Chaim Weizmann allegedly bluntly asked Crossman whether he was anti-Semitic, to which the Labourite frankly answered, "Of course." Their friendship was sealed, and Crossman's energetic crusade, partly expiation for that original prejudice, followed.

Bigotry has only been so much grist for Zionist mills. Crossman expressed it thus: "Who achieved that majority vote for partition at Lake Success? Not the terrorists of the Irgun nor the soldiers of the Haganah, but the aged leader of international Jewry [Weizmann], who could still sham and magic the Gentile world into recognizing its debt to her people."[15] It is this continued process of shaming the Christian world into accepting the guilt for the genocide of six million Jews that first brought Israel into being, and since then has been the means of rallying continued support for Israel's cause in the U.S. and in the Western world.

Parliamentarian Ian Gilmour, writing in the British magazine *The Spectator,* noted the inevitable link between Zionism and anti-Semitism:

Since the basis of Zionism is that Jewish assimilation in other countries is in the long run impossible and that anti-Semitism and persecution are bound to break out sooner or later, Zionism has almost a vested interest in racial discrimination. The Israelis mount "rescue operations" to save allegedly threatened Jews in other countries. . . . In Arab countries, Jewish difficulties and emigration to Israel were the result not of anti-Semitism, but of Zionist activities and the existence of the State of Israel. Zionism aggravated the disease that it professed to cure.[16]

This was a reecho of the words voiced earlier by Dr. Judah Magnes, the first President of Hebrew University: "We had always thought that Zionism would diminish anti-Semitism in the world. We are witness to the opposite."[17]

The separatist philosophy of Zionist dogma, staunchly supported by Organized Jewry after the holocaust, has been picked up alike by "retrogressive" conservatives and by liberal friends who would otherwise look askance at the mere mention of apartheid. And this overwhelming sentiment manifested itself, almost as if in answer to the blunt warning of Goldmann that a "current decline of overt anti-Semitism might constitute a new danger to Jewish survival. . . . The disappearance of 'anti-Semitism' in its classic meaning, while beneficial to the political and material situation of Jewish communities, has had a very negative effect on our internal life."[18] Counsel Leo Pfeffer of the American Jewish Congress voiced a similar statement: "Such discrimination may well be a blessing. It is possible that some anti-Semitism is necessary in order to insure Jewish survival."[19] In Britain, too, an article in *Blackfriars Magazine* pointed to the danger of the extinction of the Jewish community because of the absence of anti-Semitism.[20]

The large-city media came to the rescue and prevented such a catastrophe from occurring by keeping the anti-anti-Semitic pot boiling. Through its virtual control of the media, the Zionist machinery had no problems orchestrating three important themes:

1) Arab anti-Semitism: the hostility of the Arab world, and particularly of Gamal Abdel Nasser and later of Yasir Arafat and the PLO, allegedly stemming from the same kind of bigotry and hatred that was manifested in Hitlerian genocide.

2) Russian anti-Semitism: the Jews in the Soviet Union and elsewhere behind the Iron Curtain were singular victims of Communist terror and must be permitted to go to Israel.

3) Christian anti-Semitism: the bigotry that first persecuted Jews as followers of Judaism and then permitted six million Jews in Europe to be wiped out allegedly still manifested itself in continued acts of hostility toward Jews and particularly toward the State of Israel.

An attempt was made to link alleged Fascist activities in Argentina with increasing anti-Semitic overtones in Egypt. In the spring of 1975 Argentine Ambassador in Washington Alejandro Orfila asked his good friend Egyptian Ambassador Ashraf Ghorbal to briefly see a visiting writer for a supernationalist publication called *Marchar*. In response, Ghorbal received the writer for just three minutes. Patricio Kelly, this particular writer, spoke no English whatsoever and the Egyptian Ambassador speaks but a few words of Spanish and Italian. The only other person present was a photographer whom Kelly brought along; most unfortunately, no effort was made to obtain an interpreter. Several weeks after the story of the interview appeared—and the paper went out of business not long after—the Jewish Telegraphic Agency in Buenos Aires fed a long section of the alleged interview, "Extermination of Judaism in the Mideast Is Point of Departure for Arab Liberation," through its main trunk wire extending worldwide to the specialized Jewish press, which immediately picked up the story.

Jewish Week of Washington headlined its April 3 story: "Egyptian Ambassador Foresees Extermination of Judaism." An additional commentary on the alleged interview was carried by the national chauvinistic Brooklyn *Jewish Press* (April 11) with the headline: "Extermination of Jews." Letters containing clips of this alleged interview poured into the Egyptian Embassy in Washington. Even the respected and fair *Guardian* in England published a large portion of the alleged interview, but later carried a full retraction apologizing "for running a piece of black propaganda," which the newspaper admitted was obtained from "an Israeli source that was impeccable."

The opposition Herut party demanded in the Knesset that the Israeli Foreign Ministry "reprint and distribute millions of copies of the interview by one of President Sadat's principal advisers," which they claimed proved what Israelis had always contended: "The conflict is not over territories, but over the very existence of Israel and the Jewish people."

Executive Vice President of the Synagogue Council of America Rabbi Henry Siegman wrote Ghorbal: "Based on our association, I simply find it impossible to believe that you could have said the things attributed to you."[21] Chairman of the Board of the World Jewish Congress Philip M. Klutznick forwarded to Ghorbal a similar message. Evans and Novak described the defamation of the Egyptian Ambassador as "cruel and tragic and without any effort to check the accuracy of the inflammatory report in a worthless publication . . . the understandable emotions and fears of thousands of Jews have been manipulated in the rising crescendo of the propaganda battle."[22]

Every incident everywhere in the world in which a Jew or someone reputed to be of "Jewish ethnic background" was victimized was being incessantly presented by the *Times* as another example of Hitlerian anti-Semitism. (Managing editor A. M. Rosenthal early in his career wrote a sentimental piece as a correspondent in Europe following his visit to Auschwitz and admitted "that there is no news to report," but "there is merely the compulsion to write something about it," which he did.[23]) The campaign was led by Professor Seymour M. Lipset's *New York Times Magazine* article,[24] "The Socialism of Fools—the New Left call it 'Anti-Zionism,' but it's no different from the anti-Semitism of the Old Right" and by *Commentary* Editor Norman Podhoretz in an address before the American Jewish Committee warning that the "taboo on anti-Semitism is waning" and that a version of Nazism is the "in-thing" today. When there were other victims in a mass tragedy, as in the Iraq hangings, the fate of Jews was singled out as evidence of persecution of Jews as Jews, rather than as a ruthless power play to tighten control.

Every *Times* writer, correspondent, stringer, et al., with magnifying glass in hand, has undoubtedly been sworn to a Sherlock Holmes-like preoccupation with uncovering the most remote evidence of this prejudice and sending in his "find" to the news editor, who stands ever-prepared to build the remotest implication of bias into booming headlines of fact, to make atypical examples of prejudice appear typical. When Reverend George French Kempsell, Jr., of the Protestant Episcopal Church in Scarsdale, New York, condemned in a sermon the barring of Jewish escorts for debutantes going to a coming-out ball at the Scarsdale Golf Club, three lengthy stories appeared in the *Times,* two on the front page.[25]

When the winner of the Freshman First Honor prize in a letter to the *Daily Princetonian*[26] dared question the appropriateness of bringing the Warsaw Ghetto Exhibit to the university, and pointed to "the martyr image of 6 million dead" as the primary theme of the Jewish drive toward Gentile acceptance, a raging controversy took over this ivy college campus. Princeton President Dr. Robert F. Goheen stigmatized the letter as "blind prejudice." The *New York Times* promptly made national news by picking up the presidential letter from the campus paper and featuring it prominently.[27]

The *Times* continued to be the willing efficient transmittal belt in supplying the American public with constant alleged examples of Arab, Russian, and Christian "anti-Semitism" as a means of molding favorable sentiment for the Israeli state. And occasionally the trials and tribulations of a famed man of letters served the same purpose.

The death in Venice on November 1, 1972, of poet Ezra Pound, who probably did as much for English literature in the 20th century as any single individual, brought wide press reportage on the stormy life of the famed expatriot. There was little reference, however, to the final turbulent event in the hectic eighty-seven years of Pound's life in which the cult of anti-anti-Semitism gained another resounding victory, and Pound was the victim.

While still living in Italy in 1972, the poet became the center of a swirling controversy when he was awarded the annual Emerson-Thoreau medal of Boston's American Academy of Arts and Sciences by a panel of distinguished writers and critics. The Academy's governing council vetoed the panel's recommendation on what they called "moral grounds, because of other aspects of his life." What this meant was that the council, with a large number of Jewish members, was penalizing Pound for his wartime Fascist leanings and alleged "anti-Semitism."[28]

Like most incidents involving the cult, the affair was wrapped in secrecy and would have remained hush-hush had there not been a leak of the letter from Academy President Harvey Brooks (Harvard) to certain members, in which he noted that "with memories of the Holocaust so prominent, there was the unavoidable implication that the award carried special approval of life as well as work." An award to Pound, it was felt, would be "deeply offensive to many members of the Academy."

Three of this privately supported honorary society's 2,700 members resigned, protesting the relevance of social ideas in judging poetry. These were Professor Jerome Y. Lettvin of MIT; O. D. Hardison, Director of the Folger-Shakespeare Library; and Professor W. Hugh Kenner of the University of California at Santa Barbara, who perceived an inconsistency in the membership honoring Pound for his book, *The Pound Era,* while Pound the poet was not acceptable.

As Robert Reinhold's front-page article in the *Times* of July 5, 1972, pointed out, many of the most distinguished creative writers, composers, and scientists down through the ages have embraced ideologies or led lives that most people would consider despicable: "Shakespeare was a usurer, Christopher Marlowe a blasphemer and probably a homosexual, Rimabud ventured into slave trading and Baudelaire led a violent, depraved life, etc." In his letter of resignation Lettvin protested: "It is not art that concerns you but politics, not taste but special interest, not excellence but propriety." The MIT academician went on to note that to this day he himself was unable to bring himself to visit Germany, but he nevertheless felt strongly about the integrity of artistic intellectual expression.

"We are witnessing the institutionalization of a very dangerous pathology in American intellectual life," stated Martin L. Kilson, a black professor of government at Harvard, the theme which he reiterated in a letter to the *Times*. [29] He attributed the decision to a "perverse ethnic defensiveness" on the part of Jewish intellectuals, whom he likened to "ethnically defensive blacks who want opposition to white racism established as a precondition for the recognition of an intellectual's work by intellectual institutions."

Kilson went on to say that he was as outraged about anti-Negro intellectuals as a Jew is about anti-Semitic ones, but such outrage "is not a matter of intellect but of politics," and in evaluating an intellectual's work, he believed that "short of the intellectual himself committing criminal or atrocious acts against humanity under the influence of his politics, his intellectual works should stand on their own."

Who is to judge what anti-Semitism is? Those who opposed the decision of the Boston Academy pointed to Pound's generous efforts not only to promote the careers of other writers, including James Joyce, Robert Frost, and T. S. Eliot, but also to his personal warmth toward many Jewish writers. Was he an anti-Semite? Eliot, a previous Emerson winner, was also alleged to have shared Pound's anti-Semitic outlook in his earlier works.

What is this thing called anti-Semitism? Is any criticism of any Jew because he happens to be a Jew per se "anti-Semitism"? Even when Anna Pauker, a Rumanian Communist who had murdered thousands, was herself purged, certain quarters raised their inevitable hue and cry because she happened to be Jewish. If a Jewish politician is corrupt, is he to be given the protective cover of the label "anti-Semitism"?

In his Canto 52, Pound had written: "Poor yitts paying for the Rothschilds/paying for a few big Jews' vendetta on goyim." From the earliest moments of his career, Pound had criticized the vulgarity of life and the international bankers, particularly those who were Jewish. His venom expressed itself in: "Usury is the cancer of the world." The Rothschilds have been assailed from the Right and the Left for their usurious practices in building their nearly inexplicable fortune. Is all such censure automatically verboten because the persons concerned are Jewish? Since the Nazi tragedy, Jews too often have managed to take shelter under the exemption: "Don't dare incriminate a Jew lest you be taking Hitler's side."

But it took a 1973 column in the *Boston Globe* by Kevin Kelley to really expose the cult of anti-anti-Semitism. Strangely enough, this time the cultists were going after the movie industry, which has always been more than 100 percent subservient to Zionist nationalism. Certain Christians might well level the charge against *Jesus Christ Superstar* that it is irreverent (Catholics called it morally unobjectionable, but libertarian)—but that it is anti-Semitic carries this too far.

The Boston columnist quite appropriately labeled as "hysteria" the outcry and the accompanying claim that producer Norman Jewison's name might fool people into thinking that he was Jewish, thereby somehow giving the movie, magically, a Jewish blessing despite its underlying bias. "That kind of suggestion, like the charge itself, is paranoid," wrote the columnist.[30]

Particularly objectionable to the film's Israelist critics was the Jewish role in the crucifixion and the condemnation of Jesus by the high priests, whom they alleged were "libelously depicted as contemptuous, sadistic and blood-thirsty." (Amos, Ezekiel, Jeremiah, and other of the Hebrew prophets of the Old Testament had, of course, similarly described the priests of an earlier period.) These one-track-minded Jews also protested a surrealistic scene following Judas's betrayal of Jesus and the use of Israeli tanks and Phantoms (without markings). American Jews charged these damaged the Israeli image—again a case of acting "more Catholic than the Pope," as the Israelis had given their initial approval to the film.

The prerelease publicity for *Superstar* was tremendous as controversy was continuously fanned. A discussion on "Midday Live," the Channel 5 program in New York City, featured Rabbi Marc Tanenbaum's view that the film was strengthening the misconception held by many Christians, if not most, that the Jews had killed Christ. He would have history entirely rewritten. Apparently the lyrics of the song sung by Pontius Pilate made him appear all too human and shifted the responsibility for the crucifixion to the pressures of a hysterical Jewish mob. Further, the Rabbi insisted, the casting of a black actor in the role of Judas was likely to encourage black anti-Semitism.

The cultists did not cease their "anti-Semitic" branding campaign. They tried to influence reviewers. The American Jewish Committee called a press conference denouncing the musical as comparable to the "anti-Semitic" Passion Play of Oberammergau. Rabbi Tanenbaum, however, was refused a meeting by Universal Pictures President H. H. Martin to discuss the Committee's concern that *Superstar* might rouse new bigotry in West Germany and Austria, where "a strong residuum of both religious and idealogical anti-Semitism continues."

This latest effort at suppression appeared on the same page of the *New York Times*[31] as a story about a new musical based on *Molly*, the character created by Gertrude Berg on national radio and television. When would John Q. Jew stand up and protest the blind stupidity of attacking historical facts behind the crucifixion of Jesus while encouraging the dissemination of this kind of Jewish stereotype:

> Yoo-hoo, Mrs. Goldberg!
> Was that "yoo-hoo" for me, Mrs. Bloom?

Who breeds the anti-Semitism these cultists allegedly are fighting? Humorous as the Molly Goldberg series was, it contributed to building the anti-Semitic stereotype of the Jew as someone with an accent, part of a group apart from the other people of the nation in which he lives. Pressure from these same groups was responsible for bringing to an end the very popular television series "Bridget Loves Bernie," because it showed that an Irish-Jewish intermarriage can work despite obstacles. But the attempt to pressure NBC out of its scheduled showing of Lawrence Olivier in "The Merchant of Venice" failed after the cultists, joined by the magazine *Jewish Currents,* had expressed a deep dread in permitting this production "to be beamed into the homes of the mass TV audience."[32]

The anti-anti-Semitism cult is vital not only in the silencing of the opposition to Zionism and Israelism, but it also supplies a principal *raison d'être* for followers of the new modern kind of "Judaism." Many Jews insist they will remain in the faith so long as it is still unpopular to be a Jew, i.e., so long as anti-Semitism exists. This alone could account for the fact that the ADL and other "defense" organizations, with the powerful and wealthy Jewish-American community solidly behind them, have never attempted to launch one single objective scholarly study on the causes of anti-Semitism so as to make an honest effort to kill this bias.

The reasoning is obvious. Neither the religious nor the lay leaders of the many Jewish organizations wished to lose their most potent weapon. If they removed prejudice they would lose adherents to the faith. If they made strides toward eliminating bigotry, funds for Jewish nationalist activities would dry up. Hence there must be no real attempt to solve the problem of anti-Semitism. Herein lies the conspiracy between the rabbinate, Jewish nationalists, and other leaders of Organized Jewry to keep the problems of prejudice alive, just as Goldmann and Herzl had advocated. The Christian has not interfered, particularly if he carried any prejudice in his heart—the endemic anti-Semitism to which Herzl and Crossman had alluded.

No one understood these machinations better than famed journalist Dorothy Thompson. In 1938 she assumed the leadership of the country's moral mobilization against Nazism, after she risked life and limb in taking on the Nazi Bund in the famed Madison Square Garden incident. Her renowned wartime "Listen, Hans" broadcasts and espousal of the Zionist cause followed. She of course immediately became the darling of the Zionist movement.

Upon her return from visiting newly created Israel, as her biographer noted, she began voicing "concern for the plight of the Arab refugees and dismay at the tactics of Jewish refugees."[33] William Zuckerman, editor of the *Jewish Newsletter,* later wrote in a tribute to the great journalist, "Miss Thompson now saw that Zionism, which had started out as a liberal and humanitarian relief movement, was turning into a reactionary, aggressive, chauvinist movement of the same character as other European nationalisms, which she had been fighting throughout her journalistic career."

A bitter campaign of character assassination was waged against her, even to the point of attributing her new viewpoint to the influence of her "anti-Semitic" third husband, highly respected Czech sculptor Maxim Kopf. As biographer Marion K. Sanders relates:

For Dorothy, the bitterest blow was the discovery that Zionists equated criticism of their policies with anti-Semitism. "I refuse to become an anti-Semite by designation," she said, recalling not only her long record of benevolence to Jewish refugees, her steadfast battle against Hitler, and, perhaps, the fact that she had once been ridiculed for walking out of a dinner party where an anti-Semitic joke was told, with the comment, "I will not remain in the same house with traitors to the United States."[34]

The Zionist pressure directed against Thompson resulted in certain newspapers, including the *New York Post* from which she received a full quarter of her income, dropping her syndicated "On the Record" column. She was bitterly hurt: "I am crushed at the thought that this campaign has been instituted by 'liberals,' against a writer in a 'liberal newspaper' whose intolerance of an opposing or differing view leads them to character-assassination and career-assassination. It has been boundless, going into my personal life."[35]

Meyer Weisgal, the intimate associate of David Ben-Gurion and her closest friend within the Zionist hierarchy, testified:

The attacks upon her became outrageous. She was accused, among other things of having lined her pockets with the fees of Zionist organizations. This stung her deeply.... She had taken nothing for herself.... All monies accruing to her from public lectures to Zionist groups went into a trust fund, which I controlled for the German-Jewish refugees who came into her orbit.[36]

As the final word on this terrifying episode, this writer who had earlier been married to Sinclair Lewis wrote a memorable letter "On Creating Anti-Semites" for the *Jewish Newsletter:*

Really, I think continual emphasis should be put upon the extreme damage to the Jewish community of branding people like myself as anti-Semitic. It is a little beneath the dignity of anyone with my record to deny such charges in public, so they just tend to make anti-Semitism more respectable than it otherwise might be, for, rightly or wrongly, a great many people in this country respect me highly, and if it is publicized that I am an anti-Semite, anti-Semitism becomes thereby a little bit more respectable.

. . . In the same way, the State of Israel has got to learn to live in the same atmosphere of free criticism which every other state in the world must endure. If the editors of this country's press are forced to suppress critical views because of organized pressure, both in the form of masses of letters to the editor and pressures on the business side of the paper's organization, the net effect—and I know what I'm talking about—is to foment a very ugly resentment, the worse because it finds no outlet. There are many subjects on which writers in this country are, because of these pressures, becoming craven and mealy-mouthed. But people don't like to be craven and mealy-mouthed; every time one yields to such pressure, *one is filled with self-contempt and this self-contempt works itself out in resentment of those who caused it.* [Italics added.]

I often think that race relations were actually much better in this country when we took good-natured flings at the characteristics of the various national groups in our midst. People actually don't like paragons, and any group that tries to arrogate to itself all the virtues and admit none of the vices of the common run of humanity does not thereby make itself more lovable. Therefore, I am sure that anti-anti-Semitism, like anti-anti-Negroism, can reach a point where it has exactly the opposite effect from the one which it has striven for. . . .[37]

Dorothy Thompson was unable to halt the Zionist juggernaut. Scornful of the long-term effects of its anti-anti-Semitic campaign, the cult has continued its war of suppression and repression, waging an unparalleled blitz on the great and near-great to win acquiesence to its views on Israel.

XII   The Blitz

No matter whose the lips that would speak, they must be free and ungagged. The community which dares not protect its humblest and most hated member in the free utterance of his opinions, no matter how false or hateful, is only a gang of slaves.

—Wendell Phillips

Why is the subject of this book *sui generis?* A Dr. Timothy Leary could talk openly in favor of pot. Others might argue pro and con on the subject of abortion. One is quite able to attack his Holiness the Pope, or Her Majesty the Queen of England. This country carried on a lengthy, bitter, acrimonious debate on Vietnam, which finally led to the U.S. withdrawal. But why can only one side of the Arab-Israeli question be discussed in the U.S.?

In the case of every other issue of public interest, there is room for both the pros and the cons. Arguments are aired and, as befits a democratic society, disagreement is permitted to exist. Although this is the one area of foreign policy that has deep domestic as well as international implications, relating closely to the survival of the entire civilized world, no one may freely talk about it. Only when it comes to the Israeli problem is there so concentrated an attempt to crush all opposition.

At critical moments in U.S. relations with the Arab world and Israel there has invariably been some one person who has seen the problem in full perspective, bestirred himself, and attempted to tell the story to the American public. Equally invariably, like the wolf at the head of the pack, he has been forthrightly shot down, his pen or voice stilled, and the gaping vacuum once more becomes apparent. With the help of the ever-willing media, the critic of Israel or of U.S. "Israel-First" policy has been made out to be a reincarnation of Hitler. The

421

history of these personal repressions will astound Americans quite as much as did the revelations of Watergate in the spring and summer of 1973. Those who have dared break the silence barrier have paid grievously for their courage in exercising what they considered to be their democratic prerogative.

The roster of renegade libertarians, liberals and conservatives alike, who over the past thirty years have tried to buck the tide of Jewish-Zionist nationalism and then found themselves victims of a smear campaign, reads like an international Who's Who. Included in this illustrious list drawn from top educational, clerical, literary, political, and journalistic circles are: Yale's Millar Burrows, Harvard's William Ernest Hocking, Dean Virginia Guildersleeve, Dr. Henry Sloane Coffin, Henry Van Dusen, Dean Francis Sayre, Rabbi Elmer Berger, Dr. A.C. Forrest, Dr. John Nicholls Booth, Father Daniel Berrigan, Morris Ernst, Arthur Garfield Hays, Vincent Sheean, Dr. Arnold Toynbee, Norman Thomas, Howard K. Smith, J. William Fulbright, James Abourezk, Ralph Flanders, General George Brown, James Forrestal, Henry A. Byroade, Moshe Menuhin, Dr. Israel Shahak, Dorothy Thompson, Willie Snow Ethridge, Margaret McKay, Hannah Arendt, Sir George Brown, Folke Bernadotte, Dag Hammarskjold, Bruno Kreisky, Georges Pompidou, and Charles de Gaulle.

The relentless and persistent attacks waged on those who have dared raise even a note of caution, let alone a voice of protest, against the prevailing one-sided pro-Israelism line can find few parallels in a society that has not as yet extinguished free speech or opinion-expression and otherwise permits some talking out against the Establishment. It is hard to believe that such things have been taking place in this country, so persistently, for so long, and so quietly. To preserve the massive cover-up and cover-over, there has been an onslaught that can be compared only to the Nazi blitz, which sought to level London to the ground at the outset of World War II. Surveillance, harassment, character assassination, guilt by association, guilt by juxtaposition, suppression of free speech, repression of even minimal dissent—these are some of the basic techniques employed by the plethora of Zionist "humanitarian," "defense," and lobbying organizations in silencing any and all opposition to the Israeli state and its policies.

One of the earliest victims was James Forrestal, first U.S. Secretary of Defense (prior to the Truman administration the Cabinet included separate Secretaries of the Army and Navy). While other Americans were being pressured into accepting the historical necessity and validity of the State of Israel, this perspicacious man was willing to fight for what he believed to be the American national interest.

The publication of the *Forrestal Diaries* in 1950 revealed the lengths to which Forrestal went in trying to obtain an agreement from both major political parties to lift the question out of the 1948 political contest. He argued in vain to persuade Democratic National Chairman and Attorney General Howard McGrath that he would rather "lose two or three pivotal states which could not be carried without the support of people who were deeply interested in the Palestine question than run the risks which, he felt, would ensue from that kind of handling of the Palestine question." He added, "No group in this country should be permitted to influence our policy to the point where it could endanger our national security."[1]

Vilification was Forrestal's only reward for his persistent efforts. Bernard Baruch, the adviser to Presidents and a good friend, warned him that his deep involvement in this attempt to forestall the inevitable movement toward the creation of a Jewish state was already identifying him to a dangerous degree with the opposition to U.S. policy on Palestine. But Forrestal ignored such counsel. When Congressman Franklin D. Roosevelt, Jr., expressed fear that the party might lose votes should a bipartisan agreement be reached, the Secretary almost angrily retorted: "I think it is about time that somebody should give some consideration as to whether we might not lose the United States."[2]

The Defense Secretary argued in vain with Attorney General Howard McGrath, his fellow cabinet member and Chairman of the Democratic National Committee. McGrath, always the politician, would not change his mind even after he was shown the report on Palestine prepared by the Central Intelligence Agency, which underlay Forrestal's tormenting worry that the Soviet Union might take advantage of the breach of U.S. relations with the Arabs to move into the vitally strategic Middle East with its vast oil resources. It was this concern that motivated Forrestal's lonely crusade to retain a modicum of Arab friendship with the U.S. He acutely sensed the tremendous strategic importance of the area, globally and oil-wise, and his military advisers agreed that the withdrawal of the British from Palestine would result in serious troubles that could only help the Soviet Union. (History has proven how right he was in visualizing the Kremlin's "Open Sesame" to the Arab world.)

Secretary Forrestal enjoyed a short-lived triumph during the U.S. temporary shift to trusteeship, but then came President Truman's May 14 recognition of Israel.

Cries of "tool of Wall Street" and "oil hireling" greeted Forrestal's tireless efforts to divorce Middle East policy from domestic politics. Zionist lawyer Bartley C. Crum, in a widely publicized Cleveland speech, assailed Forrestal as the man "who has the power to decide whether there is a Jewish state in Palestine. 'Upon what meat does our Caesar feed that he has grown so great?' The answer is that Mr. Forrestal has found a new diet that even Caesar might envy. It is oil —Arabian oil."[3] Attacks like this, widely distributed by the American Jewish Committee, the ADL, and other Zionist groups, helped inspire the "tormenting, persecuting columns"[4] by Drew Pearson and broadcasts by Walter Winchell, aggravating the Secretary of Defense's illness.

Unfortunately Forrestal never lived to see the vindication of his judgment concerning the dire long-term consequences to the U.S. of the partition decision. This sensitive man, so deeply hurt, not so much by his failure to achieve a bipartisan Palestinian policy as by the fact that his motivations should have been impugned with the smears of "anti-Semite," threw himself from his room in the Bethesda Naval Hospital where he was being treated following a nervous breakdown. (Several articles and at least one book have hinted that he was pushed out of the window from which he allegedly fell to his death.)

It was slightly ironic that the devout Zionist and the first U.S. Ambassador to Israel, James G. McDonald, in his book *My Mission to Israel*,[5] should have been the one to come to Forrestal's defense:

He was in no sense anti-Semitic or anti-Israel nor influenced by oil interests. He was convinced that partition was not in the best interests of the U.S., and he certainly did not deserve the persistent and venomous attacks on him which helped break his mind and body. On the contrary, these attacks stand out as the ugliest examples of the willingness of politician and publicist to use the vilest means—in the name of patriotism—to destroy self-sacrificing and devoted public citizens.

When that irrepressible firebrand, Charles de Gaulle, whose pronouncements were already offensive to so many on so many grounds, added Israel in 1967 to his long list of antagonists, he really "put his foot into it." This time he took on a foe more powerful than any empire on earth, the cult of anti-anti-Semitism, and there was no American Ambassador to come to his aid.

At a press conference held at the Elysée Palace November 27, 1967, de Gaulle fired a new "shot heard 'round the world." When the information media pulled a phrase out of context from his exposition on the Middle East and gave it an inaccurate translation, they provoked pressures such as have scarcely been visited on anyone, let alone a Chief of State, since those directed at Harry Truman in 1947 to influence the final vote on the U.N. Partition Resolution. Banner headlines proclaimed that the General, who up to the very morning of the June 5 attack continued to supply the very Mystères with which the Israelis knocked out all Arab air bases, had assailed the Jews as an "elite people, sure of itself and domineering." Americans were only too ready ("Give a dog a bad name and then hang him" is an old adage) to add anti-Semitism to the long list of their grievances against the French President.

The incident caused a furor in the French press. *Le Monde* called the President "anti-Semitic," while former presidential candidate François Mitterand, interviewed in New York, labeled de Gaulle "materialistic." Some editorials accused the General not of being an anti-Semite but only of sounding like one. The *New York Times* even added yeast to the brew by noting that "some men with frankly racist views declared themselves elated."

This is what de Gaulle actually stated, as reported in the official French translation distributed by the French Information Service:

The establishment between the two world wars—for it is necessary to go back that far—of a Zionist home in Palestine, and then, after World War II, the establishment of a State of Israel, raised at the time a certain number of apprehensions. One could indeed, and people did wonder, even among Jews, if the implantation of this community on land that had been acquired in more or less justifiable conditions and in the middle of Arab peoples who were thoroughly hostile to it, was not going to produce constant and interminable friction and conflicts. Some even feared that the Jews, up to then scattered but who had remained what they had been down through the ages, that is *an elite people, sure of itself and dominating,* once they gathered on the site of their former grandeur, might come to change into a fervent and conquering ambition the very touching hopes that they had for nineteen centuries.[6] [Italics added.]

The press reportage conveniently changed "dominating" to "domineering," contradicting the official translation and thus making it simpler for the Israelist propaganda campaign to affix the heinous label. The remotest implication of bias was built into booming headlines of fact. The *New York Times* "Week in Review"[7] reported that "Jews had been described as a people with a secular inclination to seek domination."[8] One Israeli newspaper charged de Gaulle, according to the *Times,* with "surpassing the invective of Federenko"; another claimed, "There arises the stench of the 'Protocols of Zion.' "[9] Where the General was not accused of being an anti-Semite, he was condemned for "sounding like one." The Chief Rabbi of France as well as Michel Debré, the Minister of Finance and Economic Affairs (described as a rabbi's grandson), were brought into the pressuring act.

Additional reportage further embellished the case. Henry Tanner's front-page stories in the *Times* on January 6 and 10, 1968, respectively headlined "De Gaulle Assures Rabbi He Intended No Insult to Jews" and "De Gaulle Says He Praised Jews," were intended to lend further support to the thesis of neo-anti-Semitic remarks. These stories, together with his Sunday piece of January 14 under the headline "De Gaulle: He Has Some Second Thoughts on Jews," besides pointing up the tremendous influence of Jewry (no reader of the bestseller *Our Crowd* needed a reminder of this), implied that the General was retracting his statement. Tanner, David Susskind, and the Anti-Defamation League notwithstanding, there was not a single word of recantation or retraction by de Gaulle. The French President had nothing to recant.

"Informed Jewish sources" were Tanner's sole attribution for the first alleged recantation at the New Year's Day reception, where "Rabbi Kaplan told the General of his concern over the fact that the statement had been used by 'real' anti-Semites as an instrument against the Jews." (Moral to everyone: "Say nothing against Israel, Zionism, or Jews, however true, because somewhere, sometime, some real anti-Semite might pick it up and use it.") The second de Gaulle "recantation" was supposedly contained in an answer to a letter from former Prime Minister David Ben-Gurion, who had written a fifteen-page, single-spaced tome tracing Jewish suffering down through the centuries.

As in all Israelist propaganda moves, there was real purpose behind the expertly executed hue and cry. The "bad wolf" de Gaulle was pitted against "little Israel" and the "persecuted" Jews to build favorable sentiment just prior to the U.S. visit of Prime Minister Levi Eshkol, who was seeking more American planes for "defensive" purposes after the June 5 Israeli sneak attack had virtually destroyed the air arms of all Arab countries. Jewish nationalism once again sought to exploit prejudice so as to achieve political goals.

Likewise, the anti-Semitic charge shifted attention from de Gaulle's clear, concise, and unambiguous condemnation of the course taken by Israel, "whose existence and survival," according to the French President, must "depend on policies she follows, as is the case for all others." In his reply to the lengthy Ben-Gurion letter, the

President of France made crystal clear what the controversy was all about. After reviewing the "old and natural friendship France felt for Israel," de Gaulle referred to the "unfortunate blockade of the Gulf of Aqaba" and the reasonableness of Israel feeling threatened. "But," he went on:

. . . I remain convinced that by ignoring the warning given in time to your Government by the French Government, by taking possession of Jerusalem and of many Jordanian, Egyptian and Syrian territories by force of arms, by exerting repression and expulsion there—which are the unavoidable consequences of an occupation which has all the aspects of annexation [How clairvoyant the General was!]—by affirming to the world that a settlement of the conflict can only be achieved on the basis of the conquests made and not on the condition that these be evacuated, Israel is overstepping the bounds of necessary moderation.

Only in the third paragraph from the very end of his own lengthy letter to Ben-Gurion did de Gaulle allude to the controversial "elite, sure of itself" clause for which he had been so vilified, holding that "there cannot be anything disparaging in underlining the character, thanks to which this people were able to survive and to remain itself after nineteen centuries spent under incredible conditions."

This response to Ben-Gurion, far from being an apology, was a reiteration of de Gaulle's original complaint, set forth in his press conference, that Israel had ignored his May 24 warning imparted to Foreign Minister Abba Eban in Paris just twelve days before the outbreak of the 1967 hostilities:

If Israel is attacked, we will not allow it to be destroyed. But if you attack, we will condemn your initiative. To be sure, despite the numerical inferiority of your population, considering that you are much better organized, much more united and much better armed than the Arabs, I do not doubt that you would win military success. But later you will yourselves be engaged locally and on the international level in growing difficulties, all the more that war in the Middle East cannot fail to increase a deplorable tension in the world and to have very unfortunate consequences for many countries, so much that it is on you, having become conquerors, that the disadvantages would be blamed.

The General had been elevated to the rank of number-one anti-Semite because he had dared to remind Israel that "France's voice was not heard and that Israel remained in possession of the objectives it wanted to acquire." After Israel in February 1972, following the U.S. agreement to supply forty-two Phantom jets, terminated its order for fifty French Mirages, which had been fully paid for and were to have been delivered in the middle of 1967, and French-Israeli relations had further deteriorated, the *Times'* Jerusalem correspondent summarily analyzed the breach between the French and the Israelis in this manner: "President de Gaulle apparently decided that France's interests would be better served by building ties with the Arab states than by maintaining the relationship with Israel."[10]

De Gaulle had been in retirement when France joined Britain and Israel in the secret treaty of Sèvres leading to the 1956 tripartite invasion of Egypt. Despite the strong words of friendship for Israel after his return to power, he had never subscribed to the bitter anti-Egyptian sentiments of Gaullist leader Jacques Soustelle, voiced in the course of Algeria's struggle for independence. It was not too difficult for Charles de Gaulle to look beyond his nose and see where French interests lay. A leader who, when France was completely under the Nazi yoke, could envision a future for his country with grandeur, certainly could understand that the many Arab countries must eventually become infinitely more important to her interests than the State of Israel. The same vision that had carried France through its darkest moments forged a new Middle East policy after France had served for so many years as Israel's staunchest ally, not excluding the U.S.

This, and this alone, was what the Israelist case against de Gaulle was all about, and why the cult of anti-anti-Semitism pursued him relentlessly until his body was laid to rest in the small cemetery of Colombey les Deux Eglises.

From the outset of Georges Pompidou's takeover of the French Presidency, guilt through association was affixed to him by Organized Jewry. After all, he was de Gaulle's successor as well as de Gaulle's man. Few had seen fit to discredit him during the years he served with the Rothschild banking house in France. But as soon as he became Chief of State, his motives came under suspicion. Pompidou sensed this and tried to defuse it by kowtowing to the ever-present bogey of anti-anti-Semitism. The *New York Times* report on his first news conference pertinently included the following: "Mr. Pompidou described French attitudes in the Middle East in an unemotional matter-of-fact way. 'France's interest in the Mediterranean area requires good relations with the Arabs,' he said pointedly. But he added: 'France is not forgetting anything, and in particular has not forgotten the martyrdom inflicted by the Nazis on the Jews in all occupied countries, including France.' "[11]

This did Pompidou little good, however, for he found himself constantly under attack by the pro-Israelists whenever he took any position on the Middle East that did not hew 100 percent to the pure Zionist line. Perhaps the climax, at least as far as Americans were concerned, came with the French President's February 1970 trip to the U.S.

This visit, pursuant to the Nixon goal of seeking more cordial Franco-American relations, happened to follow closely on the heels of the French refusal to permit Mirages planes, contracted and paid for by Israel, to be shipped, and of the suspension of the submarine contract, which eventually was circumvented when the Israelis dramatically smuggled the ships out of the Cherbourg harbor. As a result, President Pompidou had become just about as popular with the Israelis and American Zionists as de Gaulle had been following France's major policy shift in the face of Israel's continued possession of occupied territories.

The abnormality that Israel had become was visibly demonstrated during this state visit. There were demonstrations against President Pompidou in Chicago, booing in Westchester, and picket lines in New York, which led the French Chief of State to call off the appointment that had been scheduled with Jewish leaders there. In the Windy City he had conferred with local Israelists, who used "very measured tones" and conducted themselves in sharp contrast to the demonstrators outside the Chicago and New York hotels housing the visitor from France. Mayor Daley's police treated these Zionist demonstrators with a deference not accorded to the pickets at the 1968 Democratic Convention.

President Pompidou suffered from near-physical contact with protesters who crowded in close enough to jostle him and members of his party, "shouting insults into my face and the face of my wife," to use his words. This threat of violence led to plans of Madame Pompidou to return home forthrightly, which were only reversed when President Nixon phoned from Washington to express his regrets and say that he himself was coming to New York to be present at the Waldorf Astoria Hotel dinner of the U.S.-French Society honoring the French President. That the President of the U.S. was obliged to apologize to his guest, the President of France, for the lack of manners and behavior of a small minority of Americans, constituted both a testimonial to Zionist power and also represented a damning example of the tragic Jewish dichotomy.

The indignation with which the presidents of American Jewish organizations received word of the cancellation of their New York meeting with President Pompidou can appropriately be described as "chutzpah," the Yiddish word for colossal gall. Weeks before the visit,

organized Jewry had gone into action. On January 28 a Jewish delegation visited New York's Mayor Lindsay to make certain there would be
no reception there for President Pompidou. A few days later plans
were advanced for picketing demonstrations in New York, Westchester
County, Chicago, and other cities on the Pompidou route. It was then
that certain congressmen, led by Israelists Bertram Podell and Lester
Wolff, both of New York, called for a boycott of the French President's
address to the Joint Session of Congress. A full-page advertisement
under the aegis of the American-Israel Public Affairs Committee,
which called for Phantoms for Israel to counterbalance Mirages for
Libya and was signed by 64 Senators and 243 Representatives, added
to the rising temperature.

The President of the Conference of Major Jewish Organizations,
Dr. William Wexler, responded to the Pompidou refusal to meet, in
this not-surprising, ever familiar vein: "The cancellation comes when
we have every right to be concerned with the safety of the State of
Israel. There was the holocaust. Six million Jewish men, women, and
children died."

The media headlines, if they were not so sad, further suggested
a comedy smash hit: "U.S. President Flies In; Wary Mayor Flies Out,"
and "Governor Goes Into Hiding." The *Times* photograph showed
screaming, youthful demonstrators, many recruited from Stern College of the Yeshiva University, waving Israeli flags and placards in
compliance with the Wexler theme, "Israel Must Live."[12] The same
newspaper had a full-length bannerhead, "Israelis Fascinated by
Demonstrations Against Pompidou But Deny Responsibility."

While Golda Meir was said to have been most pleased, it was the
Jewish leaders in Israel and in the U.S., rather than the Israeli government, who were directly responsible for this unsavory incident. For
decades Zionist leaders had been quietly spreading their philosophy,
and now they had persuaded their stateside followers to respond in the
correct manner to a conflict in loyalty. The abnormality that is Israel
had found its counterpart in Jewish-American reaction to this and to
every crisis involving the new state.

During the Pompidou visit the Zionists took out several full-page
ads in the *New York Times*—outrageous, screaming mouthings that led
former French Ambassador to London Ranier Massigli, in a letter to
Le Monde in Paris, to question the loyalty of Jews to France, inasmuch
as they had been behaving more like French Jews than Jewish French.

Another Israelist ad of March 1, 1970, screamed: "J'accuse." It
indicted the French President in terms parallel to those with which

Émile Zola in his historic letter had indicted France in the Dreyfus case for its "crime against humanity." President Pompidou was accused of selling out the French to Arab oil, of selling arms to Libya which he knew were destined to Egypt, of pretending to seek peace in the Middle East "while promoting war by upsetting the balance of power," and of "using Arab fanaticism against Israel to line your nation's pockets. . . . We accuse you of promoting the likelihood of war in an area that could spark a world holocaust."

At a press conference before leaving New York, Pompidou indicated that Israel could have the money back that had been advanced for the payment of the Mirages, still undelivered under the French boycott. Then, defensively, he added: "People can say what they like. I am not an anti-Semite"—an assertion that no President of France ought to have had to make, even if he had not in private life handled Jewish banking interests.

Upon his return to Paris, Pompidou found himself plagued by a remark attributed to him in his Chicago meeting with Jewish leaders to the effect that he thought Israel "must cease being a racial and religious state and must become simply a state among others." In reporting on the Cabinet meeting after the Pompidou statement, government spokesman Leo Hamon tried to draw back somewhat from what, in the words of the *Christian Science Monitor*, might possibly become "a rising problem with French citizens of Jewish descent." Public relations advisers to the President no doubt recalled the previous storm over de Gaulle's widely publicized reference to the Jewish people.

Even a Jewish head of government had not been safe from vituperative labeling at Zionist hands. In late September 1973, two Palestinians of a heretofore unknown guerrilla group calling themselves "Eagles of the Palestinian Revolution" seized three Russian Jews en route to Israel on the Moscow to Vienna train and at gunpoint held them, together with an Austrian customs guard, as hostages for thirteen hours at Vienna's Schwechat Airport. They demanded that the government close the Jewish Agency's transit camp facilities at Schönau Castle, once a royal Hapsburg hunting lodge just south of Vienna, where Jews arrived from the Soviet Union by plane and train en route to Israel. The Palestinians also demanded a plane to carry them to safety.

Austria's Chancellor Bruno Kreisky came to world attention when he defied the U.S., the Israeli government, and global pressure mounted by World Zionism and most reluctantly met the Palestinian demands, the price exacted for the lives of the four hostages. The

Eastern seaboard press accounts of the Kreisky Affair, redundant with the word "blackmail," spread worldwide hysteria. Typical was the statement of Jacob D. Stein, President of the Conference of Presidents of Major Jewish Organizations, on the second day of this Austrian crisis: "It is going to be very hard to accept the theory that Austria is closed to a single Jew without every Jew replying that it is closed to him."[13]

Although Vienna officials clearly indicated that the measures taken would not affect individual Jews passing through, only the group facilities in Vienna itself—and six months later it was revealed that actually more Jews had transited through Vienna than in the previous period—this did not stop Stein and Chairman of the National Conference on Soviet Jewry Richard Maas from sending a well-publized cable protesting the Austrian government's "refusal to grant entry to Israel-bound Jews," Added fuel to the fire was the reference by *New York Times* correspondent Terrence Smith to the Austrian cruelty to "tens of thousands of Jewish refugees from Eastern Europe and Russia."[14]

The Nixon administration, already under pressure from Capitol Hill's pro-Soviet Jewry block, made known its strong opposition to Austria's decision. Senator Jackson charged that Austria's action "represents the most serious and short-sighted submission to intimidation and blackmail." But Kreisky was not easily intimidated and resisted tremendous pressures and coercion, from abroad and home. Leaders of the opposition parties in the Austrian Parliament, even the small Freedom party with its many former Nazi members, denounced the Chancellor in a play for votes. He declared: "What we cannot accept is that Austria should become a secondary theater of the Middle East conflict with violence and confrontations of armed men from both sides. We shall maintain our humanitarian traditions." The Austrian leader issued this challenge to Washington:

Why doesn't the U.S. share the burden of assisting the Jewish émigrés? Why does not the U.S. operate an airlift? Instead of giving good advice, the U.S. might send ships to Odessa or some other Black Sea port and evacuate Jews from the Soviet Union. Ships could be sent to Leningrad. There are many possibilities.

The Chancellor firmly stood his ground and vehemently denied that Austrian borders had been closed to refugees: "This is simply untrue. All we want is for the emigrants to leave Austria as fast as possible—preferably the same day they arrive."[15]

Premier Golda Meir, always quick to recognize an opportunity to exploit an "affaire célèbre" to her own propaganda advantage, at first shrewdly only implored Vienna to keep the camp open and even praised Austria for her role in enabling Jews in the past to reach Israel. But later, in an address to 2,000 of Strasbourg's Jewish community, she charged that Austria had "betrayed her own greatness" by yielding to Arab terrorist demands, and alleged that "whoever accepts the conditions of terrorists only encourages them to pursue their criminal acts."

Meir flew to Vienna for a confrontation with the Chancellor, but came away a most disappointed woman. (The Viennese Police Code for the security during the Israeli leader's visit was "Schinkensemmel" —ham sandwich.) She stormed out of Kreisky's office, complaining, "He didn't even offer me a glass of water." Meir had made a tactical error in appealing to Kreisky, the humanist, on the grounds that he was a fellow Jew.

Chancellor Kreisky happens to be an agnostic. The Chancellor's wife is a Protestant and his two children were baptized into that faith; he resents references to himself as a Jew, preferring to be called "of Jewish origin." And he, above all, knows the meaning of the Nazi peril. Although from a wealthy family, he had joined the Socialist movement as a teenager, and after the Nazis had annexed his country, he fled to Sweden. It was thirteen years before he was permitted to return home to start his career as a diplomat, which led him to the Foreign Ministry and then to his country's highest post.

Kreisky's involvement with the Middle East hardly ended with the closing of the Schönau transit facilities. During the controversy the Israeli press had used statements of Kreisky's brother, an émigré in Israel, who had been mentally ill since his youth, to attack him. And thereafter the Israelis continued to hound him, trying to add to his embarrassment everywhere, notably at Socialist gatherings. Before leaving with members of a Socialist International delegation on a tour of the Middle East early in 1974, the Chancellor was forced to explain in an interview with the Israeli newspaper *Ma'ariv* (January 20, 1974) why they were going only to the Arab countries and not to Israel:

Because of close relations with the Israeli Labor party, we know how the solution of the problem is seen in Israel. We've heard and heard again the opinion of Golda Meir, but on the other hand, the International has no connections with the states or parties in Arab countries. Therefore, a time came at last to see the problem through the Arab eyes so that the International could arrive at a balanced position. Of course, before our eyes there will always be an approach of solidarity with a member party, the Israeli Labor party.

Further in the interview, Kreisky went out of his way to declare he did not recognize *a Jewish nationality*. He argued: "There is no Jewish race; there are only Jewish religious groups. Israel was only the ancient, religious fatherland of Jews, but not their true fatherland." Israel's Chief Rabbi Goren assailed the Austrian: "Kreisky can do what he wants, he was and will always remain a Jew." The Austrian Chancellor's reaction: "In this, Rabbi Goren does in his own way what Hitler did."

But of far greater concern to the watchdogs of Israel in the U.S. than the attitude of the French Presidents and Austrian Chancellor was the outlook of opinion molders who commanded large followings. Those iconoclasts among the clergy and media who dared direct attention to another side of the Middle East conflict soon found themselves literally under siege.

One such victim was Francis B. Sayre, Jr., Dean of the Washington Cathedral, who in his 1972 Palm Sunday sermon suggested that the "once-oppressed Israelis have become the oppressors of Jerusalem." In emphasizing his conviction that contemporary events in the Holy City were simply one of the many examples of the moral tragedy of mankind, the Cathedral dean exclaimed: "What a mirror, then, is modern Israel of that total flaw in the human breast that forever leaps to the acclaim of God only to turn the next instant to the suborning of his will for us."

Sayre asserted that Arab residents were deported, deprived unjustly of their land, and forbidden to bring their relatives to settle in Jerusalem. Arabs, he added, "have neither voice nor happiness in the city that is the capital of their religious devotion, too." To support his views, the Dean quoted from the writings in *Christianity and Crisis* of Israeli League for Human Rights Chairman, Dr. Israel Shahak.

Sayre's brief fifteen-minute sermon caused an uproar in the nation's capital when the *Washington Post* stirred up the opposition through a bitter editorial and the publication of vindictive letters. This journalistic citadel of Zionism (second only to the *New York Times*) carved two sentences out of context to build an alleged picture of bigotry: "Now the Jews have it [Jerusalem] all. But even as they praise their God for the smile of fortune, they begin almost simultaneously to put Him to death." For this, ADL cultists Forster and Epstein accused Sayre of repeating the central theme of anti-Semitism—that the Jews collectively were guilty of having killed Jesus. In the three previous sentences the Washington theologian had expressed "sympathy with the loving hope of that little state [Israel] which aspires to be the embodiment of a holy peoplehood . . . to achieve a government there is to realize the restoration of a scattered remnant; it is the fulfillment of cherished prayer, tempered in suffering. . . ."

Still seeking to bring about the removal of Sayre from his post at the Cathedral, or to force him to recant, Forster and Epstein further assailed the Washington clergyman in *The New Anti-Semitism* because he dared later to say at a memorial service in the National Cathedral that he was mourning not only the innocent Israeli athletes slain at Munich "by murderous guerrillas and ruthless revolutionaries, but also those additional victims of violence in Munich: those villagers in Lebanon and Syria whose lives have been extinguished by the Israeli Air Force even as the Twentieth Olympiad yet endures."

Praise of the Sayre sermon by Gerald L. K. Smith, widely reputed to be an anti-Semite, was adduced by the ADL as proof that the clergyman was himself a bigot.

It was slightly ironic, indeed, that Sayre should have given the eulogy at the memorial service in Washington for President Harry S. Truman three months earlier and that he should have been widely quoted for noting, "There were no wrinkles in his honesty." Sayre was the grandson of Woodrow Wilson, President at the time of the Balfour Declaration, which gave the Zionists their first foothold in Palestine. And it was President Truman without whose invaluable assistance the State of Israel would never have come into being.

One of Sayre's defenders at a Washington press conference called to counteract the charges leveled against the churchman was the Reverend A. C. Forrest, editor of the *United Church Observer,* which boasts of being the most widely read Church paper (800,000 readers) in the British Commonwealth. When the *Observer* published a special report on the Palestinian Arab refugees in the wake of the 1967 six-day war, Forrest became a victim of a campaign of hate speeches and concerted personal attacks launched by the ADL and carried out by the plethora of Canadian Zionist-oriented organizations. As Forrest explained it, "My sin was and is that I am critical of Israel's policies since the war in June. My conviction is that the pathetic refugees should be permitted to return to their homes as Israel promised last July 2 they would do . . . I said, and still say, that Israel stands condemned before world opinion."

"Monstrous allegations" and "falsehood" thundered Canadian Zionists. A Toronto rabbi repeated the falsehood that the *Observer* editor had said that "he hates Israel." Out of a sense of fairness, the *Observer,* printed a long blast by leading Rabbi W. Gunther Plaut, widely reprinted in the Zionist press. But when it refused to publish a 3,500-word diatribe by Israel Ambassador Gershon Avner, Canadian air again reverberated with cries of "anti-Semitism" against Forrest. A Zionist leader warned "we have a file on you, and it goes back twenty years." (Later, there was an apology. It seems they were talking about a previous editor, who had written critically of Israel in 1948.)

Avid Zionist Professor Emil Fackenheim of the University of Toronto demanded that Forrest be removed from the chairmanship of a teaching panel. To this the besieged editor charitably noted: "Maybe if I had gone through what Rabbi Fackenheim had in Germany, I would be a bit more irrational, too."

Hostile-looking individuals started showing up at churches and meetings when the editor spoke. They took notes. They did not hang around to shake hands. And they were not from the *Globe and Mail.* The *Globe* quoted an officer of the Jewish Congress calling Forrest "a dupe of Communist and Arab propaganda." When the *Observer* editor was not labeled anti-Semitic, he was accused of using anti-Semitic sources and thereby creating anti-Semitism. Dates for his speaking engagements were changed, if not canceled. And the Zionists left no stone unturned in their efforts to have Forrest removed from his post or, at the least, censored in his writings.

When the intrepid Canadian churchman carried the Palestinian plight to the public in 1971 through a moving book, *The Unholy Land,* readers in Canada flatly rejected a blatant attempt at censorship. Coles Bookstores, one of the largest booksellers in Canada with more than thirty outlets, suddenly cleared their shelves of the book, which was not only critical of Israel' policy vis-à-vis the Palestinian refugees but also linked the Zionist state to South Africa and Rhodesia in the "practice of apartheid." Alert public relations strategy by McClelland and Stewart Ltd., the publishers of the Forrest book, brought this attempt at book burning to the attention of the book and news editor of the Canadian press. The reaction was instantaneous. People who never heard of the book became curious. Columnists wrote that the book removal "lent color to the Forrest claim that there is a pattern in Canada of suppressing criticism of Israel." In Toronto Buckley's bookstore advertised the book by saying: "We do not suppress books however truthful they may be."

The ban led to a stormy debate in newspapers, on radio, and on television. Even as the *Canadian Jewish News* tried to quell rising interest by calling the book "political pornography" and "trash," sales mounted; the controversy pushed the book onto the bestseller list.

While the General Council of the United Church of Canada voted nearly 100 percent support of the editor of their church paper, and accorded him a standing ovation at a Toronto Dominion-wide meeting in late 1972, the persistent assault against Forrest continued. In the latest Forster and Epstein book, Forrest was described as "Canada's most notorious and perhaps most denominationally protected Christian anti-Semite." Harassment continued as a libel action was brought against Forrest and the United Church for the publication in 1972 of two controversial articles, based on sermons, by well-known Unitarian anti-Zionist minister Dr. John Nicholls Booth.

In the name of reopening dialogue with the Jewish community, Church Moderator Dr. Bruce McLeod and Secretary Rev. George Morrison jointly declared with officers of the B'nai B'rith "that we regret and disavow the insensitivity and inaccuracies contained in the article."

Forrest had repeatedly asked for proof of the alleged libelous inaccuracies, which he offered to publish. Instead, a sea of pressures —financial, political, economic, social, and otherwise, as noted in an editorial[16] by the *Canadian Churchman* (a rival journal whose circulation is second only to that of the *Observer* in Canada)—were brought to bear on his Church leaders who yielded.

The *Churchman* editorial noted how "relentless the Jewish community, especially the B'nai B'rith, can be to anyone who has the temerity to question the policies of the State of Israel."

The editorial continued: "If the Church is to enter the field of journalism, it should adopt the highest journalistic ideals rather than the bastardized journalism (public relations) that may be appropriate or inevitable in other institutions." In noting the shift in heart of the leadership, which had earlier supported Forrest but had yielded then in the name of ecumenism, the *Churchman* declared:

But what price reconciliation? The Church needs a free press, a society needs a free press, to hold before its readers a true picture of the institution. It can serve only if it is unfettered, honest and responsible. When church leaders, no matter how well motivated, diminish that freedom, we believe they diminish the freedom of Christian people to know what is being done, said and thought.[17]

This Canadian affair was closely linked to unprecedented suppression of freedom of speech in the famed Community Church pulpit in New York City, where John Haynes Holmes had once preached his renowned Voltairian liberalism. In the spring of 1971 Rev. Donald S.

Harrington, Pastor of the church, invited Dr. Booth to come East and deliver five Sunday sermons in his place during a leave of absence. The Unitarian minister, who was retiring after lengthy service at his Long Beach, California, parish, had long ago awakened the ire of the ADL through his articles in the *Observer* and in *Middle East Perspective*, including, "The Dubious Ethics of B'nai B'rith."

In his initial sermon on May 2, Wesak Sunday (honoring Buddha's birth), Booth spoke of the revulsion of Gandhi and Buddha toward warfare, violence, and armament profiteering. He described at length the U.S. as the "number-one merchant of death," naming the ten American firms that are allegedly the foremost dollar earners from this trade. No one protested this portion of the sermon, which as customary was carried on the *New York Times'* radio station, WQXR. But the eighty seconds that followed shook New York City. The station was bombarded with calls, and the church received two threats of bombing because the California Unitarian had stated that "according to a radio-cast of the previous week on KFWB, the Los Angeles Westinghouse outlet, Israel's number-one way of earning dollars was through the manufacture and export of weapons, munitions, explosives, helmets, and military uniforms."

Business Week in April had reported that Israel Aviation industries ($100 million in sales 1970) was seeking aerospace experts for its manufacturing products, including guided missiles and warplane parts. And *Newsweek* had announced that Israel was going into production with forty-ton tanks, having already manufactured 105-mm guns, not to mention the heavily exported UZI 4 and napalm widely used in the six-day war. (By 1977 U.S. officials were "expressing deep concern" over the export of Israeli armaments.[18])

What burned the Christian and Jewish Zionists most was the Booth lamentation that "it was the ultimate in desecration for present-day stewards of the Holy Land, of the Prince of Peace, of the manger and the cross, to be manufacturing and selling to other nations the instruments for killing." A large number of Unitarians are Jewish, and many of these that Sunday verbally abused Booth following the sermon.

The crisis in the church forced Harrington to fly back to New York from Chicago. Booth was asked to apologize "for his broadcast lies" to the *New York Times.* The church officially invited the Consul General of Israel in New York and the Zionist organization to send a representative to share the May 16 sermon and to broadcast with Booth. This offer was declined. The church then banned any further reference to the Middle East conflict in any of the Unitarian minister's scheduled sermons. The trustees' "Talk Back" session at the church had voted to distribute to all parishioners an explanatory statement of Booth's position as well as his reply to personal slander. But the prepared document was buried, despite the congregation's vote, so as "to prevent more trouble," according to the explanation of the church's Board Chairman. It was never pointed out that Harrington was Chairman of the heavily Jewish-dominated Liberal party in New York State; that Metropolitan Synagogue, which used the church facilities as guests, paid an annual "honorarium" of $7,000; or that Harrington had been honored with a B'nai B'rith plaque for a penultimate presabbatical sermon titled "The Miracle of Israel."

On June 21 ADL's Arnold Forster was given twenty minutes on WQXR's "Point of View" to answer the eighty-second "attack" after the *Times* had rejected the publication of a letter from Booth explaining the incident in full. Forster used this opportunity to engage in a diatribe directed against everything Booth had written or said regarding Israel, taking particular exception to the "frightful picture" conjured up by Booth in his words "Napalm from Nazareth" and "Bombs from Bethlehem." Harrington had justified censorship in his church on the grounds that these malicious phrases were "equivalent to Christian anti-Semitism."

Meanwhile, the Unitarian Church in Gainesville, Florida, which had all but reached an agreement to make Booth their new minister, was visited by an ADL representative who leveled charges of anti-Semitism against him, provided the trustees with a copy of the B'nai B'rith article, and declared that eleven Unitarian/Universalist clergymen had signed an anti-Booth protest. Booth forthrightly flew to Florida and faced his critics, pointing out that free speech was being curtailed in the guise of suppressing anti-Semitism. Despite the ADL pressure, the Florida church by a 72 percent vote designated Booth as interim minister starting September 1.

But this did not halt ADL efforts against Booth. A memo had been sent from the national offices to its representatives across the country "to alert you to possible forthcoming appearances by Dr. Booth in your area. If, indeed, he does appear, I suggest you contact friendly Christian clergy to inform them that Booth is vehemently anti-Israel and anti-Zionist, whose diatribes border on anti-Semitism. . . . We are attempting to ascertain Booth's traveling and speaking schedule. Any information about him that comes to your attention should be sent to me, quickly." (Shades of the Gestapo and the SS!)

Only after a six-week campaign of letters and phone calls from the West Coast and New York did station WQXR finally agree to permit a four-minute taped reply to the Forster attack, which Booth ended with these words:

We want peace, peace with justice for all. But it must be achieved not in terms of being pro-Arab or pro-Israel, but pro-humanity. And it will not be secured by name calling and fabrications, may I remind the Anti-Defamation League of B'nai B'rith.

Walter Neiman, Vice President and General Manager of the station, wrote Booth to ask permission to delete from the tape the words "fabrications," "character assassination," and "destroy people's character." This request was made upon advice of the station's same counsel, who without any hesitation had previously permitted ADL's Forster to smear Booth, to play down the facts about the Israeli defense industry, and to otherwise propagandize for Israel. To end the controversies, Booth had graciously consented to the deletion, although protesting the censorship. But the *New York Times* subsidiary never satisfactorily answered his query as to why the ADL had been given time to talk about articles, sermons, and matters neither germane to the original eighty-second reference to Israel nor ever heard by the listeners of station WQXR.

Booth, who had once been a journalist and whose stirring sermons and writings, including the classic *Introducing Unitarianism*, had won him wide acclaim, explained how he had become involved in the Arab-Israeli conflict:[19]

When I preached a single sermon in 1967 entitled *The Moral Case for the Arabs*, I did not realize that a turning point in my life would occur. Anyone familiar with my ministry in the metropolitan Chicago, Boston and Los Angeles areas can rattle off the issues that I have staunchly faced in pulpit and press: abortion, race, Vietnam, censorship, conservation, over-population, war, munitions manufacturing . . . and the rest.

The headaches resulting from these latter controversies paralleled those of liberal colleagues who have been unafraid to tackle prophetic issues. An occasional parishioner became inactive or resigned; some persons in the community viewed me as a "communist," a destroyer of social safeguards, or one who ought to stick to the Bible.

The reaction to the Middle Eastern sermon staggered my understanding. I learned the meaning of being defamed, isolated, threatened, and facing professional ruin for having taken a forthright stand. And it mattered little that my entire life has been fighting on many fronts for the underdog, human rights and international justice.

Rabbinical friends abruptly became abusive beyond belief. Had their reaction been framed in courteous but firm analyses of areas of disagreement, it would have been understandable and proper. But name calling, accusations of prejudice, ignorance or Hitlerism larded their letters and phone calls. . . .

A brief letter published in the *Los Angeles Times* (1/4/69), scoring our government for selling fifty jet fighters to Israel, kept my phone ringing every fifteen minutes, night and day, for about fifty-six hours. Obscenity and vilification flowed over the line. Letters and telegrams called me a "fucking bastard," "a paid agent of the anti-Semite groups," and one for whom "a gas oven would be too good."

As the months passed, our home in Southern California was splattered with rotten eggs; during a service in the First Unitarian Church of Los Angeles, while I was preaching on *American Freedom and Zionist Power,* security men were stationed in the sanctuary for my protection. I was warned that my ministerial career would fade away or be abruptly terminated. Clergymen with an idealistic view of Zionism are shocked to learn that we are not necessarily dealing with altruistic humanitarians or respecters of democratic freedoms.

Booth still bears the scars of the traumatic experience of having Rabbi Elisha Nattiv of Temple Shalom, West Covina, California, march down the aisle of the Covina Church at the conclusion of the sermon on the Middle East conflict and, after an hysterical harangue, raise his arm, point to the pulpit, and cry out: "I am going to run him out of here."

Because a clergyman's sermons are in the public domain, Booth found that his pulpit remarks directed against Zionism, particularly one on the B'nai B'rith exposing the Zionist apparatus, were picked up without his permission and reprinted by extreme right-wing, if not anti-Semitic groups. For this the California clergyman was further assailed and labeled. But it was his article in Forrest's United Church *Observer* that subjected both that editor and himself to further harassment and character assassination. Instead of trying to refute the facts, a gaggle of professors, rabbis, and editors employed vivid and personal invective against Forrest and Booth, invoking guilt by association through the appearance of the latter's heavily documented sermon in Gerald L. K. Smith's *The Cross and the Flag.*

In a widely reported speech,[20] Booth was torn apart by Catholic Father Gregory Baum, teacher of theology at the University of Toronto and a convert from Judaism, for having quoted Jean Paul Sartre in his *Observer* piece to support "the idea that Jews must invent anti-Semitism as a myth for their survival." The article actually had read: "Sartre regards some *threat of anti-Semitism* as essential to *hold Jews together.* " [Italics added.] Numerous groups in history have required an outside threat to bring about unity, and Booth had noted a common, unethical Zionist defensive strategy: "If there is no actual anti-Semitism present, then it [meaning the claim that is present] must be created. The fact that it is a falsehood and a reputation may be damaged seemingly offends few consciences." The Booth article set forth varied devastating examples of this, and the Toronto reaction provided additional substantiation of his thesis.

Ominously, stringent censorship over dissent in pulpit and press emerged as the ultimate goal of Canadian Zionists. In an acceptance address for an honorary degree from St. Andrew's College, a United Church institution in Saskatoon, Dr. Fackenheim slashed out at the host's denomination, its magazine, the editor, and this writer, and added to the astonishment of his listeners: "Merely to call the Jewish state into question is implicitly to condone the continuation of the unholy combination of anti-Jewish ideology with Jewish powerlessness. . . ."

In the Toronto *Globe and Mail* May 4, 1972, the Zionist leader disclosed his true motivation to smother a free press: "True reconciliation can come for the Jewish community and the United Church of Canada only when the church acts so as to place all anti-Jewish bias, however shabbily disguised as 'anti-Zionism' or 'concern for Arab refugees,' *firmly beyond the bounds of editorial freedom."* [Italics added.] A more total suppression of the communications media, ban on discussion of a critical subject, or disregard for the plight of refugees can hardly be imagined. Fackenheim, ironically enough, is himself a refugee from Germany.

The trials and tribulations of John Nichols Booth were heightened by an early 1973 incident that rocked the Detroit area. *South End,* the Wayne State University campus paper, reprinted in installments running from January 10 to 12 a sermon that had been delivered by Booth at the First Unitarian Church the previous November. But the articles appeared under a superimposed drawing of a swastika inside a Jewish Star of David. The articles, thus unfortunately emblemed, roused to fury the Jewish community, which otherwise probably would have paid scant attention to the ordinary writings of a well-known anti-Zionist.

College President George E. Gullen, Jr., issued a blistering statement declaring the articles "an affront to the Jewish community and an embarrassment to the University." The campus paper was supported by university funds, and it was a little ironic to hear Zionist voices raised in protest against the "misuse of government tax-free dollars." The *Detroit Free Press* had a full banner headline "WSU Head

Assails School Paper for Insulting Jews."

The *South End* editors apologized for the illustration and admitted that "the Middle East was not an issue we want to live or die for"; they merely had wished to attract attention to a different viewpoint on the Middle East. Such attention-getting tactics (also unfortunately occasionally used by the Palestinians to their grave detriment) played right into the hands of the Zionists and further victimized Booth.

Although still being subjected to an organized and thorough "tailing," Booth undauntingly sought to bring the facts to "the undecided, confused or perhaps not-yet concerned 80 percent of the American people." But he soon learned that even his own liberal Unitarian Church was no longer free. *The Journal of the Liberal Ministry,* the official organ of the Unitarian/Universalist Ministers Association, flatly rejected an article from him after they had requested contributions to a special issue on "freedom of the pulpit." In returning the piece, the editor frankly stated the reason:

We would like to publish your views on this very important topic, but frankly, after some lengthy study and thought about your article, I have concluded that it would not be to our advantage to publish material which arouses dissension among members of the association, not on matters of principle, but on ways of assuring that principles are implimented.

Apparently this was a religious editor who had little respect for Winston Churchill's observation that "it is the church's duty to lash the conscience of a guilty age"—particularly where the sensitive issue of Israel and Zionism is involved.

Another clergyman who felt the brunt of the blitz was the Catholic priest Father Daniel J. Berrigan. Ironically, he had been the idol of the liberals and radicals, including a number of Jews, for some years due to his courageous stand on the Vietnam war. But then he made the mistake of also speaking out against what he felt were wrongs in the Middle East. Admittedly, Berrigan used some strong words in his speech at the Arab American University Graduates Convention in Washington, D.C.:

It is a tragedy that in place of Jewish prophetic wisdom, Israel should launch an Orwellian nightmare of double talk, racism, fifth-rate sociological jargon aimed at proving its racial superiority to the people it has crushed. . . . The dream of Israel has become a nightmare. Israel has not abolished poverty and misery; rather, she manufactures human waste, the byproducts of her entrepreneurs, the military-industrial complex. . . . Israel has not freed the captives, she has expanded the prison system, perfected her espionage, exported on the world market that expensive, blood-ridden commodity, the savage triumph of the technologized West: violence and the tools of violence.[21]

Not words to everyone's taste or opinion, but certainly within the limits of free speech and open debate in this country. Far harsher things were said by Berrigan about his own nation during the Vietnam war years, and still far harsher things have been said by the Israelists about the Palestinians and Arabs. But the storm that broke around Berrigan was scarcely believable. His previous forthrightness and courage were totally forgotten by his liberal friends as he came in for the full repression treatment. For instance, he had been slated to receive the Gandhi Peace Award for his antiwar activities from a New Haven group. The presentation was to have been made by Rev. Harrington on January 9, 1974, but was canceled. Harrington assailed Berrigan for "aggravating Israeli fears and Arab intransigence at a time when the only hope for peace is to calm Israeli fears and to reduce Arab intransigence." (If ever a statement revealed how biased the anti-anti-Semitism cultist can become, it was this declamation, implying that Israel alone is justified in having fears and the Arabs are the only intransigent force in the Middle East.)

In a critical article in the *Times,* reporter Irving Spiegel brought to light an attack in the liberal Catholic periodical *Commonweal,* in which Michael Novak stated that Berrigan's charges "are as ominous as any tone the human voice can utter."[22] While the two attacks on Berrigan were prominently displayed up front in the *Times,* Berrigan's rejection of the award in a letter to Harrington as "a degrading consensus game" was buried away at the bottom of page 26. When the office of *Middle East Perspective* phoned the *Times* to give a wrap-up statement on the affair, attacking the cult, Spiegel, thinking that this was to be another anti-Berrigan attack, informed the caller: "Sorry, *I* can't give any more attention to that. We *have fanned that fire* as much as we can."

The power of the cult was amply demonstrated by the lengths to which syndicated columnist Peter Hamill was forced to go to disprove that he was not anti-Semitic. It is paradoxical when a "liberal" like Hamill, who only rarely deviates from the Israelist line and has never been reticent in pinning the heinous label on the Arabs, is forced to defend himself against charges of anti-Semitism. This occurred at the hands of defenders of the wretched Bernard Bergman, the ordained rabbi who had grossly exploited the aged and poor residenced in his nursing homes and was ultimately convicted for his crime.[23]

Outraged and incensed when he himself became victimized by the label callers, Hamill wrote a lengthy piece for the *Village Voice*. Both to disprove the charges, as well as to retain membership in the "club," Hamill cried out: "I am no anti-Semite, but I know one when I see one," promptly pointing his finger at the controversial Chairman of the Joint Chiefs of Staff, General George S. Brown, who had recently become the cult's latest victim.

Five weeks[24] after Brown had delivered a lecture at Duke University Law School, not one line of which was reported anywhere in the press save in the North Carolina *Anvil,* a so-called "alternative" newspaper published in Durham, a totally out-of-context parenthetical remark, made at the end of a lengthy question-and-answer period, was manipulated onto the front pages by the *Washington Post* on November 13, 1974, and built up the next day by the ever-compliant media into a national scandal. Senator William Proxmire called for Brown's resignation; Senator Jacob Javits demanded an investigation; the Jewish War Veterans insisted on an apology. In a telegram to President Ford, the President of the American Jewish Congress, Rabbi Arthur Hertzberg, stated that the General's remarks demonstrated "a degree of ignorance and susceptibility to classic anti-Semitic propaganda that cast grave doubts on his ability to serve in his presently critically important position."

Demagoguery raised its ugly head in the Congress. New York's Bella Abzug screamed: "General Brown's remarks are the kind that one would expect from a Nazi general, not from the Chairman of the Joint Chiefs of Staff." Her fellow congressman from New York, Edward I. Koch (now Mayor of New York), called the Brown words "reminiscent of . . . Charles Lindbergh, who, when leading the America First rally in New York in support of Nazi Germany, talked of Jewish money and power."

In answering the question of one student concerning whether the U.S. was contemplating force against oil-producing nations, the Joint Chiefs Chairman had replied:

I don't know. I hope not. We have no plans to. It is conceivable, I guess, it's kind of almost as bad as the "Seven Days in May" thing, but you can conjure up a situation which there is another oil-embargo and people in this country are not only inconvenienced and uncomfortable, but suffer, and they get tough-minded enough to set down the Jewish influence in this country.

It is so strong, you wouldn't believe it. We have the Israelis coming to us for equipment. We say we can't possibly get the Congress to support a program like that. They say, "Don't worry about the Congress. We'll take care of the Congress."

Now this is somebody from another country, but they can do it. They own, you know, the banks in this country, the newspapers. You just look at where the Jewish money is in this country.

Had the General's ill-considered remarks been said of some other ethnic or religious minority, they would have passed without an enormous hue and cry. But the Zionist cultists of anti-anti-Semitism desperately needed to detract attention from the U.N. appearance of Palestine Liberation Organization chieftain Yasir Arafat and the overwhelming 89–8 vote in the General Assembly declaring that the Palestinian people have both a right to nationhood and a right to return to "their homes and property."

Taken out of context and by itself, Brown's remarks may have smacked of "hoary anti-Semitism," as one writer claimed. But Peter J. Kahn, Chairman of the Duke University group that had invited the General to speak, and who is a Jew himself, said, "From the tenor of his remarks during the speech and the rest of the question-and-answer session, as well as statements throughout the course of his visit here, there is absolutely no indication that General Brown in any way holds anti-Semitic views."

Cultists everywhere gladly added to the distortion by embroidering on the story. Hamill had Brown saying that "Americans would be not only inconvenienced and uncomfortable, but suffer *unless* they get tough-minded enough to set down the Jewish influence in this country." This conveyed a totally different meaning from what the General had said.

As Air Force Chief of Staff, Brown had been in charge of the 1973 U.S. airlift that helped stave off military defeat for the Israelis. Consequently, he was only too familiar with the tremendous, unbelievable pressures then exerted by the Israelis directly on the White House, the State Department, and the Pentagon to speed this airlift, even as U.S. military strength was denuded. This was minutely described in the celebrated Marvin and Bernard Kalb biography of Kissinger.[25]

By latching onto Brown's gratuitous misstatement regarding the Jewish ownership of the banks and the newspapers—ill-advised but in no way anti-Semitic—the ADL, the politicians, Hamill, et al., hoped to divert public attention from the real thrust behind the Chief of Staff's remarks: the unabating pressure on Washington to continue to give away to a foreign country scarce American military equipment paid for by U.S. taxpayers for the defense of their own country. As Evans and Novak stated it, "quite apart from the General's inexcusable rhetoric, the Pentagon views the Middle East in terms of long-range U.S. strategic interests, a view that does not always parallel those of Israel."

It was on the very day of the bitter confrontation at the U.N. between the PLO and Israel that the media blew up this out-of-context parenthetical remark by Brown. The Zionist press had a field day for weeks with the Brown affair. James Wechsler in the *New York Post* assailed President Ford for dismissing this "anti-Semitic tirade" as "one unfortunate mistake" and administering only a mild reprimand. Calling the Brown performance "a crime and a blunder," the New York editor-columnist maintained that dismissal or resignation should have been meted out for this act of "military demagogy," all the more necessary because of the "many hidden currents of prejudice in the military."[26] And his fellow *Post* columnist, the last authority on all "liberal" subjects, Harriet Van Horne, used the uproar to take off on the military, whose "warped philosophy" is part of "an entrenched system that is doing the country no good."

A lengthy article by the *Washington Post*'s deputy editorial page editor, Meg Greenfield, "Jewish Control of the Banks is about as *Real* as Jewish Control of the Archdiocese," adroitly twisted around a few words and grossly distorted what the General had said: "[there was] need to get tough-minded with the Jews who own the banks, you know." Without a shred of evidence, she then denied the influence of an Israel lobby.

As their answer to the charge of Jewish press control, the real point behind the Brown allegation of ownership, Hamill, *Time*, Greenfield, and other cultists noted that "in 1972 of 1,748 newspapers, only 3.1 percent were owned by Jews." These ownership figures tell nothing, whatsoever, of course, about the control exercised by a large number of strategically placed Jews.

Even President Ford's rebuke of General Brown's gaffe did not halt the continuing furor, although Senator Fulbright's kindred thoughts on November 2 at Westminster College in Fulton, Missouri, where Churchill had made his famed "iron curtain" address, had drawn sketchy coverage and minor condemnation. The Arkansas Senator charged in his address, "The Clear and Present Danger," that "the majority of officeholders in the U.S." had fallen under "Israeli domination" and commented:

Neither the Israelis nor their uncritical supporters in our Congress and in our media have appreciated what is at stake in the enormous distortion of American interests in our Mideast course. Endlessly pressing the United States for money and arms—and invariably getting all and more than she asks—Israel makes bad use of a good friend. We and we alone have made it possible for Israel to exist as a state. Surely it is not too much to ask in return that Israel give up East Jerusalem and the West Bank as the necessary means of breaking a chain of events which threatens us all with ruin.[27]

But Senator Fulbright already had paid the price for his "Face the Nation" charge that the Israelis control the policy in the Congress. He had been "taken care of" in the Democratic primary by Zionist candidate Governor Dale Bumpers, while Brown was still at his desk in the Pentagon.

Two weeks before Election Day 1976, the Chairman of the Joint Chiefs of Staff was under attack again. In an interview with Israeli-born *Newsweek* journalist and cartoonist Ranan Lurie (who had served in the Israeli army), Brown had suggested that from the "pure military point of view to the United States, Israel has just got to be considered a burden."[28] As the release of the previous controversial statement had been delayed for the appropriate timing, so this new Brown gaffe was released six months after the April 12 interview and right in the midst of the presidential campaign. Aimed obviously at embarrassing President Ford—and possibly at forcing the dismissal of the General—the statement galvanized a call for Brown's resignation from every piddling Democrat—and many Republicans, too—pandering the Jewish vote. Democratic Vice Presidential nominee Walter Mondale declared the Brown statement a "vicious attack on American Jews," and he said people like the General "should not be sewage commissioners." President Ford indicated that he did not agree with his top general's "poor choice of words," but admitted that Israel had been a liability at the time of the 1973 war because of the drain the airlift caused to our military supplies, but that "her situation had since changed."

Ironically, despite the public uproar which Jewish organizations had inspired, American Jewish Committee Washington lobbyist Hyman Bookbinder is said to have admitted privately that General Brown was "an intelligent, thoughtful, civil guy who helped save Israel in 1973 by running down U.S. Air Force stocks in Germany. If he can be provoked into saying things like that, we have reason to be worried . . . We should not overreact. Getting his scalp would give credence to his charges."[29] Israel's Premier Yitzhak Rabin took a similar line, telling a December 5, 1974 Tel Aviv audience that General Brown "probably helped Israel during the last war more than anyone else did."[30]

The Zionist blitz has even attempted to impose rigid censorship over full-time working journalists. Nationally syndicated columnists Evans and Novak earned a place of honor for themselves in the Forster-Epstein epic merely by reporting that leaders of the powerful American Jewish community were annoyed with Israel over the 1973 Lebanese plane incident (Israel had intercepted a Lebanese plane and then forced it to land in Israel), which ought to be "an ominous warning to the country which controls by far the most powerful military might anywhere in the Arab Middle East." Further "anti-Semitism" was depicted in the columnists' caution against "the explosive ingredient in Israel's seeming contempt for the opinion of major U.S. allies, particularly in Western Europe, and for the U.S. itself" and for their mention of Israeli plans "to build a city for 50,000 on the Israeli-occupied (but Syrian) Golan Heights and an urban center in Israeli-occupied (but Egyptian) northern Sinai." Nothing untrue, nothing libelous, nothing bigoted, but nevertheless set forth in the ADL book annotating examples of alleged anti-Semitism.

That was in 1974, and Evans and Novak were kept under close surveillance. Indeed, they came under such continued fire for some of their independent views that by January 1975 the columnists felt compelled to devote an entire column to a defense against the *Near East Report* charge that their column "had an anti-Israel bias":

Our consistent thesis is that U.S. policy in the Arab-Israel conflict must be determined by *American* interests, not those of Israel or of the Arab States surrounding it. Our reporting on the Middle East has always sought to disentangle real American interests from claims and counterclaims of both Israel and the Arabs—making us neither pro-Israel nor anti-Israel, neither pro-Arab nor anti-Arab.[31]

Again, *Near East Report* put the finger on a correspondent. In its account of the General Brown affair, veteran CBS commentator Eric Severeid had been praised for his customary "felicity, polish, and perception," but he had apparently betrayed his trust by concluding a discussion of the remarks of the Joint Chiefs Chairman with this observation: "A growing number of American Jews are . . . torn in a soul-searching internal debate as to just where their loyalties should lie and how far they should go in honoring them."

Overnight Eric Severeid became a member of that very exclusive club made up of those vilified by the Zionists and stigmatized as anti-Semites. How the Jewish Establishment could turn on a friend and strike with the deadliness of an asp unless he crossed each "*t*" and dotted every "*i*" in accordance with their personal predilections must have been a bitter lesson to the veteran newscaster.

His younger and far more conservative colleague in CBS, Jeffrey St. John, was probably less stunned when he ran aground on the same ADL shoals, likewise for treading, among other things, on the verboten subject of dual loyalties. On the radio network program "Spectrum" St. John had this to say:

The reason, it seems to me, that we don't have an ongoing debate in this country as to whether we have been paying a high price to guarantee Israeli security, is that American public opinion is shaped largely by a pro-Israeli viewpoint. And whenever someone suggests we should begin changing our policy, as an American oil company executive did recently, *the pro-Israeli propaganda machine in America crucifies him in public.* [Italics added.] What this lop-sided state of affairs suggests is an insecurity on the part of many American Jews to thrash out in the open the issue of Arab oil and U.S. support of Israel. In fact, ever since the founding of the State of Israel, the Arabs have had precious little opportunity to present their point of view in this country.

Emotions, not reason, govern our policy toward Israel. This emotion translates itself into political support from American Jews. But I suggest that the Arab oil vs. Israel debate raises a touchy issue that American Jews don't like to talk about, especially those Jews who are devoted Zionists and support the State of Israel. *The issue is whether you are an American first and a Jew second and if forced to choose, which commands your loyalty first.* The Arab oil vs. U.S. support of Israel may be the first of many hard questions American Jews must face.[32] [Italics added.]

Cultists Forster and Epstein responded with this scarcely believable comment in their tome: "St. John's use of the word *crucified* in relation to the 'pro-Israeli propaganda machine' was a clear appeal to the hardiest of the roots of anti-Semitism. His raising of the dual-loyalty canard was in much the same category. . . ."[33] But commentator St. John added insult to injury for later stating that U.S. Middle East policy "has been and continues to be shaped in large measure by the financial and political power of American Jewry." It was shortly thereafter that CBS dropped him from this network show.

There are many others in recent years whose careers or personal lives have been subjected to the Zionist blitz. Parliamentarian Margaret McKay, who represented the constituency of Clapham and had been Britain's delegate to the U.N. Commission on the Status of Women, expressed a deep sympathy for the sufferings of the Palestinian Arabs in speeches on the floor of the House of Commons and outside. In answer to letters in London's *Evening Standard* from persons antipathetic to her views, McKay detailed the reaction to her viewpoint:

In consequence, I am being subjected to extreme pressures. I am enduring unpleasant telephone calls; receiving obscene letters (some containing excreta); I am attacked in the press; similar letters have been sent to the union which sponsors my Parliamentary candidature. I have had a death threat letter. My secretary has been physically pushed around. The police and other services have been sent on hoax bomb threat calls to an exhibition I held in Piccadilly. This exhibition was broken into. The windows of this centre were defaced. Rumours are being circulated in my constituency; pressure is being exercised through my local party; other Members have been approached as to my financial probity.[34]

Another George Brown—the one-time British Foreign Secretary and Deputy Leader of the Labor Party—also paid a price for expressing an opinion somewhat at variance with the prevailing line. Brown, never one to indulge in British understatement, caused something of an international uproar when seated at a dinner party next to Golda Meir he said, "You are merely a Jewess from Russia who came to Israel via America." The outspoken and often tactless Laborite, whose tongue was often further loosened by demon rum, was merely cautioning the Israeli leader against speaking so possessively about Palestine. Brown was never forgiven by organized Jewish interests for his independent views on Israel, which, added to other pressures, hastened his premature retirement to the House of Lords.

Even the prestigious *Christian Science Monitor* (generally regarded as the most objective and reliable U.S. paper) has come under violent attack, charged with being "anti-Israel and pro-Arab," the facile allegation so often leveled against those who displease Israel's powerful friends in this country. Like so many other U.S. newspapers, the *Monitor* has been facing financial difficulties the past several years, which had not been relieved by the change of its format to tabloid size. To broaden its subscription base, a special offer was made to the 153,000 members of the League of Women Voters. But the Zionist apparatus increased the pressures already leveled at the *Monitor* for its unbiased reporting and went to work to break up this arrangement, which would have been mutually advantageous. In a blistering attack that appeared in the Boston *Jewish Advocate,* prominent Bostonian Dr. Gerald W. Wohlberg referred to the *Monitor* as "one of the most persistent and vitriolic critics of Israel and purveyors of pro-Arab sentiment in the U.S."[35]

Referring to the paper's reaction to the 1972 Munich tragedy, the writer condemned the "mild rebuke to their Arab friends that they were doing their cause no good."

The *Monitor's* "pervasive style of liberal, pro-Palestine reporting" also came under attack, which the writer claimed was particularly damaging because of the paper's international reputation. "Bright, responsible Jewish women who have devoted enormous energies towards supporting the League" were urged "to write to League headquarters and make them aware of the potential pitfalls involved in their action, which would imply agreement with the *Monitor's* anti-Zionist declamations."

Shortly thereafter a very noticeable change began to take place in the stance of the *Monitor*. Creditable ads, which would have helped replenish the *Monitor* coffers, were rejected when presented by the Arab Information Center and *Middle East Perspective* (its controversial full-page advertisement had been run in early 1975), and the fluid, concise, on-the-spot reports of John Cooley presenting an in-depth analysis of Arab thinking were relegated to less conspicuous spots. The years of visitations by the ADL and other Zionist groups were having an effect, particularly as the *Monitor* increasingly was forced to tighten its belt and could not afford to alienate any blocs of readers.

Neither were the Quakers able to escape the tarbrush of the muckrakers. The study of the American Friends Service Committee, "Search for Peace in the Middle East," which was widely distributed,[36] was labeled by the ADL pandits a "pro-Arab document masquerading under repeated claims of objectivity in a rewrite of history." This study's gross crime was that, while it had evenly distributed blame for the six-day war on the Arabs and the Israelis, it placed the onus for the failure to bring about peace squarely on Israel. What particularly drew Zionist fire was an earlier draft of the Quaker report, which achieved some circulation:

We do appeal to the leaders of the powerful American Jewish community, whose hard work and generous financial support have been so important to the building and sustaining of Israel, to reassess the *character of their support* and the *nature of their role in American politics*. Our impression . . . is that there is a tendency for the American Jewish establishment to identify themselves with the more *hard-line elements* inside the Israeli Cabinet, to *out-hawk the hawks*, and to ignore and discount the dissident elements in and out of the Israeli government that are searching for more creative ways to solve the Middle East problems. . . .

However, the heavy-handed nature of some of these pressures and their extensiveness have served to inhibit calm and rational public discussion of the issues in the Arab-Israeli conflict. It is not a new phenomenon in American politics, but it is nonetheless disturbing to have *Congressmen complain privately* that they have signed public statements giving unqualified endorsement for Israel, even though they do not believe in those statements, or have agreed to sponsor resolutions concerning American policy toward Israel, of which they secretly disapprove—simply because they are *intimidated by Jewish pressure groups. In this situation are clear dangers of an anti-Semitic backlash. No one who is truly concerned about the long-term fate of Israel and the long-term threats to interfaith harmony and brotherhood can be indifferent to these dangers.* [Italics added.]

The deep concern only earned the Quakers further calumny, although the language in the first draft was considerably altered and all reference to congressional "intimidation" was omitted. In citing the *Christian Century*'s view that the Quaker study was "an instructive and fair-minded primer . . . , the authors undoubtedly were also implying anti-Semitism on the part of that journal, too.

The American Friends Service Committee came under further Zionist attack when they invited Israeli dissident, Retired Major General Matityahu Peled, who headed the dovish Israeli Council for Israeli-Palestinian Peace, to address its 1977 mid-February national conference in Washington. The AFSC was accused by the President of the Zionist Organization of America "of advocating Arab positions which would endanger the survival of the Jewish state."

Nor were Jews immune from the blitz. Prior to the 1973 war, moderate-minded Jewish supporters of Israel, who believed in an open-minded search for peace, formed a new organization called Breira (meaning alternative). By opposing the "Rally Against Terror" called by Organized Jewry against the 1974 U.N. Arafat appearance and favoring an "affirmation of the legitimate human and national aspirations of the Palestinian people with whom the Israeli people must eventually find a way to live," Breira found itself bitterly attacked by the B'nai B'rith and smeared by *Jewish Week,* the paper sent gratis to every UJA contributor. Two Breira members had even dared to meet with two PLO members, it was charged.

Before its first national 1977 conference convened in Chevy Chase, Maryland, Breira had been condemned by the Jewish Community Council of Greater Washington, and Israeli consulates in three cities had pressured Breira members not to attend. The Jewish Defense League called on its members to demonstrate at the convention. Bearing placards "Breira are Jew-Hating Communists," forty JDL'ers burst into the conference center, overturning tables, tearing up documents, and assaulting some attendants. One JDL member who was then permitted to address the conference harangued the audience, vowing the "destruction of Breira."

The "witch hunt," the words used by *Village Voice* columnists Alexander Cockburn and James Ridgeway to describe the campaign against Breira, did not end here.[37] Breira members who were employed by B'nai B'rith Hillel organizations on college campuses were cautioned that they would be fired if they persisted to make contacts with the PLO. Three Boston members were called in by the Israeli consulate there to receive the personal vitriol of a high-ranking member of the Israeli Foreign Office: "People who have not served in the Israeli armed forces have no right to speak out against Israeli foreign policy."[38]

Professor of political science Klaus Herrmann of Concordia University in Canada found himself facing ouster from a 26-year membership in the University Lodge of B'nai B'rith after he had written an article on his interpretation of anti-Zionism for the Protestant Student Movement of Germany and attended, with other anti-Zionist Jews from Europe and North America, a conference on Zionism and Racism in Tripoli, Libya.

If ever there was a case of the pot calling the kettle black, this occurred when the ADL leveled the accusatory finger at Walter J. Minton, President of publishing house G. P. Putnam, because of the *New York Times* advertisement on the book *Lansky*.[39] Mobster Meyer Lansky had been brought back to the U.S. from Israel under federal indictment. Admitting that the book by Hank Messick was not anti-Semitic, the cultists attacked Putnam's *Times* ad headed "Jews Control Crime in the United States" (June 24, 1971).

Minton, not so easily frightened, answered the ADL:

I've got enough Jewish, Protestant and Catholic antecedents in my own immediate background so that when I observe a Jew, a Protestant or a Catholic doing something I believe he should not be doing, I judge that action without feeling I am falling prey to prejudice.

I regret that your letter suggests that a man in your position is not capable of so doing. There are crooked Jews in America, and if you read Hank Messick's *Lansky* you will learn something about some of them.[40]

Whereas others have refused to bow to blackmail, the head of the second largest U.S. oil corporation capitulated totally to pressure, as revealed in the following correspondence between the National Chairman of the ADL and Bob R. Dorsey, Chairman of Gulf Oil Corporation:

Dear Mr. Dorsey:

As undoubtedly you are aware, there is great concern in the American Jewish community at the revelation that Gulf Oil Corporation contributed a sum of money to a source in Beirut, Lebanon, which was used for a pro-Arab propaganda campaign in the United States. One result was a critical resolution adopted on May 27 last at a plenary session of the Conference of Presidents of Major American Jewish Organizations. B'nai B'rith and its Anti-Defamation League are constituent members of this umbrella body.

Our agencies have had, and continue to receive, an increasing number of inquiries from interested citizens across the land about this Gulf gift. In order that we may more intelligently respond to these inquiries, may we have from you an official statement of explanation.

And Mr. Dorsey's reply:

Dear Mr. Graubard:

I acknowledge and thank you for your letter of August 15. We share your concern about the contribution which Gulf made abroad for educational purposes in the United States.

I must tell you that I had no knowledge of the contribution at the time it was made. It is my view that this company should not have made a contribution to support political activities for foreign interests in the United States, and I can assure you it never was our intention to do so. The contribution in question was regrettable, and you may be certain that it will not happen again.[41]

This contribution ($50,000) went to an American effort to tell the untold side of the Middle East struggle, but such has been the power and force of the anti-anti-Semitism blitz that a mighty corporation like Gulf Oil becomes a quivering mass of jelly in the face of a scolding from the Anti-Defamation League. Yet who thinks to raise even a whisper to challenge the many corporations—Jewish and otherwise—individuals, and organizations, for their multi-multi-million-dollar tax-free contributions every year for so-called "educational purposes" on behalf of Israel?

Perhaps the answer to this anomaly lies in the fact that one aim of Israel's "educational purposes" is to brainwash Americans into believing that propaganda for Israel is somehow "right" and "proper," but that in behalf of the Arabs is equally "beyond the fringe," and that whereas the Arabs pertain to something "foreign," the Israelis very much do not. As a writer for *Life* succinctly expressed it, "The net effect of pro-Israeli propaganda and relentless pressure over the past twenty-five years has been to make us all feel slightly Jewish and to feel that the Israelis are 'our kind of people,' while the Arab is our sworn enemy. It has been a masterwork of brainwashing."[42] By this peculiar, twisted logic, Israel becomes an extension of the U.S. And if that is the case, there is certainly no more glaring example of the tail wagging the dog.

This writer, no matter how hard he would try, could never present the record of repression in the U.S. in its massive entirety for the very valid reason that the more submissive victims of Zionist pressure are usually too afraid or too ashamed to publicize their experience. What has been written here is only some of the details in the more renowned cases. And there have been many other Americans from all over the country who have been similarly blitzed. That story perhaps someday will be completely unfolded.

It goes without saying that I have been one of the chief targets of the silencers for nearly thirty years, the full recital of which will be the subject of a future work. But a few select episodes may further impart to readers who have had no first-hand experience with this type of situation, the flavor of the subtle, insidious manner in which this campaign has been conducted.

From my very first lecture on December 16, 1952, in which I mentioned the plight of the Palestinian Arabs to the Women's Club of Wheeling, West Virginia, through my May 10, 1976, appearance at the College of Marin in California, there have been pressures on the sponsor, if not on the lecture agent, to cancel engagements. Where these efforts failed, there have been planned attempts to disrupt the meeting. The few of us who expressed the unpopular "other side" have never known when we started out on a lecture tour what would happen to our engagements and whether we would still have a lecture agent on our return. The Anti-Defamation League was capable of frightening them—or bribing by offering them many lucrative lectures for one of their speakers—and this they did with such long-established agencies as Keedick's Lecture Bureau.

Embarrassment often faced a lecturer from the outset of his talk. Shortly after the publication of *What Price Israel?*, the British Empire Club of Providence, Rhode Island, invited the budding young author to speak to them. Chairman Dr. Percy Hodgson in introducing me related that "a certain lady" had telephoned him saying, "Our community has lived in friendship all these years. We do not want to break that relationship." Strongly suggesting that they ought to cancel the lecture, the lady issued a veiled threat: "We will be happy to learn that you have taken the necessary action because Lilienthal's views are dangerous."

Hodgson replied that he would be happy to have one of their speakers at a later date; "We want to hear all views." The trouble was —and is—that 99 percent of the time is given to one point of view, and when by dint of perseverance one percent has been accorded the Anti-Zionist side, one is forced to split even that little time, so that the Zionist position winds up with 99½ percent of the time. This inevitable pressure, exerted even on the Rotary Club on the small out-to-sea island of Nantucket, has been a great factor discouraging program chairmen from booking any Middle East speakers.

What has been far more than a tempest in a glass of Manischewitz has occurred on the lecture circuit across the country, no matter how remote and academic the setting, in places where one might assume the blitz could not possibly reach. Read—exactly as set down in *Middle East Perspective*—from a "diary" of experiences on a trip to the West Coast in 1968:

Louisiana: Here, at McNeese State College in Lake Charles, I was rudely reminded that Zionist pressures can reach even into the deepest part of the South. The local rabbi had called the President of the College, and other interested parties had hinted elsewhere that it might be better for the school if Lilienthal's lectures were cancelled. The morning lecture to the full student body was followed by a tempestuous question period in which both the rabbi's wife and the Anti-Defamation League representative vociferously intervened. "We find democracy only in Israel and the U.S. must therefore support this small bastion of freedom," was the latter's argument. When in my rebuttal I pointed to the treatment of Arabs in Israel and to discrimination against Oriental Jews, the rabbi's wife quickly interevened: "That is a question *we* (italics mine) will solve in time." I retorted, "Who is *we?* Are you talking as an American?" Without hesitation her answer was: "I am talking as a Jew, a Zionist, and an American."

And on to California, a state that prides itself on allowing people of every persuasion and extreme to have their say:

Louis Lomax, who had invited me on his KTTV popular interview program, called to say his owners, Metromedia, insisted that I could not appear alone as originally scheduled but must share the program with a Zionist. I was forced to debate with a representative of a local Zionist organization. His charges: "Lilienthal's books are sold by the Paul Revere Society." The Paul Revere Society is "anti-Semitic, anti-Negro" and so, by inference, is Lilienthal. An attorney friend moved subsequently against this slander but the release, which you unwittingly usually sign just three minutes before recording time, as you sit in the dark wings off the set, contains in unreadable small print a waiver for any such damages.

In response to a February 7, 1974 *Wall Street Journal* ad, "Do Arms for Israel Mean No Gasoline for Americans," which I signed as Editor of *Middle East Perspective,* we received many positive letters. The vast majority of the negative letters and smut written across ad coupons were unsigned, bearing a New York City postmark. Some were amusing despite their four-letter vulgarity: "Tell the God Damn Arabs that they can stick their damn oil up their stinking ass." "Hitler killed bastards like you. Too bad he missed you." "Considering your name, you are either a German or a Jew. If you are a German, your ad is what we expect from a German, a brother of Hitler. If you are a Jew, my contempt for you is beyond expression. You are a traitor, a liar, twisting the facts which you ignore."

One letter merely listed the names of eighteen concentration camps. Another declared: "You are a Communist Jew paid by Russia to spread distrust so that the Communists can take over." A coupon signed Adolf Hitler had stapled to it a 20,000-mark Reichbanknote: "I will give $5,000 for your funeral."

While heretics naturally arouse a fury beyond all reason, the deadlier threat that unreasoned supporters of Israel pose is to human freedom. Dr. Israel Shahak, who himself has been the object of an organized campaign, from the U.S. as well as his own country, to dismiss him from his academic post at Hebrew University, in these words attributes the blitz to "areas of totalitarianism in the U.S.":

. . . In regard to anything relating to the Middle East or Jewish subjects, the USA has many of the characteristics of a totalitarian country and many of the groups who call themselves "liberal" or "peace camp" or "radical" are on that subject the most intolerant, the most totalitarian, the most dishonest and racist. . . . A totalitarian society not only does not tolerate a freedom of opinion, but it cultivates by all means in its power a "received opinion," which all have to parrot, not only without checking it, but often without any understanding of what it means. . . .

Perhaps some Americans will think that I exaggerate. But the danger of a totalitarian regime was always thought to be exaggerated before it arrived. Only afterwards, when it was too late, was it found that the society was already totalitarian in some aspects which were merely enlarged.

There is only one sure antidote to the totalitarian danger: To fight all aspects of totalitarianism in all the parts of one's society and to follow always the dictum of Socrates that the unexamined life is not worth living, and therefore with the utmost freedom and without fear of any blackmail to examine everything in the light of a universal concept of justice, applicable equally to all human beings.[43]

In forging their own brand of totalitarianism in the U.S., the Zionists continue to manipulate the victims of the Nazi holocaust as their chief weapon.

XIII   The Holocaust: Stoking the Fires

This—all this—was in the olden Time long ago.

—Edgar Allan Poe

Yad Vashem, a large compound on the Mount of Remembrance in Jerusalem, is a memorial to the Jewish martyrs and heroes of World War II. The Hall of Remembrance is a large rectangular building of basalt boulders and uneven concrete, purposely recreating the appearance of a Nazi gas chamber. Within, on a floor of inlaid tile, are inscribed the names of the twenty-one largest Nazi concentration camps. A shaft admitted through a skylight illuminates the eternal flame contained in the hollow of a colossal broken bronze urn.

Next to the hall is a large square where thousands gather annually for the ceremonies on Martyrs' and Heroes' Remembrance Day in April, the date of the Warsaw Ghetto uprising. To the left of the floor is a double-story museum, on the top floor of which are kept the names of those who perished in camps. A photographic recreation of the history of Nazi anti-Semitism is on the bottom floor.

Guarding the museum is an anguished statue of Job by the sculptor Nathan Rappaport. Circling these buildings is a small forest called the Avenue of the Righteous Gentiles, which honors Gentiles who risked their lives to save Jews. The archives contain records of rescue activities by Jewish organizations, and documents captured in Germany and satellite countries. Upon leaving Yad Vashem, one passes the Pillar of Heroism, a very modern, severe triangular shaft of stainless steel rising seventy feet on the Judean hill. Deeds of Jewish valor are carved into the surrounding stones.

This sanctification of the holocaust,[1] together with the Masada monument commemorating the Zealots who killed themselves rather than surrender to the Romans, carries out the biblical command: Tell

460

your children of it and let your children tell their children, and their children, another generation.

Yad Vashem epitomizes the last trump of the professional anti-anti-Semite. The holocaust is the weapon that hovers behind the cover-up and supplies the principal prop to the cover-over. When all else fails, the six million Jews killed during the Nazi holocaust remain the ultimate silencer. These six million are quite literally pulled from the ovens, propped up, and pushed forward to confront any who might raise the slightest question or smallest voice of dissent. Even the mere threat of this suffices to silence most people. But on many occasions, the six million are ritually brought out. Silence ensues. The line is maintained. Hitler had made reluctant Zionists out of many guilt-ridden Christians and assimilated Western Jews.

As Hitler exploited the Jews, it is paradoxical that certain Jews should have exploited and up to this very moment are still very much intent upon exploiting Hitler for Zionist propaganda purposes. There has been an almost continuing conspiracy, fostered by an unholy alliance between the media and the Zionists, to keep us all in the era of 1940–45. Since there can be only one side to any issue where the alternative would be Hitler, the aim of the game is to keep Adolf and his gang alive.

In 1952, 1967, early in 1972, and later again in November of that year, the hue and cry was raised: "He is alive." And there appeared in the world press still another widely distributed photo of someone alleged to be Martin Bormann, Nazi adjutant to Adolf Hitler. On further investigation, the stories have faded into nothingness. But this speculation, widely encouraged by the media and based on total rumor, brought on a new spate of articles and books about Nazism, further flavoring the atmosphere in which the Middle East conflict was being judged and additionally pinching the Christian conscience lest the already growing number of those disenchanted with Israel further increase.

The latest Bormann episode was by far the most elaborate. It was built around a series of articles by the writer-historian Ladislas Farago, which appeared in a six-part account in both the London *Daily Express*[2] and the *New York Daily News*.[3] Sensational articles appeared in other newspapers concerning the series on Bormann and the Nazis, until *New York Times* correspondent Joseph Novitski printed an interview with one José Velasco of the Argentine Intelligence Service, who denied ever having questioned Bormann at an Argentine checkpoint, as alleged by Farago. Velasco stated that the photograph in question showed him not with Bormann, but with a high school teacher named Rudolpho Sira in downtown Buenos Aires.

The Farago contention that Bormann, aided by the Vatican and Juan Perón, then dictator of Argentina, had escaped from Berlin and managed to smuggle out of Germany treasures in excess of $200 million in the last days of the Hitler regime, was debunked by writer Charles Dana Gibson. Putting finishing touches himself to a book dealing with German blockade-running during World War II, Gibson declared it was impossible to remove loot without the knowledge of Hitler and it was also most unlikely that Bormann "could have arranged such a cargo shipment on a U-boat."[4]

As a reply to their own correspondent, the *Times*, in line with its usual "liberal tradition," permitted Farago a three-column rebuttal, in which he rehashed the whole Nazi bit and claimed his evidence regarding Bormann was "authoritative, authentic, and accurate." He was then completing *The Aftermath*[5] for which Simon & Schuster had given him a $100,000-plus contract. The cult of anti-anti-Semitism apparently was about to be fattened anew.

A last word was had by English historian Hugh Trevor-Roper, Oxford Professor of Modern History and the author of *The Last Days of Hitler*, in a piece in the magazine section of the Sunday *New York Times*.[6] The whole past controversy was reviewed and an elaborate history of Bormann as well as some of his Nazi colleagues was added. But not one shred of new evidence had been provided to prove that Bormann was alive, even as the Hitler era was relived all over again.

All this was brought to the attention of the Sunday readers with this caption in black, bold type: "The world has never had any difficulty remembering his name, but has almost forgotten who he was." There were very few, indeed, who would bet that this would ever be allowed to happen.

Off the presses has come an unbelievable, endless spate of books pricking the world's conscience, as if there was still a Nazi peril today. Scarcely a week passes without an addition to the already imposing list of gory tomes. It would seem that writers of fiction and nonfiction, for television, the movies, and the stage alike, had no other theme than the holocaust. We should have thought Arthur Morse's *While Six Million Died*,[7] Lucy S. Dawidowicz's *The War Against the Jews, 1933–1945*,[8] Myron S. Kaufmann's *The Coming Destruction of Israel: Will the U.S. Tolerate Russian Intervention in the Middle East*,[9] Richard Chernoff, Edward Klein, and Robert Littel's *If Israel Lost the War*[10] would have been more than enough. But then along came an imposing advertisement to tell the readers of the *Times* of Eli Wiesel's *One Generation After.* [11] Wiesel's *Night* [12] and then a new spate of books in the wake of the October war and the latest "threat" of genocide to Jews followed in 1974.

Other aspects of the holocaust were set forth in *Open the Gates,* [13] *The Destruction of European Jews,* [14] and *They Fought Back,* [15] all of which with the Dawidowicz book "were reviewed together by *Libertarian* magazine. [16] The latter, referred to by the cultists as a "classic," was supplemented in 1977 by a new work by the same authoress, *The Jewish Presence,* [17] in which she assailed Hannah Arendt's *Eichmann in Jerusalem* for placing some of the blame for Jewish extermination on the leaders of the Jewish Community Councils, the Judenrat, who "cooperated in one way or another, for one reason or another, with the Nazis."

After a lengthy *Times* review of this new Dawidowicz collection of essays on a Sunday, [18] *Times* chief reviewer Christopher Lehmann-Haupt gave the book another forward push in his daily "Book of the Times" column the next day. [19] What should have appeared in the first or second paragraph of the critique, where the reviewer praised the authoress for her other writings and her habitual "do not forget the six million" thesis, was kept to the very last three lines of the two columns: *"The Jewish Presence* simply lacks what would have made it as fresh and surprising as a good collection of essays ought to be." And, of all people, the readers of the *Times* scarcely had to be told by Lehmann-Haupt: "Nor do we need to be reminded that the struggle of Israel to remain alive, particularly during the six-day and Yom Kippur wars, has served to raise the consciousness of Jews and non-Jews all over the world."

Thirty-two years after Hitler died in a Berlin bunker, and hundreds of volumes later, no book on the German Führer, no matter how trivial its contribution or how ineptly it is written, still failed to win big, bold headlines on the "Books of the Times" page. Lehmann-Haupt even apologized, "Why read yet another book about Hitler?" [20] And then he proceeded to dissect John Toland's *Adolf Hitler* [21] at length, using the gathering of "tidbits of new information" as his excuse. The real reason, of course, must be the endless compulsion that this chief *Times* book reviewer feels to lend a hand to "little Israel" by propogating the syndrome of anti-anti-Semitism.

Nor did this end it. The *Times* of July 12, 1977, carried a half-page advertisement of a "gripping, powerful portrait," the new book, *The Psychopathic God: Adolf Hitler,* [22] which was given the benefit of prepublication features in major *New York Times* and *Time* magazine stories and rave notices in Harriet Van Horne's syndicated column and in *Publish-*

ers Weekly for putting "the lie to the view that Hitler may not have known about the crimes committed against the Jews."

And Hitler himself was not the only theme pursued. A few months earlier the Howard Blum book, *Wanted: The Search for Nazis in America,* [23] had been released and was synthesized in a *New York Post* [24] series, illustrated by more horror pictures of Nazi deeds. The takeover of G. P. Putnam's Sons publishing house by Music Corporation of America (whose chairman, Lew Wasserman, was described in the Robert Scheer *Los Angeles Times* 1978 controversial series as "the most powerful Jew in Los Angeles as well as the most powerful leader of the entertainment industry") was reflected in the publication and promotion of such books as *17 Ben-Gurion.* [25] According to an advertisement in the *Times,* the book concerned "the terrorist-ridden Middle East in this big, exciting novel of a ruthless Palestinian terrorist organization plotting to destroy Israel—and Israeli Intelligence agents racing against time to trace the conspiracy to its source and smash it forever." [26] Within three weeks came the companion novel, *The Plot to Destroy Israel,* "documenting how the Arab nations intend to wipe Israel off the face of the earth." [27]

The emerging power of the PLO, the threat of OPEC, the growing recession, and the open speculation about U.S. armed intervention in the Middle East caused consternation in Jewish-American circles. Gerald S. Strober, a former staff member of the American Jewish Committee, in his book *American Jews: Community in Crisis* predicted that current trends will make "life rather unpleasant for the individual Jew" in America, and that U.S. Jews are now entering "the most perilous period" in their history. [28] Eli Wiesel claimed in the *New York Times* [29] that for the first time he could "foresee the possibility of Jews being massacred in the cities of America or in the foresteps of Europe" because of "a certain climate, a certain mood in the making." According to Cynthia Ozick in her *Esquire* piece "All the World Wants the Jews Dead," Israel's survival was in grave doubt, and with it Zionism and thus all Jews. She proclaimed "The Jews are one people. . . . You cannot separate parent from child, the Jews from Zion." [30]

The rash of hysterical articles continued: Alfred Kazin's piece in the *Atlantic Monthly;* [31] *Commentary* editor Norman Podhoretz's January 1975 article in the *New York Times* [32] and his 1976 editorial article in his own magazine; [33] Richard Reeves' *New York* magazine article, "If Jews Will Not Be for Themselves, Who Will Be for Them?" [34] All were aimed at creating panic among Jews, at linking anti-Zionism with anti-Semitism, and at crushing any stillborn opposition to the maintenance of the Middle East status quo.

The lead article in the *New York Times* Magazine of June 19, 1977 was the Helen Epstein emotional outpouring, "The Heirs of the Holocaust," in which controversy was built over whether children and grand-children should or should not feel guilty for having survived their parents and grandparents. Speculation was kept alive by the publication of eight letters the following month, which generally expressed a "deep feeling of guilt for having survived our parents and for being an heir of the holocaust. Because I am a Jew and because the suffering was so great, I can carry only an infinitesimal part of this sorrow."[35] Even obituary page headlines in the *Times*, "Rudolf Weiss, 77, Actor Who Fled Austria After Nazi Invasion, Dead," are used to fasten attention on the holocaust.[36]

The Sunday *New York Times'* Travel Section is not immune. On September 3, 1972, it carried one article on anti-Semitism in Germany and another on concentration camps in Poland over a three-page spread including a tremendous picture of a skull-capped Jew baring his Nazi tatto. Rarely has writing as contrived, platitudinous and banal as Stephen Birnbaum's "Germany: The End of Assimilation" appeared anywhere, let alone in the promotion of tourism. A visitor dropped from another planet would have believed that the Third Reich was still ruling Germany and threatening the world.

This writer, calling himself an assimilationist but referring to "Rosh Hashonah, 5372," feels forced in 1972 to make excuses for making a trip to West Germany. By his own confession he has avoided attending a synagogue for eighteen years. On this first visit to Germany, while enjoying his first meal in a German home on the North Sea coast, his eyes happen to fall upon an oil painting of the Nazi SS father of his host. He can scarcely keep down his food, and the next day he rushes to a "spiritual reunion" in a Regensburg synagogue.

Television likewise continued to keep viewers back in the unforgettable 1940s. In late 1974, for instance, a two-part documentary study of Adolf Hitler had been cunningly timed by WNET Educational Television to fall as Jews celebrated Hanukkah. According to the *New York Times*, it was "a devastating reminder and sombre warning of a madness that was able to grip a large part of the world in this century." This was followed in January on Channel 9 by "In Our Time," a 1944 drama of Nazi-shadowed Poland, starring Ida Lupino and Paul Henried; then a Sunday evening "Report on World War II" depicting the concentration camps of Belsen and Auschwitz; and then a revival of the de Sica film, *The Garden of the Finzi-Continis*, the story of Jewish persecution under Italian Fascism. This, even as the *Odessa File* with its blatant propaganda about a fictitious Nazi-Egyptian spy ring in Frankfurt, was drawing tears from thousands, who had stood in long cues to view the new hit purporting to show Egyptians and resurgent Nazis building a rocket assembly line to threaten the very existence of Israel. In short order this was followed by the appearance of *Rosebud,* the Otto Preminger film about a hijacking by Black September Palestinians of a yacht on which there are five wealthy girls, one of whom is Jewish. Among the propaganda ploys used by the film was an Israeli intelligence officer uttering, "They'll never get us in gas chambers again," as he shows off his skillful "know-how" of American equipment locating the guerrillas' Corsica hideout.[37]

This outpouring came in the wake of the PLO's appearance before the bar of international opinion and was endless. Nearly two full pages of the Sunday Arts and Leisure Section of the *New York Times* was covered by an Alfred Kazin piece, "Can Today's Movies Tell the Truth about Fascism?" The article started off with the admission, "World War II is by now the longest running movie of all time," an assessment with which no objective observer could quarrel, only hoping the writer would not further prolong it. Two tremendous pictures, each 9 × 6½ inches, evoked the immediate sympathy of the reader. One showed "a Jewish girl in occupied Paris seeking a priest's aid in the movie *Black Thursday,"* and the other was a pretty shot of a Jewish mother and her little son escaping the Nazis in the movie *Les Villons du Bal.* But the author decried the happy ending in which mother and son "manage to slip under the barbed wire and a benevolent Swiss guard looks down on them and croons 'Now you are free.' " History, he claimed, was not so kind. "For the Swiss were as gentle to 'illegal immigrants' as one of their bank tellers would be to a pauper."

French filmakers, stimulated by Marcel Ophuls' *The Sorrow and the Pity* in 1972, began to portray their countrymen in less than Resistance-hero terms, with an alleged anti-Semitism that even at times exceeded that of the Nazis. Their products were greeted with great popularity in the U.S., as in France, with the help of Zionist stimulation. But Kazin still was far from satisfied. Even when a movie did give a picture of Jews being tormented, the persecution was often not vivid or horrible enough for Kazin's taste, as was the case of Louis Malle's exceptionally interesting and intelligent film *Lacombe, Lucien.* The producer was held to be "not altogether well-informed because he was only thirteen when the war ended."

Hollywood continued to advance the cult, although not always successfully. *The Voyage of the Damned,* the film based on the story of the 1939 attempt by 937 Jews aboard the *St. Louis* to find a refuge from Hitler in Cuba, was reviewed by Vincent Canby as "clumsy, tasteless and self-righteous," another attempt to "wildly fictionalize and exploit the tragedies of real people."[38] The 1977 Alain Delon's *Mr. Klein* brought to the screen a novel aspect of anti-Semitism—an exposure of someone from the *haute monde,* who though "not an active Nazi supporter, found anti-Semitic sketches in a cabaret revue amusing and brought objects d'art at rock-bottom prices from Jews fleeing the country."[39]

Again, after the emergence of Menachem Begin in power in Israel, amidst the subsequent soul-searching by American Jews and the emerging debate over the Geneva Conference, the holocaust burst anew on the television screens of New York viewers. "The World at War: The Final Solution" was given seven hours August 1–4, 1977, on Mutual's outlet, Channel 9 (WOR-TV). On the night this series ended, an old third-rate movie, *Operation Eichmann,* was dug up out of the morgue and shown.

Later that month smatterings of the persecution theme were woven into the first of three "Jewish Tradition" series of ten Sunday half-hour shows and in "Jerusalem Lives" over Channel 13 (WNET). That station had earlier shown, as part of a network program, *L'Chaim,* the story of the Jewish people in Europe from the mid-19th century through the Nazi period to the present.

In the 1977 series *Israel: A Family Portrait,* which was unveiled as a special four-part series September 7–9, 1977, over WABC (Channel 7) "Eyewitness News" at prime 6:00 P.M. time, correspondent Joel Siegel was shown visiting relatives in the Zionist state. Here a cousin who survived "the concentration camp where 300,000 Jews were massacred" described the holocaust and his heightened feelings about Israel. In addition to such "news" outlets, a special half-hour feature picked up Siegel's narration for the September 17 season premiere of Mort Fleischer's WABC's award-winning public affairs series, "People, Places, Things."

Many television stations in all parts of the country on all networks repeatedly through 1976 and 1977 showed the half-hour United Jewish Appeal-produced film, *The Commitment,* which depicted Jewish persecution under the Nazis and closed with an appeal for funds. Israeli-American singer of note, Theodore Bikel, did the narrating. This propaganda-laden presentation was shown as a public service, at no charge whatsoever to the UJA.

In addition to keeping alive the Hitler days and the holocaust, there has been the related phenomenon of bringing to life the fear of imminent revivals of Nazism and Fascism[40] both abroad and at home. The Nazi shadow and peril were kept aglow by a plethora of *New York Times* stories and the competition between the networks in trying to magnify the importance of the U.S. Nazi party.

An NBC "Tomorrow" show interviewed American Nazi leader Frank Collin who defended his vehement anti-Jewish, anti-black position. The New Rochelle shooting spree of crazed Fred Cowan provided the excuse for focusing national attention on a fascist movement whose membership numbered little more than 1000. Not to be outdone, a CBS "Sixty Minutes" on February 20, 1977 presented another view of the U.S. Nazis. These fanatics were pictured against a background of swastikas as a growing force of hate. When asked by their Nazi parents, little children six to seven years of age responded correctly before the cameras with a quick "Kill the Jews."

The American Nazi Party claimed less than 1000 total membership, forty-one of whose members turned up at its 1978 national convention in St. Louis to reelect Collin as successor to the notorious deceased George Lincoln Rockwell. Although this conclave had already received prominent reportage, the *Times* accorded two full columns on April 18, 1978 to the "Nazis in the U.S.," with pictures of a swastika-armed Rockwell and of swastika-dominated "Nazis on parade in St. Louis last month" (all of twenty-five had marched). The article admitted bringing "American Nazis a notoriety that seems to be greatly disproportionte to their numbers."

The scheduled July 4, 1977 Nazi march through Skokie, the Chicago suburb with its fifty-seven percent Jewish population of 40,000, including 7,000 former concentration camp inmates, opened up new areas for propaganda. Through the long court fight to halt the parade, the Anti-Defamation League and other Zionist groups had a field day in picturing a "grave new threat" to America. This was heightened by media attention to the "growing" Ku Klux Klan with its 7,000 members, split into three principal vying groups, the most articulate leader of which was David Duke.

Both Collin and Duke appeared with leaders of the black community on most of the stations of National Educational Television's "Black Perspective"[41] on which the danger from these fascist groups was grossly exaggerated. The Ku Klux Klanner was given ample time to attack Jews and Zionists alike for "forcing" a pro-Israel Middle East policy on the United States.

On December 14, 1977 WNET Channel 13 avid Israelist Seymour Lipset, Anti-Defamation League representative Irwin Suall, and American Civil Liberties Union executive Bruce Ennis engaged in the pros and cons on how to cope with the threat of the Rockaway (Long Island) Klan chapter of fifty members (admittedly already reduced to twenty through an ADL campaign). Suall argued: "They are capable of perpetrating violence and constitute a real danger. It is a real obligation to point out what they stand for and what they did in our times."

To help achieve this goal, the American Jewish Committee, closely allied with the ADL, published and widely distributed a specially prepared three-article series "Nazi Groups Flourishing Throughout the U.S.A." The fearsters were determined to justify the large tax-deductible gifts given to their tax-free treasuries to fight the dangers of anti-Semitism and at the same time to spread propaganda which could only improve Israel's position in the U.S. This is why the Jewish groups rejected Collin's offer in late May 1978 to cancel the Nazi march through Skokie if the legislation barring the June 25 parade were withdrawn. The sponsors of the bill replied: "He is not the kind of person you make a deal with." And the New York organization, Survivors of Nazi Camps and Resistance Fighters, pointing to the Skokie march as "evidence that Nazi activities were not terminated with the demise of Hitler," sent out a broad mail appeal for more information on victims of the holocaust to be added to the central archives of Yad Vashem.

Earlier attention had been directed to incidents in Germany and Italy, building upon occasional rumors and unconfirmed reports of rising anti-Semitism to create an atmosphere of constant fear. After a small German extreme rightist group gained a victory in local elections in one West German state, the drums began to roll "The Nazis are coming." Old scare stories and exaggerated figures were dragged out. When the election came, this "big" threat polled less than one percent in the federal elections and won no seats.[42]

The continued spate of stories on the apprehension, release, extension of statute of limitations, conviction, and even escape of former Nazi and alleged Nazi criminals used up valuable newsprint inches. The *Times* was ever digging up Nazi terror stories, as they did in pointing the finger at the German Catholic Bishop of Munich for the alleged execution twenty-five years earlier of twenty-seven Italians in the small village of Filetto Di Camarda, running the accusation under and across the page heading: "Priest and Red in Italian Village Battle Over Role of German, Now a Bishop, in Wartime Reprisal Killing."[43]

In one single issue of the monthly *Jewish Currents,*[44] which is more broadminded in its view toward the Palestinians, there were articles on "Holocaust and Jewish Resistance," "Flight from Hitler, 1939," and "Obstacles to Nazi Hunting." When this periodical was not calling some people anti-Semitic, they were clearing others of a similar charge spread by other Jewish groups. Certain remarks had been adduced by the Yiddish and Jewish student press to prove that even Benjamin Franklin had been a pronounced bigot. And not too many days were allowed to pass without some human interest *Times* story bringing back the holocaust—a reunion of survivors of Buchenwald, Dachau or of the Cracow Ghetto which was accorded large coverage and a four-column head.[45]

The extent to which the Masada complex in Israel and its U.S. counterpart, the holocaust saga, had taken hold was illustrated in 1971, during one of the alleged Bormann "sightings." When questioned on a David Frost television show, Foreign Minister Abba Eban carelessly exclaimed that he was "hardly interested" in whether "some wretched man in Paraguay or Brazil is brought to justice." Front-page headlines in Israeli papers, from the English-language *Jerusalem Post* to Israel's Hebrew newspapers, resounded with group as well as individual castigation of Israel's most eloquent voice. Someone was threatening to put a yawning hole in the reservoir from which the anti-anti-Semitic syndrome must draw its publicity, and this was not to be tolerated. The concentration camp commemoration groups shrieked loudly and called for Eban's resignation. Golda Meir, neither publicly disavowing nor supporting her minister, refused to become involved at that critical moment in the post-Nasser period on yet another front, and as quoted, "swept the matter under the rug."

It did not end with this. An opposition party motion in the Knesset, brought by Menachem Begin's Gahal alignment and calling for Eban's resignation, failed only by a 27–22 margin. Such was the power of the syndrome that an unusually large number of Labor party coalition members abstained from voting in the face of the charge that their Foreign Minister's indifference was providing the Germans with the excuse to discontinue other planned Nazi war trials. And this was practically on the eve of a vital U.N. debate in which Eban was to assume the leading role in presenting the Israeli position.

Because it sought to link Nazi war criminals with Nasser's Egypt, *The Champagne Spy,*[46] the colorful story of the espionage work of top Israeli agent Wolfgang Lotz, found ready publishers and received favorable reviews. Operating within Cairo's *haut monde* under the cover of a wealthy German horsebreeder, Lotz was apprehended in February 1965 by Egyptian security officers after three years of sending back to Israeli intelligence such invaluble information as the disposition of Egyptian troops, which facilitated the 1967 attack. Lotz and his attractive wife, Waltrand, were arrested in February 1965 and became the center of a sensational public-show trial involving certain leading personalities in Egypt.

According to Lotz's interesting recital, he had encouraged the rumor that he was an ex-SS officer hiding from arrest for war crimes, which allegedly forthrightly opened doors for him in the Egyptian capital, particularly among the influential circle of German businessmen and scientists there who were working on the development of rockets and other lethal instruments. Described as nonfiction, it was most difficult to know where the anecdote ended and the fiction began. An Egyptian-Nazi conspiracy against "little" Israel was continuously depicted.

When the Lotzes were apprehended after they made their way into a top-secret post off the Cairo-Alexandria desert road where important secret missiles were being tested and manufactured, a phone call to an influential military friend freed them. The base commandant was quoted apologizing as follows:

Of course, Sir, if you say so, I will not pry into your affairs. Yours is a secret to be proud of. The SS, they tell me, was the *crème de la crème* of the German Reich. I have read a great deal about it. We, too, will have a great Arab Reich one day. Installations like our missile base here will help to destroy Israel soon. Now you understand why we guard it so carefully.[47]

Lotz's artificial and stilted wording failed to bring to life an Egyptian speaking this language. Whatever this book had to say in depicting inefficient, corrupt, venal, and nepotistic Egyptians, no amount of clichéd language could convincingly convey a portrait of Egyptians as Nazi-loving bigots. This was just not in line with their character. But to give his book the right flavor, the Egyptian prosecutor was alleged to have quoted from the *Protocols of the Elders of Zion* in his summation against spy Lotz, and every German introduced to the readers was insinuated to be a Nazi or neo-Nazi. Apparently the author was not acquainted with the large number of German non-Nazi scientists whose talents the U.S. had most advantageously used.[48]

Undeniably, one special objective of the persistent raking up of the Nazi past has been Germany itself. Through constant harassment Germans were not allowed to forget the Hitler days, and at all levels of society they were placed under continued pressure to redeem themselves. The ritual visits of German leaders to Israel for the purpose of unloading guilt, and the return visits of Israeli leaders to Germany for purposes of piling on more guilt, have kept the pot boiling.

On an important trip to West Germany in 1970, lengthy articles prominently placed with a photograph revealed that Foreign Minister Abba Eban had proceeded directly from the airport to the site of the Nazi Dachau crematory even before calling on his host, German Chancellor Willi Brandt. Likewise, the energetic Chancellor, when he went to Warsaw to sign the German-Polish treaty finalizing agreement on the Oder-Niesse boundary, was shown by the press of the world kneeling in front of the memorial to Jewish insurgents killed by the Nazis in the Warsaw ghetto uprising.

In 1973 the state visit of Brandt to Israel overflowed with emotion and national significance from the moment the Israeli army band struck up "Deutschland Über Alles" through his departure four days later. Wearing a dark blue suit and black homburg and accompanied by Gideon Hausner, prosecutor at the Eichmann trial and Chairman of the memorial complex, the Chancellor's first official act was to visit Yad Vashem, where he donned a yarmulka and laid a wreath. Brandt climaxed his stay with the statement that "what was done cannot be undone" but accepted the moral responsibility for Nazi genocide and declared all-out support of Israel's demand for direct negotiations and her insistence there be no substantial changes in the border of the Zionist state.

The enormous German sense of guilt, deeply felt by its postwar leadership of Konrad Adenauer, Ludwig Erhard, and Willy Brandt found expression in the words of West German editor Axel Springer: "Since the German Jewish Community no longer exists for any practical purposes, I believe it is our duty to make all possible efforts to support Israel."[49] With the payment of $3.9 billions in reparations and in restitution, Germany was second only to the U.S. in keeping Israel economically afloat.

In July 1975 Yitzhak Rabin became the first Israeli head of state to visit Germany (the 1973 October war had spared a reluctant Golda Meir this visit).[50] Scarcely had he touched down at Frankfurt Airport amidst tightest security, when he was whisked away by army helicopter to visit the former death camp of Bergen-Belsen. (The same treatment was accorded Moshe Dayan on his first visit to Germany in the fall of 1977.) A *New York Times* news story July 9, 1975, described his feelings: "Israel's first native-born premier, Mr. Rabin did not suffer directly from the Nazis. But he has described himself as 'an heir to the holocaust,' and his aides say that he felt strongly that the first official visit by an Israeli chief of government should begin with some recognition of the past."

Mrs. Rabin, who accompanied her husband, had been born in Germany and had learned German as her first language. While Bergen-Belsen today resembles more a park than "an apocalyptic vision of a vast death camp" (language of the *Times*), the reality of what happened among its green fields confronted the Rabins as they stepped into the modern museum at the entrance. The *Times* related, "On all the walls hung huge pictures of the faces and twisted bodies of the camp's thousands of victims, the faces standing out of the pictures with eyes hollowed out by anguish."

The 1976 visit to his German birthplace of Fürth by Secretary Kissinger, on which he was accompanied by his parents, his wife, his brother, and his sister-in-law, provided the *Times* with a new opportunity to spotlight attention on one of their favorite topics. Its account seemed to go far out of its way to note that "the only synagogue which the Nazis had not burned to the ground" was that which the Kissinger family had attended, and to quote the wording of a plaque in Hebrew and German inside the house of worship (which incidentally the Secretary and his family did not visit) reading: "On the 22nd of March, 1942, the last occupants of this building, 33 orphaned children, were sent to their deaths in Izbica with their teacher and director, Dr. Isaak Hallemann."[51]

In West Germany today there are more than twenty-six million men and women who were born after 1945, nearly half of the population alive today. And most of these, according to *Der Spiegel* and other sources, are beginning to question the awkward, special relationship that their parents' generation built with Israel. "After all," said a twenty-three-year-old student from Munich, "why should I feel guilty. I was not born then. I had nothing to do with it." Most of that age group feel that Germany's present relationship should be replaced by more normal balanced ties taking into account the Arab states. Virtually all Germans now insist that Germany has already paid sufficient moral and financial reparations.

It is for these in Germany and the new generations all over the world that the Zionist ploy must be advanced with gusto. "Hitler . . . ," "the Nazis . . . ," "the six million. . . ." One by one these icons have been and are today continuously invoked at any moment, into any present-day question of Jewish or Israeli affairs.

Under the impact of the holocaust, even those like sixty-nine-year-old French novelist Simone de Beauvoir, who moved in left-wing circles and would normally be alienated from Israel, assailed France's attitude toward Israel in an angry Jerusalem interview:

One of my reasons for coming here is to demonstrate the fact that some leftists have a positive attitude towards Israel and support its right to exist like any other nation. I was a witness to the Holocaust and its horrors and felt the lack of a Jewish homeland. I saw this not merely as a Jewish problem, but as something very personal.

As the one weapon that will never let "them" forget how "we" suffered, the holocaust continues to be immemorialized whenever Jews will it, and their multifold actions, exacted as many pounds of flesh, are never questioned. In 1976 the Endowment for the Humanities in Washington announced a $76,544 grant for writing a ninety-minute historical film to examine the experiences of the victims of the Nazi occupation of Poland; in 1978 a youth grant was awarded to three children of holocaust survivors to produce a documentary film on the story of their own families.

To ingrain the State of Israel more deeply into the Jewish consciousness, the International Association of Conservative Rabbis incorporated the events of the last 2,000 years in prayer. The death of the six million as well as the establishment of Israel, the June war, and the reunification of Jerusalem were all woven into the revised liturgy.

The greater the need for Israel to defend itself against pressure to yield the occupied territories, the more the holocaust was pushed before the American public. Two days before Begin's March talks with President Carter, the *Times'* Op-Ed piece, "Ein Volk, Ein Reich,"[52] illustrated with a swastika, described the takeover of a suburb of Vienna, the burning of the synagogue, and other Nazi criminal actions. At a time the Middle East was in flames over the Israeli invasion of Lebanon, the recital of this forty-year outdated, newsless, and unrelated incident could have had no other purpose than to prick the world conscience anew.

Nothing, not even Begin's first visit to the U.S. in the summer of 1977, was as widely heralded as the NBC 9½-hour, four-episode series, "Holocaust." For thirteen months the Brodkin-Green series filmed in Vienna and funded by NBC and World Vision Enterprises[53] had been promoted as a rival to "Roots." The story spanned 1933–45 and followed a Jewish doctor from his secure social and financial position in Berlin to the Warsaw ghetto. The Mauthausen concentration camp and Reinhold Heydrich's office were used as locations to inject the appropriate Nazi flavor.

Spread over three pages of *TV Guide* of April 15 was the article "A Wreath on the Graves of the Six Million" to kick off the NBC telecast April 17–20 of its series. The showings, originally scheduled for the fall, were moved up to coincide with the start of Passover and, more importantly, when disaffection with Begin was increasing in the U.S. following his most unsympathetic visit with Carter in Washington and the invasion of Lebanon. NBC's publicity department grinded out release after release during the series, claiming that 120 million had seen one or more installments, outdrawing "Roots."

The *New York Times* carried a full-page advertisement, "Six Million Jews Who Were Not Intransigent," drawing attention to the programs and paid for by Americans for a Safe Israel.[54] Taking up a good portion of the page was the ever-familiar photo of the pitiful youngster with his hands raised in the face of Nazi guns, and an awe-inspiring illustration of a burning crematorium. This page left no doubt as to the purpose of the spotlight on the holocaust. While NBC and the Anti-Defamation League were claiming merely to be imparting a history lesson, the ad sponsors were laying down guidelines for the present and the future: Support "Israel's promise to the future, send this ad to the President and Congress . . . post this in your synagogue or church . . . place this ad in your local newspaper."

The Nielsen ratings revealed that the viewing audience of "Holocaust" did not nearly match "Roots"; on the first night "Laverne and Shirley," "Three's Company," and "M.A.S.H." outdrew the televised dramatization of Jewish extermination.[55] But network officials expressed satisfaction when Part Two outdrew ABC's offbeat Western, "A Man Called Horse." The 370 phoned complaints (390 calls praised the telecasts) "appeared to be part of an organized campaign," said NBC to the *Times*.[56]

Viewers' reaction could be summed up in the words of a fifty-year-old Roman Catholic: "As I watched the show, I wanted to turn it off but couldn't. I was drawn to the story even though I am not sure if it was a true enough portrayal." At Columbia University's Furnald Dormitory some students watched "Holocaust," while in one room they waited for "Rhoda" to end before tuning in, and in another "Holocaust" was tuned out at 9:00 P.M. in favor of the James Bond film on ABC. Most metropolitan papers in New York and Washington interviewed Jewish viewers, but some Jews as well as Christians complained that the commercials—for cars, toothpaste, bandage strips, and soft drinks—proved an absurd complement to the drama. For example, immediately following a brutal rape scene involving a teenage girl, an elated Bill Cosby came on to expound the benefits of driving a Ford.

This should not have upset any intelligent viewer. The whole performance, after all, was nothing but one big commercial: "Let's support Israel or this will happen again." As *Near East Report* phrased it: "Anyone who watched NBC's 'Holocaust' this week should have a better understanding of Israel's intense preoccupation with security. The television drama and book by Gerald Green furnished six million reasons why the Jewish state's leaders insist upon defensible borders."[57]

The ensuing raging controversy among critics and viewers over the artistic merits of "Holocaust" only served to spread the propaganda message further. In the first of his two reviews, *New York Times* columnist John J. O'Connor accused writer Green of "transforming events and attitudes into a stereotypical collection of wooden characters and impossible coincidences." He called the series "less of a noble failure than a presumptuous venture."[58]

The *Times* reviewer, generally sympathetic to Zionist propaganda, added: "In a master stroke of public relations, many religious groups, Jewish and non-Jewish, were recruited to participate in related 'educational' projects effectively endorsing a program they hadn't seen and thus reducing the possibilities for their being critical. The program's content is indeed raising questions of an 'educational' nature. In searching for an upbeat angle on the story of harrowing devastation, the writer and producer settled on the Zionist cause and the founding of Israel."[59]

Elie Wiesel joined O'Connor in assailing "the trivializing of the holocaust" in his article spread over two pages of the Sunday *New York Times* the day the miniseries commenced. In calling the film "untrue, offensive, cheap—an insult to those who perished,"[60] Wiesel brought the dramatization to the attention of the 1.4 million readers, some of whom by chance might have missed the enormous, continuous publicity buildup. And the two pages of letters, pro and con, that the *Times* published two Sundays later helped realize Wiesel's final words: "The holocaust must be remembered. But not as a show."

To capture the attention of its more plebian readership, the New York *Daily News* carried that same Sunday the first of a serialization of the Green novel and a full-page story in the Leisure Section by its long-time Zionist-oriented television editor, Kay Gardella,[61] who called the film "harrowing and riveting." In her zeal to give the dramatization a boost, she let the cat out of the bag by unwittingly but pointedly linking the television program to growing Palestinian sympathy. And the more subtle *Washington Post* carried an historical piece, "Prelude to Holocaust," on 1½ pages with pictures that Sunday in its "Outlook" section.

After querying why television viewers should have been "experiencing the pain of extensive treatment of the degradation, torture, and killing of the Jews," columnist William Buckley answered his own question by noting that there "was no way of undoing retroactively what the Nazis did." He then courageously made the point that "innocent Lebanese were killed by the survivors of the holocaust in the recent operations against Lebanon. So why interest oneself in the wholesale massacres of the past?"[62]

This writer and other critics were also bothered by the "Holocaust" denigration of the Christian church and total indifference to the sufferings of others. Dr. Norbert Capek, minister of the world's largest Unitarian church, and 1,000 Catholic priests were shot at Dachau. Eastern Rite Bishop Thomas V. Dolinay boldly labeled the series "clever propaganda" in the June 8 *Wanderer*.

Following an initial 450,000 printing, Bantam sent the Green book back to the presses eight times, the ninth printing just before the series opened; the imprint total was just over 1½ million. Copies were even widely used in lobbying efforts on Capitol Hill to help congressmen who were wavering on the question of death planes for Israel, Egypt, and Saudi Arabia.

Rival networks picked up on NBC's theme. For a full week of afternoon movies ABC-TV Channel 7 showed Leon Uris's "QB VII" and "Exodus" so that the spirit of the holocaust would not be entirely lost. To CBS's "Sixty Minutes" Mike Wallace brought on April 16 the "Annual Reunion of Auschwitz Survivors," featuring actress-author Fania Fenelon, to whom the *Times* also gave a half-page story. (There is even a World Federation of the Bergen-Belsen Associations.)

To thrust the ultimate weapon, "You are either for the Jews and Israel or you are for Hitler" at every possible American, the Anti-Defamation League's sixteen-page "The Record: The Holocaust in History, 1933–1945" was distributed to some twenty million readers as an advertising supplement across the country. The National Council for the Social Studies in Washington and a staff of ten cooperated in assembling the detailed highlights of Nazi genocide and whole kit of the holocaust saga. Articles included were Otto Tolschus's "The Pogrom: Kristallnacht" (night of broken glass), Wiesel's "Teaching the

Holocaust," author and scriptwriter Green's comments on his NBC series, and such "current" news pieces as "Eichmann Directs Jewish Extermination," "Hitler Hints at New Attacks on Jews," and "Goebbels Warning to the Jews." Among the photographs were those of Anne Frank, the famed *Life* magazine Margaret Bourke-White's "The Living Dead at Buchenwald," and the Nuremberg war criminals in the docket. The myth of Albert Einstein's support of Zionist nationalism was portrayed in a piece on the "Physicist at Sixty," with a picture of the doctor, his wife, and daughter swearing allegiance receiving their American citizenship papers.

The most complete listing of source materials closed this "educational guide," which had been inserted into the regular sections of leading dailies and weeklies through the generosity of leading Zionists and advertisers—with Uncle Sam's tax-free dollars. In some cities a full-page advertisement explained that it was "being brought as a public service of this newspaper in conjunction with the Anti-Defamation League," but included three pages of ads to cover the cost of the paper's "generosity."

The week of the "Holocaust" series Christians were enlisted to wear the Nazi yellow badges. Sunday services expressing solidarity with Jews were held in many churches, and the *New York Post* of April 18 showed Michael Moriarty, who played the role of Nazi SS officer Eric Dorf in the miniseries, leaving Riverside Church with the Reverend Dr. William Sloane Coffin.

With the help of glowing press releases from the National Education Association in praise of the NBC series and the "educational follow-up," the entire American public school system was reached. In March NEA Executive Director Terry Herndon had participated with religious leaders and educators on a national televised symposium, "Man's Inhumanity to Man," which was fed by closed circuit to NBC affiliates for broadcast at their convenience as promotion for the miniseries. Nearly one million study guides prepared by the Anti-Defamation League, the National Council of Churches, the American Federation of Teachers, and NBC were distributed to schools and religious groups to aid the students as they watched "Holocaust." Schools were also sent an NEA Rozanne Weissman feature declaring the holocaust to be "an ideal ninth grade unit for teaching persecution and prejudice." To boot, Health, Education and Welfare Deputy Commissioner of the Bureau of Elementary and Secondary Education Thomas Minter pledged more coordinated federal funding for teaching about the holocaust.

Europe was not neglected either. International distribution rights for "Holocaust" were sold to ten countries including West Germany, where the two national channels competed for the purchase. But in Israel where ever financially alert Knesset Member Shmuel Flatto-Sharon had bought the rights, a debate over the sensitivity of the subject held up production.

To keep the spirit of the holocaust ablaze, the 35th anniversary of the Warsaw ghetto uprising was commemorated on April 30 with Collective Remembrance Day, marked by front-page coverage and large newspaper advertisements. Guest speakers at Temple Emanu-El included Elie Wiesel, the Israeli Ambassador, the Governor of New York, and the Mayor. As New York's Fifth Avenue synagogue was filling up, the *New York Times'* good music FM radio station WQXR shifted from the classical music of Verdi to a program of "holocaust music," including the rendition by Jan Peerce and others of such songs as "Our Town Is Burning."[63]

The public school system in the U.S. has been gradually penetrated by the holocaust. The front page of the second section of the *New York Times* on January 12, 1976, carried a six-column story headed "Students at Teaneck High Agonize Over the Holocaust." Reprinted once again was Bourke-White's famed Buchenwald photo, which had first appeared in *Life* magazine and *Time* some thirty-one years previously and innumerable times since. The article, replete with many references to the "six million," indicated that the ADL, in cooperation with the New Jersey Education Association, was sponsoring pilot projects to raise more than $1 million to make available books, clippings, films, and other teaching materials to high schools and junior high schools in many parts of the country to emphasize the holocaust and its meaning. The inspiration for this program had come from a Great Barrington, Massachusetts, high school where the holocaust was being studied in the classroom.

In an unprecedented step the New York City Board of Education designated the week of April 18–22, 1977, as the first annual "Jewish Heritage Week" for all students, Jews and non-Jews, which was kicked off with celebrations in the districts, schools, departments, and classrooms and highlighted "Solidarity for Soviet Jewry," "Israeli Independence Day," and the "Warsaw Ghetto Uprising." Included in material prepared by the Jewish Labor Committee and distributed in "instructor kits" at a teachers' workshop promoting the week on the previous Tuesday were pamphlets, including a bibliography of Zionist books and a catalog of audiovisual materials, both of which were saturated with the story of the holocaust, the history of Masada,[64] and the film *Anti-Semitism in America.*[65]

Teachers were advised to promote appearances of concentration camp survivors at classroom meetings. The students were told that the three major concerns of American Jews were "the holocaust, Soviet Jewry, and the security of Israel."

The following October a course of study on the holocaust was introduced by the New York Board of Education with the hope it would be made mandatory in all of the city high schools the following year.[66] The 461-page curriculum, "The Holocaust, a Study of Genocide," included extracts from Hitler's *Mein Kampf,* pictures and descriptions of the death camps, poems, plays, maps, and programs for class discussion. The course was to supplant, said Board President Steven R. Aiello, the brief discussion of Nazi genocide taken up in history and other social studies courses. His goal was "at least two weeks of mandatory Holocaust Study" after the initial year's experimentation (70 percent of the students in New York City schools are black or Hispanic).

In a three-column *Times* Letter to the Editor,[67] given the bold heading "Holocaust Study: The Intent Is to Inform, Not Inflame," Board of Education Chancellor Irving Anker defended the course as "part of history" from which an understanding of "prejudice and racism" will help "young people to know and respect one another's differences." The Chancellor stated that it was "never the intention to pass over the sufferings of other groups," but no plans were announced for parallel courses.

The Philadelphia secondary public schools went one step further than New York. Over the rigorous protest of the city's largest German-American organization, the school system announced in September 1977 "plans to require virtually all students in secondary public schools to study the Holocaust of the Jews in Nazi Germany."[68] The program, begun in some schools the year before, was to be expanded and introduced as part of a required world history course in the ninth grade in the city's twenty-six senior high schools and forty junior high schools.

The Chairman of the German-American Committee of Greater Philadelphia protested that the 127-page curriculum guide gave the impression "that the Jews were the only ones who suffered to any great extent and that the Nazis were the only ones who committed crimes against humanity." But this made little impact on Dr. Franklin H. Littell, Chairman of the religion department at Temple University, who developed the program after he had directed and participated in national conferences on the holocaust.

For the benefit of high school history textbooks and college texts, whose treatment of Nazism was found to be "brief, bland, superficial, and misleading," ADL pamphleteer Henry Friedlander wrote a lengthy tome, and ADL subsidized author Milton Meltzer's 217-page book *Never to Forget: The Jews of the Holocaust,* [69] published by Harper & Row and reviewed by the *Times* Sunday Book Review.[70] Widely distributed in all schools and colleges was the six-page ADL bulletin listing the publications and audiovisual material available on the holocaust. In addition to making it possible for major publishing houses to put out new tomes, the organization made available books already published. The cultists prepared new anthologies-studies on *Auschwitz,* the *Eichmann Trial, The Third Reich in Perspective,* and *The Anatomy of Nazism.* Their selected Reading List on the holocaust contained seventeen well-known titles.

Whenever all else failed and the Zionist juggernaut seemed to be stalled, Nazi pursuer Simon Wiesenthal was brought into the limelight. Although Israel has proclaimed a new relationship with West Germany, she has not been adverse to accepting any propaganda gains that might be reaped from the James Bond "007"-like efforts of manhunter Wiesenthal, whose continuing search for Nazis spasmodically erupts into healthy media coverage. "The Nazi Hunter" was the subject of a June 19, 1977, interview on CBS's "Who's Who" on "Sixty Minutes," and a vast field was opened by introducing Dan Rather to the notorious anti-Nazi.

With the announcement of a new series of children's books to be written by Wiesenthal for Raintree Publishers in Milwaukee, the very young were not to be given fairy tales—or were they?—but recitals of the Wiesenthal adventures in tracking down war criminals. The first was to deal with his search for the Gestapo police officer in occupied Holland who arrested Anne Frank, the overpublicized teenager whose diary (in twenty-six editions) told of Jewish persecution in Holland under the Nazis, but the veracity of whose saga has since come under serious question.[71]

Another Wiesenthal horror book was to describe the hunt for Adolf Eichmann, who was executed by Israel in 1961 for his war crimes. "I want to make this story alive so a young man will read and understand it," said author Wiesenthal. "It is something for society—for the new generation." Who but the Zionists would try to emulate the Nazis by capturing the minds of the young. Happily, the project was dropped.[72]

Wiesenthal's books were scarcely the first on the holocaust for the young. On one Sunday in November 1972[73] Elie Wiesel, then recently appointed Professor of Jewish Studies at City University of New York, reviewed seven books intended to add to the traumas and complexes of young readers by acquainting them with one aspect or another of the Hitler period. The books were described as "valuable, moving, and perceptible" to one degree or another. The review was illustrated with the oft-repeated 1943 photo of women and children being arrested in Warsaw.

Congress joined the act, too. Spearheaded by Representatives Joshua Eilberg, Chairman of the House Judiciary Subcommittee on Immigration, and Elizabeth Holtzman of Brooklyn, both Israel-Firsters, the publicity war against Hitler continued thirty-one years after the fact. The front page of the October 3, 1976, *New York Times* carried the story: "Nazi War Criminal Suspects in US Face Deportation as Drive Widens." Some of the "alleged" criminals had been brought to the country by U.S. intelligence agents to assist in the development of such scientific ventures as the space capsule.

But with the cooperation of the anti-anti-Semitic cult, Wiesenthal and Tuviah Friedman, Director of the Nazi war-crimes documentation center in Haifa, Israel, helped inspire a "New US Nazi Hunt," as the *Times*[74] announced in a half-page Sunday "Week in Review" spread featured by the well-known, oft-reprinted photo of the Nazi defendants in the dock, at the 1946 Nuremberg war-crimes trial. By 1976 there were pending investigations by the U.S. Immigration and Naturalization Service of some eighty-five naturalized American citizens and resident aliens for alleged atrocities in Nazi-occupied Europe and illegal entrance into the U.S. after the war. Cases involving three elderly men, two Latvians and a Lithuanian, and Rumanian Orthodox Bishop of America Valerian D. Trifa, received widespread publicity. The television programs "Sixty Minutes," "A.M. America," and the David Suskind show devoted extensive time to the war-crimes issue despite the fact that as the cameras showed, there was a definite lack of public enthusiasm for this theme. Neighbors of one of the Nazis being "pursued," Boleslaus Maikovskis, felt he should be left alone at this stage of his life. (The 73-year-old Latvian was shot, but not fatally, on August 4, 1978, ostensibly by the JDL.) But such opinions were, of course, totally ignored by the media's compulsive attraction to this subject, and nothing could halt the Nazi hunter's successful quest for funds for the new Simon Wiesenthal Center for Holocaust Studies in California.[75]

On one occasion when hard-pressed in diplomatic jousting, Prime Minister Meir audaciously declared: "You did nothing to save Jews in the holocaust. You shall not preach to us now."[76] This kind of emotional blackmail is apt to be used by anyone and to appear any place. The *New York Review of Books,* for instance, has been recognized as one of the few influential publications that has given some small space to dissenting views on the Middle East—albeit from the Left. I. F. Stone and Noam Chomsky, in particular, have been allowed in recent years to present most controversial positions on the Palestinians. Yet even in this magazine, a long piece, "Among the Israelis,"[77] by Stephen Spender, the noted British poet and critic, was climaxed with a moving but emotional account of his visit to Yad Vashem. Coming at the end of Spender's article, this served to wipe away the pros and cons that he had evidently been trying to balance in the course of his writing. All that was left was the black slate of the concentration camps. Against such atrocities, what chance had the Palestinians or the arguments of "the Arabists"[78] with whom Spender passed much of his time in the Holy Land.

No one disputes that the Nazi era was one of the lowest points, if not the lowest, in human civilization. It must not be overlooked, however, that millions of people other than Jews perished, and for these the bell does not seem to have been tolling. And it is not out of line to inquire of the cultists, these people so intent on keeping this issue of the "six million" alive, whether they have ever given any consideration to the Zionist role in the deaths of these "six million" victims? In discussing alleged Vatican indifference to the holocaust, the *Jewish Observer,* the organ of the Orthodox Agadath Israel of America, pointed out a Jewish parallel:

We are forced to realize with deep pain that this passivity had its echo on the Jewish scene, too. . . . There was not only the intrusion of politics into various aspects of the rescue efforts that were made. The writings . . . clearly prove that actual rescue opportunities were neglected or even blocked because they did not fit in with the plans of the Zionist leadership to force a showdown over the Israel state in the making.[79]

Ben Hecht's fully documented *Perfidy*[80] blatantly exposed the extent to which Zionists cooperated in the annihilation of their fellow Jews. This early supporter of Jewish statehood in Palestine described the criminal libel suit brought against Malkiel Greenwald for charging high-ranking Israeli official Rudolf Kastner of collaboration in the responsibility for the slaughter of Hungary's one million Jews. "Timorous Jewish lodge members in Zion, London and America . . . these Zionist leaders who let their six million kinsmen burn, choke, hang without protest, with indifference" is Hecht's description of the reaction of Jewish leaders who, he insisted, knew in advance the timing, method, and place of the impending annihilation, but refused to warn the victims—out of greater concern for the creation of a political state than for saving Jewish lives."[81]

Many of the Hungarian Jews, according to Hecht, were but three miles from the Rumanian border and were guarded by a very small Nazi military contingent as they were fed reassurances by Zionist leader Kastner up to the very moment they were shipped to the crematoria. He had intimate ties with such Nazis as Eichmann, Himmler, and their aide Lieutenant General Kurt Becher, in whose behalf Kastner later intervened to save from conviction at Nuremberg. But when Joel Kastner was permitted to come out of the Hungarian hell as an intermediary from the Nazis with a barter deal of trucks for human lives, President-to-be of Israel Chaim Weizmann refused to see him for weeks, and Kastner then permitted the deal to fall through.

Sixteen years later, *The Holocaust Victims*[82] by Rabbi Moshe Schonfeld corroborated Hecht's evidence that the Zionist leadership was concerned only in the creation of a state, "not the saving of Jewish lives," and had permitted thousands of their own people to go to their death so that they might advance political goals. Photostated documents and copies of letters, written by some of those accused by Rabbi Schonfeld, supported the charge of betrayal against Weizmann, Rabbi Stephen Wise, and Jewish Agency Chairman Yitzhak Greenbaum, to whom the Jewish slaughter only meant further emphasis on their insistence that the creation of a Zionist state in Israel was the only hope for surviving Jews.

Greenbaum was quoted as having said, "One cow in Palestine is worth more than all the Jews in Poland." Wise was alleged to have lobbied to make sure that relief packages of food were denied to starving Jews in Europe so that they would be forced to seek Zionist goals. At a time when money was needed to save Eastern European Jews, Greenbaum wrote, "When they asked me, couldn't you give money out of the United Jewish Appeal funds for the rescue of Jews in Europe, I said 'No,' and I say again 'No!' One should resist this wave which pushes Zionist activities, i.e. the creation of a state, to secondary importance."

In her book, *Eichmann in Jerusalem*,[83] Hannah Arendt verified the intimate connection, Lucy Dawidowicz notwithstanding, between the

Nazis and Zionist leaders, who were the only Jews in the early months of the Hitler regime to associate with the German authorities and who used their position to discredit anti- and non-Zionist Jews. According to Arendt, they urged the adoption of the slogan, "Wear the yellow star with pride" to end Jewish assimilation and to encourage the Nazis to send the Jews to Palestine. A secret agreement was reached between the Jewish Agency for Palestine and Nazi authorities to assist in Zionist plans for illegal immigration into the Holy Land, toward which end even the Gestapo and the SS were willing to cooperate, for this was another method of ridding Europe of the "hated Jews."

The cumulative effect of keeping the holocaust in the forefront of the entertainment, cultural, and political worlds can only be understood when one tries to speak on the Middle East conflict before even as impartial an audience as the American Humanist Society and emotional, near-crazed partisans wildly interrupt: "What about the six million?" To Israelis and their nationalist-minded American followers, the deaths of no one else counted.[84] Hemingway's advice to F. Scott Fitzgerald meant absolutely nothing: "We are all tragic figures . . . when you receive a damned hurt use it. . . . don't cheat with it." Yad Vashem and the holocaust keep remembrance of the tragic past aglow, blot out the growing Palestinian shadow and help hold Christians in bondage.

XIV   Christians in Bondage

It's not enough that we do our best; sometimes we have to do what's required.

—Winston Churchill

If all but a very few exceptional individuals have been silenced by the image of the Nazi holocaust and the threat of being called anti-Semitic, there still ought to have been one voice raised in conscientious protest —that of Christianity. Christians should be able to disentangle the distortions from the truth, and they ought to act without fear. After all, in sheer numbers alone Christians far surpass the Jews of this world, and granted that Jews hold a disproportionate number of positions of influence, Christians still hold many more.

The Christian voice, moreover, has become increasingly outspoken in recent years on social and economic issues, and at times even political affairs, from which the Christian church previously long shied away. While the Palestine question calls for a political solution, it is of course primarily a human problem. The dispersion into exile or subjection to alien domination of Palestinian Arabs, including many Christians,[1] poses an inescapable moral issue for the church, just as did America's treatment of its own minorities. Why have we not heard from this large and otherwise aware Christian presence?

Quite aside from general moral principles, Christians have a real and personal reason for wanting to establish the truth in this matter. The Christian experience, historically and otherwise, is most relevant to many of the matters under discussion: Palestine is also the "Holy Land" of the Christians, and Jerusalem is their Holy City, too. Who more than Christians should have a deep interest in airing the pros and cons of the conflict for control of the Holy Land, and should be expected to speak out?

But it is the irrefutability of the holocaust as a fact of the past that has hamstrung the Christian world at large, and American Christians in particular. The insinuations of anti-Semitism, backed up by threats, are manipulated to co-opt the Christian and to tie him up, signed, sealed, and delivered, for the Zionist-Israelist claque.

Christians—Protestants and Catholics alike, and from all denominations, even those who prefer not to socialize with Jews[2]—have lent their voices to the Zionist cause in varied ways. Sometimes it may be quite explicit and open, as in the case of the City Editor of a daily Rochester, New York, newspaper, who when confronted with the charge of bias in reporting said: "Sure, we feel sorry for the Jews after what happened to them. These people have to have a home of their own."

Sometimes this support even gets out of control. In 1969 Australian Christian fundamentalist Michael Rohan set fire to the Al-Aqsa Mosque, one of Islam's holiest places, in occupied Arab Jerusalem. The frenzied arsonist had been welcomed to and had lived in an Israeli kibbutz, as he rabidly preached: "There must be no mosques in this land so that the Jews may return to rebuild their temple and the final coming of Christ may be realized."

Fundamentalist Christians are victimized by the mistaken equation of modern political Israel with biblical spiritual Israel. They viewed with favor the establishment of the state as part of God's plan, the necessary precursor to the second coming of Jesus and the end of the world. Particularly in the Bible Belt, these fundamentalists have given fullest support to Israel in its conflict with the Arabs. This biblical influence undoubtedly played no small part in molding born-again Baptist Jimmy Carter's attitudes toward the Middle East.

A full-page *New York Times* advertisement of July 1, 1976, to which 105 fundamentalist churches throughout the country affixed their signatures, asserted that anyone opposing the Zionist claim to the land of Israel "isn't just fighting Israel, but God and time itself."

During the diplomatic jockeying over the Geneva Conference, this fundamentalist theme was picked up in two further full-page *New York Times* ads in November 1977. One expressed "Evangelicals' Concern for Israel" and was signed by actor Pat Boone, past President of the National Association of Evangelicals Hudson Armerding, Trinity College President Harry Evans, President-elect of the Institute of Holy Land Studies in Jerusalem and Coordinator President Emeritus of the Evangelical Free Church of America Arnold T. Olson, and President of the Institute of Holy Land Studies in Jerusalem George Giacumakis,

Jr.[3] The other, captioned "Fundamentalists Vote with Israel," was paid for, among others, by President of International Council of Christian Churches Carl McIntyre, General Secretary of the Independent Board for Presbyterian Home Missions Jack Weisenfeld, and General Secretary of American Christian Action Committee Wes Auger.[4] Similar statements of unstinting loyalty to Zionist Israel were expressed by the Southern Baptist Convention.

At times support given to the Zionist-Israelist cause is indirect and subtle, if not insidious, but certainly no less influential in the way it permeates Christian outlets.[5] The two million monthly copies of Herbert W. Armstrong's *Plain Truth* are filled with predictions of the future based on biblical interpretation favoring the return of Jews to Palestine. Oral Roberts' books and telecasts, reaching millions, have been devoted to the same end. *The Late Great Planet Earth,*[6] with its 47 printings in paperback within seven years through 1977, worked the Israeli state into the center of its apocalyptic fundamentalist-scenario and converted thousands of semi-literate Christians of Bible Belt America into rabid Zionists. "As Armageddon," readers are told, "begins with the invasion of Israel by the Arabs and the Russian confederacy, and their consequent swift destruction, the greatest period of Jewish conversion to the true Messiah will begin." The movie of the same title added further adherents.

A particularly vivid influence has been the beautiful film made by Billy Graham, *His Land,* which has been viewed by fifteen million across this country and Canada. This superbly photographed visual survey of the land of Israel, accompanied by narrated biblical prophecies and religious songs, celebrates the fact that God has kept His word to the Jew, that He has fulfilled prophetic promises[7] given 2,500 years ago by restoring Israel in the 20th century. As the film's advertisements put it: "Israel today is a living testimony to the words of the Old Testament prophets, and a portent of the triumphant return of Christ. The rebirth of the State of Israel by United Nations decree on November 29, 1947, is by far the greatest biblical event that has taken place during the twentieth century."

But as Dr. J. Calvin Keene, former head of the Department of Religion at St. Lawrence University in Canton, New York, pointed out, "the scriptural passages of supposed prediction are not numerous and upon a close inspection are found to be either very vague in their meaning and consequently unconvincing, or predictions of events which did in fact occur soon after the time of writing, or passages lifted out of context, made to imply ideas not found in their original settings."[8]

It should be made clear that *His Land* was not a scholarly dissertation. It did not develop its theme as a thesis supported by a reasoned exposition of evidence. The literal interpretation of prophecy, and the Christian's ability to identify events of modern history as prophecy fulfilled, were simply assumed to be true. It was taken for granted that the modern State of Israel *is* ancient Israel restored according to God's prophetic word. There was no hint that many Christians either totally disagree or have serious problems with this interpretation, no allusion to the possibility that other valid interpretations of prophecy and explanations for the formation of modern Israel may exist.

For example, Paul Jersild, writing in the May 10, 1975, issue of the Jesuit publication *America,* stated:

To create a "theological politics" and a nation of "chosen people" based on ethnic and religious factors is to create an immediate problem in any nation's relations with its neighbors. The Israeli claim to Palestine must be judged on the political and humanitarian realities of the 20th century, without reference to the history that took place several millenia ago. To refer to the Bible in any prescriptive sense in settling this problem *is an unhistorical and irresponsible use of scripture.* [Italics added.][9]

However, the reason that a film such as *His Land* appealed to so many Christians was that it provided a set of easy, clear answers in an area where there appeared to be only problems and question marks. Most of us are at least superficially familiar with modern Israel from the news media. All of us have been bombarded almost daily for nearly thirty years with news about the solution-defying confrontation of Israel with the Arabs. Yet a clear Christian position on this modern crisis has been largely absent. So, for many, *His Land* provided the first and only Christian explanation for the creation of modern Israel. And such a beautiful explanation, so simple: God's word come true! God has kept his promises after 2,500 years! One could walk away satisfied from a picture like that.

Although not a film about the political issues in which modern Israel is involved, it did manage to establish a correlation between biblical prophecy and 20th-century political history. It did refer to Israel's restoration of the land, her building of modern cities, and her reconquest of the site of the Temple in the 1967 war. For the rest, the film was silent about Israel's history in the Middle East. But because the identification of prophecy with modern events was made, the silence about most events and the selection of only a few resulted in a dangerously slanted portrayal of Israel. For example, the omission of the fact that the foundation of Israel in 1947 was accompanied by vehement Arab opposition (no Jordanian opposition to the conquest of the Holy City was shown or mentioned) left the audience with the impression that today's opposition by the Arab world must be unwarranted. To the viewer Israel was justified and blameless, and Arab claims on Palestine were not even worth mentioning.

The moral issues involved were totally disregarded. The Old Testament unmistakably teaches that no Jewish return save in righteousness may be countenanced and, as the true Orthodox insist, it may be only Messiah-led.

The film, as Professor Bert De Vries of Calvin College in Grand Rapids, Michigan, pointed out in his lengthy study[10] of the Graham film, advances the widely accepted American argument that "the right of ownership to the piece of property is based on industrious and correct maintenance of that property." The colonialist reasoning goes something like this: "The Arabs had their chance. They owned the land for centuries and ruined it completely. They even were incompetent and slothful stewards. Now the Israelis have transformed it from a desert to a garden. The Arabs failed; the Israelis succeeded. Therefore the Israelis have earned the right to the land." De Vries' answer to this kind of reasoning: "Should I hand over the keys of my Oldsmobile to someone else just because I allowed it to get rusty and I failed to fix the dents in the fenders?"

The assumption that Israel today is a manifestation of biblical prophecy was not an invention of Billy Graham, but there is no denying that such a film has brilliantly exploited this aspect of Jewish-American relations. The fact that so many of the Zionists who do the exploiting are atheists and agnostics indicates the cynicism with which they both manipulate the naïve religiosity of fundamentalist Christians to promote Israeli political nationalism and almost welcome its basically anti-Judaistic aim to convert all Jews to Christianity.

Zionist groups and their allied forces have gone far beyond films in their untiring efforts. From the outset of Israel's creation, they have not been satisfied merely to exert pressure upon Christian lay and clerical organizations, but rather have been intent on crushing any budding opposition in the Christian community. This they have been able to accomplish by means of meticulous organization and an alert, ubiquitous intelligence service. On August 10, 1960, Rabbi Marc Tanenbaum, then Executive Director of the Synagogue Council of America, in a "Confidential, not for Publication or Attribution" memorandum to Officers and Executive Directors of the Council of Jewish Federation and Welfare Funds (his financial backers), summarized the organization's program "in interpreting to key leaders in the national Catholic and Protestant church federations the religious aspect of American Jewry's relationship to the people and the State of Israel."

Referring to "this unpublicized chapter in Christian and Jewish relations," Tanenbaum claimed the following accomplishments over a two-year period:

1) "Forced the adoption by the National Council of Churches, representing 39 major Protestant denominations, of its first resolution acknowledging the *de facto* and *de jure* existence of the state of Israel and calling upon its 145,000 member churches and 900 local councils of churches to help safeguard the security of Israel and to assure its present frontiers."

2) Through "day-to-day contacts prevailed upon" the Council, which had begun to disseminate documents on the Arab refugees as part of their contribution to World Refugee Year, to distribute to all local councils and individual churches a memorandum, including a bibliography on the Middle East prepared by the Synagogue Council, "explaining the spiritual ties which link American Jews to the State of Israel and counteracting charges of dual loyalties." Exerted pressure simultaneously upon the Council to cease all efforts in behalf of the Arab refugees.

3) Helped block a resolution pending before the Board of Directors of the U.S. Committee for Refugees that called for a study of the Arab refugee question.

4) Won agreement from the National Council of Churches to table the strong report growing out of the Beirut Conference on Refugees, which "reflected the anti-Israel and pro-Arab sympathies of the Foreign Missions within the National Council of Churches and the World Council of Churches."

5) Intervened and testified before the House Foreign Affairs and Senate Foreign Relations Committees in favor of maintaining the status quo for Mutual Security Act grants to Israel when these in April 1959 were threatened with drastic reduction.

6) Protested use of UNESCO funds to help Arab teachers in refugee camps because they "taught their students hatred of Israel." Won adoption of a resolution denying funds to any member nation that "exploits these funds to create tensions and animosities against each other."

7) Stimulated a "Human Relations Project" in Catholic elementary high schools that was conducted by a Jewish scholar with a background in Catholic theology "to help Catholic students achieve a better image of the Jew, his religion, and his relationship to the State of Israel."

8) Brought about the delivery by Rabbi Arthur Hertzberg of a paper, "Judaism, Zionism and Israel," before both the World and National Coun-

cils of Churches, which was later published in book form as *The Zionist Idea*.

9) Blocked a World Council of Churches plan to study the question of religious liberty in the State of Israel.

10) Persuaded Dr. E. T. Dahlberg, the President of the National Council of Churches, to include Israel in his tour of world refugee camps, and had the Chief Rabbi of Israel and foreign ministry officials receive and talk to him.

11) Guided the National Council of Churches in preparing for distribution through the council educational material designed for "the average church member interpreting the Jewish community in the U.S., its relationship to Israel, etc."

In sending out this confidential memorandum, the active rabbi propagandist was not afraid to attribute much of the success of the Synagogue Council program "to the annual allocations received from various Jewish welfare funds and federations in the United States"—an admission that tax-free "religious and eleemosynary" American dollars had been used to propagandize the cause of Israel to the most potent Christian religious groups in the country.

Tanenbaum's net came up with his biggest Christian "fish" when he and Billy Graham made common cause in the fall of 1977 after Graham had been in close contact with another born-again Christian, Jimmy Carter. During the administration's first moral crisis, according to columnists Evans and Novak,[11] the President sought Graham's advice and in turn was strongly cautioned against permitting Moscow back into the Middle East diplomatic negotiations. To block such a move, an Evangelical-Zionist coalition was formed, with Graham giving the keynote address at the American Jewish Committee's National Executive Council meeting in Atlanta. The call for rededication to the existence of Israel and the end to talk of a Palestinian state made no mention of the implied secret agreement: political support for Zionism in return for Jewish conversions to Christianity.

Main-line Protestants have been more reluctant than their fundamentalist brethren to view the Middle East conflict through Zionist-tinted lenses. In fact, the National Council of Churches has been at times condemned by the Anti-Defamation League of B'nai B'rith for "pronounced anti-Israel prejudice." However, even the Protestant Episcopal church has had some of its leaders publicly espouse pro-Zionist causes—e.g., Bishops John H. Burt of Ohio, Jonathan Sherman of Long Island, and the late somewhat eccentric James A. Pike of California, who ended his life by walking out into the Judaean wilderness.

This hymn, often included in Easter Sunday services, is a reminder of the manner in which the sanctity of the State of Israel receives Episcopal approbation:

> Come ye faithful, raise the strain
> Of triumphant gladness
> God has brought his Israel
> Into joy from sadness.
> Loose from Pharaoh's bitter yoke,
> Jacob's sons and daughters
> Led them with unmoistened foot
> Through the Red Sea waters.[12]

The choice of "Israel" as the name for the new state was no accident. It further linked religion and nation; for the world, Israel, is irrevocably bound to the prayers recited on all occasions in the synagogues of all Jewish sects, as it is often in certain Christian churches.

It is fair to say that American Catholics look at the Middle East in the same manner as Americans in general look at the area, namely, with a marked partiality for Israel. This bias is also a product of the cult of anti-anti-Semitism, many such people being acutely sensitive to Jewish pressures and reluctant to be called anti-Semitic. At the outset of the Palestine question, because of their strong ties with the Holy Land, the Catholics in the U.S., as well as at the Vatican (which has never recognized the State of Israel), had been more critical of the Zionist coup in establishing its state and had continued to give tangible humanitarian support to help alleviate the plight of the Palestinian refugees. But the Catholic leadership soon found it impolitic to espouse the Palestinian cause, even if their efforts were confined to the displaced Palestinians. The full brunt of the Zionist persuasion was directed toward them as they were importuned both to accept as a fact the special "religious" link between American Jews and the State of Israel and also to equate anti-Zionism with anti-Semitism.

The fear in Catholic circles of being labeled anti-Semitic became an even more pulverizing weapon after the issuance of the declaration of Vatican II. The Council's Declaration on the Jews, adopted in 1965 by a vote of 2,221 to 88, repudiated the charge of collective Jewish guilt for the death of Jesus and rejected anti-Semitism. Rabbi Tanenbaum continued to browbeat Catholics for failing to educate their parishioners with his interpretation of the Vatican Council's declaration equating repudiation of the canard of Jewish responsibility for the death of Jesus with a blanket immunity for any criticism of Zionist-Israeli policies. Of course it remained unsaid that the declaration, according to Cardinal Augustin Bea, who headed the Secretariat that drafted it, was to have "no political implications" and thus was *not* to be interpreted as taking sides in the complicated political dispute over Palestine.

Some Catholic leaders needed no admonishment from the Rabbi. In order to advance Catholic-Jewish relations in his diocese and to overcome what some thought to be "racial" prejudice, the late Cardinal Richard Cushing spoke out clearly and passionately in favor of Israel. On one occasion, when one of his Palestinian flock called to tell the Cardinal how outrageous his remarks were to Palestinians and asked him how he could have said such a thing, the Cardinal replied in his characteristic manner of speaking, "Oh, don't pay any attention to that." While the Palestinian was shocked but felt slightly better, Boston Catholics who heard the Cardinal deliver his eulogy of Israel understood the statement only in its context. And the powerful Cardinal's words, intended only for local consumption, carried far beyond Boston environs.

Perhaps the apotheosis of Zionist nationalism among the Catholic clergy is expressed by Msgr. John M. Oesterreicher, a convert from Judaism and the Director of the Institute of Judeo-Christian Studies at Seton Hall University, South Orange, New Jersey. The institute, founded in 1953 ostensibly to promote ecumenical understanding between the Christian and Hebrew religions, has since the 1967 six-day war become a sounding board for the most blatant pro-Israel propaganda.

Oesterreicher makes support for Israel "a test for every Christian"; advocates arms aid for the Zionist state; rejects as "absolutely ridiculous" the proposition that Palestinian self-determination is essential to peace; and has publicly rhapsodized that "we must shout from the housetops that this state [Israel] has a right to live."[13]

In the wake of the 1970 bombing of a Swiss airliner by Palestinian commandos, Oesterreicher called upon Americans to impose economic sanctions against the Palestinians. On every possible occasion, using the garments of the church, the Monsignor has condemned the refugees as "terrorists." When Israel took legal steps to annex the eastern sector of Jerusalem in the face of many protesting U.N. resolutions, he maneuvered another tax-free organization, the National Conference of Christians and Jews, ostensibly established to improve relations between the two religions by opposing bigotry, to use their headquarters for launching a national campaign supporting the Israeli takeover of the Holy City.

Notwithstanding Oesterreicher's extreme Zionist chauvinism, he has enjoyed the support of Seton Hall faculty and administration, exemplified by the public purchase of $250,000 of State of Israel Bonds by the University's President.

Pro-Zionist publicity from Christian leaders continued to emanate from the National Conference headquarters, which has quickly emerged as another Zionist front organization even as its counterpart, the Council for Christians and Jews in the United Kingdom, was doing a most effective job of smothering anti-Zionist British sentiment by equating all dissent with anti-Semitism. The General Secretary of the prestigious Council, whose officers include the Archbishops of Canterbury and Westminster, the Chief Rabbi of the United Hebrew Congregation, and financiers Baring and Rothschild, was assiduously hunting down writers who, by dint of perseverance, managed to break into the letter columns of the biased press, and endeavored to make them feel guilty for their expressions of dissent. After centuries of religious prejudice against Jews, determined Christians, under astute direction, were trying to make certain that no criticism of the Israeli state, however valid, reached the surface—all this in the name of tolerance.

Seton Hall's contributions toward keeping Christians enchained were varied. On June 2, 1974, more than 400 Essex County, New Jersey, Jews joined to show their solidarity in support of oppressed Jews of the Soviet Union, staging a march from a South Orange temple to Seton Hall University for a rally. Greetings were extended by Msgr. Thomas Fahy, President of Seton Hall, where the conference had been held since 1970. In 1976 Fahy received the State of Israel Award from Joseph H. Lerner, Vice President of the Zionist Organization of America. And in 1977 University Adviser to the International Students Office John E. McLoughlin received the Justice Brandeis Brotherhood Award from the New Jersey region of the Zionist Organization of America.[14]

In February 1975 Professor J. C. Hurewitz of the Middle East Institute of Columbia University opened a series of seven lectures on "Israel, the Arabs and the World Community" at Seton Hall, sponsored by the Jewish Education Association of Metropolitan New Jersey and Seton Hall's Department of History in conjunction with the Hebrew Union College, Jewish Institute of Religion of the New York School of Education, and the Zionist Federation of Essex and Union Counties. Other Zionist spokesmen who followed were Dr. Roy Eckhardt of Lehigh University, Professor Gil Carl Al Roy of Hunter College, Professor Chaim I. Waxman of Brooklyn College, and Professor Joseph Neyer of Rutgers.

Rivaling Oesterreicher in his devotion to Israel was the Reverend Edward H. Flannery, formerly director of the U.S. Bishop's Office for Catholic-Jewish Relations and until recently head of the Office of Catholic-Jewish Relations of the Conference of Catholic Bishops. Flannery has publicly chided Catholics for being "callous" to Jewish suffering; charged that most anti-Zionists are "anti-Semitic"; suggested that "anti-Semitism" among the Roman curia was one of the reasons the Vatican has not recognized Israel. He addressed Zionist audiences on the theme "Why Israel is precious to me," and authored the book *The Anguish of the Jews: Twenty-Three Centuries of Anti-Semitism.*[15]

The Op-Ed page of the *Times* was open to Flannery for a lengthy article, "The Greatest Hatred in History," in which the Catholic priest assailed General George Brown for his "hoary lie about Jewish ownership of banks and newspapers"; President Nixon for his alleged 1972 warning to Haldeman, "The arts, you know—they're Jews—they're left-wing—stay away"; and Attorney General William Saxbe for a reference to the Jewish intellectual of the McCarthy era "who was, in those days, very enamored of the Communist party."[16] These current examples of alleged anti-Semitism were shrewdly intermixed with the history of early Catholic bigotry and deicides.[17]

But elsewhere at least some other Catholics were challenging Zionist operations. Alaska's Archbishop Joseph T. Ryan, former Director of the Catholic Near East Welfare Association and the Pontifical Mission for Palestine, called on American Catholic bishops to "speak up and speak up now." The Archbishop urged: "Make the world know that Christianity and Islam are in Jerusalem by right, not by sufferance. Make the world know that Christianity does not—cannot—accept the ethnic domination of, or political sovereignty, of one religion over another."[18]

While many Christians in the Western world continued to make reparations for crimes against the Jews in which they felt they had shared, if only vicariously, some refused to be entirely silenced regarding the plight of the Palestinian refugees. In 1968 both the National Council of Churches and the Mennonite Central Committee, following study tours, issued parallel reports that stressed the conviction of the five million Christians in the Mideast area that, as the National Council of Churches put it, "Western Christians and Churches are indifferent to their situation and even have betrayed them." The Mennonite rapporteurs decried the fact that the Arab side of the story had been so "underrepresented" and that "not only does the West not know the Arab and his cause, but the Christian West has hardly become aware of the Christians in the Arab world." The Cyprus meeting of the World Council of Churches admitted that existing programs were not "an adequate Christian response to the injustice and misery" of the Palestinians.

In 1970 still another voice was heard. The majority of British participants at the World Conference of Christians for Palestine issued a statement in Beirut declaring in part: "We consider the political creed of Zionism to be the negation of Christianity. Mankind is indivisible, and for this reason we reaffirm our belief in plural states, epitomized by the concept of a secular Palestine where Christians, Jews and Moslems can play an equal part in building a nation."[19]

This Christian "revolt" led to a fiery statement by Rabbi Tanenbaum, distributed nationally to the religious columns of all papers, accusing major Protestant bodies of "actively disseminating pro-Arab propaganda through their church structures." The response of certain Protestant denominations to church mission reports from the area, the rabbi alleged, "amount to virtual collusion with foreign Arab government representatives."

The suppression campaign had already begun with the 1969 "confidential letter" sent out under the signature of the rabbi as Director of Religious Affairs on the letterhead of the American Jewish Committee (whose chairman was Arthur Goldberg), calling for combat against growing Protestant sympathy for the Arabs. Intensified Arab propaganda had penetrated church groups and publications, Tanenbaum alleged. Expressing concern over reports from Christian church delegations to the Middle East, some of which "slide from an 'anti-Zionist' stance into 'anti-Semitism,' " the letter detailed suggested rabbinical action in organizing the Jewish community, including "monitoring of Christian publications, speakers, programs, etc., that take place in church settings." Jewish communities were urged to "organize one-day Jewish-Christian 'Institutes' " and to send letters to "public officials, general and religious press and to radio and TV program directors." The Tanenbaum letter detailed other intimate links that were necessary between Jewish "religious" and other groups so as to make the far-flung suppression operations successful.

The Vatican II goal of encouraging "study and dialogue" between Christians and Jews fits perfectly into Zionist plans. Accordingly, rabbis around the country organized one-day institutes in an endeavor to remind Christians that the Jewish concern for Israel was a religious belief and that anti-Zionism must be equated to anti-Semitism. At the same time Catholic leaders were browbeaten for failing to educate their parishioners in accordance with the Zionist interpretation of the Vatican Council's declaration.

In order to explain the presence of even a most moderate anti-Zionist speaker at an institute held in Queens, Zionist Chairman Rabbi Usher Kornblum, in a confidential widely distributed memorandum to boost attendance, made this explanation: "The meeting of December 2 is a must for every rabbi. Reverend John Sutton[20] is a 'lo m'shelaner' [not one of ours] as far as Israel is concerned. *But I had to include him to give the Institute a semblance of impartiality.* We have an opportunity to activate a number of Christian clergymen on behalf of Israel. Therefore, your presence and participation is desired." (Emphasis added.)

The report on one of the first institutes held in Long Beach indicated that about forty persons were present, of whom eight were rabbis. Rabbi Max Nussbaum of Hollywood expounded at great length to the assembled clergymen on the centrality in Jewish thought of the Holy Land and the relationship between Israel and the "Jewish people." Here is the reaction of one of the ministers who attended the institute to the kind of "dialogue" that followed:

We had been invited to ask questions or make comments after the rabbi spoke. Comments were really not wanted, only verbal questions. I challenged the rabbi courteously, but after about two minutes, the presiding rabbi broke in impatiently: "Well, what is your question?" Two or three others made comments, but none were as much as a minute long. It was obvious that there was no intent to permit a real exchange of ideas.

Dr. John Nicholls Booth had been given a place at the speakers' table next to the Israeli Consul in Los Angeles, Moshe Yegar. The Consul and the minister had a delightful chat throughout luncheon about Burma, Unitarianism, and everything but Israel. Yegar did not know or realize who Booth was until he, Yegar, started to speak and consulted his notes. When he found that he had come to Long Beach to discuss a local clergyman's sermon, "Zionist Myth-Information Examined," that was being widely distributed by "Arab students on campuses," his eyes widened and he declared, "I suddenly suspect that I have been sitting next to him all through lunch." The place rocked with laughter.

"He is such a nice fellow," Yegar continued, "I will have to destroy all, or at least some, of my notes. How could such a nice man say such terrible things?" Then the Consul politely proceeded to attack the published Booth sermon, particularly taking issue with the charge that it was difficult to criticize Israel because then one is invariably called anti-Semitic. Yegar declared—and this was most prominently picked up in the local press—"I never heard any Israeli or any American Jew who did that. It never occurred to us to call those who differed with us anti-Semitic. That is nonsense." The Consul finished his talk at nearly two o'clock, the time set for adjournment. All Booth could do with this limitation in time was to rise and say that he would be glad to provide a copy of the sermon under attack so that others could read and judge for themselves.

Reports from the Claremont-Pomona Institute and others across the country were more of the same: Only one side of the conflict was ever allowed to be aired.

In his confidential letter Tanenbaum had set forth a list of "allies" with whom rabbis and followers were advised to check when programming activities or seeking speakers. Leading the list was the organization euphemistically calling itself American Professors for Peace in the Middle East. During a speech purporting to describe the Christian response to the Arab-Israeli confrontation, which had been delivered at its national conference the previous winter at MIT in Cambridge, Lehigh University Professor A. Roy Eckardt had concluded that " 'Christian anti-Zionism' could not finally be separated from 'Christian anti-Semitism.' "

Another leader in this Zionist-oriented group is ordained Christian clergyman and Temple Professor Dr. Franklin H. Littell, under whose aegis the study of the holocaust was included in the Philadelphia school curriculum. The Reinhold Niebuhr-founded scholarly *Christianity and Crisis* had published a piece critical of Israel's treatment of Arabs, written by Dr. Israel Shahak. Littell protested the article, called its author a "renegade Jew," and said that the matter "seemed to be completely outside civilized, let alone Christian, discussion." He amplified on the theme in another article that was widely distributed, in which he indicted and linked into one group the Radical Right, Julius Streicher, Joseph Goebbels, John Nicholls Booth, A. C. Forrest, *The American Mercury, The Cross and Flag,* the *Volkische Beobachter,* and the United Church of Canada *Observer.* The obsessed professor offered "to supply [editors of *Christianity and Crisis*] appropriate paragraphs from Julius Streicher and Joseph Goebbels that attack Israel." (Both Nazi leaders died three years before the State of Israel came into being.)

At the same time as the institutes were being launched, rabbinical bodies sought to panic religion editors into full support of their drive to kill any criticism of Israel, Zionism, or Jews by linking "lack of support" among church groups with the theological "dialogue" between Christians and Jews. President of the Central Conference of American Rabbis Levi A. Olan attributed "Christian coolness" to what he described as the "church doctrine that Israel's successful existence is a Christian heresy; the people that reject Jesus, the Saviour, must fail and suffer so that their sinfulness will be proved." In a letter to the *New York Times,*[21] Rabbi Elmer Berger, the head of Jewish Alternatives to Zionism,[22] pointed out that the Olan approach failed "to distinguish between the historic concept of 'Israel' as a spiritual term in the religious cultures of the world and the State of Israel as a contemporary political entity."

The blatant distortion of the belated and weak Christian attempt[23] to present but a bit of "the other side of the coin" represented another example of thinly veiled coercion and intimidation aimed at silencing critics. Such tactics have generally been successful save for an occasional courageous statement, as by the Central Massachusetts chapter of the Universalist Ministers Association and the eight-denominational protest in the Boston area, pointing to the "selective application of the Universal Declaration of Human Rights to deprive the Palestinian people of justice."[24]

In its relentless efforts to keep the issue of anti-Semitism before the Christian conscience, the long arm of Organized Jewry had reached across the ocean and joined Roman Catholics in sponsoring courses on special religious and racial groups ever since 1962, when funds for a Chair of Tolerance were provided to Rome's Pro Deo University for Social Studies by the American Jewish Committee. The primary goal to be pursued in the announced quest for "world-wide inter-religious cooperation" was the study of "anti-Semitism as the international prototype of group hostility."[25] These "social scientists" were not to be deterred in their pursuit of uncovering "prejudice" by the 1965–66 ecumenical moves of the Vatican to ban hostility toward Judaism in religious texts. Their own study of prejudice in Catholic religious textbooks in Italy and Spain, under the auspices of the University's Sperry Center (named after an American Jewish community leader in Los Angeles), went forward and was published with a bang. A *Times* story June 26, 1967, out of Rome, filed by Robert Doty, former correspondent in Cairo, carried an eight-column headline across page 12: "Anti-Semitic Reference Found in Italian and Spanish Texts 3 Years After Ban by Vatican."

The text of the Doty article refuted the implications of this grossly distorted, inaccurate headline. It stated that in the next year four new texts, edited in the spirit of Vatican II, would replace the literally hundreds of texts under analysis and then in use containing offensive material.

This study also clearly indicated (but one had to read carefully this article to the very end to find it out) that there was a "large amount of hostility against other groups as well as against Jews," and that there were more positive references to Judaism in the texts under study than to Protestants, Orthodox Christians, Muslims, Buddhists, and Hindus combined. Once again, in the new ethos of anti-Semitism, any hostility toward Jews, even if directed equally toward others, was nevertheless to be viewed as anti-Semitism. Here was but one of many stories filed from abroad, to which Kennett Love and other former *Times* foreign correspondents can attest, that were carefully headlined, juggled, and cut to proportions to fit the predilections of the most powerful newspaper in the world.

The Italian Catholic front was further opened up with an eight-column *Times* spread[26] "Italian Jews Disturbed by a Spate of Anti-Semitism, Regard Neo-Fascist Sentiment as Major Cause." Vicious anonymous letters ("prepare your bags today, tomorrow may be too late") were alleged to have been received. At the time there were 33,000 Italian Jews, almost half in Rome. How many letters, the exact nature of them, and whether they were merely from crackpots was not revealed.

Attesting to the revived anti-Semitism in Italy was the head of the Jewish community and Sociology Professor Alfonso di Nola at the Pro Deo University, where a conference "On Religion and Prejudice" had exposed the susceptibility of the "growing lower middle class," which is "isolated alike from Marxist and Catholic cultural traditions," to the "message of power inherent in anti-Semitism." Di Nola charged: "Pro-Arab groups often confuse Zionists with Jews at large and are thus responsible for the spread of anti-Jewish propaganda, *and the Vatican has not eased the situation.*" (Italics added.)

The money had been flowing for nine years from distant coffers to this institution with its Chair of Tolerance and had brought dividends in a series of such flimsy reports, published in both the general press and in academic circles, keeping the issue of anti-Semitism before the Christian conscience. Di Nola charged that the shelves of downtown Rome bookstores were overflowing with anti-Semitic texts, such as *Protocols of the Elders of Zion* and Catholic priest Luigi Cozzi's *The Star, the Cross, and the Swastika.* As Dr. Elmer Berger pointed out at the time, the impreciseness of the term "anti-Semitism" leads to the facile labeling. But Catholics in Italy have been constantly and well alerted against saying, writing, or even thinking anything that might remotely be considered anti-Semitic.

Through the tireless efforts of Rabbi Tanenbaum, the ADL and its many supporting groups (the number of Jewish organizations advancing the Israeli cause and the anti-anti-Semitism syndrome took up thirty-two pages in the 1977 *American Jewish Year Book* compiled by the American Jewish Committee) progress continued to be made in penetrating the Catholic Church and reaching the Catholic community. Under the guise of the "altogether special dialogue," ostensibly aimed toward "a spiritual renewal of Judaic and Christian traditions," the Apostolic Delegate to Washington, Belgian-born Archbishop Jean Jadot, addressed a dinner of the Synagogue Council of America. This marked the first occasion on which a papal representative addressed a major Jewish organization in the U.S. In his remarks Jadot emphasized the struggle against anti-Semitism, which he declared "is not over." And weekly, Rabbi Tanenbaum used his WINS religious news broadcasts to broaden the scope of the definition of anti-Semitism, helping create the atmosphere in which no criticism of Israel or Zionism would be brooked.

As the pronouncements of Vatican II became increasingly warped to give a meaning never intended by the conferees, Catholic publications, which at the outset of the Palestine problem were not afraid to either denounce expansionist Zionism or express sympathy for the Palestinian Arabs, became silent. Typical of the new reportage were the articles in the *Catholic News* after the 1973 war by columnist Joseph Breig, who could talk only of "an Arab vendetta against Israel" and the need for recognition by the Arab nations of Israel's right to exist, without saying a word about Palestinian rights,[27] and by Edith Kermit Roosevelt, who blasted the Arabs for the oil boycott in a piece that literally breathed personal hatred: "If West Freezes, Arabs Could Starve."[28] Like William Buckley in *National Review,* she advocated the strongest retaliatory measures to bust the "oil producing states-Soviet Union conspiracy."

In the Holy Land itself the Catholic community was forced to adapt itself to "a recognition of the facts of life," to use the words of one Catholic writer. Apostolic delegate Pio Laghi, who showed a deep sympathy for the Palestinians, ran into many personal obstacles in carrying out his duties. And when the Greek Catholic Archbishop of Jerusalem, Hilarion Capucci, was tried and convicted in 1974 on charges of smuggling arms into the Holy City for the Palestinians, the Church was powerless to move in his behalf. Although the Vatican expressed its "pain and grief" at the Archbishop's sentencing,[29] he remained in prison for almost three years until released upon a written request from Pope Paul to Israeli President Ephraim Katzir.

The *New York Times* carried a letter by Professor Eckardt asserting, "Living today, Jesus would be called an Israeli. . . . He would condemn Archbishop Capucci to everlasting perdition."[30] Quite an attribution to the carpenter from Nazareth who declared that his kingdom was not of this world, that his spiritual message was for all mankind, and who carefully avoided even the slightest identification with the Jewish nationalists of his time.

The squeeze exerted by the Israeli government on the Catholics in the Holy Land assumed many forms. The great Basilica of the Catholic Church of the Annunciation in Nazareth, designed by the renowned Italian architect Giovanni Muzio, was built by Solel Boneh, a construction company owned by wealthy, prominent Israelis. This exposition of the growing, necessary ties between the Catholic Church and Israel was thus explained by the monograph writer:

> There are numerous signs that the Catholic Church is appraising realistically a new situation in which the Israel factor must not be underestimated. In the theological field, that situation appears more acceptable in view of the change in attitudes towards *Judaism* resulting from the memorable decisions arrived at by the Ecumenical Council. Israel's presence in East Jerusalem and throughout the Holy Land is a fact which cannot be ignored; the Church adopted a posture of remarkable correctness in its day-to-day de facto relations with Israeli authorities.[31]

In line with this development, the Israeli government began to exhibit great public relations finesse in dealing with Christians under its jurisdiction. According to the book *The Arabs in Israel*[32] by Sabri Jiryis, responsible government groups have made great efforts to establish contact with both Arab and other Christian clergymen, their eagerness bordering on flattery. The Christians have in many cases responded with enthusiasm, or at least with an acceptance of peaceful coexistence with the Israeli regime. This is quite a change from the 1950s, when a joint declaration by the two Israeli Grand Rabbis, Herzog and Nissan, referred to the Christian clergy as "emissaries of Satan, covering the land of Israel like a plague of locusts."

The efforts of Rabbi Tanenbaum and other American Jews to strengthen friendship for Israel among Christians were undercut by new "antimissionary" laws enacted in December 1977 and made effective the following April 1. The law imposed a five-year prison sentence for anyone who offers "material inducement" to change religion, and three years for anyone who accepts. Menachem Begin's latest partners in the Likud coalition, the ultra-Orthodox Agudat Israel party, responsible for the legislation, would have preferred a broader law against proselytizing. Prosecutor in the Eichmann trial Gideon Hausner, a member of the Knesset, defended the new law: "I cannot divorce myself completely from the history of compulsory conversion throughout the ages."[33]

Citizens Rights Party member Mrs. Shulamit Aloni, who vociferously opposed the new law, claimed there had been only four cases in 1974, nine in 1975, and six in 1976 in which Jews converted to Christianity; in these cases bribery was not even alleged.[34] Richard Maas, American Jewish Committee president, protested to the Israeli government that "sweeping provisions" of the Israeli law appeared "intended to intimidate the Christian community."[35] The law was so broadly written that many feared that even a gift of a Bible, rosary, or religious medal could be considered material inducement to conversion.

In the U.S. Tanenbaum, however, continued to produce Catholic support for Israel. As an answer to a statement of American bishops, calling for the inclusion of the Palestinian Arab refugees as partners in any peace negotiations, the acceptance of their right to a state and compensation for past losses, Father Donald P. Merrifield, President of Loyola Marymount in Los Angeles, wrote in the Jesuit journal *America*[36]:

I fear that the Jewish reaction to the Vatican's concerns and the echoes of those concerns by the Bishops might quite appropriately be: "Where were your concerns when the Nazis were trying to exterminate us, where is your concern about Jews in Russia, in North Africa, in other parts of the world, where was your concern about the Arab dedication to wipe Israel from the map?

. . . Among many Catholics, I'm sure there is a recognition that Jews don't share most of our concerns, don't join us in the fight against abortion or for aid to parochial schools, so why should we share their concerns?

And yet in the midst of such an apparent indifference on the part of many American Catholics, there is the continuing subtle growth of the sense of our own Jewish origins and of all that we have in common with the Jewish people. But this is low, arising from Vatican II and the more recent scriptural scholarship, and not really reaching all Catholics as yet. The challenge is upon leaders in the Catholic community to include among their other concerns a concern that the Catholic people grow in their understanding of their Jewish neighbors and in their understanding of the magnificent undertaking that is Israel and of the significance of Israel for Jewish identity and survival. And each Catholic should examine his own conscience to discover whether his own attitudes toward the Jewish people and toward Israel are in harmony with the love that the Father of both Christians and Jews bears toward these chosen people, the Jews, whom He has never rejected and from whom we, the Gentiles, have received everything including Him whom we call the Christ.[37]

The Vatican, however, had not perceptibly changed its attitude toward Israel, however strongly Cardinals Francis Spellman, Richard Cushing, and Lawrence Shehan,[38] Father Merrifield, and a myriad of staunch friends strove to help Zionism attain its goals in the U.S. Even Golda Meir, with few dismal strikeouts on her escutcheon, failed notably to bend the Holy Father to her will.

The "historic" meeting of Meir with Pope Paul in the Vatican on January 15, 1973, proved to be a colossal flop. The Israeli leader had flown in from Paris to repair some of the damage done in the French capital, where she had received a rebuke from President Georges Pompidou and found herself picketed by hundreds of Parisians in a noisy protest against her Palestine policy.

While an Israeli Prime Minister had been received by the Pope for the first time, the meeting only reaffirmed their basic disagreements and "produced irritation later on both sides." According to a *Washington Post* correspondent, the brief official communiqué after the sixty-five-minute meeting failed even to include such ritual words as "cordial" or "friendly." In fact, the Vatican went to great lengths to deny the Zionist the slightest propaganda victory from the meeting.

Both the AP and UP accounts clearly indicated that the Vatican had gone out of its way to deny that it had softened its stand on Jerusalem and on the Palestinian refugees. In an unusually blunt statement, Vatican spokesman Federico Alessandrini stated that the meeting "does not signify nor imply the least change in the attitude of the Holy See concerning the problems of the Holy Land." He contradicted an Israeli government statement that Meir had come to Rome at Pope Paul's invitation. The audience had been requested by the Israeli Premier, and there had been no previous discussion on the matter. The Vatican spokesman pointedly noted that "Pope Paul had received King Hussein of Jordan and other personalities from the Arab world and countries. And the Holy See, as is known, has warm relations with Egypt, Lebanon, and Syria, as well as entertaining diplomatic relations with various other Arab countries such as Tunisia, Algeria, Kuwait, and Iraq."

If one had read the *New York Times* account, one could scarcely imagine that the reference was being made to the same meeting. Where the press associations and other newspapers headlined the fact that the Pope and the Prime Minister were at odds (even the *New York Post:* "Pope and Golda: Tough Talk"), the *New York Times* said, "Mrs. Meir Confers with Pope in Vatican." All one could read in the front-page portion of this account was Meir's triumphal first encounter with the head of the Roman Catholic Church and reference to the problems of Arab terrorism and the condition of Jews in the Soviet Union, which she raised with him. In paragraph three attention was called to the fact that Pope Paul "recalled the history and the sufferings of the Jewish people."

Here was one of the crassest illustrations of slanting by position, in which the *Times* excels. The frosty Alessandrini statement, placing the meeting in its proper perspective, was buried away on page 6. But the truth always has a way of rearing its ugly head, and Israel itself was the source. An interview with the Premier by the newspaper *Ma'ariv* was carried on the AP wires and picked up a few days later by the *New York Post.* The *Times* could do nothing else but run the story the following morning under the caption: "Mrs. Meir Says Tension Marked Talk with Pope." This account totally blasted the impression created by the paper's previous account of a "successful meeting," laying bare at the same time an incomparable arrogance and brazenness that has rarely been displayed publicly by any individual, let alone by a head of government.

The tone and implications of the Meir remarks constituted a grave insult to the faith she claimed to represent and to the adherents of ethical, universal Judaism. Rarely had Jewish nationalism and the cult of anti-anti-Semitism so crudely exposed itself:

"I didn't like the opening at all," Mrs. Meir was quoted as saying. "The Pope said to me at the outset that he found it hard to understand why the Jewish people, who are supposed to act mercifully, respond so fiercely in their own country.

"I can't stand it when we are talked to like that. I've had previous experiences of this sort, and I won't give in to anyone who begins a conversation in this way.

"So I said to the Pope: 'Your holiness . . . do you know what my earliest memory is? A pogrom in Kiev. When we were merciful and when we had no homeland and when we were weak, we were led to the gas chambers.'

"I sat and thought to myself, here is the head of the Church, sitting face to face with the Jewess from Israel, and he's listening to what I'm saying—about the Jewish people, about their home in Israel, about their rights. . . .

"There were moments of tension. I felt that I was saying what I was saying to the man of the cross, who heads the Church whose symbol is the cross, under which Jews were killed for generations. I could not escape this feeling. It stuck with me.

"And he felt it, that a Jewess was sitting opposite him, and he said: 'This is an historic moment.'

"Everything went off in meticulous quiet, in holiness," the Israeli premier said in the *Ma'ariv* interview. "But we gazed at each other frankly. His eyes bored deep into me, and I looked back with an open, strong, honest gaze, and I decided I would not lower my eyes under any circumstances. And I didn't."[39]

Inasmuch as the Vatican persists in its policy of nonrecognition of Israel, recognition of Palestinian rights, and international control-trusteeship of Jerusalem to be administered by the three monotheistic faiths (a shift from the previous position of formal internationalization as a territorial entity), the Zionists have played their big trump card: They have sought to gain a hold over the Church of Rome by stepping up the game of blackmail through expanding on the thesis that Eugenio Pacelli, wartime Pope Pius XII, lacked compassion toward the Jews who faced death under Hitler and permitted many to be led to Nazi crematories. Action on his part, the stories intimated, could have saved those Jewish lives. The famed, highly successful play *The Deputy* by Rolf Hochhuth, which ran on Broadway in 1964,[40] was an exposition of this theme, as were the Saul Friedlaender book,[41] and the Carlo Ponti film *Reprisal*. According to the cinema story, the Nazis executed ten political prisoners for each of thirty-three soldiers murdered by a Red bomb thrown into the ranks of a German platoon in the center of Rome in March 1944. Pope Pius was alleged to have done nothing to stop the execution of the prisoners, who were mainly of Socialist, Communist, and anarchist background, previously arrested for terrorist activity, many of whom were of Jewish origin.

The defamation action brought against the producer, the director, and the film writer, American Robert Katz, by Countess Elizabeth Rossignori, niece of the Pontiff, and a newly organized committee, "Pro-Papa Pio XII," revealed for the first time the many positive actions taken by the wartime Pope on behalf of endangered Jews. In 1934, for example, as Papal Secretary of State, Pacelli had urged Pope Pius XI to open the doors of Vatican City to Italian and German dissidents, and later he prepared the 1937 encyclical *Mit Brennender*

*Sorge,** deploring the harassment of Catholics of Germany, which caused official protest from the German Ambassador to the Holy See. Shortly before his election, the Pope-to-be demonstrated his concern for Jewish intellectuals by sending a letter (dated January 12, 1939) to the four Cardinals of the U.S. and Canada, begging them to try to remedy the "deplorable reluctance" of Catholic universities in those countries to accept more German Jewish professors and Jewish thinkers on their faculties.

As Pope the following year, he founded the Catholic Refugee Committee in Rome and put in charge of this activity his own secretary, Father Robert Leiber, and his housekeeper, Mother Pasqualina. According to Monsignor G. Roche's well-documented study *Pie XII Avant l'Histoire,* this committee paved the way for tens of thousands of German Jews to enter America as Catholics, providing them with a regular and efficient service documentation, baptismal certificates, financial aid, and arrangements abroad. This French historian estimated that by 1942 over one million Jews, on Vatican directives, were being housed in convents and monasteries throughout Europe. The Holy Father himself set an example by taking care of some 15,000 Jews at Castel Gandolfo, as well as several thousand in Vatican City, where the refugees of all faiths included such famed diplomats as the future Christian Democratic Prime Minister Alcide de Gasperi and the present Socialist leader Pietro Nenni. By 1943 these refugees were overflowing into the Papal apartments themselves. The Chief Rabbi of Rome, Israel Zolli, subsequently became a Catholic convert, allegedly in gratitude for Pius's wartime protection, and took as his given name, Eugenio, Pius XII's given name.

Meanwhile, under the personal authorization of Pope Pius, Monsignor Angello Roncalli, the future Pope John XXIII, was working assiduously at his Istanbul post to help many hundreds of thousands of Eastern European Jews on their way to Palestine. In France the Pope's Deputy, Cardinal Eugene Tisserant, and his Joint Distribution Committee were doing everything in their power to facilitate Jewish emigration under the very nose of the government of Marshall Henri Philippe Pétain. An underground printing press at Nice, protected by the Archbishop and the Mayor of the city, produced 1,895 identity cards, 1,360 work permits, 1,230 birth certificates, 428 demobilization letters, and 950 baptismal certificates before it was discovered. And as far as Hungary was concerned, the Holy Father, through personal correspon-

* *With Intense Concern*

dence with Regent Miklós Horthy, won guarantees that the country's 800,000 Jews would not be deported if they submitted to mass baptism.

In their ever-constant pursuit of recalling the Nazi evil, Zionists have of course exploited the fact that Pope Pacelli, who had spent twelve years as Nuncio in pre-Hitler Germany, surrounded himself with so many Germans, including Mother Pasqualina Lehnert and his secretaries, Fathers Leiber and Hentrich. His confessor was Father Augustin Bea, and other assistants were also of that ethnic persuasion. In fact, Pius was sometimes referred to in Rome as *Il Papa Tedesco* (the German Pope). Monsignor Ludwig Kaas, who held the post of Rector of St. Peter's Basilica, had been the chairman of the Center party, suppressed by the Hitler government. And while letters, reports, and documents point to a continuous line of rebuffs to Mussolini, Hitler, and their emissaries, the Pontiff's correspondence in contrast shows warmth and cordiality where President Roosevelt, his Ambassador to the Vatican Myron C. Taylor, or Cardinal Francis Spellman was concerned. On his part, the American wartime President addressed the Pope as "My Old and Good Friend."

Because of his show of concern for the Jewish plight, often in a spectacular way, Eugenio Pacelli might rather have been accused of pro-Zionist sympathies. As a Cardinal coming into the New York harbor in October 1937 aboard the *Conte di Savoia,* he asked the ship's captain to fly, alongside the Papal flag, the six-pointed star of the future state of Israel in honor of the 600 Jewish refugees then on board. And just prior to the entrance of the German army into Rome in 1943, the Pope ordered the Papal seal to be prominently engraved on the main Roman synagogue for its protection.

It is true—and this was the main condemnatory line of attack in Hochhuth's play—that the Pope, on the basis of the evidence presented to him, refused to go along with President Roosevelt's suggestion that he make a public condemnation of the extermination of the millions of Jews at Auschwitz. The Pope's line of reasoning had been: "Up to the present time, it has not been possible to verify the accuracy of the only report available—that of the Jewish Agency in Palestine." But did that reluctance to take up the Roosevelt suggestion spell anti-Semitism? As Father Leiber wrote: "The Pope sided very unequivocally with the Jews at that time. He spent the entire fortune he inherited from his family as a Pacelli on their behalf." The Holy Father had also been silent on any condemnation of the multifold illegal actions and cruelties of the Communist regime, which was fighting the

Hitler horde, but this was in accordance with a specific promise extracted from him by the U.S. and Britain, who had meanwhile become allied with the Soviet Union.

The necessity for the utmost secrecy in the relations between the Vatican and the Allied Powers as the Nazis spread their hold on Europe was further emphasized in British documents. Whereas Jewish authors exposed the involvement of Zionist leaders in Nazi extermination, historical documentation has bared the injustice of tarring the late Pope with the anti-Semitic brush. The 1972 release of British Foreign Office papers showed that Pope Pius XII had learned of the Nazi plans for invading France and the Low Countries in May 1940, and had then tipped off the British. According to Jesuit historian Reverend Robert Graham, the Pope's information about the impending assault had come from a German spy, who was in fact a double agent. The invaluable information was forwarded to 10 Downing Street in a coded cable from the British Minister at the Holy See. The Holy Father was at the same time involved in negotiations with certain anti-Hitler officers seeking a British guarantee for nonhumiliating peace terms in the event that their planned coup d'etat should be successfully staged.[42]

After the fall of France the Pope asked the British to destroy any record of the Vatican's involvement in abortive negotiations with the anti-Hitler resistance. Apparently Foreign Secretary Lord Halifax destroyed his personal copies, but other copies were retained in the Foreign Office, documenting the Pope's activities; if uncovered, this could have meant the Nazi seizure of Vatican City. This historical exposure tore to shreds the entire thesis of *The Deputy*, charging the late Pope Pius with alleged apathy, or worse, in the face of the Nazi extermination of Jews. Hochhuth nevertheless continued to advance his thesis in other writings.

The release by the Vatican of its own documents for 1943 showed that Rome had been deeply disturbed by the growing possibility of a Jewish state in the Middle East. But opposition to statehood did not vitiate the quiet diplomacy carried on in behalf of the European Jews, as these papers revealed. The Catholic leadership had long insisted that refugeeism be distinguished from *statehood*. Cardinal Luigi Maglione, then Secretary of State, suggested "other territories which would be more suitable" for a Jewish entity, while Pope John—even when as Papal Nuncio in Istanbul helping Jewish refugees reach Palestine—was expressing fears that his efforts might lead to the "realization of the Messianic dream."

Monsignor Domencio Tardini, Deputy Secretary of State, wrote to the Papal Legate in London, Monsignor William Godfrey, that "the Holy See had never approved the plan to make Palestine a Jewish homeland." This followed in a clear line the traditional Vatican opposition to the objectives of Zionism, expressed guardedly by Benedict XV in 1921 and forthrightly by Pius X to Herzl himself in 1904.

But this same 688-page volume contained documents that the Vatican protested strongly the mass arrest of 1,027 Jews in the Rome ghetto and their transportation to death camps north of Italy. Cardinal Maglione summoned the German Ambassador to the Holy See, Baron Ernst von Weizaecker, and in the strongest language (according to the introduction to the volume) indicated that the raid on the Jewish quarter "was painful for the Holy Father, painful beyond words, that in Rome itself, under the very eyes of a common Father, so many persons are made to suffer simply because they belong to another race."

"What would the Holy See do if things were to continue like this?" asked the German envoy.

"The Holy See would not like to be faced with the necessity of voicing its disapproval," the Cardinal replied, indicating that the Pope might make a public protest, the first of the war. "For now the Holy See hopes not to say anything that the German people might consider an act of hostility during a terrible war, but there are limits."

The Ambassador indicated that the raid in Rome had been made on orders from Berlin and Hitler. He asked whether he could keep the protest to himself and not report it to Berlin, and the Cardinal agreed.

"Your Excellency has told me that you will do something for the poor Jews," the Cardinal said. "I thank you. I leave the rest to your judgment. If you think it more opportune not to make any mention of our conversation, so be it."

Secretiveness was maintained because mention of the conversation was deemed to be "dangerous and counterproductive." Of the 1,027 Jews arrested on October 6, 1943, about fifteen returned alive. But, as British Minister to the Holy See Sir Francis Godolphin D'Arcy Osborne noted in the British Foreign Office documents, the Vatican's intervention "seems to have saved a certain number of Jews," and there were no further mass arrests after the Vatican's move. The 22,-000 Jews who remained in Rome went into hiding as of that day, often helped by local Catholic clergymen, including the most famous, the Reverend Marie Benoit, a Cappucine, who became a legendary figure in rescuing Roman Jews.

Perhaps the best summation of Pius XII's efforts on behalf of the

Jews was contained in the book *Three Popes and the Jews,* by the Israeli journalist and diplomat Pinchas E. Lapide:

The Catholic Church under the pontificate of Pius XII was instrumental in saving at least 700,000, but probably as many as 860,000, Jews from certain death at Nazi hands . . . these figures exceed by far those saved by all other churches, religious institutions and rescue organizations combined.[43]

There has even been an attempt to blame Pius's predecessor, Pope Pius XI, for failure to act to prevent Hitlerian anti-Semitism. According to a 1972 story in the *National Catholic Reporter,*[44] the Pope in June 1938—fifteen months before the outbreak of World War II— had commissioned the American Jesuit editor of *America,* Father John La Farge, to write an encyclical attacking racism and anti-Semitism. For uncertain reasons the draft of the encyclical was never seen by Pope Pius before his death in February 1939. But this did not prevent the *Washington Post* from running a front-page story, under the continuation headlines on page 4: "Could Pius XI Have Saved the Jews?"[44] The article speculated through four columns on the answer to that question, and intimated that Pius XII would not have been elected had this draft encyclical been published, which "would have brought European Catholics face-to-face with anti-Semitism before Hitler got underway full swing."

In his May 1974 confidential memorandum to the Board of Governors, B'nai B'rith Washington representative Herman Edelsberg opinioned that

. . . the issue which offers by far the richest promise for a long-sustained propaganda campaign is the plight of Jews in the Soviet Union. Experience has shown that this issue can be exploited to block or at least delay agreements made at the Summit. No President or Presidential candidate can afford to brush it aside. It is therefore the opinion of the International Council that the Board should consider an increase in the budgetary appropriations earmarked for pressing this issue.

Judging by the amount of political and media attention that has been given to the question of Jews in the Soviet Union, the increased appropriation must have been a substantial one. And Christians, particularly anti-Communist ones, have been held in a tighter vise than ever.

XV   Soviet Jewry: Blackmail and Barter

> It is time that someone invented a new plot, or that the author came out of the bushes.
>
> —Virginia Woolf

Perhaps nowhere have American Christians been so tied up in the Zionist double-bind as in the matter of Soviet Jewry. Here anti-anti-Semitism, the Nazi holocaust, and Christian guilt feelings, wedded to the specter of Stalin, are manipulated to force compliance with Zionist goals. The deep-seated anti-Communist sentiment of a large number of American conservatives and moderates has made such exploitation highly successful.

One of the simplest methods of arousing sympathy for Israel has been the incessant campaign to bring Soviet Jews to the Zionist state. The Soviet refusal to allow Jews to emigrate freely to Israel, and the accompanying suppression of Jewish activities within the U.S.S.R., is presented as a continuation of Hitlerian anti-Semitism, or as a revival of traditional, pre-Soviet, Russian anti-Semitism. Effective spot ads, half-page appeals, and full-page petitions, overloaded with thousands of signatures from academic life and from the entertainment[1] and political worlds, public rallies and vigils, and dissemination of literature on the streets have all been employed by varied committees to stir up the American public against the Soviet policy toward its Jewish minority. In May 1977 Dr. William Korey, Director of B'nai B'rith's International Council, stated, "Soviet Jews have detected 'the smell of pogrom' in recent events in the Soviet Union."

The 1971 Leningrad trials of the would-be Jewish hijackers of a Soviet aircraft provided an occasion for whipping up hysteria. The emotionalism generated by Meir Kahane and his Jewish Defense League in New York swept across to the Pacific. In San Francisco the

513

Soviet Jewry Action Committee initiated a tourist boycott; all travel agencies in the Bay area were sent a letter calling on them "to help secure freedom for three million Jews unfortunate enough to have been born in the Soviet Union" and threatening those who did not respond favorably to the letter. Brochures charging that Soviet Jews were "the only minority in the U.S.S.R. who are being forced as far as possible to assimilate" were widely distributed. Offices of Aeroflot, the Soviet airline, were damaged, and in 1975 shots from a .22-caliber rifle were fired through the windows of the Soviet Mission to the U.N.[2]

The charge of Soviet anti-Semitism has been increasingly employed as Zionist propaganda ever since Israel's relations with the Soviet Union deteriorated. The Soviet Union had voted for the 1947 U.N. partition resolution, and arms from its Czech satellite were indispensable to the Israeli forces during the 1948 war for independence. As normalization of Israel-West Germany relations grew, the Nazi peril became outmoded as the principal weapon of propaganda. Kremlin "anti-Semitism" came more in vogue as Jews were depicted as "singular victims of Communist terror" who ought to be permitted to go to Israel.[3] There was, however, little evidence presented that these Jews were necessarily any worse off than any of the many other religious, ethnic, or minority groups behind the iron curtain,[4] nor was there any objective information as to how many Soviet Jews wished to be "rescued" and brought to the "promised land."

The hue and cry about persecution of Soviet Jewry is in marked contrast to the almost deafening silence[5] concerning the extirpation of the Crimean Tartars and various minor Caucasian ethnic groups, the transplanting of hundreds of thousands of Lithuanians, Latvians, and Estonians to Siberia, and the forced "conversion" of five million Eastern-rite Ukrainian Catholics to Russian Orthodoxy.

According to the *New York Post* of May 28, 1974, the twenty-five million Soviet Muslims, concentrated in the Uzbek, Kirgiz, Turkmen, Tadzhik, Azerbaidzhan, and Kazakh Republics, are considered "politically unreliable," have had their religion officially described as "poison," and are permitted but "few Mosques and few religious leaders." About these people there is little protesting.

The Soviet Jewry question presents a most complex situation that does not allow for simplistic reduction. Of the approximately 2.6 million people[6] who consider themselves Jews, probably not more than 10 percent are to any slight degree religious.[7] While the overwhelming majority of the Soviet Jews regard themselves as ethnically and culturally Jewish, most are undoubtedly atheists with the same attitudes toward Communist institutions prevailing among other Soviet nationalities. In Mother Russia all citizens are identified by nationality, including Jews.

The Jews face no residential bars nor organizational social bans, such as still persist in certain parts of the Western world, save in military and government circles. But Benyamin Dymshyts served as Vice Premier of the Soviet Union, and a number of assistant secretaries and undersecretaries in various ministries have also been Jewish.[8] David Dragunsky has held the rank of Colonel-General in the Soviet Army, while 170,000 Jews were decorated for valor in combat during World War II. And in nongovernmental endeavor, Jews in professional, intellectual, and managerial pursuits are several times as numerous as their percentage of the population.

Three times as many Jewish undergraduates attend college compared to their ratio in the Soviet population. Jews in 1961 only accounted for a little more than one percent of the Soviet population but accounted for nearly one-tenth of the country's roughly 400,000 scientific workers. While this percentage has somewhat dwindled, the Jewish share in such a highly respected and well-paid social category still hovers around 7 percent to 9 percent. Only Russians and Ukrainians are more numerous in this field.

There are certain other fields in which Jews have a share quite out of proportion to their percentage of the population. Fifteen percent of the physicians, 8.5 percent of the writers and newspapermen, 7 percent of the musicians and painters and sculptors and actors, more than 20 percent of the composers, 13 percent of the artists, 33 percent of the film industry personnel, and 10 percent of the country's jurists and lawyers are Jews.[9] The percentage of Jews among the winners of the Lenin Prize never fails to be fantastic—from 15 percent to as high as 25 percent. Out of 844 persons receiving this most coveted honor in the Soviet Union, there were 564 Russians, 96 Jews, and 184 of all other nationalities. According to statistics published in late 1975, there are 8,000 Jewish deputies in the Supreme and local Soviets.

While the number of synagogues for Jews in the Soviet Union has been greatly reduced, the post-Stalin governments have continued to heighten their campaign against all religions. Many Russian Orthodox churches have been closed to worshipers; some have reopened as atheist museums and others have been left falling to rack and ruin along the roadsides.

The U.S.S.R., it is true, has universally refused to allow citizens to emigrate freely. The emigration ban, applying also to the other 107 national-ethnic-religious groups making up the Soviet Union, helps advance the concept of national exclusiveness and achieves the single-handedness, and single-purposefulness, of state authoritarianism. But the number of Jews granted permission to leave has multiplied since the ouster of Nikita Khrushchev. His successor, Alexi Kosygin, at first allowed Jews the right to join their families in Israel, but after the 1967 war, with the Israelis refusing to yield the large amounts of occupied Arab territory in accordance with U.N. Resolution 242, and with growing protests from their Arab friends, the Kremlin was more restrictive in permitting Jewish emigration.

In the face of the war-hysteria, media exaggerations, and political propaganda, totally beclouding the verity of the facts, it is impossible to ascertain the truth about Soviet Jewry. U.S. Senate members point to the dwindling number of Yiddish publications in the Soviet Union as evidence of discrimination. But as far back as the 1959 census, Yiddish was the native language of only 21 percent of all Soviet Jews, and that number has since greatly shrunk still further.

The claim is continuously advanced that anti-Semitism in the Soviet Union can be readily evidenced by discriminatory safeguards taken only against Jewish citizens. If they have received treatment different from that accorded to other nationality groups, it is, at least in part, because of their peculiar relations, expressed openly and on all possible occasions (as when Ambassador to the U.S.S.R. and later Foreign Minister Golda Meir visited the Moscow synagogue, and pro-Israeli pamphlets were handed out), and because of other nonreligious activities related to the State of Israel, with whom the Soviet Union is engaged in a cold war. And the worldwide campaign to rescue Soviet Jewry via the emigration route certainly has not helped the status of those Jews.

There is little doubt that rising Jewish nationalism, particularly after Israel's success in the 1967 war, instilled in some of the Jewish population the same yearning for identity as other nationality groups in "protest against an atomizing, increasingly anonymous mass society, an expression of inward self-consciousness as in some of the radical youth movements in the Western world."[10] The only difference had been that their rising nationalist feeling happened to be related to Israel, a foreign state that has been at war with friends or even "wards" of the Soviet Union and is supported by the Soviet Union's big power rival, the U.S. Jews in the Soviet Union may be insisting that they have common temperamental characteristics and that they do form a special group. But, like American Jews, they encounter a problem when their separateness does not accord with the feeling of many of the people in the country, eventually leading to a tide of prejudice and discrimination, which sooner or later is labeled anti-Semitism by most outsiders. It has been said that young Jews, who have no inkling of Yiddish or Hebrew and regard themselves as atheists, nevertheless become conscious of a common bond, heightened by listening to Radio Tel Aviv, which is not jammed and can be heard in most of European U.S.S.R., and by occasional anti-Semitic remarks from uneducated Russians or Ukrainians, which only serves as a reminder of their separateness.

This raises the old familiar question: Which came first, the chicken or the egg? Did the separateness lead to the prejudicial remarks, or did the prejudicial remarks bring on the separateness? Did the strange yearning and feeling of relationship toward the State of Israel bring about discrimination, or did discrimination bring about this feeling toward Israel? The correct answer would take a great deal of probing.

In a highly controversial article, "Jews in the Soviet Union," in *Issues,* Peter Worthington, Bureau Chief in Moscow at that time of the Toronto, Canada, *Telegram,* expressed a belief that he could find little "state-sponsored anti-Semitism," and "nothing of what we would call persecution against Jews."[11] He admitted running into many examples of individual anti-Semitism, but not enough to warrant charges that the Soviet state had been following a deliberate and isolated policy against its Jewish citizens. He stated adamantly that Jews were not singled out for special abuse, but that in some ways they led better lives than most citizens. "Jews who were neither excessively religious nor ardently pro-Zionist," Worthington claimed, "stood a better chance statistically of leading a physically more comfortable life than the average Soviet citizen. . . ."

"There is no question," Worthington wrote, "that it has been the Soviet intention to liquidate Jewish culture—just as it has been their planned intent to liquidate all vigorous cultures. But this is not anti-Semitism. It is simply Sovietism, which is overrunning all minority groups alike!"

This meant, as the writer pointed out, that "charges of Soviet discrimination against Jews, while possibly valid in an absolute sense, seem less significant in a relative sense. Other groups have had it worse, are having it worse, will have it worse."

For these statements Worthington was assailed on many fronts. Moshe Decter poured invective on him, calling the Worthington article "lengthy, disjointed and laughably ignorant," published by a "discredited and irrelevent group."[12] In *Jewish Week* the Worthington piece was found to resemble "the same propagandistic technique as the Czarist bigots," and its sponsor was roundly condemned. Worthington was called an "apologist" for the Soviet Union. In the words of Rabbi Israel Miller, "Only willful ignorance or deliberate malice can lie behind the charge that Zionist elements in the U.S. might be helping to exaggerate the plight of Soviet Jews."[13]

However, Acting Director of the Columbia University Institute on Central Europe Istvan Deak wrote, "Soviet anti-Semitism has been greatly exaggerated in the United States, and this for purely political purposes." His comment on the Worthington piece: "I am grateful . . . for dissenting points of view."

In a rebuttal to his critics, Worthington pointed to a report of a six-man group sent to the Ukraine by the Communist party in Canada, which found evidence of differences in treatment of nationality groups and expressed the hope that Ukrainians would get the same privileges that Jews had been getting in the Soviet Union: "In the past few years, there has been seen the flourishing of literary creativity among Jewish writers, the emergence of new cultural forces. . . ."

State Department hearings in 1971 revealed that although Soviet Jewry had to endure special hardships, their condition had not worsened in recent years and they were not undergoing special ordeals. "All Soviet citizens—not just Jews—suffer from the Soviet government's policy of militant atheism and its refusal to consider migrating as a right rather than a rare privilege," said Richard T. Davies, Deputy Assistant Secretary for European Affairs, in his testimony before the House Foreign Affairs Subcommittee, which was holding a two-day session on "Denial of Rights to Soviet Jews" under the chairmanship of Zionist activist Congressman Benjamin S. Rosenthal (Dem.-Queens, N.Y.). He had timed the hearings just prior to President Nixon's visit to the Soviet Union.

Limitations on the emigration of Soviet Jews have undoubtedly been more stringent than those on other Russians, but as the State Department official pointed out in his testimony, it was because of certain of "their ties to the West and Israel" and because some Soviet officials regard Jewishness "as a more alien phenomenon than the fact of association with other major religious or national cultures." There could, he added, "be no comparison with Stalin's blood purge of Jewish intellectuals and the libel of the Jewish doctors' 'plot.'[14] The overwhelming majority of Jews are living in a normal fashion," and the charge that "Soviet Jews as a community are living in a state of terror seems to have been grossly overdrawn." Jews, Davies added, continued to be "eminent in the Soviet economic, journalistic, scientific, medical, and cultural world in numbers far out of proportion to their percentage of the population."

Soviet Jews, it was pointed out, still remained the best educated Soviet minority, and there was no evidence that the regime's "anti-Zionist" propaganda "had spilled over into outright, widespread anti-Semitism or deliberate, sustained efforts to fan a pogrom mentality in Soviet society at large." Davies' words were borne out by Saul Polansky, a Foreign Service officer who himself was Jewish, when he returned from a three-year tour in the U.S. Embassy in Moscow. Polansky said, "Based on my own experience and travels in the Soviet Union, it would be an exaggeration to state that Jews lived in a state of terror." He noted that synagogues in Moscow and Central Asia were usually full, and that many Jews spoke frankly with him about their situation. At this very time (November 1971), representatives of the Soviet government were seeing their wives spat upon in the streets of New York, and rifles brought into play against defenseless Soviet children by Jewish Defense League fanatics.

While thousands of Soviet Jewish immigrants have passed through Vienna on the way to Israel, there has also been a steadily growing reverse "Aliya," many seeking to return to Mother Russia. Said one returnee, a dressmaker from Odessa, "We all make mistakes for sure, but now we want to go back home."

A Tiflis shopkeeper, commenting on the reasons for the reverse migration, stated: "It's the fault of the American Jewish millionaires—they pay their money but want us to bear the brunt. A boil is good on somebody else's body." These Russian Jews were also disillusioned by the permissiveness of life in modern, secular Israel in contrast to the discipline and totalitarianism of the Soviet Union, which strangely enough they preferred. Once again it was demonstrated that the melting pot in Israel, called by Israelis "the pressure cooker," does not always melt the separate distinct nationalisms of those ingathered. Notwithstanding the great desire of Russian Jews for identification with "the Jewish people," it is hard for them, as it is for those of Czech, Chilean, American, etc., origin, to shed themselves of the culture of the many lands in which they have lived before becoming Israelis.

As *Time* magazine described it, "These immigrants suddenly sensed the loss of the double cocoon that had enfolded them. In the Soviet Union the inner layer was a comforting circle of their Jewish communities. The outer layer, even for Jews, was the paternalism of the Soviet state, which furnished everything from cheap concerts to free medical care. The result is that these emigrants disliked the democratic individualism of Israel."

Even Dr. Nahum Goldmann argued that the constant pressure being brought by Zionist propaganda against the Soviet Union endangered the position of Soviet Jewry, the overwhelming majority of whom, he admitted, wished to stay there. He was outspoken in his criticism of Israelist tactics, insisting that the emphasis should be placed on helping to improve the lives of Soviet Jews rather than sacrificing everything to get a few out.

Goldmann reasoned that in the absence of normal relations between Israel and the Soviet Union, and of peace in the Middle East, "the Soviets will not give more facilities to the Jewish minority to live as Jews because they argue that all Jews who want to live as Jews are attached to Israel. So long as they see Israel as an enemy and what they call an American satellite, why should they encourage a minority, which is more attached to their enemy than to them, to express their views?"

But Jewish leadership in the U.S. disagreed with Goldmann, and the endless hullabaloo over Zionist Jewry continued. Early on a late May 1973 morning, film actress Joanne Woodward called on the radio for a large turnout for the big annual parade on "Solidarity Sunday for Soviet Jews." The parade down Fifth Avenue, with signs "Let Our People Go," attracted 75,000 to 100,000 people.

The U.S. appearance of every artist in the U.S.S.R. who has chosen to defect or not to defect has been exploited. The famed Russian Jewish violinist Leonid Kogan was victimized by extremists when he performed at Carnegie Hall in February 1971. In an attempt to disrupt the concert, a stink bomb was dropped in the balcony during the performance, while outside pickets carried signs, "Kogan is unfair to Zionists, Israel and the U.S." (The reference to the U.S. had been hastily added to impart an appearance of American patriotism.) Russian Jews performing with the Moiseyev and the Bolshoi have also been similarly victimized, always to the tune of good publicity. A Jewish Defense League bomb, set off in the office of impresario Sol Hurok, who had sponsored the U.S. appearance of many famed Soviet artists, killed his secretary.

The fuss and cry raised in the U.S. to release ballet dancers Valery and Galina Panov to go to Israel reverberated to Britain without loss of one whit of emotionalism. A London *Times* article by Bernard Levin attacked the Lord Mayor and Corporation of Manchester at great length for permitting the Kirov Ballet to visit their city, and called upon the theatrical profession to join in the protest to bring about cancellation of the performance.

His emigration finally achieved, Valery Panov hailed the press for its role in his exodus from the U.S.S.R.[15] And well he might. Rarely has there been so much reportage-propaganda lavished as on the Panov case for more than two years. Scarcely a week passed that the media did not feature some comment/speculation on the dancers. Zionist groups even suggested that the State Department hold up the scheduled visit of the Bolshoi dance troop until exit visits were granted the Panovs.

When the Panovs ceased to make good copy, prominent space was taken up with other Soviet Jewry tales of woe, such as the trial of physicist Viktor Polsky, accused of reckless driving in hitting the daughter of a Russian General. The official Soviet press agency Tass, in its English-language commentary, condemned the editors of the New York *Times* for "literally going out of their way" to exploit the case as proof of the persecution of Jews in the Soviet Union.

The Soviet Jewry issue provided Israelists with the best club with which to maintain pressure on Washington and prevent any change in U.S. Middle East policy. During the 1972 presidential campaign, the Nixon claim (as spread by Governor Nelson Rockefeller) that his visit to Moscow had all but saved Soviet Jewry was refuted in a sensational *Los Angeles Times* article claiming that the trip had, in fact, been a disaster for them. Pro-McGovern newspapers, such as the *New York Post,* gave prominent space to this item as a means both of discrediting the Republican candidate and of helping the Zionists apply pressures on the White House—plain political blackmail—to bar trade concessions to the Soviet Union unless the schedule of payments exacted from Soviet Jews for exit permits was rescinded.

The Israel-First bloc moved on all fronts to detrain all legislation involving the Soviet Union. Spurred on by the American Israel Public Affairs Committee and encouraged by favorable press coverage, congressmen moved to amend the foreign aid bill to prohibit the use of the programs of the Overseas Private Investment Corporation and Export-Import Bank activities to assist in financing and developing trade until the Soviet Union terminated what an Ohio congressman called the "ransom" policy of the Kremlin.

Prior to the Secretary of State's departure for Moscow in late spring 1973 to arrange details for the Brezhnev visit to Washington, the Chairman of the National Conference on Soviet Jewry, the President of the Council on Jewish Federations and Welfare, and the Chairman of the Conference of Major American Jewish Organizations met with Henry Kissinger. The Jewish leadership wanted to make certain that President Nixon took up the Soviet Jewry issue with Brezhnev and that neither the Soviet Union nor the Arabs would be successful in persuading the Nixon administration to exert new pressures on Israel to yield the occupied Arab territories. The Arabs, led by King Faisal, were making ominous noises.

The Jewish emissaries brought Kissinger "fact sheets" about the cases of forty-two Soviet Jews then imprisoned and about more than 100 Jewish families experiencing unusual difficulty in getting permission to leave—an ideal diversionary weapon to use as needed counterleverage with the Soviets. And the press cooperated by providing an endless spate of stories to help push the campaign. On May 29 the *New York Post* carried a byline story that 100 Moscow Jews had appealed to world Jewish organizations to help save ailing Yevgeny Levich, a noted astrophysicist who had been sent "either to a military unit in the north or to a labor camp on the Arctic Coast." His father, a leading physicist, was the only member of the Soviet Academy of Sciences to have requested permission to emigrate to Israel. The *New York Times,* which had run a brief piece previously, now followed with a longer and more detailed story.

On June 11, based upon an AP report from Moscow, a prominently placed *Times* article was headed "7 Jewish Scientists, Forbidden to Quit Soviet, in Hunger Strike." And one week later, equally well-placed, appeared a three-columned "7 Soviet Jews Appeal for Worldwide Support" article. Whatever the news agencies or their correspondents dug up was promptly passed on to the readership as world-shaking news items.

The approaching summit meeting between President Nixon and Soviet Party Leader Leonid Brezhnev provided even a greater field day for Zionist propaganda. A large Washington rally urged Brezhnev to permit free emigration of Soviet Jewry. Similar demonstrations were held against the Soviets by the very conservative Young Americans for Freedom, who, to be truthful, probably preferred that all Jews go live in Israel rather than enjoy equal rights in the U.S. Because he refused to be stampeded into an anti-Soviet declaration supportive of academician Andrei Sakharov's sweeping attack on Moscow, even Secretary of State-designate Henry Kissinger came in for editorial criticism from the *Times.*

In the fall of 1973 the East Coast media, particularly the daily newspapers, continued negative—and sometimes abusive—reportage on events taking place within the Soviet Union. As part of the obvious campaign, the *Times* opened its letters and news column to one and all who would attack the Soviet Union. One day there was a lengthy story in the Sunday edition headed "U.S. Scholar Calls Soviet an 'Unreliable Partner.' "[16] On another morning: "Moscow Jews Demonstrate to Protest Emigration Curb,"[17] based on a UPI story about twelve demonstrators wearing yellow Stars of David as they staged their protest outside the Moscow Central Synagogue. On still another day there was an article headed "Soviet Jews Protest" plus a page 2 account under the heading "Soviet Arrests a Jew, Detains Newsman" about "a lone demonstrating Jew and an American correspondent whose film was confiscated for covering his arrest."[18] Many of these articles appeared only with the accreditation "Special to *The Times.*" The general antagonism being engendered toward the Soviet Union only added to the resounding popular support for Israel on the eve of the October 1973 war.

President Nixon did bring up the matter of the emigration of Soviet Jewry at the summit meeting with Brezhnev, which may have been another reason this U.S.-Soviet meeting was not as successful as others had been. Aside from the Soviet resentment over an intrusion into what the Russians view as an internal matter, this problem involved an additional irritant. The Arabs would be antagonized if more visas were granted so that Soviet Jews could add to the Israeli military potential, a situation about which certain Arab states had consistently complained to the Kremlin as Jewish emigration mounted in the early 1970s.

Even as the Nixon-Brezhnev Washington summit was taking place, the Syrians and Egyptians were making their final plans for their offensive to liberate their Israeli-occupied lands, and U.S.-Soviet relations faced greater strains. Following the October war, with its Arab moral victory, an even more crying need for the propaganda use of Soviet Jews developed.

Behind the heightened campaign "to rescue Soviet Jewry" was a many-faceted design. To bring Washington inexorably to her side, Tel Aviv sought the diminution or end of détente and the revival of the very dangerous polarization pitting a U.S.-Israel alignment against a U.S.S.R.-Arab world axis. The total, unalterable protection of the U.S. to supplement less firm commitments of the past was viewed by Israeli tacticians as the only way out of a vast sea of trouble engulfing the Zionist state. The Arabs were flexing their oil muscles, and certain

European countries, formerly at least partially submissive to Zionist pressures, were adjusting their policies to the new power relationship.[19] A new offensive, using Soviet Jewry as pawns, could help detract from traumatic problems at home and abroad. The task had been entrusted to the National Conference on Soviet Jewry, created and financed by the State of Israel, according to files of B'nai B'rith, and to their best friends in Congress, led by inflexible anti-Communist Senator Henry "Scoop" Jackson, who in the famed "bagel and lox" 1972 Florida primary had left no doubt about his position.

"Scoop," upset by Senator George McGovern at the 1972 Democratic Convention, still harbored strong presidential ambitions, and thus felt continuing need for Zionist votes, campaign contributions, and media support. Consequently it was Jackson who forcefully interjected an overriding concern for strengthening the demographic position of the State of Israel into the lengthy and delicate U.S.-Soviet negotiations over a sweeping trade package between the two countries.

The Soviet trade agreement was to have provided most-favored-nation treatment for the Soviet Union (the U.S. had granted similar nondiscriminatory benefits to most of its other trading power partners, both allies and nonallies, such as Poland and Yugoslavia). The agreement called for payment by Moscow of World War II Lend-Lease indebtedness of $722 million. Back in 1960 talks had broken off with a Russian offer of $300 million as a just settlement. Under the proposed agreement, total U.S.-Soviet trade would triple the $500 million rate of the previous three years. This was over and beyond the $1 billion worth of grain purchased by Moscow for delivery in 1973. Such closer ties between the U.S. and the Soviet Union were envisioned as part of the détente policy, the principal objective of the two Nixon-Brezhnev summits.

The Conference of Presidents of Jewish Organizations, the National Conference on Soviet Jewry, and other Zionist-Israelist groups, lobbying in Washington, worked closely in cooperation with Senator Jackson[20] and other members of the "Israel-First" bloc to halt passage of the Nixon trade bill. They were assisted to no small extent by the incessant press barrage of stories concerning the plight of Soviet intellectuals and dissidents. Endless statements by author Alexander Solzhenitsyn and physicist-civil rights advocate Andrei Sakharov never failed to make the front pages of the friendly East Coast press, particularly the *Times*, no matter how contrary such views may have been to the otherwise "liberal" tradition of that paper. Zionist groups latched onto every incident regarding dissidents and fully exploited their grievances, including that of Anatoly Shcharansky, despite the confirmation of the close links of his "roommate," Dina Beilin, with the CIA.[21] They were encouraged in these activities by Washington.

After the barrier of the emigration fees had been removed by satisfactory Soviet action, there still remained the obstacle posed by the sponsors of the Jackson-Vanik[22] Amendment to the trade bill. Warnings by the White House that linking improved trade relations with the Soviet Union to the emigration of Soviet Jews would endanger U.S. relations with Moscow staved off the restrictive legislation during the last days of the Nixon administration.

But the strength of the Zionist lobby was not to be denied. In the words of Stephen D. Issacs in his book *Jews and American Politics:*

Richard Perle and Morris Amitay command a tiny army of Semitophiles on Capitol Hill and direct Jewish power in behalf of Jewish interests. These young men . . . drafted the Jackson Amendment concerning Soviet emigration, denying America's most favored nation status to the Soviet Union unless it allows its citizens the right to emigrate. These two, working with a network of other Jewish and non-Jewish activists on Capitol Hill, organized support and enlisted seventy-six Senators to co-sponsor the Amendment. . . .[23]

With the help of incoming President Ford, the drawn-out three years of negotiations between the White House and members of Congress over the Soviet trade bill were brought to a climax. An exchange of unparalleled letters between Secretary Kissinger and Senator Jackson paved the way for passage of the legislation. On the basis of certain assurances allegedly received from the Kremlin, Kissinger in turn assured the Democratic presidential aspirant in writing that the Russians would permit at least 60,000 Jews to emigrate annually and would impose no punitive measures on those seeking to leave. In his familiar role as mediator, the Secretary of State had engineered negotiations to which Soviet officialdom publically acknowledged no connection. According to the senatorial triumverate Jackson, Javits, and Ribicoff, the "good faith" of Moscow was assumed or else the trade benefits were to be rescinded at the end of an initial eighteen-month trial period.

The assurances of Soviet exemplary behavior toward Jewish would-be émigrés conveyed to the legislators by the Secretary sounded like pages out of *Alice In Wonderland*. With several strokes of his pen, an American Secretary of State was seeming to guarantee for certain citizens of a totalitarian regime a so-preferential treatment, the

mere request for which constituted the grossest interference in the
internal affairs of a sovereign nation. The attempt to push any sovereign state, albeit one politically structured as the Soviet Union, to
guarantee that "applications for emigration will be processed in order
of receipt" and on a "nondiscriminatory basis," or that "individuals
holding certain security clearances who desire to emigrate" are to be
notified of the date on which they may expect to become eligible for
emigration, was scarcely believable. What was the fire and fury of *The
Gulag Archipelago,* then, all about?

As a silent partner, but allegedly privy to the negotiations, the
Kremlin leadership had indicated the extreme lengths to which it
seemed to wish to go in order to trade with the U.S. and to extend
détente. But no one ought to have been surprised when Foreign Minister Andrei Gromyko denounced this legislative attempt to swap U.S.
markets for Soviet Jewish emigration as a gross intrusion into the
internal affairs of the Soviet Union. At the same time Gromyko indicated that a letter to this effect had been given to Kissinger on
October 26 in Moscow and apparently rested inside the Secretary's
pocket for three months, even as an agreement on the legislation,
premised on alleged Soviet willingness "to increase the rate of emigration from the 1973 level of 35,000, which would continue to rise to
correspond to the number of applicants" (the words of the Kissinger
letter[24] to Jackson), was being hammered out with Congress.[25] The
last-minute passage by Congress of legislation imposing a $300 million
limitation over a four-year term on Export-Import Bank guarantees of
credit to the Soviet Union, deemed the most vital part of the trade
exchange by the Kremlin, likewise was an additional irritant to Moscow. The Soviet-American trade agreement of 1972 was nullified by an
irate Moscow.[26]

In fighting the U.N. resolution on Zionism and Racism, Israel and
friends were forced to fall back on their most reliable, readily available
ploy, "Rescue Soviet Jewry." The Zionist state faced near total isolation in the world community as the U.S., together with the apartheid
South African Republic, its only friends and allies—and even U.S.
support was under some fire at the hands of economy- and isolationist-
minded members of Congress. Moreover, a deep recession, inflation,
corruption, Palestinian unrest, and the disturbing balance between
emigration from and immigration into Israel hit the internal structure
of Israel deep and hard.

Mustering its total strength on behalf of Zionist sovereignty,
which rarely had felt itself so threatened in the twenty-four years since
the campaign for statehood had been launched at the Biltmore Hotel,

World Jewish leadership convened the 1976 Brussels Conference on Soviet Jewry. The time was ripe, for detente, under fire on many fronts, particularly as a result of the ignominious Kissinger defeat in Angola, could give way to a revival of the Cold War, ensuring the Middle East polarization, always sought by Tel Aviv.

Called just five years after the first international assembly on the "plight" of Soviet Jewry had convened in the Belgian capital, Brussels II (February 17–19, 1976) brought together top supporters of the Zionist movement from all over the world, headed by former Israeli Premier Golda Meir. The delegates gathered under the sponsorship of the National Conference on Soviet Jewry, the Conference of Presidents of Major American Jewish Organizations, the B'nai B'rith International, the European Conference on Soviet Jewry, the Israel Public Council for Soviet Jews, the Latin American Jewish Congress, the World Jewish Congress, and the World Zionist Organization. This imposing list of convenors at Brussels II told only part of the story of the importance Zionist-Israelist chieftains had given to the event. The presence of nearly a dozen members of Congress, headed by Senator Frank Church (Dem.-Idaho), a ranking member of the Senate Foreign Relations Committee as well as a presidential aspirant, was a reminder both of the fact that this was an election year in the U.S. and of the extent to which the Zionist movement had depended on vote and campaign contribution-seeking American legislators since its very inception.

At the final session of the three-day international gathering in the Palais de Congréss, the 1,200 delegates from thirty-two countries heard Meir issue a ringing call for unified action, as she declared that the meeting had been "one of the great emotional experiences of my life, and I have the feeling that I have witnessed one more period of Jewish history." Appealing to Soviet authorities to end their alleged acts of anti-Semitism, she declared:

We want the Jews there to be the masters of their own fate. We cannot accept that teaching Hebrew is counter-revolutionary, that three million Jews have no newspaper, no theatre, and a few—very, very few—synagogues are left. . . .[27]

We just refuse to disappear no matter how strong and brutal and ruthless the forces against us may be, here we are. Millions of bodies broken, buried alive, burned to death, but never has anyone been able to succeed in breaking the spirit of the people.

In her lengthy harangue to the delegates, the Israeli leader set forth the claim that Soviet restrictions on Jewish emigration were a repudiation of the pledge signed in 1975 by the Soviet Union at the

Helsinki European Security Conference to permit "a free movement of people and ideas."

While the exact strategy to be pursued by the eight large Jewish sponsoring organizations was not spelled out at the conclave, one speaker hinted at a possible course of action in making the understatement of any day: "We have grossly under-utilized our extensive business contacts." However, there was nothing vague about the closing declaration of the meeting:

We call on all men and women of conscience and all governments cherishing humanitarian ideals to speak out on behalf of the Jews in the USSR. *We have the right and duty to say to them, a generation after the Holocaust, that they dare not remain silent in the face of renewed threats confronting the Jewish people.* History has taught that these threats imperil human rights everywhere. [Italics added.]

The incessant Zionist campaign on behalf of Soviet Jewry has been disastrous to all parties concerned. Far from relaxing restrictions on Jewish emigration, these efforts proved counterproductive. In testifying before the House International Relations Committee in 1977, former U.S. Ambassador to the Soviet Union George Kennan declared that the Jackson-Vanik Amendment had served "no useful purpose, not even from the standpoint of the people it was supposed to benefit, and I see no reason to preserve it."[28] Emigration, which had reached 34,922 during the peak year of 1973, fell to 20,081 in 1974 and to 13,159 in 1975, then rose the following year to 14,138.[29] In 1977 and in the first five months of 1978 it was on the rise again, but far under the peak.

The untold story, however, has been the recital of the fate of the 3,000 Soviet Jews out of the 120,000 immigrants to Israel, who have left and have been trying to resettle themselves either in Europe or waiting to be forgiven to go back home to Mother Russia. In 1975, 200 of these hapless Jews were being housed in Westende, a tiny Belgian resort near Ostend, receiving their only assistance from a Catholic charity there. Some 600 other Russian Jewish migrants were scattered around Brussels.

Such migrants in Europe are not uncommon. There has always been a two-way traffic to and from Israel, but what makes these 800 or so Jews in Belgium newsworthy is that these were the Soviet Jews who had been portrayed by the media as martyrs, who had been ready to hazard their homes, possessions, careers, prospects, and personal safety for the joy of living in Israel. But the resurgence of that Jewish feeling, which according to Zionist dogma would flow through their veins upon their return to their "homeland," in many cases never took place.

According to a 1975 London *Observer* story, this is how a Jew from Kishinev, who was interviewed, viewed it:

I don't want to say much against Israel except that the people have had false ideas about life in their state. They treat Russians badly, no houses, no jobs, and the people were too bad. I left because I did not get anything I needed —no peace. Look at me, over fifty, and all my life I have been running, and when I got to Israel, what did I find? Darkness, blackouts, war, massacres, bombs, rockets. I suppose if you have been brought up in Israel you can learn to live with it. I could not.

The attitude of many of these Soviet migrants could be summed up in the words of a middle-aged Odessa Jew: "Things in Russia are not as bad as you think they are, and things in Israel are not as good as we thought they were."

Ironically, one of the main reasons for the size of the Israeli bureaucracy was the elaborate machine that had been set up to help the immigrants, and no immigrants have been reputed to have been helped more generously and lavishly than the Russians. They have been the so-called privileged group, and their privileges had aroused the animosity of the local population, especially the Oriental Jews, the Jews from Muslim countries. The Soviet Jews have had shouted at them on Tel Aviv streets, "Go back to Moscow." Some have formed small transitory communities in Rome, Paris, West Berlin, and Vienna in addition to Belgium. The Catholic charities have been their saviors, as there seems to have been a tacit agreement among the Israelis that these Russian Jews should not be helped. "I could pay for them myself," said a diamond merchant, "but what sort of Jews are they? They have no loyalty to Israel."

Reports of increasing Soviet Jewry "dropouts"—those who received exit visas for Israel, changed horses in the middle of Europe, and decided to emigrate elsewhere—were ignored by the pro-Israel press until the *Times* finally ran a story on December 20, 1976 (in early September a short article had appeared in the first edition but was dropped in later editions) that the number had reached 54 percent in November and 47.4 percent for the entire year. Zionists were concerned about the effect of the dropouts on the Soviets, who had been squaring themselves with their Arab friends through the fiction that they were granting Jews permission to leave so that these emigrés (many were dissidents whom the Soviet Union was happy to see depart) could be united with their families in Israel. They were even more deeply worried about the effect on Israeli manpower. Prior to the six-day war, the fate of Soviet Jewry evoked little interest. But subsequently, the need to colonize certain Arab territories, particularly East Jerusalem, forced the Israeli authorities to seek new settlers from wherever they might be obtained. Since the six million-strong American Jewish community evinced little interest in moving to Eretz Israel, the next largest bloc of potential Diaspora emigrants were those in the Soviet Union.

Many of the dropouts who came to the Italian beach resort of Ostia, outside of Rome, have been waiting for more than two years to obtain U.S. visas and have been enduring dire circumstances.[30] A bitter clash among Israeli and American Zionist "philanthropic" agencies pitted those who wished Jews to be rescued from the grasp of the Soviet Union at any cost and those who would only see them as immigration fodder for Israel. The latter won out, and a decision was reached that Soviet Jews must go to Israel and nowhere else.[31] All aid was cut off for those who dropped out. This harsh treatment also applied to Soviet Jews who went to Israel and then left. Zionists strove to deny these Russian Jews the status of refugees so that they would be unable to obtain admission into any country outside of Israel. Zionism openly and dramatically had demonstrated what their leadership had always been quietly stating: Political statemaking, not humanitarian refugeeism, is our business.[32]

This inhuman action, totally contrary to the charitable and humane tradition of Judaism, decided by the Committee of Eight, was an echo of the famed Klausner Report of post-World War II, which recommended that those Jewish displaced persons in camps "who are not interested in going to Palestine are no longer to be wards of the Jewish community or to be maintained in camps, fed and clothed."[33] But the controversy over the Soviet Jewry dropouts and émigrés[34] focused attention on the broader problem of the growing exodus from the Promised Land, whose numbers had so increased by the fall of 1976 that Premier Rabin felt forced to issue a vehement statement calling them "nemoshots"—deserters. Israel's outflow had increased from 33,000 in 1974 to close to 80,000 by the end of 1976. (It has been estimated that there are more than 85,000 Israelis in the New York area, 80,000 in Los Angeles, and 40,000 in Montreal, and few seem disposed to return to Israel, except for temporary visits.) This was accompanied by the alarming and drastic fall in the number of new settlers from 55,000 in 1973 to 32,000 in 1974, 17,000 in 1975. The rise in 1977 to 24,000 immigrants, a net gain of 8,000 over outbound, according to official figures, was made up of virtually all Soviet Jews. The forty percent annual rate of inflation, the world's highest taxes, which were taking forty-six percent of the country's gross national product, housing shortages, unemployment, bureaucratic red tape, social inequalities, violent crime, drug abuse, and prostitution accounted for what the *San Francisco Examiner* called "Israel's Modern Exodus: It Goes the Wrong Way."[35]

Washington manipulations over Soviet Jewry again illustrate the subordination of American national interests to those of Israel. Whether détente is good or bad for the U.S. is enough of an intricate and devastatingly complex issue in itself without injecting the acceptance of liberalized emigration as the criterion for deciding this question. There are overwhelming obstacles and unresolved ambiguities already blocking Super-Power understanding and agreement on the SALT disarmament talks, the success of which is necessary for the removal of the dangers of nuclear confrontation engulfing the entire world.

As a result of the nullification of the trade agreement, which had been approved in principle by both political parties two years earlier, Moscow turned to other Western countries and to Japan for the purchase of equipment and technology that otherwise would have come from the U.S. The loss of billions in trade meant the loss of many new jobs.

"The public be damned" attitude was demonstrated in still another direction. The American people have been subsidizing to date the movement of Soviet Union Jews to fulfill the manpower needs of the State of Israel through congressional appropriations of $50 million in 1973, $36.5 million in 1974, $40 million in 1975, and $15 million in 1976.[36] Zionists even succeeded in pressuring Congress to stipulate that none of the latter funds "may be used to resettle refugees in any country other than Israel."

Additional funds to move Jews from the Soviet Union, as well as from other lands around the globe, are, of course, derived from tax-deductible contributions to the United Jewish Appeal. The already intolerably overburdened American taxpayer has thus been further imposed upon through the disbursement of his monies for the political objective of building the population of a foreign state, which scarcely falls within the "religious, charitable, scientific, literary, or educational purposes" criteria set by the IRS for tax deductibility—and to boot, such expenditure of his funds has proved to be diametrically opposed to his own self-interest, his quest for peace.

Time and tide seem to have overtaken the William F. Buckley suggestion of a fifty-first-state status for Israel. America's Mediterranean ward long ago affirmed its right to be acknowledged as the first state of the Union as close examination of U.S. foreign policy will bear out.

PART FOUR

POLITICS OR POLICY

So likewise, a passionate attachment of one Nation for another produces a variety of evils. Sympathy for the favorite nation, facilitating the illusion of an imaginary common interest, in cases where no real common interest exists, and infusing into one the enmities of the other, betrays the former into a participation in the quarrels and wars of the latter, without adequate inducement or justification. It leads also to concessions to the favorite Nation of privileges denied to others, which is apt doubly to injure the Nation making the concessions: by unnecessarily parting with what ought to have been retained; and by exciting jealousy, ill will, and a disposition to retaliate, in the parties from whom equal privileges are withheld. And it gives to ambitious, corrupted or deluded citizens (who devote themselves to the favorite Nation) facility to betray, or sacrifice the interests of their own country, without odium, sometimes even with popularity; gilding with the appearances of a virtuous sense of obligation a commendable deference for public opinion, or a laudable zeal for public good, the base or foolish compliances of ambition, corruption or infatuation . . . Real Patriots, who may resist the intrigues of the favorite, are liable to become suspected and odious while its tools and dupes usurp the applause and confidence of the people to surrender their interests.

GEORGE WASHINGTON's Farewell Address

The Eisenhower, Kennedy,
and Johnson Years

A star looks down at me, And says, "Here I and you Stand, each
in our degree: What do you mean to do?"
                                                        —Thomas Hardy

Changes of administration in Washington generally made slight difference in the attitude of the White House or of Congress toward the
Middle East problem. When the House Foreign Affairs Committee
required a study on the Palestine question, the task was assigned to the
then Republican congressman (now Senator) Jacob Javits of New York.
Although his pro-Israel views were well known, Javits requested and
received this assignment with the tacit acknowledgment of his colleagues that objectivity or impartiality on this subject was impossible
—even undesirable.

President Eisenhower's administration was the exception. The
wartime military leader strove to steer the country on a neutral course
in the Middle East, and away from the Truman blatant bias toward
Israel. Ike proved to be the only American Chief Executive to stand
firm against the full brunt of Zionist pressures when, in the fall of 1956,
even though it was a national election year, he refused to yield to
political blackmail and sent his Secretary of State, John Foster Dulles,
to the U.N. to halt the tri-pronged invasion of Egypt by Israel, Britain,
and France. The long-simmering dispute over the Suez Canal had
come to a head.

On October 19, 1954, the British and Egyptian governments had
signed the Suez Evacuation Agreement, bringing Britain's seventy-
five-year occupation of the country to an end. This pact provided for
removal of British troops from the Canal Zone but left unsettled the
question of control of the Canal. The fate of that vital transportation
artery became tied to the plans of Egypt for building the High Dam
at Aswan.

On July 19, 1956, Dulles summoned Egyptian Ambassador Ahmed Hussein to his office and handed him a letter in which the U.S. government precipitately announced the withdrawal of its previous offer to contribute $56 million toward the financing of the dam (later referred to by Eisenhower as the "damn dam"). The Secretary was responding to a strange combination of political bedfellows: Southerners who feared increased competition from Egyptian cotton, election-year, economy-minded conservatives, anti-Communists resentful of Egypt's Czech arms deal and her recognition of Red China, and pro-Israeli Senators succumbing to the demands of the Zionist lobby. The next day Britain and the World Bank withdrew their promises of loans to Egypt, which were contingent upon the U.S. contribution.

Then followed President Nasser's nationalization of the Suez Canal Company, the 1956 war, and the ensuing world crisis, which came close to detonating World War III. The story of the physical occupation of the Canal by a small task force led by Mahmoud Younes, armed with a series of sealed envelopes to be opened with the utterance of the magic word by President Nasser in the course of a television broadcast from Alexandria to the Egyptian people on the fourth anniversary of the July 23 revolution, was worthy of Ian Fleming.[1] Tension mounted during the ensuing three months as Britain and France fulminated and threatened. The Users Association, a U.S. improvisation for running the Canal, aroused little enthusiasm from anyone.

Israel, armed by France and the West, had been carrying on increasing intermittent warfare through pulverizing raids against Syria, Jordan, and Egypt. Nasser's deal with Soviet satellite Czechoslovakia netted important weaponry after the U.S. refused to supply arms Egypt needed. Major General E. L. M. Burns of the U.N. Truce Supervision Organization was encountering grave difficulties in controlling border incidents. At this time the Archbishop of York declared the Jordanian-Israeli truce line "absurd," and the prelate referred to the "terrible retaliation" by Israel for isolated raids by individual Arabs, which led to the "widespread feeling that Israelis are provoking incidents." And, as Burns publicly acknowledged, infiltration was not likely to end so long as the Palestinian Arab refugees were not permanently settled. When Golda Meir succeeded moderate Moshe Sharett as Ben-Gurion's Foreign Minister, preventive war rather than further reprisal raids seemed in the offing.

British, French, and Israeli representatives met quietly in France and decided on a course of action that bound them to military action.

It took the world many years to realize "the private determination of Anthony Eden, Guy Mollet, and David Ben-Gurion to destroy Nasser,"[2] which was formalized in the secret treaty drawn up at Sèvres. In his zeal to keep the collusion with Israel a secret, the British Foreign Minister did not even disclose to his own planners and commanders that the Israelis were about to march into Sinai.[3]

The invasion followed. Israel struck at Egypt first on October 29 and, in the guise of separating the combatants, British and French forces followed after the Israeli troops had made large advances. Port Said and Ismalia were heavily bombed, the cities destroyed, and hundreds of Egyptians killed.

Then came the long, drawn-out negotiations on forcing the Israelis to evacuate the territory they had seized and held. The British and French moved out quickly when faced with a U.S.S.R. ultimatum "couched in the most brutal language and threatening the bombardment of Britain with long-range guided missiles equipped with atomic warheads."[4] But it was not until early spring that Eisenhower's determination not to let aggression pay off resulted in the Israelis pulling back unconditionally from the Sinai peninsula, Gaza, and two tiny islands in the Straits of Tiran. The Israeli demand for a prior guarantee that Egypt would cease threatening Israel's national security was answered by the President in his famed television address to the nation on February 20, 1957, in which he stated:

Israel insists on firm guarantees as a condition to withdrawing its forces of invasion. If we agree that armed attack can properly achieve the purposes of the assailant, then I fear we will have turned back the clock of internal order. We will have countenanced the use of force as a means of settling international differences and gaining national advantage. . . . If the U.N. once admits that international disputes can be settled by using force, then we will have destroyed the very foundation of the organization and our best hope of establishing a real world order.

For once the formulation of policy prevailed over domestic political expediency. This was the high-water mark in American resistance to Zionist pressure on the White House, climaxed by the Eisenhower refusal to be bamboozled by either the timing of the Israeli attack a week before Election Day or the fact that the two oldest U.S. allies, England and France, had joined together in this conspiracy to unseat Egypt's Gamal Abdel Nasser. The Eisenhower reelection sweep against the candidacy of Adlai Stevenson came in the face of the distribution of hundreds of thousands of pamphlets in New York and other large urban areas saying: "A vote for Ike is a vote for Nasser, Nixon, and Dulles."

Stalwart courage, rarely seen in public life, had paid off and made the actual existence of a deliverable Jewish vote a legitimate question. But rarely does the supine politician, who lives under the illusion that there is indeed such a deliverable vote, challenge the blackmailer, and the game of subordinating the national interest to the whims and fancies of domestic politics has continued, with this one Eisenhower exception, to the gravest detriment of the national interest. When Ike's Vice President, Richard Nixon, assumed the Presidency eleven years later, he chose not to apply the 1957 Eisenhower guidelines, preferring to follow the lead of President Johnson, who had refused to exert any pressure whatsoever on Israel to return even larger territories seized in 1967.

The disastrous British attack on Egypt brought the heretofore brilliant career of Anthony Eden to an ignominious end. Strangely enough, he earlier had seen the Middle East problem in its true perspective. But humiliated by the Israelis, he had chosen to take his sorely wounded pride out on the Egyptians.

Britain, like the U.S., increasingly molded her Middle East policy less in terms of her own interests and more to suit the predilections of the Israeli Prime Minister. The lessons of the past continued to go unheeded. In 1941 the pleas of Iraqi Prime Minister Nuri es-Said fell on deaf ears at 10 Downing Street, leading to the downfall of his pro-West government, the seizure of power by Rashid Ali al-Gailani, and the brief entrance of the Nazis into Iraq. Nuri had urged the British to reconfirm the 1939 McDonald White Paper on Palestine, limiting further Jewish immigration into the Holy Land and calling for a unitary Palestinian state in which control was to be shared by Arabs and Jews who "would both be as Palestinian as English and Scottish [living] in Britain are British." Where it was the Nazis who had initially benefited, it was the Russians who subsequently became the chief beneficiaries of the British refusal to ask themselves the question: "What Price Israel?"

Nuri, the strong, fourteen-time Iraqi Prime Minister who, more than the Hashemite rulers under whom he served, governed the country, incessantly kept urging the British Foreign Office to do something about Israel, not merely the

. . . continual and ordinary disputes about boundaries and refugees, which everyone in the West knew about and could read about. Their need related much more to the hidden dynamics of Israel's diplomacy and propaganda, to the evidence he saw that the divisions and hostilities gave Israel an opportunity of territorial gain which she intended to exploit, not defensively but in a spirit of conquest; that with this intention it was to Israel's interests to aggravate the divisions and inflame the hostilities, and that Israel's gain might inescapably be Britain's loss, if only because it would undermine Nuri and the Baghdad Pact.[5]

With the indispensable help of Western countries, Israel mastered the "divide and rule" game. The dogged, determined Nasserite opposition to the British played directly into the Zionists' hands by making it impossible for Nuri to stand up for Britain in the face of the onslaught from Iraqi nationalists.

In an October 8, 1956, interview with a correspondent of the London *Times,* Nuri sought to win British public opinion support for an Arab-Israeli settlement based on persuading Tel Aviv to negotiate with the Arab countries on the basis of the U.N. Palestine resolutions of 1947. He warned the West: "We are with you, but the ball is now in your court. I've taken the initiative, but you must come to meet me on this question of Israel. You must not leave me beating the air. If you do not make a real move now to get the Israeli and the refugee question settled while I am still in power, while there is yet time, then all will be lost." No such move was made.

When Israel shortly thereafter launched an attack on Jordan (at Qalqilya), Iraq was prepared, at the request of her then-partner in the short-lived confederated kingdom, to send troops to the Jordanian frontier. The Israeli government acted quickly and contemptuously in announcing that this would be viewed as "a threat to Israel's security."[6] And England, under Eden, cooled off in support of Nuri precisely in the same manner as the Churchill government had turned down Nuri's 1941 appeal.

These events were the prelude to the Iraqi revolution of 1958; the assassination of Nuri and young King Faisal, bringing to an end its Hashemite rule; and the demise of the British in that country. Washington and London knew the truth but continually looked the other way for fear of offending Israel. Stability in the Middle East was a possibility, but only at the risk of incurring the ill will of the potent Israeli-Zionist machine. And neither the Foreign Office nor the State Department was prepared to pay this price.

Although in the 1956 presidential election Adlai Stevenson carried traditionally Democratic New York City by a mere 65,000 votes (the usual plurality ranged from 350,000 up to 600,00) at the very time when his opponent, President Eisenhower, bore the responsibility for halting the Israeli armies at the gates of Sinai, the candidates in the next national election (1960) played the game as if there were a deliverable Jewish vote.

Nixon's running mate, Ambassador Henry Cabot Lodge, was given the particular assignment of wooing this vote. In a New York address to an important Jewish fund-raising organization, the Vice Presidential nominee declared: "A very high-level effort to settle Middle East tensions is necessary" and pledged continuing support for Israel. Nixon let it be known that if elected he intended to let his Vice President handle the "problems of Israel's relations with her Arab neighbors."

Lodge had to do some personal expiating of his own. During the Suez Canal crisis he had been the Eisenhower instrumentality at the U.N. who had carried out the "stop-Israel" action. A widely distributed piece of Democratic campaign literature quoted columnist Drew Pearson to the effect that: "There is no one in American diplomacy who is considered by the Zionists more anti-Israel than Henry Cabot Lodge." Lodge was further alleged to have "championed Nasser and favored punitive measures against Israel to halt the invasion"—a charge Cleveland's Rabbi Abba Hillel Silver, endorsing the Nixon-Lodge ticket, attempted to refute.

A key architect of this Lodge stratagem to become the spokesman on the Israeli question was Maxwell Rabb, the former Secretary to the Eisenhower Cabinet. Rabb had ingratiated himself with Organized Jewry by accepting the Chairmanship of the District of Columbia UA drive (most of which funds were going to Israel) even while serving in a most sensitive position in a Cabinet of a President who was trying to veer America's policy in a more evenhanded direction.

An unusual foreign intrusion into an American election, intended to help the Nixon-Lodge ticket, also marked the campaign. The Israeli press intervened openly and—singularly enough—attacked the Democratic presidential nominee. *Herut*, the organ of Menachem Begin's Israeli expansionist party of the same name, claimed that Senator Kennedy's father "never loved the Jews and therefore there is a question whether the father did not inject some poisonous drops of anti-Semitism in the minds of his children, including his son John's." This same newspaper further alleged that Nasser was close to Adlai Stevenson and Senator Fulbright, who were among Senator Kennedy's closest advisers: "How can the future of Israel be entrusted to these men who might come to power, thanks to Jewish votes, strange and paradoxical as this may seem?"[7]

Leaflets containing these and other partisan attacks were distributed to the Jewish-American public in a frank attempt to influence the outcome of the election. William Zukerman wrote in the *Jewish Newsletter*, "No other state which had more at stake in the election than Israel dared take such action. It revealed the curious dogmatic mentality of the Israelis, who seriously looked upon American Jews as their colonial subjects to whom they can give orders in an important election."[8]

Both of the 1960 presidential candidates, Vice President Nixon and Senator Kennedy, realized that the forty-five New York State electoral votes might be crucial to their election, and therefore at times they seemed to be conducting themselves more as candidates for the Presidency of Israel than of the U.S. Competitive pro-Israel promises filled the air, alternating with bitter attacks on the rival party as anti-Israel, if not anti-Semitic.

To keep up with Nixon's wooing of the B'nai B'rith, Kennedy did the unprecedented by coming in August to New York City to address the convention of the Zionist Organization of America. Elaborating on the Democratic platform with a four-point program, he proposed using "all the authority of the White House to call into conference the leaders of Israel and of the Arab states to consider privately their common problems."[9] The Senator noted that "the ideals of Zionism have been endorsed by both parties" so that "friendship for Israel is a national commitment."

Kennedy placed complete blame for the continued unrest in the Middle East on the Arabs, depicting "little Israel" as the innocent victim of hatred and aggression. It was almost inconceivable that the Democratic candidate, a student as well as a writer of history, could have prepared, no less presented, so partisan an account of the tensions besetting the area. The familiarity he displayed in this address with Zionist phraseology and dogma, dating from Herzl to the present day, clearly indicated that a battery of Zionist-oriented writers must have worked closely with him in preparing this talk.

In a message to the same convention, Nixon reminded the audience that Dulles had stated that the preservation of the State of Israel was "one of the essential goals of U.S. foreign policy," and he, too, pledged to use his best offices to bring about a stable Arab-Israeli relationship. At this stage of the campaign there was every indication that, faced with the choice of moving forward from the Eisenhower administration's intent to assume a more impartial posture in the Middle East struggle or of retreating to the definite bias of the Truman administration, Kennedy would be inclined to follow the well-trod path of his party with its pro-Israel orientation. There was always the chance, however, that the political pronouncements of *Candidate* Kennedy might give way to statesmanlike actions of *President* Kennedy.

This indeed was the hope of the Arab world in the fall of 1960 when I visited there. The Senator was the overwhelming favorite over Nixon. His courageous speech in the Senate on Algeria in 1957 had made many friends for him, and the Arabs could see little difference in the present behavior of the two political parties toward the Middle East. Kennedy's verve, good looks, and fine talk were personally attracting friends in this part of the world as in the rest. Likewise, the well-publicized strong opposition of former President Truman to the Kennedy nomination from the start endeared the Massachusetts Senator to Arabs, who considered the man from Independence their chief bête noire.

Before his political ambitions soared in the direction of the Vice Presidency in 1956, Kennedy had traveled to Southeast Asia, had visited the Arab refugee camps on his way back, and had subsequently expressed on television a deep feeling of sympathy for these displaced Palestinians. But not long thereafter, in his quest for second place on the Democratic ticket, he was addressing Israel Bond gatherings at a Yankee Stadium rally in support of arms for Israel. In his earlier Pulitzer Prize-winning book *Profiles in Courage,* the Senator had done a neat job of analyzing the pressures confronting the conscientious lawmaker. He listed as the first pressure "a form of pressure rarely recognized by the general public. Americans want to be liked."[10] When he assumed office, it remained to be seen whether his past actions in regard to the Middle East represented political expediency or his better judgment.

At the outset of his administration, President Kennedy threw a damper on the hope of those who were optimistic enough to believe that statesmanship might become the immediate order of the day. One of his first key appointments was Philip M. Klutznick, housing developer from Illinois, as U.S. Representative to the U.N. Economic and Social Council. Klutznick was quickly confirmed by the Senate, even though he had served as President of the pro-Israel B'nai B'rith and of the Anti-Defamation League, and was still active in their governing councils. He also had been responsible for the creation of the vital lobbying group, the Conference of Presidents of Major Jewish Organizations. And just prior to his nomination to the key U.N. position,

Klutznick had been elected Chairman of the United Jewish Appeal's 1961 drive to raise $72 million for Israel.

During the course of the hearings on his confirmation before the Subcommittee of the Foreign Relations Committee, the members went deeply into the nominee's background, which confirmed his overweaning absorption with Israel, his intimate ties both with Israel and with Jewish organizations dedicated to advancing Israeli interests, and his own necessarily strong subjectivity on the Arab-Israeli conflict. Apparently his assurance that he would divest himself of the positions he held in these pro-Israel organizations satisfied the members of the committee passing upon his nomination. They did not doubt that he could also divest himself of his close associations and strong feelings voiced over many years, expressed only weeks prior to the confirmation proceedings.

Those who anticipated a new look under Kennedy toward the Middle East were doomed to be disappointed in other directions, too. The U.S. opposed the Security Council move to censure Israel for defying the decrees of the Jordan-Israel Mixed Armistice Commission in April 1961 by parading tanks and other heavy armaments in violation of a general armistice agreement during a Jerusalem celebration of the thirteenth anniversary of the creation of Israel. And then the U.S. voted against a General Assembly Afro-Asian resolution calling for implementation of the 1948 U.N. resolution on the refugees through the establishment of a custodian over Palestinian Arab refugee property in Israel. This resolution had been supported by a 47 to 19 vote in the Special Political Committee, but without U.S. help in mustering support from the Western powers and from Latin American countries, the two-thirds needed in the General Assembly was not forthcoming. Israel had been saved "serious embarrassment" according to the London *Jewish Chronicle,*[11] because of the American insistence that the resolution would involve the U.N. in undertaking new functions that it could not legally or practicably carry out.

When the U.N. discussed the Bay of Pigs fiasco in Cuba, Saudi Arabia and four other Arab countries condemned the U.S. for giving support and military assistance to Cuban refugees who had been ousted from their country while at the same time rejecting the plight of the Palestinian Arab refugees who were similarly suffering. The Saudis, while bound closely to the Arab neutralist camp, were usually in the anti-Communist bloc when Middle East issues were not at stake. But on this occasion, to show their pique with the neophyte Kennedy administration, they had joined other Arab states in rebuking the U.S.

Prime Minister Ben-Gurion's private visit to New York, where he adroitly maneuvered himself into a meeting with President Kennedy at the Carlyle Hotel just prior to the Chief Executive's departure for his Vienna meeting with Nikita Khrushchev, forced President Kennedy to send simultaneous reassurances to the Chiefs of State of five Arab Middle East countries—U.A.R.'s President Gamal Abdel Nasser, King Saud of Saudi Arabia, King Hussein of Jordan, Prime Minister Abdul Karim Qasim of Iraq, and President Fouad Shehab of Lebanon. Through these letters, which started a personal correspondence with Nasser carried on until the Dallas assassination, Kennedy hoped to allay Arab fears resulting from the Ben-Gurion meeting. The Arab leaders were reminded that "the concepts of our founding patriots, of Abraham Lincoln, Woodrow Wilson, and Franklin Delano Roosevelt, have played such a great part in the emergence of vigorous, independent Arab states respected as sovereign equals in the international community." Kennedy, however, had said nothing new. To the Arab leaders, what the President said were so many words, and to a people who are the possessors of the richest of languages and hands-up past masters in the art of speech, it simply represented *"kellam, kellam beydoun manah* ("words, words without meaning").

However, in his correspondence with President Kennedy, Nasser made some headway in convincing the American leader that the Arab attitude "was not based simply on emotion, but on real experience," and was a result of "an agression launched in the past, of present dangers and of fears for the future." The Egyptian President explained to the American President that "continued Jewish immigration" creates a pressure within Israel that has to explode and head for expansion. "Israel," he contended, "was constantly liable to be used by 'imperialism' as a 'tool to divide the Arab nation geographically' and as a base from which to threaten the Arab liberation movement." Kennedy's subsequent peacemaking initiatives ran into a stone wall when Prime Minister Ben-Gurion categorically rejected Washington's suggestion that Israel should begin the settlement process by taking back some of the Palestinian refugees.

The contents of the Kennedy letters were not made known until much later, since the President desired a maximum of secrecy so as to avoid the counterpressures American Israelists would certainly exert against his move to build friendlier relations with the Arab leaders. The extremely politically aware Kennedy was only too familiar with the lengths to which the Israelis could and would go, as in the Lavon Affair, in order to torpedo even the slightest attempt to improve American-Arab relations.

This effort to develop a closer relationship with Arab leaders was particularly directed toward overcoming the effects of the widespread rumors that Kennedy had made important commitments to Ben-Gurion at their New York meeting, including military and political guarantees, and offers to help in financing Israeli purchases of French arms. In his letter to Arab leaders, Kennedy made a specific point regarding the Palestinians: "We are willing to help resolve the tragic Palestine refugee problem on the basis of the principle of repatriation and compensation for property."

Ben-Gurion, beset by his own domestic problems on his bid for reelection in the face of the spotlight on the Lavon Affair, had been most anxious to convey the impression that the Kennedy administration had departed from the formula of the U.N. settlement in talks with him. The 1960 Democratic campaign platform had been purposefully vague in talking of encouragement "to the resettlement of Arab refugees in lands where there is room and opportunity for them." This implied resettlement outside Israel would have been a definite contravention of the U.N. resolution giving the refugees the right to choose between repatriation and compensation.

Meanwhile, Kennedy was constantly being prodded by other politicians to take positive action to win a peace settlement favorable to Israel. New York's Governor Nelson Rockefeller, still with his eye on the White House, asked Kennedy to carry out his campaign promises to build peace in the Middle East. A member of his own party, Senator Hubert H. Humphrey, insisted that the U.S. had "the main responsibility" for fostering peace between Israel and the Arab states. Illinois Senator Paul Douglas, another Democrat close to the President, in addressing a meeting of visiting Libyan legislators, had the temerity to tell them: "Israel is here to stay, and the U.S. will see that she remains in the Middle East. It therefore behooves the government of Libya to take the necessary immediate steps to recognize Israel." In Republican New York State, everyone from Congressmen to Governor was playing domestic politics with the Middle East conflict so as to further embarrass the President.

While the President, more often through Vice President Lyndon Johnson, gave much lip service to Israelist aspirations, his administration continued to resist pressures, including a round-robin petition signed by 226 Congressmen of both parties (aided by a large *New York Times* advertisement on May 28, 1962) to initiate direct Arab-Israeli negotiations. Kennedy had decided to shelve his pledge in the Democratic platform to bring Israeli and Arab leaders together around a peace table in order to settle the Palestine question. There is little doubt that this shift was largely due to the influence and respect Kennedy had for the views of eminent columnist Walter Lippmann, who after a visit to Cairo had written that he was convinced that the "no war-no peace" status was "destined to continue."

There cannot be peace, because no Arab statesman, beginning with President Nasser himself, can afford to make a settlement which recognized the existence of Israel. Almost certainly, if he tried to do that, he would be assassinated. . . . It is as impossible for an Arab to be pro-Israel as for a Catholic cardinal to be a Communist. In Egypt and among Arab states near Israel, a permanent state of hostility to Israel is for politicians a necessity. They may think what they like, but in public they must be irreconcilable.[12]

It was not until the Kennedy administration had been in office twenty-one months that the concrete action for which Tel Aviv had been angling since the Ben-Gurion visit became a reality. On September 26, 1962, the U.S. announced that it had agreed to sell Israel short-range defensive ground-to-air Hawk missiles. "US to Sell Israel Hawk Missiles to Meet Arab Threat," sang out the *Washington Post.* The tanks, jet fighters, and long-range bombers received by the U.A.R. and Iraq in the previous months allegedly had tipped the balance of military power to the Arabs and were the justification, according to the statement attributed to "State Department officials" confirming the action. This marked the first time that the U.S. had departed from the policy of permitting France and Britain to serve as military suppliers for the Middle East.

This action had been presaged four days earlier by a widely publicized speech in Washington to 600 American and Canadian leaders of the Israel Bond Drive in which Levi Eshkol, then Finance Minister (later Prime Minister), charged that his nation's "security was imperiled by rockets possessed by the U.A.R." This was carried by the *New York Times* on September 23, 1962, and the following day a dispatch from Tel Aviv by the *Times* reported that the U.S. was "expected to make an effort soon" to restore "the balance of power in the Middle East."

The New York paper was unable to restrain itself from commenting editorially on the cynical timing of the Washington announcement. Not only had the President and his aides leaked news of the decision to leaders of Jewish groups in the U.S. before it was publicly announced—and Myer Feldman, the top Kennedy assistant in charge of Jewish affairs, had done likewise in the Israeli capital—but the action was made a matter of public record just as the campaign of the Democratic candidate for the governorship of New York was beginning to build up steam.

Washington appeared totally unconcerned about the likely repercussions from this latest action, coming at a time when a shadow could not help being cast on the sincerity of recent American efforts toward disarmament and when there was a growing trend toward complete neutralization of the southern shore of the Mediterranean, in line with the thinking of the Ben Bella government in Algeria. American bases in Morocco were to be abandoned in 1963, Bizerte was to be evacuated by the French, and everywhere new problems were being posed for NATO.

Even after the initial U.S. arms sale to Israel, Congress continued to maintain pressures on the White House. With the declaration in April 1963 of the tripartite federated United Arab Republic (which was to have comprised Egypt, Syria, and Iraq but never went beyond the intent), members of the Senate provided unmistakable evidence that another election year was coming up. The "Israel-First" bloc in the Senate attacked the administration for failing to conclude a defense pact to protect Israel and to call an embargo on all arms shipments to the Middle East. The legislators reechoed the Ben-Gurion contention that Israel had fallen behind in the arms race. Nasser, they claimed, was ready for a "push-button war. Israel is easy to pinpoint and destroy and cannot retaliate against four or five Arab states at once."[13]

With the sale of the Hawk missiles, Washington had helped give credence to the Communist propaganda picturization of an "imperialist" Uncle Sam stepping into the shoes of the old European colonialists. And those in the "liberal school" to whom President Kennedy was likely to turn for guidance on foreign policy, such as Chester Bowles and Arthur Schlesinger, Jr., who otherwise would have been so quick to note the burden of colonialism with which the U.S. was handicapping its efforts to woo the noncommitted nations, remained silent in support of this latest pro-Israel move. The Kremlin continued to label the U.S.-Israel relationship as "the last attempt by the West to maintain a colonial outpost in the Middle East."

The Arabs themselves envisioned the fledgling Israeli state alternately as a "child" who provided a continual threat, which the U.S. as "parents" could now hold against the Arabs as it grew stronger at their expense, or as a many-headed monster who held the U.S. and the Western powers by the throat and could dictate policy to them—the latter an image immeasurably strengthened by the Israeli-British-French 1956 invasion of Egypt. Whichever hypothesis was correct, the

Arabs had firmly come to regard Israel "as the prime expression of the Western aim to maintain exclusive military control over Middle East affairs."[14]

While major foreign policy adjustments had either already taken place or were being made on other fronts to woo the increasingly powerful Afro-Asian bloc, Washington did not view the quietly simmering Middle East situation with undue alarm. Perhaps the Soviet failure to move into Iraq immediately and to fill the vacuum there had inspired an optimism reflected in the equation of area stability with maintenance of the status quo. A widely disseminated report of June 1960 by the staff of the Senate Committee on Foreign Relations, of which Kennedy had been a member before becaming President, had concluded that "the gravity of the Soviet threat in the Middle East loses perspective easily. It is often exaggerated and almost as often it is foolishly minimized."[15] While carefully diagnosing the symptoms of Middle East unrest, including the 1958 revolt, which saw the crushing of the royal regime in Iraq, and calling attention to the West's need of "persuading the Arab states of their otherwise disinterested motives in their offers of assistance," this Senate report did not suggest that alteration of the U.S. policy of partiality toward Israel might provide the patient's cure. And the new President likewise was slow in moving in this direction.

There is little question, however, that Kennedy intended to move decisively in his second term. This was evidenced as far back as his personal letter of September 30, 1960, addressed to this writer in reply to a chiding for his B'nai Brith speech: "I wholly agree with you that American partiality in the Arab-Israeli conflict is dangerous both to the U.S. and the Free World"—one of the most significant and perspicacious Middle East statements made by any President.[16] It is hard to assay exactly what Kennedy would have done had he lived, but certainly the state of continued tension in the Middle East must have instilled in a President of his temperament ideas and plans for going far beyond the Kismet-like hope with which his senatorial committee had ended its Middle East study, that "the patience and ingenuity of the West will outlast the problems that have made the Middle East a chronically worrisome, dangerously unstable region."

The assassination of President Kennedy in Dallas on November 22, 1963, shattered the possibility that his second term might see Washington start to free itself from the grave burdens of U.S. partisanship on the Arab-Israeli conflict and of continuous politicking for domestic votes. President Johnson went into office with a great reputation in his legislative dealings, to use his own words, as "a compromiser and maneuverer." The 1964 campaign was approaching, and the conscious politicking for votes over the Middle East issue was stepped up. Where his predecessor drew his main political strength from the populous states of the North with their large Jewish concentrations, the new President appeared strongest in the South, and therefore his political needs required wooing of the states where the Zionist lobby was strongest.

This task was not too difficult for Johnson. As Vice President he had maintained close contact with the varied Israelist organizations, having often been delegated by Kennedy to represent the White House in bringing the administration's blessings to Zionist, UJA, and other similar conclaves. On his own, the new occupant in the White House had long been deeply committed to the Israeli cause in the U.S. During the Suez crisis in February 1957, when the Eisenhower administration was considering invoking economic sanctions against a stubborn Israel to force a withdrawal of her troops from the Sinai peninsula, the then majority Senate leader is said to have summoned his chauffeur and driven to the White House, where a heated session ensued.[17] The Republican President was bluntly told by the Texas Democrat that the Senate would never approve punitive sanctions against Israel. To Secretary Dulles and Henry Cabot Lodge, he decried such threats as "unwise, unfair, and one-sided." And on the Senate floor he charged that it was "Egyptian maintenance of a state of war and the exercise of belligerent rights . . . that resulted in Israel's military counteraction."[18]

After his election to the Vice Presidency, Johnson visited Israel and continued to give whatever comfort he could to the Zionist position. Both he and Mrs. Johnson went out of their way to demonstrate their support of Israeli philanthropic needs by a well-publicized purchase of Israel Bonds. When Lady Bird Johnson accepted the honorary chairmanship of a Washington Independence Ball to push the sale of bonds, the Iraqi Chargé d'Affaires futilely protested this action as a breach of neutrality. Both the Vice President and his wife expressed deep resentment of this Arab attitude.

The Johnson administration early announced the retention of the services of Myer Feldman, President Kennedy's Adviser on Middle East issues, who had been a key figure in bringing about the sale to Israel of the U.S. ground-to-air missiles. Feldman, dubbed by the Jewish Telegraphic Agency "the White House's Watchman for Israel," succeeded Theodore Sorensen in April 1964 as Special Counsel to the

President, and his role far eclipsed in importance that of Jewish Affairs Adviser David K. Niles[19] in the Truman administration or of Maxwell Rabb in the Eisenhower administration.

At the Weizmann Institute dinner in New York Johnson accepted on behalf of the late President a posthumous honorary fellowship, and clearly indicated that no Israeli watchman was really needed in the White House. The President disclosed that the U.S. had offered to cooperate with Israel in using nuclear power to solve the water shortage in the Middle East. He was ecstatically cheered by the Waldorf banqueters time and again for his sympathetic references to Israel and his announcement of the first joint venture by the U.S. with another country in desalinization research. One of the Arab objections to Israeli plans to irrigate the Negev by diverting Jordan River waters was the consequent salinizing effect this would have on the water flowing to Arab countries.

As Israel proceeded with its diversion of Jordan waters from Lake Tiberias, the fat was now even more than ever in the fire. The Arabs had drawn up a military plan to protect their own Jordan River diversion scheme. But even in the "era of Arab coexistence," as Robert Stephens called it in his biography of Nasser,[20] featured by U.A.R.-galvanized summit meetings and other diplomatic measures to draw the Arabs into one front, Arab leaders could reach no agreement on effective implementary action. Although Arab internecine struggles blocked any joint reaction to meet the Israeli challenge, the June 1967 war, three years away, was now in the making, and it was only a question of time. And where the U.S. had in the past done everything to sustain Nasser of Egypt in power while at the same time protecting its ward, Israel, now Johnson allowed his personal dislike of the Egyptian leader to command his policy, and he did little to avert the disaster that overcame Cairo in June 1967. The President was not idealistically motivated, as his predecessor would have been in a second term, to make a real effort to settle the Palestine question on the basis of justice for both sides. In one of his urgent messages to Kosygin concerning the impending war, LBJ referred only to "the increasing harassment of Israel by elements based in Syria," refusing to admit the slightest relationship to the worsening Palestinian plight. (Some light on Johnson's penchant for Israel is reflected in the Saul Bellow tale that the President once received Abba Eban and said, "Mr. Ambassador, Ah'm sittin' here scratchin' my ass and thinkin' about Is-ra-el."[21])

Relations between Washington and Cairo had been gradually

deteriorating since 1965. If Washington had ever been a purposeful plan, as maintained by Miles Copeland in his book *The Game of Nations*,[22] to help Nasser continue to rule Egypt since the overthrow of King Farouk in the bloodless revolution of July 1952, this was very clearly abandoned under Johnson.

At a meeting of the Palestine Council in Cairo in the late spring of 1965, Nasser cautioned the Arabs to proceed carefully, and pointed out that it was unwise to go to war at that time, with 50,000 Egyptian troops in Yemen. The Egyptian leader incurred Washington's wrath by giving moral support to the Congolese rebels in Stanleyville who were opposing the U.S.-backed Congo government under Moise Tshombe, a development the Egyptian leader viewed as blatant imperialism. This action in Africa contributed to Johnson's very sharp anti-Nasser feeling, leading the U.S. to hold back on vital wheat shipments to Cairo. Hopes for any rapprochement between the U.S. and the U.A.R. quickly faded.

On his part Nasser up to this moment had been rejecting calls from Arab extremists for war against Israel. In November 1966 Israel's near-leveling of the Jordanian village of Es-Samu'a near Hebron had put Nasser's leadership in the Arab world to the test. Jordan's Prime Minister Wasfi el-Tal, who was assassinated six years later in Beirut, blustered, "Where is the air cover Cairo promised?"

On April 7 Damascus was buzzed by Israeli planes and six Syrian jets were shot down. Still Nasser did not move. As U.S. Ambassador to the U.N. Charles Yost put it in his *Foreign Affairs* article of January 1968, "The Arab-Israeli war—How It Began": "For the second time in six months Arab forces suffered a very bloody nose at the hands of Israel without the 'Unified Arab Command' in Cairo lifting a finger." Nasser still was following his 1965 philosophy of determining when to battle and of not fighting on a new front with so many troops tied down in Yemen:

They say "drive out UNEF"; suppose that we do. Is it not essential that we have a plan? If Israeli aggression takes place in Syria, shall I attack Israel? Then Israel is the one which detetermines the battle for me. Is this the wise way? We have to determine the battle. Israel may wish us to enter a war with it now. . . . Is this conceivable while there are fifty thousand Egyptian troops in Yemen?[23]

Border warfare between Israel and Egypt and between Israel and Jordan was mounting, and Cairo found itself in a very dangerous position. Egypt needed $100 million for wheat; the local currency deal advanced by Kennedy was rejected by a thoroughly angered Johnson. At this juncture the U.S.S.R. added to the tensions by painting an alarmist's picture of Israeli intentions toward Syria. Gromyko might even have called attention to this possible threat to Syria, Stephens tells us, as part of the Soviet effort to end Cairo-Damascus feuding and to bring the two countries closer together. But certainly Nasser became convinced of a plot to bring down the Damascus regime on the basis of Syrian, Soviet, and his own reports that Israel was massing eleven to thirteen brigades on the Syrian border. Anwar el-Sadat, heading a parliamentary group on a visit to Moscow, was informed at the Kremlin that the "invasion of Syria was imminent."[24]

The situation was inflamed by public statements from both quarters (but only the Arab threats were reported to Americans). Prime Minister Levi Eshkol declared, "Israel may have to teach Syria a sharper lesson than that of the 7 of April," and then Chief of Staff General Yitzhak Rabin said that "only the overthrow of the Damascus regime could end the Fatah raids." Ambassador Yost noted both parties "had frequently proclaimed their intentions to go to war under certain circumstances" and alluded to other strong statements by Israeli Prime Minister Eshkol, including a public speech in Tel Aviv indicating that "his government regarded the wave of sabotage and infiltration gravely. . . ." James Feron in the *Times* reported from Tel Aviv (May 12) that "some Israeli leaders have decided that the use of force against Syria may be the only way to curtail increasing terrorism." "Any such Israeli reaction to continued infiltration," they argued, "would be of considerable strength, but of short duration and limited in area."

The singular Israeli decision to divert the Jordan River waters and the development of Israel's Dimona nuclear reactor were certainly prime factors leading directly to the conflict, but were scarcely reported in the 300-odd books written since 1967 by Israeli enthusiasts, apologists, crusaders, etc. Their emphasis was always on the alleged "drive-you-into-the-sea" Nasser attitude, which was reinforced by the slanted reportage on the Egyptian President's address to the Council of Trade Unions in Cairo on May 26, ten days before the outbreak of war. American headlines and news leads on radio and television quoted the Egyptian leader as saying, "We will destroy Israel." Here is exactly what the Egyptian President said in full, as translated by the Foreign Broadcasting Information Service, a U.S. agency in Washington:

If Israel embarks on an aggression against Syria or Egypt, the battle against Israel will be a general one and not confined to one spot on the Syrian or Egyptian border. The battle will be a general one and our basic objective will be to destroy Israel.

It was only the last eight words that Huntley and Brinkley, Cronkite, the *New York Times*, the *Chicago Tribune*, and other elements of the media reported at the time. (If there was ever an Oscar to be awarded for one single distortion that has been most widely used, it was this. Prime Minister Golda Meir, in an appearance in December 1971—four years later—on "Meet the Press" when she was importuning the President of the U.S. for further aid, was still repeating the canard.)

What the Western media did not report at all was only revealed seven years later when Doubleday published *The Cairo Documents* from the pen of Nasser's closest associate, Mohamed Hassanein Heikal (described in the Edward Sheehan introduction as "the most powerful journalist in the world"). In speeches on May 27 and 29 Nasser had explicitly stated: "We are not going to fire the first shot . . . we are not going to start an attack."[25] This was a public pledge to Lyndon Johnson, Charles de Gaulle, and the Kremlin, all of whom had anxiously queried Cario as to its intentions after Israeli Foreign Minister Abba Eban had gone to the State Department and told Secretary Dean Rusk that "Israel is going to be attacked and destroyed today."[26] Eban sought a public U.S. statement of support against "threatened" Nasser aggression, but the Pentagon and CIA found no evidence that Egypt was planning attack.[27]

In his meeting with President Johnson on May 26, Eban was dissatisfied with an aide-memoire assuring the "safety of Israel" and the opening of the Straits of Tiran to "free passage by vessels of all nations," but sought a declaration that "an attack on Israel would be considered an attack on the U.S." When the Israeli left the White House, Johnson is said to have turned to his advisers and stated: "I've failed; they'll go."[28]

In his report to the Security Council, U.N. Secretary-General U Thant referred to the "intemperate and bellicose utterances on both sides of the line in the Near East," and then noted that "recent reports emanating from Israel have attributed to some high officials statements so threatening as to be particularly inflammatory in the sense they could only heighten emotions and thereby increase tensions on the other side of the lines."[29] The State Department even expressed their concern to Israeli authorities.

Ambassador Yost, who certainly was in a position to know, pointed out that the dialogue between the U.S. and the U.A.R. continued right up until the outbreak of the war. As late as June 4, an agreement had been announced that U.A.R. Vice President Zahkaria Mohieddin would visit Washington within the following few days and that Vice President Hubert Humphrey would then return the visit.

Member of Parliament Christopher Mayhew interviewed Nasser on June 2. The Egyptian chieftain was asked: "If Israel does not attack, will you let them alone?"

"Yes, we will leave them alone. We have no intention of attacking Israel."

This prompted Ambassador Yost to write: "Yet even at this late date (three days before the war), despite all these verbal pyrotechnics and concentrations of force, there does not seem to have been any intention in Cairo to initiate a war."

Both sides had good reason to believe that the other was likely to attack. And Nasser, no doubt, overestimated the military strength of Egypt and Syria, augmented as it was by King Hussein, who in a last-minute dash to Cario rejoined the alliance two days after Syrian and Jordanian forces had been engaged in savage tank battles. Previously, Radio Cairo and Damascus had been heaping nightly diatribes on both King Hussein ("the Hashemite harlot") and King Faisal ("the bearded bigot").[30] As usual, the Arabs were badly fragmented.

The decision by the U.A.R., finding itself in command of the Straits of Tiran, to exercise its rights as a belligerent by imposing the blockade perhaps provided the Eshkol government with the very excuse Israel had been seeking to launch a preclusive attack. Although the blockade of the port of Eilat was hurting them little,[31] Israel chose to deem this an act of aggression and struck swiftly against Egypt and Syria with precision in the early dawn of June 5. Her fateful decision came just after Iraq had joined the Arab military pact and despite the promised exchange of vice-presidential visits, the result of tireless efforts to stave off the conflict by Ambassador Yost and Special Envoy Robert Anderson, the former Secretary of the Treasury.

The May 30 visit (under an assumed name) to Washington of the head of Israeli's intelligence service, Brigadier Meir Amit, played an important part in the later stages of Tel Aviv's debate on war and peace. Apparently the head of the Israeli CIA did not quite trust what Foreign Minister Abba Eban had accomplished in his last-minute maneuverings in the American capital, and he went to find out for himself. As Stevens expressed it: "From his opposite number in Washington,

Brigadier Amit may perhaps have gained the impression, like the killers of Thomas à Becket from the thinking-out-loud of King Henry, that a swift military victory by Israel would, in the Pentagon's view, save the United States a lot of trouble."

Israel, fearful of a possible shift in the balance of power whereby the nation might find itself at a later stage in a weaker position to resist pressure for further concessions, decided to seize this opportunity to strike a crippling blow at Nasser's military forces. Lacking deep confidence in a U.S. under Johnson, the Israelis

. . . saw themselves in a position of Czechoslovakia dealing with the Nazis at the time of Munich. Faced with what they believed to be the threat of eventual conquest, it was better to fight sooner from strength than later from a weaker position. This was an understandable analysis, given the assumption made by the Israeli government about the rightness and the necessity of the position they were defending—the political and territorial status quo that existed in the ten years after the Sinai campaign. Where the wisdom of Israeli policy may be more justly questioned is in the failure to recognize that the status quo itself was inherently dangerous and unstable, not because Arabs were vengeful fanatics, but because Israel had long been attempting by military *tour de force* to maintain a situation which imposed serious human and practical disabilities on her Arab neighbors. The real question was whether or not Israel would have been wiser to use her military power to support a search for a more stable compromise settlement rather than to rely on maintaining military supremacy alone.[32]

This same psychological cul-de-sac continued to govern Israeli policy until the present, just as it controlled individual attitudes of American and other Diaspora Jews who reacted to Middle East events purely and simply on the basis of the Hitler 1945 tragedy and the perennial Jewish persecution. The Masada complex governed Israel thinking internally and the Jewish world's outlook externally.

According to the account of Aubrey Hodes, Editor of the Israeli magazine *New Outlook,* the Israeli Cabinet at a secret meeting on the night of June 3 decided to strike first:

At the end of the week Israeli diplomats in Washington reported their conviction that, if Israel attacked Egypt the United States would not intervene and would not call for an Israeli withdrawal as it had in 1956. This was what Jerusalem was waiting for, and it set the seal on the approaching decision!

The preemptive attack was fixed for the morning of Monday, June 5. War was only thirty-six hours away. The same evening Dayan drew a red herring across the trail. He held a press conference in Tel Aviv—his first public appearance as Defense Minister. One correspondent asked him whether Israel had lost its military advantage by waiting. He replied blandly: "I would think just now it's too late and too early: too late to react right away against the blockade and too early to draw any conclusion on the diplomatic way of handling the matter! Before I became a member of the Government, it decided on diplomacy. We must give it a chance."[33]

The Israelis took advantage of each of the many Arab blunders and inherent weaknesses. Egyptian senior commanders left their command posts to go to the airfield to greet Field Marshall Abdel Hakim Amer even as the Israelis struck. They waited ten hours to put their more distant bases on the alert because "you don't pass along bad news to your superiors." And no one can forget the beautiful picture of the smug Syrian sitting tightly in the Maginot Line-type defenses on the Golan Heights.

It was quite obvious that the U.S. under Johnson (as opposed to the Eisenhower era) was not in the least inclined—and Israel knew this —to restrain Israel from attacking (nor later to force Israel back behind her original borders) unless the Egyptian leader was prepared to accede to the return of the U.N. Emergency Force. Even such an Egyptian loss of face probably would have had very little effect; U.S.-Egyptian relations had reached their lowest level, eventually to be worsened by the groundless Cairo charge that American planes had joined in the initial sneak attack on Arab airfields. The availability to the Israeli intelligence of detailed photography of Egyptian airfields provided by U.S. spy satellites, which helped make their air strike so successful, was a far more plausible explanation for the disaster than any participation in combat of U.S. planes. But, again, the Arabs proved they could be a far worse enemy to themselves and their cause than all the combined Israeli military might.

The cease-fire that ended the brief war six days later brought a humiliating defeat for Egypt, Syria, and Jordan. In addressing the Knesset on June 12, Prime Minister Eshkol related how the Arab invasion of Israeli territory had begun the war: "The very existence of the State of Israel hung upon a thread, but Arab leaders' hopes of annihilating Israel have been confounded." Three days earlier the London *Times* had been told by the Israeli Ambassador to the U.K. Aharon Remez:

In the early hours of the 5th the Egyptian attack was clearly started and the Israeli plan of defense . . . was put in operation. At that time, Egyptian planes in considerable quantities were picked up upon the radar screens. They were flying in the general direction of the Tel Aviv area, and it was not difficult to imagine their intention.

This statement in the London paper must have confused observers inasmuch as not a single Arab aircraft was ever shot down over Israeli territory, nor was a single disabled Arab tank or any other military vehicle found inside Israel.

Once again Arab public relations ineptness helped the world accept the story that "little Israel" had been in danger of being attacked, if she had not already been, and that she was engaged in but another war for Jewish survival. In a *Le Monde* interview General Yitzhak Rabin admitted: "I do not believe that Nasser wanted war. The two divisions which he sent into Sinai on May 14 would not have been enough to unleash an offensive against Israel. He knew it, and we knew it."[34]

The serious debunking of this propaganda surrounding the six-day war began with the April 14, 1971, publication in the Israeli newspaper *Al-Hamishmar* of a statement from Mordecai Bentov, a member of the Israeli coalition government during the 1967 war: "The entire story of the danger of extermination was invented in every detail, and exaggerated *a posteriori* to justify the annexation of new Arab territory." The myth that the momentous June 3 decision at the secret meeting of the Israeli Cabinet to attack Arab airports was dictated by the "necessity of military action in order to liberate Israel" after hearing reports that "the armies of Egypt, Syria, and Jordan are deployed for immediate multi-front aggression, threatening the very existence of the State," was fully exposed in the spring of 1972.

Israeli General Matetiyahu Peled, in speaking to a political literary club in Tel Aviv, stated: "The thesis according to which the danger of genocide hung over us in June 1967, and according to which Israel was fighting for her very physical survival, was nothing but a bluff which was born and bred after the war."[35] General Peled had served as Chief of Logistical Command during the six-day war, one of twelve members of the Israeli General Staff. On Israel Radio General Peled claimed the state was never in real danger and that there was no evidence Egypt had any real intention of attacking Israel: "The Egyptians concentrated 80,000 soldiers in the Sinai, and we mobilized hundreds of thousands of men against them," he said. Egypt, according to Israeli Intelligence, "was not prepared for war."

His radio debate opponent, General Haim Herzog, former head of Military Intelligence, (and after 1975 Israel's Ambassador to the U.N.), readily admitted this. He stated: "There was no danger of annihilation. Neither Israeli headquarters nor the Pentagon—as the memoirs of President Johnson proved—believed in this danger." The previous Chief of Staff, Haim Bar-Lev (later Minister of Commerce), after whom Israel's defense line on the east side of the Suez Canal had been named, confirmed this opinion by stating: "We were not threatened with genocide on the eve of the six-day war, and we had never thought of such possibility."[36]

In a later interview with *Ma'ariv*, General Peled added pertinently to his observations:

All those stories about the huge danger we were facing because of our small territorial size, an argument expounded once the war was over, had never been considered in our calculations prior to the unleashing of hostilities. While we proceeded towards the full mobilization of our forces, no person in his right mind could believe that all this force was necessary to our 'defense' against the Egyptian threat. *This force was necessary to crush once and for all the Egyptians at the military level and their Soviet masters at the political level.* To pretend that the Egyptian forces concentrated on our borders were capable of threatening Israel's existence does not only insult the intelligence of any person capable of analyzing this kind of situation, but is primarily an insult to the Israeli army. [Italics added.]

These latter observations are even more remarkable because, according to *Le Monde,* the assessments come from someone who was not a leftist and was well known for his pro-American and anti-Soviet stance.[37]

General Ezer Weizman, nephew of Israel's first President, who had been Chief of Operations during the 1967 war and is at this writing Minister of Defense, said: "There was never a danger of extermination." He added, "This hypothesis had never been considered in any serious meeting."[38] According to the Israeli Labor party weekly magazine *OT,* another respected Israeli General, Yeshayer Gavish, shared the view that "the danger of Israel's extermination was hardly present before the six-day war."

General Weizman also contended, "If the Egyptians had opened fire first, they would have suffered an acute defeat. The duration of the war would have been longer, and the Israeli Air Force would have required thirteen hours instead of three to insure its mastery of the air. The price of victory would have been higher, too."[39]

The final military witness to the real purpose of the attack was Brigadier Mordechai Hod, Commander of the Israeli Air Force, who admitted one month after the surprise attack on the Arabs had been launched: "Sixteen years' planning had gone into those initial eighty minutes. We lived with the plan, we slept on the plan, we ate the plan. Constantly we perfected it."

There has been no attempt to refute the statements of these Israeli generals, and strangely very little discussion within Israel. Several Israeli journalists allegedly approached them, before they spoke out, in an appeal to their "civic sense of duty," urging them "not to exercise their inalienable right of free speech lest they prejudice world opinion and the Jewish Diaspora against Israel." General Weizman's reply to this was interesting: "The Jews of the Diaspora would like, for reasons of their own, to see us as heroes, our backs to the wall. This desire of theirs, however, will not affect the reality of the situation."[40] And the General concluded that had Israel "refrained from attacking the Egyptians, the Jordanians, and the Syrians, the State of Israel would have ceased to exist *according to the scale, spirit and quality she now embodies.* . . . We entered the Six-Day War in order to secure a position in which we can manage our lives without the external pressures."[41] [Italics added]

With the crushing defeat in 1967, Nasser faced the darkest moment in his career. Almost all international sympathy had been concentrated on "beleaguered Israel," and on all sides derision was heaped on the Egyptians as their promise and performance did not jibe. At this stage Nasser tendered his resignation. At his home headquarters in Manshiet el-Bakri as he read the text of a speech for television on the evening of June 9, he appeared to be a broken man, looking drawn and haggard. Nasser's defense was simple. He told the Egyptians that he had listened to the warnings of President Johnson and the Soviet Union not to strike the first blow. His valedictory summed up his accomplishments since 1952, including the evacuation of "British imperialism," the independence of Egypt, the inauguration of the Socialist revolution, the recovery of the Suez Canal, and the building of the High Dam generating power networks all over the Nile Valley. No sooner were Nasser's dramatic words finished than came the amazing public response so vividly described by Eric Rouleau in *Le Monde:* "In the twilight and semi-black-out streets, hundreds of thousands, some of them still in pajamas and the women in nightgowns, came out of the houses weeping and shouting, 'Nasser, Nasser, don't leave us, we need you.' The noise was like a rising storm. Tens of thousands threatened to kill any deputies who did not vote for Nasser. Half a million people massed along the five miles from Nasser's home, millions more began to pour into Cairo from all over Egypt to make sure that Nasser stayed."

And Nasser did stay. The 1967 war accomplished nothing save to bring the world again to the brink, greater tragedy only being averted by the use of the White House-Kremlin hot line.

Moscow shared with Washington a reluctance to turn the Middle East conflict into a direct Super Powers confrontation. While the Kremlin never hesitated to pour further coals on the caldron that its support of partition had helped create, "an Arab victory, in the view of many foreign policy students, aside from the almost inevitable U.S. intervention to prevent it," would have presented the Soviet Union with extremely unpalatable alternatives.[42] The Arabs would then no longer need the Soviet Union. The U.S.S.R. wanted an Arab world reliant on her, but totally humiliated Arab clients could only drastically reduce Moscow's bargaining leverage.

There is now little doubt that Israel's unconscionable use of military power had been carried out, with the aid and abetment of Washington, under a cover of gross deceit that beguiled American public opinion and guaranteed support both for the continued Israeli occupation of Egyptian, Syrian, and Jordanian territories and for the ruthless suppression of Palestinian human rights. And in the post-conflict euphoria, a major U.S. naval disaster was totally blacked out.

XVII   The Attack on *Liberty*

Mourn not the dead . . . but rather mourn the apathetic throng
. . . who see the world's great anguish, and its wrong, and dare not
speak.

—Ralph Chaplin

When two American officers of the U.N. Security Force in Panmunjom,
Korea, were killed on August 18, 1976 by North Korean military forces
in the demilitarized zone, the U.S. replied with stern warnings and
comprehensive military preparations that were countered by the North
Koreans. When Major Arthur G. Bonifas and First Lieutenant Mark T.
Barrett were buried with full military honors at West Point and Columbia, South Carolina, the front page of the *New York Times* (August
25, 1976) carried a picture of the grieving Bonifas family. This incident
received widest, front-page coverage and comment; for a time it
seemed that the U.S. might take military action.

In contrast, the media were strangely silent about the thirty-four
American naval personnel killed and seventy-five wounded aboard the
unarmed ship U.S.S. *Liberty* on June 8, 1967. As Israel mounted its
offensive to gain the Golan Heights and added to the prize of Sinai and
the West Bank, there was no indignant press reaction to the onslaught
against this clearly marked vessel in international waters. There were
no honored and publicized burials. Israel's apology to the U.S. government for a "mistake" was accepted. Death benefits were negotiated
quietly and reported in the smallest print on the back pages of American newspapers.

On June 5, 1967, Israel had attacked Egyptian airfields and thrown
crack paratroopers against the Jordanian Legion in Jerusalem. Despite
the stubborn resistance of the Legion, the Israelis captured Jerusalem
on June 7 and completed their conquest of Jordan's West Bank on the
8th. On that same morning the *Liberty*, a World War II-vintage Victory
ship, the former *Simmons Victory*, with a sophisticated system of radio

antennae, including a "Big Ear" sonar-radio listening device with a clear capability range of over 500 miles, was steaming off the Sinai peninsula. It also carried a TRSSCOMS,[1] a radio device that could send messages directly to the U.S. by bouncing signals off the moon.

A sister ship of the *Pueblo,* which was captured by the North Koreans in 1968,[2] the *Liberty* was a spy ship, a "ferret" in Navy terms, whose movements were in fact controlled by the Joints Chiefs of Staff and the National Security Agency in Washington. She was faster than most ships of her type, with a top speed of eighteen knots; on her forecastle and deckhouse aft of the bridge she carried two pedestal-mounted .50-caliber Browning machine guns. These four guns, on open mounts without even splinter shields, were her only defenses.

The communications areas below decks—which housed intricate computers, decoding and listening devices manned by linguistic experts and other personnel who could be changed according to the ship's mission—were off limits to the crew, including the officer in charge, Commander (later Captain) William L. McGonagle. The communications areas were under direct control of a National Security Agency technician, known to the crew simply as "the Major," who had joined the ship with two other civilians at Rota, in Spain. When he first came aboard, the "Major" wore civilian clothes; later he wore khaki drill fatigues without rank insignia.

The *Liberty* had sailed from Rota on June 2 with orders to hasten to a Mideast operational area "north of the Sinai Peninsula." Off Gaza on June 8, the fourth day of the war, the crew could clearly see the minaret of the mosque at El Arish. The sea was calm, the sky blue and empty. Pillars of smoke over Sinai denoted the war.

The *Liberty* moved inshore in a "modified condition of readiness three," a normal state during operations, which meant that she had a regular steaming watch with one man on the forward machine guns and bridge lookouts ready to man the after-guns in an emergency. Shortly after daybreak on June 8, the *Liberty*'s officer of the deck spotted an airplane, identified as a French-built "Noratlas" transport, which circled the ship three times and flew off toward Gaza or Tel Aviv.

When the *Liberty* reached the eastern boundary of her operating area at 8:50 A.M. and turned on a southwesterly course, a single unidentified jet crossed her wake about three to five miles eastern, circled the ship, and flew away to the mainland. It gave no signal; neither did the ship.

The *Liberty* was cruising at ten knots, slow for a noncombatant vessel in an alien war zone but average for a civilian freighter. A standard American flag, five by eight feet, flew from her masthead on the ensign staff; the ship's name was painted clearly on her stern, and she had large U.S. Navy letters and numbers on her bows. There could be no mistaking her. At 11:30 two delta-wing jet fighters circled the ship twice and flew off toward the south. The markings could not be identified, but as Richard K. Smith indicated in his study "The Violation of *Liberty,* "[3] "since the morning of 5 June the skies over Sinai had been the exclusive property of Israel."

At 10:56 the Noratlas appeared again and circled the *Liberty* three or four times; it reappeared overhead also at 11:26 and 12:20. On each overflight, according to Officer of the Deck James G. Ennes, it circled the ship for about ten minutes and made no attempt to signal. The *Liberty* had cut speed to five knots to allow monitoring operations and radar fixings; she continued at this speed for the rest of the morning, sighting no more planes.

Although reconnaissance aircraft often study a foreign ship, McGonagle was puzzled by this surveillance, assuming (rightly) that the planes were from the Israeli Air Force. The "Major" had mentioned that transmissions monitored the previous day had caused him concern. They had worked out a careful cover story, in case the ship were challenged: They would say that the *Liberty* was monitoring Soviet radar systems used by the Egyptians.

McGonagle had received no further orders from his base and therefore assumed that he was to remain at the designated station. He did not know that three messages from the Joint Chiefs of Staff ordering him to retreat had already been sent, but they never reached him. These messages, rated "pinnacle," or highest priority, were "misrouted, delayed, and not received until after the attack."[4] They wound up back in a desk at Fort Meade, and the Navy has never vouchsafed an explanation.

The last message was sent only moments before three Mirages (fast Dassault French fighters that had destroyed the Egyptian Air Force on the ground three days before), which could carry up to seventy-two rockets, and carried two 30-mm cannon, swooped in an attack pattern at 2.05 P.M. A sudden explosion shook the ship. Electronic equipment sparked and flashed in the communications room. A seaman was thrown off his feet. Someone shouted that the boiler room had gone. McGonagle rushed up onto the deck, where men who had been working and laughing lay still, or crawled about bleeding and crying. The decks splintered under heavy-caliber bullets. McGonagle shouted to Lieutenant Stephen Toth to get to the lookout and to identify the planes. As the Lieutenant arrived at his station, a rocket wrecked the forward bridge quarter and the lookout position, killing him instantly. Lieutenant Commander Philip Armstrong was killed as he ran to jettison two blazing cans of gasoline.

The Mirages made rapid, furious, crisscross attacks on the ship for seven minutes, hitting her with more rockets and strafing her with cannon fire (shipyard examination later showed there were 821 holes on the hull and superstructure, not counting shrapnel damage). Israeli pilots with the greatest ease could "butcher a large, slow-moving, and defenseless target like the *Liberty,*" and the Mirages' ordnance, designed to penetrate the armor of tanks, "punched through the *Liberty*'s 22-year-old shell plating like a hammer against an old block of cheese."[5]

McGonagle had ordered a report to the Chief of Naval Operations, and at 2:10 P.M. he broadcast an open-channel "Mayday" distress call. Unsure of his communications, because the jets had destroyed all the ship's channels within minutes by pounding the antennae, he was fortunate that this message got through to the Sixth Fleet 600 miles to the northwest and the aircraft carrier *Little Rock:* "Mayday! Mayday! Am under attack from jet aircraft. Immediate assistance required." The rockets and machine guns silenced the radio.

The *Liberty* was still fighting fires when three motor torpedo boats bore down on the ship, riddling her with their 20-mm and 40-mm guns. One of the three torpedoes launched struck the communications room dead center in No. 3 hold, killing twenty-five of the technicians and crew, including the "Major," leaving them entombed in the flooded wreckage. The awesome consequences of the combined air and sea attacks was graphically summarized ten years later in a letter to the *Washington Star* by one of the seamen aboard:

In less than 39 minutes a fine ship was reduced to a bullet-riddled, napalm scorched and helpless floating graveyard. In those 39 minutes boys brought up in the peaceful aftermath of a horrendous world war experienced their first, and for some their last, trial by fire.[6]

In his testimony before the Naval Board of Inquiry, McGonagle stated that he thought he saw an Israeli flag through the smoke, but he could not be sure. He was incredulous when, instead of another torpedo, he saw a lamp flashing out, "Do you need assistance?" from one of the MTBs, which then drifted along with the *Liberty.* The printed record of the hearings[7] says the *Liberty* signaled "No thank you," but auditors on the spot say McGonagle shouted, "Go to hell!"

According to McGonagle, about forty-five minutes later two helicopters with the Star of David ensignia clearly visible approached the ship and "circled around and around at a distance of about 100 yards." They never made a direct approach, nor did they fire. As one of the *Liberty's* personnel later related to author Richard Smith, "These helicopters hovered off the ship as if they did not know what to do next. They were not there for rescue services; they were observed to be carrying armed troops. Neither attempted to signal the ship, and as mysteriously as they approached, they mysteriously departed."

The torpedo boats, which had left the general area of the ship and had gone to a range of about five miles, "again headed toward the ship at high speed."[8] To the Commander their intentions were unknown, and "when at about the same time, two jets approached starboard side in similar fashion to that which preceeded the initial attack, all hands were again alerted to the possibility of another attack. But none occurred and the aircraft left the scene. An hour later the torpedo boats commenced retiring."[9]

Around 6:40 P.M. while limping northward at eight knots, steering from the emergency station and by magnetic compass, the ship was approached by a helicopter bearing Star of David markings. When the request to land a man on board was refused, a message was dropped on the ship's forecastle. It was the calling card of the Naval Attaché of the U.S. Embassy in Tel Aviv, on the back of which was written: "Have you casualties?"

After fifteen minutes of unsuccessful efforts to communicate an answer, the helicopter departed. But in full view were the blood-spattered decks, and while the wounded had been removed to battle dressing stations below, three bodies, one almost completely decapitated, rested in full evidence on the forecastle to the main deck.

Somehow the remaining crew repaired the damage enough to hand-steer the *Liberty.* McGonagle, who had been badly injured in the attack, remained on the bridge and steered all night, while the ship's doctor coped with the injured. The crippled ship arrived in Malta on June 14, escorted by a destroyer, the U.S.S. *David,* and a Sixth Fleet tug.

Admiral John S. McCain, Commander in Chief of U.S. Naval Forces in Europe, conducted a naval court of inquiry, which commenced hearings in London and then went on board the *Liberty* at Malta. The court consisted of Rear Admiral I. C. Kidd (President), Captain Bernard J. Lauff, and Captain Bert M. Atkinson, of Admiral

McCain's headquarters. Captain Ward Boston served as counsel. In its findings, approved by Admiral McCain on June 18, the court said:

"From the time of the first attack onward, attackers were well-coordinated, accurate, and determined. Crisscrossing rocket and machine gun runs from both bows, both beams and quarters effectively chewed up the entire top-side including ship control and internal communications (sound powered) network. Well-directed initial air attacks wiped out the ability of the four .50-caliber machine guns to be effective.[10]

Three months later writer James Kilpatrick noted, "For the time being, there is no way for the outside observer to form an independent judgment, from the record, upon the Court's conclusions."[11]

Apart from scattered newsmagazine references, Kilpatrick's seven-page article broke the media silence about the *Liberty*. While acknowledging that some of the Israeli excuses might have been valid (the ensign hoisted by the *Liberty* might have been drooping and unrecognizable on the windless day; the side of the vessel might have been blotted out by smoke, as an Israeli naval reservist from one of the torpedo boats had claimed in an article for Associated Press on July 6), Kilpatrick expressed skepticism about the official explanation. He quoted Assistant Secretary of Defense Philip G. Goulding's refusal to "accept an attack upon a clearly marked noncombatant U.S. naval ship in international waters as 'plausible' under any circumstances whatsoever. The identification markings of U.S. naval vessels have proven satisfactory for international recognition for nearly 200 years."

Apparently shying from controversy, Kilpatrick presented his account as a "sea story; nothing more." But after describing the extreme heroism of the Captain and crew, he rejected the official explanations:

During the past month, press service interviews with survivors of the attack have turned up a uniform conviction that the attack was deliberate. Sailors point to the morning-long aerial surveillance; the presence of the flag; the known configuration of the *Liberty;* her name in English on the stern . . . her slow progression in international waters. All these factors support the crew's conclusion that the assault was no accident. . . .

Skeptical observers will continue to assume that *Liberty* was engaged upon a general mission of intelligence-gathering and code-breaking; and they will wonder what might have been received, translated, tape-recorded, and fed into computers between, say, 10 o'clock and noon on June 8 that resulted in the pinpoint destruction of the very hull compartments—frame 53 to frame 66 —where the electronic gear was housed.[12]

The American and international press preferred to forget the incident and to ignore such provocative questions. From the outset the

Israelis had insisted on minimal publicity "for the sake of the families' dead and wounded." Only the Malta *News* dared print that "the attack on the *Liberty* was no mistake." On November 4, 1967, *Newsweek* reported briefly that Israel, contrary to what had been announced June 21, would take no court-martial action against any of the pilots or seamen who fired on the *Liberty*. The Israeli Court of Inquiry had concluded that the *Liberty* had been mistaken for an Egyptian supply ship. The report made no mention of the killed or wounded, but merely stated that Israel apologized and offered compensation.

After nearly ten years, Anthony Pearson, a veteran British journalist who has covered other wars for the *Manchester Guardian,* the London *Times,* and *Paris Match,* broke this silence with two revealing articles, peculiarly enough in the magazine *Penthouse* (May and June, 1976). Pearson had wondered for years why the Arabs fought on after all seemed lost in 1967 and why the Israelis had attacked the *Liberty*. In his articles he noted the close links between Mossad (the Israeli intelligence agency) and the CIA. He also observed that during the Lyndon Johnson administration the State Department was caught between its anxiety about Soviet penetration of the Middle East and the strong pressures to support Israel, which were brought to bear at that time by U.N. Ambassador Arthur Goldberg, Eugene Rostow in the State Department, and his brother Walt Rostow, who had been appointed Special Adviser to the President on National Security just a year before the 1967 war. Rostow insisted that America should give fullest support to Israel to balance Russian aid to the Arabs, and this point of view was strongly backed by the American security agencies.

Chief of the CIA Richard Helms continued to allow all U.S. intelligence operations inside Israel to be conducted through Mossad. There was no CIA station chief in Tel Aviv; officers working under cover in the American Embassy acted in consort with Israeli intelligence officers, each supposedly having full access to the other's information.

James Angleton, head of CIA counterintelligence, had established these ties with the Israelis after the Anglo-French-Israeli attack on Suez in 1956. As part of the plan, he helped supply Israel with technical assistance for developing nuclear weapons. His partner and opposite number in Mossad was Ephraim "Eppy" Evron, Deputy Israeli Ambassador to Washington in 1967, who had been involved in the unsuccessful 1954 Lavon Affair and had disappeared from public view until May 1967, when reporters noticed that he was involved in much activity with the State Department and the White House. He "seemed to have greater significance at the Israeli Embassy than his chief, Avraham

Harman," according to Pearson, and became a vital link in a complex plan to overthrow President Nasser.

After President Nasser exposed an illegal American arms deal to Israel in 1965, James Angleton and several Mossad officers decided to oust Nasser by forcing Egypt to confront Israel. The fiery threats of the ill-starred Palestinian leader Ahmed Shukairy helped them. Following a series of secret meetings in Tel Aviv and Washington, CIA officers, the Israeli general staff, certain Israeli politicians, and inner members of Johnson's administration agreed to promote a contained war between Israel and Egypt, which would not affect territorial lines between Israel, Syria, and Jordan. Yigal Allon, Intelligence Chief Meir Amit, Aharon Yariv (head of army intelligence), Shimon Peres (Deputy Minister of Defense), Ezer Weizman (head of army operations), Mordechai Hod (air force chief), David Hacohen (head of the Knesset Committee for Foreign and Security Affairs), and Moshe Dayan (soon to be appointed Minister of Defense) organized this plan in Israel.[13] Eppy Evron was their liaison officer in Washington, dealing directly with Angleton at the CIA and with Eugene Rostow at the State Department. Nasser's increasingly hard line and the Soviet buildup in Egypt and Syria could be exploited to arouse public opinion for war, and the Israeli army would be placed on full alert to goad Damascus or Cairo into action. The Israelis assured the Americans that the ensuing war would be fought to the predesigned American plan of containment.

Knowing that American intelligence from Israel came through Mossad, Evron believed that he could tell the American government what he wished, and he assured all his Washington contacts right up to the outbreak of war that Israeli troop movements were simply precautionary. Evron did not know about the *Liberty,* but as the war began, the spy ship's listening devices tuned in to transmissions from both the Arabs and the Israelis. Its presence off the battle zone was to make sure that Israel did not overstep the objectives of the containment plan.

The observers on the *Liberty* discovered that while the Arabs failed to crack Israeli codes, the Israelis had penetrated Egyptian and Jordanian codes as soon as the war began. Somewhere between Amman and Cairo, according to Pearson, the messages between King Hussein and President Nasser were intercepted, reconstructed, and passed on by the Israelis without detection, a process called "cooking." The Israelis blocked the message from Cairo that advised King Hussein of the bad military situation on the Egyptian front, rewording it to misinform the King that three-quarters of the Israeli Air Force had been destroyed over Cairo and that he was picking up Egyptian jets raiding targets in Israel on his radar. (They were actually Israeli jets returning from the destruction of Egyptian airfields.)

The Israelis continued to "cook" messages to give the impression that the war was going well for the Arabs. They falsely informed the King that Egypt was counterattacking in Sinai and needed support in form of attacks on Israel in the Hebron area, obliging him to withdraw his forces from the planned crucial offensive designed to cut Israel in two. The Egyptians were likewise misled; thinking that the Jordanians had made a successful attack in Hebron, they counterattacked during the early hours of June 8, ignoring a U.N. call for a cease-fire. Thus the Israelis gained enough time to seize all of the West Bank they wanted, to consolidate their gains in Sinai, and to move their troops right up to the east bank of the Suez Canal.

On June 7 Eugene Rostow called Avraham Harman to the State Department and warned him that the Israeli attack must stop immediately; he informed Harman that the Americans knew about the "cooking" of communications. Four hours later in Tel Aviv the Minister of Defense and the Commander of the air force's offices ordered surveillance of the American communications ship operating off Sinai. Four hours after that, the same sources ordered that the ship be sunk. This daring and vicious plan failed only because the desperate open-channel "Mayday" message brought help from the carrier *America.* The approach of rescue planes was picked up by the Israelis, who were forced to pull back while there was still time to make the only possible excuse—mistaken identity.

In retrospect, every shred of evidence pointed to the flimsiness of Israeli contentions. June 8 was a clear day with visibility unlimited, which made the flag flying from a huge tripod mast towering almost 100 feet above the flying bridge exceedingly perceptible. According to Engineering Officer George H. Golden, an hour and a quarter before the first attack there was "a slight breeze blowing and the flag flying from the foremast was standing where it could be seen—not completely the full length, but where it could be seen."[14] When the standard was shot down early in the action, it was replaced prior to the PTB attack by a larger holiday ensign.

The large lettering on the stern in English was hard to confuse with Arabic script on Egyptian ships. The numeral "5" on the *Liberty*'s bows were almost twelve feet tall, freshly painted only a few weeks before, and quite distinctive at one or two miles in good visibility—and on this day off El Arish the visibility was excellent. The Israeli claim that the 10,000-ton, 459-foot *Liberty* was mistaken for the ancient Egyptian troopship *El Quseir* of 2,640 tons and only 275 feet was difficult to accept. The one thing that the two ships had in common was flotation. The unmistakable silhouette of the ubiquitous Victory ship, not to mention the *Liberty*'s unique antenna array and hull markings, made for immediate recognition.[15] The several hours of close reconnaissance by Israeli aircraft added to the impossibility that the Israelis did not recognize the *Liberty*. There was significant aerial surveillance, as the inquiry's findings pointed out, on three separate occasions: "five hours and thirteen minutes before the attack, three hours and thirteen minutes before the attack, and two hours and thirty-seven minutes before the attack. . . . In five of the six attacks from various angles, two or more jet aircraft at a time conducted rocket and incendiary attacks."[16]

Contrariwise, all facts indicate that the Israelis knew exactly what they were doing. The American Naval Attaché at Tel Aviv cabled the Board of Inquiry that he could not understand "how trained professionals could have been so inept as to carry out the attack," and he reasoned that "the erroneous attack resulted from trigger-happy eagerness to glean some portion of the great victory being shared by the Israeli Army and Air Force and in which the Navy was not sharing."[17]

There were two plausible motivations for this premeditated Israeli attack on an American ship. Defense Minister Moshe Dayan, according to Israeli author Zeev Schiff, had masterminded the great "befuddle plan," which called for a news blackout on Israeli victories so as to prevent the intervention of a cease-fire inspired by the U.S.S.R. or the U.N.[18] The *Liberty*, with its extremely sophisticated intelligence equipment, had been monitoring Arab and Israeli transmissions from her post off Gaza and was keeping the Joint Chiefs of Staff in Washington directly informed of the overwhelming Israeli victory that by then included Jerusalem and the West Bank. Such information gathered by the *Liberty* increased the likelihood of a cease-fire, which Dayan definitely did not want.

Alternatively, if indeed the U.S. had been party to a conspiracy to unseat Nasser, the *Liberty* had gathered definite proof that Washington had been doublecrossed and that Jordan, whose territories were to remain untouched, had been sucked into the war through Israel's code-breaking and "cooking" of false messages. More important to the Israeli Establishment even than ridding themselves of their hated Egyptian enemy was crushing the potential challenge to their very existence by seizing the West Bank and Gaza, the likely site of any Palestinian state.

The savagery of the strafing and shelling from air and sea, "the awesome combined firepower of the aircraft and torpedo boats,"[19] were indications of Israeli intent to destroy whatever vital information the *Liberty*'s complex intelligence apparatus had gathered and to kill any Americans who might in any way be privy thereto. The painstaking June 8–10 Israeli aerial search from El Arish to Rafah, ostensibly for personnel who might have been washed overboard, seemed more directed for possible incriminating evidence that might have escaped from the *Liberty*'s communications room. The helicopters with armed troops and the hovering torpedo boats appeared ready to do a mop-up job on any survivors having the slightest knowledge of what the sensitive communications antennae had carried to the communications room, but the signal of approaching American planes eliminated this option.

The communication facilities of the ship from early in the morning, according to the testimony of Chief Technician Cryptologist Carl Larkin, had been "jammed so loud that the Radioman Chief W. L. Smith thought at first it was our transmitters which were malfunctioning, but he noted, regardless of frequency, this loud jamming noise."[20] The Israelis were trying to prevent any intelligence findings or call for help from leaving the ship.

According to the findings of the inquiry, chaired by Rear Admiral Kidd, "The attack on the *Liberty* was, in fact, a case of mistaken identity,"[21] although in an appendix the Court ruled out the Israeli contention that because the Egyptian town of El Arish, then in Israeli hands, had been bombarded from the sea, it could have been the act of the *Liberty:* "It is inconceivable that either the Israeli Navy or Air Force would associate *Liberty,* with her 4.50-caliber machineguns, or *El Quseir,* armed with two 3-pounders, with a shore bombardment."[22] The ship had remained at all times in international waters and at one point was as much as 13.6 miles from the coast. And still the inquiry concluded that "there was no available indication that the attack was intended against a U.S. ship."[23] The Court significantly pointed out that "there were no Communications Officers left alive with first-hand knowledge of the missed message backlog on 8 June."[24] (One of the more remarkable aspects of the Israelis' "error" was that they jammed U.S. Navy communications frequencies, but claimed they thought they were attacking an Egyptian ship.)

The whitewash of Israel was complete. The Office of the Assistant Secretary of Defense for Public Affairs issued on the very day of the June 8 attack press release 542–67 accepting the Israeli version that the attack "was made in error" and that an apology had been received.[25]

While Rear Admiral David M. Cooney, Chief of Navy Information, maintained "that the Department of Defense endeavored to keep the American public informed of the incident through the news media,"[26] an examination of the two press releases showed a dearth of information and referred to only four deaths.

"The Committee for Immediate Action—Families and Friends of Victims of the USS *Liberty,*" formed to extract compensation from the State of Israel, encountered great problems. When the organizers, Mr. and Mrs. Thomas Reilly, sued Israel at the World Court at the Hague for $50 million, a State Department representative asked them to withdraw the claim. They did not. Writer Pearson suggested that the Court ignored the complaint under coercion of the U.S. State Department.

When Captain Joe Toth, father of Lieutenant Stephen Toth, claimed damages on behalf of his dead son and of two other officers, the State Department warned him not to make trouble. Despite a bad heart condition, Captain Toth lodged a suit against the State Department. Although supported by his friends, Admiral McCain in the Pentagon and Admiral Kidd, who had conducted the *Liberty* inquiry, no one could tell him what action the Israelis were taking against those responsible. Inquiries in Tel Aviv yielded nothing. The congressional hearings remained secret, but one or two small leaks revealed that two of the pilots in the attack were Americans. Doubtlessly, Washington had connived with the Israelis to hush things up. Even the American commendations for the ship and for Captain McGonagle's Medal of Honor were censored in behalf of the Israelis: All reference to the nationality of the attackers was deleted. McGonagle's citation simply referred to "jet aircraft and motor torpedo boats," and that of the ship's to "foreign fighter aircraft and motor torpedo boats."

The Pentagon and the State Department were not allowed to let the matter rest. Captain Toth's lawyers threatened to issue open-court writs if compensation were not quickly forthcoming. Mrs. Toth told Pearson:

They killed my husband. . . . First my son, then my husband. The harassment took the form of threats and claims that Joe was damaging national security, and there was surveillance and pressure from people like the IRS. It was too much for his bad heart. It took a year to kill him, but it did.

In May 1968 the Israeli government paid $3.3 million to the families of the thirty-four *Liberty* dead, and one year later they paid $3.5 million to the 164 injured. The U.S. government claimed $7.6

million for damage to the ship, not a farthing of which has ever been remitted, although the Israeli government had initially publicly promised to pay for all material damage.*A year later, according to a story in *Ha'aretz*[27] the Israeli government was contending that the *Liberty* had not received the instructions sent by the Joint Chiefs to move away from the fighting and was subsequently hit. The U.S. Ambassador in Tel Aviv indicated that if the matter were raised, he would point out "that whatever communications errors there may have been on the U.S. side in no way affects the Israeli Government responsibility, deriving from the fact that the ship was in international waters when attacked."[28]

After a final interview with Captain McGonagle, who, faithful to his military pledges, revealed nothing further, Pearson returned to the Middle East, where he discovered that the Israeli investigation and court-martial announced on June 21, 1967, had never taken place:

The U.S. State Department had agreed wholeheartedly with the Israelis that the entire affair be swept under the carpet. No one was eager to have the pilots involved give sworn testimony about who ordered their mission. For that matter, if there was truth to the stories that some of the pilots were American, any testimony might have been a severe embarrassment to both governments.[29]

Although the partial revelations of a most serious conspiracy on an international scale warranted some investigation at the highest level, the American press for years totally ignored the incident. It remained for the *Ledger-Gazette* (circulation 9,117), a small-town newspaper in Lancaster, California, to comment on May 5, 1976:

One does not usually associate serious purpose with a "skin" publication. This may explain the virtual absence of reaction so far among investigative journalists to a press release widely distributed by *Penthouse* magazine concerning a startling article in its current May issue. Or perhaps the allegations in the article are simply too startling for credence.

Penthouse itself soon regretted its role in publishing the two articles. Enormous Zionist pressures, about which the editors refused to talk, were brought to bear. Successful efforts to remove copies from newsstands in Canada were ascribed to the issue's "naked breasts" rather than to the "naked truth."

The failure of editors and investigative journalists to probe such a sensitive and tendentious matter has left individuals and private organizations to seek the answers to the many questions raised by the

Liberty incident. Following the publication of the Pearson articles, the American Council on the Middle East (ACME) approached the Department of State and succeeded in getting some relevant documents released. These confirmed details of the attack and the compensation paid by the Israelis, but threw no significant new light on the subject. ACME likewise obtained a censored transcript of the U.S. Naval Court of Inquiry findings, but the 532 legal-size pages and photographs, some barely legible, revealed little new information.

The organization appealed the State Department decision to retain some classified documents and continues to urge the release of all relevant material. In a letter to the Chairman of the Council on Classification Policy, ACME Secretary Eliot Sharp said:

What were apparently leaks to an author writing for a magazine of mass circulation, led to his alleging conspiracy by the Johnson administration, including President Johnson, Arthur Goldberg, Walt Rostow and Eugene Rostow, with the State of Israel in its June, 1967, attack on Egypt. The requester therefore seeks verification or refutation of these allegations, for if they are true, there has been a cover-up of a conspiracy. Disclosure of any such conspiracy is of utmost importance to the American people as revealing the United States' relations with the State of Israel, and the action of our country's leaders which might have precipitated the United States into a catastrophic war. . . .

The Freedom of Information Director in the State Department admitted there were eleven memoranda among the Rostows, Goldberg, and President Johnson at the time of the six-day war. But he refused to declassify and release four of these documents, which together with nine still classified documents of forty-eight pages dealing with the *Liberty,* might provide the answer to key unanswered questions.

UPI reported on September 18, 1977, that the American Palestine Committee had obtained CIA documents through the Freedom of Information Act revealing that Israeli Defense Minister Moshe Dayan had himself ordered the attack on the *Liberty.* One document, dated November 9, 1967, released by APC Chairman Norman Dacey, quoted unnamed agency informants:

Dayan personally ordered the attack on the ship. One of his generals adamantly opposed the action and said, "This is pure murder!" One of the admirals who was present also disapproved the action, and it was he who ordered it stopped.

The sole comment from the CIA was that the documents had been "unevaluated for accuracy." CIA Director Stansfield Turner on national television questioned the validity of the documents and asserted his belief that the Israeli attack had been an honest mistake.[30] But the accusation leveled against Dayan jibes with the theory advanced for the Israeli attack by a National Security Agency source.[31] The *Liberty,* sent to intercept details of Israeli intelligence, had learned that Dayan had ordered his victorious troops on to Damascus and Cairo, and had so informed Washington. President Johnson then brought intense pressure on Israel to halt further troop movement and at the same time warned President Kosygin against what appeared to be Soviet airborne operations aimed at Israel from bases in Bulgaria. The *Liberty* constituted a grave menace to the plans of Minister Dayan.

What is patently clear under any theory is that had the Israelis been successful in sinking the *Liberty,* the atrocity would have been blamed on the Egyptians and produced a Pearl Harbor reaction in the U.S. When the first news of the *Liberty* attack reached the Sixth Fleet, so certain was American reaction that it was the Egyptians who had struck, that a squadron of jets was sent in a threatening sweep over Cairo as if in a preliminary to war. Dayan in 1967 was determined to succeed where he had failed in the 1954 Lavon Affair—to shatter U.S.-Egyptian and eventually U.S.-Arab relations.

The *Liberty* was long ago scrapped. The discouraged survivors and their relatives remain to this day reluctant or frightened to talk about the incident, around which an iron curtain had been placed from the very outset. While the attack occurred on June 8, parents of wounded sailors did not know whether their sons were alive or dead until they finally received telegrams on June 11. The wounded, placed on board the carrier U.S.S. *America,* were immediately warned by a representative of the CIA not to talk to anyone about what had happened.[32] Those with head wounds were taken to the Landstuh, Germany, U.S. Army hospital, and while there they were kept under guard with tightest security. Inquiries from congressmen who represented the families of the deceased were never answered, and the surviving members of the *Liberty*'s crew were dispersed throughout the Navy, no two men being sent to the same place.

On June 8 at 12:02 the recently arrived U.S. Ambassador in Cairo, Richard Nolte, sent the following cable to Secretary of State Dean Rusk in Washington: "We had better get our story on torpedoing the U.S.S. *Liberty* out fast, and it had better be good."[33] For obvious reasons this advice was never followed. A total Washington blackout then and since became the order of the day; the CIA never even made an analysis on the origins of the attack. For the White House had known and understood exactly what Israel planned.

Nevertheless, despite the secrecy and the cover-up, more than enough facts had emerged to confirm suspicions that the silence masked a complex scandal and mammoth international conspiracy to which the U.S. government had been a party. And the Republicans who ousted the Democrats eighteen months later rigidly maintained this concealment.

*Spurred on by the threat of retiring Senator Adlai Stevenson III to launch an investigation into the facts behind the *Liberty* attack, Israel finally agreed to pay the U.S. $6-million for damages to the electronic surveillance vessel. But Washington officialdom continued to pretend the attack never occurred.

XVIII Oil on Troubled Waters:
The Nixon Years

An obstinate man does not hold opinions, but they hold him.
—Alexander Pope

Although elected by only a narrow margin over Hubert Humphrey in 1968, Richard M. Nixon had a golden opportunity on coming into office to bring pressure to bear on Israel for the immediate withdrawal of troops from the occupied Arab territories, as the first essential step toward peace.

The forensics with which the quadrennial bid for the Jewish vote reached new heights in this campaign had given way to the realities of a tense, fearful situation in the Middle East. The President-elect's personal message to the Arab chiefs of state, as well as the fact-finding mission to the area of former Pennsylvania Governor William Scranton, were clear-cut indications of Mr. Nixon's deep concern even before he took office.

In crossing the Allenby Bridge from Israel into Jordan, Scranton made a most significant declaration. He urged U.S. Middle East policy to be "more evenhanded"—the first time that word had been used. And he added: "I think it is important for the United States to take into consideration the feelings of all persons and all countries in the Middle East and not necessarily espouse one nation over some other." This statement following closely upon a *Life* magazine editorial that stated: "There are more hopeful avenues towards peace than a simplistic, automatic backing of Israel."

As second in command under President Eisenhower, Mr. Nixon had given at least implied consent to the halting of the Israeli-British-French invasion of Egypt in 1956, and then to President Eisenhower's firm stand forcing the unconditional Israeli withdrawal from occupied Egyptian territory. On January 5, 1969 the President-elect received a

577

personal note from Nasser calling upon him to take a more forthright position regarding Israeli withdrawal from the territories occupied since 1967. In an obvious bid for time, the reply of the victorious Republican candidate was noncommittal.

Nixon had not been obligated to the Jewish vote for his election, and yet he had already contributed to Israel's militarily impregnable position. During the campaign, candidate Nixon had confounded the world in his speech before the B'nai B'rith Convention in Washington by enunciating a policy "that would give Israel a technical military margin to more than offset hostile neighbors and numerical strength" and had called for the immediate delivery of Phantom jets for Israel:[1] President Johnson, sensing the unpopularity of his stand on the war in Vietnam, had already announced that he would not seek re-election and would retire at the end of his term. In a belated effort to push the faltering presidential campaign of his Vice-President, Hubert Humphrey, he implemented the Republican candidate's call. Under a secret informal agreement between Johnson and the Israeli Prime Minister Levi Eshkol, Israel had been assured of receiving fifty of these U.S.-made fighter bombers, the most advanced aircraft in combat in the Middle East and a more than adequate replacement for the fifty French Mirages blocked by de Gaulle's boycott imposed at the time of the six-day war. (Not too long after these U.S. aircraft had been delivered, Israeli Defense Minister Moshe Dayan was asking for additional Phantoms.)

The war of attrition across the Suez Canal and along the Jordan River mounted. The Palestinian guerrillas emerged as an important new factor following the battle of Karameh. And terrorism, sometimes threatening to burgeon into full-scale war, was on the increase. The continued failure of the mission of Sweden's Ambassador to the U.S.S.R. Gunnar V. Jarring, designated U.N. representative, to bring the Middle East disputants together, provided the White House with further incentive to act.

Middle East violence had taken a giant step forward before Nixon took his first oath of office on January 20, 1969. Just as fun-loving Lebanese were preparing to celebrate their New Year's Eve, Beirut was assaulted by Israeli planes. The apron of Khalde Airport, the pride of Israel's northern neighbor and the hub of the area's commercial air traffic, was turned into a smoldering mass of burnt-out fuselages from thirteen planes. The Israeli attack, conducted by a helicopter force, was excused by Tel Aviv as retaliation for the Arab attack in Athens in which an Israeli citizen had been killed.

The modern Hebrews had picked up the Old Testament slogan and brought it up-to-date, in true Arab fashion: "Ten eyes for an eye —ten teeth for a tooth." It was David Ben-Gurion who, as Prime Minister, had first initiated reprisals 50 to 100 times as strong as the original attack. Whenever the Israelis judged that Arab attacks had reached an intolerable level, they retaliated massively as in 1966 when they wiped out the Jordanian village of Es-Samu'a.

In their onslaught against Beirut, the Israelis had an additional motivation. They hoped to further split the Lebanese Maronite Christians, who for long had demonstrated their insistence on remaining aloof from the Arab-Israeli conflict, from the Muslims, who as fervent Palestinian supporters wished to ensure that Lebanon remained part and parcel of the Arab world. The widely disparate views of these two religious groups had led to the Lebananese civil war of 1958.

Not since American troops landed on the beaches near the same airport in July that year, in the wake of the assassination of King Faisal in Iraq, had little Lebanon been so shaken. But even the U.N. Security Council's unanimous censure of Israel, in one of the strongest of its many resolutions dealing with the Arab-Israeli conflict, had little effect on the White House, although it stirred world public opinion. When Pope Paul VI, in a telegram to Lebanese President Charles Helou, deplored the Israeli attack and expressed hope that Lebanon would refrain from violent countermeasures, Organized Jewry struck back. Led by the Synagogue Council of America, Jewish religious and lay organizations unanimously assailed the Pontifical message. Foreign Minister Abba Eban immediately interpreted the rebuke from the outside world as another instance of "anti-Semitism": "The attitude of foreign countries cannot be entirely divorced from the traditional attitude of the non-Jewish world to the Jewish world."

At his first press conference on January 27, Nixon recognized the grave danger:

We need new initiatives and new leadership on the part of the U.S. in order to cool off the situation in the Middle East. I consider it a powder keg, very explosive . . . the next explosion in the Mideast I think could involve very well a confrontation between the nuclear powers which we want to avoid.

But the new President offered no palliative. Where an undaunted Eisenhower had defied the Zionist threat in 1956, Nixon mouthed words. This was the ideal moment to have implemented the Scranton initiative for evenhandedness, but the President chose otherwise. Like President Johnson before him, Nixon ignored the declarations of their three predecessors pledging U.S. support for "the political independence and territorial integrity of *all* the nations of the Middle East." (Italics added.) Victorious Israel continued to remain undisturbed in her occupancy of captured Jordanian, Egyptian, and Syrian territory.

The basic Nixon approach during his tenure in office, despite vacillations here and there, was based on the premise that Middle East peace could only be achieved by keeping Israel stronger than all her neighbors combined, as he had pledged in the campaign. This completely ignored the fact that Israel had already been stronger than all her neighbors combined for the previous two decades, had won three wars, and yet peace was further away than ever before. This was pointed up by a group of Americans, concerned with the future of the U.S. in the area and the flouting of justice, in an open letter to the new President, which appeared in the *New York Times* as a full-page advertisement.[2] But they found this viewpoint unwelcomed at the White House.

The successful September 1969 revolution in Libya, ousting the royalist, corrupt regime of King Idris, with the consequent relinquishment of the U.S. Wheelus Air Base and the near-successful putsch against King Faisal in Saudi Arabia, shook the Capital deeply. Once again, "evenhandedness" was taken out of mothballs as the Arabs summitted at Rabat in what many predicted might be a "Council of War against Israel."[3] The Israelis had just launched their fiercest attack across the Canal—four hours of strafing, bombings, and napalm had both hurt as well as infuriated the Egyptians.

Fearful of an irrevocable Arab stand at their summit, and faced by the failure of the Big Two and Big Four power conclaves to agree on a single interpretation of the Security Council resolution, which was necessary to advance the peace momentum, Secretary of State William P. Rogers made public a new American peace initiative on December 9, the details of which had been handed to Soviet Ambassador Anatoly F. Dobrynin six weeks earlier. Speaking at the Galaxy Conference on Adult Education in Washington, Rogers called for virtual total Israeli withdrawal from occupied Arab territory and joint Israeli-Jordanian control over Jerusalem in return for negotiated and binding Arab peace commitments. The Secretary declared that "any changes in the preexisting lines should not reflect the weight of conquest and should be confined to unsubstantiated alterations required for initial security." Countervailing domestic pressures immediately came into play.

Prime Minister Golda Meir flayed the Rogers proposals as an attempt to make us "start all over again as though it were 1948," and her supporters in the U.S. picked up the familiar refrain, "It's oil that is opposing little Israel." (Where anti-Semitism could not be injected as a weapon, this secondary line of argumentation was invariably adduced and was invariably as successful.) The leak by the *New York Times* on its front page (December 22, 1969) of the secret White House meeting of a group of top bankers and industrialists, including oil company representatives, at which the President had been warned that the "U.S. was losing political and economic influence in the Arab world because of its policies," together with State Department ineptness in presenting the new Rogers initiative, provided the Zionist campaign with new momentum.[4] It did not take the pack long to latch onto the word "oil" and wage the same kind of a campaign of vilification as had been directed against James Forrestal twenty-two years previously.

Former Democratic standard bearer Senator Hubert Humphrey, who previously had been most sympathetic to the administration in its Vietnam objectives, lashed out at Rogers' suggestions. The Conference of Presidents of Major Jewish Organizations, claiming to have 4½ million members in its thirty-three constituent groups, met with Secretary Rogers, following which their President, Rabbi Herschel Schacter, announced the mobilization of American Jewry "to counter Nixon's lagging support of Israel." The Conference vehemently opposed the Secretary's proposals. Both Tel Aviv and its New York supporters viewed this new initiative, which set forth in detail for the first time terms for a peace agreement, as smacking of an imposed settlement. The stipulation for the return to Israel of an unspecified number of Palestinian refugees was likewise galling to Tel Aviv and its friends.

Marshaling of action against what was now proclaimed to be an "indefensible U.S. retreat" began. Members of the groups represented in the Conference of Presidents were requested to send telegrams to their elected representatives in Washington, to President Nixon, and to Secretary Rogers decrying "a U.S. peace proposal released without any previous knowledge of the Israeli government, as incompatible with election campaign commitments" and stressing "arms and economic aid needed by Israel to defend herself." Newspapers, radio and television stations were contacted in the all-out assault on the new Washington plan, to which the announcement of France's sale of jet fighters to Libya added more fuel.

What most aroused the spleen of these Israelists was that Washington was now insisting that Israeli-Arab bargaining was to begin on the basis of the pre-war boundaries. The counterprovisos, calling for

Arab pledges of peace and nonbelligerence, free rights of Israeli passage through the Suez Canal and the Gulf of Aqaba, and special demilitarized frontier zones to be defined by the parties, were not deemed a sufficient *quid pro quo* for the near-total Israeli withdrawal required.

The Nixon Administration was already in trouble with Israeli supporters frustrated by their failure to convince the White House to speed the release of the promised Phantoms and to permit Israel to purchase twenty-five more Phantoms and one hundred Skyhawks. A story that Israel was on the verge of producing its own nuclear missiles and launching vehicles, widely circulated by London's reliable and pro-Zionist *Jewish Chronicle,* certainly had not helped in its quest for jets. This development, although nowhere reported in the US press, together with Israel's adamant refusal to sign the Nuclear Nonproliferation Treaty, had figured in the U.S. decision heretofore not to sell more Phantoms. Where Germany and Japan had been forced to sign the treaty, Israel had thus far resisted pressures from both the Johnson and Nixon administrations. With the Japanese signature, the treaty had gone into effect. According to the 1970 *Jane's World Aircraft,*[5] Israel would have a nuclear warhead that year capable of being delivered by missiles developed for them under contract with the Dassault Aircraft Company in France. This missile, to be launched from mobile ramps, was said to have a range of 150 miles, long enough to reach and to devastate Arab capitals. If these reports were true, Israel had become the sixth nuclear power, joining the U.S., U.S.S.R., U.K., France, and China—the first of the world's small powers to develop such a potential.

In other directions, too, Israel had not helped its bid for more Phantoms. The strike and counterstrike of the war of attrition was now involving civilians as victims of the cruelest blows. The bombing of an Egyptian industrial plant at Abu Zabal, in which 80 workers were killed in February, was followed on April 8 by an Israeli aerial raid on Bahr al Bakr, 50 miles north of Cairo, which brought death to forty schoolchildren. Resentment heightened in the international community.[6]

Reporters who visited the scene of the school bombing received firsthand accounts of the "badly mutilated bodies of the dead children." Resentment spread throughout the international community. Anger against Israel mounted, and Nasser came under criticism at home for exposing Egypt to such attacks.

The entire picture then changed overnight. While Cairo still donned its blackout clothing at night and appeared to be very much at war, the Nile near where the infant Moses was found by the daughters of Pharaoh among the bullrushes was again resplendent on its Friday holiday with canoes, rowboats, and feluccas. The appearance of new SAM-3 missiles, supplied and manned by the Soviet Union, installed around Cairo and the Nile Delta to defend against low-flying Israeli fighter bombers, had given the people new confidence. President Christopher Thoren of the American University in Cairo would certainly not have felt as secure weeks earlier about entertaining me and other guests on his terrace, looking down on the burgeoning city of over five million. And not too far away, the war of attrition assumed a new look.

For the first time since Israeli airpower had virtually silenced Egyptian batteries along the Suez in July, the Egyptians had seized the military initiative. The Israelis made the serious charge that Russian pilots, who had been instructing the Egyptian air force on the new advanced SAM-3s, were now manning the Egyptian MIGs protecting Nasser's capital. Washington's anxieties mounted. Cairo's first response to the Rogers peace initiative was negative, and Amman was silent. A year earlier both President Nasser and King Hussein would have eagerly jumped at Washington's suggestions. But by 1970 the U.A.R. and Jordan had to deal with a new dynamic force that Washington scarcely recognized—the Palestinian Arabs.

While the Arab chieftains at their Rabat summit in December 1969 had publicly agreed only to disagree and the cleavage between right- and left-wing countries had widened, the Palestinian movement had emerged from the wreckage of this December Arab summit with enhanced prestige and a heightened image. But this new Palestinian phenomenon was complicating the already complex Middle East search for peace, running into the conflicting interests of some Arab states as well as bitter Israeli opposition and Washington negativeness.

Although very aware of the need for including the Palestinians in any settlement, Nasser was responding to his great losses in the war of attrition when he indicated in February in the course of his Metromedia network interview from Cairo, a strong willingness to accept a political solution in line with Security Council Resolution 242 of November 1967. The Egyptian leader went even further when he appeared in May 1970 on the National Educational Television Show "The Advocates" and, for the first time, indicated he would recognize the existence of the State of Israel if that were necessary to obtain the withdrawal of Israel from occupied Arab territories.[7]

Bolstered by the Soviet SAM defenses, the Egyptian leader made a dramatic May Day appeal to President Nixon to force the Israelis to end the occupation. And the Egyptian leader dispatched special envoys to each of the Arab capitals with the purpose of molding closer collaboration "against Israeli aggression and the United States' attitude toward it."

The Palestinians had stepped up their attacks, launched in November from Lebanon's snow-topped Mount Hermon, on Israeli settlements in East Galilee. Invariably, these led to Israeli reprisal raids against Lebanese villages, with houses of innocents demolished and many killed. When two Israelis were killed by rockets dropping into Kiryat Shemona, Israelis quickly entered six villages near the Hasbani River and carried out a massive retaliatory raid, ferreting out Palestinian fedayeen. Lebanese border villages of Bint Jbeil, Yaroun, Aitaroun, and Blida fell under heavy Israeli artillery attack after a Palestinian raid on a bus load of Israeli children from Avivim, an Israeli cooperative farm.

Nixon, who had been closely studying reports of increased Soviet involvement, including the Israeli allegation that the Soviets were flying defensive missions over Cairo, was quoted as saying that "the Middle East had taken an ominous turn." Israel was using all of its influence to further the Big Power polarization and to push her American patron into a direct confrontation with the Soviets.

The Intercontinental Hotel in Jordan, which had been relatively calm since the rejection by the government of the proposed visit of Assistant Secretary of State Joseph Sisco, became the scene in June 1970 of part one in the internecine struggle between Hussein and the Palestinians. During my stay ten days earlier at the Hotel on Jebel Amman, one still could enjoy the pleasure of the lovely site with its sparkling swimming pool, although the crackle of machine gun fire occasionally shattered the quiet of dusk as Palestinians and the Jordanian military clashed intermittently. But a fierce three days of bloody warfare saw the Palestinians seize the hotel and take sixty-two foreign guests as hostages as the Jordanian army began rounding up guerrillas elsewhere and shelled the refugee camps with artillery fire. Among the several hundreds killed in the struggle was Major Robert P. Perry, Arab-speaking U.S. Army Attaché in Amman.

This Jordanian showdown with the Palestinians came to an end with a truce arranged between Hussein and Al Fatah leader Yasir Arafat, who declared that "we will never give up Jordan as a base of operations" and gained the satisfaction of winning the dismissal of Sherif Nasser ben Jamil, the King's hated commander-in-chief of the army.

Aware of these and other grave dangers, Secretary Rogers declared it was time "to stop shouting and start talking." At a press conference June 25 he outlined a proposal for a three-month cease-fire, for Israeli withdrawal, and for Arab recognition of Israel's right to exist. This was to be accompanied by U.N. mediation and indirect peace talks under the guidance of mediator Ambassador Gunnar V. Jarring. President Nasser and King Hussein forthrightly accepted the Rogers plan. On the eighteenth anniversary of the coup that deposed King Farouk, the Egyptian leader told 1,200 followers packed into a Cairo University hall that while "in all honesty we found nothing new in this, it is an opportunity."

Prime Minister Meir, put on the spot by her foes, reluctantly accepted the proposal after the resignation from her government of the extreme right-wing Gahal party led by Menachem Begin, who had joined the Cabinet just prior to the six-day war. The Israelis were wary lest the the truce be used by the Arabs to prepare for war along the Canal. The Big Two had spoken, and when Washington and Moscow were on the same wavelength, Israel could do little to resist American pressures.

Nasser, whose May Day appeal had now been answered, had himself responded affirmatively only after a visit to the Soviet Union, which apparently also favored this truce to lessen the alarmingly increasing tensions. The Egyptian President announced, "This is a last chance. While we inform the U.S. that we have accepted its proposal, we must also tell them that our real belief is that whatever is taken by force cannot be returned except by force." The Egyptian leader also reiterated that the Arabs would yield "not one inch" of the territory seized in 1967 and still held by the Israelis.

The acceptance by Nasser and then by Hussein in August of the cease-fire signaled the end of the war of attrition but the beginning of a new internal Arab struggle. The Palestinians, while they could not afford to fight Nasser's decision to seek a political rather than a military solution, turned to meet the challenge of Hussein in Jordan, where most of the Palestinians lived and from where the fedayeen movement was then launching its attacks on Israel. Three previous showdowns between Hussein and the fedayeen had been inconclusive. Hussein viewed the armed, free-wheeling Palestinians as a continuing threat to his sovereignty that had to be faced sooner or later. When the Palestinians, determined not to be forgotten under the cease-fire, hijacked TWA, Swissair, and BOAC planes, fifty-four hostages (there were 300 originally), and then blew up the aircraft—all on a desert airstrip known by the British in World War II as Dawson's Field, twenty-five miles northwest of Amman—the Jordanian sovereign moved against them. The Jordanian civil war then erupted in earnest. The Hashemite ruler had determined this time to make himself sole ruler of his country.

After Hussein placed the country under martial law on September 15 and ordered his generals, who had replaced the previous civilian government, to destroy the commando movement, the U.S. readied itself to move militarily. The aircraft carriers *Saratoga* and *Independence* joined the Sixth Fleet in the Mediterranean; a group of C-130 transport planes carrying airborne troops flew from Europe to Turkey; helicopter carriers and Marine landing teams were readied in North Carolina.

In the ensuing crisis, when Syrian tanks moved into Jordan to assist the Palestinians and helped in the capture of the Jordanian town of Irbid, the U.S. unmistakably indicated the high priority it placed on the freedom of the small Hashemite kingdom. The 82nd Airborne was alerted and the augmented Sixth Fleet was ordered to move further eastward in the Mediterranean.

Knowing that direct U.S. intervention could both endanger any future Washington initiative as a mediator in the Arab-Israeli conflict and might bring the Soviet Union onto the scene in behalf of the Syrians, the U.S. asked the Israelis, through Prime Minister Meir (then visiting Washington), if they would agree to intervene in Hussein's behalf with planes. The wily Meir, at the time angling for $500 million in aid, in return exacted approval of her request as well as the dispatch of eighteen Phantoms ahead of schedule. The Israeli Cabinet meeting to which she rushed from her U.S. visit consented to bailing out Hussein if necessary, provided the U.S. would permit Israel to use ground as well as air forces against the Syrians and Palestinians.[8]

Israeli intervention became unnecessary when the Jordanians turned the tide in the tank battle that followed; the Syrians, persuaded by the Soviet Union, pulled back their forces across the border; and the Palestinian fedayeen proved to be no match for Hussein's 56,000-man force, the best drilled and most efficient army in the Arab world.

Three days after the Syrian retreat, the *New York Times* released maps and details of the Pentagon military plan under which U.S. and Israeli forces were to have coordinated their efforts in supporting Hussein, according to the joint design of their intelligence units. Another Big Power clash had been averted, in the course of which intimate U.S.-Jordan and U.S.-Israel ties, if not U.S.-Israel-Jordan ties, had been clearly revealed.[9]

The Arab Summit, called by President Nasser, sought to bring the fighting to an end. After arranging a shaky cease-fire between the combatants, the Egyptian President used all the prestige and persuasion he could command as he tirelessly struggled to bring about a reconciliation between King Hussein and Arafat to maintain some semblance of Arab unity. Qaddafi and Algeria's President Houari Boumedienne had wanted to send troops to join the Palestinians against Hussein. The King and Arafat flew to Cairo for a conciliatory handshake. But the effort was too much for Nasser, who had kept his ailing health a secret from all but the Russians, whose doctors had been treating him for some time.

As December 7, 1941, for Americans was a "day that will live in infamy," to use the words of Franklin Delano Roosevelt, so September 28, 1970, became for the Egyptian people a "day that will live in catastrophe." Their great and beloved leader, Gamal Abdel Nasser, suddenly succumbed to a heart attack, and was taken from them in the prime of life. Until the moment his body was buried three days later, the masses of Egypt seemed unable to accept the will of God.

Nasser, a dedicated, intelligent, resourceful man, maintained his popularity for eighteen years in a region of the world particularly noted for instability and internecine struggles. As the standard bearer of a new Egyptian-Arab consciousness, he endowed his people with a sense of dignity they never dared possess before. He was the first Egyptian to rule the land of the Pharaohs in more than 2,000 years, freeing that land from foreign domination. Both literally and figuratively, Nasser had placed the U.A.R. on the map. Even his worst enemy was invariably deeply impressed upon meeting the handsome, charismatic, solidly built six-footer with boundless energy and extraordinary personality. A master tactician in the art of balancing the U.S. against the Soviet Union, Nasser like the proverbial lucky Pierre, managed somehow to maintain himself in the middle.

Nasser's personal magnetism held Egypt under his rule while the world around him and its leadership constantly changed. His strength, undoubtedly, led to the CIA decision to help keep Nasser in power, at the same time exerting pressure on the Egyptian to temper his attitude toward Israel.[10] The Egyptian leader's problems were magnified by his worst blunder: intervention in Yemen, which he referred to as "my Vietnam."

Nasser had fallen far short of his goal of welding the 150 million Arabs of 15 countries into one spiritual nation and became the victim of his own strivings in the midst of super-strenuous efforts to end the crisis in Jordan. The cry, "Min badak, ya Gamal!" (Who will come after you, O Gamal!) echoed across the oceans and continents as the passing of Nasser left a giant void. His funeral in Cairo indicated that perhaps no world leader had enjoyed his people's adulation as much as Nasser had. Television viewers throughout the world could see endless, speechless mass demonstrations of grief for which there have been few parallels in the annals of man.

At the time, Nixon was on a European tour visiting Marshal Tito in Yugoslavia. Had he chosen to attend the funeral, he could have endeared himself and his country to the Arab masses.[11] But he would have had to face the wrath of a Zionist lobby, already exercised over Israeli charges that the Egyptians were violating the cease-fire by bringing new rockets, missiles, and other weapons into the standstill zones along the Canal.

At a special General Assembly debate on the Middle East, initiated that November by the new Sadat government, an Afro-Asian resolution was overwhelmingly adopted, calling for Israeli withdrawal from occupied territories and an unconditional resumption of Arab-Israeli peace talks under Ambassador Jarring, U.N. Secretary-General U Thant's peace representative. The U.S., supported only by Israel and fourteen other countries—but not by such normal allies as Italy, Belgium, Luxembourg, China (Taiwan), Japan, and the Philippines—opposed the resolution on the grounds that it "upset the balance between the need for withdrawal from the occupied lands and for acknowledgment of the sovereignty, territorial integrity, and political independence of all Middle East countries." This international jockeying over which comes first—Israeli withdrawal from Arab territories or Arab recognition of Israel—continues to dominate diplomatic maneuverings up to the present.

What stunned the U.N. was the announcement by Palestinian Dr. Fayez Sayegh, speaking for the Kuwaiti, Algerian, Syrian, Iraqi, Saudi Arabian, South Yemeni, and Yemeni delegations, that these countries were reluctantly abstaining in the vote on the draft resolution. The original draft recognized that "full respect for the inalienable rights of the Arab people of Palestine was a prerequisite to a just and lasting peace in the Middle East." But in the course of two revisions, the word "inalienable" disappeared and "prerequisite" became "indispensable." This, in the eyes of the Palestinians, was marked retrogression, and thus seven of the then fourteen Arab League members refrained from voting.[12] The post-Nasser Arab disunity had begun.

But the Palestinian cause received additional recognition in other directions. Within a two-week span both State Department spokesman John F. King and U.S. Ambassador to the U.N. Charles Yost were quoted as saying that peace in the Middle East depended on "taking into account the legitimate concerns and aspirations of the Palestinians." (Secretary Rogers had earlier noted that "any just settlement must take into account the desires and aspirations of the refugees.")[13] And the lengthy, scathing report of the U.N. Special Committee to Investigate Israeli Practices Affecting the Human Rights of the Population of the Occupied Territories, comprised of representatives of Sri Lanka (Ceylon), Somalia, and Yugoslavia, condemned Israel for gross violations of the 1949 Geneva Convention, which had been "adopted as an expression of the international community's sense of revulsion at the treatment accorded Jews under the Nazi regime."

Although pushed by the international community to implement the U.N. resolutions calling for Israeli withdrawal and recognition of Palestinian rights, Washington was not forgotting the Nixon campaign promise to maintain Israel's military superiority, and had rushed through the $500 million, open-ended military appropriations bill in the fall of 1970 as part of National Security Adviser Henry Kissinger's strategy to checkmate the Soviet Union challenge in any part of the globe where the free world was being challenged by proponents or wards of the East. The rivalry with Moscow in the Middle East heated up as the Soviet Union signed a twenty-year friendship agreement with Cairo, although still not giving Cairo the offensive weapons to meet the challenge of the flow of U.S. armaments to Israel.

Meanwhile, in the face of delays, charges, and countercharges regarding violation of the truce, the U.N. mediating efforts of Ambassador Jarring had floundered. The Israeli Cabinet remained badly split over the strategy to be pursued. On February 8, 1971, in identical *aides-mémoire*, Egypt was called on to commit itself to a peace agreement with Israel, and Israel was asked to withdraw its forces from occupied Egyptian territory to the former international boundary. These commitments were to be simultaneous and reciprocal, as preliminaries to a determination of other aspects of a peace settlement called for by the still extant Security Council Resolution 242 ending the 1967 war.

One week later, Egypt indicated that it would accept the specific commitments requested and would be ready to enter into a peace agreement with Israel if that nation would give commitments covering its own obligations under the resolution, including the withdrawal of its armed forces from Sinai and the Gaza Strip and achievement of a just settlement of the refugee problem in accordance with U.N. resolutions.

On February 17 the Special Representative informed Israel of Egypt's reply to his *aide-memoire.* On February 26 Israel, without specific reference to the commitment the Special Representative had sought from that government, stated that it viewed favorably Egypt's expression of readiness to enter into a peace agreement with Israel, and reiterated that it was prepared for meaningful negotiations on all subjects relevant to a peace agreement. Israel considered that both parties, having presented their basic positions, should now pursue detailed and concrete negotiations without prior conditions.[14]

On the question of withdrawal, on which Ambassador Jarring had sought a commitment, the Israeli unequivocal position was that it would promise to withdraw from the Israel-Egyptian cease-fire lines to "secure, recognized, and agreed boundaries" to be established by negotiations in the peace agreement; it would not withdraw to the lines existing prior to June 1967.[15]

To divert attention from the Israeli refusal to give Ambassador Jarring a definitive answer regarding what occupied lands Israel would be willing to relinquish, the alleged Soviet maltreatment of its Jews, as dramatized in the Leningrad hijackers, provided an excellent smoke screen for Israeli intransigency. Ted Kennedy indicated that Chappaquiddick was now far behind him as he wooed the block vote by blasting the Nixon administration for being "lax on helping Russian Jews to leave the Soviet Union."[16]

However much the media simulated progress to invent news, sell papers, and titillate the public fancy, there still remained the irreconcilable gap between Israel's goal of partial withdrawal from Arab-occupied territories and total peace, and the U.A.R. target of total withdrawal and partial peace. In agreeing to a third extension of the cease-fire, President Sadat called for a significant withdrawal of Israeli troops from the Suez Canal area. If this were done, the Egyptians would begin clearing the Canal and ready it for international traffic. The Egyptian cities on the eastern shore would of course be liberated. This new initiative had been spurred by the efforts of the committee of ten African heads of state of the Organization of African Unity.

To the trial balloon of Nasser's successor, Tel Aviv fired back the forthright question through Ambassador Jarring: "Does international traffic include Israel?" There was no direct response from Cairo.

Both sides wished to avoid renewal of the costly war of attrition, particularly in early spring, which is not good military weather. The

Middle East wars, like the tempers of the protagonists, wax warmer in higher temperatures, and the Sadat offer of opening the Suez Canal was calculated to water Western mouths, as well as to appeal to those oil companies in the U.K. and Europe that had been paying the excessively higher tolls forced by the closing of the artery. While the opening of the Canal would serve to advance the Soviet Union's naval thrust toward the Persian Gulf and Indian Ocean, this would be balanced by the savings to Western oil companies. In acquiescing to the opening of the Canal, Meir adroitly avoided any commitment as to Israeli troop withdrawal. And so the parties sparred without reaching any definite decision and continued their jockeying for support of world public opinion.

Although President Sadat's warning that April might be for the Middle East what the Ides of March had been for Julius Caesar made little impression on Washington, the Israeli Prime Minister wanted to make sure that election-minded legislators understood her goals. Going over President Nixon's head, Mrs. Meir dispatched her most talented, unexcelled orator, Foreign Minister Abba Eban, to Washington to engage in an extraordinary briefing session attended by almost one half the members of the Senate. Like so many other opponents of the Israelist machine, Secretary of State Rogers was then reduced to the degrading position of having to ask for equal time in a closed-door Senate meeting, attended by only a handful of legislators, in order to try and set the record straight.

Recruited influence was not to be halted, however. Democratic presidential aspirant Senator Birch Bayh of Indiana told a large New York audience that Washington must not pressure Israel "to rely on promises" that can be "forgotten or ignored." The conservative media gave vent to its anti-Communist sentiments by both exaggerating the extent and strength of the latest build-up of Soviet air reinforcements to Egypt, and deceiving its readership into believing that the Russian MIG-23s and the supreme interceptor Sukhoi-lls, allegedly pouring into Cairo, were capable of more than defensive potency.

The strong declaration of the newly announced Egyptian-Libyan-Syrian confederation[17] that there would be "no abandoning of one inch of Arab territory," and "no relinquishing of the rights of the Palestinians" added another obstacle for UN mediator Jarring, and provided Tel Aviv with an opportunity to wiggle out of the tight spot in which Sadat's Suez Canal offer had placed the Israelis. Although as the *Christian Science Monitor* pointed out, the Arab confederation was only "a paper alliance," which faced greater obstacles than other past, unsuccessful, similar attempts, the rising star of charismatic Libyan leader Colonel Mua'mmar Qaddafi added to Israeli concern.

Even as the media and other supporters of Israel continued to rant hysterically about alleged Egyptian infractions of the stand-still agreement, one had to read the Anglo-Jewish press to learn that Deputy Prime Minister Allon had told 300 members of a UJA mission group at a farewell dinner, "Israel has not been resting on its laurels in the Canal Zone during the past three months and is now stronger than she was before the cease-fire."[18] And Chief of Staff General Bar-Lev disclosed that "Israel's fortifications have been strengthened to withstand the heaviest bombardment, including the massive shells of the Soviet 2-03mm artillery being supplied to Egypt in large quantities." The General frankly revealed that "during the three-month truce, new roads have been constructed and fuel systems improved." This was stated even as the Nixon administration was pushing through its latest defense appropriation for Israel so as to preserve, in the words of President Nixon, "the delicate military balance."

The five-country Middle East mission by Secretary Rogers in the spring of 1971 brought little progress toward reopening the Canal, but did buy time in the form of another extension of the cease-fire. The Secretary, evenhanded at all times, drew Israeli criticism because of his alleged "supersensitivity" toward Arab feelings by refusing to drive around the occupied sector of Jerusalem with the Israeli official flag flying from his car. His arrival in Cairo coincided with Sadat's move against the leftist clique led by Ali Sabri. With the house arrest of the Ministers of War and Interior, and with other key opponents to disengagement under lock and key, the Sadat government pushed harder for a Canal agreement and Israeli withdrawal from the East Bank as a first step toward total withdrawal from all occupied territories. But as Deputy Prime Minister Yigal Allon clearly indicated to Secretary Rogers, Israel would never consent to even a partial pullback from the Canal if it were to be construed as the beginning of total Israeli withdrawal.

White House pressures on Israel to withdraw to effectuate the goals of the Secretary of State were constantly being leavened by promises of economic assistance to the faltering Israeli economy. With the next national elections looming on the horizon, the Zionist combine daily tightened its net around the President. The situation was well summed up by columnists Evans and Novak in this manner: "Thus, Nixon is caught in a bind. He must decide either to use his enormous power to back Israel down or risk losing everything he has gained in two years of hard diplomacy, with another war at the end of that road."[19]

Speaking on the eve of the anniversary, Sadat warned the members of the Arab Socialist Union, "1971 must be decisive either by fighting or by peace." While Washington had responded with fine words and proposals to the Arab insistence on near-total Israeli withdrawal from all occupied territories, there was still no indication whatsoever of when and how the U.S. would exert real pressure on Israel to force appropriate action, even though the Meir government was particularly vulnerable at this time.

Despite the interregnum of temporary peace ushered in by the cease-fire, Israel faced grave economic problems and rising internal unrest. The little-discussed Georges Friedman book *The End of the Jewish People*[20] had predicted how peace could bring deep internal frictions and even constituted a greater threat to Israel than did the Arabs.

Meir's fall 1971 visit to the U.S. saw a low watermark in U.S.-Israel relations. There seemed to be an unbreachable impasse: Israel demanded more Phantoms, Secretary Rogers wanted Israel to start withdrawing. Although Congress had been continuously resoluting for more Phantom aircraft deliveries to Israel, Rogers, according to an account in the Israeli daily *Ma'ariv,* vehemently retorted to the demand of eight Senators (and the Israeli Premier herself alluded to these alleged remarks in a major foreign policy address in the Knesset on November 25): "Israel is a state which is falling apart from within and there are elements within it who do not agree on the present policy. Even the Pope in Rome defines Israel's policy as inflexible, and, in fact, Israel is today the most isolated state in the world."

The Secretary of State and the Israeli leaders exchanged bitter words in a face-to-face confrontation. The President and the Israeli Prime Minister were at odds after an angry telephone conversation on Thanksgiving Day. And then suddenly, as happened before and since, the storm evaporated and blue skies broke through. (As on other subjects, the Nixon *Memoirs* are very selective—there is much praise of Mrs. Meir and no criticism so that little light is shed on this "family" quarrel.)

The continued pressure on the White House from Congress and from influential forces within the administration, including Detroit industrialist Max Fisher who, as a Vice Chairman of the National Committee to Re-elect the President, had been rallying Jews across the country to the President's standard, resulted in the collapse of Rogers' resistance. Kissinger's guidelines prevailed: The U.S. must support Israel because the Soviets were giving all-out help to the Arabs. This Nixonian version of the policy of containment by matching Communist strength and maintaining the so-called military balance in the area was given priority over Rogers' judgment as to what should be done in the Middle East. The rash of Soviet arms shipments were cited as justification for the decision that there now had been a shift in the arms balance requiring the U.S. to send the Phantoms demanded by Israel and to make other undisclosed commitments to Meir's government. Months earlier, at the start of the August 1970 cease-fire, when the Kremlin had rushed SAM-2s and SAM-3s into the Egyptian front lines and Israel had consequently balked at entering into the Jarring talks until she was given more security in the form of Phantoms, Washington had refused to view this an excuse for stepping up the arms escalation demanded by Israel. But at that time there was no upcoming presidential election, which, as Watergate was soon to prove, was placed above all by the Nixon administration.

There could be little doubt that Washington's shift had been inspired by concern over national politics. Six months before the Watergate break-in, initial public opinion polls were of deep concern to the White House, whose Republican occupant was not as ideologically drawn to the Zionist cause as were the several Democratic presidential aspirants. After all, it was the party of Truman and Johnson that had always so closely identified itself with the Tel Aviv-New York axis, whereas the GOP usually tagged along lest they face inevitable vital domestic political consequences. The calendar had thus invaluably assisted Israeli perseverance to gain its latest gift of air armaments.

After seeing the President and the Secretary of State in Washington, Meir spent five days in New York City and was able to say to the press: "We want aircraft. We were never happy about the necessity of bringing the subject up in the open. I've done my best to explain why additional aircraft are needed for Israel and why, if delivered, such aircraft would not obstruct negotiations for a final peace agreement or even an interim Suez Canal agreement." Despite her strenuous denials, it was all too obvious that Meir had acceded to U.S. wishes. The *quid pro quo* for the Phantoms she was to receive was the resumption of the important talks with U.N. conciliator Jarring, disrupted at the time of the Canal proposal discussions and later ground to a full halt with Israel's refusal to provide the mediator with a pledge to withdraw from the occupied territories.

Meir appeared thoroughly satisfied. But about what? Was it

merely the Phantoms, or had she won a great deal more—her longtime real primary objective of a U.S. security guarantee that would remain steady and unchanging through all political, diplomatic, and military changes and, unlike a treaty, would not be subject to legislative ratification nor public approval? The latter hypothesis was supported by the relative ease with which the U.S. was able to persuade Israel to exercise moderation in the face of the ruthless Lydda Airport slaughter (June 1972) by the Japanese hirelings of the Marxist Palestinian movement. Threats of an immediate reprisal against Lebanon were never executed, suggesting the likelihood of a U.S.-Israel relationship over and above a mere jet deal.

Incredible as it may seem, the U.S. may have involved itself in a new secret undertaking at the very moment the nation was recovering from the shock of the Southeast Asia secret commitments, revealed by the Ellsberg-stolen Pentagon Papers.

In the course of the 1971 Nixon-Meir talks in Washington, the Israeli Prime Minister's natural concern as to the U.S. position at the Moscow summit, scheduled to take place in May six months hence, had led her to exact promises to ensure the fullest protection of Israel's interests. Whatever the President of the U.S. promised the Prime Minister of Israel at that time concerning what he would say to the party leader of the Soviet Union must have been carried out, according to these exuberant comments over Israeli radio by then-Israeli Ambassador to the U.S. Yitzhak Rabin: "President Nixon's express commitment at the summit with Soviet leaders in Moscow proved he is the best friend Israel ever had at the White House."[21]

The communiqué issued after these first Nixon-Brezhnev talks was totally barren of any new peace initiatives save the agreement for resumption of the Jarring talks. The interim Suez Canal agreement was put to sleep, and other Kremlin pressures in behalf of the Arabs were resisted. The status quo preserving the Israeli position had not been impaired in the slightest.

By January 1972, after her return home, Meir completely changed her tune. The more dovish members of her Cabinet who had advocated a more flexible line (including at times Foreign Minister Abba Eban) were now overruled by the Prime Minister, Moshe Dayan, and Information Minister Galili. Meir's U.S. operation had been successful, and the Sadat's "year of decision" had run out without any Egyptian action. "No new Israeli concessions" became the Israeli order of the day.

Ambassador Jarring began his first round of renewed talks and demanded a commitment of withdrawal to the international borders of Egypt. But Tel Aviv, rejuvenated by the new Washington determination to back Israel, remained firm in its refusal to the request of the U.N. conciliator. In fact, the U.N. mediator was now openly assailed as being "biased" for having exceeded his mandate in his February 1971 memorandum by insisting upon a prenegotiations pledge from Israel.

Publicly, Israeli leadership interpreted the sale of the Phantoms as a Nixon admission of past failures in peacemaking efforts. Some quarters alleged that the Russian victory in the India-Pakistan war had forced the U.S. President to send the planes as a show of strength, a riposte prior to the Moscow summit. In the eyes of Tel Aviv, the Pakistani defeat also confirmed the Israeli viewpoint that neither U.N. nor other international guarantees could ever safeguard the security of any small state. The subcontinent war had, in addition, diverted attention from the Middle East conflict and had destroyed Sadat's plans to focus attention at the U.N. once more on Israeli intransigency.

In his February 9, 1972, message on foreign policy, Nixon expressed deep concern about the growing danger of a confrontation, and the "common interest in not becoming involved in a war." The President emphasized the dire need for Big Power restraint. The injection into the region of the "global strategic rivalry" was incompatible with Middle East peace and with the détente in U.S.-Soviet relations, he declared. White House researchers displayed an improvement over past performance in the presidential reminder that "one of the ironies of history finds that the 20th century has thrown together into bitter conflict these two peoples who had lived together and worked peacefully side by side in the Middle East for centuries." In his retirement Eisenhower had to be reminded how incorrect he was in his *Reader's Digest* article reference to "the centuries-old animosity between Arabs and Jews."[22]

The Middle East stalemate continued, however. Time and again the Nixon administration was forced to admit its inability to make any breakthrough toward peace, aside from the extension of the 1970 cease-fire. The close proximity talks between the adversaries, along the lines of the Rhodes indirect negotiations favored by Israel, were resoundly vetoed by Cairo while Israel, in turn, adamantly refused to give Jarring any magic words that would move the talks along.

Held at bay on the military front as Moscow continued to refuse to give firm backing to Cairo for any serious move across the Canal against Israeli power, Sadat decided on a new tack. A new Saudi

Arabia-Egyptian alliance had been in the making since the visits to
Cairo of Saudi Arabian Defense Minister Prince Sultan Ibn Abdul Aziz,
brother of King Faisal, and return visits to Riyadh by President Sadat.
It was obvious that the advice given Sadat by his Saudi cousins was to
move closer to the U.S., by relieving himself of the growing influence
of the Soviet Union, which Faisal feared as much or more than the U.S.
did. Apparently Kissinger's veiled remark about action "to expel" the
Russians,[23] made at a background briefing of news during the 1970
Palestinian-Jordanian struggle following the plane hijackings, had
made a lasting impression on politically aware Sadat.

The Egyptian President had failed in trips to Moscow and in
negotiations with the Russians to obtain the offensive weapons he
needed. The MIGs he was getting carried a very low bomb load with
nowhere near the speed nor maneuverability of the rival Phantoms.
These were purely defensive weapons. The Russians indicated they
would continue to supply Egypt with land-to-air defense missile systems but not land-to-land, and they were not willing to part with their
latest planes, which could outspeed the American Phantoms. The Soviet Union also rejected Egyptian requests for SS-4 Sandal missiles
with a striking range of 1,200 miles, and the SS-1C Scud short-range
missiles with a range of 185 miles, capable of delivering both conventional and nuclear warheads. Egypt's Frog-3 surface-to-surface missiles were not capable of reaching targets in Israel.

At this juncture Sadat made his famed move of July 17, 1972,
abruptly expelling the Soviet military advisers and technicians, numbering between 15,000 and 18,000. In his official announcement,
Sadat said Egypt was taking over all Soviet installations as well. He
referred repeatedly to his recent problems in securing offensive weapons from the Russians: "This is what made me say we needed to
reevaluate our position."

In the days following, experts felt Sadat was opening the door for
a direct Egyptian approach to the U.S. But in his first public speech
following the expulsion, Sadat portrayed himself as a leader misled by
the U.S., which promised help in getting peace and had never followed
through, and by the Soviet Union, which promised the means to make
war but then withheld them. He expressed frustration with both super
powers and said Egypt must turn to a policy of self-reliance, seeking
more help from the Arab world and from Western Europe. He also
hoped the latter would help pressure the U.S. toward the Arab position.

The ouster of the Russians provided Washington with a golden opportunity, coming at the most opportune moment. In the wake of the Peking and Moscow summits, there had seemed to be few further spectaculars that the Nixon administration could or needed to mount as additional reelection campaign fodder. Then came the astounding Middle East development. After a certain period of evaluation and hesitation, Secretary Rogers appealed for a forthright resumption of Middle East negotiations. The State Department chieftain clearly indicated that these did not necessarily have to be direct talks at the outset.

But this minuscule bait held out to the Egyptians was unaccompanied by other indications that at this most sensitive domestic political period Washington had any intention of prodding Israel into a more flexible mood. Neither Prime Minister Meir's extension of the olive branch in her dramatic direct appeal to Sadat nor Moshe Dayan's television announcement of the redeployment of the Suez-line Israeli troops was sufficient evidence that the U.S. President had exerted the pressure anticipated by Sadat's daring move. No one in any way was as yet speaking "harshly" to Tel Aviv, the necessary prerequisite for appropriate Israeli action.

In fact, at this juncture Nixon seemed concerned only with trying to outbid the Democrats for Zionist support at the polls. In his message to the Zionist Organization of America on July 13 on the occasion of its Diamond Jubilee Convention in Jerusalem, the President extended salutations "to a people who truly share the heritage of two great nations, Israel and the United States. Both countries are strengthened by your leadership and both share a common goal, the preservation of freedom and peace in the world." In this patent pursuit of the Jewish vote, he had endowed American Jews, the overwhelming majority of whom had never set foot in Israel, with a dual heritage. And two weeks later, in talking by telephone to Meir on July 28 for three minutes as part of the inauguration of a new Israeli satellite ground communications station, the President stated (and this was prominently publicized by his press people) that he would continue to work for "a just peace in the Mideast, which will protect the integrity of Israel."

Nixon's newly demonstrated support of Israel paid large dividends in the November 7 elections. In his overwhelming defeat of Senator McGovern, the President more than doubled his 1968 vote in the cities with Jewish population concentrations, helping to add to the Democratic rout.

On Meir's first visit to Washington after the elections, Nixon agreed not only to sell four squadrons of combat jets but also to assist the Israelis with production and technical help in manufacturing its own Super Mirage, an advanced design based on the French Mirage fighter series and powered by the same General Electric jet engines used in the sophisticated F-4 bombers. By June Israel would have received about 12 VF-4s and 200 A-4s. Delivery under the 1971 agreement between Washington and Tel Aviv was not scheduled to be completed until the end of the year.

This latest aid for Israel and the Beirut assassinations of PLO leaders deeply angered the Arab world. Widespread allegations of U.S. complicity in the Israeli raid into the heart of Lebanon, although without any proof linking the American Embassy, added to mounting Arab anti-U.S. feeling.

The summer of 1973 saw the area cold war heating up considerably. A new wave of hijacking and airport violence included the killing of fifty-five by alleged Black September Palestinians in an Athens air lounge. The Big Two's determination to avoid any conflict remained the sole constraint as the battlefield spread to the U.S. home front.

The energy crisis became more acute. Gasoline was being doled out in several parts of the country, gas stations were closing, protests were registered, and the possibility of compulsory rationing emerged. In the face of public resentment over energy shortages and the first public hints that a change in U.S. Middle East policy might help meet the crisis, Washington continued to vacillate, on the one hand trying to maintain a modicum of Arab goodwill so as not to further imperil American interests, and on the other hand responding to the same old pressures at home from politicians, liberals, and the cultists of anti-anti-Semitism. Events at the U.N. only tended to heighten the resistance of Saudi Arabia to U.S. pressures for an increase in oil production as well as strengthen the Arab world's determination to use oil as a political weapon.

In late July the Security Council meeting concluded its Middle East debate, adjourned from the previous month, and the U.S. then cast its veto to defeat an otherwise unanimous agreement—another indication of the growing isolation of the Washington-Tel Aviv alliance. The vetoed resolution, strongly deploring Israel's continued occupation of Arab lands, was supported by the U.K., France, Australia, Austria, Guinea, India, Indonesia, Kenya, Panama, Peru, the Sudan, the Soviet Union, and Yugoslavia. China abstained, protesting that the resolution failed to "strongly condemn the Israeli Zionists for their prolonged aggression against Arabs" and to "call upon all governments and people to give their firm support to the Arab peoples in their just struggle to recover their lost territory."

This was only the fifth time that the U.S. had exercised the veto in the twenty-seven-year history of the U.N., and the second time it had been used in connection with a Middle East resolution. U.S. Ambassador to the U.N. John A. Scali told the Security Council that the resolution was not balanced and would undermine "the one agreed basis on which a solution in the Middle East could be reconstructed, namely Resolution 242 of 1967."

Two weeks later, in August, after Israel had forced a Lebanese commercial airliner with eighty-one persons aboard to alter its course and land in Israel, the U.S. did join in a unanimous resolution condemning the piracy of Israel. In explaining his vote, Scali emphasized that the endorsement of the resolution "in no way represents a change in U.S. policy on the problems and possibilities for a settlement. Nor should it be interpreted as our endorsing the use of sanctions as a means of dealing with this problem." The Lebanese gratefully accepted what small blessings they could from the unanimous censure.

Washington had vigorously opposed convening the Council to hear the Lebanese complaint, coming right on the heels of its previous veto, and made it clear during the debate that the bare mention of the possibility of sanctions against Israel in the resolution, as favored by Egypt, would draw another negative American vote. The new resolution therefore avoided any language that would force two U.S. vetoes in a row.

Suddenly, two of the four parent companies of the Arabian American Oil Company (Aramco) in Saudi Arabia, largest of American oil interests in the Middle East and the largest single U.S. investment abroad, awakened to the grave dangers confronting themselves, as well as their country. Heretofore only John G. McLean of Continental Oil (Conoco), a smaller company, had mustered the courage to speak out. Full-page advertisements in January in such papers as the *New York Times,* the *Wall Street Journal,* and the *Washington Post,* and two-page spreads in four news magazines and in business publications, carried Conoco's concise message based on a speech of Board Chairman McLean. The startling copy stressed "the need for cooperation in the development of a sound framework of political relationships with the countries of the Middle East to promote stability and peace in the area," and called for both "a new look at our foreign policies with respect to the Middle East, as well as attaching to them a much higher priority than they had thus far been accorded." Guts had paid off. Continental received few of the brickbats overcautious friends had predicted and was rewarded by a flood of requests for the complete text of the McLean talk.

Prodded by the increased public criticism of oil companies for the energy shortage and by Libya's stepped-up nationalization of American oil interests, one of the major oil companies now spoke up. The 1971 takeover of the assets of British Petroleum had been followed by a 51 percent nationalization of Oasis, Amoseas, and Occidental. Although not yet affected, Mobil Oil "screwed its courage to the sticking post" with an advertisement, "The U.S. Stake in Middle East Peace," which dared to link the energy crisis with U.S. foreign policy failures.

In the light of Mobil's past performance,[24] boldness characterized their appeal to Americans to:

... understand the changed and still changing conditions in the Middle East ... that if our country's relations with the Arab world continue to deteriorate, Saudi Arabia may conclude it is not in its interest to look favorably on U.S. requests for increased petroleum supplies.... The government of that country has the power to decide how much oil is to be produced within its borders, and to what countries that oil can be shipped.

In the last analysis, political considerations may become the critical element in Saudi Arabia's decisions, because we will need the oil more than Saudi Arabia will need the money. That country could reduce oil exports three million barrels a day below present levels and, with its small population, still finance its domestic development programs with a comfortable margin for reserves ...

It is therefore time for the American people to begin adapting to a new energy age, to a vastly changed world situation, to the *realities* with which we will have to learn to live. Nothing less than clear thinking, a sense of urgency, and a grasp of what is at stake can lay the base for achieving a durable peace in the Middle East ... a settlement that will bring justice and security to all the peoples and to all the states of the region. Nobody can afford another war in the Middle East. Nobody. Nobody.[25]

Mobil's noncontroversial ads in the *New York Times* invariably appeared in a key position, generally on the Op-Ed page opposite the editorial page, where a maximum of readers could be counted on to read the message. But this "controversial" statement was relegated to inconspicuous space back on page 30. The scheduled follow-up ad never was run—a combined result of pressure and fear.

Standard Oil of California, another of the four owners of Aramco, emulated the stand taken by her sister company's ad in a letter dated July 26, 1973, sent by Board Chairman Otto N. Miller to all stockholders and employees, urging them to support closer ties between Arab countries and the U.S. in order to help solve the energy crisis. "There must be understanding on our part of the aspirations of the Arab people," he wrote, "and more positive support of their efforts toward peace with the Middle East."

Since its first oil discovery on the island of Bahrain in the Arabian Gulf in 1932, SOCAL, as this California company was called, had been an important basic supply source for Western Europe and Japan and, of course, an obvious indispensable source for the U.S. For more than forty years, since the conclusion of its historic agreement with King Abdul Aziz ibn Saud of Saudi Arabia, the company could boast of a continuous and cordial relationship with the Arab people. But it now felt forced to note with great dismay "a growing feeling in much of the Arab world that the U.S. had turned its back on the Arab people."

In response to the Miller letter, which objectively could only be deemed a constructive approach to the growing energy crisis, Los Angeles Zionists rallied American Jews to war on the company. In a statement issued from the office of President of the Jewish Federation Council of Greater Los Angeles Edward Sanders, as reported by the *Chicago Daily News,* he expressed "shock and dismay" and declared that "he still had a tankful of Standard gas in his car and a Standard credit card, but he'd decide what to do only after Standard Board Chairman Miller decides whether to send out a new letter." And Sanders added: "If he doesn't, we as a community will consider what we will do next."[26]

The Jewish War Veterans demanded a boycott of all SOCAL products. The Anti-Defamation League, the Southern California Council for Soviet Jewry, and other Jewish "defense" groups assailed the Miller letter, raising the usual cry of "anti-Semitism." SOCAL was accused of trading "Jewish blood for Arab oil."[27] American Zionist Federation head Rabbi Israel Miller said, "We are confident that the American government will not surrender to blackmail either by Arab governments or by Standard Oil of California." Simultaneously, the *Jewish News* of Los Angeles asked that California Standard's credit cards be torn in half "so we can send a ton to the company marketing Chevron gasoline." The office buildings of the company in Los Angeles and San Francisco were splashed by early morning vandals with red paint in plastic bags thrown from automobiles.

Organized Jewry across the country picked up the hue and cry, as the story was embroidered upon by the *New York Times,* the *Washington Post,* and the *Chicago Daily News.* The letter sent to an estimated 300,000 stockholders and employees did not, as reported by the media (with the notable exception of the AP), ask support for "the aspirations of the Arab people of the Middle East," only that there be an "understanding on our part of Arab efforts toward peace in the Middle East" —something quite different. And in their accounts neither the *Times* nor the *Post* referred to the last two paragraphs of the letter in which the SOCAL Chairman asked that the "legitimate interests of *all of the people* of the Middle East" (italics added) be acknowledged and that they be helped to "achieve security and a dependable economic future."

As Zionists have done customarily, they injected their Christian political supporters, members of the congressional "Israel-First" bloc, prominently into the campaign aimed to silence anyone who might link the growing energy crisis to U.S. Middle East policy and thereby bestir Americans to raise the $64 question, "What Price Israel?" Senator John V. Tunney (Dem.-Calif.) assailed the Miller letter as "counterproductive to peace," declaring, "We cannot solve our fuel crisis by selling out Israel."

One of the more ludicrous assertions in the growing controversy was contributed by the Jewish Federation Chairman's complaint that the letter "raises serious ethical and moral questions as to the utilization of a vast profit-making organization to influence American foreign policy." He insisted that such nonprofit, tax-exempt, and tax-deductible organizations as his own, or the Southern California Council for Soviet Jewry, the Anti-Defamation League, and the American Zionist Federation—all of which had been immediately mobilized and were now engaged in public battle —be solely entitled to influence foreign policy, and by way of tax-free dollars, of course.

Forced to respond to the political protests, letters, and phone calls, SOCAL Board Chairman Miller wrote the Chairman of the San Francisco Jewish Community Relations Council, explaining that his original letter had been concerned, as it expressly stated, "with the legitimate interests of all Middle East peoples," obviously including Israel.[28]

To prevent American gasoline consumers from stumbling on any linkage between U.S. pro-Israel policy and the country's energy plight, varied inspired articles and television-radio commentaries placed the blame at Washington's door for not having provided alternate energy sources. "There is no energy shortage—it is all the invention of the oil companies."[29] The salient fact being hidden from public consumption was that U.S. imports of oil, accounting in 1973 for 35 percent of its oil requirements as against 21 percent in 1970, would by 1980 reach 50 to 60 percent.

Virtually every oil analyst agreed that Saudi Arabia with reserves of more than 150 billion barrels,[30] would be the crucial single foreign source supply for the U.S. during the next decade. A Senior Vice President of Exxon publicly warned that it would take four to ten years before there could be production from new U.S. discoveries of oil and gas. And, to make matters worse, Canada indicated at this time that she would no longer tolerate the depletion of her reserves by exports to the U.S. Wishing to insulate her domestic price from the fast-changing world market price, the Canadian government planned to draw almost all the oil that Canada used from her own huge reserves rather than import or export further oil. This would cut off a daily export to the U.S. of perhaps 500,000 barrels per day, a critical loss at a critical time.

The desperate situation facing the U.S. could be seen in true perspective only through such bare facts as that the U.S., with only 6 percent of the world population, was a consumer of over 30 percent of the world's energy. Or as U.S. Energy Commissioner John A. Love phrased it: "The average American uses as much energy in less than a week as half of the world's population on an individual basis consumes in a year."

Other vital oil facts rounded out the story. While less than half of the 4.7 million barrels of oil the U.S. imported daily in 1972 came from the Middle East, 75 percent of Western Europe's 14.4 million barrel daily import and 86 percent of Japan's 5 million barrels come from the Middle East. Demand for oil by the free world had leaped far ahead of forecasts. By 1980 the U.S. alone would be importing as much as 15 million barrels daily, 11 million of which would have to come from where 60 percent plus of the proven free world reserves were located, namely the Middle East and North Africa. And these Middle East deposits would be the sole place from which the increased demand for oil might come, aside from Alaska. Europe, estimated to require 26 million barrels by 1980, and Japan, requiring 13 million, were already totally dependent on Middle East-North African oil. With its one-fourth of all middle East oil production and one-fourth of the oil reserves of the world, Faisal's Saudi Arabia assumed the command position.

During a 1973 spring visit to Washington many important new ideas were unveiled and trial balloons floated by the politically astute Saudi Arabian Minister of Petroleum, Sheikh Ahmed Zaki Yamani. Where King Faisal had previously clearly disdained the use of oil as a political weapon, his petroleum chieftain hinted at this possibility and injected this thought into his talks with congressional leaders and administration chiefs. The sheikh indicated that Saudi Arabia would not significantly expand production unless Washington moved from its pro-Israel stance to a more evenhanded policy. The Saudi Higher Petroleum Council recommended that the production/expansion program planned by Aramco, which would be the primary factor in meeting U.S. increased petroleum demands, be suspended or significantly reduced. Yamani had hinted that "if we consider only local interests, then we should not produce more oil—perhaps less." Washington was hoping for increased Saudi production from eight million to twenty million barrels daily over the next ten years. But at the same time the Arab oil leader extended the firm hand of friendship and offered a virtual partnership with U.S. industry through large capital investment in exchange for technological assistance.

In his late spring visit to Paris for a most cordial interchange with France's President Pompidou, King Faisal expressed full support of his Minister of Petroleum's refusal to expand the present oil production significantly until Washington moved toward a more evenhanded Middle East policy. As an expression of his gratitude for the increasingly pro-Arab French position, which was in vivid contrast to the attitude of the Quai d'Orsay in the 1940s and 1950s when Paris was an even closer ally of Israel than Washington, Faisal agreed to stepped-up political, military, and economic cooperation between the two countries. France would be helping Saudi Arabia in the development of a French-made color television system, already used by Egypt and Lebanon, in preference to the rival German system. The Saudis also had under consideration the purchase of two Anglo-French supersonic Concorde airliners, as well as a number of super-Mirage fighter bombers already purchased or about to be purchased by Abu Dhabi, Kuwait, and other Gulf states. With his purchase of $650 million of military hardware from Britain, Faisal further indicated the trend to push the U.S. out of its favored economic position in the Arab world until Washington accommodated itself to minimum Saudi political demands.

The visit of the ruler of Iran to the American capital that same summer could have brought little comfort to either Washington or Tel Aviv. The scene was cordial enough, pleasantries being exchanged between Nixon and Shah Mohammed Reza Pahlevi. But the essential unchanged fact affecting the oil situation was placed in focus when the Shah appeared on the "Meet the Press" television program. The

Iranian ruler indicated that by 1978 it was expected his country would be able to produce eight million barrels daily, but that production would thereafter be definitely leveled off. The U.S., therefore, could not look to that country's supply should the Saudi Arabians continue to stick to their resolve not to increase production, let alone possibly even cut back, as Minister Yamani indicated they might do.

When King Faisal called Aramco Chairman and Chief Executive Officer Frank Jungers to the palace in Riyadh, repeated Yamani's caution, and indicated that he could not long resist pressure from other Arab states, the warning was passed along to Washington, where it was promptly ignored.

Although King Faisal had always shown the friendliest disposition toward the U.S.—among other things he had sent all of his children to be educated there—he also undoubtedly still retained bitter memories of wretched treatment at the hands of American politicians under Zionist command. There had been the cancellation of the dinner scheduled in his honor at the Metropolitan Museum by New York's Mayor Lindsay in 1971 and, before that, the violent snub by Mayor Wagner to his brother King Saud in January 1957. U.S. oil shortages were already piling up when King Faisal indicated in an interview with John Cooley of the *Monitor* that increases in production would in the future be linked to "the revision of U.S. policy vis-à-vis the Arab world."[31] And on NBC's September 4 three-hour television program, "The Energy Crisis—an American White Paper," the Saudi monarch with utmost frankness warned the viewer in the Frank McGee documentary: "We do not wish to place any restrictions on our oil exports to the U.S., but America's complete support of Zionism against the Arabs makes it extremely difficult for us to continue to supply U.S. petroleum needs and even to maintain our friendly relations."

Most Washington legislators insisted that the King was bluffing. Senator Bayh claimed Saudi Arabia and other oil-exporting countries could not afford to shut the U.S. off from its marketing structure because "the supply-demand curve will shift against the oil-producing nations as new sources of oil are brought in from the North Sea and Glasgow." California's Senator Alan Cranston picked up the Zionist line on Capitol Hill with equally dangerous wishful thinking, which only helped further confuse and deceive his energy-hungry constituents.

A handful of responsible Senators appreciated the seriousness of the situation. Oklahoma Senator Dewey F. Bartlett stated that the "recent threat by Saudi Arabia to cut back if the U.S. does not change its policy is so serious that it should have been spread across the front page of every newspaper in the U.S."[32]

Senator Fulbright warned of the damaging consequences of U.S. Middle East policy:

The OPEC countries thus far have been reasonably moderate and responsible, and there remains in the Arab world, despite everything, a remarkable reservoir of good will toward the United States. But as the mounting desperation of the Palestinians shows, that reservoir is fast being drained. . . . In the service of a profound emotional commitment to Israel, we have all but kicked over the traces on our other interests in the Middle East—an economic interest in oil, a stategic interest in peace, and a perfectly ordinary human interest in the friendship of peoples who, whatever their quarrel with Israel, have never done anything to harm the United States.[33]

Others, like Congressman Richard T. Hanna from California, suddenly began to bestir themselves. Heretofore he had only reacted to the demands of Zionist pressure in support of Israel, but the energy squeeze had made him appreciate, almost for the first time, the needs of other of his constituents, including the Los Angeles Power Company, which required oil to service their many customers. Inserting a bland rebuke to the U.S. unevenhanded policy into the Congressional Record, this enterprising congressman[34] with the help of oil companies was enabled to go to Saudi Arabia and meet with the King in Riyadh, where he had the nerve to plead personally for a special allotment for his California constituents. To the bitter end, the politicians, whose misdeeds and nondeeds underlay the entire tragedy that has befallen the area, were determined to have it both ways.

That the Saudi Arabians meant business and would have to be taken seriously was indicated by Nixon at his press conference two days after King Faisal's NBC appearance, when he announced he was moving to end the deadlock in the negotiations between the Arab states and Israel and that he would use his total influence to get negotiations "off dead center." This was the first real positive U.S. response to the July 1972 removal of Soviet troops by Sadat, inspired by King Faisal. And at this White House meeting with the media, the Chief Executive for the first time linked Middle East diplomacy with the question of petroleum supplies.

Previously the administration had blinded itself to—or at least refused to acknowledge publicly—the possibility that the Saudi Arabian government might withhold oil unless the U.S. altered its policy. And the State Department, in marked contrast to the independence shown by foreign service officers in the face of the advice offered by President Truman on the Palestine problem, had been reechoing White House denials that energy shortages had anything to do with U.S. policy. In spring and early summer energy hearings on Capitol Hill, State Department representatives had told congressional committees that Saudi Arabia, in the last analysis, would be guided by their desire for increased royalties and would continue to increase their production by dipping further into their reserves so as to end the threat of a drastic U.S. oil curtailment, even should other Arab countries, closer to the Palestine question, refuse to grant a supply and hold back. The King "is only bluffing" proclaimed one State Department spokesman, who added that we can "always get the oil from Iran."

These American foreign service officers were also undoubtedly counting on past Arab weaknesses—corruption and venality, enabling almost every American oil company to have one Arab in his back pocket upon whom he could count—to throw a wrench into the works whenever Arab unity seemed to be making headway. But they underestimated Faisal's determination to right Arab honor, heightened no little both by the King's role in having encouraged Sadat to remove the Soviet influence as well as his keen awareness of the Palestinian presence that had figured in the two attempted summer conspiracies against him by officers of the Saudi Air Force. Along with many of the leading Saudi politicians and businessmen, Faisal was determined to do everything to find an end to the debilitating and dangerous Palestine question and to be able to pray once again in the Al-Aksa Mosque in occupied East Jerusalem.

In response to a press question, Nixon was now forced to admit that "we presently depend upon oil in the Middle East—we depend on it not, of course, nearly as much as Europe, but we're all in the same bag when you really come down to it." (Nixon was to find out sadly later that Europe chose not to remain in the same bag, if indeed they ever were.)

Both in this press conference[35] and in a message to Congress asking for action on seven proposals, including the Alaska pipeline, the President emphasized the importance of tackling the energy problem facing the country. The President confessed that the energy shortage was "tied up with the Arab-Israeli dispute," and that both he and Kissinger, at that time his nominee as Secretary of State, were assigning "highest priority" to making some progress toward a settlement. And deep concern was expressed over Saudi Arabia's refusal to hold production at the current level, let alone not raise it to the twenty million daily barrels sought by the West, unless the U.S. applied pressure to Israel.

Confronted with a direct question as to the possibility that "the threat of limiting the supply of oil might cause a moderation of U.S. support of Israel," the President neatly ducked a direct answer by saying it would be "highly inappropriate" for an American President to "relate our policy toward Israel" to what happens to Arab oil (a seeming inconsistency with his previous remark). Declaring that the U.S. continued to be "dedicated to the independence of Israel," the President warned:

Israel simply can't wait for the dust to settle. The Arabs can't wait for the dust to settle in the Mid-East. Both sides are at fault, both sides need to start negotiating. That is our position. We are not pro-Israel and we are not pro-Arab. And we're not any more pro-Arab because they have oil and Israel hasn't.

We are pro-peace. And it's in the interests of the whole area for us to get these negotiations off dead center. That's why we will use our influence with Israel, and we will use our—what influence we have—with the various Arab states to get these negotiations on. Now, one of the dividends of having successful negotiations will be to reduce the oil pressure.[36]

Arab oil policy was becoming more militant. OPEC in mid-September 1977 at a meeting in Vienna not only raised prices but declared support for Libya's nationalization move, warning of "appropriate measures" should oil companies take action against Tripoli's decision.[37] And even as Zionist brainwashing of the American public continued unabatingly, it was becoming more obvious that the Arab states would resort to the one sure weapon at their command—oil. While observers still contended that the Arabs could not "drink their oil" and propagandists insisted that the U.S. was only to the smallest degree dependent on their oil, the Arab states continued to raise the posted prices—the drastic increases to the oil companies being passed along to the consumer—and to lay the groundwork for the eventuality of a total petroleum cutoff if necessary.

The vision of oil as a political weapon, once held only by such Arab "radicals" as former Saudi Arabian Minister of Petroleum Abdullah Tariki, was now assuming a bandwagon movement as even moderate Arabs demanded militancy toward the West. Pressure was being exerted successfully on Faisal—and on Sadat, too—and from nonterrorist Palestinian elements. The Arab petroleum-exporting nations were described in a determined mood by Dr. Nadim Pachachi, former

Secretary-General of OPEC: "We would not be consistent with ourselves if we agreed to help a country that has no qualms or scruples
in helping our political foe. If the U.S. abandoned the policy of blind
support to Israel, there would not be any need to speak of security or
insecurity of supply."

Sadat's diplomacy was yielding rewards and new strength. He
persuaded Saudi Arabia's ruler to use oil and financial resources as a
big stick in behalf of the Arab cause and as the important bargaining
lever in whatever negotiations might develop from either the reac-
tivated Jarring mission or the fresh U.S. initiative to be undertaken by
newly-designated Secretary Kissinger. Inspired by Nixon's begrudging
recognition of the linkage between the energy crisis and U.S. policy,
the Arabs had begun to pull together for the first time since Nasser's
death.

With the new Egyptian-Saudi amity came financial backing for
Cairo's depressed economic structure and a tacit recognition of
Faisal's leadership in a realigned Arab world. Qaddafi's goal of immediate unification of Egypt and Libya was soon reduced to a proclamation of a new state, with the actual unification through a joint constituent assembly and one chief of state put off to some future indefinite
date.[38]

The healing of the breach with Amman by both Cairo and Damascus marked another important step toward mobilizing total Arab resources for a possible conflict with Israel and the recapture of Arab
territories. When Hussein began his campaign to prevent the Palestinians from operating inside his country in 1970 and the bitter internecine warfare ensued, first Syria and then Egypt had broken off diplomatic relations with the Hashemite ruler. For all practical purposes,
the eastern military front against Israel became a dead issue. Hussein's
meeting in Cairo with Sadat and Syrian President Hafez al-Assad
revived the possibilities of a common total approach against Israel.
The repaired amity had been strengthened by granting amnesty to
Palestinian guerrilla fighters, including leader Daoud Odeh, languish-
ing in Jordanian prisons.

While many Palestinians skeptically viewed the quarreling among
their brother Arabs as moves toward strengthening themselves for a
political settlement to which the refugee movement was then vehemently opposed, the new euphoria flowing from the use of oil as the
big leverage, inspired a period of internal Arab harmony.

Zionist writers, overtaken by the invariable paroxysms of fear
whenever inter-Arab cooperation replaced normal internal warfare,

overexploded with gall at the new "Faisal-Sadat axis," when the Saudi monarch included Yasir Arafat in a receiving line at a diplomatic reception in Jeddah, "forcing shocked foreign diplomats, including Nicholas Thatcher, to greet him." Of course, it remained to be seen whether Arab discipline would be developed to the point where the Arabs would, in the words of Teddy Roosevelt, really be "speaking softly as they carried a big stick."

The new Nixon peace initiative had indeed added to incipient Zionist fears that the U.S. might really be adopting a new tougher line toward Israel. In joining in the Security Council censure of Israel, the US had failed to insist upon balancing the Israeli misdeed with "the long history of terrorist activity"—the invariable standard followed by Washington in past voting at the U.N., including its July veto.

Despite the campaign of suppression, the Miller socal letter had stirred some influential stockholders, and the Zionist panic button was really pushed with the wide publicity given to Assistant Secretary of State Joseph J. Sisco's declaration over Israeli television:

We have important political, economic, and strategic interests in the entire area, whether in the Middle East, the Persian Gulf, or the Arabian Peninsula. There is increasing concern in our country over the energy crisis, and I believe that it is foolhardy to believe that it is not a factor.

To this was added the caution of former Secretary of Commerce Peter G. Peterson that the U.S. must understand "the Arab view that American policy too often sounds like an echo of Israeli policy" which drew instantaneous angry Zionist fire.[39]

While the *New York Times* and NBC spread the meaningless talk of the possibility of developing alternate sources of energy as an answer to the immediate problem,[40] Secretary of State-designate Kissinger admitted he could see "no near-term alternative to increasing imports of oil from the Middle East." Nixon, however, still preferred to describe the growing shortages as "a problem, not a crisis." To the repeated White House suggestion that an answer could be found by expanding domestic supplies and improving research, petroleum experts replied: "It is not only not true, but it is nonsense—dangerous nonsense! If you do not accept the idea that there is a valid crisis, you can hardly be expected to take the kinds of steps necessary to solve it."

By late September the new Nixon initiative seemed stalled and the Middle East status quo engrained. The ten-day visit of U.N. Secretary-General Kurt Waldheim to Israel, Egypt, Syria, Lebanon, and Jordan had yielded very little beyond expressions of hope. Upon his return to

U.N. headquarters in New York, he indicated that the Jarring mission would continue its efforts, but if the international diplomat had received any evidence that the past deadlock could be resolved, he revealed no details. Israel still refused to submit the sought-after commitment to withdraw to the borders that existed before the 1967 Arab-Israeli war.

Israel was still rejecting all prodding from the State Department that she produce some fresh ideas to break the stalemate. In a last interview in New York before returning home, Foreign Minister Eban had stuck stubbornly to the policy of "unconditional talks with the understanding beforehand that Israel would not withdraw from all territory occupied since the 1967 war." Eban contemptuously dismissed the contention that there was any connection between the energy shortage facing the U.S. and events in the Middle East. "Oil companies," the veteran diplomat noted, "should devote more attention to research and analysis rather than become amateur diplomats."

Casting further shadows on hopes for a settlement, Israel more than ever regarded the occupied territories as her own national lands. In every way the cease-fire lines were fast becoming de facto borders as Israel announced she would continue to build Jewish settlements and to sell lands to Jews in the occupied territories, a project advanced by Defense Minister Moshe Dayan. This came at the very same time as Tel Aviv was curbing the hiring of Arab farm labor by Israeli settlers in the occupied Arab territories and limiting the visitations by civilians to the new Israeli agriculture settlements, both "on security grounds."

More than a year had passed since Sadat's summary expulsion of the Soviet military advisers, and there had been as yet no honest Washington effort to pressure Israel into withdrawing from Arab territories. The national elections were long since over, and the decisive reelection of President Nixon ought to have freed the incumbent from the power of the Jewish bloc. But still there had been scarcely a move away from Washington's "Israel-First" position. The U.S. veto at the Security Council had thwarted the Egyptian effort to force Israel's withdrawal. And the Kissinger luncheon given for Arab League members the second week of the new General Assembly session brought no encouraging news, only more inconsequential language.

Its long campaign on the diplomatic front to induce an Israeli pullback having been a total failure, Cairo now moved ahead with plans to put Washington on the spot as war became inevitable.[41] The Egyptians sincerely believed that in a Middle East conflict the U.S. would be forced to stand by the principle of the inadmissibility of territory by conquest, and that a war with Israel, however painful it might be for Egypt, would force the Big Powers to intervene and bring about a settlement returning the occupied territories. Doing nothing would yield nothing.

The Egyptian leader solidified his relations with Saudi Arabia and prepared with Syria to put their war plans into effect. In the final analysis, it could be said that the October nineteen-day war had its roots in President Sadat's frustrations. He had incessantly threatened action for three years to recover Egyptian territories under Israeli occupation for six years but had done nothing until he moved, silently and precisely, on the morning of October 5, 1973.

XIX   War Again

In a world of wolves one must be a fox.

—Niccolò Machiavelli

Reports of the arrival of a large number of Soviet transport ships in Cairo and of Syrian tank movements in late September 1973 caused Washington a bit of concern. But exchanges of intelligence information between the U.S. and Israel revealed as late as September 29, a "defensive Syrian posture." And at the time in these circles, Sadat was being called a "clown," Faisal a "religious fanatic."

On Friday, October 5, the day before the war broke out, the Israelis too were sensing danger, but they were not certain. Their usually superb intelligence had learned of unusual Arab troop deployment, but apparently had failed in calculating the intentions of the enemy. Chief of Staff General David Elazer canceled all military leaves. General Ariel Sharon was recalled from retirement at his Beersheba farm, but no call for general mobilization was issued. In defense of this failure, the Israeli Establishment later contended that they had bowed to the repeated warnings from Secretary Kissinger that under no circumstances were they to "start the war—don't ever preempt." (Israelis, of course, had been similarly cautioned by President Johnson in 1967, and had then ignored Washington.) It was Meir who was said to have overruled Dayan and his Chief of Staff in maintaining the posture demanded by Kissinger.

The Secretary himself misread the evidence that war was coming.[1] He was incommunicado at the Waldorf Astoria in New York when the Department of State's Intelligence Bureau indicated the conflict was but a few hours away. The attack was launched by the Egyptians shortly before 12:00 G.M.T. on what in Israel was the Yom Kippur and in the Arab world was Ramadan. The onslaught fell on the 1,350th anniver-

614

sary of the Battle of Badr, which launched Mohammed's triumphal entry into Mecca. This was the reason the day had been chosen, even though it was in the middle of Ramadan when Arab fighters are not at their best, not because it was the holiest Jewish day of the year.

Having the advantage of surprise and having set up pontoon bridges for their tanks and heavy armaments, the Egyptians crossed the Suez Canal, then overran the defenders and the vaunted Bar-Lev line with its chain of twenty forticiations. The Syrians, too, were pushing ahead on the front they had opened on the Golan plateau. The Western press assailed the "Arab invasion of Israel"; only the *Christian Science Monitor* indicated the conflict had been launched onto Israeli-held territories.

In 1967 the Security Council had met within hours of the outbreak of fighting, but in 1973 they did not meet until the evening of the third day, and then did not adopt a resolution until seventeen days after the war had begun. Neither Big Power seemed anxious to bring about an immediate cease-fire as they had in the earlier war, each sensing some advantage in keeping the fighting going. For the Soviets, their wards —or former wards—were making progress. The U.S. perhaps saw in the initial gain of the Arabs an opportunity to exercise leverage on Israel to comply with the withdrawal provisions of Resolution 242. It was also possible that Washington delayed taking action to permit Israel to gain the upper hand after the initial retreat and the surprise Egyptian crossing of the Canal. The Pentagon was convinced that Israel would shortly gain the offensive and push the Arabs back to where they had been at the end of the 1967 war.

When the Security Council first met on October 8, the Soviet and U.S. representatives were miles apart, and hopes for a U.N. cease-fire were dim. Only Austria and Australia seemed to favor such a course. The other eight nonpermanent members, including the Sudan, were in no hurry to join in any demand for stoppage of the war. The Soviet-Arab position, supported by most of the non-permanent members, would have called on Israel to withdraw from all occupied territories as well as accept a cease-fire. But such a draft resolution was known to face a certain American veto. The Arabs, the Soviet Union, and their friends, together with most of the neutrals, were determined that the current fighting be used as a means of implementing Resolution 242 and bringing about the long sought-after Israeli withdrawal.

While calling for a halt in fighting, the U.S. did not push hard for a cease-fire. Kissinger shared the Pentagon view that Israel would win a quick victory, and he never envisioned the necessity of a massive emergency pipeline of supplies for Israel. The Secretary did intervene with the Pentagon to permit Israeli planes to land in the U.S. to pick up ammunition and spare parts (the tails of the supply planes had to be painted over to hide the identifying six-pointed star) at the Oceana Naval Air Station in Virginia Beach.

Meanwhile, massive Soviet airlifts to assist the Arabs were arriving in Arab ports and near the battlefield as relations between the Super Powers became extremely strained. At an important dinner meeting in Washington, Kissinger warned that "détente cannot survive irresponsibility in any area, including the Middle East."[2]

Upon his return from Israel on October 8, three days after the war began, Israeli Ambassador Simcha Dinitz maintained unrelenting pressure on both the Pentagon and the State Department to expedite delivery of some of the forty-eight Phantoms promised to Israel on Meir's last visit, together with replacements for both jets and Skyhawks lost in battle. Reports of further Soviet airlifts and Dinitz persistence brought a U.S. agreement on the sixth day of the war to use twenty U.S. military planes to fly emergency supplies and planes to Israel after private U.S. companies had refused to become involved in any charter arrangements.

Kissinger saw the need of correcting the "military imbalance." CIA reports on the 12th that the Russians had mobilized three airborne divisions strengthened the Secretary of State's hand in dealing with Defense Secretary Schlesinger, who at least at this stage had been resisting Ambassador Dinitz's demands for more than the sixteen Phantoms to replace losses that had taken place. His deputy, William Clements, had told Dinitz "he needed more information about American inventories before he could provide the Israelis with an exact timetable for deliveries."[3]

What to the impatient Israelis were bureaucratic difficulties accounting for the delays was actually weighted consideration of U.S. needs by the Pentagon. Secretary Schlesinger himself was said to have cautioned the Ambassador that the U.S. had to operate "in a low profile in order not to create an Arab reaction"—an unmistakable allusion to oil.

Dinitz kept prodding Kissinger to prod Schlesinger: "These delays are costing lives. Who's playing games?"[4] In his sometimes hourly telephone calls and visits to Kissinger, the Israeli diplomat never hesitated to imply that he could "always appeal to a large group of congressmen and columnists, most of whom were not Jewish" for assistance. Kissinger is said to have referred humorously to these as Dinitz's "shock troops."

Supported by varied outcries from Congress demanding all-out support for Israel, Dinitz laid down the law: "If a massive American airlift to Israel does not start immediately, then I will know that the U.S. is reneging on its promises and its policy, and we will have to draw very serious conclusions from all this."[5] The determined Israeli, in close touch with the "Israel-First" bloc on the Hill, further warned that Washington's failure to keep its word would precipitate a "crisis in Israeli-American relations." The Ambassador threatened "to go public," to carry Israel's case to the Congress and the American people, which would have been disastrous to an already badly Watergate-battered administration. Kissinger saw to it that the Israeli timetable was met.

President Nixon ordered his aide, General Alexander Haig, to make sure that at least ten of the Phantoms reached Israel by midnight Sunday, the deadline for the start of Israel's counterattack. To achieve this, giant C-5 transports were employed, the U.S. answer to the Soviet's Antonov 22s. Kissinger made certain that more planes followed, even though four out of the first fourteen had come out of America's own inventory; the Secretary was determined to match and exceed the Soviets in volume and sophistication of weapons pouring into the Middle East.

No wonder that one cynic remarked that Big Power involvement in the October war was calculated solely to test their new weapons. And U.S. officers claimed that the Pentagon learned more about Soviet weapons in the seventeen days of this combat than in seven years of Vietnam.

The Israelis had halted the Egyptian advance after an epic tank battle, in scale overshadowing the famed Alamein conflict of World War II, and were pushing back the Syrians when giant cargo aircraft, from bases across the U.S., ferried their 100-ton payloads via Lajes Airfield in the Azores to landing strips in Israel and occupied Sinai.

The tide of battle turned drastically in Israel's favor. The Egyptians had paid dearly for fatal tactical failure, allegedly Russian strategy, to move forward immediately in the Sinai and attack Mitla and Gidi passes rather than waiting to regroup, which gave the Israelis time to bring up new forces and stem the Egyptian advance. One U.S. analyst said: "The Egyptians could have overwhelmed the Israeli defenses while they were still weak, taking the desert passes and making some bold armor thrusts to annihilate the Israeli tanks and artillery."

In an address before the People's Assembly on the eleventh day of the war, Sadat declared, as an open message to President Nixon, that he was ready to accept a cease-fire based on the principle of immediate Israeli withdrawal to the pre-June 5 borders, to open the Suez Canal and to attend a U.N. peace conference. Israeli and Egyptian tanks were still locked in a bitter battle on the Sinai Peninsula. With increasing Israeli air superiority the decisive factor, Israeli ground forces under General Sharon forced their way across to the West Bank of the Canal, knocked out SAM missile sites in the Bitter Lakes region, and cleared the way for air power and a vital bridgehead. The consolidation of Israeli forces on the West Bank of the Canal drove a wedge between Egyptian forces and established a salient at Deversoir. The Third Egyptian Army on the Israeli side of the Canal was being squeezed into a pocket as the Israelis widened their bridgehead on the West Bank and poured down from the north on the east side of the Canal.

The Big Two had been moving toward a cease-fire. But before they agreed on a formula for stopping the war, Kosygin visited with Sadat and Kissinger with the Israelis. The Secretary of State offered an enticing lollipop by way of direct Arab-Israeli negotiations at a peace conference rather than through third parties. Then the two leaders met in Moscow to pin down the cease-fire. Through his trip to Moscow, Kissinger brought Israel an extra seventy-two hours to improve her military situation, which he later boasted about in his December confidential talk with Jewish intellectuals in New York.[6]

The new Security Council Resolution 338 of October 22 provided for an immediate cease-fire to take place within twelve hours in the positions then occupied, and called upon the parties concerned to start the implementation of Security Council Resolution 242 "in all of its parts" immediately after the cease-fire. However, it did not attempt to clarify the alleged ambiguity inherent in the phrase "withdrawal from occupied territories."[7]

The Palestinians, who had figured little in the war and seemed almost the forgotten people, were brought into the picture by new thinking enlarging upon the 1967 concept of Palestinians only as refugees under Resolution 242. In accepting the October 22 cease-fire, Sadat talked of the "legitimate rights of the Palestinians," and two days later in his acceptance Syrian President Assad still further broadened the concept to the "legitimate national rights of the Palestinians." Moscow, too, made its bid, and in its talks with the leaders of the PLO indicated it would accord recognition to them as the legal spokesman for the Palestinians. The Kremlin's formula was spelled out in terms of "the rights and interests of the Palestinian people." And for the first time the Palestinian leaders, with the exception of the PFLP's George Habash, seemed inclined to consider the gradualist political approach, long preached by President Habib Bourguiba of Tunisia, of starting with a possible West Bank-Gaza state as a first step toward reunifying Palestine as the homeland of both Arabs and Jews.

The October cease-fire was flouted by Israel, which stepped up the fighting between Ismailia and Port Suez in order to completely cut off the Egyptian army on the East Bank. A second U.N. resolution, 339 of October 23, called on the combatants to return to the cease-fire positions of October 22 and provided for a U.N. emergency police force to supervise the cease-fire rather than the observer group authorized by the resolution of the day before. This still did not bring an end to the fighting nor halt the advancing Israeli army. Sadat became panic-stricken as the position of his beleaguered forces worsened. In the absence of any U.N. truce supervision forces, he radioed an urgent appeal to Washington and to Moscow to send a joint Soviet-American force to police the cease-fire. Kissinger and the U.S. had long been on record as opposed to any action that would bring Soviet Union troops into the area, necessitating similar action on the part of the U.S. with all the dangers implicit therein.

The Kremlin accepted the Sadat appeal and had Soviet Ambassador Dobrynin deliver at 9:25 on the same evening, October 24, the following urgent personal note to Nixon:

Let us together dispatch Soviet and American contingents to Egypt. Israel is brazenly challenging both the Soviet Union and the United States. We cannot allow arbitrariness on Israel's part. I will say it straight, that if you find it impossible to act together with us in this matter, we should be faced with the necessity urgently to consider the question of taking appropriate steps unilaterally. Israel cannot be permitted to get away with the violations.

That same day four more Soviet airborne divisions were put on alert, and five or six Soviet transport ships allegedly were seen crossing into the Mediterranean, raising the Russian naval presence to an unprecedented eighty-five. U.S. intelligence viewed with alarm the Soviet activization of two mechanized divisions near the Black Sea. Washington could see trouble in the wind.

The National Security Council met in the White House at 11 P.M. and declared a national military alert. Nixon was upstairs in his quarters but had authorized his Secretary of State to take whatever action was necessary. Defense Secretary Schlesinger, CIA Chief William Colby, Chairman of the Joint Chiefs of Staff Admiral Thomas Moorer, White House Chief of Staff Alexander Haig, and Brigadier General Brent Scowcroft concurred in the Kissinger decision, which was relayed to Nixon. U.S. ground, sea, and air forces, conventional as well as nuclear, were placed on military alert.

Although the second Middle East cease-fire had gone into effect, the world now stood on the precipice of a nuclear confrontation. The aircraft carrier *John F. Kennedy* with dozens of A-4 attack jets was dispatched toward the Mediterranean; B-52 bombers were ordered from Guam to the U.S.; 15,000 troops of the 82nd Airborne based at North Carolina were added to the alert and were told to be ready by 6:00 A.M. The entire Strategic Air Command (SAC), with its nuclear strike forces, was likewise put on alert. At a press conference called at noon the next day and carried nationwide by television and radio, the Secretary vigorously denied that the alert might have been prompted by "domestic requirements" (Watergate), and declared the U.S. nuclear forces had been placed on a stand-by alert around the world in an effort "to dissuade Russia from taking unilateral action in the Middle East." (Nothing was said about the necessity to safeguard the U.N. cease-fire.) And Kissinger added:

We possess each of us nuclear arsenals capable of annihilating humanity. We, both of us, have a special duty to see to it that confrontations are kept within bounds that do not threaten civilized life [Note: Exactly as Metternich would have phrased it. A Secretary of State had, one would think, a special duty to avoid confrontations rather than merely keeping them within bounds.] Both of us, sooner or later, will have to come to realize that the issues that divide the world today, and foreseeable issues, do not justify the unparalleled catastrophe that a nuclear war would represent.

Then, extending the olive branch, Kissinger declared: "We do not consider ourselves in a confrontation with the Soviet Union. We do not believe it is necessary at this moment to have a confrontation." When the Security Council adopted Resolution 340 setting up a U.N. emergency police force, which specifically barred the personnel of permanent members of the Security Council, the crisis abated. The U.S. called off the military alert the next day, although Soviet airborne units had not been returned to their prealert status. Nixon in a prime-time TV news conference, in which he emotionally lashed out at the media for its Watergate coverage, still implied that Moscow had not only threatened the U.S. but that the Soviet Union "was planning to send a very substantial force into the Mideast—a military force."

Both the President and Kissinger had highlighted the infinitely dreadful implications of the alert for all peoples as the possible initial step toward doomsday for much of the world. Yet the decision was handily staged with such dreadful casualness and inadequacy.

As of two weeks earlier, at the time of the airlift to Israel, U.S. allies were given no notice whatsoever. There had been no prior consultation with NATO countries or Japan, although they could have been targets of nuclear missiles, housing as they did U.S. military forces that had been placed on military alert. The U.S. defense of Israel had left them open to attack from the Arabs and then the Soviet Union. These countries had their own interests in the Middle East and had opted for neutrality,[8] which Washington violated by shipping huge amounts of war matériel to Israel.

Philadelphia lawyer-critic Hamilton A. Long leveled an accusation against the President and Kissinger that cannot be lightly dismissed. He charged them with having acted with "criminal wanton recklessness, if not sheer madness, causing U.S. military personnel worldwide to assume that war actually threatened any moment, to stand ready for instant action, with itchy finger on nuclear triggers." Many shared the view that the alert was "a monumental fraud" to create a cover-up at a time when the Watergate disclosures were most seriously affecting Nixon.[9] A post-facto examination of the facts lends support to the view that, at the least, the administration and its several intelligence arms had misread the Russian signals and had strongly overreacted.

In the Brezhnev note to the President, the Soviet leader merely stated that if the U.S. refused to join in sending troops to enforce the cease-fire (which was certainly being ignored by Israel, if not by both sides), "we should be faced with the necessity to *consider the question* of taking appropriate steps unilaterally." [Italics added] Kissinger ignored the patent Soviet hedge and chose to interpret it as a bald threat of unilateral action. Although the Kremlin had requested a prompt reply to its proposal, none was sent before issuing the alert that night. Then the U.S. answer addressed itself only to the charge that Israel was violating the cease-fire, which the Secretary of State denied.

The Soviet message meant, at worst, a U.S.-U.S.S.R. joint enforcement of the U.N. cease-fire in Arab lands, or by the U.S.S.R. alone if the U.S. declined to act, and it had been couched in soft language, requesting U.S. cooperation. Only if this was not forthcoming would the Kremlin then "*consider* the question of taking appropriate steps." (Emphasis added.)

Prior to calling the nuclear war alert, the U.S. had made no attempt to discuss the Kremlin proposal. The Soviet Ambassador in Washington was not telephoned, although he had personally delivered his chieftain's message. Nor was the hot line used; it had served an important purpose as a direct connection between the White House and Pentagon with the Kremlin in the Cuban missile crisis of 1963 and again during the 1967 war. The meeting at which the very serious U.S. decision had been made in the White House lasted all of thirty minutes, and it was only some fifty-five minutes from the time the Kremlin message had first reached Kissinger.

At his press conference on the 25th, Kissinger had promised that within a week the full facts behind the alert would be bared to reporters and the public. Under the pretext of a reluctance to engage in further controversy with the Soviet Union, no such disclosure was ever made. At a subsequent press conference four weeks later, the Secretary of State brazenly scoffed at the value and meaningfulness of his own press statements and said he "regretted" having made this promise. No "useful purpose could be served" by telling the people these details, he concluded.

The military alert dramatically illustrated the stupendous power exercised by Israel. Kissinger had consistently maintained that his primary goal was success in the SALT talks, looking toward limiting the use and manufacture of nuclear weapons, with the immediate purpose to get the Soviet Union to "become more flexible, more sensible, more willing to engage in meaningful discussion with us." Yet his overweening concern for Israel, egged on by the "Israel-First" bloc in Congress, had forced him to endanger this most constructive goal—first through an unprecedented airlift, which dropped supplies literally on the battlefield and made the U.S. military a near appendage of the Israeli army, and which in turn brought on the foreseeable Soviet countermeasured arms escalation, and then through an alert that threatened the annihilation of mankind.

On October 7, the second day of the fighting, Iraq nationalized the 23.75 percent share in the Basra Petroleum Company held by U.S. companies Exxon and Mobil. The next day Syria and Lebanon suspended oil shipments passing through their pipelines. On October 16, the day after the U.S. airlift had begun to pour 800 tons a day of military supplies into Israel to turn the tide of battle, six Arabian Gulf producers—Abu Dhabi, Iran, Iraq, Kuwait, Qatar, and Saudi Arabia—announced an immediate 17 percent increase in the price of their crude oil. This amounted to a staggering $2 per barrel increase on light crude and marked the first time that the producers had unilaterally set the posted prices for oil. The following day the five Arab producing states announced a cut of no less than 5 percent of the September production and the maintenance of the same rate of reduction each month thereafter "until such time as the international community compels Israel to relinquish our occupied territories."[10] Countries who had helped the Arab "just cause" were not to be made to suffer, while countries who continued to "demonstrate moral and material support to the Israeli enemy" were to be subjected "to severe and progressive reduction in Arab oil supplies, leading to a complete halt."

Nixon's special message to Congress the following day requesting $2.2 million as emergency military aid for Israel was answered with further Arab production cuts. Then, on the basis "of the massive arms supplies and facilities in helping the transport of the U.S. supply of deadly sophisticated war matériel to Israel by air and sea," the Arab countries individually declared that a total embargo on oil exports to the U.S. and Holland was in effect. King Faisal's patience had become exhausted.[11] Saudi Arabia, whose daily production had reached 8.2 million barrels in September, the base to be used for the production cuts, soon lowered her oil outflow to 5.8 million barrels. In early November the Arab states agreed on further production cuts.

The Arab oil producers' decision would have been worse for the U.S. had militants prevailed over the moderate Saudi approach. Measures demanded by Iraq and Libya included withdrawal of all Arab deposits from U.S. banks, massive sales of Arab dollars on the international market to injure the American currency standing (some of which was undoubtedly done on an unofficial basis), and a total import boycott of goods from the U.S. and other pro-Israel countries. One Arab nationalist-minded newspaper reminded its readers:

It is no secret that the huge Arab reserves in the banks of Europe constitute an efficient financial weight. Such balances should be directed against the American interests in an attempt to put an end to the provocative American attitudes toward the Arabs, as well as to the false empire of the U.S. dollar. The Arab world should, without any restrictions, enter the Arab-Zionist conflict and use their effective weapon against the enemies of the Arabs and their allies.

There were even some insistent demands for a takeover of 51 percent of all American assets on Arab soil. No doubt veiled threats of U.S. intervention, hinted in certain statements and implicit in Senator Fulbright's disclosure of contingent Pentagon military plans for a takeover by American surrogates (Israel and/or Iran), were important factors moderating Arab decisionmaking at this time.

The first official energy statements, both local and federal, in concert with Zionist propagandists, belittled the effect of the Arab embargo, asserting that only about 6 percent of American imports was involved. Yet with the passage of each day of the embargo as the oil noose tightened, it became more obvious that John Doe Public had not been given the true facts. U.S. Energy Adviser John Love was forced to admit the crisis to be "far more serious than thought a week ago." The plain fact was that in 1972 Arab countries had directly supplied 9.5 percent of U.S. imports, and that did not include large quantities of Arab crude sent to Europe and then transshipped as fuel oil to the States. Thus total American dependence on Arab oil was already closer to 15 percent.

U.S. and European efforts to circumvent the effects of the embargo by creating an oil-users' cartel resulted in the same fate as had befallen John Foster Dulles' "Suez Canal Users" folly in the fall of 1956 prior to the first Suez war. Fear, always heretofore a stalwart ally of the Zionists, now became an invaluable tool of Arab economic warfare against Israel, as embargoed states carefully avoided any collaborative action that might inspire further Arab reprisals against them.

Zionist fear of an Arab oil embargo and the possible effect on Israel's position had been assuaged by Israeli Foreign Minister Abba Eban's Miami Beach reassurances prior to the outbreak of fighting: "There is not the slightest possibility that the Arab countries would withhold oil from the U.S. The oil-buying countries have alternate places in which to buy; the Arab states have no alternative but to sell their oil because they have no other resources at all. . . ."[12] This was an echo of "the Arabs can't eat their petroleum," which had been reverberating for months in the press.

The day after the war started, Jewish leaders meeting in New York's Plaza Hotel at a special emergency meeting cheered the Foreign Minister as he demanded: "Will there be a massive demonstration of Jewish solidarity? Of Jewish indignation? The answer is in your hands." In reply, Jacob Stein, Chairman of the Conference of Presidents of Major American Jewish Organizations, insisted: "The American Jewish community stands today ready for any challenge put before it to come to the aid of Israel no matter what effort or commitment."

No sooner had the oil embargo begun and the energy crisis wors-

ened than the leaders of various Jewish service organizations commenced an all-out campaign to abort any adverse American reaction
to Washington's Middle East policy. On the sixtieth anniversary of the
ADL on November 15, the group's National Chairman told a crowded
audience: "The Arab states, with the skillful assistance of the Soviet
Union, are using oil to drive a wedge between Israel and the U.S. and
to picture American Jews as those to be held responsible for empty gas
tanks and unheated homes this winter."[13]

The American Jewish Committee widely distributed pamphlets
designed to show that the Arab world embargo was only a minor factor
in the "energy crisis." The Conference of Presidents issued its own
Middle East memo in mid-February entitled "The Energy Crisis—
Who's to Blame?" They extracted articles from a *New York Times* report
that attributed the oil shortage to many causes other than the Arab
embargo.

The cover-up to prevent the American people from finding out
why they had been undergoing unnecessary hardships continued long
after the Arab oil embargo had been lifted, with gasoline rationing
ended and gas stations no longer closed on Sunday. The American
Jewish Congress, the oldest defender of Jewish nationalism in tracts
and advertisements, maintained, "It is clearly understood that Israel
is not to blame . . . the present oil shortage by the Arab oil sheikhdoms
has nothing to do with political events in the Middle East." Meetings,
letters to the editor, advertisements, and other pressure-group activities, all of which were widely covered by the media, were directed
toward this end. Almost the sole offset to this great influence on
unknowledgeable Americans were bumper stickers attainable only by
mail from a few questionable Midwest organizations, which stated "Oil
Yes—Israel No." The motivations impelling this campaign were indeed highly dubious.

The American people were deeply disturbed over the energy
crunch, and some few were even seeing the linkage to U.S. partiality
in the Middle East conflict, although there had been no campaign to
explain the motivations of King Faisal and the other Arab embargoists
to the American people. Due to the skillful Zionist-Israelist cover-up
propaganda, and the corresponding inexpert, abysmal Arab public
relations, most Americans were kept unaware of the inescapable facts.
The occasionally widely quoted remarks of charismatic Saudi Minister
of Petroleum Yamani, who obviously had a personal axe to grind,
scarcely filled the void. There were no American voices speaking out
in terms of American interests to go along with Yamani's words, and

to give emphasis to his statement: "I assure you if we can solve the Israeli problem, the price of oil will come down."

Granted that U.S. national energy planning had been grossly shortsighted and that Americans had been criminally negligent in wastage of resources, they would then still have had all the gasoline needed for their cars, all the heat for their homes, and all the oil for their industrial complex—and would not have been as threatened by a serious recession—had it not been for the U.S. "Israel-First" policy. Aside from Harvard Professor Thomas R. Stauffer, whose views went untrumpeted, very few dared adopt the slogan "interdependence" instead of "independence"[14] and admit that the sole source of meeting U.S. increasing petroleum needs for the coming decade was the Arab world, with whom the U.S. was virtually at war.

The $2.2 billion legislation in military grants/loans to cover the costs of the October airlift and to continue the military flow so as to maintain Israel's superiority had another devastating effect: The shipment of military supplies to Israel had dangerously impaired U.S. capabilities. Huge stocks of armaments were rushed out of U.S. and NATO reserves. Some 1,000 late-model M-60 tanks—an equivalent of three years production—were airlifted from U.S. military depots in West Germany and flown to the Middle East battlefield. What was given away in six weeks was found to be most difficult to replace, as American industry was unable or unwilling to manufacture castings to expand this production.[15] The concern for U.S. needs had been one of the factors behind the hesitancy of the Defense Department and of Secretary Schlesinger in meeting the Dinitz-Kissinger demands that the airlift proceed without any delay. A large number of F-4 fighter aircraft, M-48 tanks, and nearly half the highly sophisticated TOW antitank missiles were also airlifted together with other weapons.

As part of the postconflict shipment, the U.S. agreed to provide Israel advanced surface-to-surface ballistic missiles; high-performance fighter aircraft; decoy, reconnaissance, and strike remotely piloted vehicles; and tactical missiles. Additional Phantoms and new armored personnel carriers, vital to the multifronted defense system, were also on Israel's list, most of which have been since sent.

An authoritative Pentagon source later declared that "the depletion of the U.S. arsenal for the benefit of Israel during the October war left our country without a single combat-ready division anywhere." The Zionist lobby, responsible for this serious military drain, was what Chairman of the Joint Chiefs of Staff George S. Brown had been talking about in his Duke Law School controversial reference, for which he had become a member of the very exclusive "those who have been blitzed by the Zionists" club (see pages 444–448).

While the American people were unaware how vital the U.S. supply airlift had been to Israel, the military leaders in Tel Aviv never lost sight of the fact. The second cease-fire did not end the fighting; Israeli forces continued to encircle the entrapped Egyptian Third Corps, which in turn tried to break out of the Israeli encirclement. For purposes of bringing the Arabs to the negotiating table to face the Israelis, Kissinger did not wish to deprive the Egyptians of the feeling that they had won at least a moral victory in exposing the noninvincibility of Israeli military might. He insisted that the Israelis permit food, water, and medicine through the U.N. cease-fire lines to the beleaguered Egyptian forces.

Israeli Defense Minister Moshe Dayan's first response was: "This is absurd. We are at war, and you ask us to supply our enemy." But Kissinger was said to have warned: "If you don't supply them, then we will supply them. Furthermore, you will have to wage your next war alone." As Dayan told the Knesset on October 30: "The supply of the Third Army with food was undertaken by us not in a humanitarian manner but rather because we had no choice in the question. The other choices, to be more precise, were worse." Only the day before Premier Meir was quoted as saying during a visit to the troops at the Suez Canal: "It was perfectly clear that the Americans would not take with any specific pleasure our negative answer, and as it is known, we haven't got any particular surplus of friends around the world. The U.S. since 1970 has been our supplier, essential to our army. . . ." And so, once again, as in the very rare instance of the 1953 Eisenhower days when Israel had defied the U.N. edict against the diversion of waters in the demilitarized zone between Israel and Syria in the vicinity of Lake Huleh, American pressure had been forcefully and successfully brought to bear on Israel—behind the scenes, of course, lest the Zionist apparatus be aroused and seek to undermine Washington determination.

With Egyptian pride saved and a total cease-fire in effect after an agreement was finally reached at Kilo 101 on the Suez-Cairo road by the Egyptian and Israelis on November 15,[16] the momentum toward the Geneva Conference went forward under the shuttling guidance of mercurial Henry. To persuade Israel to negotiate for further disengagement of military forces along the Suez front, it was obvious that he had promised Israel more arms and security. And it was equally obvious that the Secretary had promised the Arabs on his initial trip to their world that disengagement would be but a first step in an Israeli pullback leading to total withdrawal from occupied territories. With Sadat it was "love" at first sight, and the Egyptian leader agreed to come to Geneva. However, the persuasive doctor was unable to similarly influence Syrian President Hafez al-Assad. The peace conclave opened at Geneva in the Palais des Nations on December 21 with the foreign ministers of the U.S., Soviet Union, Egypt, Jordan, and Israel in attendance, and without Syrian representation.

The conference adjourned the next day, giving way to the negotiations between Egypt and Israel conducted by the peregrinating, persistent Kissinger between Aswan and Jerusalem. Eight days later there was a signed agreement providing for Israeli withdrawal from the West Bank of the Suez and from the East Bank as far south as the Gulf of Suez, the twenty miles of Sinai territory yielded to be divided into three buffer zones.

The Nixon-Kissinger team could claim two further Middle East triumphs prior to the resignation of the President. After four weeks of shuttle diplomacy, Syria and Israel were induced to come to terms on a limited disengagement agreement on the Golan Heights. But to accomplish this, a little gentle Washington arm-twisting had to be applied in personal correspondence with Meir even as Nixon was coming under heaviest Watergate fire. According to the Israeli newspaper *Ma'ariv,* Nixon sent three personal messages to Israel asking for a show of flexibility and warning the Israeli leader not to take on itself the onus for foiling the newly presented opportunity to bring peace to the Middle East. The last private note pointedly reminded Meir that history does not repeat itself—apparently alluding to the possibility that there might not be arms to save that country the next time if Israel did not cooperate in the current negotiations. In reporting the diplomatic exchange, the Israeli journal insisted that the course of Israeli action would have been the same, but due to the frequency of the notes "and the insistence of their style, the freedom of movement of the government was certainly limited."

While the State Department and Kissinger publicly denied that any secret treaties were involved in the Golan Heights disengagement agreement, the document was scarcely signed than it was revealed that the U.S. would henceforth provide Israel with long-term arming and military procurement instead of, as previously, on an ad hoc basis. Aside from enormous military grants-in-aid, the purchases were to be made on the best possible financial terms.

At the same time the Nixon administration sought to strengthen relations with the Arab world so as to retain the image as an even-handed mediator that it was seeking. The President's enthusiastic reception on his May visit to Cairo, Aswan, and Riyadh augmented the growing ties being cemented by Kissinger. But every step forward encountered Zionist obstructionism that viewed new relations with their enemies as a setback for Israel. Israelists, on and off Capitol Hill, reacted with anger at the Nixon announcement from Cairo that Egypt would be helped toward nuclear development and that a U.S. military mission was even then visiting Egypt to discuss details.

If disengagement had reduced the ability to wage immediate further war, the possibilities of achieving real peace seemed little advanced, although both sides had suffered tremendous human and material losses. In view of her size and numbers, Israel's 2,517 killed, 7,500 wounded,[17] and $9 billion cost in the nineteen days of fighting was far greater. But a reading of translations of the Hebrew press as well as of the Arabic clearly revealed that neither side possessed even a modicum of the essential ingredient for peace: limited trust in the other party. Writer Daniel Dishon in a lengthy *Jerusalem Post* article claimed that the ultimate vision of Anwar Sadat still was a triumph over rather than friendship with Israel, and that the Arabs really had never abandoned their idea of "pushing Israel into the sea."

But it was Israel that continued to do the "pushing" and expanding. The Israeli government announced plans for the expenditure of more than $80 million for the development of settlements on the occupied Golan Heights over a two-year period, aimed to more than double the Israeli population. These cooperative industrial villages and the $20 million industrial center of Katroun in the heart of the Golan were the key projects on the planning boards. In creating another *fait accompli,* Israel was already violating the basic understanding behind President Assad's capitulation to the Kissinger urgings. The return to the Syrians of the devastated city of Quneitra never represented the ultimum to the Syrian President; it was undoubtedly the understanding that return of the bulk of the Golan Heights was to be negotiated by the parties at a reconvened Geneva Conference.

No sooner had Nixon returned from his triumphant Middle East "peace" tour than the Israelis let loose four days of the heaviest reprisal aerial raids against Palestinian camps in South Lebanon, allegedly in response to the attacks on Kiryat Shemona, Ma'alot, and Shamir. South Lebanon was devastated as Sadat declared that the "Egyptian Army could not much longer hold the peace" and in a personal note called on Nixon to take a "firm stand against Israel's repeated aggressions on Lebanon." The insecure government of Lebanese Prime Minister Takieddin Solh hesitated to bring charges against Israel to the Security Council lest he disrupt the Nixon peace momentum. Israel apparently sought some understanding with the Christian Lebanese that would seal off the borders and prevent Palestinians from mounting any future attacks.

There was precious little peace and negligible trust in view as the bomb racks seemed in the process of being rereadied for loading. Yasir Arafat charged Israel with possessing five atom bombs—not missiles —of the Nagasaki type. The Soviet Union's arms shipments to Syria and Iraq, accompanied by loud gustos, clearly indicated its intent not to relinquish her foothold, so expensively won, in the Arab world. Moshe Dayan's successor, Israeli Defense Minister Shimon Peres, sounded the alarum: Syria is being armed for further battle. The shrill Israeli warning was calculated for U.S. consumption to prepare the American people for the eventual breakdown in the peace momentum and also to serve as a reminder to UJA fund-raisers that there was another "year of crisis" ahead. New York City radio programs (WCBS, WINS, etc.) continually alluded to "Israeli fears of Arab intentions," to the arms purchases by "oil-rich Arab potentates," and to "the fragile peace."

To cap the cold war, Israel carried out a twenty-four-hour trial mobilization to test the speed with which 75,000–300,000 reservists could be called up. Syria, doubting the intentions of Israel, placed her troops on an emergency call. A wrong pushbutton, and the disengagement agreement would have been in the scrap heap, another war on the way.

These maneuverings, obviously directed toward a reconvened Geneva Conference, coincided with the resignation of Nixon in the wake of the release of the three condemnatory tapes and his admission that he had lied to the Judiciary Committee, to the Congress, and to his personal counsel. As Vice President Gerald Ford took over the reins of a deeply shaken U.S. government, the twenty-year voting record in congress of the new White House incumbent on measures relating to Israel scarcely augured well for peace in the Middle East.

XX   The Ford Interlude

I always voted at my party's call,
And I never thought of thinking for myself at all.
                    —Gilbert and Sullivan, *H.M.S. Pinafore*

No President, including Harry Truman and Lyndon Johnson, brought to the White House a more pro-Israel record and more fulsome Zionist connections than did Gerald R. Ford. If Max Fisher, Nixon's Ambassador to the Jews, could term the outgoing President a "Jewish delight," he must have viewed his successor a "super delight."

The entire four-page issue of the Zionist Establishment's weekly Washington organ, *Near East Report,* was devoted on August 14, 1974, to the views, public statements, and actions of congressman and Vice President Ford on behalf of Israel. To quote editor I. L. Kenen, "As House Republican leader, Ford consistently and vigorously urged the Executive branch to strengthen Israel . . . there were critical periods when the Nixon Administration, like its predecessors, wavered in its course and Congress moved to counteract any weakening in the traditional bi-partisan commitment to Israel." The Grand Rapids congressman helped to "develop a Capitol Hill consensus in favor of Israel," and was in the forefront on the House side of the "Israel-First Bloc," which not only favored economic and military aid to Israel and urged direct Arab-Israel peace negotiations, but also strongly opposed any Israeli withdrawal from any territory.[1]

In addition to addressing five annual policy conferences in Washington of the American-Israeli Public Affairs Committee, Ford sponsored or cosponsored many congressional resolutions and declarations from 1954 onward for Israel or against the Arabs, including an attempt to cut off surplus foods to Egypt because of what he considered to be Nasser's latent anti-American policy. He later led the hue

631

and cry against "lawless" Arab students who, with pitiful efforts, were trying to win support for the Palestinian cause on U.S. college campuses.

During the Johnson administration the new President had fought the temporary arms embargo to Israel and had helped persuade the President to sell her the first fifty Phantom jets. Congressman Ford even suggested that the U.S. lend—or give—Israel a destroyer to replace the *Elath,* sunk by a U.A.R.-directed Soviet Styx missile. On several occasions the President-to-be assailed the Soviet Union for its attitude on the Soviet Jewry emigration question, working closely with Senator Henry Jackson, and he vied with former New York Governor Averell Harriman in advancing a lend-lease concept of aid to Israel so as to ensure a continuity in the supply of jets.

In many other ways, too, the new Chief Executive had endeavored for twenty years to turn the U.S. Congress into an Israeli legislative body. All his actions, as he indicated to a Zionist conclave in the nations's capital in 1969, were dictated by his sincere belief that "the fate of Israel is linked to the national security interests of the U.S. I cannot conceive of a situation in which the U.S. will sell Israel down the Nile."[2]

One of Ford's first acts after being named by Nixon as Vice President to succeed Spiro Agnew,[3] even before he had won final congressional approval, was to fly to Hauppauge, Long Island, to attend the $250-a-plate "Dinner for Life" organized by the United Jewish Appeal. Stating that he was appearing as "a friend," the Vice President-designate spoke of "bridge building in the Middle East" and promised further administration support to Israel. To make matters worse, the new President at the outset surrounded himself with people even more committed to the Zionist dream than he, including Nelson Rockefeller, his designee as Vice President.

The Arab world's initial reaction was to view the Nixon downfall with great dismay. Their sympathies rested with the displaced Chief Executive who had so effectively projected himself on his Middle East tour three months earlier. Some writers even brought their usual keen sense of exaggeration into play, interpreting the Watergate incident as a conspiracy aimed at the President's open-minded approach to the Arabs. Few of the newspapers were the slightest bit informed as to the new President's attitude on Middle East affairs, although Beirut's *An Nahar* did point out that "President Nixon's replacement was the only American politician to have publicly recognized Jerusalem as the 'unified capital of Israel.' " (Hubert Humphrey had done likewise.)

The incoming President retained Kissinger as his Secretary of State (despite previous rumors to the contrary), appointed "even-handed" Governor William Scranton as U.S. representative to the U.N., and insisted in the first pronouncement of the new administration at his August 28 press conference that efforts "to attain a Middle East settlement and improve ties with the Arab world" would go forward.[4] The big problem was now to achieve such goals without arousing Zionist-Israeli antagonism. As Israel's insistence on "secure boundaries," which she had never defined, was shaped in terms of the Masada complex and of Zionist ideological expansionism, whatever steps the Ford administration took toward meeting Arab demands would inevitably be construed by Israel and her supporters as being at her expense.

It was difficult for the "Israel-First" bloc on the Hill to oppose Egypt's request for additional wheat and food sought early in the administration by Washington visitor Foreign Minister Ismail Fahmy and a top-expert delegation from Cairo. But when it came to sending six C-130 giant transport planes and other military supplies to Egypt, these congressmen put up a fight. At the same time the House International Affairs Committee indicated that their slogan was "Impartial but pro-Israel." The economic grant-in-aid to Israel was increased from $50 million, voted in the three previous years, to $250 million for 1974–75, although the U.S. was in the middle of a deep recession. The grant to assist the emigration of Soviet Jewry to Israel was likewise increased.

Kissinger, obviously more in charge than ever, had to come up with some answer to the Arab world's persistent demands for the return of the occupied territories in accordance with Security Council resolutions. Couldn't the U.S. sidetrack implementation of these resolutions by a new variation of the old British game of "divide and rule" by paying off Egypt and Jordan with new goodies and keeping the Palestinians at bay?

Kissinger, because of the fact and not despite the fact that he was a Jew, had been able to spark Arab postwar willingness, particularly Sadat's, to make sincere moves toward peace with Israel. But was the U.S. prepared to pay the awesome domestic political price for the kind of settlement envisioned by the Arabs, which inevitably would only lead to the mobilization of American Jewry against the Ford-Rockefeller administration, with dire consequences in 1976? What Kissinger had promised in the euphoria of his shuttle diplomacy and what the Arabs could reasonably expect were no doubt legions apart.

Unrecognized by the U.S., cynical Palestinians insisted that the principal aim of Washington was to hold off a new war as long as possible by separating the Arab and Israeli armies, meanwhile prolonging the Israeli occupation of Arab territories. The reiteration by King Faisal that the Arabs would reimpose the oil embargo if the U.S. deserted evenhandedness indicated the strong misgivings of the Saudi monarch.

What mitigated most against hopes for peace was that the American Jewish community seemed to have learned next to nothing from the lessons of the October war. Deceived by their own propaganda, Israelists in the U.S. had little understanding of the new Arab feeling of confidence and strength, permitting its leadership to consider seriously for the first time some kind of coexistence with some kind of an Israel state, albeit there was still no one common Arab approach as to what shape this should take. Blinded by their own arrogance stemming from their financial and political power, and spiritually sustained by their persecution saga—if you were not with them 100 percent you were a Nazi—Organized Jewry plotted the destruction of any U.S. rapprochement with the Arab world, particularly with the Palestinians, who to them remained nothing more than "terrorists." And this American Jewish-Israeli determination to maintain the status quo in the Middle East was no little strengthened by the knowledge that in Gerald Ford they had a far stronger supporter than Richard Nixon had ever been.

Even as Arabs and Israelis were competing as to who could make a bigger hero of Kissinger after the initial disengagement agreements, Zionism in the U.S. kept its pressure upon the State Department to obtain more planes and arms. In March the Zionist Organization of America newsletter sarcastically referred to Kissinger as "a new suitor for embracement by sheikhs, presidents and kings of Arabia." Before needed suasion could be applied to Israel to pull back, the Secretary of State was himself being subjected to the greatest pressures in the complex political chess game. Ever mindful of the larger territorial adjustments that lay ahead, the Anglo-Jewish press throughout the country took new potshots at the State Department and its chief.

In Israel an earlier feeling of compromise, exuded by the incoming government of General Yitzhak Rabin which had succeeded the repudiated Meir rule in June, soon faded under the bombardment of chauvinists and nationalists, no small part due to its exceedingly small margin of control (exactly two) in the Knesset. The National Religious party, which for the first time in Israel's history was not part of the

ruling Labor coalition, had extracted from the caretaker Meir government in the post-1973 war period the important concession that there
would be no change in status of the West Bank (to them Samaria and
Judea) without a plebiscite, and no yielding of any territory to Jordan
or Palestinians.

Trial balloons sent up by Israeli Information Minister Aharon
Yariv proved to be nothing more than that. Yariv had indicated that
Israel might negotiate with the PLO if that organization recognized
Israel's right to exist and ended its attacks against Israel. Ten days later
Prime Minister Rabin and his Cabinet revealed that while there might
be some minority support for such negotiations, the Israeli administration's viewpoint was quite contrary. "An Israeli decision today to conduct negotiations with a Palestinian delegation would be tantamount
to granting representation to Israel's chief enemies—to those who do
not want to recognize its existence and who declare their main aim is
its liquidation." While there was no official PLO response, an important "Palestinian personality" was quoted as saying: "When an apparently reasonable offer to negotiate is surrounded by impossible conditions, it is mockery. The Israelis want us to give up our goal of the
liberation of Palestine without even offering to give up their preten-
sions to the expansion of Israel."

With Syrian, Jordanian,[5] and Egyptian foreign ministers flowing
into Washington for consultations with Kissinger, the Israelis jockeyed
for position with bluster and the customary propaganda, spread by the
ever-sympathetic media, conjuring up the ever-familiar picture of
"vengeful Arabs, terrorist Palestinians, and anti-Semitic Muslims."[6]

Although all parties concerned fully appreciated the great benefits
that would flow from an honest peace, it daily became more obvious
to the student of the area that Middle East settlement was still light-
years away. While the U.S. and the Soviet Union carefully avoided a
confrontation, their continuing rivalry posed insurmountable obstacles to peace. Moscow, which had been lavishing varied help to different Arab countries to match U.S. support to Israel, had been unable
to find an alternate to the exploitation of anti-U.S. sentiment as the
means of maintaining her influence in the area. Concern over being
shut out of the area was heightened by the new U.S. role as mediator
under Kissinger's guidance, which had been accepted by not only
Israel and Egypt, but Syria as well. New Soviet strategies included
increased arms shipment to Iraq and Syria, open recognition of the
PLO, and new economic aid to South Yemen.

But Israel persisted in its policy of nonrecognition of the PLO, insisting that any negotiations for the return of the West Bank be carried on with Jordan, whose "open bridge" policy would more readily assure for Israel the Palestinian labor supply in the event of the return of any of the territory. Still financially strapped from the war despite large U.S. gifts and guaranteed securities, Israel desperately required the continued flow of people, goods, and capital between Israel and the West Bank.

Prime Minister Rabin's bare majority afforded him an excuse for inflexibility. Any attempt to give back the West Bank would brook the forthright opposition of the National Religious party and result in the fall of his government to the totally intransigent, ultranationalist, Begin-led Likud. Return to Egypt of occupied Sinai territory would involve the loss of close to $300 million in oil revenues and $50 million from the Eilat-Ashkelon trans-Israel pipeline, the substitute for the closed Suez Canal, which constituted one-third of Israel's export earnings.

The early months of the Ford administration were not the happiest for Kissinger, who in addition to allegations regarding links to past White House surveillance and wiretapping, encountered setbacks elsewhere. His intense personal dislike of Archbishop Makarios and mistrust of Soviet intentions led to the failure to take decisive action at the outset of the Greek-Turkish conflict over Cyprus, greatly weakening NATO and forcing further U.S. reliance on Israel as its "bastion" in Mare Nostrum. And the designation of the PLO as the sole representative of the Palestinian people was certainly not in line with Kissinger planning.

The lifting of the oil embargo on March 18 at the direction of King Faisal had neither provided assurances of a halt to skyrocketing oil prices nor of the flow of essential energy supplies. The Saudis had left the door open to the very real possibility of reimposition of the embargo if the peace momentum and Israeli withdrawal came to a halt.

Reacting to the danger, the speeches of President Ford to the Economic Club in Detroit and to the U.N. fairly bristled with implied threats ("End the Oil Gouging" was how the press headlined the presidential remarks), as did public echoes from Kissinger and Treasury Secretary William Simon. The President warned the General Assembly that "the two pressing world supply crises of oil and food either could be resolved on the basis of cooperation or can be made unmanageable on the basis of confrontation." The delegates of 138 nations responded most coolly.

The oil-producing countries did not remain silent. Speaking to the National Press Club in Canberra, Australia, the Shah of Iran declared his firm opposition to a reduction in oil prices unless the prices of the twenty to thirty staple commodities Middle East countries were importing from the West were likewise reduced. "No one can dictate to us—no one can wave a finger at us, because we will wave a finger back," the Iranian monarch expostulated. Kuwaiti Oil Minister Abdul Rahman al-Ateeqi similarly warned that the oil producers would fight back.

Clarifying the administration's position in a very significant and widely quoted interview with *Business Week,*[7] Kissinger declared that an American military takeover of the Middle East oil fields would be "a very dangerous course, but one which has not been ruled out." While military intervention would not be used to drive the price of oil down, it would be quite another matter "where there is some critical strangulation of the industrialized world"—an ominous warning to the Arabs not to invoke a new embargo.

The Vladivostok Summit and the Ford-Brezhnev discussions on the Middle East yielded only another agreement to disagree. The failure of Ford's inflation and energy program, growing worldwide balance of payments pressure, the downward trend in crop yields, and the rapid movement of currencies all created a mood of uncertainty and added to possibilities of military action as 1975 began. With the energy pinch tightening and the PLO-Israel impasse deepening, the war party in the U.S. grew. A renowned psychologist writing in an academic journal felt that the stage was being set for American military intervention in the Middle East because such a war could "be justified on the grounds of self-interest"—shutting off of the U.S. oil supply.[8] In an article in *Commentary,*[9] Johns Hopkins' Professor Robert W. Tucker suggested that the best area for a massive U.S. airborne assault would be the coastal strip from Kuwait to Qatar, "which accounts for 40 percent of Arab oil production and where there are few people, few forests, negligible Arab military forces" and where U.S. forces would not be harassed as they were in the jungles of Vietnam.[10]

Exuding far more hatred of the Arabs was the Andrew Tobias *New York* magazine piece, "War—The Ultimate Anti-Trust Action," which was featured by a half-page of instructions on "How to Blow Up An Oil Well." The writer asked: "Could we, technically, pull off an invasion of one of the nations belonging to OPEC? If so, should we do such a thing? And in any case, might we, or some other country, try it?"[11]

To pick up the peace momentum, Kissinger counted on his magic with Sadat and the irreparable cleavage between Moscow and Cairo, only superficially papered over by Sadat-Gromyko talks in which the Egyptian leader's request for spare parts and replacements for 1973 losses and a moratorium on the enormous indebtedness for past arms deliveries was rejected. Egypt's vulnerable military position and even more desperate economic picture impelled Sadat to take the big chance of venturing into Kissinger-conducted bilateral negotiations with Israel. Only a few months previously, Sadat had joined Assad and Arafat in announcing opposition to any idea of a partial political settlement: "The Arab cause is our cause." Now Syria and the PLO champed on the sidelines, fearful that their Arab partner might succumb to the wiles of Washington and totally isolate them. Dead set against any Egyptian-Israeli solo with no movement on the Golan Heights or the West Bank, Assad and Arafat vehemently opposed the Israeli demand of a Sadat no-war pledge for a period of three to five years. The Kissinger grant to Syria of $25 million from the previously appropriated $100 million contingency "to encourage further development of U.S.-Syrian bilateral relations," as the Secretary phrased it, did not help bridge the wide gap between the two countries.

Few weeks were more significant to the history of the Middle East than that of March 23–30, 1975, into which were crowded the failure of the latest Kissinger shuttling between Egypt and Israel, the Ford call for reassessment of U.S. Middle East policy, the assassination of King Faisal of Saudi Arabia, and the announcement by Sadat that he would open the Suez Canal to traffic on June 5.

Given the circumstances of domestic politics in the U.S., Israel, and Egypt, the outcome of Kissinger's March efforts was inevitable. The Rabin government was in a bind between its own Masada complex and its deep concern with opposition, both within and outside the Cabinet. To increase its control in the Knesset, Rabin had brought the ultrachauvinistic, unyielding National Religious party into the government. But his own Labor party, now divided into Peres, Allon, and Rabin factions, was at odds over whether a statement of the "end of belligerency" or merely "nonuse of force" should be exacted from Egypt as the *quid pro quo* for relinquishment of the Sinai Mitla and Gidi passes and the Abu Rudeis oil fields supplying 55 percent of Israel's petroleum needs. A retreat to the center of the passes was unacceptable to Cairo, and Rabin's "bull in a china shop" diplomacy did not help breach the gap between Israel and Egypt.

The U.S. media, as could be expected, laid the responsibility for the diplomatic failure to Egypt's unwillingness to end the state of belligerency rather than to the Israeli reluctance to give back territory.

But it actually had been the absence of realistic U.S. pressure on Israel that accounted for its nonsuccess. Neither the President nor his Secretary of State was truly prepared to twist Israel's arm. The personal not-too-strongly worded telegram from Ford to Rabin, allegedly drafted by the perambulating Secretary of State, asking for acceptance of Egyptian terms and vaguely warning of damaged U.S.-Israel relations was not taken too seriously. Shortly after his return from Jerusalem, Kissinger met with concerned congressional leaders and quickly dispelled the rumor that Israel had been faced with even the vaguest threat of a rejection to her newest request for $7.5 million in military aid over the next three years. Israel sought approval of a shift from year-to-year to long-term giving. Without taking action on this larger amount, the Senate Foreign Relations Committee voted Israel an additional $696 million over what had been already appropriated for the year.

The Israelis, as always, were handled with the silkiest of gloves. With the 1976 elections on the horizon, Gerald Ford was not about to antagonize the Jewish community. Washington distress signals brought no help as the White House, et al., tried to muster support for pressure from many, including Max Fisher. The off-the-record Kissinger statement placing the blame for the negotiations failure on Israel, but relieving his good friend Rabin of fault by noting that he would not have remained in office had he accepted the Sadat proposal, alerted the Conference of Presidents of Major Jewish Organizations. Ambassador Dinitz called up his "shock troops," as he had threatened during the 1973 airlift crisis, and at a New York meeting stirred 250 Jewish leaders to issue a call for "a nationwide drive to mobilize broad public support for Israel's cause among our fellow citizens." Kissinger was obliged to deny that the policy reassessment in any way implied a rejection of the Israeli request for long-term military and economic aid.[12] Secretary Schlesinger also poured soothing ointment on Israeli wounds by telling Ambassador Dinitz that Israel's safety and security would be assured through the U.S. sophisticated weaponry sought.

Following his October 1973 difficulties, the Secretary of Defense had been gaining favor in the Israeli camp ever since his January 6, 1974, television declaration that there was a "high risk" of force being used against Arab nations if they continued their oil embargo. Obviously brandishing this option, Schlesinger again reminded the Arab world that the U.S. would not readily tolerate a fresh embargo. In his reply to the question as to what action the U.S. would pursue: "That remains to be seen, but I think the reaction of the U.S. might be far more severe this time than the last."

In an atmosphere pervaded by U.S. ambivalency, or worse, rather than evenhandedness, Sadat had reasoned that it was best for him to fend for himself. Watching him in his lengthy television interview with NBC's John Chancellor, one could appreciate the "spot" in which the Egyptian President had been placed. He did not wish to be beholden to the Kremlin again; he desperately needed U.S. economic cooperation; he personally liked and trusted Kissinger very much. But he had been let down and felt forced to make a dramatic move. The opening of the Canal without an Israeli pullback from the strategic passes was a calculated risk—a bow both to Moscow and to the Western European countries that would benefit from this. But the assassination of King Faisal, Sadat's ally and "banker," no doubt largely contributed to the surprising decision.

The removal of the moderating influence of the Saudi Arabian monarch added to Middle East instability. Faisal's conservatism always balanced the "rejectionist forces" of Libya, Iraq, and Algeria, not to mention South Yemen. It was he who in 1972 and 1973 had forged the Egyptian-Saudi Arabian alliance. A staunch friend of the U.S., Faisal had reluctantly invoked the oil embargo in November 1973. (When this writer questioned the King in May 1974 in Riyadh as to the possibility of another embargo, he declared that if the Arabs were forced into another war with Israel, and if the U.S. did not remain evenhanded, he would not hesitate to invoke this weapon again. But the Saudi Arabian monarch indicated that the great confidence he felt in Kissinger would make such an eventuality unnecessary.

Faisal always seemed to have everyone in his pocket at the right time. He could moderate, he could mediate the Arab internal rivalries, even put brakes on Yasir Arafat. He was the only Arab leader since the passing of Nasser able to bring about a united Arab stand. He was the generally recognized leader of the Arab-Muslim world, challenged only by the rising prestige of Iran's Shah Pahlevi. His death at the hands of his "maddened"[13] American-educated nephew, as he sat in Majlis on the Prophet's birthday, greatly weakened the Arab cause, as well as hopes for peace in the area.

The reopening of the Canal, an imposing, globally televised spectacular, turned out to be a successful Sadat gambit, the new Suez tolls adding some small strength to the Egyptian economy. But ever since the Sadat-Ford meeting in Salzburg in May, Cairo had been prodding Washington for a meaningful Israeli pullback. Washington used Israeli's deep concern over her still-pending request for military aid and her deteriorating economic situation to force the Rabin government to yield the Sinai passes, conditional upon a U.S.—not a U.N.—presence in conjunction with electronic warning systems to be established. A number of extravagent, indispensable goodies proferred to both parties highlighted the brief twelve-day Kissinger shuttle in late August, turning the "no" of March into the "yes" of September.

The second Israeli-Egyptian agreement became a fact on September 2,[14] not so much because Israel could not afford to deny Uncle Sam its way a second time, but because of the marvelous deal Tel Aviv had wrested for itself from Washington. Sadat had not done too badly, either, once the promises of economic aid were implemented. Neither antagonist, in fact, gave up too much, as both "begrudgingly" accepted Washington's "payoff." It was John Doe, the American taxpayer, who once again was burdened with another foreign fiasco.

While headlines warned that New York City required $3.3 billion to keep its machinery going, the State of Israel was requesting that very sum for military and economic aid. Rabin's loot for only doing a minuscule portion of what was required of Israel under U.N. Security Council Resolutions 242 of 1967 and 338 of 1973 did not quite reach the figure New York sought. It was only $2.4 billion, but nevertheless considerable largesse from a government still battling a heavy inflation, a deep recession, and the threatened bankruptcy of its larger cities. Indeed, an Israel nearly fatally isolated from the rest of the world had won more U.S. concessions by yielding to so-called pressure than the previous Meir-Dayan hawk Cabinet with its intransigency had been able to squeeze out of the Nixon administration.

The new agreement was scarcely signed before Jerusalem, Cairo, and Washington were giving varied interpretations of what was contained in the pact's secret pledges. The differences, however, were solved when the *New York Times* again proved that it constituted the invisible government of the U.S. No documents, however secret, ever fail to come into possession of the scrutinizing eyes of this monolithic journal. To scoops on the Pentagon Papers dealing with Vietnam and the Watergate tapes were now added the texts of the U.S. documents accompanying the Sinai accord, published by the Sulzberger journal on September 17 and 18.

Under any view, Israel had emerged more than ever as the 51st State of the Union. Spelled out in detail in the *Jerusalem Post* were the U.S. pledges not to attempt to pressure Israel either into "any large-scale withdrawal," if and when negotiations over the Golan Heights were initiated between Israel and Syria, or into any interim agreement with Jordan; not to present any plan for any overall settlement without Israeli consent; and neither to recognize nor hold talks with the PLO. In addition to limiting U.S. options vis-à-vis Syria and Jordan, the secret covenant with Israel pledged aid and assistance in the event of an attack by another superpower, the two governments undertaking to consult promptly on the nature of such assistance. (A similar secret pledge was rumored to have been given in November 1971 by Nixon to Meir when their quarrel was healed prior to the national campaign and the successful presidential bid for the "Jewish vote.") Fearful of Soviet reaction to this covenant, Kissinger told the press upon his return from the Middle East, that the pledges made had been "qualified by references to congressional action and American resources."

There was nothing secret about the U.S. commitment to an enlarged, dangerous role in the Middle East through the presence of 200 American technicians to share in the operations of the Israeli and Egyptian surveillance stations in the Mitla and Gidi passes, and to operate six other stations in the territory from which Israel was to withdraw. The Israelis and the Egyptians had both insisted on this U.S. presence, Rabin rejecting the proposal that the U.N. fill this active role because "an attack through U.N. lines does not carry the same symbolic gravity as an attack through American stations would."

The other unchallenged U.S. commitment provided for the enlarged financial allocation to Israel and Egypt (lumped together in press reports as from $3 to $3.3 billion without any indication that at least $2.6 billion of this was for Israel, of which $1.8 billion was a military grant). In addition to this huge largesse, Israel was seeking, according to Finance Minister Yeshoshua Rabinowitz,[15] $550 to $700 million more in order to reconstruct a new Sinai defense line ($150 million), replace the oil of Abu Rudeis ($350 million), and build up her oil reserves ($50 million a year for four years).

There was little doubt that the financial aspects of the U.S. commitment—far more than the Israeli withdrawal from five kilometers of Egyptian soil, or even the return of the oil fields—were what President Sadat could not resist. Whether he had received verbal guarantees that a Syrian disengagement accord would follow or that Washington would alter its views on the Palestinians constituted another of those dark and undisclosed areas, which were of primary concern to other Arab states. But it was "Yankee dollars" that had moved Sadat, just as it had Rabin.

Even as the Egyptian leader was charged by Palestinians and other

Arab nationalists with a sellout, the American people were expressing their own doubts about this new U.S. involvement, whose small manpower beginnings paralleled the insignificant, initial undertaking in Vietnam. The mail received at the White House was running ten-to-one against sending the technicians to the Sinai, and a *National Observer* plebiscite among its readers showed 77 percent opposed. John Doe similarly informed his congressmen of his misgivings. A New York City resident voiced popular sentiment when he stated: "There is no such thing as a slight pregnancy. No American advisers to the Sinai. An American behind a computer is far more vulnerable than a soldier with a gun in hand."

Even the *New York Times* reluctantly was forced to concede editorially that "serious dialogue on the Palestinian issue in the months ahead would be far more directly to the core of the Middle East conflict than another round of bitter disputation over a few square kilometers of territory."[16]

Equally obnoxious to "energy-conscious" American was the U.S. guarantee to Israel of an adequate supply of oil as the Abu Rudeis fields were returned to Egypt after eight years of occupation. The U.S. pledged the sale to Israel of her domestic requirements and "every effort to help Israel secure necessary means of transportation." And more of the unique relationship was spelled out in the proviso whereby Israel could purchase oil from the U.S. "in accordance with the International Energy Agency conservation and allocation formula" should the U.S. be prevented from meeting Israel's normal requirements due to an embargo or otherwise. Further, it was convenanted that Congress would be requested funds both to cover any Israeli additional expenditures for the import of oil to replace the Abu Rudeis and Ras Sudar fields and for the construction and storage of oil reserves in Israel. (A Gannett News Service poll showed 64 percent opposed to U.S. compensating Israel for the loss of its formerly held Egyptian oil.)

While Democratic majority leader Mike Mansfield and some other congressional leaders indicated initial opposition to the enlarged U.S. Middle East role, the Senate soon provided the necessary green light to Kissinger's pact. The early dissent of Senator Jackson only pointed up the irrationalism of certain Israelist opposition to the pact. The Likud and other expansionists had tried to turn Kissinger's last shuttling visits to Jerusalem into street riots and violent demonstrations; the police had been forced to intervene several times. To such zealots, the so-called "peace" involvement by U.S. forces was not a sufficient *quid pro quo* for the withdrawal of Israeli forces from the passes and the return of the oil fields.

But Jackson and his Israeli cohorts could have been nothing but pleased when Foreign Defense Minister Shimon Peres arrived at the Pentagon shortly afterwards with a $2.4 billion arms shopping list. Secretary Schlesinger could voice no objection to the Israeli request for the most sophisticated weapons yet to be produced, some of which were in short—or even no—supply. The Israelis wanted more Lance missiles, laser bombs, F-15 planes, and the brand-new F-16 combat aircraft, as well as Pershing missiles with a 450-mile range, which would place Cairo and other Arab capitals within Israeli firing distance of an atomic-bearing weapon.

Speaking at Washington's prestigious Press Club on September 17, Peres claimed that Israel needed the Pershing missiles to balance the Arab's Russian-provided SCUD. Yet it was a recognized fact that the latter had a range of 150 to 175 miles, only about one-third of that of the American missile, and the Pershing assembly line had been closed down for three months. According to columnists Evans and Novak, the only immediate source for Israel was to pull the missiles down from NATO operational inventory or a training unit based in the U.S. And the U.N. Association of the U.S., heretofore always very sympathetic to Israeli goals, decreed the introduction of the Pershing into the Middle East would raise "dangerous ambiguities concerning not only Israel's nuclear capability but its nuclear intentions as well."[17]

The administration had previously indicated that it would sell to Israel for the first time 200 Lance short-range missiles, capable of carrying nuclear as well as conventional warheads, to balance the challenge of Soviet antiaircraft sites, which Egypt and Syria had used so effectively in the early stages of the October war. The Lance, a "cluster bomblet," consists of baseball-size bombs that are hurled over a wide area when the warhead strikes the ground.

While this had spurred new Arab attempts to acquire atomic weapons abroad—Sadat's bid for an atomic reactor was turned down by President Giscard d'Estaing in January 1975 just as Mua'mmar Qaddafi had been earlier rejected by President Pompidou—angry protests emanated from those who already viewed the new step-by-step accord with repugnance or skepticism, even some Egyptian leaders (notably Saed Marei, the powerful Speaker of the People's Assembly)[18] who had previously applauded the Sinai agreement. Even as the important SALT disarmament talks with the Kremlin floundered, this further escalation of the never-ending arms race with the Soviet Union went forward by way of U.S. arms shipments to Israel, Jordan, and Saudi Arabia (in exchange for good petrodollars)—all part of the pernicious madness coursed by Washington, which had brought nothing but war and near-war to the area.

In addition to the vastly enlarged U.S. commitments, the principal *quid pro quo* for Israel's relinquishment of the oil fields and of five kilometers of strategic territory (Israel retained the towering Jebel Gidi, the highest point in the region, and Israel, the U.S., and Egypt jointly shared control of the buffer zones established on the territory yielded), Israeli Chief of Staff Mordechai Gur claimed his government had even improved its position militarily because the greater distance now separating the opposing forces would require Egypt to attack on the move, a great disadvantage for the latter's accustomed type of military operations.

Arab bitterness against Egypt's disengagement mounted. Syria and the PLO attacked Cairo for going it alone; the PDFLP called for sabotage of the accord. The fear in other Arab quarters was that the Sinai accord would freeze the situation on other Middle East fronts. President Sadat's first visit to the U.S. in October 1975 only increased the venom. Although he told both the U.N. General Assembly and the Congress that "the year 1976 will be the 'Palestine year,'" Sadat made little progress in overcoming the Syrian-PLO charge that his very trip to the American capital constituted "another betrayal."

On the other hand, the "Israel-First" bloc boycotted the Egyptian President's address to Congress and demanded—and was assured—equal time for Premier Rabin on a visit scheduled early in 1976. They and other Israelists resented the goodwill the Egyptian leader was building up in the States and feared further U.S.-Egyptian rapproachement, no little of which was being advanced through the help of attractive, articulate Madame Jihan Sadat, who had accompanied her husband to the States. Everywhere Zionists strove to undermine Sadat gains and blunt a U.S.-Egyptian rapprochement.

Although building personal popularity, Sadat was not getting what he most needed: a transfusion of private American investment and technicians, far more essential to Cairo than the $1 billion in promised aid. The Sadat bid for arms was turned down with a polite, "Bring this matter up later and we'll take a second look." And Egypt had only been seeking cargo planes, trucks, and technical facilities (after a long battle Congress finally approved the shipment of six C-150s), compared to the sophisticated weaponry requested by and given to Israel.[19] The Egyptian leader spent most of his time on his first visit to the U.S. in private meetings with industrial leaders attempting to induce hesitant American companies to invest in Egypt's future, which was the theme of a major address before the prestigious Economic Club in New York City.

The Palestinians, already beset by internal strife, appeared to be even bigger losers from disengagement than the Syrians, as Kissinger continued to exploit Arab divisiveness. Lebanon, torn asunder by mounting civil strife between the haves and the have-nots, the Christians and the Muslims, the conservatives and the radicals, faced growing collapse. And in this struggle the Palestinians, intent on maintaining their position in the one country from which it could best and most freely carry on guerrilla warfare against Israel, encountered another shock upon discovery that their own interests did not always coincide with that of their heretofore staunchest friend and ally, Syria.

As a *quid pro quo* for agreeing to another six-month extension of the U.N. truce-keeping forces on the Golan Heights, Damascus however exacted the price of a full-scale U.N. Security Council debate on the Palestine question in which the PLO was to participate. This move came on top of the shattering November U.N. move against Zionism. Kissinger had done everything to defeat the resolution and block a debate, which could only enhance Palestinian prestige. The Rabin Cabinet, in an emergency session, indicated it regarded his failure as an American betrayal of the disengagement promise not to recognize the PLO, and Washington was so informed.

Apparently the Israelis were so upset that Ford felt it politically necessary to take the time during his arduous visit to Peking to send an urgent message to Jerusalem, which might be paraphrased in this way: "Look here, boys, we're still friends, and the situation has not changed as a result of any action at the U.N." Foreign Minister Allon had earlier attempted to reach him by phone aboard the presidential plane to express Israeli anger-fear, for the U.N. discussions were now going to the core of the Palestine problem and were raising the question of Israel's very right to exist. The Israelis had been exercised over a possible U.S. policy shift toward the PLO ever since Deputy Assistant Secretary of State for Near Eastern and South Asian Affairs Harold H. Saunders, in testimony on November 12, 1975, before the Special Subcommittee on Investigations of the House International Affairs Committee, had stated boldly and clearly:

... The legitimate interests of the Palestinian Arabs must be taken into account in the negotiations of an Arab-Israeli peace. In many ways the Palestinian dimension of the Arab-Israeli conflict is the heart of that conflict. Final resolution of the problems arising from the partition of Palestine, the establishment of the State of Israel and Arab opposition to these events will not be possible until agreement is reached defining a just and permanent status for the Arab peoples who consider themselves Palestinians. . . .

It is a fact that many of the 3 million or so people who call themselves Palestinians today increasingly regard themselves as having their own identity as a people and desire a voice in determining their political status . . . The issue is not whether Palestinian interests *should* be expressed in a final settlement, but *how*. There will be no peace unless an agreement is found . . . We are prepared to consider any reasonable proposal from any quarter and we will expect other parties to the negotiations to be equally broadminded.[20] [Italics added.]

The extent of Israel's alarm over the scheduled U.N. debate was demonstrated in the government's refusal to permit Rabbi Moshe Hirsch, leader of the militant anti-Zionist Neturei Karta, to come to New York and make known his group's views favoring establishment of a Palestinian state. Although possessing an American passport, the Rabbi, who considered himself and his followers to be "Palestinian Jews," was apprehended by Israeli police as he attempted to board a plane at Lod Airport. (Not a line about this shocking incident appeared in the U.S. press, although it was reported by Reuters and detailed at a well-covered U.N. press conference.[21])

The U.S. soon indicated that it was maintaining its unique relationship with Israel, first through its lone negative vote[22] out of the fifteen members on the procedural question over seating the PLO at this full-dress Security Council debate of January 12–26, 1976, and then, at the conclusion of this airing of the Palestine question, by its veto of the resolution that called for establishment of an independent Palestinian state and total Israeli withdrawal from all Arab territories occupied in the 1967 war. Although the resolution supported Israel's right to exist by providing guarantees for the "security and territorial independence" of all Middle East states, and a stronger Arab draft had been withdrawn, U.S. Ambassador Moynihan still opposed passage on the grounds that it altered the existing framework for Middle East negotiations. The Council's attempt to clarify the ambiguity in the phrase "withdraw from territories occupied" in Resolution 242 (did this mean all the territories or only some?) was resolutely resisted, as was the U.N. aim to upgrade the reference to the Palestinians as a "refugee problem" to the "political rights" of the Palestinian people. This, Moynihan insisted,[23] could only be settled by negotiations between the parties. The original resolution had been adopted at the end of the 1967 war, at which time the necessity of some reference to the national rights of the Palestinian people was not apparent.

Although civil war was raging in Lebanon, with Syria as well as Israel threatening to intervene, and Palestinian frustrations were reaching new heights in the face of continued U.S. intransigency toward them, Ford still could muster these words for his 1976 State of the Union address to the new Congress: "The key elements for peace among the nations of the Middle East now exist." Trust between the protagonists was even more lacking than five months earlier, when *Time* magazine and other periodicals were hailing the Israel-Egyptian second disengagement as "peace in our time."

The bitter internecine struggle in Lebanon proceeded to worsen, one cease-fire after another failing. In an attempt to right the balance so as to temper the demand of the Christian forces led by Pierre Geymayel and Camille Chamoun for a partition of the country, President Assad threw his forces to their side against the Palestinians. A bitter struggle took place in which Syrian and PLO forces were anomalously pitted against each other and had as their respective allies the varied Christian groups and the leftist-Druze alliance. The PLO, proving no match for the professional army of Assad, was crushed, its Beirut stronghold of Tel Zaitar wiped out in the bloodiest encounter of the war. After many innocents had been killed and much destruction added to the already devastated city of Beirut, peace was finally established under Syrian control. As Lebanon's new President Elias Sarkis gradually took over control from the Syrians, South Lebanon with its Litani waters eyed enviously as ever by Israel, remained a trouble spot.

The Israelis drew a fictional red line near the Litani River, 15 miles from the Israeli border, seeking to prevent the return of Palestinians south of this boundary. Toward this objective, they gained the immediate support of Phalangist-Christian forces. A new Israeli-Christian Lebanese alliance, featured by well-publicized excursions of Lebanese civilians across the borders into Israel for medical help and even for jobs, as well as by a flow of arms and increased Israeli-Christian military cooperation became hard fact. North of Beirut, Junieh functioned as a separate Christian center and the military capital for the opposition of the Chamounist-Gemayel forces to the central government in Beirut. President Sarkis struggled against the very real danger of partition.

In the face of Lebanon's near dismemberment and growing Israeli involvement, Washington pursued a "do-nothing" policy, particularly after the assassination of U.S. Ambassador to Lebanon Francis Melloy, who had been trying to mediate between Christian and Muslim forces. The Palestinian debacle certainly was not displeasing to the Secretary of State, as it relieved the U.S. of much of the immediate pressure to recognize the PLO. But Assad's preoccupation with the Lebanese war, and then his victory, did not encourage the Secretary to push forward with the next scheduled step, which was to have involved a withdrawal from the Golan Heights. This had been contemplated in the terms of the secret Kissinger-Sadat memorandum, part of the *quid pro quo* for the second Israel-Egyptian disengagement.

On Kissinger's last visit to Damascus en route home from Alexandria in August after the second Sinai agreement, he had faced Assad's accusation of dividing "the Arab nation" and rejection of any "cosmetic," minuscule Israeli withdrawal on the Golan Heights. Cut off from Egypt, the Syrian leader moved to forge a new alliance with King Hussein, once a bitter rival.

Sadat would have welcomed further accords to strengthen and speed implementation of the $700 million promised to him by Kissinger, which his economy desperately needed. As a dramatic step to emphasize Egypt's strategic divorce from the Soviet Union, which had begun with the expulsion of Soviet technicians in the summer of 1972, and as an appeal both to his Saudi bankers and potential U.S. investors, Sadat convened the Peoples Assembly on March 14 and unilaterally abrogated Egypt's 1971 Treaty of Friendship and Cooperation with the Soviet Union. With the end of what was to have been a fifteen-year arrangement, Egyptian ports were closed to vessels of the Soviet navy.

If Sadat's move was calculated to bring about renewed U.S. efforts to push Israel into further withdrawals, the timing was absolutely wrong. No U.S. gestures toward Egypt could be expected as the 1976 presidential campaign took over and, as usual, superseded everything else—even U.N. action.

As a replacement for the militantly pro-Israel Daniel Patrick Moynihan, whose hysterical rhetoric spawned hatred of the Arab and Third Worlds, William Scranton was making many friends in diplomatic circles that had been under blistering, insulting attacks from his predecessor. In his first remarks before the U.N. Security Council, Ambassador Scranton strongly criticized the Israeli government for its policy of establishing settlements in the occupied territories as a contravention of U.N. resolutions and the Geneva Convention. But having issued this verbal rebuke, the U.S. representative—under instructions from Washington—then vetoed the mildest kind of a resolution, which had watered down a proposed strong censure by merely "deploring" Zionist actions. Later in May when outraged Arab, African, and Asian nations, joined by a few courageous Western countries, sought to halt ruthless Israeli military actions in the occupied territories, Scranton, again upon clear instructions from his Chief in the White House, refused to approve any resolution that might offend Israel and, more importantly, that country's supporters in the U.S. Even the wording of a statement to be issued by the Security Council chairman merely as representing a "consensus" of the members, as distinct from a vote, became came a matter of many days of futile negotiations over verbiage between the overwhelming Council majority and Ambassador Scranton. The U.S. representative disassociated himself from the "consensus" statement, read by French Security Council President Louis de Guiringuad—by then a meaningless expression of nothingness—but nevertheless bitterly attacked by Israeli Ambassador Chaim Herzog. The *Washington Post* headline the next day read: "Israel Attacks U.S. Stand on Settlements." While the Israeli representative insisted he had not meant to include the U.S. in his scathing censure, Herzog had pointedly rebuffed the U.S. opposition to Israeli settlements in saying:

Any attempt to point the finger at Israel's actions and to characterize them as obstacles to peace is nothing but a cynical falsification of history. . . . We reject it out of hand.[24]

This was as direct an attack as possible on the U.S. position expressed at the U.N. in the two lengthy Council debates on settlements.

Why was the U.S. thinking one way but voting another at the U.N.? It was because Governor Ronald Reagan had won startling primary victories in Texas, Nebraska, and Indiana as well as expected wins in the South, and was threatening to go to the Republican Convention in Kansas City with more pledged votes than the President. The Jewish vote in June primaries could perhaps swing the balance. Ford could not afford to antagonize the Jewish bloc through even the mildest censure of Israel at the U.N. Republican fund-raiser Max Fisher had been unsuccessful both in making these same "Jewish fat-cats," who had poured contributions into the Nixon coffers, donate to the Ford campaign or in arousing enthusiasm among Jewish voters for the President. Nixon, who boasted he had given more military and economic aid to Israel than his three predecessors together, allegedly received 35 percent of the Jewish vote four years previously—the highest ever to be won by a Republican candidate. Ford needed those same votes on his side in the primaries, let alone in the general election. Speaking on the West Coast in Oregon two days before the important primary there, the President claimed credit for establishing "friendly relations with moderate Arab states," but noted emphatically that the U.S. was pledged as ever "to maintain the security and survival of Israel."

On the Democratic side, former Georgia Governor Jimmy Carter, with his infectious smile and clarion call for an American moral revival, seemed to have appealed to the American psyche as he won successive primaries in the North, South, and Midwest. Out of the nearly dozen serious candidates who had initially bid for the nomination of the Democratic party, by mid-May only four serious Carter rivals remained: Senators Henry Jackson and Frank Church, Congressman Morris Udall, and California's Governor Jerry Brown.

The Middle East conflict had been only scantily raised in the primaries during the first four months. In interviews and speeches, Carter made no mistake about his deep-seated religious convictions and his fervent Baptist fundamentalism. In his most important Middle East pronouncement, he attacked U.N. resolutions in behalf of the "terrorist Palestine Liberation Organization." He flatly stated that "a Palestinian state should not be recognized by Israel until the Palestinians affirmed Israel's right to exist in peace." Israel's sovereignty and security was primary to candidate Carter, but he did at least declare himself in favor of the "recognition of Palestine as a people, as a nation with a place to live and a right to choose their own leaders."

Carter, like every other politician, was surrounded in his campaign by important Jews: Campaign Treasurer R. J. Lipchutz, Advertising Chief Gerald Rafshoon, and Internal Issues Coordinator Stuart Eizenstat. When speechwriter Robert Shrum was fired, he was widely quoted in the *Jewish Press,* largest Jewish weekly in the U.S. (once edited by Jewish Defense Leaguer Meir Kahane) and an organ of the right-wing Likud movements in which Menachem Begin's weekly column appeared, accusing Carter of saying: "We have to be cautious. We don't want to offend anybody. . . . I don't want any more statements on the Middle East or Lebanon. [Senator Henry M.] Jackson has all the Jews anyway. It doesn't matter how far I go. I won't get four percent of the Jewish vote anyway, so forget it. We'll get the Christians." Eizenstat, a leader of Atlanta's Jewish community, lest these alleged remarks be construed as "anti-Semitic," instantaneously declared them to be a total "fabrication." The Carter media spokesman declared the statement regarding the Jewish votes was "totally ridiculous and contradictory to the concern Carter has felt and expressed."

When the Carter bandwagon began to falter with losses in Nebraska to ambitious, anti-big-business Senator Frank Church, and in Maryland to young, attractive Governor Jerry Brown, the move to draft Senator Hubert Humphrey as a candidate was seriously revived. The former Vice President and Democratic candidate in 1968 had announced he would not enter the primary elections and would not be an active aspirant. But he indicated he would be available if the delegates at the Convention were to honestly draft him. Humphrey's outright pro-Zionist record was unquestioned. There was a great possibility that a deadlocked convention, with Carter unable to win a majority on the first ballot, might turn to a Humphrey-Kennedy ticket, which would be far more pleasing to the political party professionals, who disliked Carter.

The threat to the Georgian from this competition was used by the Zionists to press the Democratic front runner for further commitments to Israel. Confidential reports carried this—the Jewish press boasted of it. It has always been axiomatic that the closer the November Election Day approached, the more the Middle East issue is pushed to the forefront and the blackmail intensifies.

When Brown carried his fight to Ohio and New Jersey, states with large Jewish populaces, he declared "the capital of Israel is not Tel Aviv, but in Jerusalem, and that is where our embassy ought to be." The Carter Committee for President countered with a full-page advertisement in the New York *Daily News,* the tabloid paper with the largest circulation in the U.S., also enjoying a very large number of readers in neighboring and suburban New Jersey. Here he was addressing himself to the working man and the nonintellectual community, and he talked to them in their language when he stated on June 3:

As long as I am President, the American people will never sacrifice the security or survival of Israel for barrels of oil. A lasting peace must be based on the absolute assurance of Israel's survival and security. I would never yield on that point, and it is very important for us to make this clear to the rest of the world. This country was the first to recognize Israel's existence as a country, and we must remain the first country to which Israel can turn with assurance.

Ignored in the ad were the Palestinians to whom he had referred ten days earlier in an interview with *US News and World Report:* "The legitimate interests of the Palestinians have to be recognized. But I would not favor recognition of the PLO or other government entities representing the Palestinians until they have convinced me that they recognize Israel's right to exist in peace."

Then this energetic candidate spoke to 2,000 people at the Jewish Educational Institute in Elizabeth, New Jersey, and expanded still further on his pro-Israel views, two days before the primary elections in that state. Wearing a yarmulke, the small headcap worn by Jews in orthodox houses of worship, Jimmy—as he insisted on being called—expressed "unswerving" support for Israel's right to exist as a Jewish national state. This was his principal response to the disquiet expressed by some American Jews who were fearful about the prospects of a "born again" Southern Baptist in the White House, when that church was alleged to have had a long history of "anti-Catholicism, anti-Semitism," and other bigotry. Just as the late John F. Kennedy had reassured churchmen in Dallas in 1960 about the prospect of a Roman Catholic President, so Carter had to quell the disquiet of Jews about a Baptist President. And as so many other Christians before him, Carter tried to allay fears of anti-Semitism through the most forthright protestations of support of Israel. "The survival of Israel," he stated, "is not a political issue. It is a moral imperative, and I would never yield on that point."

Carter used his total support of Israel as the weapon to calm "doubting Thomases" and to further clinch Jewish support. Jimmy noted that when the U.S. granted immediate recognition to Israel in 1948, the President had been Harry Truman, a Baptist and a Democrat. His listeners were not unmindful of the fact that Baptist dogma, with its fundamentalist literal approach to biblical **prophecy**, supports the return of the Jews to Palestine.

A summary of this address to a Jewish audience **was** carried far and near by the syndicated New York Times Service and the major television and radio stations. With victory at the convention in sight, Carter was looking forward to the general elections in November and to cutting the Jewish votes for the Republican party back to normalcy from the high that Nixon had won in 1972. A highly publicized meeting was arranged for the Georgian candidate by Washington attorney Lester S. Hyman with Israel's former Prime Minister Golda Meir at her suite at the Waldorf Towers in New York City, where she was staying before going to Wellesley College for an honorary degree (they had met during a 1973 trip to Israel). Jimmy described his position on Israel as "unshakable" and denied that the meeting had been designed to gain Jewish votes, although he pointed out that his chief Democratic rival, Senator Jackson, had had more opportunities to make his virulent pro-Israel position better known.

This blatant bid for the Jewish vote came at a time when Ford was in deep trouble due to his inability to find some solution to the critical Lebanese situation and to the very serious challenge of Governor Reagan, who was closing in on the President. Decisions that had to be made regarding the Middle East could only lose delegate votes for Ford at the August convention and gain them for Reagan, who was plunking for all-out support of Israel.

The question of additional aid for Israel in the transitional quarter period under the new fiscal-year arrangement was a source of embarrassment to Ford. Israeli proponents demanded $550 million additional to the $2.35 billion already voted the Zionist state for military and economic aid. The President contended that Israel, already assured of just over 50 percent of the total allocated to the entire world, did not need this large an increment.[25] But the Zionists, using the elections as a leverage, brought forward a new team of former Defense Secretary Schlesinger and Senator Humphrey to charge the Administration with going back on its promises to Israel and to force the inclusion of an additional $350 million.

To help recoup Ford's political losses, Governor Scranton[26] exercised the third U.S. veto on a Security Council resolution calling for implementation of the inalienable rights of the Palestinian people through the withdrawal of Israelis from occupied Arab territories and the return, in two phases, of Palestinians to their lands under their sovereignty. This occurred as the Democrats were on the verge of nominating their strongest candidate.

Jimmy Carter, former Governor and peanut king from rural Plains, Georgia (pop. 683), accomplished the politically impossible by capturing the Democratic nomination for President at the New York convention by virtual acclamation over the earlier strong opposition of the political professionals and elected public officials in his party. The political miracle of the fifty-one-year-old Georgian ranked as a greater accomplishment than the 1940 coup of another outsider, Republican Wendell Willkie. Jimmy's energy, which enabled him to survive thirty primary elections and twenty state conventions, hundreds of motel rooms, thousands of bolted meals, tens of thousands of handshakes, and hundreds of thousands of air miles, spelled success for the tireless, enterprising Georgian. Nineteen months of twenty-hour days paid off.

Carter appeared to be the right man in the right place at the right time. The only suspense at the convention revolved around the question of the Vice Presidential candidate. Minnesota Senator Walter Fritz

Mondale was chosen by the Georgian nominee from an original field of seven. The balance that swung the scales in favor of Senator Mondale, a Protestant, over Maine's better known Senator Muskie, who would have brought wide Catholic support to the ticket, was his longtime preeminent role in support of Israel and Zionism. When Israel had problems about foreign aid in the past, the Minnesota Senator, a protégé of fiery pro-Zionist Hubert Humphrey, had helped bail the Zionists out. And in his acceptance speech to the New York City Convention, the Vice Presidential candidate won a loud burst of applause when he referred to Israel's Entebbe Airport rescue: "Israel, always the bulwark of liberty, has set an historic example for freedom-loving peoples around the world by its bold and brave mission to Uganda."

Fulsome praise of Israel continued to resound from both Republican and Democratic electioneering platforms. The President, still seeking needed votes to win the Republican nomination, sent an unprecedented public message of congratulations to Premier Yitzhak Rabin for the dramatic Entebbe rescue. The insane hijacking by the Popular Front for the Liberation of Palestine proved a godsend to the heretofore very hard-pressed Zionists in Israel and in the U.S., whose fears of an immediate U.S. rapprochement with the Palestinians were now diminished and whose pride was bursting again as before the 1973 military upset.

The Democrats indicated at their convention their determination to win back that large share of the Jewish vote, the 85 percent they normally had captured until the Nixon landslide of 1972. The pressure was mounting on Carter, originally indifferent to the Zionist cause.[27] In his last interview on foreign affairs just prior to the convention, Carter had indicated that if elected he planned "to continue economic and military aid to Israel indefinitely"—President Ford was only making an annual $2.5 billion commitment for three years—although he would make "an annual judgment on the exact amount of aid that was absolutely necessary."

The chief academician for Carter on foreign affairs was Zbigniew Brzezinski, Director of Columbia University's Research Institute on International Change. A few months before the convention, Brzezinski wrote this Middle East appraisal, somewhat reminiscent of Henry Kissinger:

America has in the Middle East a combination of moral, political and economic interests—the most important one is the moral one which entails our commitment to Israel and its survival. We were instrumental in the creation of Israel, and therefore we have to be instrumental in its preservation. Our political interests are to make certain that the area is not controlled by forces hostile to us and that includes quite clearly the Soviet Union. Our economic interest is obviously the one pertaining to oil, which not only bears on our own stability, but very directly on the security and stability of our principal allies, West Europe and Japan.

The United States perhaps can continue to support both sides in the Middle East provided this support is designed to promote a settlement in the not too distant future. I do not believe that we can continue to do this in the context either of a stalemate or the absence of a settlement, neither of which, in my judgment can endure. If they do not endure, conflict again will resume, and in that context, it would be impossible for the United States to support both sides at the same time.[28]

In passing the Columbia academician mentioned that "some opportunity must be provided for the Palestinians to resolve their fate."

As Ford and Reagan continued to tear one another apart in the quest for the 1,130 delegate votes needed to win the nomination at Kansas City, giving every indication that the intraparty struggle would leave a Republican party beset by strife and bitterness, Carter used the five weeks before his opponent was chosen to get off to a big head start. And the Zionist lobby used this leverage to exert heightened pressure in all directions.

Not since 1884 had a presidential incumbent been so close to being repudiated by his party as Gerald Ford was at the hands of Reagan. That year Republican President Chester A. Arthur, who like Ford had not been elected President but had succeeded to the Presidency, was turned down by his party. The challenge posed to Ford came from the more aggressive, more outspoken, and more conservative one-time film actor, Ronald Reagan, who with his lovely wife had crisscrossed the country, effectively campaigning for nine months and rallying right-wing and some Zionist forces behind him. The outcome was in doubt when the convention opened on August 15.

Where the New York City convention that chose Carter had been a love feast, the Republican gathering in Kansas City seemed more like a council of war as charges and claims emanated from both Kansas City camps. Charges of bribery and a bitter fight over a proposed change in convention rules added to the acrimony.

On the third night of the convention, Ford beat back the challenge of the Reagan forces and won the nomination. The prestige of the White House carried the day. And then as at their rivals' earlier conclave, the suspense centered on the choice of a vice presidential candidate.

Favorite Tennessee Senator Howard Baker had eliminated himself when he revealed in a frank television interview that his wife once had a drinking problem. In the aftermath of Watergate, "Mr. Clean" was a necessary prerequisite for all candidates. In an attempt to bind the party's wounds, Reagan was consulted—if not offered the vice-presidential nomination—and agreed to the selection of Kansas Senator Robert Dole. A former Chairman of the Republican National Committee, the choice of Dole was as warmly received by the Zionists as that of his senatorial colleague, Fritz Mondale. If "Who Dole?" echoed across the country as "Who Carter?" had a year earlier, this was not so in Israelist circles. Dole had been almost as strong an advocate of Israel in the Senate as Gerald Ford had been when he served in the House. One of the Senator's closest friends and intimate advisers was a Jewish businessman who enjoyed high-ranking contacts with the Israeli government and continued even after the campaign to keep the Kansas legislator most active in Zionist propaganda activity.

The Senator himself enjoyed a very close relationship with Premier Rabin when the latter served as Israeli Ambassador in Washington. Rabin went to Kansas City to speak at a dinner during the Dole 1974 campaign when he was encountering difficulties in his reelection bid. Such important connections made the Kansan a "strong asset" to the ticket in the eyes of the President and his political managers.

In their pursuit of the critical and pivotal Jewish vote, the Republican platform declared that "the commitment to Israel is fundamental and enduring. We have honored and will continue to honor that commitment in every way—politically, economically, and by providing the military aid that Israel requires to remain strong enough to deter any potential aggression." The party platform also emphasized that "40 percent of all U.S. aid that Israel has received since its creation in 1948 has come in the last two fiscal years, as a result of Republican initiatives. Our policy must remain one of decisive support for the security and integrity of Israel." Elsewhere, the Republican policy statement praised Israel for the "daring rescue of innocent civilian hostages."

Judging by the remainder of this plank, in which the word Arab did not appear once (Israel was specifically mentioned eight times), the Republican party seemed to be concerned only with "that peace in the Middle East" that could bring "recognition of safe, secure, and defensible borders for Israel." This Republican 1976 platform probably contained the most ardent pro-Israel declarations ever adopted by the GOP.

While the Reagan forces were outspokenly critical of the Kissinger failure to end the war in Lebanon, nothing on this subject appeared in the platform. The tragedy of Lebanon, of course, only strengthened the Zionist position in the U.S. as PLO prestige plummeted and general repugnance toward the Arabs grew in the face of the unbelievable atrocities committed by both sides in the civil war.

While emphasis in the presidential campaign that followed the conventions was early placed on the economic state of the nation—both inflation and unemployment—the Middle East came in for its share of discussion, although no substantial differences separated the candidates or their parties regarding all-out support for Israel. But both Democratic nominee for the Senate in New York Daniel P. Moynihan in his race against incumbent James Buckley, and the head of his ticket, Jimmy Carter, took advantage of the administration's initial opposition to the strong anti-Arab boycott legislation pending in the Congress. The Democrats leveled charges that the Department of Commerce had been playing ball with the Arabs by advising American businessmen not to comply with the requirement that they file all information about Arab boycott demands. The "Israel-First" bloc, headed by Senators Ribicoff and Case and New York Congressmen Rosenthal and Bingham, led the fight for the enactment of legislation that would have made compliance with the Arab boycott impossible.

The Ford administration had let it be known that it did not favor legislation that might cripple U.S.-Arab business dealings, thus adding to the mounting U.S. balance-of-trade deficit. The President was trying to reconcile his desire for Jewish votes and the necessity of building friendlier relations with the oil-producing Arab countries, particularly Saudi Arabia, whose Foreign Minister, Prince Saud bin Faisal, already upset over congressional opposition to the sale of Maverick missiles to Saudi Arabia, had sternly warned against Washington challenging the economic boycott of Israel.

As Ford, according to the public opinion polls, gradually cut into the Carter lead, the critical "Jewish vote" increasingly emerged as the decisive factor. It was obvious that in a close election those extra Jewish votes, which Nixon had not needed, could put Ford over in California, New York, Ohio, Pennsylvania, and Illinois. Jewish vote-getter and fund-raiser Fisher pursued a new strategy of gaining endorsements of Ford from nationally prominent Jewish personalities to carry the day with Jewish laymen. Among those whom he had brought into camp was former Chairman of the Conference of Presidents of Major American Organizations Rabbi Israel Miller. And, of course, the principal consideration extended to these Jewish leaders were assurances of continued total support for Israel.

This was taking place even as Arab forces became bogged down once again in the mire of internecine rivalries. Israel's triumph at Entebbe, the brutality of the Lebanese conflict, and then the spectacle of the hanging of the Palestinian guerrillas in Damascus heightened pro-Israel public opinion, making it easier for the Zionist lobby to continue its blackmail of both major political parties.

The Democratic party remained the favorite of the Jewish-Zionist lobby. It was not that Nixon and Ford did little, but that Jews usually voted the Democratic line and Democrats were believed to be more reliable friends of Israel. If pro-Israel Jewish voters turned from the Democrats on Election Day, it would be only because of a mistrust of Carter and his economic fuzziness.

But the Israeli government, playing both sides, did not turn its back on the Ford candidacy. Rabin and the President were old friends, and no objections were voiced to the widespread use of Republican advertisements showing the two together and quoting the Israeli Prime Minister's words in August to the Rabbinical Council of America:

The U.S. government supports Israel in the international arena, in the supply of arms and in economic aid and almost with no precedence. The margin between what we want and what we get is very small.

The Middle East did not figure in the first of the three historic presidential television debates, featured by unplanned drama of a twenty-eight-minute mechanical breakdown in communications between the Old Walnut Theatre in Philadelphia and a national audience estimated at 100 million viewers. But three weeks later from San Francisco Ford and Carter crossed swords on foreign policy and defense issues. The Republican and Democratic candidates made little effort to conceal their principal objective. The word "Israel" was mentioned no less than thirteen times—allies Britain and France and hot spots Cyprus, Angola, Greece, and Turkey not once—and this did not include references to Prime Minister Rabin and to Jews. Each aspirant tried to outdo the other with claims of what he had done in the past and what he would do in the future for the State of Israel. The President and the former Governor shamelessly comported themselves as if they were candidates for the Presidency of the tiny Middle East state rather than of the U.S. And in the course of their sordid, competitive calls for unconditional support of Israel, the American national interest was totally, abysmally neglected.

Carter won that debate because he had the President on the defensive. In their differences over an approach to the Arab boycott, the President lacked the courage to explain forcefully to his audience the absolute imperativeness to the American economy of maintaining a semblance of an evenhandedness so as not to alienate totally the Arab world with its oil and wealth, so vital to U.S. energy supplies and to our critical balance-of-payments shortage. (By the first part of 1977 there was over $14 billion of Arab money in U.S. banks.)

The Arab boycott issue had already been reprehensibly beclouded, with the help of the media and notably the *New York Times*, by the injection of the charge of religious bigotry into what was totally a question of economic warfare. As an answer to the Carter allegations that the White House had yielded to Arab pressures, was permitting the boycott of American business companies for trading with Israel, and had encouraged the Secretary of Commerce not to reveal the names of American companies who had been subjected to the boycott, Ford noted that his administration had sold the Israelis over $4 billion in military hardware and "was dedicated to the survival and security of that country." The President also pointed out that he had already signed an amendment to the 1976 tax bill that penalized companies for cooperating with the Arab boycott.

The Ford statement in the debate that the people of Eastern Europe were not under the iron hand of the Soviet Union aroused angry outcries from Polish, Rumanian, Hungarian, and other Eastern European ethnic groups in the U.S. This biggest boo-boo of the campaign was immediately seized upon by Carter as the President vainly tried to explain away the words, which had slipped out, by pointing to his own consistent anti-Communist record in behalf of the oppressed people of that part of the world.

In an attempt to make up for important ground lost to Carter in this debate, the Republican incumbent intensified his efforts to play up to the Jewish bloc vote. The states in which offended Americans of Eastern European ancestry were heavily concentrated were the very same industrial states—New York, Ohio, Illinois, Pennsylvania, and New Jersey—in which Jewish voters were concentrated. For thirty years, as Michigan congressman and Republican Minority Leader in the House of Representatives, no one had excelled Ford in his pro-Israel, anti-Arab zeal. And now by new deeds the President was being forced to show once more how pro-Zionist he was, if not anti-Arab.

As Steven Ford, the youngest of the President's sons, was marching up New York Fifth's Avenue with other vote-seeking politicians in the Columbus Day Parade, so dear to the American-Italian, Prime Minister Yitzhak Rabin was announcing to his Cabinet that President Ford had at last agreed to a long-standing Israeli request to lift the ban on the sale of some sophisticated American military equipment and to speed up the delivery of other hardware already approved.

This politically-inspired move by Ford was given additional prominence because the President at that moment was receiving Israeli Foreign Minister Yigal Allon, and television cameras brought into American homes the picture of the beaming Israeli diplomat at the White House as he welcomed the announcement regarding the new military items, which included night-fighting electronic equipment and cluster bombs capable of causing extensive fire and concussion damage (this bomb contains fuel-air explosives and is most effective against large groups of enemy forces, because it not only causes wide incendiary damage but can create a temporary vacuum capable of suffocating the enemy). The U.S. bestowal of these arms came at a time when rebellious Arabs within Israel proper were already running up against local police armed with American weapons, and Muslim villages in South Lebanon were falling prey to Christian attackers supplied with arms bearing Hebrew markings, all made possible through the U.S. arms and dollars flowing to Israel.

Also on order to be sent to Israel were armed helicopter gun ships equipped with antitank missiles, ultramodern radar equipment, new models of the wire-guided antitank missiles, and M-160 heavy tanks, of which the U.S. was still in short supply. Much of this military equipment had not yet been made available to European U.S. allies.

The cost of the ordered military equipment was to be covered by the large amount of aid approved for Israel by the Congress just before the adjournment for the elections. Over the twenty-seven-month period from July 1, 1975, to August 1, 1977, Israel had been authorized to receive about $4.4 billion in assistance, of which nearly $3 billion was for military credits, half of which would not have to be repaid. The alleged excuse for U.S. arms shipments to Israel at this time, the Soviet arming of Arab countries, was no longer valid, as Moscow military supplies to the area had drastically declined with Egypt-U.S.S.R. relations at almost the cold war stage. And the "splendid state" of the Israeli military forces had only just been widely proclaimed in Jerusalem by Defense Minister Shimon Peres.

In response to Carter taunts of letting Israel down, the President quoted Prime Minister Rabin as saying that U.S.-Israel relations had never been better. To further emphasize to his Jewish constituents the presidential concern for Israel, Ford stated in the televised debate that the names of U.S. firms that had complied with the Arab boycott would be immediately released by the Department of Commerce. This step was intended to offset Zionist-Democratic criticism of the administration's pressure to gain congressional approval of the delayed sale of Maverick missiles to Saudi Arabia. And on the very next morning after his promise. New York City and other radio stations across the country incessantly droned forth the names of U.S. companies, released by the Commerce Department, that had complied with the Arab boycott. The *New York Times*[29] listing of the companies included the Jewish clothing firm Kayser-Roth, indicating to the careful reader that the boycott was not aimed at Jews *qua* Jews, but at all companies that aided Israel economically. (Many Muslin firms were being boycotted by the Arabs.) This Jewish firm apparently preferred to do business with the Arabs and not assist Israel's economy.

The front page of the *New York Times* (although obviously still supporting Carter) carried a three-column photo of the President visiting the Succoth booth in which religious Jews eat during their fall holiday. Ford told his Jewish audience what it wanted to hear—that he would visit Israel "in my next term when such a trip would contribute most to peace"—and he attacked terrorism, an obvious poke at the Palestinians, who at that moment were faring exceedingly badly on all sides. In a private meeting with a group of Jewish leaders, the President seemed to answer all their questions satisfactorily.

Despite these efforts, the American voters on November 2, for the first time in 128 years, sent a son of the Deep South to Washington, ousting from office the first presidential incumbent since Republican Herbert Hoover was swept into retirement by the Great Depression in 1936. The demand of the American votes for change had overpowered their fear of the unknown in one of the closest presidential elections of the century. And it was the capture of three of the five largest Electoral College states—New York, Pennsylvania, and Ohio—that carried the day for Jimmy Carter. Although Ford had run a courageous race and had come up from far behind, he could not overcome the many adverse factors that overwhelmed him. The weight of Watergate, the pardoning of President Nixon, and the floundering economy were all undoubtedly factors, as were the powerful last-minute combined efforts of the labor unions and the Democratic party chieftains. But what was most decisive was the Jewish vote in New York City, Philadelphia, and Cleveland, which went 80 percent plus for the son of Georgia and gave him the 93 big fat electoral votes to put him over the top.

In all parts of New York City, Carter ran well ahead of the Jewish vote received in 1972 by Senator George McGovern. And in the State of Ohio, Senator Robert Taft, although possessing one of the most revered American political names, went down to defeat to a staunch Zionist Jew, Howard Metzenbaum, in another "I can do most for Israel" contest. If a "beautiful new spirit," to quote the words of the President-elect, was being ushered in, it was the same old Zionist concentration in the nation's largest cities, and its traditional preference for the Democratic party that had sealed the doom of Ford, in spite of his degrading wooing of this bloc vote and a seeming reticence of certain Jews to favor a Southern Baptist with an obscure economic outlook.[30]

The number of voters who turned out—just over eighty million—was the largest in U.S. history, which surprised political observers because of the alleged apathy of the electorate toward both candidates. But the percentage of Americans either eligible to vote or registered to vote was less than it had been in 1968 and 1972. This and the very narrow Carter margin, particularly in the Electoral College count, indicated that the new President had received no mandate from the American people. And the most difficult decisions, which now had to be faced in Middle East policy, spelled real trouble ahead for the incoming Chief Executive.

XXI   Exit Henry Kissinger?

> Words are given to men to conceal their thoughts and not to
> express them.
>
> —Talleyrand

The election of Jimmy Carter not only ended the interregnum of
Gerald Ford but, of course, brought to a close the unparalleled spectacular rule over U.S. foreign policy by Henry Kissinger. In what
turned out to be his valedictory, his principal 1976 campaign speech
to the Synagogue Council of America at its Fiftieth Anniversary Jubilee
Dinner, Kissinger unequivocally stated that the principal goal of the
U.S. in its Middle East foreign policy has been "the survival and security of Israel." To the delight of his listeners, he indulged in Zionist
phraseology, talking of the "needs of the Jewish people" and the
devotion required in the "unending struggle."

Invoking Eisenhower's "there is no alternative to peace"—but
with no reference to Ike's famed fiat against the imposition of conditions for withdrawal by occupiers of conquered territory—he bestowed
fulsome praise on Israel: "No people yearn for comprehensive peace
more than the people of Israel, whose existence has not been recognized by any of its neighbors throughout its history."

While at no time a Zionist in the conventional sense of the word,
and never part of the Jewish Establishment, Kissinger had been in
close contact with its leaders and intellectual spokesmen through his
Rockefeller, Council on Foreign Relations, and Harvard connections.
There is little doubt that he was deeply affected by his experience in
Germany, where he grew up in the city of Fürth.[1] Twelve of his relatives were killed by the Nazis, and he and his family fled in August
1938, just three months before Crystal Night of November 9–10 when
so many Jews were arrested, if not killed, in raids throughout Germany.

Although he declared that "political persecutions of my childhood are not what control my life," he rarely concealed his strong concern for the Jewish state. As he told one close friend, "Look, anyone who has been through what I have been through has some very special feeling for the survival of the State of Israel."[2] Allegedly he sent a check in 1971 to the Jewish National Fund in memory of his boyhood chum, Kurt Fleischmann, who had died without going to Israel. A grove of 300 trees on the Jordan hills near Jerusalem stands in memory of his friend from Fürth.

While Kissinger could be said to be staunchly anti-Communist and very wary of Moscow's intentions, he never shared Secretary of State John Foster Dulles' view that massive retaliation was the answer to the Soviet threat. A student of nuclear development, Kissinger believed in the deterrent strategy of limited nuclear warfare, at the same time strongly advocating the broadest possible agreement with Moscow for the limitation of nuclear weapons. Long before he took over the Secretaryship, he placed a top priority on a successful culmination of the SALT negotiations. If the Big Two could delimit nuclear weapons, then they could together bring, if not impose, peace on the Middle East. It had long been his belief that Russia and the U.S. were under obligation to "foster an accommodation between Israel and the Arab states."

Although he served as National Security Adviser to the President from the outset of the Nixon administration, Kissinger's personal preoccupation with the Middle East did not begin until he had replaced William Rogers as Secretary of State in September 1973. At the time he made the surprising move of joining the administration in 1969, he had never set foot in any Arab country, and had only been to Israel twice.

The Kalbs, authors of his biography, maintained that the professor had kept out of the same personal involvement in this region that marked U.S. relations with China, the Soviet Union, and Southeast Asia at the expressed wish of the President, who preferred that he "yield the Middle East to Rogers and Sisco." His low profile in this area was calculated, we are told, "to avoid becoming a target of Arab extremist propaganda—the kind of venomous anti-Semitic propaganda that Egypt, Syria, and Iraq and some Palestinian groups had hurled at Arthur Goldberg and at Eugene and Walter Rostow."[3]

Kissinger was too good a student of history to have ever accepted this myth of Arab anti-Semitism as a reason for abstaining from earlier personal attention to the Arab-Israeli conflict. The truth was that he was overly preoccupied elsewhere, and just as he was to be wrong on many of the military aspects of the October conflict—including his miscalculation as to its approach—so he had been dead wrong in underestimating the urgency of defusing the Middle East. If fear of heightened Arab bigotry because he was a Jew had been holding him back, Kissinger would hardly have ventured so deeply into the fray after the October war, which saw a strengthened and newly rein-vigorated Arab world. On the contrary, as the almost too-brilliant student of history that he was, he knew and counted on the Arab with his tolerance to lean over backwards and perhaps accord Kissinger, the Jew, far more consideration than any Christian counterpart might pos-sibly have been accorded.

A better reason, perhaps, for not becoming deeply involved in the Middle East imbroglio until he was at the helm of the State Department on the eve of the 1973 conflict, was that he did not see eye-to-eye with Secretary Rogers' insistence on initial Israeli withdrawal from occu-pied Arab territories, with only "unsubstantial" border changes. Nor did he thoroughly share the vague sentiment of the administration for the evenhandedness recommended by Governor Scranton.[4]

But even in the period of nonparticipation in Middle East policy-making, Kissinger insisted that the U.S. had a "historical commitment" to Israel and that the preservation of that country was in the American national interest. He opposed any veering from fullest support of Israel so long as the Soviet Union was deeply entrenched in Egypt. The pro-Israelism inherent in Kissinger thinking—which became U.S. pol-icy—stemmed less from any love of Israel and an advocacy of Zionism, than from his total insistence on a 20th-century recreation of the 19th-century concept of balance of power, under which Israel, as the U.S. ward in the Middle East, must always be maintained at equal (if not greater) strength than the Soviets' Arab wards.

Kissinger patterned this thinking after that of Austria's Metter-nich, Germany's Bismarck, and England's Castlereagh, under whose guidance Europe had enjoyed a period of relative tranquility and peace from the Congress of Vienna in 1814–15 to the beginning of World War I. As set forth in his doctoral dissertation[5] at Harvard, his political philosophy was based on the successful balance of power his heroes managed to achieve:

A framework in which it was in no country's interest to escalate a war to the point of toppling the carefully balanced structure; a framework in which each of the major countries had a vested interest in stability. This "stability" was as close as mankind could come to "peace." It might not be ideal, but it offered the best chance for survival.[6]

To attain this balance of power, Kissinger believed, as the Europeans before him, that the end justified any and all means:

Statesmen must use cunning and patience. They must be able to manipulate events and people. They must play the power game in total secrecy, unconstrained by parliaments which lack the temperament for diplomacy. And they must also connive with the largest possible number of allies. They must not shy away from duplicity, cynicism or unscrupulousness, all of which are acceptable tools of statecraft. They must never burn their bridges behind them and, if possible, they must always be charming, clever and visible.[7]

This was exactly the way in which Metternich and Bismarck played the game, and a fair description of Kissinger's methodology. Any analysis of the precise admixture of these attributes, which he employed in his renowned diplomatic shuttling, would vary between admirer and detractor, and whether it came from Anwar el-Sadat, Amin al-Hafez, Golda Meir, or Yitzhak Rabin.

It was apparently Kissinger who must receive the credit for the Nixon insistence, expounded in the 1968 and 1972 campaigns, that Israel enjoy a military superiority, not a mere balance with the Arabs. Under normal conditions, "if there were two opponents of roughly equal strength," the professor would say, "you want to bring about a military balance; but a military balance is death for Israel because a war of attrition means mathematically that Israel will be destroyed."[8] The fear that the "eastern Mediterranean might become a Soviet lake" dominated Kissinger's thinking; as he expressed it, "what they are doing in the Middle East, whatever their intentions, pose the gravest threats in the long run for Western Europe and Japan and, therefore, for us."[9]

Although the former Harvard professor's apocalyptic vision fastened onto the lethal weapon of oil, he eschewed any course of action that would really have liberated the Arabs from their intermittent reliance on the Soviet Union. This would have been counterproductive to his insistence on the strategy of building Israel into a "bastion of American democracy in the Middle East," endowed with military superiority. While very cognizant of the danger, as he expressed it, that "the wealth and strategic value of the Middle East could be denied to the West, which would shift the balance of power irrevocably in Russia's favor," Kissinger's sole formula for preventing such an eventuality was to rely on Israeli strength and on the hope that the Soviets would be "expelled" from the area.

In a June 26, 1970, briefing to news editors in San Clemente, the Secretary of State-to-be let the cat out of the bag: "We are trying to get a settlement in such a way that the moderate regimes are strengthened and not the radical regimes. . . . We are trying to *expel* the Soviet military presence.[10] (Italics added.) Ironically enough, the October airlift to Israel was the very step that placed Arab oil reserves beyond U.S. and Western reach and kept the Soviet military presence, with its competitive arming of the Egyptians and Syrians, still prominently in the area. And if the Kissinger outlook was based on the threat of the Soviet Union and Communism to this most strategic of areas, it is hardly understandable how a student of world affairs, such as he, should have risked antagonizing the most obvious instrumentality toward meeting this threat—the basic conservative anti-Communism of most Arab Muslims stemming from the strong theism of Islam, which was epitomized by the Saudi Arabian monarchy. Here again, it was a case of wanting to eat as well as have the cake. If anti-Communist support was dependent on standing up to the Israelist political machinery, that support wouldn't be commandeered, as far as Kissinger was concerned. Kissinger, as had the British in World War I, very much preferred to rely on Zionist cooperation in the area rather than on Arabs in carrying out his designs.

The Secretary of State regarded Israel as a vital part of "a large strategic context" with the Soviet Union, but a special feeling towards the Zionist state was nourished by the intermittent xenophobia of some of Israel's Arab enemies, which was readily equated to Communism and thus brought into play application of his obsessive balance of power. His Israeli ties were also strengthened through a unique relationship, going back to 1964, with his special friend, Israeli Ambassador Yitzhak Rabin, the former Israeli Chief of Staff, who had ordered the air assault against Egypt and Syria opening the 1967 war. Kissinger often met Rabin off the record to discuss the Middle East crisis, but kept his distance publicly.[11]

Whenever Secretary Rogers started to exert a little pressure on Rabin to make concessions in the ongoing Jarring negotiations, even to the point of threatening to hold up the delivery of Phantom jets, it was Kissinger, at Rabin's urging, who interceded. He assured Rabin that "plane deliveries would continue and State Department pressure would stop." It was Kissinger's intercession that paved the way for Meir's second visit to the U.S. in November 1971, when the differences among her, the President, and his Secretary of State were patched up.

This led to the all-out support given to the Nixon candidacy in the 1972 elections by Ambassador Rabin (and his government), an unheard of intervention in U.S. politics on the part of a foreign diplomat. In that campaign the Secretary appeared at meetings sponsored by Max Fisher and Goldman Sachs' Gustave Levy to raise big money from Jewish sources, and he never attempted to hide from contributors his strong pro-Israel feelings, even as he was negotiating with the Arabs as a neutral mediator.

It was part of his Metternichian balancing to give the impression of primary concern both for the Israelis and the Egyptians, concealing from them his ambivalency. In 1973 he certainly had done everything he could to prevent an outright Arab victory. Spurred by a message from Prime Minister Meir the Saturday night of the second week of fighting, personally delivered by Foreign Minister Abba Eban, that Israel had only enough ammunition for about four days of continued fighting, the Secretary had galvanized final U.S. action to meet the deadline for the arms airlift, which turned Israeli defeat to near victory.

But his plan of strategy did not call for Israel winning a decisive victory as it had in 1967. Kissinger "cajoled, pressured, urged, implored, warned, threatened, and pleaded with Israeli envoy Dinitz to understand his logic and accept his policy of a non-victory for Israel.[12] Kissinger wanted a military stalemate. With Israel on the West Bank and Egypt on the East Bank, each side would have leverage over the other, which would advance his design for settlement. That is why he insisted on sending in food and supplies, blocking Israeli intended decimation of the Egyptian Third Corps, which, he felt, could not bring peace and could only create new animosities, triggering still another war. To Kissinger, a clear-cut Israeli victory through U.S. aid would only mean further isolation of Israel and encourage a new wave of anti-Americanism in the Middle East in which the oil embargo, rather than being a tactical weapon, might emerge as a permanent feature of Arab policy. He strove to use his rescue of the Third Corps as a demonstration of new U.S. impartiality, which Sadat, at least of the Arabs, accepted.

In the fall of 1975 U.S. foreign policy objectives conformed strictly to the political needs of a nonelected President struggling to win mass approval for a reelection in 1976. This required able trusted aide Henry Kissinger to maintain, above all, the status quo and to prevent any further war. Kissinger dangled new bait in front of the Arabs: "The Soviet Union can give you weapons, but only the U.S. can give you a fair and just solution through which you may regain your lands." It was a very "hungry" and desperate Sadat who had latched onto Kissinger's word "expel" and peremptorily thrown out the Russians, putting all his eggs into Kissinger's basket. And to keep the eggs there, in his talks in Riyadh with King Faisal and Prince Sultan, the Secretary stressed forthcoming continued U.S. evenhandedness toward settling the conflict. The October war of 1973 presented the U.S. with new realities that had to be faced: not only had the Arabs fielded a fighting force, which had momentarily threatened Israeli military forces, but more importantly they had developed the powerful weapon of oil, whose strength had been proven.

Kissinger's preoccupation with the Middle East was now directed toward neutralizing this political weapon and curbing the growing power of OPEC, which had defeated Kissinger's first efforts to rouse the oil producers and world public opinion against it. The realistic Secretary could not help recognize that the Arabs had come into their own. As Ghassan Tuéni, editor of *An Nahar,* expressed it:

The October war represented one great Arab achievement. They showed that they are not fossils. They are not doomed to ossify as the modern world passes them by. October showed that the Arabs are a living nation. They can develop; they can acquire the education and culture needed to handle modern technology. They can forge the social coherence, the trust in one another that alone enables men to go to war together and win. October showed that the Arabs can face the challenge of modern times. It showed that, to their quantity, the Arabs have begun to add quality.[13]

Kissinger must have been aware of the dangerous anomaly implicit in his 1975 triumphal disengagement agreement. If Arab unity was destroyed, as seemed to be one of the concomitants, if not objectives, of the second Egyptian-Israeli disengagement, the Arabs would lose their capacity to enforce progress toward peace. And for the U.S., as it had been for the British in 1958, it would be another case of "divide and lose." Those Arab countries, deprived of sharing in the benefits from the new "evenhanded" stance of the U.S., naturally opposed Egypt's unilateral approach to Israel. Sadat's signing of the disengagement agreement and his trip to the U.S. led to formation of a new anti-U.S. bloc made up of Syria, the PLO, and Libya, with Iraq standing in the wings only because of the long-standing differences between the Damascus and Baghdad branches of the Ba'ath party. (History almost exactly repeated itself two years later when Sadat went to Jerusalem in November 1977, unilaterally extended legitimacy to the Israeli state, and convened the ensuing Cairo Conference.)

Splitting the Arab world may have seemed to serve Kissinger goals of inching the protagonists through step-by-step negotiations toward a final settlement. But with the neutralization of Egypt, Syria and other Arab states turned to the Soviet Union, giving the Kremlin a new lease on life in the Middle East. Instead of the Soviet Union being effectively thrown out of the area, as Kissinger hoped, the more the U.S. strove to divide the Arab world, the more the Soviet Union seemed to work its way into these divisions, some of which fizzled on their own.[14]

In the face of the continued arms escalation, Kissinger constantly contended that U.S. arms shipments to Israel were necessary for maintenance of a military balance in the area, the alleged prerequisite for peace. In this balancing act Kissinger had to overcome certain realities by constantly creating new facts. The late Colonel William Eddy, first American Minister to Saudi Arabia, used to tell of a Dutch innkeeper who, when asked to explain the proportions of horse and rabbit in his famed hassenpfeffer, answered: "Fifty-fifty, of course. One horse and one rabbit." The balancing of an Israel against even a disunited Arab world certainly yielded a most unpalatable "stew" for the U.S., even before oil became such an important factor and marked the diminution in the qualitative differences between the two "halves" of the Middle East. A balance between twenty-two Arab states, with a population of 150 million and covering in excess of five million square miles, and one Israeli state of 3.3 million people with an area of less than 7,000 square miles, has to be arbitrary, artifical, and capricious, and must necessarily fail in its objective of bringing stability and peace to the area.

Sending Phantoms to the Israelis has only meant more Soviet MIGs for the Arabs. Sending Lance and Pershing missiles could mean only more SCUDs and other sophisticated Soviet missiles. Such a balancing act has contributed to war, not brought peace. Shattering Arab unity by treating certain Arabs as "good" Arabs and by any other possible means became a necessity to the Kissinger endeavor. While he told his Synagogue Council audience that "history teaches us that balances based on constant tests of strength have always erupted into war," the Secretary himself was guilty of failing to take concrete action to avoid these tests of strength, which instead of retarding only aggravated dangers of Big Power polarization.

During Kissinger's first visit of November 1973 to Cairo, in a conversation with Mohamed Heikal, the *Al-Ahram* editor before he was forced into retirement by Sadat,[15] Kissinger indicated the lengths to which he would go in pursuit of his "balance": "Do not deceive yourself. The U.S. could not—either today or tomorrow—allow Soviet arms to win a big victory, even if it was not decisive, against U.S. arms. This has nothing to do with Israel or with you."

In his balancing act, Kissinger blindly refused to recognize the fundamental difference between those countries whose ties with the Soviet Union stemmed from ideological compatability and the Arab world, whose links to the Kremlin primarily stemmed from the aphorism "the enemy of my enemy is my friend"—and, one might add, a damn good friend. This accounted in part for the Secretary's relentless opposition to the Palestinian and PLO aspirations. By his incessant pursuit of a fixed balance between the Superpowers, and by equating Arab ties with the Soviet Union to Israel's links with the U.S., Kissinger subjected his country to the gravest and most unnecessary risks.

A step-by-step formula, calling for separate Egyptian, Jordanian, and Syrian negotiations with Israel, was Kissinger's means of circumventing the Arab 1974 Rabat Conference decision and U.N. resolutions recognizing the PLO as the representative of the Palestinian people and a necessary negotiating party at any reconvened Geneva Conference. The veto power over U.S. recognition of the PLO, given to Israel as part of the second disengagement agreement, constituted another anti-Palestinian Kissinger move in behalf of Zionism.

If Richard Nixon was "Tricky Dick," what should Henry Kissinger be called? Despite denials to the contrary, there were secret commitments given that glued together the disengagement decisions hammered out in Cairo, Jerusalem, and Damascus; among the most important was the promise to provide Israel with long-term military assistance rather than the previous ad hoc annual grants of military aid. And who could believe that the decision announced in Washington by President Nixon shortly after his return from the Middle East, to write off an additional $500 million in military aid debts to Israel, was not part of the package deal that had led the reluctant Israeli Cabinet to change its mind and accept disengagement with Syria's Hafez Assad. And no doubt the many economic goodies promised Egypt helped bring Sadat around, including a $2 million White House helicopter, which pro-Israel Senators vehemently protested "as a policy of purchasing friendship with such a lavish and uncalled-for gift."

From the outset, students of Middle East Affairs suspected that Kissinger's goal was to buy immediate time rather than grow long-term peace-roots, and by any Metternichian means possible. The lengthy Marilyn Berger account in the *Washington Post*[16] of a Kissinger meeting on December 6, 1973 with several Jewish intellectuals scarely presented the Secretary in a much better moral light than the Watergate tapes revealed his chief. The leakage of notes about this lengthy "Pearl Harbor Day" meeting projected an image of Kissinger as more of a wheeler-dealer than a Nobel Prize winner.

The meeting had been arranged by lawyer Rita Hauser, who, before she had been active in garnering Jewish support for Nixon's reelection in the 1972 presidential campaign, had not hesitated to abuse her position as U.S. representative to the U.N. Commission on Human Rights by a blatant defense of the Israeli occupation at a Zionist conclave in California and on educational television.[17] Those in attendance were Norman Podhoretz, editor of *Commentary;* Irving Howe, editor of *Dissent;* Henry Rosovsky, Dean of the faculty of Arts and Sciences at Harvard; and Harvard Professors Seymour M. Lipset (now at Stanford), Michael Walzer, David Landes, and Kenneth Arrow. All were pronounced and active Israelists. Lipset had authored the January 1971 horrendous *New York Times* Sunday magazine piece that endeavored by every means possible to place the label of anti-Semitism on anything and everything opposed to Israel, Jews, or Zionism. Professor Arrow was one of the Harvard economic Nobel Prize laureates who warned Washington not to bow to Arab oil pressures. Irving Howe, following the meeting, likewise made his contribution in *New York* magazine in which he urged Jews to speak out against potential pressures that Kissinger and Washington might bring to bear. He concluded his piece with this warning:

A time may come when it will be necessary to turn to more dramatic and militant methods, perhaps a march on Washington. A time may come when the traditional Jewish outcry of gevalt! provoking scorn and worse may be necessary. Let us keep our voices in readiness, but meanwhile there is the work of politics, pressure, persuasion. Silence is intolerable.[18]

Lawyer Hauser ascribed the "nervousness" in the Jewish community over Kissinger's intentions as the reason for the meeting. Podhoretz told Kissinger that some Israelis were wondering whether he was a "Churchill disguised as a Chamberlain or a Chamberlain disguised as a Churchill.[19]

Kissinger emphasized that he had been instrumental in getting the arms lift to Israel approved at a time when Israel was nearly out of ammunition and when congressional support was visibly declining in the face of the energy crisis. He also detailed how he had resisted Soviet urgings to halt the war at an earlier stage, when Egypt's surprise attack was pushing the Israelis back on the eastern side of the Canal. The Secretary, adding to his acknowledged accomplishments for Israel, boasted that he had won an added ninety-six hours for the Israeli army while he went to Moscow to discuss the terms for the October cease-fire. He also claimed to have gained support of the provision for direct negotiations between Israel and the Arab states, something Tel Aviv had been seeking long before the six-day war.

In his earlier talks with Heikal in Cairo, Kissinger denied he had been taking Israel's side at any stage and insisted he had been only helping the Egyptians:

All our experts believed, if you restarted the war, you would be exposing yourselves to a decisive attack by the Israeli armed forces. It was then that I proposed a cease-fire and a return to the original lines. *I believed this measure would benefit you more than Israel.* [Italics added.]

To the Jewish intellectuals, the former Harvard professor maintained that the Israelis could not have kept going without the U.S. airlift, for which he was principally responsible, because they had run out of ammunition. He reportedly told Heikal: "Even if the Israelis had not had the arms we sent them, they would not have been in the powerless situation you imagine. They had prepared their counter-attack of the Suez Canal before even receiving our aid."

Kissinger frankly indicated why he felt that it had been necessary for the Israelis to end the war and start negotiating. He was fearful that congressional support of arms for Israel might not be forthcoming under similar circumstances again. He indicated that it was two-to-one against his being able to pull off another such airlift.

Kissinger was reported to have used extremely harsh language concerning the anxiety of European countries to placate the Arabs and obtain oil. "Craven," "contemptible," "pernicious," and "jackals"[20] were words he used to describe their behavior. And the U.S. Secretary, who shortly thereafter was embracing and holding hands with the Saudi Arabian Foreign Minister, delighted his Harvard colleagues by then labeling King Faisal a "religious fanatic, concerned mostly about Jerusalem with little interest in the Sinai or the Palestinians." Fearful that Israel was to be "Taiwanized" and sacrificed for the sake of dé-tente, his listeners pressed the Secretary for details of his immediate goals. Apparently he generally satisfied the concerns of the intellectuals, some of whom felt even more assured after his diplomatic efforts yielded the disengagement agreements.

Kissinger certainly did not start out as a Jewish nationalist,[21] but like Herzl he had been very much of an assimilationist. His second wife was Christian, as were many of his earlier female companions and close associates. But he was pressured by overwhelming Zionist, Jewish, and then Israeli connections. And he particularly wished to be both respected and loved, and to bask in the spotlight of international fame as his "every whim and quip was chronicled by a worshipful press corps."[22] (Even on his "secretive" 1974 honeymoon the press was flashed the news that Henry and Nancy were "hiding" in Acapulco.)

Kissinger sought, above all, not to cross the Jewish apparatus publicly which would have crushed his aspiration to earn a unique position in Jewish annals. Apparently his first visit to Israel had changed the viewpoint he held as a college student that the creation of a Jewish state "would be a potential and historic disaster." He became personally and professionally committed to help the state survive. Kissinger believed that Israel's best security was to get a firm security commitment from the U.S. in return for the relinquishment of the conquered territories, and from the Arabs full rights of peace, commerce and interchange.

In wanting the credit for giving Israel recognized, secure, and guaranteed boundaries as his greatest accomplishment, Kissinger aspired to follow in the footsteps of Moses Maimonides, Judah Halevi, and other Jews who perennially had served under Muslim leaders, bringing dignity and honor to Muslim-Arab-Jewish relationships during the Golden Era of Judaism. This was a challenge the Jewish side of Henry Kissinger could not resist.

Although ultraconservative Zionists assailed him and Begin's Likud railed at him when he initiated the disengagement agreements, the overwhelming majority of Israelis and American Jews loved their dynamic Henry. Not only was he their Jewish boy who had made good, but they felt he had tried to get the Arabs to accept Israel on Israel's terms. The question remains whether or not in reciprocating this love, Kissinger had betrayed his solemn pledge, given at the press conference following his swearing-in as Secretary of State, that he would "conduct the foreign policy of the U.S. regardless of religious and national heritage" and "in pursuit of the national interest."

If Secretary Kissinger's intellectual fiber was strong enough to override emotional compulsions driving him toward the Israeli camp, then it was indeed a gigantic misjudgment to have chosen Israel as the pawn on the Middle East chessboard to checkmate "the Soviet's" Arabs and their oil. Even after the inexorable burdens of the Watergate Affair were no longer directly hampering foreign policy implementation and President Ford had given him fullest latitude in foreign affairs, Israel continued to be the albatross around the U.S.

neck. And the Kissinger admixture of "balance of power" with "but Israel, too" invariably resulted in the sacrifice of American interests.

Ongoing negotiations between the U.S. and the Soviet Union were delayed or hampered in the hope that Moscow would first become more conciliatory on the Middle East issue. The U.S.-U.S.S.R. trade agreement was abrogated because the Kremlin refused to make Kissinger-sought concessions regarding Jewish emigration. As foremost expert on Soviet affairs George F. Kennan pointed out in a May 7, 1978, interview with Marilyn Berger of the *New York Times Magazine:* "The number of Jews coming abroad on the contrary has declined. I don't understand this policy on our part. I don't think it is entirely thought through."

Every external economic and political relationship that the U.S. maintained remained complicated by the unique relationship with the State of Israel. The October war, the oil embargo, and the continuing energy crisis had strained U.S. ties with France, Britain, and others of U.S. European allies as well as Japan, who opted for an "Israel Second" policy in seeking unilateral agreements to assure themselves of adequate petroleum supplies. In what was a matter of life and death for their industrial machines and civilian day-to-day living, there was little hesitation in resisting all Kissinger efforts to promote a united consumers' front against the oil-producing countries.

The failure to consult U.S. allies prior to the airlift to Israel and the all-out military alert on October 23 shattered NATO unity, already impaired by the Kissinger policy toward the Cyprus crisis, in which the U.S. managed to antagonize Greeks, Turks, and Cypriots alike. And though he left office in a burst of glory, elsewhere the Kissinger policy also proved to be a flop. On the subcontinent the U.S.-Pakistan alliance had proved to be a most unfelicitous balancing attempt. What was earlier considered enough of a triumph in Vietnam to earn him the Nobel Peace Prize turned out to be another U.S. disaster.

In the Middle East the singular Kissinger accomplishment was to avoid a major military conflict between the Arabs and Israel. What little effort had been directed toward halting the Lebanese civil war had always been tempered by an overriding regard for Israeli interests in southern Lebanon. The U.S. continued to seek to pacify rather than to solve problems, thus merely putting off a possible eviler day.

In addressing the luncheon he gave for Arab Ambassadors at the U.N. on September 25, 1973, the Secretary said:

We will show understanding, and we hope you for your part will do the same
. . . what is needed is to find ways to turn what is promptly acceptable to you
into a situation with which you can live.

These words were hardly fashioned to halt the drastic military
action Egypt and Syria launched eleven days later. While Kissinger had
declared that he was "prepared to work with all the parties toward a
solution of all issues yet remaining—including the issue of the future
of the Palestinians,"[23] the invariable impediment to implementing the
welter of fine words was his concern for Israel (and his fear of the
Zionist connection). Only a desperate Sadat, who a month before the
first failure at a second disengagement was still holding meetings with
Andrei Gromyko, allowed himself to be ruled by the proffer of Kissinger's future good intentions.

Through disengagement II, Israel had not only killed the Rogers
plan to force her back to the 1967 lines but had "wrested from the
U.S.," in the words of author Edward R. F. Sheehan,[24] "a moral,
monetary, and military cornucopia unattained by any other foreign
power." Indeed, as a senior Israeli official told *Time* magazine: "The
agreement delayed Geneva, assuring us arms, money, a coordinated
policy with Washington, and quiet in Sinai. . . . We gave up a little for
a lot."[25]

As he was waiting in late August for the Israeli government to
ratify the terms of the disengagement agreement, Kissinger spent his
last hours before leaving the Holy City on a visit to the Yad Vashem
Memorial. This paralleled the final waiting period spent in Jerusalem
the previous March, when his shuttling had failed and he had visited
Masada. While reporters and photographers were allegedly barred
from accompanying him to the Hall of Remembrance, where he laid
a wreath and lit the memorial flame, a *Jerusalem Post* story recited the
close examination by the Secretary of alleged anti-Semitic literature
printed in Arab countries (Kissinger reads neither Arabic nor Hebrew)
and study of new material on the holocaust. He asked to be sent copies
of leaflets and books printed by "Arab propagandists who claim the
killing of six million Jews never occurred." Kissinger was said to have
told his guide that "something must be done to prevent the tragedy
of the holocaust from recurring."[26]

The boy from Fürth could never forget his past. Down deep as a
Jew, he felt that he could not conduct a policy that could ever be said
to have led to any Israel setback or defeat. If he were ever forced to
that point, he had privately admitted that he would quit. In the wake

of his initial disengagement failure, Kissinger is said to have asked several of his Jewish visitors, "How could I, as a Jew, do anything to betray my people?"[27] This is why he rallied to Begin's side, despite the Israeli leader's previous antagonism toward him. Kissinger spent 70 minutes giving the Prime Minister tactical advice at the Waldorf prior to the Begin critical March (1978) meeting with Carter, which followed Israel's invasion of Lebanon. And the former Secretary of State continued to warn, "A separate Arab state on the West Bank, whatever its declarations, whatever its intentions, must have an objective that cannot have compatability with the tranquility of the Middle East."[28]

During his first audience with King Faisal in Riyadh, Kissinger was said to have pronounced words to this effect: "I arranged détente with Russia. I opened the door to China. I brought peace to the Middle East. I hate failure. I have not failed. I shall not fail."[29]

Three years later, Anwar el-Sadat endeavored to go it alone, and prove, with the blessings of the new Carter Administration, that his mentor, Henry, had made no empty boast.[30]

XXII   Enter Carter—and Then Begin

Richard sometimes reminds me of an unhappy gentleman who comes to the shore of a January sea, heroically strips to swim, and then seems powerless to advance or retire, either to take the shock of the water or to immerse himself again in his warm clothes, and so stands cursing the sea, the air, the season, anything except himself, as blue as a plucked goose.

—Christopher Fry, *The Dark Is Light Enough*

The Zionist lobby in Washington could not have been more pleased with the results of the November 1976 elections. Once again in power was the Democratic party, which had always been so closely attached to Israel and its U.S. apparatus. The Democrats had increased their hold over the lower house in the new Congress and broke even in the upper house, where the "Israel-First" bloc was greatly strengthened by the new presence of Ohio's Senator Howard M. Metzenbaum and New York's Daniel Patrick Moynihan. The latter had assiduously used his U.N. post as a platform to gain his political goal, after having declared that he should be considered immoral if he ever did this. This bombastic politician had given every indication that he would outshine even his senior New York colleague, Jacob Javits, in devotion to the Zionist cause. Along with Metzenbaum and the presiding officer of the Senate, Vice President Mondale, there was now a new, potent Israelist MMM in the Congress, and the number of Jews in the Senate had increased to five[1] and in the lower house there were now twenty-two.

The new occupant in the White House had of recent years been cultivating close ties with many Israeli and Zionist leaders. While President Ford expressed some small concern during the campaign about U.S. relations with the Arab world (which he increasingly shed as Election Day drew closer), Carter had never varied his 1,000 percent

679

pro-Israel stand. He took a much harder position on the Soviet Jewry issue, and he pledged enactment of the Bingham-Rosenthal-Stevenson anti-Arab boycott legislation early in his administration. During his drive for the White House, Carter was surrounded by important Jews, including his campaign treasurer, advertising chief, and internal issues coordinator. And Edward Sanders, president of AIPAC (the Israeli lobby), who had so fiercely assailed the president of SOCAL in 1973,[2] had resigned his post to become Deputy National Campaign Chairman.

In line with his major June 6 Middle East campaign speech before the Jewish Educational Institute in Elizabeth, New Jersey, the President was expected to move away from the step-by-step diplomacy practiced by Kissinger toward an overall settlement to be sealed at Geneva. In that speech, Jimmy listed concessions to be required of the Arabs in any peace settlement: recognition of and diplomatic relations with Israel, a peace treaty, end of the embargo, end of official hostile propaganda, open borders, economic interdependence between the West Bank and Israel, and demilitarization of the West Bank—in short, all steps required to make clear that the war was really ended once and for all.

The speech was allegedly drafted by Henry Owens of the Brookings Institute, and a memo attached to the draft was said to have indicated that some kind of input had been received by Israeli officials, who were deeply concerned that the President might be contemplating the inclusion of a Palestinian state as part of a settlement. The previous December (1975), he had stated in a college address at Medford, Massachusetts, that peace must be based on "recognition of the rights of the Palestinian people, but the PLO would have to recognize the rights of Israel, who must withdraw to the 1967 boundaries."[3]

That same December the Brookings Institute Report, prepared by a study group of sixteen including Israelist leader Philip Klutznick, six other prominent Jews, and Columbia professor Zbigniew Brzezinski, approved the principle of Palestinian self-determination in the form of a West Bank state independent or federated with Jordan, but subject to recognition of Israel by the Palestinians. The report also called for gradual Israeli withdrawal to the 1967 borders. Behind the scenes, Israeli Ambassador Dinitz vigorously fought these recommendations but had succeeded only in preventing one other Jewish member from endorsing the panel's conclusions.

Shortly after Brzezinski's appointment as National Security Adviser to President Carter, he privately informed the Israeli government and Secretary Cyrus Vance, according to columnists Evans and Novak,[4] that he no longer agreed with the 1975 proposal for "a Palestinian state next to Israel." At the same time, David Aaron, formerly Vice President Mondale's long-time legislative assistant and a fervent Israelist, was placed in charge of the Brzezinski National Security Council staff.

Carter's first significant remarks on the Middle East came in response to a question during his widely publicized town meeting in Clinton, Massachusetts. After referring to the establishment of Israel as "one of the finest acts of the world's nations," and declaring that "the first prerequisite of a lasting peace is the recognition of Israel's right to exist,"[5] with borders a matter to be negotiated between the Arab countries and Israel, the President then made his controversial statement: "There has to be a homeland provided for the Palestinian refugees, who have suffered for many, many years."[6] Immediately threatening clouds gathered. In and out of Congress, Zionists were up in arms at the mere mention of a Palestinian homeland. The Israel lobby opened its lines into the White House. Brzezinski was alerted, and told a press briefing at the U.N. prior to the President's speech on human rights the next day that the President had used the word "homeland" generically, and had intended no change in U.S. policy.

What took place in March was characteristic of Carter's moves on the Middle East during his first year in office—one step forward and one step back as he persisted on being all things to all people. Israel's political power in the U.S. had to be balanced against concern over Arab oil prices and even the possibility of an Arab shutoff in the unlikely chance of war. To assuage angered Israelists, Secretary of State Vance promised to ship "advanced technology" to Israel. This balanced Washington's cancellation of the devastatingly powerful CBU-72 concussion bombs, promised by Ford as a political gesture during the campaign, and the $500 million in aid given to Egypt as a partial answer to the January food riots in which 80 were killed, 800 hurt, and 1000 arrested. On his first swing through the Middle East in an effort to restore the peace momentum, the Secretary was told by Sadat, allegedly with the approval of Arafat, that he favored an "official link between the Palestinian state and Jordan, even before Geneva talks started." But there was still little give on either side in the struggle as to which came first: recognition and secure borders for Israel or Israeli withdrawal from all occupied territories and recognition of Palestinian rights.

Meeting in quick succession Israel's Rabin, Egypt's Sadat, Jordan's Hussein in Washington, then Syria's President Assad on May 8 in Geneva and the Saudi Arabian Prime Minister Crown Prince Fahd, the President resumed his efforts to push for reconvening of the Geneva Conference in late summer or fall. But the disaster that had overtaken Prime Minister Rabin for a domestic impropriety, forcing the May Israeli elections, complicated the process and called for another visitation to Washington by the victorious Israeli candidate.

A suave Anwar Sadat came, saw, and what he conquered in Washington was not then visible. The freewheeling, shoot-from-the-hip Carter style suited the Egyptian's own infatuation with words. The affection he felt for Kissinger was now transferred to the President, whom Sadat talked of as a "great statesman," a "sweet man," and "an inspiration." For all the flattery bestowed, Sadat seemed to come away with precious little in hand. At an intimate, final press gathering at Blair House for Middle East "experts," there was no reference to the "shopping list" of military equipment reported earlier in his visit, and he refused to divulge any details of economic aid he might have garnered during his visit.

In his appearance on the CBS show "Sixty Minutes," the Egyptian leader opposed the March 9 Carter press conference suggestion that Israel be given temporary "secure borders," which would extend for a limited undesignated period of time Israel's legal boundaries (a response to Foreign Minister Allon's demand for "defensible borders"). Sadat declared: "Sovereignty is indivisible and we can't have two borders. Sovereignty always means one border." The Egyptian leader was full of praise, however, for the presidential reference to a Palestinian homeland.

The President's meetings with King Hussein and President Assad had tempered his hopes for Geneva, and he was said to have been downcast as he saw the Jordanian King into a limousine outside the Oval Office. To Assad, Carter reiterated the need for a homeland for the Palestinians, but, as he told the press upon his return from his meeting with the Syrian President, the degree of independence of the Palestinian entity, its relationship with Jordan, and other details had to be worked out by "the parties involved. But for the Palestinians to have a homeland and for the refugee question to be resolved is obviously of crucial importance."[7]

Although the President then repeated that "it is absolutely critical that no one in our country or around the world ever doubt that our number-one commitment in the Middle East is to protect the right of Israel to exist, to exist permanently, and to exist in peace," talk of a

Palestinian homeland deeply upset the Israelis, who had to be assured by Vance that the U.S. was not planning to impose a solution but merely wanted to "help facilitate the process of peacemaking." The U.S. hoped that the parties would agree upon a five-point peace plan consisting of Palestinian recognition of Israel; Israeli support for a Palestinian state or homeland; Israeli withdrawal to roughly the 1967 lines with security lines beyond its legal frontiers; the eventual normalization of travel, trade, and other relations between Israel and its neighbors, so as to create an atmosphere of peace; and a major movement toward a settlement that year.

Almost at the same time as Carter was telling an audience at Notre Dame University (May 22) that he expected Israel would withdraw from the occupied territories west of the Jordan River and that failure to agree on peace could be disastrous, newly-elected Israeli Prime Minister Menachem Begin was telling viewers of ABC's "Issues and Answers" that Israel, quite the contrary, would not only not return the West Bank area, but that he considered this "liberated territory," open to further Israeli settlements. He called this region—and required his press to do likewise—Judea and Samaria, part of "Eretz Israel," land given by the Lord to the Jews in the covenant with Abraham. Begin had won his surprising election on the Likud platform featured by a Messianic advocacy of a Greater Israel:

The right of the Jewish people to the land of Israel is an eternal and inalienable right, and is also an integral part of the right to security and peace; thus Judea and Samaria [the entire West Bank] will never be turned over to foreign control; between the sea and the Jordan there will be only Israeli sovereignty.

At Carter's May 26 press conference covering his first four months in office, the President was asked by an obviously pro-Israeli reporter whether there was any way Israeli retention of the West Bank might be viewed as a "minor adjustment" to territorial boundaries from which Israel would not have to withdraw. The President cited U.N. resolutions in support of Palestinian rights to a homeland and compensation for losses suffered, but attributed them to the Security Council. This led to the issuance of a White House correction stating the President had been mistaken as to any such Security Council resolutions, but making no mention of the many General Assembly resolutions, where the U.S. veto does not operate, unequivocally affirming Palestinian rights, which Carter must have initially had in mind.

In addition to Resolution 194 of December 11, 1948, giving the refugees the right to return home or to be compensated, which had been reaffirmed with near unanimity every year since (and usually submitted by the U.S. delegation), there have been numerous reiterations of the "inalienable rights" of the Palestinians, of their right to political independence and self-determination in Palestine, of the legitimacy of their struggle for independence by all means available, including the use of armed force.[8] Two standing U.N. bodies, the Committee on Exercise of Inalienable Rights of the Palestinian People and the Special Committee to Investigate Israeli Practices Affecting the Human Rights of the Population of the Occupied Territories, were given permanent jurisdiction over the resoluted items. In December 1977 the General Assembly voted $456,000 for publicizing these "inalienable rights of the Palestinians."

Following a meeting with Prince Fahd at the White House in June, the President was ebullient enough to say that he and his guest "had no disturbing differences at all" on basic issues, including a Middle East settlement—a remark that disturbed the Israelis no end and again led to further pressures on the White House.

To answer growing discontent with Carter policy, Vice President Mondale was dispatched to speak in San Francisco before the affluent World Affairs Council of Northern California. He stressed the special U.S.-Israel relationship and assured his audience that Israel would never be asked to "withdraw unless it can secure in return real peace from its neighbors." The Palestinians, the Vice President asserted, "must be given a stake in peace so they will turn away from the violence of the past and toward a future in which they can express their legitimate political aspirations peacefully." If they "recognized Israel's right to exist in peace," he added, the Palestinians should be provided "some arrangement for a Palestinian homeland or entity—preferably in association with Jordan," the specifics of which "are for the parties themselves to work out."[9]

Concerned about continued reiterations by the Begin government of the "liberation of Judea and Samaria," the administration issued a statement on June 27 through the State Department reminding Tel Aviv that in return for Arab agreement for peace with Israel, Prime Minister Begin must agree "to a withdrawal from occupied lands on all fronts and to the formation of a Palestinian homeland."[10]

It was time for the administration to hold out a carrot to go with its stick. The Pentagon approved the sale to Israel of $115 million in military equipment, including 200 antitank missiles, 700 M-13 armored carriers, and 15 M-778 tank bulldozers. This was in addition to the earlier sale of $200 million in tanks in which the U.S. was still in such short supply. But this action did not spare the President from the blistering criticism of Senators Javits, Richard Stone (Dem.-Fla.), and Richard S. Schweiker (Rep.-Pa.) that the administration had been demanding far more from the Israelis than from the Arabs in outlining terms for a settlement.

Upset by the dangers stemming from the initial adverse reaction to the election of extreme nationalist Begin and what they viewed as a sterner line by the President, the Zionist lobby intensified its country-wide efforts. A thousand letters a week urging stronger support for Israel poured into the White House. Rabbi Alexander M. Schindler, who as head of the Conference of Presidents of Major Jewish American Organizations and as former President of the Union of American Hebrew Congregations (an umbrella group for 750 Reform temples with an alleged or claimed membership of 1.3 million) was emerging as the top spokesman for Zionist-Israelist interests, boasted to *Time* magazine that White House aide Hamilton Jordan seemed to reflect a change in mood over the telephone: "Then I knew that the question of American-Israeli relations had become a serious political matter and they weren't treating us as if we were part of a foreign relations department. Carter was beginning to perceive the importance of wooing the American Jewish community."[11]

Vance, Brzezinski, Jordan, and White House Issues Coordinator Eizenstat invited individual Jewish leaders to meetings or luncheons, fielding their complaints and assuring them that they had nothing to fear from Carter. Mondale had half a dozen meetings with Schindler and Washington Chief of the American Jewish Committee Hyman Bookbinder, but still leaders felt, "He's not the President." The Zionists were determined to apply more heat directly on the President prior to his meeting with Begin.

Carter, who only the week before had called for a three-week moratorium on comments about the Middle East until the Begin arrival, met at the White House on July 6 with fifty-three Jewish leaders representing all secular and relious organizations. He told them that the Arab nations should establish full diplomatic relations with Israel as part of an overall Middle East settlement. To further assuage some of the Jewish fears about his call for a Palestinian "homeland," the President stated that he did not favor a separate Palestinian state, which could be a threat to peace, but only an entity to be a part of Jordan.

No solution, he added, could be imposed; it would have to be negotiated. As the President was imparting this comfort to the Israelist leaders, the administration was announcing rejection of the second effort by Israel to sell Ecuador twenty-four Kfir fighter-bombers equipped with American engines.

Rabbi Schindler, shuttling back and forth between Israel and the U.S., assisted by flying visits to Israel of Senators Javits and Stone dispelled the "wild man" image of Menachem Begin. "He's a statesman," they insisted, "who wants to bring peace to his country." The theme was picked up by editors of the 130-odd Jewish weeklies as they depicted the new Prime Minister as a "freedom fighter" who had always sought to avoid civilian casualties in his "battle against the British." There were only a handful of iconclasts, such as Jewish chaplain at Yale and Breira National Chairman Rabbi Arnold Wolf, who persisted in criticizing Begin. "Why can't I call him a right-wing fanatic? I think it's outrageous that American Jews are supposed to suppress their feelings in the interests of the Jewish people."[12] Behind the banner "We're pledged to the security of Israel," monolithic Jewish support for Begin was mustered.

For Begin, the visit to Washington was exceedingly successful. With the help of the media, the image of a charming, kind, and flexible leader totally displaced that of an intransigent hard-nosed terrorist. The two leaders responded to each other exceedingly well, often conversing in words of the Bible. Menachem Begin and Jimmy Carter formed an instantaneous mutual admiration society. "Never in my thirty years in public life," said Begin, "have I been as impressed by a political leader." Carter called Begin "a man of truth and great dignity. I don't think the meeting could have been any better." He made clear to Begin that the U.S. goal was to achieve a comprehensive settlement to be arrived at by the parties, which suited Begin perfectly; he indicated he did not wish to negotiate an agreement with the U.S. but simply wanted to get started negotiating with the Arabs.

On a more practical level, Washington agreed to provide $106 million for the production of new Israeli Chariot tanks and to supply eighteen attack helicopters and an undetermined number of FS-16 fighters. Through military and economic grants, the U.S. was helping Israel fight its battle against inflation, worsened by a cut in subsidies on home commodities that forced a 25 percent rise in prices of such staples as bread, cheese, milk, and gasoline.

Carter softened his concept of a "homeland" for the Palestinians, but Begin would give little ground, still opposing one single Arab delegation at Geneva and insisting that under no circumstances could known members of the PLO participate, even as members of the Jordanian delegation. Through maps he had carried to the U.S., the Israeli leader attempted to show the President how vulnerable Israel would be to an Arab surprise attack should Israel be required to withdraw. And to the President's concern about the continued settlements on the West Bank, Begin responded with a most irrelevant comment: "There are eight Hebrons and four Bethlehems in the U.S."[13] And "I could scarcely refuse to let Jews settle there."

Sunday, July 24, was the last of Begin's nine days in the States, and there was more of the "Rally 'Round the Flag, Boys." His first visitor at his suite in the Waldorf Astoria was Henry Kissinger, whom I had heard in a Jerusalem square in the spring of 1974 being wildly excoriated by the Prime Minister-to-be in an outdoors emotional outpouring before thousands, with the kind of bombastic language one would not permit his mother to hear. The shuttling Secretary was, at the time, safely ensconced with his retinue at the King David Hotel, surrounded by U.S. Secret Service and Israeli Security forces.

The *Times* Sunday "Week in Review" literally glowed with the "smooth start on the high road to Geneva," which had been made by Begin in his more than five hours of face-to-face talks with Carter, although admittedly there were still wide differences over such essentials as the recognition of the PLO and its possible presence at Geneva. The Israeli reiterated that under no circumstances would he sit down with the PLO. The only Begin sop to the Palestinians was that no one would look at the credentials of the Jordanians and there would be no objection if some were Palestinians.

In his questioning on NBC's "Meet the Press," the Israeli took over totally. Before the questioning could begin, he launched into a three-minute peroration that the "Jewish people" would never face extermination again. Otherwise, Begin adroitly and totally avoided efforts of the panelists on the program to pin him down to specifics.

Carter apparently had turned "pussy cat" in the face of the iron-willed Begin. He failed to ask the Israeli his intentions regarding existing unauthorized but not as yet legalized settlements in the occupied territories,[14] although Carter had made clear that the U.S. considered these settlements illegal and that the establishment of new settlements would be "an obstacle to peace."[15] Less than a week after he left Washington, Begin gave legal status to three previously unauthorized Israeli settlements, Kadum, Ofra, and Maale Adumim in the West Bank, bringing the total of Israeli settlements to ninety—nine in the outskirts of Jerusalem, thirty-six on the West Bank, twenty-five on the

Golan Heights, and 20 in Sinai and Gaza. (By the end of 1977 there were ninety-six.)

Secretary Vance's mild censure, "this was contrary to international law and an obstacle to peace," was Washington's sole reply. Although not quoted publicly, the President himself was believed to have been infuriated. The staunch friend of Israel, the *Washington Post,* called the action "reckless, provocative and indefensible . . . a frontal assault on the American effort to arrange a settlement."[16] But there was nothing unusual about the Begin move to have surprised anyone. It was consonant both with Israel's ten-year policy of "creeping annexation" and with Herut leader Begin's oft-enunciated dogma of a "Greater Israel." But the White House continued to "waffle" on the Palestinian issue, stating that the negotiations would determine that homeland's "degree of independence."

The August swing of Secretary Vance through the Arab world and Israel resulted in a hardening of attitudes by Israel. Begin declared he would not accept a West Bank enclave under Jordanian sovereignty, a formula that the Rabin-Peres government had been prepared to accept, and the Israeli Prime Minister described the PLO philosophy as "an Arabic *Mein Kampf* which was a danger to all free nations." This was at a time the PLO seemed to have become more flexible and, under the moderating influence of Saudi Arabia, whose financial backing was always needed, was said to be contemplating some change in its attitude toward recognition of Israel, provided that Resolution 242 were amended to alter the Palestinian status from that of refugees to Palestinian nationals.

And the only carrot Washington was offering the PLO was to open talks in exchange for an acceptance of Resolution 242, but with no guarantee of a place when and if Geneva reconvened. The Vance flirtation with so-called "West Bank dignitaries" during his August visit to Jerusalem did not help relations with the Arafat-led PLO, which had been strengthened by a reconciliation with the Habash PFLP and a joint determination to push for an independent state on the West Bank and in Gaza.

Two weeks later the PLO executive committee, meeting in Damascus, ruled out "a dialogue with the Carter administration" and assailed "Zionism and American imperialism" for continuing to attempt to split the Arab world and for ignoring the "national rights of the Palestinian people." The front-page *Times* James Markham article[17] made the PLO the villains of the piece for rejecting U.S. terms requiring recognition of Israel by the PLO, without any equivalent amendment to Resolution

242 recognizing Palestinian rights.

The more intransigent and chauvinistic Begin became, the more his popularity at home, and the greater the respect for him in Washington. There was a frantic closing of ranks behind the leader. Nothing succeeds like success. Nothing dazzles more than defying the President of the U.S. By mid-October General Yael Yadin and his Democratic Movement for Democratic Change with its fifteen seats, despite its earlier opposition to the government's settlement policy, joined the government and greatly strengthened Begin's control in the Knesset. The establishment of the three additional West Bank settlements brought the mildest Washington reaction—a State Department lecture to the Israeli Ambassador, not from Secretary Vance but from Undersecretary Philip Habib.

Nor did the Begin administration seem to be embarrassed by Agriculture Minister Ariel Sharon's plan,[18] first leaked to *Ma'ariv,* for thirty additional settlements and three urban centers in the Western half of the occupied territory. The main Arab population centers would be cut off by settling two million Jews over twenty years in territories extending from Golan to Sharm el-Sheikh, at the southern tip of Sinai. Eighty-two percent of Israelis polled favored some kind of settlements in the occupied territories. In the face of these "signposts to destruction," as Lord Caradon, who had drafted Resolution 242, referred to the settlements,[19] Begin still maintained he wanted peace. "Everything is negotiable" the Israeli leader consistently proclaimed in an incessant flow of articles and interviews, which invariably depicted the Zionist state as prepared to give back its conquests for a "real peace." The announcement of the extension to the "liberated territories" of Israeli government facilities, including electric power, improved water supply, and telephone service, was hailed by the Zionist-oriented media as a conciliatory move toward the Arabs, by Israeli expansionists as indicative of the permanency of the government's control in the area.

Before the Arab Middle East foreign ministers and Dayan convened in the U.S. for unilateral meetings with Carter, the Arab League tacitly admitted Israel's right to existence as a state in calling for Israeli withdrawal from Arab territories occupied during 1967 but making no reference to Israel's 1948 boundaries.

The September State Department statement that "lasting Middle East peace will be impossible without Palestinian involvement in Arab-Israeli negotiations"[20] led to instantaneous, militant mobilization. Telegrams to the White House, telephone calls to congressmen, letters to the editor, Op-Ed pieces by Rita E. Hauser[21] and others in the *New York Times* all sounded warnings against a PLO state. Israelists had been in a state of alarm since former Ambassador William W. Scranton, a close friend of Secretary Vance, had allegedly met informally and unofficially with a PLO representative in London.

At the time Israelis were dedicating new settlements at Reihana on the West Bank near the Arab town of Jenin, the Israeli Foreign Minister was en route to the U.S. carrying in his pocket a "peace treaty," the draft of which showed that questions of a Palestinian entity and the status of East Jerusalem, in particular, were not up for discussion. By a 92–4 vote the Knesset had declared that under no circumstances was the PLO to be made a party to the negotiations. In Dayan's words, it was "less dangerous to oppose a Palestinian state and risk a war now, than it would be to accept such a state and risk a war in the future, when presumably hostile groups would be resident in a sovereign state next door." *Time* reported: "Anyone who thinks that this government is going to withdraw from the West Bank is suffering delusions."[22]

En route to the U.S. Dayan made a sudden side trip to Tangier in full disguise and met with King Hassan, from whom he allegedly received a critical message that Egypt would consider interim talks if Geneva negotiations failed and, according to *Time*,[23] the Saudis would interpose no objections. The groundwork for the startling Sadat November pilgrimage, perhaps started by Rumanian President Nicolae Ceausescu, may then have been further advanced. An earlier London Dayan secret meeting had not been productive, as King Hussein had been "carefully noncommittal"[24] to a proposal for a nonbelligerency treaty in exchange for Jordan-Israel sharing responsibility for the West Bank.

Dayan flew back to Israel for consultations before his appearance at the White House. The only concession the Israelis would make was to permit Palestinians, but not known members of the PLO, to be represented at the opening ceremonies in Geneva as members of the Pan-Arab delegation, and only within the Jordanian party. After that the Israelis would negotiate separately with the Arab states directly involved in the talks—namely, Egypt, Syria, and Jordan—and the Palestinians could attend these talks as members of Jordan's delegation. Secretary Vance at this stage announced that the new Israeli position had "added conditions that do not accurately reflect our views." Egyptian Foreign Minister Ismail Fahmy called the Israeli proposal "a nonstarter." The PLO's Farouk Kaddoumi reacted, "We reject it, full stop."

On the eve of the meeting with Dayan, the White House statement that "the Palestinians must be represented at Geneva" added to mounting pressures directed at a President already greatly weakened by the Bert Lance affair and the growing congressional opposition to the proposed Panama Canal Treaty and his energy program. And the stock market had slid to the lowest levels in twenty months.

Hoping to avoid the long-feared collision with Israel, which seemed to be increasingly inevitable in the light of Begin's inflexibility on the issue of the West Bank, the President turned to the Soviet Union. On October 1 the world was taken totally by surprise with the issuance of a three-point joint statement by the Geneva cochairmen on the desirability of reconvening the conference before the end of the year, ensuring "the legitimate rights of the Palestinian people" and enabling "normal peaceful relations in the region." The U.S. accepted for the first time the concept of Palestinian "rights" as against "interests," and the Soviet Union acquiesced in a statement that did not mention the PLO, although Moscow had long insisted that the PLO, as the legitimate spokesmen for the more than three million Palestinians, had to participate in any Geneva Conference.

The onslaught against the joint demarche was led by the media. Both the *New York Post* and the *New York Times* editorially and newswise lent their columns prominently to Israel's protests. The Zionist state was portrayed as a victim of a "Big Power-imposed settlement,"[25] and U.S. pressure on Israel was declared to be equivalent to "diplomatic isolation." The *Times* accused the President of using the "euphemism of Palestinian 'rights' to something approaching the creation of an independent Palestinian state abutting their [Israel's] borders and surrounding Jerusalem," and of wrongdoing in bringing the Russians into the negotiations "at this early stage of the negotiations."[26] The President apparently had hoped Moscow would apply pressure on the Syrians to accept less than full PLO representation at Geneva.

When Carter appeared before the U.N. General Assembly on October 4 and again declared that "the legitimate rights of the Palestinians must be recognized," the opposition to the President's program took on an open campaign. Chairman Rabbi Schindler announced that he and Dayan would visit Chicago, Atlanta, and Los Angeles to mobilize the public against the Carter administration. The 1973 threat of Ambassador Dinitz to go over the head of the U.S. Government directly to the American people was now being carried out. And in Washington the White House had already been informed, according to the *National Review Bulletin*, that any undue pressure on

Menachem Begin could result in "hard Congressional lumps on the [Panama] Canal" issue.

The seven-hour stormy meeting of Carter, Vance, and Dayan at the U.N. Plaza Hotel followed. While assuring Dayan of the U.S. commitment to Israel, the President tried to exact more flexibility on the Palestinian issue. Adamantly refusing to agree to an independent Palestinian entity or homeland on the West Bank or to accept the PLO at Geneva, the Israeli instead confronted the President with an alleged list of broken promises by U.S. Presidents who failed to give the Zionists all they wanted—from Roosevelt, who did not open U.S. gates to Jewish refugees, through even Johnson, who allegedly stated: "The U.S. is not a policeman of the world" when asked to ensure the previous Eisenhower promise of freedom of navigation through the Suez Canal.

The working U.S.-Israel paper on Geneva procedures that would permit Palestinians, but no PLO representatives, to be present at Geneva and then only to participate in any bilateral negotiations as part of the Jordanian delegation, marked another Israeli victory, although Carter continued to talk about an undefined Palestinian "homeland."[27] For Israel to go to Geneva, she did not have to accept what the administration now called the "hopes" expressed in the U.S.-U.S.S.R. statement.

For their part, the Israelis continued to demonstrate the deepest trepidation that the Palestinians would raise the issue of Zionist usurpation of land and would question the legitimacy of the Zionist state. It was much more difficult to make the Hitler label stick to homeless Palestinians, whose dispossession could be recited in moving terms, than to the Arab states, whose sole bone of contention was a piece of territory occupied by Israel through conquest. It was fear of the reaction of world public opinion, particularly in the U.S., to the moral issue that might be leveled against them that crazed the Israelis—and this at a moment when the Zionist state never felt as militarily secure. Its tremendous superiority over the Arabs in weaponry constantly increased, as the U.S. $2 million-plus military pipeline flowed continuously while Arab arming faltered and sputtered at Soviet hands or remained as unfulfilled promises of European countries.

Political pressures on the President did not cease. "I'd rather commit political suicide than hurt Israel," Carter told a delegation of Jewish members of Congress. He took the occasion to effectuate a reconciliation with New York mayoralty candidate Congressman Edward I. Koch, who was carrying forward the Lindsay-Wagner tradition of acting as if he aspired to be Mayor of Tel Aviv. Upon the President's arrival in the city to address the U.N., the Mayor-to-be handed Carter a letter denouncing the U.S.-U.S.S.R. communiqué, as media cameras ground away and all newspapers headlined the incident. (Previously Congressman Koch had called for the dismissal of General Brown and accused the Syrian government of anti-Semitism, despite the thrice-repeated Mike Wallace program on CBS's "Sixty Minutes" exposing this charge as pure propaganda.)

As Washington pressed for Geneva "this year," the Israeli Cabinet and Knesset accepted the U.S.-Israel working paper, with Dayan emphasizing that there would be a walkout from the conference if there was any insistence upon a Palestinian state. Syria's President Assad indicated: "No PLO, no Geneva for us." The White House attempted through personal assurances to assauge Sadat, who opposed the working paper because of the elimination of the PLO. In the wake of Arafat meetings with Sadat, PLO spokesmen indicated formation of a provisional government was under consideration.

The President was still very much on the defensive. Although the administration had unmistakably indicated its opposition to Israeli settlements in the occupied territories, the U.S. abstained in the 131-to-1 October 28 U.N. vote on the Egyptian-sponsored resolution censuring Israel for "changing the legal status, geographical nature, and demographic composition" of the territories in violation of the U.N. Charter and of the Geneva Convention. If Washington was exerting any pressure on Israel behind the scenes, up front Carter was now maintaining a very pro-Israel posture as Israel's press allies joined the fray.

A Pranay Gupte-prepared article rehashed Stanford's Dr. Seymour M. Lipset's thesis from *Commentary* magazine[28] that Carter's call for the "legitimate rights" of the Palestinians "would have a devastating effect on President Carter's chance for re-election." Lipset closed with the warning that "because the political and financial support of this portion of the electorate is usually significant in a presidential election, any move on the part of Mr. Carter perceived as detrimental to Israel would adversely affect his political future."[29]

Far more subtle than any editorial critical of the President for insisting on a greater voice in peace negotiations for the Palestinians, this lengthy, contrived "news piece" two days after a lengthy front-page Sunday article, "Growing Alarm Among U.S. Jews Threatening Carter's Mideast Policy,"[30] placed additional pressure on the White House and added incentive to the Zionists, already steamed up after unsatisfactory talks with Secretary Vance,[31] to war on the President.

In early November Carter addressed a gathering of 800 Jewish leaders from forty-one countries who were attending a Washington meeting of the World Jewish Congress. The President begged for support of the "best opportunity for a permanent Middle East settlement in our lifetime," and assured these Zionists that Israel would never be forced to deal directly with major officials of the PLO.[32] Senator Howard H. Baker (Rep.-Tenn.), who also addressed this conference, pursued the partisan tactics of the Republican party Chairman, former Senator William Brock, in accusing the administration of breaking with past U.S. policy established under presidents of both parties. The ugly and perennial quest for "the Jewish vote" was not even subtly concealed. And Andrew Young's statement that the U.S. was "bolstering Israel" in its Mideast policy represented the latest political bid of the ambitious U.S. Ambassador to the U.N.

While his appointment had been greeted with great enthusiasm by Arab and black African nations, the handsome one-time aide to Dr. Martin Luther King soon indicated on which side of the street he was going to walk. At his first press conference on January 3 before the Senate had confirmed his appointment, Young defended his viewpoint toward the Rhodesian crisis by stating: "I would no more want the 400,000 whites in Rhodesia to be driven into the sea than the three million Jews of Israel." Following this gratuitous remark, the Ambassador further indicated the depth of his feelings (or more precisely, his political attachment) toward Israel. After being sworn in as Ambassador by the President in Washington and presenting his credentials to Secretary-General Kurt Waldheim, his very first act was to rush over and pay a courtesy call on "his old friend" Israeli Ambassador Chaim Herzog—this was prior to any call on any other Ambassador, African or otherwise.

Two months later in a New York City meeting with members of the Conference of Presidents, Young declared that he had experienced in 1966 "a brutal awakening" to the hatred of Jews by Arabs, an experience that "brought terror to my heart." As a result, Young told the visiting Zionists, "I saw the need for Israel to be strong and secure to cope with the hatred of its neighbors."[33]

The meeting had been closed to the press, but Young's presentation had been leaked to the New York Post by a spokesman for the organization. Young had gone on to say that he had experienced "the Ku Klux Klan mentality of hatred in the South," but the first time he ever saw hatred by "intellectuals" was during a 1966 visit to Jordan—

a hatred aimed at the Jews, Young reported. The Ambassador's peace formula was to make Israel as "secure as possible militarily, as strong as possible politically, and as adventurous diplomatically" as the Israelis wish.

A candidate who could sew up the Jewish as well as the black vote would make an ideal Vice Presidential running mate for Walter Mondale in 1984. And then in 1992, who knows? The first black in the White House?

As Washington was weighing the effect of vying Geneva "peace" formulas on Carter's political future, the scene in South Lebanon scarcely reflected tranquillity. As a means of further intimidation of the Palestinians and of improving its bargaining position, Israel flexed its military muscle in fierce "reprisal" aerial onslaughts on refugee camps and civilian sites, with more than 100 casualties—the first Israeli strike into South Lebanon in nearly two years. This may have helped divert Israeli attention from intolerable economic problems at home wrought by the moves away from Israel's socialist-oriented past toward free enterprise. The subsidy-cutting, instituted by Finance Minister Simha Ehrlich and resulting in 10 to 30 percent price rises, led to demonstrations and strikes.

Inflexibility of both sides over the Palestinian issue was proving to be an insurmountable obstacle to any Geneva reconvening. Talk—and rumor—of American Arab professors representing the PLO came to nothing. The meeting of Arab Foreign Ministers in Tunis resolved no problems, only bared new internecine rifts.

Sadat faced mounting economic problems, and the only solution seemed to be the speediest possible peace. American investment had not flowed to Cairo, as he hoped after the second disengagement agreement. His 1975 and 1977 trips to the U.S. and long talks with businessmen indicated that the risks of area war would have to be removed before there was a serious flow of American capital. At one point he even considered reopening his option of dealing with the Soviet Union again in the hope of persuading the Kremlin to reschedule Egypt's debt payments, estimated at close to $4 billion, and to resume desperately needed arms deliveries.

His own military, aware of the overwhelming Israeli superiority, strongly pushed for a Geneva settlement. It was Minister of War Mohammed el-Gamasy who allegedly had hinted to his opposite number in September 1975 at the Kilo 101 disengagement initialing that there might be a way out other than war, but Meir had paid no attention when this was reported to her.

There had been other Egyptian peace soundings. A forty-member delegation of the Zionist-oriented American Professors for Peace in the Middle East had been given the red-carpet treatment during a spring 1975 visit and had met with the Minister of Information. At Kissinger's insistent urging, Sadat had received Zionist columnist Joseph Alsop in Alexandria, rejecting all other interviewers after the May 1975 opening of the Suez Canal, and helped in the composition of the *New York Times Magazine* piece, "An Open Letter to an Israeli Friend,"[34] portraying a moderate Sadat seeking peace. The Egyptian leader was not unmindful of the great financial advantages that could flow from the same Jewish coffers that were keeping Israel afloat, if he could find ways of agreeing with Begin's formula. To boot, he was very aware that it would take months, if ever, to overcome procedural obstacles and get the Geneva talks underway.

Meanwhile there was the real possibility of an Israeli preemptive strike against which General Gamasy conceded there could be little defense. He pledged to back Sadat in any move he would make. According to *Times* military expert Drew Middleton, Egypt's forces were weak in major areas and faced an acute shortage of spare parts, particularly for the Soviet bombers, fighter-bombers, and interceptors and for Soviet antitank and antiaircraft missile systems.[35] Egypt had not received its Mirage F-15 and Crotale surface-to-air missiles from France. It was accepted that no combination of Arab countries, with or without Egypt, could stand up to Israel's military might.

Quite suddenly, Middle East politics were revolving around on everyone's axis in a world that seemed to have gone from mad to madder. A Sadat challenge, enunciated to the Egyptian National Assembly that he would be ready "to come to the Israeli Parliament in order to prevent a single Egyptian soldier from being wounded,"[36] at first considered to be a theatrical gesture, was picked up by Menachem Begin. With a formal invitation then extended and accepted through the U.S. embassies in Tel Aviv and Cairo, the way was paved for the most dramatic turn in Middle East affairs since the creation of Israel: the unprecedented November 19–20 Anwar el-Sadat pilgrimage to Jerusalem and the return December 25 summit visit of Begin to Ismailia.

It was Sadat, who in the past had so often said things that he more than often did not mean, and there he was in Jerusalem. All Americans were glued to television to view the thirty-six-hour amazing visit of the Egyptian leader to Israel. Sadat was warmly greeted by Prime Minister Begin, prayed at the Al-Aqsa Mosque, visited the Yad Vashem memorial, laid a wreath at the Eternal Flame monument to Israel's war dead, addressed the Knesset (his entrance into the Israeli parliament was heralded by the sounding of trumpets), and held private talks with his Israeli host. In the receiving line of Israeli VIPs at the airport, the exuberant Sadat nearly kissed Golda Meir, whom he used to call "that old lady," and particularly sought to clasp the hand of Ariel Sharon, one of the five generals in the Israel "peace" Cabinet, who in the 1973 war had nearly crushed the Egyptian Third Corps with his brilliant maneuverings.

The euphoric euphoria, which swept over the U.S. and all of the West, reached new heights as CBS's Walter Cronkite, ABC's Barbara Walters, and NBC's John Chancellor competed with one another in advancing the new "diplomacy of television" to show the "love" that radiated in the Holy City. The press accounts were as ecstatic in describing the cordiality prevalent in the unprecedented Jerusalem meeting as they were merciless in their mockery of those Arabs, principally the PLO and the Syrians, who were critical of the unilateral Sadat approach. The media relented not one whit in their customary slantings and distortions, the unbridled enthusiasm only providing an excuse for being more than ever totally anti-Palestinian. While the *New York Post* carried an elegy, "On a Day of Hope, Memories of Death," detailing onto two pages the sorrows of the family of one of the two victims of a Palestinian rocket attack on Nahariya, its readers were told nothing about the reprisal assault that leveled the Lebanese village of Hazziye and once again hit the Palestinian refugee camp at Nabatieh, killing close to 120 people in all. Only author Edward Sheehan, appearing on Channel 11 in New York, was allowed to cast the slightest shadow on "the television pax" in suggesting that the isolation of the Palestinians could lead to new problems and that a violent division in the Arab world could be counterproductive to any reconvening of Geneva.

The euphoriacs poured forth their fantasies regarding the "new peace." Rabbis piously intonated from their pulpits: "The dialogue we have sought is now at hand"—this from the very voices who either individually or organizationally had done everything in their power for thirty years to ruthlessly crush the opinions of any and all who refused to view the Israeli state as less than the Messiah come. Even the novitiate on Middle East affairs must have been puzzled to read in print the glowing reams of praise for Sadat from the pens of such chauvinists as the *New York Post*'s Max Lerner, who referred to Sadat's mission as the "impossible dream," where only a few days earlier all Arabs, including the Egyptian leader, were either filthy bedouins or intransigent extremists who could never appreciate the uplifting from neighboring "Jewish culture" and wished to "throw all Israelis into the sea."

For months the press, TV, and radio, in the guise of news reportage, had been engaged in the grandiose task of reconstructing a new Menachem Begin for public consumption. Now they speedily fashioned a different Anwar Sadat, who with his pledge "no more war" (at that moment as much a statement of military inability as a promise) tactily was admitting that the Arabs had been the aggressors, was hailed for breaking down the "psychological barriers" to peace.

Overnight, Israelis and Egyptians had become fellow Semites, whom Begin declared had in the past and could in the future live peaceably together. And he claimed he, too, was a Palestinian. As the second disengagement had been hailed in 1975, so now "peace" was universally acclaimed and every critic or sceptic damned, even after Begin's contemptuous reply in the Knesset following Sadat's speech. Aside from graciously accepting the Egyptian's peace offering, the Israeli leader offered not the slightest concession, while vigorously expounding Zionist dogma of a land first given to Jews by God and later consecrated to Zionism by the holocaust.

The Egyptian solo initiative was attacked by the PLO, Syria, Iraq, Libya, Algeria, and South Yemen. Saudi Arabia, Kuwait, and the Gulf States remained uncommitted. King Hussein, following the lead of President Assad, declined to participate in the mid-December Cairo conference that was announced to the Egyptian National Assembly by an exhilarated Sadat on his return from Jerusalem. Nor did the Jordanian ruler go to the Tripoli rejectionist summit called by Qaddafi and attended by al-Assad, Arafat, and Boumedienne as well as top Iraqi and South Yemeni representatives.

Sadat stated that "all parties involved in the Middle East conflict"[37] were being invited to the conclave, and specifically mentioned "Secretary Waldheim, the two Super Powers, Israel as well as other *Arab countries."* (Italics added.) In both his Jerusalem and Cairo speeches Sadat had carefully avoided any mention of the PLO, although he had talked of Palestinian rights. Before the names of the invitees could even be released, a PLO spokesman in Damascus declined the invitation and assailed Sadat. While the flags of the nonattendant PLO, Syria, Jordan, Lebanon, and the U.S.S.R. were all flown, prior to protests of the Israeli delegation, on the first day at the Mena House, scene of the conference near the Pyramids, there was no indication that Sadat had ever intended to include the Arafat-led group in the conclave. Israel had made it perfectly clear that she would never sit down around any table with this feared enemy, which Begin certainly had emphasized privately to Sadat. And Washington had never recognized the existence of the PLO. This spotlighted the importance of the provision in the secret annex to the second Sinai disengagement agreement, where Kissinger had seen to it that the Israelis were given the right of veto over any such move by any American President until the PLO recognized Israel's existence. Foreign Minister Ismail Fahmy, who resigned when Sadat informed him of his peace initiative, had at the time asked the U.S. Secretary of State: "How could you have mortgaged your future to a piece of paper like that?"

The name of the game seemed to be "Bypass the PLO," and the U.S. appeared to be more than an innocent bystander. Despite vigorous Washington denials as to its involvement in the Jerusalem meeting, Hamilton Jordan was quoted as saying, "Now that we brought them together, they are on their own." Carter admitted being in almost daily touch with Sadat, and with Begin only to a lesser extent. The smooth manner with which U.S. Ambassador Hermann Eilts in Cairo acted as intermediary for the formal invitation from Begin to Sadat, and in which other communications were set up between Cairo and Jerusalem, suggested a little more than casual participation by Uncle Sam.

While Carter drew some sharp criticism for taking his time before accepting the invitation and designating Assistant Secretary of State Alfred L. Atherton instead of Secretary Vance to attend Sadat's Cairo conclave, many in the administration shared with their Israeli friends the satisfaction of seeing the Arab world torn asunder by the surprising Sadat move. As long as Saudi Arabia appeared to be playing it safe and to be not too disturbed by the Sadat initiative (remaining quiet until the late December statement from the Foreign Ministry calling for full withdrawal and implementation of Palestinian "rights"[38]), Washington was not upset.

Kissinger had kept in close touch with the fast-moving events. The former Secretary of State had met Anwar, his protégé, during his spring visit and had an introductory meeting with Begin at the Waldorf on the last day of the Israeli leader's summer visit. He talked by phone to both leaders during the weekend of the Sadat visit to Jerusalem, and hailed the mission as "one of those historic events that cannot be permitted to fail." It represented the fulfillment of his efforts, his dreams come true. While denying that he had anything to do with the initiative, the former Secretary of State again reiterated his opposition to efforts seeking "a comprehensive Middle East settlement"[39]—something which, coincidentally, Begin had long indicated he greatly feared.

To Begin, so long as Cairo and Damascus thought along the same lines, there was a threat to his West Bank policy of legalizing existing settlements and authorizing further new ones. He reasoned that the Arabs, if not fragmented, would eventually be forced to go to war over this and the other occupied territories. Even though they knew they could not win, it would be the lesser of two evils for them.

But once Sadat had broken the Arab freeze by coming to Jerusalem, Begin could and did assume an increasingly tougher position toward the Arabs and Washington. The legitimacy of the Zionist state had been given the recognition of the largest Arab state, obfuscating the "original sin" and Palestinian grievances. The Israeli leader refused to permit key military or security issues to be discussed in the initial phases of the Cairo conference. Director General of the Prime Minister's Office Eliahu ben-Elissar and Legal Adviser to the Foreign Ministry Meir Rosenne were not to operate at the level of a "piece of territory for a piece of peace."[40] Before the Mena House conference convened, the *Jerusalem Post* carried the names of Givon and Bet Heron, the two latest Israeli settlements in Judea and Samaria.[41]

After Carter had been further softened up by the Zionist lobby and the "Israel-First" bloc in Congress, Begin announced to Washington that he was flying in to "show" Carter his peace plan before presenting it to Sadat on Christmas Day in Ismailia. He had not come, Begin averred, to win presidential support of the plan, only his non-disapproval. What the canny Israeli chieftain most wanted was another chance to reach the American public—which the media, in particular "Face the Nation," afforded him—and to further encourage his pressure boys on the Hill. The White House made no statement, nor did it dispute the claim of the Israeli leader that Carter viewed the Israeli plan as a "fair basis for negotiations." (It was not until the day after Begin left that it was leaked that Carter had "reportedly" cautioned the Israelis that his plan as to the Palestinians "won't satisfy Sadat and suggested new packaging"[42] another instance of Carter's fear of antagonizing the Zionists.)

When Sadat opened up his Santa Claus gift from his Israeli guest, he found a very "old hat"—the proposal for so-called Palestinian "self-rule" on the West Bank, which combined features of the extant Allon and Dayan plans maintaining Israeli military and strategic control while permitting the Palestinians limited civil government, and retaining the Israeli settlements strategically placed around Arab towns and villages. The twenty-six-point plan giving the Palestinians, referred to as "residents of Judea, Samaria, and Gaza," no right of self-determination, only the option to choose Israeli or Jordanian citizenship, and maintaining Israeli sovereignty over all of Jerusalem, was to be subject to review after a five-year period.

Begin at his press conference in Ismailia again excoriated the PLO as the "vilest organization of murderers in history with the exception of the Nazi armed organizations." Under his plan the immigration of Palestinians into the "territories" would be closely regulated—a means of barring entry from Lebanon and Syria of PLO members. But Israeli Jews could without restriction settle in the "territories" and would be under direct Israeli, not Arab authority.

No joint communiqué followed the Ismailia summit. After the terms of the Israeli "peace" plan were announced, Jordan flatly rejected the proposal, and Sadat asked Israel to reconsider its stand. When Carter in a television interview prior to his year-end trip to six countries, including Iran and Saudi Arabia, praised the Israeli leader for taking a "long step forward" and expressed opposition to a Palestinian state, the Egyptian leader declared that he was "disappointed" and "embarrassed" by the President's statement. (On a stopover in Aswan the following week, Carter tried to patch over the differences.)

Screaming headlines in the *New York Post*[43] translated the Sadat reaction into "Sadat Slams Carter's Stand" and played up Begin's determination not to "surrender" to international pressure. The media's honeymoon with Sadat quickly evaporated as full-scale anti-Arab slanting was resumed. And in Israel as the tumultuous year 1977 wound up, the media there was alternately attacking Sadat because "his appetite has grown instead of diminishing" and Begin for making "too many concessions too soon."

The man whom Kissinger had transformed from an ally of the Soviet Union into an ally of the U.S. faced the danger of being caught in a squeeze of his own making, unless he was seeking a separate peace, which he vigorously denied. (Sadat claimed that while in Jerusalem he had been offered by Begin a separate peace pact in exchange for complete withdrawal from Sinai, which he had summarily rejected.) All Arabs, including Sadat and particularly the Saudis, could see no indication in the Begin-Dayan plan of any Israeli turnabout from its "creeping annexation." And the deteriorating PLO position, compounded by its totally inept image-building, was adding to the dangers of the situation through frustrated flirtations with Moscow and Red China.

On the basis of the Palestinians' alleged negativism and radicalism, Carter joined Israel in closing the door to any recognition of or negotiating with the PLO. Israel's desire for further Big Power polarization was being realized.

The Sadat boldness placed everyone on the spot, no one more than Carter, as Israel was forced for the first time to detail its concept of a Palestinian settlement. The President, it appeared, had been responsible for imprecise utterances as to a Palestinian "homeland" and "legitimate rights" so as to stave off the Arabs, particularly the Saudis, while encouraging Sadat to make his move and become Begin's first Arab "waltzing partner." The Carter New Year's Day meeting with Hussein in Teheran was calculated to overcome previous Hashemite reluctance to join the "dance" but failed as other similar efforts had in the past and up to this writing.

The Saudis somehow had to be kept happy. There was an estimated 39 billion plus of OPEC monies, nearly three-quarters Saudi, in Treasury securities, banks, bonds, stocks, and other investments in the U.S. A further oil price increase could bring economic chaos and usher in Paul Erdman's *Crash of '79.*

It remained Washington's constant hope that Saudi preoccupation with its own long-range economic development would make them more flexible—and hence make Sadat more amenable to what had been practically presented, through Begin's maneuverings, as a U.S.-Israeli plan for a solution to the West Bank problem.

While the Israeli-Egyptian talks in Cairo on the military aspects of a peace settlement were reporting some limited progress in resolving differences over the future of Israeli settlements around the Rafah Salient in the Sinai and the fate of Israeli airfields at Bir Gifgata, Eitam, and Etzion, the Jerusalem political talks were abruptly broken off in mid-January by Sadat. Foreign Minister Mohammed Ibrahim Kamel was recalled, after the latter's airport arrival declaration that "Israel must give up Jerusalem" and Begin's subsequent insulting dinner toast, the Israeli leader attempting to draw a parallel between Arab demands for Palestinian rights and Hitler's misuse of Sudeten self-determination.

In meeting later with Egyptian editors before their departure, Begin called Kamel's Jerusalem remark "the most preposterous ever made by a guest—pure 'chutzpah' " (colossal impudence). When reminded by one Egyptian that he should have been impressed by Sadat's acceptance of Israel's existence, the Israeli leader exploded:

We have never asked anybody to recognize our right to exist. We exist, my dear Egyptian friends, without your recognition for 3,700 years. Our right to exist was given by the God of Abraham, Isaac and Jacob. We never asked your President or your Government to recognize our right to exist. What we expect from you is to recognize our right to our land.[44]

The negotiations had already been floundering with vast differences over the set of principles on which the comprehensive Middle East settlement was to be based. The Sadat move was intended to emphasize his insistence on complete Israeli withdrawal and Palestinian self-determination. In place of the previous euphoria and goodwill, a war of words was waged between the Egyptian and Israeli press, in which even the charge of "anti-Semitism" was hurled at Cairo editors.

As Dayan warned "Egypt cannot put a pistol to Israel's head" and Secretary Vance tried to bridge the differences, the U.S. became the principal battleground. Sadat flew to Washington for a Camp David weekend with the President, and ensuing public relations efforts presented his case to key members of Congress, to some Jewish leaders, and principally to the American people. On the heels of what was a most successful visit for Sadat—particularly the National Press Club luncheon where he most favorably impressed newsmen and Washington dignitaries—came Moshe Dayan, who under the guise of UJA fund-raising, once more rallied American Jews around the country and the "Israeli-Firsters" in Congress to the Zionist cause. Sadat was pressing his case in a swing through Western Europe, where Begin also was striving for support.

Intent on reviving the peace process, which had ground to a near-total halt, Carter found himself haunted by his temporizing attitude toward the Israeli settlements on the West Bank and fear of Israel's supporters. Despite unaltering U.S. opposition to these settlements as violations of the Fourth Geneva Convention and as provocations to the Arabs, the Israelis continued to establish new ones and to claim that the U.S. "does not object seriously" to these actions. Exasperated by the announcement of a new settlement on the site of ancient Shiloh (in the guise of an excavation dig), Vance protested, and upon instructions from the President, the State Department on February 7 released the chronology (just covering the previous month) of U.S. reiterations of its position in communications between the President and the Israeli Chief of State, including a sharp note of January 27 regarding Tel Aviv's actions.

Begin, then in Geneva, arrogantly and contemptuously "rejected"[45] the U.S. position that the settlements were illegal and negative, and later added that the Vance remarks were "in complete contradiction" to the comments made by Carter at their December meeting in Washington. Once more the White House, this time through Press Secretary Jody Powell, ignominiously attempted to clarify the record —"reluctantly and with no desire to prolong the argument," as he stated—to indicate that the U.S. view of these settlements has been repeated "publicly and privately by various American officials since 1967" and that there had been no "contradiction at any time between that position and any presidential statement any time."[46]

When the Israeli cabinet on February 26, after two days of debate, decided not to change its policy and approved the plan to expand Jewish settlements in northern Sinai and establish three new ones[47] on the West Bank, the U.S. withheld immediate comment pending the Begin March visit to Washington.[48] But a head-on collision between Washington and Tel Aviv seemed unavoidable. Carter was under incessant pressure to shift the U.S. role in the negotiations from moderator to Zionist protagonist, even as totally consistent evenhandedness appeared to be his principal weapon in persuading the Arabs to continue to believe that the only road to peace led through the White House. The words of Lebanon's *An Nahar* served as a serious reminder to Washington: "The Arab world has heard enough brave words from various American leaders. What is wanted now is concrete evidence of the U.S. collective determination to put its power where its mouth is."[49]

Since the President came into office, the noose around his neck had gradually been tightened, as it had been in the past around the necks of his predecessors, under the meticulously manipulated weight of the Zionist connections through the Jewish connectors and their Christian affiliates. No one was more important to the President than his Chief Staff Aide for Domestic Affairs, Stuart Eizenstat, "The Man the President Listens To."[50] Then there was Counsel Lipshutz, with his intimate B'nai B'rith ties, former Democratic National Committee Chairman and Chief Trade Negotiator Robert S. Strauss, and the Secretaries of the Treasury, Defense, and Energy, who were particularly pervious to Zionist pressures. Visiting Israel in October 1977 for the signing of the agreement establishing an $80 million agricultural research fund (an increase of $20 million over last year's U.S. contribution), Treasury Secretary Blumenthal told the Israelis that "Egypt's disastrous economic situation will force it toward a peace settlement with Israel within three years."[51]

The 1978 congressional elections were around the next corner, and pro-Israel pollsters were warning Washington that Carter's falling popularity was due to his Middle East policy. The *Times* came up even with a selected poll among "those who were informed on the Middle East"[52] to show disapproval of the new Carter approach. A poll of 300 people taken at random among Jews was also used as a weapon to show that Carter was losing his support because of his Mideast policy and his election might be endangered. CBS Newsradio 88 intoned the doom of the Democratic candidate—"American Jews do not like Carter's turnabout on Israel." An Israeli editorial writer commented, "God's gift to Israel is that the U.S. has this type of election cycle," and a noted American Jewish scholar remarked, "It's as if we are fifty million strong in this country—it's unbelievable."[53]

Of no small contribution to such exuberance was the continued performance of the *New York Times*. As the new year dawned, the Sulzberger paper sparkled with slantings by headlining[54]; letters to the editor weighted by size and placement[55]; myth-information of Flora Lewis columns[56]; and editorial support for the latest Tel Aviv-Washington fall-back position that *a radical Palestinian state* alongside Israel could not be tolerated.[57]

But with the peace momentum stalled in late February, primarily over the West Bank-Gaza issue, and U.S. Ambassador Atherton shuttling to break the deadlock, the *Times* ran a surprising, moderately objective three-part series on the Palestinians and the PLO,[58] and the columns of the "new" Anthony Lewis increasingly continued to present a more balanced look "at reality."[59] Everyone concerned—the Israelis, Egyptians, Americans, Palestinians, other Arabs, and the media, too—seemed to be reconciled to settling down to long-protracted maneuverings over the peace negotiations.

To help offset Israel's request, presented in Washington by visiting Defense Minister Weizman, for a long-term U.S. armaments commitment of some $12 billion over a ten-year period (in addition to what was already in the pipeline for 1978 and 1979), the White House proposed a $4.8 billion package plane deal. Egypt was to be sold fifty F-5E jet interceptors, Saudi Arabia sixty F-15 fighter bombers, and Israel was to be given by grant-credit fifteen F-15s and seventy-five of the most advanced F-16 fighters. Zionists emitted the wildest howls of opposition to supplying the Saudis a replacement for their force of British-built Lightning interceptors. This, they maintained, would upset the military balance, even though the planes would not be delivered before 1982, and it was very doubtful that Saudi Arabia, with 100 trained fighter pilots and equally limited ground personnel, could handle such sophisticated planes. They would be sent, the Israelis averred, to Arab confrontation states. But the Saudis had indicated they were making the sale of these jets the test of professed U.S. friendship.

The Israel-First bloc in Congress, impressed by the Zionist argumentation that the F-15s would be based at the Saudi base of Tabuk, only 275 miles from Tel Aviv, persisted in their opposition to the package deal, which would have blocked approval of planes for Israel without a similar assent for Saudi Arabia and Egypt. The White House countered, à la Rodgers and Hammerstein, "With us, it's all or nothing."

As intensive lobbying on Capitol Hill went forward against this Carter proposal, the publicity spotlight centered on the resignation of Mark Siegel, White House liaison with the American Jewish community, who declared he could no longer defend a policy that he had little voice in shaping and with which he often disagreed. This coincided with Begin's hardened position; he insisted that no withdrawal from the West Bank was required under his interpretation of Resolution 242, whatever partial withdrawal in the Sinai and Golan Heights might be agreed to in the negotiating process—an interpretation characterized by William Buckley as "so idiosyncratic that even true believers had difficulty keeping a straight face."

In rallying a united Jewish front behind Begin prior to his scheduled March visit to Washington for the thorny discussions on settlements and withdrawal, Rabbi Schindler insinuated that Security Adviser Brzezinski was "anti-Semitic." The President himself, not immune from attack, was now declared "a question mark in the eyes of American Jews"—ploys even the *New York Times* was obliged to decry as "scurrilous" and "insulting."[60]

The deep divisions over Begin's policy within Israel and among her U.S. supporters all but vanished with the March 11 raid into Israel in which thirty-seven Israelis were killed and some seventy-five wounded by a PLO band of guerrillas that landed from rubber boats and hijacked a tourist bus. The abortive Palestinian fedayeen intended to capture hostages in exchange for companions held in Israeli raids. As *Time* magazine pointed out, "the bloody massacre that ensued, unfortunately, may have been as much the result of Israeli incompetence as Palestinian menace. . . . The police commander at the roadblock gave a blanket open-fire order to terrified traffic cops, and their wild fusillade when the bus was finally halted probably killed more hostages than did the terrorists."[61]

Three days later, in Israel's largest military operation since the 1973 war and by far her deadliest retaliatory raid, 15,000 combined air, naval, and land forces swept across the borders into Lebanon and rained death on innocent Palestinian refugees and Lebanese civilians alike. Begin, returning to the tactics of his Irgun days, called it "a purification of Lebanon," a drive to "cut off the arm of evil," the PLO. Pro-Zionist papers, such as the *New York Post,* labeled it "REVENGE"[62] in large letters across the front page. The operation claimed close to 2,000 lives, and some 265,000 refugees fled northward toward Sidon and Beirut.

Most of the casualties were civilians with no affiliation whatsoever with the PLO. No military targets were struck, and what had been hit hard were civilian dwellings. Military correspondents calculated that the Israelis fired an average of a dozen 155-millimeter shells for every guerrilla known to have been in the area (some 220 were killed and 23 captured), and dropped at least twenty tons of high explosives per bunker and village.[63] *Time* could only conclude that this had been "deliberate counterterror on the part of the Israelis."[64]

Under the pretext of establishing a six-mile *"cordon sanitaire"* between Lebanon and Israel, "Stone of Wisdom," the plan long on the military establishment's drawing board, was updated and put into effect. Within six days the overpowering Israeli forces had subdued Palestinian resistance and swept to the long-coveted Litani River; all of southern Lebanon was in their hands before the U.N. cease-fire could take effect and the international peacekeeping force (UNIFIL), under the command of Ghanian General Emmanuel Alexander Erskine, could assume its duties. As U.N. forces moved in, there were few signs the Israelis intended to leave, the digging of trenches and placing of barbed wire indicating the contrary. Despite the U.N. Security Council Resolution 425 calling for forthright and total withdrawal, it was not until June 14 that Israel finally completed its removal from Lebanese soil. But just as they had deliberately encouraged turmoil in the south by refusing to allow the Syrian peacekeeping troops there at the end of the Lebanese civil war in 1976, now the Israelis turned over twenty of the most vital portions along a forty-mile border front, three to five miles deep, to their allies, the right-wing Lebanese Christian militia commanded by Major Saad Haddad, instead of to General Erskine's U.N. forces. Israel was determined not to surrender control of fully fortified villages, maintained as forward bases for its potential operations.

As Begin flew to Washington on March 19 for his week-delayed meeting with Carter to iron out existing differences, to which was added the critical occupation of southern Lebanon, the Israeli leader's philosophy about the West Bank could be summed up in these words of Robert Frost: "The land was ours before we were the land's."[65]

The Carter-Begin talks were a total failure. To avoid an open confrontation, the customary joint communiqué was not issued by the White House. As Begin returned home "to put his house in order," reports that the White House was out to unseat the Israeli leader, vehemently denied in Washington, were widely spread through media sources closest to the Israelis. Banner front-page *New York Post* headlines screamed one day: "U.S. vs. Israel: Worst Crisis,"[66] and the following day: "U.S. Presses for Ouster of Begin."[67] The alleged attempted sandbagging of Begin was another means of rallying Jews against Carter. And Begin himself added fuel to the rumors by curtly declaring, "The Premier of Israel is elected by the people of Israel, not by the President of the United States."

Although General Weizman had called for new directions, the Cabinet unanimously supported Begin's position, and a parliamentary vote of confidence was carried 64 to 32. As the Arab states struggled to reach an agreement on the necessity of a summit conference to close their divided ranks and face the consequences of the latest disaster in Lebanon, Yasir Arafat pledged observance of the U.N. cease-fire. But it was unreasonable to believe that the PLO would give up the war of liberation it had been waging for fourteen years, and that the more moderate Al Fatah could stop the more radical Habash group from attacking Christian positions in the south or crossing in forays into Israel. Guerrilla warfare, à la Vietnam, loomed ahead.

The Palestinians on the West Bank and Gaza did not remain quiet during the invasion of Lebanon, once more strongly indicating their PLO affinity, although this was not reported in the U.S. until much later. For five days the region seethed with unrest, "schools were closed and youths roamed the streets, throwing stones and setting fires."[68] The retaliation of Israeli soldiers was severe, and in one incident two boys of eight and sixteen were killed when an army truck ran into them. At a school in Beit Jala, five miles south of Jerusalem, fifty Israeli troops rolled up in trucks, ordered the pupils—all in their early teens—to close their windows, then hurled beer-can-size canisters of U.S.-made antiriot gas into the packed classrooms. Several severe accidents followed.[69] Raymonda Taweel, Palestinian activist,[70] was seized in her home by seven Israeli soldiers and plainclothes officers and thrown into prison. The charge: "Terrorist activities and creating public disturbances."

Sadat criticized both the PLO and Israel for their actions, which complicated the waning peace momentum. He indicated he would not yet desert his initiative and still favored further efforts to reach some sort of an agreement with Begin. Whatever the final outcome, the Egyptian leader could at least boast that he had "flushed" his Israeli adversary out into the open and for the first time had bared Zionist aspirations for the world to see.

While Carter's attention was momentarily diverted from the Middle East to other problems on his four-country trip to Venezuela, Brazil, Nigeria, and Liberia, the Zionist lobby was struggling to maintain both its inordinate influence in Congress and its monolithic control over the Jewish community in the face of growing criticism of Israeli intransigency being voiced publicly by such leaders as Senator Abraham Ribicoff,[71] foreign trade negotiator Robert Strauss and, more surprisingly, Dr. Nahum Goldmann, who allegedly had told White House officials that the Conference of Presidents, the spearhead of Jewish political lobbying, had become a "destructive force," a "major obstacle to peace in the Middle East."[72] To silence the dissent, the leaders of organized Jewry stoutly insisted that open criticism of Israel amounted to heresy. "The strength of Israel depends on the strength of the American Jewish community and its unity in support of Israel," Rabbi Schindler contended.

The Zionist lobby continued to pull every possible string on its powerful congressional bow to block the plane package deal and to prevent the President from using aid in any way as leverage in dealing with Israel. In a similar 1975 test of strength, when President Ford tried to exert a little pressure, he was speedily reminded in a letter signed by seventy-six Senators "to be responsive to Israel's urgent military and economic needs." At that time the Israelis received what they wanted. Carter, facing a bitter and possibly losing fight in Congress, softened his language about treating the $4.8 billion sale of planes to the three countries as a package to permit separate congressional consideration of each sale, but at the same time declared that if planes for one country were voted down, he would withdraw the proposal to sell to the other two countries. To further mollify the "Israel-First" bloc and avoid a confrontation, the White House agreed to increase by twenty the number of jets for Israel, in line with Kissinger's proposal in testifying before the Senate Foreign Relations Committee.

Using Israel's thirtieth anniversary as an excuse, Begin came to the U.S. again on April 30, the fourth visit within ten months. At the State Department and the White House he received the warmest welcomes. Afterward, at a reception and ceremony on the White House lawn attended by Jewish leaders and rabbis from across the country, the President pledged "total, absolute commitment to Israel's security." In response, Begin called Carter's speech "one of the greatest moral statements ever."

Traveling on his own Israeli Boeing 707, Begin flew coast to coast. He spoke before enthusiastic audiences in Los Angeles (and politicked with ambitious Governor Jerry Brown), Chicago, and New York, where overflow crowds greeted him at an Israel Bond luncheon, a parade up Fifth Avenue, and a festival in Central Park. At Northwestern University in Evanston, Illinois, an honorary degree was bestowed on the Israeli leader, although the student body had voted 1,199 to 907 against this action. (The university's public relations action was not unrelated to its refusal to remove Arthur Butz, the professor who had written *The Hoax of the 20th Century*, the very controversial book denying any holocaust had taken place.)

Not only did Begin raise money and sell bonds for Israel, but he asked American Jews to support his opposition to relinquishing Arab territories and to the three-way jet sale. No foreign chief of state, as one news magazine put it, had ever "so unabashedly ventured out into the hustings, as it were, to drum up support for his policies."[73] And American Jewry had been programmed for top receptivity to Begin through the holocaust frenzy into which the NBC miniseries and vast accompanying propaganda had cast them. While the media reported little else but exuberant reaction to the Begin exhortations, the U.S. and the Begin government were on a confrontation course.

Refusing to accept advice from House Speaker Thomas P. O'Neill for a delay, the President sent the controversial package to Congress. Following a tie vote in its Foreign Relations Committee, the Senate in a stunning upset refused to block the plane deal. The Israel lobby combine of American-Israel Policy Affairs Committee director Morris Amitay and chairman of the Conference of Presidents Rabbi Alexander Schindler hoped that their magic, which had never before failed with Congress, would bring victory over the administration. But the President was upheld in a 54–44 vote in which there were untold surprises.

Senator Abraham Ribicoff was joined by other stalwart Israel supporters such as Mike Gravel (Dem.-Alaska), Tom Eagleton (Dem.-Mo.), and Adlai Stevenson, Jr. (Dem.-Ill.) in support of the package because, as heretofore staunch Zionist Ribicoff explained it, "The Saudis are essential to the search for peace. They have a moral and economic force in the Islamic world."

The White House packed a lobbying wallop of its own by persuading Hubert Humphrey's widow through a combined Carter-Mondale effort to support the program in the committee and in winning over Republican Senate House leader, Howard Baker. The Tennessee Senator, although presidentially ambitious, shifted drastically from his past record of catering to the Zionists and carried twenty-five other critical votes from his party. This upset the strategy of National Chairman William Brock, who had hoped to play further domestic politics with this serious issue.

Many of the Senators agonized over their votes. In the end, anti-Communist sentiment and the necessity of keeping OPEC on a course of moderate pricing prevailed. King Khalid's letter citing the need to halt potential Communist dangers in the region had been effective, although Foreign Minister Prince Saud bin Faisal had made clear he would accept only limitations on deployment of its F-15s that are of "general applicability and not aimed at Saudi Arabia for a specific requirement." Moshe Dayan had made it easier to support the President by indicating that rather than Israel not receive her planes, he would prefer the passage of the package even if this meant aircraft for the Saudis and the Egyptians as well.

Only three Democratic Senators who were running for reelection in six months voted for the proposal. Votes and campaign funds from Jewish backers have always been decisive to their party, and the Israel lobby was very far from vanquished.

In addressing the two-day annual conference of the American Israel Public Affairs Committee in Washington a week before the crucial Senate vote, Republican presidential aspirant Connecticut Senator Lowell P. Weicker, Jr., attacked the Carter Middle East stand. He suggested that the administration was trying to make Jews the scapegoats for its foreign policy difficulties and noted that "time and time again" in history "when national leaders ran into difficulties, they found it convenient to blame problems on the Jews. We know the results." This insinuation of anti-Semitism against the President and Brzezinski was calculated to rouse the deep-seated fears of his 1,000 listeners, who interrupted his remarks twenty-six times with applause, including his statement, "If I were President, I would have his (Brzezinski's) resignation before sundown, and his reputation for break-fast."[74]

The Senator declared that the NBC "Holocaust" program "helped put into perspective Israel's concern for security." He added: "Mr. Carter and Mr. Brzezinski see Menachem Begin as an agent of reaction. I see him as a guardian and one of the principal architects of one of the greatest acts of redemption in the history of man."

Presidential Counsel Robert Lipshutz was immediately granted the right to reply to Weicker. He attacked "with sorrow" this gross demagoguery, as did subsequently Senators Ribicoff, Javits, and Percy. (Weicker's Press Secretary, Rebecca Lett, later stated that the Senator stood by his speech.) The divisions among American supporters of Israel were drastically widening. The solidarity of American and Israeli Jews was very much in question.

Die-hard Zionists such as Senator Javits considered the sale of planes for Egypt and Saudi Arabia "a grave threat to the special U.S.-Israel relationship." To them the plane vote was a test of their ability to break the Saudi connection before it blossomed into another competing special relationship. They ought to have taken much comfort from what Vice President Mondale stated in seeking to calm the bitterness in the American Jewish community: "Of the total U.S. military aid abroad in next year's budget, 42 percent of the supporting assistance, 48 percent of military sales credits, and 56 percent of all military grants go to Israel. Moreover, repayment of about half of those $1 billion worth of credits is consistently forgiven."[75] (Since 1974, $3 billion out of $5.5 billion in military purchases have been turned into outright grants.)

While a Senate rejection of the plane deal would have been a death blow to what was left of the Sadat initiative, the positive benefits seemed to be minimal as the roadblocks to a Middle East settlement remained. Doors to peace have seldom been opened by a flow of deadly weaponry. The refusal of the Begin cabinet on June 18, despite Washington pressure, to give any commitment regarding the permanent status of the West Bank and Gaza until after the end of the five years of so-called Palestinian self-rule, indicated just how far away the end of the conflict was. Washington very quietly registered its displeasure and called on Sadat to come up with a detailed plan for the Palestinians. The Egyptian President was already wallowing in domestic troubles brought on by his suppression of opposition parties, continued economic woes, and growing popular discontent, particularly in the military, which was heightened by the defection of former Chief of Staff Lt. General Saad Eddin el-Shazli, who from his exile abroad wrote his searing book, *The Crossing of the Suez*,[76] and led the opposition outside the country.

After attempting to dilute support of Begin by meeting with Defense Minister Weizman and Opposition Leader Peres, Sadat sought to satisfy his internal critics by expelling the Israeli military mission based in Cairo since January. As the Arabs quietly tried to close their ranks and find means of persuading Sadat to gracefully drop his peace initiative, the U.S. endeavored to impart an illusion of progress through staged conferences, such as at Leeds Castle in England, where Secretary Vance and Foreign Ministers Dayan and Kamel held their inconclusive talks, and by the resumption of shuttle diplomacy by Ambassador Alfred Atherton.

It was declining public approval of his conduct as President, at a time the autumn Congressional elections were quickly approaching, that induced Carter to assume the grave hazards of a summit. Only a visit to Jerusalem and Alexandria by the Secretary of State, armed with personal letters from the White House, persuaded the stalemated Israeli and Egyptian leaders to agree to join President Carter in a Camp David summit on September 5.

Washington's fears, based on reports of Egyptian military preparations or a possible Sadat move into the Sinai by refusing to agree to an extension of the 1975 disengagement agreement, prompted Carter to schedule the Camp David spectacular. Israeli plans to establish five new settlements in the Jordan Rift, only temporarily shelved until after the summit, added to U.S. imperatives for keeping the dialogue open. The Gush Emunim, Begin's most enthusiastic supporters, announced a plan which would provide a Jewish majority in "Judea and Samaria" (the West Bank), by the end of the century. Begin held a midnight, clandestine meeting with Lebanese anti-Palestinian leader Camille Chamoun in Jerusalem.

The media continued its slanted reportage, particularly misleading regarding the nature of the Lebanese war. Endless misleading headlines, "Christians Attacked," "Beirut's Christians Return to Streets," etc., misrepresented the conflict as a religious one. Hidden from the public were the pernicious efforts of the Israeli-supported Phalangist forces of Pierre Geymayel and Chamoun, representing only a portion of the Maronite Catholics and bitterly opposed by the Greek and Syrian Orthodox, Melkites, as well as other Catholic and Protestant groups, to bring about a partition of the country. Lebanon's Major Haddad, who refused to accept dismissal by Beirut from his army post, continued both to harass the U.N. forces and to block the deployment of units of the regular Lebanese army, thus preventing them from taking over the 60-mile border strip which remained subservient to Israel. In his efforts to stabilize the country by maintaining a balance of power, Syria's Hafez Assad remained caught in a military-political quagmire.

The Camp David negotiations between Sadat, Begin and Carter, shrouded in complete secrecy, were long and intensive. At one point, Sadat threatened to leave and had a helicopter ready unless all of the Sinai, not part, as the Israelis envisioned, were returned and all Israeli settlements abandoned. In return for Sadat yielding on his Palestinian position, Begin gave way on the Sinai. Sharon, then Minister of Agriculture, indicated that there were "no security risks in giving up the Sinai provided that there was a firm hold on the West Bank."

After twelve days, the talks were successfully concluded and two accords initialed by Egypt and Israel on September 17. A nationwide television audience was treated to the unusual picture of Sadat and Begin embracing one another, with a beaming Carter looking on. "A framework for peace in the Middle East" covered the future of the West Bank and Gaza, and "a framework for the conclusion of a peace treaty between Egypt and Israel" covered Sinai and bilateral relations between Egypt and Israel.

With Cairo and Tel Aviv in disagreement on many points, the three-months deadline for signing the treaty passed. Just when it seemed that certain defeat faced him, Carter flew to the Middle East, and shuttling back and forth between Cairo and Tel Aviv, he miraculously bridged the differences and brought the Egyptian and Israeli leaders to Washington for the signing of the treaty in a widely publicized extravaganza on March 26. Almost with one voice the press in the Arab world vehemently assailed the treaty as a "sell-out."

The flexibility of both parties to the treaty had been molded by the additional goodies Carter dished out to turn the tide at the breakfast meeting with Begin, followed by the airport conclave with Sadat. All concerned were deliriously happy. Begin had the peace he so cherished with his most powerful Arab foe; Sadat had iron-clad guarantees for the return of the Sinai; and Carter triumphantly returned to Washington to stem his decline in the public opinion polls.

The unwitting American taxpayer, of course, picked up a little chit for the treaty. Israel received supplementary assistance of $2.2-billion in military credits and $800-million in grants for construction of two air bases in the Negev to replace the Sinai bases being surrendered. Egypt was given an additional $1.5-billion in military credits, $200-million in economic grants, and $100-million in economic loans. For regular foreign assistance for fiscal year '79 Israel received $1.79-billion and $1.79-billion for fiscal year 1980. Egypt received $902-million for fiscal year '79 and $971-million for fiscal year '80. The U.S. also agreed to raise aid to Israel up to $2-billion for fiscal year '81 and $2.2-billion for fiscal year '82. Egypt would receive $1.4-billion for fiscal year '81 and $1.6-billion for fiscal year 1982. This brought the total amount under the treaty to a mere $17.5 billion.

The Egyptian Cabinet voted unanimously to approve the treaty, and there were only two opposing votes in the Israeli Cabinet. Begin assured the Knesset that there would "never be a Palestinian state on the West Bank" and that Jerusalem would "never be divided again." What was more important to the Israelis was the U.S. commitment both to strengthen its forces in the area to prevent any treaty violations which threatened the security of Israel and to veto any U.N. Security Council action which would be detrimental to the accord.

What helped induce Sadat to sign was the promise by the U.S. that it would both supply some troops to the Sinai peace-keeping forces and would be a partner in future peace negotiations—and, of course, the hope of additional economic rewards. The Egyptian leader was still seeking meaningful American investment to help alleviate the ever-worsening economic plight which had so seriously plagued the land of the Pharaohs since the days of the Khedive Ismail, who was forced to sell the Suez Canal to the British government and French private interests.

Arab opponents of Camp David met in Baghdad to take action to limit the effects of the accords and the treaty. A fifteen-billion dollar offer to Sadat to change his mind was rejected. All the Arab countries, save Sudan, Oman and Somalia, severed relations with Cairo and withdrew their diplomatic representatives. The headquarters of the Arab League were moved from Cairo to Tunis.

The attitude of the Palestinians and Arab intellectuals could best be summed up in the words of Palestinian scholar Dr. Fayez Sayegh:

Under the Camp David accords, a fraction of the Palestinian people (under one-third of the whole) is promised a fraction of its rights (not including the national right to self-determination and statehood) and a fraction of its homeland (less than one-fifth of the area of the whole); this promise is to be fulfilled several years from now, through a step-by-step process in which Israel is able at every point to exercise a decisive veto power over any agreement. Beyond that, the vast majority of Palestinians is condemned to permanent loss of its Palestinian identity, to permanent exile and statelessness, to permanent separation from one another and from Palestine—to a life without national hope or meaning! [77]

In negotiations for a fruitful definition of autonomy, Sadat found Begin even more than at Camp David to be obdurate, obstinate and intransigent in his insistence that the West Bank was Biblical Judea and Samaria, which had been given to the Jewish people by God. Autonomy, he contended, applied to West Bank and Gaza inhabitants—not to the territory—and was to be limited to administrative control of local affairs. The Palestinians would exercise no right of self-determination, with a review of the status of the occupied territories only after the five-year transition period.

Washington tried to help out. Roving Ambassador Robert Strauss, although an inveterate Zionist who, as a former chairman of the Democratic National Committee, had been steeped in domestic politics, was given the difficult task of putting Cairo and Tel Aviv on the same wavelength regarding Palestinian autonomy. When he left this thankless job, another Zionist took over this important negotiating post, former Xerox chairman Sol Linowitz. He was no more successful.

The input of private citizen Henry Kissinger, who at all times has visibly demonstrated that he has never really exited from Washington, was far more important than either of these two official negotiators. The former Secretary of State had done all he could to encourage both Sadat and Begin in the final moments to come to terms and sign the treaty. Although most critical of other aspects of the foreign policy of the Carter Administration, he told *Newsweek's* Arnaud de Borgrave:

On the Middle East I would give the Administration high marks. The basic strategy is correct, Camp David was the right approach in the sense that it represented a solution by stages. [78]

Kissinger could not but have been a little pleased and even flattered to see to what extent his Democratic successors, Vance-Brzezinski-Carter, carried forward his divide-and-rule policy. Arab disunity became a joint goal of U.S. and Israel foreign policy in response to the Arafat conciliatory visit to King Hussein in Amman and the truce in the twelve-year-old feud between the Syrian and Iraqi Ba'ath Parties (only temporary, as union efforts between these two countries failed, and Syria soon supported Iran in the war against Iraq).

The concession the Israeli Labor government wrested from Kissinger in 1975 as a price for signing Disengagement II, namely, that the United States would not dialogue with the PLO until Israel was recognized, continued to plague American diplomatic efforts. This was dramatically highlighted by the Andrew Young affair. The U.S.

Ambassador to the U.N. met secretly at the home of Kuwaiti Ambassador Abdulla Bishara where PLO Observer at the U.N. Zehdi Terzi was present. They discussed the postponement of the Security Council debate which would have resulted in a certain U.S. veto of an Arab-Third World resolution favoring Palestinian self-determination, an action Washington wished to avoid. Young was fired for doing the verboten, talking to the PLO. Sentimental Arabs did not press for the resolution at the resumed Security Council meeting so as not to force the retiring Ambassador to exercise a veto as his last act as U.S. representative.

As an aftermath to the Young resignation, the Southern Christian Leadership Conference, under the chairmanship of the Rev. Joseph Lowery as well as black leader Jesse Jackson, moved to closer ties with the PLO. Jackson and Lowery visited Arafat in Beirut, where they issued strong statements denouncing the continued bombing of Lebanon and otherwise indicated support for the Palestinians. But this shift of some of its leaders had little affect on the total black sentiment largely expressed through organizations which continued to ally themselves closely with Organized Jewry.

The 1975 disengagement agreement contained still another Kissinger gift for Israel. Iran's Shah Pahlevi, totally impervious to the needs of his people, was driven from his peacock throne and flew to Aswan in Egypt on January 16, 1979. In one of their first moves, the Ayatollah Khomeini and his fundamentalist mullahs turned the Israeli Embassy over to the PLO for its headquarters. (The Khomeini-Arafat empathy lasted long enough for the PLO leader to arrange the early release of seven American hostages.)

The fall of the Shah emphasized other dangers for Israel. Iranian oil production was the source for sixty percent of the Israeli state's supply. But with his foresight, Kissinger had made sure in a side accord to the agreement that the U.S. assumed the responsibility for making up to Tel Aviv any petroleum shortages she might incur from Iran or elsewhere.

Very cognizant of the importance of their many American connections and connectors, the Israelis moved to strengthen these ties for the battle over autonomy. At a Spring (1979) luncheon, Finance Minister Simcha Erlich reminded guests at a Greater New York Committee for Israel Bonds gathering: "We must mobilize the tremendous reserves of Arab oil and money."[79] Begin told the several thousand Jewish leaders from all over the U.S. "how powerful was their clout in Washington, and their strength is such that Washington quails before them." (Subsequently, he tried to tie the hands of rebel leaders in Organized Jewry by urging them to "consider whether the public statements of dissent from Israeli policy would strengthen or weaken those who negotiate for Israel.")

Sadat increasingly became only too aware of just how enormous this power was. He underestimated the strength of Zionist pressures over the White House. Ambiguities in the accords, never resolved at Camp David, were resolved by Israeli faits accomplis. Less than four weeks after the treaty signing, Israel announced the establishment of two new West Bank settlements as Begin claimed that the freeze was to take place only during the three-month period during which the treaty was being negotiated. He assured settlers at Hebron that they represented "only the start of the development of the land."

Originally, Sadat insisted that he could never accept Jewish settlements on the West Bank and an Israeli military presence there, which Begin contended was not merely to assume public order, but to guarantee the "permanent security of the borders."

The autonomy talks which began in Alexandria and then were moved to the Netherlands and Herzlia in Israel, with the U.S. intermittently present, failed to resolve basic differences. The Israelis still insisted that the Palestinians be given only inconsequential administrative powers, while matters of security, water, land and other more important aspects of self-rule were to be left in the hands of the Israeli government. The Egyptian Parliament strongly insisted on the return of East Jerusalem to Arab hands.

The talks were called off by Sadat, only to be resumed when Carter intervened by telephone. Once again, they were terminated, only to be resumed, although Israel made clear that it would never agree to the creation of a Palestinian state and that East Jerusalem was not to come under the autonomy plan.

There was little help from within Israel to move the autonomy talks along. The leaders of Israel's Peace Now movement, doves if judged by a strong reluctance to go to war and opposition to further settlements, were, however, equally reluctant to oppose Zionist nationalist philosophy. Their own widely distributed major pamphlet expostulated: "Now, for the first time in over thirty years, we have the opportunity to move from negative Zionism, the enforced concern with defense, to positive Zionism." In a letter to the *Jerusalem Post* defending its position, the group claimed that nothing which it advocated had not already been advocated "by Israeli leaders whose Zionist credentials cannot be doubted." The image of the state rather than justice for the Palestinians seemed to be its primary concern.

The Knesset voted to permit further new settlements on the West

Bank, even over the protests of Washington. Minister of Defense Weizman, labeled a moderate simply because he was not as extreme as Begin or Sharon, announced plans for six para-military settlements. Even in the face of some opposition at home, he permitted the establishment of new settlements at Elon Moreh near Nablus and the construction of religious and field schools in Hebron, the largest Arab city on the West Bank.

Angered by the successful Arafat-Bruno Kreisky-Willi Brandt meeting with its strong statement of support for Palestinian rights and by the new European initiative to push toward Palestinian self-determination, Begin lashed out in continuous vehement denunciations of the PLO to whom he invariably referred as "a murderous neo-Nazi organization."

To the March U.N. 1980 call to dismantle existing settlements and cease construction and planning of new ones, the Israelis answered arrogantly and defiantly. Although Washington—both the White House and the President—made it clear that it considered such settlements illegal and contrary to the Camp David accords, Begin strongly denied any controvention in letter or spirit of the treaty he had signed with Sadat.

The foment in the occupied territories increased when gunmen near the Israeli settlement in Hebron killed four Israelis and one American Jew and wounded seventeen others as they returned home from Sabbath worship. This ugly incident had followed in the wake of a night raid into Hebron by Israeli settlers (many, followers of Meir Kahane) in which cars were destroyed, doors smashed down, hundreds of homes entered, and all that was glass—radios, televisions, windows—broken so that one commentator referred to it as the West Bank's "Kristalnacht." For allegedly encouraging the attack on the Israelis, Halhoul Mayor Mohammed Milhem, Hebron Mayor Fahd Qawasmeh, and chief of the Hebron Religious Court Sheikh Rajab Bayyoud Tamimi were summarily deported.

To add to the unrest, a seventeen-year-old-boy in the small village of Anabta was killed and two other students wounded when the Israeli military governor and his aides entered the yard of a secondary school where a peaceful May Day demonstration was being held, words were exchanged, stones were thrown and shots fired. When the three deportees, backed by hundreds of supporters, attempted to push their way across the King Hussein Bridge, Israeli soldiers blocked the path with steel barriers, causing considerable violence over the River Jordan. In ensuing clashes between Israeli troops and demonstrating West Bank students, six youngsters were hospitalized. Bir Zeit University was intermittently opened and closed as the campus was rocked by demonstrations and Israeli military interventions.

With the arrest and imprisonment of Nablus Mayor Bassam Shaka, all the other twenty-five mayors on the West Bank resigned in sympathy. Israeli soldiers raided and attacked the Jalazoun refugee camp. From their exile in Amman and Beirut, the deported leaders called on the Palestinians in the occupied area to revolt as a curfew was imposed on a large portion of the West Bank and Gaza as demonstrations spread. Efforts through near-unanimous U.N. resolutions to stem the violence were of no avail.

In support of its settlement plans, the Israeli government ended the regulations which had heretofore prohibited Israeli citizens and businesses from buying land in the occupied Arab territories. In response to Cairo's protests, Tel Aviv upbraided Egypt for its failure to proceed with the normalization of relations as provided by the Camp David accords.

Although election day was some eighteen months away, the quadrennial Presidential campaigning had begun, and Sadat's quiet prodding of Washington to exert pressure on Israel to show more flexibility went unheeded. In stating that there should not be "a fairly radical, new, and independent nation in the heart of the Middle East," Carter accepted Tel Aviv's fiat for limited autonomy and disappointed his Egyptian friend.

Sadat flew to Washington, but had to retreat from his position, fearful of alienating the White House and of endangering his public image. As the man who had brought "peace," he was more popular than any Western leader, a position which could be seriously endangered by Begin's repeated accusation that "the Egyptians were resorting to notorious anti-Semitic expressions." The Zionist groups saw to it that the contestants in the on-going presidential sweepstakes were made very aware of Begin's words and views.

President Carter early amassed a seemingly unbeatable lead in his battle for renomination by the Democratic Conclave in New York City. But a presidential flip-flop presented Ted Kennedy with a golden opportunity to exploit the Jewish vote and cut heavily into delegates pledged to Carter.

The U.S. had joined other U.N. Security Council members in a unanimous vote on a resolution calling upon Israel to dismantle existing settlements and to cease the construction and planning of new settlements in the "Arab territories occupied since 1967, including Jerusalem." The resolution further requested member states to provide

Israel with no foreign aid "to be used specifically in connection with the settlements."

Prior to the vote, unbelievable pressures were exerted on the White House to alter its position, and even afterwards the condemnations continued to roll in. Other presidential aspirants from both major political parties and independent Congressman John Anderson joined Kennedy in upbraiding the President for the position he had taken. Once more, as in previous presidential campaigns, the air was filled with a new version of Rodgers & Hammerstein's hit song from *Annie Get Your Gun*. Recklessly echoing everywhere was "I can do more for Israel than you can."

Two days later, Carter stated that the U.S. voted in favor of the resolution with the understanding that all references to Jerusalem would be "deleted" and that a "failure to communicate" with Ambassador Donald McHenry had resulted in a U.S. vote disregarding the original intent to abstain.

This vote change after the fact had no effect whatsoever; it did not help Mr. Carter with the insatiable Zionists and only lowered the President's image in the Arab world, as it did Uncle Sam's.

By early 1979 Organized Jewry had already clearly indicated that the vital Jewish vote would not go its traditional Democratic way in the 1980 elections. Carter had been the subject of attacks because of his gestures, however vacillating, to the Palestinians. The Zionists were also mindful of Washington's promise to the Saudis. In return for its moderation in the face of demands by other OPEC members for further price increases and their refusal to cut production, the house of Saud had been assured there would be some movement towards relinquishment of Israeli-held territories.

Carter also gained further Zionist enmity by siding with Sadat in the interpretation given to Israeli settlements in the Camp David accords. This led to bitter Zionist attacks on Carter, which accelerated after the Security Council flip-flop. Presidential hopes were also further hamstrung by the unfortunate Billy Carter affair, the exceedingly well-publicized stories about his brother's ties with Qaddafi and Libya.

On the Republican side, former Secretary of the Treasury John Connolly evinced seeming sympathy for the Palestinian-Arab position by urging the return of all Israeli-held territory and the right of the Palestinians to determine their own fate. Immediately, he came under heavy pressure from the Zionists, who barred him from a speaking engagement in New York.

In announcing his formal candidacy for the Republican nomination at the Washington National Press Club and becoming the sixth aspirant (not counting Gerald Ford), the three-time former governor of Texas showed himself to be an inveterate master of doubletalk. In the course of discussing the Middle East and the serious situation in Iran, he swung into euphoria over the Zionist state:

I have long looked on Israel not only as a nation that deserves our support from the moral standpoint, but from a strategic standpoint...that it clearly brings into sharp focus the importance of the preservation and strength of the State of Israel today. Nothing could be more important at this moment.

Only a few minutes earlier, in responding to certain questions, Connolly had defended the role of his large Houston law firm (208 lawyers), which had several Arab countries as clients. The Republican aspirant declared that this would create:

no conflict of interest because as a candidate I won't be a member of the firm.... Let me assure you, the Arab clients have our professional abilities, but they do not have our philosophy or our conscience.

Naturally, this was carried by the Jewish Telegraphic Agency. When well-known New York attorney Rita Hauser, one of Connolly's earlier ardent supporters, failed to commit him to further public support of Israel, she resigned from the campaign and soon joined others in attacking him.

Carter had not made himself more popular with the Zionists by telling a Washington press conference that the U.S. "considers the creation of Israeli settlements to be inconsistent with international law." However, he had prudently added: "There is a limit to what we can do to impose our will on a sovereign nation." Senator Kennedy slammed Carter for his rebuke to Israeli settlements and claimed that he alone was the hope for maintaining "our sacred alliance with Israel."

To bolster his image with the Jewish community, sagging despite his rescue of the peace treaty, the President even attended a Seder. This night was indeed "different from all other nights," because for the first time the President was at the home of Assistant Stuart Eizenstat for this Jewish holiday.

The 96th Congress certainly did not help to stem the continuing politicalization of the Middle East section when it rejected legislation to do away with the antiquated Electoral College system. Forty-two senators under the leadership of Birch Bayh, supported by President Carter, bowed to the power and pressures of well-entrenched minority interest groups led by the powerful Zionists.[80]

With the exception of Connolly's vacillating position, all of the twelve extant Democratic and Republican aspirants bowed completely to Zionist power. As one indication of Ronald Reagan's determination to consolidate his hold on the Jewish Republican vote and break into Democratic strength, he appointed ardent Israelist Maxwell Rabb[81] as vice chairman of his campaign committee. The initial Connolly nod to the Palestinians had provided the Reagan forces with the opportunity to push their bid for Zionist votes and accompanying dollars even further. The independent candidacy of Anderson, marked by his vigorous and blatant support of Israel, markedly affected the campaign tactics of his rivals, President Carter and Governor Reagan, who had emerged victorious at their conventions.

The shattering, overwhelming defeat of President Carter at the hands of his California rival sent the Republican Party into the White House without any obligation to the Jewish vote. Nonetheless, in a statement which appeared November 17, President-elect Reagan told *Time* magazine: "The Muslims are returning to the idea that the way to heaven is to lose your life fighting Christians or Jews." Such a distortion of why Muslims and Arabs were opposing U.S. policy could only have been written for Reagan by his pro-Israel staff advisors, who included Joseph Churba (the old friend of JDL leader Meir Kahane), Robert Tucker, Edward Lutwak, and Uri Raanan, the latter two Israeli citizens.

The Republican sweep into the White House and control of the Senate was marked by the deepest anti-Soviet sentiment, which further manifested itself in a discernible antipathy toward the Palestinians in general—and the PLO in particular—who were viewed as an integral part of the Communist vortex. Such a polarization, however dangerous to the rest of the world, could not but be most pleasing to Tel Aviv.

XXIII   Reagan and Still Begin

He that will not reason is a bigot; he that cannot reason is a fool; and he that dares not reason is a slave.

—Sir William Drummond

The Reagan Administration gave unmistakable signs that it would be primarily concerned at the outset with domestic affairs, principally in winning the battle of the budget and fighting inflation. Foreign affairs were well down on the list of presidential priorities, all the more so due to a most pleasant inauguration present, the final release of the American hostages in Teheran.

The hostage crisis following the Soviet invasion of Afghanistan had tended to whip up a near-war fever among Americans. In such an atmosphere in which Arabs were equated with Muslims and red-baiting was most stylish, Israel flourished in its role as the sole dependable U.S. friend in the Middle East." Begin was counting on the Palestine problem and certainly the Jerusalem question remaining on a Washington back burner, barring a grave crisis, until after more Arab disunity had been sown and the PLO further isolated.

Begin's continued intransigency on Palestinian autonomy was encouraged by Reagan's early stand that his Administration did not consider the settlements illegal, contrary to the previous position of the White House and the State Department. The upcoming Israeli elections also helped forge Washington acquiescence.

Reagan's personal long-term ties with conservative Jews and Zionist publications (including the _Jewish Press_ of Brooklyn in which in past years his syndicated articles had often appeared side-by-side with those of Begin when the paper was edited by Meir Kahane) were reflected in the roster of important appointments. Although the President did not name one Jew to his cabinet—this is the first time this has happened since the Eisenhower Administration—there was no shortage of Jews at the critical sub-cabinet level, particularly at the State Department, where vital policy-making decisions affecting Israel are made. From the Zionist point of view, having people in these slots was far more important than having a Jewish cabinet minister who remained out of Middle East diplomacy.

Sherwood (Woody) Goldberg, who worked for Secretary of State Alexander Haig in Vietnam, now served as his right-hand man and office chief of staff. Dr. Harvey Sicherman of the Foreign Policy Research Institute in Philadelphia also was helping the Secretary, along with Dr. David Korn, formerly of Howard University. Likewise, importantly placed in the State Department was Undersecretary for Economic Affairs Myer Rashish and Paul Wolfowitz as Director of the Policy Planning Staff—and, of course, Mrs. Jeane Kirkpatrick, U.S. Permanent Representative at the U.N. Although a Christian, her devotion to Israel is unsurpassed by anyone. The President also was receiving advice on matters affecting the Jewish community from invaluable fundraisers, Detroit's Max Fisher and Ted Cummings of Los Angeles.

Richard Perle, formerly Senator Jackson's principal liaison with the Zionists in the important work done on the Hill for the Israeli lobby,[1] was designated as Assistant Secretary of Defense for International Security Policy. Perle promptly appointed as consultant Stephen Bryen, who had been forced to resign his post with the Senate Foreign Relations Subcommittee on Middle Eastern Affairs after leaking material to the Israelis.[2]

Taking advantage of Reagan's reluctance to antagonize members of Congress while he was seeking to win support for important domestic programs, Israeli planes continued to attack targets in southern and central Lebanon. Begin claimed the right of reconaissance over Lebanese territory and arrogantly threatened to wipe out Syrian anti-aircraft missile emplacements in Lebanon's Bekaa Valley near the border. Long a strong advocate of Israel, Security Council Advisor Richard Allen's "hot pursuit" allusion on television supported the massive aerial "retaliatory" attacks on alleged PLO bases.

The U.N. was unsuccessful in efforts to halt the continued raids, bombing attacks and incursions on Lebanon by Israel. Internecine Arab warring added to the woes of the beleaguered Lebanese. The cease-fire following the March 1978 Israeli mammouth thrust into Lebanon had been incessantly broken by warfare between the Syrian peace-keeping forces and the Lebanese Maronites; between Chamounites vs. Geymayel Phalangists; between the PLO and allies and the Israelis; between the

Palestinian forces and those of Israel's ally, Major Saad Haddad, operating from his 60-square mile enclave in south Lebanon. Added to this was the unbelievable slaughter of innocents at the hands of private Lebanese armed bands and freelance gunmen. Even UNIFIL (United Nations International Forces in Lebanon) suffered considerable losses in repeated clashes with the Israelis.

War, bombing, terror and devastation were sealing the doom of Lebanon. Only an eyewitness can appreciate the irreparable tragedy that has befallen Beirut. As the crackling of artillery could be heard on an August afternoon from suburban Hadith, the scene of the latest conflict between the Syrian peace-keeping forces and the Phalangists, I examined the past years' devastation of this once uniquely beautiful city. On top of destruction has been added the influx of refugees from south Lebanon, many squatting in the apartments of other Lebanese in the finest residential areas or ensconced on the famed corniche in huts, shanties and shacks overlooking the nearly deserted beaches. For these Beirutis who have remained, the fear of tomorrow has been added to the torment of yesterday.

The Syrians strove to prevent the partition of Lebanon. As the peace-keeping forces of the Arab League, they attempted with little success to stabilize and strengthen the Lebanese government so that it would be able to take over policing duties in south Lebanon. Trumpeted by the media, Israel warned that it would never permit "the annihilation of Lebanese Christians by Syrians" as the Maronite separatists moved further away from any reconciliation with the central government in Beirut. Begin strengthened his ties with Maronite leaders[3] in the north, secretly meeting with Chamoun and signing an accord[4] with Major Haddad who increasingly ruled his enclave as a separate country.

Secretary of State Alexander Haig's first venture into hazardous Middle East waters came with his Spring trip. He did not visit the West Bank and was at least spared the embarrassment of Cyrus Vance's futile quest to find a substitute for the PLO. Returning from his tour, the Secretary of State tried to convey the impression—with the help of the ever-obliging media—that he had been most successful and that the Arabs would adopt his priority, a containment of Soviet expansionism.

In fact, his reception at Riyadh, his most important stop, had been very cool. Saudi Foreign Minister Prince Saud bin Faisal had made it very clear that, consonant with the position taken at the Foreign Ministers Islamic Conference at Taif three months earlier, Israel was considered the number-one danger to the Arab world, and that Jerusalem—at the very least, East Jerusalem—was the center of Saudi concern. The Secretary was told that the implementation of U.N. resolutions on Palestinian rights was essential. Neither the fall of the Shah nor the siege of the mosque in Mecca by politically-motivated zealous Muslims had instilled sufficient fear in the Saudi royal family to drop its anti-Zionism and seek the shelter of Washington's anti-Communist umbrella. Israel's surprise aerial assault against Iraq had quite the opposite effect.

At 18:37 hrs. Baghdad local time, Sunday, June 7, Israeli Prime Minister Menachem Begin's eight F-16 jet fighter-bombers, newly acquired from American factories and escorted by six F-15's, flew from their Etzion airbase in the Sinai and struck a deadly blow at global security.

Dramatically illustrating once again the swift, uncanny prowess and devastating accuracy of Israel's innumerable earlier "surgical" strikes and blitzkriegs north, south and east of its own expanding frontiers, "Operation Babylon," as it was dubbed, hit the Tammuz 17 $260-million nuclear reactor complex, known to Europeans as Osirak at Tuwaitha, about ten miles southwest of Baghdad and more than 500 miles distant from the borders of their own country.

The mission was widely hailed by military analysts as a masterpiece of precision in the era of the supersonic jet and the "smart bomb." The pilots, crack veterans of the Israeli-Arab air battles of the sixties and the seventies, had rehearsed their task for months, complete with a mockup of their ultimate target. Expressions of admiration, ranging from the grudging to the enthusiastic, were widespread from Western strategists and analysts for the pinpoint targeting and the hundreds of miles of elusive flight which preceded it.

In attempting to justify his actions, Begin alluded to a secret chamber 40 meters beneath Tammuz 17, where the Iraqis allegedly engaged in clandestine nuclear armaments research. The mysterious "room," first put at a depth of 130 feet by Begin, was later raised to a level of only 13 feet below the reactor. Israeli authorities abandoned the claim after American intelligence politely found that "evidence for its existence could not be verified."

Although French and American analysts estimated an Iraqi nuclear weapons capacity years in the future, possibly not before the end of the decade, much media ink was spilled in the wake of Israel's nuclear blitz, on the question of Iraq's nuclear intentions: Was Baghdad going for the nuclear bomb, and if so, when? Discussion was shifted to center on Iraqi potential and intentions rather than on the bombing by Israel: "Iraq is the potential aggressor and Israel the potential victim" was the theme of the swelling chorus of the Israeli lobby, which succeeded in surpassing, in sheer decibel volume, the actual bombing itself.

At a news conference three days later, President Reagan stated: "I do think one has to recognize Israel had reason for concern with Iraq." He declared that Israel may have sincerely believed the raid was a defensive move, adding: "It is very difficult for me to envision Israel as being a threat to its neighbors."

A widely publicized nuclear threat against Israel by Iraqi President Saddam Hussein, allegedly published in the official Iraqi newspaper, *Al-Thawra*, was soon exposed as a hoax despite the fact that such diverse reputed foreign policy "experts" as New York's Mayor Edward I. Koch and *New York Times* columnist William Safire had attested to the remarks. Safire later apologized, blaming the error on a "mistranslation of a loose paraphrase" by the Israeli Foreign Minister. (The *New York Times* editorially called the attack "an act of inexcusable and short-sighted aggression.") [5]

Dr. Sigvard Eklund of Sweden, Director-General of the International Atomic Energy Agency, stated on June 9 that there was "a very high probability" (in the Iraqi case, a "full guarantee," according to the *New York Times)* that the diversion of any highly enriched uranium reactor fuel or the unreported production of plutonium for weapons would have been spotted during inspections. Iraq, it was agreed, could not have obtained a meaningful amount of fissionable material for use in nuclear weapons without France or the International Atomic Energy Agency knowing and abrogating its treaty commitments.

To offset this expert opinion, ardent Zionist-minded California Senator Alan Cranston brought Roger Richter, a junior-level inspector, who had worked in Vienna for the IAEA, but had never been to Iraq, to testify at the Senate Foreign Relations hearings dealing with the possible Israeli violation of the law governing foreign military sales. He alleged that Iraq had the ability to develop a bomb dangerous to Israel and that he had earlier tried to warn the State Department of this danger.

The White House had expressed shock at the Israeli attack, following which President Reagan placed a temporary hold on the shipment of four F-16's scheduled for delivery to Israel that week. Claiming total surprise, the State Department's spokesman Dean Fischer also declared that the Israeli action might be a "possible violation" of the U.S.-Israel agreements under which procured U.S. arms may be used only for defensive purposes.

Inasmuch as the two intelligence services, the CIA and Israel's Mossad, are as close as two peas in a pod, it was hard to believe that

Washington was not aware of Israel's intent to attack the Osirak reactor. The exact timing was kept a top secret even from Israeli cabinet members until a special meeting was convened when the attackers were well on their flight to Baghdad.

The Israeli daily, *Maariv*, alleged that American officials had visited Israel several times in 1980 to keep Israelis informed on Iraq's alleged progress towards producing a bomb. Another Israeli newspaper reported that Israel relied on U.S. intelligence data before deciding to carry out its bombing attack.

The nuclear fallout from Operation Babylon may have been negligible, but the political and military fallout was considerable. Shimon Peres' planned visit to Cairo was indefinitely delayed; the Philip Habib mission, on behalf of Israel, to get Syrian anti-aircraft missiles removed from Lebanon was rendered even more hopeless. "Moderate" Anwar Sadat of Egypt voiced his outrage, having conferred with Begin at Sharm el Sheikh only three days before; "moderate" Jordanian Prime Minister Mudar Badran reportedly wrote a despairing letter to President Reagan; and the Saudis sternly warned the U.S. at the highest level to reconsider its pro-Israeli orientation. The Haig-Reagan policy goal of knitting the Arabian Gulf area countries together in an anti-Soviet alliance appeared more elusive than ever.

For its part, "The Iraqi Government vowed ... to press ahead with its nuclear program despite the threat by Israel's Prime Minister to order a new attack if the nuclear reactor raided last Sunday was rebuilt." Information Minister Latif Nusayyef Jassem announced that his country was capable of establishing new and better nuclear installations and would do so after the French made it clear that they would favorably view a request to aid in the reactor's reconstruction.

Whatever Iraq's original nuclear intentions may have been, it became clear that its timetable had now been speeded up by the very operation purporting to thwart it. In his first public reaction to the raid, Iraqi President Hussein called on "all peace-loving nations to help the Arabs acquire nuclear weapons to balance Israel's nuclear capacity." He said it was a "rational move for Arabs to try to acquire a bomb" and described it as "a remedy for an existing situation in Israel" with its possession of nuclear arms.

Apparently, at home the raid on the Iraqi reactor had worked to Begin's advantage. In an election many earlier feared he might lose, his party squeezed by on July 30 with a one-vote plurality over Labor Alignment's Peres, who had bested the incumbent in the big television debate. To form a government, Begin had to rely on the votes of the

National Religious Party and two smaller splinter groups, Tami and Tleme, with their five seats.

Undaunted by the strong unanimous Security Council condemnation,[6] the wording of which had been worked out in lengthy U.N. Delegates Lounge horsetrading (a call for sanctions certainly would have drawn a U.S. veto) between Iraqi Foreign Minister Saadoun Hammadi and American Ambassador Jeane Kirkpatrick, Israel's American bombers struck again five weeks later—this time into the heart of Lebanon. Seeking to forestall PLO raids on Israel, the Israelis bombed civilian areas of Beirut on July 17, allegedly to wipe out PLO headquarters, killing 385 and wounding in excess of 600—more casualties in this one raid than Israel suffered at the hands of the Palestinians since the creation of the state. Lengthy Israeli-U.S.-Saudi-PLO negotiations, which resulted finally in a cease-fire, constituted the nearest thing to a Tel Aviv recognition of the Palestinians.

The Zionist influence over Reagan was severely tested by this latest aerial onslaught against Beirut. Secretary of Defense Casper Weinberger attacked Begin in a nationally televised interview, and Deputy Secretary of State William Clark joined in the criticism. Even as Secretary Haig was holding his fire during a breakfast meeting with reporters, other lower echelon diplomats were accusing the Israelis of trying to split the U.S. from its moderate Arab friends.

The President's very special affection for Israel, strongly manifested during the campaign, came to the fore. Calling Israel "an oasis of democracy in the area and a loyal ally," the President was alleged to have personally ordered an end to the short-lived campaign by his aides to condemn Begin for the attack on civilian Beirut. It was concluded that everybody was mad as hell at Begin—except one man—"and he was the one who counted."

In meting out "punishment" to Israel for its bombing raids on the Baghdad facility and on Beirut, Reagan behaved like most of his predecessors—the mildest chastisement administered to Begin in the form of a temporary embargo, first on four F-16 attack planes and then after "the escalating level of violence" on an additional fourteen F-16's and two F-15 fighter-interceptors scheduled for delivery.

The embargo was lifted in August amid contradictory reports in the press. First came a trial balloon that Israel would have to agree to the customary limitations on the use of weapons for defensive purposes which accompany any sale of U.S. weaponry. This only encouraged further spirited verbal Israeli assault on the embargo as "unjust and unjustifiable." Administrative spokesman Larry Speakes was credited with the report that Israel had now agreed to the normal conditions imposed on arms sales. But Begin declared he had no intention of making any promises on the use of any weapons received from the U.S.

Haig was forced to admit that the U.S. had neither sought nor received any assurances from Israel. The Secretary stated that the arrangements "under which military assistance to Israel is provided are clearly recognized on both sides," and that the decision had been reached following extensive "candid discussions" between them both.

As required under the terms of the Arms Export Control Act, Secretary Haig reported the bombing of the Iraqi reactor to Congress, and requested a response as to whether Israel had misused its weapons and disregarded the conditions of sale. During his press conference dealing with the lifting of the embargo, the Secretary had been asked whether there had been an answer from Congress on the possible Israeli violations. To this Haig simply said "there had never been one in the past, and we do not feel it was necessary on this occasion. It's just that simple." [7]

However outraged the rest of the world may have been over the latest Israeli attack, Secretary Haig wished to close the incident before Begin's visit, apparently to avoid antagonizing the Israel lobby and, even more expressly, the Congress at that particular time, although he emphatically denied any linkage between the end of the suspension and the projected sale to the Saudis of five AWACS. The sale also included ground stations and spare parts for the sophisticated surveillance planes as well as equipment for enhancing the performance of the sixty-two F-15's purchased by the Saudis in 1978, for a total of $8.5-billion.

Begin's Washington September meeting with Ronald Reagan netted the Israeli Prime Minister his greatest triumph—not only what was hailed as the start of a strong friendship between the two chiefs of state, but, more pragmatically, the new agreement for "strategic cooperation." Such recognition of Israel as a strategic asset (the late Chief of Staff General Brown had labeled Israel a "military burden," see *supra*, p. 448) was far more to the liking of the Israelis than any defense pact requiring Senate ratification and hence open to public purview and debate.

In the aftermath of world repugnance over the Israeli bombing of Beirut and at a time the Reagan Administration was desperately striving to bring federal expenditures closer in line with income, Begin's gains were all the more astounding. Little wonder that he hailed "a new U.S.-Israeli era" and boasted that Reagan had made no mention of the two outstanding sensitive issues, the distinction between offensive and defensive Israeli use of American weapons and the West Bank.

While specifics of the U.S.-Israeli arrangements were to be kept under total secrecy and spelled out later by military committees, there was little doubt that Israel was provided with infinite new benefits and many additional goodies. Openly included were the holding of joint naval exercises, the stockpiling of military stores, the pre-positioning of medical facilities in Israel, U.S. use of Israel for servicing and repairs of military equipment, and joint planning to counter the Soviet Union.

Areas of cooperation, which both governments announced were better left unpublished, included arrangements for the emergency stationing of forward elements of the U.S. Rapid Deployment Force at Israeli bases and a more significant exchange of intelligence with all super-technology intelligence operations to be bared to the Mossad. Already in possession of more American-supplied electronic warfare gear than any of our European allies, Israel was allegedly granted access to the top secret in the American technological arsenal: how to launch so-called countermeasures against American-built aircraft, missiles and reconnaissance systems that the Arabs had or were planning to buy from U.S. manufacturers.

Israel, unlike other countries, would also enjoy the right to use U.S. military aid dollars in support of its own military complex rather than to make purchases from U.S. companies, which would bring desperately needed dollars into the family. An additional figure of $2 to 3-billion was reportedly to be tucked away for Tel Aviv somewhere in the defense budget. No wonder the jubilation of Begin. Henceforth, Israel was not to be the 51st state, as critics had complained, but the first state of the Union.

Begin was allegedly urged to soft-pedal his opposition to the AWACS sale in a pre-departure airport meeting with Secretary Haig, who left a National Security Council meeting in Washington to speak to him. The strategic alliance, however, did not deter the Zionist lobby from doing its utmost to defeat the sale. Although the Senate earlier had overwhelmingly supported a resolution opposing the sale, President Reagan was upheld on October 28 by an astounding 54 to 48 surprise vote.

No president ever worked so assiduously on the Congress as did Reagan, who over a period of weeks met personally at the White House, on a one-to-one basis, with many senators, some of whom were deeply committed to the opposition to the sale and others who had not made up their minds. All of his charm and personality went into a prodigious job of persuasion and arm-twisting. The Administration's promise to the

Saudis had to be kept, he insisted, for the sake of "regional peace and the security" for all countries, including Israel.

Reagan for the first time experienced what every one of his predecessors, beginning with Truman through Carter, had undergone since Israel's creation: inordinate lobbying pressures imposed on both the executive and legislative branches, bolstered by simultaneous outpourings on the theme of anti-Semitism. At the height of the battle, the *New York Times* took the President severely to task in an editorial, "Mr. Reagan Blames Mr. Begin":

The President did not quite say 'choose Begin or Reagan,' or accuse the opponents of his AWACS deal of putting Israel's interests ahead of America's. But those are the *repugnant implications of his prepared statement that 'it is not the business of other nations to make American foreign policy.'* [8]

The editorial ended with a less subtle evocation of the charge of anti-Semitism:

To suggest that Congress is under foreign influence merely makes a bad predicament worse. *To raise the spectre of undue Israeli influence, with all the ugly echoes that this scene can have in American society, risks turning a bad deal into a disaster.* [Emphasis added.]

Hitler may have died in a Berlin bunker in 1945, but vital elements of U.S. foreign policy were nevertheless still being decided on the basis of the total human revulsion towards Nazism. The role of anti-Semitism was, strangely enough, primary for both many who voted to uphold the President and some who opposed. (Coincidentally, the AWACS vote came on the day of the final session of the first International Liberators Conference, organized by the U.S. Holocaust Memorial Council, in Washington.) Maine's William S. Cohen voted with Reagan because he felt the defeat of the sale would cause a backlash against both Israel and American Jewry.[9] Fundamentalist Iowa's Roger W. Jepsen dramatically switched sides under impact of this reasoning and secret security information divulged to him by the President. On October 1, Reagan had broadened the American commitment in the Persian Gulf by declaring, "Saudi Arabia we will not permit to be another Iran."[10] The U.S., he said, would bar a takeover by forces, inside or outside, that imperiled the flow of oil to the West.

Opponents to the sale feared that weapons in the hands of the Saudis constituted a threat to Israel which could usher in a new Holocaust, despite Presidential assurances that "Israel's edge in armaments, quantitatively and qualitatively, would be maintained."[11]

Alleged Reagan pledges to senators that there would be joint U.S.-Saudi crewing of the planes and that the delivery of the planes was conditional upon Saudi Arabia's contribution to the peace effort remained a matter of ambiguity and dispute.

The final outcome of the AWACS battle provided convincing proof of crass American materialism. For the first time, forty business institutions, who had been (and still are) earning billions from Saudi petro dollars, banded together and met the challenge of the Israeli lobby. Neither altruism, concern for the national interest nor alarm over growing Zionist power had prompted U.S. and Saudi business interests to act. With Mobil as their spokesman, they ran full-page advertisements in eleven major newspapers and in *Time*, noting that 700 non-petroleum companies had a $35-billion stake in business with Saudi Arabia.

Unlike at any time during the long history of the Palestine question,[12] these companies lobbied, placed pressure on senators and had their friends do likewise. They also persuaded their subcontractors and suppliers to follow suit.

Their action was supplemented by that of thirty-four organizations under the leadership of the American Security Council. Right-wing and conservative, they had strong ties with junior GOP senators and envisioned a grave blow to Reagan's image in his possible defeat on this issue, even damaging the manner in which he would be able to function in the future. And these total efforts challenged for the first time the heretofore omnipotence of the Zionist lobby and won. The shocking passing of Anwar Sadat earlier in the month had also played a role in the Senate vote.

While reviewing a military parade commemorating the 1973 war with Israel, Sadat was assassinated on October 6 by a group of Egyptian soldiers led by Lieutenant Khalid Ahmad al-Islambuli, who was a member of a clandestine religious organization. Intermittent fighting between security forces and religious militants followed in Assuit and elsewhere, but order was restored as all public demonstrations were barred.

World political leaders, mostly from Western countries (only four Arab states were represented), including former Presidents Nixon, Ford and Carter, attended the Sadat burial in Cairo. (Upon their return, Ford and Carter jointly called for a policy of mutual recognition between the PLO and Israel and for American dialogue with the PLO.)

Eight days later following elections, Vice President Hosni Mubarak was sworn in to succeed the slain leader and promised to follow his predecessor's policies.

The death of Sadat in no way stirred his people as had Gamal Abdel Nasser's passing eleven years earlier. In Cairo, silence and closed doors prevailed, even as Mayor Koch, who, as congressman during the '73 war, had unmercifully assailed the Egyptian leader, now paid tribute to him for whom he predicted there will be "a deep outpouring of grief on the streets of Cairo." But wire associations and the *New York Times* were equally hard put to come up with photos of mourners, save in Mit Abul Kum, Sadat's hamlet birthplace.

Still at war with Qaddafi after the August shooting down of two Libyan planes over the Gulf of Sidra and repeated charges that the Libyan leader was plotting the death of Reagan, Washington at first encouraged the media to attribute the assassination to a Libyan-Soviet-PLO conspiracy, thus to cover up the widespread Egyptian discontent with Sadat's policies.

Clearly, Sadat was out of step with his own people. His last months were increasingly stormy, marked by domestic unrest. The Egyptian leader rarely brooked personal criticism, and he vindictively repressed the increasing number of dissidents. These represented a wide spectrum: the right and the left—religious militants, Nasserites, and intellectuals—Christians and Muslims—journalists, lawyers and politicians.

In early September he cracked down and arrested 1,600 of his critics, prominent among whom was famed journalist Heikal. He declared the Muslim Brotherhood illegal and cancelled the choice of Pope Shenuda III as head of Egypt's Copts. A correspondent of ABC television was thrown out of the country because of an interview not to the President's liking. As an answer to what he deemed an important question by a foreign reporter, Sadat stated: "In other times I would have shot you, but it is democracy I am suffering from as much as I am suffering from the opposition." No wonder the *New York Times* in its eulogy, "One Extraordinary Man," was forced to confess that "Anwar Sadat was also a skillful despot."

After launching his attack on Muslims and Copts as a threat to the unity of the country, Sadat accused a dozen former Egyptian officials of "conniving" with the Soviet Union to destabilize his regime, and expelled the Soviet ambassador, six members of his staff, two journalists and more than 1,000 technicians working on projects throughout the country. The Egyptian President claimed they tried to undermine the regime, and the Cairo media thereafter ascribed the opposition to him to communist subversion.

Although professing to protect Palestinian rights, Sadat's

pragmatism led him to give up his earlier insistence on a timetabled linkage between Palestinian rights and treaty ratification for concessions on the Sinai. His acceptance of a "piece"—the Sinai—as a substitute for genuine peace won him acclaim and American euphoria because he was able to so thoroughly convince the Western media that he was a "seer endowed with almost mystical serenity." The far-reaching consequences of his role are described by two British writers in their new book, *Sadat:*

The international order which, since his pilgrimage to Jerusalem, Sadat had built and come to personify is still in place. But that his violent end, so eminently foreseeable, should be regarded as having dealt such a devastating blow merely illustrates how fragile and unnatural that order has always been. Rejoicing in the Arab world was certainly in poor taste, but it was no more out of place than the official grief and extravagant obituaries in the West.[13]

As Lebanon's Prime Minister Shafik al-Wazzan noted:

Ill-fated Camp David involved the Arab world in a series of divisions and conflicts and gave room for continuous arrogance, arbitrariness and aggression. It inflicted victims and destruction on Lebanon. It was Camp David that killed Sadat.[14]

In a move billed by the Israelis as a step towards implementation of autonomy for Palestinians, Menachem Milson was designated civilian administration director on the West Bank. A colonel in the Israeli Army for many years, Milson's sole claim to civilian status rested on a short period spent as a lecturer at the Hebrew University.

Milson sought, as reported in his article in *Commentary,* to restructure the political loyalties in the occupied territory by neutralizing all local authority and leadership as a prerequisite for carrying out the Israeli interpretation of the autonomy commitment under Camp David. His avowed purpose was to strengthen "moderate" Arabs of the Village Leagues (the first such league was set up in Hebron in 1978 when he served as Arab Affairs Advisor to the military government) to counter the influence of the "pro-PLO" elected mayors of the West Bank, whom he claimed represented a minority view. According to the *Jerusalem Post:* "Leaders chosen for the Village League were some of the most discredited persons in the West Bank community (one had been convicted by the Jordan government of embezzling municipal funds) even before they agreed to collaborate with Israel, and their adjutants regular ruffians who commanded plain loathing."

The people of the West Bank were placed in the position of having to choose between municipalities impoverished because of their support of the PLO and shunned by the Zionist authorities on the one hand, and collaborators who were able both to dispense funds, supplied by Israel, and were given access to the occupation forces for the permits required for a wide range of everyday activities. For example, those needed for travel abroad, formerly obtainable from the occupying authorities via the municipality, could now only be secured through the Village Leagues. Aid from Arab Gulf states and elsewhere, and from Palestinians abroad to West Bank villages was frozen while Zionist authorities showered favors on their Village League sycophants.

Viewed as a prelude to annexation, the institution of the civilian administration set off violent demonstrations on the West Bank and the University of Bir Zeit was closed once again. Within three weeks, President of the Village League of Ramallah Yusuf el-Khatib and his son were killed in an ambush set by Palestinians. The National Committee of Arab Local Council Chairmen announced a general strike to protest Israeli government failures to fund Arab councils adequately. Israeli troops disbanded demonstrations, two bombs exploded in Jerusalem, and several homes were demolished on suspicion that sons of the owning families had thrown home-made Molotov cocktails at Israeli troops. Demonstrators were arrested in Ramallah for protesting the demolitions and the closing of Bir Zeit.

In December, Gaza businessmen began a general strike in protest of an Israeli twelve per cent value-added tax on the income of doctors; in the ensuing demonstrations one Arab teenager was killed and three others were wounded by the Israeli army. Two days later, Army forces welded shut two hundred merchants' doors in retaliation for the demonstrations, and Israeli troops entered the Women's Training Center in Ramallah for having conducted an illegal demonstration.

It was later that month that the Israeli Knesset voted to annex the Golan Heights, a move unanimously condemned by the U.N. Security Council, which called on Israel to rescind the annexation. The following day the U.S. suspended the U.S.-Israeli Memorandum of Understanding on strategic cooperation which had been signed by Sharon and Weinberger the month before.

Begin literally frothed at the mouth: "What kind of talk is this, 'punishing Israel'?" He railed: "Are we a vassal state of yours? Are we a banana republic? Are we fourteen-year-olds, that if we misbehave we get our wrists slapped?" The Israeli Prime Minister likened measures of the Reagan Administration to those of an anti-Semitic British general in pre-Israel Palestine.

As 12,000 Syrian Druze of the Golan Heights, with a few exceptions, refused to accept Israeli identity cards, the Syrians failed to gain support for a draft Security Council resolution that would have imposed sanctions on Israel. However, they won a Phyrric victory when the General Assembly adopted an ineffectual resolution calling for *voluntary suspension* of diplomatic and trade relations with Israel. (Emphasis added).

The Israeli announcement of the establishment of two new settlements on the Golan Heights brought Druze protests and a curfew was then imposed on their principal town of Majdal Shams. The Druze continued to oppose the annexation by refusing to pay Israeli income taxes or to sell lands to Israelis, by rejecting Israeli social security and medical help, and by resisting new attempts to impose Israeli identity cards. They insisted on identifying themselves as Syrians. Four of their leaders were arrested for leading the protests, a general strike followed, and schools were closed. The Israelis retaliated by firing several hundred Druze employees and businesses.

For forty days the Israeli Army sealed off four Druze villages, preventing food or people, including American and Israeli journalists, from coming in or out. Ironically, heretofore, since the inception of Israel, the Druze had been given greater privileges than any non-Jews and even served in the Israeli Army, as they had always been considered loyalists.

Israeli jurist members of the Association for Civil Rights in Israel documented that troops had clubbed a three year-old Druze child, shooting his mother when she tried to intervene; that troops had vandalized village schools; that residents had refused emergency medical care; that Druze telephone links were cut periodically; and that several of them had been sentenced to prison in summary trials without representation by counsel.

With the massing of Israeli troop forces along the Lebanese border following the Golan annexation, rumors were rife of an Israeli invasion of southern Lebanon. The U.S. government sent Philip Habib back to the Middle East to receive assurances that Israel would not attack.

It was at this time that the turmoil escalated on the West Bank, spearheaded by Milson's firing of Mayor Ibrahim Tawil of El-Bireh for refusing to cooperate with the Israeli civilian administration. Following a similar dismissal of Mayors Kareem Khalef of Ramallah, Bassam Shaka of Nablus and Wahid Hamdallah of Anabta and replacement by Israelis, the worst violence since 1967 erupted on the West Bank in the course of which fifteen Palestinians were killed, most of them teenagers. A Security Council resolution aimed at forcing Israel to reverse the dismissal of these elected mayors was vetoed by the U.S.

Violence and disturbances further accelerated when on Easter Sunday U.S. citizen Alan Goodman, who was serving in the Israeli Army, opened fire at the Dome of the Rock, killing two Arabs and wounding eleven others. Answering an appeal from Saudi Arabia's King Khalid, the Muslim world staged a general strike to protest Israel's failure to safeguard Jerusalem's holy places. Again, it was the U.S. that vetoed a U.N. Security Council resolution which would have condemned the sniper's attack.

With the approach of April 25, the date for the final portion of the Sinai to be turned back to Egypt, the opposition of Jewish settlers increased. Reinforced by militant ultra-nationalists, including supporters of Rabbi Meir Kahane, who had moved into the region to fight the evacuation, some Jewish settlers, particularly at the large settlement of Yamit, rejected the huge offer of compensation (an average of $245,000 for 1183 families), burned a government office and otherwise resisted eviction notices with threats of suicide. The Israeli government itself threatened to renege on its withdrawal commitment, alleging Egyptian infractions of the agreement, but differences with Cairo were straightened out.

Even as Israeli troops were engaged in the south, battling die-hard Yamit settlers who resisted evacuation, sixty Israeli war planes struck Beirut suburbs, killing twenty-five and wounding scores of others, thus breaking the ceasefire that had been in effect since July. The U.S., concerned lest Israel launch a full scale invasion of Lebanon which would endanger the Sinai evacuation, urged the PLO not to retaliate.

To emphasize the great sacrifice the Israelis were making for peace, American television and newspaper front-page photos depicted Jew struggling against Jew, as the Israeli army rooted the last of Yamit settlers out of underground fortresses and a synagogue on April 24. After blowing up every building in Yamit, the Israelis handed the last slice of the Sinai, as scheduled, over to Egypt the following day. To assuage the opposition, Begin announced that he would introduce legislation in the Knesset barring any further surrender of settlements or territory in any part of occupied Arab lands.

In place of legislation, because of Labor Party opposition, the Prime Minister delivered an exceedingly tough statement at the opening of the Parliamentary summer session on May 3, in which he referred to Israel, the West Bank and the Gaza Strip as "western Eretz Israel," thus reviving the notion of his hero Jabotinsky and the Revisionist Zionist movement that its historical land included the east bank of the Jordan River on which the Hashemite Kingdom is located. Begin served notice that at the end of the transition period under autonomy, Israel would raise its demands for "sovereignty over Judea, Samaria and the Gaza district." Meanwhile, he declared that "the government will act to strengthen settlements, to expand and consolidate them." His government was determined to raise the population of Jewish settlements on the West Bank from 25,000 to 100,000. In any future negotiations over the signing of a peace treaty between Israel and its neighbors, Begin added, "any proposal for the removal or evacuation of Jewish settlements would be rejected." Opposition leader Shimon Peres did not fail to try and make political points by noting that Begin earlier had pledged never to dismantle Israel Sinai settlements.

Regarding the autonomy talks, Begin insisted that sessions would have to be held in Jerusalem, his capital city, as well as in Cairo and Washington, despite the reluctance of his treaty partners to recognize Israel's annexation of East Jerusalem.

Faced by an Israel determined to strengthen its hold on the occupied West Bank and Gaza and to keep PLO forces subservient to Tel Aviv's omnipotent aerial power, ever-reinforced by new U.S. shipments, a helpless PLO faced its darkest hour. Non-implemented, futile U.N. resolutions censuring Israel or affirming the inalienable rights of the Palestinians were of little avail. The Arab states in hopeless disarray, with internecine rivalries never so bitterly fragmenting and the continuing Iran-Iraqi war sapping their strength, seemed unable to use their enormous wealth (slightly depleted by falling oil prices) to help.

The Arabs were incapable of uniting or disuniting around Saudi Arabian Crown Prince Fahd's eight-point peace plan. This called for the return of territory captured by Israel in 1967, the establishment of a Palestinian state with East Jerusalem as its capital and a guarantee of the right of all countries in the Middle East to live in peace, a tacit recognition of Israel.

PLO chieftain Arafat stated that the Fahd plan contained positive aspects and told an interviewer that the plan was "a good beginning."[15] But it was attacked by some rejectionist Palestinian groups. The November (1981) Arab summit in Fez, called to discuss the proposal, adjourned after its very first session when it was apparent that important absences, notably Syria's, and wide disagreement made a consensus impossible.

The European initiative, once a vibrant hope, was no longer even on a back burner. The gradual return of Egypt under Mubarak to the Arab fold could be predicted, but its immediate effect on the balance of power in the area remained to be seen.

Despite an occasional demonstration by the Peace Now movement, the overwhelming majority of Israelis gave full support to Begin's policies, and some even voiced preference for the tougher line of Defense Minister Sharon. They overwhelmingly approved of the new settlements being activated on the West Bank and the Golan Heights.

The media could not avoid reporting the mounting violence in the occupied territories and the aerial assaults on Lebanon. But the press still cast its spotlight on Nazi genocide, and featured articles and endless Holocaust television films absorbed the attention of America's brainwashed. Whereas American public opinion had improved, it remained unled and inarticulate. Holocaustomania, in full bloom across the United States, stultified effectual action. As novelist George Steiner expressed it, "Any man can say *Auschwitz*, and if he says it loud enough, everyone has to cast their eyes down and listen. Like smashing a glass in the middle of dinner."[16]

Presidential spokesman Larry Speakes refused to speculate whether the use of U.S.-made planes in the April Israeli strike at Lebanon violated foreign military sales provision: "It serves no useful purpose at a time like this to examine that question." But he claimed that the Administration was "looking into every aspect of this action."

In his syndicated column Pete Hamill was indeed looking at the deeper implications of the tragedy:

With every new outrage, Begin separates the U.S. from the Arab world. We have become his accomplices, partners in his unbridled violence, collaborators in his racist assumptions about the inferiority of Arab lives. We do not have to condone the terrorism of the PLO in order to oppose Begin. That is the trap. Begin wants every proposition to become either/or. If you oppose Begin's policies, you oppose Israel, and if you oppose Israel, you are an anti-Semite. Or so the Begin reasoning goes.

Reagan's reaction to Begin's fanatical policies has been limited and mild. He slaps Begin on the wrist, then gives him more weapons that are used to kill more children. In a way, this is the most patronizing form of anti-Semitism. It is time for the U.S. to start acting like a great nation and make its international positions coherent. Reagan wouldn't tolerate Begin-like behavior in Central America. He can't condone it in the Middle East.[17]

Reagan found himself, whether he liked it or not, forced to accept "Begin-like behavior." After the April (1982) raid on Beirut, vast pressures were exerted not to interfere. Reminding the President that Congressional elections were approaching and the budget problem remained unresolved, Chairman of the Presidents of major Jewish Organizations Howard Squadron stated while a request from Jordan for planes was under consideration: "There is a deep and growing concern in the U.S. Jewish community at the direction of U.S. policy in the Middle East."

Reagan's most ardent supporters, the neo-conservatives based around the magazine *Commentary*, pressed for an acceptance of this Podhoretz precept:

The relentless assault on Israel in the U.N. and elsewhere is more than a matter of calling the legitimacy of Israel into question. It represents a covert attack on the political culture of the U.S. and the entire democratic world. In this perspective the willingness to defend Israel (ideologically and politically no less than through military aid) becomes a subtle measure of our willingness to defend ourselves.[18]

And there was little resistance from the White House to accepting this.

It is virtually impossible for any historian to provide a definitive analysis of events that are daily so swiftly unfolding as he rushes copy for this updated edition to the printer. Many questions remain to be answered by time, some final judgments to be made independently of the instantaneous coloration imparted by the media and vested interests. Only one thing is reasonably certain: the U.S. will never "start acting like a great nation" as long as Begin—or any successor—can instantaneously rally Jews in the U.S. behind him, regardless of American national interests, with the call: "The unity of the Jewish people is a second line defense for the State of Israel." And rally they did, with some very few exceptions, on each and every occasion, including the ever-mounting crisis in Lebanon.

The chips were down, and Jews were faced with the dilemma they had so assiduously sought to avoid. If Jewish Americans permitted their total transformation from a religious grouping into a political movement dedicated to the interests of a foreign state and sanction the awesome gross display of Zionist power in their name toward bringing successive occupants of the White House to terms, it will exact a price that many innocents—Americans as well as Middle Easterners—will have to bear. It is certainly not inappropriate to inquire whether such an injustice is consonant with the mission for which the claimed forebears of the Zionists were allegedly made the Chosen of God.

XXIV   The Ultimate Dichotomy:
Israel Über Alles?

There is no room in this country for hyphenated Americanism.

—Theodore Roosevelt

In a controversial 1970 *Commentary* article, Robert Alter raised a most basic question:

Does a Jewish State belong in an area where, even as late as 1947, the majority of the population was Arab? How can Israel be imagined, even in the most diffuse sense, as a continuation of the moral heritage of Judaism if its existence depends upon a manifest historical injustice?

That Judaic heritage is clear and unmistakable and has been unwavering. Where Zionism is particularist and segregationalist, Judaism has been universalist and integrationalist. Judaism, like its offspring monotheistic faiths, Christianity and Islam, has always represented a moral choice, a spiritual link between man and his Creator in whose ethos there is little room for narrow chauvinism. Whereas Zionism staked its claim to a land that had not belonged to Jews for 2,000 years, Judaism's power to survive has always depended on its being unrelated to any particular geographic tract. The Jews were chosen by the Lord neither to possess a specific piece of land nor to be favored over others of his children. They were selected for the task of spreading the message that there is one and only one God.

In exchanging their birthright for the "mess" of statehood, and staking the future of American Judaism on the roulette of power politics, Jewish leaders surrendered to the noxious dualism of religion and nationalism.

Fifty years ago these same Jews had vigorously opposed being classified with Italians, Germans, Czechs, French, etc., on an ethnic basis rather than with Baptists, Catholics, Methodists, Muslims, etc., as a religious community. But with the triumph of the Zionist revival in Palestine, the ethnicity of the Jew elsewhere shifted; and without protest the subtle transmutation from Jewish Americans, a religious grouping, into American Jews, an ethnic-national entity, was accomplished.

To conceal the dual national attachment, the link with Israel was passed off as a religious tie, the worship of Israelism increasingly supplanting Judaism. It was much simpler to write a check to the UJA, and pleasanter than to attend synagogue services. The new idolatry had no time for immutable principles and universal values. Jews accepted situations they otherwise would have rejected, but now welcomed in the name of Israel.

Opposed to violence and war, Jews accepted Israel's acts of military might and aggression. Opposed to union of church and state, they accepted such a unity wherever Israel was involved. Long dedicated to integration into the body politic, they moved toward separateness and segregation.[1] Judaistic tradition had placed its followers alongside those who struggled against the limitation of human and civil rights. In the name of Israelism, they sanctioned the suppression of Palestinian Arab civil and human rights within Israel proper and in the occupied territories. Expressed another way, Jews have come to lose their own traditional universal, human ethos through their identification with Israelism. Intellectual and staunch defender of Israel Arthur Waskow noted pertinently: "And it's not just politics the Jewish institutions want to avoid; it's God, too. Try talking of God to a rabbi!—he's too busy trying to raise money for Israel or the synagogue mortgage."[2]

No Fourth of July was ever celebrated in the manner that Israel's Atlantic capital, New York City, exuberantly commemorated the state's twenty-fifth anniversary. The press, radio, and television joined together in proclaiming Israel "the hope of Jews all over the world." In three laudatory Sunday magazine articles,[3] "Israel at 25," and in its editorial entitled "Shalom" (the *Daily News* ended its own rapturous editorial with this same word), the *Times* dropped all pretense to any claim of being non-Zionist as it fervently extolled the twenty-fifth year of the existence of the Zionist state as representing but "a small milestone in 4,000 years of a people's recorded history."[4] A fashion show, with a prestigious lineup of models drawn from filmdom, the theater, the arts, politics, and society, sold out to purchasers of a $500 or more Israel Bond. An elaborate Sunday parade featured high school bands from the eastern seaboard, lured by a national band competition and the opportunity to march on America's most famed Fifth Avenue, and floats from which little children waved hundreds of Israeli flags. In the line of march, in front of each unit, the American and Israeli flags were balanced, but behind the standard bearers there were hundreds of the Star of David for every Stars and Stripes.

During Israel's twenty-sixth anniversary parade the following year, I talked to two Brooklyn teenagers who said they belonged to the International Conference of Synagogue Youth. They would give me no more than their initials—B.D.K. and G.W. One wore a "Jewish Power" button, the other "Jewish Poverty: It's No Myth." This helped encourage bystanders to throw American dollars onto Israeli flags being used as collection baskets.

Our tape-recorded interview proved most interesting:

"If Israel and the U.S. get into the war, which side will you be on?"

"This will never happen—it couldn't happen."

"Do you consider yourself an American or a Jew?"

"I am an American and a Jew."

"But which do you consider first?"

"I am a Jew before I am an American."

"Do you have a dual loyalty? Some people insist that you do."

"No, but we do have strong connections with Israel as well as with the U.S., and we have more connections with Israel because this is *our* state." (Italics added.)

"What do you mean? I thought the U.S. was your state?"

"We live in the U.S. We are proud, however, that Israel is our state— Israel is our homeland, and our final goal is to settle there."

"Why don't you go there now?"

"We're not ready to go."

"Then why do you stay in the U.S. and use the U.S.?"

"We must have a country powerful and strong, and we want to build up the U.S. because while we are here it can help Israel. We are here because this is a powerful country and we want to use our influence."

"Influence the U.S. in behalf of Israel?"

"Not only influence the U.S., but influence other American Jews, many of whom we feel are not doing as much as they could."

"What is your feeling toward Israel?"

"Israel is ours. The U.S. is not our state. We are making it our home, but a home is not a state." (Ironically this lad, in reverse, used the identical verbiage that anti-Zionists use against the Balfour Declaration.)

"What happens when people say there are Jews here who are using the U.S. and imply that it is time you get out?"

"They would want us to get out—that is anti-Semitism."

"But you have dual loyalties."

"What's wrong with that? Israel can help the U.S. and the U.S. can help Israel. . . . We don't use the U.S. as a base. We're supporting the U.S., we pay taxes. We don't want to emigrate right now. And don't get the idea we are living off the fat of their land and taking it away—that's bigotry, that sounds like anti-Semitism."

"Well, maybe it is, but don't you feed this anti-Semitism with your ideas?"

"No. If the U.S. asked us to serve in the army and it didn't involve Israel, we would serve. But we can't trust the U.S. completely to do what we want. If the U.S. does not have a favorable policy to Israel, it's up to us to help build that, and we *wouldn't be able to do for Israel* what is necessary if we weren't living in the U.S." (Italics added.)

The behavior of Jewish oldsters was not distinguishable from that of the youngsters. On the occasion of the U.S. Bicentennial, when one might logically expect words of concern for the welfare of the country in which he and his fellow Jews were living, Chairman of the Miami 1976 Combined Jewish Appeal-Israel Emergency Fund Drive L. Jules Arkin kicked off the effort with this prominently publicized statement:

We are a community of 250,000 Jewish people, and *our concern is the people of Israel, the quality of their lives, their welfare, their ability to survive and grow in a time of staggering economic pressure.* What is happening at the United Nations is a clear signal that the world is challenging democracy as we know it in America.

. . . As Jews, we must come together like a real family to make sure all Jews can live with social justice and dignity. That is our responsibility in 1976.[5] [Italics added.]

Adherence to Judaism was judged by financial support of the State of Israel, as the sale of Israel Bonds and the raising of UJA funds in synagogues on the highest Holy Days of Rosh Hashanah and Yom Kippur went forward. During the October war Jews were rallied to the cause of Israel from the synagogue pulpit. A series of advertisements called on Jewry to "Give a bond for Hanukkah," implying that the spirit of this holiday imposed on Jews everywhere the support of Israel. There was no longer even a pretense of distinguishing between the humanitarian and the propaganda dollar, as the UJA with 90 percent of its funds going to Israel and the local Federations of Jewish Philanthropies ran joint fund-raising campaigns.

The "Rally for Humanity Against Arab Terror," called in New York City by the Conference of Presidents to protest the Arafat U.N. appearance brought out a vast hysterical crowd, many coming in buses from nearby states. Religious schools let their children off; New Yorkers came on their lunch hour; union members were given time off; judges were said to have closed down their courts. Judge Alfred H. Kleinman of the Criminal Court of New York expostulated, "It is very difficult to sit in judgment of persons accused of crimes when we open the doors of our country to international criminals." The claimed-to-be 100,000 protestants were harangued by Senator Javits, who declared that the U.S. "must honor the refusal of Israel to negotiate with the PLO."

On every occasion since Israel's creation, American Jews reacted to the continuing Middle East crisis as Israeli leaders conditioned them to do from the very outset. There was not the slightest concern over the dangers of dual loyalty. David Ben-Gurion was never afraid to express most candidly his views about the role of American Jews in helping to carry out the foreign policy goals of the State of Israel:

It was *always* my view that we have always to consider the *interests* of Diaspora Jewry—any Jewish community that was concerned. But there is one crucial distinction—not what *they* think are their interests, but what *we* regarded as their interests. If it was a case vital for Israel and the interests of the Jews concerned were different, the vital interests of Israel came first—because Israel is vital for world Jewry.[6]

An assistant Director General of Israel's Foreign Office presented this candid and persuasive rationale as the justification for exploiting the Jewish duality:

The Almighty placed massive oil deposits under Arab soil and the Arab states have exploited this good fortune for political ends during the past half century. It is our good fortune that God placed six million Jews in America. And we have no less a right to benefit from their influence with the U.S. government to help us survive and to prosper.[7]

Ben-Gurion often reiterated his inexorable view that "the State of Israel is a part of the Middle East only in geography . . . from the decisive standpoint of dynamism, creation, and growth, Israel is a part of World Jewry."[8]

Writing about his first visit to the U.S. after his election, Ben-Gurion noted that whenever Jews speak of "our country" they mean Israel, and whatever the Israeli Ambassador says, they know he is representing them.[9] When Zionist lobbyist I. L. Kenen was quoted as saying, "Israeli diplomats are accredited not only to the U.S. government but also in a sense to the American Jewish community,"[10] he was only echoing the sentiments of Walter Eytan, who as Israeli's Permanent Undersecretary of the Foreign Office proclaimed, "It is a commonplace of our Foreign Service that every Envoy Extraordinary and Minister Plenipotentiary has a dual function: "He is Minister Plenipotentiary to the country in which he is accredited and Envoy Extraordinary to its Jews."[11]

Moshe Sharett, who succeeded Ben-Gurion, proudly declaimed to the World Jewish Congress:

From the standpoint of constitutional law and formal sovereignty, Israel does not differ from any normal state in the world. It claims political loyalty only from its own nationals. But in a deep historic sense which, however, receives a most tangible expression both in long-term policy and in day-to-day life, Israel is a common possession of the entire Jewish people, that is to say of all the Jews in the world. Every Jew can claim a share in it. . . . They can, as Jews, no longer imagine their own existence without it. . . . Therefore, they must do everything they can—materially, politically, whatever and whichever way is practical, effective and legitimate—to preserve it, to strengthen it.[12]

In denouncing the 1970 Rogers plan calling for Israeli withdrawal, Prime Minister Meir called on Jews everywhere to help resist: "This is not the border of the U.S.A. we are talking about but of *the Jewish people.*" (Italics added.) Once again, the abnormality of Israel was being proclaimed to rally the loyalty of nationals of other countries. And when asked what boundaries Israel intended to accept, Meir replied: "Israel is where Jews are. It is not a line on a map."

When Ben-Gurion declared that Zionism demanded "an unconditional love of Israel, a complete solidarity with the state and its people,"[13] this was not just the conduct expected of those who by a conscious act of dedication have pledged their allegiance to the State of Israel. In the eyes of all Israeli Prime Ministers, from himself to Begin, all Jews all over the world are implicitly Zionists, the task of the ubiquitous Zionist apparatus being merely to make this fact explicit.

Despite other differences, Dr. Nahum Goldmann was in accord with Ben-Gurion as to the duties and responsibilities of Diaspora Jewry toward Israel. To the earlier blunt interdiction that "Jews have to overcome the conscious or unconscious fear of so-called double loyalty,"[14] Goldmann later added in 1959:

American Jews must have the courage to openly declare that they entertain a double loyalty, one to the land in which they live and one to Israel. Jews should not succumb to patriotic talk that they owe allegiance only to the land in which they live . . . they should live not only as patriots of the country of their domicile, but also as patriots of Israel.[15]

Speaking to a conclave of the World Jewish Congress in Jerusalem on February 3, 1975, Goldmann warned that "the honeymoon between Israel and the non-Jewish world has come to an end," and boldly declared:

At the time of crisis for Israel when its policies are rejected by many countries in which Jews live, conflict is bound to occur. The only solution is to acknowledge the existence and fight for the recognition of double loyalties. The real test of our solidarity with Israel will come when we support it against the views of the States in which we live.[16]

In many lectures across the country, Abba Eban, former Israeli Foreign Minister, encouraged Jewish implementation of the Goldmann thesis. In declaring on the campus of William Patterson College (Wayne, New Jersey) that "Israel could never be a normal state because its memories were not normal—with six million wiped out, centuries of persecution," Eban expostulated, "Israel could master the burdens facing it, but not alone. Why should we? All we built—*you and I* built together in a common responsibility and common pride. Whether the Jew will carry this burden is up to you. The answer is in your hands."[17]

Frenzied New York students who harassed President Pompidou on his 1970 visit, the anti-Arafat mob outside the U.N. in 1974, and the synchronized emotional March 1977 Jewish outpourings through the media, featured by full-page ads of Elie Wiesel and the Au Revoir to France Committee[18] when Palestinian Abu Daoud, suspected of masterminding the Munich Olympics affair, was released by the Giscard d'Estaing government, were all responses to leadership calls for dual loyalty. And the American media served as a catalyst in stirring hatred against America's oldest ally.[19]

One had to go back to the post-Hitler days of 1946, 1947, and 1948 to find a parallel to these outbursts of Jewish nationalist emotionalism. Then Organized Jewry moved as a cohesive unit in a violent "Hate Britain" campaign. A concerted effort was made to mobilize American public opinion behind an Israelist boycott of British goods. Signs were plastered in stores throughout New York City as the Sons of Liberty Boycott Committee was formed. From the pulpit and in resolutions, support was given to this anti-British activity.

At the time, the recovery of Europe through the Marshall Plan was the fundamental keystone of American bipartisan foreign policy, and the heart of an envisoned reconstructed Europe was to be Britain. Strong Communist parties in Italy and France were doing all in their power to interfere with the operations of the plan, while the Russians were creating obstacles by means of the air-block of Germany. In practical effect, this was as much an attempt to sabotage U.S. foreign policy as were any of the Communist efforts in Europe. While Uncle Sam was pouring out hundreds of millions from the national coffers to place her closest ally in a better financial position, there were many Jews who dropped England from their travel plans so as not to leave U.S. dollars there.

On another prominent occasion the Jewish duality revealed itself. It was not easy to reach the decision that Germany should be rearmed as part of the defense against Communism and integrated into the Western European Community. The specter of a remilitarized Germany was frightening enough in itself without adding to it Israeli prejudices toward Hitler's successors. Zionism injected the issue of the special Jewish peril, even coupling the indemnification rights of Israel against Germany. When the Knesset recessed as a protest against the signing of the peace treaty between West Germany and the Western Allies, no Jewish group stepped forward to disassociate itself from what was publicly stated to be *"the* Jewish position."

What American Jews would not see was that their acceptance of Israel's abnormal nationalism, viewing them as inchoate Israeli citizens, was linked to the inflexible Israeli policy of expansionism, the principal obstacle to peace.

When Jews who were congressmen, rabbis, and leaders of large organizations in the U.S. insisted that relationships between Israel and France and/or England were their personal responsibility, little wonder that the Arabs were so reticent to accept their neighbors as an accomplished fact. Emotional blindness prevented Jews from seeing the total incongruity of their demands that Arabs be prevented from boycotting companies doing business with Israel while Zionists could impede U.S. trade with France, Britain, Mexico, etc., because of differences between those countries and Israel.

In an infinite number of other ways, American Jews have betrayed the pervading Jewish dichotomy. Moshe Brilliant, long-time stringer of the *New York Times* in Israel, disclosed in December 1972 that more than 11 percent of the investments in residences in Israel in 1971 was made by foreign Jews, mostly Americans purchasing second homes. The $45 million estimated to have been spent did not include the substantial investments by those who have moved there, but merely represented purchases by guilt-feeling Jews for remaining outside and not sharing the fate of their coreligionists. This further flight of American dollars came at a time when the U.S. deficit balance of payments continued to mount perilously.

More than 3,000 U.S. banks, including 300 of the largest, have been influenced to buy Israel Bonds, a major prop in that state's struggle for financial viability. Because one of the directors of the Pacific Bank of Nantucket, also the president of a large bank in Providence, Rhode Island, has been pressured to buy a considerable amount of bonds, a small purchase was made even on this island forty miles out in the Atlantic.

New York City's Jewish-dominated Teachers Union put up $30 million for the purchase of Israel Bonds.[20] Teachers' pension funds in major cities followed suit. And a New York State law, pushed through by Majority Senate Leader Stanley Steingut, enabled savings banks, savings and loan associations, and credit unions to invest up to 5 percent of their net worth in Israel Bonds. According to 1976 figures of net worth, this could result in a total of more than a quarter of a billion dollars, belonging to innocent depositors, being invested in one of the world's worst credit risks. (Similar legislation passed the lower house of the Texas legislature but was bottled up in committee in the upper house.)

Faced with defections, conversions, intermarriages, and other flights from Judaism, Jewish religious leaders have been only too happy to use the pulpit for advancing the dichotomy through calls to "man the barricades" to meet the threats from outsiders. Any and all

Israeli crises are invariably presented as if they were the crises of Jews all over the world, and as if they were members of an extra-territorial entity, "the Jewish people." Lacking a God with a face in its competition with Christianity, Jewish lay and rabbinical leadership increasingly relied on the concept of Jewish peoplehood and naked tribal chauvinism to keep its flock intact.

But there is no "Jewish people," save in the sense of a religious grouping, whose actions can justifiably be permitted to extend beyond national sovereign lines, flaunting the verboten of dual loyalties. Representatives of Israel have spoken many times at the U.N. in behalf of the "Jewish people" and have seldom been challenged. Hungary's Permanent Representative Karoly Csatorday during a 1968 debate on Jerusalem told the Security Council:

We thus categorically reject the attempt of the representative of Israel to speak here on behalf of what he calls "the Jewish People." Let us take only one example, the Hungarian delegation alone, speaking here on behalf of the Hungarian citizens of the Jewish faith, no one is entitled to abrogate this right of ours. I would add that my delegation has no knowledge that any other Government whatsoever has given authorization to the representative of Israel to represent their citizens of the Jewish religion.

Four years earlier the U.S. government had made its position regarding "the Jewish people" concept very clear in a letter from Assistant Secretary of State Phillips Talbot to Rabbi Elmer Berger, in which it was stated *inter alia* that the Department of State

. . . does not recognize a legal-political relationship based upon religious identification of American citizens. It does not in any way discriminate among American citizens upon the basis of religion. Accordingly, it should be clear that the Department of State does not regard the "Jewish people" concept as a concept of international law.[21]

This fundamental legal principle has been included in the official U.S. codification of international law,[22] although it has never been invoked by the American government or its representatives to challenge Zionism's nationality claims adherent in the separatist "Jewish people" concept.

The concept of peoplehood[23]—that amalgam of religion, nation, race, culture, and heritage—brought the deep national consciousness of *being a Jew*, in contrast to simply *believing in Judaism*, into a command position. This nationalist pride commanded the spontaneous support of even the most minimal Jews, causing many so-called "liberals" in the West, as well as dedicated socialists among the first pioneers in

Palestine (many living in the collective kibbutz or cooperative moshav) to look the other way and cast aside deeply held principles.

In "New, Instant Zionism" in the *New York Times Magazine* February 3, 1974, reprinted three weeks later in the *Miami Herald,* editor Norman Podhoretz hailed the total conversion of Jews to Zionism, and pointed to Jewish editors and other intellectuals who had "never yielded to the claims of religion" and "felt contempt for nationalist or chauvinist sentiments," but who, with the body of American Jews, had responded to Israel's fate at the time of the 1973 war "as though their own lives, their own families, and their own homes were immediately and imminently at stake."

Podhoretz could indeed point exultantly to the "near dwindling into invisibility" of organized anti-Zionism by way of the decline of the American Council for Judaism.[24] Nevertheless, many Jews who were members of no group still subscribed to the principles of universalism and integration but were too frightened to speak up and disclaim the asserted Zionist link to all Jews. More important, there were Christians whose resentment of the narrow, arrogant particularism expressed by Podhoretz caused them to erupt in Letters to the Editor, as did Harvard's Professor Martin Kilson:

> Though one is accustomed to a certain grossness in the sensibilities of the author of *Making It,* I was not quite prepared for the display in "Now, Instant Zionism." The nakedly crass and vulgar ethnic chauvinism surrounding "his we-are-all-Zionists-now" pronouncement to his fellow Jews is more than I expected, even from Norman Podhoretz.
>
> A decade ago I had thought that this pathological level of neo-ethnicity in American life would remain restricted to separatist black militants, but it is clear I was mistaken. Jews have now acquired the new ethnic chauvinism and, alas, are outdoing all of us at it: as much as 99 percent are Zionists now, Podhoretz gleefully informs us.
>
> The most distressing feature of Mr. Podhoretz's article is the revelation that his new ethnic chauvinism has chipped away at his intellectual capacity for objectivity, restraint, and common-sense—just as it has among separatist black intellectuals. For example, in referring to the argument for joint Arab-Jewish control of Israel, he places quotation marks around the term "binational," suggesting that such a solution is intrinsically unacceptable. But I would have thought common sense dictates just the opposite—namely, there is neither a viable nor progressive solution to the claims for a Jewish presence in Israel without some variant of binationalism and the separation of church (Judaism) and state. . . .
>
> I suspect, too, we can soon look forward to a new wave of ethnic chauvinism among the Protestant majority—an event many Jews in their current

ethnocentric craze ironically welcome. But I would like to suggest to Norman Podhoretz and his supporters that they think again. For a new Nativism among Protestants (their variant of ethnic chauvinism) will have horrendous consequences for all of us—Jew and non-Jew alike. Mr. Podhoretz's celebration of the new Jewish chauvinism is as politically dangerous as it is intellectually revolting.[25]

Rabbi Jacob Neusner also raised his voice in opposition to Zionist-Israeli absolutism:

There can be no "center of Judaism," but where we find ourselves and live Jewish lives. . . . How can American Jews focus their spiritual lives solely on a land in which they do not live? The underlying problem which faces both Israeli and American Jews, is understanding what the ambiguous adjective "Jewish" is supposed to mean when the noun "Judaism" has been abandoned.

Conceding that supplying funds, encouragement, and support for Israel seem to be the primary commitments of American Jews, the Rabbi added, "One wonders whether one must be a Jew at all in order to believe and practice in that form of Judaism. What is 'being Jewish' now supposed to mean?"

Even more pertinently, because he himself is an Israeli, Dr. Israel Shahak proclaimed that undeviating devotion to the State of Israel was "both immoral and against the mainstream of Jewish tradition":

I am a Jew living in Israel, and consider myself a law-abiding citizen. I serve in the army every year, in spite of being nearly forty years old. But I am not "devoted" to the State of Israel or to any other state or human organization! I am devoted to my ideals. I believe in speaking the truth and in doing something for securing justice and equality for all human beings. I am devoted to the Hebrew language and poetry, and I like to think that I follow in my small way some of the values of our ancient prophets.

But to be devoted to the State? I can well imagine Amos or Isaiah splitting their sides with laughter if somebody had demanded of them to be "devoted" to the Kingdom of Israel or the Kingdom of Judah. "Hate evil and love good and establish judgment in the gate," says Amos (Chapter 5, verse 15), who does not spare a word of devotion to the great, warlike and successful Kingdom of Israel of his times.

In fact this new doctrine preached as a Jewish duty, is nothing but Jewish apostasy. All Jews used to believe, and say it three times a day, that a Jew should be devoted to God, and God alone.[26] A small minority still believes it. *But it seems to me that the majority of my people has left God, and has substituted an idol in its place, exactly as happened when they were so devoted to the Golden Calf in the desert that they gave away their gold to make it. The name of this modern idol is State of Israel.*

We should understand a little more closely what forms this "devotion" of

Diaspora Jews to Israel take. The main form it takes is money—enormous sums of money, which are given to the government of Israel and to Israel political parties, without any control whatsoever. Two consequences follow: First, the Israeli government has much greater power over its citizens than any other, for a great part of its money does not come from Israeli citizens. Because of this, any democratic attempt to change the government in Israel becomes most difficult, if not impossible, for a great part of the power of the Israeli government is not derived from any sources inside Israel: it is derived from the pockets of Disapora Jews by means of their idolatrous "devotion" to the State of Israel.

The second necessary consequence is that since as a matter of proven experience, Diaspora Jews give more money when the danger of war is greater, therefore the Israeli Government has a great financial interest in not making peace: it would receive so much less "easy" money . . .

Ask a Jew in the Diaspora, who proclaims his devotion to the State of Israel, who usually knows no Hebrew, is ignorant about Jewish culture and history, participates only in some religious Jewish ceremonies which he does not understand, to what exactly he is devoted; and he will answer that without Israel, or strong Israel, he will not be able to carry his head high, that he will feel low and insulted, or similar answers.

Nevertheless this situation where, for all practical purposes, the Diaspora Jews think that they can buy our blood with their money and feel good and devoted, cannot last. *It cannot last, for it has a corrupting effect on both the giver and the receiver. As an Israeli, I would say that the Diaspora Jews are being corrupted more than we. In the Middle East, it promotes a perpetual state of war, and outside promotes anti-Semitism.* [27] [Italics added.]

When a Russian diplomat is attacked on the streets of New York, or Soviet-American culturalists are bombed, who can claim any rational let alone any national interest was served, least of all that of Israel? Such an expression of nationalist affinity only highlights the aged Jewish dichotomy of being both a nation and a religion. So long as the U.S.-Israel honeymoon, consecrated by overweening domestic political realities, continued happily, the purposeful intermixing of nationalism with religion might be tolerated and even encouraged. But in time another Dean Acheson in an autobiography may also expose the secret that he opposed the creation of a Zionist state in the heart of the Arab world because it "would vastly exacerbate the political problem and not only imperil American, but all Western interests in the Middle East." And suddenly the once-bigoted libel, "These Jews are foreigners—they don't belong here," may assume a reasonableness with the realization that vital American interests have been sacrificed in the face of indescribable pressures and financial power. If and when Americans add up the inordinate price they have been paying so that a Golda Meir or Menachem Begin might be the Prime Minister of a sovereign nation-state, a dozen anti-Defamation Leagues will be unable to suppress the ensuing storm.

It could no longer be claimed that the dichotomous nature of the Jew, wherein he lived on for centuries under the discipline both of the sovereign state in which he was physically located and of the religio-political community to which he belonged, was rooted in circumstances beyond his control. In that past, prior to Jewish political emancipation in the 18th century, religious and political ties were necessarily intimately and politically linked. Today the duality stems from his voluntary association with Israel. Even in the face of the deep fear of being blackmailed by the anti-Semitic label, it is not likely that Christian America will continue to permit, in the guise of religious duty, the political problems of Israel to remain the political responsibility of American Jews. Sooner or later it will be deemed totally abhorrent that the policies and politics of a sovereign foreign state are being underwritten by nationals of this country. Americans are bound to discern the price that is already being paid for assuming that the enemy of Israel is necessarily the enemy of the U.S. In an October 9, 1977 *Miami Herald* article, Arthur Miller admitted that American Jews were confronted with a conflict of loyalties when their president proposes policies that do not coincide with those favored by Israel.

In the U.S. a number of people may indeed achieve something of a separate group identity merely by believing they belong together, but American tolerance toward separation ceases when group thought and group action run counter to the mores and interests of America. In plain words, why should Jews be permitted the unique status of being part of a worldwide Jewish nation with its center in Israel to which they are bound by a system of rights and obligations, while freely implanting this idea of Jewish nationhood throughout the U.S. in the guise of religion?

As the American Jew sits around the Passover table and repeats the ancient prayer, "Next Year in Jerusalem," he ought to consider appropriate action to free metaphysical practices essential to worshipping God from his nationalist activities related to the foreign State of Israel. The Middle East crisis might once more threaten to become another Vietnam, and some of his exasperated fellow Americans might then one day be asking him: "Why next year? Why not this year? There are almost daily El Al flights to Israel."

No other group in the U.S. dares don a garment of such duality.[28]

The continuing conflict in Ireland exposed on what quicksand the clichéd Zionist defense to the charge of dual loyalty rested. "Look how the Irish display their special passions for Ireland," Israelists argued. But the very muted activity of Irish Americans has shown that there is little analogy between the abnormal feelings/activities of Jewish Americans toward Israel and the one-day exuberant enthusiasm for Eire that shamrock-wearing Irishmen effect on St. Patrick's Day. The sentimental affection that Irish (or Italian, French, etc.) Americans have for their country of origin offers no analogy to the feeling toward Israel exhibited by American Jews. The Irish who are in the U.S. left Ireland only in recent generations. While some Jews left Roman Palestine two millenniums ago, centuries before the first Angles and Saxons set foot in England, they have come to America not from Israel but from every country in Europe.

Irish Americans have shown that they are not American Irish (they are never referred to in this way, just as Jews are invariably called American Jews) and that their deep, sentimental tie to the motherland from which they had come (most Jews and even their remotest ancestors could not trace their way back to the land of Canaan) is kept within bounds of permissive cultural pluralism. Not even an Eamon de Valera would ever have dared demand from Irish Americans one one-hundredth of the allegiance the Israeli government demands from Jewish Americans as a matter of course, or claimed one one-hundredth of the sovereignty over "Diaspora Irish" that the Israeli government has exercised over Diaspora Jews. The resolute disavowal of IRA terrorism by Senators Kennedy and Moynihan, Governor Carey, and other Irish Americans provided an example of detachment from "motherland," which Jewish Americans unfortunately in no way have ever followed.

Whether cognizant of it or not, the average Jew has been made to feel so much a part of Israel that he scarcely regards the abnormal treatment accorded that country by the U.S. as anything more than a most natural act, not as one extracted by massive pressures. He is therefore unconscious of the dangers in permitting a foreign country to become the special concern of a special group of Americans. This has nothing to do with cultural pluralism, which has rarely been questioned. But under the universal system of nation states, any American is precluded from being saddled with rights from, and with corollary duties and obligations to, a foreign state, whether called religious, humanitarian, communal, brotherly, or racial.[29]

The failure to appreciate that Israel must be regarded as much a foreign state as Italy or Sweden has led Jews into pitfalls that others, not afflicted with the aged duality, would more easily have seen. Dual loyalties do not necessarily involve the conscious process of choice: *"This* is in the interests of the U.S., *that* is in the interests of Israel, and I choose *that."* Such is the rare case. For more common is the unconscious choosing of *that* without any consideration being given to *this.*

Whatever responsibility is taken for the security of the State of Israel can only be assumed by the U.S. as a whole and not by Zionists or any other segment of the population acting apart. The destiny of those who call themselves Jews in the U.S. should depend on the security of but one country. Their "to be or not to be" ought to be inflexibly interwoven only with the fate of the U.S. Giving away something that belongs entirely to their country is wrong under any circumstances and can even be disastrous in moments of crisis. Those who preach this doctrine of insecurity—"It can happen here as it has everywhere, and therefore let us guard well the State of Israel"—are sadly hastening to bring about the very tragedy they imagine they are preventing.

The U.S. differs from all other nations in that it is not based either on common descent, centuries-old rootedness in a common ancestry or on a religious unity. The universal idealism of the 18th-century awakening gave America a very special ideology. As a substitute for those elements the U.S. lacked, a steadfast devotion to the principle of the melting pot was needed. It takes no superpatriot or chauvinist to suggest that conflicting loyalties only vastly complicate the ends sought. It is possible to experience different kinds of emotions. Support of the fullest participation of the U.S. in such international organizations as the U.N. or its subsidiary agencies does not create any problem of duality. The child has a different feeling toward his mother than toward his father or brother. But this is certain: Just as you cannot have two fathers, you cannot have two "Uncle Sams."

However much American Israelists belittle the problem of dual loyalties, attempting to dismiss the dichotomous phenomenon as a mere expression of determined unanimity toward the survival of Israel, the herding of Jews together in support of Zionist goals and the service of some in the Israeli armed forces[30] have raised anew the hazards of self-segregation, the dangers of arousing bigotry. The perennial Zionist-Israeli answer to "Why are the Jews always persecuted?" invariably has attributed the entire blame to "them"—the other guys. They exclaim, "We're perfectly innocent—what have *we* done to bring this on?" It never occurs to them that by thinking—and living—in terms of "we" and "they," the "goys" and the "kikes," they are bound to bring down upon themselves the natural reaction to self-segregation and apartheid—and even more so when the combustible element of foreign entanglements has been added.

To hold that prejudice directed against them stems today solely from their belief in Judaism—if they do believe—or from the simple fact that they hold themselves out as Jews, indicates the extent of the hypnosis under which Jews have allowed their leaders and organizations to place them. Jews disregard the vital, all-important fact that their singular and abnormal relationship to a foreign state called Israel has given validity to the centuries-old charge that they can never become assimilated, "part and parcel," into the country in which they are living. Their partnership role, both through organic ties between the State of Israel and the Jewish Agency and day-to-day organizational activities advancing vital interests of the State of Israel, only confirms the existence of a dual loyalty that in the end can bring not mere prejudice and discrimination, but total disaster.

It was the trauma sparked vicariously by Nazi genocide that caused Jews to be so totally blinded that they readily forsook their heritage of tolerance in accepting the Zionist shadow for the Judaistic substance. Dr. Arnold Toynbee expressed this painful reversal in these terms:

In A.D. 1948, the Jews knew from personal experience what they were doing and it was their supreme tragedy that the lessons learned by them from their encounter with Nazi German Gentiles should have been not to eschew but to imitate some of the evil deeds that the Nazis had committed against the Jews. On the Day of Judgment the gravest crime standing to the German National Socialist account might be not that they had exterminated a majority of Western Jews, but that they had caused the surviving remnant of Jewry to stumble.[31]

It was not only the Nazis who caused Jews to stumble, but their own intellectual lights to whom they turned for guidance, such as Nobel Literature Prize winner Saul Bellow. In his eloquent outpouring *To Jerusalem and Back,*[32] dealing with a 1975 visit to Jerusalem, Bellow early informed his readers that he had been brought up in a Yiddish-speaking family and had married out of the faith, thus making more understandable both his idolatry of Zionist Israel and his hatred of Arabs. Simplistically, he dismissed the French government's attitude in the 1973 war, and its recognition of Arafat and the PLO, as a revival of French anti-Semitism going back to the Dreyfus Affair and the Vichy government.

Overflowing with references to the Warsaw Ghetto, the concentration camps, and other Jewish tragedies, the Bellow recital depicted

Israeli novelist David Shahar pounding on the table literally shouting: "The West doesn't know the Arabs. They will not let us live." The fundamental right of Jews *qua* Jews to exist has never been under challenge in the Middle East conflict, save in the imagery of cultists like Bellow, who cover up the long intrepid fight of progressive forces to accord Jews as individuals equal and secure rights, and rewrite history so as to prove that statehood can be the only safe repository for Jewish rights.

Special Bellow disdain was reserved for George Steiner, author, critic, and Fellow of Churchill College at Cambridge University, for his charge that "Zionism was created by Jewish nationalists who drew their inspiration from Bismarck and followed a Prussian model.[33] This viewpoint was further expanded by Steiner at the Sixth American-Israel Dialogue in Jerusalem during the summer of 1968:

The existence of Israel is not founded on logic. It has no ordinary legitimacy. There is neither in its establishment nor present scope any evident justice— though there may be an utter need and wondrous fulfillment.

What irked Bellow most was Steiner's universalist reminder to his audience of the existence nearby of Palestinians in refugee camps and shanty towns whose families for generations had lived in Jerusalem, while in the room with him were Jews who were brought up in Vilna, Hamburg, or Manchester. The critic pressed the painful question, "By what right are we here, while others are dispossessed?"

The Nobel Prize winner claimed that Jews were "alone amongst the peoples of the earth [who] had not established a natural right to exist unquestioned in the lands of their birth." Aside from the fact that the land for more than nineteen centuries has been inhabited overwhelmingly by Arabs, is Israel in fact the homeland of Herzl, Weizmann, Ben-Gurion, Meir, Rabin, Begin, and Bellow, as they have unhesitatingly maintained?

Arthur Koestler answers this question with an emphatic "No." In his 1976 bestseller *The Thirteenth Tribe,*[34] the Author of *Darkness at Noon, Promise and Fulfillment,* and *The Roots of Coincidence* dropped another bombshell by proving that today's Jews were, for the most part, descendants of the Khazars, who converted to Judaism seven centuries after the destruction of Jerusalem in 70 A.D. and the dispersion of the small original Judaic Palestine population by Roman Emperor Vespasian and his son Titus.

The Khazars, a seminomadic Turko-Finnish people who settled in what is now southern Russia between the Volga and the Don, spread to the shores of the Black, Caspian, and Azov seas. Jews who had been banished from Constantinople by Byzantine ruler Leo III[35] found a home among the pagan Khazars and then, in competition with Muslim and Christian missionaries, won Khagan Bulan, the ruler of Khazaria, over to the Judaic faith around 740 A.D.[36] His nobles followed suit, and somewhat later so did his people. Some details of these events are contained in letters exchanged between Khagan (King) Joseph of Khazaria and R. Hasdai Ibn Shaprut of Cordova, doctor and quasi-Foreign Minister to Sultan Abd al-Rahman, the Caliph of Spain.[37]

When Khazaria fell to Mongols in the 13th century, its population of "Jewish"-convert Khazars fled northwest to become the progenitors of Ashkenazim (Russian/German/Baltic/Polish/) Jewry. These Khazar Jews greatly outnumbered racially Jewish Jews who had reached Europe by other routes and at other periods of history. Therefore, the great majority of Eastern European Jews are not Semitic Jews at all, and as most Western European Jews came from East Europe, most of them also are not Semitic Jews. Thus, maintains Koestler, the veins of 45 percent of Israelis (save only the Arab and the Sephardic Jews), plus a big majority of Jews around the world, are utterly vacant of corpuscular links to the tribe of Moses and Solomon. This nullifies Zionism's strongest claim to Palestine/Israel, the author's codicil to his fine book not withstanding.[38]

The Koestler thesis, however startling, is in no wise a new one. The genetic Khazar derivation of most Jews—only the Sephardic may be accounted Hebrews by blood—has been long if not *widely* known. Dunlap at Columbia, Bury in England, and Poliak at Tel Aviv University have researched this "cruelest of jokes" and won research acceptance over the past half-century. It remained for Koestler to popularize Khazars as the thirteen tribe—"lost" only to the memory of most Jews, especially *Zionist* Jews. Naturally, the *Times* review of the Koestler thesis by Fitzroy Maclean was squeezed into two unobtrusive columns on page 4 of its Sunday book section.[39]

What Price Israel?, published twenty-three years before the Koestler work, pointed out that the lineal ancestors of Eastern and Western European Jewry were these 8th-century Khazar converts, and noted how this was being kept a dark secret because it tended to vitiate the principal prop of the Zionist claim to Israel:

For all that anthropologists know, Hitler's ancestry might go back to one of the ten Lost Tribes of Israel; while Weizmann might be only a descendant of Khazar converts to Judaism who were in no anthropological respect related to

Palestine. The home to which Weizmann, Silver, Ben-Gurion and so many other Ashkenazim Zionists have long yearned to return has most likely never been theirs. "Here's a paradox, a paradox, a most ingenious paradox": in anthropological fact, many Christians may have much more Hebrew-Israelite blood in their veins than most of their Jewish neighbors.

Ironically enough, too, Volume IV of the Jewish Encyclopedia (as of the time of research, 1952), because this publication spelled Khazars with a "C" instead of a "K", is titled "Chazars to Dreyfus." And it was the famed trial of Captain Alfred Dreyfus, as interpreted by Theodore Herzl, that made the modern Jewish Khazars of Russia, most of the intrepid Zionist leaders, forget their descent from converts to Judaism and accept anti-Semitism as proof of their Palestinian origin—the heartstone of their right to establish the State of Israel.[40]

Despite his legal weaseling about the Zionist claim to Palestine, a furious Zionist onslaught was directed against Koestler for exposing Israel's Achilles' heel and giving prominence to another upsetting point: If the majority of Jews surviving the Hitler holocaust are of Caucasian rather than Semitic origin, then "the term 'anti-Semitism' would become totally void of meaning, based on a misapprehension shared both by the killers and their victims." And without the hue and cry, "anti-Semitism," pray what happens to the Zionist movement?

Khazar conversion was not unique. There is additional history that has not been hidden from public purview which also casts serious doubts on the legitimacy of the effort to endow Jews with a common ethnicity, namely that of the Hebrew nation of twelve tribes, the remaining two of which had inhabited the Holy Land at the time of Jesus and were fully dispersed around the world with the destruction of the Temple by the Romans. One must note that the Jewish Diaspora had begun more than two centuries before this Jerusalem tragedy. We find, according to Philo, that by 250 B.C. Alexandria, Egypt, contained by far the largest number of Jews in the world, far outstripping Jerusalem. By the time of the Romans there already were more people of the Judaic faith throughout the world than in the Holy Land. Judaism, then the sole monotheistic religion in a pagan world, had made converts in the Roman Empire and in many lands. The universal aims of the second Isaiah found expression in great missionary activities.

Judaism became a tremendous proselytizing force in the pagan world. Those who carried the religion of Yahweh to other parts of the globe were hardly more than a drop in the ocean of foreign peoples who had never possessed any racial, lingual, or cultural affinity with Israel and nevertheless became members of the Judaic monotheistic faith. These converts included such diverse peoples as Yemenites and Greeks, the Queen of Sheba, the people of Adiabene, the Hellenistic state on the Tigris. Judean traders carried their faith eastward as far as India and China. Conversions to Yahweh in Rome carried Judaism through Italy into France, the Rhone Valley, and the Rhine Basin. Mass conversions of Germanic tribes spread Judaism into Central and Eastern Europe, particularly Poland and western Russia. Frederick Hertz in *Race and Civilization* notes, "in the Middle Ages and in modern times, notwithstanding all obstacles,"[41] there have been occasional conversions in Slavic countries, which accounts for unmistakable Slavic facial characteristics of Polish and Russian Jews. There were even conversions in Hungary as late as 1229.[42] Whole peoples of varying ethnic strains became proselyte Judaists, especially during the two centuries before the birth of Christ. Judeans migrated to the Arabian desert and converted Semitic peoples in Yemen. Pagans as distant as those of the Kerch Strait and the Crimea accepted Yahweh, the Hebrew God.[43]

The Hebrews then were indeed a light unto the other nations and were spreading monotheism, the task given to them by God. Many Romans, including members of the nobility, embraced the simple teachings of Judaism, won by the appeal of what Jewish historians have referred to as a "system of morals, anchored in the veneration of the One and Holy God," and the "purity of Judean home life." For the most part the proselytes accepted the idea of monotheism and the moral law without the ceremonial precepts.[44]

With the advent of Christianity, the parent faith ceased proselytizing. Monotheism was now carried to the pagan world by the disciples of Jesus (and later by Islam). The Apostle Paul, born Saul of Tarsus, removed the ceremonial law and freed those who were willing to accept Christianity from the minute formalization of the ancient worship of Yahweh.

In a debate with Palestinian journalists on a June 1977 Public Broadcasting System telecast of an interview show made outside the walls of Jerusalem, editor of *Davar* Hannah Semer vehemently declaimed her 3,000-year right to Israel and the exclusion of the Palestinians.

But the "historic connection" upon which Zionists have staked their claim that Palestine belongs to them—and to them alone—turns out to be but a racial myth, which a further glance back into history exposes. Twelve tribes started in Canaan thirty-five centuries ago; not only did ten of them disappear, more than half of the other two never returned from exile in Babylon. How can anyone claim descendancy directly from that relatively small community that inhabited the Holy Land at the time of Abraham's covenant with God? (And if there was such a covenant, Arabs are part of the seed of Abraham through Hagar, who gave birth to a son, Ishmael.) Who can say for sure that many Christian readers of this book might not in fact have a better claim, which they do not choose to exercise, to go back "home" to Palestine than Hannah Semer, Menachem Begin, or Golda Meir? Queen Victoria herself belonged to an Israelite society that traced the ancestry of its membership back to the lost tribes of Israel.

The descriptive name "Judaism" was never heard of by the Hebrews or Israelites; it appears only with Christianity. Flavius Josephus was one of the first to use the name in his recital of the war with the Romans[45] to connote a totality of beliefs, moral commandments, religious practices, and ceremonial institutions of Galilee that he believed superior to rival Hellenism. When the word "Judaism" was born, there was no longer a Hebrew-Israelite state. The people who embraced the creed of Judaism were already a mixture of many nations, races, and strains, and this diversification was rapidly growing.

This story and the authoritative Koestler evidence ought to persuade American non-Zionist Jews of the folly flowing from the blind, emotional support they have been giving the Israeli state. It should make them pause before making further commitments, which can only greatly endanger their status as Americans, and the security of other Americans.

Those who would step forward today to advance the heritage of Judaism and battle the mighty Zionist-Israelist array will have to do so without the warmth and comfort that tribalism affords. They will be forced to look beyond narrow confines and strive to impart perspective from the larger, total picture. But they will have great figures who came before them to light the road on which they must make their way. Like many of God's more fortunate human beings, anti-Zionist Jews have had excellent forebears of whom they may justly be proud. The roots of anti-Zionism go back to the very beginnings of Judaism.

The writings and preachments of the great Hebrew prophets Amos, Jeremiah, Micah, Hosea, and the two Isaiahs, and Elijah (in whose exalted number Jesus properly belongs), unfortunately were never accorded the same position of honor and respect that Christianity has accorded to the Apostles of Jesus—Paul, Peter, John, Luke, Mark, and Matthew.

It was Jeremiah who spoke out to the Judaeans in the midst of their Babylonian captivity in 586 B.C. with these words of advice:

Build ye houses and dwell in them and plant gardens and eat the fruit thereof;
take wives and beget sons and daughters. . . . And seek the peace of the city
whither I have caused ye to be carried away captives and pray unto the Lord
for that city, for in the peace thereof shall ye have peace. [Jeremiah 29:5–7.]

These Hebrew prophets were not interested in the restoration of
political power. But they were passionately concerned with the injus-
tices of their day, and the remedy, they insisted, could be found only
in a universal God of mercy, justice, and righteousness, who demanded, above all, an undeviating code of moral values.

The second Isaiah, writing circa 536 B.C., endowed the burgeoning faith with a vision of the Messianic coming. His "next year in
Jerusalem" referred to a Kingdom of God and was unrelated to any
particular nation or sovereignty. To this prophet, the mission of the
Judeans was to open blind eyes and to serve as a light to the Gentiles.
(Isaiah 42:6.) "For my House shall be called a House of prayer for all
people." This recognition of the universality of man was echoed by the
prophet Amos when he thundered forth: Are ye not as children of the
Ethiopians unto me, O Children of Israel? (Amos 9:7.)

These preachments are in contrast to those of the unknown
psalmist from whose words "If I forget thee, O Jerusalem, let my right
hand forget her cunning" (Psalms 137:5) has grown the seed of nation-
alist-segregationalist Zionism. The history of the peoples who came
after the Judeans and who became known only many generations later
as "Jews" represents a continuous struggle between conflicting ideologies: nation versus faith, chosen people versus universality, segregation versus integration.

Following the 1791 Edict of Emancipation by the French Chamber
of Deputies endowing Jewish citizens, for the first time, with full and
equal rights. Berr Isaac-Berr wrote a significant letter on September
28 of that year to his coreligionists (then numbering 60,000):

We must then, dear brethren, strongly bear this truth in our minds: that, till
such a time as we work a change in our manner, our habits, in short, our whole
education, we cannot expect to be placed by the esteem of our fellow citizens
in any of those situations in which we can give signal proof of that glowing
patriotism so long cherished in our bosoms. *We must divest ourselves entirely of
the narrow spirit of corporation and congregation in all civil and political matters not
immediately connected with our spiritual laws.* [46] [Italics added.]

In 1917 when Zionism, in its first bid for Palestine, pressed for the
promulgation of the Balfour Declaration, it was a most perspicacious
anti-Zionist Jew who spoke out courageously, but unfortunately his

government was not prepared to heed him. Edwin S. Montagu, Secretary of State for India[47] in the Lloyd George World War I Cabinet, would accept the declaration calling for a Jewish national home in Palestine only conditionally as "a military expedient" (the Allied Powers were then losing World War I to the Central Powers), and only after the wording of the policy statement had been rephrased. Montague informed his chief that he had "striven all his life to escape from the ghetto," to which he now faced possible relegation as a result of the proposed policy paper.

Montagu did not wish to endanger the hard-won status of Jews as an integrated religious community enjoying equal rights, privileges, and obligations in countries in which they lived, and he deeply resented the efforts of Zionist nationalists to persuade unwitting coreligionists that they were an ethnic-racial group, one of superior stock entitled to rule over Palestine. Believing that without a deep sense of righteousness there was little left to Judaism, Montagu appreciated the patent injustice in turning over control of a land to those who then constituted but 7 percent of the population.

The British Cabinet records of 1915 to 1920, made public by the British government only in 1970, contained voluminous references to the Balfour Declaration, including three memoranda by this sole Jewish Cabinet member that revealed his remarkable foresightedness. Whereas today it is the critics of Zionism who are the ones labeled anti-Semitic, Montagu in a memorandum circulated to other Cabinet members pinned that very label on the sponsors of Zionism's charter. The document of August 23, 1917, titled "The Anti-Semitism of the Present Government" and marked "Secret" bears looking into:

I have chosen the above title for this memorandum, not in any hostile sense, not by any means as quarreling with an anti-Semitic view, which may be held by my colleagues, not with a desire to deny that anti-Semitism can be held by rational men, not even with a view to suggesting that the Government is deliberately anti-Semitic, but I wish to place on record my view that the policy of His Majesty's Government is anti-Semitic in result and will prove a rallying ground for anti-Semites in every country in the world. . . .

The war has indeed justified patriotism as the prime motive of political thought. It is in this atmosphere that the Government proposes to endorse the formation of a new nation with a new home in Palestine. This nation will presumably be formed of Jewish Russians, Jewish Englishmen, Jewish Roumanians, Jewish Bulgarians, and Jewish citizens of all nations—survivors of relations of those who have fought or laid down their lives for the different countries which I have mentioned, at a time when the three years that they have lived through have united their outlook and thought more closely than ever with the countries of which they are citizens. [Note the precise manner in which Montague refers to Jewish Russians, etc., rather than Russian Jews, etc.]

Zionism has always seemed to me to be a mischievous political creed, untenable by any patriotic citizen of the United Kingdom. If a Jewish Englishman sets his eyes on the Mount of Olives and longs for the day when he will shake British soil from his shoes and go back to agricultural pursuits in Palestine, he has always seemed to me to have acknowledged aims inconsistent with British citizenship and to have admitted that he is unfit for a share in public life in Great Britain or to be treated as an Englishman.

I have always understood that those who indulged in this creed were largely animated by the restrictions upon and refusal of liberty to Jews in Russia. But at the very time when these Jews have been acknowledged as Jewish Russians and given all liberties, it seems to be inconceivable that Zionism should be officially recognized by the British Government, and that Mr. Balfour should be authorized to say that Palestine was to be reconstituted as the "national home of the Jewish people." I do not know what this involves, but I assume that it means that Mohammedans and Christians are to make way for the Jews, and that the Jews should be put in all positions of preference and should be peculiarly associated with Palestine in the same way that England is with the English or France with the French, that Turks and other Mohammedans in Palestine will be regarded as foreigners. . . .

I assert that there is not a Jewish nation. The members of my family, for instance, who have been in this country for generations, have no sort or kind of community of view or of desire with any Jewish family in any other country beyond the fact that they profess to a greater or lesser degree the same religion. It is no more true to say that a Jewish Englishman and a Jewish Moor are of the same nation than it is to say that a Christian Englishman and a Christian Frenchman are of the same nation—of the same race. . . .

. . . I certainly do not dissent from the view, commonly held, as I have always understood by the Jews before Zionism was invented, that to bring the Jews back to form a nation in the country from which they were dispersed would require Divine leadership. I have never heard it suggested, even by their most fervent admirers, that either Mr. Balfour or Lord Rothschild would prove to be the Messiah. . . . [This was a view similarly held today by the Neturei Karta in Jerusalem.]

I claim that the lives that British Jews have led, that the aims that they have had before them, that the part that they have played in our public life and our public institutions, have entitled them to be regarded, not as British Jews, but as Jewish Britons. I would willingly disfranchise every Zionist. I would be almost tempted to proscribe the Zionist organization as illegal and against the national interest. . . .

I deny that Palestine is *today* associated with the Jews. It is quite true that

Palestine plays a large part in Jewish history, but so it does in modern Mo-
hammedan history, and, after the time of the Jews, surely it plays a larger part
than any other country in Christian history. The Temple may have been in
Palestine, but so was the Sermon on the Mount and the Crucifixion. I would
not deny to Jews in Palestine equal rights to colonization with those who
profess other religions, but a religious test of citizenship seems to me to be
only admitted by those who take a bigoted and narrow view of one particular
epoch of the history of Palestine, and claim for the Jews a position to which
they are not entitled.

I am not in the least surprised that the non-Jews of England may welcome
this policy. I have always recognized the unpopularity, much greater than some
people think, of my community. We have obtained a far greater share of this
country's goods and opportunities than we are numerically entitled to. We
reach, on the whole, maturity earlier, and therefore with people of our own
age we compete unfairly. Many of us have been exclusive in our friendships
and intolerant in our attitude, and I can easily understand that many a non-Jew
in England wants to get rid of us. . . .

*I would say to Lord Rothschild that the Government should be prepared to do
everything in their power to obtain for Jews in Palestine complete liberty of settlement and
life on an equality with the inhabitants of that country who profess other religious beliefs.
I would ask that the Government should go no further.* [48] [Italics added.]

Here in the 1917 words of Edwin Montagu, a Jewish Briton, is the
forerunner to the Arafat-PLO secular, binational state, enunciated at
the U.N. in November 1974, to which concept Israelist-Zionist leadership adamantly refuses to even discuss.

On this side of the Atlantic, too, during this same period, virulent
opposition to Zionism manifested itself. The *New York Times* of March
5, 1919, featured a lengthy story on San Francisco Representative
Julius Kahn and his presentation of the views of thirty-one prominent
Jewish Americans in a petition to President Woodrow Wilson. Fearful
that the appeal of the Zionists (who only claimed to represent 150,000
of the then 3½ million Jewish populace) to the Paris Peace Conference
might be the opening wedge toward the creation of a Jewish state,
these presidential petitioners warned against any commitment "now
or in the future to Jewish territorial sovereignty in Palestine. This
demand," these anti-Zionist Jews stated, "not only misinterpreted the
trend of the history of the Jews who ceased to be a nation 2,000 years
ago, but involves the limitation and possible annulment of the larger
claims of Jews for full citizenship and human rights in all lands in which
those human rights are not yet secure."

The thirty signees of the petition, in addition to Congressman
Kahn, included such outstanding leaders of the Jewish community as

Henry Morgenthau, Sr., ex-Ambassador to Turkey; Simon W. Rosendale, ex-Attorney General of New York; Mayor L. H. Kampner of Galveston, Texas; Cleveland's E. M. Baker, President of the Stock Exchange; R. H. Macy's Jesse I. Straus; *New York Times* publisher Adolph S. Ochs; Judge M. C. Sloss of San Francisco; and Professors Edwin R. Seligman of Columbia and Morris Jastrow of the University of Pennsylvania. Wilson brought the petition to the Peace Conference.

This broad-based leadership strongly rejected the Zionist project of a "national home for the Jewish people in Palestine." They viewed the concept with suspicion because they foresaw it might be applied not only to Jews living in countries in which they were oppressed, but to Jews universally. "No Jew," they wrote, "wherever he may live, can consider himself free from the implications of such a grant." Distinguishing, as their successors have never been able to do, between "haven" and "state," these leaders heartily approved of "aid in redeeming Palestine from the blight of centuries of Turkish misrule," while at the same time vigorously opposing "the Zionist project to segregate Jews as a political unit and to reconstitute a section of such in Palestine or elsewhere."

Declaring the political segregation of Jews in Palestine or elsewhere as "necessarily reactionary in its tendency, undemocratic in spirit, and totally contrary to the practices of free government," these outspoken voices repudiated "every suspicion of a double allegiance, which is necessarily implied in, and cannot by any logic be eliminated from, the establishment of a sovereign state for the Jews in Palestine." Observing sagely that those who favor a restoration of such a Jewish homeland in the Holy Land, "advocate it not for themselves, but for others . . . those who act thus, and yet insist on their patriotic attachment to the countries of which they are citizens, are self-deceived in their profession of Zionism and under the spell of an emotional romanticism or of a religious sentiment fostered through centuries of gloom."

Unlike Dr. Chaim Weizmann and other Zionists, these American visionaries were very aware of the Arab presence in Palestine and of the dangers of an ensuing struggle between the two groups:

It is not true that Palestine is the national home of the Jewish people, and of no other people. . . . To subject the Jews to the possible recurrence of such bitter and sanguinary conflicts, which would be inevitable, would be a crime against the triumph of their whole past history and against the lofty and world-embracing visions of their great prophets and leaders. . . . Whether the

Jews be regarded as a "race" or as a "religion," it is contrary to democratic principles for which the World War was waged to found a nation on either or both of these bases. . . .

Before the Hitlerian emotionalism and vicarious guilt engulfed them, there were Jewish leaders who did not flinch from expressing themselves in this vein:

We object to the political segregation of the Jews because it is in error to assume that the bond uniting them is of a national character. A Jewish State involves fundamental limitations as to race and religion, else the term "Jewish" means nothing. To unite Church and State, in any form, as under the old Jewish hierarchy, would be a leap backward of 2000 years.

The great Jewish families of the Western world, whose Judaic traditions made philanthropy the crowning justification of their wealth, likewise totally rejected political Zionism. In a speech at the Menorah Society Dinner in December 1917, Chief Judge Irving Lehman, brother of Governor Herbert H. Lehman, declared:

I cannot recognize that the Jews as such constitute a nation in any sense in which that word is recognized in political science, or that a national basis is a possible concept for modern Judaism. We Jews in America, bound to the Jews of other lands by our common faith, constituting our common inheritance, cannot as American citizens feel any bond to them as members of a nation, for nationally we are Americans and Americans only, and in political and civic matters we cannot recognize any other ties. We must therefore look for the maintenance of Judaism to those spiritual concepts which constitute Judaism.[49]

In his autobiography, Henry Morgenthau, Sr., stated: "Zionism is the most stupendous fallacy in Jewish history. It is wrong in principle and impossible of realization; it is unsound in its economics, fantastical in its politics and sterile in its spiritual ideals. I speak as a Jew."[50]

Neither he, Jacob Schiff, Julius Rosenwald, or Felix Warburg would have permitted all the Hitlers in the world to change their basic philosophy. These men were not just non-Zionists, they were passionate antinationalists. But their viewpoint was soon overridden through new demographic factors and a different leadership.

The earliest Jewish settlers had no concern for group rights and had disdain for even a segregated cultural existence. In 1897, when Herzl's Zionism was beginning to fascinate Europe, the Central Conference of American Rabbis adopted a resolution disapproving of any attempt to establish a Jewish state. The resolution stated: "Zion was a precious possession of the past . . . as such it is a holy memory, but it is not our hope of the future. America is our Zion."[51] In 1904 the *American Israelite* noted, "There is not one solitary prominent native Jewish-American who is an advocate of Zionism."[52]

Between 1881 and 1924 the third wave of Jewish immigration brought 2½ million Jews from Central and Eastern Europe to settle in the larger eastern cities. Most of these new immigrants were Orthodox and inclined toward Zionism. They had not only lived as a separate nationality, but had voted as Jews for other Jews to represent them in governments. They mostly had spoken a language other than their environment's, and had lived in a mental ghetto to "balance the physical ghetto around them."[53] The Jews from these countries had been a nation within a nation so that, when they came to the U.S. as emancipated persons, the nation complex came with them.

By sheer numbers these newcomers soon began to dominate their American coreligionists, taking over some older organizations and starting new groups of every variety. In 1918, with the creation of the nationalist-minded American Jewish Congress, the hegemony of the earliest Jewish settlers, the Sephardic and German Jews ended, and Zionism made its entrance. The philanthropic-minded antinationalists in the Jewish Agency, the official liaison between Palestine Jews and Jewry in the Diaspora, were soon outvoted and either surrendered their seats, to be filled by fervent Zionists, or were neutralized as non-Zionists.

It is most unfortunate for everyone that descendants of those who took an inspiring antinationalist stand should today be found either in Zionist ranks or among the numerous fellow travelers, tongue-tied by fear to speak up. But others have picked up the standard and have held the universalist banner aloft. They know how both "to be 'a Jew' at home and a man in the world," as author Alan Taylor expressed it.

Denmark's Chief Rabbi Marcus Melchior responded to the Ben-Gurion call for "complete solidarity with the State of Israel" in this manner:

We Danish Jews do not usually air our patriotism. Why on earth should we shout "hurrah" more loudly than all the other Danes? But we take an opportunity like this to state that no one, however big he may be or from wherever he may come, has the right or is able to change even one jot of what for 150 years has been the status of Danish Jews under which there has been established a relationship in Denmark of which we are all just as happy on the Christian side as on the Jewish side.

If Premier Ben-Gurion really claimed that in order to be a Jew every minute of one's life, one has to live in Israel, then according to my view, two questions arise. The first is whether to be a Jew every minute is of imperative necessity and whether Jewishness and being a general human being did not equate each other so completely that one at the same time could be Jewish and a human being in other places than in the few square kilometers which form the territory of Israel.[54]

It was Moshe Menuhin who dug up the old 1919 *Times* clipping. In his postscript, "Quo Vadis Zionist Israel?" to his book, *The Decadence of Judaism in Our Time,* the father of the famed violinist, Yehudi Menuhin, wrote: "I am an integrated citizen of the United States. I am a Jew by my religion and by nothing else. Prophetic Judaism is my religion." An early advocate of Zionism, when he lived in Palestine, Moshe Menuhin has since waged a relentless crusade against the Zionists who, he considers, "only use and abuse their religion to promote Jewish nationalism, the new religion of so many subverted and brainwashed Jewish people."

However much courage it takes to oppose Zionism in the Diaspora, it requires much more to stand up and be counted inside Israel. Dr. Judah Magnes, the first President of the Hebrew University, was forced to end his days out of the country when he urged closer collaboration and understanding between Jews and Arabs as a basis for the "creation of a bilingual and biracial state in Palestine along lines similar to the Swiss Confederation, with Palestine participating as one of several states in an Arab federation."[55]

With unparalleled fearlessness, Dr. Israel Shahak has followed in Magnes's footsteps through his solo fight against the "grave social discrimination visited upon any Israeli citizen every day of his life if his mother is not a Jewess."[56] And the living testimonials to the inseparable chasm between Zionism and Judaism are those religious Jews of the Neturei Karta who have been a continuing thorn in the side of the Israeli Establishment as they live their daily lives in accordance with the precepts of the Torah and persist in their refusal to recognize the existence of the Israeli state under whose jurisdiction they are ruled, because it was not Messiah-created. It is Israeli Jews who epitomize the resistance of all who refuse to countenance: "Israel Über Alles" (Israel Above All).

While I have tried to interject myself and my own experiences into this volume as little as possible, there are personal feelings that must be expressed at this juncture. I believe that I am articulating the voices of many, many Jews who wish to think American, but who will not volunteer an expression of their innermost feelings, even though they will cheer from the sidelines the expression of these deeply felt sentiments.

I cannot tolerate Israel turning me and others, who regard ourselves as Americans of the Jewish faith, into second-class citizens in our own country. For today my relations to the State of Israel are different from that of Christian Americans—of John Jones, my neighbor. If I wish to retain my religious affiliation, I am bound, whether I like it or not, to help, assist, give, lend, etc., the foreign State of Israel in a manner in which other American non-Jewish citizens do not have to do.

I insist, if I wish to worship or identify with the Judaic God—and that may be only for one minute a year—that I be able to do so without going through the State of Israel or any other intermediary. Whether a man be a good Jew or better still Judaist—a word I prefer as a follower of Judaism—ought in no way be judged by his attitude toward the State of Israel. I absolutely refuse to substitute fealty to a foreign state for the worship of Yahweh, and I insist on the doctrine of separation of church and state for which progressive-minded peoples have so long fought.

To add to my negative affirmations, as I declared twenty-eight years ago when I first wrote in the *Reader's Digest,* I refuse to be a hyphenated American. I am neither an American-Jew nor a Jewish-American. I am an American of the Jewish faith, and Israel's flag is not, has not, and never will be mine.

The final judgment as to whether Israelists and Zionists can be considered good Americans should come from Woodrow Wilson who, about sixty years ago, said:[57]

You cannot become true Americans if you think of yourselves in groups. America does not consist of groups. A man who thinks of himself as belonging to a particular national group has not yet become an American, and the man who goes among you to trade upon your nationality is not worthy to live under the Stars and Stripes.

But as Eric Sevareid observed during the 1976 election campaign, "The country is becoming the home of the ethnics—a country of groups sharing hyphenated names and candidates wandering among them promising what they'll do for their homelands across the sea."[58] And the Jew, above all others, should realize that his future security rests in his record as an individual, not as part of any group, let alone one abnormally tied to a foreign state.

Various Jewish organizations in 1954 elaborately celebrated the

300th anniversary of the first communal settlement of the Jewish people in the U.S. But Elias Legardo, who arrived aboard the *Abigail* in Virginia in 1621,[59] Solomon Franco, who arrived in Boston in 1649, and Jacob Barsimson, who was already a resident of New Amsterdam in 1654—the anniversary of whose arrival on American shores went totally unobserved—might well have been puzzled at the significance of the "Jewish people" and well might have queried: "Didn't we leave all that behind in unemancipated Europe?"

Imagine their even greater surprise if they could see how this term "the Jewish people" is being used to further the ends of a foreign state. They had made the hazardous journey across the ocean to escape group segregation, to leave behind forever the idea that the rights of a "Jew" depended upon his rights as part of a group rather than as an individual. Like other immigrants then arriving, they had no intention of transplanting any national allegiances, but to shake off the old for a new one. Three centuries later some of their forebears who had followed in their footsteps to this country were intent on transferring to the new soil of America this outmoded and archaic concept that had long since received a decent burial in most of Old Europe.

From Haym Solomon of the American Revolution through Judah P. Benjamin, Secretary of State for the Confederacy, down to the present, there have been many who have made vital contributions to the American melting pot: Flexner, Einstein, Brandeis, Cardozo and Frankfurter; Gershwin and Berlin; Pulitzer and Ochs; Louis Untermeyer, Fannie Hurst, and Edna Ferber; Heifetz, Elman, Zimbalist, Milstein; Horowitz, Rubinstein, and Serkin; George S. Kaufman, Moss Hart, and Elmer Rice; the Guggenheims, Schiffs, Strauses, Lewisohns, Warburgs, and Rosenwalds. Some of these were born here and others were not, but the attainments of all these men and women were as individual Americans and not as part of a separate people.

The Jew in America should have continued to struggle for integration, not segregation, and to seek to be judged for himself, if only because "Jews are such a mass of contradictions and encompass such extremes of human behavior that they are simply beyond the reach of pat formulas, casual generalizations, or prophetic clichés." The same writer further pointed out:

They are both the "People of the Book" and the inventors of the strip tease. They were pioneers of plutocracy and communism. They originated and lived by the concept of the "Chosen People," yet are presently the most vociferous of anti-racists. They are the most God-fearing and God-hating, the most straitlaced and the most permissive, the most cosmopolitan and most narrow-minded, the most cultivated and the most vulgar of peoples. Jewish sabras in Israel fight like ten thousand Lawrences of Arabia, but in Germany their brethren went like lambs to the slaughter. The same racial dynamics which has sporadically propelled Jews to the top of the social heap has also cast them down into the abyss. The penduluming, rags-to-riches swing of Jewish history may lead to the fairyland castles of the Rothschilds, but it also leads to the gas chambers of Auschwitz. When viewed objectively, the story of Jewish wanderings through time is both fascinating and repulsive, ennobling and degrading —in part comic, in great part tragic. The only last word that can be said about Jews is that there is no last word.[60]

For Judaism as a religious faith, there have been and will be few problems in the U.S.—for Judaism as a nationalist commitment the road ahead can only become thornier. The corresponding allegiances to religion and to state, long before the heightening of emotions under Carter and the impact of Sadat peace initiatives, have become so confused that it would require the Hebrew wisdom of a Jesus for Jewry to be able to apply to the present conflict the spirit of his answer to the Pharisees: "Render therefore unto Caesar the things which are Caesar's, and unto God the things that are God's." (Matthew 22:21.)

If Jews could only be this wise, they would clearly discern that peace can only be achieved through the binationalist thinking of Albert Einstein, Martin Buber, Judah Magnes, and other universalists, which was so succinctly stated in the conclusion of that remarkable 1919 document presented to President Wilson by the thirty-one sages:

As to the future of Palestine, it is our fervent hope that what was once a "promised land" for the Jews may become a "land of promise" for all races and creeds, safeguarded by the League of Nations. . . . We ask that Palestine be constituted as a free and independent state, to be governed under a democratic form of government, recognizing no distinctions of creed or race or ethnic descent, and with adequate power to protect the country against oppression of any kind. We do not wish to see Palestine either now or at any time organized as a Jewish State.

Such a mandate from any number of Jews and Christians today would enable President Carter, the Soviet Union, the Arabs, and the Israelis to move, through a reconvened Geneva Conference or otherwise, on a steady path toward true justice and lasting peace in the Middle East.

XXV   Conclusion: Toward Justice
and Then Peace

> I shall no longer ask myself if this or that is expedient, but only
> if it is right. I shall do this, not because I am noble or unselfish,
> but because life slips away, and because I need for the rest of my
> journey a star that will not play false to me. . . . a compass that will
> not lie . . . I do it because I am no longer able to aspire to the
> highest with one part of myself and deny it with another.
>
> —Alan Paton, *Cry, The Beloved Country*

With sacrifices by all parties, the impossible dream of peace in the
Middle East may yet be achieved before further disaster overruns the
area and the world. But this depends on the true intent of the Israelis
and the Arabs, and on banishment of the guile to which the Old
Testament refers: They speak peace to their neighbors, but mischief
is in their hearts. (Psalms 28:3.)

In the course of the Christmas Day luncheon during the 1977
historic visit of Menachem Begin to Ismailia, the Israeli leader defended his refusal to grant sovereignty to the Palestinians of the West
Bank and Gaza with one of his customary history lectures, which traced
the persecution of Jews from Roman times through the holocaust and
included the Arab attack on the newly established state in 1948 and the
1973 "surprise strike." Sadat's only answer was: "No, no, let's not start
all that again. That happened before November 19 and my trip to
Jerusalem."

The Egyptian leader ought never have let the record stand as
Begin recited it and as the myth-informed world accepted it. Sadat
might have seized the opportunity to cite the "original sin," the dispossession of the overwhelming majority of the indigenous Arab inhabitants of Palestine, which made these innocents pick up the bill in
expiation for what Hitler and others had done to the Jews of Europe.

776

At the risk of displeasing a guest who was making his first visit to Egypt, he also could have quoted Israeli humanist Rabbi Benjamin:

In the end, we must come out publicly with the truth: that we have no moral right whatever to oppose the return of the Arabs to their land. . . . Until we have begun to redeem our sin against the Arab refugees, we have no right to continue the in-gathering of the exiles. We have no right to settle in a land that has been stolen from others while the owners of it are homeless and miserable.

We had no right to occupy the house of an Arab if we had not paid for it at its value. The same goes for fields, gardens, stores, workshops. We had no right to build a settlement and to realize the kind of Zionism with other people's property. To do this is robbery. Political conquest cannot abolish private property.[1]

During the thirty-year step-by-step occupation of Arab Palestine, the demand of the dispossessed for their human and political rights has never ceased. But in this period Golda Meir's "What Palestinians?" had only given way to "Why the Palestinians?" Far more needed for a lasting Middle East settlement than any Sadat Jerusalem pledge of "no more war," was the Israeli admission: "We have committed a grave wrong to the Palestinians." The failure to recognize even partial guilt for the tragedy militates against hopes of a settlement. Until an Israeli head of government makes this declaration, peace can never be any more than illusory. For the crux of the bitter Middle East conflict, the struggle between the Zionists of Israel and the Arabs of Palestine, will have remained unresolved.

The long years of double-talk engendered by Hitler's specter concealed the true nature of the Zionist state and its purposefulness in denying recognition to the Palestinians, who are an independent people fully entitled to exercise the right of self-determination in their own land. Their existence as an independent nation was provisionally recognized by the League of Nations in the 1922 grant of the Palestine mandate—long before there was any corresponding international rec- ognition of a Zionist state. The same time as the U.N., successor to the League, recommended establishment of the Zionist state, it sanctioned establishment of a Palestinian state on Palestinian soil. Nothing has occurred since 1947 in any way invalidating this title to a national state. In population size, in sense of national identity, and in capacity for self-government and independence, the Palestinians are fully as well qualified for membership at the U.N. as many of the existing member states, including Israel.

The rights of the Palestinian people to exist as an independent

national entity and the rights of the people of Israel to a secure existence are two sides of the same coin. As a man of the Bible who has
made the quest for human rights the keystone of his administration,
who better than President Carter could have led the way toward ending the anguish of Palestinian exile and the hell of Israeli occupation?
If a sense of justice constitutes the basis for U.S. support of Israel, the
cake must slice in both directions. Justice must come for those who
have an equal, if not a superior, legal and moral claim to the same land
of Palestine. The right of the Palestinian people to statehood and of
all Palestinians to make their home in their own land ought no longer
be questioned.

Staunch American friends of Israel called for the end of the occupation of the West Bank and Gaza for the benefit of the Israelis themselves:

It is corrupting to hold and govern another people by force. This is one of the
arguments mounted against slavery by Thomas Jefferson. Slavery not only
wronged the slave, it coarsened and brutalized the master.[2]

Highly respected Israeli journalist Boaz Evron points to the price
the occupation was causing his own people:

. . . Through the creation of a semi-colonial regime and the rise of a class of
small omnipotent despots who tyrannize a submissive population by using
weapons . . . the ruler is bound to develop all the loathsome traits of arrogance,
corruption and oblivion of the humanity of the ruled. The ruler may in time
transfer these conditions to his own people. . . . Oppression of the conquered
population will turn into interior terror against dissenters among Jews. This
is an unavoidable process, by which the poison and rot spread. Oppression has
no limits.[3]

Presidents Johnson, Nixon, and Ford all failed in their quest for
the "just and lasting peace" envisaged in Resolution 242 by ignoring
Palestinian rights and adhering to the false premise that this goal could
best be achieved by keeping Israel unilaterally stronger than all her
neighbors combined. Israel has been so militarily endowed by the U.S.
for two decades, and yet the Arab-Israeli conflict continues.

Carter seemed to be seeking a more evenhanded approach during
the early months of his administration by becoming the first U.S.
President to talk of a "Palestinian homeland." But he continually wavered, as others before him had, in the face of Zionist pressure and
power. He abandoned the goal of an overall settlement for the dramatic Israeli-Egyptian version of Kissinger step-by-step diplomacy,

leading to the Begin-Dayan plan for the occupied West Bank, in which PLO participation was totally ruled out and a mockery was made of Palestinian rights. While sharply disagreeing with Begin over the settlement issue and the necessity of some withdrawal from all occupied territories, Carter's negativeness toward Palestinian statehood for the West Bank and Gaza persisted.

By what right does the U.S., Egypt, Israel, or any other party lay down the rules for the self-determination of the Palestinian people and decide whether they shall live in a Palestinian state, a Jordanian-Palestinian federation, a unified Jordanian kingdom, a republic, or otherwise? The overwhelming Palestinian sentiment against the Israeli plan was expressed by Mayor Mohammed Hassan Milhem of the West Bank town of Halhoul: "Our people should be given the right of self-determination and the full right of an independent state without being under the patronage of anybody. We condemn any effort or attempt to go around and try to create alternatives.[4] As Dr. Walid Khalidi, Palestinian professor of political studies at the American University in Beirut stated to Anthony Lewis of the *New York Times* June 15, 1978, "the cornerstone" of an acceptable solution is a sovereign state, not one with "ersatz sovereignty" or an Indian reservation sprinkled with "armed archeologists," but "only a true state" that could give Palestinians "a national anchorage."

Palestinians of the West Bank became increasingly dejected and angry as they remained unconsulted and negotiations stalled. From an irate Christian in Ramallah came this comment: "Mondays, Wednesdays, and Fridays Carter is for the Arabs. Tuesdays, Thursdays, and Saturdays he's for the Israelis, and on Sundays he goes to church." They are convinced "no one can force Israel to do anything." As a businessman told a *Washington Post* correspondent (January 15, 1978): "We want the PLO—warts and all—to represent us." Termination of occupation is the key demand.

Ambiguous promises of autonomy under alien supervision and control in another Bantustan with the exercise of self-determination after five years—and not positively then—is no answer to the Palestinian claim to nationhood in a national state of their own. While there could be no objection to a very brief, temporary, and transitional period of international administration to help prepare the way for full exercise by the Palestinians of their right of self-determination in an orderly representative manner, this was a far cry from Israeli intent.

The number-one step on any peace agenda is for the U.S. to grant immediate and forthright recognition to the PLO as the legitimate representatives of the Palestinian people and to lend every possible assistance to the establishment of a Palestinian state on the West Bank and in Gaza. Such action would be consonant with the inalienable right of self-determination, inexorably proclaimed by all American statesmen. It is for the Palestinians—and the Palestinians alone—to choose their own leaders and representatives. However militant and intractable they may be, there is little alternative to dealing with the effective leaders of a people in revolt. U.N. General Assembly resolutions, the Arab states at Rabat, and the 1976 West Bank elections all affirmed the PLO leadership.

Such an act of recognition by the U.S. admittedly would breach the once-secret Kissinger covenant given as an inducement to Israel to enter into the second disengagement agreement. Not only has the situation totally changed with the Sadat initiative, but Israel herself violated her agreement with the U.S. by employing American weapons, in particular the CBU-72 cluster bombs, during the 1978 invasion of Lebanon, contravening the Arms Export Control Act and additional pledges of use only in case of full-scale war (such as 1967 and 1973) against well-entrenched emplacements.[5]

Recognition by the U.S. would place the Palestinian leadership under a sense of obligation to Washington, which could be balanced against any promissory notes that might be due to Moscow for assistance rendered in achieving this essential goal. As Arnold Toynbee expressed it some years ago: "The question is whether the Arabs are going to attain their acceptable objectives with the goodwill and assistance of the West, or whether they are going to attain their objective, in the teeth of Western opposition, thanks to Russian support. . . . The way in which they will win will decide whether they join our or Russia's camp."[6] And this applies particularly to the Palestinians after their long struggle.

As an excuse for its boycott of the PLO, the U.S. points to Begin's assertion that he would negotiate anything but Israel's destruction, which he insists is the Palestinian aim. Syrian President Hafez al-Assad told Arnaud de Borchgrave, senior foreign correspondent of *Newsweek*, in January 1978: "Let Begin address himself to the PLO. Let him say to the PLO executive committee: 'I want to negotiate with you, but not on the destruction of Israel,' and let him hear their answer."

Next in importance, Washington must persuade Israel through Jewish-American leadership that the State of Israel must de-Zionize by giving up its abnormal nationalism, which extends inchoate citizenship to nationals of other countries because they share a common faith. It has been Zionism, never Judaism, that has been the intruder in the area and the harbinger of animosity between the two peoples of Palestine. It was fear of this political ideology, striving for an exclusivist state, not hatred or bias toward Jew *qua* Jew, that ushered in the awesome conflict. Arabs and Jews lived peacefully together for centuries before the advent of Zionism, and they could do so in the future.

What we today know as anti-Semitism never existed in the Arab world. Moses and Abraham, as well as Jesus, are recognized as prophets in the Islamic faith, the Koran refers to Jews as "people of the book," and one of the holiest places in Islam is the Rock of Jerusalem where Abraham was prepared to sacrifice his son Isaac. It is difficult for the seeds of bigotry to grow in such an atmosphere. The Jews had originally been brought to Babylon (now Iraq) by Nebuchadnezzar after the destruction of the Kingdom of Judah. It was there that the Babylonian Talmud had been written and the captives had found the "peace of the city" prophesized for them by Jeremiah. It was in the ensuing great Islamic empires that they served as counselors and advisers to sultans and pashas, gaining civic prestige and financial position while enjoying for centuries economic and religious freedom. In Iraq there had been Jewish finance ministers in various Cabinets, and 125,000 Jews who attended some sixty synagogues.[7]

The situation was the same in Egypt, where the Jews had lived for millennia side by side with the followers of Islam. Some of them were descendants of ancient Hebrews whom Moses left behind in his exodus. Others had fled to Egypt following the first destruction of the Temple in Jerusalem at the hands of the Babylonians in 250 B.C. Jews gained sanctuary in Egypt from Christian persecutions in Spain and Portugal in the 15th century, from Soviet excesses at the time of the Russian Revolution, and from Hitler's racial persecutions in the 1940s. And the invasion of Egypt by Israel on October 29, 1956, calculatingly brought an end to this Egyptian sanctuary for the Jews of the world, some of whom I had encountered in the Great Synagogue in the middle of Cairo, when as a World War II GI I attended the Rosh Hashanah services.

As one Oriental Jew expressed it: "We sang together and wept together. It was only after Zionism and Israel appeared on the scene that this human structure collapsed. . . ." Today the Jewish community in Iraq numbers less than 1,000 and is even smaller than that in Egypt. It was Zionism that brought an end to peaceful coexistence; a well-organized Zionist campaign led by agents sent into the country produced the trouble between Jews and Muslims, resulting in a most reluctant Jewish exodus despite the opposition of Iraq's chief rabbi, Sassoon Kheddoury.[8]

The holocaust has caused a total misreading of history and has blocked out the reality of the long, intimate relationship under which Jews and Judaism thrived in the Arab-Muslim world. Almost totally ignored by the U.S. media was the magnanimous act of Yasir Arafat in sending food and water to nearly 150 Jewish Lebanese trapped in a Beirut synagogue during the Lebanese civil war. Wadi Abu Jamil, the Beirut neighborhood that housed many of the city's 1,500 Jews, had been a no-man's land between the warring Christians and Muslims. Acting on a request from attorney Salim al Maghrebi, who heads the Jewish community there, the PLO rushed in the necessary aid. Maghrebi was quoted as saying: "The Lebanese Jews are grateful to Mr. Arafat. We have no need of any outside protection because no one has touched a hair on our heads. We reject Israeli reports that the community is in any danger. We want no outside protectors, Israeli or otherwise. We simply plan to go on living as we always have, as Lebanese."[9] After sending in food for those in need, the Palestinian commandos became the guardians of this community during the remainder of the strife.

Jews, Muslims, and with Christians all have an equally deep spiritual and emotional attachment to Jerusalem and can share a Holy City that is internationalized. This would be consonant with the 1947 U.N. partition plan, and depoliticizing this most sacred of cities would return it to the three monotheistic faiths to whom it justly belongs.

Five years before Begin came to power, *Guardian* correspondent David Hirst refuted Zionism's unique claim to Jerusalem:

They cannot challenge the Arab claim to Jerusalem by the only criterion which would count in modern law—centuries of continuous residence and ownership of the land; so they have to erect another one in its place, the intensity of the sentimental attachment, the strength of the mystic bond which binds them to it. The world is asked to have a sense of history and to appreciate what it means to the Jews to return to the Holy City from which they were expelled 1900 years ago. It is asked to find no undue presumption in the recent assertion of Ben-Gurion that "Jerusalem has been the Jewish capital for 3000 years since King David."[10]

For their part, the Arabs must prove that their record of tolerance toward Jews is not just past history and that they sincerely intend to implement present words regarding coexistence in the area on an equal basis with Jews. By not making a mere shibboleth of the deep abyss between Judaism and Zionism, they can do much to overcome the deep-seated recent mistrust that has grown up between two Semitic "cousins." There are many Israelis who would respond positively to a resumption of fraternal relations with Arabs.

What hopes there are for a more reasonable Israeli attitude rest in the hands of Israel's youth and future generations. Many young Sabras (the native-born were given this name because their resilience makes them resemble the cactus fruit—tough on the outside, sweet on the inside) are not afflicted with the Masada complex. What desire they may have for a "Greater Israel" stems not from support of worldwide Jewish nationalism but from overbearing pride in their country, which would constitute no menace to their neighbors. Prime Minister David Ben-Gurion openly admitted that the Eichmann trial had been used not only to win world sympathy for the new state but to indoctrinate his youngsters with an understanding of the true meaning of Hitler and the holocaust. But this new generation of Israelis never developed any love of Zionism and, in fact, holds the deepest disdain for nonimmigrating Jews living outside. Israeli youth deeply resent the price exacted for their insecure living in Israel: the inordinate taxes, rampant inflation, and the ever-present threat of an Arab attack. They cannot help feel the increasing hostility of an outside world in which their only real friend and ally, aside from the U.S., is South Africa, with its blatant racism and apartheid, and with whom military-economic ties have vastly escalated.

The desire for peace was expressed in the gigantic April 1, 1978, rally outside Jerusalem's City Hall when more than 30,000 Israelis responded to a call by 300 military reservists and university students, who had sent a letter to Prime Minister Begin criticizing the government's conduct of negotiations. Huge placards, "Better Peace in Israel than a Greater Israel," supplied the keynote for the demonstration. The pessimistic realism of the youthful strata of Israel is reflected in the ever-increasing exodus from their country, including the more than 2,000 Israeli taxi drivers on the streets of New York City.

An independent U.S. policy based on the development of a sound framework of evenhanded political relationships with all Middle East countries is a prime necessity. This alone can serve vital U.S. interests as well as the world community's desire for peace and stability in the region. Israel, as President Eisenhower required her to do after the 1956 aggression, must be made by Washington to give up the occupation of all Egyptian, Syrian, and Jordanian territories, save for minor border rectifications, in accordance with the most reasonable interpretation of Resolution 242. The long-extant U.S. guarantee of the territorial integrity of all nations of the Middle East, flouted since the 1967 war, should be replaced by a U.S.-U.S.S.R. security pledge, under U.N. auspices, to Israel, to the new Palestinian entity, and to the other Arab states.

There is little prospect of Middle East peace, and certainly no hope of ending the dangerous and escalating arms race without the cooperation of the Kremlin. Between 1973 and 1976 $20 billion in armaments were poured into the area; $11 billion from the U.S., $6 billion from the U.S.S.R., and $3 billion from Britain and France. (On his March 1978 visit to Washington, Israel's Defense Minister Weizmann sought a long-range arms commitment in excess of $12 billion.) It is not in the cards for military establishments to be long in possession of such great arsenals without finding some good excuse to use them. Israel's nuclear capability, which the Arab countries were constantly striving to match, has added to the dangers. Washington must both find means other than the sale of instrumentalities of death to overcome a portion of its huge deficit balance of payments stemming from oil imports and abandon the anomalous use of armaments, such as the $4.8 billion jet sale to Saudi Arabia, Egypt, and Israel, as the way to peace.

As for Israel, a genuine peace with its neighbors should prove more satisfactory than an amorphous U.S. commitment to its security. So long as the Israelis felt they could rely on Washington's security commitment—expressed or implied—they could always reply to a demand for concessions: "We cannot give that territory back. It endangers our security."

Whatever commitment may have been given was certainly intended by the American people for the people of Israel, not for an Israeli state bent on expansionism, be it by conquest or ideology. No commitment covering Israel as well as its conquests has ever been constitutionally ratified. No President, let alone any number of members of Congress, ever had the right to guarantee the Zionist policy of bringing in Jews from all over the world, the "ingathering of the exiles" as it is called, or the concomitant establishment of settlements in the occupied territories. Why should it still be considered blasphemous to call for clarification and redefinition by Washington of the exact nature of the extant U.S. security commitment to Israel?

These recommended drastic U.S. foreign policy steps might be accompanied by important internal measures. The entire question of the Middle East must be taken out of the domestic political arena, a goal for which James Forrestal gave his life, and made part of the bipartisan foreign policy Senator Arthur H. Vandenberg first envisaged. Nothing but national harm has been wrought by the continual Republican sniping, led by National Committee Chairman William Brock and Senator Howard Baker, to which ex-President Ford lent a conspicuous hand by addressing a New York meeting of the National Council of Young Israel in April 1978 and assailing the Carter administration for insisting on significant Israeli territorial concessions. His 1976 running mate, Senator Robert J. Dole, made it known that he did not intend to "fade away"; he began addressing Zionist rallies, including a large gathering in Jerusalem where he exhorted the Israelis not to give up an inch of territory. Still maintaining his popularity among Conservative Republicans, Ronald Reagan, who always had been "gung-ho" for Israel, did a weekly column for the *Jewish Press* of Brooklyn and took intermittent pokes at the Carter administration for not doing enough for Israel.

Bipartisanship could be realized, and the sordid campaigning for votes over this issue best brought to an end, through the elimination of the Electoral College system and the popular election of the President and Vice President. This would drastically reduce the reliance of any President, or nominee for that office, on the so-called "Jewish vote," the wooing of which has so plagued the development of policy in the national interest. Such direct elections of the Chief Executive would drastically curtail the ability of Zionism and other special interest groups to gain preferential treatment for themselves and for their friends abroad. Several Presidents, including Carter, have submitted legislation in this direction, but all have encountered overwhelming obstacles to date.[11]

Everyone has played domestic politics with the Arab-Israeli conflict—Republicans, Democrats, and the politicians of other Western countries—and have brought only more chaos to the scene. The Arab countries competed with one another in being more anti-Israel, the Israeli political parties vied as to degree of anti-Arab sentiment. At a critical stage in April during the 1978 Middle East negotiations, Senator Howard Baker appeared on "Face the Nation" to make political capital of Carter's position by strongly defending Begin against the charge of intransigency. In a bid to return to power, former Canadian Prime Minister John Diefenbaker visited Israel, planted 750 trees in behalf of Canadian Jews, and criticized the Trudeau government for not moving its embassy to Jerusalem in recognition of the "true capital of Israel."

Next in importance is removal of the word "anti-Semitism" from political and public discussion of the Middle East problem. This throttling label is totally irrelevant to the debate over the rights of two Semitic-speaking peoples. A free and open expression of opinion is needed so that Americans may understand why their President can rarely say "no" to Israel, why their representatives in Washington are not serving the totality of American interests, why the media is afraid to report the news fairly, and why their sons may one day be forced to fight in a new, more horrible Vietnam. The Great Middle East Debate, totally untethered and uninhibited, must be permitted to go forward to avoid the overwhelming catastrophe that otherwise lies ahead. And just as judges disqualify themselves in cases where they cannot be impartial because of a conflict of interests, so likewise should the many media commentators whose Zionism pervades their outpourings to millions.

What is required is that all Americans face the Middle East crisis courageously and participate in helping to find a solution. All fear of speaking out must be banished. To tell the truth as he sees it, a George Ball ought not have to be abjectly apologetic, as in his *Foreign Affairs* article, "How to Save Israel in Spite of Herself!"[12] Nor should a competent political-economic observer be forced to employ a pseudonym, to turn to Vanity Fair publishers, and then have to resort to the title "Goldstein Explains How Jews Control American Policy Toward Israel"[13] in order to set forth the thesis that international Zionism has played on "latent racism and pathological anti-Communism" to achieve its ends in the U.S. The author tellingly puts these words in the mouth of his Mr. Goldstein:

It really upsets us to see that the Palestinians have been as nationalistic as Jews. We have a mandate from God and Americans to be so. I never read in any Bible about God's having given a similar mandate to the Palestinians. God, are they unreasonable bastards! Can you imagine Americans being like that? If Israel annexes New York State because it is mostly Jewish owned, Gentiles in America will never become as unreasonable as the Palestinians and fight the Jews. Well, it's only a hypothetical situation anyway. Why would Israel want only New York State when it has all the United States?[14]

The potent American business community, which has a tremendous stake in the region but has displayed abysmal cowardice to date on this issue, must join the struggle for justice. U.S. companies have not only refrained from anything but superficial involvement in the contest for American public opinion, but have failed to protect even

their own selfish interests. Large, powerful corporations have countenanced the distortion and embellishment of the actual Arab economic boycott of Israel into a "shadow boycott"[15] so as to give all the
appearances of an Arab "anti-Semitic" campaign. This helped spur the
passage by Congress of antiboycott legislation handcuffing vital U.S.
trade in the area.

It is difficult to estimate how many billions of dollars of trade and
hundreds of thousands of jobs may be lost due to adoption of the
Stevenson-Rosenthal bill and companion enactments designed to curtail Arab economic warfare against companies giving economic and
financial assistance to Israel. As pointed out in the 1976 testimony
before the House Committee on International Relations by representatives of the Associated General Contractors of America,[16] part of
what was at stake was more than $200 billion in construction programs
expected over the following five years, of which the American market
ought to have captured at least 15 percent or $30 billion. (By April
1978 far more of the top 400 American contracting firms were doing
business in Saudi Arabia than in any other foreign country.)

Conceivably, as Congressman Robert H. Michel (Rep.-Ill.)
warned the House during the 1977 debate over the pending legislation, the U.S. could lose "$16 billion in outstanding service and con-
struction contracts in Saudi Arabia alone this coming year plus another
$4 billion a year in sales of direct civilian exports, and $9 billion in
military goods and services."[17] As many as half a million jobs could be
lost if all eighteen Arab countries were taken into account, according
to the study of MIT Professor Richard D. Robinson, cited by Congressman Michel.[18]

The long, tedious, complex, and confusing regulations now required for Middle East traders by the Department of Commerce under
the new legislation have imposed a frightening, restrictive burden,
particularly on smaller business firms. For many it is better not to
attempt to do any business rather than to record and justify not only
transactions but motivations in order to protect themselves against
unfounded charges and heavy penalties for compliance with the Arab
boycott. As the U.S. deficit trade balance dangerously mounts, detri-
mentally affecting the American people and economy, serious thought
should be given to repealing the crippling antiboycott legislation. The
Zionist legislators who convinced their colleagues that American contractors and major business suppliers to the Middle East would still win
their share of petrodollars because the U.S. is the "only country"
supplying "what the Arab countries need"[19] unfortunately have been

proven wrong. The fantastic rise in U.S.-Arab trade since 1973 is beginning to reverse itself, and West European and Japanese competitors are speedily replacing their American counterparts.

In the past the U.S. has employed economic sanctions and/or boycotts against the Soviet Union, China, Cuba, North Vietnam, Cambodia, North Korea, and Rhodesia. Not to be forgotten was the Zionist 1946 boycott of Britain, nor their more recent acts of economic warfare: boycotting 970 Japanese companies that preferred to do business with twenty Arab countries rather than with Israel, boycotting Mexico in 1976 for her vote on the U.N. resolution equating Zionism with racism, and France for releasing Palestinian Abu Daoud.

A heavy price has already been exacted for the failure to heed the warning of John F. Kennedy against American partisanship in the Arab-Israeli conflict. As Americans continue to view the fast-moving Middle East scene through Israeli spectacles and to judge Palestinian rights according to the terrorist syndrome, the extent to which the security of every American is linked to the attainment of stability in the Middle East has been very much kept from public purview.

Infinitely more necessary than the much-discussed normalization of relations between Israel and the Arab states is the normalization of U.S.-Israeli relations. An end must be put to the unique relationship, unparalleled between two sovereign nations, that has been an albatross around the U.S. neck in its execution of foreign policy, not to mention an incredible burden on the American taxpayer. For example, the Israeli government's 1974–75 budget totaled $8.6 billion, the largest item of which was $3.8 billion—44 percent—for defense. This was almost as much as had been spent during the October war, the bulk of which was covered by the special $2.2 billion U.S. military aid bill enacted to cover the cost of the arms airlift.

From the very outset, Uncle Sam had come to the rescue in crucial moments in Israel's history. No loan was more vital than the first $135 million Export-Import Bank loan granted by President Truman in 1949 when the new state faced instant bankruptcy. But no help had been better timed than the gigantic flow of U.S. arms in the midst of the 1973 war. The huge Galaxy transports droning in over Tel Aviv's shorefront every hour during the last two weeks of the conflict, delivering forty-four tons of armaments, were a visible demonstration of the extraordinary American-Israeli relationship.

In testifying against the special aid bill, Senator James Abourezk stated: "It is ludicrous that this Congress should be asked to permit the Administration an additional $1.2 billion over and above the $1 billion costs of the Israeli supply effort for undisclosed 'imponderables.' " Another view of this extraordinary aid bill for Israel came from an American teaching at the University of Beirut:

$1.5 billion is being planned as capital budget for New York City with its 11 million population, and now $2.2 billion military aid is given for a country of 2.5 million. On the basis of that arithmetic, I think it would be much cheaper all the way around to transfer all Israelis to New York City. The United States would be about a couple millions ahead, and they would live within "safe and secure" borders!

Originally only $1 billion had been declared an outright grant, but when President Nixon was in Moscow[20] he exercised the discretion under the legislation to sign an authorization converting a half-billion of the remaining amount to an additional grant. This was done at the request of Israeli Defense Minister Shimon Peres, then on a visit to Washington seeking an additional $7.5 billion for the ensuing five years, almost all in grants rather than "loans" because of Israel's "flagging economy," according to the *New York Times.*

Israel's per capita arms expenditure for 1974 was more than 2½ times that of any other nation.[21] Her expenditure amounted to more than $1,110 per person, the nearest comparable per capita figure being that of Russia's $428, with a yearly expenditure of $119 billion. The U.S. expenditure was $91 billion, per capita only $390. On an absolute dollar basis, only ten other nations spent more for military might than Israel.[22] The armament expenditures by nine Arab states (the United Arab Emirates, Saudi Arabia, Kuwait, Libya, Iraq, Syria, Egypt, Jordan, and Lebanon) totaled some $6 billion for a population of 71.1 million. Those nine countries spent $84 per capita, 8 percent of the Israeli per capita expenditure.

In the ten years ending in 1974, the Israeli armaments figure reached a staggering $15.48 billion, most from government or private sources in the U.S. The Zionist state was expending 34.60 percent of its G.N.P. on the military, compared to 6 percent by the U.S. Israel's growing war industry, responsible for its Kfir fighters and Chariot tanks, was backed by U.S. investments and U.S.-Israeli technology. In order to keep its aircraft industry viable, Israel coproduced a portion of the F-16s received from the Pentagon and in 1978 was seeking authority to manufacture components of U.S. weapons that it did not wish to acquire, such as subassemblies of Gruman A-6 tactical bombers.[23] But Israel continued to draw on American advanced armaments and supplies—and billions.

Half of the development budget of $1.6 billion in 1974 was covered by the sale of Israel Bonds abroad, additional sums from Jewry in the Diaspora being necessary to cover other foreign loans. Various health, education, and social welfare programs were financed in this critical postwar year by roughly $1 billion the government received in other donations, primarily from United Jewish Appeal and Jewish welfare funds—all tax deductible to the donor.

While a handful of objectors fearfully[24] expressed objections to the dollar drain for Israeli Bonds, the purchase of large amounts of Israel Bonds continued to come from the most curious sources.

In May 1973 Teamsters President Frank E. Fitzsimmons received the Israel Silver Anniversary Award for his efforts in the investment of $26 million of Teamster pension and health and welfare funds in Israel bonds. According to news reports, present and participating in the praise of the Teamster leader was Secretary of the U.S. Treasury George Shultz. Fitzsimmons is an Irishman, but the dinner for 2,500 Teamsters and Teamster employees was declared his "Bar Mitzvah" by Herbert Stein, Chairman of the President's Council of Economic Advisers. A telegram from President Nixon was read to the diners. Not only did it not seem strange for trust funds of American organized labor to be invested in a foreign nation, but two of the administration's top economic advisers, who were otherwise expressing public concern over inflation and the credit crunch, apparently gave their approval.

Israeli Ambassador Simcha Dinitz, substituting for Foreign Minister Abba Eban, presented the medal and stated that the Teamsters' investment had made it possible for Israel to "not only support war, but to launch peace." What the members of the International Brotherhood of Teamsters certainly did not appreciate was that this pension fund management, which had brought them $26 million of Israel 5½ percent Bonds due in twenty years, could have bought at the same time the exact number of U.S. bonds, which would have yielded a return of 6.9 percent for each of the next twenty years. The difference of 1.40 percent annual return on $26 million is $364,000, or $7.28 million over twenty years—the amount the pension funds lost because their management had chosen the foreign country of Israel over the U.S.

American taxpayers continue to pay the piper for Israel on many fronts. Under pressure from Speaker Stanley Steingut and Assemblyman Irwin J. Landes, the Board of Regents of the State of New York appropriated $225,000 as a grant to the Sachler School of Medicine in Tel Aviv to pay the tuition for forty New Yorkers to study medicine there, and to put ten Israeli students through medical college in the

U.S. at no cost.[25] The plain fact is that tax-free, tax-deductible monies given as charitable dollars are simply a gift to the Israeli national budget. When sums needed for various services by an Israeli government agency are provided through American charity, other monies are freed to help meet that portion of the Israeli defense budget for which there have not been grants or loans. Instead of listing these under charitable contributions, they ought to be listed under the category, "Taxes Paid to Foreign Governments." The IRS provides that only those contributions that are wholly (not holy) humanitarian, charitable, or educational are deductible to the donor. U.S. tax-deductible funds given for humanitarian purposes have gone into the purchase of jets and the manufacture of napalm bombs to subdue the Palestinians or to defray the expenses of Moshe Dayan rallies against efforts to win increased Israeli flexibility.

The U.S. has been Israel's largest trading partner, and private investments of American business have played a major factor in the Israeli post-1967-war economic boom. U.S. investments approach an annual average of 55 percent of the total foreign investments in the Israeli economy.

It is significant that Americans in their relations with Israel lag behind other national groups in only one area—immigration. In 1973, for example, only 4,393 Americans moved to Israel, while over 35,000 Soviets immigrated there. Of the 1.5 million who came to Israel between 1948 and 1974, only 30,000 Americans remained. The Israelis resent their dependence on both the U.S. and American Jews who only visit but do not settle in Israel. Despite the continuous urging by Zionist leaders to emigrate, American Jews draw the line here. They will give money and all else, but to send Jews other than themselves to Israel. The contributing nonimmigrating American has frequently been the butt of sarcastic jokes. A manager of Jerusalem's King David Hotel used to carry a few bills in his pocket so that, whenever a visiting American complained of Israel's shortcomings, he could thrust the note into his hands and say, "We're even."[26]

The box score on the capital that has poured into the tiny Mediterranean state from its benefactors, the U.S. government and the American people, scarcely constitutes a joke. It is staggering: $42 billion or $10,700 per Israeli citizen. (See table on next page.)

Contributions from West Germany to Israel by way of reparations, restitutions, and loans reached an additional figure of $4.314 billion, which were only made possible by the U.S. forgiveness of $2 billion in reparations from Germany. In every way possible, Hitler has done

U.S. AID TO ISRAEL (IN MILLIONS)[27]

SOURCE	FISCAL YEARS			
	1948–1975	1976-1977	1978-1981	1948-1981
U.S Government Assistance (Military & Economic)	$6,562.3	$4,525.0	$10,531.9	$21,619.2
Private Institutions	3,363.0	[3]1,013.0	1,987.0	6,363.0
Private Individuals	[1]2,301.0	[4]578.0	[4]1,935.0	4,814.0
Israel Bonds*	[2]2,611.0	[5]546.0	[5]1,619.2	4,776.2
Loans (commercial)	2,060.0	[6]240.0	[6]480.0	2,780.0
Investments	1,410.0	[7]139.0	[7]157.0	1,706.0
TOTALS	$18,307.3	$7,041.0	$16,710.1	† $42,058.4
	(or $10,700 per Israeli citizen)			

1. This figure represents the minimal U.S. 75% of all private individual transfers worldwide.
2. This figure represents the minimal U.S. 75% of total Israel Bond purchases worldwide.
3. Principally UJA. According to the Library of Congress research, a spokesman stated these sums represented pledges not yet fully collected or transmitted.
4. Figures supplied by Russell Misheloff, Near East Bureau A.I.D.
5. According to a spokesman, the U.S. purchases represented 85% of total worldwide sales, which figures were set forth in the *New York Times*, January 9, 1978.
6. Figures not available . . . this represents a minimal based on the average of investments during the 1948–1975 period, which is exceedingly low.
7. Israel Central Bureau, Monthly Bulletin of Statistics, Supplement May 1978 and May 1982.
*Not subject to the Interest Equalization Tax as are other foreign securities.
†This is exclusive of $1.24 billion given to UNRWA, the agency that provides Palestinian refugees with a bare minimum of subsistence. And the closure of the Suez Canal cost the U.S. and the Free World an estimated $3.4 billion annually from 1967 to 1975.

more than his share for the State of Israel.

This accounting does not of course, include other vital benefits to Israel given on a scale proportional to her share in financial and military aid, as Harvard's Nadav Safran pointed out:

Hundreds of American technicians and Israeli trainees who have been exchanged; dozens of Israeli cultural, educational and philanthropic institutions who enjoyed American assistance from counterpart funds. Likewise, the Israeli public has been able to buy American cultural and educational material payable in Israeli currency at the official rate. In short, Israel has been given the status of a most favored nation, and not only in the technical sense in which the word is used in international trade. . . . There is scarcely one important educational, cultural, social or philanthropic institution in Israel which is not supported to some degree by Jewish-American, as well as US Government aid. . . .[28]

The majority of Israel's doctors, professors, scientists, and other professionals receive part of their training, if not most, in the U.S. At the Hebrew University in Jerusalem, sixty-one of the ninety-three visiting professors in 1976 were from the U.S., and some 1,400 American undergraduates attended courses in 1974, the largest of about fifty national groups.

Not only did the American taxpayer carry the financial burden of the 1973 war, but statistics prove that the U.S. emerged the only loser. The Arabs gained new confidence and self-respect from their surprising near-victory. The Israelis took consolation in the fact that by virtue of the American arms lift they managed to pull off a military comeback, almost wiping out the Egyptian Third Corps. General Ira C. Eaker, who commanded Allied Air Forces in the Mediterranean in World War II, pertinently noted that the 1973 war:

. . . cost this country at least $4 billion. It used up scarce reserves of weapons and supplies and lost the critical Arab oil. General Motors, during the embargo, laid off 65,000 workers and put 5,700 more on temporary furlough, and the entire U.S. economy was affected inasmuch as this move had repercussions on GM's 13,000 dealers and 45,000 suppliers. There was hardly a company or person in the U.S. who did not suffer in some way from the shortage of materials, rising costs or even unemployment stemming from the embargo. Completely forgotten, too, was the cost to the United States and Europe of the closing of the Canal from 1967 to 1975, well over $10 billion.[29]

Losses to the U.S. from its Middle East foreign policy cannot be calculated in dollars alone. There has been a vast nonmonetary price paid for the government's inordinate support of Israel, although the Zumwalt-Keegan-Churba school of thought vociferously argues that the U.S. pays a very small price for having the Zionist state perform as our Middle East watchdog, preventing the area from going Communist. Retired Admiral Elmo Zumwalt remained Israel's great champion in military circles; in a 1977 speech at Chapel Hill, North Carolina, the former Chief of Naval Operations advocated annexing Israel and sending a large U.S. force to be stationed permanently to defend that country if necessary. General George Keegan stated in an interview that "for every dollar of support this country has given Israel, we have gotten a thousand dollars worth of benefits in return—access to equipment, access to documents, etc., which prepare us to cope with the Soviet forces and equipment around the world. The data is of incalculable value."[30] And Joseph Churba played the same tune whenever and wherever he could.

Such reasoning is a gross perversion of the truth. The gravest dangers to U.S. interests in the Middle East have arisen from creation of the Israeli state, forcing certain Arab countries to turn to the Soviet

Union for help against demonstrated Zionist expansionism.

The many warnings that the creation of a Zionist state in the heart of an Arab world against the will of the majority would bring the Soviet Union into the area were totally ignored. Russia, which had striven for warm water ports and an "open sesame" to the region as far back as Peter and Catherine the Great, only needed one big opportunity. And when America's "Israel-First" stance and the Arabs' "Not-at-all" policy gave Moscow that big chance, Israelists and anti-Communist pundits alike cried out with a perfectly straight face: "Communism is threatening us through the Arabs. We must give Israel all-out support, military and otherwise, to save the area and U.S. interests."

This kind of ludicrous reasoning has not only prevailed but has rarely been prominently challenged until the appearance of the article on the Arab-Israeli military balance, "How Much Is Too Much?" in the October 1977 issue of *Armed Forces Journal.* Written by Anthony H. Cordesman, former civilian assistant to Deputy Secretary of Defense Robert Ellsworth and Secretary of the Defense Intelligence Board, the article claimed that "Israel has become a militaristic state whose military buildup has gone far beyond the requirements of defense." On the other hand, he wrote, the Arabs "still lack effective air training and command, control and communications systems," and their "vast amounts of air defense weaponry" have not been organized into an effective system. They still "cannot train effectively for armored maneuver warfare," and their aircraft generally lacks modern air-to-air missles.

With the emergence of the Likud Begin government, Cordesman contended:

The U.S. may no longer be supplying an Israel whose military struggle would lead to Israeli willingness to compromise for peace. It may now find itself aiding a country which may use its military strength to take permanent control of former Arab territory in direct opposition to U.S. policy, and be locked into an indefinite cold war with the Arabs. At worst, the U.S. may find itself tied to an ally which will use military force in a pre-emptive attempt to settle the PLO problem, or to destroy Arab military forces while they are weak.[31]

The article cited the advice of several of Begin's senior advisers to provoke Syria into war (which Israel nearly accomplished five months later during the March invasion of South Lebanon, but President Assad exercised the greatest restraint, out of respect for Israel's military might) "as an excuse to destroy its improving forces before they became threatening"[32] and to launch "attacks in support of Lebanese Christians against the PLO."

Before Cordesman could even prove how remarkably accurate a crystal ball he possessed, the Anti-Defamation League charged that he had used classified information gained during his employment in the Defense Department and that the article contained an anti-Israel and anti-Jewish slant; the League called for a Pentagon investigation. Most of the five-page ADL press statement contained attempted refutations by Keegan and Churba of the Cordesman allegation that "new Israeli attitudes threaten the strategic interests of the U.S. and its allies," which could lead to war, oil embargo, and inestimable damage to the dollar and the world monetary system.

What particularly inflamed the Zionists was the article's careful documentation, invaluable military statistical charts, and refutation of the large Israeli military requirements for assistance called for by their "Matmon B" plan. Cordesman claimed that the U.S. has never taken into account the "qualitative differences between Israeli and Arab forces and has chosen instead to set aid requirements based on the U.S. view of the future strength of Arab confrontation forces or the threat." The charts, he maintained, proved that planned U.S. aid exceeded "far beyond the limit necessary to assure Israel's security" and created an Israel "which has all of the capabilities necessary to wage offensive warfare."

The ADL was so exercised by publication of the article that, in addition to their demand for a Defense Department investigation, which resulted in an ambiguous refutation of the premise on which the protest was based, they harassed the editors of *Armed Forces Journal* into accepting a lengthy rebuttal by Churba, in which "none of the data are referenced,"[33] and flooded the magazine with letters.

Prior to Sadat's peace initiative, other sources confirmed Israeli preparations, in the event of the failure of Carter's efforts, for a "war of annihilation" against the Egyptian and Syrian armies before the Big Powers could intervene to bring about a cease-fire as in 1973. Israel by the end of 1977 had already "stockpiled enough weapons, ammunition, and fuel to fight a three-front conventional war for thirty days before needing fresh supplies from the U.S., according to estimated American arms exports.[34] The idea was to destroy the Arabs militarily for seven to twelve years, thus getting through the period when Arab oil and money could be used to squeeze concessions from Israel. Through its existing eighteen-month, $2 billion military pipeline of new equipment, Israel was said by American officials to be in a position to do what it wanted. On a scale of 100 equaling their military capabilities in 1973, Israel in October 1977 stood at 160, Syria at 100, and Egypt at 80 to 90.[35]

The basic American fear of Communism and the danger of the U.S.S.R. making further inroads into the Middle East has been fully exploited by Israel and her friends. U.S. policy makers, wittingly or unwittingly, have turned their backs on the best possible ally against any Communist threat, namely the strong theism of Islam. Deep Muslim spirituality is rooted in natural repugnance of a totalitarianism that wipes out religion. If the strengthening of anti-Communism is deemed to be a primary aim of U.S. foreign policy, then U.S. behavior in the Middle East has certainly been totally counterproductive.

Close American ties to the Free World have invariably been subordinated to concern for Israel. At the critical moment of the Hungarian uprising, which coincided with the 1956 Suez war, U.S. hands were tied by "Israel First." With the exception of Portugal, relations with our NATO allies were strained almost to the breaking point during the 1973 airlift by their refusal to allow landing rights for U.S. planes carrying arms to Israel. When the oil embargo was imposed, the subsequent energy problems and differences over the solution further mired relations with Europe, and with Japan as well.

Since the early 1960s when the U.S. prodded West Germany to serve as an arms supply depot for Israel, differences between Bonn and Washington have intensified, the chasm widened by denunciatory full-page *New York Times* ads charging "the bell of danger was tolling in Germany for the third time in this century."[36] Many of the problems between Washington and the France of de Gaulle, Pompidou, and D'Estaing stemmed from America's deep obsession over Israel. The whipped-up hysteria after the sale of jets to Libya and the Abu Daoud affair, scarcely served American national interests.

The campaigns of Zionism against India and Japan, complicated American relations as did Israel's harmful tourist boycott of Mexico. The list could go on and on. There is scarcely a country with whom U.S. relations have not been adversely affected over Israel. The U.S. no longer had French-U.S. relations; it had French-U.S.-Israeli relations. And at the U.N. America virtually isolated itself, frequently standing alone in defense of Israeli actions and policies. By 1978 this fact further complicated the brand-new problems Washington was encountering in the East African region known as the Horn, caused by the Somali-Ethiopian strife in which Israel was sending U.S.-made weapons to Ethiopia, who was being backed by the Soviet Union and

Cuba, against assistance being given to the former by the U.S., Egypt, and Saudi Arabia.

Little wonder that by September 1977 President Carter was cautioning: "Dozens of other foreign policy matters have suffered to some degree because I've expended so much effort on this issue. If our efforts fail this year, it will be difficult for us to continue to devote that much time and effort to the Mideast."[37]

There are many other reasons dictating that the U.S. sever the unique umbilical cord attaching it to the Zionist state and alienting invaluable Arab connections. Propagandists and idealists summarily dismiss any consideration given by Washington to her relationship with Saudi Arabia as purely an immoral and commercial interest. But more objective Americans cannot help feeling how ungrateful the Israelis must be to think that the U.S. will be a continuing source of infinite remittances and of policies winning enemies and losing friends for itself so as to keep the Israelis alive in the style and territory to which they have grown accustomed. There is a growing realization that we need Arab friendship, too!

If Israel is to be made an exception to our first President's admonition against "favored nations," U.S. national interests cry out for an equally special relationship with the Saudis (or other oil-rich Arabs), however Washington may have committed itself to the security of the Israelis. The U.S. 1977 trade deficit was $23.5 billion, and oil imports amounted to $41.5 billion. The trade deficit of $4.5 billion for the month of February 1978 was the worst in U.S. history. In its 1977 report the CIA revealed that worldwide oil demands were likely to outstrip the supply within five to ten years. The U.S., already importing 1.2 million barrels of oil daily from Saudi Arabia, was hoping to double these imports by 1980.

The Arab oil-rich states have a minimum of $34 billion in our largest banking institutions—Bank of America, Chase, First National, and Morgan Guaranty. The Saudis, helping to alleviate the world energy crisis, have been producing far more oil than their revenue needs, and hence piling up surpluses of investments in the U.S. In the heated dispute over the advisability of such investments, Chairman Howard G. Blauvelt of Continental Oil Company noted:

Resistance to Arab investments in the U.S. is understandable, but misquoted. There already are thousands of businesses in the U.S. owned or controlled by foreigners with an estimated book value of more than $40 billion. On the other hand, the book value of American investments overseas is now more than $100 billion. For example, some economists have projected a short-fall of $650 billion investment capital in the U.S. alone over the next ten years, a gap which OPEC investments in this country can in small part help close.[38]

The Saudis likewise have been the restraining force in OPEC on price increases, and in 1976 when other OPEC nations decided on a 10 percent increase, they refused (along with the United Arab Emirates) to raise prices. The condition behind forgoing this increase was, as Zaki Yamani expressed it, some "forward movement toward peace," the achievement of which would not preclude the use of American pressure on Israel. The Saudis were worried, of course, about the rising inflationary costs for the purchase of their imports, which they claimed did not match any comparable rise in oil prices. There was an admitted reluctance on both sides, the Saudis and the U.S., to exacerbate the differences that already exist. As Carter warned in late May 1977, failure to act quickly could "mean disaster not only for the Middle East, but for the international political and economic order as well." The Saudis wanted peace, no break in their financial and commercial ties with the U.S., and certainly not another war. However, when pressed, they have not hesitated—without specifying the use of the oil boycott as a weapon—to talk of using "every effort or every capability towards achieving peace," as phrased by Foreign Minister Prince Saud bin Faisal on the CBS show "Face the Nation" in May 1977.

The Saudis and other Gulf states certainly have not forgotten the contingency Pentagon plans for an invasion of Arab oil fields. They must also realize that in the event of another embargo, their accounts would be frozen in this country. Weakened by the death of King Faisal, the new Riyadh government has since been striving to unite the Arab world as a means of avoiding another ravaging conflict, if for no other reason than to protect its own economic well-being.

If the Sadat initiative should lead not to a general settlement but only to another Israel-Egyptian separate agreement, area unrest is bound to mount as the PLO and the Palestinians press for their rights. In a fifth war Israel is almost certain to emerge victorious. Aside from the bloodletting and the risk of the possible use of nonconventional weapons, what then? A just, lasting peace would be further away than ever, and additional rounds inevitable until justice was done.

The growing financial power of the Arabs, and the decreasing technological gap between them and their enemy, must eventually bring them victory. The Arabs can afford to lose another round or two

—the Israelis cannot afford to lose one. In addition, the support for Israel in the international community has been rapidly vanishing. Indeed, from the outset this was greatly exaggerated and always minimal. The alleged historical connection of the Jewish people did sway the U.N. General Assembly in November 1947, only two years after Hitler's downfall. But Rabbi Silver's brilliant rhetoric in his call for "the reconstitution of our national home"[39] would fall totally flat today, particularly after the Koestler disclosure that the "home" for which the Zionist has yearned had never indeed been theirs.

The world never did give its approval to the Palestine partition plan in 1947. There were then only fifty-seven member nations in the U.N.; thirty-three, or 58 percent, of these voted favorably for the resolution while thirteen were opposed, ten abstained, and one was absent. There are now 152 members, and a vote on the same resolution would scarcely gain ten supporters. As far as world public opinion is concerned, today there would be little objection to returning to the 1948 borders provided there were ironclad international guarantees safeguarding the lives of the Israeli people.

What about the U.S.? Does Israel enjoy the deep-seated support among Americans that Zionists claim? The polls show that Americans strongly favor Israel over the Arabs, but there is an even more overwhelming sentiment against any commitment to Israel involving military forces, and a growing reluctance to provide further military and financial support.

According to an opinion poll conducted for *Time* magazine by Yankelovich, Skelly, and White (March 1975), Americans by two-to-one opposed sending arms to either Israel or the Arabs; 41 percent favored a cutback while 37 percent backed continued support, and only 8 percent favored an increase. An NBC poll January 31, 1975, showed 78 percent opposing and only 13 percent approving a U.S. guarantee of Israel's security. The February 1975 issue of *US News & World Report* ran opinion research figures showing 57 percent opposition to U.S. military aid to Israel with 27 percent in favor. A January 1976 survey by NBC reported that less than one in five would back a move to send troops to Israel. And the Foreign Policy Association survey, "Great Decisions '76," approved the right of Palestinian Arabs to an independent state by 66 percent to 19 percent. Even in heavily Jewish populated New York City, a *Daily News* opinion poll in late March 1978 registered by 44 to 42 percent disapproval of sending more planes to Israel, while 52 percent opted against selling arms or aircraft to any Middle East country.

The Gallup Poll found that Israel was losing considerable ground. While the sympathies of 46 percent of a 1500-person sample in the previous October before the Sadat initiative had been with Israel, this had shrunk to 33 percent in its latest survey of 654 people, according to *Newsweek*, February 27, 1978. Compared to a year ago, 42 percent of those questioned stated they were more sympathetic to Egypt and 20 percent less, while 27 percent admitted to be more sympathetic to Israel and 34 percent less.

Bias has placed the shoe on the wrong foot. As if they had committed the original grievance and were the party at fault, it is the PLO from whom Israel and the U.S. demand recognition of "the right of Israel to exist" as a prior condition for participation in a process aimed to produce a mutually acceptable definition of Israel's permanent frontiers. It is as if a thief, who has stolen property, refused to return it until his existence as an American citizen was recognized and his great-great-grandfather's residency in the house he had just robbed had been confirmed.

As academician and member of the Palestine National Council Dr. Fayez Sayegh expressed it:

The right of a state to exist cannot be divorced from its location and frontiers. France has a right to exist: but does it have a right to exist on Algerian soil? Will those who exhort the PLO to "recognize the right of Israel to exist" be good enough to tell the PLO just *where* that "right" is supposed to be exercised? And are they prepared to guarantee that Israel itself will accept that territorial stipulation?[40]

Hardly. Zionist expansionist aspirations are limitless. Even during the Sadat-Begin negotiations, the cabinet voted to expand the existing settlements in Sinai by putting more acreage under cultivation and moving in more settlers to Jewish communities near the Rafah salient and Sharm el Sheikh.

Furthermore, the requirement of recognition should be one of mutuality. Yet Carter never has demanded that Israel recognize the right to existence of an independent Palestinian state, let alone ever considered Israel's lack of compliance with that hypothetical demand a barrier to U.S. recognition of Israel. Is it not more reasonable to consider mutual recognition an end result of a settlement rather than an *a priori* condition for participation in the negotiating process?

The Western world and the Christian conscience has been asked to accept Israel's existence unreservedly and to force the Palestinians to do likewise. "You cannot turn the clock back" is the stock argument advanced against righting past wrongs. But it is not a question of turning the clock back; it is a question of winding the clock up properly so that it will work. The Hitler tragedy moved the world in 1948 to turn the clock back 2,000 years by establishing in the heart of the Middle East a Jewish state where none had existed since 70 A.D. Can it be wrong to try to correct a grievous error, thirty years later, if this will be beneficial to all peoples concerned?

In the face of the total dependence of Israel for its viability and existence, no U.S. President should hesitate to apply all the necessary leverage at his command, both to reach a just settlement and to resist efforts to disrupt U.S. relations with Arab countries. It would not be unreasonable for Carter to remind Zionists and Israelists in this country that rarely has a people so deeply in debt exacted conditions for reasonable behavior from its patron and banker, as has the arrogant-minded Zionist leadership, supported by a fear-ridden, Masada-complexed Israeli people. To hear the words of Senators Javits and Jackson, one would imagine the shoe was on the other foot and the U.S. was deep in debt to Israel.

Any close, objective study of the history of the conflict should inspire the President to say to the Israelis, as one writer has put it:

For the U.S. to have aided and abetted the dispossession of the greater part of the Palestinian population is an act of barbarism. For American Jews to continue to edge the U.S. into the Middle East imbroglio where America has everything to lose and nothing to gain is an act of sheer ingratitude to the nation which has given them more wealth, freedom and power than any other in the long curve of their history. Americans have more constructive and more moral things to do than to expend their money, their arms and perhaps their lives on a racial dream that is not even their own.[41]

Although the Arab's congenital incapacity for collaboration constantly plagues himself and his friends alike, the many Arab minuses do not add up to a Zionist plus in terms of the American national interest.

If necessary, Carter can carry out the recommendations made to President Truman in 1949 by the State Department when the Israelis balked at returning territories won by conquest, and refused to do the just thing for the new refugees they had created.[42] By action that every one of his predecessors would have liked to have carried out but lacked the intestinal fortitude to accomplish, the man from Georgia could make the greatest contribution toward geniune peace in the Middle East.

Any solution of the differences between the Arabs and the Israelis must be based not only on the resolutions of the U.N. that created Israel, but on the universal demand for a just settlement of a problem that had its origins in the Western world. To justify the right of the West to gain expiation of the crimes of Hitler at the expense of the Arab world remains unconscionable. Justice for Palestine, in the words of Professor Toynbee, "requires vindication of people's rights and the righting of wrongs and the least possible suffering of the least possible number of people."[43]

It has been Zionism and its philosophy, not the particular leadership in power, that has molded Israeli intransigency and inflexibility. The fall of Begin (alleged by the Israeli Establishment in March 1978 to be Carter's aim) would not solve the basic problem.

Golda Meir indicated a mentality quite incapable of winning the correct Arab response to peace: "After we have signed peace treaties with our neighbors and agreed on the borders, the nature of the State of Israel will be Jewish with a large Jewish majority so that we don't have to get up every morning afraid to ask, 'Who was born last night —was it a Jew or an Arab?' "[44] The entreating Arab phone call for which she and other Israeli leaders waited for six years never was made. Instead, in October 1973 came the Egyptian and Syrian armies.

Opposition leader Shimon Peres attacked his successor for inflexibility on the issue of settlements during the peace talks with Sadat. But as Defense Minister in April 1976, he planned "to develop a vast area of two million dunum (about 800 square miles)." He proposed to set up "110 settlements in the future in the Rafah-Beersheba-Kadesh Barnea triangle."[45] Before Ezer Weizman wrested an agreement from Begin by threatening to resign unless further settlements were suspended until after the March 1978 talks in Washington, the Israeli Defense Minister himself had his own plans for setting up two large Jewish urban centers in the West Bank that would plant 100,000 Israelis in the disputed region within two years.[46] Directly after the Israelis failed in May to upset the Carter jet plane package deal, Weizman proposed that six controversial Israeli settlements on the occupied West Bank be expanded into solid urban centers—a move hardly calculated to clear the atmosphere for a resumption of the stalled peace negotiations. While General Sharon emphasized in his plan the necessity of setting up a wedge of Jewish settlements extending from the Golan down to Sharm el-Sheikh, the two generals differed only as to detail and timing. UJA funds were to make the settlements possible. (The cost of existing settlements in all the occupied territories, made possible through UJA tax-deductible funds, was estimated by *Time* magazine of June 19, 1978, at $2 billion, the fifty-one West Bank communities having alone received half of this amount.)

To enlarge their settlements, the Israelis moved in 1978 to confiscate further West Bank property owned by Arabs abroad. Bethlehem Mayor Elias Freij was informed in April that 80,000 acres around his town owned by Arabs living in the U.S., Canada, and Latin America would be handed over to the Israeli "custodian of absentee property," which since 1967 has controlled all property owned by persons residing in Arab countries.[47] Anthony Lewis of the *New York Times* reported from Ramallah that as many as 11,000 houses were involved, including many owned by Arab-Americans. West Bank Palestinians, he noted, viewed this latest action as further humiliation designed to make them get out and to ease the way for a permanent Israeli hold on the territory. A surgeon told the reporter: "By hook or crook they want us to leave the country."[48]

The hour for truth has almost passed us. History will someday certainly record that it was far from heretical to have declared that there was neither a need for a state for the "Jewish people," and certainly little justification for establishing such a state in its present locale.[49] Meanwhile, there is little sense in further meaningless talks about Israel's legitimate right to exist unless we define precisely what Israel we are talking about. A normal Israel propagating Israeli nationalism in behalf of the people living within its borders could gain coexistence with a Palestinian state and all other Arab nations in the exact same manner in which Arabs and Jews lived together side by side for centuries before the advent of Zionism. But an abnormal Israel promulgating worldwide Jewish nationalism means only perpetual warfare. More than physical boundaries, the limitless nationality base of the present Israeli state obstructs all hope of a peaceful tomorrow and underlies much of Arab fear. The "lebensraum" the Zionist state requires for its ingatherees poses a perpetual threat of limitless expansion.

Contrary to what most people believe, neither the Israeli occupation of Arab territory nor even the settlements are the most serious obstacle to a solution. These are merely manifestations of an ideology that constitutes the greatest hazard to peace. Israel's abnormality commenced with its self-promulgation on May 15, 1948, as the state not of Israeli people living in the territory, but of the "Jewish people" everywhere. The Law of Return provided a built-in expansionism that no boundaries, however they may be drawn at Geneva or elsewhere, can ever control. No sanction can be found for this kind of an exclusivist, racist state upon which the present Israeli leadership insists under the pretext of security. The representatives of the thirty-three nations who in 1947 recommended Israel's creation were moved totally by humanitarian considerations in giving approval to a small refugee state. They never contemplated a nation with an ever-expanding nationalism depriving the indigenous populace of its rights as well as spilling over into the territory of its neighbors. Under the boundaries drawn up, the Jewish state was to have had a 42 percent Arab minority, and there was no guarantee whatsoever that the original Jewish majority was to be maintained in the face of the far higher Arab birthrate. The international organization thus provided the basis for a *binational* Arab-Israeli state, which was to be joined in economic union with an Arab Palestinian state and the holy city of Jerusalem internationalized.

Is the sovereignty of the Israeli state so sacrosanct that the mere suggestion of its dimunition to fit the original U.N. concept is automatically *verboten*? Who can deny that the real concern of Americans and of the international community is and has always been for the lives of the people of Israel rather than for the size or form of the entity in which they live. Whether it is called "dismantling" or "remantling" of the state, what is so destructive about Jewish Israelis sharing a whole country with the original Palestinian Arab inhabitants? This is the way one can reconcile the vast number of Jewish settlements imposed upon the Arab-occupied territories. This is how the "original sin" may be righted. And this is the only way, rather than through armed might or guileful encouragement of Christian forces in furthering the partition of Lebanon, to obtain the security about which there has been so much loose talk.

As Israeli Hebrew University professor Avigdor Levontin expressed it:

A secure border—to the extent that such a thing exists in our world—is not a "natural" boundary, like a mountain range or a river. That is an anachronistic conception. Nor is it a border mentioned in signed documents. A border is secure when those living on the other side do not have sufficient motivation to infringe on it. No matter how banal this may be, we have to remind ourselves that the roots of security are in the minds of men and that is where the source of insecurity also lies. We have fallen into a vicious circle: since there is no trust in the Arabs' desire for peace, people emphasize the need for "security" apparently for a substitute, and even say that one really couldn't rely on the peace agreement with the Arabs even if they agreed to it since it wouldn't be a "true peace. . . ."

I would go on to say about the term "secure" borders that it has to face not only the test of reasonableness, but also the test of the inherent integrity of the concept itself. The term ceases to be honest one when you expand settlements up to the new border so that in order to make the new line "secure" you need still another strip of some tens of kilometers, and in that way things are liable to continue in what may perhaps be described as a salami method in reverse.[50]

The Zionist movement should not be permitted to exploit indefinitely the holocaust, its ultimate and final weapon, so as to obstruct the final hope of assuring true justice and real security for all peoples of the area, of ending the dangerous duality for American and other Diaspora Jews, and of removing the number-one threat to world peace.

Last Word

These words are being written as Israeli bombs from American planes are again raining death and destruction on Beirut, its environs and south Lebanon. Begin timed the combined air, land and sea invasion to coincide with Reagan's economic summit meeting at Versailles with his six industrial partners and his European tour.

Calling it a reprisal raid against the PLO for the near-fatal shooting in London of Israeli Ambassador to the U.K. Shlomo Argov, the media (most particularly CBS Newsradio 88) indulged in its customary slanting by giving scant attention to either the fact that the assailants were Jordanian, Iraqi and Syrian or that the PLO had denied responsibility from the very outset. Ignored or underplayed by all the media was Margaret Thatcher's announcement that a hit list found on the assailants included the name of the head of the London PLO office.

Anticipating (or knowing) the worst, the President immediately ordered the evacuation from Beirut of half of American diplomatic personnel and dispatched a letter to Begin with Ambassador Habib urging moderation.

After the Security Council twice had called for a cease-fire and withdrawal of Israeli forces from Lebanon, which Israel ignored, a third resolution demanded that Israel and the Palestinians halt hostilities in six hours and said, if they did not, the Council would "consider practical ways and means" to enforce this proposal approved by the fourteen other Council members.

In his unprecedented speech in Whitehall before a joint session of both houses of Parliament, Reagan echoed Israel's point of view in placing the blame for Middle East war on the "scourge of terrorism," which, he indicated, had to be "stamped out ." He refused to view the conflict in its fullest perspective.

The administration's behavior was further evidence of what one Middle East writer has called Washington's permanent "calculated non-settlement" policy of not really making an honest effort to resolve the

806

problem, but simply "maneuvering to protect our interests in Middle East oil and to assure the well-being of Israel."

Only such a non-policy could account for the near-fatal collapse of the Palestine autonomy talks, the war in Lebanon, the unrest on the West Bank and the nonsensical inconsistencies in the U.S. treatment of Iran. Aid was being given to Iranian exiles battling the Ayatollah while Israel was permitted in 1981 and 1982 to ship U.S. arms to assist the Khomeini regime in its war with Iran. "Tango November," a chartered Argentinian CL 44, carried 360 tons of tank spare parts and ammunition to Iran before the plane mysteriously crashed in Soviet Armenia. (Israel also sent arms to Argentina during the Falkland Islands war.)

Washington gave covert approval to Israel's support of Teheran in the long Iraqi-Iranian war and to Tel Aviv's goal of downing the Sadaam Hussein regime until Washington became alarmed lest an impending Iraqi defeat endanger other "moderate" friendly Arab Gulf regimes.

Public opinion has been swinging toward recognition of Palestinian rights, some polls indicating that a majority, including a fair sampling of Jews, even favor the establishment of a Palestinian state. But most sentiment for justice for the indigenous people of Palestine still remains very muted with the few illustrious exceptions.

Visiting the U.N. for sixty-two minutes as a high-light of his two-day visit to New York City in October 1979, Pope John Paul II told assembled diplomats:

Any attempt made to settle the conflict would have no value if it did not truly represent the first step of a general, overall peace in the area. Peace, being necessarily based on equitable recognition of the rights of all, cannot fail to include a consideration and just settlement of the Palestinian question.

The subsequent summer, scarcely noted amidst the heat and the national political campaign, was *L'Osservatore Romano's* major review of the "history and contemporary reality of Jerusalem" whose 'uniqueness requires for all three religions a level of parity without any of them feeling subordinate with regard to the others." The voice of the Vatican emphasized that all three religions must be "partners in deciding their own future.... We cannot reduce the question to mere free access to the holy places .... The significance of Jerusalem surpasses the interests of a single state." The viewpoint concluded that what was required was an "appropriate juridicial safeguard that does not derive from the will of only one of the parties interested."

Of course, a George Ball in a *Foreign Affairs* article or a Zbigniew

Brzezinski speaking to a small group of Washington reporters might urge the U.S. to start dealing with "the reality of the PLO." But foreign policy molders will not stick their chins out lest they be called anti-Semitic. John Doe, spellbound by myth-information, still bows to the Jewish-Zionist connectors. In the absence of respectable American leadership galvinating this sentiment into a broad-based popular movement, there is not likely to be any change in U.S. policy, particularly in the light of the continuing terrorist PLO image. Who is strong enough to remove the gun ever-pointed at the White House by the combined hands of supine politicians, the controlled media and the Zionist lobby?

With the April 25 Israeli turn-over to Egypt of the last portion of the Sinai, U.S. ground-combat troops for the first time became involved in Middle East peace efforts since Lebanon in 1958. Eight-hundred paratroops from the 82nd Airborne Division became the heart of the 2,500 eleven-nation force patrolling the buffer zone between Israel and Egypt following the Sinai evacuation and 400 at Eitam Airbase headquarters in nothern Sinai as part of the peacekeeping force, MFO. These soldiers were ready to be used as part of the U.S. Rapid Deployment Force to intervene anywhere in the Gulf area wherever needed.

The U.S. military presence in the Middle East has dangerously expanded from the 200 technicians monitoring surveillance stations in the Sinai's Mitla and Gidi passes. Without a miraculous breakthrough, the tragedy of nuclear war could envelope this area and the world as the arms race continues to dangerously escalate.

The June 6 Israeli invasion of Lebanon, which fell on the 15th anniversary of the 1967 war, brought new dangers and new horrors alike—not only the most extensive bombing of Beirut, Tyre and Sidon, but the total destruction of small towns, villages and refugee camps. The Israeli Army systematically blew up and bulldozed Palestinian homes that survived the battle, completely leveling the camp at Ain el-Halweh in the same manner as it had fifteen years earlier the Golan Heights capital, Quneitra.

Forty-thousand Palestinians and Lebanese were killed or wounded and upwards of 600,000 people were left homeless. The Israelis, supported by the Phalangist militia of Beshir Geymayel, laid siege to west Beirut, the last Palestinian stronghold, which was subjected to both unmerciful and mock air raids to force an unconditional PLO surrender.

The Israelis were still proclaiming "Peace for Galilee" as their sole war goal—the freeing of northern villages from the constant threat of

Palestinian guns. "We do not want an inch of territory" intonated both Begin and Sharon who in the quick conquest of Lebanon had once more demonstrated his military acumen.

In the midst of the on-going genocide in Lebanon, Reagan received Begin in the Oval Office at the White House. In refusing to rebuke the Israeli leader, the President overruled the advice of Vice President George Bush, Defense Secretary Weinberger, National Security Advisor William Clark and other White House aides, and sided with Secretary of State Haig, whose resignation he accepted a few days later. With his shameful surrender Reagan was contradicting Begin's angry response to Washington's suspension of the strategic cooperation agreement: "No, we are the banana republic. We are your vassal state!"

At a nationally televised press conference, the President claimed "we were not warned or notified of the invasion that was going to take place." Despite this denial, there was little doubt that Israel's unconscionable use of miliary power, as in the 1967 war, had been carried out with the aid and abetment of Washington and the media, under a cover of gross deceit that beguiled American public opinion and guaranteed support for the continued ruthless suppression of Palestinian rights. But it remained to be seen whether, out of the crushing military defeat, the political and diplomatic struggle for an independent Palestinian state would be advanced.

At Senate confirmation hearings Secretary of State-designate George P. Shultz stated: "The crisis in Lebanon makes painfully clear a central reality of the Middle East: the legitimate needs and problems of the Palestinian people must be addressed and resolved—urgently and in all their dimensions." At the time the Israelis were heightening their repression and moving toward annexation of the West Bank and Gaza.

The sad and tragic realities of the Middle East conflict were further exposed at a top-secret summit held by Brezhnev, Reagan and Begin with the Lord. The Soviet leader asked God: "Do you think there will ever be detente between the Soviet Union and the United States?" The Lord replied, "Yes, but not in your lifetime."

Then Reagan queried: "Do you think it will ever be possible for the U.S. to achieve a balanced budget and at the same time maintain a defense establishment strong engough to contain the threat of communism?" The Lord's response was "Yes, but not in your lifetime."

Begin then put this final question to God: "Do you think there will ever be peace between Arabs and Israelis?" To this the Lord answered: "Yes, but not in *my* lifetime."

Alfred M. Lilienthal
New York, July 14, 1982

Notes

Bibliographical Note: FR is used in the References as an abbreviation for *Foreign Relations of the United States, Diplomatic Papers,* cited by year and volume. These volumes are publications of the Department of State, and contain diplomatic correspondence, cables, memorandums, reports of conversations, etc. Usually, they are published twenty-five years after the events to which they pertain. The U. S. Government Printing Office in Washington, D.C. may issue several in any given year. All bear the title *Foreign Relations of the United States, Diplomatic Papers.*

Chapter I: Sixty-seven Words: One Man's Dream, Another's Nightmare

1. H. G. Wells, *Outline of History* (New York: Doubleday, 1956).
2. Their literature indicated real nationalist thinking: "Sleepest thou, O our nation? What hast thou been doing until 1882. Sleep and dream the false dream of assimilation." Walter Lacqueur, *The Israel-Arab Reader* (New York, Bantam, 1943), p. 3.
3. The Sultan was willing to receive Jewish emigrants in all his Asian provinces save Palestine, provided they became Ottoman subjects, accepted military service, and settled "in a disbursed manner, five families here and five families there."
4. See Theodor Herzl, "Tagebücher" (Tel Aviv, 1934) and Nevil Barbour, *Palestine: Star or Crescent?* (New York: Odyssey Press, 1947).
5. Herzl was also interested in the possibility of a Jewish colony in the neighborhood of El Arish on the Egyptian-Palestine frontier. (This village figured importantly in the 1956 warfare between Egypt and Israel.) But Lord Cromer, the British High Commissioner in Cairo, scotched this proposal. Later, during the World War II period, a Jewish state or colony in vastly underpopulated Libya was advocated but the idea died quickly.
6. Desmond Stewart, *Theodor Herzl* (New York: Doubleday, 1974). This fascinating book was well displayed in the book windows of Jerusalem during the spring and summer following its publication.
7. Alex Bein, *Theodor Herzl* (Philadelphia: Jewish Publication Society of America, 1941), p. 89.
8. Quoted by Barbour, *op. cit.,* p. 56, based on N. M. Gelber, *Hatshart Balfour Vatoldoteha* (The Balfour Declaration and Its Coming Into Being) in Hebrew (Jerusalem, 1939) p. 190.
9. From Memorandum of Board of Deputies of British Jews and the Anglo-Jewish Association, published in the London *Times,* May 24, 1917.
10. As David Lloyd George relates in *The Truth About the Peace Treaties* (London: Victor Gollancz, 1938), pp. 1133–34, Edwin Montagu said he had "striven all his life to escape from the Ghetto," and the Cabinet minister therefore would not accept the original wording of the Balfour Declaration.

11. At the insistence of U.S. Supreme Court Justice Louis Brandeis, who was active in Zionist circles, the original draft referring to "the Jewish race" was softened to "the Jewish people."

12. Albert M. Hyamson, *Palestine: A Policy* (London: Methuen, 1942), p. 110.

13. Arab historian George Antonius called McMahon's reply "a curious example of official evasiveness." *The Arab Awakening* (Philadelphia: Lippincott, 1939), p. 45.

14. Letter of Professor William Yale to the author, August 14, 1957. Yale was military observer at General Allenby's headquarters of the Egyptian Expeditionary Force. Expert on Arab affairs to the Paris Peace Conference and adviser to the King-Crane Commission, Yale served both the Department of State and the U.N. as a specialist on the Middle East. Later he taught history at the Universities of New Hampshire and Boston and in 1958 authored *The Near East*, part of the University of Michigan's fifteen-volume *History of the Modern World.*

15. Dr. Fayez Sayegh first released the documents in the bimonthly magazine *Hiwar*, January–February 1964 (Beirut, Lebanon). The article was quoted at length in articles of April 17, 1964, and May 6, 1964, in the London *Times.*

16. The Memorandum and the Appendix were both prepared in 1919 by the Political Intelligence Department of the Foreign Office for use by the British Delegation to the Paris Peace Conference. In Section IV the Memorandum states: "With regard to Palestine, His Majesty's Government are committed by Sir Henry McMahon's letter to the Sherif [Sharif] on October 24, 1915, to its inclusion in the boundaries of Arab independence." The Appendix declares: "The whole of Palestine, within the limits set out in the body of the Memorandum, lies within the limits which H.M.G. have pledged themselves to Sherif Hussein that they will recognize and uphold the independence of the Arabs." On both documents appears the legend: "This Document is the Property of His Britannic Majesty's Government." Along with several others, these two documents are part of the *Westermann Papers*, a prized portion of the Middle East Collection of the Hoover Institution on War, Revolution and Peace, founded originally as the depository for the papers of President Herbert Hoover, situated at Stanford University, Stanford, California.

17. The *Century*, July 1920.

18. *Al Sharq*, January 23, 1917, as noted in George Antonius, *Arab Awakening* (Philadelphia: Lippincott, 1939), p. 208.

19. David Lloyd George, *The Truth About the Peace Treaties, op. cit.*, pp. 1131–41.

20. Arab fears were further allayed by leaflets dropped by British planes over Palestine early in 1917 addressed to "Arab officers and soldiers in the Turkish Army" assuring them that the British were fighting for "the freedom of Arabs generally."

21. Philip P. Graves, *Palestine, The Land of Three Faiths* (Westport, Conn.: Hyperion Press, 1976). This is a reprint of the 1923 edition published in New York by G. H. Doran, pp. 5–6.

22. Appended to the agreement was this proviso: "Provided the Arabs obtain their independence as demanded in my Memorandum dated the fourth of January, 1919, to the Foreign Office of the Government of Great Britain, I shall concur in the above articles. But if the slightest modification or departure were to be made, I shall not then be bound by a single word of the present Agreement, which shall be deemed void and of no account or validity, and I shall not be answerable in any way whatsoever." Antonius, *op. cit.*, p. 439.

23. *Ibid.*, p. 440–41.

24. T. E. Lawrence, *Seven Pillars of Wisdom* (London: Jonathan Cape, 1935), p. 275.

25. Emanuel Neumann, *The American Zionist*, February 5, 1953. The British Government did feel some gratitude to Weizmann for his process of developing TNT, vital in the manufacture of cordite needed in the war effort.

26. Royal Commission Report of July 1937. British Command Paper 5479.

27. According to Professor William E. Yale, who had been sent by the State Depart-

ment to the Middle East to gather information concerning "the Arab situation," the famed T. E. Lawrence indicated that Britain was "supporting the Zionists for the help it was thought they could be to us in Russia and because they brought America into the war." Lawrence stated: "The Arabs had great faith in the U.S. and they believed in America's political honesty." Report 18 of March 11, 1918, Document 763.7211/1741, Diplomatic Branch (NNFD) National Archives and Records Service.

28. J. W. V. Temperley, *History of the Peace Conference*, IV, p. 170.

29. Parliamentary Debates, House of Commons, Vol. 326, col. 23330. Weizmann himself describes an interview with Lord Robert (later Viscount) Cecil of Chelwood, the Assistant Secretary of State for Foreign Affairs, in which the Zionist leader stressed the point that a "Jewish Palestine would be a safeguard to England, in particular in respect to the Suez Canal." Chaim Weizmann, *Trial and Error* (New York: Harper & Brothers, 1949) p. 192.

30. Lloyd George, *op. cit.*, p. 1137.

31. Curzon went on to state: "If this is Zionism, there is no reason why we should not all be Zionists, and I would gladly give my allegiance to such a policy, all the more that it appears to be recommended by considerations of the highest expediency and to be urgently demanded as a check or counterblast to the scarcely concealed sinister designs of the Germans."

32. British Command Paper No. 1700, *A Survey of Palestine, 1945–1946*, Vol. I, pp. 87–90.

33. *Ibid.*

34. H. L., June 27, 1923: O.R., Col. 676. This was a negation of the suggestion that Weizmann made in his statement to the Council of Ten at the Peace Conference, February 1919, that Palestine was destined to become "as Jewish as England is English."

35. Albert M. Hyamson, *Palestine: A Policy* (London: Methuen, 1942), footnote p. 112.

36. Before the Council of the League of Nations. See Charles H. Levermore, *Third Year Book of the League of Nations* (1922), p. 137.

37. Hyamson, *op. cit.*, p. 110.

38. Weizmann, *op. cit.*, p. 261.

39. In April before the issuance of the Balfour Declaration, Weizmann said, "The Jews could work for one or two generations under British protection endeavoring to develop the land as far as possible and counting upon a time when a just Tribunal would give the rest of Palestine to which they have a historical claim." Barbour, *op. cit.*, p. 214.

40. Barbour, *op. cit.*, footnote p. 118.

41. Paul Goodman, ed., *Chaim Weizmann: A Tribute on His Seventieth Birthday* (London: Victor Gollancz, 1945), p. 199.

42. *Trial and Error: The Autobiography of Chaim Weizmann* (New York: Harper, 1949), p. 100.

43. Bert de Vries, *The Reformed Journal* (Grand Rapids, Mich.), "His Land and History," April, 1971.

44. J. N. Jeffries, *Palestine: the Reality* (Westport, Conn.: Hyperion Press, 1976), pp. 177–78.

Chapter II: America Picks Up the Torch

1. *Papers Relating to the Foreign Relations of the United States, the Paris Peace Conference, 1919*, XI, 150–55.

2. For the best and fullest exposition on the King-Crane Commission, see Harry N. Howard, *The King-Crane Commission: An American Inquiry in the Middle East* (Beirut: Khayat's, 1963).

3. *Ibid.*, p. 350.

4. British Command Paper No. 5479.

5. Nevil Barbour, *Palestine: Star or Crescent?* (New York: Odyssey Press, 1947), footnote p. 240.

6. British Command Paper No. 6019.

7. "The Palestine Mandate," *The Fortnightly* (London), December 1944; reprinted in *Middle East Perspective* (New York), April 1970.

8. *FR: 1943, The Near East and Africa*, Vol. IV (Washington, D.C.: 1964), pp. 776–77.

9. For a full discussion of the refugee problem, see Morris L. Ernst, *So Far So Good* (New York: Harper, 1948), pp. 170–77.

10. *Ibid.*, p. 176.

11. *FR: 1942*, Vol. IV, pp. 538–44.

12. *FR: 1945*, Vol. VIII, p. 699.

13. *FR: 1943*, Vol. IV, p. 798. See enclosure to letter of July 19, 1943, from Cordell Hull to President Roosevelt.

14. *Ibid.*, p. 809. Memorandum of Colonel Harold B. Hoskins of August 31, 1943.

15. *FR: 1944*, Vol. V, p. 588. Telegram 56, March 21, 1944.

16. *FR: 1945*, Vol. VIII, p. 679.

17. *Ibid.*, pp. 680–82.

18. *Ibid.*, pp. 688–89. One of the suggestions made by Rabbi Stephen Wise and Dr. Nahum Goldmann in their lengthy meeting with Acting Secretary of State Joseph C. Grew was that the Department appoint an officer who might specialize exclusively in Jewish interests abroad. Grew rejected the proposal, replying that existing Department officers had a "good grasp of the Jewish and Palestine question."

19. *Ibid.*, pp. 2–3.

20. *Ibid.*, p. 702.

21. For a full first-hand account of the meeting, see William A. Eddy, *F.D.R. Meets Ibn Saud* (New York: American Friends of the Middle East, 1954); also John S. Keating, "Mission to Mecca: A Postscript," *U.S. Naval Proceedings*, Vol. 104, No. 902 (April 1978).

22. *FR: 1945, The Near East and Africa*, Vol. VIII (Washington, D.C.: 1969), p. 690.

23. *Ibid.*, p. 689.

24. *Ibid.*

25. *Ibid.*, pp. 694–95.

26. The FDR message to King Ibn Saud was dated April 5 but was not actually transmitted until April 10, two days before his death in Warm Springs, Georgia.

27. Joseph P. Lash, *Eleanor and Franklin* (New York: W. W. Norton, 1971).

28. Richard H. S. Crossman, *A Nation Reborn* (New York: Atheneum, 1960), p. 14.

29. Lash, *op. cit.*, p. 214.

30. *FR: 1943*, Vol. IV, p. 809.

31. In a similar vein Libyan President Muammar Qaddafi, at the World Conference on Zionism and Racism held in Tripoli on July 24–27, 1976, suggested that the Jews who have come into Israel be resettled in the lands from which they were driven or enticed, in Europe and Arab countries. He offered to take back the Libyan Jews and called on the leaders of other Arab countries to accept back those who had left their ancestral homes under the impact of Zionism's ingathering campaign.

32. "Roosevelt, in his appointment of Morgenthau as Secretary of the Treasury, with the important part played in his administration by Sidney Hillman and other Jews, showed that he had no prejudice against Jews. Yet in the matter of Israel, FDR had earned no laurels." *The Jewish Press* (Omaha), December 29, 1972.

33. Dr. Emanuel Neumann, writing in *The American Zionist*, February 5, 1953.

34. *Ibid.*

35. *FR: 1945*, Vol. VIII, pp. 704–5.

36. *Ibid.*, p. 705.

Chapter III: The Creation of Israel Revisited

1. *The American Zionist*, February 5, 1953.
2. *FR: 1945*, Vol. VIII, p. 707.
3. *Ibid.*, pp. 708–9.
4. *Ibid.*, p. 709.
5. Henderson, on whom the Zionist leader was calling, had invited Wilson and the Chief of the Division of Near Eastern Affairs, Gordon Merriam, to be present during the call, and asked Wilson to act as the officer reporting the conversation.
6. *FR: 1945*, Vol. VIII, p. 714.
7. *Ibid.*, pp. 716–17.
8. *Ibid.*, p. 722.
9. *FR: 1945*, Vol. VIII, pp. 725–26. Moose reported that extreme nationalists looked to the Soviet Union for help against Zionism and that the Kremlin's "secret weapon has been its ability to maintain silence while retaining full liberty of action."
10. *Ibid.*, pp. 727–33. In this memorandum Ambassador Henderson predicted the probability of the Arab oil embargo that followed twenty-eight years later.
11. *Ibid.*
12. Anglo-American Committee of Inquiry, Report to the U.S. Government and His Majesty's Government of the United Kingdom (Washington, D.C.: Department of State, 1946).
13. *FR: 1945*, Vol. VIII, pp. 749–50.
14. The British referred to this as the Anglo-American Committee of Enquiry.
15. *FR: 1945*, Vol. VIII, pp. 771–79.
16. *Ibid.*, p. 771.
17. *Ibid.*
18. *Ibid.*, pp. 777–78.
19. *Ibid.*, p. 775.
20. Eugene Meyer was married to a Christian, as was his daughter, which left him doubly open to Jewish guilt feelings, leading to submission to Zionism.
21. *FR: 1945*, Vol. VIII, p. 795. For Niles's role in advancing Israel's interests while still in the White House, see Alfred M. Lilienthal, *What Price Israel?*, (Chicago: Henry Regnery, 1953), pp. 94–95.
22. *Ibid.*, p. 780: "I had to see Eugene Meyer. Then when I walked out of the White House, Dave Niles asked me what the news about Palestine was. That made me mad, that fellow stopping me when I was so busy."
23. *Ibid.*, p. 814.
24. *Ibid.*, p. 819.
25. *Ibid.*, pp. 828–29. Cable November 20, 1945, from Cairo, where Minister Eddy sent his message to the Secretary of State. He told Emir Faisal that "consultation would be meaningless if the results were predetermined, but that my personal understanding is that it assures full consideration of Arab opinion and local conditions."
26. *Ibid.*, p. 829.
27. *London Times*, November 15, 1945.
28. Anglo-American Committee of Inquiry, *Report to the United States Government and His Majesty's Government of the United Kingdom* (Washington, D.C.: Department of State, 1946), preface.
29. Crossman was said by his Prime Minister to have been chosen "because he was a man of common sense and integrity who had not committed himself in any way on the Palestine question." Within no time after his service on the committee, he committed himself to Zionism and emerged as one of its leading advocates.
30. Three of the signers of these unanimous recommendations later became the most ardent Christian supporters of Jewish nationalism. Bartley Crum, R. H. S. Cross-

man, and James G. McDonald reversed their position completely, even before Israel became a political reality.

31. Anglo-American Committee of Inquiry, *op. cit.*, Recommendation No. 3, p. 4.

32. *Ibid.*

33. Henry F. Grady, Dean of the College of Commerce of the University of California, who because of exceptional knowledge and abilities was called in from time to time by the State Department to carry out special missions, and Herbert Morrison, one of the leaders of the British Labor Party and later Foreign Minister.

34. Telegram, Fitzpatrick to Truman, August 2, 1946. Official File 204 Miscellaneous, Truman Papers, Harry S. Truman Library.

35. In fiscal year 1942 only 10 percent of the quotas were used; 5 percent in 1943; 6 percent in 1944; 7 percent in 1945.

36. Speech of Rabbi Abba Hillel Silver before the 49th Annual Convention of the Zionist Organization of America, *New York Times*, October 27, 1946.

37. *Yiddish Bulletin*, Free Jewish Club, May 19, 1950. Rabbi Philip S. Bernstein, who had served in 1946 as Adviser on Jewish Affairs to the U.S. High Commissioner in Germany, lied to President Truman in an October 11, 1946, meeting when he said that 90 percent of the displaced Jews still in European displaced persons camps wanted to go only to Palestine. Opinion voiced by these unfortunates indicated they preferred to go to the U.S. or elsewhere.

38. H. C. Hansard, *Parliamentary Debates*, Fifth Series, Vol. 433 (London: His Majesty's Stationary Office, 1948).

39. Official File 204, Truman Papers, Harry S. Truman Library.

40. Margaret Truman, *Harry S. Truman* (New York: Morrow, 1973).

41. The Arabs missed an opportunity for achieving a unitary Palestine at the U.N. in 1947 when the minority report supported by India, Yugoslavia, and Iran, which called for a single state with a federal structure rather than the partitioning of Palestine, inspired little enthusiasm. Prince Faisal of Saudi Arabia was willing to meet with U.S. Secretary of State George Marshall to discuss a possible reconciliation with the majority, but the meeting never took place.

42. Harry S. Truman, *Memoirs*, Vol. II, *Years of Trial and Hope* (New York: Doubleday, 1958), p. 225.

43. Margaret Truman, *op. cit.*, p. 385.

44. New York *Daily News*, December 31, 1972.

45. Binghamton (N.Y.) *Press*, December 13, 1972.

46. *Near East Report* (Washington, D.C.), December 20, 1972.

47. Walter Millis, ed., *Forrestal Diaries* (New York: Viking Press, 1951), p. 346.

48. Dean Acheson, *Present at the Creation: My Years at the State Department* (New York: W. W. Norton, 1969), p. 169.

49. Robert J. Donovan, *Conflict and Crisis: The Presidency of Harry S. Truman, 1945–1948* (New York: W. W. Norton, 1977), p. 330.

50. *Forrestal Diaries, op. cit.*, pp. 346–47.

51. *Ibid.*, p. 346.

52. *Ibid.*

53. Donovan, *op. cit.*, p. 331

54. United Nations, *Official Records of the 2nd Session of the General Assembly* (Lake Success, 1947), Plenary Meetings, II, p. 1312.

55. *FR: 1947, The Near East and Africa* Vol. V (Washington, D.C.: U.S. Government Printing Office, 1971), p. 1321 for message to Cairo; *FR: 1948*, Vol. V, p. 571, footnote 3, for message to Jeddah.

56. *FR: 1947, The Near East and Africa*, Vol. V (Washington, D.C.: U. S. Government Printing Office, 1971).

57. *Ibid.*, p. 1309.

58. *Washington Post*, December 29, 1976. The headline of this story was backed up by the *Jersey Journal* of December 29: "Truman Disobeyed on Israel."

59. Margaret Truman, *op. cit.*, p. 387.

60. *Ibid.*, p. 388.

61. Identified as White 4 and marked "urgent and secret," according to the copy in the George M. Elsey Papers in the Harry S. Truman Library at Independence, Mo. *FR: 1948*, Vol. V, Part 2, p. 637, footnote 1. Elsey was assistant to Special Counsel to the President Clark Clifford.

62. *Ibid.*, pp. 637–40.

63. *Ibid.*, p. 640.

64. *Ibid.*, p. 645.

65. *Ibid.*, pp. 679–85.

66. *Ibid.*, p. 697. Tel. 116 from Marshall to Austin.

67. *Ibid.*, editorial note, pp. 748–49.

68. Telegram of February 22, Truman to Marshall: "Your working draft of recommended basic position for the Security Council discussion received. I approve in principle this basic position." *Ibid.*, p. 645.

69. There was an exchange of correspondence between former Secretary of State Dean Rusk, who is now Professor of International Law at the University of Georgia Law School, and the author. After reading this chapter, Rusk sent his letter of July 27, 1977, which appears on pp. 95–96. After a telephone conversation in September 1977 and receipt of a Xeroxed copy of this chapter, former Undersecretary of State Robert A. Lovett in a letter of October 3, 1977, wrote: "You are correct in relying heavily on the documentation as issued by the State Department in FRUS, Vol. 5, Part 2, and avoiding the myths that are being offered for a number of reasons." Lovett referred to the Robert Donovan book on Truman, "Conflict and Crises," as a "readable and fair-minded account of the extraordinary confusion which was in large part compounded by political pressures and the multiplicity of agencies trying to get into the act." Interviews of April 14, 1977, and of March 1, 1978, and an exchange of letters in that period with Loy Henderson, former Director of the Office of Near Eastern and African Affairs, further confirmed the loyalty of State Department officers to the President. As Henderson expressed it, "As I look back, I realize at times I have made errors either in judgment or in action. More criticism has been aimed at me for what I did during my three years as Director of NEA than what I did in all of my other years in service [nearly forty]. I can take criticism for bad judgment, for poor performance, and for inadequacy. But attacks on my motives, charges of disloyalty and lack of honor, leave scars that are slow to heal." Henderson letter of March 13, 1977, to author.

70. *Washington Post*, December 29, 1976.

71. *FR: 1947*, Vol. V., pp. 1153–58. In the transmittal of his memorandum, Henderson assured Secretary Marshall that despite the views expressed, "the staff of my office is endeavoring loyally to carry out the decision [the majority partition report] . . . and will continue to endeavor to execute the decision in a manner which will minimize as far as possible the damage to our relations and interests in the Near Middle East" (p. 1158, footnote 1).

72. Letter of Loy H. Henderson to author, July 29, 1977.

73. *American Jewish Historical Quarterly*, December 1968, pp. 215–16.

74. John Snetsinger, *Truman, The Jewish Vote and the Creation of Israel* (Stanford: Hoover Institution Press, 1974) p. 88.

75. Set forth in a memorandum of March 22 from Secretary Marshall to State Department Counselor Charles Bohlen. *FR: 1948*, Vol. V, Part 2, p. 750, footnote 3.

76. *Ibid.*, p. 746.

77. Harry S. Truman, *Years of Trial and Hope, op. cit.*, p. 163.

78. Donovan, *op. cit.*, p. 377. See the Papers of Eban A. Ayers, Box 12, Vice-Presidency folder, Diary Note of March 20, 1948, Harry S. Truman Library, Independence, Mo.

79. David Lloyd George, *Memoirs of the Peace Conference*, Vol. II (New Haven, Yale University Press, 1939), p. 722.

80. From the Austin statement to the Security Council, March 2, 1948. Reported *FR: 1948*, Vol. V, Part 2, pp. 675–76.

81. Clifford's handwritten notes of May 4 outline the background of Ambassador Austin's March 19 speech setting forth the trusteeship proposal. Clifford admitted that "Austin and Rusk were not instructed to delay the speech until final vote in Security Council." Clifford Papers, Harry Truman Library, Independence, Mo. Quoted *FR: 1948*, Vol. V, Part 2, editorial note, p. 746.

82. *FR: 1948, The Near East and Africa*, Vol. 5, Part 2 (Washington, D.C.: 1976), p. 729. Dean Rusk on March 17 reported from the U.N. the impasse in seeking to conciliate the irreconcilable differences between the Jewish Agency and the Arab Higher Committee, and Ambassador Austin's view of the urgent necessity of bringing about both a cease-fire and the establishment of a "temporary trusteeship for Palestine under the Trusteeship Council of the U.N." (p. 736).

83. *Ibid.*, Telegram 309 of March 17, New York, to the Secretary of State, "EYES ONLY FOR MCCLINTOCK FROM RUSK."

84. *FR: 1948*, Vol. V, Part 2, p. 657.

85. *Ibid.*, pp. 637–41. Top-secret message to the President of February 21.

86. Snetsinger, *op. cit.*, p. 82.

87. *Forrestal Diaries, op. cit.*, p. 346.

88. *FR: 1948*, Vol. V, Part 2, pp. 666–75.

89. This report was concurred in by the intelligence agencies of the Department of State, Army, Navy, and Air Force on February 19. *Ibid.*, p. 666, footnote 1.

90. *Forrestal Diaries, op. cit.*, p. 387.

91. See, for example, memorandum of September 22, 1947, from Director of the Office of Near Eastern and African Affairs Loy Henderson to the Secretary of State, *FR: 1947*, Vol. V, pp. 1153–58. Henderson claimed that his views were "also those of nearly every member of the Foreign Service or of the Department of State who had worked to any appreciable extent on Near Eastern problems."

92. Harry S. Truman, *op. cit.*, Vol. II, p. 163.

93. The U.S. objection to an international police force because it would mean Soviet military presence in the area similarly underlay Washington's calling a military alert during the October 1973 war.

94. *FR: 1948*, Vol. V, Part 2, p. 767. Telegram 550 of U.S. Ambassador Walter Bedell Smith in the Soviet Union to Secretary Marshall, March 26, 1948.

95. *Ibid.*, pp. 741–42. Top-secret telegram 144 of March 18, Thorp (Acting Secretary of State) to Austin. According to a marginal notation by Charles Bohlen, this paragraph had been cleared by phone with Secretary of Defense James Forrestal.

96. *Ibid.*, footnote 1, p. 760. Lovett in a marginal notation indicated that "the White House does not approve" of a U.S. commitment "to contribute armed forces along with other U.N. members, if troops become necessary."

97. This vague language followed Clifford's reluctance to supply the President with a direct answer to Ambassador Austin's direct question as to whether the U.S. would contribute armed forces to maintain truce and trusteeship. The undated Clifford memorandum to the President (as set forth in the Clifford Papers, *FR, 1948*, Vol. V, Part 2, pp. 760–61), emphasized that the purpose of the trusteeship was only "to obtain a peaceful implementation of the U.N. decision for the partition." Clifford wished to make certain that U.S. action would be viewed in no way other than as "the preservation of the peace in aid of partition."

98. *FR: 1948*, Vol. V, Part 2, p. 759.

99. *Ibid.*, pp. 759–60.

100. A check with the State Department Archives indicated that the research had been done by two "young men" including Harold P. Luks, to whom thanks were extended by Clifford in the revised version of his paper, "Recognizing Israel: The 1948 Story," published by *American Heritage*, April 1977. (Luks also coauthored with Editor

Emeritus I.L. Kenen an article for the Israel lobby's *Near East Report*, August 2, 1978.) The magazine also carried a lengthy exclusive interview with Clifford by Contributing Editor Bernard A. Weisberger.

101. Clark M. Clifford paper, "Factors Influencing President Truman's Decision to Support Partition and Recognize the State of Israel," presented to the American Historical Association, December 28, 1976.

102. In an *American Heritage* reprint copyrighted by the American Jewish Historical Society, Jessup and Ross were correctly substituted for Henderson and Wadsworth. An editor's note explained that "the senior officer" was identified in *FR: 1948*, Vol. V, Part 2 on page 967 (actually page 965) as Dean Rusk.

103. *FR: 1948*, Vol. V, Part 2, p. 967.

104. *Ibid.*, note 3, p. 750.

105. This is the same limited choice that the Zionist propagandists had incessantly placed before American Jews and the public in general during the 1947 U.N. battle over partition.

106. *New York Times*, February 11 and 16, 1948.

107. *FR: 1948*, Vol. V, Part 2, editorial note, p. 906.

108. Snetsinger, *op. cit.*, pp. 103–4.

109. Lowenthal sent another memorandum the same day; one each on May 8, 9, and 11; and two on May 12. Clifford Papers, Truman Library, Independence, Mo. When Lowenthal could not reach Clifford, he worked through his assistant, George M. Elsey.

110. Only two days before his appointment, the General in a speech before the Jewish Welfare Board declared that he unmistakably favored partition.

111. Congressman F. D. Roosevelt, Jr., warned Forrestal of loss of funds unless the Democrats took a strong, aggressive pro-Israel stand.

112. From notes of George M. Elsey, *FR: 1948*, Vol. V, Part 2, p. 976.

113. *Ibid.*

114. Patrick Anderson, *The President's Men, White House Assistants of Harry S. Truman, Dwight D. Eisenhower, John F. Kennedy and Lyndon B. Johnson* (Garden City, N.Y.: Doubleday, 1968), pp. 118–19.

115. *FR: 1948*, Vol. V, Part 2, p. 976.

116. Anderson, *op. cit.*

117. Memorandum of conversation by Secretary of State George Marshall. *FR: 1948*, Vol. V, Part 2, pp. 972–76, at page 975.

118. *Ibid.*

119. These are the words used by Clifford in his December 28, 1976, address at the American Historical Association meeting in Washington.

120. *Ibid.*

121. *FR: 1948*, Vol. V, Part 2, p. 960.

122. According to the memorandum of May 13 by Legal Adviser Ernest A. Gross, "the deciding criteria which have in the past been employed in granting or witholding of recognition are: (a) *de facto* control of the territory and machinery of State, including the maintenance of public order; (b) the ability and willingness of a government to discharge its international obligations; (c) general acquiesence of the people of a country in the government in power." *FR: 1948*, Vol. V, pp. 964–65. Naturally after the creation of a new state such as Israel, it required some time to ascertain whether these criteria were being met by the government in power. A prerequisite for all criteria was receipt of the request for recognition from the government itself.

123. Chaim Weizmann, *Trial and Error* (New York: Harper & Brothers, 1949), p. 477.

124. Snetsinger, *op. cit.* Snetsinger in his version, p. 109, declares this was done by telephone. But in 1952 George Elsey, assistant to Clark Clifford, informed this writer in an interview that Epstein had come to the White House in person.

125. According to the undated George M. Elsey notes on the May 12 White House

meeting, "Clifford spent the afternoon getting arrangements made, including arrangement that Epstein would send in the request to the U.S. Government for recognition." George M. Elsey Papers, Harry S. Truman Library, Independence, Mo.

126. Dan Kurzman, *Genesis 1948* (New York: World Publishing Co., 1970), p. 252.

127. *Ibid.*

128. In one Zionist account Niles claimed credit for calling Epstein, but naturally it was to his own interest to magnify his role. According to another story, the President only notified his aide late in the afternoon of the impending recognition, telling him he was the first to whom the good tidings had been relayed.

129. In a later communication to Eleanor Roosevelt, who had been incessantly spurring her husband's successor to support partition and then to recognize the Israeli state, President Truman told a different story: "Since there was a vacuum in Palestine and since the Russians were anxious to be the first to recognize the new state, General Marshall, Secretary Lovett, Dean Rusk, and myself worked the matter out and decided the proper thing to do was to recognize the Jewish Government." Harry S. Truman, *op. cit.* According to the widow of Weizmann, in her book *The Impossible Takes Longer: The Memoirs of Vera Weizmann as told to David Tutaev* (London: Hamish Hamilton, 1967), p. 233, "The President told Marshall and Lovett during their discussion the day before, 'I'm the boss here, and I'll make the decisions.'"

130. *FR: 1948*, Vol. V, Part 2, pp. 1005–7. Memorandum of conversation by Undersecretary of State Robert Lovett. Clifford in his December 28, 1976, American Historical Association speech, alleged that "Lovett was the moving force that changed the White House position. . . ." I believe he persuaded Marshall to alter his opinion despite the implacable opposition of the NEA to the very end." Both Lovett's attitude at the May 14 luncheon with Clifford and his later recollection contradicts this. In a letter of October 3, 1977, to the author, Lovett writes: "That doesn't coincide with the facts as I know them. I was not the 'moving force' but one of a number of advisers consulted by the Secretary."

131. Letter of Dr. Forrest C. Pogue, Director of the Dwight D. Eisenhower Institute for Historical Research, to the author, February 10, 1978.

132. *FR: 1948*, Vol. V, Part 2, p. 1007.

133. Despite continuous Zionist pressures, Truman held off with de jure recognition until Israel held elections and the government became permanent on January 31, 1949.

134. Vera Weizmann, *op. cit.*, p. 234.

135. *FR: 1948*, Vol. V, Part 2, editorial note, p. 993.

136. *Ibid.*, p. 1015, footnote 2. In her letter to Secretary Marshall, Eleanor Roosevelt stated she "would not have wanted the recognition done without the knowledge of our representative at the U.N." In response, Secretary Marshall wrote on May 18, "All I can say is that Ambassador Austin was advised shortly before the recognition was to be made public, but unfortunately he was not present with the Delegation at the time the public announcement became known and Mr. Sayre had not been advised of the situation by Mr. Austin. We were aware of the unfortunate effect on our situation with the U.N., which is much to be regretted. *More than this, I am not free to say.*" (Italics added.)

137. *FR: 1948*, Vol. V, Part 2, editorial note, p. 993.

138. Margaret Truman, *op. cit.*, p. 387.

139. *Jewish Telegraphic Agency* daily news bulletin, December 27, 1972, in which Acheson referred to Truman's deep feeling of "moral and emotional" obligation to the Jewish refugees.

140. *Jewish Telegraphic Agency* story in *The Jewish Press* (Brooklyn), December 29, 1972.

141. *Ibid.*

142. Maurice Bisgyer, *Challenge and Encounter* (New York: Crown Publishers, 1967), p. 195.

143. Edward E. Grusd, *B'nai B'rith: The Story of a Covenant* (New York: Appleton-

Century, 1966), p. 244. In a message in June 1965 to the B'nai B'rith Convention in Tel Aviv, former President Truman stated: "It is a fact of history that Eddie Jacobson's contribution was of decisive importance." *Ibid.*, p. 245

144. In his *Memoirs* the President referred to "Eddie Jacobson who had never been a Zionist," but "was deeply moved by the sufferings of the Jewish people." Like his daughter, President Truman was confused semantically.

145. Snetsinger, *op. cit.*, p. 76.

146. Merle Miller, *Plain Speaking* (New York: Berkley Publishing, 1966), p. 217.

147. Memorandum, Jacobson to Dr. Josef Cohn, April 1, 1952, Weizmann Archives, Harry S. Truman Library, Independence, Mo.

148. Merle Miller, *op. cit.*, pp. 217–18. Loy Henderson in his letter of July 29, 1977, to the author wrote: "I have doubt that the President told anyone in the State Department in advance that he was to receive Dr. Weizmann. I am confident that none of us in the Department who at the time was working on the Palestine problem had any idea that Weizmann was in Washington, that he was planning to talk to the President, or that the President was likely to change his mind with regard to the policies relating to Palestine.

149. Memorandum Jacobson to Cohn, *op. cit.*

150. Miller, *op. cit.*, p. 218.

151. *Ibid*, p. 216.

152. *Ibid*, p. 216.

153. Miller, *op. cit.*, pp. 216–7. This reference to other matters that might preoccupy a President was repeated in the warning that President Carter issued in early fall 1977 that he was giving an undue amount of time to the Middle East while neglecting other important problems.

154. Harry S. Truman, *op. cit.*, p. 130.

155. *U.S. Foreign Policy, Compilation of Studies Prepared Under the Direction of Committee on Foreign Relations,* United States Senate, Pursuant to S Res 335, 85th Congress and S Resolution 31 and S Res. 250, 86th Congress, (Washington: U.S. Government Printing Office, 1960), Study No. 13 of June 9, 1960, pp. 1308–9.

156. *FR: 1949, The Near East, South Asia, and Africa,* Vol. VI (Washington, D.C.: 1971), p. 1074.

157. *Ibid.*, pp. 1104–5.

158. *Ibid.*, p. 1107.

159. *Ibid.*, p. 1110. An adaptation of this 1949 State Department proposal could have been most useful in U.S. efforts to overcome the intransigency of Israel under the leadership of Begin to yield all Arab territories, including the West Bank.

160. McDonald, *My Mission to Israel* (New York: Simon and Schuster, 1951), p. 184.

161. William Eddy, *FDR Meets Ibn Saud* (New York: American Friends of the Middle East, 1954), p. 37.

162. *FR: 1948,* Vol. V, pp. 665–66.

163. *Ibid.* Marshall told the press that "this comment could not be made public" because "we had enough troubles already." *Ibid.*, footnote 1.

164. Alfred Steinberg, "Mr. Truman's Mystery Man," *Saturday Evening Post* (December 24, 1949).

165. When Myron C. Taylor, personal representative of the President at the Vatican, warned of the possible dangers in antagonizing King Ibn Saud, a David Niles memorandum to President Truman cited "considerable help" given by the Jews to the Allies and none from the Arabs. Donovan, *op. cit.*, p. 316.

166. Acheson, *op. cit.*, p. 176.

167. Donovan, *op. cit.*, p. 319.

168. *Ibid.*

169. Margaret Truman, *op. cit.*, pp. 384–85.

170. Memorandum, Truman to Niles, May 13, 1947, File of President's Secretary:

Palestine, 1945–1947 folder, Box 184. Harry S. Truman Library, Independence, Missouri.

171. Letter of Secretary Dean Rusk to the author, July 27, 1977.

172. Arnold Toynbee, *A Study of History*, Vol. VIII (London: Oxford University Press, 1954), p. 308.

173. Frances Williams, *A Prime Minister Remembers* (London: Heinemann, 1961), p. 181.

174. *Ibid.*

175. Almost up to the October 1973 War and the ensuing Arab oil embargo.

176. Titled, influential Jewish Zionists in Britain have been successful, for example, in arranging a joint benefit for the Jewish National Fund and for the pet charity of Prince Phillip, the Royal Consort, which was protested by a few voices. In 1973 there were some objections to the gift by Israel and acceptance by Her Majesty of a forest in Israel as a commemorative gift to the Royal Family, but the pro-Arab bloc still did not pack enough of a wallop, save to kick up a slight storm in the press.

177. For the political storm created in a by-election in which 7,000 votes in Whitechapel plagued the Labor Party following the introduction of the 1939 Passfield White Paper limiting Jewish immigration into Palestine, see Allan Bullock, *The Life and Times of Ernest Bevin*, Vol. I (London: Heinemann, 1960), pp. 455–56.

178. H. C. Hansard, *Parliamentary Debates*, Fifth Series, Vol. 347 (London: His Majesty's Stationary Office, 1939), Column 1967.

Chapter IV: Inside Israel

1. Without essential military assistance from Israel, Idi Amin would never have successfully executed his military coup and come to power. Israeli military advisers, including General Chaim Bar-Lev, guided the irascible African leader in the move that overthrew Milton Abote, his predecessor. Israel trained Ugandan troops, and the closest economic ties existed between the two countries until the 1973 Arab-Israeli war, when powerful Arab forces persuaded Amin to shift loyalties. The thorough knowledge of Uganda and its military establishment is what made possible the swift, paralyzing, and spectacular Israeli commando raid at Entebbe Airport in July 1976.

2. Moynihan declared the resolution to be "symbolic amnesty—and more—to the murderers of the six million European Jews" and added that "the abomination of anti-Semitism has been given the appearance of international sanction." The Moynihan-Herzog combine could not halt a series of continuing condemnations of Zionism: the International Women's Year Conference in Mexico (July 1975), the Organization of African Unity in Kampala (July 1975), and the Non-Aligned Conference in Lima (August 1975).

3. Only Joseph C. Harsch of the *Christian Science Monitor* dared write: "Very few countries in the U.N. are in a position to accuse anyone else of racism. Offhand, I can't think of any ethnic group entirely free of the notion of its own superiority. But the Israelis will not be free of it either until or unless the Arabs in the occupied territories are free and the Arabs inside Israel can enjoy all the rights belonging to any citizen." November 13, 1975.

4. Gary V. Smith, ed., *Zionism: The Dream and the Reality* (New York: Harper & Row, 1974), p. 212. Ben-Gurion quote was also used by I. F. Stone in *New York Review of Books*, August 3, 1967.

5. R. Patai, Ed., *The Complete Diaries of Theodor Herzl* (New York: Herzl Press, 1960), Vol. 1, p. 88.

6. *Jerusalem Post*, July 20, 1976.

7. *Revised Standard Version* (RSV), Leviticus 19:34.

8. William Zuckerman, *Jewish Newsletter* (New York), October 16, 1961.

9. Joseph Badi, ed., *Fundamental Laws of the State of Israel* (New York: Twayne Publishers, 1961), p. 10.

10. *Israel Government Year Book 1952* (Jerusalem: Government Printing Press), p. 29.

11. *Israel Government Year Book 1953–54* (Jerusalem: Government Printing Press), p. 57.

12. London *Times,* February 22, 1962.

13. Joseph Raya resigned as Greek Catholic Archbishop in September 1974 following a break both with his superior, Patriarch Maximos V, and with the Vatican. After his unsuccessful campaign in behalf of the villagers of Baram and Ikrit, he faced great pressures. Soon the Archbishop was most vocal in pronunciations of loyalty to Israel and even vociferous in denunciation of fellow Archbishop Hillarion Capucci, who was convicted by the Israeli High Court of smuggling weapons to Palestinian commandos and sentenced to twelve years. Raya's stand made him persona non grata with other Arab churchmen.

14. *Yediot Aharonot,* July 14, 1972.

15. *New York Times,* August 29, 1977.

16. *Ibid.*

17. London *Times,* February 22, 1962.

18. *Christian Science Monitor,* October 5, 1961.

19. *Ner* (Jerusalem, Ihud Association), January–February 1962.

20. Quoted in *Ner,* August 1962.

21. Cooperatives, differentiated from kibbutzim, which are collective settlements.

22. *Ner,* July–August 1962.

23. John Hope Simpson, *Palestine Report on Immigration, Land Settlement and Development,* Command 3686, (London: His Majesty's Stationary Office, October 1930).

24. Quoted by Noam Chomsky, "An Exception to the Rules," *Inquiry* (San Francisco, April 17, 1978).

25. *U.S. News & World Report,* June 10, 1968.

26. *Report of U.N. Special Committee to Investigate Israeli Practices Affecting the Human Rights of the Population of the Occupied Territories,* December 1970.

27. Christopher Sykes, *Crossroads to Israel* (Cleveland and New York: World Publishing Co., 1956), p. 354.

28. London *Times,* July 27, 1967.

29. Alfred M. Lilienthal, *There Goes the Middle East* (New York: Devin-Adair, 1958), p. 49.

30. Sabri Jiyris, *The Arabs in Israel* (New York: Monthly Review Press, 1976), p. 208.

31. *Jewish Newsletter,* September 18, 1961.

32. *New York Times,* September 23, 1961.

33. *Al-Hamishmar,* September 7, 1976, as translated in *Swasia* weekly news digest in Washington, D.C., October 15, 1976. This Hebrew-language paper was published by Israel's Mapai party, aligned in 1973 with the Labor party as part of the Rabin coalition government.

34. *Swasia, ibid.*

35. *Ibid.*

36. Israel Shahak, "The Racist Nature of Zionism and of the Zionist State of Israel," *Pi-Ha-Aton* (weekly student paper, Hebrew University, Jerusalem), November 5, 1975.

37. Confirmed by the negative opinion handed down by the Israeli Supreme Court in the 1969 case of Professor George Tamarim. The court refused to permit Tamarim to change his nationality designation from Jew to Israeli on his identity card.

38. For further details of this and other riots, see Alfred M. Lilienthal, *The Other Side of the Coin* (New York: Devin-Adair, 1965).

39. *Time,* June 21, 1971.

40. *Le Monde,* October 15, 1971.

41. Earlier the Jewish reform movement agreed "not to perform black conversions as it would cause U.S. blacks to flood Israel." *Ma'ariv,* June 4, 1973.

42. *Jewish Journal,* January 28, 1977.

43. Letty Cottin Pogrebin, "Feminist Goes to Israel," *Ms Magazine,* October 1977.

44. *Jewish Journal,* April 19, 1974.

45. *Ha'olam Hazeh,* Israeli weekly news magazine, December 25, 1974.

46. *The Scotsman,* April 26, 1977 (Edinburgh, Scotland).

47. Wilfred A. Beling, ed., *The Middle East: Quest for an American Policy* (Albany, State University of New York Press, 1973), p. 160.

48. Malcolm Kerr, "The Middle East Conflict," *Foreign Policy,* October 1968, p. 47.

49. Published in the Israeli weekly *Ha'olam Hazeh,* as reported in the London *Times,* June 25, 1969.

50. *Ha'aretz,* March 25, 1975.

51. *Commentary* magazine (New York), September 1976.

52. Moshe Dayan, "A Soldier Reflects on Peace Hopes," *Middle East Reader* (New York: Pegasus, 1969), p. 417.

53. At least three other non-Cabinet generals played key roles in the Begin Establishment: Israel's Ambassador to the U.N. Chaim Herzog, Israeli Ashkenazi Chief Rabbi Shlomo Goren, and Tel Aviv Mayor Shlomo Lahal.

54. From the eulogy delivered at the funeral of Roy Rotenberg, a member of the Nahal-Oz kibbutz as quoted by Uri Avnery, *Israel Without Zionism* (New York: Collier Books, 1971), pp. 153–54.

Chapter V: What Palestinians?

1. *Davar,* January 24, 1969.

2. Golda Meir, March 8, 1969.

3. Golda Meir, June 15, 1969.

4. Amos Elon, *The Israelis: Founders and Sons* (New York: Bantam Books, 1972), p. 272. (Originally published by Holt, Rinehart & Winston, 1971).

5. *Ibid.,* p. 196.

6. *Ibid.,* p. 146.

7. *Ibid.,* p. 206.

8. Published in Jerusalem, November–December 1974, Vol. 17, No. 9.

9. Dr. Julius Morgenstern, *As a Mighty Stream* (Philadelphia: Jewish Publication Society of America, 1949), p. 525.

10. Quoted by Hans Kohn, "Zion and the Jewish National Idea," *Palestine: A Search for Truth,* Alan Taylor and Richard Tetlie, eds. (Washington, D.C.: Public Affairs Press, 1970), p. 68.

11. *Ner* (Jerusalem, Ihud Association), September–October 1953.

12. Joseph Weitz, *My Diary and Letters to the Children* (Tel Aviv: Masada, 1965–1973), 6 vols., in Hebrew.

13. From a diary entry made in 1940, reiterated as still valid in *Davar,* September 29, 1967. Quoted by Noam Chomsky, "Israeli Jews and Palestinian Arabs: Reflections in a National Conflict," *Holy Cross Quarterly,* Summer 1972, p. 9.

14. Joseph B. Schechtman, *Rebel and Statesman: The Vladimir Jabotinsky Story—The Early Years* (New York: Thomas Yoseloff, 1956), p. 104.

15. Eliezer Schweid, "New Ideological Directions After the Six Day War," *Dispersion and Unity,* No. 10 (1970), p. 48.

16. *Jewish Newsletter* (published in New York), February 9, 1959.

17. The minority report was presented by representatives of India, Yugoslavia, and Iran. While Saudi Arabia's Prince Faisal was willing to meet with Secretary of State George Marshall to discuss a possible reconciliation with the majority report, the meeting never took place.

18. The figure 254 dead was the number declared by International Red Cross representative Jacques de Reynier, who was at the scene. Thirty-five of the women killed were pregnant.

19. This was the observation of David Shaltiel, Jerusalem's Haganah commander.

Larry Collins and Dominique Lapierre, *O Jerusalem!* (New York: Simon and Schuster, 1972), p. 272.

20. Harry Levin, *Jerusalem Embattled* (London: Victor Gollancz, 1950), p. 57.

21. *New York Times,* April 12, 1948.

22. John Kimche, *Seven Fallen Pillars* (New York: Praeger, 1953), p. 217.

23. William R. Polk, David M. Stamler, and Edmund Asfour, *Backdrop to Tragedy* (Boston: Beacon Press, 1957), citing *New Judea,* p. 291.

24. Collins and Lapierre, *op. cit.,* p. 275.

25. *Ibid.*

26. *Ibid.*

27. *Ibid.*

28. Polk, Stamler, and Asfour, *op. cit.,* p. 291.

29. *Ibid.*

30. Jacques de Reynier, *A Jérusalem un Drapeau Flottait Sur La Ligne de Feu* (Neuchâtel: La Bacconnierre, 1950), p. 213.

31. Collins and Lapierre, *op. cit.,* p. 279. According to the account of Harry Levin, once Middle East correspondent of the *Daily Herald* and then Israeli chargé d'affaires in Australia, "the muchtar of Deir Yassin, his womenfolk and children were in one truck." Levin, *op. cit.,* p. 57.

32. J. Bowyer Bell, *Terror Out of Zion* (New York: St. Martin's Press, 1977).

33. *Ibid.,* p. 295.

34. Collins and Lapierre, *op. cit.,* p. 279.

35. Bertha Spofford Vester, *Our Jerusalem: An American Family in the Holy City (1881–1969)* (New York: Doubleday, 1950). The more controversial portions of the manuscript submitted by Mrs. Vester were deleted by the publisher.

36. Polk, Stamler, and Asfour, *op. cit.,* p. 291.

37. *The Christian Century,* March 16, 1949.

38. Kimche, *op. cit.,* p. 228.

39. Don Peretz, *Israel and the Palestine Arabs* (Washington, D.C.: The Middle East Institute, 1958), p. 6.

40. Arthur Koestler, *Promise and Fulfillment, Palestine 1917–1949* (London: Macmillan, 1949), p. 160.

41. James G. McDonald, *My Mission to Israel* (New York: Simon and Schuster, 1951), p. 176.

42. Fred V. Winnett, "Why the West Should Stop Supporting Israel," *Macleans Magazine,* January 18, 1958.

43. *The Spectator* (London), May 12, 1961.

44. Maxime Rodinson, *Israel and the Arabs* (New York: Random House, 1969), p. 50.

45. *Jewish Newsletter,* February 9, 1959.

46. Menachem Begin, *The Revolt: The Story of the Irgun* (New York: Henry Schuman, 1951), pp. 164–65. *The Revolt* was translated from Hebrew for the American edition in 1951 by the same Shmuel Katz who became Begin's personal representative to the U.S. in June 1977, and who had been a member of the Command of the Irgun. The revised 1976 edition published in California carried an introduction by the Jewish Defense League's Rabbi Meir Kahane. But after his election in 1977 another edition was put on the market by Nash Publishing and a paperback by Dell. Kahane's introduction was dropped for a short foreword by former *Jewish Chronicle* (London) editor Ivan Greenberg. The *New York Post* serialized the book in July 1977.

47. Twenty-eight years later in an article in the May/June 1976 issue of *The American Zionist,* Mordechai Nisan of the Truman Research Center of the Hebrew University in Jerusalem expressed concern with the failure to understand "the major significance of terrorist groups and guerrilla tactics in the struggle for Jewish sovereignty in the 1940's. Without terror it is unlikely that Jewish independence would have been achieved when it was."

48. London *Times*, April 23, 1948.

49. Jon and David Kimche, *A Clash of Destinies, The Arab-Jewish War and the Founding of the State of Israel* (New York: Frederick Praeger, 1960), p. 160.

50. First published in mimeographed form, February 15, 1973, by Dr. Israel Shahak in Jerusalem; smuggled out of Israel and printed in London and Washington in 1975.

51. *Ha'aretz*, April 4, 1969.

52. U.N. Document A/8089, Annex VI, p. 6.

53. Amos Kenan, *Israel—A Wasted Victory*, translated by Miriam Shimoni (Tel Aviv: Amikam, 1970).

54. Quoted in Michael Adams, "Signposts to Destruction," published by the Council for the Advancement of Arab-British Understanding (London, 1976).

55. *Ha'aretz*, October 3, 1975.

56. *Ibid.*

57. The former Jordanian Cabinet Minister and Ambassador indicated that "in the present confusing circumstances, I find it impossible to talk to journalists as I used to in the past." *New York Times*, January 29, 1974.

58. *Siah* magazine (Jerusalem), January 1975, pp. 17–18.

59. London *Times*, June 1, 1974.

60. *Ibid.*

61. *New York Times*, February 11, 1975.

62. The author has visited Israel many times. The travels referred to were in 1973 and 1974.

63. *Manchester Guardian Weekly*, January 26, 1968.

64. *Le Nouvel Observateur*, July 3, 1972; *Christian Science Monitor*, December 21, 1972.

65. Cited by Rev. L. Humphrey Walz, *Report to the U.N. Committee to Investigate Israeli Practices Affecting the Human Rights of the Population of the Occupied Territories*, October 10, 1977, p. 3.

66. *Ibid.*, p. 5.

67. Amnon Kapeliouk, *New Outlook*, November–December 1968.

68. Those expelled were: Ab dal-Jawad Saleh, Mayor of El-Bireh; Jeryis Uda, teacher, of El-Bireh; Jamil Hussein Uda, of Ramallah; Dr. Walid Kamhawi, gynecologist, of Nablus; Hussein Jarub, of Nablus; Arrabi Musa, of Nablus; Shaker Muhammad Abu Khajla, of Nablus; and Abdul-Mohsen Abu Meizer, lawyer, member of the Superior Muslim Council, of Jerusalem (presently member of the PLO Executive Committee).

69. Dr. Walid Kamhawi writing in *Middle East International* (London), July 1974.

70. Mayor Saleh was part of the delegation that accompanied PLO Chieftain Yasir Arafat when he came to the United Nations to present the case of the Palestinians in November 1974.

71. Felicia Langer, *With My Own Eyes: Israel and the Occupied Territories 1967–1973* (London: Ithaca Press, 1975), pp. 62–3.

72. Ann Lesch, American Friends Service Committee Report No. 35, "Deportations from the West Bank and Gaza Strip, 1967–1976," April 1977.

73. Langer, *op. cit.*, pp. 62–63.

74. For nearly a year (1974–75), Mr. and Mrs. Thomas Noreuil of Chicago endeavored in five letters to Senator Edward Kennedy and in correspondence with other Judiciary Subcommittee and staff members to obtain a copy of the so-called De Haan staff report. This had been compiled by three staff members after a fact-finding mission to the Middle East to review the "situation of the Palestinian refugees, the effects of the October 1973 war on civilians, and to find ways of enhancing peace negotiations." Senator Kennedy finally answered their request and refused to release the report. When Senator James Abourezk intervened on behalf of the Noreuils, he was told that the report was made for the staff only and would not be released to the public. It was said to contain "sensitive" information.

75. U.N. Document E/CN4/1016/Addendum 2, February 11, 1970.

76. International Committee of Red Cross, report of December 5, 1968.

77. *Le Monde*, November 27, 1969.

78. London *Sunday Times*, November 23, 1969. Foreign Editor of the London *Times* E. C. Hodgkin also reported "grim and severe repression, multiplying acts of resistance and deportations," London *Times*, October 28, 1969.

79. *The Economist*, March 21, 1970.

80. U.N. Special Committee on Human Rights in the Occupied Territories, U.N. Document A/8089, Annex VI, p. 5.

81. *Al Fajer* (Jerusalem paper), January 16, 1974.

82. "Report on Israeli Methods of Torture," *Amnesty International*, April 12, 1970.

83. The charge of a "torture camp" at Sarafand was first heard in August 1969 testimony before the U.N. Commission to Investigate the Treatment of Arabs under Israel Occupation. Thirty witnesses appeared at an Amman hearing, a report of which was carried by the London *Times* August 20, 1969. Bedouin witnesses before the same committee in Cairo the next day charged Israeli soldiers with the use of violence and repression to force residents of the peninsula to abandon their homes and flee across the Suez Canal. *New York Times*, August 21, 1969.

84. Eric Moonman, MP and Chairman of the Zionist Federation, told the *Jewish Chronicle* in London that the letter received from Harold Evans, London *Sunday Times* editor, explaining why the Israeli answer had not appeared in the same issue as the "Insight" report, was unacceptable. The Zionists were taking their grievance to the Press Council and otherwise exerting pressure on the *Sunday Times*.

85. *Christian Science Monitor*, March 1, 1977.

86. The very hospital Jordan's Queen Alia was about to visit when her plane crashed in 1977.

87. *Austin Daily Herald* (Austin, Minnesota, population 25, 074), October 27, 1977.

88. *Country Reports on Human Rights Practices*, February 3, 1978. Report submitted to the Committee on International Relations U.S. House of Representatives and Committee on Foreign Relations U.S. Senate by the Department of State (Washington: U.S. Government Printing Office, 1978).

89. *Comparative Survey of Freedom* (New York: Freedom House, 1978), p. 9.

90. The progressive attitude taken by some of the new Jewish settlers on the West Bank must have come as a shock to more hawkish elements. In the words of the wife of a rabbi living in Qiryat Arba, the Jewish settlement outside the large Arab town of Hebron, "We, Jews, have always lived together in this land with other nations. We were never here alone. God said to go and live in Israel. I see no other reason why we can't live with the Arabs peacefully in Hebron." Here was another Jewish call for binationalism for which the Zionist Establishment, and its supporters in the U.S., completely and utterly refuse any consideration, using the ever-present fear of the holocaust to justify their intransigence.

91. Michael Adams, "Signposts to Destruction: Israel Settlements in the Occupied Territories" (London: Council for the Advancement of Arab-British Understanding, 1976).

92. *New York Times*, November 13, 1975.

93. *Ma'ariv*, September 26, 1971.

94. *Ha'aretz*, September 16, 1971.

95. *New York Times*, December 26, 1972.

96. Mohamed Hassanein Heikal, *The Road to Ramadan* (New York: Quadrangle/New York Times Book Co., 1975), p. 205.

97. Walz, *op. cit.*, p. 7

98. *Ha'aretz*, September 3, 1973.

99. *Washington Post*, September 14, 1973.

100. Five years later, Israeli youth in rallying against Begin plans for new settlements expressed an entirely different viewpoint. See p. 754.

101. *Jerusalem Post,* February 18, 1975.

102. *Ha'aretz,* May 9, 1974.

103. *New York* magazine, June 14, 1976, p. 46.

104. *New York Times,* September 6, 1977.

105. *Ibid.,* September 27, 1977.

106. In *U.S. News & World Report,* November 18, 1974, Arafat was described as "fighting against British and French forces that invaded Egypt in 1956." The writer somehow omitted any reference to the fact that Israel also was a part of this invasion.

107. For fuller details see articles in the London *Guardian,* May 14, 1976, a special supplement compiled by Louis Eaks, editor of the monthly journal *Free Palestine.*

108. *New York Times,* January 26, 1975.

109. *Time* magazine, November 11, 1974.

110. Alistair Cooke, *Six Men* (New York: Knopf, 1977), p. 180.

Chapter VI: The Jewish Connection: Numbers Don't Count

1. To the nonobservers, the majority of Jews, these have become holidays rather than Holy Days—a day, of course, to stay home from work and go to a ball game or a movie.

2. Advertisements in the *Wall Street Journal* from groups wishing to oppose U.S. policy in the Middle East or criticize Israel were increasingly rejected after 1974, and the editorial policy in the paper's "Review and Outlook" became more blatantly pro-Zionist. On March 16, 1978, "The Use of Force" depicted Israel's invasion of Lebanon as "operating with some restraint . . . [her] response seems preferable to past retaliations. . . . The Israelis seem to be observing strict territorial guidelines." "We have come a long way," says the *Journal* gloatingly, "since 1974 when PLO leader Yasir Arafat got a fawning reception at the U.N.," and the Israeli action undoubtedly will curb the Palestinians' "independence of action . . . for stable peace to come, something like the present raids has to take place." In a May 17, 1978, post-mortem on the arms sale package, the *Journal* denied "the vote was any sort of mandate for Carter Mideast strategy," and predicted there would be no "general erosion of support for Israel."

3. UJA advertisement, *New York Times,* May 15, 1961, covering seven-eighths of page 13.

4. The five-page memorandum, "Tasks Confronting B'nai B'rith," described as of "the most sensitive nature," discussed the wide range of Washington activities that B'nai B'rith was undertaking after the "heavy losses suffered by Israel in men and equipment . . . since it is our duty to maintain pressures to secure the greatest possible U.S. support for Israel's needs."

5. The American Zionist Council report noted that "in one recent week, for example, we were forced to research and prepare communications in reply to three extremely inimical articles appearing in the Columbia University (Quarterly) *Forum, Cosmopolitan* magazine, and *Editor and Publisher;* all three were handled with dispatch, and it is hoped the replies will shortly appear. In any case, the publications are alerted to the fact that we are prepared to answer any unwarranted attacks of this kind. In an average month about twenty-five letters to newspapers and magazines are written or sent, either directly from the National Office or through our Field Offices or by our community contacts after consultation with our National Office. . . ."

6. The Zionist Council report claimed "that in 1969 2,240 engagements were made through the Speakers Bureau; this does not mean 2,240 speakers, but rather 2,240 engagements. In addition to our own roster of speakers, we utilized speakers engaged by commercial bureaus (booking them in those cities to which they are traveling for their own bureaus, or in a city en route), as well as speakers based in the local communities, in order to save on transportation costs. When we send speakers out, we don't send them for a single appearance. Our speakers average from four to seven appearances in a single

day. In a typical community, a speaker may talk to a Rotary Club, a World Affairs Council, a church group, a high school assembly or college group, a women's club, a TV or radio appearance, a background session with a local editor or commentator, etc. (We believe the speaker should do p.r. work in addition to making public appearances, and many of them are capable of doing this type of job.) Speakers often remain in a community for several days."

7. The commission, under the chairmanship of Dr. Judah Nadich, was made up of important rabbis, representing all levels of religious opinion. Strangely enough most of them were Reform or Conservative, and the chairman was seeking more Orthodox representatives.

8. The committee consists primarily of professional producers and writers under the initial leadership of a professional public relations woman.

9. Leonard Slater, *The Pledge* (New York: Simon and Schuster, 1970), pp. 120–21.

10. Robert St. John, *The Boss* (New York: McGraw-Hill, 1960).

11. Harry Golden, *The Israelis* (New York: Putnam, 1971).

12. Amos Elon, *The Israelis: Sons and Founders* (New York: Holt, Rinehart and Winston, 1971).

13. Gerold Frank, *The Deed* (New York: Simon and Schuster, 1963).

14. In a March 2, 1978, editorial, "Egypt's Ungrateful Friends," the *Washinton Star* attacked the PLO and called on the Palestinians to take another look at their "official" leadership. In a May 5, 1978, editorial, "Planes and Oil," the *Star* called for defeat of the plane deal since "to the extent that the U.S. is put in the position of being a supplicant for 'enlightened' oil production policies in Riyadh, we mortgage future freedom of action, politically and diplomatically."

15. *Parade,* June 26, 1977.

16. *The Zionist Connection* represents the first publication of an anti-Zionist (and pro-Palestinian) book by a major American publishing house.

17. *New York Post,* October 24, 1977. Cindy Adams, wife of Joey, in her October 28, 1977, column in *Our Town,* reprinted the Redgrave misquotation and claimed, "Columbia, who produced her current film *Julia,* is in deep shock." Producer Richard Roth and scriptwriter Alvin Sargent, according to *Soho Weekly News* of October 27, 1977, refused to attend a screening in Los Angeles of the PLO documentary.

18. *Show Business,* October 20, 1977. The vendetta against Redgrave was still being carried on months later. In an open letter of July 26, 1978 in *Variety,* Israeli-born Equity President Theodore Bikel attacked the actress for her "insensitivity and pronouncements," charging her with "distorting history and pretending that there is a difference between those Jew-haters who destroyed Jerusalem 2000 years ago and those who seek to destroy it now." And Publisher Leo Shull of *Show Business* in a lengthy front-page diatribe, August 3, 1978, assailed Bikel for being too kind to Redgrave.

19. *New York Times,* March 5, 1978.

20. *Between the Lines* (bimonthly newsletter, Princeton, N.J.), Charles A. Wells, ed., December 1, 1973.

21. *New York Times,* May 31, 1975.

22. *Sacramento Bee,* November 7, 1976.

23. William Attwood, *Look,* "Position of the Jews in America Today," November 29, 1955.

24. *New York Times,* July 10, 1977.

25. *Ibid.,* June 26, 1974.

26. On the same wavelength in praising New York City investment in Israeli securities were long-time avid supporter of Israel, former City Council President Paul O'Dwyer, a Trustee of the City's Pension Board, and Israeli Ambassador to the U.N. Yosef Tekoah. They both hailed the investment as "a significant contribution in support of democracy."

27. In November 1969 the President of the Zionist Organization of America ap-

pealed to American Jews to support President Nixon and criticized Reform Jewish leaders for urging an "immediate cease-fire" in the Vietnam War.

28. *New York Times*, January 24, 1971, "The Complex Past of Meir Kahane."

29. The first sentence of the *New York Times* article of November 10, 1976, on Churba's resignation said he was "stripped of his special security clearance because he talked to a *New York Times* reporter." Three paragraphs later, an Air Force spokesman was quoted as saying that when Churba took the post, he was told he would be unable to speak publicly.

30. Sisco had been a student at the University of Chicago of Professor Hans Morgenthau, long-time Zionist. On October 10, 1976, he was guest speaker at Technion's Annual Dinner Dance in the Grand Ballroom of New York's Hotel Pierre.

31. *Jerusalem Post*, August 2, 1977.

32. Joseph Churba, *The Politics of Defeat: America's Decline in the Middle East* (New York: Cyrco Press, 1977).

33. *Book World*, October 30, 1977. Mark Bruzonsky is an associate editor of *World View* magazine.

34. Lilienthal has never allowed himself to be used by the Zionist movement.

35. The late Admiral Strauss was an inveterate anti-Zionist.

36. The economic coordinator was born of Jewish parents and is a member of the nondenominational Fountain Street Church in Grand Rapids, whose minister, Reverend Duncan Littlefair, happens to be one of the most fanatical Christian Zionists in the U.S. See *Middle East Perspective*, June–July 1971.

37. A protest to Exxon, one of the sponsors of the MacNeil/Lehrer Report and widely publicized as a key member of the so-called pro-Arab "oil lobby," was rejected. Leonard in August 1978, was serving as deputy U.S. Representative to the U.N. and as U.S. Ambassador on the Security Council.

Chapter VII: Whose Congress?: Thwarting the National Interest

1. In all, U.S. Presidents have been elected twelve times with an actual minority of the votes: 1824, 1844, 1848, 1856, 1860, 1876, 1880, 1884, 1888, 1892, 1912, and 1916.

2. As quoted by David S. Broder, "Congressional Whims in Foreign Policy," *Washington Post*, April 26, 1978.

3. House Resolution 163 on March 19, 1975, changed the name of the House Foreign Affairs Committee to the House International Affairs Committee.

4. In seeking the Democratic nomination for John Tower's seat in the Senate, Texas Congressman Bob Krueger sent out a form letter of November 2, 1977, itemizing seventeen votes vitally concerning Israel since March 1975 and boasting that on each and every occasion he had voted for all requests of funding to Israel, in favor of the resolution condemning the U.N.'s anti-Zionism resolution, and in support of the $20 million appropriation for resettlement of Jewish refugees from the U.S.S.R. His record certainly entitled Krueger to a seat in the Israeli Knesset, if not in the U.S. Senate.

5. *New York Post*, February 10, 1970.

6. General Ira C. Eaker, *Strategic Review*, Winter 1974 issue (U. S. Strategic Institute, Washington, D.C.).

7. H.R. 17123, Title V, Section 501.

8. See p. 59–60.

9. George D. Aiken, *Aiken: Senate Diary, January 1972 through January 1975* (Brattleboro, Vt.: Stephen Greene Press, 1976), pp. 170–71. In his diaries Aiken showed an optimism in March 1973 as to the possibilities of developing better understanding between the Arabs and the Israelis, which events did not bear out; six months later the 1973 October war occurred.

10. *New York Times Sunday Magazine*, November 23, 1975.

11. The Conference of Presidents of Major Jewish Organizations has been con-

stantly used in pressuring Congress on behalf of Israel. Although six oᶠ the original nineteen participating organizations were chartered for religious or fraternal purposes, their leaders did not hesitate to represent American Jews on such foreign policy issues as the sale of arms to Israel, withholding arms from the Arabs, a security pact between the U.S. and Israel, barring of the United Arab Republic from a seat in the U.N. Security Council, etc. Since December 29, 1953, this lobby, now combining thirty-three Zionist and non-Zionist groups, has engaged in a continued, carefully planned campaign. Half of the Conference's budget was subsidized by the Jewish Agency through tax-free UJA funds. See "Activities of Nondiplomatic Representatives of Foreign Principals in the United States," *Hearing Before the Committee on Foreign Relations, United States Senate*, Part IX, May 23, 1963, Part XII, August 1, 1963 (Washington, U.S. Government Printing Office, 1963), p. 1757.

12. The usual Zionist names came from both parties and included such stalwarts as Case of New Jersey, Church of Idaho, Jackson of Washington, Javits of New York, Mondale of Minnesota, Ribicoff of Connecticut and Scott of Pennsylvania.

13. *Aviation Week & Space Technology*, December 13, 1976.

14. *Near East Report*, March 23, 1977.

15. Letter of Senator Hubert H. Humphrey to Dr. C. W. Fairbanks of St. Paul, Minnesota, dated October 5, 1976.

16. *Los Angeles Times*, May 28, 1974.

17. *Hearing Before the Committee on Foreign Relations, United States Senate*, 93rd Congress, First Session, on S. 2692 and H.R. 11088, December 13, 1973, p. 128.

18. Russell Warren Howe and Sarah Hays Trott, *The Power Peddlers / How Lobbyists Mold America's Foreign Policy* (Garden City, N.Y.: Doubleday, 1977), p. 282. This was an increase from $250,000 in 1973.

19. *New York Times*, August 8, 1975.

20. *Ibid.*

21. The document had been classified by Adolph Dubs, Deputy Assistant Secretary of State.

22. Eventually, after looking in the Soviet Union, Jordan did purchase the U.S. systems—with Saudi money.

23. *New York Times*, August 8, 1975.

24. When Carl Marcy, former staff member of the Senate Foreign Relations Committee and editor of *Foreign Affairs Newsletter*, contemplated devoting an issue to the lobby, which he felt had been ignored in press analysis, "he was promptly persuaded otherwise by friends who warned him of economic consequences." Marcy's conclusion: "The subject of Arab-Israeli relations is so fraught with emotions that it cannot be discussed rationally," even in the world's oldest democracy. This desperate fear has stymied even the merest thought of any probe of the Israel lobby.

25. Norman F. Dacey, Chairman of the American Palestine Committee; Rabbi Elmer Berger, President of American Jewish Alternatives to Zionism; and Dr. Alfred M. Lilienthal, Chairman of *Middle East Perspective*.

26. Bryen, who was an aide to New Jersey's Senator Clifford Case and was assigned to matters dealing with the Senate Foreign Relations subcommittee on Middle East affairs, was accused by North Dakota businessman Michael Saba of "improperly offering advice and classified material" to the Israelis regarding Saudi Arabian military bases. A conversation between Bryen and Israeli officials at Washington's Madison Hotel was overheard from a nearby table by Saba, who took notes. Bryen was given a long "leave of absence." *Newark Star-Ledger*, April 2, 1978.

27. Stephen D. Isaacs, *Jews and American Politics* (New York: Doubleday, 1974), p. 255.

28. *Cleveland Jewish News*, January 24, 1975.

29. Robert Keatley, "Potent Persuaders," *Wall Street Journal*, July 5, 1977.

30. *Ibid.*

31. *Ibid.*

32. *Ibid.*

33. See "Activities of Nondiplomatic Representatives of Foreign Principals in the United States," *Hearings Before the Committee on Foreign Relations, U.S. Senate,* Part IX of May 23, 1963, and Part XII of August 1, 1963 (Washington: U.S. Government Printing Office, 1963).

34. *Congressional Quarterly,* July 1976, p. 1509.

35. *New York Post,* May 16, 1977.

36. Leo Mindlin, editor of the *Jewish Floridian* (Miami Beach), June 26, 1959.

37. $1.2 million in contributions to Senator Muskie included large givers Arnold Picker, Vice President of United Artists Corporation; Matthew Lifflander, former President of Uniworld Corporation; Lionel Pincus, President of E. M. Warburg & Company; Norman Redstone, theater chain owner; Milton P. Semer, lobbyist and lawyer; Mr. and Mrs. Fred Morgan, *Hudson Review.*

38. $500,000 in contributions to Senator McGovern included gifts from Henry L. Kimmelman, New York and Virgin Islands real estate owner; James Kerr, President of Avco Industries; Robert J. Bernstein, President of Random House; Carol Weil Haussamen; Max Palevsky.

39. $750,000 was given to Senator Bayh by contributors including Milton Gilbert, Gilbert Carrier Corporation, and Richard Adler, Broadway producer. After spending some $500,000, Bayh withdrew, allegedly because of his wife's health.

40. Prominent among the givers of $250,000 to Senator Harold Hughes were Eli Sagon, New York Girl Coat, Inc.; Robert S. Pirie, Boston attorney; Joseph Rosenfield, department store magnate. Subsequently the Iowa Senator abandoned the race.

41. *New York Times,* May 17, 1971.

42. *Congressional Record,* 95th Congress, Second Session, June 16, 1970, p. S. 9078.

43. *Congressional Record,* 95th Congress, Second Session, June 2, 1970, p. S. 8122.

44. *Rocky Mountain News,* March 27, 1977.

45. *Rocky Mountain News,* March 24, 1977.

46. *Washington Post,* October 24, 1977.

47. *Congressional Record,* 86th Congress, Second Session, April 29, 1960, p. S.8979.

Chapter VIII: Slanting the Myth-Information

1. The demographic makeup of Israel has shifted drastically since founding of the state in 1948 from an overwhelming European to Oriental (Middle East and Arab) composition, and in the future the country will be even more preponderantly non-European. However, the cultural and political patterns are still dominated by Israel's European bloc.

2. Edmund Ghareeb, "The American Media and the Palestine Problem," *Journal of Palestine Studies,* Vol. V, Nos. 1 and 2, Autumn 1975-Winter 1976. (Published jointly by the Institute of Palestine Studies and Kuwait University, Washington, D.C.).

3. *New York Times,* August 11, 1977.

4. At the Century Club in November 1972, where Tom Wicker had taken the author for lunch.

5. Ghareeb, *op. cit.*

6. *Ibid.*

7. Ayad Al-Qazzaz, "Stereotypes and Images of the Arab in America," Study for California State University, 1974; published in *Middle East Perspective,* January 1975.

8. CBS Special on Saudi Arabia, March 28, 1975.

9. There is a daily average of 106 column inches of international news. Studies indicate that the adult reader takes in approximately 12 column inches, devoting about 2 1/3 minutes to this reading, most of which Professor Ayad al-Qazzaz describes as "political in nature and by-and-large of an exotic and immoral nature." Al-Qazzaz, *op. cit.*

10. A study examined eighteen textbooks taught in Ohio elementary schools. Of the 202 pictures appearing in these books, 82 were connected with different phases of bedouin life, such as oases, date picking, camels, and camel caravans; 22 depicted the primitive aspects of Arab farm life and farming; 36 showed Arab city life, but only 7 of those were of modern cities. Al-Qazzaz, *op. cit.*

11. A paper, "Television's Distorted Image of the Arab," covering partial monitoring during 1974–76 by Dr. Jack G. Shaheen, Associate Professor of Mass Communications at Southern Illinois University, was delivered at the Annual Conference of the Arab American University Graduates at the Biltmore Hotel in New York City, October 2, 1976.

12. *Ibid.*

13. A good example was "Cannon," May 27, 1976.

14. "The Six Million Dollar Man," ABC, March 21, 1976.

15. "Medical Center," NBC, June 28, 1976.

16. "Weekend," NBC, January 3, 1976.

17. "To Tell the Truth," a syndicated Goodson-Todman production, June 11, 1976.

18. NBC's "Mystery Theater," "McCloud," January 11, 1976, and "Columbo," May 16, 1976.

19. I.BC's "The Little Drummer Boy" has been telecast for several years during the Christmas season.

20. The Anti-Defamation League has been most successful in persuading television stations to present their views as a public service in many parts of the country.

21. Letter dated July 26, 1977, from William B. Ray, Chief of Complaints and Compliance Division, to Harriet Karchmer, American Council on the Middle East.

22. J. C. Hurewitz, *The Struggle for Palestine* (New York: Greenwood, 1950).

23. *Time* magazine, November 25, 1974.

24. A further example of the media's refusal to discuss the question of Zionism vs. Judaism was the lengthy article filed from Cairo by H. D. S. Greenway (August 15, 1977). Normally the *Washington Post*'s regular correspondent in Israel, Greenway had switched with his alter ego in Cairo for two weeks. The article was riddled with anti-Israeli, anticolonial phrases attributed to Nasser, as well as the assertion that Israel "never originally intended to keep the spoils of war." Not one word about Egyptian attitudes toward Zionism and anti-Zionism found its way into print.

25. Other stations have done likewise. In early 1969 a minister and a priest—both total unknowns—returned from Israel. From early morning to late evening, WCBS Newsradio 88 and Channel 2 in New York City prominently featured their defense of Israel and their criticism of the U.N. censure for the attack on the Beirut Airport. Returnees from the Arab world, however knowledgeable, are never given such an opportunity.

26. With all due respect to Mehdi's sincerity, he usually played right into Zionist hands. As one Zionist once remarked, "If we didn't have a Mehdi, we would have to create him." Mehdi speaks with a decided accent, and no matter how calmly he might state his case, viewers can never relate to him as they might to the Zionist leaders who were on the program, or to the numerous Israelis—particularly Abba Eban, who over the years has been given an enormous amount of TV exposure. The former Foreign Minister of Israel has few peers in his command of the English language and his gift for oratory. What CBS did on this program has been the constant practice of the other major networks, that is, present the Middle East problem solely in terms of two positions: the Israel-U.S.-Zionist and the Arab positions, while the third point of view, that of the American national interest as represented by pro-Arab Christians (non-Arab Americans) and anti-Zionist Jews is scarcely ever aired.

27. This result was in line with polls, including that of the Foreign Policy Association in June 1976, which indicated very strong public opinion against further arming of Israel. This is detailed in the concluding chapter.

28. Other constant manipulations of the news have similarly given the American public myth-information. WCBS Newsradio 88 financial expert Ray Brady exhibited much glee in predicting that new Mexican oil discoveries would relieve the U.S. energy crunch and "send the Arabs back into the desert." There was no retraction by Brady when Mexico announced it was going to sell its oil at OPEC prices, and that Cuba and Latin American countries, not the U.S., would receive special treatment in the dispensation of the new oil. Later, Brady broadcast that "the Arabs were not only raising oil prices, but that Morocco, Libya, and Syria were responsible for the new high sugar prices. . . ."

29. Russell Warren Howe and Sarah Hays Trott, *The Power Peddlers / How Lobbyists Mold America's Foreign Policy* (Garden City, N.Y.: Doubleday, 1977), p. 321. Wallace was not the only one to be swamped by the Zionist machine. In April 1974 *National Geographic* carried an article, "Damascus, Syria's Uneasy Eden," by Robert Azzi. Under an indescribable barrage of pressure and threats, in its November issue for the first time in its eighty-six years of publishing, the magazine was forced to tell its readers that the small Syrian Jewish community has been existing since 1948 under "harsh conditions." For this purpose, the *National Geographic* instituted a new monthly column.

30. *Christian Science Monitor*, March 19, 1976. Reporter Arthur Unger allowed his bias to show through at the end of his article on the Wallace controversy: "But most observers in the news gathering profession—Mike Wallace included—will probably agree that there is a certain unreliability inherent in man-in-the-street, or at-home, interviews audited by Ministry of Information personnel in a totalitarian state. The danger is that what sets out to be a clarification of truth may turn out to be an oversimplification of truth."

31. *Voice*, "The Review of Arab Affairs," London, October 20, 1977. Parliament Member Mayhew announced that any claimant not satisfied could take him to court and, if he lost, he would "pay up." One Zionist produced a genocidal threat attributed to the first Secretary-General of the Arab League, Azzam Pasha, but which was an apparently deliberate mistranslation. Mayhew forced this Israelist to go into the High Court of Justice and apologize.

32. In my opening remarks I said: "First, I would like to point out that I am not talking from an Arab perspective but an American one. . . . Americans have been stirred up on this issue because there is an American interest in the boycott. There are jobs at stake. And this antiboycott legislation is likely to affect the average American businessman, taking away maybe 100,000 jobs involving eventually twenty to twenty-five million dollars worth of dollars that would flow to the U.S. from the purchase of goods."

33. The Arab League has observer status at the U.N., and its Ambassador and other staff members receive their diplomatic status from being attached to one of the twenty-one Arab League members, all of whom are fully accredited to the U.N. save the PLO, which has observer status.

34. The week before my appearance on "Firing Line," *TV Guide* asked my office to rush over a bio, a record of past television appearances, and any other relevant material on my views. Within half an hour of the request, the material was sent by messenger. When *TV Guide* appeared containing the programs for Saturday, November 29, all it had was "Channel 13, Wm. F. Buckley, Jr., Firing Line." A call to Miss Herma Rosenthal of *TV Guide* brought an astonishing response: "Oh, we wanted that not for the current issue but only in case the program was shown at a later date elsewhere." It was shown around the country, but the material was never used. The *New York Times* and the *Post* did even better in their Saturday TV/Radio column. Their listing ran: "Wm. F. Buckley, Jr., Firing Line: The Zionist Vote." If anything, the subject ought to have been "The Anti-Zionist Vote." What they would not put in print was the real subject: "The U.N. Resolution Equating Zionism with 'Racism and Racial Discrimination.' "

35. *Chippewa Herald Telegram*, April 30, 1969.

36. *Independent Press Telegram*, March 4, 1969.

37. Aside from the *New York Times,* the *Washington Post* has been the most blatant and consistent purveyor of myth-information regarding the Middle East. It was this paper which, six weeks after General George Brown had made a controversial statement with regard to Jewish ownership of banks and media, had reporter Michael Getler dig up the incident and present it as a front-page national news story. It was this same *Post* that in January 1976 purposely sabotaged a *Middle East Perspective* full-page ad so that, under cover of a newspaper strike making normal supervision by advertisers difficult, what ought to have read "Zionism Is Racism and Anti-Zionism Is Not Anti-Semitism" in fact appeared, "Zionism Is Racism and Zionism Is not Anti-Semitism." More about this incident in a later book with other personal anecdotes.

38. *Sunday News,* Ridgewood N.J., "New Policies in Middle East Should Aim at Peace," September 1, 1968. Gregg ran for Congress that fall on the Republican ticket, was defeated, and in 1969 became a registered Democrat.

39. The community's influence over the University of Utah, for example, was powerful enough to discourage sponsorship for a lecture appearance at the University. Arab students finally managed to sponsor the lecture after other groups mysteriously withdrew their offers. I subsequently learned that the fifty Jewish families had provided a gift of $425,000 for teaching of the Hebrew language at the Center, as well as for classes in Jewish history (interlaced with Zionism), whereas courses given on Islam and Arab history avoided discussion of the Arab political position for fear that the slightest drift into politics would spell the elimination of both courses from the curriculum and of funds to the University.

40. *Salt Lake Tribune,* October 28, 1973.

41. *Deseret News,* Jim Fiebig column October 26, 1973.

42. *Broadcasting* magazine, January 14, 1974.

43. While the wealthy Arab countries certainly have the means of bringing hundreds of writers, commentators, and news analysts to their countries, they do not believe in such public relations efforts, although the marked change in attitude toward the Arab-Israeli conflict as a result of seeing for oneself has been brought to their attention. In the spring of 1974 Editorial Page Editor Pat Murphy of the Phoenix *Arizona Republic* spent two weeks traveling thousands of miles to visit seldom-seen areas of Saudi Arabia, and in a series of articles attempted to overcome false impressions held by his readers about this important Arab country. Murphy wrote: "By default or design, Americans have shaped a distorted impression of this oil kingdom."

44. *Sacramento Bee,* May 30, 1976.

45. *Ibid.*

46. When it comes to coverage of the Middle East, distinctions between liberal and conservative have little meaning. Conservative publications were at one time more inclined to give space to anti-Zionist, pro-Arab positions (see *Human Events,* 1953–60), even as citadels of liberalism turned their back on the Voltairian credo, "I may disagree with you, but I will defend with my life your right to speak." After the Soviet military infiltration of the United Arab Republic under Nasser, conservative publications veered sharply to the Israeli camp, whose staunch anti-Communism provided a mutuality of interest. *Human Events, National Review,* and other like-minded magazines today almost invariably support the Israeli position, both because of its "anti-Communism" and also because they wish to compensate for the soupçon of anti-Semitism they may be harboring.

47. J. Bowyer Bell, *Terror Out of Zion* (New York: St. Martin's Press, 1977), p. 296.

48. Richard Reeves, *A Ford, Not a Lincoln,* 1975; *Old Faces of 1976,* 1976; *Convention, 1977* (New York: Harcourt Brace Jovanovich).

49. The release read: "Save Our Israel" is sponsoring a demonstration in solidarity with the Arab refugees at the Lebanese Consul, 76th Street and Fifth, on Wednesday, January 1st, at 1:30 P.M. Demonstrators will demand repatriation for Arab refugees incited to flee from their homes in '48 by Arab leaders. They will demand an end to the

deliberate perpetuation of the refugee problem by the Arab States. They also note that a 'Palestinian people' do not exist. The absurd Arab myth that the Jews came in and usurped Arabs from their homes and land must be countered by historical fact. Arab refugees were created by Arab leaders in order to be exploited as a weapon against the State of Israel."

50. *The New York Review of Books,* March 9, 1978.

51. Larry Collins and Dominique Lapierre, *O Jerusalem!* (New York: Simon and Schuster, 1972).

52. Richard Z. Chesnoff, Edward Klein, and Robert Littell, *If Israel Lost the War* (New York: Coward-McCann, 1969).

53. For the distortion of President Nasser's remarks before the six-day war, see p. 552–53. This was the most widely exploited slanted quote of all.

54. September 13, 1968, letter of McCloskey to *Look* magazine.

55. James Michener, *The Drifters* (New York: Random House, 1971), p. 180.

56. *Look,* August 8, 1967.

57. The responsibility for this rested with Editor Eugene Lyons, an escapist Jew who refused to have the *Digest* give any more attention to the subject of Jews and Zionism lest the spotlight on this call attention to himself.

58. *Reader's Digest Almanac* (1972), p. 623.

59. In December 1977 David Holden was mysteriously murdered shortly after he arrived in Cairo to cover the Begin-Sadat summit meeting in Ismailia.

60. *Life,* November 22, 1968.

61. *American Jewish World* (Minneapolis, Minn.), November 29, 1968.

Chapter IX: Numero Uno: The New York Times

1. *Chicago Tribune,* July 6, 1977, syndicated by King Features.

2. The writer has had to queue up for over forty-five minutes outside The Hub during the summer at Nantucket to get the Sunday *Times* so he can read the paper and angrily tear out examples of slanting.

3. *New York Times,* April 23, 1968.

4. This is a technique employed by the *Times* to editorialize on many issues, including national ones, to denigrate the views of opposing groups and individuals.

5. *Ibid.,* March 23, 1968.

6. *New York Times,* November 9, 1976; *Christian Science Monitor,* November 9, 1976.

7. When Israeli military attaché Colonel Yosef Alon was murdered (or assassinated) in his home in suburban Maryland, the same picture of the bereaved family used earlier in the week was blown up for the "Week in Review" and used again as a three-column photo lead for the article. *New York Times,* July 2 and July 8, 1973.

8. May 7, 1971.

9. *New York Times,* November 10, 1977.

10. *Ibid.,* November 13, 1977.

11. *Ibid.,* April 20, 1977.

12. *Ibid.,* February 15, 1978. The use of the word "Christian" was most misleading inasmuch as many Maronite Catholics, virtually all Greek and Syrian Orthodox, Greek Catholics, among other Christian denominations, were siding with the Palestinians— Muslims—leftist Lebanese.

13. The text of the pertinent portions of the Nasser 1970 May Day appeal follows:

"I address all this to President Nixon, for this is a crucial moment and the consequences are very dangerous.

"I say to President Nixon that there is a forthcoming decisive moment in Arab-American relations. There will be either rupture forever, or there will be another serious and defined beginning.

"Despite the facts that there are no diplomatic relations between our two countries, there is nothing that stops us from addressing one another in a last appeal for peace in the Middle East.

"We want President Nixon to ask Israel just two questions. The answer, if he receives any, will place at his disposal the whole truth. We want him to ask them:

"First, are they prepared to withdraw from all the Arab territories in accordance with the Security Council resolution and the United Nations principles?

"Secondly, are they aware that there is a people that were born free and master of themselves, namely, the people of Palestine, and that this people has rights, pointed out in the Security Council resolution, the United Nations' resolutions and the principles of its Charter—the principles that men have believed in and struggled for?

"Their answer has been clear to us from the beginning. They are not prepared to withdraw; they are not prepared to use the word 'withdrawal' even for mere consumption in the face of world opinion. This is what the Prime Minister of Israel said a few days ago, because they seek expansion. They are against the rights of the people of Palestine; they even deny that there is a people called the people of Palestine.

"President Nixon should have a look at what is going on in Israel itself in order to see the picture in its true perspective. There are many voices, even in Israel itself, which have begun to warn against the difficult and dangerous road along which the military ruling clique in Israel is drifting and to which it wants to drag the whole of the Middle East and perhaps others bigger than the Middle East.

"This is the appeal I make to U.S. President Nixon."

14. *Time,* May 7, 1973.

15. Purely by accident, an attractive member of the Dominican delegation to the U.N. poured out her heart to the author over a cup of tea in the Delegates' Lounge and revealed the extent of the Zionist pressures brought to bear on her country.

16. *New York Times,* October 15, 1974.

17. *Ibid.,* February 7, 1970.

18. *Ibid.,* October 5, 1974.

19. *Ibid.,* December 1, 1974.

20. *Ibid.,* June 26, 1973. American architect Arthur Kutcher also assailed the sacrifice "of the city's visual and spiritual character," and wrote protesting in a critical book: "The matchless, delicate, poignant landscape is utterly without defense and is being bulldozed randomly throughout its length and breadth." *New Jerusalem: Planning and Politics* (Cambridge, Mass.: MIT Press, 1975).

21. *Ibid.,* November 25, 1976.

22. *Ibid.,* June 26, 1974.

23. *Rolling Stone* magazine, November 15, 1977.

24. *Ibid.* Also *New York Post,* October 24, 1977.

25. *Newsweek,* January 9, 1978.

26. *New York Times,* November 6, 1977.

27. *Newsweek,* January 9, 1978.

28. *Washington Star,* March 23, 1978.

29. Colonel Mua'mmar Qaddafi of Libya on his 1973 harmonious and otherwise successful visit to Paris had baldly asked President Pompidou if he could buy a nuclear bomb and was told that such "were not for sale."

30. *New York Times,* August 23, 1974.

31. *Ibid.,* July 22, 1976.

32. Monroe H. Freedman, Professor of Law at Hofstra Law School, and Alan M. Dershowitz, who teaches law at Harvard and has been a fervent supporter of Israel through contributions to the *New York Times* and appearances on National Educational Television. On June 15 the *Times* did publish a long letter, "On the Israelis' Trial of Sami Esmail" by John Masterson and Barbara Thibeault, cochairpersons of the National Committee to Defend the Human Rights of Sami Esmail.

33. The *Los Angeles Times* in its editorial called the occupation among "the most benevolent, humane and progressive in history. Israel has interfered only nominally with the life of the area."

34. Aziza E. Wilson survey, "Stands on the Arab-Israel Conflict: Letters to the Editor and Op-Ed Articles Published by *The New York Times*" (Letters: January through December 1975; January through June 1976; January through September 1977. Articles: January through September 1977), prepared for *Middle East Perspective.*

35. For example, *New York Times* letter "Wrong PLO Contact" by Hadassah President Bernice S. Tanenbaum, dated December 20 and appearing January 4, was a lengthy reply to Op-Ed piece of December 16, while "Middle East Abnormality" was the answer to a short letter dated December 23 and appearing January 6 from Abdelwahab M. Elmissiri, Office of the League of Arab States. Also, January 16 pro-Israeli letter by S. Godick as opposed to that of B. Ferencz.

36. *New York Times,* April 13, 1977, pro-Israel letter by G. S. Jeremias as opposed to that of Gay Mize on the same date.

37. *New York Times,* January 4 and January 6, 1977 letters by B. S. Tanenbaum and by Abdelwahab Elmissiri.

38. *New York Times,* July 5, 1977, letters: M. T. Mehdi and M. B. Schub.

39. *New York Times,* letters of January 16 and 18 and of February 28, 1977.

40. Aziza E. Wilson survey, *op. cit.* Code for multiple-letter days, January through September 1977: 1 pro-Israel; 2 pro-Arab; 3 neutral.

1 1			—	two days
1 1 1			—	one day
1 1 3			—	one day
1 2			—	four days
1 2 1			—	one day
1 2 2 1			—	one day
1 3			—	one day
1 3 1 1			—	two days
2 1			—	three days
2 2			—	one day
2 3			—	two days
3 1			—	three days

41. *New York Times,* September 2, 1977. A. V. Martin's letter is an example: "Obviously Recognition of the PLO Is Not Open to Negotiations." Also March 26, 1977, F. Badr's letter.

42. Another *New York Times* method is to give prominent position by itself to a pro-Israel letter, as on November 10, 1977, to the very strong letter of District Attorney Carl A. Vergari, which attacked a *Times* ad by the Arab Information Center, without any indication that the ad in its entirety consisted of quotations supportive of the charge of terrorization of the Palestinians in the occupied territories and in Israel, from Amnesty International, International Fact Finding Delegation of National Lawyers Guild, Israeli League for Human and Civil Rights, Sunday *Times* of London, and the Swiss League for Human Rights.

43. *New York Times,* January 16, 1977.

44. *New York Times Magazine,* November 7, 1971.

45. Albert Einstein: *Out of My Later Years* (New York: Philosophical Library, 1950), p. 263.

46. *New York Post,* March 13, 1955. The *New York World-Telegram* on his death April 18, 1956, referred to him as "an ardent Zionist." Among a full page of pictures in the Scripps-Howard paper was one showing the late professor buying the 200,000th State of Israel bond.

47. Teddy Kollek with Amos Kollek, *For Jerusalem* (New York: Random House, 1978).

48. Eitan Haber, *The Legend and the Man* (New York: Delacorte, 1978).

49. *New York Times*, October 27, 1946.

50. Gay Talese, *The Kingdom and the Power* (New York: World, 1969).

51. *Ibid.*, p. 92.

52. While the *Times'* owners would vehemently deny any Zionist affiliation, the record clearly bears out the newspaper's Israelist, if not Zionist, orientation.

53. *Time*, "The Kingdom and the Cabbage," August 15, 1977.

54. For example, see James Markham's piece in the *Times* of August 27, 1977, and several Flora Lewis articles the following fall.

55. The *Minneapolis Tribune*, May 19, 1977, had this to say about Begin:

" 'You call me a terrorist, but I call myself a freedom fighter.' These words, or words like them, have been spoken by Palestinian terrorists for years in defiance of world disapproval of terrorism.

"But this specific quote is not from a Palestinian terrorist, but from a man whom Tuesday's election placed first in line to become Israel's next prime minister. Menachem Begin founded the Irgun terrorists in pre-Israel Palestine; the group's atrocities against Arabs were justified, in Begin's eyes, by the struggle to achieve a Jewish homeland.

"President Carter has spoken of the need for a Palestinian homeland. But 29 years after the creation of Israel, the Palestinians still have no homeland.

"And if one of them says, 'You call me a terrorist, but I call myself a freedom fighter,' what will Begin say in response? That the end justified the means for his Irgun terrorists, but doesn't for the Palestinians?"

56. As a balance to an article excerpting a July 31, 1946, pro-Zionist speech in the House of Lords by Lord Victor Rothschild, the *Times* ran on its December 6, 1977, Op-Ed page a picture of rescue workers at the King David Hotel after the bombing, with this sized caption:

Rescue workers at the King David Hotel, Jerusalem, in July 1946 after the underground Irgun Zvai Leumi, then headed by Menahem Begin, blew up a wing, killing 91 persons and injuring 45. The hotel was headquarters of the British Secretariat for Palestine. Mr. Begin, now Prime Minister, is currently on an official visit to Britain.

57. *Village Voice*, June 6, 1977.

58. *Human Events*, July 23, 1977.

59. Ranan Lurie was the Israeli journalist who interviewed Chairman of the Joint Chiefs of Staff George S. Brown and "exposed" his statement calling Israel a "military burden."

60. *New York Times*, May 19, 1977.

61. *Ibid.*, Sunday, July 24, 1977, by correspondent Marvine Howe.

62. *Ibid.*, June 7, 1977.

63. *Ibid.*

64. "Give Vision a Chance in the Middle East," *New York Times*, June 29, 1977.

65. *New York Times*, June 21, 1977.

66. *Ibid.*, June 22, 1977.

67. *Ibid.*, June 27, 1977.

68. *Ibid.*, July 18, 1977.

69. *Ibid.*, July 17, 1977.

70. *Jerusalem Post*, June 21, 1977.

71. *Chicago Daily News*, December 8, 1948.

72. The Coffin-La Farge-Lazaron letter was attacked from his pulpit by Rabbi Emanuel Neumann, who then held the post of official U.N. observer for the Central Conference of American Rabbis, as "only another attempt to sabotage the progress of Palestine Jew . . . in direct succession to the other anti-Jewish monuments of the last several years organized by Lazaron." Alfred M. Lilienthal, *What Price Israel?* (Chicago: Henry Regnery, 1954), p 107.

73. *New York Times*, August 11, 1977.

74. *Ibid.*, September 9, 1976.

75. *Philadelphia Inquirer*, May 29, 1977.

76. *New York Times*, December 21, 1977.

77. Philip E. Davies, letter to editor, *New York Times*, January 7, 1978.

78. *New York Times*, February 10, 1978.

79. *Ibid.*, March 16, 1978. On March 24 the editorial page, in the face of unsuccessful Carter-Begin talks, pushed its viewpoint further: "What Carter should seek is return of captured territory to all who grant Israel recognition, genuine security, and real peace. It is not too much to ask."

80. The Chief Justice said that "the large media conglomerates" had amassed "vast wealth and power" and that there was "no basis for saying" that their leaders "are more or less sensitive to the views and desires of minority shareholders" than are other corporation officials. *New York Times*, April 28, 1978. In an editorial the following week, the *Times* answered Justice Burger by warning against "venturing down a tricky theoretical path . . . and rushing to embrace indiscriminate solutions." *New York Times*, May 7, 1978.

Chapter X: Terror: The Double Standard

1. After Munich, correspondent John Law, who had by then reported for nineteen years from the area, indicated that the Palestinian terrorists were striving to win "attention" to their problem, even though "they realize they lose world sympathy by acts of terror. They are bitter and very desperate men who feel they have a real cause, and nothing to lose. They are in many instances college-educated men. These are people who believe that what they are doing is right, even though it is vicious." *U.S. News & World Report*, September 18, 1972.

2. Janis Terry and Gordon Mendenhall, *Journal of Palestine Studies*, "1973 U.S. Coverage on the Middle East," Vol. IV, No. 1, Autumn 1974.

3. *Washington Post*, April 12, 1973.

4. "Open Letter to Christians in the West" signed by sixty-six American clergymen serving as missionaries and pastors in Lebanon for the United Presbyterian Church in the USA, United Church Board of World Ministries, Reformed Church of America, Near East Baptist Mission, Southern Baptist Convention, Lutheran Church, Community Church of Beirut, Mennonite Board of Missions, and L'Action Chretienne en Orient. Reprinted in *Middle East Perspective*, October 1968.

5. For a full, itemized report of the Zionist record on the use of violence and terrorism from 1939 through September 1974, see U.N. General Assembly Document No. A/9801, October 11, 1974.

6. *Morning Journal*, November 27, 1950.

7. The Stern Gang was organized in 1939 by Abraham Stern, one of the Irgun's commanding officers, who left the parent organization to build up his own group of 250–300 more extreme fanatics. Stern, said to have written Hebrew poetry between acts of violence, was killed in 1942 by Palestine police.

8. Stanton Griffis, *Lying in State* (New York: Doubleday, 1952), p. 213.

9. *Yediot Aharonot*, February 28, 1977. This second volume of the Ben-Gurion series appeared in the U.S. as a 1977 Signet book.

10. Ghassan Kanafani, Palestinian editor and novelist, and his sixteen-year-old niece were killed on July 8, 1972, when a bomb planted by Israeli agents exploded in his car. Emile Khayyat, a Rif Bank employee in Beirut, was seriously injured on July 18, 1972, by a letter bomb; intellectual Dr. Anis Sayegh was blinded the next day, and Bassam Sherif, a young Palestinian writer, was seriously maimed a week later by letter bombs in Beirut. Two Import-Export Bank employees were later seriously wounded, also by a letter bomb (October 26, 1972). In the famed raid in which the Israeli assassins were landed from sea craft, PLO leaders Yusuf Najjar, Kamal Adwan, and Kamal Nasser (one of Palestine's foremost poets) were gunned down in their Beirut apartments on April 10, 1973. Four Lebanese civilians, three Syrians, and an Italian were also killed, and

twenty-nine Lebanese were wounded in the course of this operation, for which Israel was unanimously condemned by the Security Council.

11. Los Angeles accountant Mohammed Shaath and child badly injured by a bomb placed by agents in his home (September 14, 1972).

12. Noel Zuaiter, Palestinian scholar and PLO representative, gunned down by the Mossad (Israel's CIA) at his apartment entrance (October 16, 1972).

13. Mustafa Awad Zaid blinded and paralyzed by a letter bomb (October 25, 1972).

14. Omar Suffan, Representative of the Red Crescent, lost his fingers when a letter bomb exploded (November 29, 1972).

15. Palestinian student lost his arm with the explosion of a letter bomb, allegedly the work of the Mossad (November 30, 1972).

16. When an electronically detonated bomb, allegedly installed by the Mossad, exploded in his Paris home, Palestinian leader Mahmoud Hamshari lost a leg and died a month later (January 8, 1973). Iraqi political science professor Dr. Bassel Kubaissy was gunned down on a Paris street (April 6, 1973). Algerian poet and friend of the Palestinians, Mohammed Boudaisu, was killed by the explosion of a bomb in his car.

17. Palestinian Hussein Abul Kheir was killed in his hotel room in Cyprus.

18. Ahmed Bouchiki was gunned down by Israeli agents in Oslo.

19. See *Time* magazine, July 14, 1975, for specifics on the June 11 raid directed against key members in the Popular Democratic Front for the Liberation of Palestine (the Hawatmeh group), and of the Popular Front for the Liberation of Palestine (the Habash group).

20. Chaim Weizmann, *Trial and Error* (New York: Harper Bros., 1949), pp. 437–38.

21. Anglo-American Committee of Inquiry, *Report to the United States Government and His Majesty's Government of the United Kingdom* (Department of State, 1946), Recommendations No. 10, p. 12.

22. Gerold Frank, *The Deed* (New York: Simon & Schuster, 1963) pp. 307–8.

23. In remarks to the press on August 3, 1970, President Nixon lamented "the tendency of some to glamorize those identified with crime." *New York Times*, August 4, 1970. The day before the presidential remark was reported in the *Times*, there appeared on page 2 a photo and a profile of Menachem Begin in which the Israeli was described as an "Israeli hawk," whose "admirers felt that his exploits had a Robin Hood quality."

24. For a thirty-eight-page account of the Lavon Affair and the Cairo spy trial, see Howard M. Sachar, *From the Ends of the Earth: The Peoples of Israel* (New York: World, 1964).

25. Eli Ben-Hanan, *Our Man in Damascus: The Story of Elie Cohen, Israel's Greatest Spy* (New York: Crown, 1969).

26. Joshua Tadmor, *The Silent Warriors* (New York: Macmillan, 1969).

27. The letters, according to a William Sherman story in the New York *Daily News* of October 11, also contained a message signed by the Black September movement. A third bomb addressed to another Hadassah executive, because she had moved, wound up in the Fordham Post Office and badly injured a clerk when it exploded. While the envelope was totally destroyed, the "terror note" was miraculously found intact on top of a file eight feet from where the bomb exploded. The postal station had been vandalized on the night between the explosion and the discovery of the note two days later. A carrier was quoted, "It is possible that the note had been planted by vandals."

28. Wolfgang Lotz, *The Champagne Spy* (New York: St. Martin's Press, 1972), p. 174.

29. *Boston Globe*, September 7, 1972. p. 1.

30. *New York Post*, February 23, 1973.

31. New York *Daily News*, February 23, 1973.

32. *New York Times*, September 7, 1972.

33. February 23, 1973 *New York Post's* editorial was scarcely believable: "Sometime before 2:00 P.M. local time yesterday, a Libyan commercial airliner due in Cairo with 112 persons apparently flew past the Egyptian capital for some reason and within a few

minutes was over the Suez Canal—an Israeli military position. No pretense is being made that the airliner was armed or that it engaged in any menacing maneuvers; *it may even have been off course.* [Italics added; this was an established fact hours before the editorial was written.] Yet it was set upon by some of the most sophisticated warplanes now flying, and if not actually shot down, forced to make a catastrophic crash landing."

34. Miles Copeland, *The Game of Nations* (New York: Simon and Schuster, 1969).

35. *National Review*, "Dirty Tricks and All," October 26, 1973.

36. *New York Times*, "Terror in Khartoum," March 4, 1973.

37. The *Times* referred to the "airspace of Israeli-occupied Egyptian territory." The *Christian Science Monitor* declared, "Sinai is not Israel . . . the deed carries the appearance of defiance of world opinion and the interest of other peoples and nations."

38. New York *Daily News*, February 23, 1973.

39. In Boston, at special funeral services in the chapel of the Associated Synagogues of Massachusetts on Tremont Street, attended by Governor Francis W. Sargent, the "mourners" were harangued by Mayor Kevin H. White and others who denounced the Arab terrorists to the cheers of those in attendance, according to the September 7, 1972, *Boston Globe* account, "A Time to Mourn and a Time for Anger," featured by a four-column, six-inch-deep picture of the mourners.

40. *New York Times*, September 7, 1972.

41. *Washington Post*, September 7, 1972.

42. In December 1974 Mr. and Mrs. Berger were again used as props, brought from Cleveland to New York for radio-television appearances to remind the American public of the Munich incident just after the U.N. had heard Yasir Arafat and was about to take decisive action regarding the PLO.

43. *New York Times*, February 24, 1973.

44. In a June 2, 1977, editorial, "Red Carpets and Blood Stains," the *New York Post* hit at the "lavish official welcome" given King Juan Carlos and Queen Sophia of Spain on their visit to Washington, pointing to the "reported steadily mounting evidence that arrests and torture of political prisoners in post-Franco Spain are again as common as they were under the Caudillo at his worst." Also quoted at length was the charge of the International League for Human Rights that torture of political prisoners was taking place in India, and similar allegations of such acts in Chile. But this editorial writer failed to mention one word about the illegal arrests and torture inflicted upon the Palestinians under the Israeli occupation, substantiated, even before the London Sunday *Times* exposé, by the U.N. Commission on Human Rights, the U.N. Special Committee to Investigate Israeli Practices Affecting the Human Rights of the Peoples of the Occupied Territories, the International Committee of the Red Cross, Amnesty International, and the Swiss League for Human Rights.

45. The *Christian Science Monitor*, at that time the notable press exception to the caliber of reportage, carried the Pierpoint commentary in full on March 9, 1973.

46. This brings back memories of the kind of protest that was raised during the summer of 1971 on the faraway island of Nantucket, Massachusetts, with the appearance of a single anti-Zionist letter in the local *Inquirer and Mirror*, and the sudden inundation of Zionist supporters in the middle of summer at a meeting held in the Unitarian Church there.

47. The Nahal is an Israeli paramilitary organization from which recruits are taken for paratroop corps or other military service.

48. London *Times*, May 18, 1974.

49. *New York Post*, May 17, 1974. The European press joined in: "Monstrous cowardice that nothing could justify," cried *Figaro*. "Revolting means used to block the way to peace," wrote *Les Echos*. Even before the facts were all in, London's *Daily Telegraph* on May 16 bitterly condemned the Palestinians in an editorial, "Murderers of Children."

50. Judith Coburn, "Israel's Ugly Little War," *New Times*, March 7, 1975.

51. *New York Times*, editorial, June 22, 1974.

52. Much of the detail regarding the comparative coverage of the attack on southern

Lebanon comes from the fine pen of Alexander Cockburn's "Press Clips" in *The Village Voice*, March 27, 1978.

53. *New York Times*, March 14, 1978.

54. *New York Post*, March 15, 1978.

55. *New York Times*, March 19, 1978.

56. *Washington Post*, March 18, 1978.

57. *New York Times*, March 18, 1978.

58. *Time* magazine, March 27, 1978.

59. *Washington Post*, November 10, 1977.

60. Thomas Kiernan, *The Arabs* (Boston: Little, Brown, 1975), p. 8.

61. *Jerusalem Post Weekly*, May 14, 1974.

62. Irene Beeson, *Guardian*, July 22, 1974.

63. George Petersen, "The Town That Used to Be," *Nation Review* (Australia), July 29, 1974.

64. Stewart West, "The Destruction of Quneitra," *Scoop* magazine (Australia), July 24, 1974. West has since been elected to Parliament.

65. *New York Times*, August 26, 1976.

66. Meir Kahane, *The Story of the Jewish Defense League* (Philadelphia: Chilton Book Co., 1975).

67. *New York Times*, June 8, 1975.

68. Bombs have been thrown at Mehdi's residence, employees have been beaten and stabbed. In the fall of 1974, when the Jewish Defense League was particularly on the rampage due to Yasir Arafat's imminent arrival at the U.N., a peaceful demonstration by Medhi and nine other people had to be guarded, according to then U.S. Ambassador to the U.N. John A. Scali, by 150 New York City policemen.

69. During the lecture two young men first pelted me with eggs and then, mounting the platform, hit me in the head with gloved hands. I was taken to the hospital for treatment of minor head injuries. Metromedia Channel 5 news that night interviewed a JDL official who declared that "the attackers did not do a good job, because he [Lilienthal] deserved a lot more."

70. *New York Times*, June 4, 1974.

71. Beirut *Daily Star*, October 15, 1972.

72. *New York Times*, October 31, 1974, shortly before Arafat's speech at the U.N.

73. "Terrorists' Techniques Improve and So Do Efforts to Block Them," *New York Times*, July 23, 1974.

74. The attack by the splinter Palestinian group, Popular Front for the Liberation of Palestine, General Command, timed to coincide with the visit of President Nixon to the area, was directed against the border kibbutz of Shamir, eleven miles from Kiryat Shemona, which previously had been attacked. In a battle with the kibbutz residents, four fedayeen slew three women before being killed themselves.

75. Winston Churchill, *History of the English Speaking Peoples*, Vol. 1 (London: Cassell, 1956), p. 21.

76. *Parade*, January 18, 1976.

77. *Ibid.*, October 3, 1976. The article abounded with Israeli expressions of peace and hostile Arab responses. Peace, concluded the writer, could be advanced through a student exchange between Cairo and Tel Aviv.

78. *Ibid.*, February 6, 1977. This same Sadat picture with a rose in his hand was used as a full-page *Parade* advertisement in the *New York Times* on November 29, 1977, after the Egyptian leader's visit to Jerusalem.

79. *Ibid.*, "This is the West Bank—The Hottest Piece of Real Estate in the Middle East," February 19, 1978. The writer details the emotional and political Israeli reasoning for keeping this territory through an interview with the 21-year-old settler he sympathetically presented in his 1976 article on the same subject. Inquiry at the magazine revealed that Michaelson was "Jewish, but non-practising."

80. *Congressional Record*, 93rd Congress, Second Session June 21, 1974, p. S. 20500.

Chapter XI: Exploiting Anti-Semitism

1. *Jewish Newsletter*, (New York), January 9, 1961.

2. *Newsweek*, March 1, 1971.

3. A confidential memo (December 26, 1967) from Joseph Sklover to B'nai B'rith President William Wexler, impounded in the U.S. District Court in Washington in the Joftes case, states that the Jewish organization provided $557 toward the trip to Israel of *New York Times* writer Irving Spiegel.

4. Rabbi Solomon Bernards of the ADL distributed on June 26 and July 20, 1967, Israel Information Services pamphlets carrying the official Tel Aviv version of the six-day war.

5. Leonard Slater, *The Pledge* (New York: Simon and Schuster, 1970).

6. *Ibid.*, pp. 120–21.

7. Larry Collins and Dominique Lapierre, *O Jerusalem!* (New York: Simon and Schuster, 1972), p. 271.

8. *Presbyterian Life*, July 1, 1967, p. 27.

9. Arnold Forster and Benjamin R. Epstein, *The Troublemakers* (Garden City, N.Y.: Doubleday, 1952); *Cross-Currents* (Garden City, N.Y.: Doubleday, 1956); *Some of My Best Friends* (New York: Farrar, Strauss, 1962); *Danger on the Right* (New York: Random House, 1964); *Report on the John Birch Society* (New York: Random House, 1966); *The Radical Right: Report on the John Birch Society and its Allies* (New York: Random House, 1967).

10. *New York Times*, March 6, 1974.

11. *New York Post*, March 8, 1974.

12. Desmond Stewart quotes Herzl's reference to anti-Semitism in this metaphor: [as] "steam power which is generated by boiling water in a tea kettle and then lifts the lid." *Theodor Herzl* (New York: Doubleday, 1974), p. 217.

13. M. Lowenthal, ed., *The Diaries of Theodor Herzl* (New York: Grosset & Dunlap, 1962), p. 7.

14. Richard H. S. Crossman, *A Nation Reborn* (New York: Atheneum, 1960), p. 21.

15. *Ibid.*

16. *The Spectator* magazine (London), June 27, 1960.

17. Statement of October 27, 1947, quoted in *Council News* (New York: American Council for Judaism), December 1956, and in Alfred M. Lilienthal, *What Price Israel?* (Chicago: Henry Regnery, 1954), p. 52.

18. *New York Times*, July 24, 1958.

19. *National Jewish Post and Opinion*, November 6, 1959.

20. *Blackfriars Magazine*, Monthly Review (London: Blackfriars Publications, January 1957). Charles Solomon wrote: "When to proclaim oneself a Jew may mean hardship, even death, the indomitable spirit of man—or perhaps his sheer obstinacy—asserts itself. . . . But when to be a Jew is merely inconvenient, it is difficult to maintain this mood of high resolve."

21. Amidst the euphoria immediately following the Sadat visit to Jerusalem and the invitation to Begin to come to Cairo, this same rabbi and same organization eighteen months later warmly welcomed Egyptian Ambassador Ashraf Ghorbal at a New York meeting on December 6, 1977, at which the Hanukkah candles were lit. All smiles, Ghorbal assured his former detractors, now exuberant admirers, that there would be only peace, no more war between Israelis and Egyptians.

22. *Washington Post*, April 21, 1975. Argentina with its 400,000 Jews has in the past three years become a focal point of Zionist propaganda activity. See Morton M. Rosenthal, "Argentinian Jews in Danger," *Anti-Defamation League Bulletin*, November 1976, New York.

23. Quoted by Gay Talese, *The Kingdom and the Power* (New York: World, 1969), p. 270.

24. *New York Times Magazine*, January 3, 1971.

25. *New York Times*, January 14, 1961, p. 6, "Lichtenberger Hails Rector in Scarsdale"; January 16, p. 24, "Rector Is Praised for Stand on Bias"; January 24, p. 1, "Scarsdale Golf Club Reverses Guest Rules."

26. *Daily Princetonian*, February 24, 1964, carried President Robert F. Goheen's letter. The biting letter of student Paul J. Ponomarenko, class of 1966, appeared on February 20, and there were other letters on the 21st and 24th. Most unusual was the frank and remarkable perception of Frank C. Strasburger, class of 1967, who decried "the continual carping, which serves only to remind people of what they already know, . . . Jews may find persecution if they look for it (and they do look for it), but those Jews who assume their equality (that they are neither lesser nor greater than those of other faiths), find that they need not assert it."

27. *New York Times*, February 26, 1964.

28. The lengthy *New York Times* evaluation of the man and poet boldly referred to Pound as a "persistent anti-Semite," while the *New York Post* more conservatively reported "the charge that he was an anti-Semite."

29. *New York Times*, July 16, 1972.

30. *Boston Globe*, November 7, 1971.

31. *New York Times*, August 9, 1973.

32. *Jewish Currents*, March 31, 1974. The international edition of the *Jerusalem Post* of March 28, 1972, carried an article by drama critic Mendel Kohansky calling "The Merchant of Venice" an anti-Semitic play, even in its contemporary Hebrew rendition in Jerusalem.

33. Marion K. Sanders, *Dorothy Thompson: A Legend in Her Time* (New York: Houghton Mifflin, 1973), p. 322.

34. *Ibid.*, p. 327.

35. *Ibid.*, p. 326.

36. *Ibid.*, p. 323.

37. *Jewish Newsletter* (New York), April 6, 1951.

Chapter XII: The Blitz

1. Walter Millis, ed., *Forrestal Diaries* (New York: Viking Press, 1951), p. 363.

2. *Ibid.*

3. Arnold A. Rogow, *James Forrestal: A Study of Personality, Politics and Policy* (New York: Macmillan, 1963), p. 187.

4. *Ibid.*

5. James G. McDonald, *My Mission to Israel* (New York: Simon and Schuster, 1951), p. 17.

6. When Israeli Deputy Premier Yigal Allon declared in 1969, "Our late victory, as the previous ones, was mainly thanks to our quality of superiority," he was uttering the equivalent of President de Gaulle's "an elite people sure of itself and dominating." But when Allon said this, it was an appropriate expression of pride.

7. *New York Times*, December 3, 1967.

8. *Ibid.*

9. *Ibid.*

10. *New York Times*, February 7, 1972.

11. July 11, 1969.

12. Recruits from this same college were promoting the NBC "Holocaust" miniseries of April 1978 and were photographed distributing circulars in the *New York Post*, April 19, 1978.

13. *New York Times*, September 30, 1973.

14. *Ibid.*

15. *Newsweek*, October 15, 1973. In a tedious propaganda account replete with

pictures of weeping Soviet Jewish women and children as well as an "adamant" Kreisky, Wisconsin University historian George L. Mosse was quoted as contending that the incident proved how "unreconstructedly anti-Semitic Austria remains."

16. Hugh McCullum, "Freedom of the Press" (editorial), *Canadian Churchman*, June 1973.

17. *Ibid.*

18. The *New York Times*, January 15, 1977, broke the story on its front page: "U.S. Officials Expressing Concern About Rising Israeli Arms Exports." Apparently, since the October 1973 war, Israel had increased its military exports five-fold and was supplying certain countries with American jet engines and other sophisticated military equipment in contravention of American law. Such action if committed by other countries would instantaneously bar further military aid to them, but in the instance of Israel only raised a question from the media.

19. *Middle East Perspective*, January 1973.

20. Including the *Toronto Star*, April 17, 1972.

21. Arab American University Graduates Convention, October 19–21, 1973.

22. The title of the Novak article, "The New Anti-Semitism," had its antecedents in the *New York Times Magazine* article of January 3, 1971, by Professor Seymour M. Lipset, upon which Forster and Epstein also drew for the name of their 1974 book.

23. Federal Judge Marvin Frankel gave Bergman an initial light four months sentence, and he was placed, like Rabbi Meir Kahane, in the "country club" prison. The Judge no doubt had been deeply moved by the Bergman plea that he would atone for his sinfulness by "giving courses on the holocaust to educate the uninformed."

24. The lecture was delivered before some 150 persons at the Duke University Law School forum in Durham, North Carolina, on October 10, 1974. The story by Michael Getler broke on November 13 in the *Washington Post*, and on the next day nationally just as Arafat was addressing the U.N.

25. Marvin and Bernard Kalb, *Henry Kissinger* (Boston-Toronto: Little, Brown, 1974), pp. 473–78. This book is discussed at length in Chapter XXI.

26. Wechsler also accused Brown's hostility and the atmosphere at the U.N. of killing "serious reflection and even reappraisal of past positions. Both tend to vitiate thoughtful debate—both here and within Israel—about difficult alternatives." Again, the pot was calling the kettle black. *New York Post*, November 20, 1974.

27. San Francisco *Examiner*, November 3, 1974; UPI, November 4, 1974.

28. *New York Times*, October 19, 1976.

29. Quoted by Russell Warren Howe and Sarah Hays Trott, *How Lobbyists Mold America's Foreign Policy* (New York: Doubleday, 1977), p. 317.

30. *Ibid.*

31. *New York Post*, January 15, 1975.

32. CBS (radio), "Spectrum," September 10, 1973.

33. Arnold Forster and Benjamin Epstein, *The New Anti-Semitism* (New York: McGraw-Hill, 1974), p. 313.

34. *Evening Standard* (London), July 29, 1969. The pressures against Mrs. McKay became so great that she was denied renomination by her party and did not return to Parliament.

35. *Boston Jewish Advocate*, December 28, 1972.

36. *Search for Peace in the Middle East* (Philadelphia: American Friends Service Committee, 1970), reprint Fawcett, 1971.

37. *Village Voice*, March 7, 1977.

38. *Ibid.*

39. Hank Messick, *Lansky* (New York: G. P. Putnam, 1971).

40. Letter of Walter J. Minton to Justin Finger, national director, Department of Fact Finding, ADL, July 19, 1971, quoted in Forster and Epstein, *op. cit.*, p. 103. According to *Publishers Weekly*, September 1, 1971, Minton placed the matter with his attorneys for possible action.

41. Letter Seymour Graubard to Bob R. Dorsey, August 15, 1975; Dorsey reply August 24, 1975.

42. Donald Weadon, speaking at St. Mary's College in California, April 16, 1970.

43. Dr. Israel Shahak, "What Price Totalitarianism?" *Middle East Perspective*, October 1977.

Chapter XIII: The Holocaust: Stoking the Fires

1. According to Lucy Dawidowicz in *The War Against the Jews, 1933–1945* (New York: Harcourt, Brace & World, 1975; Bantam, 1976), the word "holocaust" comes through the Greek from the Hebrew word "olah," literally meaning "what is brought up," but signifying in biblical texts a "burnt offering." When used in connection with Nazi genocide, it brings to mind pagan sacrifices to placate angry gods.

2. *London Daily Express*, November 27 through December 2, 1972.

3. New York *Daily News*, November 27 through December 2, 1972.

4. Charles Dana Gibson, *The Ordeal of Convoy* (New York: South Street Museum, 1973).

5. Ladislas Farago, *The Aftermath* (New York: Simon and Schuster, 1974). On the same subject, see William Stephenson, *The Bormann Brotherhood* (New York: Harcourt Brace Jovanovich, 1973).

6. *New York Times Magazine*, January 14, 1973.

7. Arthur Morse, *While Six Million Died* (New York: Ace Publishing, 1967).

8. Dawidowicz, *op. cit.* The book was glowingly reviewed on the front page of the Sunday *Times* Book Review of April 20, 1975, with a terrorizing photo.

9. Myron S. Kaufmann, *The Coming Destruction of Israel: Will the U.S. Tolerate Russian Intervention in the Middle East?* (New York: New America Library, 1970).

10. Richard Chernoff, Edward Klein, and Robert Littel, *If Israel Lost the War* (New York: Coward-McCann, 1969).

11. Eli Wiesel, *One Generation After* (New York: Random House, 1970).

12. Originally published by Hill and Wang, New York, 1960.

13. Ehud Avrie, *Open the Gates* (Chicago: Quadrangle, 1961). This was picked up by the ADL, making a new edition possible.

14. Raul Hilberg, *The Destruction of European Jews* (New York: Quadrangle, 1971).

15. Yuri Suhl, *They Fought Back* (New York: Crown Publishers, 1967). Another ADL book edited, then translated by the author and placed in paperback.

16. *Libertarian*, Vol. 5, No. 3, May–June 1976.

17. Lucy S. Dawidowicz, *The Jewish Presence* (New York: Holt, Rinehart and Winston, 1977).

18. *New York Times* Book Review, July 24, 1977, by Edward Rothstein, described as a "free-lance critic who writes on a variety of cultural topics."

19. *New York Times*, July 25, 1977.

20. Christopher Lehmann-Haupt Book Review, *New York Times*, October 12, 1976.

21. John Toland, *Adolf Hitler* (New York: Doubleday, 1976).

22. Robert G. L. Waite, *The Psychopathic God: Adolf Hitler* (New York: Basic Books, 1977).

23. Howard Blum, *Wanted: The Search for Nazis in America* (New York: Quadrangle/New York Times, 1971).

24. *Wanted: The Search for Nazis in America*, *New York Post*, February 14–18, 1977.

25. Jack Hoffenberg, *17 Ben-Gurion* (New York: G. P. Putnam's Sons, 1977).

26. *New York Times*, April 7, 1977.

27. Alvin Rosenfeld, *The Plot to Destroy Israel* (New York: G. P. Putnam's Sons, 1977). This book indicted President Sadat, too, and contended he sought only nonbelligerency, not a real peace. This book was published in the spring before the Sadat peace initiative.

28. Gerald S. Strober, *American Jews: Community in Crisis* (New York: Doubleday, 1974).

29. *New York Times,* December 28, 1974.

30. Cynthia Ozick, "All the World Wants the Jews Dead," *Esquire,* November 1974.

31. Alfred Kazin, "What Do We Do Now?" *Atlantic Monthly,* April 1974.

32. *New York Times Magazine,* February 3, 1974.

33. Norman Podhoretz, "Abandonment of Israel," *Commentary,* July 1976. That December the magazine published twenty letters from readers, including Congressman Edward I. Koch and Clare Boothe Luce, all but one of which expressed overwhelming agreement with the article.

34. *New York Magazine,* December 23, 1974.

35. *New York Times Magazine,* July 24, 1977. See also Michael Selzer, "The Murderous Mind—A First Look at the Psychological Drawings of Adolf Eichmann," *New York Times Magazine,* November 27, 1977, in which a political scientist analyzes the doodlings of the Nazi leader in attempting to prove pathological sadomasochism.

36. *New York Times,* April 8, 1978.

37. Making his debut in *Rosebud* was none other than former New York Mayor John Lindsay, who in playing the role of a U.S. Senator, father of one of the girls, had difficulty with his few lines and did not seem to know what to do with his hands. After viewing the politician turned actor, one TV commentator noted, "A star was not born tonight."

38. *New York Times,* December 23, 1976.

39. Judith Crist review of *Mr. Klein* in the *New York Post,* November 9, 1977. Months after the film had been first shown in Boston, the *Globe* of June 28, 1978, carried a two-column article by Steven Erlanger, "The Real Terror of a 'Mr. Klein,'" which also discussed the value of NBC's miniseries "Holocaust" in educating "60 percent of Americans about the persecution and murder of Adolf Hitler."

40. Noting on April 30, 1973, that hundreds of persons, including former inmates of Dachau, assembled at the Nazi death camps site to mark the day, the *Times* also carried at the bottom of the same page this headline: "Italian Neo-Fascists Are Linked to a Synagogue Fire in Padua" (p. 3, column 1).

41. Seven PBS stations rejected this episode of "Black Perspective on the News," which was shown by the other stations in the network sometime after September 30, 1977, when it was sent out nationally.

42. *New York Times,* September 29, 1969.

43. *Ibid.,* July 25, 1969. Also see "Freeing of Man East Germany Called Ex-SS Officer," *New York Times,* June 24, 1977.

44. *Jewish Currents,* April 1977.

45. *New York Times,* March 14, 1977.

46. Wolfgang Lotz, *The Champagne Spy* (New York: St. Martin's Press, 1972).

47. *Ibid.,* p. 106. Just how false a picture Lotz drew of Egyptian feelings toward Jews was revealed in an interview of Nasser with a British journalist: "I have never been anti-Semitic on a personal level. It is very difficult for a thinking Egyptian to be so. We have so many basic links—after all, Moses himself was an Egyptian. My feelings and actions against Israel later were inspired solely by the Israelis' actions as a state." Robert Stephens, *Nasser: A Political Biography* (New York: Simon and Schuster, 1971), pp. 436–37.

48. When in New York on a book promotion trip in 1972, author Lotz admitted in a telephone interview with the author that "most Egyptians were not anti-Semites nor even anti-Jewish. They were great admirers of the Germans and their achievements." Editor Mohamed Heikal and others questioned in Cairo denied the Lotz charge as to the use of the *Protocols* at the trial of the spy.

49. Quoted in *New York Times,* January 7, 1968.

50. Meir during her visits abroad had developed a good relationship with Willy Brandt, but had stated in an interview that she was "unable to set foot on German soil." Brandt angrily retorted, but the quarrel was healed, and only the October war and then the fall of her government prevented the Meir visit.

51. *New York Times,* December 16, 1975.

52. *New York Times,* Sunday, March 19, 1978. The article was written by Hans Knight, columnist for *Discover,* the Sunday magazine of the *Philadelphia Bulletin.* In a letter of April 6, Knight noted that the news-peg for the article was the fortieth anniversary of the Anschluss, although it appeared a week later, and that he had written a similar piece for the *Bulletin* ten years previously.

53. *Variety,* June 15, 1977.

54. *New York Times,* April 18, 1978.

55. *New York Post,* April 18, 1978.

56. *New York Times,* April 18, 1978.

57. *Near East Report,* April 19, 1978.

58. *New York Times,* April 14, 1978. NBC admitted that a former Nazi officer had been paid as a technical consultant for the series, as he had been for work on the film *The Odessa File.*

59. *Ibid.,* "Art Versus Mammon," April 20, 1978.

60. *Ibid.,* April 16, 1978. The implausible situations about a gentile woman who is forced to sleep with an SS guard in order to be able to smuggle letters to her imprisoned Jewish husband led some to call the series "Mr. and Mrs. Miniver Go to Auschwitz."

61. As far back as 1962, Kay Gardella was writing favorable commentary in the New York *Daily News* for Zionist propaganda television films as she did that year on April 23 (late edition) and April 24 for the thirty-minute historical documentary "Years of Destiny," prepared by the Jewish National Fund and presented as a public service over Channel 11 in New York and elsewhere around the country. Few films have had as many half-truths, innuendos, distortions, and slantings as this presentation, which Ms. Gardella hailed as a "splendid history of the rebirth of Israel and of the life of the prophet of the Jewish state, Theodor Herzl."

62. *New York Post,* April 20, 1978.

63. In 1977 the Warsaw Ghetto commemoration had only received a three-column picture and no story on page 35 of the *New York Times* of April 18. On April 20 the *New York Times* devoted a full-page column to Israel Shenker's "Holocaust Survivors Remember."

64. At a purchase price of $175 or rental of $10, a twelve-minute color film "explains why Masada has come to symbolize resistance against oppression for Jews the world over."

65. A twenty-five-minute black-and-white film study cleared for TV on the attitudes and motivations behind anti-Semitism, prepared by Dr. Melvin Tumin, professor of sociology and anthropology at Princeton University, for adult and secondary school levels.

66. *New York Times,* October 7, 1977.

67. *Ibid.,* October 8, 1977.

68. *Ibid.,* September 18, 1977.

69. Milton Meltzer, *The Jews of the Holocaust* (New York: Harper & Row, 1976; Dell, 1977). In its Children's Catalogue for spring 1978, the Book-Of-The-Month Club listed the Meltzer book for "ages 12 and up." The title was slightly altered to *Never to Forget: The Jews of the Holocaust.*

70. *New York Times,* May 2, 1976.

71. Bestseller, *The Diary of Anne Frank,* translated into many languages and printed in multifold editions, may be a fraud. It was sold as the actual diary of a young Jewish girl who died in a Nazi concentration camp after two years of abuse and horror. Any informed literary inspection of this book would have shown it could not possibly have been the work of a teenager. Writer Meyer Levin won a suit in the New York Supreme Court against Otto Frank, Anne's father, for $50,000 as an "honorarium for his work" on the diary.

72. According to a telephone conversation with Raintree editor Russ Bennett in

August 1978, the publication of the Wiesenthal series had only been in the talking stage, but somehow the publicity had been leaked to the press.

73. *Ibid.*, November 5, 1972.

74. *Ibid.*, November 28, 1976. The article was written by Ralph Blumenthal, described as a *Times* reporter "who has followed the cases of war-crimes subjects in this country." The very day the *Times* and the rest of the media were playing up this "old-hat" story, they were totally blacking out the important press conference of Israeli Jewess lawyer and civil rights defender Felicia Langer, where she produced irrefutable evidence of the Israeli government's ruthless suppression and persecution of Palestinian Arabs in the occupied areas. This was eight months before the startling page-one revelations of torture in the Sunday London *Times.*

75. See *New York Times*, April 18, 1978, for a quarter-page advertisement asking funds for the Simon Wiesenthal Center for Holocaust Studies and featuring George Santayana's "Those who cannot remember the past are condemned to repeat it." Wiesenthal waged war in Austria against Bruno Kreisky, accusing the Austrian Chancellor of condoning anti-Semitism to advance his political career.

76. Compare this Meir show of arrogance with the tone of her conversation with Pope Paul, pp. 506–7.

77. *New York Review of Books,* March 6, 1975.

78. Spender refers to spending much of his time in Israel with "Arabists." The substitution of that word for "Arabs" helped serve as a subtle warning to his readers to expect that his views might have been colored by this fact, and hence that he was not as pro-Israel as otherwise might be expected.

79. The Agudath Israel has since changed its view considerably and is a member of the Begin ruling coalition.

80. Ben Hecht, *Perfidy* (New York: Julian Messner, 1961).

81. Reviewing the Hecht book in the September 1962 issue of *Freeland* (published in New York City by the Freeland League for Jewish Territorial Colonization), Michael Astour noted: "If any of his [Hecht's] statements are erroneous, the Zionist leaders can easily defend their honor in the normal manner. They are not doing this. . . . They are silent." According to Faris Glubb (writing as Faris Yahya) in *Zionist Relations with Nazi Germany* (Beirut: Palestine Research Center, 1978), the Eichmann trial provided the Israeli government with the opportunity "of burying once again all the unpleasant things which the Kastner case had brought to light" (p. 70). Witnesses who might have spoken up on the affair were not called by prosecutor Gideon Hausner (pp. 70–71). This small but excellently researched book is replete with recitals of close Zionist-Nazi ties.

82. Rabbi Moshe Schonfeld, *The Holocaust Victims* (Brooklyn: Neturei Karta, 1977). Much of the Schonfeld study was based on material of Rabbi Michael Ben Weisseman, published in Hebrew in the untranslated *Min Ha Metzar (From the Depths).*

83. Hannah Arendt, *Eichmann in Jerusalem* (New York: Viking Press, 1963).

84. In an October 25, 1977, letter to the *New York Times*, Yehuda Bauer, professor of Holocaust Studies and Chairman of the Institute of Contemporary Jewry at the Hebrew University in Jerusalem, explained why the murder of 30,000 Jews at Babi Yar in Kiev was far worse than that of hundreds of thousands of gypsies, Asiatics, Communists, and others whom the Nazis liquidated. There are "gradations of evil," the writer insisted, and what happened to "an endless list was evil, but not holocaust." The professor was commenting on an earlier announcement that the Soviet Union was constructing a monument on the site of Babi Yar to commemorate its victims. By some twist of convoluted logic, the writer makes the holocaust the sole property of the Jews.

Chapter XIV: Christians in Bondage

1. Some 10 percent of the Palestinian Arabs are Christian. In the entire Middle East, Arab Christians number five million. There are an additional one to two million scat-

tered throughout the world. Sometimes figures as high as eleven million are used by those who include Christians of all ages and degrees of loyalty in the Arab and non-Arab Middle East.

2. Supporting Herzl's thesis that Zionism could expect support from anti-Semites anxious to be rid of Jews were Polish anti-Semites in the interwar period. See Celia S. Heller, *On the Edge of Destruction, Jews of Poland Between the Two World Wars* (New York: Columbia University Press, 1977).

3. *New York Times*, November 1, 1977.

4. *Ibid.*, November 15, 1977.

5. For a detailed study of Christian movements emphasizing prophecy, see Calvin Keene's "Prophecy and Modern Israel," *Quaker Life*, December 1972.

6. Hal Lindsey with C. C. Carlson, *The Late Great Planet Earth* (Grand Rapids, Mich.: Zondervan, 1970).

7. The prophecies are contained, among other places, in Genesis 17 and 35, Deuteronomy 30:1–5, and Ezekiel 11:17. The Ezekiel passage reads: "Thus says the Lord God, I will gather you from among the peoples and assemble you out of the countries wherein you are scattered, and I will give you the land of Israel."

8. Letter of Mr. J. Calvin Keene to the author, June 5, 1976. See also Keene, *op cit.*

9. A letter written to *America* (June 7, 1975) by six Arab Christians in response to the Jersild article stated: "We have observed that, while American Jews almost solidly support Israel simply because it is Jewish, American Christians do not support us, or even understand our position, and in many cases are unaware of our very existence . . . we find this tendency of American correligionists to ignore our legitimate rights and disregard our deep-felt sense of moral grievance not only scandalous but incomprehensible."

10. Bert DeVries, *The Reformed Journal* (Grand Rapids, Mich.), " 'His Land' and History," April 1971 and " 'His Land' and Prophecy," November 1971.

11. *New York Post*, December 8, 1977. Out of fear of further angering American Jews, who were still angry over the sale of jets to Egypt, Ruth Carter Stapleton, the President's sister, canceled her appearance at a scheduled Long Island convention of a Hebrew-Christian group, B'nai Yeshua. The group was engaged in converting Jews.

12. The words appear in the Episcopal hymn book and commonly in Protestant hymnals. The words come from John of Damascus, circa 750 A.D., and the usual tune is from Arthur S. Sullivan.

13. Oesterreicher's Zionist chauvinism has been so extreme that he was bitterly criticized in a Catholic publication by Jewish writer Dr. Norton Mezvinsky, associate professor of history, Central Connecticut State College, for his "crude, unsophisticated, and misleading approach to some of the crucial problems and facts underlying the Arab-Israeli conflict." Letters to the Editor, *The Commonweal*, September 25, 1970.

14. *Newark Star-Ledger*, May 15, 1977.

15. Edward H. Flannery, *The Anguish of the Jews: Twenty-Three Centuries of Anti-Semitism* (New York: Macmillan, 1965).

16. *New York Times*, June 30, 1974.

17. In his book *Honor the Promise—America's Commitment to Israel* (New York: Doubleday, 1977), Congressman and Roman Catholic priest Robert F. Drinan followed the Oesterreicher-Flannery line. Two weeks before publication, the *Miami Herald* of October 9, 1977, carried a three-quarter-page feature by Drinan with bold headlines addressed to Christians. After visiting Israel as "guest of the government," according to an editorial introductory footnote to his April 9, 1963, article in *America*, Father Drinan wrote: "In January 1963, Israel's Ministry of Religious Affairs organized a course for Muslims aspiring to the clergy." Islam, of course, has no clergy!

18. *Link* (New York: Americans for Middle East Understanding), October, 1972. Another Ryan, the Reverend Joseph L., from Beirut, has been on the U.S. lecture circuit for several years expounding the claims of the Palestinians.

19. May 9, 1970 in most Beirut papers.

20. Dr. John Sutton served as executive director of the educational group, Americans for Middle East Understanding, which published the newsletter, *Link,* directed principally at educating church people.

21. *New York Times,* July 19, 1969.

22. After a battle of many months for control of the American Council for Judaism, Berger "resigned" from the organization he had spearheaded and organized American Jewish Alternatives to Zionism. This new, smaller group was more anti-Zionist and openly critical of Israeli policies than the ACJ had ever been.

23. For similar cowardice on the part of the Church of England, see Michael Adams and Christopher Mayhew, *Publish It Not* (London: Longman, 1975).

24. The ministers were from Unitarian Universalist, Protestant Episcopal, United Presbyterian, Catholic, Society of Friends, Antiochan, Orthodox, and United Church of Christ Churches. The statement appeared in the *Church Herald,* official organ of the Reformed Church in America, the oldest Protestant denomination on the North American continent (with a continuous ministry since 1628).

25. *New York Times,* January 20, 1962.

26. *Ibid.,* August 27, 1972

27. *Catholic News,* November 15, 1973.

28. *Ibid.,* November 29, 1973.

29. *New York Times,* December 11, 1974.

30. *Ibid.,* December 13, 1974.

31. Dr. Sam P. Colby, monograph, "The Growth and Development of Christian Church Institutions in the State of Israel" (Jerusalem: Israel Economist, 1975).

32. Sabri Jiryis, *The Arabs in Israel* (Beirut: Institute of Palestine Studies, 1968).

33. *Washington Post,* January 13, 1978.

34. *Washington Post,* January 13, 1978.

35. *Washington Star,* March 18, 1978. Widespread opposition in Jewish and Christian circles was revealed in the *Christian Science Monitor*, April 26, 1978.

36. This is the publication that in its 1954 annual book issue voted *What Price Israel?* one of the six best books of that year.

37. *America,* April 27, 1974.

38. Cardinal Shehan, the Archbishop of Baltimore in 1969, made public a document, allegedly with the approval of the Vatican Secretariat, recommending among other things that Catholics should recognize the significance of the State of Israel for the Jews. The document was subsequently *not* approved by the Holy See.

39. *New York Times*, January 20, 1973.

40. The charges contained in the play were strongly refuted in a lengthy letter to the editor of the *New York Times* by Cardinal Spellman.

41. Saul Friedlaender, *Pius XII and the Third Reich* (New York: Knopf, 1966). Friedlaender owed his life to the fact that he was sheltered during World War II in a Catholic convent in France.

42. See Peter Hoffmann, *The German Resistance* (Cambridge, Mass.: M.I.T. Press, 1977).

43. Pinchas E. Lapide, *Three Popes and the Jews* (New York: Hawthorne Books, 1967), pp. 214–15.

44. *Washington Post,* December 10, 1972.

Chapter XV: Soviet Jewry: Blackmail and Barter

1. The "Free Anatoly Shcharansky" November 8, 1977, *New York Times* ad carried signatures of such Zionist stalwarts as Senator Daniel P. Moynihan, New York Mayor-elect Edward Koch, Father Edward Flannery, Rev. Michael Harrington, Elie Wiesel, M.P. Winston Churchill, Saul Bellow, Paddy Chayefsky, Professors Seymour Lipset (Stan-

ford) and Dershowitz (Harvard) as well as a large number of prominent English and American actors, including Glenda Jackson, John Gielgud, Wendy Hiller, Trevor Howard, Emlyn Williams, Terry Thomas, and Claudette Colbert.

2. Asked about this incident, Alan Rocoff, National Jewish Defense League College Director, stated: "I have no information about that. However, as in the past, the JDL applauds such actions as helping to emphasize the conditions we're protesting against."

3. Books such as *Spiritual Genocide—Soviet Outrage* and *Anti-Semitism: Political Weapon* appeared describing in graphic terms the special harassments and cultural strangulation said to be meted out to Jews in the Soviet Union and in its Eastern European satellites.

4. Some Zionists have alleged that greater harassment is exerted against Jews because they, alone among Soviet nationalities, have no officially designated territorial entity of their own—the Jewish autonomous region of Birobidzhan being described as a fraudulent facade. However, one might reasonably ask just how much protection the Lithuanian Soviet Socialist Republic affords the Lithuanian people, when hundreds of thousands of Lithuanians are deported from its territory and colonization by Russian settlers is promoted.

5. Perhaps the epitome of the Zionist "concern" about Soviet persecution in general was the reported statement of Golda Meir that dissident Soviet Jews should devote full attention to remedying the grievances of their own group and avoid diffusing their efforts by seeking to ameliorate the problems of non-Jews.

6. This figure is hard to establish because many of Jewish background do not wish to identify themselves as such.

7. Estimate of Theodore Shabad in the *New York Times,* March 3, 1965, at the time he served as the Moscow correspondent. The figure for Jewish religiosity may be even lower now.

8. Members of the original Soviet leadership were largely Jewish—Trotsky, Kamenev, Zinoviev, Bukharin, among others.

9. William M. Mandel, *Russia Reexamined* (New York: Hill & Wang, 1967), revised edition.

10. Paul Wohl, "Soviet Jews in Search of Their Image," *Issues* (American Council for Judaism, New York), Summer 1968.

11. *Issues* (American Council for Judaism, New York), Autumn 1967.

12. *Congress Biweekly,* February 5, 1968.

13. *Jewish Post and Opinion,* February 2, 1968.

14. In January 1953 six Jews among nine physicians were indicted and charged with being in league not only with American and British agents but with Zionist spies. The U.S.S.R. shortly thereafter broke off relations with Israel. After Stalin's death on March 5, 1953, these charges were dropped.

15. Once freed, the Panovs touched base most momentarily in Israel and proceeded to Europe and the U.S. to exploit their dancing careers, which had blossomed under the spotlight of the enormous global publicity. When the dancers made their belated New York City debut with the Berlin Opera Ballet, the three-quarter-page *New York Times* July 2, 1978, article (with picture) carried forward Israel's propaganda war against the Soviet Union.

16. This *New York Times* article of October 23, 1973, covered the views of Professor Hans Morgenthau, which had appeared in a piece in *New Leader* magazine.

17. *New York Times,* September 2, 1973.

18. *Ibid.,* September 24, 1973.

19. Spain, of course, had never been submissive to Zionist pressures—it does not even have diplomatic relations with Israel. President Charles de Gaulle had shifted French policy in a pro-Arab direction since the termination of the Algerian war. Probably the European countries most susceptible to Zionist pressure were West Germany, because of the Nazi stigma, and Holland, the homeland of *The Diary of Anne Frank.*

20. "Scoop" received some singular Zionist plaudits for his efforts when he was

named "Man of the Year for 1974" by the Judaic Heritage Society, which went so far as to strike a commemorative medal in his honor, available at $32 in "gold on sterling" and $25 in "solid sterling silver."

21. *New York Times,* March 8, 1978.

22. Charles A. Vanik is a Czech-American Republican House member from Ohio's 22nd District.

23. Stephen D. Isaacs, *Jews and American Politics* (New York: Doubleday, 1974), p. 254.

24. In his letter to Senator Jackson, Secretary Kissinger had stated that he has been "assured that harassment of would-be Soviet emigrants would cease, and he assumed emigration could therefore rise." On his part, the Senator declared that he would regard 60,000 emigrants, almost a 90 percent rise over 1973, as a test of Soviet compliance.

25. The release by Tass of the Gromyko denunciation, in the form of a letter, was timed as a counterpart to the public demand of Egyptian Foreign Minister Ismail Fahmy that Israel curtail further immigration.

26. When Ford declared that he wished to work with Congress to eliminate the problems that precipitated the Soviet action, the presidential aspirant from the State of Washington snapped back, "This unfortunate reaction suggests that we should reward the egregious Soviet breach of good faith with increased largesse and a weakening of our insistence that they move toward freer emigration."

27. The extent to which Meir and other Israeli leaders, who are principally agnostics in their personal religious habits, are sincerely interested in how many Hebrew houses of worship exist in the Soviet Union—or anywhere else—remains an unanswered question.

28. Hearings before the Subcommittee on Europe and the Middle East of the House International Relations Committee, September 27, 1977, p. 78. In an interview with Marilyn Berger, this expert on Soviet affairs was even more blunt: "We have pressed for increased Jewish emigration from the Soviet Union, and the result is that we neither have the trade agreement which we could have had with that country, nor have we achieved an increase in the number of Jews coming abroad. On the contrary, it has declined. I don't quite understand this policy on our part. I don't think that it is entirely thought through." *New York Times Magazine,* May 7, 1978.

29. *New York Times,* January 22, 1978.

30. *Ibid.,* January 30, 1977.

31. One American Zionist spokesman reportedly stated that if the Soviet Jews did not want to go to Israel, then "let them rot in Russia."

32. The *Jewish Journal* of November 19, 1976, bared the internal friction between forces led by Chairman of the International Committee on Soviet Jewish Emigration Max Fisher, the Jewish fund-raiser for Presidents Nixon and Ford, and Zionist groups aligned to the Israeli government, which favored cutoff of U.S. funds to needy emigrants not proceeding to or exiting from Israel. World Zionist Organization new chief, Leon Dulzin, stated that "Russian Jews who choose not to go to Israel are morally inferior and neither need nor deserve the help of Jewish people." Quoted by *Special Interest Report* (New York: American Council for Judaism), May 1978.

33. For more details on the Klausner Report see Alfred M. Lilienthal, *What Price Israel?* (Chicago: Henry Regnery, 1953), pp. 194–96. This report and the decision of the Committee of Eight followed the same racist line of the 1976 Koenig Report, in which the Israeli Sub-Minister of Interior for the Galilee District proposed a plan to force out the Arab population so as to prevent it from becoming a majority. See p. 124.

34. Those Soviet Jews who reemigrated from Israel were no longer regarded by the U.S. Justice Department as refugees from racial or political persecution and have found it difficult to obtain U.S. visas. Facing harsh conditions, they rely for financial support upon Roman Catholic organizations.

35. San Francisco *Examiner,* March 21, 1976.

36. One letter-writer protested: "If Mr. Javits and Mr. Jackson who are sponsoring this bill wish to be so generous, let them pay from their own pockets and not from that of the taxpayers. People who pay taxes have the right to know where their money and why their money is going."

Chapter XVI: The Eisenhower, Kennedy, and Johnson Years

1. The events of 1955–57 are skillfully and reliably detailed in Kennett Love's *Suez: The Twice Fought War* (New York: McGraw-Hill, 1969). Well known for his reliable and impartial reporting as *New York Times* correspondent in the Middle East from 1953 to 1956, the author failed to ingratiate himself with the cable desk back in New York. His book also gave a brief picture of the June 1967 six-day war, for which, noted the author, "the 1956 war served as a rehearsal." The Russian arms deal, the Anderson secret mission, the Aswan Dam renege, the nationalization of the Suez Canal Company, the abortive Canal Users Association, and the British-French-Israeli conspiracy all excitingly unfold in meticulous detail. The Love book might well be read in conjunction with Miles Copeland's *The Game of Nations* (New York: Simon and Schuster, 1969), since they both cover CIA activities in Egypt under the direction of Kermit Roosevelt, particularly the story relating to the Russian arms deal and the thwarted Dulles ultimatum delivered to President Nasser by George Allen. Both authors fail to give an assessment, however, of this ubiquitous organization's Middle East activities, or to mention even a word about its role played on the U.S. domestic scene in helping to keep the American public ignominiously uninformed.

2. Love, *op. cit*, p. 3.

3. This revelation was made in a BBC/2 television interview twenty years later by General Hugh Stockwell, the overall commander of the joint land forces that captured Port Said on November 6, 1956. Only on October 26, three days before the Sinai campaign, did Stockwell learn from French commander General André Beaufre "that the Israelis were in on the act."

4. Paul Johnson, *The Suez War* (New York: Greenberg, 1957), pp. 115–16.

5. Michael Ionides, *Divide and Lose* (London: Geoffrey Bles, 1960), p. 165.

6. *Ibid.*, p. 168.

7. *Herut*, September 9, 1960.

8. *Jewish Newsletter*, November 28, 1960.

9. *New York Times*, August 26, 1960.

10. John F. Kennedy, *Profiles in Courage* (New York: Harper Bros., 1956), p. 4.

11. *Jewish Chronicle*, April 28, 1961.

12. *New York Herald Tribune*, December 9, 1959. Almost eighteen years later, Egypt's Anwar el-Sadat broke with tradition and flew to Israel to recognize the Zionist state and, for the moment, end the state of Egyptian-Israeli hostility.

13. *Ibid.*, May 22, 1963.

14. Ionides, *op. cit.*, pp. 249–50.

15. *U.S. Foreign Policy: Compilation of Studies.* Prepared under the Direction of Committee on Foreign Relations, U.S. Senate, Pursuant to S. Res. 335, 85th Congress, and S. Res. 250, 86th Congress (Washington: U.S. Government Printing Office, 1960), Study No. 13, June 9, 1960, p. 1312.

16. Complete text of this important John F. Kennedy letter: "Dear Alfred: I appreciated having the benefit of your comments upon my talk to the Liberal Party and the Zionist Organization. I wholly agree with you that American partisanship in the Arab-Israeli conflict is dangerous both to the United States and the Free World. My program merely calls for using the power of the President to bring the parties themselves to an agreement. For too long a time, this dispute has been a bitter cause of friction between the Arab nations and Israel. I would hope that both would be friends of the United States. Your sobering analysis of my speeches is provocative of additional thought. [signed] John."

17. *Congressional Record*, 88th Congress, First Session, December 23, 1963, p. S. 7818.

18. *Ibid.*

19. See Alfred M. Lilienthal, *What Price Israel?* (Chicago: Henry Regnery, 1954), pp. 70, 83, 93–95, for role played by David K. Niles in the creation of Israel.

20. Robert Stephens, *Nasser* (New York: Simon and Schuster, 1971), pp. 411–31.

21. Saul Bellow "Reflections," *The New Yorker*, July 12, 1976. Part of LBJ's solicitude for Israel stemmed, according to his brother Sam Houston Johnson, from political advice given to him by his old Aunt Jessie, who wrote to her nephew: "I want you to tell Lyndon something else for me. Tell him to stick with the Jews and never do anything against them. Now they're God's chosen people, you know. Says so right in the Bible, and don't you ever doubt it. The best thing Harry Truman ever did was to create the State of Israel . . . why, when he did that, Sam Houston, whether he figured on it or not, he had that next election right in the bag. Tom Dewey didn't have no more chance than a pig in a dog race." Sam Houston Johnson, *My Brother Lyndon* (New York: Cowles, 1969, 1970), p. 132

22. Copeland, *op. cit.*

23. Stephens, *op. cit.*, p. 454.

24. Mentioned in speech of Gamal Abdel Nasser on the anniversary of the Revolution, July 23, 1967. British Broadcasting Co., SWB NE/523/A/1–17.

25. Mohamed Hassanein Heikal, *The Cairo Documents* (New York: Doubleday, 1973), p. 245.

26. *Ibid.*, p. 240.

27. William P. Quandt, *Decade of Decisions: American Policy Toward the Arab-Israeli Conflict, 1967–1976* (Berkeley: University of California, 1977), p. 50.

28. *Ibid.*, p. 54.

29. U Thant came in for a great deal of criticism for withdrawing the U.N. troops, but under the terms of the U.N. arrangement with Nasser, once Cairo had requested the United Nations Emergency Force (UNEF) to leave, the Secretary-General had little option other than to delay and refer the matter to the General Assembly, which he deemed unwise. It had never been Nasser's original intent to close the Gulf of Aqaba to shipping. He had asked U Thant to stay in Gaza and Sharm-el Sheikh, but the Secretary-General insisted that either all the troops be kept or all withdrawn. When the Secretary-General raised the possibility of stationing UNEF on the Israeli side of the line (since 1957 this force had been on the Egyptian side), the Israeli U.N. representative replied that this would be "entirely unacceptable to his Government," reaffirming the position Israel had taken ever since the establishment of the peace-keeping force in 1956.

30. *Time* magazine, June 2, 1967.

31. According to the *Statistical Abstract of Israel, 1967*, the "relative importance of Eilat to the total number of ships arriving at the four other principal Israeli ports (Haifa, Tel Aviv, Jaffa, and Ashdod) was 2.20%, 2.46%, 2.75%, and 2.91% for the years 1966, 1965, 1964, and 1963 respectively; while the percentage of net tonnage registered at Eilat to the net tonnage registered at the other four ports was 1.90%, 2.48%, 1.71%, and 1.55% for the same years respectively."

32. Stephens, *op. cit.*, p. 491.

33. Aubrey Hodes, *"Dialogue with Ishmael: Israel's Future in the Middle East"* (New York: Funk & Wagnalls, 1968), p. 93.

34. *Le Monde*, February 28, 1968.

35. *Ibid.*, June 3, 1972, article by Israeli intellectual Amnon Kapeliouk.

36. *Ma'ariv*, April 4, 1972.

37. *Le Monde*, June 3, 1972.

38. *Ma'ariv*, April 4, 1972.

39. *Ha'aretz*, March 29, 1972.

40. *Le Monde*, June 3, 1972.

41. Quoted by Noam Chomsky, "An Exception to the Rules," *Inquiry* (San Francisco, Calif., April 17, 1978). This was in the MIT professor's review of Michael Walzer's *Just and Unjust Wars.*

42. Quoted by George Heitmann, *Survey* (London), October 1969.

Chapter XVII: The Attack on Liberty

1. Technical Research Ship Special Communications System.

2. In warning of the need for restraint in the *Pueblo* affair, Senator Fulbright recalled that "our friends, the Israelis, shot a similar ship of ours almost out of the water at great loss of life. We didn't threaten them with atom bombs. I understand it is agreed informally to sell them more planes." This account in the first edition of the *New York Post* of February 5, 1968, was "yanked out" of later editions and appeared nowhere else in the New York or Eastern press.

3. Richard K. Smith, "The Violation of *Liberty,*" *U.S. Naval Institute Proceedings,* Vol. 104, No. 904, June 1978.

4. *Time,* July 7, 1967.

5. Smith, *op. cit.*

6. Joseph C. Lentini of Oxon Hill, Maryland, letter to the editor, *Washington Star,* October 4, 1977.

7. Board of Inquiry "Record of Proceedings on the Attack on the USS *Liberty,*" June 6, 1967, held in London June 10, 1967, and then continued on board the *Liberty* at Malta through June 16. Its top-secret findings were pronounced on June 18, 1967, and the documents were declassified June 21, 1976.

8. *Ibid.,* p. 41.

9. *Ibid.*

10. *Ibid.,* p. 166.

11. James Kilpatrick, "June 8, at 1400 Hours," *National Review,* September 5, 1967.

12. *Ibid.*

13. Three of these, all generals, were in the Menachem Begin Cabinet of 1977: Moshe Dayan as Foreign Minister, Ezer Weizman as Minister of Defense, and Meir Amit as Minister of Communications.

14. Board of Inquiry "Record of Proceedings," *op. cit.,* pp. 63–64.

15. *New York Times,* June 10, 1967, commented upon this editorially.

16. Board of Inquiry "Record of Proceedings," *op. cit.,* Finding of Facts 19.

17. Messages, Department of Defense, National Military Command Center, Message Center, June 13, 1967.

18. Zeev Schiff, *A History of the Israeli Army* (New York: Simon and Schuster, 1974), pp. 159–60.

19. Words of Counsel to Board of Inquiry Captain Ward Boston, Board of Inquiry, "Record of Proceedings," p. 159.

20. Board of Inquiry, "Record of Proceedings," p. 93.

21. *Ibid.,* Findings of Fact 1, p. 161.

22. *Ibid.,* Appendix VI.

23. *Ibid.,* Findings of Fact 6.

24. *Ibid.,* Findings of Fact 33.

25. "The Israeli attitude toward the *Liberty* incident was one of studied indifference," according to Richard Smith's "The Violation of *Liberty,*" *op. cit.* In vivid contrast to the incident in which the U.S.S. *Panay* was sunk in 1937, when only three men were killed, individual Japanese called on the U.S. embassy in Tokyo to express personal regrets, Japanese schoolchildren collected money for the survivors and next of kin, and the government within five months of the incident remitted its monetary compensation.

26. Letter of August 30, 1976, from Admiral David M. Cooney to Eliot Sharp, Secretary of American Council on the Middle East (ACME).

27. *Ha'aretz*, July 23, 1968.

28. Airgram, July 23, 1968, U.S. Embassy Tel Aviv to Department of State.

29. Anthony Pearson, "Conspiracy of Silence," *Penthouse*, June 1976.

30. Letters of American Palestine Committee Chairman Norman Dacey to Admiral Turner and the White House, demanding release of documentation allegedly refuting the previously released CIA document that incriminated Moshe Dayan, have been ignored.

31. P. Fellwock (writing under the pseudonym of W. Peck), *Ramparts*, August 1972.

32. For further details of the Defense Department's lid that was tightly placed on the *Liberty* incident, see *Herald of Freedom*, July 28, 1967 (Zarephath, N.J.), reprinted in the Congressional Record, Vol. 113, No. 147, September 19, 1967.

33. Richard Nolte actually never had an opportunity to present his credentials as Ambassador. The 1967 war began before he could be received by President Nasser, and then the U.A.R. broke relations with the U.S.

Chapter XVIII: Oil on Troubled Waters: The Nixon Years

1. This suggestion had first been advanced by Senator Javits who, while campaigning for reelection at resort hotels in Sullivan County (the area known as the "Borscht Belt"), had called on President Johnson to deliver seventy-five Phantoms immediately to Israel. Strangely, the *New York Times* derided the Nixon proposal to tip the military scales permanently in Israel's favor as a "new, dangerous, open-ended and ultimately self-defeating commitment." The long, bitter feud between the *Times* and Richard Nixon had begun. At this juncture, apparently it was more important to the newspaper to try to defeat the Republican nominee than bow to Tel Aviv's immediate wishes.

2. Full-page *New York Times* advertisement by Friends of *Middle East Perspective*, January 20, 1969.

3. Not only was the media describing the Rabat Arab Summit as a war meeting, but such staunch Israelists as writer Paddy Chayefsky were openly predicting that "the Arabs were again planning to drive us Jews into the sea."

4. Because his brother, Chase Bank president David Rockefeller, was in the group that allegedly advised President Nixon to alter his Middle East course, New York Governor Nelson Rockefeller quickly disassociated himself from any connection with the call for change. From the outset, Nixon himself was most cynical about the Rogers initiative. As he wrote in his *Memoirs*, "I knew that the Rogers Plan could never be implemented, but I believed that it was important to let the Arab world know that the United States did not automatically dismiss its case regarding the occupied territories or rule out a compromise settlement of the conflicting claims. With the Rogers Plan on the record, I thought it would be easier for the Arab leaders to propose reopening relations with the United States without coming under attack from the hawks and pro-Soviet elements in their own countries." Richard Nixon, *The Memoirs of Richard Nixon* (New York: Grosset & Dunlap, 1978), p. 479.

5. *Jane's World Aircraft*, March 20, 1970.

6. The *New York Times* on page 3, April 2, 1970, reported the Israeli claim that the children (ages seven to thirteen) had been undergoing prearmy training. It was not until the fourth day after the incident that the *Times'* readers were told the truth, and then it was tucked away on page 9 under the ambiguous headline: "No Arms Evident in Egyptian Town/Site *Reportedly* Bombed by Israelis Housed School." [Emphasis added.]

7. For other aspects of this telecast, see pp. 285–86.

8. This suggests that Israel, if she had been forced to enter a conflict within Jordan, already had its eyes focused on certain territories such as the West Bank, whose occupancy would be made possible through the participation of ground forces.

9. The revelation early in 1977 that the Jordanian monarch had been annually receiving $1 million since 1957 from the CIA caused quite a stir and confirmed the

closest U.S.-Israel relations. Hussein declared that he had not personally benefited from the funds, which were directed to worthwhile development projects. Close CIA ties with successive Israeli Prime Ministers were also subsequently revealed. When newly designated Prime Minister Menachem Begin came to the U.S. in July 1977, he gave President Carter a lengthy document recounting the details of Israel's involvement during the 1970 Jordan-Syria crisis, and of other intelligence operations allegedly carried out by Israelis on behalf of the U.S. government. While the media carried little of the story, Israel had been receiving $80 million yearly from the CIA, much of which had been used for underwriting Israel's aid program designed to win black African support.

10. For details, see Miles Copeland, *The Game of Nations* (New York: Simon and Schuster, 1969). Nixon himself showed a lack of understanding of the Egyptian leader's motivations as he ascribed to Nasser "a blind intolerance of the Jews." Nixon, *op. cit.*, p. 249.

11. President Nixon's presence induced Tito not to attend. Nixon did not even send Secretary Rogers; Welfare Secretary Eliot Richardson represented the U.S. But the NATO Sixth Fleet naval maneuvers were canceled.

12. It was the first time that Saudi Arabia and Kuwait had lined up on the Palestinian issue with the rejectionist Arab bloc, and Libya had voted with the conservatives. Sayegh expressed their thinking: "While some elements and features make it unthinkable for us to vote against it [the resolution], other positions make it impossible for us to vote for it."

13. William P. Rogers, "A Lasting Peace in the Middle East: An American View." Address before the 1969 Galaxy Conference on Adult Education at Washington, D.C., on December 9.

14. U.N. Office of Public Information, *Yearbook of the United Nations, 1971*, Vol. 25, New York, 1974, p. 168.

15. Subsequently Secretary-General U Thant reported that the talks under Ambassador Jarring's auspices had lapsed. Jarring resumed his post as Sweden's Ambassador to the U.S.S.R. on March 25. Although he returned to headquarters from May 5 to 12 and from September 21 to October 27, and held certain consultations elsewhere, the Ambassador found himself faced with the same deadlock, and with no possibility of actively pursuing his mission. *Yearbook of the United Nations, 1971, op. cit.*, p. 169.

16. When he visited Moscow in 1974, the Massachusetts Senator did not hesitate to ask for increased emigration of Soviet Jews in his meeting with Leonid Brezhnev.

17. The agreement signed in Bengazi (Libya) by President Anwar el-Sadat, Libyan Chief of State Colonel Mua'mmar Qaddafi, and Syrian President Hafez al-Assad called for a council made up of the Presidents of the three countries with a federal President to be chosen by a majority vote in a national assembly for federal legislation. According to Sadat, the union was to have "one president, one flag, one anthem, and one federal capital." Less than seven years later Egyptian air forces were attacking Tobruk, the old royalist capital, in another and most serious of the border conflicts between Egypt and Libya.

18. *Jewish Press*, November 13, 1970.

19. Evans and Novak, *Washington Star* Syndicate, April 12, 1971.

20. Georges Friedmann, translated by Eric Mosbacher, *The End of the Jewish People* (New York: Doubleday, 1967).

21. UPI article datelined Tel Aviv. August 17, 1972.

22. Dwight D. Eisenhower, "A Proposal for Our Time," *Reader's Digest*, June 1968.

23. This diplomatic rumination was quickly explained away by the State Department lest it unduly jeopardize U.S. relations with the Soviet Union. But this remark might be said to have initiated the strange Sadat-Kissinger honeymoon that was to follow.

24. For example, during the first Suez crisis this same company, fearful of antagonizing certain of its prominent stockholders, resorted to an elaborate subterfuge in

order to contribute the paltry sum of $300 to the work of an anti-Zionist organization.

25. *New York Times*, "The U.S. Stake in Middle East Peace," June 21, 1973.

26. *Chicago Daily News*, August 16, 1973.

27. Some years previously, House Foreign Affairs Committee member Mrs. Francis P. Bolton of Cleveland, Ohio, had shown some concern for loss of U.S. prestige in the oil-laden Middle East and had promptly been taken to task by Zionist Organization of America President Rabbi Abba Hillel Silver: "Madame, apparently oil, not blood, courses through your veins."

28. *Near East Report* editor I. L. Kenen gloatingly inferred a Miller retraction because the oil executive in his second letter had not again referred to his call for "more positive support of Arab efforts toward peace in the Middle East"—as if any conclusion could be drawn from the fact that everything that appeared in the first letter of the SOCAL Chairman was not repeated in the second.

29. MIT Professor M. A. Adelman, who earlier had called the Arab oil threat "a bogus" in *Foreign Policy*, No. 9, Winter 1972/73 (New York: Foreign Policy Association), contended in an Op-Ed piece, "There Is No Energy Crisis," in the *New York Times* of April 21, 1973, that it was only a "pinch" manufactured by the oil companies to increase their profits. For another attack on the oil companies, see John M. Lee, "Backfire for the Oil Men," *New York Times*, July 29, 1974.

30. An article, "The Oil Crisis: This Time the Wolf Is Here," in the Spring 1974 issue of *Foreign Affairs* by James E. Akins, who had been State Department Director of the Office of Fuels and Energy, and consultant to the White House on oil problems before his appointment as Ambassador to Saudi Arabia, maintained that country's reserves exceeded the 150 billion barrels previously estimated. He declared: "With the possible exception of Croesus, the world will never have seen anything quite like the wealth which is flowing and will continue to flow into the Arabian Gulf." Fuel experts projected the cumulative earnings of the Gulf States between 1973 and 1980 at more than $210 billion.

31. This supported the previous Yamani warning that Saudi Arabia would not "significantly expand its production unless Washington changes its pro-Israel stance." *Washington Post*, April 19, 1973.

32. *Congressional Record*, 97th Congress, First Session, September 5, 1973, p. S. 15900.

33. *Congressional Record*, 97th Congress, First Session, May 21, 1973, p. S. 16263.

34. This same congressman was later indicted and jailed for accepting a bribe in the Tongsun Park South Korean case.

35. It was at this press conference that President Nixon referred to the U.S. using its influence with "the various Arab states and a non-Arab state like Egypt." The White House later admitted this gross error. Could this have been a Freudian slip of things to come, which only made sense in terms of continued U.S. efforts after the first disengagement to separate Egypt from the other Arab countries?

36. Nixon press conference, September 6, 1973.

37. The nationalization had been announced on the fourth anniversary of the Libyan Revolution and was followed the next day by a price increase of more than one dollar for the standard 42-gallon barrel.

38. The intrepid Libyan leader never stopped trying. But such Qaddafi maneuvers as the civilian march on Cairo to catapult his Egyptian ally into a precipitate unification failed. Even a gradualist approach to union was doomed to die in the post-Suez disengagement world. Sadat and Qaddafi's views were worlds apart, and the incessant war of words between the two in 1974, 1975, and 1976 erupted into the bitter border clashes of 1977. Diplomatic relations were totally disrupted in November 1977 after Sadat's heralded November visit to Jerusalem.

39. *Near East Report*, August 27, 1975, reached the desk of every member of Congress with the lead story drawing the parallel between alleged current efforts of the oil

industry to alter U.S. policy and its 1948 pressures on the Truman administration to reverse the U.S. partition decision. Revived was one of the greatest of all Middle East myths, which had figured monumentally in the early debate on the Palestine question in the 1940s. Oil companies, whose closet skeletons reeked of depletion allowances and tax advantages, had always been lamentably half-hearted and pathetic in protesting U.S. pro-Israel moves despite their tremendous personal stakes in the area, and in its opposition to partition. They had been—and were still—so subject to Zionist blackmail that they totally refused to play the game even though they had been fully given the name. See also Alfred M. Lilienthal, *The Other Side of the Coin* (New York: Devin Adair, 1965), pp. 199–203.

40. Most of the three-hour NBC September 4, 1973, energy program on which King Faisal briefly appeared was devoted to the thesis that the search for alternate energy sources was the answer to the growing shortages.

41. Former Undersecretary of State George W. Ball stated that the failure of Washington "to compel an Israeli withdrawal from occupied Arab territory made the October war inevitable." *New York Times*, March 24, 1974.

Chapter XIX: War Again

1. A few imaginative scenarists have insisted that Kissinger was aware of the Arab plans to launch a surprise attack and push the Israelis back, which for purposes of later bargaining with Israel is what he was supposed to have wanted. The fact that the Arabs' goal was a limited rather than total war against Israel, aimed to recover occupied lands rather than destruction of the enemy, could explain Sadat's military strategy of stopping to consolidate his gains rather than pushing on to the Gidi and Mitla passes, which were thirty-five miles from the Canal and might then have fallen to his forces. But the intimate Kissinger-Sadat relationship did not commence until after the war, although there is some evidence of an earlier intelligence interchange.

2. *Pacem in Terris* dinner, October 9, 1973.

3. Marvin and Bernard Kalb, *Kissinger* (Boston-Toronto: Little Brown, 1974), p. 469.

4. *Ibid.*, p. 472.

5. *Ibid.*, p. 475. Apparently President Nixon took the Dinitz threat most seriously. He told Kissinger: "Goddamn it, use every one [plane] we have. Tell them to send everything that can fly." *The Memoirs of Richard Nixon* (New York: Grosset & Dunlap, 1978), p. 927.

6. *Washington Post*, Marilyn Berger story, February 9, 1974.

7. The absence of the definitive article "the" before "occupied territories" in the English version (but not in the French and Spanish versions) of Resolution 242 of November 22, 1967, has been used by the Israelis to justify their contention that they do not have to fully withdraw. But the preamble to the resolution as well as the U.N. Charter itself, as George Ball pointed out in *Foreign Affairs* (April 1977), bars the "inadmissibility of the acquisition of territory by war." Israel continually pointed to the article as indicating U.N. intent that she was not obliged to relinquish all of the occupied territories. Since the resolution did not call for withdrawal from "part" of the territories or "some" of the territories, but called for "withdrawal of Israeli armed forces from territories occupied in recent conflict," the intent was perfectly clear that the withdrawal was to be from all occupied territories without exception, save minor mutually agreed border rectifications.

8. Kissinger was furious over the attitude of our Western allies when they dared think of their own interests and refused to adopt Washington's "Israel-First" policy.

9. Nixon personally defended the alert at the same press conference at which he vigorously attacked the media for biased Watergate reportage. A radio interview in which I was participating while lecturing in Salt Lake City was interrupted to permit listening to the President's remarks.

10. Resolution by the Ministers of Petroleum of member states of the Organization of Arab Petroleum Exporting Countries meeting in Kuwait October 17, 1973.

11. As Faisal told Kissinger in Riyadh on November 8, 1973, "It was very painful for me to have been forced to take this action against our American friends." Edward R. F. Sheehan, *The Arabs, Israelis, and Kissinger* (New York: Reader's Digest Press, 1976), p. 72.

12. David Hirst, "Israel—A Wasting US Asset?", *Manchester Guardian Weekly*, September 15, 1973.

13. *New York Times*, November 16, 1973.

14. Statement by Thomas R. Stauffer, Lecturer on Economics and Research Associate in Middle Eastern Studies at Harvard University, before the Federal Energy Administration Hearings on "Project Independence," Boston, Massachusetts, August 29, 1974. Stauffer stated: "The proposal for 'Project Independence,' irrespective of whether desirable or practicable in the long run, is irrelevant for the crucial five years to come. Indeed, false emphasis upon the long-run, as implied in even the less naïve versions of 'Project Independence,' could be harmful or even dangerous if it diverts our attention from the more immediate perils."

15. According to a *New York Times* Washington story of September 29, 1974, "The Defense Department, which had supplied Israel with 1,000 tanks last fall, is running into unexpected difficulties in expanding production to replenish the depleted tank inventories of the United States Army." The Pentagon had wanted to more than double the production of the M-60 tank, in large measure to offset the transfer of a large number of the Army's latest tank to Israel. Because of the combination of economic, environmental, and safety reasons, the Defense Department was finding industry either unwilling or unable to expand production to meet its goals. Domestic foundries could not be found to handle the huge castings that make up the turrets and holds of the tank. Secretary Schlesinger publicly questioned in mid-September whether American industry was capable of living up to its traditional role as "the arsenal of democracy."

16. The Israelis resisted moving back to the original October 22 cease-fire lines, as called for by the second Security Council resolution of early morning October 24, using the excuse that it was impossible to delineate exactly where the armies had been on the day of the first cease-fire. While the Egyptians were being pictured in the U.S. media as intransigent and the Israelis as generous for allowing supply trucks with medicine and food to get through to Suez, the *Jerusalem Post* printed a map showing where the armies actually stood on the 22nd, and also one three days later to show their delighted readers the great advance made in the encirclement of the Egyptian Third Army.

17. Figures based on a list released in late October 1974 by the Israel Defense Ministry, plus ten missing.

Chapter XX: The Ford Interlude

1. In St. Louis in 1970 Congressman Ford said: "Israel should not withdraw from a single inch of occupied territory unless there is a real peace treaty and creditable evidence that the Arabs will normalize relations." *Near East Report*, August 14, 1974.

2. Speech at the Annual Conference of the American-Israeli Public Affairs Committee in Washington, April 24, 1969. *Near East Report*, August 14, 1974.

3. As Vice-President, Spiro Agnew appeared at many Jewish functions to bring the greetings of President Nixon and performed as other politicians were obliged to do until his resignation. Two and a half years later, in his first television appearance promoting his novel, *The Canfield Decision*, Agnew told Barbara Walters on NBC's "Today" show that "Zionist influences are dragging the U.S. into a rather disorganized approach to the Middle East problem. . . . I do think the media are sympathetic to the Zionist cause." *Washington Post*, May 12, 1976. In *New York Times* Op-Ed pieces his speechwriter, William

Safire, called him a "bigot" (May 24, 1976) and his press secretary, Victor Gold, accused him of selling out (May 28, 1976). The Zionist blitz had struck again.

4. When asked by avid Zionist correspondent Rev. Lester Kinsolving, known as "the most notorious baiter in the Nixon press room," about a 1972 statement in which he called it unreasonable to preserve the fiction that Jerusalem is not the capital of Israel, the President replied: "That particular proposal ought to stand aside. We must come up with some answers between Israel and the Arab nations in order to achieve a peace that's both fair and durable."

5. Jordan's Zaid Rifai served as both Prime Minister and Foreign Minister.

6. On the CBS radio's *Newsfeed,* a "Tel Aviv Report" by Bruno Wasserthiel quoted "an Israeli newspaper" as the source for reports of alleged Syrian and Egyptian violations of the disengagement agreements, of Russian arms flow to Syria, and of possible use of Arab oil to purchase new shipments of planes and armaments to be used against Israel. WINS "Religion" commentator Rabbi Marc Tanenbaum interwove plugs for Israel's position and abstract references to biblical Israel while never failing to push the persecution theme. A call to the CBS offices in New York could elicit no further details as to the source of these reports. The American people were being prepared for some possible drastic new Israeli move.

7. *Business Week,* January 13, 1975.

8. Professor David C. McClelland, former Chairman of Howard University's Social Relations Department, in the January 1975 issue of *Psychology Today.* "Wars," he declared, "stem from certain motivation patterns within a nation: The need for power and the need for affiliation. But to run the great risk involved in a Middle East war, the country must be motivationally prepared to act violently and self-righteously on behalf of the oppressed—in this case Israel."

9. *Commentary* magazine, January 1975.

10. According to the author's conversation at the U.N. with Foreign Minister Omar Saqqaf, shortly before his sudden death in New York, the Arabs had in readiness elaborate emergency plans for the destruction of oil facilities in the event of an external attack, which would result in an oil flow shutdown of from six to seven months. This was known to the U.S. and no doubt helped put the brakes on the war party.

11. *New York* magazine, October 8, 1974.

12. The original Israeli request was for $1.5 billion in military credits for three years and $2.5 billion in military purchases over the same period. At that time a Pentagon spokesman called an arms expenditure of $4 billion annually by a country with a gross national product of less than $10 billion "totally ridiculous."

13. After careful examination by alienists and psychologists in Saudi Arabia, assassin Prince Faisal Ibn Musaed Ibn Abdul Aziz was declared to be sane and in complete control of all of his faculties "at the time of the murder." He was put to death in June 1975 in Riyadh. But this did not end the speculation that surrounded this politically important event. A. A. Milne's "who killed Cock Robin?" was revived. Hypotheses advanced had implicated CIA, Soviet, Israeli, and even Arab agents. Was the assassin a committed leftist, taking upon himself the cleansing of the country from monarchial rule? Was he still obsessed by the very unfortunate death of his brother, a fanatical conservative who, like some Saudis of the strict Wahabi orthodox sect, believed television represented a criminal deviation from the preachments of the Koran, and joined an armed attack on the Saudi television station in which he was killed? Was he avenging this brother, or was he the tool of some foreign power?

14. The accord, initialed in Cairo and Jerusalem on September 2, was signed on the 23rd by Israeli and Egyptian representatives in Geneva, without any U.S. or Soviet presence.

15. *Jerusalem Post,* September 2, 1975.

16. *New York Times,* September 6, 1975.

17. *New York Post,* "Limit Sought on Arming the Israelis," April 13, 1976.

18. Saed Marei's son was married to Anwar Sadat's daughter; Marei, in key positions during the Nasser regime, claimed that Kissinger had misled the Egyptians during the disengagement negotiations by not telling them he had promised that Washington would give sympathetic consideration to supplying Israel with the Pershing missiles. (*New York Times*, September 27, 1975.) Marei's distrust of the Israelis was further strengthened by the September announcement, after the disengagement agreement, that the Israeli government would build a new kibbutz on occupied Egyptian soil south of Gaza in the Sinai, hardly indicating an intention of returning lands taken in 1967.

19. Secretary of Energy Schlesinger, on "Meet the Press," admitted that the Pershing missiles Israel sought would not be available until at least 1979, but other Israel requests were being met.

20. Department of State Selected Documents No. 4, "U.S. Policy in the Middle East: November 1974–February 1976," Bureau of Public Affairs, Office of Media Services (Washington, D.C.: U.S. Government Printing Office, October 1976).

21. The PLO called a press conference on January 23 at the U.N. As the debate on Palestine was nearing its last stages and a Palestinian statement could be expected, there was a capacity turnout to hear PLO Observer Chief Dr. Zehdi L. Terzi introduce the author of this book as editor of *Middle East Perspective*. The continued, ruthless campaign to crush the expression of anti-Zionism and support of the PLO, both in the U.S. and in Israel, was detailed, including the astonishing case of Rabbi Hirsch. There was a total media blackout, as there had been to documented accounts of torture administered to Palestinians in Israel. Nine months later, Israeli lawyer Felicia Langer's recital to a sparsely attended Biltmore Hotel press conference of the Arab-American University Graduates also drew a blank. It was not until the first-page story in the London Sunday *Times* (June 19, 1977) that anything on this subject was allowed to appear in the Western media.

22. The veto enjoyed by permanent members of the Security Council does not apply to procedural questions, only to substantive issues.

23. While Moynihan was setting forth his views on the inviolability of Security Council Resolution 242 and 338, the eyes of other U.N. delegates were focused on Jacqueline Kennedy Onassis in the guest gallery. If she had come to hear the accustomed vitriolic rhetoric for which this U.S. diplomat was renowned, the widow of President Kennedy must have been disappointed. The Ambassador was unusually moderate and mild-mannered, and the famed pyrotechnics were absent on this occasion (January 12, 1976).

24. *Washington Post*, May 27, 1977.

25. The administration had budgeted Israel $225 million for the interim period.

26. After his strong statement against Israeli settlements in occupied territories, Scranton told a Chicago *Sun-Times* columnist that he personally might support "some permanent Israeli settlements." "Something along the line of the Allon Plan makes sense" were his words as he tried to backtrack, with Ford's primary race against Reagan at its height, from his rebukes to Israel at earlier Security Council meetings.

27. Party Chairman Robert Strauss was Jewish with strong Zionist connections, and one of Carter's closest foreign policy advisers had been Columbia Law School Professor Richard Gardner, who was more zealously Zionist after marrying an Italian Catholic. (Gardner was later appointed Ambassador to Italy by President Carter.)

28. *Sceptic* magazine (Santa Barbara, Calif., March–April 1976).

29. *New York Times*, October 19, 1976.

30. When I entered the polling booth and reached for the lever to record my choice, I was still angered by last-minute blatant Ford advertisements appealing to Jewish voters to remember all the military aid given to Israel by his administration. But reason tempered emotionalism, as I recalled how it has always been the Democratic party of Presidents Truman and Johnson, of Senators Hubert Humphrey and Henry Jackson, that has been the Zionist stronghold, and I pulled the lever for the loser as the lesser

of two evils. Had other resentful New York voters, anti-Zionists or pro-Arabs, followed my example and not cast a spite vote for Carter, or for independent candidate Eugene McCarthy, the final result might have been different.

Chapter XXI: Exit Henry Kissinger?

1. Kissinger's childhood was characterized by brightness, but not the brilliance which was later to shine through. Marvin and Bernard Kalb, *Henry Kissinger* (Boston-Toronto: Little, Brown, 1974), p. 33.

2. *Ibid.*, p. 188.

3. *Ibid.* This is one of the infinite number of pro-Zionist biases of the Kalb biography, which particularly shows through in gross oversimplification of the events leading up to the 1967 war: "Nasser tried to block the Israeli port of Elath after evicting the U.N. supervisors in the Sinai" (p. 187). In writing about the Israeli air onslaught in January 1970, the Kalbs referred to "a series of lightning attacks against missile sites and other military targets deep in the Egyptian heartland, bombing the outskirts of Cairo," but said nothing about the nonmilitary targets struck, including the factory at Abu Zabal and the school at Bahr el Bakr. In referring to Soviet help in supplying Nasser with military and economic aid and in keeping him in business, the Kalbs never mentioned the similar role of the CIA in earlier maintaining Nasser in power so as to serve as an example of stability to other Arab regimes in the area (see Miles Copeland, *The Game of Nations*, New York: Simon and Schuster, 1969). Nasser had so successfully played East off against West that both superpowers at one point were assisting him to stay in power.

4. U.S. support for evenhandedness never remotely approached the definiteness of these words: "It is high time that the U.S. stopped acting as Israel's attorney in the Middle East," a remark attributed by the Kalbs to "one of Nixon, Rogers, Richardson, Laird, Helms." Kalb and Kalb, *op. cit.*, p. 188.

5. Henry A. Kissinger, "A World Restored: Castlereagh, Metternich, and the Restoration of Peace, 1812–1822," Harvard University, 1957.

6. Kalb and Kalb, *op. cit.*, p. 47. Note how Kissinger's behavior in the Soviet Jewry affair and the Jackson Amendment, marked by total deceit, so well fits this yardstick for "statesmanship."

7. *Ibid.* Few can accuse Kissinger of not practicing what he earlier preached.

8. *Ibid.*, p. 191.

9. *Ibid.*, p. 192.

10. Two days later the *Washington Post* (June 28) picked up this word "expel," which Kissinger had used again the following day, and built a first-page story around the endeavor by "high administration officials" to "expel the Russians from the Middle East." The White House quietly had to let the Soviets and Egyptians know that this was a "mistake" of Henry's—"inadvertent, completely inadvertent." Two years later, Sadat picked up these signals from San Clemente and threw out the Soviet military advisers.

11. During the fall of 1972, a few weeks before the presidential election, Kissinger and Rabin did appear publicly in the presidential box (without Nixon) at the Kennedy Center for a performance of the Israeli Philharmonic Symphony Orchestra in celebration of the twenty-fifth anniversary of Israeli independence. According to the Kalb biographers, "No one in the concert hall missed this public display of the special Israeli-American relationship." Kalb and Kalb, *op. cit.*, pp. 208–9.

12. *Ibid.*, p. 487.

13. Ghassan Tuéni, *An Nahar*, March 19, 1974. This theme was picked up and expanded in "After October: Military Conflict and Political Change in the Middle East," *Journal of Palestine Studies* (Beirut), Vol. III No. 4, Summer 1974.

14. As brought out in the investigation of the CIA, in 1975 Kissinger armed the Kurd rebels in northern Iraq with millions of dollars of weapons to fight the Iraqis and to help Iran in its dispute with its Soviet-supported neighbor. This ploy, enthusiastically

endorsed editorially by the *New York Times*, turned out to be a miserable failure when the Iranians and Iraqis reached an agreement to settle their border dispute, mostly centering on the Shatt-al Arab River, and the Iranians ceased support of the Kurds, virtually ending their rebellion.

15. During Sadat's crackdown on political opposition in the late spring of 1978, Heikal, who had been writing most critically of the Egyptian president, was barred from continuing to do so.

16. *Washington Post,* February 9, 1974.

17. This was at the time that the first Phantoms negotiated by the previous Johnson administration were delivered, and the Special Committee of the U.N. had brought to light evidence substantiating the Arab charge of the harsh, inhumane rule in the occupied territories.

18. *New York* magazine, December 24, 1973.

19. *Washington Post, op. cit.*

20. *Ibid.*

21. His speech of November 3 before the World Jewish Congress could not have been more nationalist had a doctrinaire Zionist written it: "All Jews have seen too much suffering and too many people killed to be able to abandon their own judgment as to what is necessary for peace and survival." *New York Times,* November 4, 1977.

22. These words came from the acid pen of columnist Mary McGrory, who wrote as Kissinger departed that "the torch of American foreign policy has passed from the most imperial and theatrical secretary of state in history to a calm, gray-haired professional who apparently expects to be treated like an ordinary mortal, not a super-celebrity or a sovereign power." *New York Post,* February 1, 1977. In *The Memoirs of Richard Nixon* (New York: Grossett & Dunlap, 1978), the former President is less than worshipful of his Secretary of State. He refers early in 1973 to the Kissinger reluctance "to get going on the Mideast . . . Henry has constantly put off moving on it each time, suggesting that the political problems were too difficult. . . . He agreed that the problem with the Israelis in Israel was not nearly as difficult as with the Jewish community here. . . . The Mideast he just doesn't want to bite, I am sure because of the enormous pressures he's going to get from the Jewish groups in this country." (pp. 786–87).

23. Quoted by Harold H. Saunders in his testimony before the House International Affairs Committee. Department of State Documents No. 4, "U.S. Policy in the Middle East: November 1974–February 1976," p. 62. Bureau of Public Affairs, Office of Media Services (Washington, D.C.: U.S. Government Printing Office, October 1976).

24. Edward R. F. Sheehan, *The Arabs, Israel and Kissinger* (New York: Reader's Digest Press, 1976), p. 192.

25. *Ibid.*

26. *Jerusalem Post,* August 24, 1975.

27. Sheehan, *op. cit.,* p. 173.

28. From November 3 Kissinger speech in Washington before the World Jewish Congress, *Jewish Journal,* November 11, 1977.

29. Sheehan, *op. cit.,* p. 203.

30. Both President Sadat and Prime Minister Begin publicly referred to Secretary Kissinger during their Jerusalem-Ismailia meetings. When the talks broke down in January 1978, Sadat is said to have approached Kissinger "requesting him to act as secret intermediary between Egypt and Israel," which role he declined. *Arab Report and Memo* (Zurich, *An Nahar*), February 6, 1978.

Chapter XXII: Enter Carter—and Then Begin

1. Omaha Mayor Edward Zorinsky, the first Nebraska Democratic Senator elected since 1934, was the fifth Jew to join Javits, Ribicoff, Metzenbaum, and Richard Stone in the upper house.

2. See p. 602.

3. Robert L. Turner, *I'll Never Lie To You: Jimmy Carter in His Own Words* (New York: Ballantine Books, 1976).

4. Evans and Novak syndicated column, *Dallas Times Herald,* January 19, 1977.

5. Presidential Documents, Jimmy Carter, 1977, Volume XIII, No. 12, Clinton Town Meeting, March 16, 1977. The question had been posed by Rev. Richard Harding.

6. *Ibid.*

7. *Ibid.,* No. 20, May 20, 1977.

8. Resolutions 2535B (XXIV Session), December 10, 1969; 2672 (XXV Session), December 8, 1970; 2792D (XXVI Session), December 6, 1971; 2963E (XXVII Session), December 13, 1972; 3089D (XVIII Session), December 7, 1973; 3236 (XXIX Session), November 22, 1974; 3376 (XXX Session), November 10, 1975; 31/20 (XXXI Session), November 24, 1976; 32/40 (XXXII Session), December 2, 1977.

9. Department of State, Office of Media Sources, June 17, 1977 (San Francisco).

10. *New York Times,* June 28, 1977.

11. *Time,* July 18, 1977.

12. *Ibid.,* September 5, 1977.

13. *Ibid.,* August 1, 1977, pointed out that there are at least twelve Hebrons and six Bethlehems in the U.S.

14. At a subsequent press conference Carter admitted this had been an oversight on his part.

15. *Time* interview, August 8, 1977.

16. *Washington Post,* July 28, 1977.

17. *New York Times,* August 27, 1977. Later in an October 9 *Times* dispatch Markham took a further poke at the PLO as "the Palestinian commandos whose disdain of Lebanon's tattered sovereignty helped provoke the Lebanese war."

18. Sharon, according to an Evans and Novak column in the *Washington Post* of July 15, 1977, had advised a U.S. Senator ten days prior to the Begin visit not to let worry over Arab oil affect U.S. peace plans for the area, stating that Israel itself was in a position to "handle" the oil question if the need ever arose.

19. In a letter to the *New York Times,* February 12, 1978, Lord Caradon answered a very emotional *Times* advertisement of February 3, which denied the Palestinians the right to self-determination: "I give my testimony from my long experience in the Middle East and frequent recent visits that the Palestinians crave a home of their own—small though it would be—in which they can make their own decisions and elect their own leaders and run their own government and regain their self-respect. I also give my testimony that they dearly want to live in peace with all their neighbors."

20. UPI, September 12, 1977.

21. October 5, 1977.

22. *Time,* September 19, 1977.

23. *Ibid.,* October 3, 1977.

24. *Ibid.*

25. *New York Post* editorial, October 2, 1977.

26. *New York Times* editorial, October 3, 1977.

27. According to *New York Post* columnist Sidney Zion's account of the long bargaining session, Carter asked Dayan where he was going next. Dayan indicated he was leaving for Chicago to speak to Jewish leaders, and Carter said, "Do me a favor. Don't attack me." That even a Zionist writer could impute such a request to the President of the U.S. reflects the power of the Israelist apparatus and the arrogance of its supporters. *New York Post,* November 1, 1977.

28. *Commentary* magazine, November 1977.

29. *New York Times,* November 1, 1977.

30. *Ibid.,* October 30, 1977. The article began on page one and continued over onto three-quarters of page 34.

31. *Ibid.*, October 27, 1977.
32. *Ibid.*, November 3, 1977.
33. *New York Post*, March 30, 1977.
34. James Alsop, "An Open Letter to an Israeli Friend," *New York Times Magazine*, December 14, 1975.
35. "Egypt's Forces Reported Weak," *New York Times*, November 20, 1977.
36. Extracted from Menachem Begin statement beamed by Israeli radio and television networks to neighboring Arab countries. *New York Times*, November 12, 1977.
37. *Ibid.*, November 27, 1977.
38. *Ibid.*, December 29, 1977.
39. *Ibid.*, November 20, 1977.
40. *Ibid.*, December 6, 1977.
41. *Jerusalem Post*, December 6, 1977.
42. *New York Times*, December 21, 1977.
43. *New York Post*, December 28 and 29, 1977.
44. *New York Times*, January 20, 1978.
45. *Ibid.*, February 10, 1977.
46. *Ibid.*, February 14, 1977.
47. Silt-a-Dahar, Tel Kharis, and Tapuach, all in the neighborhood of Nablus, the largest Arab city on the West Bank.
48. *New York Times*, February 27, 1978.
49. "Arab Report and Memo," *An Nahar*, Beirut, February 6, 1978, Vol. 2, No. 6.
50. The title of Hedrick Smith's article in the *New York Times*, November 6, 1977.
51. *Washington Post*, October 26, 1977.
52. *New York Times*, November 2, 1977.
53. Quoted by Mark A. Bruzonsky, "Middle East Policy: Carter's Year of Decision," *Dissent* (New York), Winter 1977.
54. *New York Times*, January 2, 1978. Front-page subhead, "Hussein *Hints* at a Failure in Teheran" (italics added). Correspondent James T. Wooten from New Delhi in paragraph 3, page 1, wrote: "King Hussein indicated that Mr. Carter had failed to persuade him to join Middle East negotiations," and on page 3 a long Flora Lewis story from Teheran in its first sentence stated: "King Hussein made it clear today that President Carter had failed . . ." etc.
55. Letters to the Editor of January 2, 1978, included a two-column bold-head contribution from Associate Director of the American Jewish Congress (4½ inches in width) with an opposing single-column light-type-headed letter from Ted Swedenburg of Middle East Resource Center (two inches in width and 20 percent less in length).
56. In the Sunday *Times* "Week in Review" of January 1, 1978, Flora Lewis writing from Cairo: ". . . With the exception of the Palestinians themselves, emotional satisfaction is what the Arabs have always wanted most from Israel. But the Israelis no longer equate emotions so easily with the hard facts of life." [Syria wants back their territories, too.] ". . . and war broke out again—with an Israeli first strike in response to *dire provocation—* in 1967." [Italics added. The statements of the four Israeli generals, see pages 557–59, refute this Lewis fairy tale.] ". . . The 1973 war, launched by Egypt . . ." [not mentioned was that Egypt attacked on Israeli-occupied Egyptian territory] ". . . the PLO, which never renounced the goal of eliminating the Jewish state. . . ." [There is an Israeli state, no Palestinian state and the PLO covenant called for a secular binational Palestinian state for Arabs and Jews to replace the Zionist state of Israel.] In her piece of January 3, 1978, from Teheran, Lewis by sentence structure attributed words to King Hussein which the Jordanian ruler did not utter: "Despite the recent belligerent statements of Yasir Arafat, leader of the PLO, the King said he was convinced that 'the overwhelming majority of Palestinians seek a life of dignity under conditions of peace.'"
57. The *Times* January 2, 1977, editorial, "Peace and the Palestinian Entity," mis-

represented Sadat's primary objections to Carter's television interview of December 28, which were not directed solely against the Palestinian entity (referred to as the "so-called Palestinian entity") being joined to "either Israel or Jordan," but more importantly to the failure to give the Palestinians the right of self-determination. At the same time the editorial found an excuse for the Begin cover-over, "everything is negotiable but the destruction of Israel," and asked for "credible assurances that self-determination for the Palestinians—which ultimately might mean an independent state—would not jeopardize the security of Israel." An earlier editorial of November 6 had strenuously defended the right of the Zionist lobby, "dedicated not for narrow profit or group interest, but for their humanity, indeed sanity" to take any and all steps to prevent "American betrayal of Israel." The right to exercise multiple loyalties was also stoutly defended in this *Times* editorial.

58. *New York Times*, February 19–21, 1978.

59. Anthony Lewis, "Looking at Reality," *New York Times*, February 23, 1978; subsequent Lewis columns March 6 and March 27, 1978. The new Lewis outlook was also expressed in a series of articles during the columnist's April–May trip to the area, particularly his May 4 article in which he stated that "most Palestinians seem to regard the PLO as their collective voice."

60. *New York Times*, March 12, 1978, Sunday editorial. In his *Times* column the same day, Tom Wicker also warned that the attitude of White House liaison aide Mark Siegel and of Rabbi Alexander M. Schindler implied that "some Jews think the only 'square deal' for Israel is to give Israel what it wants," and that anyone who differed with Israeli policy lacked "support for the survival of Israel." This latter tactic paralleled the 1947–48 Zionist accusation that those who did not go along with the partition plan and the creation of the State of Israel wished "to drive the Jews into the sea."

61. *Time*, March 27, 1978.

62. *Boston Globe*, March 15, 1978, in its headlines across the front page called it a "Retaliatory 'Purifying' Act." As the Sadat peace euphoria gradually evaporated, the near-paranoia of *New York Post* editorial page editor James A. Wechsler became increasingly apparent in editorials either bemoaning the "lost dream," assailing PLO "terrorism," or eventually tearing apart "undemocratic" Sadat, and in the publication of endless pro-Zionist, anti-Arab diatribes in the letters column. All this tied into the Murdoch paper's screaming yellow journalism in the selling and reselling of Israel.

63. *New York Post*, March 25, 1978.

64. *Time*, March 27, 1978.

65. Quoted by James Reston in the *New York Times*, March 19, 1978.

66. *New York Post*, March 23, 1978.

67. *Ibid.*, March 24, 1978.

68. The details of the uprising in the occupied West Bank, Gaza strip, and East Jerusalem were first reported in the *New York Times* on March 30, 1978, tucked away in a page 12 story under the misleading caption: "Israel's Invasion of Lebanon Kills Hope on West Bank for End of Occupation."

69. Confirmed by *Time* magazine's Jerusalem Bureau Chief Donald Neff (*Time*, April 3, 1978).

70. See Chapter V, p. 173.

71. According to *New York* magazine of April 24, 1978, the Connecticut Senator told the *Wall Street Journal* that "the official leaders were simply self-appointed spokesmen who try to give the impression they speak for the Jews . . . they do a great disservice to the U.S., to Israel, and to the Jewish community."

72. Quoted by Sol Stern, "Menachem Begin vs. the Jewish Lobby," *New York* magazine, April 24, 1978.

73. *Time*, May 15, 1978.

74. *New York Times*, May 9, 1978.

75. *Christian Science Monitor*, May 22, 1978.

76. General Saad el Shazly, *The Crossing of the Suez* (San Francisco: American Mideast Research, 1980).

77. Fayez Sayegh, *Camp David and Palestine* (New York: Americans for Middle East Understanding, 1978), p. 16.

78. *Newsweek*, December 11, 1978. On his trip to the Middle East shortly after the Reagan election, although neither the President-elect nor the State Department would hold him out as representing them, the former Secretary kept insisting that his views actually represented those of the incoming Administration.

79. To show how strong they were, the Zionists even threatened civil rights leader District of Columbia delegate Walter D. Fauntleroy with defeat by the Maryland legislature of his District of Columbia Voting Rights Amendment unless he publicly rescinded his openly avowed support of the PLO.

80. For attitude of Zionist groups toward Electoral College reform, see infra, p. 874, footnote 11.

81. See supra, p. 236.

Chapter XXIII: Reagan and Still Begin

1. See supra, p. 260.

2. See footnote 26, p. 831.

3. U.S. weaponry has flown steadily from Tel Aviv to north and south Lebanon.

4. This fulfilled the goal of Moshe Dayan, which Prime Minister Moshe Sharett had rejected in 1954. See Livia Rokach, *Israel's Sacred Terrorism: A Study on Moshe Sharett's Personal Diary.* (Belmont: AAUG, 1980), p. 28.

5. *New York Times*, June 9, 1981. "When Prime Minister Begin cries out that he is 'not afraid of any reaction by the world,' he embraces the code of his weakest enemies, the code of terror. He justifies aggression by his profound sense of victimhood. And he assumes that even commitment to allies—like those governing the use of American weapons—can be twisted to suit any purpose.... Israel's ever-widening definition of self-defense is illusory.... It argues for unrelenting attack in pursuit of an unsustainable superiority."

6. In his lengthy, documented presentation to the Security Council, Iraq Foreign Minister Saadoun Hammadi quoted directly from pp. 329-332 of this book as to Israel's nuclear capacity and the White House cover-up.

7. *New York Times*, August 18, 1981.

8. *New York Times*, October 4, 1981.

9. Mary McGrory column, *Washington Post*, October 29, 1981.

10. *New York Times*, October 2, 1981.

11. The AWACS were not to be delivered until '85, and Saudi crews were to continue training through '90. In fact, Israel was far more concerned about the enhancements being supplied for the sixty F-15's sold to Riyadh in 1978 than they were about the ultra-sophisticated planes. Military correspondents raised questions about the effectiveness of the AWACS and its threat to Israel. Two F-106 fighters in a demonstration had come within 150 feet of the AWACS "undetected by the airplane's highly-touted sensors," according to the *Chicago Tribune* (James Coates, September 20, 1981). The highly-publicized debate over the AWACS to a great measure was "much ado about nothing."

12. At the outset of the Palestine question in 1947, when the fate of the U.N. partition resolution hung in balance, forthright action, such as was manifested in behalf of the AWACS sale, might have netted a different result. See Alfred M. Lilienthal, *The Other Side of the Coin* (New York: Devin-Adair, 1965), p. 201 etc.

13. David Hirst and Irene Beeson, *Sadat* (London: Faber & Faber, 1981), p. 15.

14. *New York Times*, October 7, 1981.

15. *New York Times*, August 16, 1981.

16. George Steiner, *The Portage to San Cristobal of A.H.* (New York: Simon & Schuster, 1980), p. 114.

17. *Rocky Mountain News*, (Denver), May 2, 1982.

18. Norman Podhoretz, *New York Times Magazine*, May 2, 1982.

Chapter XXIV: The Ultimate Dichotomy: Israel Uber Alles?

1. "And what is happening today is that for the first time in American history, American Jews feel secure enough in their Jewishness and their Americanism to challenge major aspects of this country's foreign policy with regard to both the Middle East and the Soviet Union." Stephen D. Isaacs, *Jews and American Politics* (New York: Doubleday, 1974), pp. 244–45.

2. *New York Times,* January 27, 1974, in review of the Eugene Borowitz book, *The Mask Jews Wear.*

3. *New York Times Magazine,* May 6, 1973.

4. *New York Times,* May 7, 1973.

5. *Miami Herald,* January 5, 1976. The story appeared in five columns on the first page of Section 2 and continued with photos on an inside page.

6. Michael Brecher, *The Foreign Policy System of Israel* (New Haven, Connecticut: Yale University Press, 1972), p. 232 and footnote 4.

7. *Ibid.,* p. 503, footnote 3.

8. David Ben-Gurion, *Rebirth and Destiny of Israel* (New York: Philosophical Library, 1954), p. 489.

9. David Ben-Gurion, "Jewish Survival," *Israel Government Year Book, 1953–54,* p. 35.

10. While this expression of dual loyalites caused Kenen no concern, the duality on the part of Jews and Greeks worried Mike Mansfield enough to cause the Senate Majority Leader to comment on NBC's "Meet the Press," July 27, 1975. This was prominently reported in the *Jerusalem Post,* July 29, 1975.

11. Walter Eytan, *The First Ten Years: A Diplomatic History of Israel* (New York: Simon and Schuster, 1958), pp. 192–93.

12. World Jewish Congress, Stockholm, August 1959.

13. Action Committee, World Zionist Organization, Jerusalem, April 25, 1950.

14. Zionist Ideological Conference, Jerusalem, Spring 1957.

15. *Jewish Daily Forward,* January 9, 1959.

16. In the lengthy *New York Times* two-column account of Goldmann's remarks, this was buried away at the very end, 104 lines into the story.

17. Abba Eban speech, "Prospects for Peace in the Middle East," William Patterson College (Wayne, N.J.), November 20, 1974.

18. Advertising blasts against France by the Au Revoir Committee carried the signatures of such "foreign policy experts" as Buddy Hackett, Jerry Stiller, and Anna Meara (the famed Stiller & Meara), Abbe Lane, Jack Carter, Herschel Bernardi, Paddy Chayefsky, Jan Sterling, Steve Lawrence, Eydie Gormé, and former Anti-Defamation League head Dore Schary, whose fine non-Italian hand could be seen in the composition of the ad and of the committee. Some of these with such distinguished additions as Richard Burton, Colleen Dewhurst, Estelle Parsons, and Beverly Sills joined a more permanent organization, Writers and Artists for Peace in the Middle East, which crusades for a settlement on Zionist terms and ran full-page ads in the *New York Times* and *Washington Post* under the heading of "REMEMBER," attacking the PLO for its terrorism.

19. The press, television, and radio had likewise built anti-French hatred in its coverage of the 1970 purchase by Libya of 114 French Mirages, which Zionists alleged would be transferred to Egypt for use against Israel.

20. At a 1968 Waldorf Astoria dinner honoring Israeli Prime Minister Levi Eshkol, UJA Chairman Edward Ginsberg exhorted his listeners to renew their commitment to Israel by more gifts and more Bond purchases, "as the greatest insurance for *our* future as Jews as well as for the future of Israel" (italics added). *New York Times,* January 12, 1968.

21. April 20, 1964, letter from Talbot to Berger quoted in "A Letter from an American Rabbi to an Arab Ambassador," full-page advertisement, *New York Times,* November 23, 1975.

22. Marjorie M. Whiteman, editor, *Digest of International Law* (U.S. Government Printing Office, 1967), Vol. 8, pp. 34–35.

23. Everyone in Israel is required to carry a "leumi" card, signifying "peoplehood" or "nation." Interestingly, the "leumi" corresponds to the "volk" card carried by Germans, also to identify them as members of a particular volk who believed in myths about a common ancestry, origin, and fatherland. These legends imparted a sense of superiority over other "volk" groups, expressed fear of contamination by associating with them, and fed basic Nazi dogma.

24. The Zionist infiltration of the American Council for Judaism, going back several years, finally succeeded following the 1967 war in ousting Rabbi Elmer Berger and in totally neutralizing the organization thenceforth. Mouthing an occasional mild criticism of Zionism, the Council has placed any censure of Israel on the *verboten* list. While keeping the Zionists from entering the front door, they left the back ajar to Israelists, despite warnings from Berger, Moshe Menuhin, and other staunch anti-Zionists.

25. *New York Times,* March 24, 1974.

26. "And thou shalt love the Lord thy God with all thy heart and with all thy might." Deuteronomy 6:5.

27. Letter, Israel Shahak, "A Jewish Duty or Jewish Apostasy?", London *Times,* January 27, 1973.

28. A classic example of an open avowal of dual loyalty was brought to public attention during the Sacramento hearings in March 1975 on the confirmation of Arnold Sternberg as California State Director of Housing and Development. Opposed by a group of Arab-Americans because he had served with the Haganah, Jewish underground forces during the British mandate, and had participated in driving Palestinian Arabs from their homes, Sternberg stated, as reported in the San Francisco *Jewish Bulletin* of May 9, "If forced to choose in a crisis, there is no question about it—my choice lies with my people—the Jewish people." Although an Israel-Firster by his own words, he was confirmed by the State Senate to his post.

29. The saddling of special rights as well as duties and obligations on Jews in the Diaspora is, among other things, a negation of the protective guarantee set forth in the Balfour Declaration.

30. In a 5–4 decision in the case of Afroyim vs. Rusk, the Supreme Court decided that Americans could be deprived of their American citizenship only on personal renunciation, thus permitting military service by private American citizens in foreign armed forces. This encouraged enthusiastic young American Jews to volunteer in the Israeli armed forces before and during the 1973 war, despite the statement of the U.S. Mission to the U.N. declaring its strong opposition to such service as "contrary to the foreign policy interests of the U.S. and because it risks involvement by American citizens in hostilities with countries with which we are at peace."

31. Arnold Toynbee, *A Study of History* (London: Oxford University Press, 1954), Vol. VIII, pp. 290–91.

32. Saul Bellow, *To Jerusalem and Back* (New York: Viking Press, 1976). In commenting on the book, Noam Chomsky stated that Bellow is a "propagandist's delight. He has produced a catalogue of 'What Every Good American Should Believe,' as compiled by the Israeli Information Ministry. Everything is predictable. No cliché is missing . . . Bellow has an engaging ability to skim the surface of ideas and a craftsman's talent for capturing a chance encounter or an odd circumstance. Beyond that, his account of what he has seen and heard is a disaster." Noam Chomsky, *The New Arab* (New Delhi, India), November 1977.

33. George Steiner, *The Listener* magazine (London: British Broadcasting Corp.), September 18, 1975.

34. Arthur Koestler, *The Thirteenth Tribe: The Khazar Empire and Its Heritage* (New York: Random House, 1976).

35. Constantine VI, the son of Leo III, married the Khazar Princess Irene.

36. For details see Alfred M. Lilienthal, *What Price Israel?* (Chicago: Henry Regnery, 1953), pp. 220–22.

37. This correspondence (circa 936–950 A.D.) was first published in 1577 to prove that Jews still had a country of their own—namely, the Kingdom of Khazaria. Judah Halevi knew of the letters even in 1140, and their authenticity has since been verified.

38. Author Koestler strains to conclude that the "Khazar" point does not dilute the Zionist legal claim to Palestine. He insists that the U.N. 1947 resolution decided *de jure* Israel's right to exist, which is now a fact that cannot be undone, except by genocide. Yet the Zionists themselves, plus their U.S. backers, were so fearful that the U.N. was not legally competent to confer sovereignty upon Jews even in *part* of the Holy Land, that they mercilessly pressured the U.N. Ad Hoc Committee on Palestine, November 1947, to vote down by the narrowest margin Arab demands for a ruling on this question from the International Court of Justice. Jurists worldwide, including some Jews, who have studied the legality of the right of the U.N. to give portions of Palestine to the Zionist Jewish Agency, are largely in accord that no such authority existed.

39. *New York Times*, August 29, 1976.

40. Lilienthal, *op. cit.*, p. 223.

41. Friedrich Hertz, *Race and Civilization* (London: Kegan Paul, Trench, Trubner & Co., Ltd., 1928), p. 134.

42. William Z. Ripley, *Races of Europe* (New York: Appleton, 1898), p. 392.

43. Max C. Margolis and Alexander Marx, *A History of Jewish People* (Philadelphia: Jewish Publication Society of America, 1927), p. 525.

44. A small number, called "proselytes of righteousness," accepted the initiatory rites of Judaism as well as other laws and customs.

45. Flavius Josephus, *History of the Jewish War*, written in both Hebrew and Greek, in seven volumes.

46. Berr Isaac-Berr, "Lettre d'un citoyen, 1791," *Transactions of Parisian Sanhedrin*, M. Diogene Tama, ed. (London: Charles Taylor, 1807).

47. The Secretary of State for India had jurisdiction over British colonial interests in the Near and Middle East as well.

48. Edwin Montagu, Cabinet No. 2A/24, August 13, 1917. Montagu felt that no matter what safeguarding rights might be provided in the declaration, "the civil rights of Jews as nationals in the countries in which they lived might be endangered." He asked, "How could he, for example, be able to negotiate with the peoples of India on behalf of His Majesty's Government, if the world had just been told that the Government regarded his national home as being in Turkish territory." David Lloyd George, *Memoirs of the Peace Conference* (New York: Howard Fertig, 1972), Vol. II, p. 733.

49. Originally published in *Menorah Journal*, February 1918; reprinted in *Menorah Journal*, Autumn 1950, pp. 116–18.

50. Henry Morgenthau, Sr., *All in a Lifetime* (New York: Doubleday, Page & Co., 1921/1922), p. 385.

51. Naomi Wiener Cohen, *The Reaction of Reform Judaism to Political Zionism (1897–1922)* (Philadelphia: Publications of the American Jewish Historical Society, June 1951), p. 365.

52. *Ibid.*, p. 368.

53. Solomon Grayzel, *A History of the Jews* (Philadelphia: Jewish Publication Society of America, 1947).

54. *Issues*, American Council for Judaism (New York), October 1962. At the commemoration in Bagdad of the 20th anniversary of the overthrow of the monarchy, the author was told by a Danish journalist that Rabbi Melchior's son and successor is a Zionist.

55. Judah Magnes, "Problems of Today," *The Call* (New York), July 3, 1942.

56. Israel Shahak, "The Racist Nature of Zionism and the Zionist State of Israel," *Middle East Perspective*, April and May 1976.

57. Address in Philadelphia, May 10, 1915, *Public Papers of Woodrow Wilson*, Vol. II, Part 1 (New York: Harper Bros., 1925).

58. *New York Post*, October 14, 1976.

59. Anita Libman Lebeson, *Pilgrim People* (New York: Harper & Brothers, 1950), p. 62.

60. Wilmot Robertson, *The Dispossessed Majority* (Cape Canaveral, Fla.: Howard Allen, 1972), pp. 191–92.

Chapter XXV: Conclusion: Toward Justice and Then Peace

1. NER, summer issue, 1955 (Jerusalem: Ihud Association).

2. Gary Wills, syndicated columnist, *The Dispatch* (Bayonne, N.J.), February 18, 1978.

3. *Yediot Aharonot*, May 14, 1976. Uri Avneri, former Knesset member and editor of the Tel Aviv weekly magazine *Ha'olam Hazeh*, has stated: "The occupation is an unmitigated disaster for Israel. The fact that the Palestinians remain without their dignity poses a greater danger to Israeli security than any long-range benefit Israel could have from the military side of things." *Time*, June 19, 1978. Also Harold R. Piety, "Israel's Trouble on the West Bank," *Journal Herald* (Dayton, Ohio), May 21, 1976. He referred to the "corrosive relationship brutalizing the oppressor as well as the oppressed."

4. *New York Times*, January 5, 1978.

5. Secretary of State Cyrus R. Vance admitted that Israel *"may have"* violated American law limiting use of these weapons to legitimate self-defense. *New York Times*, April 6, 1978. [Italics added.]

6. Arnold J. Toynbee, "The West and the Arabs," *Encyclopedia Britannica Yearbook*, 1959.

7. When Rabbi Benjamin of Tudela visited Baghdad in 1170 A.D., he found ten rabbinical schools and 238 synagogues in the land. The Chief Rabbi, he wrote, was held in highest esteem, being regarded as a descendant of David. Philip Hitti, *The Arabs* (Chicago: Henry Regnery, 1956), p. 178.

8. For Zionist tactics employed to stampede Iraqi Jews into flight, see Alfred M. Lilienthal, *The Other Side of the Coin* (New York: Devin-Adair, 1965), pp. 37–38.

9. See Paul Martin's story in the London *Times*, November 4, 1975.

10. *Manchester Guardian Weekly*, April 27, 1972.

11. That the entrenched Zionists, as well as other special interest groups, will continue to resist pending Electoral College reform legislation, sponsored by forty-two Senate members and being pushed by Senator Birch Bayh (Dem.-Ind.) as Chairman of the Senate Judiciary Committee on Constitutional Amendments, was indicated in a lengthy March 23, 1978, *Washington Star* article, "The Electoral College: An Antique that Works," by coeditor and columnist Edwin M. Yoder, Jr. The writer's principal defense of the outmoded and sometimes undemocratic Electoral College system rests in the words of Lord Falkland, once quoted by John F. Kennedy during a Senate debate on the subject: "When it is not necessary to change, it is necessary not to change." Under the Bayh amendment, the Electoral College would be eliminated and the presidential and vice-presidential candidates who jointly received the most votes in all states combined would be elected. If no ticket received 40 percent or more of the vote, a run-off between the top two would take place. Judah Shapiro, head of the Labor-Zionist Alliance, told a meeting of the group's National Council at New York's Biltmore Hotel: "President Carter's proposal to eliminate the Electoral College could strip the country's Jews of their political influence and hurt the liberal community." She noted that "in states with a substantial Jewish population, the Jewish vote can help deliver the states through the Electoral College." *Christian Science Monitor*, March 28, 1977.

12. *Foreign Affairs*, April 1977. An April 4, 1976, London *Times* editorial was afraid

to criticize Israeli leadership for the turmoil then going on in the occupied West Bank in Israel proper, preferring to place the blame on the "indulgence" of friends of Israel, "which has encouraged self-righteousness in Israel," and to attribute the "heady dream of a 'Greater Israel' " to "extremist groups." Thirteen months later, Menachem Begin was elected with this slogan as Prime Minister.

13. Timothy R. Attwood, *Goldstein Explains How Jews Control American Policy Toward Israel* (New York: Vantage Press, 1976).

14. Attwood, *op. cit.*, p. 69.

15. For a full study, see Nelson T. Joyner, Jr., *Arab Boycott/Anti-Boycott—The Effects on U.S. Business* (McLean, Virginia: Rockville Consulting Group, Inc., December 1976).

16. The Associated General Contractors of America is a national trade association representing 8,000 general contracting construction firms and an associate membership of some 17,500 subcontractors. The association, based in Washington, is responsible for 60 percent of the total annual U.S. contract construction and about one-third of all international construction undertaken by American firms.

17. Remarks by Congressman Robert H. Michel (Rep.-Ill.), *Congressional Record*, 95th Congress, First Session, April 20, 1977, p. H.3274.

18. After the study had appeared in a two-page advertisement in the *Wall Street Journal* placed by Dresser Industries, Professor Robinson was told by an active Zionist member of the faculty that had the piece been written prior to his appointment as a tenured professor, he would never have received the appointment. In his letter to the author, September 5, 1977, the professor adds: "Given his position at MIT, I believe he could have made good on that threat. One wonders what sort of message comes through to junior members of the faculty when such a statement is made."

19. Senator Abraham Ribicoff's contention as related in "Squelch the Boycott and Cut Petrodollar Income," the syndicated Evans and Novak column, September 13, 1976.

20. *New York Times*, July 1, 1974.

21. *World Military Expenditures and Arms Transfers 1966–1975*, U.S. Arms Control and Disarmament Agency (Washington, D.C.: U.S. Government Printing Office, 1977).

22. In addition to the two superpowers, these were China, Iran, Japan, Italy, Czechosolovakia, France, the U.K., and Poland.

23. *Southside News* (Orlando, Florida), March 16, 1978.

24. One objector wrote the author requesting anonymity, "not because of the persecution we have suffered ourselves, but because of that extended to our children and other family members. The children, in particular, have children of their own or are in various stages of education. Their parents cannot afford to have business opportunities withheld. Isn't all of this sickening? I know that you will heed my request and not mention my name."

25. When Board of Regents member Mrs. Genevieve Klein opposed this giveaway of taxpayer funds, Stanley Steingut, Jr., Democratic leader in the New York State Assembly, wrote to Warren Anderson, Republican leader in the State Senate, calling Mrs. Klein "an anathema to my people." Her refusal to admit that Israel was the fifty-first state of the Union was an important factor in her defeat for reelection by the legislature.

26. *New York Times*, June 16, 1974.

27. Clyde R. Mark, *Foreign Assistance to the State of Israel: A Compilation of Basic Data*, Foreign Affairs and National Defense Division, Congressional Research Service, Library of Congress, September 28, 1976; *U.S. Overseas Loans and Grants and Assistance from International Organizations*, Bureau for Program and Policy Coordination, A.I.D., March 1982.

28. Nadav Safran, *The U.S. and Israel* (Cambridge: Harvard University Press, 1963), p. 278. What Safran wrote at that time is even much more true today. In his article "The U.S. and Israel: Conflicts of Interest," *Issues* (New York: American Council for Judaism, Summer 1964), Dr. Harry Howard, formerly of the U.S. Department of State, pointed out that the U.S. had given $877.7 million in economic and military aid to Israel between 1946 and 1962. This was a per capita rate of $39.70, the highest in the U.S. foreign assistance program.

29. General Ira C. Eaker, *Strategic Review* (Washington, D.C.: U.S. Strategic Institute, Winter 1974).

30. Wolf Blitzer interview of General George Keegan, "The Arab Plan to Destroy Israel," *Jerusalem Post*, August 9, 1977; reprinted in *Near East Report*, August 10, 1977.

31. *Armed Forces Journal International*, October 1977.

32. *Ibid.*

33. *Ibid.*, December 1977. See p. 21 for editor's comments on the Churba piece, "Weighing the Middle East Balance on a Different Set of Scales," which appeared in that issue. The same issue also described the "grilling" to which Cordesman's former secretary was subjected in the course of the investigation by the over-conscientious agents of the Defense Department, who forced the opening of a safe containing old Cordesman papers and messed up the combination.

34. Jim Hoagland, "War of Annihilation," *Washington Post*, October 26, 1977.

35. *Ibid.*

36. *New York Times*, February 18, 1965.

37. *Time*, September 19, 1977.

38. Howard W. Blauvelt speech, Town Hall, Los Angeles, California, February 11, 1975.

39. "The historical connection of the Jewish people with Palestine" first appeared in the preamble of the League of Nations mandate for Palestine and was incessantly repeated by fervent Zionist supporters during the 1947 U.N. debate as the "reconstituting of our national home."

40. Dr. Fayez A. Sayegh, "The Mideast's Other Side: What the Palestinians Want," *Boston Globe*, July 24, 1977.

41. Wilmot Robertson, *The Dispossessed* (Cape Canaveral, Fla.: Howard Allen, 1972), p. 493.

42. See p. 92.

43. Arnold Toynbee, "The West and the Arabs," *Encyclopedia Britannica Yearbook*, 1959.

44. *The Times* (London), October 23, 1972.

45. *Jerusalem Post*, April 19, 1976.

46. *New York Post*, March 9, 1978.

47. *New York Times*, May 24, 1978.

48. *Ibid.*, May 25, 1978.

49. The Kurds, with close to 3½ million people scattered through East Turkey, Soviet Armenia, Northeast Iraq and Northwest Iran in a contiguous area of 74,000 square miles (Israel covered 8,050 in 1951 with a population of 1.8 million) that could be carved out for them with little displacement, have never been accorded a state of their own.

50. Avigdor Levontin, "The Possible Instead of the Ideal," *New Outlook* (Tel Aviv), June-July-August 1969.

Index